LITERACY IN MEDIEVAL AND EARLY MODERN VILNIUS

UTRECHT STUDIES IN MEDIEVAL LITERACY

55

LITERACY IN MEDIEVAL AND EARLY MODERN VILNIUS

FORMS OF WRITING AND RHETORICAL SPACES IN THE CITY

Jakub Niedźwiedź

BREPOLS

British Library Cataloguing in Publication Data

A catalogue record for this book is available from the British Library

This publication was financed under the Polish Ministry of Science and Higher Education's 'National Programme for the Development of Humanities' in 2018-2022 Uniwersalia 2.1 nr 21H 17 0289 85

NATIONAL PROGRAMME
FOR THE DEVELOPMENT OF HUMANITIES

This book is made open access with funding support from the Faculty of Polish Studies of the Jagiellonian University under the Excellence Initiative – Research University programme.

D/2023/0095/34

ISBN 978-2-503-60430-5

e-ISBN 978-2-503-60431-2

DOI 10.1484/M.USML-EB.5.132178

ISSN 2034-9416

e-ISNN 2294-8317

Printed in the EU on acid-free paper

To my beloved wife Dominika

Contents

Preface xiii
Abbreviations xvii
Images xix
Chronological Table xxix
List of the Grand Dukes of Lithuania and the Kings of Poland Who Controlled Vilnius in 1323-1655 xxxix
Maps xli
Transcriptions, Translations, and Spellings xlv

Introduction 1

Why Vilnius? 6
The State of Research and Sources 12
The Methodological Approach 26
The Structure of the Book 35
Terminology and Other Explanations 37
The Name of the City, The Politics of Memory, and Linguistic Issues 41

Part 1: *Loci Textuales* in Late Medieval and Early Modern Vilnius

1. Chanceries, Courts, and Their Writing Staff 47

Legal Settings 47
Chanceries 61
Professionals of the Written Word: Scribes and Secretaries 74

2. The Preservation of Texts 83

Archives 83
Libraries 92

Book Collections of Orthodox Churches; The Cathedral Library; Libraries of Churches, Monasteries, and Convents; The Library of the Academy of Vilnius; Private Book Collections (Libraries of the Clergy; Libraries of People in Power; Book Collections of Wealthy Town Dwellers and the Nobility)

What Was the Purpose of Possessing Books? 126

3. Schools 131

Introduction 131
The Cathedral School – A Bridge of the University of Cracow 133
St. John's School 140
Other Schools in Vilnius: Monastic and Conventual 144
The Jesuit College and Academy of Vilnius 144
Student Life 161
The Orthodox Brotherhood's School 164
The Uniate School 169
Protestant Schools 171
The Jewish School 178
The Tartar School 179
Summary 180

4. *Loci Textuales* of Women 183

The City 183
The Castle 199
The Nunneries 205
Conclusion 222

Part 2: Languages and Scripts: Materiality, Writing and Reading

5. Reading and Writing in Early Modern Vilnius 225

The Levels of Pragmatic Literacy and Illiteracy 225
Reading and Power 233
Popular Reading and Elite Reading 236
The Production of Texts 239

6. The Materiality of Texts 247

Texts of Vilnius 247
Materials for the Production of a Text 250
Spoken and Written Languages 254
The Shape of Script 266

7. The Book 281

The Manuscript Book 281
Printers 285
Bookbinding 301
The Book Trade 308
The Price and Value of Books 313

Part 3: *Genera Scribendi*

8. *Genus Deliberativum*: Letters and Testaments 321

Preliminary Remarks 321
The Legal Contracts: Transactions and Donations 329
The Rhetoric and Use of Letters 335
The Rhetoric of a Private Document: The Will 351

9. Texts in a Dispute 365

The 'Open' City vs. the 'Closed' City 365

Agonistic Culture 369
The Methodology of a Dispute: Jesuit Polemical Theology 370
Polyphonic Texts of Dispute (the 'Closed' City) 372
The Texts of Religious Polemics (the 'Open' City) 381
Disputations in Vilnius: Between Rhetorical Action and Dialogue 384
Polemic Treatises: Between Tumults and Disputations 394
Polemic Discourses I (Protestants vs. Catholics): Between a Treatise and a Pasquil 406
Polemic Verses: Between Pasquils and Riots 412
Polemic Discourses II (Orthodox Christians vs. Catholics and Uniates) 417
Polemic Sermons: Between Positive-Controversial Theology and Riots 424

10. Epideictic Texts 429

The Epideictic Art 429
Demonstrative Texts in the 'Closed' City: Literature on Display 436

Epitaphs; The Style of Christian Funerary Inscriptions; Mausolea; Votive Offerings; Other Inscriptions: Foundations, Pious and Parenetic); Epigraphic Ephemera; Inscriptions: Memory and Competition

Panegyrics in Vilnius: The Creation of Memory and Prestige 471

The Jesuit *Res Publica Litteraria* in Vilnius at the Turn of the Sixteenth and Seventeenth Centuries; Panegyrical Sermons in the First Half of the Seventeenth Century

Religious Theatre and the Theatre of Power 484

The Art of Epideictic Art in the City; Theatre and Drama; The Theatricalisation of Religion and Power; The Royal Entry into Vilnius of 24 July 1611; The Other Side of the Coin, or Bills

Is A Scholarly Text Demonstrative? 512

The Building of Lithuanian Identity (The Panegyrical Art of the 'Open' City) 517

A Panegyrical History; Historiography in Vilnius

11. Religious Texts 525

The Religious Identity of Vilnius 525
Holy Texts and Their Interpretations 530

Holy Books; Explaining Holy Books

Prayers 545

Everyday and Festive Prayers and Songs; The Prayer as Poetry; Liturgy and Liturgical Texts

Basic and Advanced Religious Teaching: Catechisms and Sermons 570

Catechisms; Sermons; Preachers; Postils; Orally Performed vs. Written Sermons

Recapitulation 592

Conclusion: The City of Memory 595

The Lost Voices of the Inhabitants of Vilnius 607

Bibliography 615

Indices 715

Index of Personal Names 715
Index of Place-Names and Ethnic Names 743
Subject Index 749

Preface

The first version of this book was the monograph *Kultura literacka Wilna (1323-1655): Retoryczna organizacja miasta miasta* [The Literary Culture of Vilnius 1323-1655: The Rhetorical Organisation of the City]. At first, the book was to be only translated from Polish. The preliminary version of the translation was made. However, during the editorial work, the book's editor Anna Adamska and the author decided that the translation had to be thoroughly revised. There were several reasons to do so. Firstly, the Polish version was designed for Polish readers, for whom many facts, terms, and data were obvious. An international audience required additional explanations related to the history of the Polish-Lithuanian Commonwealth. On the other hand, the readers of *Utrecht Studies in Medieval Literacy* (*USML*) would not need some information which it had been necessary to provide a Polish audience with. Secondly, the Polish book was written between 2005 and 2010. Over the last twelve years, a large number of relevant new publications has appeared: editions of unknown sources, important monographs and articles. They had to be taken into consideration. Finally, after twelve years, the author changed his views on several matters expressed in the original book. All this resulted in designing a new book, although it obviously remains based on materials and large fragments translated from the Polish book.

The methodological background, scope, and questions presented in the English version are new (cf. the Introduction). The book has an entirely new structure and logic. Three chapters from the Polish version were only moderately revised (chapters 2, 7, and 9). Five chapters were thoroughly revised and changed (chapters 3, 4, 5, 6, and 10). They were redesigned, extended and in many places rewritten. Five chapters (the Introduction, Chapters 1, 8, and 11, and the Conclusion) are wholly new. Apart from that, the author added new illustrations, maps and explanatory materials at the beginning of the book. The final English shape of the book is the result of meticulous and thorough revisions made by Marco Mostert.

The list of people and institutions to whom I owe the possibility of writing and finishing this book is long. In 2004-2006 I carried out research financed by the Polish Committee of Academic Research under grant H01C 073 26 *Kultura literacka Wilna do 1655 roku* [The Literary Culture of Vilnius until 1655]. The result of this research was a book published in 2012. The present book has been translated thanks to the support of the Polish Ministry of Science and Higher Education, that financed the editorial project Uniwersalia 2.1 0289/NPRH6/H21/85/2017 *Tłumaczenie na język angielski i publikacja książki Kultura literacka Wilna (1323-1655): Retoryczna organizacja miasta*; it is published in English as *Literacy in Medieval and Early Modern Vilnius: Forms of Writing and Rhetorical Spaces in the City*. The publication of this new version of the book in the series *Utrecht Studies in Medieval Literacy* (USML) was made possible thanks to Brepols Publishers and the invaluable help of Guy Carney. I am grateful to Kaja Szymańska for the translation of the first version of the book and to David Lilley for its proofreading, and to Maria Szajna from the Jagiellonian University (Cracow) for her help in financial matters related to the grant. I am also grateful to Jan Mostert for proofreading the Cyrillic texts in the book.

I would like to convey my sincere gratitude to Anna Adamska and Marco Mostert, as editors of this volume of *USML*, who supported me in writing the new book. Anna devoted a huge amount of time to revise the former version thoroughly. She applied her immense knowledge to improve the new book and in every way encouraged me to deepen my knowledge about medieval and early modern European culture. Marco revised all chapters and used his research, linguistic, and editorial expertise to elucidate any unclear passages. Thank you, Anna and Marco!

I am grateful to the staff of the Jagiellonian University, Maria Łada-Palusińska, Aleksandra Ryś, Małgorzata Trębusiewicz, and Tomasz Job for dealing with the financial, administrative, and legal issues of the grant and publication. I am also grateful to the Dean of the Faculty of Polish Studies, Professor Jarosław Fazan, for his help in completing the endeavour. I got welcome support from Brepols, especially from Guy Carney, who patiently assisted me during the whole process of making the book. Thank you Guy!

I would also like to extend my thanks to the friends and colleagues who provided me with valuable advice, inspiration, and materials, as well as with opportunities for discussion. First of all I would like to thank Joanna Orlik, Aleksandra Wojda, and Elżbieta Żak for monthly meetings in which the concept of the first version of the book emerged. I could discuss the problems of early modern textual culture with Prof. Andrzej Borowski, Prof. Tadeusz Bujnicki, Paweł Bukowiec, Grzegorz Franczak, David A. Frick, Beata Kalęba, Justyna Kiliańczyk-Zięba, Emiliano Ranocchi, Andrzej Romanowski, Magdalena Ryszka-Kurczab, and Aleksander Sroczyński. I also appreciate the suggestions and advice of Professor Eugenia Ulčinaitė, who has supported my research in Vilnius for many years. I am thankful to the reviewers of the first version of the book, whose comments were valuable for its new version: Piotr Borek, Mirosława Hanusiewicz-Lavallee, and Janusz Gruchała.

My colleagues and acquaintances from different parts of the world provided me with valuable information, sources, and advice. I am especially grateful to Darius Antanavičius, Dariusz Chemperek, Maria Cieśla, Mintautas Čiurinskas, Karin Friedrich, Radosław Grześkowiak, Jakub Koryl, Margarita A. Korzo (Маргарита А. Корзо), Joanna Kunigielis, Piotr Lasek, Karol Łopatecki, Dorota Malec, Maciej Mikuła, Mirosława Mycawka, Mikalai Nikalaeŭ (Мікалай Нікалаеў), Anna Paulina Orłowska, Wioletta Pawlikowska, Beata Piasecka, Izabela Pisarek, Andrzej Probulski, Oleksii Rudenko (Олексій Руденко), Andrzej T. Staniszewski, Eleonora Terleckien, Leonid Tymoshenko (Леонід Тимошенко), and Andrzej B. Zakrzewski. I also received much help from Mirka Bialecka and Maria Zadencka, Professor Sergei I. Nikolaev (Сергей И. Николаев) and Aliaksandr I. Hrusha (Аляксандр І. Груша) during my research in Uppsala, St. Petersburg, and Minsk respectively.

Finally, I would like to express my gratitude to my wife Dominika Niedźwiedź, who encouraged me to publish this book in English and apply for the grant. She supported me during the whole process of translation, writing, and publication and showed a great deal of patience (all researchers and their partners know what I mean). I cannot thank you enough, Gizka.

Abbreviations

AGAD Warsaw, Central Archive of Historical Records (Archiwum Główne Akt Dawnych w Warszawie).

AIZR *Акты относящіеся к исторіи западной Россіи собраные и изданные Археографическую комиссею*, 4 vols. (St. Petersburg, 1846-1851).

APPD Cracow, Archive of the Polish Province of the Dominican Fathers (Archiwum Polskiej Prowincji Dominikanów w Krakowie).

ARSI Rome, Archivum Romanum Societatis Iesu.

AS The Archives of the Republic of Slovenia in Ljubljana, Slovenia (Arhiv Republike Slovenije)

AVAK *Акты, издаваемые Виленскою Археографическою коммиссиею,* 39 vols. (Vilnius, 1865-1915).

BJ The Jagiellonian Library in Cracow, Poland

BK Kórnik, Library of the Polish Academy of Sciences.

BN Warsaw, National Library (Biblioteka Narodowa w Warszawie).

BRAN St. Petersburg, Library of the Russian Academy of Sciences (Библиотека Российской академии наук в Санкт-Петербурге).

CR Uppsala, University Library Carolina Rediviva (Uppsala universitetsbibliotek).

CZART. Cracow, Czartoryski Library (Biblioteka Książąt Czartoryskich w Krakowie).

EJ *Encyclopaedia Judaica*, second edition, ed. F. SKOLNIK, 22 vols. (Detroit, 2007).

IMBRAM Imbramowice, Norbertine nunnery.

IS PAN Warsaw, Institute of Art of the Polish Academy of Sciences (Instytut Sztuki Polskiej Akademii Nauk).

JEBE *Еврейская энциклопедия Брокгауза и Ефрона*, 16 vols. (St. Petersburg, 1908-1913) <http://brockhaus-efron-jewish-encyclopedia.ru/>.

LDKVR Vilnius, National Museum – Palace of the Grand Dukes of Lithuania (Nacionalinis muziejus Lietuvos Didžiosios Kunigaikštystės valdovų rūmai).

LNMB Vilnius, Martynas Mažvydas National Library of Lithuania (Lietuvos nacionalinė Martyno Mažvydo biblioteka).

LVIA Vilnius, Lithuanian State Historical Archives (Lietuvos valstybės istorijos archyvas).

MAB Vilnius, Wróblewski Library of the Lithuanian Academy of Sciences (Lietuvos mokslų akademijos Vrublevskių biblioteka).

MNK Cracow, National Museum (Muzeum Narodowe w Krakowie).

MNW Warsaw, National Museum (Muzeum Narodowe w Warszawie).

MPSI *Monumenta Pedagogica Societatis Jesu: Nova editio penitus retractata*, ed. L. Lucács, 5 vols. (Rome, 1965-1986).

MS Manuscript.

NGAB Minsk, National Bielarusian Archive (Нацыянальны гістарычны архіў Беларусі).

PSB *Polski słownik biograficzny* [The Polish Biographical Dictionary], 53 vols. (Cracow, 1935-2021).

RGADA Moscow, Russian State Archive of Ancient Documents (Российский государственный архив древних актов, РГАДА).

SLUB Dresden, Saxon State and University Library (Sächsische Landesbibliothek – Staats- und Universitätsbibliothek Dresden).

Statut *Statut Wielkiego Księstwa Litewskiego naprzód, za najjaśniejszego hospodara Zygmunta III, w Krakowie w roku 1588, drugi raz w Wilnie, w roku 1619, z pokazaniem zgody i różnice Statutów Koronnych i W. Ks. L., trzeci raz za najjaśniejszego Władysława IV, w Warszawie, w roku 1648, z przydaniem konstytucyj od roku 1550 do 1647, czwarty raz, za najjaśniejszego Jana Trzeciego, w Wilnie w roku 1698, z przyłożeniem pod artykuły konstytucyj sejmowych od sejmu roku 1550, aż do sejmu roku 1690 obojgu narodom służących, tekstu samego w niczem nie naruszając, piąty raz za najjaśniejszego Augusta Trzeciego, po dwakroć za najjaśniejszego króla Stanisława Augusta, z przydatkiem summaryjuszów, praw i konstytucyj od roku 1764 do roku 1786, teraz za szczęśliwego panowania najjaśniejszego cesarza i samowładcy Wszechrossyi, króla polskiego Aleksandra I* (Vilnius, 1819).

Images

Fig. 1 Vilnius at the beginning of the seventeenth century. T. Makowski, *Vilna, Magni Ducatus Lithuaniae caput* (Vilnius, *c.* 1604). The copperplate shows Vilnius before the great fire in 1610 with its main buildings described in the cartouches: "1. The palace of the Princes Radziwiłł of the Biržiai branch; 2. The bridge over the Neris River called the Stone Bridge; 3. St. Barbara church [in the lower castle]; 4. The Armoury called Cekhauz [in the lower castle]; 5. The Catholic cathedral of St. Stanislas in the lower castle; 6. The Royal Castle; 7. The upper castle; 8. St. George church; 9. The Franciscan (Bernardine) monastery; 10. The nunnery [of the Bernardine Sisters and St. Michael's church]; 11. The Calvinist school; 12. The Orthodox (Ruthenian) cathedral of the Holy Virgin; 13. The parish church of St. John; 14. The Bishop's Manor; 15. The Jesuit University (the Academy of Vilnius); 16. The Dominican convent; 17. The town hall; 18. The Orthodox Trinity church; 19. The conventual Franciscan monastery; 20. The Orthodox Saviour church; 21. SN (?); 22. The mausoleum of Bekiesz; 23. The Holy Cross church; 24. St. Nicolas church in the upper castle". Original of the copperplate lost during World War II. IS PAN, Zbiory Fotografii i Rysunków Pomiarowych Instytutu Sztuki PAN (Collection of Photographs and Measuring Drawings), negative 17174. Reproduced with the permission of IS PAN. 8-9

Fig. 2 The seal of the bench (aldermen's) court of Vilnius from 1536 put on the document from 1588. MS Vilnius, LVIA, F22, ap. 1, nr 5344, f. 662r. Photo J. Niedźwiedź. 55

Fig. 3 Seventeenth-century copies of the oldest records from the bench (aldermen) court of Vilnius (1481). MS Vilnius, LVIA, F22, ap. 1 b. 1, nr 5333, f. 9r. Photo J. Niedźwiedź. 62

Fig. 4 Codicil (will) of Jan Czarny from 1573. A fragment of the aldermen court registers. The judge was *Voigt* Augustyn Rotundus. MS Vilnius, LVIA, F22, ap. 1 b. 1, nr 5333, f. 74r. Photo J. Niedźwiedź. 63

Fig. 5 A fragment of the city council registers from 1654. MS Vilnius, LVIA, F23, ap. 1, nr 5096, f. 656r. Photo J. Niedźwiedź. 67

Fig. 6 A fragment of the aldermen court registers from 1588. MS Vilnius, LVIA. F22, ap. 1, nr 5344, f. 661r. Photo J. Niedźwiedź. 68

Fig. 7 List of books of the mayor of Vilnius, Jakub Kiewlicz. A fragment of the copy of the post-mortem inventory from the city council court records, 20 June 1630. MS Vilnius, LVIA, F694, ap. 1, no. 3322, f. 6r. Photo J. Niedźwiedź. 118

Fig. 8 Fragment of an inventory of books of the mayor of Vilnius, Stefan Lebiedzicz, 1649. MS Vilnius, LVIA, F23, ap. 1, nr 5096, f. 441r. Photo J. Niedźwiedź. 120

Fig. 9 A fragment of an inventory of the library of Salomon Rysiński, 1625. MS Minsk, NGAB, Ф 694 оп. 1 ед. 450, f. 58r. Reproduced with the permission of NGAB. 123

Fig. 10 The Academy of Vilnius at the beginning of the seventeenth century. A fragment of a view of Vilnius by Tomasz Makowski from *c.* 1604 (cf. Fig. 1). The buildings of the Academy (with a tower) are marked as number 15, the big Gothic parish church of St. John is number 13. The buildings of the Academy were significantly extended after the fire in 1610. 145

Fig. 11 Manuscript of lectures on Thomas Aquinas's *Summa theologica* given by M.K. Sarbiewski in the Academy of Vilnius in 1633: *In primam partem Summae Thelologicae divi Tomae Aquinatis doctoris Angelici*. MS Vilnius, VUB, F3-2037, f. 2r. Reproduced with the permission of VUB. 160

Fig. 12 The Calvinist church and school (number 11) at the beginning of the seventeenth century. Other buildings: 10. the nunnery of the Bernardine Sisters and St. Michael's church; 12. the Bernardine convent; 14. the Bishop's Manor. A fragment of the view of Vilnius by Tomasz Makowski from *c.* 1604 (cf. Fig. 1). 173

Fig. 13 Register of the Archconfraternity of St. Anne, entries of women from 1581. MS Vilnius, LVIA, F1135, ap. 4, nr 472, ff. 66v–67r. Reproduced with the permission of LVIA. 185

Fig. 14 Signature of Dorota Demerówna Balaszkowa, 1631. MS Vilnius, LVIA, F23, ap. 1, nr 5096, f. 64r. Photo J. Niedźwiedź. 189

Fig. 15 Signature of Anna Dygoniowa, wife of Marcin Dygoń, a councillor of the city, 1649. MS Vilnius, LVIA, F23, ap. 1, nr 5096, f. 418r. Photo J. Niedźwiedź. 190

Fig. 16 A prayer book and a pendant watch of a noblewoman. A fragment of the funeral monument of Dorota Firlejówna (*c.* 1550-1591), wife of chancellor Lew Sapieha. St. Michael's curch of the Bernardine Sisters in Vilnius, *c.* 1633. Photo J. Niedźwiedź. 198

Fig. 17 Letter of Queen Barbara Radziwiłłówna to her mother, Barbara Radziwiłłowa (Vilnius, 1547?). Signature and a postscript of the Queen: "with her own hand, Barbara, the daughter and servant of Your Grace". [Postscript:] "My dear mother, please, send me some ceruse [*bielidło*] because I do have not a speck of it; then please, do not forget me, Your Grace, as your servant and daughter" (original in Polish). MS Warsaw, AGAD, 1/354/0/3/29, p. 67 <https://www.szukajwarchiwach.gov.pl/jednostka/-/jednostka/17873161> (accessed: 29.05.2022; public domain). 200

Fig. 18 Contract of selling a plot of land by a tailor Jan Myszkowski, an inhabitant of the bishop's *jurydyka*, 1543. MS Vilnius, VUB, F4-18345, f. 3r. Reproduced with the permission of VUB. 227

Fig. 19 Seals of the witnesses who confirmed the inventory of the house of Paweł Mydlarz and Mikołaj Mydlarz, 1621. MS Vilnius, LVIA, F22, ap. 1, nr 5344, f. 605v. Photo J. Niedźwiedź. 228

Fig. 20 Signature of Tomasz Rządziewicz in place of the signature of his semi-illiterate father: "I sign [this testament] in place of my father, Mr. Jędrzej Siemiaszko, who cannot write – Thomas Rządziewicz the merchant and citizen [*mieszczanin*] of Vilnius" (original in Polish). MS Vilnius, LVIA, F23, ap. 1, 5096, f. 212r. Photo J. Niedźwiedź. 230

Fig. 21 Late medieval stylus excavated in the Lower Castle of Vilnius. Vilnius, LDKVR. Photo J. Niedźwiedź. 253

Fig. 22 Orthodox prayer book published in 1638 in the printing house in Vievis (Jewie) for the Vilnian Orthodox Brotherhood. The title, in Polish and Ruthenian, says: *The Psalter of the Blessed Prophet and King David translated from Greek into Slavonic and from Slavonic into Polish* (Vievis, 1638). However, the psalms in the prayer book were taken from the Polish Catholic translation of the Latin Vulgate, i.e. from the second (1575) or third (1577) edition of the so-called Leopolita Bible (Biblia Leopolity): *Biblia to jest księgi Starego i Nowego Zakonu na polski język z pilnością według łacińskiej Biblijej od Kościoła krześcijańskiego powszechnego nowo wyłożona* (Cracow, 1575). The editors of the prayer book were guilty of a dissimulation similar to that of Smotrycki in his *Thrēnos*. Photo M. Nikalaeŭ. 261

Fig. 23 Signatures in Arabic script of the warrant officer (*chorąży*) Mehmet Jakubowicz and Obdulach Jakubowicz under a Ruthenian document written in Montowtyszki (Lithuania) on 29 May 1571. Similar Arabic signatures must have been used by the Tartar inhabitants of Vilnius. MS Vilnius, MAB, F264-27, f. 3r. Reproduced with the permission of MAB. 267

Fig 24 Polish *cancellaresca* script and Ruthenian *skoropis*. Document written by the Vilnius notary Krzysztof Wobolewicz, 1661. MS Vilnius, LVIA, F23, ap. 1, nr 5099, f. 28r. Photo J. Niedźwiedź. 268

Fig. 25 Latin italic and Ruthenian *skoropis.* Testament of Paweł Michajłowicz Sznipka in the Vilniuis municipal registers, 1594. MS Vilnius, LVIA, F22, ap. 1, nr 5333, f. 90v. Photo J. Niedźwiedź. 269

Fig. 26 Gothic *textualis* script and a judge writing a sentence. Fragment of a monumental polychrome, showing the Passion of Christ on the north wall of the Franciscan Observant (Bernardine) church (St. Francis and St. Bernard's church) in Vilnius, *c.* 1530. Photo J. Niedźwiedź. 270

Fig. 27 Gothic script on the *półgrosz* (half-grosch) of King Sigismund I the Old, minted at the Vilnius mint in *c.* 1512: "MONETA SIGISMUNDI IZ". Photo J. Niedźwiedź. 272

Fig. 28 Renaissance script on the *półgrosz* (half-grosch) of King Sigismund II Augustus, minted at the Vilnius mint in 1565: "MONETA MAG[NI] DUCAT[US] LITU[ANIAE]". Photo J. Niedźwiedź. 272

Fig. 29 The confirmation and signature of a Jew, Zelman Jakubowicz, in the Hebrew alphabet below a Polish-language document of lending money from 1648. MS Vilnius, LVIA, F23, ap. 1, nr 5096, f. 379r. Photo J. Niedźwiedź. 277

Fig. 30 A sloppy Polish *cancellaresca* script and Yiddish in Hebrew cursive. Confirmation of paying off a debt, 1634. MS Vilnius, LVIA, F23, ap. 1, nr 5096, f. 81v. Photo J. Niedźwiedź. 278

Fig. 31 Albert of Prussia (Albrecht Hohenzollern), *Księgi o rycerskich rzeczach a sprawach wojennych z pilnością zebrane a porządkiem dobrem spisane*, trans. M. Strubicz (Vilnius, 1561). MS Cracow, CZART., 1813 IV, f. 9r. Photo J. Niedźwiedź. Reproduced with the permission of MNK. 284

Fig. 32 *Agenda, sive exsequiale divinorum sacramentorum*, ed. Martinus canonicus Vilnensis (Gdańsk, 1499). Warsaw, BN, SD Inc.Qu.141 <https://polona.pl/item/agenda-sive-exsequiale-sacramentorum-ed-martinus-canonicus-vilnensis,NDA3OTU0/3/#info:metadata> (accessed: 29.05.2022; public domain). 286

Fig. 33 F. Skaryna, *The Little Travel Book* (Vilnius, *c.* 1522). Wrocław, University Library. <https://www.bibliotekacyfrowa.pl/dlibra/ doccontent? id= 89330> (accessed: 26.05.2022; public domain). 287

Fig. 34 Manuscript copy of the *Apostle* by F. Skaryna (Vilnius, 1525). The manuscript was made in the second half of the sixteenth or at the beginning of the seventeenth century for an unidentified Orthodox monastery of St. Michael the Archangel in the Ruthenian Voivodeship (*województwo ruskie*, part of the Kingdom of Poland). Warsaw (Poland), BN, MS 11907 III, p. 1r. <https://polona.pl/item-view/88c8bfab-9056-47ba-ad6d-9a306b8c8429?page=4> (accessed: 18.07.2022; public domain). 288

Fig. 35 Colophon of the *Chasoslovec* (*Chasovnyk*) printed by Mamonicz (Vilnius, 1572): "This book called *Chasovnyk* was printed with the help of God and with the permission of our Lord His Royal Majesty Sigismund Augustus, by the grace of the Lord King of Poland and Grand Duke of Lithuania, Ruthenia, Prussia, Samogitia, Masovia, Livonia, etc., with the blessing of Archbishop Ioan, by the grace of the Lord Metropolitan of Kyiv, Halych, and all Rus' in the famous city of Vilnius, in the house and with funds of Their Graces Mr Ivan and Mr Zenobii Zaretski" (original in Church Slavonic). Cracow, BJ, Cim. 1878. Public domain. Photo J. Niedźwiedź. 290

Fig. 36 M. Smotrycki, *Threnos* (*ΘΡΕΝΟΣ*), *to jest lament jedynej św. powszechnej apostolskiej wschodniej Cerkwie… pierwej z greckiego na słowieński, a teraz z słowieńskiego na polski przełożony* (Vilnius, 1610), title page. Cracow, BJ, I 40951 <http://neolatina.bj.uj.edu.pl/neolatina/page/show/id/10609.html> (accessed: 26.05.2022; public domain). 292

Fig. 37 The front cover of a book from the collection of King Sigismund Augustus with his supralibros made in Vilnius. Johannes Herold, *Originum ac Germanicarum antiquitatum libri* (…) (Basel, 1557). Warsaw, BN <https:/polona.pl/item-view/a311b15d-a76d-4ca0-a2dc-cf78e672c09f?page=0> (accessed: 15.07.2023; public domain). 302

Fig. 38 The back cover of a book from the collection of King Sigismund Augustus with his supralibros made in Vilnius in 1560: "The monument of King of Poland Sigismund Augustus, 1560 AD". Francisco Alvares, *Historiale description de l'Ethiopie, contenant vraye relation des terres et pais du grand roy et emperor Prete Ian* (Antwerp, 1558). Warsaw, BN <https://polona.pl/item-view/af21318a-426b-48f2-ba6c-20fdc9997de0?page=0> (accessed: 15.07.2023; public domain). 303

Fig. 39 A binding of the book made probably in Vilnius after 1582: P. Skarga, *Artes duodecim sacramentariorum seu Zvingliocalvinistarum* (Vilnius, 1582), Cracow, MNK. Photo J. Niedźwiedź. 305

Fig. 40 Document of selling a garden confirmed by *Voigt* Augustyn Rotundus. MS Vilnius, LVIA, F22, ap. 1, nr 5333, f. 75r. Photo J. Niedźwiedź. 332

Fig. 41 Receipt in Polish, in which Katarzyna Kanecka Wakania renounces any money from a royal secretary and doctor Sebastian Szperkowicz, Vilnius, 12 November 1636. MS Vilnius, LVIA, F23, ap. 1, nr 5096, f. 334. Photo J. Niedźwiedź. 333

Fig. 42 Example of a text of the 'open' city and of spreading news in letters. An English paper informing about anti-Calvinist riots in Vilnius in 1640, based on letters sent from Vilnius by the Radziwiłłs (cf. Chapter 9): Eleazar Gilbert, *Newes from Poland, wherein is declared the cruell practice of the Popish clergie against the Protestants and in particular against the ministers of the city of Vilna* (London, 1641). MS Warsaw, BN <https://polona.pl/preview/437b35b6-e0d9-481a-bbf1-0f95c44abf03> (accessed: 31.05.2023; public domain). 336

Fig. 43 Latin formulary of letters and other documents written mainly in Vilnius in the royal chancery, 1556. MS Vilnius, LVIA, F1135, ap. 2, nr 30, f. 1r. Photo J. Niedźwiedź. 338

Fig. 44 Letter of the rector of the Academy of Vilnius, Jan Grużewski, to Prince Krzysztof II Radziwiłł, Vilnius, 3 September 1619. MS Vilnius, LNMB, F93-1690, f. 1. Reproduced with the permission of the LNMB. 345

Fig. 45 Testament in Polish of Rev. Jan Gawecki, 1655. MS Vilnius, LVIA, F23, ap. 1, nr 5099, f. 8r. Photo J. Niedźwiedź. 350

Fig. 46 The beginning of the testament of Mrs. Anna Czyżowa, 1652, in Polish. Vilnius, LVIA, MS F23, ap. 1, nr 5096, p. 606r. Photo J. Niedźwiedź. 356

Fig. 47 A page from the court register of the Vilnius burgrave (the *horodniczańska* or burgrave *jurydyka*), 1620. Vilnius, LVIA, MS F20, ap. 1, nr 4563, f. 44r. Photo J. Niedźwiedź. 375

Fig. 48 D. Mikołajewski, *The Vilnan Disputation* (Vilnius, 1599). <https://dbc.wroc.pl/dlibra/publication/13385/edition/11901> (accessed: 31.05.2022, public domain). 387

Fig. 49 M. Śmiglecki, *The Vilnan Disputation* (Cracow, 1599). <https://dbc.wroc.pl/dlibra/publication/4958/edition/ 4779> (accessed: 31.05.2022, public domain). 388

Fig. 50 An excerpt from the registers of the Tribunal of the Grand Duchy of Lithuania. A Ruthenian document related to the trial concerning anti-Calvinist riots, Vilnius, 6 June 1611. Vilnius, LNMB, MS F93-1732, p. 1. Reproduced with the permission of the LNMB. 396

Fig. 51 Title page of an anti-Calvinist book in which the Jesuit Piotr Skarga attacked the Calvinist Andrzej Wolan as "the arch-minister of this heretic plague". P. Skarga, *Artes duodecim sacramentariorum seu Zvingliocalvinistarum, quibus oppugnant et totidem arma Catholicorum quibus propugnant praesentiam corporis Domini nostri Iesu*

Christi in Eucharistia contra Andream Volanum, huius hereticae pestis in Lituania archiministrum (Vilnius, 1582). Photo J. Niedźwiedź. 404

Fig. 52 Andrzej Wolan's response to the Catholic attacks: *Apologia Andree Volani* (Vilnius, 1587). Wrocław, OSSOL. XVI.Qu.2214 <https://www.dbc.wroc.pl/dlibra/doccontent?id= 4172> (accessed: 31.05.2022, public domain). 405

Fig. 53 Example of an epideictic print from the end of the sixteenth century. A Polish epithalamy written on the wedding of Piotr Kroszyński and Anna Sokolińska. The author was a certain Krzysztof Kiernowiski, a student of the Academy of Vilnius and client of the newly-weds. Dozens of similar books were printed in Vilnius at the time. K. Kiernowiski, *Epithalamium na wesele wielmożnego książęcia jego mości pana pana Piotra Kroszyńskiego, dzierżawcy poniewieskiego, szadowskiego etc. i jej mości księżnej paniej paniej Anny Sokolińskiej, dobrodziejom swym miłościwym* (Vilnius, 1595). BJ <https://jbc.bj.uj.edu.pl/dlibra/publication/709734/edition/671874> (accessed: 31.05.2022, public domain). 435

Fig. 54 Latin commemorative inscription on the outer wall of the chapel of St. Casimir in Vilnius cathedral, 1636. Photo J. Niedźwiedź. 439

Fig. 55 Latin cenotaph of bishop Benedykt Woyna in Vilnius cathedral, 1615. Photo J. Niedźwiedź. 444

Fig. 56 The monument of Barbara Tyszkiewiczowa (née Naruszewicz) in her mausoleum in the Holy Trinity Uniate church in Vilnius, *c.* 1627. The project by the royal architect Matteo Castello. Photo J. Niedźwiedź. 454

Fig. 57 Tombstone of the mayor of Vilnius, Atanazy Braga, and his son Antoni Braga, after 1580 (?), Holy Trinity Uniate Church in Vilnius. Photo J. Niedźwiedź. 455

Fig. 58 Muslin cover made by Helena Wiekowicz, wife of Dawid Blinstrub, 1647. *Album zabytków ewangelickich w Wilnie wydany przez Towarzystwo Miłośników Reformacji Polskiej im Jana Łaskiego* (Vilnius, 1929), picture XXII. 466

Fig. 59 Silver coin minted after the recapturing of Polatsk and Livonia by King Stefan Bátory in 1579: "Livonia and Polatsk recuperated". Probably such coins were disseminated among the viewers of the triumphal entrance to Vilnius and other cities in Lithuania and Poland. Cracow, MNK. Photo J. Niedźwiedź. 469

Fig. 60 Panegyric for Marcin Śmiglecki, written by his students in 1594. *Gratulationes in promotione doctissimi et eruditissimi R.D. Martini Smiglecii Societatis Iesu artium et philosophiae magistri a studiosis Philosophiae amoris ergo et officii in amantissimum Praeceptorem conscriptae* (Vilnius, 1594). Uppsala, CR, Carmina Latina et Graeca gratulat. IV. Script. lat. rec., nr 2; 59:42. Public domain. 475

Fig. 61 Polish and foreign officials during the ceremony of the entry of Queen Constance of Austria into Cracow on 4 December 1605. In the front, Bartłomiej Nowodworski in a coat with the Maltese Cross. Probably he was dressed in a similar way at the entry into Vilnius, six years later. A fragment of the *Stockholm Scroll*, 1605. Warsaw, The Royal Castle Museum. <https://www.zamek-krolewski.pl/strona/wizyta-archiwum-wystaw-czasowych/894-krol-sie-zeni-rolka-sztokholmska-skarb-zamku> (accessed: 31.05.2022; public domain). 499

Fig. 62 Royal standard-bearer (*chorąży*) Sebastian Sobieski during the ceremony of the entry of Queen Constance of Austria into Cracow on 4 December 1605. A fragment of the *Stockholm Scroll*, 1605. Warsaw, The Royal Castle Museum. <https://www.zamek-krolewski.pl/strona/wizyta-archiwum-wystaw-czasowych/894-krol-sie-zeni-rolka-sztokholmska-skarb-zamku> (accessed: 31.05.2022; public domain). 500

Fig. 63 Latin epos commemorating the canonisation of St. Casimir in 1604. Jan Krajkowski, *Epos de S. Casimioro Iagellonide Poloniae ac Lituaniae principe et patrono* (Vilnius, 1604), f. A3r. Warsaw, BN. <https://polona.pl/preview/493caa51-8467-4446-b353-700f1ac4508> (accessed: 06.06.2023; public domain). 505

Fig. 64 Marginal note of a reader of the Protestant New Testament (a fragment of the Radziwiłł Bible) published in Vilnius in 1580 by Jan Karcan. Warsaw, BN, 996 I Cim <https://polona.pl/preview/db0a90aa-33db-4abb-ba6e-90a7d62776e2> (accessed: 26.06.2023; public domain). 534

Fig. 65 *Prayer for The Town* in a prayer book belonging to the Lithuanian chancellor Olbracht Gasztołd, *The Shield of the Soul* (*Szczyt duszny* or *Clypeus spiritualis*), p. 82. Munich, Universitätsbibliothek der Ludwig-Maximilians-Universität, Cim. 89, <https://epub.ub.uni-muenchen.de/11772/> (accessed: 26.06.2023, public domain). 546

Fig. 66 F. Skaryna, *The Little Travel Book* (Vilnius, *c.* 1522). On the inferior margin of the left page the colophon of the printer; on the right, the start of the Canon of the Virgin Mary. Cracow, BJ, Cim 561. Public domain. Photo J. Niedźwiedź. 548

Fig. 67 The title page of the emblemata collection of H. Bildziukiewicz, *Divi Tutelaris Patrii Casimiri insigne virtutum hieroglyphicis emblematum figuris adumbratum. Poloniarum Reginae Constantiae … deusta observantia humiliter oblata* (Vilnius, 1610). CZART. (MNK) 28066 II <https://cyfrowe.mnk.pl/dlibra/publication/9670/edition/9494/content> (accessed: 26.06.2023, public domain). 552

Fig. 68 Orthodox prayer book in Polish and Church Slavonic: *Wykład liturgiej świętej i modlitwy z doktorów świętych według Świętej Wschodniej i Apostolskiej Cerkwie zebrane i na wielu miejscach z pilnością poprawione* (Vilnius, 1624). CR. Public domain. 556

Fig. 69 J. Kochanowski, Hymn *What Do You Want from Us, Lord, for Your Generous Gifts* (*Czego chcesz od nas, Panie*) in the Polish Calvinist *Katechizm* (Vilnius, 1594). Uppsala (Sweden), CR. Public domain. 558

Fig. 70 *Agenda, sive exsequiale divinorum sacramentorum*, ed. Martinus canonicus Vilnensis (Gdańsk, 1499), Warsaw, BN, SD Inc. Qu. 141 <https://polona.pl/item-view/2f9e6052-f97f-43a5-be72-0be52a0516ee?page=3> (accessed: 15.07.2023; public domain). 563

Fig. 71 Rite of baptism in three languages (Polish, Lithuanian, and German) in the Catholic *Agenda parva in commodiorem usum sacerdotum Provinciae Polonae conscripta* (Vilnius, 1630), p. 21. <https:// www.europeana.eu/pl/item/776/_nnsf8fk> (accessed: 15.07. 2023; public domain). 565

Fig. 72 The Catholic catechism in Church-Slavonic: *Кітехизм или наоука всемъ православнымъ хрстїяномъ* … (Vilnius, 1585). Uppsala, CR, Litt. Slav. Kyrkslav. 157 (4). <https://www.alvin-portal.org/alvin/view .jsf?dswid=7054&searchType=EXTENDED&query=Litt.Slav.Kyrkslav.+157.4&aq=%5B%5B%7B%7B%22A_FQ%22%3A%22Litt.Slav.KKyrkslav.+157.4%22%3A%22Litt.Slav.Kyrkslav.+157.4%22%7D%5D%&aqe=%5b%5D&af=%5B%5D&pid=alvin-record%3A413166&c=8#alvin-record%3A413166> (accessed: 15.07. 2023; public domain). 572

Fig. 73 Latvian translation of the *Catechism* of Petrus Canisius, *Catechismus catholicorum* (Vilnius, 1585). Uppsala, CR, Utl. Rar. 174 <https://www.alvin-portal.org/alvin/view.jsf?dswid=348&searchType=EXTENDED&query=catechismus+catholicorum&aq=%5b%5b%7B%22A_FQ%22%3A%22catechismus+catholicorum%22%7D%5D&aqe=%5B55D&af=%5B%5D&pid=alvin-record%3A146019&c=2#alvin-record%3A146019> (accessed: 15.07. 2023; public domain). 574

Fig. 74 Title page of a Polish Calvinist catechism by Krzysztof Kraiński, published in Vilnius in 1605 (K. Kraiński, *Dziennik, to jest modlitwy o krześcijańskie potrzeby należące ludziom powszechnej wiary apostolskiej na każdy dzień* (Vilnius, 1605)). Warsaw, BUW, <https://polona.pl/item/dziennik-to-iest-modlitwy-o-krzescianskie-potrzeby-nalezace-ludziom-powszechney-wiary,MTE4MTUxMTA/3/#info:metadata> (accessed: 21.05.2022; public domain). 578

Fig. 75 Konrad Götke, *Andreas Schonflissius Thorunensis Borussus aetatis suae 62 anno Domini 1652* [*Andrzej Schönflissius, A Prussian from Thorn Aged 62 in 1652*], a copperplate (Vilnius, 1652), in: A. Schönflissius, *Postylli chrześcijańskiej z Biblijej świętej i z doktorów kościelnych według starożytnej nauki i zwyczajnego porządku Kościoła Bożego zebranej na niedziele doroczne część pierwsza. Od Adwentu aż do Trójcy Świętej* ([Vilnius?], 1652). Reproduced with the permission of the Museum of Protestantism in Cieszyn. Photo Marcin Gabryś. 585

Fig. 76 Signature of Jan Kolenda, notary of Vilnius castle court, 11 July 1611. Vilnius, LNMB, MS F93-1734, p. 2. Photo J. Niedźwiedź. 608

Chronological Table

Year	Events in and outside the country	Events in Vilnius
second half of the thirteenth century		Foundation of the castle and the borough (The Castle Mountain and lands along the river Neris)
25 January and 26 May 1323		Duke Gediminas' letters to the Hanseatic cities written in Vilnius
2 October 1323	A peace treaty with the Livonian Brothers of the Sword signed in Vilnius	
Mid-fourteenth century		The development of urban settlements around the castle, on the Hill of Three Crosses as well as of the Ruthenian Town (Miasto Ruskie) and the German/Polish Town (Miasto Niemieckie/Lackie – Polish Town); the construction of the Orthodox church of the Theotokos
second half of the fourteenth century		The completion of the Catholic St. Nicolas' church
1365		The burning of the settlements surrounding the castle
1365		The first starosta (governor) of Vilnius established by Grand Duke Algirdas
1377		Most of the town burnt down by the Teutonic Knights
1383		Part of the town burnt down by the Teutonic Knights

Year	Events in and outside the country	Events in Vilnius
14 August 1385	Union in Kreva between the Kingdom of Poland and the Grand Duchy of Lithuania	
17 February 1387		The foundation of the Vilnius bishopric. The beginning of the construction of the cathedral church. The beginning of the organisation of the episcopal chancery and of the cathedral school.
22 March 1307		The city is granted the Magdeburg law by King Jogaila (Władysław II)
1387		King Jogaila granted lands to St. John's parish church; the construction of the Franciscan monastery
1390	A major invasion the Teutonic Knights	The burning of a settlement by the river Neris as well as of the castle and of the settlement on the Hill of Three Crosses; the town centre is moved towards today's Town Hall Square
1392	A Teutonic invasion	
1394	A Teutonic invasion	A siege of Vilnius by the Teutonic Knights
1399		A huge fire in Vilnius; the rebuilding and unification of the German and Ruthenian parts of the town
1402	A Teutonic invasion	A siege of Vilnius by the Teutonic Knights
1413		A description of Vilnius by Gilbert de Lannoy on his way back from Veliky Novgorod
1415		The Theotokos Orthodox church is elevated to the rank of the cathedral (*sobor*)
23 September 1432		The confirmation of the former privileges granted to the city by Duke Sigismund Kęstutaitis

YEAR	EVENTS IN AND OUTSIDE THE COUNTRY	EVENTS IN VILNIUS
1441		The renewal of the Magdeburg law by King Casimir IV Jagiellon
1447/1448, 1451, 1452, 1457, 1461, 1475		Assemblies of the Lithuanian nobility in Vilnius
1480?		The arrival of the Bernardine friars to Vilnius
1492-1506	The ruling of Alexander I Jagiellon	Vilnius becomes one of the main residences of the ruler; the city was surrounded by the defence walls (completed in 1522); the foundation of the mint office
1492		The confirmation of privileges by Duke Alexander I Jagiellon
1501		Foundation of the Dominican convent in Vilnius by King Alexander I Jagiellon
1506-1548	The rule of Sigismund I the Old	The development of the city; the foundation of the waterworks, glass works and of a foundry
1509/1510		A church council convened by the Orthodox Kyiv Metropolitan Bishop Joseph II Sołtan
1514		A session of the Polish-Lithuanian Parliament (*Sejm*) in Vilnius
1522		Francysk Skaryna opens a printing house
1524		A paper-mill is founded
1524-1530	A dispute between the Polish and Lithuanian Bernardine friars	The appointment of the Lithuanian province of Bernardine friars in 1530 with its capital city in Vilnius
1528/1529	A session of the Polish-Lithuanian Parliament (*Sejm*) in Vilnius	
1529	The coronation of Sigismund II Augustus as the Grand Duke of Lithuania	
1529	The first Lithuanian Statute	

Year	Events in and outside the country	Events in Vilnius
9 September 1536		A new privilege for the city granted by King Sigismund I; confirmation of the principle of the confessional parity between the Catholics and the Orthodox in the municipal authorities
1536		The completion of the Stone Bridge (*Kamienny Most*)
1534–1541		Vilnius Cathedral rebuilt in the Renaissance style after a fire
1541–1542		The foundation of the humanist Protestant school by Abraomas Kulvietis
1542		Anton Wied draws a map of Muscovy in Vilnius
1547		The foundation of the Catholic hospital
6 October 1544	Sigismund II Augustus seizes power over Lithuania; Vilnius Castle becomes the main residence of the ruler	
1547	A Sejm in Vilnius	
1547	Sigismund II Augustus marries Barbara Radziwiłłówna	
1551		The city council issues the first document in Polish
1554	A session of the Polish-Lithuanian Parliament (*Sejm*) in Vilnius	
1555	The spread of the Reformation	Foundation of the first Protestant church in Vilnius
1559-1563	Sigismund II Augustus' stay in Vilnius	Vilnius Castle rebuilt in the Renaissance style
April 1544 -1565		The establishment of Sigismund II Augustus' library in Vilnius, the librarians ("the senior management of the library"): S. Koszutski and Ł. Górnicki
1561	A session of the Polish-Lithuanian Parliament (*Sejm*) in Vilnius	
1562	The introduction of postal service between Vilnius–Cracow–Vienna–Venice	
4 October 1562	Catherine Jagiellon marries John Vasa, the Duke of Finland and the brother of King Eric XIV of Sweden, in Vilnius	
1563	A session of the Polish-Lithuanian Parliament (*Sejm*) in Vilnius	

YEAR	EVENTS IN AND OUTSIDE THE COUNTRY	EVENTS IN VILNIUS
1562-1582		A. Rotundus becomes the *Voigt* (*wójt*) of Vilnius
1565	A Sejm in Vilnius	
1565	The death of Voivode Mikolaj Radziwiłł 'the Black'; the income from the sales of the Brest Bible allocated to the foundation of a Calvinist school in Vilnius	
1566	The publication of the second Lithuanian Statute	
1568		The first mentions of the Jewish community
1569	The Union of Lublin	
1570		The foundation of the Jesuit collegium
1571-1572		Famine and plague in Vilnius
7 July 1572	The death of King Sigismund II Augustus	
28 January 1573	The Warsaw Confederation	
1573		The construction of a wooden synagogue
1574		The beginning of the controversy between Piotr Skarga and Andrzej Wolan
1574-1595		The installation of several printing houses, by the Mamonicz and Karcan families, by the academic, Protestant and Orthodox communities. Vilnius becomes the centre of Lithuanian printing
1579		King Stephen Báthory's ceremonial entry into the city
1579		The foundation of the Academy of Vilnius by Stephen Báthory (on the basis of the papal bulle of Gregory XII, from 29 October 1579).
1579-1582	The Livonian War between the Polish-Lithuanian Commonwealth and Muscovy	Vilnius – one of the command centres during the war with Moscovy
1579-1584		Piotr Skarga becomes the chancellor of the Academy of Vilnius

YEAR	EVENTS IN AND OUTSIDE THE COUNTRY	EVENTS IN VILNIUS
1582	The end of the war with Muscovy	King Stephen Báthory's ceremonial (triumphal) entry into the city
14 April 1585		The Lutheran-Calvinist dispute on the Eucharist
1585		The publication of the first book in Latvian
1588	The third Lithuanian Statute	
1589		King Sigismund III Vasa's ceremonial entry into Vilnius
1588		The foundation of the Orthodox Brotherhood
1591-1593		Annual convocations (general assemblies of noble Lithuanian legates and senators)
7 May 1592		The Anti-Jewish tumult, devastation of the synagogue
3 June 1592		Sigismund III Vasa's first privilege for the Jews of Vilnius
24 and 25 January 1594	A dispute between M. Śmiglecki and J. Licyniusz in Navahrudak	
1594-1607	The ordering and copying of the Lithuanian *Metrica*	
1595 and 1599		The publication of Mikołaj Dauksza's (Daukša) Lithuanian translations of the *Catechism* by Canisius and *Postil* by Wujek
1596	The Union of Brest between the Orthodox and Catholics. The beginning of the Uniate Church	
2 June 1599		A dispute between Marcin Śmiglecki and Daniel Mikołajewski
1599	A Protestant–Orthodox congress; an agreement on cooperation	
January 1602	Muscovite legation to Sigismund III Vasa and negotiations in Vilnius	
1604		The installation of M.K. Radziwiłł 'the Orphan' as the Voivode of Vilnius
10 April 1604		The festive canonisation of St. Casimir
1605		Convocation (a general assembly of noble Lithuanian legates and senators)

Year	Events in and outside the country	Events in Vilnius
January 1609		The seizure of the Orthodox churches by the Uniates supported by the soldiers of Mikołaj Krzysztof Radziwiłł 'the Orphan'; the citizens' anti-Uniate demonstrations
12 August 1609		An unsuccessful assassination attempt of the Uniate Metropolitan bishop Hypatius Pociej
1609	The beginning of a war between the Polish-Lithuanian Commonwealth and Muscovy	The triumphal entry of the hetman Jan Karol Chodkiewicz, returning from the war campaign in Livonia
2 July 1610		The destruction of the major part of the city and of the castle by the huge fire
1610		The publication of *Thrēnos* by Meletius Smotrycki; the closure of the Orthodox Brotherhood's printing house
30 June 1611		The execution of an Italian, Franco de Franco, for the profanation of the Communion bread during the feast of Corpus Christi
3 July 1611		The anti-Calvinist riots; the burning of the Calvinist church, as well as of the houses of teachers and ministers, one of them is killed; the convictions of the perpetrators suspended by the King, debates of the Royal investigative committee
24 July 1611		King Sigismund III Vasa's triumphal entry after the capture of Smolensk
1611-1613		The construction of new Jesuit schools
1613-1615 and 1617		Convocations (general assemblies of noble Lithuanian legates and senators)

Year	Events in and outside the country	Events in Vilnius
3 April 1621		The mass arrest of town dwellers and municipal officials supporting the Orthodox church
1623		Anti-Protestant riots
1624		Convocation (a general assembly of noble Lithuanian legates and senators)
1630		A fire and plague in the city
14 October 1631		The enthronement of Bishop Abraham Woyna
1632	The death of Sigismund III Vasa The election of Władysław IV Vasa	15-16 May. A convocation (a general assembly of noble Lithuanian legates and senators)
15 February 1633		Władysław IV Vasa's privilege for the Vilnian Jews; permission for the building of the Great Synagogue
1633		A privilege allowing the organisation of two fortnight-long fairs, starting at the Day of The Assumption of Virgin Mary and at the Epiphany
1633	An act of homage of the Duke of Courland Wilhelm Kettler	
1634		A convocation (a general assembly of Lithuanian noblemen)
1634	Victory at Smolensk	Władysław IV Vasa's ceremonial entry into the city
3 March 1634		An anti-Jewish riots, destroying the Jewish cemetery
14 August 1636		The ceremonial transfer of the relics of St. Casimir to side-chapel in the Cathedral founded by the Vasa family
17 February 1639	An act of homage of the Duke of Courland Jacob Kettler before Władysław IV Vasa	
October 1639		Anti-Calvinist riots
1640	A Sejm court verdict: liquidation of a Calvinist church at St. Michael Street (Zaułek Świętomichalski) and its relocation outside the city walls	

Year	Events in and outside the country	Events in Vilnius
1642		The reconstruction of the synagogue (Jews transporting bricks via the Stone Bridge exempted from the bridge toll)
600541	The death of Queen Cecilia Renata in the Vilnius castle	
1648	The Khmelnytsky Uprising	King Władysław IV Vasa's visit; the decision on the building of new fortifications
May 1650		The enthronement of Bishop Jerzy Tyszkiewicz
1652		The inclusion of a representative of the Vilnius Jews in the *Vaad* (the Lithuanian Jews' parliament)
1653		A plague and evacuation of the city
16 May 1653		The enthronement of the Voivode of Vilnius Prince Janusz Radziwiłł
1654	The beginning of the war between Muscovy and the Polish-Lithuanian Commonwealth	
Summer 1655	Swedes' and Muscovites' invasion in Lithuania ("the Deluge")	The exodus of the inhabitants of the city; the capture of Vilnius by the Muscovite army on 8 August; the destruction of the city; the beginning of the six-year long occupation.

List of the Grand Dukes of Lithuania and the Kings of Poland Who Controlled Vilnius in 1323-1655

Rulers	Years of rule	
	The Grand Duchy of Lithuania	The Kingdom of Poland
Gediminas (*c.* 1275-1341)	1316-1341	
Jaunutis (*c.* 1308 - after 1366)	1341-1344	
Algirdas (*c.* 1296/1304-1377)	1345-1377	
Jogaila (Władysław Jagiełło, *c.* 1362 or *c.* 1352-1434)	1377-1381 and 1382-1434	1386-1434
Kęstutis (*c.* 1308/1310-1382)	1381-1382	
Vytautas (*c.* 1354/1355-1430)	1401-1430 (governor of Lithuania since 1392)	
Žygimantas Kęstutaitis (*c.* 1365-1440)	1430-1440	
Casimir IV Jagiellon (1427-1492)		
Alexander I Jagiellon (1461-1506)	1492-1506	1501-1506
Sigismund I the Old Jagiellon (1467-1548)	1506-1548	
Sigismund II Augustus (1520-1572)	1529-1572	1530-1572
Henry of Valois (1551-1589)	1573-1575	
Anna Jagiellon (1523-1596)	1575-1587	
Stephen Báthory (1533-1586)	1576-1586	
Sigismund III Vasa (1566-1632)	1587-1632	
Władysław IV Vasa (1595-1648)	1632-1648	
John II Casimir Vasa (1609-1672)	1648-1668	

Map 1. The Polish-Lithuanian Commonwealth ca. 1640

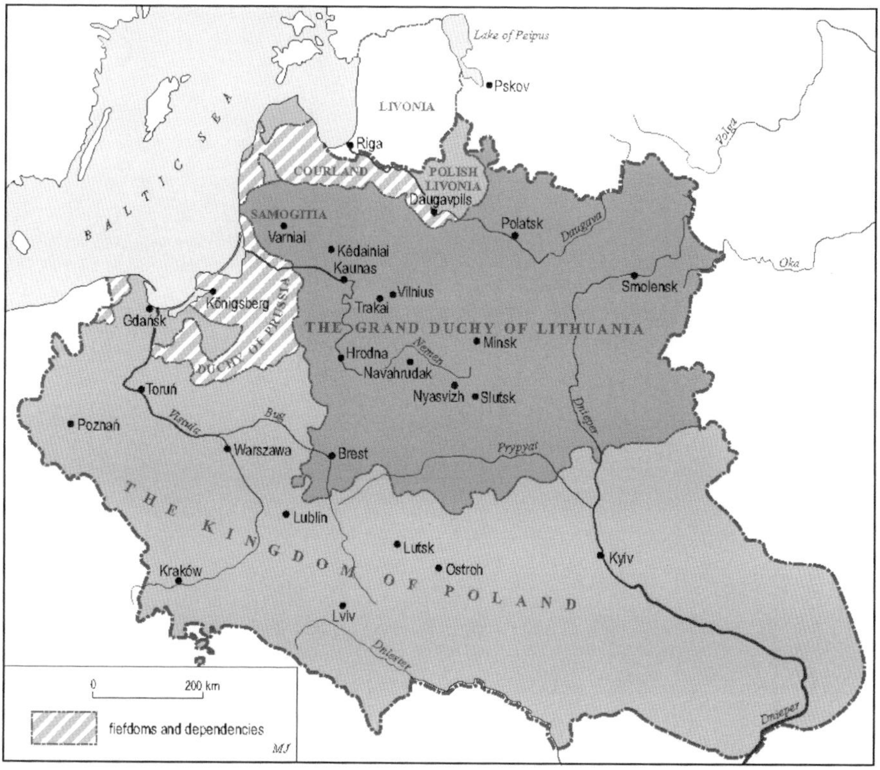

Map 2. Vilnius in the first half of the 17th century

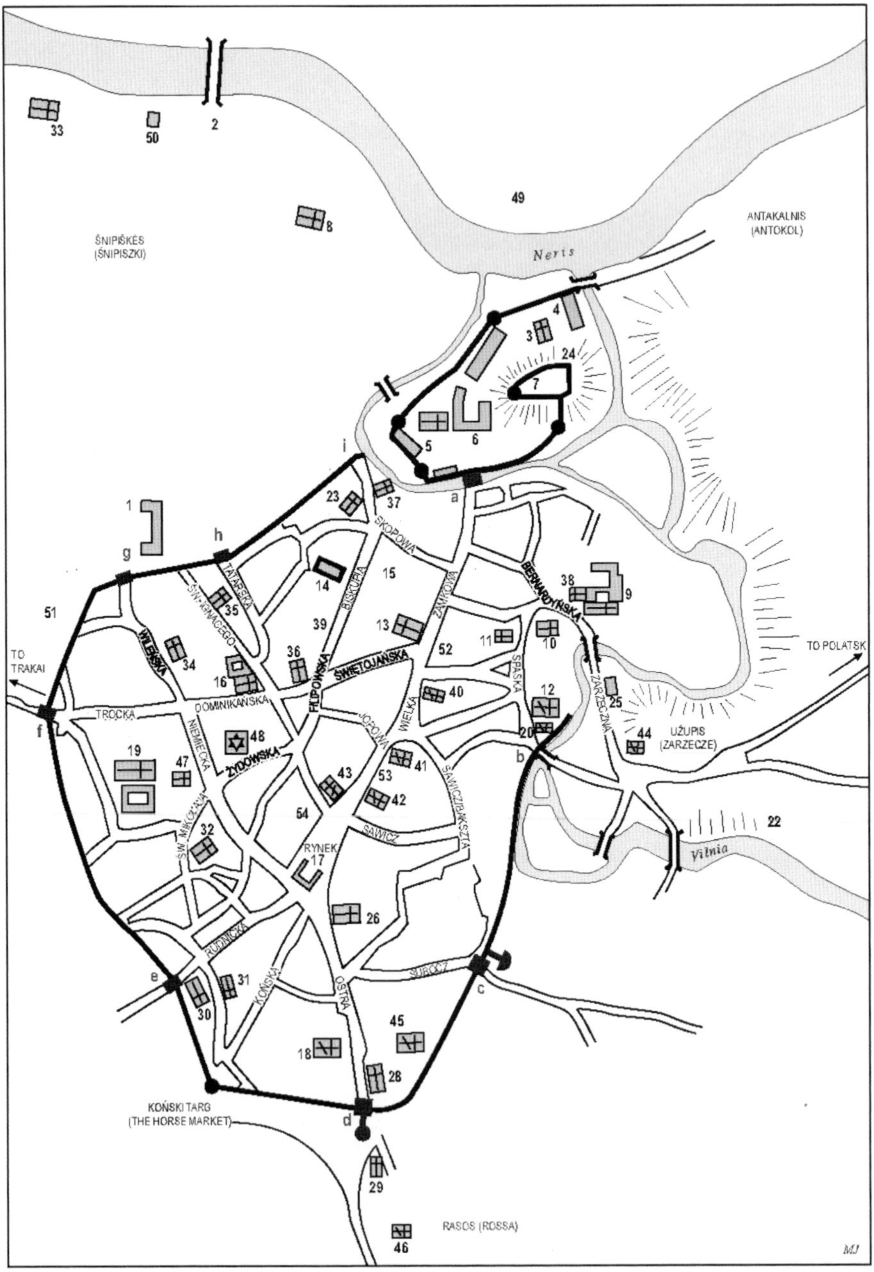

Numbers 1–24 correspond to the view of Vilnius by Tomasz Makowski from 1604 (cf. Fig. 1 at p. 8).

Makowski's View:

1. Palace of the Radziwiłł princes of the Biržiai (*Birże*) branch (Calvinist)
2. Stone Bridge over the Neris River
3. St. Barbara church in the lower castle (Catholic)
4. Armoury (Cekhauz) in the lower castle
5. Cathedral of St. Stanislas in the lower castle (Catholic)
6. Royal palace in the lower castle
7. Upper castle
8. St. George church (Catholic)
9. St. Francis and Bernardine church and the Observant Franciscan (Bernardine) convent (Catholic)
10. St. Michael Archangel church and the nunnery of the Bernardine Sisters (Catholic)
11. Calvinist church and school
12. Cathedral of the Holy Virgin (Orthodox, later Uniate)
13. Sts. John the Baptist and John the Evangelist parish church (Catholic)
14. Bishop's Manor
15. Jesuit Academy of Vilnius
16. Holy Spirit church and the Dominican convent (Catholic)
17. Town hall and the Market Square
18. Trinity church (Orthodox, later Uniate) and the Basilian monastery
19. Assumption of Mary church and the Franciscan convent (Catholic)
20. Saviour church (Orthodox, later Uniate)
21. -
22. Mausoleum of Kasper Bekiesz (Gáspár Békés de Kornyát, *c.* 1520–1579)
23. Holy Cross church and the hospital of the Brothers Hospitallers of Saint John of God (*Bonifratrzy*) (Catholic)
24. St. Nicolas church in the upper castle (Catholic)

Other Catholic Churches and Institutions:

25. Franciscan observant (Bernardine) nunnery on Užupis (*Zarzecze*)
26. Casimir church and the Jesuit residence
28. St. Therese church and the convent of the Discalced Carmelites
29. Sts. Josef and Nicodemus church
30. All Saints church and the Carmelite convent
31. St. Joseph church and the nunnery of the Discalced Carmelites
32. St. Nicolas church
33. Sts. James and Philip church and the residence of the Jesuits
34. St. Catherine of Alexandria and the nunnery of the Benedictine nuns
35. St. Ignatius church and the residence of the Jesuits
36. Trinity church
37. St. Mary Magdalene church
38. St. Anne church
39. Papal seminary

Other Orthodox and Uniate Churches and Monasteries:

40. St. John the Baptist church
41. St. Paraskeva church
42. St. Nicolas church
43. Resurrection church
44. St. Peter church
45. Holy Spirit church and Orthodox Brotherhood monastery and school
46. St. George church

Other Religious Buildings and Places:

47. Lutheran church and school
48. Synagogue and the Jewish school
49. Jewish cemetery
50. Mosque and the Tartar school
51. Calvinist cemetery and a new Calvinist church (after 1640)

Other Places:

52. Palace of the Radziwiiłs of the Nyasvizh (*Nieśwież*) branch (Catholic)
53. Palace of the Chodkiewiczs
54. Mamoniczs printing house

The Municipal Fortifications:

a) Castle Gate (Pol. *Zamkowa*)
b) Saviour (*Spaska*) Gate
c) Subocz Gate and the bastion of King Władysław IV
d) Gate of Dawn (Pol. *Ostra Brama*, Lit. *Aušros Vartai*)
e) Rudninkai Gate (Pol. *Rudnicka*)
f) Trakai Gate (Pol. *Trocka*)
g) Neris Gate (Pol. *Wileńska*)
h) Tartar Gate
i) Mary Magdalene Gate

Transcriptions, Translations, and Spellings

Transcriptions of the Polish-language historic sources are based on rules proposed in *Zasady wydawania tekstów staropolskich. Projekt* [The Rules of Editing Old-Polish Texts], ed. K. Górski and J. Woronczak (Wrocław, 1955).

Translations of the Bible after the King James Version <https://www.kingjamesbibleonline.org/ (access 31.05.2022)>.

The main vernacular language of early modern Vilnius was Polish. As the result, the Polish words, names and terms often appear in this book. Since the Polish phonetic and orthography significantly differs from the English, I put below some simplified rules of spelling Polish words.

ą	*/on/*	like **con**tinued; e.g. kąt /kont/ – angle.
c	*/ts/*	like **tz**ar; e.g. ulica */ulitsa/* – street.
ć	/ts'/	like tset**se** fly; e.g. pracować */pratsovats'/* – to work.
ch	*/h/*	like **h**ome, e.g. chować /howatsh'/ – to hide.
cz	*/tsh/*	like bu**tch**er; e.g. czarny */tsharny/* – black.
dż	*/j/*	like **J**ames; e.g. dżdżysty */jjisti/* – rainy.
e	*/e:/*	like **el**ectricity; e.g. elementarz */e:le:me:ntash/* – primer.
ę	*/en/*	like **ten**dency; e.g. wędka /ventka/ – fishing rod.
ł	/w/	like **w**oman; e.g. łowić */wovits'/* – to fish.
ń	*/n'/*	like **n**ickname; e.g. wileński */vilen'sky/* – of Vilnius.
ó	/oo/	like pr**oo**f; e.g. wół */voow/* – ox; *ó* souds the same as *u*.
rz	*/sh /*	like me**s**ure; e.g. rzeka */sheka/* – river; *rz* sounds the same as *ż*.
sz	*/sh/*	like **sh**adow; e.g. mysz */mish/* – mouse.
ś	*/sh'/*	like **s**ure; e.g. śnieg */sh'niek/* – snow.
u	*/oo/*	like pr**oo**f; e.g. kura */koora:/* – hen; *u* sounds the same as *ó*.
w	*/v/*	like Vilnius; e.g. Wilno */vilno/* – Vilnius.
ż	*/sh/*	like mea**s**ure; e.g. chorąży */horonshy/* – a standard bearer; *ż* sounds the same as *rz*.
ź	*/sh'/*	like mea**s**ure, e.g. źródło */sh'roodwo/* – a source.

Introduction

This story begins with the Wolf. Once upon a time Duke Gediminas and his companions hunted the aurochs. After the hunt, it grew dark and the hunters decided to spend the night in the Šventaragis Valley by the Neris River. The duke fell into a deep sleep and had a strange dream. He dreamt about a huge iron wolf which stood on the high hill and howled loudly. When the duke woke up, he asked his dream-interpreter Lizdeika what was the meaning of the dream. Lizdeika explained, that the wolf meant the new capital city which was to be built on this spot, and that the howling signified the fame of the deeds of its future inhabitants. Shortly afterwards Gediminas began the construction of the castle and city of Vilnius.

This story, which is known to every Lithuanian and to many Poles and Belarusians, was first written down in the 1520s and 1530s in *The Chronicle of the Grand Duchy of Lithuania*,[1] almost two hundred years after Duke Gedminas' death. We have no possibility to check if this account is true.[2] Still, it might be trustworthy. Why?

[1] The Ruthenian chronicle (*letopis*) was the third version of the official history of the Grand Duchy of Lithuania. Its predecessors were two historiographical works: the *Letopis of the Dukes of Lithuania* written in Smolensk in the 1420s and the *Belarusian-Lithuanian Letopis of 1446*. The *Chronicle of the Grand Duchy of Lithuania* from the 1520s is known from seven sixteenth-century copies. The legend is copied in five of them. See *Летапісы і хронікі Беларусі. Средневечча і раньемодэрны час* (Smolensk, 2013), pp. 213, 244, 272, 293-294, 334-335; В. ВАРОНІН, "Прадмова", in: *Летапісы і хронікі Беларусі*, p. 4.

[2] Until today there is a saying in Polish 'a fairy tale about the Iron Wolf' (*bajka o żelaznym wilku*), used when somebody dismisses some story as incredible. The saying was noted in dictionaries in the mid-eighteenthth century, but with a slightly different meaning. See "*Jakoby mi o żelaznym wilku bajał. – Er redet mir von böhmischen Dörfern vor. – C'est du Grec (du Breton) pour moi*" (M.A. TROTZ, *Nowy dykcyjonarz, to jest mownik polsko-niemiecko-francuski – Nouveau dictionnaire polonois, allemand et françois (...)*, 3 (Leipzig, 1764), col. 2561.

The *Chronicle* was written at the demand of the Vilnius political elites of the time and expressed their political aspirations.[3] The prophecy in the story about the Iron Wolf tells a truth, but rather about the way of thinking of the Lithuanian elites at the beginning of the sixteenth century than about the circumstances of the foundation of the city. The author of the *Chronicle* almost certainly knew the *Aeneid* and the legend about the beginnings of Rome.[4] Thus, he made the Iron Wolf into a Lithuanian equivalent of the Capitoline Wolf. The legend provided him with a suitable occasion to start the official written narration about the past of Vilnius, linking as it did a local history-to-be with universal history. In Lithuania, in the 1520s there must have been a high demand for such narratives. Since the 1490s, Vilnius had been growing into an important economic, political, juridical, and religious centre in the east of Europe, and by the 1520s the city had become the real capital of the Grand Duchy of Lithuania, one of the Eastern European empires ruled by the Jagiellonian dynasty (cf. Map 1 and 2).

Creating local history, however, is only one aspect of the interpretation of the legend about the Iron Wolf. Other interpretations seem to be no less important from the point of view of the topic of this book. Let me mention some of them.

1. The legend was a literary text with all that implies. The legend of the Iron Wolf is not only yet another realisation of a mythopoeic pattern and a narration about the *translatio imperii* or *translatio studiorum*. It was also a written narrative, composed in according with the rules of rhetoric of the genre, and it was transmitted in a form of book. In the historical circumstances of the sixteenth century, it could form part of collective memory only as a written text. It grew in popularity because of the many versions of the story, firstly in a manuscript form, later also in print. In other words, if the story was to be an effective narrative, it had to be written down. Without the text – a written object, its rhetorical organisation and interpretations – the story would not

[3] Probably it was Lithuanian chancellor Olbracht Gasztołd who may have decided about writing a new version of the chronicle.

[4] In the same chronicle the writer put a legend about the ancient origins of Lithuanians. From the second half of the fifteenth century it was believed that the Lithuanians were descendants of Roman refugees who in Antiquity had navigated the Baltic Sea and had settled on the Lithuanian shore. The legend became extremely popular in the sixteenth century. See M. ZACHARA-WAWRZYŃCZYK, "Geneza legendy o rzymskim pochodzeniu Litwinów", *Zeszyty Historyczne Uniwersytetu Warszawskiego* 3 (1963), pp. 5-35 and E. KULICKA, "Legenda o rzymskim pochodzeniu Litwinów i jej stosunek do mitu sarmackiego", *Przegląd Historyczny* 71.1 (1980), pp. 1-21.

have power, and the capital would not have its history and destiny. Because it was written down, the story remained an active part of the cultural memory of Lithuanians until the present day. The Iron Wolf is still the symbol of Vilnius and constitutes the core of the identity of the city. In 1996, in the very centre of Vilnius, on the Cathedral Square, a monument to Gediminas and the Iron Wolf was erected.
2. It was a response to the political aspiration of the Lithuanian ruling class.
3. It constituted the identity of the capital of the Grand Duchy of Lithuania.
4. It was closely related to those texts whose purpose was the modernisation and reorganisation of the state in the first half of the sixteenth century (in this case, the Lithuanian Statute). In this way, too, it was a political text.
5. It was deeply rooted in a long literary tradition and was one of the links between the Grand Duchy of Lithuania and Mediterranean civilisation.
6. The legend was written down by a professional of the written word, maybe an Orthodox *diak* ('scribe') or a secretary employed in the Lithuanian chancery. If so, his everyday duties were to compose or copy various types of documents. This means that his *Chronicle* was a text immersed in a sea of texts with other rhetorical functions, such as charters, property registers, sermons, court sentences, last wills and testaments, prayers, etc.

To fully understand the meaning of a literary work such as the legend of the Iron Wolf, it must be seen within the contexts of all texts mentioned above. Its various interpretations epitomise the main topics of this book, which is an answer to the following question: how did literature work in late medieval and early modern Vilnius? The answer makes use of three assumptions. To explain this, I refer both to the legend and to an example of another type of written texts: last wills and testaments.

a) The materiality of a literary text such as the narrative about the Iron Wolf did not differ significantly from the materiality of a legal document, such as a last will. In the sixteenth century, similar textual procedures were followed to produce both kinds of texts. What is more, literary texts and documents were usually written by the members of the same group of professionals of the written word – or even by the same person. Consequently, I assume that *literature has to be understood as a particular case of the use of script and text.* A narrative and a last will have the same textual nature; their difference lies in a modality of the use of script. If a historian of literature wants to understand what the meaning of a literary text was, what its genesis was and how it functioned in some historical period, he or she has to interpret it in the context of other written records present at the time, even those that are not usually associated with literature. One's research should not merely be a simple structural comparison of two texts, e.g. a narrative and a last will, but one should examine the scribal and textual procedures of the time in their social context. In other words, if we want to know how a Renaissance narrative was written, how its meanings were produced, and how it was interpreted, we should also take into account the ways of writing, disseminating, and interpreting documents such as last wills. In his or her research, a historian of literature should consider the methods applied to written culture by historians of literacy.

b) In Europe, from the thirteenth century urban settlements have been the main centres of the use of script and text production.[5] In medieval towns writing was used on an unprecedented scale. Even though until the end of the eighteenth century Europe remained rural and most its inhabitants lived outside the towns, it was in towns that the culture of text was cultivated on an increasingly huge scale. A town is a complex organism, socially, economically, politically, etc. It could not exist without writing[6] and the use of different genres of texts. Towns may have been different from one another, but all towns were based on similar textual procedures. A town, as a textual entity, can be compared to a rhizome: it accumulated, preserved, produced, and reproduced the substance necessary to sustain the life of the organism and, when circumstances were favourable, multiplied the organism. In the case of the town its substance consisted of texts, and each European urban community relied on the perpetual consulting and producing of records. These records consisted of privileges, municipal law, legal transactions, registers of the town institutions, tax registers, urban statutes, last wills, sentences, professional literature (herbals, codices of law), etc. etc. In each urban settlement there were many people whose everyday activity was dealing in script. Towns were also the natural environment of the production and dissemination of literature. *Literature was an intrinsic part of the textual rhizome of the town.*[7] It was the town that enabled

[5] A. ADAMSKA and M. MOSTERT, "Introduction", in: *Writing and the Administration of Medieval Towns: Medieval Urban Literacy I*, ed. M. MOSTERT and A. ADAMSKA (Turnhout, 2014), pp. 2, 5-6.

[6] J. GOODY, *The Logic of Writing and the Organization of Society* (Cambridge and New York, 1996).

[7] I use the organic metaphor of the rhizome because it enables me better to explain the nature of urban textuality. The rhizome accumulates the energy of a plant, making it grow and survive. It also allows the plant to reproduce. A small part of a rhizome can be the beginning of a new plant. Premodern urban textuality worked in a similar way. It accumulated the necessary knowledge which enabled the city to function, survive and grow. In convenient circumstances urban textuality multiplied quickly and evolved. The town grows from such a textual rhizome. In late medieval and early modern towns written texts, including literature (e.g. epitaphs, church songs, plays, romances, didactic poems etc.) was part of this rhizome. Literature was as necessary as notarial acts, court sentences, the town registers, liturgical books, codices of the Magdeburg

literary institu-tions to exist: groups of professional copyists, printing houses, universities and humanistic Latin schools, bookshops, large literary audiences, the institution of modern authorship, etc. The town was an engine which, from the thirteenth century onwards, drove literary production. Since the Autumn of the Middle Ages all of literature has been conditioned – directly or indirectly – by urban textuality.[8]

c) In medieval and early modern times, probably all written texts were based in one way or another on rhetoric. This concerned not only the structure of some documenta (as, e.g. last wills) or literary texts (as, e.g. the narration about the Iron Wolf), but also the procedures by which these texts were produced. This was always a kind of rhetorical performance, called *actio* or *pronunciatio*. If somebody sold a house, the document of the transaction always had a rhetorical structure, since the European Latin law has been from the very beginning rooted in rhetoric.[9] Furthermore, several legal actions were 'performed', among others the reading aloud of the document, its sealing, presenting it in the office, and paying for it. The axis of these procedures was a legal and rhetorical text, and the procedures performed were a kind of *actio*. If the town worked because of the constant use of rhetorical texts, *the town can be seen as a rhetorical organism*. Rhetorical theory can be useful to understand how this organism was built and which rhetorical processes occurred when texts were produced, exchanged, preserved, etc. Urban rhetoric was itself the subject of perpetual change and evolution.

law etc. This means that it cannot be treated as a kind of superstructure over the basis of other textual genres.

[8] This assertion does not mean that literature was produced *only* in towns. We can enumerate many writers who worked outside urban settlements, e.g. Michel de Montaigne. He started his education in a rural environment, but his literacy was anchored in the town: his father was a wealthy merchant, his German tutor came from the city, and he got the final stage of his education in the city of Bordeaux. His professional career as a royal lawyer was also urban. Another example are the poems written by Polish noblemen who usually lived in their manor houses. Their literary output is called 'rural literature (Polish: *literatura ziemiańska*); this was anti-urbanistic. See J.S. GRUCHAŁA and S. GRZESZCZUK, "Staropolska poezja ziemiańska", in: *Staropolska poezja ziemiańska: Antologia*, ed. J.S. GRUCHAŁA and S. GRZESZCZUK (Warsaw, 1988), pp. 6-7, 20, 30-31, and especially pp. 43-44. However, these poets' use of script and literacy background was entirely urban. Probably all of them got their education in towns (in humanist colleges and universities, often in Italy, Germany, and the Netherlands) and their financial, political, and juridical dealings – always textual – were usually associated with a nearby town. What is more, urban institutions (e.g. bookshops, printing houses) and activities (e.g. buying ink and paper, acquiring new books) determined the way in which Montaigne and the Polish rural writers carried on their literary activities.

[9] H. LAUSBERG, *Handbook of Literary Rhetoric: A Foundation for Literary Study*, Foreword by G.A. KENNEDY, trans. M.T. BLISS, A. JANSEN, and D.E. ORTON (Leiden, Boston, and Cologne, 1998), pp. 63-64.

In short, in this book I aim to show that a) a medieval and early modern town was a textual rhizome; b) literature was a part of this rhizome and literary texts grew from it; c) rhetoric was a matrix which enabled all types of texts occurring in medieval and early modern towns to function. I will attempt this by examining the case of the city of Vilnius.

Why Vilnius?

Vilnius is a city in Eastern East-Central Europe, the capital of the Republic of Lithuania, and since 2004 one of the capitals of the European Union. As the legend about the Iron Wolf has it, from its very beginning the city was destined to be a capital. In fact, the historical sources confirm this assertion. Vilnius is relatively young, because it was founded in the first decades of the fourteenth century. The first documents which confirm its existence are the letters which Duke Gediminas sent in 1323 to the Hanseatic cities.[10] At that time, even by Eastern-European standards Vilnius was a small settlement, but it was predestined to be the capital of an empire.

In the mid-fourteenth century the Grand Duchy of Lithuania was among the largest European countries, encompassing the territory between the Baltic and Black Seas. It was ruled by the last non-Christian rulers of medieval Europe, the Lithuanians Gediminas and his son Algirdas. They took control of vast parts of the Eastern-Slavic lands (the former Kyivan Rus'), inhabited by the Orthodox Ruthenians. As a result, a multi-ethnic, multi-religious, and multilingual state was formed. In 1385, Gediminas' grandson Jogaila issued the Act of Krevo, which established a personal union between the Grand Duchy of Lithuania and the Kingdom of Poland.[11] Jogaila, who married Queen Jadwiga of Poland, became king of Poland and decided to baptize his country according to the Catholic rite.[12] The union and the introduction of Catholicism dramatically changed the political, religious, economic, and cultural situation of Lithu-

[10] These letters will be discussed in Chapter 1.

[11] For the history of the Polish-Lithuanian unions and its consequences see a recent monograph by R. Frost, *The Oxford History of Poland-Lithuania*, 1, *The Making of the Polish-Lithuanian Union, 1385-1569* (Oxford, 2018).

[12] D. Baronas and S.C. Rowell, *The Conversion of Lithuania: From Pagan Barbarians to Late Medieval Christians* (Vilnius, 2015), pp. 221-260.

ania.[13] These changes also influenced Vilnius, which was for the first time put on the map of the Latin Christendom.[14]

The first town-like settlement was established in the middle of the fourteenth century.[15] It consisted of two settlements, an Orthodox and a Catholic one; it was inhabited by Ruthenian and German merchants and craftsmen. At that time, the first Christian churches were built. The actual foundation (or 'location') of Vilnius as a city took place in 1387, when King Jogaila granted Vilnius the privilege of Magdeburg law. Vilnius became the seat of a Catholic diocese as well. The first Poles settled in the town, and their number increased in the following decades. The town was destroyed by the Teutonic Knights in 1390, and after that its centre was moved to the area of the later Market Square. At the turn of the fourteenth and fifteenth centuries, the present street network began to take form.[16]

[13] *Ibid.*, pp. 261-326.

[14] It is supposed that an anonymous illuminator who worked in Poland in 1380-1390 put the name of Vilnius on the so called Bohemian road-map'. This parchment is currently kept in The Archives of the Republic of Slovenia in Ljubljana, MS AS 1080, fasc. 1, 48/11. See J. HÖFLER, "Še enkrat o tako imenovanem 'češkem cestopisu' v zbirki Arhiva Republike Slovenije", *Acta historiae artis Slovenica* 6 (2001), pp. 17-31.

[15] W. SEMKOWICZ, "Hanul, namiestnik wileński (1382-1387) i jego ród", *Ateneum Wileńskie*, 7.1-2 (1930), pp. 3-4; J. JURGINIS, V. MERKYS, and A. TAUTAVIČIUS, *Vilniaus miesto istorija (nuo seniausių laikų iki Spalio revoliucijos)* (Vilnius, 1968), pp. 35-36; J. MAROSZEK, "Ulice Wilna w XIV-XVIII wieku", *Kwartalnik historii kultury materialnej*, 47.1-2 (1999), p. 168. Archaeologists who have conducted excavations in Vilnius in recent decades have found traces of a medieval settlement in the castle, which received its first fortifications already in the second half of the thirteenth century, and north of Gediminas Hill over the Neris River, which they also date to the thirteenth century. See K. KATALYNAS, *Vilnaius plėtra XIV-XVII a.* (Vilnius, 2006), pp. 26-46; *Vilniaus žemutinės pilies rūmai, (1996-1998 metų tyrimai)*, ed. V. URBANAVIČIUS (Vilnius, 2003), p. 11.

[16] The first larger urban settlements date only from the middle of the fourteenth century. At that time, there were three settlements there: one around Gediminas Hill, another one in the area of the Hill of the Three Crosses, and a further one in the area of today's Old Town, where. along the trade routes, the Ruthenian Town with the Orthodox churches of Theotokos and St. Paraskeva were built, as well as the German Town or Polish End (*Lacki*, mentioned in 1471), the current German Street, next to which St. Nicholas's church was built. See MAROSZEK, "Ulice Wilna w XIV-XVIII wieku", p. 168; K. KATALYNAS and G. VAITKEVIČIUS, "Rozwój Wilna w XIV wieku w świetle badań archeologicznych", *Kwartalnik Historii Kultury Materialnej*, 1.50 (2002), pp. 3-9; KATALYNAS, *Vilnaius plėtra XIV-XVII a.*, pp. 53-58; L. BEDNARCZUK, "Nazwy Wilna i jego mieszkańców w dokumentach Wielkiego Księstwa Litewskiego (WKL)", *Annales Universitatis Paedagogicae Cracoviensis: Studia Linguistica* 5 (2020), p. 7.

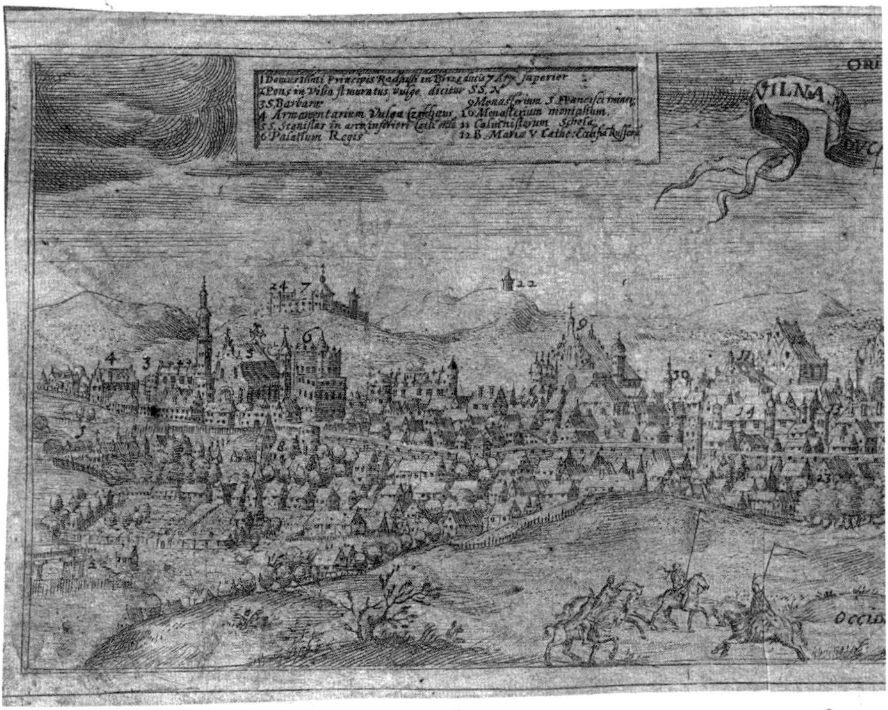

Fig. 1 Vilnius at the beginning of the seventeenth century. T. Makowski, *Vilna, Magni Ducatus Lithuaniae caput* (Vilnius, *c.* 1604). The copperplate shows Vilnius before the great fire in 1610 with its main buildings described in the cartouches: "1. The Palace of the Princes Radziwiłł of the Biržiai branch; 2. The bridge over the Neris River called the Stone Bridge; 3. St. Barbara church [in the lower castle]; 4. The Armoury called Cekhauz [in the Lower Castle]; 5. The Catholic cathedral of St. Stanislas in the lower castle; 6. The Royal Castle; 7. The upper castle; 8. St. George church; 9. The Franciscan (Bernardine) monastery; 10. The nunnery [of the Bernardine Sisters and St. Michael Church]; 11. The Calvinist school; 12. The Orthodox (Ruthenian) cathedral of the Holy Virgin; 13. The parish church of St. John; 14. The Bishop's Manor; 15. The Jesuit University (the Academy of Vilnius); 16. The Dominican convent; 17. The town hall; 18. The Orthodox Trinity church; 19. The conventual Franciscan Monastery; 20. The Orthodox Saviour church; 21. SN (?); 22. The mausoleum of Bekiesz; 23. The Holy Cross church; 24. St. Nicolas church in the upper castle". Original of the copperplate lost during World War II. IS PAN, Zbiory Fotografii i Rysunków Pomiarowych Instytutu Sztuki PAN (Collection of Photographs and Measuring Drawings), negative 17174. Reproduced with the permission of IS PAN.

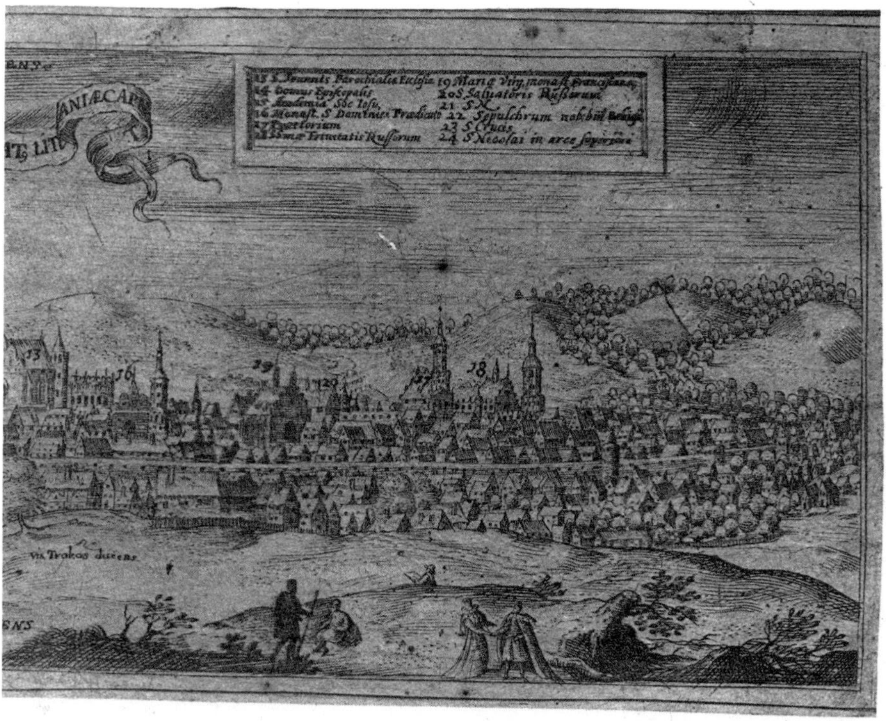

As early as the first half of the fifteenth century, merchants from Gdańsk and other cities in Prussia engaged in brisk commerce with their Vilnius counterparts.[17] This activity would benefit the city in the future. However, it took almost a hundred years until Vilnius really earned its place on the map of significant urban settlements in this part of Europe. Before the 1480s, Vilnius was a political, religious, and military centre rather than a fully established medieval town.

It was not until the rule of Alexander I Jagiellon (since 1492) that Vilnius gained the status of a true – and not only a titular – Lithuanian metropolis. The city bloomed in the first half of the sixteenth century. The rulers granted the city new privileges, which facilitated an economic boom. Since 1543 Vilnius

[17] S.C. Rowell, "Vilniaus pirklių partnerių tinklas XV a. viduryje: Šaltiniotyrinis aspektas", *Vilniaus istorijos metraštis* 1 (2007), pp. 19-28; A.P. Orłowska, "Kontakty handlowe Gdańska i Wilna w świetle piętnastowiecznej księgi kupieckiej", *Rocznik Lituanistyczny* 7 (2021), pp. 59-91.

became the residence of King Sigismund II Augustus, who built a new Renaissance-style residence there. In the next hundred years, Vilnius blossomed as an economic, political, and cultural centre. The capital witnessed many important political events (e.g. sessions of the Lithuanian Parliament and visits of foreign envoys), and the kings often visited the city or resided there. In 1579 the university was founded: the Academy of Vilnius. The city became a major centre of information exchange (the postal service between Vilnius, Cracow, and Venice was established in 1562; there were dozens of printing houses and bookshops). The prosperity of the city ceased by the destruction of the city by the Muscovite army on 8 August 1655 and the following occupation, which lasted for five years.

Vilnius has always been a borderland city in the geographical and cultural sense. To some degree it reflected the status of the Grand Duchy of Lithuania, which was a multi-ethnic and multi-religious country. Eastern and Western Christianity met here, and Christians lived alongside Jews and Muslims. In one and the same house in Vilnius its inhabitants could speak Polish, Yiddish, and Ruthenian. Inter-confessional marriages among Christians were not unusual.

In the sixteenth and seventeenth centuries, Vilnius' inhabitants were mainly Poles (or rather Polish-speaking Catholics and Protestants) and Ruthenians. But Lithuanians, Germans, Jews, and Tartars lived there as well.[18] All these communities spoke their own languages. The religious situation was also complex. In the fourteenth century, Lithuanians cultivated their pre-Christian polytheistic religion, the Ruthenians were Orthodox and the Germans and Poles Catholic. After the conversion of Lithuania, the Lithuanians converted to Catholicism. In the fifteenth century, in the suburb called Šnipiškės, the Muslim Tartars settled, and in the next century the Jewish *qahal* (*kehila*, *kahal*) in Vilnius was established. The Reformation caused further religious diversification of the city. Protestants of the Augsburg confession (Lutherans) and Reformed Church (Calvinists) made Vilnius their main seat in Lithuania. After the Union of Brest in 1596, the Uniate Church got a strong position in Vilnius.[19] In short, the map of Vilnius confessions at the turn of the sixteenth and

[18] About the relationships in the multi-ethnic Vilnius David A. Frick published a fascinating study: D.A. Frick, *Kith, Kin, and Neighbors: Communities and Confessions in Seventeenth-Century Wilno* (Ithaca and New York, 2013).

[19] In 1596 a part of the Orthodox Church in the Polish-Lithuanian Commonwealth subordinated to the Roman Catholic Church. The new Uniate Church kept the Orthodox rites but accepted the Catholic dogmas and supremacy of the Pope. See *Unia brzeska: Przeszłość i teraźniejszość. 1596-1996: Materiały międzynarodowego sympozjum, Kraków 19-20 listopada 1996*,

seventeenth centuries was rich and complex, which inevitably led to many conflicts.[20]

The cultural opulence and social diversity of the city are undoubtedly two of the main reasons why it is worth to be investigated. Along with such cities as Amsterdam, Istanbul, or Venice, Vilnius was a predecessor of the contemporary multi-ethnic metropolises. It is not an accident that since the middle of the twentieth century Vilnius, as an urban cultural network, has been an object of interests for historians, historians of literature, philologists, and anthropologists from many countries.[21]

Vilnius, as a borderland city, might be seen as a fascinating as well as a unique phenomenon. It shows a unique set of ethnic and religious groups inhabiting the city, different languages and scripts, the kaleidoscopic functions of the city, which was both an urban settlement and the political, religious, and administrative centre of a vast country. There were many towns, but only a few were multifunctional in a similar way, in that they were simultaneously commercial centres, capitals of a state, seats of a university, ecclesiastical and local authorities, and administration. As a consequence, the set of *loci textuales* ('textual places'), that is the places of the production, use and preservation of texts, was unique. They were many, and their output was often untypical. Finally, the social processes in the city and their dynamics make a unique story.[22]

However, Vilnius was also a typical urban settlement, similar to thousands of other towns and cities which functioned in late medieval and early modern Europe. It worked accordingly to the Magdeburg law and its urban institutions:

ed. P. Natanek and R.M. Zawadzki (Cracow, 1998).

[20] Conflicts as a cause of text production will be discussed in Chapter 9. The problem of religious conflicts in early modern Vilnius was thoroughly discussed by Tomasz Kempa in his valuable book T. Kempa, *Konflikty wyznaniowe w Wilnie od początku reformacji do końca XVII wieku* (Toruń, 2016).

[21] Among them are: В.Н. Топоров, "Vilnius, Wilno, Вильна: город и миф", in: *Балто-славянские этноязыковые контакты*, ed. Т. М. Судник (Moscow, 1980), pp. 3-72; M. Kvietkauskas, *Vilniaus literatūrų kontrapunktai: Ankstyvasis modernizmas 1904-1915* (Vilnius, 2007); Frick, *Kith, Kin, and Neighbors*; Kempa, *Konflikty wyznaniowe w Wilnie*; Л. Тимошенко, *Руська релігійна культура Вільна: Контекст доби. Осередки: Література та книжність (XVI-перша третина XVII ст.)* (Дрогобич, 2020).

[22] An example is the history of the religious conflicts by Kempa, *Konflikty wyznaniowe*. Another fine example is a paper by David A. Frick about measuring time in Vilnius in early modern times. Since each religious confession used its particular calendar, their members had to negotiate the temporary circumstances in which they lived. See D.A. Frick, "The bells of Vilnius: keeping time in a city of many calendars", in: *Making Contact: Maps, Identity, and Travel*, ed. L.B. Cormack, N. Pylypiuk, G. Berger, and J. Hart (Edmonton, 2003), pp. 23-59.

the city council, the *Voigt*, the aldermen court, etc., reflecting the administrations of many, if not all other towns in Poland and Lithuania. In many respects, the use of script and the textual culture of Vilnius did not differ significantly from what we can encounter for instance in Warsaw, Lviv, Prague, or Leipzig. Their inhabitants could validate their financial agreements in the municipal chancery, study the *Disticha Catonis* in the parish school, listen to sermons in church, buy a prayer book from the bookbinder and dictate their last wills in the presence of a public notary. As a consequence, Vilnius can also be treated as a typical example of urban textuality. The way in which it functioned can be easily compared to other urban settlements of the time, and an examination of Vilnius textuality can shed new light on how the textual rhizome of the town helped forge the early modern literary field in Europe generally.

The State of Research and Sources

This book shows the unique and typical features of the textual background of a city. Some subjects presented here, especially those related to medieval urban literacy, have been quite well researched, for instance the role of urban chanceries,[23] the programme of cathedral and parish schools,[24] the ways of shaping collective memory,[25] the urban *theatrum ceremoniale*,[26] etc. Other subjects seem to have been less thoroughly examined. Among them there are multi-scripturality (that is, the use of many alphabets)[27] in the town; rhetorical

[23] A. BARTOSZEWICZ, *Urban Literacy in Late Medieval Poland*, trans. A.B. ADAMSKA (Turnhout, 2017), pp. 89-173.

[24] K. STOPKA, *Szkoły katedralne metropolii gnieźnieńskiej w średniowieczu: Studia nad kształceniem kleru polskiego w Wiekach Średnich* (Cracow, 1994), pp. 132-185; P.F. GRENDLER, *Schooling in Renaissance Italy: Literacy and Learning, 1300-1600* (Baltimore and London, 1991), pp. 111-117; BARTOSZEWICZ, *Urban Literacy in Late Medieval Poland*, pp. 51-57.

[25] O.G. OEXLE, "Die Gegenwart der Lebenden und der Toten", in: *Gedächtnis, das Gemeinschaft stiftet*, ed. K. SCHMID (Munich, 1985), pp. 74-107; A. ZAJIC, "Texts on public display: Strategies of visualising epigraphic writing in late medieval Austrian towns", in: *Uses of The Written Word in Medieval Towns: Medieval Urban Literacy II*, pp. 389-426.

[26] J.A. CHROŚCICKI, *Sztuka i polityka: Funkcje propagandowe sztuki w epoce Wazów, 1587-1668* (Warsaw, 1983). K. FRIEDRICH, "Royal entries into Cracow, Warsaw and Danzig: Festival culture and the role of the cities in Poland Lithuania", in: *Europa Triumphans: Court and Civic Festivals in Early Modern Europe*, ed. J.R. MULRYNE, H. WATANABE-O'KELLY, and M. SHEWRING, 1 (Cambridge, 2004), pp. 386-387.

[27] The term of multi-scripturality was invented by David A. Frick and was for the first time used in his translation of a paper: J. NIEDŹWIEDŹ, "Multiscripturality in the Grand Duchy of

genres as the matrix of the urban textuality; literary texts as vehicles of managing the conflict in early modern town; etc. Against the background of the research on urban literacy in other parts of Europe, that in the Grand Duchy of Lithuania and Vilnius has rarely been examined.

The lack of a modern monograph, based on serious research, on the history of Vilnius, is a major impediment. Vilnius is probably the last metropolis in the Polish-Lithuanian state whose history has not yet been covered in a modern multi-volume study, from many perspectives. This is somewhat paradoxical, as the three oldest historical monographs on Vilnius, written by Michał Baliński and Józef Ignacy Kraszewski, were published as far back as the 1830s and 1840s, that is, before any of the other Polish and Lithuanian cities had been investigated so thoroughly.[28] Most of the later accounts of the late medieval and early modern history of Vilnius, however, are very concise and were intended for a wide audience, often as part of a touristic guide, as for instance the studies by Adam Honory Kirkor (1856, 1880), Władysław Zahorski (1921), Iwo Jaworski (1929), Saulius Žukas (2002), Tomas Venclova (2001, 2008), A.R. Čaplinskas (2010), and L. Briedis (2021).[29] Most of these publications rely on the works by Baliński and Kraszewski and a study of Łowmiańska published in 1929. In 1968, a monograph in Lithuanian by Juozas Jurginis, Vytautas Merkys, and Adolfas Tautavičius was published, which covers the history of Vilnius from its origins up to the October Revolution.[30] Finally, in 2008 Joachim Tauber and Ralph Tuchtenhagen provided a good introduction

Lithuania: New research approaches", *East European Politics and Societies and Cultures* 33.1 (2019), pp. 3-16. This is an English version of a Polish term *wielopiśmienność*, used in the Polish version of the paper: ID., "Wielopiśmienność Wielkiego Księstwa Litewskiego: Nowe perspektywy badawcze", *Wielogłos* (2014), 2, pp. 11-21. See also ID., "Cyrillic and Latin script in late medieval Vilnius", in: *Uses of the Written Word in Medieval Towns: Medieval Urban Literacy II*, ed. M. MOSTERT and A. ADAMSKA (Turnhout, 2014), pp. 99-116.

[28] M. BALIŃSKI, *Historia miasta Wilna*, 2 vols. (Vilnius, 1836); ID., "Wielkie Księstwo Litewskie opisane", in: M. BALIŃSKI and T. LIPIŃSKI, *Starożytna Polska pod względem historycznym, jeograficznym i statystycznym opisana* (Warsaw, 1846), pp. 123-200; J.I. KRASZEWSKI, *Wilno od początków jego do roku 1750*, 1-2 (Vilnius, 1840), 3 (Vilnius, 1841), and 4 (Vilnius, 1842).

[29] A.H. KIRKOR, *Przechadzki po Wilnie i jego okolicach* (Vilnius, 1856); ID., *Przewodnik historyczny po Wilnie i jego okolicach* (Vilnius, 1880); W. ZAHORSKI, *Przewodnik po Wilnie* (Vilnius, 1921); I. JAWORSKI, *Zarys historii Wilna* (Vilnius, 1929); S. ŽUKAS, *Vilnius: The City and its History*, trans. L. BLAŽEVIČIŪTĖ (Vilnius, 2002); T. VENCLOVA, *Vilnius: City Guide* (Vilnius, 2001); EAD., *Vilnius: A Guide To its Names and People* (Vilnius, 2008; Lithuanian edition: Vilnius, 2006); A.R. ČAPLINSKAS, *Vilniaus istorija: Legendos ir tikrovė* (Vilnius, 2010); L. BRIEDIS, *Vilnius: City of Strangers* (Vilnius, 2021).

[30] JURGINIS, MERKYS, and TAUTAVIČIUS, *Vilniaus miesto istorija*.

to the history of Vilnius from its beginning to the present times.[31] The authors recognised several functions of the city as the residence of non-urban authorities and as a 'civil town' (*Bürgerstadt*).[32] In 2007, a yearbook devoted to the history of Vilnius was launched; unfortunately, only one issue was published.[33]

Although there is no exhaustive study that covers all aspects of the history of the pre-1655 city, there are several major studies about particular topics or periods.

Among the older publications, a crucial role is played by a doctoral thesis published in Polish in 1929 by Maria Łowmiańska, the title of which translates as *Vilnius before the Muscovite Invasion in 1655*.[34] Based on extensive archival research, the author shows how the city functioned in the late 1640s and early 1650s. Łowmiańska examines the topography of Vilnius, its inhabitants, authorities, and economy. The last aspect is especially interesting, because there are only a few smaller studies that deal with the economic life of the city before the mid-seventeenth century.[35] Only one comprehensive book discusses the topic of the socio-topographical development of Vilnius in medieval and early modern times.[36]

There are several publications about the Vilnius religions published in the nineteenth and the first half of the twentieth centuries. Valuable publications about the history of the Vilnius diocese were published by Jan Kurczewski.[37] The history of the Vilnius Calvinists was discussed in the works of Józef Łukaszewicz (1842-1843) and W.G. Studnicki (1932).[38] Only a few publica-

[31] J. Tauber and R. Tuchtenhagen, *Vilnius: Kleine Geschichte der Stadt* (Cologne, Weimar, and Vienna, 2008).

[32] *ibid.*, pp. 32-66, 73-84, 124-137.

[33] *Vilniaus istorijos metraštis*, 1 (2007). This publication contains many valuable papers by the leading Lithuanian historians.

[34] M. Łowmiańska, *Wilno przed najazdem moskiewskim 1655 roku* (Vilnius, 1929). The book was republished in the twenty-first century: M. Łowmiańska, "Wilno przed najazdem moskiewskim 1655 roku", in: *Dwa doktoraty z Uniwersytetu Stefana Batorego w Wilnie: H. Łowmiański, Wchody miast litewskich; M. Łowmiańska, Wilno przed najazdem moskiewskim 1655 roku* (Poznań, 2005), pp. 149-330.

[35] C.S. Rowell, "Vilniaus pirklių partnerių tinklas xv a. viduryje", pp. 19-28; A.P. Orłowska, "Kontakty handlowe Gdańska i Wilna", pp. 59-91; Kunigielis, *Organizacja funkcjonowania mostów*, pp. 45-46.

[36] M. Klovas, E. Meilus, A.K. Urmański, and O. Valionienė, *Vilniaus sociotopografijos metmenys XIV-XVIII a.* (Vilnius, 2022).

[37] J. Kurczewski, *Biskupstwo wileńskie od jego założenia aż do dni obecnych, zawierające dzieje i prace biskupów i duchowieństwa diecezji wileńskiej oraz wykaz kościołów, klasztorów, szkół i zakładów dobroczynnych i społecznych* (Vilnius, 1912).

[38] J. Łukaszewicz, *Dzieje kościołów wyznania helweckiego w Litwie*, 2 vols. (Poznań,

tions deal with the history of Lutheran culture in the city.[39] The Tatar settlement in Vilnius was mentioned in works by Jakub Szynkiewicz and Stanisław Kryczyński.[40] Very informative are the studies by Sergei A. Bershadski (1882, 1883, 1886, 1887) about the Jewish community.[41] In 1943, Israel Cohen published a new book on this topic, basing himself in part on the works by Bershadski.[42] These valuable publications are the basic reference works concerning the beginnings of the Jewish settlement in the city, especially because almost all the Jewish sources got lost during World War II.

During the Soviet period (1940-1990), research on the history of Vilnius was limited because of political reasons, both in the People's Republic of Poland and in the Lithuanian Soviet Socialist Republic. The situation has changed after the fall of the communism in 1989-1990.

In the twenty-first century three important monographs were published. All three deal with the social-cultural history of Vilnius in the sixteenth and seventeenth centuries. In his vast study from 2013, David A. Frick mapped most aspects of the social life of the inhabitants of the city in the seventeenth century: the multi-ethnic character of Vilnius, religious relations, everyday life, the most important events in life of the inhabitants (birth, marriage, death), education, the measuring of time, conflicts, marital life, etc.[43] In 2016, Tomasz Kempa published his book in Polish, whose title translates as: *The Religious*

1842-1843); W.G. STUDNICKI, *Zarys historyczny wileńskiego kościoła ewangelicko-reformowanego i jego biblioteki* (Vilnius, 1932).

39 A.F. ADAMOWICZ, *Kościół augsburski w Wilnie: Kronika zebrana na obchód trzechwiekowego istnienia Kościoła w roku 1855 w dzień św. Jana Chrzciciela* (Vilnius, 1855); A. ŚNIEŻKO, *Cmentarz ewangelicki w Wilnie 1806-1956* (Wrocław, 1972); A. KASPERAVIČIENĖ, *Evangelikų liuteronų ir evangelikų reformatų kapinės Vilniuje* (Vilnius, 1996).

40 J. SZYNKIEWICZ, "Literatura religijna Tatarów litewskich i jej pochodzenie", *Rocznik Tatarski* 2 (1932); S. KRYCZYŃSKI, *Historia meczetu w Wilnie (próba monografii)* (Warsaw, 1937); ID., *Tatarzy litewscy: Próba monografii historyczno-etnograficznej* (Warsaw, 1938).

41 С.А. БЕРШАДСКИЙ, *Документы и регесты к истории Литовских евреев* (St. Petersburg, 1882); ID., *Литовские евреи: История их юридического и общественного положения в Литве, 1388-1569* (St. Petersburg, 1883); ID., Бершадский, "История виленской еврейской общины с 1593 до 1648 гг.", *Восход* 6.10 (1886), pp. 125-138, 6.11 (1886), pp. 145-154, 7.3 (1887), pp. 81-98, 7.4 (1887), pp. 65-78, 7.5 (1887), pp. 16-32, 7.6 (1887), pp. 58-73, and 7.8 (1887), pp. 97-110.

42 I. KOHEN, *Vilna* (Philadelphia, 1943).

43 FRICK, *Kith, Kin, and Neighbors*. This beautifully written book is based on many papers and a book which Frick published earlier. In the course of my book I also cite these previous publications, especially the book *Wilnianie: Żywoty siedemnastowieczne*, ed., introduction, and comments D.A. FRICK (Warsaw, 2008). This is a selection of valuable sources gathered by Frick during his longstanding research in many countries.

Conflicts in Vilnius since the Beginning of the Reformation until the End of the Seventeenth Century.[44] Kempa meticulously examined an impressive amount of sources and constructed a vast panorama of the religious diversity in Vilnius in early modern times. Another monograph was published in 2020 in Ukrainian by Leonid Tymoshenko under the translated title *The Ruthenian Religious Culture of Vilnius: The Context of the Epoch, Hubs, Literature and Book (From the Sixteenth to the First Third of the seventeenth Century)*.[45] This is the first publication in which the culture of the Orthodox and Uniate inhabitants of Vilnius was examined in all its complexity. The book is important especially because earlier research favoured the 'Latin' texts of the city. Tymoshenko focused on the religious institutions, schooling, the religious life of the Eastern-Christian communities, the production and the use of Cyrillic books, and religious conflicts.

Apart from these monographs, many smaller studies discuss particular aspects of the history of Vilnius and its inhabitants.[46] The city is often mentioned in publications whose scope is broader than the history of this particular city. From the point of view of the topic of this book, most useful are works about late medieval and early modern cultural production in Vilnius: about literature and theatre, the history of book, literacy, schools, communication, and history of the ecclesiastical institutions.

It was Kraszewski who first discussed the history of literature in Vilnius.[47] Later publications on the topic came from the interwar period (1922-1939), when Vilnius belonged to the Republic of Poland[48] and the city and its culture

[44] T. Kempa, *Konflikty wyznaniowe w Wilnie od początku reformacji do końca XVII wieku* (Toruń, 2016).

[45] Л. Тимошенко, *Руська релігійна культура Вільна: Контекст доби: Осередки: Література та книжність (XVI-перша третина XVII ст.)* (Дрогобич, 2020).

[46] A.R. Čaplinskas, *Vilniaus gatvių istorija*: *Šv. Jono, Dominikonų, Trakų gatvės* (Vilnius, 1998); id., *Vilniaus gatvių istorija: Valdovų kelias: Pirma knyga: Rūdninkų gatvė* (Vilnius, 2001); id., *Vilniaus gatvių istorija: Valdovų kelias: Antra knyga: Didžioji gatvė* (Vilnius, 2002); id., *Vilniaus gatvių istorija: Valdovų kelias: Trečia knyga: Pilies gatvė* (Vilnius, 2005); A. Ragauskas, *Vilniaus miesto valdantysis elitas XVII a. antrojoje pusėje (1662-1702 m.)* (Vilnius, 2002); R. Ragauskienė, *Vilniaus "aukso amžius": Miesto gyventojai XVI a. 67-ajame deš. (Vilniaus vietininko teismo knygų duomenimis)* (Vilnius, 2021).

[47] Kraszewski, *Wilno od początków jego*, 4, pp. 3-112, and Chapter 3, *Kronika bibliograficzna*" (The Bibliographical Chronicle), pp. 113-365.

[48] In 1918-1939 a conflict between the Republic of Poland and the Republic of Lithuania about Vilnius broke out. In 1920 the Polish army took control over the disputed territories and in 1922 the Vilnius Region (*Wileńszczyzna*) was formally incorporated into the Republic of Poland. Since then, the Lithuanians considered the city to be their capital under the Polish

was the object of intensified research. Valuable works appeared in *The Vilnian Atheneum*.[49] Among them there were Maria Baryczowa's dissertation about a sixteenth-century humanist, writer and advocate (*Voigt*) of Vilnius Augustyn Rotundus,[50] Henryk Łowmiański's paper on the oldest paper mills in Vilnius,[51] Wacław Gizbert Studnicki's history of the library of the Calvinist church,[52] Jan Fijałek's paper about medieval and early modern descriptions ('choreographies') of Vilnius,[53] etc.

After the Second World War Vilnius became an awkward topic for researchers from countries under Soviet domination. Censorship, especially in Soviet Lithuania and Belarus, did not allow researchers to do wide-ranging research or publication on the past of the Grand Duchy of Lithuania. Nevertheless, some studies about politically less sensitive matters were carried out, about the history of printing houses, paper mills, book-binding in Vilnius, and early modern literary theory in the Jesuit colleges of Lithuania.[54] Among them

occupation. The break of the Second World War ceased the dispute. After the Yalta Conference (1945), Vilnius was granted to the USSR and became the capital of the Soviet Lithuania. In 1944-1947, *c*. 170,000-200,000 Poles were expatriated from the Lithuanian Soviet Socialist Republic, most of them from Vilnius. After 1990, when Lithuania declared its independence, the city has been the capital the Republic of Lithuania. See T. SNYDER, *The Reconstruction of Nations: Poland, Ukraine, Lithuania, Belarus, 1569-1999* (New Haven and London, 2003), pp. 52-89; P. ŁOSSOWSKI, *Konflikt polsko-litewski 1918-1920* (Warsaw, 1996); S. CIESIELSKI and A. SREBRAKOWSKI, "Przesiedlenie ludności z Litwy do Polski w latach 1944-1947", *Wrocławskie Studia Wschodnie* 4 (2000), pp. 227-253.

49 *Ateneum Wileńskie: Czasopismo Naukowe Poświęcone Badaniom Przeszłości Ziem Wielkiego Księstwa Litewskiego*. The journal appeared from 1923. Its authors were mainly professors of the Stefan Báthory University in Vilnius. Until 1939, 285 articles appeared in the *Ateneum Wileńskie*. The last issue was published a couple weeks before the outbreak of the Second World War. See H. ŁOWMIAŃSKI and J. TUMELIS, "Bibliografia zawartości *Ateneum Wileńskiego*", *Pamiętnik Biblioteki Kórnickiej* 20 (1983), pp. 227-259.

50 M. BARYCZOWA, "Augustyn Rotundus Mieleski, wójt wileński, pierwszy historyk i apologeta Litwy", *Ateneum Wileńskie* 10 (1935), pp. 71-96 and 11 (1936), pp. 117-172.

51 H. ŁOWMIAŃSKI, "Papiernie wileńskie XVI wieku: Przyczynek do ich dziejów", *Ateneum Wileńskie* 2.7-8 (1924), pp. 409-422.

52 W.G. STUDNICKI, "Biblioteka Wileńskiego Synodu Ewangelicko-Reformowanego", *Ateneum Wileńskie* 8 (1931-1932), pp. 205-214.

53 J. FIJAŁEK, "Opisy Wilna aż do połowy wieku XVII", *Ateneum Wileńskie* 1.3-4 (1923), pp. 313-336 and 2.5-6 (1924), pp. 121-158; *Teksty opisowe Wilna*, ed. J. FIJAŁEK, *Ateneum Wileńskie*, 1.3-4 (1923), pp. 506-526.

54 E. LAUCEVIČIUS, *Popierius Lietuvoje XV-XVIII a.* (Vilnius, 1967); *Encyclopedia wiedzy o książce*, ed. A. KAWECKA-GRYCZOWA, H. WIĘCKOWSKA, and S. PAZYRA (Wrocław, 1971); E. LAUCEVIČIUS, *Knygų įrišimai Lietuvos bibliotekose* (Vilnius, 1976); K. ČEPIENĖ and I. PETRAUSKIENĖ, *Vilniaus Akademijos spaustuvės leidiniai 1576-1805: Bibliografija* (Vilnius, 1979); Z. STOBERSKI, *Między dawnymi i młodszymi laty: Polsko-litewskie związki literackie*

there is a fundamental work, *The Printers of Ancient Poland*, vol. 5, *The Grand Duchy of Lithuania*.[55] Some topics, deemed useful to Communist ideology, were allowed, but always subject to scrutiny and censorship: the Reformation, education, and the activities of some sixteenth-century humanists.[56] Vilnius was not allowed to be the topic of any Polish monograph, but it appeared in case studies and articles and was mentioned in many books on the history of Polish literature.[57] As the city played a crucial role in the history of early modern Polish literature, it was mentioned in innumerable publications, for instance about writers who lived there: Pedro Ruiz de Moros, Barbara Radziwiłłówna, Piotr Skarga, Daniel Naborowski, etc. Usually, scholars did not go into details about how the city and its culture influenced the literary output of early modern writers.

Among works printed behind the Iron Curtain, the most important is the history of the Academy of Vilnius by the Polish Jesuit Ludwik Piechnik.[58]

The blossoming of studies of Vilnius literary culture began in the times of Perestroika in the Soviet Union in the late 1980s and continued after the fall of communism and the Soviet Union in the 1990s. Many publications of Belarusian, Lithuanian, Polish, Russian, and Ukrainian researchers appeared. Among the most often discussed topics were: neo-Latin literature in Vilnius; the literature of the Protestants, Jesuits, and Orthodox; writing and languages; book history and the history of libraries; and legal texts and their use.

(Łódź, 1981); M.B. Topolska, *Czytelnik i książka w Wielkim Księstwie Litewskim w dobie Renesansu i Baroku* (Wrocław, 1984); E. Ulčinaitė, *Teoria retoryczna w Polsce i na Litwie w XVII wieku* (Wrocław, 1984); I. Lukšaitė, "Salomono Risinskio bibliotekos Vilniuje sąrašas", in: *Iš lietuvos bibliotekų istorijos*, ed. V. Bulavas (Vilnius, 1985); В. Шматаў, *Мастацтва белорускіх старадрукаў (XVI-XVIII стст.)* (Minsk, 2000).

[55] *Drukarze dawnej Polski od XV do XVIII wieku*, 5, *Wielkie Księstwo Litewskie*, ed. A. Kawecka-Gryczowa, K. Korotajowa, and W. Krajewski (Wrocław, 1959).

[56] I. Lukšaitė, *Lietuvos publicistai valstiečių klausimu XVI a. pabaigoje-XVII a. pirmojoje pusėje* (Vilnius, 1976); ead., *Radikalioji reformacijos kryptis Lietuvoje* (Vilnius, 1980); J. Kubilius, *A Short History of Vilnius University* (Vilnius, 1979); H. Baranowski, *Uniwersytet Wileński 1579-1939: Bibliografia za lata 1945-1982* (Wrocław, 1983); Е.Л. Немировский, *Франциск Скорина. Жизнь и деятельность белорусского просветителя* (Minsk, 1990).

[57] See, e.g. J. Nowak-Dłużewski, *Okolicznościowa poezja polityczna w dawnej Polsce: Pierwsi królowie elekcyjni* (Warsaw, 1969); id., *Okolicznościowa poezja polityczna w dawnej Polsce. Zygmunt III* (Warsaw, 1971); id., *Okolicznościowa poezja polityczna w dawnej Polsce. Dwaj młodsi Wazowie* (Warsaw, 1972); Cz. Hernas, *Barok* (Warsaw, 1972); J. Ziomek, *Renesans* (1973); J. Ochmański, "Najdawniejsze szkoły na Litwie od końca XIV do połowy XV wieku", in: id., *Dawna Litwa* (Olsztyn, 1986), pp. 113-133.

[58] L. Piechnik, *Początki Akademii Wileńskiej 1570-1599*, preface J.W. Woś (Rome, 1984); id., *Rozkwit Akademii Wileńskiej w latach 1600-1655* (Rome, 1983).

In studies on the literary culture of Vilnius the work of Eugenija Ulčinaitė plays a special role. She not only edited and translated works of many neo-Latin authors (among others Maciej Kazimerz Sarbiewski and Andrzej Wolan)[59] and published valuable papers about early modern literature,[60] but also trained three generations of Lithuanian historians of literature who carried out research on the literary culture of the Grand Duchy of Lithuania. Most of them focused on neo-Latin literature in Vilnius. Their output includes the catalogue of Lithuanian Latin books printed in the fifteenth, sixteenth and seventeenth centuries;[61] studies about the Lithuanian Latin book;[62] and editions of works by Pedro Ruiz de Moros, Jan Radwan, the *Lives* of St. Casimir, and of sources for the history of the Reformation in Lithuania.[63]

A second large group of studies about literature in Vilnius is closely connected to the Reformation. The city was mentioned many times in publications about history of the Reformation in Lithuania,[64] the literary culture of the court of the Radziwiłłs,[65] and anti-Protestant literature.[66] Introductions and commen-

[59] M.K. SARBIEWSKI, *Lemties žaidimai: Poezjijos rintkinė: Ludi Fortunae: Lyrica selecta*, ed. E. ULČINAITĖ (Vilnius, 1995);

[60] ULČINAITĖ, *Teoria retoryczna*; EAD., *Kalbų varybos: Lietuvos Didžionsios Kunigaiktystės valdovų ir didikų sveikinimai – Competition of Languages – The Ceremonial Greetings of the Grand Duchy of Lithuania's Rulers and Nobles – Concert josikaea: Pozdrowienia władców i magnatów Wielkiego Księstwa Litewskiego* (Vilnius, 2010); E. ULČINAITĖ and A. JOVAIŠAS, *Lietuvių literatūros istorija. XIII-XVIII amžiai* (Vilnius, 2003).

[61] *XV-XVI a. lietuvos lotyniškų knygų sąrašas: Index librorum Latinorum Lituaniae saeculi quinti decimi et sexti decimi*, ed. D. NARBUTIENĖ and S. NARBUTAS (Vilnius, 2002); *XVII a. lietuvos lotyniškų knygų sąrašas*: *Index librorum Latinorum Lituaniae saeculi saeculi septimi decimi*, ed. ID. (Vilnius, 1998).

[62] D. NARBUITENĖ, *Lietuvos Didžiosios Kunigaikštijos lotyniškoji knyga XV-XVII a.* (Vilnius, 2004).

[63] *Ankstyvieji šv. Kazimiero "Gyvenimai"*, ed. M. ČIURINSKAS (Vilnius, 2004); *Du laiškai: popiežiaus nuncijaus Luigi Lippomano ir kunigaikščio Mikalojaus Radvilo Juodojo polemika (1556) – Two Letters: a Controversy between Papal Nuncio Luigi Lippomano and Duke Nicolaus Radvilas the Black (1556)*, ed. D. POCIŪTĖ (Vilnius, 2015).

[64] I. LUKŠAITĖ, *Reformacija Lietuvos Didžiojoje Kunigaikštystėje ir Mažojoje Lietuvoje XVI a. trečias dešimtmetis – XVII a. pirmas dešimtmetis* (Vilnius, 1999), EAD., *Reformacja a przemiany kulturowe w Wielkim Księstwie Litewskim* (Poznań, 2003); D. POCIŪTĖ, *Maištininkų katedros: Ankstyvoji reformacija ir lietuvių-italų evangelikų ryšiai* (Vilnius, 2008); EAD., *Nematomos tikrovės šviesa: Reformacijos Lietuvoje asmenybės ir idėjos* (Vilnius, 2017), Italian translation: EAD., *La Riforma in Lituania*, trans. E. RANOCCHI (Turin, 2021)); E. BUOŽYTĖ, "Kodėl vystyklėliuose jo kiaulės nesurijo: Balcerio Wilkowskio laiškas sūnui (1584)", *Literatūra* 60.1 (2018), pp. 142-160.

[65] M. JARCZYKOWA, *"Papierowe materie" Piotra Kochlewskiego: O działalności pisarskiej sekretarza Radziwiłłów birżańskich w pierwszej połowie XVII wieku* (Katowice, 2006); "Kopie

taries to four editions of works by Protestant writers, Salomon Rysiński, Andrzej Wolan, Abraomas Kulvietis, and Andrzej Schönflissius, bring much information about Protestant literature in Vilnius.[67]

The Vilnius Jesuits were mentioned in some publications,[68] often in editions of works of the members of the Academy of Vilnius (among others Kacper Pętkowski, Jakub Olszewski, Maciej Kazimierz Sarbiewski, Walenty Bartoszewski, Wojciech Wijuk Kojałowicz, and students of the Academy).[69]

listów jezuity Sarbiewskiego oraz księcia Janusza Radziwiłła (1612-1655)", ed. M. JARCZYKOWA, trans. A. GOLIK-PRUS, *Terminus* 12.1 (2010), pp. 231-242.

[66] J. NIEDŹWIEDŹ, "Strzała w nodze świętego Michała: Daniel Naborowski i wileńskie narracje sądowe z XVII w.", in: *Daniel Naborowski: Krakowianin – Litwin – Europejczyk*, ed. K. GAJDKA and K. FOLLPRECHT (Katowice and Cracow, 2008), pp. 83-101; D. CHEMPEREK, "Wileńscy luteranie w świetle XVII-wiecznych satyr jezuickich (1620-1642): Wydarzenia, bohaterowie, autorzy", *Terminus* 19.2 (2017), pp. 277-308.

[67] S. RYSIŃSKI (S. RISINSKIS), *Trumpas pasakojimas apie garsiuosius šviesiausiojo didiko, Biržų ir Dubingių kunigaikščio Kristupo Radvilos žygius*, ed. S. NARBUTAS (Vilnius, 2000); A. WOLAN, *De libertate politica sive civili: O wolności rzeczypospolitej albo ślacheckiej*, ed. M. EDER and R. MAZURKIEWICZ (Warsaw, 2010); A. KULVIETIS, *Pirmasis Lietuvos Reformacijos paminklas – The First Recorded Text of the Lithuanian Reformation: Abraomo Kulviečio* Confessio fidei *ir Johanno Hoppijaus* Oratio funebris *(1547) –* Confessio fidei *by Abaromas Kulvietis and* Oratio funebris *by Johann Hoppe (1547)*, ed. D. Pociūtė (Vilnius, 2011); *Dwa kazania wygłoszone po śmierci Katarzyny Habsburżanki i Zygmunta III Wazy*, ed. J. NIEDŹWIEDŹ (Warsaw, 2016).

[68] R. JURGELĖNAITĖ, *Lotyniškoji laidotuvių poezija: XVI amžiaus pabaigos Vilniaus Akademijos tekstų retorinė analizė* (Vilnius, 1998); *Motiejus Kazimieras Sarbievijus lietuvos, lenkijos, europos kultūroje: Tarptautinės mokslinės konferencijos, skirtos poeto 400-ųjų gimimo metinių jubiliejui, medžiaga, Vilnius, 1995, spalio 19-21*, ed. E. ULČINAITĖ (Vilnius, 1998); J. NIEDŹWIEDŹ, *Nieśmiertelne teatra sławy: Teoria i praktyka twórczości panegirycznej na Litwie w XVII-XVIII w.* (Cracow, 2003); *Maciej Kazimierz Sarbiewski i jego epoka: Próba syntezy*, ed. J.Z. LICHAŃSKI (Pułtusk, 2006); E. BUSZEWICZ, *Sarmacki Horacy i jego liryka. Imitacja – gatunek – styl: Rzecz o poezji Macieja Kazimierza Sarbiewskiego* (Cracow, 2006); *Alma Mater Vilnensis: Vilniaus universiteto istorijos bruožai: Kolektyvinė monografija* (Vilnius, 2012); Ž. NEDZINSKAITĖ, "'Finis epigrammatis est anima eius': Transformations of the content of the Latin epigram in the epoch of the Baroque", *Interlitteraria* 19.2 (2014), pp. 276-292; EAD., "A quest for originality in Latin poetry of the Grand Duchy of Lithuania observed in manuscripts of the seventeenth-eighteenth centuries", *Interlitteraria* 23.2 (2018), pp. 278-294; O. DAUKŠIENĖ, "Sigismundus Laetus – Žygimantas Liauksminas? Apie kai kuriuos paslaptingus Sarbievijaus odžių adresatus", *Senoji Lietuvos Literatūra* 44 (2017), pp. 53-72.

[69] K. PĘTKOWSKI, "Dialog o pokoju dla króla Stefana", trans. H. SZCZERKOWSKA, in: *Dramaty staropolskie: Antologia*, ed. J. LEWAŃSKI, 4 (Warsaw, 1961); ID., *Łacińskie dialogi Kaspra Pętkowskiego*, ed. A. SOCZEWKA (Niepokalanów, 1978); *Dwa kazania wygłoszone po śmierci Katarzyny Habsburżanki*; M.K. SARBIEWSKI, *Epigrammatum liber: Księga epigramatów*, ed. M. PISKAŁA and D. SUTKOWSKA (Warsaw, 2003); W. BARTOSZEWSKI, *Utwory poetyckie*, ed. M. KARDASZ (Warsaw, 2019); W. WIJUK KOJAŁOWICZ (A. VIJŪKAS-KOJALAVIČIUS), *Lietuvos istorijos įvairenybės*, 1, ed. D. KUOLYS, trans. D. ANTANAVIČIUS and S. NARBUTAS (Vilnius,

Researchers focused mainly on Jesuit sermons, drama, and panegyrics. Among papers about other institutions of the Catholic Church in Vilnius, those about the Vilnius chapter should be mentioned. They give important information about the cultural role of the diocesan clergy in Vilnius (among other things on education, text production, and libraries).[70]

The literary culture of the Orthodox and Uniate communities were less discussed. Among the most interesting studies are articles and monographs about catechisms,[71] the Vilnius Orthodox Brotherhood,[72] printing houses,[73] the Union of Brest of 1596, and Orthodox-Uniate polemics.[74]

The use of texts in Vilnius was not the topic of any separate publication, but was dealt with as part of larger studies. Some remarks on the use of documents can be found in papers and books about the Vilnius magistrate and the state authorities that operated in the city (especially the Lithuanian chancery) and about the law.[75]

2003); ID., *Lietuvos istorijos įvairenybės*, 2, ed. D. KUOLYS, trans. R. JURGELĖNAITĖ (Vilnius, 2004); ULČINAITĖ, *Kalbų varybos: Lietuvos Didžiosios Kunigaiktystės valdovų ir didikų sveikinimai*; J. KAL, "Religionis, Reipublicae, Vilnae, Collegii et omnium ordinum ex fortunatissimo Sacrae Regiae Maiestatis adventu laetitia et gratulatio – Radosne powinszowania Religii, Rzeczypospolitej, Wilna, Kolegium oraz wszystkich stanów z okazji najszczęśliwszego przybycia Jego Królewskiej Mości", ed. E. BUSZEWICZ and J. NIEDŹWIEDŹ, in: *"Umysł stateczny i w cnotach gruntowny": Prace edytorskie dedykowane pamięci Profesora Adama Karpińskiego*, ed. R. GRZEŚKOWIAK and R. KRZYWY (Warsaw, 2012), pp. 17-39.

70 W. PAWLIKOWSKA-BUTTERWICK, "Księgozbiory prywatne w Wielkim Księstwie Litewskim XVI stulecia. Postulaty metodyczne w rozpoznaniu problemu", *Nasze Historie* 8 (2007); EAD., "Księgozbiór biblioteki katedralnej w Wilnie z końca XVI wieku", *Odrodzenie i Reformacja w Polsce* 56 (2012), pp. 162-191.

71 M.A. КОРЗО, *Украинская и белорусская катехетическая традиция конца XVI-XVII вв. Становление, эволюция и проблема заимствований* (Moscow, 2007).

72 A. MIRONOWICZ, *Bractwa cerkiewne w Rzeczypospolitej* (Białystok, 2003).

73 A. MIRONOWICZ, "Drukarnie bractw cerkiewnych", in: *Prawosławne oficyny wydawnicze w Rzeczypospolitej*, ed. A. MIRONOWICZ, U. PAWLUCZUK, and P. CHOMIK (Białystok, 2004); I. KAŽURO, *Vilniaus bazilijonų vienuolyno spaustuvės veikla 1628-1839 m.* (Vilnius, 2019) (a doctoral thesis).

74 D.A. FRICK, *Meletij Smotryc'kyj* (Cambridge, Mass., 1995); *Unia brzeska: Przeszłość i teraźniejszość: 1596-1996: Materiały międzynarodowego sympozjum, Kraków 19-20 listopada 1996*, ed. P. NATANEK and R.M. ZAWADZKI (Cracow, 1998); *Między Wschodem a Zachodem: Prawosławie i Unia*, ed. M. KUCZYŃSKA (Warsaw, 2017).

75 A. DUBONIS, D. ANTANAVIČIUS, R. RAGAUSKIENĖ, and R. ŠMIGELSKYTĖ-STUKIENĖ, *The Lithuanian Metrica: History and Research* (Boston, Mass., 2020); A. RACHUBA, "Kancelarie pieczętarzy WKL w latach 1569-1765", in: *Lietuvos Metrika: 1991-1996 metų tyrinėjimai* (Vilnius, 1998), pp. 256-270; A.B. ZAKRZEWSKI, *Wielkie Księstwo Litewskie (XVI-XVIII w.): Prawo – ustrój – społeczeństwo* (Warsaw, 2013).

There is also a study devoted to private documents in late medieval Lithuania.[76]

Languages and scripts were the subject of studies carried out by linguists, historians, and historians of literature. Researchers focused especially on the problem of the Ruthenian written language.[77] The features of spoken and written Polish were discussed by linguists.[78] Several Belarusian, Lithuanian, and Polish researchers focused on Latin and Ruthenian palaeography.[79]

Two important German monographs shed new light on the role of Vilnius in building the early modern national identity of the Lithuanians.[80] There are also some other publications about the construction of Lithuanian collective memory in the sixteenth and seventeenth centuries in historical works, poetry, and education.[81] In these studies the role of the literary milieu of Vilnius was noted.

[76] M. KLOVAS, *Privačių dokumentų atsiradimas ir raida Lietuvos Didžiojoje Kunigaikštystėje XIV a. pabaigoje – XVI a. pradžioje (1529 m.): Daktaro disertacija* (Vilnius, 2017).

[77] Б.А. УСПЕНСКИЙ, *История русского литературного языка (XI-XVII вв.)* (Budapest, 1988); A. DANYLENKO, "A missing chain? On the sociolinguistics of the Grand Duchy of Lithuania", *Acta Baltico Slavica*, 41 (2017); С.Ю. Темчин (S. TEMČINAS), "Функционирование руськой мовы и иерархия церковных текстов", *Studia Russica* 23 (2009), pp. 226-234; ID., "Języki kultury ruskiej w Pierwszej Rzeczypospolitej", in: *Między Wschodem a Zachodem*, pp. 81-120; J. NIEDŹWIEDŹ, "Cyrillic and Latin script in late medieval Vilnius", in: *The Uses of the Written Word in Medieval Towns*, pp. 99-116.

[78] Z. KURZOWA, *Język polski Wileńszczyzny i kresów północno-wschodnich XVI-XX w.* (Warsaw, 1993); EAD., *Ze studiów nad polszczyzną kresową: Wybór prac* (Cracow, 2007); M.T. LIZISOWA, "O języku kancelarii Wielkiego Księstwa Litewskiego", in: *Wilno i kresy północno-wschodnie: Materiały II Międzynarodowej Konferencji w Białymstoku 14-17 IX 1994 r. w czterech tomach*, 3, *Polszczyzna kresowa*, ed. E. FELIKSIAK and B. NOWOMIEJSKI (Białystok, 1996).

[79] A.I. ГРУША, *Белоруская кірылычна палеаграфія: Вучэбны дапаможнік для студэнтаў гістарынага факультэта* (Мінск, 2006); ID., "Гісторыя вывучэння беларускай і ўкраінскай кірылычнай палеаграфіі да 1928 гг.", *Беларускі археаграфічны штогоднік* 7 (2006); R. ČAPAITĖ, *Gotikinis kursyvas Lietuvos dzidžiojo kunigaikščio Vytauto raštinėje* (Vilnius, 2007); K. PIETKIEWICZ, *Paleografia ruska* (Warsaw, 2015).

[80] H.-J. BÖMELBURG, *Frühneuzeitliche Nationen im östlichen Europa: Das polnische Geschichtsdenken und die Reichweite einer humanistischen Nationalgeschichte (1500-1700)* (Wiesbaden, 2006); M. NIENDORF, *Das Großfürstentum Litauen 1569-1795: Studien zur Nationsbildung in der Frühen Neuzeit* (Wiesbaden, 2006).

[81] K. PUCHOWSKI, *Edukacja historyczna w jezuickich kolegiach Rzeczypospolitej 1565-1773* (Gdańsk, 1999); D. ANTANAVIČIUS, "*Cnotliwy Litwin* z 1592 roku: Autorstwo i proweniencja tekstów źródłowych", *Miscellanea Historico-Archivistica* 21 (2014), pp. 63-91; D. CHEMPEREK, "Jan Karol Chodkiewicz – *miles Christianus* i obrońca ojczyzny: Wstęp historycznoliteracki", in: F. Małkot, *Tureckich i iflanskich wojen o sławnej pamięci Janie Karolu Chodkiewiczu głos – Karųsu turkais ir Livonijoje balsas apie šlovingo atminimo Joną Karolį Chodkevičių*, ed. D. ANTANAVIČIUS, D. CHEMPEREK, and E. PATIEJŪNIENĖ (Warsaw, 2016), pp. 47-61.

This survey of publications about literary culture reveals several gaps. We lack modern and thorough discussions of the economic aspects of Vilnius literate culture in the time under consideration (for instance of lists of prices and services).[82] Our knowledge of the book trade, schooling, the writings of women, Tartars and Jews, political propaganda in the city, the relationships between architecture or other arts and literature, libraries, the literacy of the inhabitants, the religious use of texts, texts in the public domain, etc. is still insufficient. In this book I raise these points, but one should bear in mind that in many cases the answers I give are only provisional and require further full-scale studies.

This state of research is partially caused by the poor state of the historical sources. Only some of the texts relating to Vilnius from before the mid-seventeenth century have survived, and some of them only in later copies and editions. Others were lost in the many calamities that befell the city.

The first disaster was the fire of 2 and 3 July 1610, when most of the city was consumed by fire. The Muscovite occupation in the years 1655-1661 was even worse: on 8 August 1655 the entire municipal archive, which had kept *c.* 200-300 volumes of registers from the fifteenth century onwards was destroyed.[83] In 1707, the original royal privileges for the city got lost in another fire. And after the third partition of the Polish-Lithuanian Commonwealth the Russian authorities tried to destroy memory of the Grand Duchy of Lithuania. This was especially effective after the November Uprising (1830-1831) and during the period of Russification in the second half of the nineteenth century.[84] Finally, the Second World War brought considerable losses of historical

[82] Such catalogues of prices in other cities of the Polish-Lithuanian Commonwealth (Cracow, Lublin, Lviv and Warsaw) were published in the first half of the twentieth century. They can be used for reference in the next parts of the book. See W. ADAMCZYK, *Ceny w Lublinie od XVI do końca XVIII wieku* (Lviv, 1935); ID., *Ceny w Warszawie w XVI i XVII wieku* (Lviv, 1938).

[83] The content of this destroyed archive is discussed in Chapter 2.

[84] After the third partition of the Polish-Lithuanian Commonwealth in 1795, the Russian Empire occupied the Grand Duchy of Lithuania and a part of the Kingdom of Poland. The November Uprising against Russian rule was unsuccessful, and Lithuanian society fell victim to Russian repressions. They took the form of ethnic cleansing, especially in the territory of contemporary Belarus and Ukraine: many patriots were executed, fifty thousand families were deported to the interior of Russia or Siberia, Russian became the official language in the administration and education, the University of Vilnius was closed, all the Catholic monasteries and nunneries were dissolved, the Uniate Church was abolished etc. Part of the repressions was the systematic annihilation of the social and historical memory of the Grand Duchy of Lithuania. The central Lithuanian archives were transferred to Russia (mainly to Moscow, where they are

documents (for instance when the Central Archives of Historical Records in Warsaw was burnt in 1944 and most of the Jewish records and historical monuments were destroyed). Vilnius is probably the least fortunate city in the Polish-Lithuanian Commonwealth when it comes to losses of early historical records.

Researchers of the past are constrained by the remains of the historical sources and sometimes have to make conjectures from the tenuous traces of information. To do so, it is necessary to travel much, because the existing sources are scattered over many European archives and libraries. Fortunately, from the second half of the eighteenth century onwards many historical sources have been published.

The remnants of the registers of the magistrate, aldermen and *Voigt* are kept in the Lithuanian State Historical Archives in Vilnius. They contain copies of a couple of hundred documents from the 1480s onwards.[85] David A. Frick published a collection of the seventeenth-century documents from these registers.[86] Part of the registers of the burgrave (*horodniczański*) court are kept in the same archive.[87] Some of the municipal documents were entered into the registers of the Lithuanian chancery (*Metrica*), which is currently kept in the Russian State Archive of Ancient Acts in Moscow (RGADA).[88] Since 1980 the relevant volumes have been published in the series *Lithuanian Metrica*.[89] The privileges of the city were printed in 1788 by mayor of the city, Piotr Dubinowski, in the volume *The Collection of the Laws and Privileges Granted to the Capital City of the Grand Duchy of Lithuania, Edited and Printed on Demand of Many Towns of the Polish Crown and the Grand Duchy of Lithuania*.[90] Most of these documents have not survived. In 1843 some of them were reprinted with the addition of several other charters.[91]

kept until today), but the vast majority of private, municipal, educational, ecclesiastical, or juridical documents were destroyed.

[85] Lietuvos valstybės istorijos archyvas (LVIA), especially MS F. 23, Ap. 1 b. 1, nr 5096 and F. 22, Ap. 1 b. 1, nr 5333; F. 22, Ap. 1, nr 5335; F. 22, Ap. 1 b. 1, nr 5344; F. 694, ap. 1, nr 3322.

[86] *Wilnianie. Żywoty siedemnastowieczne*.

[87] MS LVIA F20, ap. 1, nr. 4563.

[88] Российский государственный архив древних актов (РГАДА), фонд 389.

[89] DUBONIS, ANTANAVIČIUS, RAGAUSKIENĖ, and ŠMIGELSKYTĖ-STUKIENĖ, *The Lithuanian Metrica*, pp. 38-57.

[90] *Zbiór praw i przywilejów miastu stołecznemu Wielkiego Księstwa Litewskiego Wilnowi nadanych, na żądanie wielu miast koronnych jako też Wielkiego Księstwa Litewskiego ułożony i wydany*, ed. P. DUBINOWSKI (Vilnius, 1788).

[91] *Собрание древних грамот и актов городов: Вильны, Ковна, Трок, православных монастырей, церквей, и по разным предметам: с приложением трех литографированных*

Many valuable sources were edited in the second half of the nineteenth and in the first decades of the twentieth centuries in volumes published by the Vilnian Archeographic Committee (*AVAK* – cf. the list of abbreviations at pp. XVII-XVIII) and the Archerographic Committee (*AIZR*).[92] Especially important are the volumes of *AVAK* with the acts from the castle court (vol. 8), the land court (vol. 9), and the Magdeburg court as far as they relate to the city (vols. 10 and 20), post mortem inventories (vol. 14), documents related to history of the Jews (vol. 28 and 29) and the Tatars (vol. 21). The creation and activity of *AVAK* and *AIZR* were part of Russian politics of history of the time. The documents were selected to prove the everlasting relations of the Lithuanian Ruthenians with Muscovy and stressed the role of the Orthodox Church in Lithuania.

Collections of the historic sources relative to several institutions were published in the twentieth and twenty-first centuries: the *Codex diplomaticus* of the Vilnius bishopric,[93] the acts and privileges of the Vilnius guilds (1495-1759),[94] the statutes of the Vilnius chapter,[95] the acts of the Lithuanian Protestant Reformed (Calvinist) church (1611-1637),[96] and documents related to history of the printing house of the Academy of Vilnius.[97]

A valuable collection of manuscripts and old prints is kept in the Wróblewski Library of the Lithuanian Academy of Science in Vilnius. In this library are preserved the archives of the Vilnius chapter and the Vilnius bishopric from the fifteenth century onwards.[98] The Manuscript Department of the University Library in Vilnius keeps some original documents from the sixteenth and seventeenth centuries issued by the Vilnius magistrate. Collection F-3 contains a

рисунков – Zbiór dawnych dyplomatów i aktów miast: Wilna, Kowna, Trok, prawosławnych monasterów, cerkwi i w różnych sprawach, z przyłożeniem trzech rysunków litografowanych, 1 (Vilnius, 1843).

92 *Акты, издаваемые Виленскою Археографическою коммиссиею,* 39 vols. (Vilnius, 1865-1915); *Акты относящіеся к исторіи западной Россіи собраные и изданные Археографическую комиссею*, 4 vols. (St. Petersburg, 1846-1851).

93 *Kodeks dyplomatyczny katedry i diecezji wileńskiej*, 1, *(1387-1507)*, ed. J. Fijałek and W. Semkowicz (Cracow, 1938-1994).

94 *Akty cechów wileńskich 1495-1759*, ed. H. Łowmiański, M. Łowmiańska, and S. Kościałkowski (Poznań, 2006).

95 W. Pawlikowska-Butterwick and L. Jovaiša, *Vilniaus ir Žemaičių katedrų kapitulų statutai* (Vilnius, 2015).

96 *Akta synodów prowincjonalnych Jednoty Litewskiej 1611-1625*, ed. B. Grużewski and H. Merczyng (Vilnius, 1915); *Akta synodów prowincjonalnych Jednoty Litewskiej 1626-1637*, ed. M. Liedke and P. Guzowski (Warsaw, 2011).

97 *Vilnius akademijos spaustuvės šaltiniai XVI-XIX a.*, ed. I. Petrauskienė (Vilnius, 1992).

98 Especially important is fonds MAB F 43.

rich collection of commonplace manuscript books from the seventeenth century, some of which have been written in Vilnius.

Many interesting manuscripts and early printed books which I consulted are preserved in the Jagiellonian Library (Cracow, Poland), the Czartoryski Library (Cracow, Poland), the Central Archives of Historical Records (Warsaw, Poland), the University of Warsaw Library (Warsaw, Poland), the University of Latvia Academic Library (Riga, Latvia), and the National Historical Archive of Belarus (Minsk, Belarus).

Very useful sources are bibliographies and catalogues. Most important is the Polish bibliography of Estreicher (*Bibliografia Estreichera*), the most complete description of printed books published in Poland and the Polish-Lithuanian Commonwealth. In 1979 a bibliography of the printed books of the Academy of Vilnius appeared[99] and in 2019 a doctoral thesis was defended about the printing house of the Basilian Order.[100] Two volumes contain the list of Lithuanian Latin printed books of the fifteenth through seventeenth centuries.[101] A valuable index of seventeenth-century Lithuanian books in Polish was published in 1998.[102] There is also a beautifully edited catalogue of the preserved books from the *Bibliotheca Sapiehana*.[103] Finally, a catalogue of sixteenth- and seventeenth-century last wills from the municipal books in LVIA was published in 2017.[104]

I based this study on a couple of hundred old printed editions of literary works written or published in Vilnius in the fourteenth through seventeenth centuries. The full list of them can be found in the Bibliography.

The Methodological Approach

There are two factors which strongly determined the methodology used in this book. Firstly, this is the first comprehensive study about literature and

[99] K. Čepienė and I. Petrauskienė, *Vilniaus Akademijos spaustuvės leidiniai 1576-1805: Bibliografija* (Vilnius, 1979).

[100] Kažuro, *Vilniaus bazilijonų vienuolyno spaustuvės veikla 1628-1839 m.*

[101] *XV-XVI a. lietuvos lotyniškų knygų sąrašas*: *XVII a. lietuvos lotyniškų knygų sąrašas.*

[102] *XVII a. lietuvos lenkiškos knygos: Kontrolinis sąrašas (Polska książka na Litwie w XVII w. Wykaz kontrolny)*, ed. M. Ivanovič (Vilnius, 1998).

[103] *Bibliotheca Sapiehana Vilniaus universiteto bibliotekos rinkinys: Katalogas*, ed. A. Rinkūnaitė (Vilnius, 2010); cf. Chapter 2.

[104] *Testamenty w księgach miejskich wileńskich z XVI i XVII wieku: Katalog*, ed. K. Frejlich (Warsaw, 2017)

textuality in any late medieval and early modern Eastern-European city, so it was difficult to find a publication that could offer a ready methodology. Secondly, the book deals with very different subjects, such as literary genres, book production, libraries, the literacy of the inhabitants, the economic aspects of the texts production and their exchange, the professionals of the written word, social and interpersonal tensions that gave rise to text production, legal texts, religions and confessions, the *loci textuales* of women, political events, education, etc. To deal with such a complex research task, a new approach had to be developed. This required application and adaptation of methodologies of several disciplines and sub-disciplines developed in the humanities and social sciences.

First of all, I rely on literary studies and the history of literature, especially in four fields: historical rhetoric and poetics; the sociology of literature; gender studies; and borderland studies.

The book discusses the rhetorical organisation of the city. The idea that the city reflects the theory of rhetoric is derived from a long tradition of rhetorical discourse carried out since the times of Aristotle, Cicero, and Quintilian. Accordingly to them, the city (*polis*, *res publica*) was based on textual communication between the *oratores* or *homines rhetorici*. Ever since Antiquity this communication was believed to be guided by rhetorical rules, functions of the text, and the ethos of the *orator*.[105] Roman rhetoric lived on, evolved, and changed in the Middle Ages,[106] but remained a matrix of textual production in Europe. The concept of the rhetorical organisation of the city has been introduced in this book for the first time. I assume that most of the social relations in urban settlements were more or less arranged by texts (juridical, political, epideictic, and religious texts) and the ways of using them. The third part of the book is inspired by the rhetorical functions of these texts. Historical rhetoric, poetics, and philological methods were also used in the interpretation of several texts quoted elsewhere in the book.

I will often refer to the term 'literary culture', borrowed from the vast field of the sociology of literature. In the 1970s and 1980s, in Poland the term was widely discussed by literary critics, among others by Janusz Sławiński, Stefan

[105] LAUSBERG, *Handbook of Literary Rhetoric*.

[106] Many publications show the transmission of rhetoric in the Western Europe, a.o. E.R. CURTIUS, *European Literature and the Latin Middle Ages*, trans. W.R. Trask, introduction C. BURROW (Princeton and Oxford, 1983) and *Renaissances Before the Renaissance: Cultural Revivals of Late Antiquity and the Middle Ages*, ed. W.T. TREADGOLD (Stanford, 1984).

Żółkiewski, and Krzysztof Dmitruk in their many studies.[107] These studies were highly theoretical, inspired by semiotics, structuralism, and the Marxist methodologies then prevalent in the humanities. Accordingly to Dmitruk, literary culture consists of a literary system based on a 'sign community' (*wspólnota znakowa*). This system allowed literary communication,[108] that is its constituent literary institutions (for instance scribes, printing houses), the sign community, and the net of cultural centres allowed society (or parts of it) to benefit from literature as a mean of communication.

The author and the audience were perceived as the main instances in this literary communication. Sławiński defined 'literary culture' in the following way:

> It is a relatively unified 'orienteering system' [*system orientacyjny*] which decides about the character of the [literary] audience. It enables the members of the audience an effective communication through the literary works, i.e. it provides them with the reciprocal sender codes [*kody nadawania*] and receiver codes [*kody odbioru*]. It also guarantees, that the individual interpretations of the members of the audience can be equivalent.[109]

Afterwards significant changes took place in the field of the sociology of literature in the 1990s,[110] and literary culture is now researched in new ways.

[107] J. Sławiński, "Socjologia literatury i poetyka historyczna", in: *Problemy socjologii literatury*, ed. J. Sławiński (Warsaw, 1971), pp. 45-52; S. Żółkiewski, "Badania kultury literackiej i funkcji społecznych literatury", in: *Problemy socjologii literatury*, pp. 53-77; *Kultura literacka 1918-1932* (Warsaw, 1973); id., *Kultura, socjologia, semiotyka literacka* (Warsaw, 1979); id., *Wiedza o kulturze literackiej* (Warsaw, 1980); id., "Kultura literacka: instytucje", in: *Słownik literatury polskiej XX wieku*, ed. A. Brodzka *et al.* (Wrocław, 1995), pp. 499-518; K. Dmitruk, *Literatura – społeczeństwo – przestrzeń: Przemiany układu kultury literackiej* (Wrocław, 1980); id., "Kultura literacka", in: *Słownik literatury staropolskiej: Średniowiecze, renesans, barok*, ed. T. Michałowska, B. Otwinowska, and E. Sarnowska-Temeriusz (Wrocław, 1998), pp. 426-440.

[108] K. Dmitruk, "Kultura literacka", pp. 426-431.

[109] J. Sławiński, "Socjologia literatury i poetyka historyczna", pp. 45-46. Sławiński's definition of literary culture relies on the Shannon-Weaver model of communication. His definition of the literary culture is similar to the concept of the interpretive community introduced a couple of years later by Stanley Fish in S. Fish, *Is There A Text in This Class? The Authority of Interpretative Communities* (Cambridge, Mass., and London, 1980), pp. 1-17, 147-174.

[110] W. Griswold, "Recent moves in the sociology of literature", *Annual Review of Sociology* 19 (1993), pp. 455-467; G. Jankowicz and M. Tabaczyński, "Socjologia literatury jako nieodzowne źródło cierpień", in: *Socjologia literatury: Antologia*, ed. G. Jankowicz and M. Tabaczyński (Cracow, 2015), pp. 12-13.

However, in contemporary literary studies the term usually remains without definition and authors assume that it is understood by itself.[111] Almost always it is connected to a concrete place and a specific historical period, for instance in titles such as *Literary Culture of the Cracow Region in the Times of Enlightenment*, *Literary Culture of Renaissance Silesia*, or *Literary Culture of Antwerp in the Sixteenth Century*.[112] The term 'literary culture' basically means the way in which people used literature in the communication process. An instructive example is a recent study by Ingo Berensmeyer about literary culture in early modern England:

> In order to understand early modern literary culture, we need to reconstruct the conditions of literary communication prior to the modern concept of literature as aesthetic (fictional) discourse. How did literature work? What were the functions of reading and writing in seventeenth-century England? My suggestion is to describe literary forms in relation to, and at times in conflict with, socio-cultural formations or arrangements in which these forms are negotiated, modified, and continued. The aesthetic, then, is not an independent realm that can be taken for granted or posited as given. If we want to come closer to an idea of what literary communication might mean, we will have to question and explore more closely the (historically specific) modes of access to (literary) texts.[113]

Scholars dealing with literary culture in the 1970s and 1980s and often even today (such as Berensmeyer) assume that literary culture is a kind of superstructure over a primordial communication system used in a society. This theoretical approach, based on Marxist theory, does not take into account the fact

[111] There are many examples of this attitude, e.g. L. BUEL, *New England Literary Culture: From Revolution through Renaissance* (Cambridge and New York, 1986); M. INGLOT, *Polska kultura literacka Lwowa lat 1939-1941: Ze Lwowa i o Lwowie: Lata sowieckiej okupacji w poezji polskiej: Antologia utworów poetyckich w wyborze* (Wrocław, 1995); *Literary Cultures and Public Opinion in the Low Countries, 1450-1650*, ed. J. BLOEMENDAL, A. VAN DIXHOORN, and E. STRIETMAN (Leiden and Boston, 2011); J. NIEDŹWIEDŹ, *Kultura literacka Wilna 1323-1655: Retoryczna organizacja miasta* (Cracow, 2012); B. NOWOROLSKA, *Kultura literacka Podlasia: Szkice* (Białystok, 2017).

[112] J. SNOPEK, *Prowincja oświecona: Kultura literacka Ziemi Krakowskiej w dobie Oświecenia 1750-1815* (Warsaw, 1992); J. MALICKI, *Kultura literacka renesansowego Śląska* (Katowice, 1985); R. SZMYTKA, "*Kultura literacka Antwerpii* w XVI wieku", in: *Literatura renesansowa w Polsce i Europie: Studia dedykowane Profesorowi Andrzejowi Borowskiemu*, ed. J. NIEDŹWIEDŹ (Cracow, 2016), pp. 274-291.

[113] I. BERENSMEYER, *Literary Culture in Early Modern England, 1630-1700: Angles of Contingency* (Berlin and Boston, 2020), p. 13. See also the section about literary culture, pp. 23-27.

that the European societies were shaped by the use of all kinds of different types of texts. The organisation of any complex religious, financial, juridical, and political (think of the state) national and regional organisation or community is fully integrated with its textuality.[114] Without literacy and literate communication European societies would not exist at all. Since literature is an integral part of this textuality, the model of the base and superstructure cannot work in this instance.

In this book, 'literary culture' has a specific meaning. It refers to all activities, artifacts, people, institutions, and social networks which facilitate some community to benefit from literature.[115] Literary culture relies on written texts, although the oral residue is still valid. Its essence is literacy, that is literary culture exists only in literate societies. To understand how literary culture works in a society, it is necessary to examine also literacy generally, such as the procedures of the use of script by the members of this society. Literary culture is an indispensable part of the entire 'textual culture' (textuality) which since the early Middle Ages increasingly constituted European communities: urban, religious, political, state, ethnic, and other communities.

The first part of the book strongly relies on the gender studies, especially Chapter 4, '*Loci Textuales* of Women'. This part of literary studies is now one of its main fields, which is shown in countless publications, for instance about women's literacy in the Middle Ages and in early modern times.[116] Women's writing in early modern Poland and Lithuania was the subject of research by Joanna Partyka, Karolina Targosz, Jolanta Gwioździk, Anna Struska, and others.[117] Agnieszka Bartoszewicz devoted a part of her research to women's liter

[114] GOODY, *The Logic of Writing*.

[115] Thus, literary culture includes: a) activities and rituals: production of texts, their copying, preserving, storage, memorising, validation, and dissemination; b) artifacts: books, letters, coins, public inscriptions, styluses, royal privileges, sermons, primaries, quills, maps, codices of law etc.; c) people: teachers, printers, professionals of written word, nuns, judges, engravers, readers, students, priests, etc.; d) institutions: schools, offices, churches, guilds, nunneries, Holy Scripture, the royal court, printing houses, etc.; d) social networks: commerce (including the book trade), the mail, the Hansa, a parish, friendships, local church structures, singular events (such as a coronation or urban riots), political assemblies, etc.

[116] A good introduction to this vast topic are two companions: *The Cambridge Companion to Medieval Women's Writing*, ed. C. DINSHAW and D. WALLACE (Cambridge, 2003), and *The Cambridge Companion to Early Modern Women's Writing*, ed. L. LUNGER KNOPPERS (Cambridge, 2009). Both publications contain vast bibliographies on the topic.

[117] J. PARTYKA, *Żona wyćwiczona: Kobieta pisząca w kulturze XVI i XVII wieku* (Warsaw, 2004); K. TARGOSZ, *Piórem zakonnicy: Kronikarki w Polsce XVII w. o swoich zakonach i swoich czasach* (Cracow, 2002); J. GWIOŹDZIK, *Kultura pisma i książki w żeńskich klasztorach dawnej*

acy in late medieval towns in Poland,[118] but comprehensive studies about practices of reading and writing by women in early modern towns in the Polish-Lithuanian Commonwealth are still lacking.

This book is rooted also in 'literary borderland studies' (*studia pograniczne*), which form part of postcolonial studies. This approach has been developed from the 1990s onwards. At first, it was focused on cultural production in multi-ethnic East-Central Europe;[119] recently it has also been applied to other territories.[120] Borderland studies do not possess an explicit methodology. What first triggered this approach was the notion that East-Central Europe did not always fit the methods concerning the study of cultural production in other parts of Europe. As a result, the term 'borderland' was coined.

A borderland is a space of a heterogeneous culture, which is constituted by groups of people that differ ethnically, linguistically, religiously, legally, or in other ways. Each group has developed its own 'habitus', which interacts with other 'habituses' within the borderland. This interaction is visible in the results of cultural production. For example, in early modern Vilnius Catholics, the Jews, and the Orthodox could live in the same home. In the same printing

Rzeczypospolitej XVI-XVIII wieku (Katowice, 2015); *Kobiety za murem: Antologia tekstów lubelskich karmelitanek bosych XVII i XVIII wieku*, ed. A. NOWICKA-STRUSKA (Lublin, 2021).

118 A. BARTOSZEWICZ, "Kobieta a pismo w miastach późnośredniowiecznej Polski", in: *Per mulierem… Kobieta w dawnej Polsce – w średniowieczu i w dobie staropolskiej*, ed. K. JUSTYNIARSKA-CHOJAK and S. KONARSKA-ZIMNICKA (Warsaw, 2012), pp. 117-126; and EAD., *Urban Literacy in Late Medieval Poland*, pp. 383-392.

119 Most publications on borderland culture are devoted to literature in the nineteenth and twentieth century. Among them are: T. BUJNICKI, *W Wielkim Księstwie Litewskim i w Wilnie* (Warsaw, 2010); ID., "Miasto w tyglu kultur", in: *Wilno literackie na styku kultur*, ed. T. BUJNICKI and K. ZAJAS (Cracow, 2007), pp. 5-10; P. BUKOWIEC, "Mała tożsamość: Esej na marginesie *Leśnika* Marii Kuncewiczowej", in: *Etniczność, tożsamość, literatura*, ed. P. BUKOWIEC and D. SIWOR (Cracow, 2010), pp. 246-258; ID., "O potrzebie ujęć subwersywnych w badaniach nad pograniczem", *Wielogłos* 20.2 (2014), pp. 81-90; ID., *Różnice w druku: Studium z dziejów wielojęzycznej kultury literackiej na XIX-wiecznej Litwie* (Cracow, 2017); B. KAŁĘBA, *Rozdroże: Literatura polska w kręgu litewskiego odrodzenia narodowego* (Cracow, 2016); M. KVIETKAUSKAS, *Vilniaus literatūrų kontrapunktai*; E. PROKOP-JANIEC, "Kategoria pogranicza we współczesnych studiach żydowskich", in: *Na pograniczach literatury*, ed. J. FAZAN and K. ZAJAS (Cracow, 2012), pp. 134-146; A. ROMANOWSKI, *Młoda Polska wileńska* (Cracow, 1999); B. SPEIČYTĖ, *Poetinės kultūros formos: LDK palikimas XIX amžiaus Lietuvos literatūroje* (Vilnius, 2004). Recently Katharina N. Piechocki in her valuable monograph used border (-land) studies to examine the Renaissance concepts of Europe, cf. K.N. PIECHOCKI, *Cartographic Humanism: The Making of Early Modern Europe* (Chicago and London, 2019), pp. 68-106.

120 P. BUKOWIEC, "From Baranowski to Baranauskas, from James to Ngũgĩ: Post-colonial aspects of linguistic switch", *Studia Interkulturowe Europy Środkowo-Wschodniej* 13 (2020), pp. 219-243.

house, Calvinist and Orthodox books were printed. Within the city walls, there were the Uniate, Calvinist, and Lutheran churches. In public spaces four different languages could be heard on a daily basis. The borderland cultural system can be compared to an emulsion: its components are in a state of dispersion and never make a homogeneous solution. The borderland exhibits one more important feature. It is not found in the outskirts of two or more cultural zones, it is rather a relatively autonomous cultural system that is a centre for itself.[121] Thus, early modern Vilnius was not a result of a cultural clash, interference, or other interactions between Polish and Lithuanian lands, between Orthodox and Catholic religious zones, western and eastern influences, etc. It was (and still is) a cultural space in its own right, just like contemporary London and Paris, and like early modern Istanbul or Venice. All these cities I call borderlands.[122]

The second methodological basis of this book is provided by historical studies, especially those concerning the history of literacy. This important field in contemporary humanities was initiated by fundamental publications by Jack Goody (1963, 1977, 1987), Michael Clanchy (1979) and Walter Ong (1982).[123] Among the more recent studies which also strongly influenced my methodological approach are several volumes published in *Utrecht Studies in Medieval Literacy*.[124] I borrowed from these studies many inspiring concepts and termi-

[121] In this respect borderland studies differ from transcultural, transnational, or intercultural studies, which strongly rely on the division between centres and peripheries. In the latter perspectives borderlands are simply the peripheries, where interactions between two well-defined, monolithic, centrally positioned, and strong cultures occur. D. REICHARDT. "On the theory of a transcultural Francophony: The concept of Wolfgang Welsch and its didactic interest", *Novecento Transnazionale: Letterature, arti e culture* 1 (2017), pp. 40-56; A. KÖRNER, "Transnational history: Identities, structures, states", in: *Internationale Geschichte in Theorie und Praxis – International History in Theory and Practice*, ed. W.D. GODSEY, B. HAIDER-WILSON, and W. MUELLER, (Vienna, 2017), pp. 265-290.

[122] I write about the towns, but the term 'borderland' can be applied also to wider territories, e.g. Volhynia in Ukraine, to literary works, e.g. *Pan Tadeusz* by Adam Mickiewicz (1832), or to people, e.g. Meletius Smotrycki (*c.* 1577-1633). Smotrycki's identity and his multi-dimensional activities are a topic of a brilliant study by David A. Frick: D.A. FRICK, *Meletij Smotryćkyj* (Cambridge, Mass., 1995).

[123] J. GOODY and I. WATT, "The consequences of literacy", *Comparative Studies in Society and History* 5.3 (1963), pp. 304-345; J. GOODY, *The Domestication of the Savage Mind* (Cambridge, 1977); ID., *The Interface Between the Written and the Oral* (Cambridge, 1987); M.T. CLANCHY, *From Memory to Written Record: England 1066-1307*, 2nd edn. (Oxford, 1993); W.J. ONG, *Orality and Literacy: The Technologizing of the Word* (London and New York, 1982; reprinted 2013).

[124] From 1999 in the series published by Brepols more than fifty volumes appeared. For this book the most important for us are: *New Approaches to Medieval Communication*, ed. M.

nology, which proved especially useful in the fist part of the book. Among them there are: the intersection of administrative texts and literature; pragmatic literacy; levels of literacy; professionalisation of the written word; the use of different languages in administration; the mechanisms of the use Latin and vernacular languages; and others.

Literacy in medieval towns is the subject of several important works. An essential book from 1984 gives an overview of the history of the urban settlements in medieval and early modern Poland and Lithuania.[125] Several sections of this book are devoted to administration, education, and culture in the towns. Three recent volumes about medieval towns significantly contributed to the topic of the book: two volumes of *Medieval Urban Literacy* edited by Anna Adamska and Marco Mostert and a monograph by Agnieszka Bartoszewicz about literacy in late medieval Polish towns.[126] Adamska, Bartoszewicz, and Maciej Ptaszyński also edited an important volume of essays *Loca Scribendi: Places and Circles of the Production of the Culture of the Written Word in the Polish-Lithuanian Commonwealth in the Fifteenth-Eighteenth Centuries*.[127] This volume inspired me to coin the term *loci textuales*: the places of the production, copying, preserving, and using of texts.

Many historical studies that contributed to my research belong also to other fields of humanities, especially cultural,[128] urban,[129] communication,[130] and

MOSTERT (Turnhout, 1999); *The Development of Literate Mentalities in East Central Europe*, ed. A. ADAMSKA AND M. MOSTERT (Turnhout, 2004); *Along the Oral-Written Continuum: Types of Texts, Relations and their Implications*, ed. S. RANKOVIĆ, L. MELVE, and E. MUNDAL (Turnhout, 2010); *Vernacularity in England and Wales, c. 1300-1550*, ed. E. SALTER and H. WICKER (Turnhout, 2011); and *Cultures of Religious Reading in the Late Middle Ages*, ed. S. CORBELLINI (Turnhout, 2013); <http://www.brepols.net/Pages/BrowseBySeries.aspx?TreeSeries=USML>.

125 M. BOGUCKA and H. SAMSONOWICZ, *Dzieje miast i mieszczaństwa w Polsce przedrozbiorowej* (Wrocław, 1986).

126 *Writing and the Administration of Medieval Towns: Uses of the Written Word in Medieval Towns: Medieval Urban Literacy II*, ed. M. MOSTERT and A. ADAMSKA (Turnhout, 2014); and BARTOSZEWICZ, *Urban Literacy in Late Medieval Poland*.

127 *Loca scribendi: Miejsca i środowiska tworzące kulturę pisma w dawnej Rzeczypospolitej XV-XVIII stulecia*, ed. A. ADAMSKA, A. BARTOSZEWICZ, and M. PTASZYŃSKI (Warsaw, 2017).

128 *Kulturowa teoria literatury: Główne pojęcia i problemy*, ed. M.P. MARKOWSKI and R. NYCZ (Cracow, 2006).

129 D. JĘDRZEJCZYK, *Geografia kulturowa miasta* (Warsaw, 2004).

130 D.R. OLSON, *The World on Paper: The Conceptual and Cognitive Implications of Writing and Reading* (Cambridge, 1994).

memory studies,[131] and the history of education.[132] In Chapters 2 and 7 I widely used the findings of historians of book.[133]

The concept of literary culture presented here is similar to the concepts of 'graphosphere' and the 'literary field'. The graphosphere was defined as the "totality of graphic devices used to record, store, display, and disseminate messages and information, and the social and cultural spaces in which they figure".[134] While the term graphosphere is still a relatively new, the literary field is well established in the humanities. This is one of the central categories developed by the French sociologist Pierre Bourdieu. In *The Rules of Art* he explained how literature works in the social context.[135] Bourdieu argues that the literary field emerged as an autonomous field only in the capitalist culture of the second half of the nineteenth century.[136] Even if we agree with this state-

[131] In Chapter 10, I use the concepts 'cultural memory' of Jan Assmann and *memoria* of Otto Gerhard Oexle. See J. ASSMANN, *Cultural Memory and Early Civilization: Writing, Remembrance, and Political Imagination* (Cambridge, 2011); O.G. OEXLE, "Die Gegenwart der Lebenden und der Toten: Gedanken über Memoria", in: *Gedächtnis, das Gemeinschaft stiftet*, ed. K. SCHMID (Munich, 1985), pp. 74-107; ID., "Memoria als Kultur", in: *Memoria als Kultur*, ed. O.G. OEXLE (Göttingen, 1995), pp. 9-78.

[132] L. PIECHNIK, *Początki Akademii Wileńskiej*; J. OCHMAŃSKI, "Najdawniejsze szkoły na Litwie", pp. 113-133; P.F. GRENDLER, *Schooling in Renaissance Italy: Literacy and Learning, 1300-1600* (Baltimore and London, 1991); K. STOPKA, *Szkoły katedralne metropolii gnieźnieńskiej w średniowieczu: Studia nad kształtowaniem kleru polskiego w wiekach średnich* (Cracow, 1994).

[133] *Drukarze dawnej Polski od XV do XVIII wieku*, 5, *Wielkie Księstwo Litewskie*, ed. A. KAWECKA-GRYCZOWA, K. KOROTAJOWA, and W. KRAJEWSKI (Wrocław, 1959); E. LAUCEVIČIUS, *Knygų įrišimai Lietuvos bibliotekose* (Vilnius, 1976); E. POTKOWSKI, *Książka rękopiśmienna w kulturze Polski* (Warsaw, 1984); J.S. GRUCHAŁA, *Iucunda familia librorum: Humaniści renesansowi w świecie książki* (Cracow, 2002).

[134] S. FRANKLIN, "Mapping the graphosphere: Cultures of writing in early nineteenth-century Russia (and before)", *Kritika: Explorations in Russian and Eurasian History*, 12.3 (2011), p. 531. The term was expanded by Franklin in his later study S. FRANKLIN, *The Russian Graphosphere, 1450-1850* (Cambridge and New York, 2019), pp. 1-9. Although Franklin's approach seems to be attractive, the book lacks a connection with current research on the sociology of literature and on medieval and early modern literacy (e.g. there are no references to the seminal books by T.M. Clanchy or P. Bourdieu). The book only minimally discusses the transcultural position of the Russian graphosphere, especially in the second half of the seventeenth and the first half of the eighteenth century. Early modern Russian literary culture in many respects mirrors the borderland features of the literary culture of the Hetmanate and the eastern parts of the Polish-Lithuanian Commonwealth.

[135] P. BOURDIEU, *The Rules of Art: Genesis and Structure of the Literary Field*, trans. S. EMANUEL (Stanford, 1996).

[136] G. SAPIRO, "The literary field between the state and the market", *Poetics* 31 (2003), pp. 441-464.

ment, many findings and terms proposed by Bourdieu are useful in research on late medieval and early modern literary culture as well, especially the concepts of the 'habitus' and of different forms of capital, such as 'cultural capital'.[137]

The Structure of the Book

The book consists of nine chapters, subsumed under three parts. They could be described by five words or categories: people, places, objects, procedures, and networks.

The first part concerns the *loci textuales* and the legal settings of the use of texts. In this part I will try to answer two questions: what were the centres of textual production in Vilnius and what were their legal frames? Like other urban settlements in this part of Europe, Vilnius was founded accordingly to Magdeburg law. Consequently, one of the main 'textual places' of the city was the municipal chancery.

In the first chapter I examine how the Vilnius town hall functioned as a place where legal texts were produced, used, and archived. To be able to do so, I had to reconstruct the main legal settings that enabled this activity. To this end the royal privileges (of 1387, 1432, 1536 and others), the city statute (1552), and other documents were examined. However, since the city was also a political, religious, and administrative centre, several other chanceries and courts operated within the city walls. They are presented in the second section, which discusses among others the chanceries of the Grand Duke (the Lithuanian chancery), the Vilnius Catholic chapter, the Protestant Churches, the Jesuit Province, etc. Finally, the staff of these institutions is presented: notaries, secretaries, and scribes.

Chapter 2 will be entirely devoted to the preserving texts, that is to the archives and libraries. Even though the remaining sources are far from complete, we can see Vilnius as a great depository of texts. Apart from the city archive, which in 1655 counted *c.* 300 volumes of records, the state archive (the Lithuanian *Metrica*) was kept in the city. In the sixteenth and seventeenth centuries, dozens of book collections were located in Vilnius, both ecclesiastical and private. Their history and content is presented in this chapter as well.

[137] Bourdieu distinguished several forms of capital available to a member of society: economic, social, educational, and cultural capital. See P. BOURDIEU, *Distinction: A Social Critique of the Judgement of Taste*, trans. R. NICE (Cambridge, Mass., 1984), pp. 13-14.

Among the most important *loci textuales* in each town are schools. In Chapter 3, history of the Vilnius schools is presented. The first school of which we have knowledge was the cathedral school, founded in the 1380s. In the sixteenth century other schools were established, such as St. John's parish school, several Orthodox, Protestant, Jewish, and Muslim schools, and finally the Jesuit college and the Academy (University) of Vilnius. At the turn of the sixteenth and seventeenth centuries Vilnius became the major educational centre in the Grand Duchy of Lithuania and in this part of Europe generally.

In early modern times, women formed a special group of users of texts. Chapter 4 is entirely devoted to their *loci textuales*. They could be traced from the end of the fifteenth century only; earlier data are missing. All women who lived in Vilnius were pragmatically literate, but only a few of them gained higher levels of literacy. In the first section I examine the lay female inhabitants of the city and their literary education, legal activities, and constraints related to the use of texts. The second section is devoted to nunneries, which in the seventeenth century were important *loci textuales*. The most prolific were the Franciscan Observant (Bernardine), Benedictine, and Carmelite nunneries. The literary activities of nuns and their literary output is presented. The final section brings some observations about the chanceries and courts of the queens and princesses. During their long stays in Vilnius, their secretaries operated in the royal castle. In this chapter I focus on the correspondence of Helena of Moscow, Bona Sforza, Elisabeth of Austria, and Barbara Radziwiłłowa.

The second part of the book concerns the materiality of texts and procedures of their use.

Chapter 5 is devoted to reading and writing. I focus on pragmatic literacy, levels of literacy, and cultural, economic, and social capital of readers and writers. The sources from the sixteenth and seventeenth century examined in this chapter usually concern economic and religious matters. They allow us to establish the social circumstances in which literature could function in early modern Vilnius.

In Chapter 6 I focus on the material aspects of textual production: utensils and their production (such as paper, quills, wax, etc.), the languages used in Vilnius, and multiscripturality. The inhabitants of the city spoke seven languages and used four alphabets. Most sources were written in Latin and Cyrillic script, in the Latin, Polish, German, Lithuanian, Ruthenian, and Church Slavonic languages. In this section some 'minor' scripts are also examined, to wit Arabic and Hebrew script.

Chapter 7, the last chapter in this part, is devoted to the printed book, its production (printing houses, bookbinders), and bookselling. The topic is important, because early modern Vilnius was one of the main centres of book production in Eastern Europe, printing books both with Cyrillic and Latin characters.

Part 3, *Genera scribendi* ('The Genres of Writing') consists of four chapters. They show how rhetoric permeated all the aspects of urban textuality. I decided to order them according to their rhetorical functions. They are based on the classical division of texts into rhetorical genres (*genera dicendi*),[138] that is deliberative (for political and administrative purposes; Chapter 8), judicial (for litigation; Chapter 9), and epideictic (Chapter 10). This last rhetorical genre includes texts whose fundamental purpose was to be pleasant for the reader, but also to shape hierarchy and thereby providing order to the surrounding world. Chapter 11, the last chapter of the book, deals with the religious function of texts. This was not mentioned in rhetorical theory, but the texts studied here are also highly rhetoric.

It turns out that, through the use of seemingly archaic rhetorical categories, one can write about early modern Vilnius from many perspectives that sometimes exclude and sometimes complement each other.

In the Conclusion, once again I focus on the significance of the multicultural texts that formed a borderland city. I also make some final remarks about the city as a space of linguistic, literary, ritual, and other translations.

Terminology and Other Explanations

Since the book is intended for an audience from several fields within the humanities, some terms used here need to be explained more thoroughly. Some of them may be ambiguous, while others belong to the specific historical conditions of the Polish-Lithuanian Commonwealth and are familiar only to historians of the region understand them, and some others still belong strictly to Polish literary studies. Finally, there is some terminology coined especially for this book. The most important of these words have already been explained above: the literary rhizome, literary culture, borderland, the rhetorical organisation of the city, and *loci textuales*. Below I present the others.

[138] LAUSBERG, *Handbook of Literary Rhetoric*, pp. 30-39.

Applied literature. This term (*literatura stosowana* or *użytkowa*) has been widely used by Polish literary critics since the 1930s, when Stefania Skwarczyńska used it for the first time.[139] It describes those literary genres and works whose purpose is not primarily aesthetic, for instance letters, sermons, conversations, journals etc.[140] In her theory of literature, Skwarczyńska extended literature to genres or texts that had been absent from traditional poetics. The term is particularly important in Chapters 8 and 11, where the applied texts (*teksty użytkowe*) are presented: charters, testaments, letters, and prayers. Part of them belongs to the register of pragmatic literacy.

Church. In Polish and Ruthenian, the languages which since the sixteenth century dominated in Vilnius, the main Christian confessions have names for specific 'churches': *kościół* (a Catholic church), *cerkiew* (an Orthodox or Uniate church), and *zbór* (a Protestant church). These names are also applied to the names of ecclesiastical organisations (written with capital letters, for instance *Cerkiew* – the 'Orthodox Church'). There are also adjectives formed from these nouns (for instance *ulica Zborowa* – 'Protestant Church Street'). In English, this rich vocabulary is replaced by the single word 'church', which not always renders the nuances of the Polish words.

City. I call Vilnius a city, although it was not a big urban settlement. In the fifteenth century it can be compared to the Polish towns of the second category, that had no more than 3000 inhabitants (such as the Polish cities of Lublin, Sandomierz or Kalisz).[141] According to estimates, in the sixteenth century Vilnius counted *c.* 5,000-10,000 inhabitants.[142] It is estimated that just before the Muscovite invasion in 1655, *c.* 20,000 inhabitants lived there.[143] By the

[139] S. SKWARCZYŃSKA, "O pojęcie literatury stosowanej", *Pamiętnik Literacki* 28.1.4 (1932), pp. 1-24.

[140] S. SKWARCZYŃSKA, *Teoria listu* (Białystok, 2005).

[141] In the second half of the fifteenth century, Polish cities were divided into four classes, which facilitate the state tax policy. Vilnius, as a Lithuanian city, was not included in these registers, so our comparison is just a conjecture. M. BOGUCKA and H. SAMSONOWICZ, *Dzieje miast i mieszczaństwa w Polsce*, pp. 109-133. However, in the fifteenth century, Vilnius almost certainly could not be as large and wealthy an urban settlement as Cracow, Gdańsk, Prague, Vienna, and Wrocław, or even Poznań and Lviv.

[142] for reasons of comparison: in the sixteenth century the Cracow agglomeration had from *c.* 23,000 to *c.* 28,000 inhabitants and its size was similar to Prague (*c.* 30,000). In the first decades of the seventeenth century, more than 36,000 people may have lived in Cracow. L. BELZYT, *Kraków i Praga około 1600 roku: Porównanie topograficznych i demograficznych aspektów dwóch metropolii Europy Środkowo-Wschodniej* (Toruń, 1999), pp. 95-96, 130.

[143] There are no accurate data to estimate the number of inhabitants of Vilnius. Researchers vary in their calculations. Łowmiańska, e.g., estimated the number of the inhabitants at 14,000,

South- and Western-European standards, Vilnius was rather a town. However, in less densely populated countries of Europe, such as Sweden, the Polish-Lithuanian Commonwealth, Muscovy, Moldova, Transylvania, Brandenburg, or Pomerania, not only the numbers of the population decided calling an urban settlement a city, but also its political, religious, cultural, and symbolic functions. In the sixteenth and seventeenth centuries metropolises such as Cracow, Königsberg, Prague, Stockholm, Suceava, Vilnius, and Warsaw were (in their local contexts) cities.

'Closed' city and *'open' city*. In a 'closed' city, events take place on a micro-scale, limited by the space of the city walls, and the activities of those who live or stay there are directed inwards. The influence of an 'open' city can be felt in other places as well. It draws the outside world into its own life but it is also pulled back into external affairs. It is an integral, though separate, part of its surrounding reality. Both spaces activate and stimulate each other. Both types of city, 'open' and 'closed', form a complex network of interconnections. The texts usually associated with the 'closed' city are for instance last wills, epitaphs, and other public inscriptions, court registers, the 'city statute' (*wilkierz*), etc. Among the texts of the 'open' city we can count letters, printed sermons, political and religious pamphlets, lives of local saints, etc. The concept of the 'closed' and 'open' city will be discussed mainly in part 3 of the book.

The Grand Duke of Lithuania and King of Poland. The ruler of the Grand Duchy of Lithuania was the Grand Duke. However, since 1386 most of the Grand Dukes were also Kings of Poland. Thus, in the sources the rulers of Lithuania were simply called 'kings'[144] and the adjectives for 'royal' (*królewski*, *regius*) were usually applied. I also use these titles and call Sigismund III Vasa, for instance, 'king'. However, some rulers were only Grand Dukes of Lithuania, for instance Jogaila before 1386, Vytautas, Casimir Jagiellon in 1440-1447, and Alexander Jagiellon in 1492-1501. In these instances I call these rulers 'Grand Dukes'. In the historical sources in Polish and Ruthenian

Paknys gave the number as 25,000 and Frick as 20,000. All of them agree, though, that during the war in 1655-1661 Vilnius lost *c.* 50% of its population. See M. ŁOWMIAŃSKA, "Wilno przed najazdem moskiewskim", pp. 219-224; M. PAKNYS, *Vilniaus miestas ir miestiečiai 1636 m. Namai, gyventojai, svečiai* (Vilnius, 2006), pp. 16-18; FRICK, *Kith, Kin, and Neighbors*, pp. 7, 428-429.

[144] E.g. "Sigismund Augustus, by the Grace of the Lord King of Poland, Grand Duke of Lithuania, Ruthenia, Prussia, Samogitia, Masovia, etc.". The title of King of Poland was always put in the first place, as the most important.

the Grand Duke is often called *hospodar*. The adjective *hospodarski* was used in some names of the grand ducal institutions, for instance *sąd hospodarski* (the court of the Grand Duke).

Grosz ('groat', *Groschen*). The *grosz* was a silver coin which from the mid-fourteenth century was used in the Kingdom of Poland and later also in the Grand Duchy of Lithuania. Its value changed, but it remained the main monetary unit. For larger sums of money, the term *kopa groszy* was used, which meant one 'shock' (60) of *grosz*. Another monetary unit of account that was widely used in the Polish-Lithuanian state was the *złoty*, worth 30 *grosz*. However, the monetary system was complex and intricate, because the value of the *grosz* changed over the time. Other monetary units used in Lithuania were *grzywna* (48 *grosz*), *szeląg* ('shilling', 1/3 *grosz*), *czerwony złoty* ('ducat' or 'florin', a golden coin whose value varied over the time; in 1501 it was worth 32 *grosz*, by the end of the century 58-60 *grosz*, and in 1655 180 *grosz*); *talar* ('thaler', a silver coin worth in 1501 30 *grosz*, by the end of the sixteenth century 36 *grosz*, and in 1655 90 *grosz*).[145]

Humanist. In this book, the term humanist is understood in the way Paul Oskar Kristeller understood it in his works.[146] The humanists were professionals of the written word who were trained in humanities, that is in grammar, poetry, and especially rhetoric.[147] They were *oratores* or rhetorical men, in the sense explained by Quintilian in his *Institutio oratoria* (Institutes of Oratory). Their proficiency was the result of practising *imitatio* in its fifteenth- and sixteenth-century meanings.[148] The humanists were specialists in interpretation, transformation, and in composing different types of texts: they were teachers, notaries, secretaries, scribes, diplomats, politicians, scholars, clergy, printers etc.

[145] W. ADAMCZYK, *Ceny w Lublinie od XVI do końca XVIII wieku – Les prix à Lublin dès le XVIe siècle jusqu'à la fin du XVIIIe siècle* (Lviv, 1935), pp. 22-26, 57-63; A. JEZIERSKI, and C. LESZCZYŃSKA, *Historia gospodarcza Polski* (Warsaw, 1998), p. 61.

[146] P.O. KRISTELLER, "Humanism and scholasticism in the Italian Renaissance", *Byzantion* 17 (1944), pp. 346-374. See P. BAKER, *Italian Renaissance Humanism in the Mirror* (Cambridge, 2015), pp. 6-10.

[147] At a first glance, the curriculum of the humanist schools in the fifteenth-seventeenth centuries was the continuation of the medieval *trivium*. However, as Peter Burke pointed out, important shifts were made and the content, ways, and purpose of teaching in humanist *trivia* differed significantly from the earlier schools. See P. BURKE, *The Italian Renaissance: Culture and Society in Italy* (Princeton, 1986), pp. 54-56.

[148] B. OTWINOWSKA, "Imitacja", in: *Słownik literatury staropolskiej: Średniowiecze – Renesans – Barok*, pp. 344-349.

Middle Ages and *early modern times*; 'medieval' and 'early modern'. I do not dare to draw a line between these epochs and to make any stable distinctions. The terms should be understood as a part of a process of change. The literary culture of the end of the fifteenth century in Vilnius and the end of the sixteenth century differed significantly – I try to catch the change but I do not label something as either 'medieval' or 'early modern'.[149]

Text. My understanding of the word 'text' is quite general. By texts I mean objects that were created by means of writing. I will be interested in all types of texts, although I will not devote the same amount of space and attention to all of them. Most of them can be classified into specific categories, types, or genres, and can be distinguished using functional and structural criteria. Since my intention is not to describe or catalogue, but to try to understand, I will not devote too much space to traditional historical-literary genre classifications. However, I will use them to create a map-like overview of a fairly large scale.

The chronological scope of my book spans the period from 1323, when Gediminas wrote his first letters known to us, up to 1655, that is, the destruction of the city by the Muscovite army. These dates are of course arbitrary, as they usually are in such cases. On the one hand, it cannot be precluded that some chancery clerks worked for Gediminas in Vilnius before he sent his letters to the Hanseatic cities. On the other hand, the year 1655 is an even less clear caesura because, despite the fact that the city had been devastated and had lost a vast number of its inhabitants, the continuity of textual procedures was still maintained. Designating the mid-seventeenth century as a convenient finish (as such a point must needs be designated) is supported by the fact that both the number and variety of texts, that is, their types, subjects, alphabets and languages, reached their climax in the first half of the seventeenth century and declined in the first decades after the catastrophe. The situation was not worse, but it was different.

The Name of the City, the Politics of Memory, and Linguistic Issues

In Polish, my native tongue, the city is called Wilno, but in this book I call it Vilnius.

[149] cf. A. ADAMSKA and M. MOSTERT, "Introduction", in: *Writing and the Administration of Medieval Towns*, p. 3.

Vilnius is the official contemporary Lithuanian name of the capital of the Republic of Lithuania. However, the city has had several names in several languages which render its rich and complex history: Belarusian *Вільня*, Polish *Wilno*, Hebrew וילנה, Yiddish ווילנע, German *Wilna*, Latin *Vilna*, Russian *Вильно*, Ukrainian *Вільнюс* and *Вильно*. This polyonomy, however, is apparent because each of these names refers in fact to a slightly different referent, that is, a Vilnius of a different language, creed, or social group. It is therefore hard to imagine a transparent and objective language in which to write about this city, covering the entire diverse range of perspectives. David A. Frick chose the Polish name Wilno:

> The *acta* of the city magistracy, a central source for this book, were kept largely in Polish with occasional formulaic prologues and colophons in Latin and a phrase or two in Ruthenian. As most of the source material for a study of seventeenth-century Wilno burgher life – perhaps 85 percent – is in Polish garb, I have given all names in Polish form (with variant forms in parentheses where needed). This has nothing to do with the nationalist (and thus anachronistic) fights between proponents of one orthography over another.[150]

However, in the case of East Central Europe (and many other parts of the world), the choice of language – even if it is well motivated, as in the case of Frick – determines the choice of perspective. History is always involved in politics. This involvement, known from ancient times and sometimes less visible, in the last thirty years got its own name: the "politics of history" (memory) or "history politics", derived from German *Geschichtspolitik*.[151] There are many instances of international cooperation and research groups seeking a common language and common interpretations of historical events in Central and Eastern Europe.[152] Nevertheless, all the Eastern- and Central-European states,[153] research communities, and individual scholars are taking part – some

[150] D.A. Frick, *Kith, Kin, and Neighbors*, p. xxiii.

[151] *Geschichtspolitik und demokratische Kultur: Bilanz und Perspektiven*, ed. B. Bouvier and M. Schneider (Bonn, 2008); M. Saryusz-Wolska, *Pamięć zbiorowa i kulturowa: Współczesna perspektywa niemiecka* (Cracow, 2009). In English there exists also a concept of 'politics of memory'.

[152] One such institutions is the Lithuanian Committee (*Komisja Lituanistyczna*) in the Institute of History of the Polish Academy of Sciences in Warsaw. Since 1990, the Committee has organised annual conferences, which are a forum for the international community of researchers working on the Grand Duchy of Lithuania.

[153] The most controversial topics are related to history of the Second World War: responsibility for the war crimes and ethnic cleansings, involvement in the Holocaust, col-

times even involuntarily – in a competition for the past. The history of the Grand Duchy of Lithuania is also an object of politics of history (memory), and many instances of this process can be shown.[154]

The personal experience and cultural horizons of a historian always determine his or her research and publications. Thus, despite the fact I tried to avoid partiality, my Polonocentric perspective was in some degree inevitable. Taking it into account, I tried to avoid this perspective as far as possible.

Whenever it was possible, I decided to use English terminology, for instance the *voivode*, the *Voigt*, but 'the city council', 'aldermen', etc. When it was possible, I translated Polish, Ruthenian or Latin terms into English and added the original version in brackets. In many instances I chose Polish, and sometimes Ruthenian, because in this languages the names and terms were used in medieval and early modern sources (for instance *diak*, *hetman*, *grosz*, *kopa*). The use of Polish terminology established by historical sources also

laboration with the Nazis and the Soviet occupants, mass deportations, territorial disputes, etc. For example, in 2015 the Polish authorities launched the Strategy for the Polish Historical Policy. See "Andrzej Duda inauguruje prace nad powstaniem Strategii Polskiej Polityki Historycznej: *Pytanie, jak to robić?*" [przemówienie prezydenta]", *wPolityce*, 17.11.2015 <https://wpolityce.pl/polityka/272108-andrzej-duda-inauguruje-prace-nad-powstaniem-strategii-polskiej-polityki-historycznej-pytanie-jak-to-robic-przemowienie-prezydenta> (accessed on 2.02.2022).

[154] I give three examples. At the blog of the *Universal Short Title Catalogue: An Open Access Bibliography of Early Modern Print Culture* of the University of St. Andrews (Scotland), there is a section devoted to Lithuanian early modern printed books. The author of the essay suggests that the contemporary Republic of Lithuania is the direct heir of the Grand Duchy of Lithuania; cf. A. DER WEDUWEN, "USTC Adds Coverage of the Print Culture of the Grand Duchy of Lithuania, 1522-1650; Wednesday March 4, 2020" < https://pwrb.wp.st-andrews.ac.uk/ustc-adds-coverage-of-the-print-culture-of-the-grand-duchy-of-lithuania-1522-1650-5/> (accessed on 5.02.2022). And in March 2021 a facsimile of the *Desatiglav* of Matvei Desatyi was published as a joint project of Belarus and Russia by the Standing Committee of Union state: *Библия Матфея Десятого 1507 года. Из собрания Библиотеки Российской академии наук*, 2 vols. (Санкт-Петербург, 2020) <https:// www.postkomsg.com/reading_room/227714/?fbclid=IwAR1BpDrq5H5X5V5a7K4SPNjsSfAvfjgzCFuvS7TE0iVAYsX1Aq7t0CoKdIE> (accessed on 5.02. 2022). The project has its political dimensions and links the memory of the Orthodox culture of the Grand Duchy of Lithuania with Moscow rather than with Vilnius. Finally, in the Introduction to the edition of a polemic between Stanisław Orzechowski (1513-1566) and the *Voigt* of Vilnius Augustyn Rotundus, Krzysztof Koehler wrote: "The debate between Stanisław Orzechowski and Augustyn Rotundus Mieleski, which we present in this publication, belongs to the most interesting polemics that took place in Renaissance Poland" (K. KOEHLER, "Wstęp", in: *Stanisława Orzechowskiego i Augustyna Rotundusa debata o Rzeczypospolitej*, ed. K. KOEHLER (Cracow, 2009), p. 7). The author missed the fact that it was not an internal Polish debate, and that Augustyn Rotundus had constructed a Lithuanian discourse of an independent country. Of similar examples of incorporating early modern Lithuanian, Ruthenian, or Livonian texts into Polish literature (in its modern sense) we can find many from the nineteenth century onwards.

concerns the numbering of rulers; hence the second ruler of the Polish-Lithuanian Commonwealth from the Vasa dynasty is here called Władysław IV, although Lithuanian scholars name him Vladislovas Vasa or Vladislovas II in accordance with the numbering of Lithuanian dukes.

The use of names is most troublesome, and some choices were necessary.

Geographical names are usually put in their contemporary versions, i.e. in the language of the state to which a town or village belongs today. This is why I chose Vilnius instead of *Вільня*, Navahrudak instead of Nowogródek, Gdańsk instead of Danzig. Cyrillic names are rendered in English transcription, for instance Kyiv, Minsk, Hrodna etc. Some places have their well-established English versions, for instance Cracow, Moscow, and Warsaw. Only in the case of Königsberg I used the historical toponym instead of its contemporary name, Kaliningrad.

The names 'Lithuania' and 'Poland' are used in their historic meanings and refer to two states that have not existed since the end of the eighteenth century, that is the Kingdom of Poland (or the Polish Crown) and the Grand Duchy of Lithuania. The adjectives 'Polish' and 'Lithuanian' are derivatives of these names, with the exception of the Polish language (one of the Western Slavonic languages) and the Lithuanian language (one of the Baltic languages). By analogy, if any Lithuanians or Poles are mentioned in this book, they cannot be identified with the citizens of today's Republic of Lithuania or the Republic of Poland respectively, nor with the members of the Lithuanian or Polish nations of today, even if present-day Poles or Lithuanians would like to regard them as their ancestors. The early modern Lithuanians and Poles cannot usually be equated with the contemporary ethnic meaning of these names. A sixteenth-century Pole, for instance, could be a German-speaking Catholic burgher from Royal Prussia, such as cardinal Stanisław Hozjusz, or a Ukrainian-speaking seventeenth-century Orthodox nobleman from Ukraine, such as Bohdan Khmelnytsky.

In accordance with the terminology used at least until the end of the seventeenth century, I use the names 'Muscovy' and 'Muscovites' and not 'Russia' or 'Russians'. The name 'Ruthenians' mostly refers to the ancestors of the contemporary Belarusians and sometimes to Ukrainians, Orthodox and Uniate eastern Slavs. In the sixteenth and seventeenth centuries the Ruthenians from the Grand Duchy of Lithuania were sometimes called Lithuanians. The Ruthenian (spoken) language refers to various variants of the old-Belarusian language. The complex question of the written Ruthenian language (*prosta mova*) and the Cyrillic alphabet is discussed in Chapter 6.

The spellings of persoanl names are based on historical sources, usually in a Polish version, for instance Akwilina Stryludzianka Dorofiejewiczowa, Maciej Vorbek-Lettow, Maciej Stryjowski, etc. The reader has to bear in mind that in other languages, especially in contemporary Lithuanian, the same names have other spellings. This is why in some instances I put also the variants in brackets, for instance in the case of Olbracht Gasztołt (Albertus Gastold, Albertas Goštautas) or Wojciech Wijuk Kojałowicz (Albertas Vijūkas-Kojelavičius; cf. the Index of personal names). Some names are already present in the English-language studies, for instance King Jogaila, Grand Duke Vytautas, Queen Anna Jagiellon, Krzysztof II Radziwiłł, Mikalojus Daukša, Abraomas Kulvietis, Martynas Mažvydas, Fracysk Skaryna, Piotr Skarga, Queen Constance of Austria, etc. There are a couple of exceptions, for instance Pedro Ruiz de Moros (instead of Piotr Rojzjusz or Roiziusz, widely used in Polish since the sixteenth century).

Nearly all quotations featured in the main text of this book are translated into English from the sources in Polish, Ruthenian, Latin, Church Slavonic, German, and Hebrew. This is for the reader's convenience. When citing, I add, whenever necessary, explicit information about the language of the original text.

Chapter 1

Chanceries, Courts, and Their Writing Staff

The institutions of the written word are important from the point of view of the literary culture of the city because they were the hubs of textual production in the city. With schools, the university, and printing houses, chanceries and courts were the most prolific centres where texts were developed, written, copied, and preserved. What is more, in these hubs dozens of specialists of textual production were employed. As we will see below, many of them produced and validated not only legal documents but also wrote poetry and rhetorical prose. Consequently, to understand the city as a place and space of textual production, the chanceries, their staff, and the legal settings in which these institutions worked must be examined. Most of these institutions were similar to those which operated in other urban settlements in Europe at the time. The uniqueness of Vilnius lies not in the institutions themselves and their functions, but rather in their setting and number.

Legal Settings

The basis of most of texts produced in any urban settlement in the late medieval and early modern Kingdom of Poland and the Grand Duchy of Lithuania (as in most towns of Latin Europe) were legal regulations, such as royal privileges, the municipal (German) law, statutes, and state law. Without these fundamental legal texts, the urban settlements could not function on any level. The legal settings were mainly derived from ancient tradition and deeply set in the textual context of other written sources: political, religious, philosophical, juridical, scientific, and poetical. The consequence of their introduction was a growth in the use of script on a large scale, that is the production and use of subsequent texts. In this process of massive production of texts one can observe the development of collective literacy and the "emergence of literate mentalities".[1] Since this process was embedded in rhetorical theory and practice, an intersection occurred between legal culture and belles-lettres: to some degree the legal settings constituted a frame for artistic texts.

Vilnius was a place where legal regulations were not only applied or used, but were also created. This process started in the fourteenth century, but its heyday was the sixteenth century. The representatives of the Lithuanian elites, who were involved in this process, many times expressed the significance of legal regulations in the proper functioning of the commonwealth (*res publica*) and society (*societas*). This applied both to the Grand Duchy of Lithuania and to its capital, which was also called a commonwealth (the *res publica Vilnensis*).[2]

The royal secretaries and other officials who were in the service of the state, and who were mostly residents of Vilnius, either created or applied the legal regulations that served the state and the city. Thanks to them, and contrary to the grumblings of the sixteenth-century lawyer Pedro Ruiz de Moros,[3] Vilnius can be considered as a communal space formed by legal texts. Already at the beginning of the sixteenth century, many graduates in law, experts legal matters, worked in the state chancery and the chancery of the cathedral chapter, such as chancellor Olbracht Gasztołd, canon Mikołaj Wiżgajło, Jerzy Taliat, and Wacław Czyrek.[4] Later, especially during the reign of King Sigismund II Augustus (1548-1572), even more humanist-lawyers were active in Vilnius. The task faced by these elite circles was to create and put into writing the law of the Grand Duchy of Lithuania. These activities accompanied the social and political transformations of the state, and resulted in several collections of laws

[1] A. ADAMSKA and M. MOSTERT, "Introduction", in: *Writing and the Administration of Medieval Towns*, p. 2.

[2] *Zbiór praw i przywilejów*, p. 144.

[3] Pedro Ruiz de Moros criticised the lack of efficient law and jurisprudence in Vilnius in his epigram *Facies urbis Vilnae* (The Face of the City of Vilnius). See P. Ruiz de Moros (Petrus Royzius), *Petri Royzii Maurei Alcagnicensis Carmina: Pars II carmina minora continens*, ed. B. KRUCZKIEWICZ (Cracow, 1900), pp. 17-18 (Nos. XXII, XXIII), p. 270; ID. (Petras Roizijus), *Rinktiniai eilėkraščiai*, trans. R. KATINAITĖ, E. PATIEJŪNIENĖ, and E. ULČINAITĖ (Vilnius, 2008), p. 171.

[4] S. GODEK, *Elementy prawa rzymskiego w III Statucie litewskim (1588)* (Warsaw, 2004), p. 29.

that are of prime importance for the history of legal literature, especially the *Statute of the Grand Duchy of Lithuania*.

One of these people was the aforementioned Pedro Ruiz de Moros (Piotr Rojzjusz, *c.* 1505-1571), the provost of St. John's church in Vilnius, lawyer and one of the co-authors of the second Lithuanian statute. He was also the author of a well-respected treatise on property law entitled *Decisions in the Appeal Cases in the Grand Ducal Lithuanian Court*, published in 1563 in Cracow.[5] The dissertation resulted from the experience Ruiz de Moros had gained while working at the grand ducal assessorial (appellate) court (*asesorski sąd hospodarski*), where he dealt with issues of the Lithuanian urban settlements governed by the Magdeburg law, including Vilnius.[6] In an extensive subtitle, the author or publisher wrote that it is "a work most worthy of reading and learning, both by those who preside in the courts and by those who teach or study true philosophy, that is the art of goodness and justice", and that it is a work "particularly necessary for all those involved in the administration of justice".[7] The ban on pirated reprinting of the work on pain of thirty *grzywna* of pure silver, as well as the phrasing quoted above, allow us to presume that the author and publisher believed that the work would enjoy great popularity, probably also among those inhabitants of Vilnius who dealt with the law. Later editions in Venice (1570) and Frankfurt (1572) testify to the accuracy of these assumptions.

A similar opinion on the usefulness of the codified law was expressed by chancellor Lew Sapieha in his Ruthenian dedicatory letter, published in the first printed edition of the Statute of 1588 and addressed to the Estates of the Grand Duchy of Lithuania:

[5] P. Ruiz de Moros, *Decisiones Petri Royzii de rebus in sacro auditorio Lituanico ex appellatione iudicatis* (Cracow, 1563). On Ruiz de Moros' work see: M. Dyjakowska, "*Decisiones Lituanicae* Piotra Rojzjusza – przykład renesansowego źródła poznania stosowania prawa rzymskiego przed sądem asesorskim w Wilnie: Problemy badawcze i translatorskie", *Krakowskie Studia z Historii Państwa i Prawa* 13.1 (2020), pp. 1-15; ead, "Prawo rzymskie jako kryterium interpretacyjne w *Decisiones Lituanicae* Piotra Rojzjusza", *Z Dziejów Prawa* 12 (2019), pp. 109-123.

[6] J. Tazbir, "Roizjusz Piotr", *PSB*, vol. 31, p. 501.

[7] *"Opus lectu dignissimum atque cognitu tam iis, qui iuridicundo praesunt, quam qui veram philosophiam hoc est artem boni et aequi vel tradunt, vel addiscunt, ob multiplicemque earum rerum tractationem exactamque ac diffusam definitionem, quae in scholam et forum incidere cottidie solent. Iurisprudentibus omnibus apprime necessarium*" (P. Ruiz de Moros, *Decisiones*, title page).

> So this curb, bit, and tack was invented for the suppression of every daredevil, so that, fearful of the law, he would refrain himself from any kind of violence and prodigality, and that he would not torment the weaker and poorer, and could not oppress them, as the law was enacted so that the mighty and powerful could not do all they wished. As Cicero said, we are slaves of laws so that we can exercise freedom. [...] And we rightfully take it for truth, for which we thank the Lord, that under the rule of kings and grand dukes, our lords, we have this power and freedom in our own hands and we can make our own laws, we seek our own freedoms in everything, because neither our neighbour, nor our fellow citizen in our homeland, nor our ruler, our lord can have any authority over us except that which is allowed by the law.[8]

Sapieha's preface implied that all the inhabitants of the State had knowledge of the law. This does not mean that all inhabitants of Vilnius read and understood legal collections on a regular basis, but we can assume the constant presence of texts of this type among them. This assumption is confirmed by posthumous inventories of the possessions of town dwellers, which included various editions of the Magdeburg law (*Ius Saxonicum*) and the Lithuanian statutes.[9] Legal books were also collected in the libraries of all Vilnius institutions, including the library of the cathedral chapter.[10]

Copies of the Magdeburg law must have been kept in the town hall, because they were indispensable for the city, aldermen, and the *Voigt* offices in their everyday legal proceedings. It is almost certain that in the second half of the fifteenth century some manuscripts which usually contained the Magdeburg law, collections of 'legal advice' (*Urteile*), and sometimes other legal regulations as well were in the possession of the aldermen's court, because we know it was in operation as early as 1484.[11] Such manuscripts, usually produced in Cracow, were often used by the municipal authorities and urban elites of the Kingdom of Poland in the late Middle Ages.[12] In the sixteenth century they

[8] *Статут Велікого Князства Літовского от наяснейшего господаря короля его мости Жикгимонта Третего на коронацыи въ Кракове выданы року 1588* (digital editions: <https://pravo.by/pravovaya-informatsiya/pomniki-gistoryi-prava-belarusi/kanstytutsyynae-prava-belarusi/statuty-vyalikaga-knyastva-lito-skaga/statut-1588-goda/po-naya-versiya-tekstu-pdf/> and <http://starbel.narod.ru/sapeh1.htm> accessed 8.12.2021).

[9] ZAKRZEWSKI, *O kulturze prawnej*, p. 44.

[10] See Chapter 2.

[11] A. RAGAUSKAS, "1650 m. kovo 30 d. Vilniaus suolininkų teismo įrašų knygų aprašas", in: *Lietuvos miestų istorijos šaltiniai*, 3, ed. A. DUBONIS (Vilnius, 2001), pp. 262-264.

[12] On the importance of these (sometimes made on demand) collections of urban and land law see: A. ŁOSOWSKA, *Kolekcja Liber legum i jej miejsce w kulturze umysłowej późnośrednio-*

were certainly replaced by printed editions of the Magdeburg law; it formed part, for instance, of a legal collection by Polish chancellor Jan Łaski in 1506,[13] there was the Latin version by Mikołaj Jaskier (1535),[14] and the Polish translations by Bartłomiej Groicki (in the 1550s)[15] and Paweł Szczerbic (in the 1580s).[16]

A particularly large number of legal books were held in the university library. King Sigismund Augustus bequeathed to the Vilnius Jesuit college his library, containing a couple of hundred legal books. In 1644, Kazimierz Lew Sapieha founded a chair of civil and canon law and bequeathed his library to the university as well. These legal collections were referred to by judges who sat in Vilnius courts of different administrative levels, sometimes mentioning specific regulations in their sentences.

The need for legal texts in Vilnius had a significant impact on the entire textual culture of the city. David A. Frick showed how the rhetoric of the protestations before the Vilnius courts was reflected in the polemical works of Meletius Smotrycki.[17] And this was not the only example of the osmosis between legal literature or 'juridical' texts and other types of text, often classified as belles-lettres. To understand the social history of literature in late medieval and early modern towns, one needs to take into account the legal framework,

wiecznego Przemyśla (Warsaw-Przemyśl, 2007) and BARTOSZEWICZ, *Urban Literacy in Late Medieval Poland*, pp. 17, 139-154. The topic was thoroughly discussed by Maciej Mikuła in his recent work M. MIKUŁA, *Municipal Magdeburg Law (Ius Municipale Magdeburgense) in Late Medieval Poland: A Study on the Evolution and Adaptation of Law* (Leiden and Boston, 2021).

[13] J. ŁASKI, *Commune incliti Polonie Regni privilegium, constitutionum et indultuum publicitus decretorum, approbatorumque cum nonnullis iuribus tam divinis quam humanis per serenissimum principem et dominum dominum Alexandrum, Dei gratia Regem Poloniae, magnum ducem Lithwanie, Russie, Prussieque dominum et haeredem etc.* (Cracow, 1506).

[14] M. JASKIER, *Iuris municipalis Maideburgensis liber vulgo Weichbild nuncupatus ex vetustissimis exemplaribus vigilanti opera nuper latinitate datus* (...) (Cracow, 1535); ID., *Promptuarium iuris provincialis Saxonici, quod Speculum Saxonum vocatur tum et municipalis Maideburgensis summa diligentia recollectum* (Cracow, 1535).

[15] B. GROICKI, *Artykuły prawa majdeburskiego, które zowią Speculum Saxonum* (Cracow, 1558); ID., *Ustawa płacej u sądów w prawie majdeburskim tak przed burmistrzem a rajcami, jak przed wójtem* (Cracow, 1568), ID., *Porządek sądów i spraw miejskich prawa majdeburskiego w Koronie Polskiej* (Cracow, 1559); ID., *Postępek sądów około karania na gardle* (Cracow 1559).

[16] P. SZCZERBIC, *Speculum Saxonum albo prawo saskie i magdeburskie porządkiem abecadła z łacińskiego i niemieckich egzemplarzów zebrane* (Lviv, 1581); ID., *Ius municipale, to jest prawo miejskie magdeburskie nowo z łacińskiego i niemieckiego języka z pilnością i wiernie przełożone* (Lviv, 1581).

[17] D.A. FRICK, "*Słowa uszczypliwe, słowa nieuczciwe*: The language of litigation and the Ruthenian polemic", *Paleoslavica* 10.1 (2002), pp. 133-138.

that is the legal texts which formed the rhetorical organisation of any urban settlement.

The legal regulations of an urban settlement were never introduced in a single act. It was a never-ending process of issuing new documents and their confirmations, supplements, elaborations, and alterations. The case of Vilnius was no different. From 1387, when King Jogaila granted the first privilege to the city, dozens of other documents regulating its life were issued. Among the most important were the confirmations of the previous privileges on the basis of the Magdeburg law, the privileges for merchants and guilds, the great privilege of 1536 issued by King Sigismund the Old, the 'statute' (*wilkierz*) of 1552, the Statutes of the Grand Duchy of Lithuania (1529, 1566 and 1588), and to some degree the 'parliament bills' (*konstytucje sejmowe*). In some parts of the city the ecclesiastical law, *Halakha*, and *pinkases* of the *Vaad* (the parliament of the Lithuanian Jews) and local legal regulations (such as the Statute of the Vilnius chapter) were applied.

We do not know how the inhabitants of Vilnius dealt with legal issues before the 'location' (the foundation) of the city in 1387, but Duke Gediminas's letters, written in Latin on 25 January and 26 May 1323 and addressed to the Hanseatic cities[18] imply the use of the Western European law in Vilnius already by the mid-fourteenth century. These few texts, similar to thousands of other letters written at that time all over Europe, are widely treated as the beginning of the city's history. Although some kind of urban settlement already existed at the place of the future city, the 1323 letters show that by the 1320s this settlement was constituted in a new legal sense.

Gediminas's letters to the Hanseatic cities were not a single and random event, because we know about a group of professionals of the written word in his entourage. Catholic friars (probably Franciscans) who served him, and who probably came to Lithuania from the State of the Teutonic Order, took part in

[18] *Kodeks dyplomatyczny Litwy*, p. 27-32; *Gedimino laiškai*, ed. V. Pašuta and I. Štal (Vilnius, 1966) (online: <http://viduramziu.istorija.net/ru/s1283.htm>, accessed 22.11.2021); *Chartularium Lithuaniae res gestas magni ducis Gedeminne illustrans – Gedimino laiškai*, ed. S.C. Rowell (Vilnius, 2003). The editor of the latest edition of Gediminas's letters (*Chartularium Lithuaniae*), S.C. Rowell, lists all documents known to have been issued or received by Gediminas; apart from the letters to the Hanseatic cities and the Dominicans, he also mentions correspondence with Pope John XXII. The first known letters, sent from Vilnius, were written in the summer of 1322. Most of the preserved letters are dated 1323, but there are also later ones, e.g. from 2 June 1325 and from 1 November 1338. See S.C. Rowell, *Pratramė*, in: *Chartularium Lithuaniae*, pp. XV-XXVIII, and Nos. 14-25, 54, 60, 69.

a meeting in 1324 devoted to his acceptance of Christianity.[19] Although this group of clerics cannot be described as the grand duke's chancery, their work introduced to the city-to-be to Western standards of the use of the written word for the purposes of administration and communication. The 1323 letters promised the German merchants or artisans who would settled there favourable conditions – also in legal terms – to carry on their businesses.

Although we do not know what the direct response of German merchants and craftsmen to Gediminas's letter was, over the next decades Vilnius began to be considered as one of the growing markets on the trade routes. This was not due not only to its convenient location but also to its political and administrative functions. By the mid-fourteenth century Vilnius was already an urban settlement with two churches, one Catholic and the other Orthodox. We may suppose that at least the German inhabitants of Vilnius used the Magdeburg law or one of its local adaptations, such as the Culm law. Still, we do not have any documents with which to confirm this hypothesis.

The actual location of the city took place on 21 March 1387.[20] The charter issued by King Jogaila was succinct. Its disposition states only that Vilnius was granted the Magdeburg law ("*ius Theutonicum quod Magdeburiense dicitur damus et conserimus*"); the status of Vilnius was no different from that of the towns in the Polish Crown: the authority over the town belonged to the *starosta* of Vilnius castle and the inhabitants were obliged to defend the castle as long as the city walls were standing.[21] In the fifteenth century, however, the grand duke held the supreme legal position in the Grand Duchy of Lithuania, and his power was not restricted by any written law.[22] He could interfere in the matters of Vilnius without any regard for the city's Magdeburg laws, for instance by granting his people parts of the city and consequently to exempt these parts from the city's jurisdiction. In the 1480s, for example, King Casimir Jagiellon gave the Lithuanian chancellor Olehna Sudymantowicz a plot of land. The plot was located in the very centre of the city in front of the Orthodox church of St.

[19] M. KOSMAN, *W kancelarii wielkiego księcia Witolda*, in: ID., *Orzeł i Pogoń*, p. 109; L. KORCZAK, *Litewska rada wielkoksiążęca w XV w.* (Cracow, 1998), p. 14; see also ROWELL, *Pratramė*, pp. XXXVI-XXXVIII.

[20] *Zbiór praw i przywilejów*, pp. 1-2; *Собрание древних грамот и актов городов*, pp. 1-2.

[21] *Zbiór praw i przywilejów*, p. 1; *Собрание древних грамот и актов*, p. 1. See I. JAWORSKI, "Przywileje miejskie na prawo niemieckie w Wielkiem Księstwie Litewskiem", *Rocznik Prawniczy Wileński* 3 (1929), pp. 48-49.

[22] L. KORCZAK, *Monarcha i poddani: System władzy w Wielkim Księstwie Litewskim w okresie wczesnojagiellońskim* (Cracow, 2008), pp. 31-32.

Nicolas. The document was not copied into the city registers, but in a book of the Lithuanian *Metrica.*[23]

In the following decades of the fifteenth century other privileges were given to the town, among others exemptions of paying tolls (1432, confirmed in 1440), exemptions from the obligation to give the monarch free transport services (Polish: *podwody*; 1451, confirmed in 1492), privileges on fairs (1441), the city scales (1432, 1441), and for free commerce in the cities of Poland and Lithuania (1448, 1496, 1514).[24] From 1495 privileges were granted to the Vilnius guilds.[25] The oldest of these guilds were those of the goldsmiths (1495), tailors (1495), barbers (1509), smiths, caldron makers, and locksmiths (1516), tanners (1519?), and shoemakers (1522).[26]

Every time the new ruler ascended to the throne of the Grand Duchy of Lithuania, the inhabitants of the city received confirmations of their privileges (Sigismund Kęstutaitis in 1432, Casimir Jagiellon in 1441, Alexander Jagiellon in 1492, Sigismud the Old in 1506, Sigismund Augustus in 1547, Stephen Báthory in 1576, Sigismund III Vasa in 1588, Vladislaus IV Vasa in 1633, and John Casmir Vasa in 1649). From 1432 particular regulations relative mainly to city commerce were included in to the main privilege. The legal immunity of the city was confirmed several times by the kings in the sixteenth and seventeenth centuries, especially when the burghers had to defend their rights and freedoms against the bishop and chapter of Vilnius, the mayor (*Burgermeister*; *horodniczy*) of Vilnius castle, state officials (the chancellor and the *voivode* of Vilnius), and the nobility.

Two documents issued in the sixteenth century were particularly important for the organisation of the city: the privilege of 1536 and the 'city statute' (*wilkierz*) of 1552. These long documents dealt with many topics, and merit meticulous examination. Here I will present only those parts which had an impact – either directly or indirectly – on how different types of texts were produced and used in Vilnius.

[23] *Lietuvos Metrika: Knyga Nr. 4 (1471-1491): Užrašymų knyga 4*, ed. L. ANUŽYTĖ (Vilnius, 2004), pp. 113-114, No. 71.

[24] *Zbiór praw i przywilejów*, pp. 2-18, 23-25; *Собрание древних грамот и актов*, 1, pp. 2-7, 10-16, 23-24; JAWORSKI, "Przywileje miejskie", p. 58.

[25] The collection of Vilnius guild documents was edited by the distinguished historian Henryk Łowmiański: *Akty cechów wileńskich 1495-1759.*

[26] *Ibid.*, pp. 1-14.

Fig. 2 The seal of the bench (aldermen's) court of Vilnius from 1536 put on the document from 1588. MS Vilnius, LVIA, F22, ap. 1, nr 5344, f. 662r. Photo J. Niedźwiedź.

On 9 September 1536 King Sigismund the Old issued, in Ruthenian, a great privilege for the city.[27] In the arenga it was explained that the document was a response to demands of the inhabitants of the city which were supported by Queen Bona Sforza. Its main purposes were to confirm the Magdeburg law, to finish the long-standing feuds between the council and the common people, and to legitimise the way in which the city was to administered. The king agreed that the city council would consist of 12 *burgermeister* ('mayors') and 24 councillors, half of whom were to be Catholics and the other half Orthodox (Ruthenians). Each year two burgermeisters and four councillors were elected as the annual council.[28]

Apart from this, the king stated that the city budget was to be administered by four tax collectors (*szafarz*): two were to be elected from the members of the city council and two from the commoners. Once a year the expenses were to be checked by the collectors and two representatives of the guilds. It is obvious the tax collectors had to have good literacy and numeracy skills. We can assume that large numbers of financial registers must have been kept in the

[27] *Zbiór praw i przywilejów*, pp. 53-60; *Собрание древних грамот и актов*, 1, pp. 51-60. The original was burnt in the fire of 1706 and only the Ruthenian transumpt issued 7 June 1607 by King Sigismund III Vasa is known.

[28] *Zbiór praw i przywilejów*, p. 54. The privilege stated that parity in the city council was a much earlier tradition ("*z starodawna*", *ibid.*).

town hall. A separate chamber was designated there for the treasury, privileges and other documents (certainly including the financial ones).[29] The privilege stated that the budget data were to be confidential.

According to this privilege, the city council had to gather once a week on Thursdays.[30] They gained some legislative rights: they could adjust the Magdeburg law according to their needs and could issue their own ordinances (*wilkierz*; 'by-laws').[31] The king granted the city a new seal.[32]

In the privilege, there are some remarks about the use of documents by the inhabitants of the city. In cases of epidemics, the city authorities were to encourage the Vilnians to make their last wills. The privilege also stated that depositions were to be put in the city registers. Excerpts from the registers were always to be issued to both sides. There are also some remarks about charges for the services of the scribes.

The legislative prerogative of the city was exercised sixteen years after the privilege of King Sigismund the Old. On 18 November 1552 the council, the ordinary people (*pospólstwo*) and the *Voigt* (from the German *Vogt*) issued a city ordinance (*wilkierz*) in the Ruthenian language.[33] This document was partially based on a decision issued by the Polish supreme court of the Magdeburg law (*Iudicium commissariorum sex civitatum*) and had been published in Cracow in 1547.[34]

By far the largest part of the ordinance was devoted to procedures in civil and criminal cases, the forms of documents, and introducing official charges for preparing them. The ordinance simplified the legal procedures and the form of sentences and other legal statements. They shortened arengas and removed "all useless splendours or ceremonies",[35] allowed putting several decisions in one sentence, and recommended avoiding repetitions in the court registers. All these regulations allowed to save time, paper, and money.

[29] *Ibid.*, p. 55.

[30] *Ibid.*, p. 57.

[31] *Ibid.*, p. 56.

[32] The oldest known seal of the city was made in 1444. On the history of the seals of the city council and the bench court see a thorough study of Edmundas Rimša, E. RIMŠA, *Lietuvos Didžiosios Kunigaikštystės miestų antsapudai* (Vilnius, 1999), pp. 579-634.

[33] *Zbiór praw i przewilejów*, pp. 91-100;

[34] *Abrogatio abusuum in iudicio scabinali* (Cracow, 1547). The text was translated into Polish by Bartłomiej Groicki and was for the first time published in 1568; see B. GROICKI, *Ustawa płacej*.

[35] *Zbiór praw i przywilejów*, p. 92.

The charges for reading in court and issuing documents were fixed: they were basically reduced. For instance, before 1552 parties had had to pay 1 *grosz* for each document read at the trial. The statute ordered that this sum would be paid for reading all the documents.[36] This solution was probably caused by the fact that by the middle of the sixteenth century all participants in legal actions presented to the court many written testimonies, probably many more than a couple decades earlier. The charge for reading each document caused a rise in the expenses of the process as a whole, which must have been inconvenient for all clients of the municipal courts.

The ordinance of 1552 is an interesting example of how the city authorities managed the problem of the flood of written records which resulted from the growth of pragmatic literacy among the Vilnians.

The inhabitants of the city were subject to the Magdeburg law. Many royal privileges confirmed that the municipal law prevailed in the city.[37] Several times the kings had to admonish the state and church authorities that the inhabitants of Vilnius were not exempt from their jurisdiction as well. In 1538 King Sigismund the Old forbade the nobility to take away from the city those of their former serfs who had lived in Vilnius for at least six years.[38] In the same year the king admonished the Vilnius *voivode* not to try subjects of the Magdeburg jurisdiction.[39] This was repeated in 1559 by King Sigismund Augustus.[40] In 1540 the Sigismund the Old guaranteed the protection of the city's pastures against the nobility, senate, and the royal court.[41] In 1543 the king demanded from all the estates of the Grand Duchy of Lithuania (but especially from the nobility) to recognise the privileges of Vilnius.[42] In 1556 Sigismund Augustus forbade to make any appeals against municipal sentences in the royal court. In 1618 King Sigismund III secured the city rights to the taxes from the city manors which were contested by the nobility – etc.[43]

However, several parts of the city were not subject to the jurisdiction of the town hall and the Magdeburg law.[44] They were called *jurydykas* and usually

36 *Ibid.*, p. 94.
37 *Ibid.*, pp. 31, 63, 67, 103.
38 *Ibid.*, p. 60.
39 *Ibid.*, pp. 62-63.
40 *Ibid.*, pp. 107-108.
41 *Ibid.*, pp. 66-67.
42 *Ibid.*, p. 76.
43 *Ibid.*, pp. 170-172.
44 K. Frejlich, *Pod przysądem horodnictwa wileńskiego: O jurydyce i jej mieszkańcach v XVII wieku* (Toruń, 2022), pp. 13-18.

consisted of several houses. The biggest *jurydykas* belonged to the Vilnius chapter, the bishop, the burgrave (*horodnictwo*), the *voivode* of Vilnius, and the Orthodox Metropolitan (and since the beginning of the seventeenth century the Uniate Metropolitan).[45] Sometimes a single house belonging to a member of nobility could become a *jurydyka*. The convents, nunneries, and the Academy of Vilnius were also exempt.[46]

Inhabitants of *jurydykas* were subject to other courts than the Magdeburg court: the castle court (*sąd grodzki*), the bishop's court, the chapter's court, the land court (*sąd ziemski*), or the burgrave's court (*sąd horodniczański*).

The proprietors and inhabitants of *jurydykas* often profited from their special legal status. Many artisans worked in the bishop's, chapter's or burgrave's *jurydykas* and competed with the artisans under the Magdeburg court's jurisdiction. Obviously, this caused conflicts between the municipality and the proprietors of the *jurydykas*. The courts and other institutions had to solve these problems. For example, in 1567 King Sigismund Augustus admonished bishop Paweł Holszański not to obstruct the municipal court in its efforts to try and punish the stallholder living in the bishop's *jurydyka*.[47] In 1604 the chapter ordered the tailors from their *jurydyka* to become members of the Vilnius tailors' guild, which operated under the magistrate's jurisdiction.[48] The next year the tailors' guild had to pay a fine and apologise to the chapter for attacking a house of a chapter tailor and violating its jurisdiction.[49] Interesting examples are the attempts of the city authorities to prohibit the Jews to settle in Vilnius. The regulations were evaded because some noblemen let parts of their houses to Jews, for instance the Słucki House (*Kamienica Słucka*) which was not subject to Magdeburg law.[50]

In the non-urban courts (of the land, castle, burgrave, bishop, or chapter) and the Tribunal of the Grand Duchy of Lithuania state law was used.[51] The

[45] MAROSZEK, "Ulice Wilna w XIV-XVIII wieku", p. 167. In his recent work about the burgrave's *jurydyka*, Kamil Frejlich established that in early modern Vilnius there were fifteen *jurydykas* (FREJLICH, *Pod przysądem horodnictwa wileńskiego*, pp. 104-118).

[46] *Ibid.*, p. 171.

[47] *Zbiór praw i przywilejów*, pp. 88-89.

[48] *Akty cechów wileńskich*, pp. 136-137.

[49] *Ibid.*, p. 141.

[50] *Wilnianie. Żywoty siedemnastowieczne*, p. 268; FRICK, *Kith, Kin, and Neighbors*, p. 37.

[51] Apart from that, in the *jurydykas* of the Catholic Church canon law and some other regulations were used, such as the statute of Vilnius cathedral (since 1515). See W. PAWLIKOWSKA-BUTTWERWICK, "Regarding the sixteenth-century statutes of the cathedral chapters of Vilna and

first comprehensive set of regulations governing legal relations in Lithuania, *Subiednik*, was issued by Casimir IV Jagiellon in 1468.[52] However, the real revolution took place in the sixteenth century, when much more extensive legal texts were put together in Vilnius in the three subsequent versions of the *Statute of the Grand Duchy of Lithuania*.[53] Its origins are associated with Alexander I Jagiellon, who in 1501 intended to codify the law, but this project was carried out only during the reign of his younger brother Sigismund I the Old.[54] The first Lithuanian statute was drafted by a committee chaired by chancellor Olbracht Gasztołd. The text was approved by Sigismund the Old during the session of Parliament in Vilnius on 29 September 1529. It was written in Ruthenian (the written version of old-Belarusian with elements of Church Slavonic and other Slavonic languages, including Polish), but was translated into Latin soon after, in 1530, and in 1532 into Polish.[55]

The next statute was created in the mid-1560s and was confirmed by the privilege of Sigismund II Augustus on 1 March 1566. Chancellor Mikołaj Radziwiłł 'the Black' was the patron of the committee that elaborated the code, but the main role was played by lawyers from Vilnius. The most important person in this team was the *Voigt* of Vilnius, Doctor of Law Augustyn Rotundus. He worked with two canons from the Vilnius cathedral chapter, Stanisław Narkuski and Jan Domanowski (from 1553 bishop of Samogitia), as well as with a judge of the Vilnius land court, Paweł Ostrowicki.[56] Pedro Ruiz de Moros (Piotr Rojzjusz), an auditor of the grand duke's assessorial court, who knew Rotundus not only professionally, was another Doctor of Law, who had

Samogitia", in: W. PAWLIKOWSKA-BUTTERWICK and L. JOVAIŠA, *Vilniaus ir Žemaičių katedrų kapitulų statutai*, pp. 133-141.

[52] KORCZAK, *Litewska rada wielkoksiążęca w XV w.*, p. 21, A.B. ZAKRZEWSKI, "O kulturze prawnej Wielkiego Księstwa Litewskiego XVI-XVIII wieku – uwagi wstępne", in: *Kultura i języki Wielkiego Księstwa Litewskiego*, p. 34.

[53] See ZAKRZEWSKI, *Wielkie Księstwo Litewskie (XVI-XVIII w.)*, pp. 215-231.

[54] The history of the statutes has recently been thoroughly discussed by Sławomir Godek in GODEK, *Elementy prawa rzymskiego w III Statucie litewskim (1588)*, pp. 21-67 (with an extensive bibliography on the subject, including also Lithuanian, Belarusian, Ukrainian, and Ruthenian publications). See also F. PIEKOSIŃSKI, "Statut litewski, 1, Powstanie trzech redakcyj Statutu", in: *Rozprawy Akademii Umiejętności: Wydział Historyczno-Filozoficzny*, Series 2, 14 (Cracow, 1900), p. 76.

[55] For a facsimile edition of all three versions (the Ruthenian manuscript and two translations) and a transcription with a commentary, see: *Pirmasis Lietuvos Statutas*, vol. 1, *Dzialinskio, Lauryno ir Ališavos nuorašų faksimilės*, 2, *Tekstai senąja beltarusių, lotynų ir senąja lenkų kalbomis*, ed. S. LAZUTKA, I. VALIKONYTĖ, and E. GUDAVIČIUS (Vilnius, 1991).

[56] GODEK, *Elementy prawa rzymskiego w III Statucie litewskim (1588)*, pp. 41-42.

sat on the committee since 1563. In his *Decisiones* he described Rotundus as "my friend, Augustyn Rotundus, the *Voigt* of Vilnius, whom I mention because of the favours I have received from him in the past".[57] Rotundus prepared the Latin version of the statute, which was accepted by King Stephen Báthory in 1576.[58] Perhaps Rotundus also translated the second statute into Polish. His manuscripts would be used, among other things, to draw up the Polish version of the last statute.[59]

The third Lithuanian statute was prepared in the 1580s by chancellor Lew Sapieha and his collaborators. The code was approved at a solemn parliamentary session (the Coronation *Sejm*) in January 1588 in Cracow, by King Sigismund III Vasa, and was published in Vilnius by the printing house of Kuźma Mamonicz that same year.[60] It was the first printed edition of this collection of laws, as the earlier statutes were only published in manuscript form. Over the following three decades, it was republished by the same printing house in Ruthenian and also in a Polish translation in 1614. The third Lithuanian Statute was a cutting-edge legal instrument. It was used in the Lithuanian lands until 1840,[61] and some its remnants were even on the statute book until the October Revolution in 1917.

The Statute played an important role in the whole legal system of the country and also strongly influenced municipal law. Although the Magdeburg law dominated in the city, one must remember that its legal situation was complex.

[57] "*Qua re cum apud familiarem meum Augustinum Rotundum, praetorem urbanum, quem honoris veterumque eius in me meritorum gratia nomino, iudicium susceptum esset, et post multam disceptationem, quid statuendum foret, ambigeretur. Ille, ut est homo iuris prudens et minime arrogans, cuius ego verecundiam hac parte non possum non laudare, licet animadverteret, quamobrem de viribus testamenti merito dubitaretur, lecta tamen principali confirmatione, regium auditorium adeundum maiestatis causa et inde rescripti interpretationem petendam, modestissime pronunciavit: ne alius rescripti conditor fuisset: alius interpres. quod fieri vetat constitutio*" (P. RUIZ DE MOROS, *Decisiones*, p. 14).

[58] M. BARYCZOWA, *Augustyn Rotundus Mieleski, wójt wileński, pierwszy historyk i apologeta Litwy* (Vilnius, 1936: offprint from *Ateneum Wileńskiego* 10-11 (1935-1936)), p. 21; EAD, "Rotundus Augustyn", *PSB*, vol. 32, p. 317.

[59] S. ESTREICHER, commentary on the entry on *Statut litewski*, in: ID., *Bibliografia polska*, 33 (Cracow, 1933), pp. 234-235.

[60] The most recent comprehensive study about the 1588 edition of the Statute was published by Vladimir Mikiashev; see В. МЯКИШЕВ, *Кириллические издания Литовского Статута 1588 года* (Cracow, 2014). In 2018 an anniversary conference devoted to the 1588 Statute took place in Minsk. The papers were published in the same year: *Статут Вялікага Княства Літоўскага, Рускага і Жамойцкага 1588 г.: да 430-годдзя выдання. Зборнік навуковых артыкулаў па матэрыялах канферэнцыі. У аўтарскай рэдакцыі* (Minsk, 2018).

[61] F. KONECZNY, *Dzieje administracji w Polsce w zarysie* (Vilnius, 1924), p. 284.

The main causes for this were the many *jurydykas* in Vilnius and the status of the city of capital of the state, Catholic bishopric, Orthodox and Uniate archdiocese, voivodeship, etc. As a result, different laws were exercised next to one another. This also resulted in a multiplicity of legal institutions, that is places where texts were produced and used.

Chanceries

The municipal chancery undoubtedly played the central role in issuing documents related to the management of the city. However, it was not the only *locus textualis* in Vilnius. Apart from the fact that Vilnius was a town, it was also the seat of a Catholic bishopric, a cathedral chapter, an Orthodox and later Uniate Metropolitan, two noble courts (the land court and the castle court), the state's appeal court, and the monarch's residence with its administrative institutions. Several churches, monasteries, and nunneries operated in Vilnius, some schools, and later also the university. Since the city was the capital of the state, the chancery of the Grand Duchy of Lithuania (temporarily) and the state archive (continually) operated there. All these institutions had their chanceries or scribal offices and were important *loci textuales*.

Researchers have pointed out that the municipal chancery played the most important role in the uses of the written word in medieval urban settlements.[62] This statement is generally true in relation to most medieval towns and cities, but in the case of Vilnius the situation was probably more complex than in other towns. The non-municipal *loci textuales* in Vilnius were many; they were closely connected to the city and in most instances operated within the city walls.[63] As a result, in the sixteenth and seventeenth centuries the municipal chancery was one of many public institutions in which texts (especially documents) were issued, preserved, copied, etc.

Its history is still to be written, and the remarks presented below should be treated as preliminary. The main obstacle is the fragmentary nature of the city archives from before the 1660s: they are virtually non-existent, having been

[62] On the central role as the of the municipal chanceries in medieval urban settlements in Europe, see comments of ADAMSKA and MOSTERT, "Introduction", in: *Writing and the Administration of Medieval Towns*, p. 4.

[63] It would be useful to study in a comparative survey Gdańsk, Poznań, Wrocław, Cracow, Warsaw, Riga, Tallin, Vienna, and Prague.

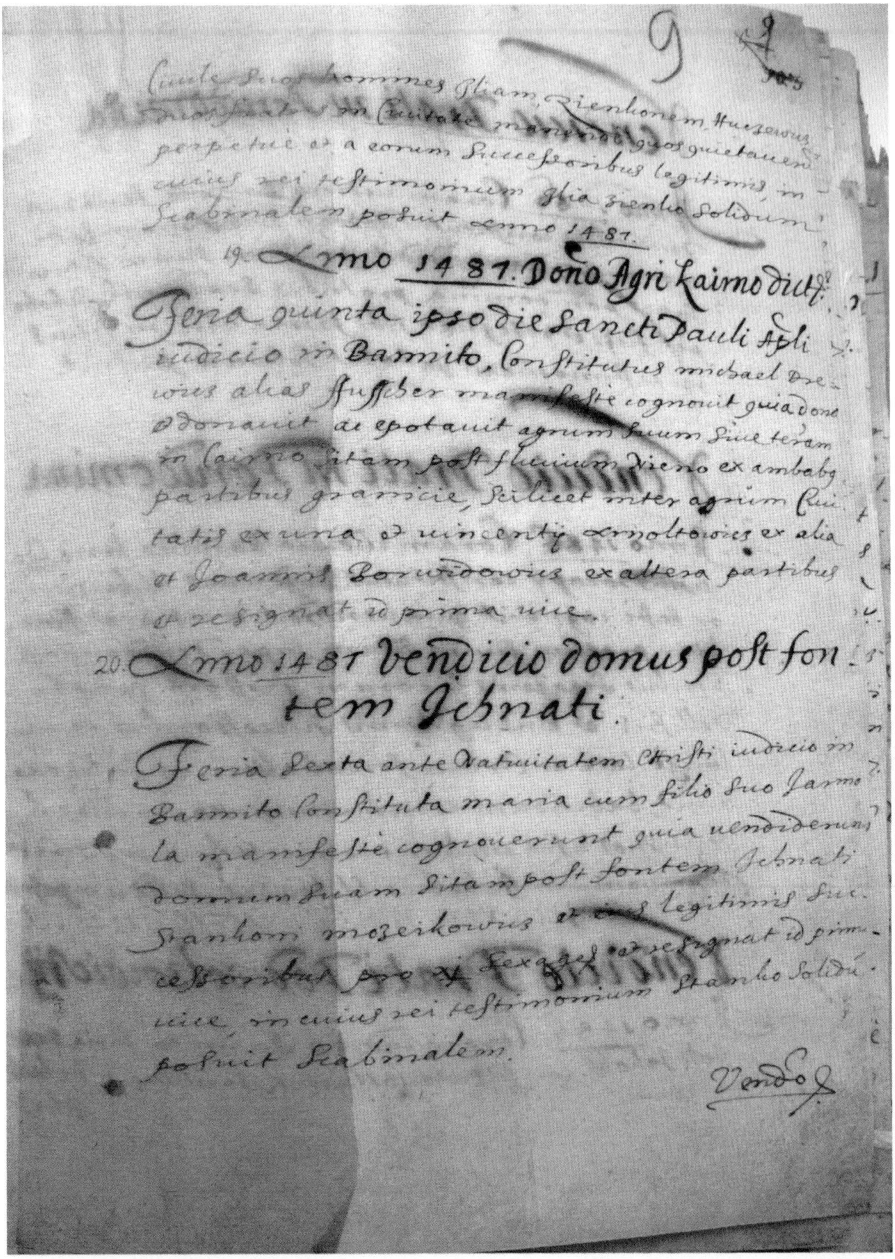

Fig. 3 Seventeenth-century copies of the oldest records from the bench (aldermen) court of Vilnius (1481). MS Vilnius, LVIA, F22, ap. 1 b. 1, nr 5333, f. 9r. Photo J. Niedźwiedź.

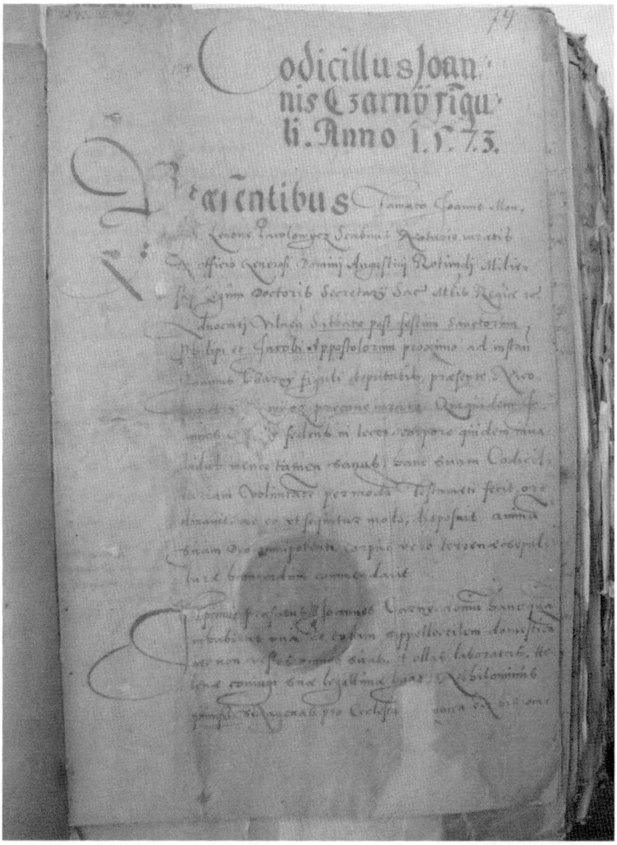

Fig. 4 Codicil (will) of Jan Czarny from 1573. A fragment of the aldermen court registers. The judge was *Voigt* Augustyn Rotundus. MS Vilnius, LVIA, F22, ap. 1 b. 1, nr 5333, f. 74r. Photo J. Niedźwiedź.

destroyed by fire in 1610, 1655 and 1707.[64] The privileges published in the eighteenth and nineteenth centuries and some still existing documents produced in the municipal chancery nevertheless allow us to sketch an outline of how it worked.

The municipal authorities knew two major institutions: that of the *Voigt* (*wójt*, *advocatus*) with the aldermen and the city council, that is the *burgermeisters* (*burmistrz*, mayors) and the councillors.

[64] KRASZEWSKI, *Wilno*, 2, p. 84, and 3, p. 316; ŁOWMIAŃSKA, "Wilno przed najazdem moskiewskim 1655 roku", p. 157. See also Chapter 2.

The office of the *Voigt* was established in the location privilege of 1397. He was the grand duke's governor of the city and the chairman of the court of the aldermen. We know some names of fifteenth-century *Voigts*,[65] who were lawyers from the Kingdom of Poland. The most notable among them were Feliks Langurga from Cracow (*Voigt* 1527-1551), doctor of law Augustyn Rotundus Mieleski from Wieluń (1552-1582) and doctor of medicine Stanisław Sabinka from Stradom (1582-1588).[66] Most of the *Voigts* in the sixteenth and seventeenth centuries were royal secretaries, that is specialists in administrative matters and confidants of the king. The independent status of *Voigts* led to conflicts between them and the city council, for instance in 1532.[67] This organisational problem was solved when, on 11 November 1610, King Sigismund III Vasa granted the city a privilege according to which the *Voigt* became a municipal official, but the king kept the right to name the *Voigt* from four candidates presented by the city council.[68] The *Voigt* had his own chancery, but nothing is known of its registers.[69]

We do not know much about activities of the aldermen's court in the fifteenth century. More information is available from the sixteenth and seventeenth centuries. It examined criminal and civil cases, and in this respect it did not differ from other aldermen's courts in the Polish-Lithuanian Commonwealth.[70]

The city council certainly existed already in the fifteenth century, but it is unclear what its competences were or how it worked. The privileges of the grand dukes were addressed to the city of Vilnius or its citizens (*cives Vilnenses*, "the burgers of Vilnius of Roman and Greek faith"[71]) without any mentions of the city council. Its councillors were mentioned for the first time in the 1490s, in the privilege of Grand Duke Alexander Jagiellon: "*famosi et circum-*

[65] *Urzędnicy Wielkego Księstwa Litewskiego: Spisy*, 1, *Województwo wileński* XIV-XVIII *wiek*, ed. H. Lulewicz, A. Rachuba, and P.P. Romaniuk (Warsaw, 2004), p. 204.

[66] *Ibid.*, p. 204-205.

[67] M. Baliński, *Historia miasta Wilna*, 2 (Vilnius, 1836), p. 129.

[68] *Zbiór praw i przywilejów*, pp. 167-168.

[69] A. Ragauskas, "Źródła do historii urzędu wójta wileńskiego (koniec XIV w.-koniec XVII w.): Czy istniały księgi sądu wójtowskiego?", in: *Lietuvos Didžiosios Kunigaištystės istorijos šaltiniai: Faktas: Kontestas: Interpretacija*, ed. A. Dubonis *et al.* (Vilnius, 2006), pp. 396-397.

[70] M. Bogucka and H. Samsonowicz, *Dzieje miast i mieszczaństwa w Polsce przedrozbiorowej* (Wrocław, 1986), pp. 58, 68, 74-76; Bartoszewicz, *Urban Literacy in Late Medieval Poland*, pp. 110-113, 120-127.

[71] *Zbiór praw i przywilejów*, p. 6.

specti advocatus, magistri civium et consules civitatis nostrae Vilnensis".[72] In the next century the role of the city council grew significantly.

The *Voigt*'s office, the aldermen's court and the city council had to issue and use growing numbers of documents. As they worked in the town hall on Market Square, as early as the last decade of the fourteenth century it became a major *locus textualis* in the town. It certainly existed at the turn of the fourteenth and fifteenth centuries, as it was mentioned for the first time in 1503.[73] Although the current building was built in 1785-1799 by architect Wawrzyniec Gucewicz,[74] its underground rooms are medieval. The archaeologists who led their excavation in 2017 suppose that these rooms were built in the 1390s, shortly after the Magdeburg location of the city.[75]

The earliest written sources relative to the city chancery, however, date from the end of the fifteenth century. The oldest known documents of the Vilnius aldermen's registers are Latin copies of land sales from 1491 and 1495.[76] A register of the aldermen's court books from 1650, however, informs us that they were carried as early as in 1484 (see Fig. 4).[77]

It is almost certain that the registers of the city council also existed at that time, because we know the names of the municipal scribes (or rather notaries?). Before he moved to Warsaw in 1496, Cyryl of Głubczyce was a Vilnius scribe.[78] One of his successors in 1505 was a man called Rey.[79] It is difficult to say if they worked both for the council and the aldermen's court, but they were certainly not the only professionals of the written word in the municipal office. Cyryl of Głubczyce, who had studied at the University of Cracow, knew Latin and probably German, but it is almost certain that he could not write in Ruthenian, another language of writing in Vilnius. It is therefore probable that in the urban chancery there was a clerk (*diak*?) responsible for managing Ruthenian charters. This has an important consequence: city documents could

72 *Ibid.*, p. 11.

73 A.R. Čaplinskas, *Vilniaus gatvių istorija*, 2, *Didzioji gatvė* (Vilnius, 2011), p. 25.

74 Łowmiańska, "Wilno przed najazdem moskiewskim 1655 roku", p. 192.

75 B. Łapszewicz, "Ratusz wileński, który pamięta średniowiecze", *Kurier Wileński* 52.18, 11-17.05.2019 <https://kurierwilenski.lt/2019/05/18/ratusz-wilenski-ktory-pamieta-sredniowiecze/> (accessed: 7.11.2021).

76 LVIA, F. 22, Ap. 1 b. 1, nr 5333.

77 Ragauskas, "1650 m. kovo 30 d. Vilniaus suolininkų teismo įrašų knygų aprašas", pp. 262-264.

78 Bartoszewicz, *Urban Literacy in Late Medieval Poland*, p. 276.

79 *Ibid.*

be written in Latin, Polish, or Ruthenian and maybe in German as well.[80] This set of languages distinguished Vilnius from other cities of the Hansa region.[81]

In the first half of the sixteenth century each office (the *Voigt*, the aldermen, and the city council) had their own notaries (*pisarz*). Because the city council was divided into a Latin and Ruthenian one, either one had its own notary, one for Latin and one for Ruthenian. The *Voigt* and aldermen also had their own notaries which were responsible for documents issued in either script. This suggests that by the second half of the sixteenth century at least four notaries worked in the town hall, together with several other scribes (*podpisek*). Apart from them, the *Voigt*, who could judge some cases in his home, must have had his own scribe as well.

In the seventeenth century the staff of the municipal chancery grew in numbers. In 1647 there were three municipal notaries,[82] and in the 1650s four.[83] Maria Łowmiańska noted that at that time the same notaries assisted both institutions, the aldermen's court and the city council.[84] However, the sources confirm that these institutions had separate notaries.[85]

The role of the Vilnius municipal chancery was crucial for the management of the city. It issued charters and wrote correspondence on behalf of the city council and aldermen. Unfortunately, it is impossible to reconstruct fully how the chancery operated. Probably it was similar to other municipal chanceries in the cities and towns of the Polish Crown and the Grand Duchy of Lithuania. There are only a few documents which shed light on this matter. For example, in 1584 the king had to decide about the rules for electing the Latin notary.[86] Some *burgermeister* and councillors, mainly the Ruthenian ones, protested against the decision of some members of the Latin part of the city council about electing "a certain Benedict, a bachelor of an unknown promotion". According to the complaint, Benedict was "inexperienced in law and without any merits for the city of Vilnius". The election was made "with violation and

80 *Zbiór praw i przywilejów*, p. 54.

81 M. GRULKOWSKI, "Definicja i klasyfikacja ksiąg miejskich: Księgi w kancelariach miast obszaru Hanzy", in: *Nauki pomocnicze historii: Teoria, metody badań, dydaktyka*, ed. A. JAWORSKA and R. JOP (Warsaw, 2013), pp. 119-148.

82 *Zbiór praw i przywilejów*, p. 214.

83 ŁOWMIAŃSKA, "Wilno przed najazdem moskiewskim 1655 roku", p. 283.

84 *Ibid.*

85 RAGAUSKAS, "1650 m. kovo 30 d. Vilniaus suolininkų teismo įrašų knygų aprašas", pp. 260, 264, 266.

86 *Zbiór praw i przywilejów*, pp. 143-145.

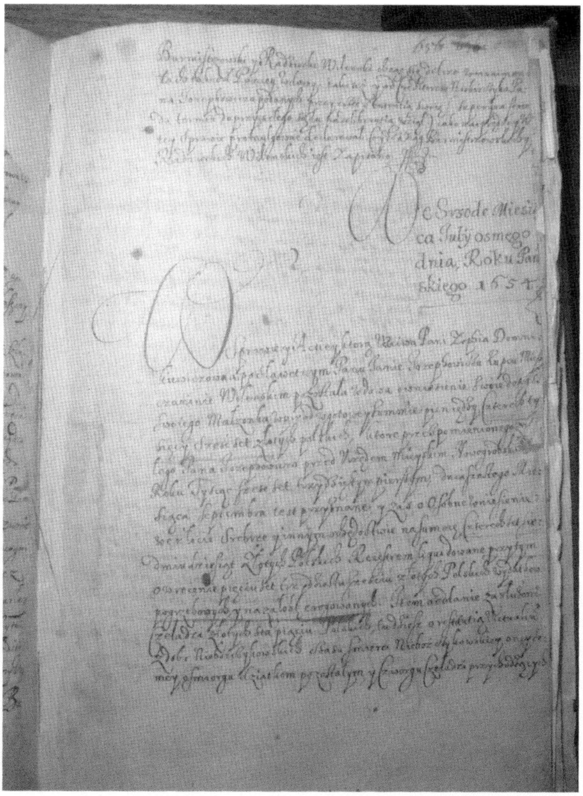

Fig. 5 A fragment of the city council registers from 1654. MS Vilnius, LVIA, F23, ap. 1, nr 5096, f. 656r. Photo J. Niedźwiedź.

disrespect for the privileges of the freedom of the city and caused harm to the mutual love, fraternal relationship and severely worsened the state of the Commonwealth of Vilnius ('*Reipublicaeque Vilnensis haud mediocre detrimentum*') and saint concord".[87] This case shows that the city elites clearly understood how important was control over the municipal chancery.

The number of documents produced by this chancery rose each year. This can be confirmed by the aldermen court's register[88] and the extant books from

[87] *Ibid.*, p. 144.

[88] RAGAUSKAS, "1650 m. kovo 30 d. Vilniaus suolininkų teismo įrašų knygų aprašas", pp. 264-266.

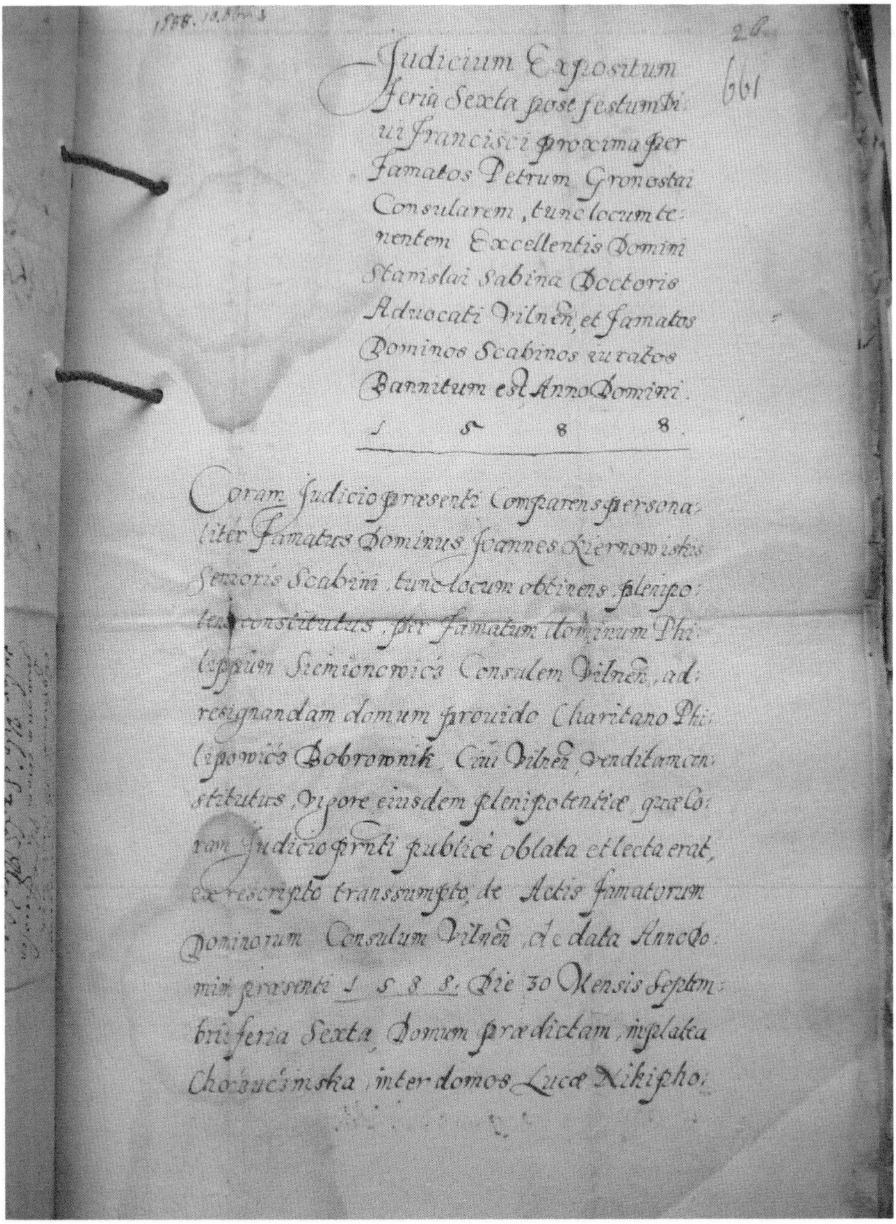

Fig. 6 1.5. A fragment of the aldermen court registers from 1588. MS Vilnius, LVIA, F22, ap. 1, nr 5344, f. 661r. Photo J. Niedźwiedź.

the second half of the seventeenth century. In the fifteenth century one book contained cases from several years, for instance "The first volume contained the years 1484, 1486, 1487, 1488 and 1499".[89] In the sixteenth century one register contained usually cases from two years. From 1606 there was one volume registering cases for any single year.[90]

Another important chancery in the city served the bishop. It was probably the oldest such institution in Vilnius, established just after the creation of the Vilnius diocese in 1488.[91] We may suppose that bishops used rather their own scribes than hired public notaries. The oldest known document issued by bishop Andrzej of Vilnius is dated 30 August 1391.[92] Unfortunately, only a few documents of the Vilnius bishops from the fourteenth and fifteenth centuries survived, so we cannot say much about the activity of the bishop's chancery during that time. As in case of other Vilnius *loci textuales*, the last decade of the fifteenth century brought a dramatic change in their use of writing and functioning. The bishop's chancery grew in importance as the number of issued documents confirms. This chancery was responsible for issuing and preserving documents of the diocesan curia and the consistory court. The office played also an important role in the city, because it was the main *locus textualis* of the bishop's *jurydyka*.

In the privilege for the Vilnius bishopric from 1388, King Jogaila granted the bishop and the chapter a vast part of the city.[93] This caused two major *jurydykas* in the city, that of the bishop and of the chapter. As a result, the curia had to deal with municipal matters. In the bishop's *jurydyka* many artisans lived, among them many goldsmiths. In the sixteenth century this caused tensions between the magistrate, the bishop, the guilds, and the artisans. All these conflicts had to be solved, for instance by the consistory court. Apart from that, the curia and consistory court dealt with the usual legal matters of the inhabitants of the *jurydyka*. This resulted in a growing number of texts produced by the bishop's chancery: verdicts, contracts, last wills, and transumpts. In the sixteenth and seventeenth centuries the bishop's chancery worked in the Bishop's Manor (*Dwór Biskupi*, today the Presidential Palace); it employed several clerks: the notary and some scribes. In some documents, especially in last wills, we find information that a document was written in the Bishop's

[89] *Ibid.*
[90] *Ibid.*
[91] *Kodeks dyplomatyczny diecezji wileńskiej*, pp. 1-9.
[92] *Ibid.*, pp. 36-37.
[93] *Ibid.*, pp. 1-9.

Manor. For example, the last will of the chancellor of the Grand Duchy of Lithuania Mikołaj Radziwiłł (1470-1521) was made there.[94]

The chancery of the Vilnius chapter operated elsewhere, near the cathedral in the lower castle. We have preciously little information about the chapter's writing activities before the end of the fifteenth century. It was created together with the diocese and is mentioned in the sources since 1391.[95] On 1 December 1398, the chapter issued its first known document, about the election of the Franciscan Jakub Plichta as bishop of Vilnius.[96] We do not know if the chapter had its own scribe or that the same person worked for both the chapter and the bishop. In the 1490s, Grand Duke Alexander Jagiellon granted some of his trusted men positions as canons of the Vilnius chapter. Among them was a brilliant and ambitious humanist, Erazm Ciołek (1474-1522), a master of arts of Cracow University and the secretary of the grand duke.[97] Ciołek, who was quickly promoted to the post of the provost (*praepositus*) of the chapter (1499), reformed this institution in the first years of the sixteenth century, among other things starting registers, organising the archive and preparing the rules for the capitular scribe.[98]

Luckily, the registers of the chapter were evacuated before the Moscovite attack in 1655 and are still extant today. They confirm that the chancery of the chapter was very active. At the beginning of the sixteenth century, the chapter had only one notary, but in the second half of the century the number had risen to two.[99] The registers contain detailed records of the chapter's proceedings, copies of important court documents, reports, decisions of the chapter, and financial matters. Just as the bishop's court, the chapter regulated the life of the inhabitants of the chapter's *jurydyka* and of the manors which belonged to the canons.

In the lower castle several other chanceries or *loci textuales* worked. The office of the burgrave (*horodniczy*) operated probably from the last decades of the fourteenth century onwards. In the sixteenth and seventeenth centuries it

[94] KLOVAS, *Privačių dokumentų atsiradimas ir raida*, p. 198.

[95] *Kodeks dyplomatyczny diecezji wileńskiej*, p. 36.

[96] *Ibid.*, pp. 60-62.

[97] A. BRZOZOWSKA, *Biskup płocki Erazm Ciołek (1474-1522)* (Cracow, 2017); EAD., "Erasmi Vitellii, episcopi Plocensis et oratoris regis Poloniae, litterae binae ad Bernardinum Clesium nunc primum editae", *Humanistica Lovaniensia* 62 (2013), pp. 281-283.

[98] MS MAB F43-210/01 (*Akta kapituły wileńskiej 1502-1533*), ff. 46v-47r. J. KURCZEWSKI, *Kościół zamkowy, czyli katedra wileńska w jej dziejowym, liturgicznym, architektonicznym i ekonomicznym rozwoju*, 1 (Vilnius, 1908), p. 17, and 3 (Vilnius, 1913), pp. 11.

[99] *Regestr kapituły roku 1579 i roku 1580*, MS MAB, F43-452, vol. 26r.

had several tasks. Its first purpose was the administration of the lands and properties which belonged to the Vilnius castle. Secondly, the burgrave had juridical power over the burgrave's *jurydyka*. The burgrave registers (*księgi horodniczańskie*) contain depositions of witnesses which offer valuable information about everyday events in the life of the middle class and the poor in early seventeenth-century Vilnius.[100]

For a long time, in the lower castle and later in the city three courts worked: the land court (*sąd ziemski*), the castle court (*sąd grodzki*), and the Tribunal of the Grand Duchy of Lithuania (the appeal court). All three courts had their offices, scribes, and registers. Basically, they were the courts of the nobility; this was especially true of the land court. They did not differ from other such courts in the Polish-Lithuanian Commonwealth in the fifteenth through eighteenth centuries.[101] In the case of Vilnius, not only Lithuanian noblemen and noblewomen brought their cases to these courts. In the castle and Tribunal registers we encounter many entries relative to the inhabitants and institutions of the city: the nobility, clergy, burghers, Jews, religious institutions, and the city council.

The largest chancery operating in Vilnius was that of the Grand Duchy of Lithuania. It was the main state institution responsible for the production, copying, and keeping of the documents issued by the grand duke.[102] In the fifteenth century it also played some role in exercising power in the Grand Duchy of Lithuania.[103] From the sixteenth century the Lithuanian chancellors were responsible for the diplomatic relationship of the Polish-Lithuanian commonwealth with Muscovy.[104]

[100] See FREJLICH, *Pod przysądem horodnictwa wileńskiego*, pp. 39-41. Fragments of the burgrave registers will be quoted in Chapter 9.

[101] J. Bardach, B. LEŚNODORSKI, and M. PIETRZAK, *Historia ustroju i prawa polskiego* (Warsaw, 2005), p. 239; J. ŁOSOWSKI, "Akta sądów i urzędów szlacheckich w XIV-XVIII wieku", in: *Dyplomatyka staropolska*, pp. 256-260, 270-288.

[102] J. BARDACH, "O praktyce kancelarii litewskiej za Zygmunta I Starego", in: *Studia z ustroju i prawa Wielkiego Księstwa Litewskiego, XIV-XVII w.* (Warsaw and Białystok, 1970), pp. 351-378; M. KOSMAN, "W kancelarii wielkiego księcia Witolda", in: ID., *Orzeł i Pogoń*, pp. 122-130; RACHUBA, "Kancelarie pieczętarzy WKL w latach 1569-1765", pp. 256-270; K. JABLONSKIS, "Lietuvos rusiškųjų aktų diplomatika", in: *Istorija ir jos šaltiniai*, ed. V. MERKYS (Vilnius, 1979), pp. 219-298; W. CHORĄŻYCZEWSKI, "Kancelarie centralne państwa w XIV-XVIII wieku", in: *Dyplomatyka staropolska*, ed. T. JUREK (Warsaw, 2015), pp. 173-174; DUBONIS, ANTANAVIČIUS, RAGAUSKIENĖ, and ŠMIGELSKYTĖ-STUKIENĖ, *The Lithuanian Metrica*, pp. 38-57.

[103] KORCZAK, *Monarcha i poddani*, pp. 40-41.

[104] BARDACH, LEŚNODORSKI, and PIETRZAK, *Historia ustroju i prawa polskiego*, p. 227.

In the fifteenth century the Lithuanian chancery did operate only in Vilnius, because its members travelled with the monarch, especially before the sixteenth century. Several semi-independent scribes constituted the chancery officials.[105] Most of them belonged to the Orthodox or Catholic clergy[106] and some of them lived and worked in Vilnius. In the next century the chancery was anchored in the capital, in part because the chancellor was usually also the *voivode* of Vilnius. In that time the city became the place for keeping the Lithuanian *Metrica*, the central archive of the state.[107] At least since the 1630s the chancery's core operated mainly in Warsaw, which meanwhile had become the actual (but not formal) capital of the Polish-Lithuanian Commonwealth.[108] Still, the Lithuanian chancery was rather a group of the offices of five 'great notaries' (*pisarz wielki*) than a single centralised office.

From the very beginning, the Lithuanian chancery knew sections. In Duke Vytautas's chancery, which was the first chancery of the state (*c.* 1400-1430), there were two teams of scribes, a Ruthenian one which wrote charters and letters in Cyrillic script (and in Ruthenian language), and a Latin one, producing the same in the Latin and German languages;[109] several Tartar scribes also worked here.[110] There are fifteen names known of secretaries and scribes employed by Vytautas. The most important were Mikołaj Cebulka and Mikołaj Małdrzyk, who were also members of the grand duke's council.[111] In the times of Casimir IV Jagiellon, in the 1440s, the reorganised Lithuanian chancery became completely independent from the Polish one, and the grand duke appointed a separate chancellor to manage it.[112] From that time onwards, members of the chapter played an important role in the chancery, for instance Mikołaj of Błażejowice, who served as chancellor. In 1477, Alekhna Sudzimontavych (Olechno Sudymuntowicz) became chancellor[113] and used his experience

[105] CHORĄŻYCZEWSKI, "Kancelarie centralne państwa", p. 173.
[106] *Ibid.*, p. 174.
[107] See Chapter 2.
[108] RACHUBA, "Kancelarie pieczętarzy WKL", p. 260.
[109] In the second half of the fifteenth century the grand ducal chancery exchanged several letters in German with the authorities of the Teutonic Order. Most of them were sent from Vilnius. They were published in KORCZAK, *Monarcha i poddani*, pp. 163-176.
[110] KOSMAN, *Wpływ unii jagiellońskiej*, p. 18.
[111] M. KOSMAN, "W kancelarii wielkiego księcia Witolda", in: ID., *Orzeł i Pogoń*, pp. 122-125 and 129-130; KORCZAK, *Monarcha i poddani*, p. 130.
[112] KORCZAK, *Litewska rada wielkoksiążęca w XV w.*, pp. 41-42; KOSMAN, "W kancelarii", p. 114.
[113] KORCZAK, *Monarcha i poddani*, p. 119.

of the chancery of the Polish Kingdom, among other things by introducing Polish chancery practice and forms of documents.[114] During the reign of Alexander I Jagiellon (1492-1506), the aforementioned Erazm Ciołek became the main figure in the chancery. From the beginning of the sixteenth century, it began to rely on well-qualified humanists (laymen and clergymen alike), such as Ciołek or Adam Jakubowicz of Kotra.[115] The new office of the vice-chancellor (*podkanclerzy*) had been introduced in the second half of the fifteenth century.[116]

From 1522 chancellor Olbracht Gasztołd tried to centralise the office, subordinating semi-independent scribes and introducing the scribe's oath.[117] At that time there were *c.* 10-20 secretaries, each of whom had his own scribes (*diaks*). In 1566 the number of secretaries was reduced to six and in the late 1570s to five.[118] One of the most accomplished Lithuanian chancellors was Lew Sapieha, who held the office in 1589-1623. The experience he gained in his early years in the chancery allowed him to undertake a number of reforms. It was thanks to him that the Lithuanian *Metrica* was copied and put in order. This task, supported by Parliament, lasted for several years and required the employment of group of appropriately qualified scribes. At the beginning of the seventeenth century Sapieha introduced specialisation among the members of staff: two *regents* (the most experienced secretaries who were the personal assistants of the chancellor and vice-chancellor), secretaries of the seal, two registrars (*metrykant*, responsible for preparing the documents), and many scribes.[119] The chancery now employed dozens of people at any one time. Probably many of the employees lived in Vilnius.

In the sixteenth and seventeenth centuries, when the king stayed in Vilnius, the (Polish) royal chancery, which accompanied him, also operated in the capital. The peak of the activity of this central scribal office was the rule of Sigismund II Augustus (1548-1572). According to Mirosław Korolko, the Polish

[114] KOSMAN, *Polacy na Litwie*, p. 31.

[115] *Ibid.*, p. 32.

[116] *Urzędnicy centralni i dygnitarze Wielkiego Księstwa Litewskiego XIV-XVIII wieku: Spisy*, ed. H. LULEWICZ and A. RACHUBA (Kórnik, 1994), p. 155.

[117] CHORĄŻYCZEWSKI, "Kancelarie centralne państwa", p. 174.

[118] *Urzędnicy centralni i dygnitarze Wielkiego Księstwa Litewskiego*, p. 118; RACHUBA, "Kancelarie pieczętarzy WKL", p. 257; A. ZAKRZEWSKI, *Wielkie Księstwo Litewskie (XVI-XVIII w.): Prawo – ustrój – społeczeństwo* (Warsaw, 2013), p. 147; CHORĄŻYCZEWSKI, "Kancelarie centralne państwa", p. 174.

[119] RACHUBA, "Kancelarie pieczętarzy WKL", p. 261-267; ZAKRZEWSKI, *Wielkie Księstwo Litewski (XVI-XVIII w.)*, p. 147.

royal chancery then employed 222 secretaries.[120] Many of them used to work at the Vilnius castle, especially when the city featured as the main residence of the monarch. In these periods, the royal chancery residing in Vilnius used the services, for instance of Piotr Myszkowski, Jan Przerębski, Walerian Protasewicz, Augustyn Rotundus, Mikołaj Trzebuchowski, Wacław Agryppa, Maciej Strubicz, Andrzej Wolan, Łukasz Górnicki, Stanisław Koszutski, Jan Kochanowski, and others. They were people with a thorough humanistic education. The condition for their employment was university education, often obtained in Germany and Italy, especially at Padua.[121] They were fluent in foreign languages and, above all, they had a very high level of competence in the field of composing various kinds of texts. They were the intellectual elite of the commonwealth and their literary works belong to the canon of Renaissance literature.

This outline of chanceries must be supplemented by smaller scribal offices. The central offices of the state had their own chanceries, especially the treasurer (*podskarbi*),[122] the great *hetman* ('commander'), the field *hetman*, and the marshal of the Grand Duchy of Lithuania. Apart from that, there were offices of the *voivode* of Vilnius and the magnates. The institutions of the Church had their larger or smaller offices as well, especially the Jesuits and their Academy of Vilnius, the provincials of the Dominicans and Franciscans, the Orthodox and later also the Uniate Metropolitans, the Calvinist and Lutheran communities, nunneries and convents. As a result, Vilnius was a city where several dozens and sometimes hundreds professionals of the written word lived and worked.

Professionals of the Written Word: Scribes and Secretaries

The beginnings of Vilnius are closely connected to the presence of men who were not only literate, but could also produce different types of complex documents. First among them were the Catholic clergymen, such as those who wrote the letters of Gediminas in 1323.[123] Later on, Orthodox clergymen also

[120] M. KOROLKO, *Seminarium Rzeczypospolitej Królestwa Polskiego: Humaniści w kancelarii królewskiej Zygmunta Augusta* (Warsaw, 1991), p. 6.

[121] *Ibid.*, p. 75-76.

[122] A. FILIPCZAK-KOCUR, "Kancelaria podskarbich litewskich w pierwszej połowie XVII wieku", in: *Dzieje biurokracji na ziemiach polskich*, 1, ed. A. GÓRAK (Radzyń Podlaski, 2008), pp. 47-64.

[123] S.C. ROWELL, "Pratramė", in: *Chartularium Lithuaniae*, pp. XV-XXVIII.

worked for the grand dukes, especially after the incorporation into the Grand Duchy of Lithuania of vast parts of the Ruthenian lands. By the end of the fourteenth century, not only professionals of the written word employed by the rulers lived in Vilnius but also professionals who offered their literate services to a broader clientele: to the bishop, the chapter, and the inhabitants of the city. A testament of a bishop of Vilnius, Andrzej, sheds some light on this issue.

This testament was written on 27 October 1398 by "a public notary, Nicolas, son of Nicolas of Cracow" ("*Nicolaus Nicolai de Cracovia clericus publicus ... manu propria scribens, signo*").[124] This short note implies several interesting things. Firstly, it informs the reader that already in the first years after the location of the city relationships between Vilnius and the capital of the Kingdom of Poland, Cracow, were established. The migration of the professionals (clergy, mercenaries, merchants, and artisans) from Poland to Lithuania began shortly after the union between the two monarchies of Krevo (1385). Professionals of the written word were among them. Secondly, a couple of years after the destruction of the city by the Teutonic Knights and the Western crusaders in 1390 and 1394,[125] it had become again a vivid commercial centre. At least some of its inhabitants found writing indispensable in the management of their properties. Consequently, they needed a public notary.

Probably from as early as the 1470s the need to produce and copy documentation continuously involved the inhabitants of the capital, and therefore the demand for people able to produce them grew steadily. Such a demand was even greater in the institutions of the state and the Churches.

Since the city archives from the fifteenth century did not survive, we have only scarce information about the activity of notaries and scribes in Vilnius at that time. Only a few private documents produced in the city survived in the Lithuanian *Metrica*,[126] and this prevents us to draw any conclusions about the activities of public notaries and scribes in the city. We only know the names of two Vilnius scribes (or notaries?) we have mentioned before: Cyryl of Głubczyce (until 1496) and Rey (1505).[127] Probably they belonged to a large group of itinerant scribes who offered their services to the various municipal

[124] *Kodeks dyplomatyczny diecezji wileńskiej*, pp. 54-59.

[125] H. ŁOWMIAŃSKI, "Agresja zakonu krzyżackiego na Litwę w wiekach XII-XV", *Przegląd Historyczny* 45.2-3 (1952), p. 362.

[126] KLOVAS, *Privačių dokumentų atsiradimas*, p. 61.

[127] BARTOSZEWICZ, *Urban Literacy in Late Medieval Poland*, p. 276.

institutions in the Jagiellonian monarchies. They probably worked in ways similar to other professionals of the written word in the Hanseatic territories.[128]

In addition to full-time scribes and chancery clerks with permanent positions in municipal, state, and religious institutions, there was a large group of occasional scribes or 'proletarians of the written word' who supported themselves by lending their quills to those in need of them. We know very little about this group. Nor do we have any information about scribes employed by the city or private individuals, or about secretaries who served state and church dignitaries. More is known about the castle, burgrave, and land scribes.[129] So far, however, researchers have devoted most attention to the chanceries of the grand dukes, and to the staff employed there.[130]

Service in the Lithuanian chancery offered the possibility of promotion to higher state offices. Such was the career of for instance Lew Sapieha, who started as secretary in the 1580s, under King Stephen Báthory, and eventually achieved the dignity of chancellor of Lithuania.

Other institutions active in the sixteenth and seventeenth centuries employed a smaller number of secretaries and scribes, but their competences were similar: "to write down and read documents".[131] The key competence possessed by a scribe or secretary was proficiency in calligraphy. In the case of some institutions, such as the castle court or the grand duke's chancery, the ability to write in two alphabets, Latin and Cyrillic, knowledge of three languages, Ruthenian, Latin, and Polish, and the ability to use appropriate formularies for different types of charters were usually required.

Not always did the qualifications of the professionals of the written word serve legitimate purposes. On the one hand, cases are known of forged document,[132] even of the Lithuanian dukes' conferments (of titles, rights, etc.), or of

[128] Grulkowski, "Definicja i klasyfikacja ksiąg miejskich", pp. 119-148.

[129] *Urzędnicy Wielkiego Księstwa Litewskiego. Spisy*, 1, pp. 133-136, 139-140.

[130] Kosman, *W kancelarii wielkiego księcia Witolda*, pp. 122-130; Bardach, "O praktyce kancelarii litewskiej za Zygmunta I Starego", pp. 351-378; A. Rachuba, "Kancelarie pieczętarzy WKL w latach 1569-1765", in: *Lietuvos Metrika: 1991-1996 metų tyrinėjimai* (Vilnius, 1998), p. 256; Jablonskis, "Lietuvos rusiškųjų aktų diplomatika", pp. 219-298; Dubonis, Antanavičius, Ragauskienė, and Šmigelskytė-Stukienė, *The Lithuanian Metrica: History and Research*, pp. 38-57.

[131] M. Kromer, *Polonia, czyli o położeniu, ludności, obyczajach, urzędach i sprawach publicznych Królestwa Polskiego księgi dwie*, trans. S. Kazikowski, introduction and elaboration R. Marchwiński (Olsztyn, 1984), p. 142.

[132] *Kodeks dyplomatyczny diecezji wileńskiej*, 1, pp. 42-45 (No. 27), 116 (No. 88), 118-119 (No. 91), and 187-188 (No. 165), 2, pp. 341-345 (No. 293), and 422-423 (No. 362).

donations and legacies. It happened that this activity was effective, but it required a great deal of know-how of writing a document and the ability to imitate *skoropis* (a Cyrillic cursive), which had been used earlier on. On the other hand, the officials had the task to examine the authenticity of the documents.[133]

Since the beginning of the sixteenth century, notaries or secretaries in municipal, church, and state offices swore an oath to correctly perform their duties and not betraying the trust put in them. Chancellor Olbracht Gasztołd introduced the oath in the grand duke's chancery in 1522;[134] the oath of the municipal notaries is mentioned in city documents from the sixteenth century.[135] The text of the oath taken on the Gospel by the notary of the Vilnius chapter spoke of

> the secrets and other statements and actions of the chapter and of not revealing them, to the extent that they are to be kept confidential according to the law [...] and of faithful performance of other such duties proper to the office of secretary.[136]

The formula for the appointment of a scribe was only preserved in the books of the chapter, but notaries of other institutions were subject to a similar appointment procedure, at least in the municipal and ducal chancery.[137]

Appreciation of the efforts of scribes is visible in the last will of canon Tomasz Szeliga from 1640, who asked his colleagues: "if you, the priests of the chapter and my benefactors, decide that your servant, the capitular scribe (needed by you and this church) should live in this apartment of mine, then he should celebrate *sacrum pro anima mea*".[138] Other evidence of the high status of official scribes is found in the sermon published under the title *The Light-*

[133] I owe the information concerning the forgery of documents in the Grand Duchy of Lithuania to Prof. Aleksander I. Grusza, who shared the results of his research with me. See A.I. Груша, "Гісторыя вывучэння белорускай і ўкраінскай кірылычнай палеаграфіі да 1928 гг.", *Белорускі археаграфічны штогоднік* 7 (2006), pp. 95-98.

[134] Chorążyczewski, "Kancelarie centralne państwa", p. 174.

[135] *Zbiór praw i przywilejów*, pp. 143-145.

[136] "De secretis et caeteris dictis et factis Capitulae, qua merito venient celanda non revelandis; imo sub silentio et sigillo secreti retinent. Et alias officias huiusmodi notariatus fideliter exercendo". MS MAB F43-215 (VKF449: *Akta kapituły wileńskiej 1585-1601*), f. 1v; see also MS MAB F43-210/01 (*Akta kapituły wileńskiej 1502-1533*), ff. 46v-47r.

[137] Mirosław Korolko points out that in the times of Sigismund II Augustus there was probably a diploma confirming the appointment to the position of the royal secretary (Korolko, *Seminarium*, p. 72).

[138] As cited in: M. Borkowska, *Dekret w niebieskim ferowany testamencie: Wybór testamentów z XVII-XVIII wieku* (Warsaw, 1984), pp. 120-121.

weight Quill That Carried the Heavy World.[139] This sermon was written by the archimandrite Aleksy Dubowicz in the church of the Holy Trinity church for the funeral of Jan Kolenda, who had served for thirty-two years, first as a castle scribe in Vilnius and then as a land scribe.[140] Father Dubowicz used traditional *vanitas topoi*: kings, *hetmans*, chancellors, and marshals cannot take the attributes of their power (crowns, maces, seals, and staffs) with them into the hereafter.

> These ornaments, which cannot go beyond the end of our lives, do not help and must remain on earth. However, I will go so far as to call it a paradox that "only the quill has the privilege that it continues to accompany the deceased on his way" and does not make pilgrimages from hand to hand in this world. Because the deceased official does not give his quill to the next scribe, but rather transfers the virtues tempered by his own hand to the heavenly chancery. Therefore, this is why we cannot see his quill on the coffin of the late scribe, we do not display the symbol of his office there, because he took it with him to the other world. St. Paul, a scribe of the Orthodox Church – the chancery of Christ – being close to death [said]: [...] "As they are to offer me and the time of my end is coming, bring me books, and especially parchment". Note, please, how this great scribe embarks on his journey and what he takes with him to heaven: [...] particularly parchments.[141]

The Superior of the Holy Trinity monastery used a metaphor originating from Holy Scripture – a practice frequent in his times – translating the reality surrounding him into sacred history by picturing the Orthodox Church as the chancery of Jesus Christ himself. But this metaphor works also in the opposite direction: in his sermon, the scribe's office and the very act of writing became a sanctified activity by quoting relevant passages from the Bible about the creation of the text and by evoking religious phraseology related to writing. For a moment, giving a sacral dimension to the act of writing once more takes place.

Only a few notaries, secretaries, or scribes gained such a high status as, for example Jan Kolenda, or Jan Wieliczko, a castle scribe in 1606-1626. Some of them gained secretarial positions at the courts of magnates, for instance Daniel

[139] A. DUBOWICZ, *Pióro lekkie ciężki świat noszące na pogrzebie jego mości pana Jana Kolendy, województwa wileńskiego, trybunalskiego, ziemskiego pisarza, w Wilnie, w cerkwi Św. Trójce ojców bazylianów w jedności św. będących, roku 1636, dnia 18 miesiąca decembra wystawione* (Vilnius, 1637).

[140] *Urzędnicy Wielkiego Księstwa Litewskiego. Spisy*, 1, pp. 135, 139.

[141] DUBOWICZ, *Pióro lekkie ciężki świat noszące*, ff. B1v-B2r.

Naborowski or Salomon Rysiński, who worked as secretaries for Krzysztof II Radziwiłł (1585-1640). Such positions could give a secretary or scribe an opportunity to further his career.

There are many example of such promotions, which help to establish – to a degree – the hierarchy of the scribal offices in Vilnius in the sixteenth and seventeenth century. A job as notary of the aldermen's court was less profitable than an office of the city council. Thus, in 1650 Stefan Karol Byliński, a notary (*pisarz*) of the aldermen's court moved to the post of notary of the city council.[142] It is worth to add that he and his successor in the post, Krzysztof Wobolewicz, were both noblemen. This means that the job was both lucrative and prestigious, even for members of the nobility. It could be also a step up to even higher positions. In 1649 a nobleman called Józef Piotrowicz became the *Voigt* of Vilnius. Previously, he had been a royal secretary and afterwards a notary of the city council.[143]

Jan Kolenda probably started his career as a scribe in one or another of Vilnius' offices. In 1604 he was appointed notary of the Vilnius castle court (*sąd grodzki*), and in 1608 he was promoted to the more prestigious post of notary of the Vilnius land court (*sąd ziemski*).[144] Marcin Tur (†after 1548) was the notary of the Vilnius castle court (actually, he was the scribe of the *voivode* of Vilnius) between 1523 and 1537. Afterwards he got a job in the chancery of the Grand Duchy of Lithuania where he was mentioned between 1540 and 1545 as a notary or secretary.[145] The scribes in the office of the treasurer (*podskarbi*) of the Grand Duchy Lithuania were often promoted to the post of administrator of the treasury (*skarbny*).[146] In 1631, for example Stanisław Beynart was promoted from the post of scribe to the post of administrator. In 1645 he resigned in favour of his nephew Samuel Beynart, who previously had been a scribe in the office.[147] Daniel Naborowski, who had first been a secretary of Prince Krzysztof Radziwiłł, in 1637 became judge of the castle court in Vilnius (*sędzia grodzki*).

Most professionals of pragmatic literacy, especially those who did not belong to the nobility, had to work hard to find employment even in the lower

[142] RAGAUSKAS, "1650 m. kovo 30 d. Vilniaus suolininkų teismo įrašų knygų aprašas", pp. 262, 264-265.

[143] *Urzędnicy Wielkiego Księstwa Litewskiego. Spisy*, 1, pp. 205-206.

[144] *Ibid.*, pp. 135, 139, 670.

[145] *Ibid.*, pp. 133, 742.

[146] FILIPCZAK-KOCUR, "Kancelaria podskarbich litewskich", p. 54.

[147] *Ibid.*, p. 52.

positions of copyists in the offices mentioned above. Many occasional scribes, not directly connected to any institution, were involved in the production of documents. They composed protestations, wills, and other documents for the inhabitants of the city, which were then validated by the relevant authorities. This required some knowledge of the law, legal rhetoric, and of the forms appropriate to this type of text.

The demand for such services was high. A qualified scribe drafted the text, and after its approval prepared a clean copy of it, as well as making extracts from it. A document that was not prepared at any office, for instance a deed of purchase or a will, was sealed and later on also signed, and was then brought to the office, where it was entered into registers and authenticated, or copies of it were made. For properly qualified people the production of documents therefore could have been quite a profitable business.

Information about the costs related to the production of documents and scribes' salaries is incomplete.[148] We have mentioned the rather high salaries of chapter scribes, who in the second half of the sixteenth century initially earned eight and then twelve Lithuanian *grosz*. It may be assumed that a similar remuneration was received by land or castle notaries, especially as their salaries were comparable to the salaries of similar clerks working in the municipal chanceries of Warsaw and Lublin.[149] Surely, this was not the only source of their income, because they supplemented their salaries by producing texts outside their office. The notaries of the city council or the aldermen courts were probably earning very handsomely. We do not have data about their salaries, but they should have been comparable to the earnings of the secretaries in the chancery of the Grand Duchy of Lithuania or those of the scribes of the treasurer of the Grand Duchy. A famous lexicographer, Jan Mączyński (1520-*c.* 1587), who was a royal secretary and a notary in the Lithuanian chancery, in 1562 got an impressive annual salary of 100 *grzywnas*.[150] In the first half of the seventeenth century each of the four scribes was paid 503-577 *zlotys* from the royal treasury,[151] which was a high sum.

Very little is known about the fees charged for the services provided by the scribal offices of the various institutions in the Grand Duchy of Lithuania. The city statute of 1552 (*wilkierz*) listed prices for services and documents offered

148 RACHUBA, "Kancelarie pieczętarzy WKL", p. 267.

149 ADAMCZYK, *Ceny w Lublinie*, pp. 103, 105; ID., *Ceny w Warszawie*, pp. 65, 108.

150 RACHUBA, "Kancelarie pieczętarzy WKL", p. 270.

151 FILIPCZAK-KOCUr, "Kancelaria podskarbich litewskich", p. 54.

by the municipal court.[152] They were based on the aforementioned decision of the supreme court of the Magdeburg law issued in 1547.[153] The price for reading all the documents at one court session was one *grosz*.[154] Half a sheet of extract (*minuta*, *wypis*) without the municipal seal was one *grosz*; with the seal – two *grosz*. A whole sheet of a document written on both sides was two *grosz*, with the seal three *grosz*. The same prices applied to entries in the municipal registers.[155] Last wills validated by the aldermen's court were the most expensive. The *Voigt* received fifteen *grosz*, the notary twelve *grosz*, and each alderman six *grosz*.[156] Other documents produced by the representatives of the office were cheaper: the notary or the *Voigt* received six *grosz* and an alderman three *grosz*.[157]

We do not have information about the fees in the castle and land courts, but the sources from the voivodeships of Sieradz, Cracow, Łęczyca, the Duchy of Zator and the county (*powiat*) of Sochaczew from 1607 and 1613, reflecting prices in other areas of the Polish-Lithuanian Commonwealth, may shed some light on this problem.[158] In 1607, for most of the rather simple entries, such as a protestation or an entry in a court register, one paid one *grosz*, for the more complicated ones five *grosz*. From 1613 official copies of the most common documents registered in the castle and land registers, such as "receipts, protestations, decrees, intromissions and manifestations, medical reports and post mortem examination reports" cost five *grosz*. An extract from an institutional register cost seven and a half *grosz* ("*groszy pułósma*").

The registers of the Vilnius chapter from the second half of the sixteenth century confirm the amounts of these fees:

> 14 September [1578] for entering in the castle books the plenipotentiary powers authorising me to talk with Hurin before the Minsk office and explaining that I am

[152] *Zbiór praw i przywilejów*, pp. 91-94, 98-100.

[153] In 1568 Bartłomiej Groicki listed the same fees in his Polish translation of this decision; see Groicki, *Ustawa płacej*, p. 7v.

[154] *Zbiór praw i przywilejów*, p. 94.

[155] *Ibid.*, p. 98.

[156] *Ibid.*, p. 100.

[157] *Ibid.*

[158] *Volumina legum: Przedruk zbioru praw staraniem księży pijarów w Warszawie od roku 1732 do roku 1782 wydanego*, 3 (St. Petersburg, 1859), p. 87. See A. Moniuszko, "Wybrane aspekty ekonomicznego funkcjonowania sądownictwa grodzkiego i ziemskiego na Mazowszu w pierwszej połowie xvii wieku", in: *Nad społeczeństwem staropolskim*, 2, pp. 54 and 58-60.

> not subject to the secular law, I gave 2 *grosz*; for the copy of this document I gave 0 *kopa* 6 *grosz*.

For special tasks, however, one had to pay dearly: "I paid the scribe of Mr Wojewodziński two thalers, each worth 28 *grosz*; and 0 *kopa* 56 *grosz* for writing a letter to the soldiers about the Viciebsk inn".[159]

The prices of producing documents were, all in all, rather high,[160] and the trade in texts belonging to the registers of pragmatic literacy accounted for a major share in the sixteenth- and seventeenth-century Vilnius economy. Quite a large number of its inhabitants made a living from the production and reproduction of such texts, and the possibility of generating a significant income and the high social usefulness of their profession maintained their prestige. This raised the status of *homines litterati*, many of whom were identical with the humanists able to create complex texts.[161]

If we look at sixteenth- and seventeenth-century Vilnius from the perspective of the groups of professionals of literacy, the clerks employed by the various institutions should be placed next to the students of the schools and the university, as well as the clergy. Both the quill of an official scribe and that of preachers played a role in creating the textual map of the city and fuelled its economic development. A sermon printed by the Mamonicz publishing house and an extract from the municipal records of Vilnius were produced by professionals who offered their scribal services both to the inhabitants of the capital and to the whole of Lithuania. The scribe Jan Kolenda and the preacher Aleksy Dubowicz used the same "lightweight quill that carried the heavy world".[162]

[159] *Regestr kapituły roku 1577 i roku 1578*, MS MAB F43-451; *Regestr kapituły roku 1579 i roku 1580*, MS MAB F43-452, f. 21v.

[160] RACHUBA, "Kancelarie pieczętarzy WKL", pp. 267-268.

[161] From the beginning of the sixteenth century most jobbing clerks in Vilnius had a humanist background. This was required especially in the municipal, ecclesiastical, and state institutions. Later, in the second half of the sixteenth century, every man who had got some level of schooling possessed the typical humanist literary devices. See the Introduction and Chapter 3 on schools.

[162] DUBOWICZ, *Pióro lekkie ciężki świat noszące*, title page.

Chapter 2

The Preservation of Texts

Archives

As the capital, the main city, and the cultural centre of the Grand Duchy of Lithuania, Vilnius almost naturally became place for amassing large collections of texts in archives and libraries that belonged either to institutions or individuals. As entries in administrative and legal registers and other books concerned the interests of many people, there was constant movement in the relatively small area within the city walls, inspired and caused by copies of documents which were in turn copied into registers. Processing, exchanging, and producing them occupied not only the permanent residents of the city, but also people who came from other Lithuanian urban settlements and villages. It was the presence of the archives in Vilnius that kept the administrative and legal registers that, in turn, determined to a large extent the open nature of the city. Four large archival fonds were located in the lower castle.

From the 1540s, copies of documents issued by the grand duke's chancery were collected and later evolved into the Lithuanian *Metrica* (the *Metrica* of the Grand Duchy of Lithuania), that is the central archive of the state.[1] Initially, it was stored in the treasury at Trakai castle (on the island in Lake Galvė). From there, it was transported to Vilnius in 1511 and was placed in the treasury in the lower castle. Due to the poor condition of the books, chancellor

[1] From 1996 the journal *Lietuvos Metrikos naujienos* is published by the Institute of History in Vilnius, <https://www.istorija.lt/leidiniai/mokslo-zurnalai-ir-testiniai-leidiniai/lietuvos-metrikos-naujienos/668#tab-about_magazine> (accessed 18.02.2021). See KRAWCZUK, "Metryka Koronna i Metryka Litewska", p. 206-212; DUBONIS, ANTANAVIČIUS, RAGAUSKIENĖ, and ŠMIGELSKYTĖ-STUKIENĖ, *The Lithuanian Metrica*.

Lew Sapieha ordered that they should be ordered anew and copied; this work took from 1594 to 1607. Sapieha's efforts to arrange the main Lithuanian archive coincided with similar efforts in Europe in the second half of the sixteenth century.[2] After they had been finally revised in 1621, the copied books were to be placed in a new room. However, they were not put there until 1636, when their transfer was eventually ordered by chancellor Albrycht Stanisław Radziwiłł. They were moved to Jan Kluczata's house, purchased for this purpose on Wielka (Didžioji) Street near the Rynek (the Market Square), while the oldest books were left in the castle.[3] Until the middle of the seventeenth century, the Lithuanian archive consisted of at least 130 volumes, which contained tens of thousands of entries of documents from the grand duke's chancery. After the taking of Vilnius by the Muscovite army in 1655, the Lithuanian *Metrica* was transferred from Vilnius to Moscow and was returned only after the Truce of Andrusovo in 1667. In the period we are interested in, the records of the *Metrica* were kept mainly in Ruthenian and much less frequently in Latin.

The lower castle housed the seat of the castle court (*sąd grodzki*), which also had its own archive. In the municipal books, as in the registers of other institutions, various documents, such as transactions or wills, could be registered. The sentences of the Tribunal of the Grand Duchy of Lithuania (founded in 1581) were also entered into the registers of the castle court when it sat in Vilnius. Ruthenian was the official language of the municipal books, although entries could also be made in Polish and (much more rarely) in Latin.

A separate institution that kept its own books was the burgrave's court (*horodniczański* or the castle supervisor's court), that is a court run by the administrator of the castle and the part of the town which was subordinate to it, in other words the burgrave's *jurydyka*.[4] The burgrave's (*horodniczy*) books usually contain records of court cases between the inhabitants of the burgrave's *jurydyka*, although there are also registers in which one could enter, for exam-

[2] K. POMIAN, *Przeszłość jako przedmiot wiedzy* (Warsaw, 2010), pp. 158-161.

[3] S. PTASZYCKI, *Описание книгъ и актовъ Литовской Метрики* (Санкт-Петербург, 1887), pp. 8-11; E. BANIONIS, *Pratramė*, in: *Lietuvos Metrika (1427-1506)*, Knyga No. 5, *Užrašymų knyga 5*, ed. E. BANIONIS (Vilnius, 1993), pp. 28-29; P. KENNEDY GRIMSTED, "Introduction", in: *The "Lithuanian Metrica" in Moscow and Warsaw: Reconstructing the Archives of the Grand Duchy of Lithuania: Including An Annotated Edition of the 1887 Inventory Compiled by Stanisław Ptaszycki*, ed. P. KENNEDY GRIMSTED and I. SUŁKOWSKA-KURASIOWA (Cambridge, Mass., 1994), p. 11.

[4] About *jurydykas*, see Chapter 1.

ple, a will or a contract concerning a purchase. A separate part of the castle supervisor's archives concerned the documentation regarding the properties subject to the castle. The official language in the few preserved books was Polish.

The fourth and last collection of documents then stored in the lower castle contained the documentation of Vilnius cathedral and the bishopric; this dated back to the end of the fourteenth century. Among the documents there were charters, royal privileges, testaments of the members of the chapter, and records of the chapter's daily activities. Both the originals and copies of these documents, especially if they were in any way related to the chapter and the cathedral, were kept in the cathedral archives. In 1520 bishop John of the Lithuanian Dukes ordered the making of a list of charters and a cartulary. After the great fire of Vilnius in 1610 the archive was divided into two parts: the archive of the cathedral chapter and the archive of the bishopric of Vilnius.[5] The registers of the chapter were kept in Latin. The seat of the archive and the library was the cathedral. The bishop of Vilnius also had his own archive. It contained documents relative to his property and his *jurydyka*. At least until the beginning of the seventeenth century it was located at the Bishop's Manor (the present Presidential Palace).[6]

The main archive of the city was located in the town hall on Market Square. There, the privileges of the city, the registers of the city council and of the aldermen's court (acting according to the rules of the Magdeburg law) were preserved. The registers were kept here at least from the middle of the fifteenth century.[7] The location of the archive was confirmed by the privilege of King Sigismund the Old in 1536.[8] The king ordered that the documents were to be kept together with the municipal funds in a place secured with four locks with four keys. The keys were shared between the two mayors, one Catholic and one Orthodox.[9] Though the king's privilege stated that the municipal archive should be properly protected in the town hall,[10] most of the oldest records did

[5] J. MAROSZEK and W.F. WILCZEWSKI, "Archiwa kapituły i kurii diecezjalnej wileńskiej, dzieje i współczesne miejsca przechowywania w zbiorach litewskich i polskich", *Białostocczyzna* 4 (1998), p. 3.

[6] I am grateful to Dr Wioletta Pawlikowska for information about the places where the cathedral archives were.

[7] See Chapter 6.

[8] *Zbiór praw i przywilejów*, p. 55. See M. BALIŃSKI, *Historia miasta Wilna*, 2 (Vilnius, 1836), p. 72.

[9] *ibid.*, p. 206.

[10] In 1646 it is mentioned as "the Archive or rather a vaulted room where the privileges are

not survive. Even though they had been saved from the 1610 fire, they got lost as a result of the Muscovite invasion in 1655.[11]

In April 1655 the delegates of Vilnius to the parliament (*sejm*) session took the most valuable documents to Warsaw, among them the privileges of the grand dukes and kings. Later, the documents were evacuated to Gdańsk. However, most of the municipal registers, which were left in Vilnius, were not secured and were looted or destroyed after the city was taken by the Muscovite troops on 8 August 1655 (just like most of the archives of the Vilnius nunneries and monasteries). In a statement (*protestacja*) made by the Vilnius magistrate in Vilnius' castle court (*sąd grodzki*) on 30 December 1661, the lost documents were listed:

> We regret the loss of the municipal fortunes, but most regretful is the loss of the documents of both courts, the council's and the *Voigt* and aldermen's. We lost the royal privileges, apart from those, which – thanks to Providence – were taken to the parliament session before the capture of the City of Vilnius [...]; the verdicts of the Parliament and the Courts: *relacyjny*, assessors', commissioners'; the verdicts of the Tribunal of the Grand Duchy of Lithuania; the fiscal documents, the responses of the kings, the documents confirming purchase of lands, manors, homes, gardens and Lukiškės, which belonged to the city; various documents of transactions, exchanges, agreements, bequests, receipts; all the matters and documents related to the ecclesiastical homes and hospitals, their registers of incomes and expenses; the documents of the municipal scales and the *Communitas Mercatoria Vilnensis*; the receipts of the war taxes (*popisowe i poborowe*). [...] In essence, when the enemy wreaked havoc on the city on 8 August 1655 all the archive and collection of the matters and privileges of the city of Vilnius became the spoils of war or got lost when the city and the town hall were burnt down.[12] (original in Polish)

This list can help – to some extent – to imagine the content of the archive.

Another document, issued five years before the invasion, suggests that in the archive there may have been a couple of hundred of manuscript volumes. On 10 March 1650 Stefan Karol Byliński, a notary (*pisarz*) of the aldermen court, was promoted to the position of notary of the city council. A nobleman,

kept" (*Zbiór praw i przywilejów*), p. 206. BALIŃSKI, *Historia miasta Wilna*, 2, p. 72, and Chapter 1.

[11] RAGAUSKAS, "1650 m. kovo 30 d. Vilniaus suolininkų teismo įrašų knygų aprašas", p. 262.

[12] *Zbiór praw i przywilejów*, p. 229-230. It is worth adding that the original privileges, among them the privilege of King Augustus II and many municipal registers, were burnt in the fire in 1706. Another fire in 1749 caused further losses. See KRASZEWSKI, *Wilno*, 2, p. 84.

Krzysztof Wobolewicz, was appointed as a new notary of the aldermen's court. In the acceptance protocol, Mr Byliński handed over to Mr Wobolewicz 100 books of the aldermen's court, which covered the period between 1484 and 1649.[13] Aivas Ragauskas, who published the document, supposes that in the following five years another five books must have been produced.[14] As in the town hall also the books of the city council and various financial registers were kept, we may assume that just before the Muscovite invasion in the city archive there were 200-300 registers (volumes) of different character and an unknown number of original charters and other unbound documents.

The Jesuit archives were among the largest in the city, as a result of the extensive bureaucracy of the Society of Jesus. Usually, three copies of each major document were drafted, one of which remained on site, another was transferred to the archives of the province, and the last one was sent to Rome. From the beginning of the seventeenth century, Vilnius was the capital of the Lithuanian Province of Society of Jesus; earlier on, its documents had been sent to Cracow, the capital of Polish Province. There were several Jesuit institutions in Vilnius, each with its own archives: the office of the province (in the building of the Academy); the college which later became the Academy of Vilnius; the papal seminary, that is the Alumnat on Biskupia (Vyskupai) Street; several residences, among others at St. Casimir's church on the Market Square, and at St. Raphael's church on Šnipiškės.[15] Most of the Jesuit documents were produced in Latin.

The archives of the other religious orders and churches were smaller. Those that have been (at least partially) preserved include the archives of the Franciscans, Bernardines, Dominicans, Basilian monks, and the parish church of St. John.[16] As early as 1440 is mentioned the existence of the necrologium (*liber mortuorum*) kept by the Franciscans of Vilnius. On 21 October of that year, Alexander Muntholt, his wife Helena, and sons Michał, Jan, Bartłomiej, and Konrad agreed to offer each year 20 barrels of rye and one cow in exchange for listing them in the book of the dead and prayers: "after our death,

[13] RAGAUSKAS, "1650 m. kovo 30 d. Vilniaus suolininkų teismo įrašų knygų aprašas", pp. 262, 264-265.

[14] *ibid.*, p. 262.

[15] *Encyklopedia wiedzy o jezuitach na ziemiach Polski i Litwy 1564-1995*, ed. L. GRZEBIEŃ (Cracow, 1996), pp. 745-746.

[16] See the collection of documents from St. John's church, MS LVIA F694, ap. 1, no. 3322.

our souls should be entered into the book of the dead to be read aloud after the sermon on holidays".[17]

At the beginning of the sixteenth century a Bernardine, Jan of Komorowo, mentions some old documents he placed in a coffer: "*et hec Vilne habentur in cista litterarum, quia ego, qui hec scripsi, ea reposui*" ("and these are kept in Vilnius in the chest of letters, because I, who have written them, have put them there").[18]

The parish churches of Vilnius, especially St. John's church, must have had rich collections of documents. The second edition of the *Small Agenda* of the Vilnius bishopric (from 1630) sheds some light on this issue. In the book there is an instruction on how to keep records of marriages and baptisms.[19] This can be interpreted in two ways: either not all parish priests kept such records and the *Agenda* informed them how to do it properly, or the diocesan authorities wanted the records to be uniformly kept. We may suppose that in the Vilnius parish churches records of baptisms and marriages had been introduced before 1630. Unfortunately, all of them perished in the great fires in 1610 and 1655.

In the first half of the seventeenth century the Calvinists, too, began to organise their documents and keep church registers:

> According to the old resolution and custom of God's churches, each [Protestant] church shall keep a church book, into which the foundations of [Protestant] churches are to be entered, as well as ministers' ordinations, baptisms, communicants and marriages, and a senior pastor in each district shall look after it diligently and especially during visitations.[20]

In their archive on Zborowa Street documents were kept that referred not only to local matters, but also to the whole Evangelical community in Lithuania.

[17] "[...] *post obitum vero nostrum animas nostras suis libris asscribere et eas diebus festivis post sermonem pronunciare*" (*Kodeks dyplomatyczny katedry i diecezji wileńskiej*, 1, *1387-1507*, ed. J. Fijałek and W. Semkowicz (Cracow, 1938-1994), p. 190.

[18] Jan of Komorowo, *Memoriale Fratrum Minorum a fr. Ioanne de Komorowo compilatum*, ed. K. Liske and A. Lorkiewicz, in: *Monumenta Poloniae Historica*, 5 (Lviv, 1888), p. 250.

[19] *Agenda parva in commodiorem usum sacerdotum Provinciae Polonae conscripta* (Vilnius, 1630), pp. 43-44, 142. See Hołodok, "Źródła do dziejów liturgii sakramentów", p. 199.

[20] Canon 8 of the Vilnius synod of 1635, *Strony ksiąg kościelnych*, ms mab F40-1157 (*Akta synodów litewskich prowincjonalnych 1611-1637*), f. 153v. Three years later, the synod ordered the Vilnius minister Jurski to prepare a book of wages (*ibid.*, f. 1r).

Most of this archive was destroyed by a fire in 1611.[21] In 1641, together with the library, it was transported from Vilnius to the Radziwiłł estate in Alanta, and hence to Kėdainiai,[22] in this way avoiding destruction during the Muscovite invasion. Thanks to the surviving inventories, it is possible to get an idea of the contents of this collection.[23] It consisted mainly of royal privileges (the privilege for the Vilnius Protestant church [*zbór*] issued by King Stephen Báthory on 28 September 1579 was always listed first), property documents, records concerning legal proceedings (for instance on anti-Calvinistic tumults) and regulations that governed the functioning of Lithuanian *Unitas* (mainly files of provincial synods), as well as correspondence, including a letter from John Calvin dated 9 October 1561 and addressed to the Vilnius Evangelical community.[24] The documents were arranged by category and carefully catalogued, and the brief descriptions on the reverse enabled a quick search of the collections.

Some church institutions, however, did not take proper care of their documents. In the long run this resulted in legal problems, because it was difficult to prove the ownership of their property. The Metropolitan bishop Josyf Velamyn Rutsky from the Uniate monastery of the Holy Trinity, who began to organise its archive only in 1618, had to face such difficulties. His work was facilitated by a letter from King Sigismund III addressed to the city council with a request to make the registers available and to issue copies of the relevant documents because

> through the negligence of the clergy, they [the Uniates] lost much of their funds and properties that, searching with great effort in our *Metrica* in the Lithuanian Tribunal, land and noble court books [the Metropolitan Bishop] must obtain them".[25]

[21] M. Liedke, "Wykorzystanie akt synodów prowincjonalnych Jednoty Litewskiej z XVII wieku w badaniach historycznych", *Białostocczyzna* 59-60.3-4 (2000), p. 9.

[22] W. Gizbert-Studnicki, "Biblioteka Wileńskiego Synodu Ewangelicko-Reformowanego (I)", p. 209; Id., "Biblioteka Wileńskiego Synodu Ewangelicko-Reformowanego (II)", in: *Biblioteki wileńskie*, ed. A. Łysakowski (Vilnius, 1932), pp. 99-101; the canon of the fifteenth Synod of 1642, MS MAB F40-1136 (*Akta synodów litewskich prowincjonalnych 1638-1675*), p. 36.

[23] MS MAB F40-12 (*Rewizje archiwum prowincjalnego* 1669-1753).

[24] Gizbert-Studnicki, "Biblioteka (I)", p. 206; W. Saks 1928, "Zbiory rękopiśmienne synodu ewangelicko-reformowanego w Wilnie", *Reformacja w Polsce* 5.1 (1928), pp. 151-155. Currently, the archive of the Lithuanian Evangelical-Reformed Synod is located in the MAB and is marked with reference number F93.

[25] *AVAK*, vol. 9, p. 158.

The archive of the Jewish community included, among other things, court registers dating back at least to the middle of the sixteenth century. Scholars working before the Second World War used them, but we cannot say much about the content of this archive.[26] Most of it disappeared in the first half of the nineteenth century, after the liquidation of the of the communal Jewish courts (quahal courts) in Lithuania in 1844.[27] Some of the records had been destroyed even earlier during various cataclysms. The oldest surviving *pinkas* (minute book) of *chevra kadisha*, that is the 'sacred society' which provided correct burials to the members of the Jewish community, dates from 1747; it also recorded deaths from the end of the sixteenth century and the seventeenth century. Earlier *pinkases* burned in a fire in the first half of the eighteenth century.[28]

The Vilnius guilds also kept their own archives. They contained royal privileges and "regulations issued by the mayors and town councillors", as well as lists of members, of fees, and court documents. Most of these documents had to be recreated after the Russian invasion, but there is evidence that allows us to assume that in the first half of the seventeenth century the guild archives functioned similarly to the later ones. In 1664, King John II Casimir Vasa issued a new privilege for the goldsmiths' guild,

> because our subjects, masters of goldsmithing who live in our capital city of Vilnius, regretfully complained that because of the faithless Muscovite enemy they lost their privileges granted and established by the most gracious Polish kings, grand dukes of Lithuania, our antecessors, in which they were allowed to have their own guild with all rights and freedoms, as is stipulated in the Lithuanian *Metrica*.[29]

The goldsmiths' documents were destroyed despite the great importance attached to their storage. Each guild had a common coffer in which membership fees were mentioned in "properly bound registers, written in Polish and including such information as who gave how much, with the name and nickname of the payer"[30] as well as "letters and privileges, brotherhood's registers".

[26] Дубнов, *Разговорный язык*, pp. 10-11.

[27] P. KON, "Odnaleziona część archiwum dawnego kahału wileńskiego", *Ateneum Wileńskie* 15.5 (1928), p. 152.

[28] COHEN, *History of the Jews in Vilnius*, p. 124-125.

[29] Privilege of John Casimir for the guild of goldsmiths from 30 June 1664, *AVAK*, vol. 10, p. 62.

[30] The statute of the guild of glaziers of 8 September 1668, *AVAK*, vol. 10, p. 41.

> Such a coffer shall be carefully guarded by supervisors elected on an annual basis. It should not be transferred anywhere outside the city but kept in a safe place under the supervision of the town hall's *jurydyka*. There shall be two keys for the coffer, one kept by the Catholic supervisor and the other one by the Orthodox [supervisor], and neither of them should open the coffer without the other.[31]

Not only the guilds, but also the *communitas mercatoria*, an association of the richest merchants, next to its headquarters, that is the merchants' chamber in the town hall, had a room where documents were kept in a box.[32]

The magnates' archives were not permanently kept in Vilnius. Instead, they were either kept in family residences, for instance in the Radziwiłł's Nyasvizh, or travelled with the owner's chancery (something Bogusław Radziwiłł used to complain about).[33]

Wealthy townsmen, nobility, and clergy who lived in Vilnius also collected documents. The inventory of the possessions of mayor Stefan Lebiedzicz of 27 September 1649 contains, among other things, a section on "Miscellaneous matters and registers" ("*Sprawy różne i regestra*"), which contained ten different fascicules and debt records,[34] and there are plenty of similar lists that have survived. As has been already mentioned, the poorer inhabitants of the city also kept some documents. They provided a guarantee for money, goods, buildings, and other forms of ownership, so it was crucial to ensure they were kept safely. Inventories, not only from Vilnius, mention that documents were carefully stored in safe boxes, and in order to make them more durable, they were also recorded in the registers of the institutions mentioned above. However, we know little about how private individuals kept and arranged documents, and only further research can shed some light on this problem, which is interesting from the point of view of the circulation of texts.[35]

[31] The statute of the guild of saffian makers of 6 March 1666, *AVAK*, vol. 10, p. 76.

[32] M. ŁOWMIAŃSKA, "Udział *communitatis mercatoriae* w samorządzie wileńskim", *Lituano-Slavica Posnaniensia* 9 (2003), p. 76.

[33] M. JARCZYKOWA, *"Papirowe materie" Piotra Kochlewskiego: O działalności pisarskiej sekretarza Radziwiłłów birżańskich w pierwszej połowie XVII wieku* (Katowice, 2006), pp. 94-95.

[34] MS LVIA F23, ap. 1, no. 5096, ff. 441r-441v; *AVAK*, vol. 9, p. 483; *Wilnianie*, p. 194. There is an inventory of the objects left by Anastasia Witkowska Janowa Gilewiczowa from 1684, in which there are sections *Obliga i sprawy* and the *Registers of the late Mr Gielewicz* (*Regestra nieboszczyka pana Gielewicza*). They list thirty-six different documents and booklets, mainly registers and records of debt. See *ibid.*, pp. 205-208.

[35] K. SYTA, "Archiwa szlachty żmudzkiej w II poł. XVI wieku", in: *Studia o bibliotekach i zbiorach polskich*, 7, ed. B. RYSZEWSKI (Toruń, 1997), pp. 29-30.

Libraries

Before the second half of the fifteenth century, the Eastern Orthodox and Catholic church libraries were the only ones in the city. Their origins are connected with the appearance of the first Orthodox churches in Vilnius, as liturgical texts were necessary for conducting the divine service It would appear that the first collection of manuscripts was created at the church of the Theotokos, which, according to tradition, was founded in the middle of the fourteenth century by one of the Orthodox wives of Duke Algirdas, Maria of Viciebsk or Uliana of Tver.[36] This was the most important Orthodox church in the capital, which in 1415 gained the status of a cathedral (*sobor*) when the Lithuanian Orthodox metropolis was established along with the Metropolitan bishop's capital in Navahrudak.

The number of books needed in the cathedral was large, but even minor Orthodox churches were equipped with smaller or larger book collections. At the end of the fourteenth century there must have been at least a few libraries in the Orthodox and Catholic churches. They were growing in number. At the beginning of the sixteenth century there were as many as sixteen Orthodox and eight Catholic churches in Vilnius, and at the turn of the sixteenth and seventeenth centuries there were seven Orthodox, twelve Uniate, and thirteen Catholic churches.[37] In 1650, the Jesuit historian Wojciech Wijuk Kojałowicz remarked:

> There are Catholic churches in this city: twenty-three of the Roman rite and nine of the Greek rite (excluding schismatics), many of which are wonderfully built and amply equipped with precious items. There are nineteen religious houses and eight hospitals. Such support for the Christian religion is necessary in this city not so much because of its size, but because of the number of sects. For Calvinists, Lutherans, Ruthenian schismatics, Jews, and even Tartar Mohammedans have their places of worship in the city, the latter on the outskirts on the bank of River Neris.[38]

At the time when Kojałowicz described the diocese of Vilnius, there were at least 29 libraries that belonged to religious institutions; they ranged from a few

[36] BALIŃSKI, *Historia miasta Wilna*, 1, pp. 20-21; V. DRĖMA, *Vilniaus bažnyčios: Iš Vlado Drėmos archyvų* (Vilnius, 2008), p. 956.

[37] M. PAKNYS, *Vilniaus miestas ir miestiečiai 1636 m.*, pp. 39-40.

[38] W. WIJUK KOJAŁOWICZ, *Miscellanea rerum ad statum ecclesiasticum in Magno Lituaniae Ducatu pertinentium collecta* (Vilnius, 1650), p. 76. Maria Łowmińska confirms that there were thirty-seven places of worship and provides a detailed list of them. Cf. M. ŁOWMIŃSKA, "Wilno przed najazdem moskiewskim 1655 roku", in: *Dwa doktoraty z uniwersytetu*, pp. 194-207.

books to tens of thousands of volumes. The ecclesiastical regulations, especially those relating to Catholic orders and congregations, required that each monastery and monastery have a library and regulated their operations,[39] so that these institutions were the largest depositories of books in early modern Vilnius. It should be mentioned that one monastery or nunnery could have several book collections. A similar situation is encountered in the Academy of Vilnius, which had one common library and a number of specialised libraries, including those of individual professors, the rector, the preacher, and the pharmacy.[40] Other Jesuit residences and homes in Vilnius also had two or more book collections. The libraries of the Orthodox Brotherhood, as well as those of the Lutheran and Calvinist churches and schools, had similar regulations.

Book Collections of Orthodox Churches

The Orthodox churches' book collections contained works necessary for conducting the divine service. Among them were biblical and liturgical texts, as well as combinations of them, and Orthodox regulations.[41] In smaller churches, the number of texts could be reduced to a minimum, while in major places of worship, such as the cathedral of the Theotokos or the Orthodox monastic churches, there could be several books of each type. At the beginning of the sixteenth century, libraries of large Lithuanian monasteries possessed on average about fifty volumes. For example, in 1494 there were 45 volumes in the Holy Trinity monastery in Slutsk.[42] In the middle of the sixteenth century there may even have been more than a hundred of them, as is suggested by the inventory of the library of the monastery in Supraśl from 1557, which mentioned 129 volumes from the old collection.[43]

Very little is known about the content of the libraries of Orthodox churches and monasteries, because no inventories could be found that describe them.

[39] M. PIDŁYPCZAK-MAJEROWICZ, *Biblioteki i bibliotekarstwo zakonne na wschodnich ziemiach Rzeczypospolitej w XVII-XVIII wieku* (Wrocław, 1996), pp. 52-55.

[40] *Ibid.*, p. 88; L. GRZEBIEŃ, "Organizacja bibliotek jezuickich w Polsce od XVI do XVIII wieku", part 1, *Archiwa, Biblioteki i Muzea Kościelne* 30 (1975), pp. 246-264.

[41] O. NARBUTT, *Historia i typologia ksiąg liturgicznych bizantyńsko-słowiańskich: Zagadnienie identyfikacji według kryterium treściowego* (Warsaw, 1979), p. 51. See Chapter 9, "Holy texts and liturgical texts".

[42] A.I. ГРУША, *Белоруская кірылычна палеаграфія*, p. 82; M.B. НІКАЛАЕЎ, *Гісторыя беларускай кнігі*, 1, p. 67.

[43] ГРУША, *Белоруская кірылычна палеаграфія*, p. 82.

However, many references to the practice of copying Orthodox books in Vilnius at the turn of the fifteenth and sixteenth centuries have survived. Due to growing demand they also had to be imported from other urban settlements of the Grand Duchy of Lithuania where scriptoria operated, for instance from Kyiv, Smolensk, Polatsk and Slutsk, as well as from scriptoria outside Lithuania. Entries in several manuscripts provide information about pious bequests and donations of precious books. In the 1580s, the court's marshal Alexandr Alexandrovych Soltan donated an *Acts of the Apostles* to the Holy Trinity Orthodox church, while in 1594 councillor Jakub Iwanowicz handed over to the cathedral of the Theotokos a gospel book in a velvet binding reinforced with silver.[44]

The most famous gift to the Vilnius Orthodox library known today is the richly illuminated *Kyiv Psalter*, copied by the monk Spiridon in Pechersk Lavra in Kyiv in 1397, which is one of the most beautifully decorated Ruthenian manuscripts. Over a century later, in 1518, Jan Abraham Ezofowicz, the Lithuanian treasurer, donated it to the Orthodox St. Nicholas's church in Wielka (Didžioji) Street, perhaps in connection with the renovation of that church by *hetman* Konstanty Ostrogski. The dedication on the parchment added to the psalter reads:

> I, a servant of God christened Jan and called by the name of Abraham Ezofowicz, the treasurer of the Grand Duchy of Lithuania, of the Sovereign and King Sigismund Kazimirowicz, I presented this book called a psalter, laboriously written in gold and ink on parchment, to the Orthodox church of the great Christian saint, Nicholas the Worker of Miracles and of the Transfer of His Venerable Reliquaries in Vilnius, in the city of Vilnius, which remained in the care of God for the salvation of the soul and eternal life.[45]

[44] Г.Я. Галечанка, *Невядомыя и малавядомыя помнікі духоўнай спадчыны і культурных сувязей Беларусі XV-сярэдзіны XVII ст.* (Minsk, 2008), pp. 102-103; М.В. Ніколаеў, *Палата кнігопісаная: Рукапсная кніга на Беларусі ў X-XVIII стагоддах* (Мінск, 1993), p. 127.

[45] As cited in: Г. Вздорнов, *Исследование о Киевской псалтыри* (Москва, 1978), p. 10; facsimiles of dedication: *Киевская псалтырь 1397 года из Государственной Публичной библиотеки имени М.Е. Салтыкова-Щедрина в Ленинграде [олдп F 6]* (Москва,1978), ff. 1ar-13v.

It is possible that other Orthodox Vilnius churches received similar donations, as the treasurer mentioned in his will of 28 September 1519 that "Orthodox holy objects and books" are to be handed over to designated churches.[46]

From the 1520s onwards, book collections held at Orthodox churches and monasteries were supplied with books printed in Vilnius, first by Skaryna, then by Mstislavets, the Mamonicz family, and the Othodox Brotherhood's printing houses, as well as with imported Orthodox prints. Liturgical handwritten books were also still handed over to the churches.

At the beginning of the seventeenth century, the libraries of the Orthodox Brotherhood at the church of the Holy Spirit, as well as those of the Uniate church of the Holy Trinity and the Basilian monastery, were enriched thanks not only to the publishing activity of these institutions, but also to bequests. This is shown, for instance by four volumes of works of St. Augustine given to the Uniates by the Metropolitan bishop Hipacy Pociej, accompanied with the following note:

> Executing the last will of the late Metropolitan bishop of Kyiv, Halych, and all Rus, the *vladyka* [bishop] of Volodymyr [Volynskyi] and Brest, our master and father, we present these books to the monastery of the Holy Trinity in Vilnius, provided that they are not moved from this monastery to any other place.[47]

The constitutions of the Basilian Order, drafted by Josyf Velamyn Rutsky and adopted by the general chapter in 1624, regulated the functioning of monastic libraries. Special attention was devoted to the assurance of financial support for the book collection and to the duties of the librarian. He was mainly charged with guarding the entire collection of books and preventing the volumes from being taken out of the reading room,[48] which was probably a worry for all librarians in Vilnius. The problem of disappearing books is mentioned in the records produced by the Jesuits, by the chapter, and by the Calvinists, while the dedication of the *Kyiv Psalter* of 1518 even contained an elaborate curse on a putaqtie thief: "Let his days be short, let his bishopric be taken by

[46] *Русскоеврейский архив: документы и материалы для истории евреев в России*, 1, *Документы и регесты к истории литовских евреев (1388-1550)*, ed. С.А. БЕРШАДСКИЙ (Санкт Петербург, 1882), p. 98.

[47] Augustinus Aurelius, *Opera*, 1 (Leiden, 1586) (MAB V 16/2-471/4).

[48] M. PIDŁYPCZAK-MAJEROWICZ, *Bazylianie w Koronie i na Litwie. Szkoły i książki w działalności zakonu* (Warsaw, 1986), pp. 144-145.

another, and his prayer be in sin, let his sons be orphans and his wife a widow", and so on.[49]

The library of the Orthodox Brotherhood of the Holy Spirit used books borrowed from other Orthodox brotherhoods that operated in the commonwealth. In 1619, its representatives asked the Lviv Brotherhood to lend them a codex of a collection of biblical texts written in Greek (the *Menaion*, *Triodion*, *Shestodnevets* and *Octoechos*) through their envoy Joseph Berezhsky. "By this letter, we promise our brothers and assure you that after their proper use in our church, we will send them back in their entirety to you with a fraternal blessing", the brothers of Vilnius promised.[50] This loan was probably for the purpose of copying the manuscript for use at the school run by the Brotherhood. Manuscripts must have constituted a rather important part of this book collection. For example, Melecjusz Smotrycki mentions that his unpublished texts were stored in the Brotherhood's library.[51]

The Cathedral Library

Among the earliest documents that provide evidence for the existence of the library at the Catholic cathedral in Vilnius and of private collections belonging to Vilnius canons is a legal sentence of 22 September 1486, issued by arbitrators appointed by Casimir IV Jagiellon, resolving a dispute between the chapter and bishop Andrzej Szeliga. Among other things, this concerned the belongings of deceased members of the chapter.[52] If there were any books left – the verdict stipulated – the more valuable ones should be given to the cathedral library, as well as those which had not been in it before. The others were

[49] See the dedication in Вздорнов, *Исследование о Киевской псалтыри*, p. 10.

[50] *AIZR*, 4, *1588-1632*, p. 506.

[51] "Even now, the library of the brotherhood in Vilnius contains a treatise on the origin of the Holy Spirit composed by means of syllogisms often explained by the Orthodox and the Catholics to one another, written in Polish and given to the archimandrite who preceded me in reading" (M. Smotrycki, *Apologia peregrinatiej do krajów wschodnich przez mię, Meletiusza Smotrzyskiego, M.D. archiepiskopa połockiego, episkopa witebskiego i mścisławskiego, archimandrytę dermańskiego roku P<ańskiego> 1623 i 24 obchodzonej przez fałszywą Bracią słownie i na piśmie spotwarzonej do przezacnego Narodu Ruskiego obojego stanu duchownego i świetskiego sporządzona i podana A<nno> 1628 Augusti die 25 w Monasteru w Dermaniu*, (Lwów, 1628), p. 105.

[52] Kurczewski, *Kościół zamkowy, czyli katedra wileńska*, 1, pp. 30-31; M. Kosman, "Episkopat litewski XV-XVIII w.", in: id., *Orzeł i Pogoń*, p. 228.

to be assigned "to pious works and for the consolation of friends in accordance with the custom provided by law" ("*na dzieła pobożne i dla pocieszenia przyjaciół zgodnie z przewidzianym przez prawo zwyczajem*").[53] The friends who demanded such consolation probably included the canons of Vilnius.

However, the cathedral library was much older than the ordinance quoted above, as it was founded at the time of the formation of the diocese of Vilnius. As in the case of Orthodox churches, its book collection consisted of texts that served the liturgy.[54] In addition, there were books on canon law, theology, lists of revenues, and, although in a smaller amount, literature, such as historiography and the Latin classics. Queen Hedwig (Jadwiga) played a special role in supplying the cathedral with books. In the 1390s she employed at least three scribes (*kathedrales*, professional copyists of books),[55] who produced manuscripts for Lithuanian churches, including for Vilnius' cathedral church, as is mentioned by the Polish historian Jan Długosz.[56] An inventory from 1458-1460 recalls a great donation to Vilnius cathedral made by the Queen and King Jogaila in 1398. They ordered the deputy chancellor Klemens of Moskorzew to purchase or make (*comparare*) a book with the *Aurea legenda* (the *Golden Legend*) by Jacob of Voragine and the *Gospel of Nicodemus*. The book was sent to Vilnius with several liturgical codices: two missals (one with musical notation – "*missale magnum notatum*") and a breviary.[57] Another copy of the *Golden Legend* was bequeathed to the cathedral by its first custodian Marcin, whose task was to take care of the treasury and library.[58] The first bishop of Vilnius, Andrzej, also donated his books to it:

> Therefore, first of all we give and bequeath to our church in Vilnius and to the chapter itself for eternal possession two better pontificals, written on parchment, one of which is new, the other is old with the same title as the former one, and the

[53] *Kodeks dyplomatyczny katedry i diecezji wileńskiej*, p. 409.

[54] See Chapter 9, "Holy texts and liturgical texts".

[55] E. POTKOWSKI, "*Kathedrales* at the court of Queen Hedwig", *Codices Manuscripti* 13 (1987), p. 79-85.

[56] E. POTKOWSKI, "Produkcja książki rękopiśmiennej w Polsce w XV stuleciu", in: *Z badań nad polskimi księgozbiorami historycznymi: Książka rękopiśmienna XV-XVII w.*, ed. B. BIEŃKOWSKA (Warsaw, 1980), p. 27.

[57] This information is given by an inventory record of 1498, which concerns the capitular library, in the entry in the crown *Metrica* of 1459-1460; cf. *Kodeks dyplomatyczny katedry i diecezji wileńskiej*, p. 57.

[58] J. FIJAŁEK, "Kościół rzymskokatolicki na Litwie: Uchrześcijanienie Litwy przez Polskę i zachowanie w niej języka ludu po koniec Rzeczypospolitej", in: *Polska i Litwa w dziejowym stosunku* (Warsaw, 1914), p. 127.

> third one is ancient and treats about the authority of the Roman curia, and, in short, all the other books that we have, according to how they are listed in the register of the said chapter.[59]

King Jogaila was also among the benefactors of the chapter's library. Długosz recalls that in 1410, after the conquest of the castle Brodnica (Strasburg in Westpreußen), belonging to the Teutonic Knights, part of the loot, including manuscripts, was given to the cathedral.[60] It may be assumed that the original library consisted of several dozen volumes.

In the second half of the fifteenth century, the bishop and the chapter decided to enlarge the cathedral library. Manuscripts were ordered to be produced by the professional copyists and jobbing clergymen in Cracow.[61] In 1483, the acolyte of St. Mary's church, Bartłomiej of Biecz, made an antiphonary commissioned by the *starost* of Navahrudak, Marcin Gasztołd.[62] The Polish *kathedrales* also made "one Cracow parchment missal", kept in 1598 in the Manvydas chapel.[63] Such "old missals" were mentioned on the list a few more times.

Unfortunately, the medieval collection of the library did not survive the sixteenth century and was probably burnt during the fires of 1513, 1530, or 1542.[64] Thanks to the efforts of various benefactors, for instance Olbracht Gasztołd (Albertas Goštautas) and bishop John of the Dukes of Lithuania,[65] it was regularly rebuilt. Again unfortunately, apart from some general information about its existence or about restrictions on taking books from it (formu-

[59] The testamentary legacy of brother Andrzej, bishop of Vilnius of 27 October 1398, in: *Kodeks dyplomatyczny katedry i diecezji wileńskiej*, pp. 56-57; KURCZEWSKI, *Kościół zamkowy*, 2, p. 20;

[60] E. POTKOWSKI, "Monarsze dary książkowe w polskim średniowieczu – pogrunwaldzkie dary Jagiełły", in: *Ojczyzna bliższa i dalsza*, pp. 369 and 371.

[61] E. POTKOWSKI, *Książka rękopiśmienna w kulturze Polski średniowiecznej* (Warsaw, 1984), pp. 103-108.

[62] *Cracovia impressorum XV et XVI saeculorum*, ed. J. PTAŚNIK (Lviv, 1922), pp. 8-9 (item 20); POTKOWSKI, "Produkcja książki", p. 30; НІКАЛАЕЎ, *Гісторыя беларускай кнігі*, 1, p. 71.

[63] *Regestr apparatów i inszego sprzętu, złota i srebra w kościelie św. Stanisława katedralnym na zamku wileńskim spisany i rewidowany*, 1596-1626, MS VUB F4- 35808 (A2472), p. 77.

[64] One of Sigismund I the Old's letters from 1531 informs us that "last year [...] the church and the Bishop's Mouse along with a major part of the town [...] burnt down". See A. WALAWENDER, *Kronika klęsk elementarnych w Polsce i krajach sąsiednich w latach 1450-1586*, 2, *Zniszczenia wojenne i pożary* (Lviv, 1932), p. 305. The other two fires are discussed *ibid.*, pp. 288 and 317.

[65] KURCZEWSKI, *Kościół zamkowy*, 1, p. 28.

lated in the statute of 1561), we do not know the precise contents of the collection, although we may surmise what works were kept there. The library was probably similar to the cathedral libraries in Poland, for instance the Wawel cathedral in Cracow,[66] but the number of its volumes was certainly smaller. There must have been missals, breviaries, psalters, bibles, lives of saints, collections of sermons, vocabularies, and *exempla*. In the middle of the sixteenth century, the library was already large enough to support the collections of the newly established Jesuit colleges with single copies. Among other things, the library of the college in Braniewo (Braunsberg) received from the Vilnius chapter comments on Aristotle's *Physics*, published in Cologne in 1506.[67]

At that time, donations to the cathedral included not only its main library as a beneficiary, but also individual altars and chapels. A description of the items of the foundation of the altar (*altaria*) of the main cathedral has also survived. The cathedral was dedicated to the Holy Cross; the Holy Cross founded in the 1570s by bishop Walerian Protasewicz survived. The bishop and other donators, apart from chalices, crosses, and liturgical vestments, also donated to the cathedral a rich collection of eighty-one (or seventy-nine) works in 101 volumes.[68] It contained liturgical books, and for instance a Vulgate, a Roman missal, biblical commentaries and indices, works of theologians and Church Fathers such as Origen of Alexandria and St. Jerome, St. Ambrose, St. John Chrysostom and St. Augustine, synodical resolutions (for instance the *Confessio fidei Petricoviana*), polemical books, anti-Protestant books, anti-Jewish books, and books that related to the post-Tridentine reform (for instance

[66] The inventory, that covered only part of the library of Wawel cathedral from the end of the fifteenth century, listed as many as 244 volumes; see "Katalog rękopisów kapitulnych Katedry Krakowskiej", ed. I. Polkowski, in: *Archiwum do Dziejów Literatury i Oświaty w Polsce*, 3 (Cracow, 1884), pp. 7-23.

[67] The copy is currently in Uppsala (CR 29.23; Script. Graeci): Aristoteles, *Commentaria in libros Physicorum Aristotelis in gymnasio Coloniensi quod Bursam Laurentii vocant novissime edita* [per Joannem de Nurtingen]. *Divi Alberti Magni sententias et interpretationes in eodem una cum questionibus disputabilibus ac dubijs textualibus*, Coloniae, Liberorum Quentell officina, 1506. Provenance notes: D. Stanislai Cathedralis Vilnen<is> and Collegÿ Brunsbergensis. See *The Catalogue of the Book Collection of the Jesuit College in Braniewo Held in the University Library in Uppsala / Katalog księgozbioru Kolegium Jezuitów w Braniewie zachowa nego w Bibliotece Uniwersyteckiej w Uppsali*, 2, ed. J. Trypućko, M. Spandowski, and S. Szyller (Warsaw, 2007), p. 40, item 1111.

[68] *Altare S. Crucis In Ecclesia Cathedrali Vilnensi in medio templi situm, fundationis et erectionis S. Reverendissimi in Christo patris d. Domini Valeriani Dei gratia Episcopi Vilnensis*, MA BK 71, f. 11r. See U. Paszkiewicz, *Inwentarze i katalogi bibliotek z ziem wschodnich Rzeczypospolitej (spis za lata 1553-1939)* (Warsaw, 1996), p. 64.

by Hozjusz or Konrad Braun (Conradus Brunus)), as well as many collections of sermons (such as the *Homiliae Ioannis Loiardi in Omnes epistolae*), and works for religious education (for instance the *Loci communes* by Conrad Clingius and the *Cathechismus Friderici Nauseae* and *Imagines mortis*), and the *Sentences* by Peter Lombard. There were only a few non-religious books, including Ambrogio Calepino's dictionary, the *Chimera* by Stanisław Orzechowski, Paul the Deacon's *Longobard History*, and the *Speculum Saxonum*.[69] Much free space was left in the inventory for entering books that were intended to expand the library. Among all these works, one particularly stands out. It is related to a bequest for the altar of Holy Cross:

> For this altar a parchment missal, hand-calligraphed and exquisitely decorated with gold and coloured miniatures, in a bronze binding with gold-plated silver clasps and fasteners, as well as the coat of arms of the venerable founder placed above, with an index bound in silk and adorned with pearls.[70]

In 1598, the cathedral book collection consisted of 126 volumes[71] and was reminiscent of Protasewicz's bequest. However, these were not the only books in the cathedral, because each chapel was provided with its own books. Most of them were in the royal chapel (of St. Casimir): ten "books on chains where priests sing in the choir stalls".[72] Other chapels had several books each, for instance in the chapel of bishops there was, among other things, an "old Cracow missal".

Such a large library was created mainly thanks to the bequests of various clergymen, mostly members of the chapter. In 1570, most of the books from the late suffragan of Vilnius, bishop Jerzy Albinus,[73] were handed over by the

[69] This is probably a work that contained the famous woodcuts of Hans Holbein entitled *Imagines Mortis: His Accesserunt Epigrammata, e Gallico idiomate a Georgio Aemylio in Latinum translata. Ad Haec, Medicina Animae tam iis, qui firma, quam qui adversa corporis valetudine praediti sunt, maxime necessaria* (Cologne, 1555; or a later edition).

[70] "*Id. altari missale pergameneum manu artificialiter scriptum et figuris auro et variis coloribus subtiliter ornatur in veluto brunatino cum bullis et clausuris ar genteis deauratis et armis Reverendissimi Domini Fundatoris desuper aplicatis cum regestro serico filato, margaritis exornato*". *Altare S. Crucis*, f. 13r.

[71] Two copies of the *Index Librorum in Bibliotheca Ecclesiae Cathedralis Vilnensis* have survived. 1598: MS LVIA F1135, ap. 4, No. 471, pp. 36-40; MS VUB F4-35808 (A2472), pp. 78-80. See PAWLIKOWSKA-BUTTERWICK, "Księgozbiór biblioteki katedralnej w Wilnie z końca XVI wieku", pp. 162-191.

[72] MS VUB F4-35808 (A2472), f. 65r.

[73] Some of them were identified by Edmundas Laucevičius (E. LAUCEVIČIUS, *Knygų įrišimai*

chapter to the Jesuit college library, but four of them were left in the chapter library: two whose titles are not mentioned, because their valuable velvet binding with silver ornaments attracted all attention, and the other two being a pontifical and a missal.[74] Canon Mikołaj Koryzna left 51 books to the chapter. His colleague, the canon of Vilnius and Samogitia Ambroży Bejnart, who died in 1603, bequeathed the same number of volumes to the library.[75] Three years later, in 1606, the cathedral library received 47 books from archdeacon Jan Ryszkowski.[76] In 1617, his successor, the Vilnius archdeacon Grzegorz Święcicki bequeathed the "missal, which is in Smarhon" and paintings "for the grave of St. Casimir".[77] In 1638, canon Olaus Alginus left to the cathedral "one missal with the liturgy of masses for the Polish patrons. My altar will receive a breviary with a diurnal and a crucifix".[78]

After the donation of bishop Protasewicz was made, many Catholic printing houses started to work in Vilnius and the number of booksellers increased. This made it easier to supply the library with books. In 1603 it was decided that one of the members of the chapter would be its librarian.[79] However, the catastrophes of the seventeenth century destroyed the book collection almost entirely. At the end of the inventory of the bishop's chapel mentioned previously there is a note: "Everything burnt *anno 1610 Julii 1a in communi incendio urbis et Ecclesiae Cathedralis* [in 1610 on 1 July in the general fire of the city

Lietuvos bibliotekose (Vilnius, 1976), e.g. p. 84, item 390).

74 MS MAB F43-212 (VKF446: *Acts of the Vilnius Chapter 1561-1570*), ff. 251v-252r (item 746), 12.05.1570; ff. 253v-254r (item 749), 12.05.1570.

75 *A.D. 1603 Libri reverendi domini Ambrosii Beynarti canonici Vilnensis et Samotitiensis post mortem eiusdem Bibliothecae Ecclesiae Cathedralis Vilnensis donati*, *in Regestr apparatów i inszego sprzętu*, ff. 86r-87r. See U. PASZKIEWICZ, *Inwentarze i katalogi libraries z ziem wschodnich Rzeczypospolitej (spis za lata 1510-1939)* (Warsaw, 1998), p. 167. However, these were not all the books that Bejnart possessed, as the posthumous inventory of his belongings includes e.g. a Ruthenian breviary and a Lithuanian statute in Ruthenian, which are not listed in the register of the chapter. See *Inwentarz wszytkich pozostałych rzeczy nieboszczyka księdza Ambrożego Beinarta kanonika wileńskiego*, MS MAB F43-492, ff. 2r-2v.

76 *Regestr apparatów i inszego sprzętu*, ff. 88r-89r: "A.D. 1606 16 Junii post mortem admodum reverendi patris Joannis Ryszkowski archidiaconi Ecclesiae Catheralis Vilnensis libri bibliothecae cathedrali donati". See PAWLIKOWSKA, "Księgozbiór biblioteki katedralnej w Wilnie", p. 176.

77 MS MAB F43-26717.

78 "*Missale unum, missas patronorum Polonorum. Breviarium cum diurnali pro meo altari constat et crucifixus*". MS MAB F43-218 (VKF452; *Acts of the Vilnius Chapter 1632-1643*), ff. 427v-428v (item 1205), 16.05.1642.

79 OCHMAŃSKI, *Najdawniejsze księgozbiory na Litwie*, p. 75.

and cathedral church]". The Muscovite occupation brought similar devastation half a century later.

This outline of the history of the cathedral library helps us to imagine its content in the first few centuries of its existence. It was far less fortunate than other cathedral libraries, such as the library of Wawel cathedral in Cracow, which was not only much larger, but has also largely survived to the present day. Knowledge of the Vilnius chapter book collection, although fragmentary, is a valuable help in determining the content of other, usually far more modest Catholic church and monastic book collections in the Lithuanian capital, of which we have less knowledge for the period discussed here.

Libraries of Churches, Monasteries, and Convents

At the end of the fifteenth century and during the sixteenth century, one of the largest monastic book collections in Vilnius belonged to the Bernardines, not only because it was an order of scholars who brought books with them into the city, but also because they created and copied them in Vilnius for the use of their monastery. This library contained manuscripts, incunabula, and old printed editions that were kept in the Bernardine library in the nineteenth century and were later transferred to Vilnius' University Library and to the National Library of Lithuania. However, it is probable that the earliest book collection had been destroyed during the fire of 20 June 1560, which claimed the monastery and 200 houses.[80] It was recreated thanks to purchases and donations. Archdeacon Jasiński, mentioned above, for instance donated a copy of the chronicle of Marcin Kromer.[81]

The Franciscans and Dominicans probably had quite extensive book collections. We know that the library of the Vilnius Franciscan convent was supplied by the book collection of the Vilnius canon Jan Makowiecki (see below). More information is available about the Dominican library, which at the beginning of the seventeenth century consisted of 550 volumes.[82] Apart from liturgical and theological books, religious polemics, etc., the inventory includes titles of texts on secular matters, such as works on rhetoric, medicine, astronomy,

[80] WALAWENDER, *Kronika klęsk elementarnych w Polsce*, p. 328.

[81] PIDŁYPCZAK-MAJEROWICZ, *Biblioteki i bibliotekarstwo*, p. 96.

[82] *Libri Conventus Vilnensis*, 1604, a manuscript in the archive of the Polish Province of the Dominican Fathers in Cracow, ref. Wd. 1. See K. ZAWADZKA, "Źródła bibliotek dominikanów w Polsce", *Nasza Przeszłość* 39 (1973), pp. 216, 218.

and geography (works by Cicero, Quintilian, Aphthonius, Hippocrates, Pedacius, Vadianus, and Pliny). Maciej Vorbek-Lettow says in his diary that in 1610 his half-brother Paweł Katerle was interested in the explanation why the Catholic Eucharist should not be served under both kinds (*sub utraque specie*). Although he was a Lutheran, he was allowed into the Dominican library, where he consulted the decisions of the Council of Constance. This was possible because "he was on friendly terms with the Dominican librarian, so that *praetextu alio* [using another excuse] he entered the library, having received permission".[83] Vorbek-Lettow added that "all the Dominican books were chained to the desks".[84]

In the second half of the sixteenth and the first half of the seventeenth century, the collections of Catholic churches ranged from a dozen to several dozen or so items, but the monastic libraries were larger. In March 1656, the library of the Discalced Carmelites numbered 774 volumes in Latin and Polish, which were plundered by Muscvovite soldiers. The robbers who tried to sell the loot were apprehended and the Muscovite *voivode* Mikhail Shakhovsky, who resided in Vilnius, ordered the books to be returned to their rightful owners.[85] The book inventory of the library of the Carmelites of the Ancient Observance's monastery of St. George from 1677, is less rich and resembles the Dominican inventory from the beginning of the century, although it comes from a later period not covered by this study. It contains some 70 items grouped not by subject, but by format: *in folio*, *in quarto*, *in octavo*, *in sedicesimo*.[86] The library contained bibles and their parts (gospel books), biblical commentaries, liturgical books, lives of saints, theological works, sermons, and meditations. Among them there are non-religious works such as Calepino's dictionary, Kromer's *Chronicle*, and Johannes Sturm's *Partitiones oratoriae*.

Vilnius' monastic libraries from the middle of the sixteenth century were usually housed in their own rooms; books were catalogued and numbered.

[83] M. VORBEK-LETTOW, *Skarbnica pamięci. Pamiętnik lekarza króla Władysława IV*, ed. E. GALOS and F. MINCER (Wrocław, 1968), p. 36.

[84] *Ibid.*, p. 36.

[85] E. MEILUS, "Życie codzienne w Wilnie w czasie okupacji moskiewskiej 1655-1661", in: *Litwa w epoce Wazów*, ed. W. KRIEGSEISEN and A. RACHUBA (Warsaw, 2006), p. 133.

[86] *Liber magistralis in quo fundationes, confirmationes, summae tam capitales, quam censuales, lapideae, domus, fundi, iurisdictio, incolae necnon inventaria munimentorum totiusque suppellectilis ecclesiae et conventus S. Georgii Vilnae cura et diligentia reverendi ac venerabili patris Francisci Gorzynski interea v. Prioris per r.p. Anselmum Smieszkowic sanctae theologiae baccalaureati, concionatori ordinis conscripta, ordinata et confecta anno Domini 1677*, MS MAB F43-21018 (VKF1637).

Monasteries had their own librarians, whose task was to follow procedures and, first and foremost, to keep an eye on the whole collection.[87]

The libraries of the Lutheran church (of the Augsburg confession) and the Calvinist church (Evangelical Reformed) were particularly extensive. In the first half of the seventeenth century, the Lutheran library became of such a large size that it not only had its own librarian, but in 1644 it was decided to sell off doublets. The Lithuanian superintendent and outstanding author of postils Samuel Dambrowski, who died in 1625, as well as the preacher of the church, father Jędrzej Schönflissius, who died during the plague of 1653, bequeathed their book collections to this institution.[88]

Books and the library were also at the heart of the interests of the Calvinists, who attached great importance to a solid education and to educational reading. Despite the fact that it refers to the church in Smarhon' (Smorgonie), the will of Krzysztof Deszpot Zenowicz validated in the Vilnius municipal court in 1614, reflects the Protestant love of knowledge and wisdom contained in the books:

> The collection of books that, with God's help, I have gathered over the course of my life, I leave to you, my son Mikołaj, and to your descendants. And I ask you not to tear it apart, but to expand it, God willing, and to keep it always in one place in Smarhon' (without giving it away or lending it), near the brick church (for which I built the library in the tower), because there are more of them *in theologia*. And when, with God's help, you reach a more mature age, I ask and admonish you, my dear son, to sharpen and practise your conscience and your reason in studious reading for the sake of the true evangelical religion, which you should support, refining your soul *in spiritu et veritate* and following good examples, with the help of our father's God, Jehovah, and to hand it down to your sons by the working of the Holy Spirit. And so that you are able to serve both your mother the Commonwealth and your neighbour *in spiritu et veritate*, as I have said before.[89]

Zenowicz's attitude follows from his humanistic belief in the wisdom derived from contact with books. Collecting them was to serve the glory of God, as

[87] PIDŁYPCZAK-MAJEROWICZ, *Biblioteki i bibliotekarstwo*, pp. 56-71.

[88] A.F. ADAMOWICZ, *Kościół augsburski w Wilnie*, pp. 46 and 56.

[89] "Testament Krzysztofa Despota Zenowicza, wojewody brzeskiego, Głębokie, 1611 rok", ed. in: U. AUGUSTYNIAK, *Testamenty ewangelików reformowanych w Wielkim Księstwie Litewskim*, (Warsaw, 1992), p. 111.

well as the benefit of the Church, the Commonwealth and one's own neighbours.[90]

The Vilnius Calvinist church, where the library was established, was the centre of the religious and cultural life of the Lithuanian evangelicals: a humanist school was in operation there, and many donations and bequests allowed it to prosper. The library was probably established in 1557 and was destroyed in the fire of 1610. One of the few books saved was a Bible printed in 1480. The collection was reestablished thanks to successive donations and bequests in wills. In 1616 the church received the books of father Salinariusz; in 1623 it was expanded with the collection of superintendent Jakub Kostecki, purchased by Krzysztof II Radziwiłł for 350 *złoty*; and in 1634 it was further enlarged thanks to the bequests of Wacław Pakosz and Andrzej Welzjusz.[91] In 1634, the synod ordered a catalogue to be compiled:

> The synod appoints certain persons who work with Father Superintendent, that is father Tomaszewski and father Jurski, to arrange and catalogue the library at the Vilnius [Evangelical] church. Following the synod, they shall begin their work and prepare three registers of the books, one for the archive, another one for Father Superintendent, and the third one for the Polish minister in Vilnius. This system is to be introduced in all churches And during the visits, the superintendents of these books are to act according to the register, so that the library does not deteriorate.

In 1641, the book collection together with the archive was transported to Alanta, where it was catalogued again.[92] Since the church in Vilnius and the church

[90] The main protector of Calvinism in Lithuania in the first half of the seventeenth century, Krzysztof II Radziwiłł, assigned a similar function to his library. U. AUGUSTYNIAK, *Dwór i klientela Krzysztofa Radziwiłła (1585-1640): Mechanizmy patronatu* (Warsaw, 2001), p. 340.

[91] *Akta synodów prowincjonalnych Jednoty Litewskiej 1611-1625*, p. 36; GIZBERT-STUDNICKI, "Biblioteka (I)", pp. 206-207.

[92] "We wish to exercise the canon of the annual synod in order to revise and catalogue the library in Alanta. To which end *reverendum dominum Joannem Hulesium ecclesiae Kieydanenesis pastorem* together with father Marcin Bitner, we decide that, being informed by the senior of Vilnius, they shall go there, make an inventory of the collection in accordance with the register that is kept *in archivo*, and then bring it to Kėdainiai. For which purpose the Vilnius senior undertakes to provide horses and charts. As pertains to the registers of the books in the future, one shall be in the hands of the Vilnius senior, another one in the Vilnius church, yet another one will go to the Samogitian senior, and the last one shall be in the hands of the person who will manage the library" (canon 4 of the synod from 1642, MS MAB F40-1136 (*Akta synodów litewskich prowincjonalnych 1638-1675*), p. 48).

schools did not regain their former significance, it was decided to transfer the library to the *gymnasium* in Kėdainiai.

The Library of the Academy of Vilnius

The Jesuits had libraries in each of their institutions in the city, as required by the regulations contained in the *Ratio studiorum*.[93] Among these libraries, the most important one belonged to the college which later became Vilnius University. It was created in 1570 thanks to the testamentary donations of canon Jan Makowiecki and a nobleman, Jan Oborski, and also thanks to the transfer "*ad contubernium Societatis Iesu*" of the collection of the deceased bishop Jerzy Albinus, provided that the Jesuits prepare a proper catalogue.[94] Soon afterwards two other clergymen made significant additions to the library. Bishop Walerian Protasewicz gave it books specially purchased for this purpose from an old library, while Stanisław Warszewicki brought part of his book collection from Poznań.[95] At that time it must have been already the largest library in the city, but soon afterwards it was to grow even further. After the death of Sigismund II Augustus in 1572, according to his wishes included in his will, his sister Anna Jagiellon handed over a large part of his book collection to the Jesuits.

Thanks to these and later donations that enriched the library throughout the first half of the seventeenth century, as well as through regular purchases,[96] it grew to become one of the largest book collections in the Polish-Lithuanian Commonwealth. It was supplied with books bequeathed, for instance, by bishops Protasewicz, Bendykt Woyna (250 volumes) and Eustachy Wołłowicz, by members of the Vilnius chapter, and by former graduates. Several people also

[93] L. PIECHNIK, "O bibliotekach i najważniejszych podręcznikach u początku działalności Towarzystwa Jezusowego", in: *Librorum amatori: Księga pamiątkowa ofiarowana ks. Czesławowi Michalunio SJ na 50-lecie ofiarnej pracy w Bibliotece Filozoficznej Towarzystwa Jezusowego w Krakowie*, ed. A.P. BIEŚ (Cracow, 2004), p. 106.

[94] *Tractatus et conclusio occasione librorum post mortem olim reverendi domini Georgii Albini iuris utriusque doctoris Dei gratia episcopi Metonensis suffraganei et cantoris Vilnensis intestati decessi*, MS MAB F43-212 (VKF446: *Akta kapituły wileńskiej 1561-1570*), ff. 251v-252r. See L. VLADIMIROVAS, "Georgijaus Albiniajaus knygų kolekcijos likimo klausimu", in: *Apie knygas ir bibliotekas: Straipsnių rinkinys*, ed. A. GLOSIENĖ and G. RAGUOTIENĖ (Vilnius, 2002), p. 115.

[95] PIECHNIK, *Rozkwit Akademii Wileńskiej*, pp. 203-205.

[96] GRZEBIEŃ, *Organizacja bibliotek jezuickich*, 1, p. 270-277.

donated significant sums of money for the maintenance and development of the library, including the Jesuit provincial Mikołaj Łęczycki and King Władysław IV Vasa, who in 1636 gave it 3,000 *złoty*.[97]

Only members of the order had access to the library of the Academy, so it was located in the cloistered part of the building, on the first floor above the refectory.[98] This had fatal consequences during the fire of Vilnius that broke out on 1 July 1610 and became a disaster not only for the city, but also for the university library:

> Because of this fire, not only the whole city (of which only a fifth remained), not only seven magnificent places of worship and monasteries, as well as Catholic hospitals, including three or four Ruthenian ones, and the royal castle itself, but also our novitiate and college with schools were completely burnt down and destroyed. [...] In the college, although some books survived, having been thrown into the vaulted rooms and cellars, many others, particularly some very fine ones, which could not be saved so quickly from the library located on the top floor, were lost in the fire.[99]

The oldest inventories of the book collection of the Vilnius Academy have not been preserved; the only known list dates from 1773.[100] However, the organisation of the library certainly resembled a typical collection of Jesuit colleges. The books were stored in wardrobes and divided according to subject. Individual sections contained holy books (bibles), writings of the Fathers and doctors of the Church, theological works, decisions of the Church councils, synods, etc., canon and secular law, homiletics, historical works, works on

[97] *Ibid.*, p. 206-208.

[98] J. PASZENDA, "Pomieszczenia biblioteczne u jezuitów polskich", in *Librorum amatori*, p. 111; L. GRZEBIEŃ, "Organizacja bibliotek jezuickich w Polsce od XVI do XVIII wieku", part 2, *Archiwa, Biblioteki i Muzea Kościelne* 31 (1975), pp. 225- 226, 247-248.

[99] "*Hoc incendio non solum tota fere ciuitas (vix enim quinta illius pars remansit), non solum templa praecipua ac monasteria atque hospitalia catholica septem, Ruthenica tria vel quatuor, arx ipsa regia, sed etiam nouitiatus noster et collegium cum scholis plane exusta et vastata sunt.* [...] *In collegio vero licet aliqua in fornices et subterranea cellaria iniecta seruata sunt, plurima nihilominus et maxime libri praecipui, qui tam cito ex biblioteca, quae in suprema contignatione erat, erupi non poterant, incendio perierunt*". *Historia seu succincta narratio de origine ac fundatione Collegii Vilnensis Societatis Iesu ab anno 1569 usque ad annum 1611 in Julio*", MS ARSI Lit. 38F, f. 12v.

[100] KOCHANOWICZ, "Inwentarze bibliotek jezuickich 1570-1820: Próba rekonstrukcji", in: *Librorum amatori*, pp. 177-178.

catechetics, liturgical regulations, devotional and meditation books, medicine and rhetoric, grammar and books in foreign non-classical languages.[101]

Before 1610, the academic library must have contained several thousand volumes, probably not less than four or five thousand.[102] After the fire, it was rebuilt quickly and efficiently. Shortly before the Muscovite invasion, it was to be enriched by a collection of 3,000 books that belonged to Kazimierz Lew Sapieha, the great benefactor of the Academy. Luckily, the donation was transferred after the mid-seventeenth-century wars and did not become part of the university library until 1666 under the name *Bibliotheca Sapiehana*. Part of this splendid collection survived and today it is held in Vilnius University Library.[103]

In the early summer of 1655, the university library was packed in boxes and sent to Königsberg, because information had been received about approaching Muscovite troops. Despite losses, a large part of the library probably returned to Vilnius in 1661.[104]

[101] GRZEBIEŃ, "Biblioteki jezuickie w Krakowie", in: *Librorum amatori*, pp. 33-34, 45, 49-50; ID., *Organizacja bibliotek jezuickich*, part 2, pp. 270-277.

[102] For comparison, the library of the Jesuit college in Braniewo, transferred to Uppsala in 1626 by the troops of Gustavus Adolphus, possessed about 2,500 manuscripts and printed books. Four years earlier, in 1622, the Swedes had treated a collection belonging to Jesuits from Riga in a similar way. The catalogue of these books is preserved in Uppsala, compiled shortly after they were brought there by Johannes Bothdivius; it includes about 900 items. See MS CR U 271; *The catalogue of the book collection of the Jesuit College in Braniewo*, 1-3. The book collection of the novitiate house at St. Stephen's church in Cracow consisted of about 1,000 books, and in 1621, in the Professors' House at St. Barbara's church in the same city there were over 5,000 works (MS BJ 177; MS BJ 2626). See GRZEBIEŃ, "Biblioteki", p. 33; KOCHANOWICZ, "Inwentarze", pp. 168-169.

[103] The history and richness of the Sapieha library have recently been remembered in a masterly and beautifully published catalogue; cf. A. BRAZIŪNIENĖ, "*Bibliotheca Sapiehana* – europinės LDK kultūros veidrodis: Bibliotheca Sapiehana as a mirror of European culture of Grand Duchy of Lithuania", in: *Bibliotheca Sapiehana Vilniaus universiteto bibliotekos rinkinys: Katalogas*, ed. A. RINKŪNAITĖ (Vilnius, 2010), pp. VII-XLIII; D. PIRAMIDOWICZ, *Feniks świata litewskiego: Fundacje i inicjatywy artystyczne Kazimierza Leona Sapiehy (1609-1656)* (Warsaw, 2012), pp. 236-242.

[104] A. KAWECKA-GRYCZOWA, *Biblioteka ostatniego Jagiellona: Pomnik kultury renesansowej* (Wrocław, 1988), pp. 36, 82.

Private book collections

Libraries of the Clergy

The oldest private book collections in Vilnius in the fourteenth and fifteenth centuries belonged to the clergy of the Orthodox and Catholic churches. There is some evidence confirming the assumption that representatives of the Orthodox clergy collected religious and liturgical books.[105] They include, for example, the testament from 1522 of Matvei, *ierei* (a lower clergyman) of St. George's church in Vilnius, which lists eleven books that belonged to the priest.[106]

The situation has dramatically changed in the sixteenth century, when printed books became more available in Vilnius.[107] This affected the number and size of the private libraries of clergymen of all denominations. Unfortunately, the sources rarely speak about their libraries. For example, the Calvinist clergy must have possessed collections of tens, if not hundreds of volumes, but the only traces of them are single volumes that have been identified, such as *Novi testamenti catholica expositio ecclesiastica* (Geneva, 1564), which in 1578 belonged to the superior of the Vilnius Protestant church, Stanisław Sudrowski.[108] There is relatively rich information about the collections of the Catholic clergy.

The most numerous and richest sources speak of the libraries that belonged to the members of the Vilnius chapter. This is not surprising, considering the canons were the elite of the secular clergy. Most of them were well educated people, and usually half of them had graduated from universities, mostly from Cracow University. For example, the list of the members of the chapter of 1502 includes fourteen people, six of whom had a master's degree and one even a doctorate.[109] A group of

[105] Catholic and Orthodox priests often owned liturgical books. Apart from that, all parish churches were equipped with the liturgical books that belonged to the church.

[106] Topolska, *Czytelnik i książka w Wielkim Księstwie Litewskim*, p. 203.

[107] See Chapter 7.

[108] Laucevičius, *Knygų įrišimai*, p. 61, item 225.

[109] "*Albertus, episcopos Vilnensis; Erasmus Vitellinus, praepositus; Magister Jacobus de Kuczyno, decanus; Martinus, episcopos Medniczensis, archidiaconus; Magister Stanislaus, custos; Prelati et canonici: Martinus de Radom; Magister Georgius; Magister Andreas Szwÿrskÿ; Doctor Joannes Philipowicz; Magister Bernardus; Joannes de Dobrzÿnÿcze; Casparus de Varschowia; Nicolaus Zukowskÿ; Valentinus Kucharskÿ*". ms mab F43-210/01 (*Akta kapituły wileńskiej 1502-1533*), f. 2r. Its author, provost Erazm Ciołek (Vitellinus) also had a master's degree not mentioned in the list. Bishop Albertus, or Wojciech Tabor, also studied with his

such learned men had to use books not only because they were needed to celebrate Mass or canonical hours.

As was mentioned in the first chapter of this book, the oldest information of books that were in the possession of an individual, the first bishop of Vilnius, Andrzej, who bequeathed his books to the cathedral library, dates from 1398. According to the decree of 22 September 1486, mentioned above, the books of deceased members of the chapter were to be sent to that library. It may be assumed that the canons possessed mainly liturgical codices, that is missals, bibles, and the lives of the saints, and, from the end of the fifteenth century, also liturgical textbooks, such as the *Agenda* of 1499.

This did not change much in the sixteenth and seventeenth centuries. Few members of the chapter had large personal libraries, such as canon Mikołaj Decjusz and bishop Jerzy Albinus, whose book collections were handed over to the university library,[110] archdeacon Jan Makowiecki,[111] canons Stanisław of Niemenczyn (*c.* 1470), Adam Jakubowicz of Kotra (1516), Wawrzyniec Międzyleski (1529), Stanisław Rozbicki (1529), Józef Jasiński (1550; he possessed the *Chronicle of the Grand Duchy of Lithuania*, copied into the so-called *Kodeks olszewski*),[112] Maciej Stryjkowski (canon of Samogitia), Jan Grodzicki, Piotr Rojzjusz, and Jan Wiewiórka. The few wills mentioned mainly liturgical books. In 1625, canon Mikołaj Gałązka Kołodziński drew up the following legacy:

> To Wojciech Ugoski, my niece, I bequeath the breviary-diurnal bound in black leather, with red *marinis*, the lives of the saints, *praedicationes* Simonis Verpei and litanies *tomus*.[113]

A year earlier, in 1624, the Vilnius penitentiary, canon Jan Makowiecki, distributed his books in such a way that most of them were given to the Vilnius Franciscans:

> I also wish to include in the monastery of these fathers or their libraries my book collection, which is small but not worthy of contempt, a list of whose books has

brother at the University of Cracow, cf. W. URBAN and S. LŪŽYS, *Cracovia Lithuanorum saeculis XIV-XV: Lietuvių Krokuva XIV-XVI amžiais* (Vilnius, 1999), p. 46.

110 N. FEIGELMANAS, "Apie Vilniaus universiteto bibliotekos XV-XVII a. knygų proveniencijas ir jų mokslinę reikšmę", in: *Iš lietuvos bibliotekų istorijos*, ed. V. BULAVAS (Vilnius, 1985), p. 14.

111 MS MAB F43-26648.

112 OCHMAŃSKI, *Najdawniejsze księgozbiory na Litwie*, p. 76.

113 MS MAB F43-26613, f. 2r.

> been catalogued on a card and included in the Polish Bible. [...] Also the Roman missal from Antwerp with copperplate prints and silver clasps, as well as other necessary decorations.[114]

Three inventories of libraries that belonged to Vilnius canons at the turn of the sixteenth and seventeenth centuries have survived. They are catalogues of the book collections of Mikołaj Koryzna, Ambroży Bejnart, and Jan Ryszkowski. According to these catalogues, the canons' book collections each consisted of about 50 volumes and contained mainly theological and liturgical works, as well as some texts on other subjects, mainly in the humanities.

As was said before, the bishops of Vilnius had much more extensive libraries. The bishop and humanist Paweł Holszański's attachment to books is in evidence in a letter from 1542 addressed to his close collaborator, Archdeacon Józef Jasiński:

> You also wrote to me that you could not find in our treasury those books in which there is the *vita sancti Adalberti*, nor master Valentine, so I cannot contain my surprise as to where they have disappeared and I grieve over them.[115]

In the collection of the Jagiellonian Library in Cracow, one book, a Counter-Reformation work by Johann Eck, *Opera contra Ludderum* (Augsburg, 1530-1532), has survived with the *supralibros* of bishop Holszański on the binding. Bishop Protasewicz had a significant collection of books, which has already been mentioned. Edmundas Laucevičius identified several books that formed part of this library.[116]

Unfortunately, we do not know the inventories and provenance records of the books that belonged to other Catholic clergymen who worked in Vilnius in the sixteenth and in the first half of the seventeenth centuries, neither of the monastic nor of the secular clergy. Probably their book collections did not differ much from those of the Vilnius canons and contained from a few to a

[114] "*Eorundem patrum caenobio seu bibliothecae eorum incorporare volo (quod et favo) licet parvam non tamen contemnendum bibliothecam meam, quorum librorum indicem in charta ordine descriptam et in libro Bibliorum Polonicorum insertam ictam. [...] Missale quoque Romanum Antverpianum cum figuris aeneis cum clausulis et aliis requisitis argento ornatis. Idque ut iugis mei memoria sub sacro missae sacrificio esse non desinat perpetuo*" (MS MAB F43-26648, ff. 1v-2r).

[115] KURCZEWSKI, *Kościół zamkowy*, 2, p. 113-114.

[116] LAUCEVIČIUS, *Knygų įrišimai*, inter alia, p. 49, item 112; p. 65, item 247; pp. 70-71, items 291, 391, 392.

dozen or so items, mainly on religious and liturgical topics (missals, breviaries, bibles, theological works, and lives of saints). For example, when he was a student in the 1650s, Michał Woyniłłowicz, the future father superior of the Dominican convent and a valued preacher, had a precious fifteenth-century parchment Bible in French.[117]

Some priests owned professional literature other than that used for liturgy. There is no inventory of the books that belonged to St. John's parish priest and canon Pedro Ruiz de Moros, called Doctor Spaniard, but they must have included legal works on the basis of which he prepared his *Decisiones ... de rebus in sacro auditorio ... Lithuanico ...* Another canon (and a colleague of de Moros), Wojciech Grabowski, did not mention in his will from 1570 any books, but the quotation below contains hints about their contents:

> I have also learnt that it is rumoured that when I wrote about the future, I used necromancy. In this last will of mine, I declare that I have never had anything to do with this abominable practice because I have always assumed that a man who uses it is despised by God. And when I wrote *de rebus futuris* [about future things], I did it *iuxta praecepta astronomica ex constellationi motum caelestium atque cursum planetum* [according to the principles of astronomy from the motion of celestial constellations and the paths of the planets].

Father Grabowski learnt the principles of astrology during his studies at Cracow University (to which, by the way, he bequeathed part of his assets), but *praecepta astronomica* may also refer to books on this discipline.[118] Besides, he would not have been the first scholar to bring books and knowledge gained while a student in Cracow to Vilnius, since several decades earlier he was preceded, among others, by the doctor of Alexander I Jagiellon, Wojciech of Brudzewo (in Vilnius in 1495-1497) and by Bernardine monks such as Marian of Jeziorko, about whom it was written in the chronicles of the convent that "during the reign of Casimir IV in Poland, Marian, a Bernardine, who once

[117] A damaged provenance record says that "*Fr Michael Woyniłowicz studens*" offered it to his Vilnius convent on 18 October 1660. A later note confirms the presence of the codex in the Dominican library, first in Vilnius and then in Hrodna. See MS BK 2673, f. 1r.

[118] Father Grabowski began studying astrology and published several prognostics during his studies. The lack of data concerning his library is highlighted by the author of his biography, W. PAWLIKOWSKA-BUTTERWICK, "Kanonik Wojciech Grabowski z Sierpca – zapoznana postać szesnastowiecznego Krakowa i Wilna", *Lituano-Slavica Posnaniensia* 11 (2005), pp. 177-179, 231, 236; "Testament kanonika wileńskiego Wojciecha Grabowskiego z Sierpca", ed. W. PAWLIKOWSKA-BUTTERWICK, *Studia Pedagogiczno-Artystyczne* 4 (2004), pp. 116-131.

received a master's degree at Cracow University and later was the most humble, chaste, and vigilant guardian of the rule of St. Francis, died in Vilnius on 14 August 1492".[119] Unfortunately, although we have a relatively large amount of information about the work of the Vilnius Bernardines, we know nothing about their private book collections.

Libraries of People in Power

Private libraries were owned by the grand dukes and by members of their families who resided in Vilnius. There are references to the fact that Grand Duke Vytautas's wife, Princess Uliana Olshanska, collected liturgical and paraliturgical texts. The sons of Casimir IV Jagiellon, Alexander and Sigismund, acting as grand dukes of Lithuania, and Prince Casimir showed even greater interest in books. They acquired a good humanist background, including the ability to read in Latin, thanks to their training under the direction of, among others, Jan Długosz and Filippo Buonaccorsi (Callimachus).[120] The book collection left by Prince Casimir (who died in 1484) contained mainly religious works, including a collection of hymns and a personal prayer book.[121] There was a dispute over this inheritance between the Vilnius chapter and bishop Andrzej Szeliga, which was settled in 1486.

The library of Alexander I Jagiellon was part of his treasure, inventoried by chancellor Jan Łaski in June 1506 shortly before the king's death. Probably this is the oldest known 'catalogue' of library that can be associated with the Polish-Lithuanian rulers. Łaski recorded thirty-four books in the register of church items. Seven of them were exceptionally beautifully decorated and had

[119] "*Eodem Casimiro IV regnante in Polonia Marianus bernardinus, quondam magister in Academia Cracoviensi postea humillimus innocens ac Regularum S.Francisci vigilantissimus custos obiit Vilnae anno 1492 14 Augusti. Manuscripta Conventus Vilnensis*" (E. KRZEMYCKI, *Descriptio Poloniae*, written in Tuchów in 1723, MS BK 62, f. 33r). In fact, Marian of Jeziorko was only a bachelor and died in Vilnius in 1491.

[120] PIETKIEWICZ, *Wielkie Księstwo Litewskie*, p. 205 U. BORKOWSKA, "Edukacja Jagiellonow", *Roczniki Historyczne* 71 (2005), pp. 99-119; A. ADAMSKA, "The Jagiellons and the written word: Some preliminary remarks about royal literacy in the later Middle Ages", in: *Hofkultur der Jagiellonendynastie und verwandter Fürstenhäuser – The Culture of the Jagiellonian and Related Courts*, ed. U. BORKOWSKA and M. HÖRSCH (Ostfildern, 2010: *Studia Jagiellonica Lipsiensia* 6), pp. 159-160.

[121] U. BORKOWSKA, *Królewskie modlitewniki: Studium z kultury religijnej epoku Jagiellonów (XV i początku XVI wieku)* (Lublin, 1999), p. 59.

valuable bindings, but even those less lavishly decorated were valuable enough to be placed in the treasury:

> A prayer booklet bound in red velvet, illuminated with gold; then six books bound in silver; then ten books without silver; then a booklet written in Ruthenian without gold; then three large and three small codices; [...] then eight smaller codices; then four large codices.[122]

Among these books it was possible to identify only the illuminated prayer book (*oracionale*) mentioned at the beginning, produced in Cracow in 1491 by the professional copyist Jan Złotkowski.[123]

In the sixteenth century, probably all Jagiellonian dynasty members who resided in Vilnius for a long time had their book collections here, especially Bona Sforza[124] and her husband's natural son, bishop John of the Lithuanian Dukes. The content of notes about the libraries of Prince Casimir and King Aleksander and copies of books that belonged to other members of the dynasty may shed new light on the reading practices, the collecting, and the use of books among the third generation of the Jagiellons.[125]

The list of books included in the Lithuanian *Metrica* from 1510 and 1511, which contained seventy-one volumes in Ruthenian, Serbian, Polish, Latin, and Czech, is quite a mysterious matter. It was assumed that they belonged to Sigismund I the Old.[126] However, research conducted by Lithuanian scholars provides strong arguments that they were collected by Olbracht Gasztołd (Albertas Goštautas).[127] The list includes volumes with different purposes and themes.

[122] *Akta Aleksandra króla polskiego, wielkiego księcia litewskiego itd. (1501-1506)*, ed. F. Papée (Cracow, 1927), pp. 544-545; cf. Laucevičius, *Knygų įrišimai*, p. 111; M. Gębarowicz, "Na śladach polskich bibliotek królewski", *Roczniki Biblioteczne* 14 (1970), p. 1-2, 114.

[123] The manuscript has survived in the collections of the British Library. See Borkowska, *Królewskie modlitewniki*, pp. 89-90.

[124] In 1556 Bona took to Bari (Italy) *c.* 100 books. See U. Borkowska, *Dynastia Jagiellonów*, p. 387.

[125] Adamska, "The Jagiellons and the written word", pp. 158-159.

[126] Baliński, *Historia miasta Wilna*, 2, p. 86; J.I. Kraszewski, *Wilno od początków*, p. 78; J. Lelewel, *Bibliograficznych ksiąg dwoje*, 2 (Vilnius, 1826), p. 97; K. Hartleb, *Biblioteka Zygmunta Augusta* (Lviv, 1928), pp. 135-137 (the census printed there); Gębarowicz, "Na śladach polskich bibliotek królewski", pp. 116-121; Laucevičius, *Knygų įrišimai*, p. 111; Kawecka-Gryczowa, *Biblioteka ostatniego Jagiellona*, p. 29-30.

[127] K. Jablonskis, "1510 m. Albrechto Goštauto biblioteka", in: *Lietuvių kultūra ir jos veikėjai* (Vilnius, 1973), pp. 353-357; D. Narbutienė, "LDK latyniškoji knyga asmeninėse XVI-XVII a. bibliotekose", *Knygotyra* 37 (2001), p. 2; Ochmański, *Najdawniejsze księgozbiory na Litwie*, pp. 79-80; А. Рычков and Л. Каралюс (L. Karalius), "О принадлежности списков книг и

The majority of them were liturgical and religious works (the Bible and its parts, missals, prayer books, sermons, and exempla), a total of thirty-three items. Other books concerned canon and secular law (for instance the Code of Roman law and Łaski's *Statute* from 1506), lexicography (three books of maxims, and a Latin dictionary by Reuchlin), medicine, history (for instance a Ruthenian chronicle and Paul the Deacon's *History of the Lombards*). The inventory also mentions Regiomontanus's almanac[128] and the Polish translation of the *History of Alexander the Great* by Leonard of Bończa. In 1510 and 1511 the library was probably kept in Hieraniony (today Belarus),[129] the estate of Gasztołd. However, it is quite likely that at least part of this book collection was used by Gasztołd in Vilnius.[130]

The registers reveal also which books were of interest to the political elites of the Grand Duchy of Lithuania at the time, not only to the rulers, but also to others, especially those with higher cultural aspirations, such as Olbracht Gasztołd, Mikołaj Mikołajewicz Radziwiłł or Michał Gliński, who resided in Vilnius. Later, libraries of magnates were located in residences outside Vilnius. Perhaps such a library was acquired by bishop Protasewicz in order to become part of the newly established Jesuit college.

However, the largest collection of books belonged to King Sigismund II Augustus. The beginnings of the library date back to at least 1547,[131] when the first known purchases were recorded. On the order of the king they were made by Jan of Koźmin, and afterwards by Andrzej Trzecieski the Older and his son Andrzej Trzecieski the Younger, humanists and people perfectly acquainted with contemporary literature and the book market. But this was not the only source of books for the library. The king designated Vilnius lower castle as its accommodation, to which the volumes purchased were packed off, often by

других списков имущества 1510–1511 гг. будущему канцлеру Великого княжества Литовского и виленскому воеводе Ольбрахту (Альберту) Гаштольду", *Древняя Русь. Вопросы медиевистики* 1 (2022), pp. 66–88. Albertas Goštautas possessed manuscript canonical hours, calligraphed and decorated with miniatures by the painter Stanisław Samostrzelnik in 1528. See *Modlitewnik Olbrachta Gasztołda kanclerza wielkiego litewskiego 1528 r. Facsimile*, introduction W. Wydra (Poznań, 2015).

[128] Johannes Müller von Königsberg, called Regiomontanus (1436-1476), was an astronomer and mathematician. His work, mentioned in the register, is probably an incunable: *Calendarium*, printed in Venice by Erhard Ratdolt in 1485.

[129] Рычков and Каралюс, "О принадлежности списков книг", pp. 76-77.

[130] Adamska, "The Jagiellons and the written word", pp. 158-159.

[131] Hartleb, *Biblioteka Zygmunta Augusta*, p. 69; Kawecka-Gryczowa, *Biblioteka ostatniego Jagiellona*, p. 33.

way of Cracow, where they were usually bound. The king attached great importance to his collection, devoting considerable resources to enlarging it systematically. At the beginning of the 1550s, purchases reached over 300 volumes per year.[132] At the end of Sigismund's life, the library consisted of about 4,000 printed books and manuscripts;[133] it was among the largest book collections in Europe.

To take care of the library, the king created the position of librarian. The first one was Stanisław Koszutski, appointed in 1551. He immediately started to prepare a catalogue. The register of books on law from 1553 has survived, while the catalogue of grammar books has been lost. After Koszutski's death in 1559, he was succeeded by Łukasz Górnicki. The library was kept in Vilnius until 1565, when it was moved to the castle in Tykocin. The volumes belonging to the royal book collection were provided with valuable bindings with supralibros, some of which were made in Vilnius after the fashion of Cracow bindings.[134]

The library was the king's private property and served various functions. Certainly, it reflects the "insatiable hunger" for acquiring and possessing books characteristic of humanists.[135] It was a representative and valuable collection, and the way it was maintained was guided by the Renaissance conviction that the use of books is essential for one's actions to be effective. One of its main objectives was to provide people in the royal entourage with books necessary (or considered necessary) for administering the state, conduct religious services, and develop intellectual life. Among the people using it were chaplains, courtiers, dignitaries of the royal chancery. One of them was Andrzej Patrycy Nidecki, to whom Górnicki made available a rare edition of *De civitate Dei* by St. Augustine, which was necessary for preparing an edition of Cicero's *Excerpts*.[136] Presumably other members of the humanist elite of mid-sixteenth-century Vilnius, such as Rojzjusz or Rotundus, humanists who held the post of king's secretary, also had access to it.[137]

[132] HARTLEB, *Biblioteka Zygmunta Augusta*, p. 71.
[133] *Ibid.*, p. 111. KAWECKA-GRYCZOWA, *Biblioteka ostatniego Jagiellona*, p. 41-43.
[134] This will be discussed in Chapter 7.
[135] GRUCHAŁA, *Iucunda familia librorum*, pp. 89-90, 119-120.
[136] K. MORAWSKI, *Andrzej Petrycy Nidecki: Jego życie i dzieła* (Cracow, 1892), pp. 99-100.
[137] KAWECKA-GRYCZOWA, *Biblioteka ostatniego Jagiellona*, p. 57.

The library contained works in all fields of knowledge,[138] including a number of works imported at the king's special request, manuscripts and translations prepared especially for the library, such as Duke Albrecht of Prussia's *Kriegsordnung* (Polish *Księga o rycerskich rzeczach a sprawach – The Book on Knightly Things and Affairs*), translated and copied in the sophisticated hand of the secretary of the royal chancery Maciej Strubicz.

In his will, Sigismund II August bequeathed his entire book collection, whose estimated value was 10,000 *złoty*, to the Jesuit college in Vilnius; this bequest was basically honoured a few years after the death of the ruler.

In the middle of the seventeenth century another big library was donated to the Academy of Vilnius: the library of the Lithuanian vice-chancellor Kazimierz Lew Sapieha.[139] This splendid collection counted no less than 3,000 books, which Sapieha had collected during his studies abroad and after his return to Lithuania.[140] He kept his library in his residence in Ruzhany (Różana). An Italian architect, Giovanni Battista Gisleni, who in 1652 worked in Vilnius, designed a building for his library.[141] The two-storey pavilion had to house the library and a small study (*gabinetto*) on the ground floor, and a hall and a restroom on the first floor.[142] It is not clear if the building was actually completed before the Muscovite invasion or whether it was designed for the palace of Sapieha or the Academy of Vilnius.[143] Nevertheless, it is the first known project of a private library building in Vilnius or indeed in all of the Grand Duchy of Lithuania. If other magnates, such as the Radziwiłłs, possessed large book collections, they were rather kept in designated rooms. The smaller libraries of the merchants or the nobility did not need to have a special spaces to store them, although there was at least one exception.

[138] HARTLEB, *Biblioteka Zygmunta Augusta*, pp. 107-120; KAWECKA-GRYCZOWA, *Biblioteka ostatniego Jagiellona*, pp. 47-50.

[139] BRAZIŪNIENĖ, "*Bibliotheca Sapiehana* – europinės LDK kultūros veidrodis", pp. VII-XLIII.

[140] Sapieha belonged to the best educated Lithuanian magnates of the time. He studied in Vilnius and from 1621 to 1628 in Munich, Ingolstadt, Leuven, Brussels, Bologna, and Padua. He was a patron of arts, music, and literature and financed many Catholic churches. See PIRAMIDOWICZ, *Feniks świata litewskiego*, pp. 55-232.

[141] A version of the project of the library by Gisleni survived to our times. See M. KARPOWICZ, "Giovanni Battista Gisleni i Francesco de'Rossi", in: *Lietuvos dailė europiniame kontekste*, ed. E. ALEKSANDRAVIČIUS, M. KARPOWICZ, and R. JANONIENĖ (Vilnius, 1995), pp. 176-190.

[142] *Ibid.*, p. 176; PIRAMIDOWICZ, *Feniks świata litewskiego*, p. 192.

[143] PIRAMIDOWICZ, *Feniks świata litewskiego*, p. 193.

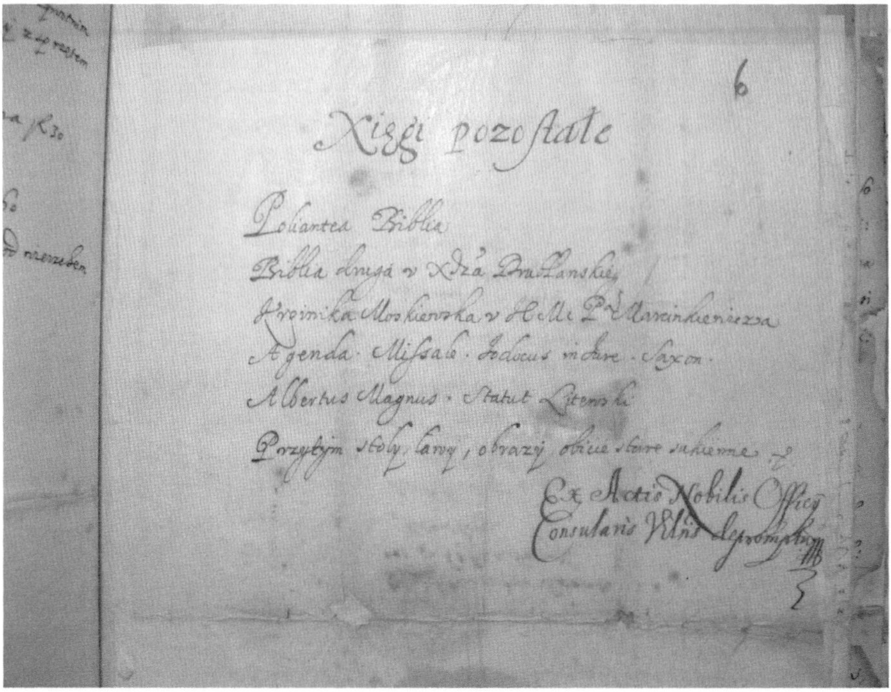
6

Xięgi pozostałe

Poliantea Biblia

Albertus Magnus · Statut Litewski

Ex Actis Nobilis Officii Consularis Viln. depromptum

Fig. 7 List of books of the mayor of Vilnius, Jakub Kiewlicz. A fragment of the copy of the post-mortem inventory from the city council court records, 20 June 1630. MS Vilnius, LVIA, F694, ap. 1, no. 3322, f. 6r. Photo J. Niedźwiedź.

Book Collections of Wealthy Town Dwellers and the Nobility

Although the Cyrillic printed books of Skaryna, Mstsislavets, and the Mamonicz family were essentially intended for the clergy, we also find them in the houses of the most wealthy inhabitants of the city. Data on this subject come from seventeenth-century wills and posthumous inventories copied into the registers of the municipal council. For example, in 1604 an Orthodox burgher from Vilnius, Ivan Rabka, mentioned "*Psałterz druku Skoryny*" ("a psalter printed by Skaryna") in his will.[144] In 1636, Semen Ivanovich Azarich bequeathed a copy of the gospels decorated with silver "and all the other books that belong to me" to the Orthodox church of the Holy Spirit.[145] As we learn from a later inventory of things left after Teodor Kochański's death (1668), he

[144] НІКОЛАЕЎ, *Гісторыя беларускай кнігі*, 1, p. 253.
[145] *AVAK*, vol. 9, p. 472.

left behind a "Ruthenian psalter" and two other books, "an old jagged Ruthenian statute" and "a Ruthenian *semi-ustav*, well worn".[146]

The number of books in rich urban houses in the seventeenth century (we do not have earlier data) usually did not exceed a few items. On 20 June 1630, an inventory of items left by the deceased mayor of Vilnius, Jakub Kiewlicz, was recorded in the city books. It contains, among other things, a list of eight books:

> Polyanthea Bible, the second Bible of Father Drublański, the *Kronika moskiewska* [Muscovy Chronicle] of Mr Marcinkiewicz, *Agenda*, *Missale*, Iodocus *In Iure Saxonico*, Albertus Magnus, and the Lithuanian statute. As well as tables, benches, paintings, and old cloth upholstery.[147]

Much later wills mention similarly equipped libraries. In 1673, a wealthy Orthodox town dweller left to the refectory of the Orthodox church of the Holy Spirit "my books, Polish and Ruthenian, that is: the Bible translated by the Jesuit theologian Jakub Wujek, Baronius, Stryjkowski and others, all Polish and Ruthenian works of any title".[148] In his turn, in 1689 Paweł Kossobucki mentions in his will the book *Żywoty ojców świętych i Biblia polska* (The Lives of the Holy Fathers and the Polish Bible) and unspecified books lent to Mr Józef Kossobudzki.[149] Individual books from the libraries of Vilnius townsmen, including mayor Jackowicz and notary Józef Piotrowicz, have survived.[150]

As in other cities of the Commonwealth, larger libraries were owned by members of the local elite,[151] for example doctors, clerks, pharmacists, and teachers.[152] Only a few more extensive inventories have survived and all of

[146] *Wilnianie*, p. 254.

[147] MS LVIA F694, ap. 1, no. 3322, f. 6r.

[148] *AVAK*, vol. 8, p. 523.

[149] *AVAK*, vol. 9, p. 517.

[150] TOPOLSKA, *Czytelnik i książka*, p. 219.

[151] The role of these professionals in the spread of the pragmatic literacy in late medieval towns in Poland is discussed in BARTOSZEWICZ, *Urban Literacy in Late Medieval Poland*, p. 57-59.

[152] M. KRAMPEROWA and W. MAISEL, "Księgozbiory mieszczan poznańskich z drugiej połowie XVI wieku", *Studia i Materiały do Dziejów Wielkopolski i Pomorza*, 11.1 (VI) (1960), p. 259; R. ŻURKOWA, "Księgozbiory mieszczan krakowskich w XVII wieku", *Rocznik Biblioteki PAN* 13 (1967), pp. 21-51; E. RÓŻYCKI, *Z dziejów książki we Lwowie w XVII wieku* (Katowice, 1991), pp. 45-46; E. Torój, *Inwentarze księgozbiorów mieszczan lubelskich z latach 1591-1678* (Lublin, 1997), pp. 12-15; A. Wnuk, *Mieszczanie lubelscy przełomu XVI/XVII wieku a książka*, in: *Lublin a książka: Materiały z konferencji naukowej Lublin – Pszczela Wola, 6-7 listopada 2002 roku*,

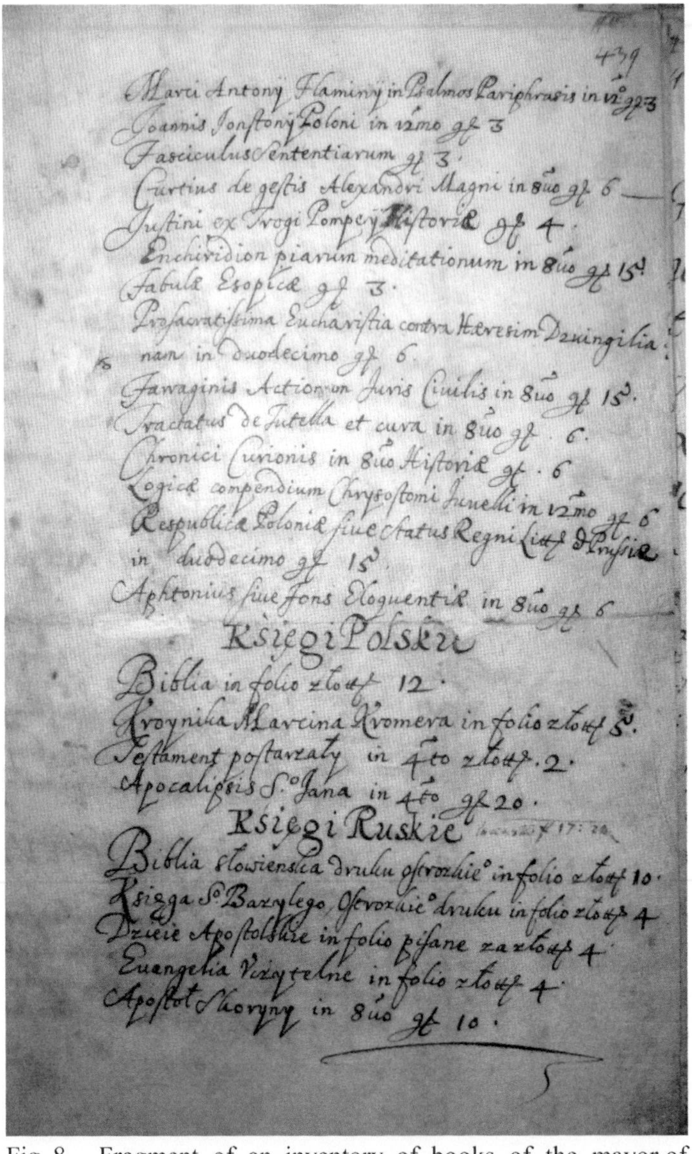

Marci Antonij Flaminij in Psalmos Pariphrasis in 12° gr 3
Joannis Jonstonij Poloni in 12mo gr 3
Fasciculus Sententiarum gr 3.
Curtius de gestis Alexandri Magni in 8uo gr 6
Justini ex Trogi Pompeij Historiae gr 4.
Enchiridion piarum meditationum in 8uo gr 15.
Fabulae Esopicae gr 3.
Prosacratissima Eucharistia contra Haeresim Dzuingilianam in duodecimo gr 6.
Fawaginis Actionum Juris Ciuilis in 8uo gr 15.
Tractatus de Tutella et cura in 8uo gr 6.
Chronici Curionis in 8uo Historiae gr 6
Logicae compendium Chrysostomi Junelli in 12mo gr 6
Respublicae Poloniae siue status Regni Litt. et Prussiae in duodecimo gr 15.
Aphtonius siue Fons Eloquentiae in 8uo gr 6
Księgi Polskie
Biblia in folio złotych 12.
Kroynika Marcina Kromera in folio złotych 5.
Testament postarzały in 4to złotych 2.
Apocalipsis S. Jana in 4to gr 20.
Księgi Ruskie
Biblia słowienska druku ostrozkie in folio złotych 10.
Księga S. Bazylego Ostrozkie druku in folio złotych 4
Dzieie Apostolskie in folio pisane za złotych 4
Euangelia Vczytelne in folio złotych 4.
Apostoł Skoryny in 8uo gr 10.

Fig. 8 Fragment of an inventory of books of the mayor of Vilnius, Stefan Lebiedzicz, 1649. MS Vilnius, LVIA, F23, ap. 1, nr 5096, f. 441r. Photo J. Niedźwiedź.

ed. A. Krawczyk and E. Józefowicz-Wisińska (Lublin, 2002), pp. 85-86; A.T. Staniszewski, *Historyje krakowskie: Funkcjonowanie narracyjnych tekstów popularnych we wczesnonowożytnej aglomeracji krakowskiej* (Cracow, 2020), pp. 201-233.

them confirm this. The inventory of objects left by the *Voigt* of Vilnius, Feliks Langurga, dated 15 May 1551, includes 43 bound volumes in a chest and additionally 24 other books, mostly unbound, in folio format.[153] Among the latter there were as many as eight items by Erasmus of Rotterdam, several works by Aristotle, one by St. Thomas Aquinas, the poetry of Seneca, the letters of St. Paul, dictionaries, two books on history, a poetic anthology, and a textbook on physiognomy. In the light of this inventory, Feliks Langurga appears as a humanist with versatile interests.

The most extensive Vilnius book collection from the first half of the seventeenth century known to us was described in the previously mentioned list of objects left by the Uniate (or Orthodox) mayor Stefan Lebiedzicz, inscribed into the municipal register on 27 September 1649. The catalogue includes 112 volumes, of which 94 are in Latin, twelve in Cyrillic, four in Polish, and two in Greek and Latin; this testifies to the exceptionally wide reading interests of its owner.[154] Among the books there are mainly printed books and three manuscripts. Each of them is priced, which is particularly valuable information for us, because we do not know the inventories of the Vilnius booksellers from the sixteenth and seventeenth centuries. The inventory was not well organised and divided books according to the language in which they were written, but there without distinction between Church Slavonic and Ruthenian ones. Reading it, one can nevertheless distinguish several sections.

Religious texts formed the most numerous group, which included 27 liturgical, theological, and prayer books (for instance *Apostol* (The Apostle) of Skaryna, printed in Vilnius in 1525; an anthology *Flores theologicarum quaestionum* by Josephus Angles; *Summa doctrinae Christianae* by Petrus Canisius; commentaries on the Psalms by Marcantonio Flaminio; Ruthenian catechisms and prayer books; and meditations). This section also contained Holy Scripture, which accounted for eight items (the Bible in Polish, and the Church Slavonic Ostroh Bible and individual books of the Bible, among them the Psalter, Acts of the Apostles, the Book of Revelation, and the gospels).

[153] *Materiały do historii drukarstwa i księgarstwa w Polsce*, ed. A. BENIS, in: *Archiwum do Dziejów Literatury i Oświaty w Polsce*, 7 (Cracow, 1892), p. 223.

[154] MS LVIA F23, ap. 1, no. 5096, ff. 441r-441v; *AVAK*, vol. 9, pp. 481-483; *Wilnianie*, pp. 185-186 and 189-192. Antoni Mironowicz states that Lebiedzicz was of the Orthodox faith and bequeathed as many as two (!) book collections of the Brotherhood of the Holy Spirit, but does not mention the source of this information (cf. A. MIRONOWICZ, *Bractwa cerkiewne w Rzeczypospolitej* (Białystok, 2003), p. 39). David A. Frick (FRICK, *Wilnianie*, p. 187) believes that Lebiedzicz was rather an Uniate.

Philosophy was represented by as many as thirteen works (for instance the *Bibliotheca philosophorum clarissimorum* by Jean Jacques Boissard; works of Cicero and Aristotle; an *Introductio ad dialecticam*; a book on dialectics by Rudolf Agricola; and a *Logicae compendium*).

The third group concerned the liberal arts, that is school literature: nineteen works of rhetoric (for instance works by Cicero; Aphthonius' *Progymnasmata*; Philippus Melanchthon's speeches; two issues of Álvares's rhetorical treatises; Lipsius' work in the field of 'sacred philology'; rhetorical commonplace books; *Orationes in variis actionibus dicendae*; and Ioannes Ravisius' *Epithetorum opus absolutissimum*), six collections of poetry (only classical poems, for instance *Poemata veterum poetarum*; Aesop's fables; the comedies of Terence; the *Odyssey* in Greek with a Latin translation), ten historical works (for instance Caesar, Curtius, Jonston, Kromer, Herburt and Antonio de Guevara's *Horologium principum*) and eight dictionaries (Latin-Hebrew, Greek-Latin, Polish-Latin, Calepino's dictionary, the *Lexicon historicum ac poeticum*, and Johann Philipp Pareus' *Calligraphia Romana, sive thesaurus linguae Latinae*).

Other subjects included in the collection were eleven works on law and political science (for instance *Iustiniani Institutiones*; *Introductiones in respublicas Ioannis Angelii*; Andreas von Gail, *Practicarum observationum libri duo*; Gregorius Richter, *Axiomata politica*; Erasmus of Rotterdam, *Institutio principis*), two works on medicine (Hieronimus Marcurialis, *Variarum lectionum medicina* and the *Pharmacographia naturalis*), four works on astrology and alchemy (a handbook on the use of astrolabes; a dream book by Artemidorus Daldianus; *Ephemerides et vaticinium*; and Bernardus Trevisanus' *De chymico miraculo*). The collection was completed by two best-selling Latin guides (M.K. Radziwiłł 'the Orphan', *Hierosolymitana peregrinatio* and Franciscus Schottus' topography of Italy). One work could not be identified, and finally there was one blank notebook.

Lebiedzicz's library could have been the pride and joy of any seventeenth-century European humanist. What distinguishes his collection from other contemporary book collections and determines its Eastern European specificity is the large number of works in Ruthenian and Church Slavonic.[155] A humanist book collection composed in such a way could have been put together only in the cities of the Grand Duchy of Lithuania or in the eastern territories of the Kingdom of Poland (for instance in Lviv), but in comparison with other Vilni-

[155] *Ibid.*, p. 186.

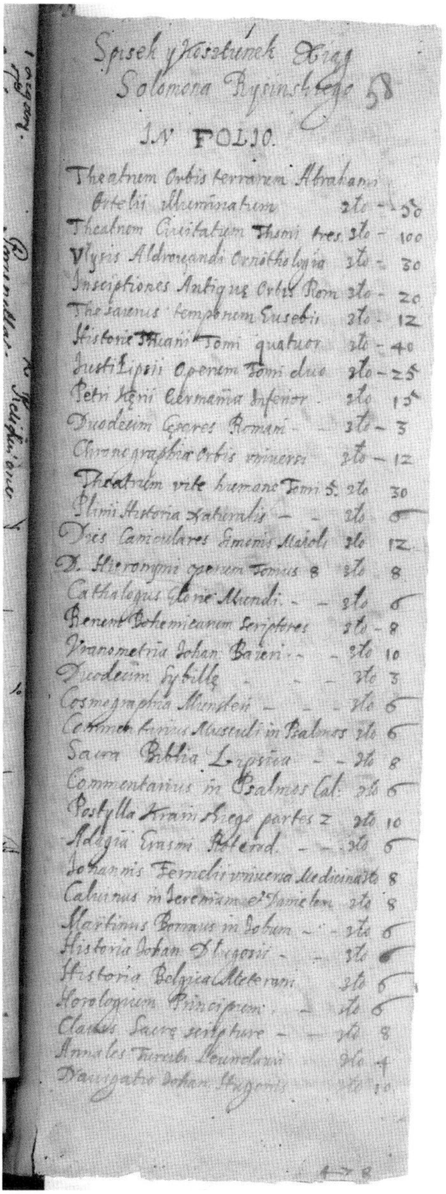
Spisek y Resstunek Xiąg
Solomona Rysinskiego 58
IN FOLIO.
Theatrum Orbis terrarum Abrahami Ortelii illuminatum — zło — 30
Theatrum Civitatum Tomi tres — zło — 100
Vlysis Aldrovandi Ornithologia — zło — 30
Inscriptiones Antiquae Orbis Rom — zło — 20
Thesaurus temporum Eusebii — zło — 12
Historiae Thuani Tomi quatuor — zło — 40
Justi Lipsii Operum Tomi duo — zło — 25
Petri Kerii Germania Inferior — zło — 15
Duodecim Caesares Romani — zło — 3
Chronographia Orbis universi — zło — 12
Theatrum vitae humanae Tomi 5 — zło — 30
Plinii Historia Naturalis — zło — 6
Dies Caniculares Simonis Maioli — zło — 12
D. Hieronymi operum Tomus 8 — zło — 8
Cathalogus Gloriae Mundi — zło — 6
Rerum Bohemicarum Scriptores — zło — 8
Uranometria Johan Bayeri — zło — 10
Duodecim Sybillae — zło — 3
Cosmographia Munsteri — zło — 6
Commentarius Musculi in Psalmos — zło — 6
Sacra Biblia Lipsiae — zło — 8
Commentarius in Psalmos Cal. — zło — 6
Postylla Krain Szęgo partes 2 — zło — 10
Adagia Erasmi Roterod. — zło — 6
Johannis Fernelii universa Medicina — zło — 8
Calvinus in Ieremiam et Danielem — zło — 8
Martinus Borrhaus in Jobum — zło — 6
Historia Johan Sleidani — zło — 6
Historia Belgica Meterani — zło — 6
Horologium Principum — zło — 6
Clavis Sacrae scripturae — zło — 8
Annales Turcici Leunclavii — zło — 4
Navigatio Johan Hugonis — zło — 10

Fig. 9 A fragment of an inventory of the library of Salomon Rysiński, 1625. MS Minsk, NGAB, Ф 694 оп. 1 ед. 450, f. 58r. Reproduced with the permission of NGAB.

us private collections this one is the largest one known and it is hard to say to what extent it can be treated as a typical example of a library of a rich Vilnius townsman.[156] From the same time we only have one more mention of a comparable library that belonged to the former doctor of Władysław IV Vasa, a Vilnius resident and nobleman, Maciej Vorbek-Lettow. In his diary, he mentions that during the evacuation from Vilnius on 8 August 1655 he lost his property "with a library worth several thousand due to the excellent authors [it contained]".[157] This book collection may have resembled the collections of two Lublin doctors from the seventeenth century, Adam Majer and Piotr Kliczewski. They consisted mainly of works in the field of medicine and related arts.[158]

In the first decades of the seventeenth century, probably the largest private book collection in Vilnius belonged to a courtier of the Radziwiłłs of Biržai and a Calvinist activist, Salomon Rysiński (*c.* 1565-1625), known mainly for his work on proverbs.[159] A catalogue from the 1620s compiled by the owner for Krzysztof II Radziwiłł, who purchased the whole collection, listed 952 works in 1,152 volumes,[160] but Rysiński mentioned numerous "books in unbound sexternions with psalms, texts by Cato, *paraeneses*, parables, funeral texts and diverse writings by me and others".[161] Its main part was kept in Słutcki House (Kamienica Słucka), owned by the Radziwiłłs, in German Street, while a smaller part was kept by Rysiński in his house at the ducal manor house near the Vilnius Gate.[162] Compared to other private libraries, Rysiński's book collection was completely unique in Vilnius at the time, due to its abundance and the diligence in his selection of works. The abundance of this library can be explained by the fact that it was collected by a scholar, lecturer, and religious activist.

[156] TOPOLSKA, *Czytelnik i książka*, p. 219.

[157] VORBEK-LETTOW, *Skarbnica pamięci*, pp. 241-242. This book collection may have resembled the collections of two Lublin doctors from the seventeenth century, Adam Majer and Piotr Kliczewski.

[158] WNUK, *Mieszczanie lubelscy*, p. 85.

[159] H. LULEWICZ, "Rysiński Salomon", *PSB*, vol. 33, p. 553-557. The main work of Rysiński was a dictionary of 1800 Polish proverbs: S. RYSIŃSKI, *Proverbiorvm Polonicorvm collectorum centuriae decem et octo* (Lubcha, 1618).

[160] MS NGAB Ф 694 оп. 1 ед. 450, ff. 58r-71r. This is meticulously discussed by I. LUKŠAITĖ, "Salomono Risinskio bibliotekos Vilniuje sąrašas", in: *Iš lietuvos bibliotekų istorijos*, pp. 17-45. AUGUSTYNIAK, *Dwór i klientela*, p. 341.

[161] MS NGAB Ф 694 оп. 1 ед. 450, f. 59r.

[162] I. LUKŠAITĖ, "Risinskis – lietuvos reformacijos veikėjas ir humanistinė kultūra", *Lietuvos Istorijos Metraštis* 1984, p. 7; EAD, "Biblioteka Salomona Rysińskiego", *Odrodzenie i Reformacja w Polsce* 30 (1985), p. 193.

As in other libraries, there are many religious and polemical works, as well as books on history, geography, astronomy, mathematics, linguistics, rhetoric, and poetry. Ancient literature was also well represented. It is impossible to discuss all of it here; as examples, we will mention those works that would be difficult to find in other Vilnius book collections, to wit: *Sielanki* (Idylls) by Szymonowic, the atlas of Ortelius, *Amorum emblemata* by Otto Vaenius, *Fraszki* (Trifles) by Kochanowski, *Dworzanin polski* (Polish Courtier) by Górnicki, *Poemata* by George Buchanan, religious works of Calvin and Melanchthon, *Meteororum liber by* Giovanni Pontano, the *Psalter* by Eoban Hessus, *Navigatio* [...] *Lusitanorum Indiam* by Johannes van Linschoten, and *Thesaurus numismatum Romanum* by Abraham Gorlaeus.

As in the case of Lebiedzicz's book collection, the books were priced. On the basis of the information provided at the end of the inventory it can be assumed that Rysiński wrote down the sums he actually paid for the books. The cost of the entire book collection reached the staggering sum of 2,136 *złoty* and 6 *grosz*. The most expensive items were the three volumes of Braun and Hogenberg's *Civitates orbium terrarum*, which cost 100 *złoty*, while most other items were worth from one to several *złoty*, such as the *Annales* by Orzechowski, bought for one *złoty*. Against the background of inventories known today from all over the Commonwealth, Rysiński's library appears to be exceptionally versatile, especially when it comes to *litteraria*.

There were also large libraries of Jewish scholars working in Vilnius, mainly in the field of Jewish law. They contained manuscripts and printed books of religious Hebrew texts and commentaries. We learn about the existence of these libraries mainly from reports of their destruction by the Muscovite army. Aaron Samuel ben Israel Kaidanover and Moses ben Naphtali Hirsch Rivkes[163] lost their very valuable collections of books in 1655.

The data on Vilnius private book collections are quite modest, but even a comparison of this evidence with findings from other cities of the Commonwealth allows us to make a few hypotheses. The libraries of Vilnius residents were probably smaller than those of the citizens of Lublin, Lviv, Poznań, or Cracow.[164] The largest collections of books in the Lithuanian capital, as in

[163] *Кайдановер Арон*, <http://be.wikipedia.org/wiki/Кайдановер> (accessed on 20.08. 2011); COHEN, *History of the Jews in Vilnius*, p. 42 (cf. the 'Epilogue' of this book (at pp. 611-612),, where a fragment of Rivkes's account about the occupation of Vilnius can be found).

[164] KRAMPEROWA, and MAISEL, "Księgozbiory mieszczan poznańskich z drugiej połowie XVI wieku", p. 259; ŻURKOWA, "Księgozbiory mieszczan krakowskich w XVII wieku", pp. 21-51; RÓŻYCKI, *Z dziejów książki we Lwowie*, pp. 45-46; TORÓJ, *Inwentarze księgozbiorów mieszczan*

other large cities, belonged to the elite, first of all to the clergy, then to doctors, lawyers, barbers, pharmacists, city officials, and teachers. The content of the collections were similar in all cities. Religious and professional books, usually medical or legal, dominated. Belles-lettres (rhetorical prose and poetry) was represented mainly by school classics and constituted only a small fraction of any book collection. Libraries that belonged to wealthy town dwellers consisted of several volumes, for the most part religious books, which matched the needs of the readers in this period better than belles-lettres. We do not know how popular romance and the street literature (the penny histories) diffused in chapbooks were in Vilnius, because their presence has left no clear traces.

What Was the Purpose of Possessing Books?

The main reason why the inhabitants of early modern Vilnius possessed books was their usefulness. Books were probably selected for similar purposes for large and small libraries alike, and that is why in the secular ecclesiastical and monastic catalogues as well as in private collections which contained only a few volumes we find basically the same texts. The most common are liturgical, theological, legal and historical books, such as the Bible, the Lithuanian statute or comments on the *Sachsenspiegel*. These three works could be found both in the collections of Lebiedzicz and Kiewlicz, and in the library of the chapter.

Throughout the period we are interested in, owning books also testified to any special devotion or more general religious needs of their owners. Neither King Alexander I Jagiellon, nor the treasurer Jan Abraham Ezofowicz, nor mayor Kiewlicz were clergymen, and yet they possessed bibles and missals. Although they could not celebrate Mass, they could ask a priest to do it for them. It is highly probable they could read the Latin Bible. From the *Chronicle* by Marcin Kromer (1555) we know that Sigismund I Old used to read the Bible and knew fragments of it by heart.[165] The presence of such books was the pres-

lubelskich, pp. 12-15; WNUK, *Mieszczanie lubelscy przełomu XVI/XVII wieku*, pp. 85-86; STANISZEWSKI, *Historyje krakowskie*, pp. 201-233.

[165] "He made a great progress in his literary studies [*in litteris*]. Without an interpreter or translator he understood people reading or speaking Latin and without any problems he spoke this language. He knew German well because of the vicinity [of German countries] and because many Germans live in our country. Then, he possessed so great expertise in Holy Scripture, that even in his old age he remembered its many fragments." M. KROMER, *Oratio in funere optimi et maxi-*

ence of the *sacrum*. Still, they could have used them in other ways as well. Prayer books and hymn books, which were mainly utility books, were a sign not only of piety (which is why the dead on tombstones often hold such a prayer book in their hands), but they also gave a signal that one was a member of the exclusive club of those who prayed using books.[166] Lavish design, for instance in the prayer book of St. Casimir or the *Kyiv Psalter*, as well as a costly binding, as in the case of the volumes that belonged to the bishops and canons of Vilnius, increased the value of these books when they became gifts for Catholic and Orthodox churches. Collecting liturgical books was an act of piety, which can be clearly seen in Semen Ivanovich Azarich's will:

> I bequeath to the Orthodox church of the Holy Spirit all the church fittings that I have purchased for the decoration of the Lord's church and that I have always had with me in a separate chest, that is a golden-silver cross encrusted with a gem stone; a copy of the gospels bound in velvet and silver; a goblet, some incense, a paten, a star, a spoon, a jug or pot with a cover, and two apples, all made of silver.[167]

Liturgical books are part of the ecclesiastical equipment (*apparatus ecclesiae*), precious both for their material and spiritual value. Collecting religious books was therefore an activity similar to collecting other holy objects, such as icons, paintings, or relics, and contributed to the 'spiritual capital' of their owners.

Amassing a book collection in one place, irrespective of the expense, raised the status of its owner. The library of Sigismund II Augustus provides a good example. From the fifteenth century onwards, collecting precious books was one of the requirements of an ambitious ruler.[168] In addition to being functional, it was similar to the collections of Jagiellonian tapestries or jewels,

mi principis Sigismundi, eius nominis primi, Polonorum, Lituanorum, Russorum, Prussorum et Masoviorum regis etc. 1548 Calendis Aprilis defuncti, in: ID., *De origine et rebus gestis Polonorum libri XXX* (Basel, 1555), p. 679.

[166] M. CLANCHY, *Looking Back from the Inventing of Printing: Mothers and the Teaching of Reading in the Middle Ages* (Turnhout, 2018), p. 87, 90-98.

[167] *AVAK*, 9, p. 472.

[168] Book-collecting became popular among the rulers in Renaissance Italy. The most famous library belonged to duke of Urbino, Federico da Montefeltro (1422-1482). This fashion was quickly adopted by the rulers in Central Europe. The king of Hungary and Bohemia Matthias Corvinus (1444-1490) was the owner of an impressive book collection. See J. BURCKHARDT, *The Civilization of the Renaissance in Italy*, trans. S. MIDDLEMORE (New York, 2010), p. 116; P. BURKE, *The Italian Renaissance: Culture and Society in Italy* (Princeton, 1987), p. 119; J.S. GRUCHAŁA, *Iucunda familia librorum*, pp. 109-110.

which the last of the Jagiellons loved so much.[169] Ecclesiastical institutions treated book collections, especially liturgical books, in much the same way. They considered them to be part of their wealth, which also consisted of robes and other items of ecclesiastical garb, and relics. The seventeenth-century inventories of the libraries of Stefan Lebiedzicz and Salomon Rysiński, as well as the information gleaned from the diary of Maciej Vorbek-Lettow, show that book collection had a high and very specific price.

However, the value of a book collection could be calculated not only in terms of the number of *kopas* of Lithuanian *grosz* it was worth, as its social value should also be taken into account. The books served not only their owner but also his friends and acquaintances. Although we do not know what the collection of Augustyn Rotundus' books may have looked like, because we only know one title from it, Ioannes Faber's *De missa evangeli* (printed at Cologne in 1557),[170] we can guess that the humanists who met in his house also had access to them. We do know the horizon of books read and used by Rotundus' friend Andrzej Wolan, which constituted the basis of his treatise *De libertate politica sive civili* (1572). In this text, Wolan refers to about fifty ancient and modern works in the field of political theory.[171] Some of them he cannot have known first-hand, but he could base his deliberations on excerpts, notes, and what he remembered from works he had read previously. However, he did have direct access to most of them, hence the conclusion that either he himself had a large library, which must have been much larger than fifty volumes, as it is difficult to imagine that it consisted only of works on political science, or that he used books borrowed from other book collections.

[169] Prince Albert of Prussia, a cousin of King Sigismund Augustus, exhibited a similar attitude towards collecting books. In his book collection, he joined together the Jagiellonian loves for books and jewellery. The most valuable part of his library he ordered to be bound in precious silver bindings. Most of the Silver Library is preserved in the Nicolaus Copernicus Library in Toruń (Poland). See *Srebrna biblioteka i inne cymelia królewieckie ze zbiorów Biblioteki Uniwersyteckiej w Toruniu* (Toruń, 2005), pp. 3-8.

[170] Laucevičius, *Knygų įrišimai*, p. 58, publishes a reproduction of the binding of the work, with the initials A:R, the Rola coat of arms, the year 1559 and the following title: "DE MISSA EVANGELI" (Fig. 202; currently in BUW, call number 28.20.2.1416).

[171] R. MAZURKIEWICZ, "Wstęp", in: A. WOLAN, *De libertate politica sive civili: O wolności rzeczypospolitej albo ślacheckiej*, ed. M. EDER and R. MAZURKIEWICZ (Warsaw, 2010), pp. 44-47. Roman Mazurkiewicz's research shows that to some extent we are able to answer the questions posed by Wioletta Pawlikowska-Butterwick, who asked what kind of literature was used by authors in the Grand Duchy of Lithuania in the sixteenth and seventeenth centuries. See PAWLIKOWSKA-BUTTERWICK, "Księgozbiory prywatne w Wielkim Księstwie Litewskim XVI stulecia", p. 7.

Later on, Andrzej Wolan engaged in religious polemics with two Catholics, father Piotr Skarga and canon Andrzej Jurgiewicz. When preparing their responses to his writings, his two opponents could use institutional libraries that belonged to the university and the chapter. Wolan, as a Calvinist, had no access to them, so he must have acquired his material from his own private collection or from those of his friends, as well as from the library of the Protestant church. The question of how private libraries functioned becomes even more interesting when we consider the richness of Rysiński's book collection. Did anyone borrow books from him? Or did he make his books available in the Slutsk tenement house? Did his library only serve academics and was it a gloomy "grave of books"?[172]

Records from Kaunas from the first half of the seventeenth century provide information on a dispute over the appropriation of a borrowed *Speculum Saxonum*,[173] and it can be assumed that people in Vilnius also exchanged books and sued each other for them. Unfortunately, we have little information on this subject. The list of books left by Jakub Kiewlicz mentions the Bible (probably in Polish translation) and the *Historia moskiewska* (Description of Muscovy) by Alessandro Guagnini, owned by father Drublański and Mr Marcinkiewicz We can speculate that Kiewlicz borrowed both books from his acquaintances. In this way, book collections contributed to the development of another network of relations between Vilnius residents, which is unfortunately difficult to study and describe. It was based on the transfer of books as items. The owner of even a few titles became more 'attractive' in the eyes of a neighbour or relative, because even a modest library increased the chance of entering into new relations of exchange. The status of people who not only had a book collection but also knew how to use texts in different ways was of course higher, especially if they could not only read but also write texts. And in the seventeenth century there were quite a few people with such competences in Vilnius.

The least measurable, though not the ultimate reason why the inhabitants of Vilnius collected books was the pleasure of dealing with them. The book was an inseparable component of the humanist model of life.[174] Therefore, by exploring the utilitarian dimension of possessing books and examining their social functions we must not lose sight of the personal and very intimate need

[172] Gruchała, *Iucunda familia librorum*, pp. 123-125.

[173] Z. Kiaupa, "Kauniečių knygų rinkiniai xvi-xviii a.", in: *Iš lietuvos bibliotekų istorijos*, pp. 5-12.

[174] Gruchała, *Iucunda familia librorum*, pp. 89-90.

to read and own them. Many South and West European humanists were bibliophiles, and their Vilnius colleagues had similar passions. Salomon Rysiński and Stefan Lebiedzicz selected items for their libraries with great care, like many other early modern collectors.[175] It was probably important for them for which purpose particular titles would be useful, but there is no doubt that their collections also grew out of their humanist love for books.

[175] K. POMIAN, *Collectors and Curiosities: Paris and Venice, 1500-1800*, trans. E. WILES-PORTIER (Cambridge, 1991), pp. 9-10; GRUCHAŁA, *Iucunda familia librorum*, pp. 89-92, 108-125; POMIAN, *Przeszłość jako przedmiot wiedzy*, pp. 133-134.

Chapter 3

Schools

Introduction

The ethos of the school and its tasks were described by the Calvinist delegates, gathering for a synod in Vilnius in 1653, as follows:

> The good education of young people is the foundation of the whole state and even the pagans themselves have recognised that well organised schools are a very special instrument. Reverend Superintendent, together with teachers and other servants of God and patrons, shall ensure that not only provincial, district, and local schools that are already well managed are provided with exemplary and well-educated teachers, but also that schools can be erected where they are not present but are needed. And they shall strongly encourage the patrons and auditors of each [Protestant] church with the word of God and righteousness itself.[1]

Not only the Protestants would sign their names to such a programme of educational development.

The significance of schools lies not only in the fact that they taught reading and writing. It was equally important that they played a formative role in the creating of certain reading and writing habits. Therefore the development of educational institutions in Vilnius not only contributed to the rising number of people who had higher literacy skills, but also to change in the ways they used texts. This change was mainly qualitative in nature. Thanks to education, texts

[1] Canon 49: *O szkołach* in genere, MS MAB F40-1136 (*Akta synodów litewskich prowincjonalnych 1638-1675*), p. 179.

and writing gained new functions and created new, previously unknown domains of culture in Vilnius.

At least from the first half of the sixteenth century, a greater number of new literary forms and genres were discussed in Vilnius schools, teachers began to reflect on the nature of texts (that is, on literary theory based on rhetoric and poetics), texts were introduced into the public sphere to a greater extent, and the practice of translation was being developed. Besides, schools, especially humanist ones, not only taught how to create texts, but also how to use them effectively, for instance in giving speeches, composing epitaphs, winning someone's favour with the help of panegyrics, or insulting opponents with the help of letters called *epistolae offensivae*. At the same time, they taught the inhabitants of Vilnius how to interpret texts on different levels.

At the time, the Academy of Vilnius propagated a new approach to text as a basic tool for action in. It was the most important educational institution in the city and perhaps in this part of Europe. Possibly this was why it overshadowed the other schools in Vilnius, especially those established earlier. This hegemony of the university manifests itself not only in the role it played in early modern Vilnius and in the whole Polish-Lithuanian Commonwealth, but also in the number of sources relating to the history of education in the city. There exists a large documentation concerning Jesuit schools, as well as many studies devoted to them, with father Ludwik Piechnik's four-volume work taking pride of place.[2] The Calvinist and Lutheran schools were less fortunate with regard to the scope of Piechnik's interests, although there are many references to them in his work as well. We have less information, however, about the school that was in operation at the synagogue. Nor do we have any trustworthy information on teaching at Orthodox church schools in Vilnius in the sixteenth century.

The earliest sources speak of the Catholic schools, the cathedral one, organised in 1387, and the municipal one, which opened at St. John's parish church in 1513.[3] Conventual schools were probably opened at the same time at by the Bernardines and Dominicans. From at least as early as the beginning of the fifteenth century onwards, a school must have existed for the training of clergy at the Orthodox cathedral of the Theotokos, and perhaps there were

[2] PIECHNIK, *Początki Akademii Wileńskiej*; L. PIECHNIK, *Rozkwit Akademii Wileńskiej w latach 1600-1655* (Rome, 1983).

[3] OCHMAŃSKI, "Najdawniejsze szkoły na Litwie od końca XIV do połowy XV wieku", pp. 122-125.

schools as well at the Orthodox churches of the Holy Spirit or the Holy Trinity by the first half of the sixteenth century. The first humanist (Lutheran) school, situated at the castle, was established by Abraomas Kulvietis (Abraham Kulwieć) in the early 1540s. It presaged the rapid development Vilnius education was to undergo in the second half of the century.

From the 1560s onwards, there was a Calvinist school and, probably at about the same time, a school was also established at the Lutheran church. One of the creators of the Vilnius Jesuit college, the Czech Baltazar Hostounský, described the situation of Vilnius' religious denominations and schools in a letter to general Francesco Borgia dated 12 September 1570 as follows:

> There are many nationalities in this city of Vilnius [...], namely Lithuanians, Ruthenians, Poles, Tartars, Germans, Jews, rather numerous Italians, and Armenians. The Germans have their own school with a Lutheran church, the Tartars also have their own place of worship and school where they teach Arabic. On feast days, sermons are given for the Italians in a school. The Ruthenians also have their own schools and churches. The Lithuanians and Poles have churches and schools. The Zwinglians [i.e. the Calvinists] also have their own church and school.[4]

The Jesuit collegium, whose aim was to prevent the spread of Protestantism and to strengthen Catholicism in Lithuania, was established in 1569, and ten years later it was transformed into a university. The Jesuits also established a papal seminary and contributed to the creation of a diocesan seminary. The Orthodox Brotherhood's school was established as a response to the expansion of the Protestants and Catholics. To the image of the first half of the seventeenth century presented by father Hostounský we should add a Jewish school, a Uniate one at the Holy Trinity church, and a school for women at the Benedictine nunnery.

The Cathedral School – A Bridge of the University of Cracow

Vilnius' cathedral school was for a long time the most important Latin school in Lithuania. Its foundation in 1387 is connected with the establishment of the Vilnius bishopric. It certainly ceased to work during the Teutonic invasions of 1390, 1392, and 1402, but it was rebuilt each time, as one year after

[4] MS ARSI Germ. 151, f. 286r, as cited in: PIECHNIK, *Początki Akademii Wileńskiej*, pp. 32.

the first invasion, in 1391, a legate of the Teutonic Knights noted that Franciscans taught there.[5] Until 1513, when the parish school was established, it was the only school available for the sons of the inhabitants of Vilnius.

Successive rulers took financial care of the cathedral school, although, as one may suppose, they had various motifs in mind. In a document issued in Trakai on 24 May 1409, Grand Duke Vytautas made it compulsory for "the bishop of the cathedral [...] to support and finance the cleric or master of the school from his own income".[6] King Casimir Jagiellon accepted the responsibility for supporting the rector and, in a charter of 23 April 1452, allowed him a salary of eight *kopas* (three scores) of *grosz* per year, financed from a tax paid by the Vilnius inns.[7] Two days later, on 25 April, he ordered the *horodniczy* (burgrave) of Vilnius castle to pay this sum. The document has survived in a Ruthenian version and in a contemporary translation into Polish with the fifteenth-century spelling:

> Casimir, by the Grace of God, King of Poland, Grand Duke of Lithuania, etc., orders the burgrave of Vilnius castle Ivashko and his successors to carry out the following: We have stipulated at St. Stanislaus's church [that is, the cathedral] eight *kopas* from the Vilnius inns annually to be given without any delay every year. Dated Vilnius, twenty fifth of April, fifteenth indiction.[8]

Most fifteenth- and sixteenth-century Vilnius bishops and canons were well educated; often they were university graduates (mainly from Cracow),[9] and it is probable that they paid attention to maintain a high level of education in the cathedral school of Vilnius.

As has already been mentioned, the cathedral school was at that time the most important Latin educational institution in Lithuania. Its programme and teaching methods probably did not differ from the standards of the time. It

[5] KURCZEWSKI, *Kościół zamkowy*, 1, p. 8.

[6] *Kodeks dyplomatyczny katedry i diecezji wileńskiej*, p. 76.

[7] *Ibid.*, p. 236. *Biskupstwo wileńskie od jego założenia aż do dni obecnych*, p. 159; J. FIJAŁEK, "Kościół rzymskokatolicki na Litwie", p. 189.

[8] *Kodeks dyplomatyczny katedry i diecezji wileńskiej*, p. 237.

[9] M. Antoniewicz, "Pochodzenie episkopatu litewskiego XV-XVI wieku w świetle katalogów biskupów wileńskich", *Studia Źródłoznawcze* 59 (2001), p. 56; W. PAWLIKOWSKA, "A 'foreign' elite? The territorial origins of the canons and prelates of the cathedral chapter of Vilna in the second half of the sixteenth century", *Slavonic and East European Review* 92.1 (2014), p. 80; EAD., "Znaczenie szlachectwa i wykształcenia przy obejmowaniu przez cudzoziemców wyższych godności kościelnych na Litwie w drugiej połowie XVI wieku", *Wschodni Rocznik Humanistyczny* 12 (2015), pp. 25-26.

must have been similar to the other cathedral schools in the Gniezno archdiocese.[10] The school must have had at least two levels, teaching both the programme of an elementary school[11] and that of the liberal arts. The registers of the chapter confirm that in 1557 there were three classes in the school.[12]

Just as in other urban schools in the late Middle Ages, the students of the elementary school must have been taught basic literacy skills. They also learned liturgical chant, as is confirmed by the chapter's registers.[13] They learned by heart Latin prayers (the *Pater noster*, *Credo*, *Ave Maria*) and the psalter, and many texts in verse, for instance the *Distichs of Cato* and mnemotechnic verses, and they possessed knowledge about some elements of the art of memory.[14]

The teaching of people from the higher classes was probably at the level of *trivium* with some elements of the programme of the *quadrivium*.[15] They studied Latin grammar (probably from the manuals of grammar of Donatus or Alexander of Villedieu), elements of rhetoric useful for teaching the writing of various texts (possibly including some *ars dictaminis*). Probably they also learned the art of writing letters (the *ars epistolandi*).

It was a grammar school which also prepared boys for service in the cathedral.[16] Its level must have been high, because it provided a basis for its alumni

[10] Krzysztof Stopka thoroughly examined the program of cathedral schools in the medieval Kingdom of Poland; see K. STOPKA, *Szkoły katedralne metropolii gnieźnieńskiej*, pp. 132-185. See also FIJAŁEK, *Kościół rzymskokatolicki na Litwie*, p. 190; A. MANGUEL, *A History of Reading* (London, 1997), pp. 76-77; K. STOPKA, "Zakres i program nauczania septem artes w szkołach katedralnych", in: Septem artes *w kształtowaniu kultury umysłowej w Polsce średniowiecznej: Wybrane zagadnienia*, ed. T. MICHAŁOWSKA (Wrocław, 2007), pp. 125-136.

[11] Krzysztof Stopka pointed out that cathedral schools in Poland never abandoned the teaching of basic literacy skills. See STOPKA, *Szkoły katedralne*, p. 136.

[12] OCHMAŃSKI, "Najdawniejsze szkoły na Litwie", p. 123.

[13] *Ibid.*

[14] In his valuable work Rafał Wójcik examines the heyday of the art of memory in Poland at the turn of the fifteenth and sixteenth century (cf. R. WÓJCIK, *Opusculum de arte memorativa Jana Szklarka: Bernardyński traktat mnemotechniczny z 1504 roku* (Poznań, 2007), pp. 9, 55). Studies on the *ars memorativa* must have been known among the canons of the Vilnius chapter. In the fifteenth-century Kingdom of Poland much mnemotechnic verse was written in Polish and Latin; see M. WŁODARSKI, "Wstęp", in: *Liryka polska XV wieku* (Wrocław, 1997), pp. XC-XCVI; Polish examples of such texts with commentaries can be found in *Liryka polska XV wieku*, pp. 121-144; WŁODARSKI, "Wstęp", pp. LXXXIV-LXXXVI; examples of texts in Polish translation with commentaries in: *Liryka polska XV wieku* pp. 167-174.

[15] STOPKA, *Szkoły katedralne*, p. 133.

[16] We do not know the exact curriculum of the school, but it must have been similar to other cathedral schools in the Jagiellonian monarchy. See STOPKA, *Szkoły katedralne*, pp. 154, 169.

to start studies at the University of Cracow. In the fifteenth century it became a kind of 'branch' of Cracow. It was usually run by graduates of the Academy, who prepared its future Lithuanian students. Among its alumni were later functionaries of the State and of the Church, the latter being involved in the administration of the Latin diocese of Vilnius. The education of future staff should therefore be considered the reason why King Casimir IV decided to co-finance the cathedral school.

The studies of Lithuanians at the University of Cracow[17] had already been given the support of Jogaila and Vytautas, as they pointed out in a letter to Pope Martin V in 1418, emphasising that the university "teaches newly baptised Lithuanians all knowledge".[18] Professors, especially those previously connected with the milieu of Queen Hedwig (Jadwiga), tried to support them, including the rector. Mikołaj Gorzkowski,[19] and professor Jan Isner. In his last will (1410) Isner donated among other things part of his property to fund the Dormitory of the Poor. This was supposed to ensure first of all lodgings for students from Lithuania enrolled in the faculties of theology and liberal arts. Isner also ordered that two talented students from Lithuania be paid eight marks each year from the dormitory funds.[20]

Among the Lithuanian students was Jan of Vilnius, who obtained the degree of *baccalaureus* in 1422.[21] Another Jan of Vilnius was matriculated in 1442 and earned the degree of bachelor four years later. He has been identified as Jan Łosowicz, later bishop of Lutsk and in the years 1468-1481 bishop of Vilnius.[22] Bernard of Vilnius received the baccalaureate degree in 1487 and returned to Lithuania, where he received the title of canon of Vilnius in 1493. In the fifteenth century there were many such Andrzejs, Jans, Mateuszes, Marcins, or Piotrs of Vilnius, students, bachelors and masters. The *album studiosorum* of Cracow University lists seventy students who signed themselves "of Vilnius", although many of them actually came from other places.[23] This might

[17] The University of Cracow was founded by King Casimir III the Great in 1364. The foundation was resumed in 1400 thanks to the bequest of Queen Hedwig (Jadwiga). See P.W. KNOLL, *A Pearl of Powerful Learning: The University of Cracow in the Fifteenth Century* (Leiden and Boston, 2016), pp. 11-41.

[18] URBAN and LŪŽYS, *Cracovia Lithuanorum saeculis XIV-XV*, p. 24.

[19] M. KOSMAN, "Polacy na Litwie (do połowy XVI w.)", in: ID., *Orzeł i Pogoń*, p. 13.

[20] URBAN and LŪŽYS, *Cracovia Lithuanorum saeculis XIV-XV*, p. 22.

[21] *Ibid.*, p. 25.

[22] M. KOSMAN, "Episkopat litewski XV-XVIII w.", in: ID., *Orzeł i Pogoń*, p. 228.

[23] *Metryka Uniwersytetu Krakowskiego z lat 1400-1508: Biblioteka Jagiellońska rkp. 258*, 2, *Indeksy*, ed. A. GĄSIOROWSKI, T. JUREK, and I. SKIERSKA (Cracow, 2004), pp. 544-545.

mean that for most of them the cathedral school in Vilnius was the first step on their long educational path. Occasionally there were also people who had acquired their basic education elsewhere, such as Grzegorz de Guraw (Grzegorz of Góra), from the Franciscan convent, whom Pope Martin V allowed in a document of 27 May 1426 to obtain the degree of bachelor and master of theology in the *studium generale* of the University of Cracow.[24] In fact, that year "brother Grzegorz, lector of the Vilnius convent of Friars Minor" matriculated at the university.[25] Some other students may have come from a parish school in Trakai or Senoji Trakai.[26]

In the second half of the fifteenth century ever more Lithuanians were gaining a university education in Cracow, thanks to which they made careers if not in academia or literature, then in the church and state administrations. The previously mentioned dormitory for the poor hosted the Samogitians Bartłomiej Tabor and his twin brother Wojciech, later bishop of Vilnius.[27] Adam of Vilnius also studied with his brother. Adam obtained the degree of bachelor in 1482 and a master's degree in 1487.[28] A year later, as an *extraneus magister*, he lectured in Cracow on Horace's poetry, but soon abandoned his position and returned to his hometown, where he found a job as a notary in Alexander I Jagiellon's chancery and obtained the dignity of canon of Vilnius.[29]

Although Adam lived in Vilnius permanently, after 1508 one of his books made its way back to Cracow. On the endpaper of the large lexicon of 1477, there is a Latin epigram and a handwritten provenance note in Ruthenian:

According to Jerzy Ochmański, from 1401 to 1550 at least 101 students "from Vilnius" studied at the University of Cracow. See OCHMAŃSKI, "Najstarsze szkoły na Litwie", p. 132. See also KNOLL, *A Pearl of Powerful Learning*, p. 198.

[24] *Kodeks dyplomatyczny katedry i diecezji wileńskiej*, pp. 122-123.

[25] *Metryka Uniwersytetu Krakowskiego*, vol. 1, p. 132 (item 26/181).

[26] In the fifteenth century Trakai (Polish: Troki), a town *c.* 30 km to the west of Vilnius, was one of main residences of grand dukes of Lithuania. Senoji Trakai (Stare Troki; Old Trakai) is a village near to Trakai. The parish schools at this location are among the oldest in the Grand Duchy of Lithuania. They were founded in Senoji Trakai in 1400 and in Trakai in 1409. The first students from Senoji Trakai and Trakai were matriculated at the University of Cracow in 1413 and 1419 respectively. See OCHMAŃSKI, "Najdawniejsze szkoły na Litwie", p. 117.

[27] In 1473, he slandered *magister* Abraham of Seliszewo; the contention was settled by the superior of the dormitory, Piotr of Zambrzec; see URBAN and LŪŽYS, *Cracovia Lithuanorum saeculis XIV-XV*, p. 46.

[28] *Ibid.*, pp. 60, 62.

[29] KOSMAN, "Polacy na Litwie", p. 32.

> The book of Adam Jakubowicz from Kotra in Lithuania, in the Hrodno (Grodno) Volost, a brother of Zbroshko; his maintenance from his childhood in a Vilnius school as well as his ten-year-long studies in Cracow were funded by the late Prince (*Knyaz*) Andrzej [Świrski], once a canon and custodian of the Vilnius church of St. Stanislaus.[30]

Above the note the Latin signature of the owner can be seen ("*Certe sum Ade Lithuani*" – "In sooth, I belong to Adam of Lithuania"), and on the strip that strengthens the binding the same is repeated, but in Cyrillic: "АДЕ ЛИБЕР", which allows the hypothesis that a longer narrative was added to the two shorter signatures later on. Adam of Kotra must have believed that, if he noted something about himself and his benefactor in such a useful book, his memory would survive. He was also proud of his multilingual and multiscriptual skills.[31] These few lines of text about his studies in Cracow and Vilnius and about canon Świrski[32] are the oldest known autobiographical note written by a resident of early modern Vilnius.[33]

Sending more talented students of the cathedral school to Cracow was a common practice until the Academy of Vilnius was established in the second half of the sixteenth century. In 1563, the chapter funded a scholarship amounting to seven thalers in silver for a young man, Peter (Petrus) of Kaunas, to study at the University of Cracow, at the faculty of liberal arts.[34] For this to be

[30] "Книга Адамова Іакоубовича съ Котьри съ Литвы зь волости городенскоє Згрошкова бр<а>та. Емоуж накладал на наоуку до Кракова болеи дєсять лѣтъ, изь дєтинства єстъ при щолє вилєнскои ласкавє ховалъ нєбошьчикъ князь ѡндрѣи, нєгьды каноникъ и коустошъ костола вилєнского святого Станислава". See G. Maggio (Iunianus Maius), *De priscorum verborum proprietate* (Trewir, per Bernardum de Colonia, 1477), BJ Incunab. 1824. See W. Wisłocki, *Incunabula typographica Bibliothecae Universitatis Jagellonicae Cracoviensis inde ab inventa arte imprimendi usque ad A. 1500* (Cracow, 1900), p. 308; Fijałek, "Kościół rzymskokatolicki na Litwie", p. 173. The book later had only one more private owner, professor of theology Mikołaj Mikosz from Cracow, who in 1528 bequeathed it in his will to the Collegium Maius library.

[31] J. Niedźwiedź, "Multiscripturality in the Grand Duchy of Lithuania: New research approaches", trans. D.A. Frick, *East European Politics and Societies and Cultures* 33 (2019), pp. 7-8.

[32] Prince Świrski, who died in 1508, appears on the list of members of the Vilnius chapter in 1502; see MS MAB F43-210/01 (*Akta kapituły wileńskiej 1502-1533*), f. 2r; J. Tęgowski, *Rodowód kniaziów Świrskich do końca XVI wieku* (Wrocław, 2011), pp. 62-64, 179-180; G. Błaszczak, "Regestry dokumentów diecezji wileńskiej z lat 1507-1522 Jana Fijałka i Władysława Semkowicza", *Lituano-Slavica Posnaniensia* 9 (2003), p. 252.

[33] J. Niedźwiedź, "Autobiografia Biernata z Lublina (1516)", in: *Biernat z Lublina a literatura i kultura wczesnego renesansu w Polsce*, ed. J. Dąbkowska-Kujko and A. Nowicka-Struska (Lublin, 2015), pp. 19-21.

[34] MS MAB F43-212 (VKF446: *Akta kapituły wileńskiej 1561-1570*), f. 35, items 123, 1562

possible, the cathedral school had to teach, to a greater or lesser degree, the syllabus of the humanist gymnasia of the time.

This change of its programme probably took place in the time of bishop John of the Dukes of Lithuania. In 1522 he appointed the first *scholaster*, that is a representative of the chapter responsible for the school, as well as a cantor,[35] and two years later the chapter provided the school with additional income.[36] Bishop John, himself a humanist educated in Bologna who led the life of a Renaissance 'prince', certainly contributed to the reform of the school in the spirit of Renaissance humanism, although one of its main tasks remained to teach the service of the liturgy. The position of teacher was then occupied by Marcin Lwówek, who held a master's degree in the liberal arts.[37] In 1539, twenty-eight young men studied at the school, twelve of whom sang and sixteen served at Mass.[38]

Initially, the classes took place in the building where the schoolmaster's quarters were also located. It stood in the row of buildings that formed the lower castle and surrounded the cathedral from the south and west. In 1563 the rector, canon Wojciech of Stopnica, complained about the poor condition of the school and his quarters ("*schola et sua mansio seu habitatio* [...] *ruinatae*" ("the school and his apartment, or flat [...] are ruined"), and funds were allocated to repair the building.[39] The most difficult times of the cathedral school began after the Jesuits opened their free college in 1570. In that year the number of pupils of the cathedral school diminished to such a degree that there were not enough boys to chant during the services in the cathedral. The bishop and chapter had to negotiate with the Jesuits, 'hiring' their competitors' students to sing at the Masses. In 1572 there were no students at the school, and some researchers even supposed that the chapter ceased its very existence.[40] However, later documents confirm that the cathedral school was renovated. In

(Veneris tercia mensis Octobris).

[35] KURCZEWSKI, *Kościół zamkowy*, 1, p. 28; *Biskupstwo wileńskie*, p. 159; FIJAŁEK, "Kościół rzymskokatolicki na Litwie", p. 191.

[36] MS MAB F43-210/01 (*Akta kapituły wileńskiej 1502-1533*), f. 77v (item. 289).

[37] *Biskupstwo wileńskie*, p. 160.

[38] A. PACEVIČIUS, "Szkolnictwo", in: *Kultura Wielkiego Księstwa Litewskiego: Analizy i obrazy*, ed. V. ALIŠAUSKAS, L. JOVAIŠA, M. PAKNYS, R. PETRAUSKAS, and E. RAILA, trans. P. BUKOWIEC, B. KALĘBA, and B. PIASECKA (Cracow, 2006), p. 724.

[39] *Propositio magistri scholae occasione deffectum eiusdem scholae*, MS MAB F43-212 (VKF446: *Akta kapituły wileńskiej 1561-1570*), ff. 101v-102 (item 378), 5.10.1563; f. 103v (item 387), 22.10.1563.

[40] OCHMAŃSKI, "Najdawniejsze szkoły na Litwie", p. 123.

1632 a new building was erected, or at least the old one was essentially rebuilt, as is reported in the list of expenses relative to this investment.[41] At the same time, the salaries of its teachers were also taken care of.[42]

We do not have detailed information on the school's curriculum. In 1633, several canons shared the cost of wax tablets meant to teach writing and to take notes during lessons,[43] but the teachers certainly did not limit themselves to teaching basic literacy skills in Polish and Latin and to singing. Fiedorek Andrzejewicz enrolled at the cathedral school in 1639 as a fifteen-year-old after four years of education in two other schools in Vilnius.[44] After such a period he should have reached the level of the rhetorical class (in accordance with Jesuit standards). A certain unification in the field of education in the Vilnius Catholic schools of the seventeenth century is suggested by the fact that in all of them the school year started at the beginning of September.

St. John's School

St. John's School was the main (Catholic) parish school, even though it had been under Jesuit rule since 1570. As in other European towns, the process of transforming St. John's school into a municipal school began,[45] but it seems it was never concluded. It offered elementary education (writing, reading, Latin, and memorisation of various texts), sufficient for conducting transactions and commercial interests.

At the beginning of the sixteenth century, the cathedral school apparently seemed to be ever less suitable for fulfilling the educational aspirations of the

[41] *Przychód pieniędzy na budynek szkoły katedralnej w zamku wileńskim, 7 marca 1632*, MS MAB F43-19840. It mentions bricks, bricklayers, shingles, stoves, windows, a blacksmith, nails, and so on. The last entry comes from 16 October 1632. It is signed by Marcin Żagiel, the provost, and Paweł Lewicki, the Vilnius scholaster.

[42] *Pro bacalaureo scholae Cathedralis*, MS MAB F43-218 (VKF452; *Akta kapituły wileńskiej 1632-1643*), ff. 142r-142v (item 393), 5.01.1635.

[43] "*De scamnis pro schola cathedrali. Pro sua liberalitate asseres seu tabulas siccas promiserunt, specifice vero R. Dominus Decanus unum asserem, R. D. Nieborski duos, R. D. Szulc unum, R. D. Sczyt unum. Reliqua R. D. Cantor obtulit se propositurum*". MS MAB F43-218 (VKF452; *Akta kapituły wileńskiej 1632-1643*), ff. 18v-19 (item 56), 8.04.1633.

[44] *Kopia relacji miesckiej o wyznaniu niektórych burzycielów zboru wileńskiego 1639 d. 9 Octobra*, MS LNMB F93-1701.

[45] BOGUCKA and SAMSONOWICZ, *Dzieje miast i mieszczaństwa*, pp. 260-262; BARTOSZEWICZ, *Urban Literacy in Late Medieval Poland*, pp. 60-65.

Vilnius patricians, since in 1513 efforts were made to establish a school at St. John's church. Its creation must have been influenced by events and developments such as the elevation of Vilnius to the rank of official capital of the Grand Duchy of Lithuania during the reign of Alexander I Jagiellon, the economic development of the city, and the increase in the development of pragmatic literacy, together with the greater spiritual needs of the inhabitants, whose knowing how to reading enabled an increase in their religious activity, for instance in the brotherhoods that developed in the city at the time.[46] Literacy was necessary to run the businesses of the merchants and craftsmen. The guilds or master craftsmen did not provide teaching in reading and writing, so the parish school had to do so.[47] In addition, the school was intended to educate boys who could serve in the church and improve the quality of the liturgy.

For this reason the parish priest, Leonard Rodian, and the townspeople asked the chapter for permission to open a school, and despite initial resistance they were eventually granted permission on 13 December 1513. The school was supposed to educate six clerics (for singing in the choir) and sixteen pupils, and it was in the care of the magistrate and the fraternity of St. John the Baptist, which operated at the parish church.[48]

There must have been two levels of teaching in the school, the elementary one and the *trivium*, and it did not differ from hundreds of similar Latin schools in the towns of late medieval Europe.[49] The documents produced by the Jesuits, who took over the school in 1571, indirectly inform us about it. Judging from the programme of the Jesuit *infima*, that is the lowest form of the Jesuit college, we can draw some conclusions regarding the curriculum of the parish school. In the first years of the Vilnius college, its *infima* programme

[46] Michael T. Clanchy points out that the development of reading was connected with private prayer and that during the Enlightenment reading was a skill most frequently found among the inhabitants of rural Protestant countries. Prayer is therefore at the heart of modern literacy. See M.T. Clanchy, *From Memory to Written Record*, p. 14.

[47] The main goals of teaching in the workshops in Vilnius were *mores* and the craftsmanship. The statutes of the guilds in Vilnius do not tell much about the teaching of future masters. See B. Manyś, "The pupil in handicraft guilds: The education and development system of boys in craft guilds of Vilnius in early modern times, in light of guild bylaws", *Biuletyn Historii Wychowania* 40 (2019), pp. 7-22.

[48] Kurczewski, *Kościół zamkowy*, 1, p. 27; Fijałek, "Kościół rzymskokatolicki na Litwie", p. 190.

[49] On the programme of late medieval urban schools, see P.F. Grendler, *Schooling in Renaissance Italy*, pp. 111-117; Bartoszewicz, *Urban Literacy in Late Medieval Poland*, pp. 60-65.

was based on the forms of a typical late medieval urban grammar school.[50] It is highly probable that the programme of the *infima* and the elementary programme of St. John's school were similar in may respects. The boys probably studied the beginnings of the *Grammar* of Donatus, the *Distichs of Cato*, and *A Little Catechism* by Peter Canisius. They were also taught liturgical chant. Only in the 1580s did the Jesuits introduce the *infima* to modern manuals of grammar and replaced the *Distichs of Cato* with Cicero and other classics.[51] They probably did the same at St. John's school.

Vladas Drėma supposes that apart from Latin and singing, reading and writing in German may also have been taught there at the school's start.[52] The position of German was strong in Vilnius even in the 1570s.[53] The Jesuits provided classes of German on Mondays "to respond to the universal demands [of the parents]".[54] It is probable that German had previously been taught at St. John's school.[55] From the very beginning, St. John's school was supervised by the parish priest and the city council. On 17 March 1527 King Sigismund I the Old issued a privilege in which he confirmed the conditions of cooperation between the parish church and the city. Among other things, the privilege stated that the rector of the school would always be selected by the parish

[50] The Jesuit *infima* offered the following classes: "7 AM: The beginnings of the grammar of Donatus. Repetition and revisions of the learnt material. 9 AM: *A Little Catechism* by Canisius. 1 PM: Continuation of the grammar of Donatus. 2 PM: Inflection of nuns and verbs; 3 PM: Explanation of *Distichs of Cato*". I cite after PIECHNIK, *Początki Akademii Wileńskiej*, p. 82. The *longue durée* of the classics of grammar in Renaissance Europe is confirmed also in other places, e.g. in Italy. See GRENDLER, *Schooling in Renaissance Italy*, pp. 166-202.

[51] PIECHNIK, *Początki Akademii Wileńskiej*, p. 80. The Jesuits followed the changes in teaching grammar introduced in sixteenth-century Italy.

[52] I am quoting after V. DRĖMA, *Vilniaus Šv. Jono bažnyčia* (Vilnius, 1997), p. 12.

[53] On the use German in Vilnius, see Chapter 1.

[54] I cite after PIECHNIK, *Początki Akademii Wileńskiej*, p. 81.

[55] There were at least three reasons why German was taught in Vilnius schools. Firstly, from the fourteenth century Vilnius merchants had strong relationships with German-speaking areas and cities in Royal and Ducal Prussia and Livonia (Gdańsk, Riga, and Königsberg). Secondly, a German-speaking community existed in Vilnius until the Second World War. Thirdly, Vilnius was an attractive place of study for German-speaking students from Prussia, Livonia, and other regions. Similarly, Polish was important for the German-speaking inhabitants of Gdańsk, Königsberg, and Riga. In the Academic Gymnasium in Gdańsk, Polish was taught from 1589. By the end of the seventeenth century Stanisław Jan Malczowski, a priest and graduate from the Academy of Vilnius, was a teacher of Polish, interpreter, translator, and lexicographer in Riga. His clients were merchants of the city. See J. NIEDŹWIEDŹ, "Report of research in the Latvian Academic Library and the Latvian National Library in Riga, 2005", in: *Absent Culture: The Case of Polish Livonia*, ed. K. ZAJAS (Frankfurt am Main, 2013), pp. 377-389.

priest together with the city council. In case of disobedience, the priest could remove the rector from his office.[56] There are no mentions about the cost of teaching as the existing sources do not give any information about fees.[57]

After less than twenty years after its foundation it turned the new school completely satisfied the Vilnius Catholics' need for education. In 1533, Jan Wilamowski, the secretary of chancellor Olbracht Gasztołd, asked the Vilnius chapter for permission to establish a private school for the sons of noblemen, in which a master of liberal arts, Grzegorz of Ejszyszki, would be the teacher. The chapter refused, mainly because the two schools that already existed in Vilnius had difficulties maintaining an adequate number of pupils (which was something of an exaggeration, as in 1539 as many as twenty-eight pupils studied at the cathedral school). Additionally, there were fears that the Reformation might be spreading in an institution over which the clergy had no control.[58] The ban on opening a new school probably did not bring many new pupils to Catholic schools, all the more so because Lutheranism was indeed gaining ever more popularity among the town dwellers.

Despite troubles in finding a greater number of pupils, in the second half of the sixteenth century things improved for both the parish and cathedral schools. The Jesuits obtained St. John's church in 1571 and established their collegium there. In 1574, they reported to their superiors in Rome that in St. John's school, which was not part of the collegium, one bachelor taught more than a hundred boys.[59] To what extent the school was controlled by the parish, the city, or the Jesuits was still an open question.

[56] *Zbiór praw i przywilejów miastu stołecznemu Wielkiego Księstwa Litewskiego Wilnowi nadanych*, p. 42.

[57] In a document dated 11 March 1529 from the fifteenth book of the Lithuanian *Metrica*, there is a mention that Małgorzata Słowakowa paid for teaching her son by her first marriage, Jan Stanisławowicz Kowalowicz, 30 *grzywnas*, i.e. 24 *kopas* of Lithuanian *grosz*. Unfortunately, the document does not say anything about the period of teaching. The editor or the document, Artūras Dubonis, suggests that Jan Kowalowicz was taught in St. John's school, the cathedral school, or privately ("а того сына Яна давала на науку, и выдала на него трыдцать грывен своих властъных пенязеи"). See A. Dubonis, "Duomenys apie mokslo kainą Vilniuje (XVI a. pradžia), in: *Lietuvos miestų istorijos šaltiniai*, 3, pp. 255, 257. However, in the sixteenth century the phrase "давать на науку" meant not only "to send someone for learning", but "to send someone for apprenticeship" as well. This may mean that Jan Kowalowicz rather learned some craft than the liberal arts.

[58] Adamowicz, *Kościół augsburski w Wilnie*, p. 10; Kurczewski, *Kościół zamkowy*, 1, pp. 27-28. Drėma, *Vilniaus Šv. Jono bažnyčia*, p. 12.

[59] Piechnik, *Początki Akademii Wileńskiej*, p. 51.

Other Schools in Vilnius: Monastic and Conventual

Educational activities were pursued in all monasteries in Vilnius, where male and female novices were trained. The education of nuns will be discussed in the next chapter. Of the most important male monastic schools we should mention the Bernardine, Carmelite, and especially the Dominican one. Shortly after the convent was founded by Alexander I Jagiellon, in 1501 the Dominicans opened a theological department. However, the school at the church of the Holy Spirit was also open to boys of no faith.

Two seminaries operating in Vilnius had the character of humanist schools. They were the diocesan seminary (which educated six to eight clerics), established on 12 January 1582,[60] and the papal seminary (from a dozen to thirty alumni), established by Gregory XIII on 5 February 1583. The papal seminary, subordinate to the Jesuits, was intended for Ruthenians and Muscovites. From 1625 it prepared mostly priests who were to carry out missionary work in non-Catholic areas.[61] This is why so many foreigners studied at the alumnat on Bishop Street. They included Swedes, Finns, Danes, Englishmen, and Germans.[62] Jesuits also taught in the diocesan seminary, which caused conflicts with the chapter. Eventually, the Jesuits stopped managing it in 1652. In the 1590s, Nuncio Malaspina's envoy Alexander Comuleus required it to educate Lithuanian-speaking priests.[63] Both institutions should be credited with the publication of Peter Canisius' *Catechism* in Latvian in 1585, translated by Erdman Tolgsdorf, and the translation of Jakub Wujek's *Postilla* into Lithuanian by Mikalojus Daukša in 1599.

The Jesuit College and Academy of Vilnius

The Jesuit *collegium*[64] and the Academy of Vilnius which grew out of it,

[60] KURCZEWSKI, *Kościół zamkowy*, 1, p. 77; PIECHNIK, *Rozkwit Akademii Wileńskiej*, pp. 254-255.

[61] J. POPLATEK, "Powstanie Seminarium Papieskiego w Wilnie (1582-1585)", *Ateneum Wileńskie* 6.1-4 (1933-1934), pp. 47-71 and 429-455; ID., "Alumnat Papieski w Wilnie", in: *Z dziejów szkolnictwa jezuickiego w Polsce*, pp. 97-112; *Encyklopedia wiedzy o jezuitach*, pp. 741-742.

[62] J. POPLATEK, "Wykaz alumnów seminarium papieskiego w Wilnie 1582-1773", *Ateneum Wileńskie* 11 (1936), pp. 218-282.

[63] KURCZEWSKI, *Kościół zamkowy*, 1, pp. 87-88.

[64] It is worth remembering that a *collegium* meant a house of Jesuits, not a school. However,

Fig. 10 The Academy of Vilnius at the beginning of the seventeenth century. A fragment of a view of Vilnius by Tomasz Makowski from *c.* 1604 (cf. Fig. 1). The buildings of the Academy (with a tower) are marked as number 15, the big Gothic parish church of St. John is number 13. The buildings of the Academy were significantly extended after the fire in 1610.

vastly changed the image of the city, which gained a more Catholic character. However, the Jesuits paid attention not only to the "Vilnius urban metropolis" itself, but also to its function as capital city: they designated it as their headquarters in this part of Europe. Vilnius was to serve as a basis for ambitious missionary work, which was to consider the dominance of the Orthodox Church in Lithuania, the growing role of the Calvinists, the weakening position of Catholics, and the prospects for expansion in Muscovy and Livonia.[65] Francisco Sunyer, the superior of the Polish Jesuit vice-province, wrote: "And we cannot ignore the fact that a wide door opens here to Muscovy, and from there through Tartary we will be able to get to China. In addition, we should not forget about Sweden and Livonia".[66] Previously, capital of the Jesuits in the

the Jesuits established schools at almost all their *collegia* in Europe. In the secondary literature the terms *collegium* (college) and school are used interchangeably; see P.F. GRENDLER, *Jesuit Schools and Universities in Europe 1548-1773* (Leiden and Boston, 2019), p. 13.

[65] The mission of the Jesuit diplomat Antonio Possevino to Muscovy in 1581-1582 and the papal seminaries organised by him, e.g. in Vilnius in 1583, were intended mainly for Muscovites and Ruthenians (cf. *Encyclopedia wiedzy o jezuitach*, p. 742); they testify to these far-reaching plans of the Society of Jesus.

[66] *Informatio*, ARSI Pol. 75 f. 316 (as cited in PIECHNIK, *Początki Akademii Wileńskiej*, p. 90).

Polish-Lithuanian Commonwealth had been Cracow, but considering these plans, Vilnius was more convenient than the capital of Poland.

In making the decision to settle in Vilnius, the Jesuits operating in the territory of the Polish-Lithuanian Commonwealth were well aware of the role played by the city and, despite objections of the authorities in Rome, they strove hard to maintain a strong position in the capital of the Grand Duchy, as evidenced by the letter of Baltazar Hostounský quoted above. The arrival of Jesuits in the city, where many religious communities, each with its own schools, lived next to each other, became a necessity for Catholics. It also raised the status of the order, which had arrived in the Polish-Lithuanian Commonwealth only a few years earlier, in 1564. Father Sunyer, who was mentioned before, and his companions made serious efforts in Rome[67] and at the court of Sigismund Augustus. Initially, the religious authorities were not inclined to establish a new institution, due to the lack of an adequate number of Jesuits in the Polish vice-province. In the end, however, thanks to the financial and logistical support of bishop Protasewicz, their efforts were successful. The Jesuits arrived in Vilnius on 28 September 1569, before the official announcement of the foundation of their college, and in October of that year they set up two grammar classes in which sixty pupils learnt Latin and Greek.

In Vilnius, the Jesuits obtained support from two prominent personalities, bishop Walerian Protasewicz and the *Voigt*, Augustyn Rotundus.[68] The bishop offered them a significant estate, which consisted of several villages.[69] For the needs of the order, he also bought a tenement house between Bishop and Zamkowa (Pilies) Streets (Fig. 10). The Austrian provincial of the order, Laurentius Maggio, wrote emphatically that, after the castle and the Bishop's Manor, it was the most magnificent building in the city, which could not be matched by the collegia in Italy.[70] The foundation was officially approved on 18 July 1570. A few days earlier, on the 10 July, a welcoming ceremony for bishop Protasewicz took place in the collegium. The opening ceremony continued from 15 to 18 October of that year, and the lessons started on 23 October. The inauguration was preceded by an extensive propaganda and information campaign. Both the Jesuits and bishop Protasewicz promulgated letters in

[67] The correspondence between Hostounský and General Borgia in 1565, discussed by PIECHNIK, *Początki Akademii Wileńskiej*, pp. 42-43.

[68] BARYCZOWA, "Rotundus Mieleski Augustyn", in: *PSB*, 32, p. 317.

[69] On the details of the foundation of the *collegium*, see PIECHNIK, *Początki Akademii Wileńskiej*, pp. 42-49.

[70] *Ibid.*, p. 43.

which they announced the opening of the Vilnius school.[71] It may be assumed that interest was high, as in the first official year of teaching 160 boys enrolled at the collegium,[72] which made it the largest school in the city. A year later, however, the number of pupils decreased significantly as a result of a plague (1571-1572),[73] and it took thirty years before the number of pupils increased to its original size.

As announced in bishop Protasewicz' and the order's letters, the Jesuit authorities sent a select international teaching staff to Vilnius, including Stanisław Warszewicki as rector, the Croat Thoma Zdelarič as the prefect of studies and professor of rhetoric, the Scot John Hay, the Belgian Franciscus Fabritius, the Irishman David Dymus, two Czechs, Matthias Haslerus and Baltazar Hostounský, mentioned above, as well as Martinus Suabius and Joachim Petronell. Accepting help from foreigners was inevitable, as in Lithuania and Poland the order experienced ongoing problems caused by a lack of personnel. Only a few decades later, thanks to an intensified educational campaign in ever more collegia and in the Academy, the situation was to improve.

From the beginning, five classes were created in accordance with the existing legislation on the organisation of Jesuit colleges in Europe: three grammar classes, a rhetoric class, and a poetics class (*humaniorum litterarum*).[74] Over time, with the Academy established, teaching was extended to four grammar classes and syntax, poetics, and rhetoric classes. There is no doubt that the great importance attached to rhetoric and to the literary education based on rhetoric testifies to the willingness of the school authorities to prepare the students of the collegium for public work.

Soon after the collegium was launched in 1571, faculties of philosophy and theology were opened. This kind of teaching was necessary, because the Jesuits did not have any other institution in the Polish-Lithuanian Commonwealth where both subjects were taught. The philosophy lectures posed many problems, because there were not enough permanent teachers available. The situation normalised only after two years. More important, it seems, was the start of a polemical theology course, meant to demonstrate the superiority of Catholic over Protestant doctrine. This was run by father Hostounský from 1571; it was open to philosophy students, students of the senior collegium classes, and

[71] The content of both writings was published by PIECHNIK, *ibid.*, pp. 201-208.

[72] *Ibid.*, p. 49.

[73] WALAWENDER, *Kronika klęsk elementarnych w Polsce*, pp. 278 and 284.

[74] LUCÁCS, "Introductio generalis", in: *MPSI*, 5, pp. 1*-9*. On the organisation of a Jesuit college, see GRENDLER, *Jesuit Schools and Universities in Europe*, pp. 12-19.

extramural students.[75] Despite temporary financial problems the collegium grew, and in 1578 there was a full course in theology in Vilnius, while polemical theology still played a very important role in the theological department.

From 1574 onwards, the collegium had a department of mathematics, which was run by an English Jesuit, the outstanding mathematician James Bosgrave, who resided in Vilnius, apart from some absences, until 1580. Mathematics was part of the philosophical studies curriculum. In a letter addressed to general Claudio Aquaviva, Bosgrave reported that about forty talented students studied mathematics and would be suitable for employment in the collegia of the Polish province and beyond.[76] As mathematics was part of higher education, its teaching was limited to a rather narrow circle of people.

A few years after the founding of the college, its governors and the Jesuit authorities began to make plans to transform it into a university. The collegium's property did not provide adequate income, so it was necessary to increase its sources of income as much as possible. It was necessary to obtain not only the consent of the religious authorities in Rome and the favour of the Pope, but also to secure the help of King Stephen Báthory. These efforts met resistance from the University of Cracow, whose professors believed that they had a monopoly on higher education in the Polish-Lithuanian Commonwealth, and of Protestants who were not happy about the extension of the property of the Jesuits. In the end, on 7 July 1578, in Lviv, after long and complicated procedures, the king issued a charter that elevated the collegium to the rank of university.[77] Subsequent documents were issued during the following year. On 1 April 1579, the king, who was preparing in Vilnius for the first expedition against Muscovy, issued a solemn charter and confirmed the foundation of Protasewicz' institution, while on 30 October of that year Pope Gregory XIII promulgated a bull in which he made the Academy independent of any secular and ecclesiastical power.

The organisation of the Academy as outlined in both documents was based on models taken from other Jesuit academies, especially from the Collegium

[75] PIECHNIK, *Początki Akademii Wileńskiej*, pp. 51-53.

[76] S. BEDNARSKI, "Bosgrave Jakub", in: *PSB*, 2, p. 374; PIECHNIK, *Początki Akademii Wileńskiej*, pp. 125, 132-133; S. ALEXANDROWICZ, *Rozwój kartografii*, p. 83.

[77] The establishment of the Vilnius Academy has long attracted the attention of researchers; see P. RUBIKAUSKAS, "Przywileje fundacyjne Akademii Wileńskiej", in: *Z dziejów Almae Matris Vilnensis: Księga pamiątkowa ku czci 400-lecia założenia i 75 wskrzeszenia Uniwersytetu Wileńskiego*, ed. L. PIECHNIK and K. PUCHOWSKI (Cracow, 1996), pp. 19-31; PIECHNIK, *Początki Akademii Wileńskiej*, pp. 53-65.

Romanum.[78] All matters were to be decided by the rector, who was subject to the direct authority of the general of the order and the provincial. The Vilnius Academy resembled the previously established collegium, but had an extended curriculum. In addition to the university, two additional Jesuit schools were soon established and were connected with the main educational institutions, the theological seminary and the papal seminary (Alumnat). Several decades after the foundation of the university, in 1644, thanks to the efforts and donations of the chancellor Kazimierz Lew Sapieha, a faculty of canon and civil law was established. At the same time, attention started to be given to the training of staff, with the establishment of a Jesuit seminary for teachers. This was transferred from Polatsk, where it had been destroyed by fire; it operated in the city between 1641 and 1647.[79]

The success of the Academy was measured by the rapid increase in the number of students. In the 1570s, numbers rose to 500 boys; in the early 1590s the number of students was about 600, and in 1596 it had reached 800, with 290 students in the infima class. In its later years, the Academy educated no less than 800 students.[80] In the second decade of the seventeenth century, the number of students exceeded 1000. In 1618, there were 1210 of them, of whom 110 were in higher education and the others studied the *humaniora*.[81] This number places the Academy of Vilnius among the largest European universities. If there were colleges in France where up to 2000 students studied, they were very rare.[82] In the Polish-Lithuanian Commonwealth, the larger collegia taught about 300 students, such as the collegia in Sandomierz and Polatsk.[83]

During the first twenty years of the university's existence, the Jesuits of Vilnius devoted themselves to improving the education system by taking part in the preparation of the first version of the *Ratio Studiorum*, a curriculum that was to apply to all the schools of the Society of Jesus in Europe, America, and

[78] GRENDLER, *Jesuit Schools and Universities in Europe*, pp. 27-29.

[79] B. NATOŃSKI, "Szkolnictwo jezuickie w dobie kontrreformacji", in: *Z dziejów szkolnictwa jezuickiego w Polsce: Wybór artykułów*, ed. J. PASZENDA (Cracow, 1994), p. 41.

[80] PIECHNIK, *Początki Akademii Wileńskiej*, p. 113.

[81] PIECHNIK, *Rozkwit Akademii Wileńskiej*, p. 87-88.

[82] About the number of students in the Polish-Lithuanian Jesuit schools, see J. NIEDŹWIEDŹ, "Jesuit education in the Polish-Lithuanian Commonwealth (1565-1773)", *Journal of Jesuit Studies* 5.3 (2018), pp. 443-444.

[83] *Ibid.* Paul F. Grendler quotes the number of students in some Jesuit colleges in France, Northern Italy, Austria, and Upper Hungary (contemporary Slovakia); see GRENDLER, *Jesuit Schools and Universities in Europe*, pp. 32-33.

Asia. Versions of this document were published in 1586, 1591, and 1599.[84] The Academy of Vilnius was one of the institutions where the curriculum was tested and improved, especially the variant of 1591. Reading the regulations included in the *Ratio* allows us to understand the aims and principles of Jesuit pedagogy, and they are an additional source for the study of the paradigm of Catholic culture in the Polish-Lithuanian Commonwealth and in other Catholic countries. The *Ratio Studiorum* shaped the way of thinking and the attitudes of a large number of young Catholics who passed through the Academy of Vilnius and other Jesuit schools. The text also indirectly influenced the way in which Orthodox Christians and Uniates (who were often Jesuit alumni) thought and wrote. To some extent, the document influenced the Protestants as well, who had to compete, at least to some extent, with the categories of thought of their adversaries when engaging in polemics with Catholic authors.[85] And these categories were not that different from their own categories of thought, because both Catholics and Protestants relied on the humanist (literary) model of education.

In the *Ratio studiorum*, the individual areas of education were arranged hierarchically, from the most important and most difficult, that is those that were studied in the highest classes, to the most rudimentary elements of education in the lowest classes, that is reading and writing, especially in Latin.[86] The *Ratio studiorum* divided education into two levels of study, higher studies (*studia superiora*) and lower studies (*studia inferiora*). The higher studies consisted of theology and philosophy. Of the exact sciences, which at the time were grouped under philosophy, only mathematics was taught at a higher level at the Jesuit university. The other exact or natural sciences were not appreciated until the eighteenth century. In this respect, the Jesuit universities in their

[84] For a critical edition of all the versions, see *MPSI*, 5. The Polish edition of the final version of 1599: *Ratio atque institutio studiorum, czyli Ustawa szkolna Towarzystwa Jezusowego (1599)*, ed. K. Bartnicka and T. Bieńkowski (Warsaw, 2000).

[85] Before any dispute involving Jesuits and Protestants, the conditions under which it would take place were drawn up. Often one condition, usually proposed by the Catholic side, was the use of the rules of dialectical discourse, implemented in the colleges. This subject has been elaborated by Magdalena Ryszka-Kurczab in her doctoral thesis, M. Ryszka-Kurczab, *Retoryka polskich dialogów polemicznych doby Renesansu* (*The Rhetoric of Polish Polemic Dialogues of the Renaissance Period*), defended at the Faculty of Polish Studies of the Jagiellonian University in 2009, Chapter 11.1.3: "Reguły sztuki: Argumentacja", pp. 194-202. I would like to thank the author for making this unpublished work available to me.

[86] D. Julia, "Généalogie de la *Ratio studiorum*", in: *Les jésuites à l'âge de baroque (1540-1640)*, ed. L. Giard and L. de Vaucelles (Grenoble, 1996), p. 129.

Polish and Lithuanian provinces differed significantly from those in Western and Southern Europe, where Jesuits dealt on a larger scale in the non-humanist domains, especially from the second decade of the seventeenth century onwards.[87]

As at the medieval universities, the most important subject and queen of all sciences were the *studia divina*, that is theology based on philosophical studies.[88] The aims of Jesuit education are briefly summarised in chapter XII of the Constitution of the order:

> [...] in the universities of the Society the principal emphasis ought to be placed upon [theological studies] [...]. Moreover, since both the learning of theology and the use of it require (especially in these times) knowledge of the humanities and of the Latin, Greek, and Hebrew languages, there should be capable professors of these languages, and, furthermore, in a sufficient number. [...] The humanities should be understand to include not only grammar, but also rhetoric, poetry, and history.[89]

Even such fields of knowledge as philosophy and theology were subject to the exigencies of literature and the rhetoric-based humanities, that is the first stage of learning, in which, according to *Ratio Studiorum*, rhetorical thinking was intensively instilled into the students. However, the Jesuits did not only aim to teach techniques of effective persuasion or of speaking and writing beautifully. Theological and literary studies were closely intertwined, and the emphasis was placed on the ethical and religious aspect of rhetorical education. By modifying Quintillian's commonly known definition of an orator, one can say that, according to the Jesuits, a speaker-orator, that is a citizen, politician, scholar, clergyman, etc., is a *vir Christianus (vel Catholicus) dicendi peritus* ('a Christian (or Catholic) man who is expert in speaking').[90] In the third decade of the

[87] L. GIARD, "Le devoir d'intelligence ou l'insertion des jésuites dans le monde du savoir", in: *Les jésuites à la Renaissance: Système éducatif et production du savoir*, ed. L. GIARD (Paris, 1995), pp. LVIII-LX; S.J. HARRIS, "Les chaires de mathématiques", in: *Les jésuites à la Renaissance*, pp. 244-251.

[88] GRENDLER, *Jesuit Schools and Universities in Europe*, p. 25.

[89] *The Constitutions of the Society of Jesus and Their Complementary Norms: A Complete English Translation of the Official Latin Texts* (Saint Louis, 1996), pp. 180-181.

[90] LAUSBERG, *Handbook of Literary Rhetoric*, p. 502; M. KOROLKO, *Sztuka retoryki: Przewodnik encyklopedyczny* (Warsaw, 1998), p. 43.

seventeenth century, this idea found its embodiment in the development of *eloquentia sacra* ('ecclesiastical rhetoric').[91]

The majority of boys studied at the faculty of humanities, as this prepared them to a large extent for a life in the world. They could continue their studies as lay people after graduating in the humanities, but most of the students of the faculties of philosophy, theology, and law probably belonged to the clergy. They were mainly members of the Society of Jesus. A large number of the students were probably Catholics, but the Jesuits were keen to accept Orthodox Christians and Protestants as well. For this reason, the latter introduced bans on the enrollment of their followers in Jesuit schools.[92]

The lack of enrolment lists of students from the initial period of the existence of the Vilnius Academy makes it impossible to state how long the average alumnus studied in the faculty of humanities. The full course included a seven-year education in five classes. Each student started with three and later four grammar classes, the first two of which were called *infima* and *infima maior*, the third *grammatica*, and the fourth *syntax*. Next, students moved on to a class called poetics and finished his education in a two-year rhetoric class. They could continue their studies at the academic faculties, either in philosophical studies, which included two departments, or theological studies, which included initially four and later six departments.[93]

In grammar classes, catechism was taught, knowledge of Latin grammar was consolidated, and the fundamentals of Greek language were introduced. After the final version of the *Ratio studiorum* was introduced, the main textbooks in the lower classes were the catechism of Peter Canisius and a grammar book by Manuel Álvares[94] and Jacob Gretser. Both classical languages were taught on the basis of rhetorical prose and poetry, although education started with writing letters in Polish. In the early years of the Academy, the teaching

[91] R. GRZEŚKOWIAK and J. NIEDŹWIEDŹ, "Wstęp", in: M. MIELESZKO, *Emblematy*, ed. R. GRZEŚKOWIAK and J. NIEDŹWIEDŹ (Warsaw, 2010), pp. 9-10; GRENDLER, *Jesuit Schools and Universities in Europe*, pp. 19-23.

[92] However, it is impossible to prove that "in 1578 about one third of the students enrolled in the Academy of Vilnius were said to be sons of dissenters" (J. TAZBIR, "Państwo bez stosów", in: ID., *Państwo bez stosów i inne szkice* (Cracow, 2000), p. 138), if only because we do not have lists of students who studied there. The synods of the Lithuanian Evangelicals forbade members of the Church from sending their sons to Jesuit *collegia*. See ŁUKASZEWICZ, *Dzieje kościołów wyznania helweckiego*, p. 152.

[93] PIECHNIK, *Początki Akademii Wileńskiej*, p. 65.

[94] L. PIECHNIK, *Powstanie i rozwój jezuickiej "Ratio studiorum" (1548-1599)* (Cracow, 2003), pp. 124-125.

of the Ruthenian language also found a place, but with time this practice was abandoned.[95] Instead, at least from the beginning of the seventeenth century, all students, many of whom had little knowledge of the Polish language, developed their ability to speak Polish. The visitor recommended:

> That students in the three lowest classes be able to compose letters in Polish and later in Latin. As Lithuanians, as well as indigenous Poles, do not speak Polish well and do not have good pronunciation, it is necessary for them to learn to write and speak Polish, especially since parents only occasionally use the standard Polish language.[96]

In the higher classes, students' knowledge and skills were expanded to include the theoretical basis for structuring texts. The graduate was supposed to know Latin grammar, the theory of rhetoric and poetics, and to be able to apply them in practice. The basic grammar textbook used was the one of Manuel Álvares, the book of poetics was Jacobus Pontanus' (Spanmüller) *Poetices libri III*, and rhetoric was taught with the aid of Cypriano de Soarez's *Institutiones rhetoricae libri III*. The latter was initially taught in the rhetoric class, and later also in the lower poetics class.

Teaching poetics and rhetoric at the Academy of Vilnius served to develop several competences, first and foremost composing and delivering Latin texts of various functions. In the lower classes, progymnasmatic forms were taught, that is texts such as descriptions, stories, praises, reprimands, fables, and theses.[97] The most popular form was *chreia*, a kind of short dissertation. In the lower classes students also learned humanist epistolography and stylistics appropriate for different types of letters, for instance by memorising appropriate phrases, creating dictionaries of useful phrases, the forms of addressing the recipient, etc.

From the beginning of the students' education, translation exercises were introduced. Almost every day they translated a fragment of a text of a Latin classical author into Polish and from Polish into Latin, usually a paragraph or several verses. The translation was checked by the teacher and rewritten in a

[95] *Ibid.*, p. 85.

[96] *Proposita provinciae Lithuaniae de studiis humanioribus promovendos anno 1609*, MPSI, 7, p. 414.

[97] B.B. Awianowicz, *Progymnasmata w teorii i praktyce szkoły humanistycznej od końca XV do połowy XVIII wieku: Dzieje nowożytnej recepcji Aftoniosa od Rudolfa Agricoli do Johanna Christopha Gottscheda* (Toruń, 2008), pp. 308-310.

notebook. In poetics classes, they continued to learn epistolography, as well as writing shorter poetic forms, such as epigrams, epitaphs, emblems, and artistic forms, like odes or elegies. Latin metrics and strophic systems were discussed separately.[98] In the rhetoric class, poetics was not completely abandoned, but the focus was on prose. Students learned the rules of writing different genres of speech. As in the poetics class, much time was devoted to practical stylistics, based on the available classification of styles.[99]

Practice was supported by theoretical considerations. Theory, which systematised the knowledge of poetry and prose, was adapted to the age of the students and to its practical application. In some sentences long definitions of different terms were given, followed by many examples illustrating the argument.[100] Because of the practical objectives, some genres, such as epic or tragedy, although highly regarded, were given relatively little space compared to odes or epigrams. During the classes students practised epigrammatic and lyrical forms, while longer and complex ones were only objects of analysis and interpretation.

Rhetoric and university poetics were of a scholarly rather than speculative nature and usually boiled down to the rules of constructing a text and the principles of expressing oneself correctly and beautifully in Latin and Polish. The considerations could also not be too complicated, in view of the relatively young age of the students. Those in the rhetoric classes were usually sixteen or seventeen years old.

Cicero had a prominent place among the authors read at school. His texts served the teaching of reading, and the *Ratio studiorum* ordered that Latin stylistics be modelled on him. His speeches as well as his philosophical and rhetorical works were studied, although the latter only in the rhetoric class. Other Roman writers selected for school education included Caesar, Sallust, Tacitus, Livy, and Curtius. Among the poets read were Horace, Virgil, Ovid, Martial, and Seneca. It can be assumed that Greek was taught at a good level.[101] In the rhetoric classes, education began with the speeches of St. John Chrysostom and the letters of St. Gregory of Nazianzus. In the higher classes, students

[98] T. MICHAŁOWSKA, *Staropolska teoria genologiczna* (Wrocław, 1974), p. 19.

[99] Z. RYNDUCH, *Nauka o stylach w siedemnastowiecznych retorykach polskich* (Gdańsk, 1967); E. ULČINAITĖ, *Teoria retoryczna w Polsce i na Litwie w XVII wieku: Próba rekonstrukcji schematu retorycznego* (Wrocław, 1984), pp. 113-116.

[100] MICHAŁOWSKA, *Staropolska teoria genologiczna*, p. 45.

[101] T. VETEIKIS, *Greek Studies and Greek Literature in Sixteenth-Seventeenth Century in Lithuania: A Summary of Doctoral Dissertation* (Vilnius, 2004), p. 15.

moved on to quite difficult texts, like Isocrates' and Demosthenes' speeches, Homer's *Iliad*, and Hesiod's *Works and Days*. Reading matter in Jesuit education clearly embraced the works of the classics. This trend was initiated in the last decade of the sixteenth century by Antonio Possevino's *Bibliotheca selecta de ratione studiorum* and was strengthened during the pontificate of Pope Urban VIII.[102]

The choice of readings can be traced in the reports on the activity of the faculty of humanities of the Academy of Vilnius,[103] in the *Ratio Studiorum*, and also in Possevino's book. Of course, the texts suggested by the lecturers were properly prepared and carefully selected so as not to scandalise young students.[104] For example, those fragments of the *Aeneid* in which the sensual figure of Dido appeared too often were carefully omitted. The same happened with the choice of odes by Horace or odes in Polish by Jan Kochanowski (*Pieśni*). In one of the copies of Kochanowski's poetry, which in the seventeenth century belonged to the collegium in Kražiai and is now kept in the Library of Vilnius University, someone carefully tore out or blurred the indecent parts of the text.[105]

Apart from classical authors, the Academy of Vilnius also taught Polish literature, in both poetry and prose. The teaching of the Polish language flourished in the second half of the seventeenth century, when the canon of Polish literature was shaped, but in Vilnius its beginnings are noticeable earlier. Originally, Polish and the other modern languages were to be used at Vilnius University for catechetical and missionary purposes. The graduates of the Academy learned the languages of the Grand Duchy of Lithuania and the provinces adjacent to Lithuania, that is Ruthenian, Estonian and Latvian, in order to promote and strengthen Catholicism in this area. Over time, however, the importance of the Polish language in Jesuit education increased to such an extent that

[102] T. BIEŃKOWSKI, "'Bibliotheca selecta de Ratione studiorum': Possewina jako teoretyczny fundament kultury kontrreformacji", in: *Wiek XVII: Kontrreformacja – Barok: Prace z historii kultury*, ed. J. PELC (Wrocław, 1970), p. 299; M. FUMAROLI, *L'età dell'eloquenza: Retorica e 'res literaria' dal Rinascimento alle soglie dell'epoca classica*, trans. E. BAS, M. BOTTO, and G. CILLARIO (Milan, 2002), pp. 208-217.

[103] "Aneks", in: PIECHNIK, *Rozkwit Akademii Wileńskiej*, pp. 269-280.

[104] P.A. FABRE, "Dépouilles d'Egypte: L'expurgation des auteurs latins dans les collèges jésuites", in: *Les jésuites à la Renaissance*, pp. 55-73.

[105] The censored fragments were reconstructed with the same care several decades later. The missing pages were pasted in, and a seventeenth-century hand filled in the missing parts of the text, writing it above the blurred verses.

Polish literature became one of the three literatures taught and practised in the Jesuit schools.

Originally, the recommendation to use Polish was based on the need to unify the language used as a support for Jesuit education, which was conducted predominantly in Latin. The student environment was multilingual, so the choice of one vernacular language was a typical normalising measure. The religious regulations allowed the use of the mother tongue only as an auxiliary tool, in the lower classes in the teaching of catechism and in the higher classes in the translation of classical texts. Teachers at the Academy of Vilnius gradually devoted more attention to the Polish language, as in checking the work of the students they were obliged to correct not only Latin but also the Polish translations. In 1614, the visitor to the Jesuit Lithuanian Province, Giovanni Argenti, recommended that teachers pay attention to Polish spelling.[106] In the long run, this resulted in the (linguistic) Polonisation of Lithuanian literary culture.

Among the models of rhetorical texts prepared at the Vilnius Academy are examples of Polish-language speeches suitable to be pronounced during local assemblies (*sejmiki*). It is likely that students of the faculty of humanities had to practise writing texts in Polish as early as the first phase of the university's existence, as this was recommendations by its superiors. Students probably wrote mostly prose (epistolography and speeches), but there is also testimony that in poetry was taught and written in Polish as well.

The Jesuit schools were the places where a first Polish literary canon was established. It was probably the famous neo-Latin poet Maciej Kazimierz Sarbiewski who introduced Jan Kochanowski, the most important Polish Renaissance poet, into the curriculum of Jesuit studies. Sarbiewski quite often referred to Kochanowski in the lectures on poetics he gave in Polatsk in 1626/1627 and which he repeated in 1627/1628 within the walls of the Academy of Vilnius, where he had assumed the chair of rhetoric. His admiration for Kochanowski forced Sarbiewski to compare him to Horace in ways appropriate for people in the seventeenth century.[107] Gradually, the Academy as well as the

[106] PIECHNIK, *Rozkwit Akademii Wileńskiej*, p. 75.

[107] M.K. SARBIEWSKI, *Wykłady poetyki (Praecepta poetica)*, ed. and trans. S. SKIMINA (Wrocław, 1958), p. 38. Perhaps Sarbiewski's role in seventeenth-century literary culture is much more important. His importance as a poet and theoretician of literature has been emphasised. Sometimes, although rarely, his achievements in the field of theology were mentioned in the interwar period. Meanwhile, his personality and authority clearly marked the teaching of literature in Jesuit education, which in the long run is perhaps Sarbiewski's most enduring achievement. His

other colleges of the Lithuanian province adopted the view that Kochanowski was a classic. This opinion can be traced in the poetry textbooks of the second half of the century. In the collegia, Polish poetry clearly liberated itself from the shadow of Latin literature. Although a student of the collegium would leave school having been well trained in Greek and Latin literature, one also considered that an ability to write poetry in Polish could come in handy. As far as the subjects and the construction of texts was concerned, Latin models provided enough material, but in the case of stylistic and metrical issues it was necessary to introduce the teaching of writing poems in Polish as well. The earliest studies of this type that have been preserved date from the mid-1660s. They were written at the Academy of Vilnius.[108] It can be assumed, however, that the teaching of writing poems in Polish began even before the Muscovite invasion, perhaps in the 1640s. Manuscript poetics textbooks from Vilnius from the 1680s described 'Types of poems in *Polish odes*' as the second part of the chapter devoted to metre and Latin versification. They were classified according to the model of Latin poems, taking account of the position of the caesura, the number of syllables, and the number of metrical feet. Fragments of Jan Kochanowski's poems were given as examples, while the authors of the lectures assumed that students had solid knowledge of his works.

The Jesuit schools in Vilnius were practically orientated, so a graduate's literary competences would be useful in everyday public life. Much attention was paid to the presentation of the texts the students had written. This was usually done through public declamations. On holidays and Sundays, students delivered their texts before other students, and, on the occasion of particularly important festivities, before invited guests as well, such as parents, patrons, benefactors of the Academy, etc. A special variant of such declamations were theatrical performances at the end of the academic year. The Jesuit theatre in Vilnius was inaugurated the year after the collegium was opened. On the day

accomplishments in pedagogy may well have had more to do with the inclusion of Polish poets into the school canon than his views on poetry and the rules of writing it. Shortly after his death, he himself became one of the Polish classics. See J. NIEDŹWIEDŹ, "Twardowski w szkole XVII i XVIII wieku. (Quae rapiet sub nubae vetustas minimae molles Tvardovii Musas?)", in: *Wielkopolski Maro: Samuel ze Skrzypny Twardowski i jego dzieło w wielkiej i małej Ojczyźnie*, ed. K. MELLER and J. KOWALSKI (Poznań, 2002), pp. 352-359.

[108] MICHAŁOWSKA, *Staropolska teoria genologiczna*, pp. 129-130; J. NIEDŹWIEDŹ, "Sylabotonizm Jana Kochanowskiego i teoria wersyfikacji polskiej w XVII w.", *Terminus* 8.1 (14) (2006), pp. 173-187.

of the start of the new school year, on 18 September 1570, students staged the *Hercules*.[109]

Another way of presenting the students' texts was to publish them. If they were panegyrics, they were printed by the university printing house, while other texts were published in manuscript form, as so-called *affixiones*:

> Every second month the best verses written by the pupils are to be posted on the walls of the classroom to lend colour to the celebration of some special day, or to the announcement of class officers, or to some similar occasion. [The poems should be carefully selected and rewritten by students.] Local custom may sanction the posting of even shorter pieces, such as inscriptions for shields, churches, tombs, gardens, statutes, or descriptions of a town, a harbour, an army, or narratives of a deed of some saint, or, finally, paradoxical sayings.[110]

This review of the Vilnius catalogues of lectures (*catalogus lectionum*) leads one to conclude that, over the course of a century, the model for teaching humanities at the Academy of Vilnius was quite stable. It was, of course, subject to some improvement and modification, but its objectives remained unchanged. The improvements aimed at greater effectiveness "in knowing and stimulating the love for our Creator and Redeemer"[111] and in literary education. Differences between successive lists of recommended lectures mainly boiled down to modifying the list of textbooks and reading matter.[112] This immutability, or even conservatism, of the humanist curriculum in Vilnius resulted from fidelity to the *Ratio studiorum*. Successive generations of Jesuits raised in the spirit of this document were attached to tradition and only slowly absorbed any literary innovations. This is clear in the lectures on poetry and rhetoric from the first half of the seventeenth century. The humanities described in the successive versions of the *Ratio studiorum* were based on the classical canon of Latin and Greek literature, which was formed during the late Renaissance.[113] The

[109] J. POPLATEK, *Studia z dziejów jezuickiego teatru szkolnego w Polsce* (Wrocław, 1957), p. 167; PIECHNIK, *Początki Akademii Wileńskiej*, pp. 98-99. The theatre at the Academy of Vilnius is discussed in more detail in Chapter 10, *Epideictic texts*.

[110] The Jesuit *Ratio Studiorum* of 1599, trans., introduction and explanatory notes A.P. FARRELL SJ, p. 84.

[111] *Ratio atque institutio studiorum Societatis Iesu* (1599), *MPSI*, 5, p. 367.

[112] PIECHNIK, *Rozkwit Akademii Wileńskiej*, pp. 71-74 and 269-280, discusses the list of readings in detail.

[113] It may be assumed that the second phase of the dispute between the Ciceronians and the Anti-Ciceronians, which took place in the 1530s, contributed to the formation of this version of the canon. However, the reasons why Catholic reformers referred to the domesticated Ciceronian

core of this canon included the works of Cicero as far as prose was concerned, and of Virgil, Horace, and Ovid for poetry. The influence of Ciceronianism gradually decreased, especially when Justus Lipsius and the Spanish *conceptismo* began to gain popularity. However, until the end of the order's existence, Cicero was held to be the proper model for rhetorical prose, at least at the school level.

Until the middle of the seventeenth century the Vilnius Academy was in the vanguard of European educational institutions, mainly thanks to its excellent staff. Almost all Jesuits who worked in Vilnius had studied humanities, philosophy, and theology, so they were prepared to write various texts in their mother tongue (which was not necessarily Polish) and in Latin, and sometimes in Greek as well. Among them were authors of European calibre, including Piotr Skarga (a preacher, hagiographer, and Catholic polemicist), Jakub Wujek (a postillographer and translator), Antonio Possevino (a writer, polemicist, and cultural theoretician), Stanisław Grodzicki (a polemicist), Mikołaj Dauksza (Mikalojus Daukša; a translator), Wawrzyniec Bojer (Laurentius Boyer; a poet), Marcin Śmiglecki (a philosopher, polemicist, and speaker), Grzegorz Knapiusz (Cnapius; a lexicographer and playwright), Maciej Kazimierz Sarbiewski (a poet, theologian, and theoretician of literature), Konstanty Szyrwid (Konstantinas Sirvydas; a lexicographer), Jakub Olszewski (a preacher), Zygmunt Lauksmin (Sigismundus Lauxmin; a theoretician of literature), Kazimierz Wijuk Kojałowicz (Kazimieras Kojalavičius-Vijūkas; a panegyrist and theoretician of literature), and Wojciech Wijuk Kojałowicz (Albertas Kojalavičius-Vijūkas; a historian and heraldist). Thanks to these and other authors, lecturers, and scholars, as well as to the printing house that published their works, Vilnius became one of the most important cultural and humanist centres of Eastern Europe.

The importance of the Academy was significant not only in the broader perspective of Lithuania, the Polish-Lithuanian Commonwealth, or indeed of the *Christianitas* as a whole, but also on a micro-scale, that is for the city and for individual students. As has already been mentioned, the university influenced the city's economy, contributing, for example, to the increase in the trade

humanist tradition still need to be thoroughly examined. It is significant that among the representatives of Anti-Ciceronianism were, *inter alios*, Giovanni Pico della Mirandola and Erasmus of Rotterdam, who did not inspire confidence among representatives of the Counter-Reformation. See FUMAROLI, *L'età dell'eloquenza*, pp. 76-108; A. FULIŃSKA, *Naśladowanie i twórczość: Renesansowe teorie imitacji, emulacji i przekładu* (Wrocław, 2000), pp. 116-154.

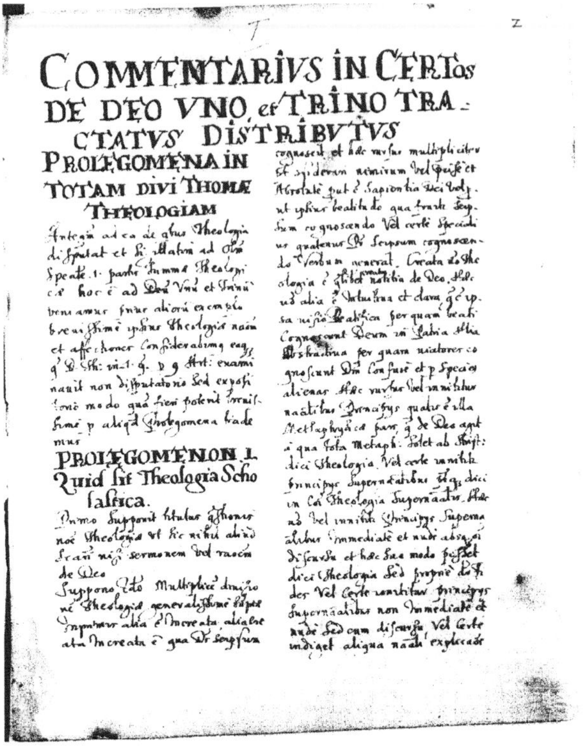
COMMENTARIVS IN CERTos DE DEO VNO et TRINO TRACTATVS DISTRIBVTVS

PROLEGOMENA IN TOTAM DIVI THOMAE THEOLOGIAM

PROLEGOMENON I. Quid sit Theologia Scholastica.

Fig. 11 Manuscript of lectures on Thomas Aquinas's *Summa theologica* given by M.K. Sarbiewski in the Academy of Vilnius in 1633: *In primam partem Summae Thelologicae divi Tomae Aquinatis doctoris Angelici*. MS Vilnius, VUB, F3-2037, f. 2r. Reproduced with the permission of VUB.

in books and stationery, as well as to the city's culture generally. All major events connected with the functioning of the State or the Catholic Church, such as the arrivals of monarchs and magnates, processions, canonisation ceremonies, the inauguration ceremonies of offices, anniversaries, funerals, and meetings of the nobility took place with the involvement of the Academy. These events were always accompanied by the production of texts such as speeches, poems, panegyrics, as well as theatrical and para-theatrical performances.

Every student of the Academy had the opportunity to acquire rare and valued skills that facilitated his public career, regardless of whether a student belonged to the nobility, to the town dwellers, or to the clergy. Literacy cannot be reduced to the ability to produce a large number of various types of text. After years of intensive rhetorical training, 'a rhetorical man', who had completed the full cycle of studies in the humanities and left the walls of the Academy of Vilnius, read texts through the prisms of Roman poetry and prose and schemata that forced a humanist interpretation. This way of reasoning was subject to the principles of building enthymemes and syllogisms, while sentences had the form of rhetorical periods. The grammar and style of his mother tongue was also strongly influenced by Latin. A graduate of the Academy was a poet but also an actor, able to perform a rhetorical act in court, at a council meeting, or at a wedding. Several years of effort had been required to learn by heart numerous texts and created in his mind an extensive humanist library, and this considerable memory repository was a highly valued treasury. One always viewed the world in relation to one's library. A literary text itself inspired no less respect than a feat of memory. In Jesuit education the appreciation of literature and authors was axiomatic. The Jesuit pupil was instilled – usually very effectively – with the need to write and express himself through a rhetorised text.

Without being aware of the marks left by the humanist Jesuit school we are unable to read and understand certain layers of the texts written in Vilnius in the second half of the sixteenth century and the first half of the seventeenth century. Even though relatively few graduates of the Academy remained in the capital after their studies, traces of Jesuit textual culture gradually permeated the vast majority of works created in this city.

Student Life

The large numbers of students certainly had an impact on the city's economy. Most of them came from outside Vilnius and lived not only in the dormitories but mainly in private lodgings. In the city they bought food, clothes, books, and paper. Probably some of them worked. Through their presence, the city took on a student atmosphere which is difficult to describe. Superiors, especially Jesuits, tried to impose a certain organisational framework on students' lives, for instance through establishing student religious confraternities. However, the academic life was not always orderly.

Theodor (Fiedorek) Andrzejewicz came to Vilnius at the age of eleven and for the first four years he studied at St. John's Catholic parish school and at the Dominican school at the church of the Holy Spirit. At the age of fifteen, he went to the Catholic cathedral school and was henceforth under the jurisdiction of the bishop. His testimony given before the bishop's court at the beginning of October 1639 after anti-Protestant riots, sheds some light on the life of Vilnius students in the seventeenth century:

> And when the *pauperes* [students from the Dormitory for the Poor] from the castle school and St. John's parish school went to the Calvinist church [*zbór*] to demolish it, I was there with them. But I do not know and I cannot name any of them, neither by first name nor by nickname, although I would recognise their faces. And when the subsacristan of St. John's church, killed by a shot from a fiery shotgun at the wall of the Vilnius Calvinist church, was brought to St. John's cemetery, I also went there. There, the elder from the dormitory commanded us to return to demolish the tenement house, where, having reached the stalls, some took various things and goods and took them home or to the schools. With these goods I was arrested by the city guard and taken [to the magistrate].[114]

Jesuit students were regularly accused of assaulting Calvinists, which the fathers of the Society of Jesus consistently denied. In 1619, the rector of the Academy Jan Grużewski reassured the *voivode* of Vilnius, Krzysztof II Radziwiłł, a Calvinist, with these words:

> Intending to satisfy the request of Your Grace, I ordered schools to introduce a fierce ban *sub gravissimis poenis* [under the gravest pains] that are possible *in Academia* [in the Academy], so that no person would dare to violate the peace or attempt to riot.[115]

The student unrest occurred after the traditional Marian pilgrimages to the town of Trakai, which took place annually at the beginning of July and September. In 1611, there had been a dispute between a Calvinist and some Jesuit students:

> Now again, on the night from Saturday to Sunday, there was a fresh brawl that, if it is true, was caused by a small spark. At first, Mr Radzymiński's apprentice [...],

[114] *Kopia relacji miesckiej o wyznaniu niektórych burzycielów zboru wileńskiego 1639 d. 9 Octobra*, MS LNMB F93-1701.

[115] MS LNMB F93-1690.

seeing a procession returning from Trakai, took a student aside, I do not know whom precisely, and told him "you were supposed to serve me and you did not come to me". Seeing this, other students are said to have hurled themselves at them, torn that student, and taken the man himself to the prison in the town hall.[116]

Sometimes altercations involving students ended extremely badly. From a verdict of the bishop's court of 18 March 1633, we learn how much the life of a pupil of the cathedral school was worth. For the murder of one of them, a man called Haydonenius was sentenced to a wergild of one hundred *kopas*, three months in prison, and spending two weeks confessing his ungodly deed at the entrance to the cathedral.[117]

Court records are our basic source of knowledge about the students of Vilnius in the seventeenth century. However, to some extent they distort their image. We can supplement this with much more praiseworthy achievements, especially of the Jesuit alumni, whose work includes many literary texts published from the late 1560s by the academic printing house. This does not alter the fact that these texts (poems, letters) and court documents provide totally different kinds of testimony of the actions of the head boys and those who were a nuisance to their teachers and educators.

Another image of student life in Vilnius at the beginning of the seventeenth century is outlined in the diary of Maciej Vorbek-Lettow, who in 1603, at the age of ten, finished the grammar school at the Evangelical-Augsburg (Lutheran) church. Then, after about three to four years of study in Königsberg, Elbląg, and Gdańsk, he returned to Vilnius where he continued his studies, first at the church school and then at the Academy of Vilnius. Although he originally came from Vilnius, he did not live in his family home but stayed with an Evangelical preacher, Christian Bruno, who ran a kind of dormitory for Lutheran boys, keeping an eye on their educational progress, morals, and fidelity to Lutheranism. Every morning, father Bruno examined his pupils, checked whether they had completed their homework correctly,

and on Sundays, at the table *inter colloquia sacra* [when discussing sacred things] and always *articulum fidei ex catechesi explicare* [explained an article of the faith from the catechism].[118]

[116] *Z listu pana Siesickiego, podwojewodziego mego wileńskiego de data z Wilna 3 Julii 1611*, MS LNMB F93-1729.

[117] MS MAB F43-218 (VKF452; *Akta kapituły wileńskiej 1632-1643*), f. 17r.

[118] VORBEK-LETTOW, *Skarbnica pamięci*, p. 241-242.

Lettow studied in Vilnius until the age of seventeen. Just after the fateful fire of 1610 he went to study abroad. He was undoubtedly a talented student, though probably not the most outstanding one. In any case, thanks to his education, he was to achieve significant successes afterwards. This evidence is exceptional; we have only little information about the most numerous group of ordinary and average students, to which the Fiedorek Andrzejewicz belonged who was mentioned above, who was not clever enough to escape the city guards.

The Orthodox Brotherhood's School

During the first two centuries of Vilnius urban community, Orthodox education was the responsibility of the clergy. Teaching, presumably quite rudimentary, was intended to prepare future priests and lower clerics. The earliest schools were established at Orthodox churches and monasteries. We can name two such places with a high degree of probability. They were the church of the Theotokos, the oldest church in Vilnius, which according to tradition was founded by one of the Orthodox wives of Duke Algirdas, Maria or Uliana, and the church and later the monastery of the Holy Spirit, whose origins date from the fourteenth century. At the beginning of the next century, the role of the Theotokos church was particularly important, because in 1415 it was elevated to the rank of *sobor* (cathedral) and for a short period became the capital of the Lithuanian patriarch. In the fifteenth century, Orthodox schools taught Church Slavonic, reading and writing in the Cyrillic alphabet, and singing religious chant (*Octoechos*).

In the sixteenth century, at least some churches kept small parish schools. One of them existed until the fire of 1610 at St. Peter and Paul's church in Great (Didžioji) Street: "the whole tenement house and the building was built on a plot of land that belonged to the Orthodox Church, where before the fire there was only the Orthodox school".[119]

A Vilnius brotherhood of a new type was founded at the Holy Trinity church in 1588. This was the first institution of this type in the Polish-Lithuanian Commonwealth after the Lviv Brotherhood had been reorganised in 1586.[120] The Brotherhood's activity was based on a privilege of 1588 issued by

[119] *Rewizyja gospód dworu*, p. 214.
[120] BARDACH, "Bractwa cerkiewne na ziemiach ruskich Rzeczypospolitej", pp. 78-79.

the Patriarch of Constantinople, Jeremiah II, who gave it the status of a stauropegic brotherhood, that is, it was directly dependent on the patriarch and thus independent of a local *vladyka* (bishop).[121]

The school at the monastery of the Holy Trinity is mentioned for the first time in the privilege of King Stephen Báthory of 27 May 1584, issued to the Orthodox mayors, councillors, and burghers of Vilnius, which gave them control over the monastery after the death of the Kyiv Metropolitan Onisiphor Devochka. The revenue from the monastic property was to be used to maintain the archimandrite (the abbot superior), monks, and monastic servants, and "to build schools and educate people with expertise in writing so that they would teach children of the Greek faith who would live in and by this monastery".[122] We may suppose that the school was established four years later.[123] In the privilege issued by Sigismund III Vasa on 21 June 1589, which approved the rules governing the Brotherhood's existence and operations, the tasks of the Brotherhood were defined, including:

> At the Brotherhood's school, the children of members of the Brotherhood and poor orphans should learn for free at the expense of the Brotherhood the following things: speaking and writing in Ruthenian, Greek, Latin, and Polish according to the Brotherhood's arrangements.[124]

On 9 October 1592, at a session of the Parliament (*Sejm*) in Warsaw, the king granted two more privileges, in which he agreed to the opening of a school and printing house and to exempt the house of the Brotherhood from municipal taxes. In addition, the Brotherhood was to have two tax-exempt houses with a school and a dormitory for poor students, as well as a printing house.[125] A few days later, on 15 October, a similar privilege was issued to the Lviv Brother-

[121] *Собраніе древнихъ грамотъ и актов городовъ: Вильны, Ковна, Трокъ, православныхъ монастырей, церквей и по разнымъ предметамъ*, part 2, Вильно 1843, pp. 6-8.

[122] *AIZR*, vol. 3: *1544-1587*, pp. 286-288, item 144.

[123] Antoni Mironowicz mentions 1584 as the date of the foundation of the Vilnius Brotherhood's school, indicating Báthory's charter mentioned above. However, the school could not be established until after the monastery was taken over by the Orthodox burghers following the death of the Metropolitan. See A. MIRONOWICZ, "Szkolnictwo prawosławne na ziemiach białoruskich w XVI-XVIII wieku", *Беларускі Гістарычны Зборнік – Białoruskie Zeszyty Historyczne* 2.2 (1994), p. 22.

[124] *Собраніе древнихъ грамотъ*, p. 10.

[125] *AVAK*, vol. 9, pp. 144-153. See J. JURGINIS, V. MERKYS, and A. TAUTAVIČIUS, *Vilniaus miesto istorija nuo seniausių laikų iki Spalio revolucijos* (Vilnius, 1968), pp. 137-139.

hood. Here, the king referred to provisions concerning the Vilnius institutions (schools, printing houses, hospitals).[126] In this way the statutes of the Vilnius Brotherhood became a model for other brotherhoods in the Polish-Lithuanian Commonwealth. The Orthodox synod held in Brest in 1594, devoted to the activities of Orthodox schools, approved the principles of their functioning, including those of the Vilnius school.[127]

At the turn of the sixteenth and seventeenth centuries, due to the growing conflict between Orthodox Christians and Uniates,[128] and also due to the hostile policy of Sigismund III Vasa towards the Orthodox Church, the Vilnius Brotherhood experienced several problems. In 1609, the Brotherhood lost the church and monastery of the Holy Trinity and moved to the church of the Holy Spirit on the opposite side of the street. Over time, the Brotherhood adopted the Holy Spirit as its patron in order to distinguish themselves from the Holy Trinity Uniates. The school continued to operate as one of the main points of resistance to the expanding influence of the Union. In a letter to the Lviv Brotherhood dated 21 January 1619, the representatives of the Vilnius Brotherhood reported that two years earlier (1617) a new brick school building had been built and asked for teachers (*didaskals*) to be sent.[129] After the restitution of the church in the 1620s and the pacification act (*punkty uspokojenia*) had been passed in 1632,[130] on 26 February 1635 King Władysław IV Vasa confirmed the privileges granted by his father, finally allowing the launch of the school of the Brotherhood of the Holy Spirit.[131] According to the statute of the Brotherhood's school, education knew three stages and resembled the model developed for Jesuit and Protestant humanist education. The emphasis was placed on multilingualism and the ability to use different types of text. However, the set of languages, texts, and writings noticeably distinguished the Broth-

[126] *Privilegia typographica Polonorum: Polskie przywileje drukarskie 1493-1793*, ed. M. JUDA (Lublin, 2010), p. 108 (item 77).

[127] MIRONOWICZ, "Szkolnictwo prawosławne", p. 22.

[128] In 1596, in Brest (Brześć), part of the Orthodox hierarchy from the territory of the Polish-Lithuanian Commonwealth accepted the Catholic dogmas and the authority of the Pope, but could keep their own language and liturgy. The Uniate Church was the result of the Brest Union. See: *Unia brzeska: Geneza, dzieje i konsekwencje w kulturze narodów słowiańskich: Praca zbiorowa*, ed. R. ŁUŻNY F. ZIEJKA, and A. KĘPIŃSKI (Cracow, 1994).

[129] *AIZR*, vol. 4: *1588-1632*, p. 506.

[130] The pacification act was issued by the election *Sejm* on 11 November 1632. See A. MIRONOWICZ, *Józef Bobrykowicz, biskup białoruski* (Białystok, 2003), <http://kamunikat.org/download.php?item=4255-4.html&pubref=4255> (accessed 24.02.2021).

[131] *AVAK*, vol. 9, pp. 169-172.

erhood's school from other humanist schools in the city. The letter to the Lviv Brotherhood from 1619 provides some information. At that time, the school was divided into five branches. In the first three Latin was taught, in the fourth Ruthenian, and in the fifth Church Slavonic and Greek. Because of a lack of Orthodox teachers of Latin, the services of "German infidels", presumably Lutherans, were used.[132]

The statute of the Vilnius school is not preserved, so we can only guess what the curriculum looked like. The statute of the Lutsk school from around 1624, based on the Lviv and Vilnius models, speaks of the teaching of basic literacy skills:

> Article 9
>
> Children at school should be divided into three groups: one that learns to recognise and compose letters; another one that learns to read and learn many things by heart; and a further one that learns to explain, reflect and understand. Because, as St. Paul says, "when I was a child, I talked like a child, I thought like a child, I reasoned like a child. When I became a man, I put the ways of childhood behind me".[133]

The first stage of learning therefore corresponded to the Jesuit class called *infima*: here, pupils learnt to read and write in the Latin and Cyrillic alphabets.[134] The main handbooks used for this purpose, as in Catholic parish schools, were primers, prayer texts, and the psalter. Initially, Orthodox Christians had Church Slavonic elementary books at their disposal, for instance the one by Laurentius Zizany (Wawrzyniec Zizani) published in 1596,[135] and later also Polish ones. In 1633, an Orthodox primer was published in Vilnius with the title *Dla dziatek nauka czytania pisma polskiego* (For Children, Learning to Read Polish). This was probably intended for the Brotherhood's school and other primary schools that operated at Orthodox churches.[136] The first part is a

[132] *AIZR*, vol. 4: *1588-1632*, p. 506.

[133] *Памятники изданные временною коммиссіею для разбора древнихъ актовъ высочайше учрежденною при Кіевскомъ военномъ, Подольскомъ и Волынскомъ Генералъгубернаторъ*, 1.1 (Кіевъ, 1845), pp. 103-104.

[134] Ё.О. Флеров, *О православных церковных братствах, противоборство-вавших Унии в югозападной России, в XVI, XVII, XVIII столетиях* (St. Petersburg, 1857), pp. 111-113. Mironowicz, "Szkolnictwo prawosławne", pp. 27-28.

[135] M.C. Bragone, "Introduzione", in: *Alfavitar radi učenija malych detej: Un abbecedario nella Russia del Seicento*, ed. M.C. Bragone (Florence, 2008), pp. 13-15.

[136] *Dla dziatek nauka czytania pisma polskiego* (Vilnius, 1633).

typical textbook for reading words. Pupils acquired the alphabet written in *Schwabacher* and *Antiqua*, then learned to put together two, three, and finally four syllables. The second part of the primer contained texts for the exercises. They were Church Slavonic prayers translated into Polish and the basics of Christian dogma, including the Orthodox profession of faith.[137] The book was richly illustrated with woodcuts based on Orthodox iconography.

The psalter could also serve as a textbook. In the afterword to the Church Slavonic psalter published by the Kuźma Mamonicz publishing house in 1593, the publisher wrote that it was to be used by young people to learn to read.[138] This use did not change over the next few decades, as the inventory of things of the left at the demise of Teodor Kochański from 1668 indicates that "the Ruthenian psalter was given to the sons of the deceased for learning".[139] During the lessons, wax tablets were used, similar to those funded by the canons of Vilnius for the cathedral school. After returning home, pupils copied texts from the tablets into notebooks. On Saturdays, the whole week's material was revised and pupils received education in Christian ethics, and on Sundays catechesis was the subject, consisting of explaining the Gospels and the Acts of the Apostles.[140]

The higher stage of education was the equivalent of the Jesuit grammar class. The teaching of Church Slavonic grammar was aided by textbooks prepared especially for this purpose. In 1596, the printing house of the Vilnius Brotherhood published a book by Laurentius Zizany, *Grammatyka słowieńska* (Slavonic Grammar), and in 1618 the very popular *Grammatike slovenskiya* by Meletius Smotrycki appeared in Vievis, printed by the same publisher.

Education in the last year of school, the rhetorical class, was based on knowledge of Latin, Church Slavonic and, to some extent, Greek.[141] As in the Lviv school, dialectics, arithmetic, geometry, astronomy, and geography were also taught at this level. The teaching methods were similar to those in primary schools (memory exercises, copying of the texts), supplemented by declamations and para-theatrical performances, imitating the methods of the Jesuits. The quality of the education of several dozen pupils was guaranteed by teach-

[137] "And [I believe] in the Holy Spirit, the reviving Lord, who comes from the Father, and with the Father and the Son is glorified and worshipped"; *ibid.*, f. B6v.

[138] T. ILJASZEWICZ, *Drukarnia domu Mamoniczów w Wilnie (1575-1622)* (Vilnius, 1938), p. 55.

[139] *Wilnianie*, p. 254.

[140] *Памятники изданные временною коммиссіею*, p. 104-105; ФЛЕРОВ, *О православных церковных братствах*, pp. 112-113.

[141] MIRONOWICZ, "Szkolnictwo prawosławne", p. 27.

ers (*didaskals*) of the same rank as Zizany, Smotrycki, and Teofil Leontowicz, mentioned above.[142] Nevertheless, in 1629, Melecjusz Smotrycki rated its achievements in the field of the education of young Ruthenians as quite low:

> Where are the schools of Ostroh, Lviv, Brest, and others? What progress has the youth in your Vilnius [school] made, considering your expenses were so huge? This as if you tried to push it through some small slit; the result is as if you tried for many years to squeeze from a stone some water of fire. And it is not because of a shortage of money or your carelessness, because it lacks neither the sensitivity of the teachers nor funding, but because God did not bless the Ruthenian nation in this country. God did not allow anything good either inside or outside. The reason of this is that this nation lost their faith and love, which is so pleasant to God.[143]

We must remember, however, that Smotrycki was already a convert and an opponent of the Orthodox Church when he wrote these words, so it is possible that his criticism is one of many characteristically rhetorical tricks that he used in the polemic that he fought for several decades.[144] The impressive library of mayor Stefan Lebiedzicz, presumably a graduate of the Vilnius Brotherhood's school and its later benefactor, testifies against Smotrycki's severe judgment.[145]

Among the more remarkable graduates were the Orthodox polemicist and archimandrite of Vilnius Józef Bobrykowicz and printer Leon Mamonicz.[146]

The Uniate School

In the first years of the seventeenth century, the Uniates were in a much worse situation than the Orthodox Christians, whose strongest bastion was the Brotherhood with its own printing house and humanist school. There was an urgent need to educate the clergy, but despite the efforts of the Kyiv metropoli-

[142] *Ibid.*, p. 23.

[143] M. SMOTRYCKI, *Paraenesis abo napomnienie od Bogu wielebnego Melecyjusza Smotrzyskiego, rzeczonego archiepiskopa połockiego, episkopa witepskiego i mścisławskiego, archimandryty wileńskiego i dermańskiego do Przezacnego Bractwa Wileńskiego Cerkwie Św. Ducha a w osobie jego do wszystkiego tej strony Narodu Ruskiego uczynione* (Cracow, 1629), p. 32.

[144] D. FRICK, *Meletij Smotryc'kyj* (Cambridge, Mass., 1995), pp. 173-180 and 204-205.

[145] MIRONOWICZ, *Bractwa cerkiewne*, p. 39.

[146] A. MIRONOWICZ, *Józef Bobrykowicz – biskup białoruski* (Białystok, 2003), p. 83; ID., "Drukarnie bractw cerkiewnych", in: *Prawosławne oficyny wydawnicze w Rzeczypospolitej*, ed. A. MIRONOWICZ, U. PAWLUCZUK, and P. CHOMIK (Białystok, 2004), p. 56.

tan bishop Hipacy Pociej, it was not possible to set up a seminary, although from 1601 clerics were educated at the monastery of the Holy Trinity.[147] It was not until 1603 that Józef Welamin Rutski, a humanist and graduate of several Western universities, was sent from Rome to Vilnius and established a Uniate school there.[148] Despite the fears of the Metropolitan bishop Pociej, who resided in Vilnius, that the school run by Rutski would undergo strong Latinisation, it retained its Ruthenian character. In 1608, Rutski published *Theses, to jest pewne przełożenie z nauki o sakramentach cerkiewnych* (Theses, That Is a Certain Explanation of the Doctrine about Ecclesiastical Sacraments), a textbook for the fifty students who were staying in the monastery at that time. One of Rutski's successors was another significant person in the history of the Uniate Church, Leon Kreuza Rzewuski, a graduate from a Jesuit college in Rome. In 1617 he became the archimandrite of the monastery and the rector of the school.[149]

Initially, before the establishment of the seminars kept by the Basilian monks, the Uniate school was more focused than the Orthodox Brotherhood on educating priests and monks, the future staff of the Uniate Church. The teaching methods and the curriculum were similar to those of the Brotherhood's school, with some elements taken from Jesuit education. The subsequent stages of learning included classes in grammar, syntax, and rhetoric, and philosophy and theology.[150] Theology, especially positive-controversial theology, was practised to a relatively great extent. Pupils learned Latin, Greek, Polish, and Church Slavonic from the same textbooks as their adversaries from the Orthodox church of the Holy Spirit. A copy of Smotrycki's grammar book kept in the Jagiellonian Library comes from the library of the Holy Trinity monastery.[151]

[147] J. DZIĘGIELEWSKI, "Pociej Adam", in: *PSB*, 27, p. 31; W. WALCZAK, "O kształceniu duchowieństwa unickiego w Rzeczypospolitej w XVII-XVIII wieku", in: *Nad społeczeństwem staropolskim*, 1, *Kultura – instytucje – gospodarka w XVI-XVIII stuleciu*, ed. K. ŁOPATECKI and W. WALCZAK (Białystok, 2007), p. 486.

[148] M. SZEGDA, "Metropolita Józef Welamin Rutski (1613-1637)", in: *Unia Brzeska: Przeszłośći i teraźniejszość 1596-1996: Materiały niędzynarodwego sympozjum, Kraków 19-20 listopada 1996*, ed. P. NATANEK and R.M. ZAWADSKI (Cracow, 1998), pp. 291-339, at p. 293.

[149] B. STRUMIŃSKI, "Foreword", in: L. KREVZA, *A Defense of Church Unity*, Zakharia Kopystens'ky, *Palinodia*, 1, ed. and trans. R. KOROPECKYJ, D.R. MILLER, and W.R. VEDER (Cambridge, 1995), p. XIV.

[150] PIDŁYPCZAK-MAJEROWICZ, *Bazylianie*, p. 32.

[151] M. SMOTRYCKI, *ГРАММАТІКН Славенския правилное Сунтагма* [...] (Jewie, 1618), BJ 311216 I ("Monasterii Vilnensis S. Trinitatis OSBM Uniae").

In 1615, thanks to Rutski's efforts, in his breve *Piis et elevatis* Pope Paul V gave to the schools kept by the Uniate Basilian Order the same rights as those possessed by the Jesuit collegia. In this way, approval was given to the humanist nature of teaching in Basilian schools, one of the main objectives of which was to shape a 'rhetorical man'.

Protestant Schools

The Vilnius chapter probably sensed the atmosphere in the city, as it did not want to agree to the foundation of a school by Jan Wilamowski. In 1535, in a privilege of Sigismund the Old, the king banned the spread of new ideas, including the sale of Protestant books.[152] However, the royal ban failed to take effect, and only four years later Abraomas Kulvietis decided to establish a new school. He was a humanist, outstanding in Greek and Hebrew studies. He also translated Luther's prayers and psalms into Lithuanian. He had studied in Cracow and at the German universities of Wittenberg and Leipzig, where he had attended lectures given by Martin Luther himself.[153] He started out in Vilnius in 1541 by preaching at St. Anne's church in the lower castle,[154] and as interest in his sermons was significant, in the spring of the same year he decided to open an Evangelical-Augsburg (Lutheran) gymnasium.[155]

Kulvietis' energetic approach, like Wilamowski's earlier attempts, earned him the support of Olbracht Gasztołd (Albertas Goštautas) and he found his greatest ally in the person of Queen Bona, who, at the time lived in the city.[156] For obvious reasons, the bishop was not asked for his consent. From the very beginning, the chapter tried to put an end to Kulvietis' activities, but thanks to the queen's endorsement for a long time this was not possible. Only after Bona's departure from Vilnius did bishop Paweł Holszański and members of the chapter ask the king for help in silencing Kulvietis. The school was closed in

[152] *Potestas episcopo Vilnensi circa fidem in haereticos*, MS MAB F43-426 (VKF5938).

[153] STOBERSKI, *Między dawnymi i młodszymi laty*, p. 98.

[154] P. ŚLEDZIEWSKI, "Kościół św. Anny-św. Barbary intra muros castri vilnensis", *Ateneum Wileńskie* 9 (1933-1934), p. 17.

[155] See D. POCIŪTĖ, "Abraomas Kulvietis and the first Protestant Confessio fidei in Lithuania", in: *Abraomas Kulvietis, Pirmasis Lietuvos Reformacijos paminklas*, p. 47.

[156] STOBERSKI, *Między dawnymi i młodszymi laty*, p. 98; H. BARYCZ, "Kulwieć Abraham", in: *PSB*, 16, pp. 165-166; POCIŪTĖ, "Abraomas Kulvietis and the first Protestant Confessio fidei", pp. 49-50.

1542 and its rector moved to Königsberg, where he obtained the position of professor of Greek at the university.

His school may have been short-lived, but its importance was lasting. It was not only the first Protestant school in the city, but also the first humanist Latin school in Lithuania, with which none of the Catholic schools could compete. It offered a high level of education, as in addition to Kulvietis teaching was provided among others by Stanislaus Rapagelonis (Stanisław Rafajłowicz), a graduate of the universities in Cracow and Wittenberg and later the successor of Kulvietis in the chair of Greek studies at Königsberg.[157]

With such a competitor, the Catholic clergy were well aware of the danger. However, the Catholics' success turned out to be of short duration, as several years later the Protestants made new attempts to establish their schools in the Lithuanian capital, this time successfully thanks to the support of the *voivode* Mikolaj Radziwiłł 'the Black'. Probably in 1555, the Protestant church, which still exists today, was built in German Street. Soon afterwards, a school must have been established there, This was mentioned in the charter issued by Sigismund II Augustus, confirmed by subsequent rulers.[158] The school operated continuously during the period we are interested in and is mentioned in the *Rewizyja* of 1633: "the Saxon Protestant church and the school where the ministers live".[159] The language of instruction was Latin, although it also taught pupils how to read and write German and Polish texts. The level of teaching offered at the turn of the sixteenth and seventeenth centuries was described by Maciej Vorbek-Lettow in the following words:

> At that time, there was a famous school at the Evangelical church, in which my tutor and their alumnus Adamus Rassius, *vir literatissimus*, was employed as the vice-rector. He convinced my parent that I should go to that school, and I was ordered to listen to various *lectiones*. Under priest Baltazar Krośniewicki, *theologiae doctorem, sacra et logicam*. Under Marcin Chmieleski *phisicam et ethicam*. Under my inspector *rhetoricam*.[160]

[157] STOBERSKI, *Między dawnymi i młodszymi laty*, p. 98.

[158] ADAMOWICZ, *Kościół augsburski w Wilnie*, p. 63.

[159] *Rewizyja gospód dworu jego królewskiego mości w mieście Wilnie pod bytność króla jego mości w roku 1636 i w roku 1639*, MS BJ B Slav F 12 and B Slav F 15; Lithuanian edition and translation: M. PAKNYS, *Vilniaus miestas ir miestiečiai 1636 m. Namai, gyventojai, svečiai* (Vilnius, 2006), p. 250, No. 239. *Rewizyja* (Review) became the basis for David Frick's book, cited here many times, see FRICK, "Wstęp", in *Wilnianie*, pp. XXV-XXVII.

[160] VORBEK-LETTOW, *Skarbnica pamięci*, pp. 241-242.

Fig. 12 The Calvinist church and school (number 11) at the beginning of the seventeenth century. Other buildings: 10. the nunnery of the Bernardine Sisters and St. Michael's church; 12. the Bernardine monastery; 14. the Bishop's Manor. A fragment of the view of Vilnius by Tomasz Makowski from *c.* 1604 (cf. Fig. 1).

As a Reformed Evangelist, Mikołaj Radziwiłł 'the Black' significantly contributed to the spread of Calvinism in the Grand Duchy of Lithuania. Among other things, he supported the school at the church in Vilnius. It was located in the quarter of buildings that belonged to the Calvinists at Zborowa Street (today's Volano gatvė). In his will, made at Lukiškės on 27 May 1565, he wrote that "to this church, where my body will be buried, and to the school, I bequeath all the Bibles printed at Brest at my expense".[161] It is not known whether the Calvinist school had been situated before. Initially, it was quite modest, and it was not until the end of the 1580s that it started to grow.

In June 1588 bishop of Vilnius and cardinal Jerzy Radziwiłł reported to King Sigismund III Vasa and *nuncio* Annibale a Capua about the Calvinists' synod, where the Protestants decided to

> organise funds for the establishment of a collegium that would compete with the Jesuits. They have already chosen the location of the school and they are collecting contributions for it. They are bringing lectors from Germany and they have sent a

[161] "Testament Mikołaja Radziwiłła "Czarnego", ed. in: AUGUSTYNIAK, *Testamenty ewangelików reformowanych*, p. 20.

letter to Your Majesty in which they ask Your Majesty for his consent, as it is rumoured, through the help of Your Majesty's sister.[162]

The General Synod, which was attended by sixty representatives from the Polish Kingdom and the Grand Duchy of Lithuania, was held under the patronage of Krzysztof Radziwiłł 'The Thunderbolt', Jerzy Radziwiłł's Protestant cousin. The cardinal expressed his concern that, if the king consented to their actions, it could lead to a weakening of the position of the Jesuit university.[163] Unsurprisingly, Sigismund III, who was hostile towards the Calvinists, did not grant permission, but this did not stop the Vilnius school from operating. In the 1590s, it offered the curriculum of a humanist Latin school.

A letter of 21 June 1595, addressed to the participants of the synod in Toruń, was among others signed by five lecturers from Vilnius: Joannes Moravus *Gymnasii Vilnensis Rector* and four *Collegae Scholae Vilnensi*: Joannes Groterus Rostochensis, Ciriacus Mollerus Leutschovius, Mathias Schmissius Silesiacus Glogoviensis, and Abraamus Wysocki.[164] This means that the school probably offered the programme of a five-year humanistic *gymnasium* (each teacher teaching one cohort), and at least forty pupils were educated there. The student register of the five-year *gymnasium* at Slutsk says that it was attended in the second half of the seventeenth century by about forty to fifty pupils.[165] However, in the second half of the sixteenth and the first two decades of the seventeenth century, the Vilnius school was larger, and it cannot be ruled out that the number of pupils could have reached a hundred. After 1611, the school ran four year-groups, one of its rectors before 1616 being Piotr Siestrzencewicz.[166] In the 1620s, the school fell declined and for some time it did not even have a rector. It was only in 1631 that a "Mr Hartlib" was appointed to this position.[167]

162 Annibale a Capua, *Listy Annibala z Kapui nuncyjusza w Polsce o bezkrólewiu po Stefanie Batorym i pierwszych latach panowania Zygmunta III do wyjścia arcyksięcia Maksymiliana z niewoli*, ed. and trans. M. CYTOWSKA (Warsaw, 1852), pp. 181-182. The royal sister mentioned in the letter was Anna Vasa of Sweden (1568-1625), a Lutheran.

163 LUKŠAITĖ, *Reformacija Lietuvos Didžiojoje Kunigaikštystėje*, pp. 468-469.

164 The letter was published by J. ŁUKASZEWICZ, *Dzieje kościołów wyznania helweckiego w Litwie*, 1 (Poznań, 1842), p. 100; see LUKŠAITĖ, *Reformacija*, p. 471.

165 MS MAB F40-148 (*Album profesorów i studentów gimnazjum słuckiego, 1640-1782*), ff. 39r-54r.

166 *Akta synodów prowincjonalnych Jednoty Litewskiej 1611-1625*, p. 38.

167 Canon 16 and 17 in MS MAB F40-1157 (*Akta synodów litewskich prowincjonalnych 1611-1637*), f. 136v.

The curriculum included grammar and rhetoric classes, but, first of all, learning to read and write in Latin, knowledge of Latin grammar, and Latin stylistics. Joannes Moravus wrote a Latin grammar textbook for the second year of the Vilnius *gymnasium*, which was published in 1592 by Jan Karcan.[168] At a higher level of education, students interpreted classical poetry and rhetorical prose, and also prepared and read texts in Latin and Polish. The school also taught some of the other liberal arts, such as dialectics, elements of arithmetic, geometry, geography, and astronomy. An important element was catechisis, reading the Bible and the teaching of basic evangelical theology, as well as memory exercises, as in all contemporary educational institutions. Much importance was devoted to checking the pupils' progress. From the report of 1693 of the public examination of the Slutsk school one can conclude that the exams lasted several days and consisted of four parts. Students recited fragments of texts, then explained them, wrote essays, and demonstrated their ability to use sentences and excerpts from classical works.[169]

Concern for the state of Evangelical education as a whole, especially at the Vilnius *gymnasium*, was expressed in the decisions of the synods of the Evangelical-Reformed Church, held in Vilnius every year. At the synod of 1 July 1612, it was declared that a contribution for the reconstruction of the school that had burnt down a year earlier was to be made, with six *grosz* to be paid by a peasant and one *złoty* by a nobleman.[170] In 1617, a dormitory for poorer students was established (in the former hospital building).[171] The synod of 1625 adopted measures to support *gymnasia* in Vilnius and Slutsk.[172] At the same time, from 1614 bans were repeatedly issued on sending sons to Jesuit colleges under the threat of exclusion from the community. However, according to Józef Łukaszewicz they do not seem to have been very effective.[173]

[168] J. MORAVUS, *Quaestiones de primis grammatices rudimentis, ex quibusque probatis autoribus in usum secundae classis gymnasi Wilnensis apud orthodoxos collectae*, (Vilnius, 1592). The only known copy, which probably belonged to the seventeenth-century Gdańsk councillor and bibliophile Adrian Engelke, can be found in the Library of the Polish Academy of Sciences in Gdańsk, ref. Dm 1925.8 (I would like to thank Radosław Grześkowiak for inspecting and describing this old printed book).

[169] *Specimen profectuum I classis me Johanne Cień rectore a die 11 Augusti ad diem 14 Novembris factorum exhibitum examine publico, quod anno 1693 post festum S. Martini diebus 17, 18, et 19 Novembris habebatur in illustri Gymnasio Radziwilliano Słucensi*, MS MAB F40-148, ff. 67r-68r.

[170] ŁUKASZEWICZ, *Dzieje kościołów wyznania helweckiego*, p. 152.

[171] *Akta synodów prowincjonalnych Jednoty Litewskiej 1611-1625*, p. 26.

[172] ŁUKASZEWICZ, *Dzieje kościołów wyznania helweckiego*, p. 168.

[173] E.g. canon 3 of the Vilnius synod of 1628: "Since Evangelical parents, having no fear for

Nonetheless, this problem also worried other Protestant communities in the Polish-Lithuanian Commonwealth, not only the Lithuanian one.[174]

Calvinist education found considerable support from the powerful branch of the Radziwiłłs clan of Biržai. In the will of Krzysztof II Radziwiłł, written on 15 September 1619, there is a reference to church schools on his estates: "[there should be] a teacher for young children at every [Protestant] church, *habita proportione loci* [depending on the place]; he should have a decent salary".[175] A year later, his brother Janusz donated "three thousand [złoty] to the church, school, and hospital of the Vilnius Evangelical religion, which were to be given to them *post decessum meum* [after my death]; they were to be given on a one-off basis".[176] In 1629, the Vilnius synod issued an instruction that regulated the functioning of all schools subject to the Calvinist Church, first that of the *gymnasia* in Vilnius and Slutsk then of that in Kėdainiai.[177]

The Vilnius gymnasium attracted respected humanists. Joannes Moravus, mentioned above, the rector of the Vilnius school at least from the early 1590s, corresponded with the Flemish cartographer Abraham Ortelius, sending him information about Lithuania used later in the well-known atlas *Theatrum Orbis Terrarum*.[178] At the turn of the sixteenth and seventeenth centuries, the rector of the school was Quirinus Cnoglerus (Kwiryn Knogler), a lecturer in logic and rhetoric, who in 1602 converted to Catholicism and became known as a Catholic theologian and a courtier of bishop Benedykt Woyna.[179] In 1617, Melchior

God or respect for synodical canons, send their children to the schools of our adversaries, reassuming the canon of 1621 we decide that each priest who feels obliged to fulfil the duties arising from his post shall urgently inquire into this matter in his parish and execute *admonitione prima et secunda adhibita paenam excommunicationis cum scitu superintendentis*, as *contra inobedientis*". MS MAB F40-1157 (*Akta synodów litewskich prowincjonalnych 1611-1637*), f. 107r.

[174] ŁUKASZEWICZ, *Dzieje kościołów wyznania helweckiego*, p. 152. See also LIEDKE, *Wykorzystanie akt synodów*, p. 12.

[175] "Testament Krzysztofa II Radziwiłła", ed. in: AUGUSTYNIAK, *Testamenty ewangelików reformowanych*, p. 145.

[176] "Testament Janusza Radziwiłła", ed. in: AUGUSTYNIAK, *Testamenty ewangelików reformowanych*, p. 174.

[177] Canon 21 from the synod in 1629: *Leges scholarum Lithuanicarum*, MS MAB F40-1157 (*Akta synodów litewskich prowincjonalnych 1611-1637*), f. 115r-115v. Copies of this ordination are, e.g.: MS MAB F40-546, ff. 123r-124r; F40-546, ff. 157r-163r.

[178] S. ALEXANDROWICZ, *Rozwój kartografii Wielkiego Księstwa Litewskiego od XV do poł. XVIII wieku* (Poznań, 1989), pp. 80-81; *Iter Italicum. Accedunt Alia Itinera: A Finding List of Uncatalogued or Incompletely Catalogued Humanistic Manuscripts of the Renaissance in Italian and Other Libraries*, 5, ed. P.O. KRISTELLER (London, 1993), p. 205.

[179] B. NATOŃSKI, *Humanizm jezuicki i teologia pozytywnokontrowersyjna od XVI do XVIII*

Pietkiewicz, the author of a popular catechism, and Salomon Rysiński[180] were appointed examiners at the school. It is also known that the school was supported by another client of Radziwiłł clan, the Vilnius castle judge [*sędzia grodzki*] Daniel Naborowski, who was one of the church's elders in the 1620s. Both sons of the Calvinist nobility and of commoners were educated there.[181] Among its most renowned alumni one finds Józef Welamin Rutski, the later Uniate Metropolitan bishop of Kyiv, who was educated there in the 1580s.[182] Probably no girls were educated at this school.[183]

The school, like the Calvinist church and hospital, was burnt and destroyed several times by Catholics in 1591, 1611, and 1623. The end of its existence on Zborowa Street was brought about by the events of 5 October 1639 which were discussed at the beginning of this chapter.[184] The following year, a royal decree ordered the Calvinist institutions to be placed outside the city walls. In this situation, the Evangelists decided to increase financial support for the Kėdainiai *gymnasium*, established in 1637. The school in Slutsk had already been a significant competitor for the Vilnius school. From the 1630s the Vilnius school, together with the one in Kėdainiai, took over the functions of the main Evangelical educational institutions in Lithuania.[185] After 1640 the Vilnius school still existed, although at the primary level only. The synod of 1643 ordered that

> the catechist *cum domino cantore tam in artibus, quam in pietate sincere* [with the Choir-Master] teach children [both the liberal arts and piety]. They will conduct monthly examinations and exams before the Vilnius synod together with brother minister.[186]

wieku. Nauka i piśmiennictwo (Cracow, 2003), pp. 148 and 164; E. OZOROWSKI, "Knogler Kwiryn", in: *Słownik polskich teologów katolickich*, 2, ed. H.E. WYCZAWSKI (Warsaw, 1982), p. 308.

[180] *Akta synodów prowincjonalnych Jednoty Litewskiej 1611-1625*, p. 44.

[181] *Ibid.*, p. 27.

[182] SZEGDA, "Metropolita Józef Welamin Rutski (1613-1637)",, p. 293.

[183] *Porządki kościelne*, 1648, MS LNMB F93-16.

[184] B. ZWOLSKI, *Sprawa zboru ewangelicko-reformowanego w Wilnie w latach 1639-1641* (Vilnius, 1936), p. 18.

[185] ŁUKASZEWICZ, *Dzieje kościołów wyznania helweckiego*, p. 252.

[186] MS MAB F40-1136 (*Akta synodów litewskich prowincjonalnych 1638-1675*), p. 60.

The Jewish School

The evidence concerning the other schools that operated in Vilnius is rather scarce. First of all, we should mention the school of the Jewish community. As Maciej Vorbek-Lettow recalls, in the middle of the seventeenth century this school was located in the 'Jewish district' on Szklanna Street (Stiklių Street), adjacent to the Słucki tenement house (which was located on German Street).[187]

According to the extant sources, in the second half of the seventeenth century a pious foundation was established for boys from poorer families, who were to start their education in the Talmud Torah primary school (*heder*), which prepared them for later studies at the yeshiva.[188] Vorbek-Lettow's mention of the school proves that it had existed previously, especially as several outstanding authors of rabbinical literature from Vilnius are known, including the Talmud scholar Joshua Heschel Zoref (1633-1700), who was active in the first half of the seventeenth century. The famous rabbi Joshua Heschel ben Joseph, born in Vilnius around 1578, completed his rabbinical education in Przemyśl and in other towns of the Polish Crown, but he may have acquired basic knowledge and skills before he left his hometown. This means that the level of teaching at the Vilnius *heder* must have been higher than that at the typical Jewish schools of the time.[189]

The Vilnius school presumably performed the same functions as the schools in other Lithuanian Jewish communities.[190] If the curriculum resembled that of a lower-level school operating in Kazimierz near Cracow, then one may assume that it taught the Hebrew alphabet, reading, translation of the Torah into Yiddish, exegesis of the Holy Scriptures according to Beer Moshe's Yiddish translation and Rashi's Hebrew commentary, as well as ethics and principles of good behaviour, writing in Hebrew, and arithmetic.[191] It is possible that

[187] VORBEK-LETTOW, *Skarbnica pamięci*, p. 244.

[188] I. KLAUSNER, "Vilnius", in: *EJ*, 20, p. 529.

[189] M. SAPERSTEIN, "Education and homiletics", in: *The Cambridge History of Judaism*, 7, *The Early Modern World, 1500-1815*, ed. J. KARP and A. SUTCLIFE (Cambridge, 2018), p. 415.

[190] On early modern Jewish education in Central-Eastern Europe, see I. FISHMAN, *the History of Jewish Education in Central Europe, from the End of the Sixteenth to the End of the Eighteenth Century* (London, 1944), pp. 104-109; SAPERSTEIN, "Education and homiletics", p. 416. Unfortunately, the author does not refer to the one of the most important sources, the statute of the Cracow yeshiva from 1595.

[191] *Statut krakowskiej gminy żydowskiej z roku 1595 i jego uzupełnienia*, ed. and trans. (on the basis of a copy made by M. Bałaban) A. JAKIMYSZYN (Cracow, 2005), pp. 95-96; J. SCHALL,

shortly before the Muscovite invasion a higher-level institution, a yeshiva, was founded as well. This is suggested by the presence of significant numbers of suitably qualified scholars who could support such an institution.

As in the case of the fifteenth-century cathedral school, the alumni of the Vilnius Jewish school went to major schools, for instance to the yeshivas at Cracow and Lublin. The Cracow yeshiva was attended, among others, by Moses ben Isaac Judah Lima (*c.* 1615-*c.*1670) and Shabbatai ben Meir HaKohen (1621-1662).

The Tartar School

There was a Tatar school in Vilnius at least from the middle of the sixteenth century, although the only mention of it is Hostounský's letter quoted previously. It is possible that it was located near the mosque in Lukiškės (Łukiszki),[192] and was mentioned in 1651 by bishop Tyszkiewicz.[193] There are two additional reasons to assume its existence. The first was, that in such a large community there was a need for religious education for young followers of Islam. In 1631, there were 32 Tatar houses in Lukiškės. This means that several hundred Muslims lived there.[194] The second is the evidence for the ability of

Historia Żydów w Polsce, na Litwie i Rusi z 25 ilustracjami (Lviv, 1934), p. 120; Sz.A.A. CYGIELMAN, "Zagadnienia organizacji i programów nauczania szkolnictwa podstawowego w krakowskiej gminie żydowskiej na przełomie XVI i XVII w.", in: *Żydzi w dawnej Rzeczypospolitej: Materiały konferencji "Autonomia Żydów w Rzeczypospolitej szlacheckiej": Międzywydziałowy Zakład Historii i Kultury Żydów w Polsce: Uniwersytet Jagielloński, 22-26 IX 1986*, ed. A. LINK-LENCZOWSKI and T. POLAŃSKI (Wrocław, 1991), pp. 284-296.

[192] The Tartar settlement in Lukiškės was founded by Duke Vytautas at the turn of the fourteenth and fifteenth centuries, and it is probable that the mosque was built at that time. For the first time it was mentioned in 1558. Its detailed description can be found in a letter from an anonymous Pole to David Chytraeus written in 1581: "Ex epistola a Polono ad Davidem Chytraeum, scripta anno 1581", in: *Russia seu Moscovia itemque Tartaria commentario topographico atque politico illustratae* (Leiden, 1630), p. 322. See KRYCZYŃSKI, *Historia meczetu w Wilnie*, pp. 8, 15. The wooden mosque was built in the seventeenth century and considerably rebuilt in the nineteenth century. In the 1960s the Soviet authorities completely destroyed the mosque and the old Tartar cemetery. There are several iconographical sources depicting the mosque (the oldest from 1781, by Franciszek Smuglewicz.

[193] A.B. ZAKRZEWSKI, "Osadnictwo tatarskie w Wielkim Księstwie Litewskim – aspekty wyznaniowe", *Acta Baltico-Slavica* 20 (1991), p. 138.

[194] "Tartars who lived in Lukiškės near Vilnius upon Neris in a total of twenty-two houses shall provide four horses", quoted after: P. BORAWSKI, W. SIENKIEWICZ, and T. WASILEWSKI, "Rewizja dóbr tatarskich 1631 r. – sumariusz i wypisy", *Acta Baltico-Slavica* 20 (1991), p. 95.

Lithuanian and Vilnius Tatars to use Arabic writing.[195] Learning usually took place at a mullah's house. This was a religious school and probably not a large one. It taught pupils how to read the Quran using special textbooks called *tajweed*[196] and writing in the Arabic alphabet. Perhaps it was also meant to train future Muslim clergy, but in the 1580s Possevino reported that candidates were sent "to Arabia" for study.[197]

Summary

While in the first half of the sixteenth century education in Vilnius could be compared neither with Cracow nor with other major cities of the Polish Crown such as Gdańsk, Poznań, or Lviv, in the second half of the century it became the most important educational centre of the Polish-Lithuanian Commonwealth alongside Cracow.

The number of people involved in educational activities in Vilnius in the first decades of the seventeenth century may have reached as many as 1,500 persons. At the Academy of Vilnius alone, there were from 1,000 to 1,200 students, to which at least a dozen or so professors should be added.[198] The other schools were smaller and numbered 30 students in the case of the cathedral school, up to perhaps 50 or even 70 at the Orthodox Brotherhood and Calvinist schools, and about 100 at St. John's school. The teachers, examiners, tutors, and supervisors of these schools, as well as bookkeepers whose clients were also students, must also be taken into account. With a population of 20,000 people before the Muscovite invasion, they formed a significant percentage of the urban population.

In the first half of the seventeenth century, those who had attended Christian schools in Vilnius acquired (or at least had a good chance of acquiring) extensive literacy skills based on a few common elements. In all of them, the fundamental language of writing was Latin. Learning to read was based on reading biblical books (usually the psalter). Great importance was attached to developing one's memory and storing texts in it. The most important subjects

[195] *AVAK*, vol. 31, pp. 185-186, item 122; A. KONOPACKI, *Życie religijne Tatarów na ziemiach Wielkiego Księstwa Litewskiego w XVI-XIX wieku* (Warsaw, 2010), pp. 127-128.

[196] KRYCZYŃSKI, *Tatarzy litewscy*, p. 217.

[197] Quoted after KRYCZYŃSKI, *ibid.*, p. 212.

[198] In 1644, humanist schools employed nine lecturers; see PIECHNIK, *Rozkwit Akademii Wileńskiej*, p. 10.

were grammar and rhetoric. Similar methods and teaching aids were employed, and a similar Latin reading canon was used. Thanks to the diversity of several Christian communities, the pupils of different schools were able to co-create the Vilnius 'cultural crossroad' (or *Kulturbund*)[199] and to participate at different levels in the negotiation and exchange of its components.

[199] I coined this term following the term *Sprachbund*. The *Sprachbund* (a linguistic area or language crossroads) is a group of several languages which belong to different linguistic groups but share many similarities caused by they geographical proximity and mutual interactions. The *Kulturbund* is as an analogous phenomenon to the *Sprachbund* on a territory where several different cultures interact and influence each other. The existence of the *Sprachbund* in the Grand Duchy of Lithuania is a arguable (cf. DANYLENKO, "A missing chain? On the sociolinguistics of the Grand Duchy of Lithuania", p. 38).

Chapter 4

Loci Textuales of Women

Although in an early modern city men dominated in the written word, women also constituted a specific group of text users. And they also took part in the production of texts. On the following pages, I will answer the question how they managed to participate in the rhetorical organisation of the city. The chapter is divided into three parts. The first two will discuss the texts created and used by lay women; next we will turn to those written and used by nuns. The following issues will be at the centre of attention. Which types of sources speak of women's literacy? How did women acquire competence in reading and writing? And for which purposes did women use their reading and writing skills in early modern Vilnius?

The City

There are no objective criteria that allow us, even approximately, to estimate the level of literate skills and the use of texts by men living in medieval and early modern Vilnius. With regard to women, this task is even more difficult.[1] The problem is important, many sources inform us that women were users of texts and had a wide range of literary skills. Some of them exhibited the skills of pragmatic literacy, while others were fully literate. How can we deal with the participation of women in the literary culture of late medieval and early modern Vilnius?

[1] J. Partyka, *"Żona wyćwiczona": Kobieta pisząca w kulturze XVI i XVII wieku* (Warsaw, 2004), p. 85.

In the late fifteenth century and later, in early modern times, many members of the male elites were also active members of the reading and writing communities, and the clergy were losing their monopoly of literacy.[2] Women had fewer opportunities to become fully or even partially literate persons, because reading and writing were not activities that were primarily considered to be feminine. Their access to education and obtaining literary skills were limited. What is more, their legal status prevented them to perform many social roles reserved in practice to males (for instance being a priest, an urban official, or a scholar).

Women reached for the pen less frequently than men, timidly and shyly, and their access to texts was limited. Basically, a literate or semi-literate Vilnius woman was not supposed to boast about her contact with texts and the pen; if she did, it was supposed to be an act of her obedience or piety: prayer or the reading of admonitions intended for a pious Christian or Jewish woman.[3] Reading and writing were supposed to reproduce the role designated to her by the dominant cultures.[4] Furthermore, what a woman read or wrote was under constant control and self-control, as will be discussed later in this chapter. As a consequence, the surviving sources of information about the literacy of Vilnius women are not only modest but are also silent about many more things than in the case of men.[5]

However, in an urban space, especially in such a city as Vilnius, women had to deal with many financial matters. This required the production and use of a wide range of texts. What is more, the religious culture of the time required from all people, women as well as men, to be in contact with the word of God or other religious texts.[6] This specific position of women, whose literate activity was at the same time dubious and mandatory, is the main reason why I distinguish women as a separate group of text users, despite the fact that they belonged to different social strata.

[2] CLANCHY, *Looking Back from the Invention of Printing*, p. 27.

[3] SNOOK, *Reading Women*, p. 41.

[4] M.E. BURKE, J. DONAWERTH, L.L. DOVE, and K. NELSON, "Introduction", in: *Women, Writing and the Reproduction of Culture in Tudor and Stuart Britain*, ed. M.E. BURKE, J. DONAWERTH, L.L. DOVE, and K. NELSON (Syracuse, 2000), p. XXIV.

[5] S. FISHER and J.E. HALLEY, "Introduction: The lady vanishes: The problem of women's absence in late medieval and renaissance texts", in: *Seeking the Women in Late Medieval and Renaissance Writings: Essays in Feminist Contextual Criticism*, ed. S. FISHER and J.E. HALLEY (Knoxville, 1989), pp. 3-4.

[6] See Chapter 9.

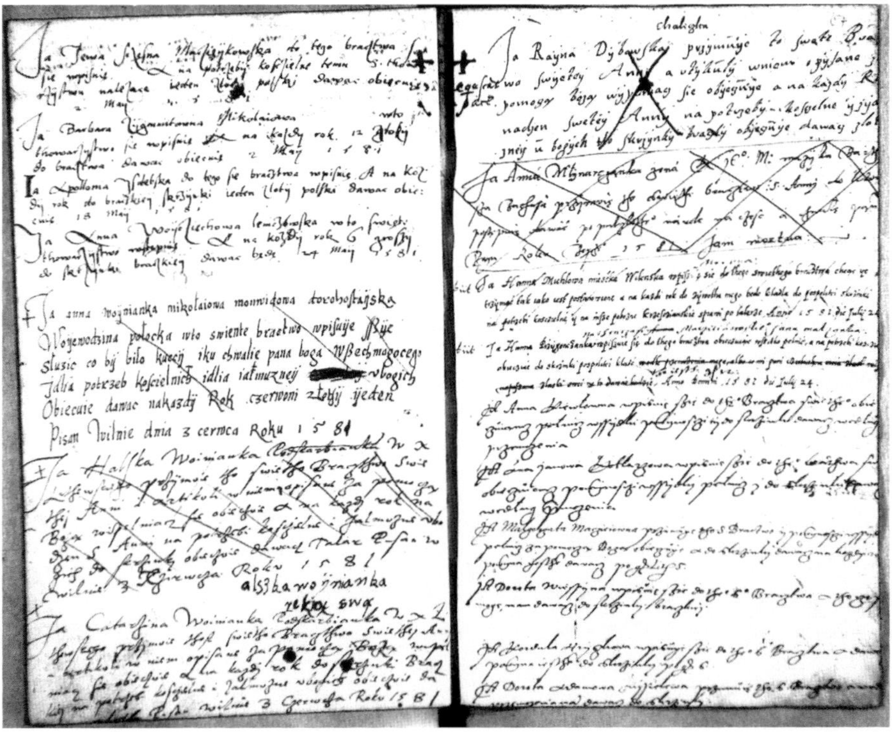

Fig. 13 Register of the Archconfraternity of St. Anne, entries of women from 1581. MS Vilnius, LVIA, F1135, ap. 4, nr 472, ff. 66v–67r. Reproduced with the permission of LVIA.

For the Polish-Lithuanian Commonwealth, statistical data concerning any historical problem appear only in the second half of the eighteenth century, and the value of richer source materials from other urban settlements and regions needs to be methodically questioned.[7] We can, however, analyse individual cases of using texts by the female citizens of early modern Vilnius.

The level of female literacy was generally low, but it also depended on social status.[8] Studies that focus on the Polish Crown, chiefly on Lesser Poland, as well as on other European countries, show that in the case of both men

[7] PARTYKA, *"Żona wyćwiczona"*, p. 85. István G. Tóth stressed the fact that research on the level of literacy in early modern Central Europe should be carried out in different way than in Western Europe (I.G. TÓTH, *Literacy and Written Culture in Early Modern Central Europe* (Budapest, 2000), pp. 47-48).

[8] Tóth pointed out a similar situation in Hungary (TÓTH, *Literacy and Written Culture*, p. 123).

and women reading and writing skills were shown by the nobility and wealthy town dwellers.[9] This does not necessarily mean, however, that women from other social groups were completely deprived of opportunities to take part in the circulation of texts and ideas.[10] This holds true also for Vilnius.

The main sources for our investigation are the records of the administrative and legal institutions, which kept various types of documents whose preparation involved women. First of all, there were women who possessed significant property; the urban poor usually were not in need of cultural and educational capital,[11] although there were exceptions as well. The archival documents mostly come from the first half of the seventeenth century and include wills, financial transactions, and donations. An interesting source is the register of the Archconfraternity of St. Anne, kept from 1580, to which both Catholic men and women belonged. Every member joining the confraternity had to put their name in the book, but in those many of members who could not write their admission was recorded by a secretary. In exceptional instances, we come across entries made by women personally or at least their signatures. Almost all of them were made by women originating from the families of magnates or from the urban elites. 72 entries referring to women accepted into the confraternity in the years 1582-1605 are accompanied by their signatures, such as that of Katarzyna Laskowska, who left her personal trace in the confraternity book in January 1582, undertaking to pay an annual fee of 12 *grosz*, or Halszka Grajewska, the wife of the pantler (*stolnik*, a servant in charge of bread on the table) of Podlasie, who promised to pay 1 red (i.e. gold) *złoty* in June of the same year.[12] The signatures in this book were executed by the wealthiest of women. They could put their signatures there because their social background and their material wealth had allowed them to acquire the skill of writing. The use of signatures in this register informs us about two things. Firstly, high social status and property were unconditionally related to the use of texts, and literacy was conditioned mostly economically.[13] Secondly, in the two last de-

[9] W. URBAN, "Umiejętność pisania w Małopolsce w II połowie XVI wieku", *Przegląd Historyczny* 68.2 (1977), pp. 245-246; FISHER and HALLEY, "Introduction: The lady vanishes", p. 9; A. KARPIŃSKI, *Kobieta w mieście polskim w II pol. XVI i w XVII wieku* (Warsaw, 1995), p. 295.

[10] S. PEYRONEL RAMBALDI, "Introduzione: Per una storia delle donne nella Riforma", in: R.H. BAINTON, *Donne della Riforma in Germania, in Italia e in Francia*, trans. F. SARNI (Turin, 1992), p. 37.

[11] The concept of cultural and educational capital is borrowed here from a classic conception of the social field of Pierre Bourdieu (BOURDIEU, *Distinction*, pp. 13-14).

[12] MS LVIA F1135, ap. 4, no. 472, f. 68v.

[13] As was already pointed out in Chapter 1.

cades of the sixteenth century putting one's signature became a common practice to validate documents, at least among the literate elite of the Grand Duchy of Lithuania and its capital. Literate and pragmatically literate women were aware of the meaning of a signature.[14] Documents, also those issued by women, tended to include clauses written by witnesses that were stamped with their seals, and, from the second half of the sixteenth century also signatures are found. They are very valuable for us, even though they do not tell us everything about the writing competence of their authors; a person able to sign a document was not necessarily capable of writing anything else, while a person utterly incapable of writing, including their name, could have been able to read. There were many more people who read individually or listened when others were reading out aloud than those who could sign for themselves. Even though signatures cannot be used to measure the level of literacy skills in early modern Vilnius, they are valuable indications of pragmatic literacy nevertheless and of the development of ways of validating documents.[15]

A rather large number of men in early modern Vilnius were able to write their signatures by hand.[16] They were sometimes lopsided, misshapen, and childlike.[17] Many men never got a proper education, or during their life they

[14] The rising role of signatures in the Grand Duchy of Lithuania is still a research problem to be examined. Probably Vilnius was a leading place where signatures became common among users of script relatively easy. A similar situation can be observed in Little Poland and Cracow. See W. URBAN, "Umiejętność pisania w Małopolsce", pp. 231-257. In Hungary, signatures were a standard form of validating documents only in the seventeenth century (TÓTH, *Literacy and Written Culture*, pp. 96-97).

[15] In his paper, Wacław Urban used signatures as an indication of literacy among Lesser Poland nobility in the second half of the sixteenth century. He assumed that if somebody could put his or her signature under a document, he or she could write (URBAN, *Umiejętność pisania w Małopolsce*, pp. 233-234). This simple equation of "nice signature" ("ładny podpis") = "literacy" led him to the too optimistic conclusions that majority of the Lesser Poland noblemen (more than 96-98%) and many noblewomen (49%) could write in the third quarter of the sixteenth century. The data presented by Urban (*ibid.*, p. 238) was later used by other researchers (e.g. by TÓTH, *Literacy and Written Culture*, pp. 206-207). Anna Adamska sensibly explained why a signature or its lack cannot be proof of somebody's ability to writing or reading. See A. ADAMSKA, "Stąd do wieczności: Testament w perspektywie piśmienności pragmatycznej na przełomie średniowiecza i epoki nowożytnej", *Kwartalnik Historii Kultury Materialnej* 61.2 (2013), p. 196.

[16] In the last decades of the sixteenth century, in Lithuania signatures became a common way of validating documents alongside seals.

[17] I.G. TÓTH, "Illiterate and Latin-Speaking gentlemen: The many faces of the Hungarian gentry in the early modern period", in: *The Development of Literate Mentalities in East Central Europe*, ed. A. ADAMSKA and M. MOSTERT (Turnout, 2004), p. 526.

may have rarely written anything,[18] but most of them displayed a greater or lesser skill in handling a pen. With regard to women, this was different. The acts of the Vilnius cathedral chapter contain an extract from the municipal registers: the last will of Regina Lewonowiczówna Frezowa about a bequest to the chapter. At the end of the document the donor confirms:

> This is why I gave my dear husband, Mr Jachim Frez, this sheet bearing my seal. And since I myself cannot write, I asked the honourable seal-bearing gentlemen and my friends, whose names are expressed in the signatures beneath, to affix their seals and signatures. Written in Vilnius in the year one thousand six hundred and thirty seventh on the fourteenth day of July.
>
> Five seals are affixed to the sheet, as well as handwritten signatures with the following statements:
>
> Being orally asked to affix my seal to this sheet by a woman not skilled in handwriting – Symon Łachmowicz, the undersigned. Orally asked in front of witnesses by Mrs Regina Lewonowiczówna Jachimowa Frezowa not being capable of writing herself to affix my seal – Kazimierz Giedroyć, with my own hand. Being asked by the aforementioned person incapable of writing to affix my seal – Franciszek Szystowski, *manu propria*. Orally asked by Mrs Regina Lewonowiczówna Jachimowa Frezowa not capable of writing herself to affix my seal – Maciej Daubor Markiewicz, *manu propria*.[19] (original in Polish)

The legacy of the illiterate Mrs Frezowa was by no means an exception. Two years later, a Mrs Wasilewska authenticated her legacy in a similar manner: "This is, therefore, my last will. Sealed and signed on my request, due to my lacking the skill of writing, by the gentlemen named beneath next to their signatures".[20] Regina Parkiewiczówna Bartłomiejowa Gilowa affixed her own

[18] ADAMSKA, "Stąd do wieczności", p. 196.

[19] *"I na tom dała małżonkowi memu miłemu, panu Jachimowi Frezowi ten mój list z pieczęcią moją. A że sama pisać nie umiem, prosiłam o przyłożenie pieczęci i podpis rąk ich mości panów pieczętarzów przyjaciół moich imiony na podpisach niżej wyrażonych. Pisan w Wilnie roku tysiąc sześćset trzydziestego siódmego miesiąca Junii czternastego dnia.*
U tego listu pieczęci przyciśnionch pięć, a podpis rąk tymi słowy:
Ustnie proszony pieczętarz do tego listu od osoby pisać nieumiejącej ręką swą podpisał Symon Łachmowicz. Ustnie oczewisto proszon i pieczętarz od pani Reginy Lewonowiczówny Jachimowej Frezowej jako pisać nieumiejącej Kazimierz Giedroyć ręką swą. Proszony pieczętarz od osoby wyż mianowanej pisać nieumiejącej Franciszek Szystowski manu propria. Ustnie proszony pieczętarz od pani Reginy Lewonowiczówny Jachimowej Frezowej jako pisać nieumiejącej Maciej Daubor Markiewicz manu propria". MS MAB F43 – 218 (VKF452; *Akta kapituły wileńskiej 1632-1643*), f. 318v.

[20] MS MAB F43-218 (VKF452; *Akta kapituły wileńskiej 1632-1643*), f. 360r.

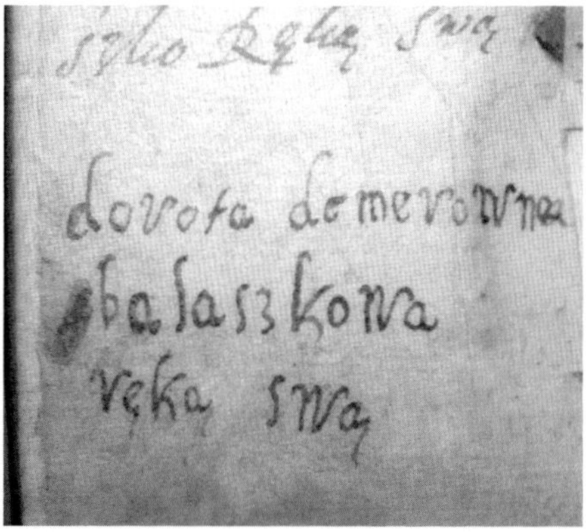

Fig. 14 Signature of Dorota Demerówna Balaszkowa, 1631. MS Vilnius, LVIA, F23, ap. 1, nr 5096, f. 64r. Photo J. Niedźwiedź.

seal to a document of 3 February 1630, but as she was unable to put her signature she asked witnesses to do it for her: "Simon Narkiewicz was asked orally to affix his seal to this sheet by a woman not capable of writing, with his own hand".[21] Under the last will from 1652 of Anna Prokopowiczówna Aleksandrowa Czyżowa, who could not write, a signature was put in her name by Michał Czyż,[22] and under a similar document of Marta Janówna Marcinowa Kiewliczowa from 1634 there are the signatures of two witnesses, but not her own.[23] We should add that these women belonged to the group of wealthy town dwellers. In this respect, Vilnius was not extraordinary: as late as the mid-seventeenth century there was a high percentage of illiterate Cracow patrician ladies.[24]

When women's signatures finally do begin to appear, they deserve increased attention. They were usually written with a rather unskilled hand and resembled the signature of Dorota Demerówna Balaszkowa (Fig. 14).[25] These may have been the only words she was able to write. And Akwilina Stryludzianka Dorofiejewiczowa signed herself in Ruthenian despite the fact that her will was drawn up in Polish.[26]

21 MS LVIA F23, ap. 1, no. 5096, f. 62r.

22 MS LVIA F23, ap. 1, no. 5096, fol. 607r.

23 MS LVIA F22, ap. 1, no. 5333, f. 173v.

24 KARPIŃSKI, *Kobieta w mieście polskim*, p. 295.

25 MS LVIA F23, ap. 1, no. 5096, f. 64r.

26 MS LVIA F22, ap. 1, no. 5333, ff. 257r-257v. The analysis of other documents, not only written by female authors, suggests that most of the literate inhabitants of Vilnius were able to write in only one alphabet and only one language. The exceptions are some professional scribes, officials, and Orthodox and Uniate clergymen and monks. Writing with many scripts by one person is a topic to be investigated in future research.

Fig. 15 Signature of Anna Dygoniowa, wife of Marcin Dygoń, a councillor of the city, 1649. MS Vilnius, LVIA, F23, ap. 1, nr 5096, f. 418r. Photo J. Niedźwiedź.

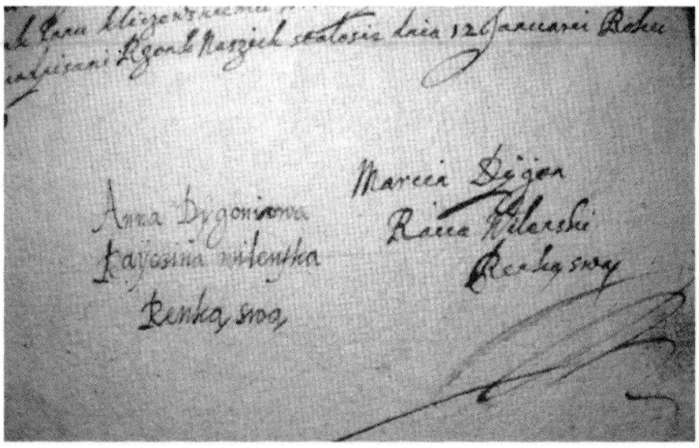

There are, nonetheless, exceptions such as the documents and letter of Anna Giblowa,[27] whose female author must have learnt to read and write in her childhood or early youth. They were issued as early as the second half of the seventeenth century. Her handwriting provides evidence of skill of a high level and is in no way worse than that of men or nuns taught to read and write from childhood.[28] We should mention that Mrs Giblowa could not have been destined for a nunnery, as she came from the notable Vilnius Lutheran Engelbrecht family. And this may be the key to the secret of her education. In Vilnius and in other parts of the Polish-Lithuanian Commonwealth, the Protestants paid much more attention to the education of women than Catholics did[29]

Seventeenth-century female handwriting is usually based on chancery script (*cancellaresca*), as in the case of this signature from 1649: "Anna Dygoniowa, [wife of Marcin] Vilnius councillor, with her own hand" (Fig. 15).[30] Similar clumsy signatures, or the lack of them, may point to the different roles of men and women in the world of texts in early modern Vilnius.[31] Women did not attend either parish or grammar schools, and therefore their

[27] *Wilnianie*, p. 68.

[28] Church regulations (Catholic, Orthodox, Protestant, and Uniate ones), the *Ratio studiorum*, municipal or ecclesiastical documents, books, primers, etc. tell us that most male inhabitants of Vilnius in the sixteenth and seventeenth acquired their writing skills in their childhood. These sources are discussed in Chapter 3.

[29] PARTYKA, "Żona wyćwiczona", pp. 81-82.

[30] MS LVIA F23, ap. 1, no. 5096, f. 418r.

[31] In the generally illiterate society of early modern East-Central Europe, men also could write a clumsy hand. I.G. Tóth quoted examples of seventeenth-century semi-literate noblemen and burghers from western Hungary who could not sign any documents or their signatures reveal a lack of fluency in writing (TÓTH, *Literacy and Written Culture*, p. 98-101). However, Vilnius was a city where the average level of literacy was higher than in the rural territories of western Hungary. The existing documents suggest the members of the city elite (wealthy burghers, nobility, and clergymen) exhibited good writing skills, sometimes in several languages.

handwriting is often unrefined.[32] A woman's hand was rarely sufficiently adapted for handling a pen or signing a document, and in the sixteenth and seventeenth centuries it was not even believed to be created for this purpose. Nevertheless, most or maybe all of the women in Vilnius were pragmatically literate, evidence of which we find in the documents from the municipal registers or in the registers kept by other offices.

According to the Magdeburg law, which was introduced to Vilnius by the privilege of King Jogaila (Władysław Jagiełło) in 1387, a woman could represent herself in a number of legal actions.[33] This meant that the women could and had to deal with legal texts such as documents of transactions, last wills, donations, etc. Researchers pointed out a high percentage of female clients of the municipal courts in late medieval Poland, especially when it comes to making the last wills.[34] Although the Vilnius municipal archives from the fifteenth century do not survive, a similar situation may have occurred in this city as well. However, in practice the legal position of women and men in the municipal court was not equal. The main causes of this situation were two: women did not exhibit such literary skill as men did; and the law favoured men as legal subjects.

For example, Anna Stor, a widow of the Vilnius goldsmith Jan, would not have been able to read her own testament of 1572 because it was written in Latin.[35] However, she had to know its content, since there was a strong legal requirement that a will would be read aloud and translated to the testator before validation.[36] In this instance, Mrs Stor could be counted among the semi-literates, and she had to hire a professional scribe who not only wrote but also orally translated the document for his client. There was a common practice to hire a lawyer in such situations but men, especially from the city elite (and the

[32] H. Wolfe, "Women's handwriting", in: *The Cambridge Companion to Early Modern Women's Writing*, pp. 27-35.

[33] The Magdeburg law states that in court a woman should have her guardian with her: "It is not decent that women presented their cases or sued somebody in the court without her guardian" (P. Szczerbic, *Speculum Saxonum, albo prawo saskie i majdeburskie porządkiem obiecadła z łacińskich i niemieckich egzemplarzów zebrane, a na język polski z pilnością i wiernie przełożone*, 1, ed. G.M. Kowalski (Cracow, 2016), p. 41, No. 33). *Promptuarium iuris provincialis Saxonici quod Speculum Saxonum vocatur, tum et municipalis Maideburgensis summa diligentia recollectum et ad communem editum utilitatem*, ed. M. Jaskier (Cracow, 1535), p. 48 v.

[34] A. Bartoszewicz, *Urban Literacy*, pp. 387-388; Adamska, "Stąd do wieczności", p. 190.

[35] ms lvia F22, ap. 1, no. 5333, ff. 77r-787r; a copy by Michał Baliński, manuscript bj, sign. 2926, pp. 37-38.

[36] Adamska, "Stąd do wieczności", p. 191.

late goldsmith Jan Stor had belonged to that group) could have had more opportunities to learn Latin and consequently be able to read and understand the content of the document without professional help. Anna Stor almost certainly could not do that.

Later, by the end of the sixteenth and in the seventeenth century, when wills were also written in Ruthenian or Polish, a woman herself could – if she was capable of reading and writing – read and sign a will. The Magdeburg law, other regulations, and local legal traditions allowed women to do so, if only because men and women had equal rights to the inheritance.[37] However, there were some legal actions from which women were excluded. This meant that a woman – unlike a man – could not take an active part in issuing or even using certain legal texts in the Grand Duchy of Lithuania.

An example of such a situation prevented women from being witnesses of the last wills. This role was always reserved for men, for instance relatives, sons, neighbours, and friends. Inheritance law in Vilnius was based on regulations in use in Poland since 1530.[38] The privilege of King Sigismund I the Old for Vilnius from 1543 stipulated:

> From this time, that is from the date of issuing our document, those testaments which were validated by the burgers of Vilnius in other offices than the municipal office (as the Magdeburg law states), do not have any legal validity. From that time all burghers and citizens of the city of Vilnius are obliged to validate their last wills in the municipal office accordingly to the customs of the Magdeburg law.[39] (translation from Polish)

[37] J. WYSMUŁEK, "Urban testaments in Poland: Research present and future", in: *Uses of the Written Word in Medieval Towns: Medieval Urban Literacy II*, ed. M. MOSTERT and A. ADAMSKA (Turnhout, 2014), p. 302; J. WYSMUŁEK, *Testamenty mieszczan krakowskich (XIV-XV wiek)* (Warsaw, 2015), p. 185.

[38] M. MIKUŁA, "Statuty prawa spadkowego w miastach polskich prawa magdeburskiego (do końca XVI wieku)", *Z Dziejów Prawa* 7 (2014), pp. 33-63; ID., "Tradycje prawne w regulacjach testamentowych w miastach Królestwa Polskiego XIV-XVI wieku: Prawo sasko-magdeburskie, prawo kanoniczne i rzymskie oraz prawodawstwo lokalne", *Kwartalnik Historii Kultury Materialnej*, 68.2 (2020), pp. 131-158.

[39] The original of the document was issued in the Ruthenian language. *Zbiór praw i przywilejów*, pp. 75-76. The content of the document and other privileges given by King Sigismund I the Old to the city council, in which he ordered applying the Magdeburg law in the city, suggests that the process of consolidation of municipal authorities in Vilnius was concluded only in the first decades of the sixteenth century.

We do not know the municipal statute (*wilkierz*) issued by the Vilnius authorities which regulated the procedures of issuing last wills in detail. However, in Polish commentaries to the Magdeburg law from the sixteenth century, used also in the towns of the Grand Duchy of Lithuania, there is a strict regulation about who can assist validating a testament as a witness:

> If somebody wants to give somebody something from his or her goods, he or she must do that being in good health in attendance of seven men, to whom he or she reveals his or her will. He or she must tell this also to his or her heir in their presence. And this handing over will be valid. And these witnesses shall give their evidence about the will of the testator and it shall be testified – if necessary – with the seal of the judge or another official. The witness of such a document cannot be a woman, the heir, the deaf nor the blind, a convict, an excommunicated person, an outlaw, nor a man in infamy (Polish *bezecny*, Latin *infamis*). (original in Polish)

The regulations of the *Statute of the Grand Duchy of Lithuania*, which was also the legislation used in Vilnius, also contained detailed regulations about last wills. The third version of the *Statute* (1588) stipulated that

> at the drawing up of a will the following persons may not act as seal bearers or witnesses. First of all, those who are unfit to make their will, secondly women, thirdly, executors of the will or its protectors, fourthly, also those who will inherit according to the will.[40] (translated from Polish)

And in fact, from the sixteenth and seventeenth centuries in Vilnius, there are no wills signed or sealed by female witnesses.

The aforementioned example reveals that the use of texts by women, even those from the urban patriciate, was even more restricted than in the case of common men. The existing social and legal system continued to keep them in a state of functional illiteracy or semi-literacy. This, in turn, resulted in a strong dependence on men. A woman who could not write or who was not allowed to

[40] *Statut*, p. 235, chapter 8, art. 5. This was due to the different status of men and women. For most of her life, a woman was under the sway of a man, and her self-dependence in legal actions was limited. This pertains both to inheritance, trading assets, and even the raising of children. G. PERCZYŃSKA, "Kobiety Iszkołci, czyli dzieje zarządzania majętnością", in: *Administracja i życie codzienne w dobrach Radziwiłłów XVI-XVIII wieku*, ed. U. AUGUSTYNIAK (Warsaw, 2009), pp. 42-43; A. LESIAK, "Kobiety z rodu Radziwiłłów w świetle inwentarzy i testamentów (XVI-XVIII w.)", in: *Administracja i życie codzienne*, pp. 131-138.

put her signature on a document had to rely on the help of literate men, not on women.

Against this background, the lay female inhabitants of Vilnius in the second half of the sixteenth century and the first half of the seventeenth century who belonged to the nobility, the aristocracy, or were members of the royal family were exceptionally privileged. Presumably, many of them were literate, which may be deduced from the letters and legal documents that have been preserved.[41]

From the second half of the sixteenth century, many women exhibited good literary skills and took an active part in 'written conversation'.[42] One of them was Zuzanna Nonhartówna Chreptowiczowa (who died in 1646), the wife of the *voivode* of Pärnu (Parnawa), who, "in her young age, behaved gracefully with respect to maidens' virtues, which blossomed in her heart as beautiful flowers in a pleasure garden".[43] Her father, the burgrave (*horodniczy*) of Vilnius castle Piotr Nonhart, made every effort to equip her with a solid literary education, traces of which are found in the fragments of her correspondence that have survived. More frequent examples of the epistolography of Lithuanian wives and daughters of magnates, created both by themselves and their secretaries, survive from the second half of the seventeenth century. There are only remnants of the female correspondence from earlier times, for instance a letter of Zofia Rotundusowa Mieleska (died *c.* 1604), the wife of *Voigt* Augustyn Rotundus Mieleski, dated on 18 June 1585, to Katarzyna Radziwiłłowa, the wife of the *voivode* of Vilnius Krzysztof Radziwiłł 'the Thunderbolt':

> Your Grace,
>
> As your servant I sincerely recommend your grace my services and wish you and your husband, his grace the *voivode*, all the best and happiness.
>
> Apart from all the aforementioned, I inform you that the children of your grace are not bad. Mr Krzysztof, thank God, is all right now and miss Halszka during the day

[41] A pioneering study devoted to the correspondence of female Lithuanian aristocrats and members of the ruling house in the sixteenth century was published by R. RAGAUSKIENĖ and A. RAGAUSKAS, *Barboros Radvilaitės laiškai Žygimantui Augustui ir kitiems* (Vilnius, 2001).

[42] RAGAUSKIENĖ and RAGAUSKAS, *Barboros Radvilaitės laiškai*, p. 83-87.

[43] J. SCHÖNFLISSIUS, *Legat prętko przychodzący i zbawienne poselstwo przynoszący. Na pogrzebie niegdaj cnej i pobożnej matrony, Wielmożnej Pani, Jejmości Pani Zuzanny Nunhartównej Chreptowiczowej w roku 1645 9 Decembra w Wilnie zmarłej kazaniem pogrzebnym pokazany* (Lubecz, 1646). The sermon has been published by FRICK, *Wilnianie*, p. 49.

catches a fever which lasts at night but not as high as previously. Thanks to the grace of the Lord, she is joyful and eats well. And now, I do not have anything more to write to your grace and only again recommend your grace my services. In return, I ask not to be forgotten.

Datum in Haszeny, on the Monday after Holy Trinity anno Domini 1585.

The humblest servant of your grace.

The misses [Regina and Elżbieta, i.e. Zofia's daughters] send your grace and his grace the *voivode* their best wishes of good health and recommend their services.

Zofia Mieleska *wójtowa wileńska*.[44] (original in Polish)

Zofia Mieleska (née Montanówna) probably got her literacy skills in her family home in Cracow. She was a descendent of an Italian family Montana and daughter of a doctor of medicine, Jakub Montanus (*c.* 1524-1580), which certainly influenced her education.[45]

In this period, the ability to read and write was mostly acquired by Vilnius women in their family home, that is, in "informal educational spaces".[46] Michael Clanchy suggests that in late medieval Western Europe it was the mother who could teach their children reading.[47] A similar situation may have been found in Vilnius, also in later times. In the second half of the sixteenth century, there was only one school in Vilnius in which – maybe – girls were taught, namely the Calvinist school. It is also plausible that they were later taught at the Lutheran school at the Lutheran church in German Street. Education in Calvinist schools was regulated by the decisions of synods,[48] but the Lithuanian canons do not mention girls being given access to schools. Girls did how-

[44] "The letter of Zofia Rotundusowa, the wife of the *Voigt* of Vilnius to Katarzyna Radziwiłłowa, the wife of voivode of Vilnius", in: R. Ragauskienė and A. Ragauskas, "Vieną ar dvi žmonas turėjo Augustinas Rotundas Meleskis (apie 1520-1584 m.)? Nauji duomenys įžymiojo Vilniaus vaito biografijai", *Lietuvos istorijos metraštis* (2000), pp. 31-32.

[45] The high social status of Zofia Mieleska is confirmed by her later activities and the good marriages of her daughters Regina and Elżbieta (mentioned as "misses" in her letter). J. Tęgowski, "Rodzina Łoknickich herbu Nieczuja na Podlasiu i w powiecie brzesko-litewskim do połowy XVII wieku", *Rocznik Lituanistyczny* 5 (2019), pp. 126, 135.

[46] C. Bowden, "Women in educational spaces", in: *The Cambridge Companion to Early Modern Women's Writing*, pp. 90-91.

[47] Clanchy, *Looking Back from the Invention of Printing*, pp. 31-35, 189-191.

[48] Karpiński, *Kobieta w mieście polskim*, p. 292.

ever obtain basic literary skills, learned to read in Polish, which was supposed to enable them to read the Holy Scriptures, and in so doing acquired the skill of reading. This is why the average literacy of Protestant women was higher compared to that of Catholic women.[49]

The foundation of new nunneries in Vilnius from the 1590s (heretofore there had only been the Bernardine nunnery in Užupis) also allowed young Catholic girls to obtain a systematic education. We only have information about one school for girls from the period, which operated at the Benedictine nunnery. In Catholic nunnery schools, more emphasis was placed on upbringing and religious formation than on intellectual development. The teaching of crafts predominated: embroidery, spinning, sewing, textile weaving, and sometimes cooking and laundering.[50] However, on occasion they indirectly learned to read and, to a lesser extent, write.

The data concerning the Benedictine school are scarce, so we may only suppose that, as in other schools of this kind, the number of female pupils was between ten and twenty. We only know the names of three of them. In a letter of 21 March 1627, Halszka z Podolskich Milewska, a noblewoman from Zaborze (probably in the Oszmiana district) wrote to abbess Kuczkowska, mostly about storing cereals in the nunnery. But not only about that:

> And since I ordered them to purchase certain things in Vilnius in accordance with my register, please allow my daughter [Aleksandra Milewska] to go to the stalls with my servant so she can buy these things and send a maiden with her. (original in Polish)

This paragraph sheds some light on using written word among noblewomen in the Grand Duchy of Lithuania at the beginning of the seventeenth century. Not only did Mrs Milewska write a letter but she also sent a register (a list) of goods which were to be bought in Vilnius. This suggests it was not a unique example of women using such texts on property management. Other sources inform us that women belonging to the Lithuanian aristocracy wrote or ordered their servants to write similar shopping lists,[51] but there are no such documents

[49] PARTYKA, "Żona wyćwiczona", pp. 81-82; KARPIŃSKI, *Kobieta w mieście polskim*, p. 295.

[50] M. BORKOWSKA, *Panny siostry w świecie sarmackim* (Warsaw, 2002), p. 78; PARTYKA, "Żona wyćwiczona", p. 80; KARPIŃSKI, *Kobieta w mieście polskim*, pp. 290-291.

[51] An example of such a shopping list is the *Regestr spisania towarów jej mości paniej wileńskiej pokupionych* (Register of things bought by Mrs Voivode of Vilnius), written at the turn of the sixteenth and seventeenth centuries for Zofia Chodkiewiczowa (†1618), wife of Jan

related to the middle nobility. What is more, Miss Aleksandra Milewska must have known the procedure of buying goods with a list, which allows us to deduce two things. Firstly, she must have gained her writing skills at home, before she was enrolled to the Benedictine school. And secondly, the purpose of Miss Aleksandra's education (at home) was to gain necessary competences, among them literacy, to become a good property manager.

Should abbess Kuczkowska have consented to the noblewoman's request and should Miss Aleksandra have had the opportunity to do the shopping at the capital city stalls, it would have meant that the strict Benedictine regulations of the Chełmno rule, which prescribed the creation of a separate enclosure for female pupils, were not strictly followed in Vilnius.[52] Maybe Mrs Milewska dared to ask if her daughter could go shopping due to rather intimate relations between her, her family and the abbess, which follows from the postscript under the letter:

> I send you, my dear Miss, a bottle of fine liqueur. Please deign to accept it and look kindly on my Alesieńka, both you and all the other sisters. I have heard she suffers from coughs. Please, my dear Miss, have regard for her poor health. My daughters pay dear Miss and all the other Ladies their respects and ask for your grace.[53] (original in Polish)

We do not know whether Miss Aleksandra Milewska's sisters also attended the Benedictine school, but there has been preserved a letter written by King Sigismund III Vasa to abbess Kuczkowska dated 30 June 1626 concerning the admittance to the novitiate of a daughter of a barber and Vilnius town dweller, Jakub Kal (Koll), who had spent a considerable time being raised by nuns from the nunnery of St. Catherine in Vilnius. Several years previously, on 26 May

Karol Chodkiewicz, the *hetman* of the Grand Duchy of Lithuania and the *voivode* of Vilnius. The long register (four pages) lists mainly different kinds of fabrics (velvet, linen fabric), spices, and sweets. MS VUB F4-11440 (A-157). The registers of the food expenses of the court of Queen Barbara Radziwiłłówna from 1549-1550 are examined by A. JANUSZEK-SIERADZKA, "Dwór królowej od kuchni, czyli o zaopatrzeniu stołu Barbary Radziwiłłówny (1548-1551)", in: *Jagiellonowie i ich świat*, ed. B. CZWOJDRAK, J. SPERKA, and P. WĘCOWSKI (Cracow, 2015), pp. 75-77. It is an open question to what extent Ms. Chodkiewiczowa and Queen Barbara played an active role in keeping their own financial registers.

52 M. BORKOWSKa, *Życie codzienne polskich klasztorów żeńskich w XVII-XVIII wieku* (Warsaw, 1996), p. 60.

53 M. BORKOWSKA, "Problemy siedemnastowiecznych fundacji benedyktynek na Litwie w świetle korespondencji. Wybór listów", *Nasza Przeszłość* 80 (1993), pp. 288-289.

Fig. 16 A prayer book and a pendant watch of a noblewoman. A fragment of the funeral monument of Dorota Firlejówna (*c.* 1550-1591), wife of chancellor Lew Sapieha. St. Michael's church of the Bernardine Sisters in Vilnius, *c.* 1633. Photo J. Niedźwiedź.

1622, bishop Eustachy Wołłowicz had asked the abbess to admit Anna Zenowiczówna, a daughter of the Castellan of Polatsk, to the school.[54] The school admitted girls from noble and aristocratic families from outside Vilnius and, exceptionally, the local urban elite.

However, when discussing female literacy, we cannot limit ourselves to the evidence concerning the Benedictine school. Far more women learned to read through schooling at home, as can be indirectly concluded from the analysis of Polish and Ruthenian signatures mentioned above. The women who wrote them surely did not acquire the skill of writing in any formal educational institution, so the only possible solution was education in the home.[55] The scope of their education is unknown, but presumably it included mostly arithmetic and familiarity with simple documents, and, with regard to literature, the ability to read religious books, for instance a prayer book, a hymn book, or a catechism. In this respect, Vilnius was not that different from other regions of the Polish-Lithuanian Commonwealth or indeed from Europe generally.[56] We have very scarce data concerning such home education in the first half of the seventeenth century. In his diary, under the date of 14 November 1653, a young Lutheran from Zamość, Jan Golliusz, a recent graduate of the University of Leipzig, noted the following: "Mrs Bergmanowa entrusted me with Krzysia, the daughter of Daniel, to teach her reading and writing, but with respect to these skills she was very thick-headed".[57] We may suppose that many of the alumni and

[54] *Ibid.*, pp. 284 and 288.

[55] CLANCHY, *Looking Back from the Invention of Printing*, p. 163.

[56] W. URBAN, "Szkolnictwo małopolskie od XVI do XVIII wieku", in: *Nauczanie w dawnych wiekach*, p. 69; S. PEYRONEL RAMBALDI, "Introduzione: Per una storia delle donne nella Riforma", p. 38; BOWDEN, "Women in educational spaces", p. 90.

[57] *Pamiętnik Jana Golliusza, mieszczanina polskiego (1650-1653)*, ed. J. KALLENBACH, in: *Archiwum do Dziejów Literatury i Oświaty w Polsce*, 7 (Cracow, 1892), p. 98.

students of Vilnius schools earned a living providing similar educational services.[58]

The Castle

An important *locus scribendi* for women in Vilnius was the royal court. Vilnius was a temporary residence of the queens and grand duchesses of Lithuania: Helena of Moscow (1476-1513), wife of King Alexander Jagiellon, Barbara Zápolya (Szapolyai, 1495-1515),[59] and Bona Sforza (1494-1557), wives of King Sigismund I the Old, Elisabeth of Austria (1526-1545), Barbara Radziwiłłówna (1520/1523-1551) and Catherine of Austria (1533-1572), the wives of King Sigismund Augustus, and princesses: Sophia Jagiellon (1522-1575), Anna (1523-1596, since 1576 Queen of Poland) and Catherina (1526-1583),[60] daughters of Queen Bona; Constance of Austria (1588-1631), the second wife of King Sigismund III Vasa and Cecilia Renata of Austria (1611-1644), the wife of King Władysław IV Vasa. The queens and the members of their courts were very active in the field of text production, especially epistolography.[61]

The first queen of whose letters sent from Vilnius we know was Helena of Moscow, a daughter of Grand Prince of Muscovy Ivan III of Russia.[62] There is

[58] BARTOSZEWICZ, *Piśmienność mieszczańska*, p. 272.

[59] There are known three Latin letters of Barbara Zápolya to Sigismund the Old and twenty four sent by the king to the queen. The author of the queen's letters was her secretary Andrzej Krzycki. See D. KERŠIENĖ, "Desiderium videndi: Barboros Zapolijos ir Žygimanto Senojo korespondencija", *Senoji Lietuvos Literatūra* 47 (2019), pp. 15-55.

[60] Anna and Catherine Jagiellon visited Vilnius several times. Their longest stay in the city lasted six years (1556-1562). At that time they had their separate courts. See R. RAGAUSKIENĖ, "The marriage of Catherine Jagiellon and John III Vasa in Vilnius (1562)", in: *Lithuania – Poland – Sweden: European Dynastic Unions and Historical-cultural Ties*, ed. E. SAVIŠČEVAS and M. UZORKA (Vilnius, 2014), pp. 112-113.

[61] In her thorough study Urszula Zachara-Związek showed the ways in which correspondence of the first and the third wives of Sigismund Augustus, Elisabeth of Austria and her sister, Catherine, was produced. U. ZACHARA-ZWIĄZEK, "Dwór królowej jako locus scribendi: Analiza wybranych aspektów funkcjonowania na przykładzie korespondencji Elżbiety Habsburżanki z Zygmuntem Augustem", in: *Loca scribendi: Miejsca i środowiska tworzące kulturę pisma w dawnej Rzeczypospolitej XV-XVIII stulecia*, ed. M. PTASZYŃSKI, A. BARTOSZEWICZ, and A. ADAMSKA (Warsaw, 2017), pp. 171-182.

[62] J. GARBACIK, "Helena (1476-1513)", in: *Polski slownik biograficzny*, 9 (Cracow, 1960-1961), pp. 359-362.

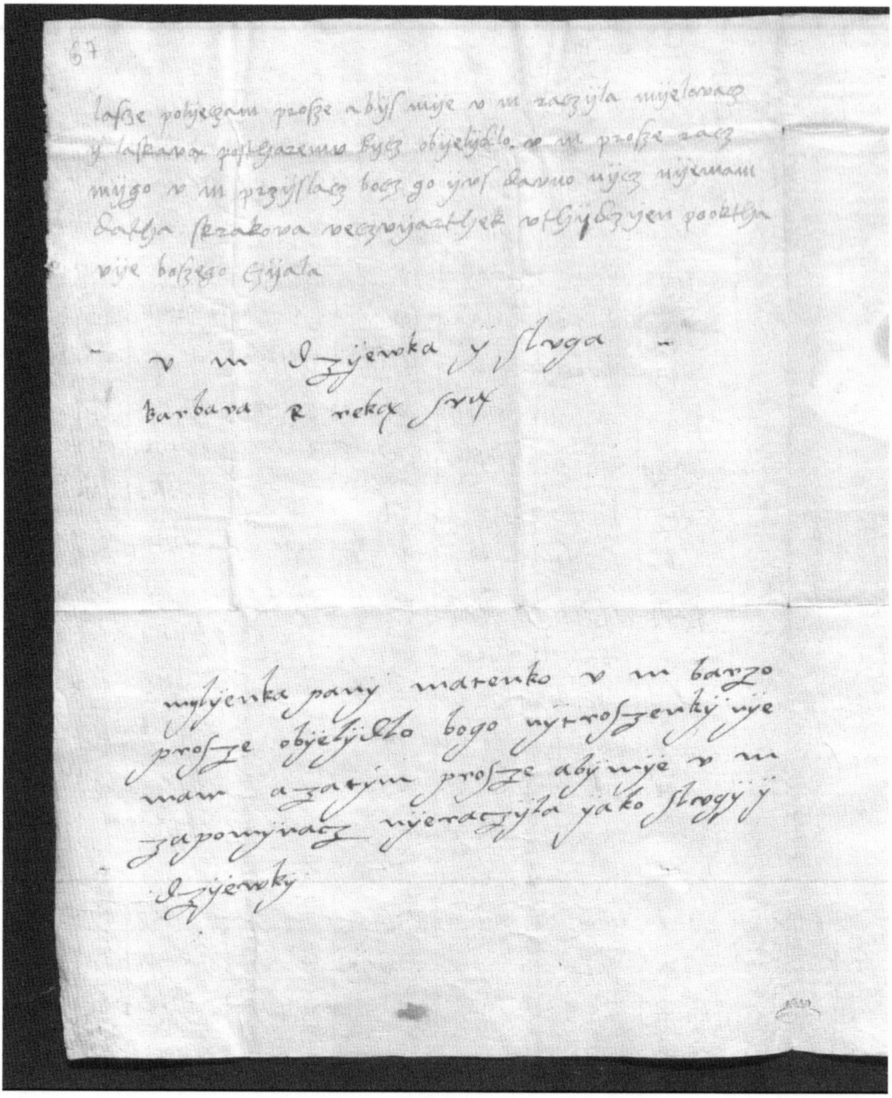

v m dzyewka y sluga
barbara z reky swey

mylyenka pany matenko v m barzo
prosze obyelydlo bogo nytrosyenky nye
mam a zatym prosze aby mye v m
zapomynacz nyeraczyla yako slugy y
dzyewky

Fig. 17 Letter of Queen Barbara Radziwiłłówna to her mother, Barbara Radziwiłłowa (Vilnius, 1547?). Signature and a postscript of the queen: "with her own hand, Barbara, the daughter and servant of Your Grace". [Postscript:] "My dear mother, please, send me some ceruse [*bielidło*] because I do have not a speck of it; then please, do not forget me, Your Grace, as your servant and daughter" (original in Polish). MS Warsaw, AGAD, 1/354/0/3/29, p. 67 <https://www.szukajwarchiwach.gov.pl/jednostka/-/jednostka/17873161> (accessed: 29.05. 2022; public domain).

no separate study devoted to the texts written on behalf of Helena of Moscow. We do not even know if she was able to read or write herself,[63] but she often used the written word and this might confirm she was at least pragmatically literate in a high degree. The queen possessed her own library. In 1497 her father sent her thirteen books, and later she bought some books in Hrodna.[64] She exchanged a number of letters with her father, her family, and with Polish politicians, both in Ruthenian and Latin.[65] At her court, she hired highly qualified *diaks* (clerks, scribes) who wrote her letters. In 1495 her father sent to Vilnius a scribe (*poddiachyi*), Ivan Kotov, who was expected to write secret letters to Moscow on behalf of Helena.[66] In 1499 her *diak* was Grisha Ivanovych, and between 1502 and 1509 her chancellor was an accomplished diplomat, Iwan Semenowicz Sapieha (*c.* 1431-1517).[67] Probably he was responsible for preparing some of the documents issued by the queen. Among them, there are three letters sent to her father on 2 January 1503 and identical letters sent to her mother Sophia Palaiologina and to her two brothers Vasili (later Vasili III of Russia) and Yuri.[68] She also exchanged Latin letters with her brother-in-law cardinal Frederic Jagiellon.[69]

The best known Vilnius 'female epistolographer' from the first half of the sixteenth century was Queen Barbara Radziwiłłówna, the second wife of King

[63] On the lack of sources about the education of Helena, see G. RUTKOWSKA, "Kościół w życiu Heleny moskiewskiej, żony Aleksandra Jagiellończyka", ed. A. KOZAK, *Średniowiecze Polskie i Powszechne* 12.16, (2020), p. 275.

[64] F. PAPÉE, *Aleksander Jagiellończyk* (Cracow, 1949), p. 32; RUTKOWSKA, "Kościół w życiu Heleny", p. 275.

[65] Helena's letters are mentioned in A. WINIARSKA, "Rola Heleny Rurykowiczówny w świetle stosunków litewsko-moskiewskich na przełomie XV i XVI w.", *Rocznik Naukowo-Dydaktyczny WSP w Krakowie: Prace Historyczne IV*, 32 (1968), pp. 5-30, and see also RUTKOWSKA, "Kościół w życiu Heleny", pp. 261-307.

[66] WINIARSKA, "Rola Heleny", p. 14.

[67] K. PIETKIEWICZ, *Wielkie księstwo litewskie pod rządami Aleksandra Jagiellończyka Studia nad dziejami państwa i społeczeństwa na przełomie XV i XVI wieku* (Poznań, 1995), p. 110.

[68] *Сборник Русского исторического общества,* 35, *Памятники дипломатических сношений древней России с державами иностранными: 1, Памятники дипломатических сношений Московского государства с Польско-Литовским государством в царствование Великого Князя Ивана Васильевича, 1 (годы с 1487 по 1533)*, ed. Г.Ф. КАРПОВ (Санкт-Петербург, 1882), pp. 368-376 (No.75 IVa, б, в, г); *Lietuvos metrika: Knyga Nr. 5 (1427-1506). Užrašymų knyga 5*, ed. A. BALIULIS, A. DUBONIS, D. ANTANAVIČIUS (Vilnius, 2012), p. 317 (No. 511); WINIARSKA, "Rola Heleny", p. 25-26; RUTKOWSKA, "Kościół w życiu Heleny", pp. 285-286.

[69] *Akta Aleksandra króla polskiego*, pp. 155-156; WINIARSKA, "Rola Heleny", p. 25; N. NOWAKOWSKA, *Church, State and Dynasty in Renaissance Poland: The Career of Cardinal Fryderyk Jagiellon (1468-1503)* (London and New York, 2007), p. 135-137; R. FROST, *The Oxford History of Poland-Lithuania*, 1, *The Making of the Polish-Lithuanian Union, 1385-1569* (Oxford, 2015), pp. 309-310.

Sigismund II Augustus.[70] At the beginning of their marriage (1547) she wrote her letters by herself. After she moved from Dubingai to Vilnius in April 1548, her chancery was established.[71] In September 1548 Jerzy Podlodowski (*c.* 1510-1555), a royal secretary and priest, was appointed as her chancellor.[72] Most of her letters to the king and her brother Mikołaj Radziwiłł 'the Red' were drafted by her secretary, the brilliant humanist Stanisław Koszutski (†1558). After his studies in Wittenberg he became a royal secretary, and he was also a poet, translator and, after the queen's death, the royal librarian in Vilnius.[73] The marriage of Sigismund and Barbara caused political turmoil in Poland, and Koszutski was one of a few authors who defended the couple.[74]

[70] Barbara Radziwiłłówna was a member of a powerful Lithuanian aristocratic family of the Radziwiłłs. In 1546 she met the king and later became his mistress, when he was still married to Elisabeth of Austria. After Elisabeth's death, in secret, the king married Barbara in 1544. The marriage was inspired by a cousin of Barbara, Mikołaj Radziwiłł "the Black" and her brother Mikołaj "the Red". This move outraged the vast majority of the Polish nobility. The opponents of the king declared the marriage unlawful and invalid. In a number of pamphlets they attacked the queen and openly called her a prostitute. Ultimately, the king forced the nobility to agree to her coronation, which took place in Cracow on 6 December 1550. Half a year later Barbara died. FROST, *The Oxford History of Poland-Lithuania*, 1, pp. 435-439.

[71] The queen's chancery was established in a very short time. For a long time the first wife of Sigismund Augustus, Elisabeth of Austria (1526-1545) did not have her private secretary. ZACHARA-ZWIĄZEK, "Dwór królowej jako locus scribendi", pp. 173-174.

[72] I. KANIEWSKA, "Jerzy Podlodowski", in: *PSB*, 27 (Cracow, 1982-1983), pp. 130-131; BORKOWSKA, *Dynastia Jagiellonów*, p. 196; M. KOROLKO, *Seminarium Rzeczypospolite Królestwa Polskiego: Humaniści w kancelarii królewskiej Zygmunta Augusta* (Warsaw, 1991), p. 227-228; RAGAUSKIENĖ and RAGAUSKAS, *Barboros Radvilaitės laiškai*, p. 155.

[73] After the queen's death he lived in Vilnius, where he translated Reinhard Lorich's *De institutione principum loci communes* and Cicero's *De officiis*. R. LORICH, *Księgi o wychowaniu i o ćwiczeniu każdego przełożonego*, trans. S. KOSZUTSKI (Cracow, 1558); M. Tullius Cicero, *O powinnościach wszech stanów ludzi... księgi troje*, trans. S. KOSZUTSKI (Łosk, 1583). Features of the Polish language of Koszutski have been recently analysed by Zofia Zając-Gardeła in her doctoral thesis Z. ZAJĄC-GARDEŁA, *Wariantywność i normalizacja polszczyzny literackiej XVI wieku na podstawie Ksiąg o wychowaniu i o ćwiczeniu każdego przełożonego, nie tylko panu ale i każdemu ku czytaniu barzo pożyteczne: teraz nowo z łacińskiego języka na polski przełożone Reinharda Lorichiusa w tłumaczeniu Stanisława Koszuckiego: Fonetyka i fleksja: Praca napisana pod kierunkiem prof. dra hab. Bogusława Dunaja* (Cracow, 2020). I am grateful to prof. Mirosława Mycawka for making the manuscript of this work available to me.

[74] Koszutski wrote a Latin epithalamium for Sigismund and Barbara, which was in fact a political pamphlet in which he defended their marriage. S. KOSZUTSKI, *Epithalamion in nuptiis Sigismundi Augusti Regis Poloniae et Barbarae*, in: *Epitalamia łacińskie w Polsce*, ed. J. NIEDŹWIEDŹ, trans. J. BROŻEK (Cracow, 1999), pp. 318-341.

Koszutski was not the only employee in the chancery of the queen. Since 1550 she had also a Ruthenian scribe, Jan Hajek (Gajka).[75] Probably there were other people responsible for managing her correspondence. However, even if others were responsible for managing Barbara's correspondence in Vilnius, it was the king, Radziwiłł 'the Red', and the queen herself who established her Vilnius *locus scribendi* as an important place of exchanging texts.

60 letters written by Barbara have survived, most of them addressed to her brother Mikołaj 'the Red' (39) and her husband Sigismund (9).[76] Fifteen of them were written in Barbara's hand, the others in that of Koszutski. The letters written by Koszutski are often provided with her personal additions and signatures. Only one Latin letter known today was sent to the duke of Prussia, Albert. Scholars suppose that her correspondence must have been by far larger than suggested by the extant letters, and from historical sources we know about other people she exchanged letters with.[77]

Barbara could read and write in Polish and maybe she also knew Latin and Ruthenian to some degree. She was an active user of written word and she exploited every opportunity to make use of her own and her secretary's reading and writing skills. She was encouraged by her husband to be an active and competent writer. In 1549 he gave her an expensive silver inkwell.[78]

The king, the queen, and the staff of their chanceries paid particular attention to the rhetorical form of queen's letters. In a letter of 25 June 1548, the king asked Mikołaj 'the Red' to admonish Barbara and her chancery on how to fashion the queen in her correspondence. The king advised her not to use her official royal titles at the beginning of her letters and use only a simple signature at the end. On the other hand, the king ordered her to write in her letters the majestic *we* instead of singular *I*.[79] Based on these meticulous recommenda-

[75] RAGAUSKIENĖ and RAGAUSKAS, *Barboros Radvilaitės laiškai*, p. 155-156; BORKOWSKA, *Dynastia Jagiellonów*, p. 196.

[76] Forty-four of them were published by A. PRZEŹDZIECKI, *Jagiellonki polskie w XVI wieku*, 1 (Cracow, 1868), pp. 301-344. A new transcription of a part of Barbara's correspondence is printed in: *Listy polskie XVI wieku. Listy z lat 1525-1548*, pp. 90-3, 431-434, 442-443, 453-459, 490-491. See also RAGAUSKIENĖ and RAGAUSKAS, *Barboros Radvilaitės laiškai*, pp. 137-145.

[77] *Ibid.*

[78] In the register of expenses of the royal court we find a note: "*[20 Februarii 1549] S[acrae] Maiestati Reginali pro atramentario argenteo et cingulo fl 36*" (For a silver inkwell with a belt for Her Majesty the Queen 36 florins). *Materiały do historyi stosunków kulturalnych w XVI w. na dworze królewskim polskim*, ed. S. TOMKIEWICZ (Cracow, 2015), p. 12.

[79] A letter of King Sigismund Augustus to Mikołaj Radziwiłł "the Red", Cracow 25.06. 1548, in: *Listy polskie XVI wieku*, 2, ed. K. RYMUNT, *Listy z lat 1548-1550 ze zbiorów Władysława Pociechy, Witolda Taszyckiego i Adama Turasiewicza* (Cracow, 2001), p. 52.

tions some historians suggest that Barbara did not know how to write her letters to the officials of the Kingdom of Poland properly.[80] However, this is a more complex issue.

The Renaissance *ars epistolandi* was a set of rules, but their knowledge among literate people was not the only condition for writing letters. No less important than skills were practice, experience, and literary talent. They were necessary to structure and nuance the rhetorical form of a letter properly. Some rulers and politicians had a good humanistic background and were accomplished writers, for instance King Stephen Báthory, Polish chancellor Jan Zamoyski, or the *voivode* of Trakai Mikołaj Krzysztof Radziwiłł 'the Orphan' (a son of Barbara's cousin, Mikołaj 'the Black'). However, even they hired the best humanists as secretaries for their chanceries, specialists in the production and managing of information. One of the main tasks of the secretaries was to compose letters in which they often played a complex, multi-layered, and intertextual game with the reader.[81]

In the letter to Mikołaj 'the Red' we notice a glimpse of the rhetorical rules of such a game. The king advised Barbara to avoid to use her royal title so as not to give their political enemies a weapon against her; and to use the grammatical forms reserved for the royals to wind them up and to show her royal position. It is rather doubtful that the king alone came up with the idea of how to construct the image of the queen in her letters by himself. It must have been someone else from among his trusted secretaries who noticed the problem with Barbara's titles and found a solution on how to deal with it rhetorically.

In the process of production Barbara's letters, several people were engaged: the queen, her secretary Koszutski, Mikołaj 'the Red', the king, and the members of his chancery. Such a situation was normal among the rulers and aristocracy of the period. The royal correspondence, even the so-called 'private' correspondence, was the collective work of at least two people: the king and a secretary. The image of the 'author' of a letter was the result of the literary activity of several people.[82] The admonition of King Sigismund to Queen

[80] RAGAUSKIENĖ and RAGAUSKAS, *Barboros Radvilaitės laiškai*, p. 138.

[81] An example of such a game was analysed by J. Axer in his brilliant interpretation of a letter from 1580 of the royal secretary and poet Jan Kochanowski to chancellor Zamoyski, cf. J. AXER, "Problemy kompozycji makaronicznej. Poprzedzający 'Pieśni trzy' list Kochanowskiego do Zamoyskiego", *Pamiętnik Literacki* 76.3 (1985), pp. 123-134.

[82] It is worthwhile remembering here that the modern concept of authorship only began to germinate among the humanists. Many texts were multi-authored or their authorship was concealed. This was mixed up with the practice of the *imitatio auctorum*. In the sixteenth century,

Barbara should be examined in terms of the collective authorship of royal epistolography and the network in which this took place. The participants of the process of letter production were fully aware of the necessity of co-operation. For example, the first wife of Sigismund Augustus, Elisabeth of Austria, had also relied on help from royal secretaries, and in one of her letters she asked an unidentified secretary to send her formulas for Polish-language official letters.[83]

Even though most of the letters were written by secretaries, queens and princesses took an active role in their preparation. Apart from Bona Sforza, who had received a thorough humanist education, other queens and princesses sometimes experienced problems with writing letters according to the rules of the Renaissance *ars epistolandi* and chancery customs, especially when it came to Latin letters. A similar situation was encountered among noblewomen and female members of the city elite.

The Nunneries

By the mid-seventeenth century, seven female nunneries had been founded in the city. The oldest one, the Bernardine nunnery in Užupis, was built as early as 1495; the second was the Orthodox nunnery at the church of the Holy Spirit, established in the sixteenth century. In 1594, chancellor Lew Sapieha founded another Bernardine nunnery and the church of St. Michael the Archangel, founfded in 1629, opposite the Calvinist church, which later was to result in considerable problems.[84] In the next half-century, four more nunneries were founded in Vilnius: the Benedictine nunnery at the church of St. Catherine of Alexandria (1622), that of the Carmelite sisters at the spot of the later St. Joseph's church (1638), the Basilian sisters at the Uniate Holy Trinity church, and that of the Bridgettine Sisters (*c.* 1650).[85] This rise in the number of nunneries was a sign of the remarkable flourishing of the conventual movement in all provinces of the Commonwealth.[86]

writing meant to imitate and to put other writers' voices in one's text. On the idea of imitation, cf. FULIŃSKA, *Naśladowanie i twórczość*.

[83] ZACHARA-ZWIĄZEK, "Dwór królowej jako locus scribendi", pp. 177-178.

[84] See Chapter 7.

[85] WIJUK KOJAŁOWICZ, *Miscellanea rerum*, p. 76; ŁOWMIAŃSKA, *Wilno*, pp. 195-200; KURCZEWSKI, *Kościół zamkowy*, 1, p. 240; TARGOSZ, *Piórem zakonnicy*, p. 79.

[86] PARTYKA, *Żona wyćwiczona*, p. 179.

Nuns were those among the Vilnius women who had the most contacts with texts and their production. Texts were necessary for daily life of the nunnery, for instance a mother superior was elected by way of secret ballot. However, most of all, reading aloud religious works was a common practice.[87] Nuns in all female orders were required to use texts. The rules formed the frame of most of their textual practices.[88] The rules of some nunneries did not allow illiterate maidens to take religious vows.[89] The Benedictine rule stipulated after the Chełmno reform, for example,[90] stipulated that every nun joining the order had to contribute her own breviary as part of her dowry.[91] Nuns were first and foremost supposed to pray, meditate, and sing, so it was only natural that books were constantly present and used within the conventual walls. The rule of the Bernardine Sisters of St. Michael from the years 1629-1633 says the following about the necessity of reading and practising reading by novices:

> The teaching of the novices is entrusted to the due diligence and care of sister vicaress, whose role is to train them in all virtues and monastic activities, in the spirit of piousness by way of spiritual exercises and meditation, as well as to examine every day their knowledge of sermons, readings, and meditations, and teach them to say the Divine Office.[92]

But was this literacy the same as in the case of the friars from the nearby Bernardine monastery?

[87] GWIOŻDZIK, *Wileńskie mniszki w kręgu kultury słowa w dobie staropolskiej*, *Kultura i języki Wielkiego Księstwa Litewskiego*, pp. 265-266.

[88] Research has thoroughly examined the rules of female orders in the Polish-Lithuanian Commonwealth in relation to the reading and writing practices of nuns. BORKOWSKA, *Życie codzienne polskich klasztorów żeńskich*, pp. 295-303; TARGOSZ, *Piórem zakonnicy*, p. 9; GWIOŻDZIK, *Kultura pisma i książki*, p. 93-140; H. PAULOUSKAYA, *Grodzieńskie kroniki klasztorne XVII i XVIII wieku: Formy gatunkowe i aspekty komunikacyjne* (Warsaw, 2016), pp. 34-35.

[89] BORKOWSKA, *Panny siostry*, pp. 307-314; PARTYKA, *Żona wyćwiczona*, p. 173.

[90] In the first half of the seventeenth century, the abbess of the Benedictine nunnery in Chełmno (Kingdom of Poland) Magdalena Mortęska implemented a reform inspired by the changes undergone by the Catholic Church after the Council of Trent. The reform introduced, among other things, the development of the sisters' intellectual life. What is more, reformed nunneries (almost twenty) ran schools for girls.

[91] J. GWIOŻDZIK, "Kultura umysłowa benedyktynek kongregacji chełmińskiej", in: *Sanctimoniales: Zakony żeńskie w Polsce i Europie Środkowej (do przełomu XVIII i XIX wieku)*, ed. A. RADZIMIŃSKI, D. KARCZEWSKI, and Z. ZYGLEWSKI (Bydgoszcz, 2010), p. 484.

[92] *Konstytucje panien zakonnych klasztoru wileńskiego przy świętym Michale*, MS CZART. 3705 I, p. 91.

If we take into account the social context of their literacy, it turns out that among Catholic nuns it was to some extent the result of their social status. According to Małgorzata Borkowska, as many as 70-80% of nuns came from the nobility, 20% from the town dwellers, and less than 1% from the peasantry.[93] A closer look at the Catholic nunneries in the Lithuanian capital city reveals that they were also elitist in terms of whom they accepted, as the nunneries were often inhabited by women from the aristocracy, such as the Radziwiłł, Chalecki, Tyszkiewicz, or Zenowicz families.

In nunneries, liturgical texts and religious literature predominated, carefully selected in accordance with the rule of a given order. We do not have catalogues of the libraries of the Vilnius nunneries from before the mid-seventeenth century, but we do know that they possessed their own book collections, and maybe they had several libraries, for instance one for the nuns, one for the novices, a separate book collection for the chaplain (if such a person resided at the nunnery), and finally the private books of individual nuns.[94]

The main library of a nunnery may have resembled the libraries of the male monasteries, although it was probably smaller and less diverse.[95] In the seventeenth century, the Bernardine sisters' library contained 209 books.[96] A chapter from the Rule of the Benedictine sisters of the Chełmno reform informs us which spiritual books were supposed to be read in the refectory by a "weekly reader":

> 1. The Life of Jesus by Granatens, 2. The Life of Holy Mary, 3. The Lives of the Saints, 4. The Imitation of Christ, Thomas à Kempis, 5. *Collationes Patrum* written by the eremite John Cassian and other fine things in the volume, 6. Hieronim Plat on the benefits of the monastic life, 7. Writings of Desiderius [Pope Victor III], 8.

[93] M. Borkowska, "Córki chłopskie w polskich klasztorach epoki potrydenckiej", *Nasza Przeszłość* 101 (2004), pp. 315-330. These data are confirmed by research conducted by Marzena Baum. In the first half of the seventeenth century, more than half of the Benedictine sisters in Poznań, or even as many as three quarters of them, came from the nobility; cf. M. Baum, "*Struktura społeczna wspólnoty benedyktynek poznańskich w XVII-XIX wieku*", in: *Nad społeczeństwem staropolskim*, 2, *Polityka i ekonomia – społeczeństwo i wojsko – religia i kultura w XVI-XVIII wieku*, ed. D. Wereda (Siedlce, 2009), p. 255.

[94] Borkowska, *Życie codzienne*, pp. 305-309; Gwioździk, *Wileńskie mniszki*, pp. 272-273.

[95] Gwioździk, "Kultura umysłowa benedyktynek", pp. 497-498.

[96] See Topolska, *Czytelnik i książka*, p. 194; Gwioździk, *Kultura pisma i książki w żeńskich klasztorach*, p. 46.

Giulio Fatio on self-mortification, 9. A companion,[97] 10. A speculum,[98] 11. The Polish Baronio,[99] and anything similar to these books.[100] (original in Polish)

In the first half of the seventeenth century, nuns' contact with books developed significantly in comparison to the preceding period, but it was still limited. First of all, they only used to read in the vernacular language, that is in Polish. There is much evidence of this situation. When they listened to the readings during their meals or read books as an act of private piety, there were exclusively Polish texts. Many of them were translations from the Latin, designed especially for nuns.[101] The vast majority of volumes in their libraries, however, were in Polish.[102] Polish was also the only language of written communication in nunneries: we find it used in correspondence, registers, manuscripts of devotional or mystical texts, chronicles, poems, etc.

Nuns knew Latin only to some degree, and this knowledge can be called 'phonetic literacy'.[103] They were obliged to say or sing the Latin prayers ordered by their monastic rules, so they had a pragmatic competence in using this language. However, they did not read works in Latin which required advanced knowledge of Latin. Even if such texts were present in their library, reading them was virtually impossible. If any Latin text was necessary for the use of nuns, it was translated into Polish, mainly by the male members of the religious

[97] It is not known what kind of companion the author had in mind.

[98] Speculum literature; the precise work referred to here is unknown.

[99] Cesare Baronio's *Annales ecclesiastici*, translated by Piotr Skarga SI.

[100] As cited in Baronio, *Annales ecclesiastici*, pp. 486-487.

[101] In her valuable book about the use of books and the written word among nuns, Jolanta Gwioździk gives a list of books sponsored by or published for the female orders in early modern Poland and Lithuania *c.* 1600-1800). The list contains 485 entries. The author stresses that the nuns were important patrons of the culture of print. Since her register lists only printed books, it does not mention the many books which circulated in the nunneries as manuscripts. GWIOŹDZIK, *Kultura pisma i książki*, pp. 231-292, 373-375.

[102] "Apart from the Visitation Sisters and the Benedictine Nuns of Perpetual Adoration of the Blessed Sacrament, in the 'conventual' libraries there were only a few books in foreign languages. The sisters did not study e.g. philosophy or speculative theology" (BORKOWSKA, *Życie codzienne polskich klasztorów żeńskich*, p. 305). See also GWIOŹDZIK, *Kultura pisma i książki*, pp. 46-47.

[103] GWIOŹDZIK, *Kultura pisma i książki*, p. 30; A. NOWICKA-STRUSKA, "Za murami klasztoru: Historiografia lubelskich karmelitanek bosych", *Acta Universitatis Lodzensis: Folia Litteraria Polonica* 53.2 (2019), p. 100. About two types of literacy, phonetic and comprehension literacy, see P. SAENGER, "Books of Hours and the reading habits of the later Middle Ages", in: *The Culture of Print*, ed. R. CHARTIER (Cambridge, 1989), p. 142; CLANCHY, *Looking back*, p. 29-30.

orders or by diocesan priests. Among these texts were the monastic rules,[104] works by Fathers of the Church or the saints (for instance St. Bernard, St. Bonaventure, and St. Teresa of Ávila),[105] psalters, hymns and sequences,[106] ascetic writers (for instance Juan de Jesús María or Thomás de Jesús),[107] etc. Even the Benedictine sisters of the Chełmno rule (this included the nuns from St. Catherine's nunnery), who put particular emphasis on the development of intellectual skills,[108] could not match the alumni of the Academy of Vilnius, of the diocesan and papal seminaries, or of any of the Vilnius monastic schools, who for many years were trained in Latin. The sisters' attitude towards Latin books can be described as utilitarian. They had liturgical books which were necessary for the chaplain, but not theological writings nor even devotional Latin literature. Quite often the nuns did not hesitate to destroy expensive books of emblems published abroad from which they cut out the pictures. These pictures were reused in Polish manuscript translations or paraphrases of the destroyed Latin printed books. We know many examples of such adaptations of Herman Hugo's *Pia desideria*[109] and Jean David's *Paradisus sponsi et sponsae*.[110]

[104] *Reguła świętego ojca Benedykta z łacińskiego przetłumaczona i z reformacyją porządków chełmieńskiego, toruńskiego, żarnowieckiego nieświeskiego i inszych wszystkich w Królestwie Polskim tejże refromacyjej i reguły św. Benedykta, które teraz są i na potym zjednoczone będą klasztorów panieńskich*, (Cracow, 1606).

[105] St. Bernard, *Sposób mądrego i dobrego życia... dla pożytku zakonnych osób napisany, a teraz nowo dla osobiliwie zakonnic na polskie przegłumaczony*, trans. M. BROKARD MELECIUS (Cracow, 1630); St. Bonaventure, *Zegar nabożnej oblubienice Chrystusowej... Przydany jest do niego Psałterz św. Bonawentury* (Poznań, 1624).

[106] *Hymny, prozy i cantica kościelne cokolwiek sie ich w brewiarzach i we mszałach rzymskich teraz znajduje i niektóre insze z dawniejszych co przedniejsze, zwłaszcza prozy i hymny*, trans. S. GROCHOWSKI (Cracow, 1599). This is an enlarged version of the edition of 1598; the book, several times reprinted, at the beginning of the seventeenth century was present in probably each library of nuns in the nunneries in the Polish-Lithuanian Commonwealth.

[107] Juan de Jesús María, *Zegar serdeczny, w którym Jezus godziny wybija w sercu grzesznika, aby go do pokuty nawrócił*, trans. P. DOMIECHOWSKI (Cracow, 1651); Thomás de Jesús, *Modlitwy wnętrznej droga krótka i bezpieczna... z łacińskiego przetłumaczona* (Vilnius, 1640). Both were translated for the Carmelite nuns).

[108] GWIOŹDZIK, *Kultura pisma i książki*, p. 483.

[109] R. GRZEŚKOWIAK, J. GWIOŹDZIK, and A. NOWICKA-STRUSKA, *Karmelitańskie adaptacje* Pia Desideria *Hermana Hugona z XVII i XVIII w.* (Warsaw, 2020), p. 70.

[110] The work by the Jesuit Jean David (1546-1613) was translated into Polish probably in the male Norbertine monastery in Hebdów (Lesser Poland Voivodeship): J. DAVID, *Raj oblubienica i oblubienice, w którym żniwo miry i kwiatków z tajemnic męki Chrystusowej jest zebrane, łacińskim stylem przez wielebnego księdza Jana Dawida S.J. w roku Pańskim 16*[0]*7, a zaś w roku Pańskim 1671 na polski język przetłumaczone* (MS in the Norbertine nunnery in Imbramowice,

The readings from which they could choose were strictly regulated. The monastic rules precisely pointed out the books which nuns were allowed or obliged to read.[111] Reading material was carefully selected and controlled by the church authorities. This also concerned the reading of the Bible. In some Polish nunneries, nuns were allowed to read only the New Testament.[112] An interesting note about the purpose of reading the Bible is expressed in the title of a Polish version of the psalter translated by the Jesuit Jakub Wujek. His translation, first published in 1594, was provided with many theological and philological commentaries. On the margins of his translation Wujek, who compared three versions of the psalter (in Latin, Greek, and Hebrew), gave explanations about his interpretation of Scripture and added alternative solutions of the translations.[113] However, its three consequent editions, published in the first half of the seventeenth century, which were designated for the use of the Polish and Lithuanian nuns, were deprived of Wujek's learned comments:

> David's Psalter, with diligence translated from Latin, Greek, and Jewish into the Polish language, now at the demand of many nuns who do not know the Latin language, who wish to say the psalter, anew reprinted without any explanations and annotations.[114] (original in Polish)

The church authorities, among them the authorities of the female orders, allowed sisters to read the Bible, but the purpose of this reading was primarily prayer and not the exegesis or any deeper understanding of Holy Scripture. Reading and creating texts served first of all the spiritual formation of nuns and

without shelfmark). The source of the translation was an edition printed in the Officina Plantiniana in Antwerp (edition princeps, 1607). After the translation was completed, the Polish text was carefully transcribed (maybe by a nun from Imbramowice) and the original text destroyed by cutting out all its copper plates, including the title page. The Polish manuscript was designed in this way to imitate the Latin printed version (its format, the title page, and the places where the pictures were to be pasted).

[111] GWIOŻDZIK, *Kultura pisma i książki*, p. 27.

[112] *Ibid.*, p. 99.

[113] *Psałterz Dawidów: Teraz znowu z łacińskiego, z greckiego i z żydowskiego na polski język przełożony i argumentami i annotacyjami objaśniony… Z dozwoleniem starszych: Pod rozsądek Kościoła świętego powszechnego rzymskiego wszystko niech podlęże*, trans. J. WUJEK (Cracow, 1594); FRICK, *Polish Sacred Philology*, p. 165.

[114] *Psałterz Dawidów z łacińskiego, z greckiego i żydowskiego na polski język z pilnością przełożony… teraz znowu na żądanie wiela panien zakonnych łacińskiego języka nieumiejących a Psałterz mówić pragnących bez argumentów i annotacyj przedrukowany*, trans. J. WUJEK (Cracow, 1616). This edition was reissued under the same title in 1626 and once again without the year of publication.

the liturgy, rather than foster their intellectual development.[115] Until the eighteenth century rhetoric, philosophy, astronomy, geography, and poetics were not accessible to nuns. In practice, though, the side effect of their reading activities was the creation of vast female intellectual centres, reaching far beyond the limitations imposed on them by the official rules of the church authorities. In the late seventeenth century, Vilnius nuns broke the glass ceiling that had previously precluded them from elite education, although evidence for this exists only in the remains of the book collection of the Vilnius Visitants;[116] they include the 'novel-like' lives of their French spiritual sisters translated from French.

Sisters dealt not only with reading, but also with the production of texts. First of all, they copied prayers, sometimes rhymed ones, meditations, songs, etc. This kind of activity is also known to have taken place in other nunneries of the Commonwealth, as well as in Vilnius in a later period. The manuscripts that were for instance produced by friars and priests who worked with the nuns, were circulated among nunneries[117] and may also have been gifts donated by benefactors. Some texts were 'copied' in printed form. We know some instances of such practices in Vilnius from the first half of the seventeenth century. For example, in 1647 the Bernardine sisters of St. Michael reissued, for their own use, an extensive work by Luis de la Puente *Meditations on the Mysteries of Our Holy Faith, the Life and Passion of Jesus and Holy Mary, the Saints and the Gospels*.[118] The book consisted of six parts containing several dozens of meditations. Each meditation contained a brief introduction (usually a quotation from the Bible) and, on average, three points that provided an insight into the chosen subject. That the collection was designed for women follows from the fact that the form of verbs in the first person is consistently feminine (in Polish, verbs inflect according to the grammatical gender of their

[115] See. GWIOŻDZIK, *Kultura pisma i książki*, p. 30.

[116] The nunnery of Visitant Sisters was founded in Vilnius in 1694. This order was under strong influence from French culture of the seventeenth century. The nunnery was closed in 1863 as part of Russian anti-Polish repression. The Russian authorities handed over the buildings to the Russian Orthodox Sisters of Saint Mary Magdalene (Марие-Магдалининский монастырь). The library of the Visitants Sisters was confiscated. Its remains are now held in the library of the University of Vilnius.

[117] PARTYKA, *Żona wyćwiczona*, p. 185-186.

[118] BORKOWSKA, *Życie codzienne*, p. 310. The full Polish title (provided in footnote 119) may be a specific take on the original title of the work. Furthermore, it may also indicate that the Polish edition included not only Pontanus' text but also additions, some or all of which could have been authored by other people.

subject): "*O Mistrzu niebieski, daj mi klarowne oczy, bym trumy swoje obaczyła, a w cudze się źdźbła nie wdawała*" ("Oh, Heavenly Master, give me clear sight so I can see the beam in my eyes and would not point out the motes in the eyes of others").[119]

The aim of copying was not only to reproduce certain texts but also to choose those that were proper for Catholic female spirituality. When copying them, nuns aimed to make an appropriate selection according to what was needed to function well in a nunnery. The book by Pontanus mentioned above proved useful precisely because of the many recommendations that sisters could internalise. For instance, the meditation *O niewieście od fluxu uzdrowionej* ('On a woman healed from flux') provides an explication of the reasons for which Jesus wanted people to learn about this miracle:

> Thirdly, so the woman was raised from her wretched shame as she knew she was detested by all people because of her condition. What I should learn from this story is that I should not be ashamed during my confession, but I ought to reveal before the confessor all my faults and everything shameful about me for the sake of my spiritual health. And that even though I have been granted the absolution of sins through my internal repentance, the confessor needs to confirm what God did for me.[120] (original in Polish)

One question that still to be answered is to what extent this selection was under the control of men, as was the case of the books selected for the nunnery's library and of printed works targeted mainly at nuns.

In the manuscript writings of the nuns in Vilnius and other nunneries in the Polish-Lithuanian Commonwealth, there are many characteristic features of what I call the 'female customisation of settings'.[121] It is discernible both in

[119] L. PONTANUS (Luis de la Puente), *Rozmyślania o tajemnicach wiary naszej, żywocie i męce Pana Jezusowej i błogosławionej Maryjej Panny, świętych bożych i ewangelijach przypadających: Z naukami dostatecznymi około nich i około rozmyślnej modlitwy, na sześć części rozdzielone* (Vilnius, 1647), p. 74.

[120] "*Trzecia, aby niewiastę z marnego wstydu wywiódł, która rozumiała, iż dla swej sprośnej choroby od wszytkich odrzucona była. Abym się stąd uczyła, nie bać się wstydu na spowiedzi, ale defekty i co mię zawstydać może dla duchownego zdrowia objawiać spowiednikowi. I potrzeba tego, chociem przez skrytą skruchę otrzymała odpuszczenie, aby spowiednik potwierdził, co Bóg uczynił*" (Pontanus, *Rozmyślania*, pp. 82-83).

[121] A single feature of the nuns' using the written word is not characteristic for female writing only and can also be found also in texts written by men. However, when we take into account the whole set of features of texts written or copied by nuns, a kind of pattern becomes clear. This pattern is called here the 'female customisation of settings': the nuns used to write only in Polish;

texts that are copies and in original works written by the nuns. For example, from other parts of the Commonwealth we know of autobiographies compiled at the behest of a spiritual guide, or lectures[122] and meditations. We may presume that such marks also characterised the writings of a Vilnius Carmelite sister, Katarzyna of Christ, née Felicjanna Tyszkiewiczówna (1625-1683), a daughter of the *voivode* of Brześć and a sister of the bishop of Vilnius, Jerzy Tyszkiewicz.[123] A Carmelite friar and confessor, father Ludwik of St. Florian, who lived many years later, mentions a volume of religious meditations received from her, one of many she authored:

> The Lord also decided that I should receive this manuscript book of our honourable sister Katarzyna [...]. I thank the Lord for the willingness of this saintly soul and her ability to note such important and needful things.[124]

Rafał Kalinowski, an eminent Carmelite friar and future saint, who at the end of the nineteenth century saw her other manuscripts, stated that they amounted to *c.* 400-500 pages of dense writing and that each of them ended with a commemorative appeal to future female readers:

> By virtue of God's mercy, I, Katarzyna, the most unworthy daughter of my mothers, ask for prayer. My dears, help my soul now and after death, so I will not be eternally rejected by God's mercy for my sins, as I have deserved. I ask you humbly, all my mothers and sisters, both living now and those who will come in the future, for help.[125]

they copied texts and changed male grammatical forms into female (in nouns, verbs, and pronouns; cf. GRZEŚKOWIAK, GWIOŹDZIK, and NOWICKA-STRUSKA, *Karmelitańskie adaptacje*, p. 68-69); for copying they chose a specific texts allowed or required by the Church or their order's authorities (similar to the choice of books in the libraries of male convents); the syntax of the sentences in their literary output is simpler than in similar male texts, because nuns did not have a formal education based on rhetoric and imitation rules (cf. TARGOSZ, *Piórem zakonnicy*, p. 15); in many of their texts they applied the rhetoric of self-humiliation; their writings are often based on mystical texts translated into Polish; their texts often reflect emotional relationships between nuns or with people from outside the nunnery; the nuns often exhibit their emotions in their chronicles, personal notes, or poems. They almost never wrote about political matters.

[122] Pl. *konferencje*: utterances given by a priest or a secular person during a mass or at other times on a religious, ethical, etc. subject.

[123] R. KALINOWSKI, "Klasztor karmelitanek bosych pw. św. Józefa w Wilnie: Pogląd ogólny", in: *Klasztory karmelitanek bosych w Polsce, na Litwie i Rusi: Ich początek, rozwój i tułactwo w czasie rozruchów wojennych w XVII w.*, 1, *Wilno*, ed. R. KALINOWSKI (Cracow, 1900), p. 7.

[124] Quoted *ibid.*, p. 8.

[125] *Ibid.*, pp. 8-9.

We may surmise that Sister Katarzyna was not the only Vilnius female author of this type of works, but all possible evidence for this was destroyed during the Muscovite occupation in the mid-seventeenth century.

We know that in the same nunnery sisters used to write religious poetry.[126] Among the Carmelite poets there is Eufrazja of St. Casimir (Helena Sanguszkówna, 1617-1679), since 1656 the mother superior of the Vilnius Carmelite nunnery. She wrote 41 Polish songs (*pieśni*, *kantyczki*), most of which were devoted to newborn Jesus.[127]

There are other texts that witness to the well-developed literary culture of the Benedictine, Bernardine and Carmelite sisters that have survived, namely correspondence and nunnery chronicles. Unfortunately, only vestiges of private

[126] For a long time the literary output of early modern Polish and Lithuanian nuns was neglected by the male-dominated research community. The most important anthologies of early modern Polish poetry, monographs, and university handbooks devoted to early modern Polish literature do not mention any poem written by a nun. This situation has been changed since the late 1970s, when several publications devoted Carmelite poetry were published. See B. KRZYŻANIAK, *Kantyczki z rękopisów karmelitańskich (XVII-XVIII w.)* (Cracow, 1977); S. NIEZNANOWSKI, "Barokowe kolędy polskie", in: *Necessitas et ars: Studia staropolskie dedykowane Profesorowi Januszowi Pelcowi*, 1, ed. B. OTWINOWSKA *et al.* (Warsaw, 1993), pp. 113-121; H. POPŁAWSKA, "Zabawa wesoło-nabożna przyszłych obywatelów nieba: Nad siedemnastowiecznymi sylwami karmelitanek bosych", in: *Literatura polskiego baroku w kręgu idei*, ed. A. NOWICKA-JEŻOWA, M. HANUSIEWICZ, and A. KARPIŃSKI (Lublin, 1995), pp. 133-159; A. GLIŃSKA, "Przyczynek do dziejów poezji karmelitańskiej: Charakterystyka i wybrane wiersze z rękopisu o sygn. 3643 I ze zbiorów Biblioteki Jagiellońskiej", *Barok* 5.2 (1998), pp. 185-194; M. HANUSIEWICZ, *Święte i zmysłowe w poezji religijnej polskiego baroku* (Lublin, 1998), pp. 335-348; EAD., "Wyobraźnia i erudycja w karmelitańskich pieśniach o Miłości Bożej", *Barok* 5.1 (1998), pp. 191-201; M. NAWROCKA-BERG, "Dziwne światy karmelitanek: Próba czytania zakonnych kantyczek", in: *Koncept w kulturze staropolskiej*, ed. L. ŚLĘK, A. KARPIŃSKI, and W. PAWLAK (Lublin, 2005); H. POPŁAWSKA, *Kultura literacka karmelitanek bosych w Polsce* (Gdańsk, 2006); M. HANUSIEWICZ-LAVALLEE, "Prywatność w rękopiśmiennej poezji polskich karmelitanek", *Barok* 18.2 (2011), pp. 11-22; L. STERCZEWSKA, "Głośny rezon ... Edycja kolęd z osiemnastowiecznych rękopisów Biblioteki Karmelitanek bosych w Krakowie na Wesołej", TERMINUS 12.22 (2020), pp. 151-177. A number of female texts written in nunneries were published from manuscripts. Among them there are writings by the Benedictine mother superior Magdalena Mortęska (1554-1631) and by a Carmelite mystic, Marianna Marchocka (Teresa of Jesus, 1603-1652). Research upon their writings contributed in the second decade of the twenty-first century to initiating the process of beatification of both writers by the Catholic Church. M. MORTĘSKA, *Rozmyślania o Męce Pańskiej*, ed. M. BORKOWSKA and M. MRÓZ (Cracow, 2020); M.A. MARCHOCKA (Teresa od Jezusa), *Autobiografia mistyczna i inne pisma*, ed. Cz. GIL (Cracow, 2010).

[127] The authorship of this collection of poems was established by H. POPŁAWSKA, "Rękopiśmienne Kantyczki po polsku z XVII wieku – problemy proweniencji i autorstwa", *Napis* 9 (2003), pp. 79-91.

correspondence, in particular particularly that of nuns, have been preserved,[128] and we can study what remains mainly on the basis of intermediary accounts. One of them is the Rule of the Vilnius Poor Clares in its Latin and Polish versions, approved by bishop Wołłowicz in 1629. Communicating by letter must have been quite popular, since the sisters were even explicitly forbidden to do so. In fact, they were not allowed to write to anybody without the consent of the mother superior; one's closest family was an exception, but only in exceptional situations:

> From this time on, no sister will be allowed to write to her relatives or to any other ecclesial or secular persons, or to send notes without mother superior being notified and having put to them the nunnery seal. [...] They may, however, write to their parents and first-degree relatives if they need to and obtain the consent of mother superior without her reading the letters, which, nonetheless, cannot be frequent, but only if the need be clear.[129]

Despite the fact that in all Vilnius nunneries the sisters wrote letters, I was able to find back only those connected with the Benedictine nunnery.[130] Its superior, abbess Marianna Kuczkowska, engaged in correspondence with the bishop of Vilnius Eustachy Wołłowicz, mothers of the pupils of the nunnery school, and the abbesses of other nunneries. The letters mostly concern the administration of properties and legal issues. However, mothers superior were not the only ones to write letters. They sometimes used the assistance of other sisters, who acted as their secretaries,[131] and during their absence they were replaced by other nuns. Their letters are characterised by a knowledge of the fundamental rules of epistolography of the first half of the seventeenth century.

The chronicles are no less interesting. They were written by nuns and monks from the central Middle Ages onwards, and belong to the most popular

[128] PARTYKA, *Żona wyćwiczona*, p. 186.

[129] *Konstytucje panien zakonnych*, pp. 110-111. The change in reading habits after leaving the external world and entering enclosure was noticed by H. WOLFE, "Reading bells and loose papers: Reading and writing practices of the English Benedictine nuns of Cambrai and Paris", in: *Early Modern Women's Manuscript Writing: Selected Papers from the Trinity / Trent Colloquium*, ed. V.E. BURKE and J. GIBSON (Burlington, 2004), pp. 135-136. We may presume that for a young noblewoman in the first half of the seventeenth century in Lithuania commencing a cloistered life entailed much more contact with written texts than life at home.

[130] BORKOWSKA, "Problemy siedemnastowiecznych fundacji", pp. 264-307.

[131] PARTYKA, *Żona wyćwiczona*, p. 129.

type of texts produced by monastic communities.[132] In most nunneries in the Polish-Lithuanian Commonwealth, nuns followed this long tradition and wrote down the histories of their nunneries.[133] This was also the case of Vilnius.[134] However, the seventeenth-century female chronicles written in Polish and Lithuanian nunneries gravitate towards a new literary genre: memoirs.[135] Researchers noticed that their authors take a clear stance, show their emotions, express their opinions, and are strongly subjective.[136] Male chronicles from that time are much more close to historiography, and in these texts "there is hardly any information on life inside the monastery or relationships between the monks".[137]

Two handwritten female chronicle-memoirs have been preserved, that of the Discalced Carmelite sisters and the Bernardine sisters of St. Michael.[138] The latter of these manuscripts, although it was begun only in 1671, also refers to events that happened before the 1650s which its female author witnessed and which replaced the original chronicle destroyed in the Muscovite attack.

The first, Carmelite, chronicle, of which we only have fragments, was initiated by mother Magdalena of the Saviour and discusses the origins of the nunnery in 1638. The other, newer one is an intriguing and vivid narrative of the history of the Vilnius Carmelite sisters in the years 1644-1659, who must have escaped a plague, the Muscovite assailants, and Mrs Hanna Radziwiłło-

[132] An example of a late medieval male chronicle is the *Chronicle* by the Bernardine Jan of Komorowo, written in Vilnius at the beginning of the sixteenth century.

[133] Karolina Targosz was able to identify *c.* 30 names of nuns who were the authors of the chronicles in the seventeenth-century nunneries in Poland and Lithuania. See TARGOSZ, *Piórem zakonnicy*, pp. 290-291.

[134] TARGOSZ, *Piórem zakonnicy*, pp. 91-92; PAULOUSKAYA, *Grodzieńskie kroniki klasztorne*, pp. 11-12.

[135] NOWICKA-STRUSKA, *Za murami klasztoru*, p. 102.

[136] TARGOSZ, *Piórem zakonnicy*, pp. 13, 171; PAULOUSKAYA, *Grodzieńskie kroniki klasztorne*, p. 148; NOWICKA-STRUSKA, *Za murami klasztoru*, pp. 90-99.

[137] H. PAULOUSKAYA, "O czym milczą kroniki klasztorów grodzieńskich (II połowa XVII-XVIII wiek)", *Rocznik Lituanistyczny* 2 (2016), p. 97. See also N.P. NEUMANN, "Kronikarze poznańskiego klasztoru karmelitów bosych i ich dzieło w okresie staropolskim", *Karmelitańskie Studia i Materiały Historyczne* 1 (1993), pp. 113-146; I. PIETRZKIEWICZ, "Teksty historiograficzne w środowisku dominikanów Prowincji Litewskiej – wybrane przykłady", *Annales Universitatis Paedagogicae Cracoviensis. Studia ad Bibliothecarum Scientiam Pertinentia* 14 (2016), pp. 328-346.

[138] "Krótka kronika fundacyi karmelitanek bosych klasztoru św. Józefa w Wilnie, która stanęła w roku 1638, 18 Decembra", in: *Klasztory karmelitanek bosych w Polsce, na Litwie i Rusi*, pp. 19-124; "Kronika bernardynek świętomichalskich w Wilnie", ed. M. KAŁAMAJSKA-SAEED, *Nasza Przeszłość* 101 (2004), pp. 331-435.

wa, the wife of the castellan of Vilnius, who wanted, regardless of whether it was right or wrong, to snatch her daughter Zofia Konstancja from the nunnery who had chosen the veil against her mother's will. The author of the book may be sister Katarzyna of Christ (Felicjanna Tyszkiewiczówna),[139] whom we encountered above. The account of their exile during the Swedish and Muscovite invasion, when they wandered all around the Commonwealth, Upper Hungary, and Moravia, is one of the most interesting narratives about the events of the mid-seventeenth century, and it may be regarded an antithesis to the well-known male memoirs from the seventeenth century, which were praised by scholars, such as Jan Chryzostom Pasek's memoirs (*c.* 1690-1695).[140] The comparison of both texts allows us to understand the individual quality of the Carmelite sisters' memoir better.

There are distinct differences between the two memoirs, not only because Pasek was a soldier and sister Katarzyna of Christ a civilian. They also had different educational backgrounds since Pasek – unlike Sister Katarzyna – studied in a Jesuit college and spoke and wrote Latin fluently. The differences affect the stylistic form of both texts. Pasek wrote long and complex periods, interlaced with Latin phrases or words; he was trying to amuse his readers with funny or curious stories. Sister Katarzyna's sentences are shorter and in pure Polish. She did not care about the rhetorical refinement of her story but focused on facts and did not avoid writing about everyday matters.

Sister Katarzyna was keeping a close watch on other people's fortunes and misfortunes. She was compassionate and easily expressed her emotions. Even though sister Katarzyna and her companions experienced many difficulties during the war, in her memoirs we can notice close relationships, emotions, and traces of self-reflection.[141] Writing about emotional relationships occurs in

[139] KALINOWSKI, "Klasztor karmelitanek bosych pw. św. Józefa w Wilnie", p. 7.

[140] J.Ch. PASEK, *Pamiętniki*, ed. R. POLLAK (Warsaw, 1987). Karolina Targosz was the first scholar to suggest a comparative interpretation of the chronicles-memoirs by nuns and Pasek's memoirs. TARGOSZ, *Piórem zakonnicy*, p. 14.

[141] The main difference between the two narratives lay in the construction of the narrator. In his memoirs, Pasek was completely focused on his self-fashioning. In these memoirs it is difficult to find any warm emotions towards other people. He rarely recalled his comrades in arms, and the only creatures he loved were his animals (the horse and the otter). After ten years of his military career he may have suffered PTSD. At this stage of research, it can be only speculated if the difference between memoirs by Pasek and the chronicle by sister Katarzyna mirrors the difference between the female and male way of writing in the Polish-Lithuanian Commonwealth in the seventeenth century. This problem will be discussed in another study.

many chronicles written by nuns, not only in Vilnius.[142] I shall quote from sister Katarzyna again later on.

The chronicle of the Bernardine nunnery also reveals significant stylistic skills of its anonymous female author. She consciously used rhetoric and rhetorical topoi, although she could not have known them from a formal education, as might have been the case of a man writing a similar text, but only from her own reading experience. The Bernardine sister aimed at recording past events in a text which was supposed to serve as an 'external memory' for the nun and her readers. Accordingly, she describes the history of her nunnery going back even to before she took the veil, of which she only learned from a previous chronicle destroyed by the Muscovites. As for many later events, she herself participated in them, knew the characters of the narrative, and used the aid of her companions' memory. Her story is thus a "collective diary", as Karolina Targosz has put it,[143] and one of the few seventeenth-century narratives written from a woman's perspective and for women.

Chronicle-diaries were a type of text nuns usually were not obliged to write. It was different when it came to financial and economic documentation.[144] The need to manage a nunnery property required the constant use of writing. Notwithstanding the fact that women in the world outside were quite often engaged in business operations, financial and economic issues were usually the domain of men. In a nunnery this was not possible; administrative matters and most other legal issues had to be taken care of by the nuns. Nunneries kept registers of the sisters, that is books of vows containing brief biographical entries concerning the nuns of a given nunnery.[145] This was a medieval tradition, which has been continued in monasteries and nunneries until

[142] Hanna Paulouskaya. who thoroughly examined six seventeenth and eighteenth-century chronicles from five male monasteries and one nunnery of the Bridgettines, in Hrodna (Grodno) in the Grand Duchy of Lithuania (now Belarus), noted: "The *Dzieje kapitulne* [History of the chapter] is the unique 'feminine' text examined here. Its form and structure are similar to the construction of chronicles containing excerpts from the documents. Its female author [*autorka*] also quotes many other texts (speeches of the prioress) and makes comments upon them. Sometimes these comments are concise and neutral. However, in a large part of her chronicle the author openly expresses her stance, which is subjective and emotional. This feature distinguishes her text from the 'male' ones. [...] In another comment quoted *supra* the author describes her own experiences in the nunnery and her relationships with the prioress, something which never occurs in the chronicles from male monasteries" (PAULOUSKAYA, *Grodzieńskie kroniki klasztorne*, p. 148).

[143] TARGOSZ, *Piórem zakonnicy*, p. 13-14.

[144] BORKOWSKA, *Panny siostry*, pp. 317-324; PARTYKA, "Żona wyćwiczona", p. 190.

[145] GWIOŹDZIK, *Kultura pisma i książki*, p. 168.

today.[146] Two such books have survived, the *Księga żywota, w której się wpisują imiona sióstr karmelitanek bosych, które czynią professyją w tym klasztorze św. Józefa w Wilnie od roku 1640 do roku 1668* (The Book of Lives, Which Registers the Names of those Discalced Carmelite Sisters Who Took Their Vows in This Nunnery of St. Joseph)[147] and a book containing longer biographies of pious nuns, *Życia i przykłady wielmożnych karmelitanków bosych konwentu wileńskiego* (The Lives and Examples of the Honourable Discalced Carmelite Sisters of the Vilnius Nunnery).[148]

Rich economic documentation testifies to well-developed pragmatic literacy in the Vilnius nunneries. To a large extent, this category also includes texts written by mothers superior. The mother superior and / or the sister steward (*subprzeorysza* or *ekonomka*) were the persons responsible for the financial matters of the nunnery.[149] They had to show not only high literate skills but also be skilful businesswomen. They were responsible for supervising the registers of incomes and expenses, which were maintained in all nunneries.[150] The remains of the archives of the nunneries and the court registers (the registers of the municipal, castle, and land courts and of the Lithuanian Tribunal) reveal large numbers of documents concerning financial and property matters

[146] E.g. in the Norbertine nunnery in Imbramowice (Lesser Poland Voivodeship, Poland) founded in the twelfth century, the nuns keep a *liber mortuorum* (or *necrologium*), a calendar-like register containing names of Norbertine nuns and fathers and benefactors of the nunnery. The purpose of the register was to recall people on the anniversary of their death to pray for their souls. The register was initiated by mother superior Zofia Grotówna in 1718, but there are mentioned also names of people who died in the first half of the seventeenth century. The last record found in this register in 2018 is in the page marked on 12 October: "*Obiit Virgo Hugona (Marianna Prawda), iubilaria huius loci 2005, anno aet[atis] 86, prof[essi] 55*". Previous records, written by four different hands, remember people who died on that day in 1842, 1806, and 1620: *Poczet imion w Panu Bogu odpoczywających braci i sióstr po wszytkich klasztorach premonstratu polskiego zmarłych pod szczęśliwą władzą najprzewielebniejszej w Chrystusie panny jej mości panny Zofii z Przyłęka Grotówny, zakonu przeświętnego Norberta św. konwentu przewielebnych panien imbromowskich zasłużonej ksieni przez wielebne księdza Hermana Zawarskiego, tegoż zakonu profesa Chebdowskiego* (sic!) *a na ten czas wikaryjego zwierzynieckiego z pilnością należytą sporządzany i dla wspólnego tych dusz poratowania konwentowi imbramowskiemu aplikowany 1718* (MS without shelf-mark), p. 142.

[147] *Klasztory karmelitanek bosych w Polsce, na Litwie i Rusi*, pp. 15-17.

[148] The manuscript is mentioned by Rafał Kalinowski in KALINOWSKI, "Klasztor karmelitanek bosych pw. św. Józefa w Wilnie", p. 128.

[149] BORKOWSKA, *Życie codzienne w polskich klasztorach żeńskich*, pp. 162-171.

[150] GWIOŹDZIK, *Kultura pisma i książki*, p. 163-169, 184-191.

in which the nuns were engaged. This preoccupation with property management is also visible in the chronicles of nunneries and convents.[151]

The smallest group among texts written in nunneries includes *litterae*, which in this case meant chronicles and collections of meditations. The status of these sets of texts, seemingly similar to those written by men, changes if we take into account their function in a different interpretative community – different because they were regulated by different laws and were subject to rules stricter than those that were binding for monks, priests and secular men.

> And be kind to her too because you will thus prevent her from getting married; as despite my knowledge of *nocivam et inimitabile feminam* [the female harmfulness, which is beyond compare], I am convinced that she will pray to the Lord so that He does not punish her in order to denigrate her sobriety and age. But do not force her with anger because *nihil est atrocitas et severitas femina* [there is nothing stronger than the atrocity and severity of a woman] and every woman *et suo malo ulciscitur iniuriam* [avenges misdeeds, even if it were to inflict damage to herself].[152] (original in Polish)

Thus did Jan Hlebowicz, the *voivode* of Trakai, caution his sons in his testament written in Vilnius in 1599 against their own mother. And although Hlebowicz was a 'Calvinist heretic', his opinion – which had much in common with medieval misogynous statements[153] – would have found supporters not only among his Catholic neighbours, but probably also among the Carmelite sisters from St. Joseph's Nunnery. This text is permeated with the language of weakness and his own helplessness, as well as humility – mostly with regard to the (male) God, but also to other men. The first abbess of the nunnery, mother Eufrazja of St. John (Teodora Piaseczyńska),

> used to say the following about our honourable fathers [that is the Carmelite fathers]: they are our greatest benefactors, the guardians of our souls. If it were not for them, there would be no Carmelite sisters whatsoever. They are our shepherds, our judges, often adding that our honourable fathers, albeit sons of the same holy mother of whom we are daughters – not through any obligation but because of the

[151] PAULOUSKAYA, *Grodzieńskie kroniki klasztorne*, pp. 118-121.

[152] "Testament Jana Hlebowicza, Wilno, 28 lipca 1590 roku", ed. in: AUGUSTYNIAK, *Testamenty ewangelików reformowanych*, p. 67.

[153] A. CLASSEN, *The Power of a Woman's Voice in Medieval and Early Modern Literatures. New Approaches to German and European Women Writers and to Violence Against Women in Premodern Times* (Berlin and New York, 2007), pp. 13-16.

> pure love they have for our holy mother – because of the same love, they take care of us. And what would we do should they leave us?[154] (original in Polish)

A similar spirit permeates the praise of the founder and "fertile father" of the nunnery of St. Michael, chancellor Lew Sapieha:

> But here we cannot be silent about the fact that our first founder, guardian, patron, father, and benefactor made a name for himself in the Lord's eyes as he initiated the foundation of so many nunneries. Indeed, happy and fertile is our father because he shall not cease to give birth to chaste maidens for both the earthly and eternal service of our Lord Jesus and His immaculate Mother.[155] (original in Polish)

The topos of *humilitas*, that is to belittle oneself, derives from classical rhetoric,[156] but its use in the two Vilnius chronicles and in the letters of the nuns seems to be characteristic of nunnery rhetoric. At a first glance, it may appear that this rhetoric comes from the humiliation recommended by the monastic rules from the Middle Ages.[157] Therefore, nuns – as the lowest of creatures – are obedient, timid and unsure, for instance as to whether they will manage to build a church without any help from wealthy founders, or whether or not they are in danger of being attacked by the heretic Prince Janusz Radziwiłł, who wishes to free his relative under the pretext that they have deluded her. However, what shows very clearly through this fear of God and people is the rhetoric of a lack of independence, which is directly rooted neither in the Rule nor in trusting to God's will. A comparison of a chronicle written by an anonymous Bernardine sister with a Latin work of a sixteenth-century conventual annalist, Jan of Komorowo (Komorowski), reveals the following contrast: the rhetoric of *humilitas* of the Bernardine friar is of a different kind from the rhetoric of fear (or lack) of independence of the Bernardine sister. The difference between the construction of the narrative subjectivity of Jan of Komorowo and the Bernardine sister lays in the rhetorical strategies related to their gender roles. Jan of Komorowo, as a man, priest, and provincial, was allowed to present – at least to some degree – his power, while the Bernardine nun, as a woman, was supposed to present her obedience and uncertainty.

[154] *Krótka kronika fundacyi karmelitanek bosych*, p. 26

[155] *Kronika bernardynek świętomichalskich w Wilnie*, p. 338.

[156] E.R. CURTIUS, *Literatura europejska i łacińskie średniowiecze*, ed. and trans. A. BOROWSKI (Cracow, 1997), pp. 90-92.

[157] C. CANNON, "Enclosure", in: *The Cambridge Companion to Medieval Women's Writing*, ed. C. DINSHAW and D. WALLACE (Cambridge, 2003), pp. 136-138.

The rhetorical nature of such a construction of the subject in the female chronicles is visible when we take into account other types of discourse the sisters were involved in. In her letters, abbess Kuczkowska negotiates hard; she firmly defends the properties of the Benedictine sisters and threatens her adversaries with a trial when necessary.[158] In 1639, the Bernardine sisters of St. Michael protested before the castle courts of Vilnius and Hrodna (this is why they used the services of Jan Górski, the legal adviser of the Vilnius Bernardine friars) against the Evangelical Protestants who shot an arrow into the image of St. Michael on the façade of their church.[159] Therefore, despite being the weaker and inferior participants in a game in which the object is to circulate texts, the sisters were not passive. This does not alter the fact, however, that at least until the mid-seventeenth century the rules of using texts were predominately regulated by men,[160] and in Vilnius nobody would dare to even think about questioning this status quo.

Conclusion

The remarks on female literacy in early modern Vilnius which have been presented here show that women's use of writing was strictly conditioned by their social status. Reading and writing skills were more common among women who belonged to the aristocracy, the nobility, or the wealthy urban 'middle class' than among those from other social groups. In this respect, Vilnius is not much different from other cities of the time. However, we should also take into account additional factors, which make the situation of women's literacy in Vilnius different from other cities in the Polish-Lithuanian Commonwealth. The literacy of lay Catholic women was mainly limited to eco-

[158] "Marianna Kuczkowska do Stanisława Wolkanowskiego", Vilnius, 5 May 1635, in: BORKOWSKA, *Problemy siedemnastowiecznych fundacji*, pp. 279-280. Mothers superior of all nunneries had to defend the properties of their congregations in various ways. In the acts of the Vilnius cathedral chaplain, there is a letter from the abbess of the Benedictine sisters in Nyasvizh, Dorota Brądzberska, from 9 August 1616, in which she explains to canon Szydłowski why she is sending him a sum lower than required. MS MAB F43-443/8.

[159] The events of the year 1639 are discussed in Chapter 9, 'Polemic treatises: Between tumults and disputations'.

[160] Contradictions of female literary activity in the seventeenth-century Poland were recently discussed by Andrzej Staniszewski when analysing the memoirs (from 1685) by Anna Stanisławska (Zbąska). A.T. STANISZEWSKI, "Nieobecna 'książka białogłowskiego konceptu': Kobiety, kanon i badania literatury dawnej", *Terminus* 16.2 (31) (2014), pp. 205-208.

nomic and, to some extent, religious purposes. Lay women used documents, bills, and probably prayer books. Some of them were able to write simple utility texts, for instance signing a document or making a list of the goods offered in their stores. Presumably, many women from the social elite of all Christian confessions read prayer books, hymn books, religious books, or the Bible.

The best educated women in the city, who produced or processed more complex texts, were Catholic nuns: Bernardines, Benedictines, and Carmelites. The Vilnius nunneries had a major impact on the rhetorical shape of the city, even though the nuns lived in many respects separated from other social groups.[161] Nuns created economic texts (bills, inventories), wrote many letters, historical-diarist texts (chronicles), prayers, poems, texts for meditations, and spiritual exercises. Nuns read much and, unlike the majority of lay women, books accompanied their daily life. Sometimes, the Vilnius nunneries initiated printed editions of books. Therefore it is reasonable to say that nuns were also patrons of literature. The events of the mid-seventeenth century, to wit the destruction of the city by the Muscovite army, also proved that the Vilnius nunneries were important 'places of memory' and depositories of collective memory. All these circumstances made seventeenth-century Vilnius the most important centre of women's literature in the Grand Duchy of Lithuania.

[161] The relationship between the nunnery and the outer world in early modern Poland and Lithuania is an issue to be investigated in the future. The sources prove that nuns had a dense net of contacts with lay people, members of the ecclesiastical structures, priests, fathers from male monasteries, and nuns from other nunneries. Sometimes nuns belonging to different orders visited each other. For example mother superior Zofia Grotówna from the Imbramowice Norbertine nunnery noted in her diary visits of nuns from the Order of Saint Clare, and from the Dominican, Norbertine, Bernardine, and Benedictine Orders from Grodzisko, Cracow, Racibórz, Zwierzyniec, and other places. "16 July 1716. Four Dominican sisters from the nunnery in Racibórz arrived. The same day came also two Bernardine sisters from the nunnery of St. Joseph in Cracow: Miss Łącka and Miss Grotówna. They remained here for five days" (Z. GROTHÓWNA, *Kronika klasztorna sióstr norebertanek w Imbramowicach, 1703-1741*, ed. W. BIELAK and W.W. ŻUREK (Kielce, 2011), p. 93. All these contacts resulted in the production and exchange of texts (mainly letters and devotional literature).

Chapter 5

Reading and Writing in Early Modern Vilnius

The Levels of Pragmatic Literacy and Illiteracy

Those who dealt with script can be divided into 'users' and 'producers' of texts, or 'readers' and 'scribes', because reading and writing are not the same competences[1] and in the past, clearly, more people possessed the skill of reading than this of writing. We must bear in mind, however, that the competences of the 'users' and 'producers' of texts varied within each of these groups: from those who recognised the letters IC XP on the icons of Christ Pantocrator, to those who read the Latin commentaries to St. Thomas Aquinas, to those who carved letters in stone that formed someone's epitaph, to those who were able to write such an epitaph in Latin dactylic hexameters or Polish alexandrines.

Almost certainly all city dwellers were users of script and texts, as almost everyone had to deal with different kinds of texts. In this sense, there were no illiterate people in the city, that is people who had no idea what writing was for.[2] However, it is difficult to determine to what extent the use of texts can be identified with reading them, because the degree of pragmatic literacy[3] varied

[1] FRANKLIN, *Writing, Society and Culture*, pp. 3-4.

[2] M. MOSTERT, "Forgery and trust", in: *Strategies of Writing: Studies on Text and Trust in the Middle Ages*, ed. P. SCHULTE, M. MOSTERT, and I. VAN RENSWOUDE (Turnhout, 2008), pp. 48-49; J. BURGERS and M. MOSTERT, "O fałszerstwach dokumentów w średniowiecznej Holandii", *Roczniki Historyczne* 69 (2003), p. 65. These researchers list four main levels of literacy: illiteracy, semi-illiteracy, semi-literacy and literacy.

[3] The concept of pragmatic literacy (*pragmatische Schriftlichkeit*) was introduced in 1979 by Brigitte Schlieben-Lange. This means using writing and text either for practical action or to

significantly. It could mean the simplest competences, that is the recognition of writing and its functions by semi-illiterates, then the more complex ability to identify individual letters and words, next the semi-literates' limited ability to read printed books and manuscripts, and, in the case of fully literate people, the ability to read and write texts, including texts in Latin, and possibly in other foreign languages of similar difficulty, for example in Greek. The possession of certain reading competences was directly connected with membership of particular groups (estates, guilds, etc.), which emerged from the hierarchical divisions characteristic not only of Vilnius, but of the whole of Europe at that time. The higher the social status of the text user, the greater his or her practical literacy skills and the wider the range of varieties and genres with which he or she came into contact.

Reading skills can be compared to a device or a driver that allows one to perform texts. The degree of technological advancement of this tool could vary, and the ability to replay a text depended on it. As a result, not every 'device' was able to read every text, as some 'drivers' only supported texts in Ruthenian, while others were intended for Latin texts, and yet others had universal functions. The ability to read / replay various texts was highly valued, mainly because of its social usefulness, especially if combined with writing skills.[4] Many users of texts in early modern Vilnius had little competence in deciphering them, let alone in writing them, that is in encoding information. As a result, they had to use the services of specialists who made their competences (that these 'devices / drivers') available, either for a fee or, in a different type of exchange, for instance for neighbourly help.

The main source that allows us to assess how the inhabitants of early modern Vilnius used other people's writing skills is formed by documents relative to debts, sales, purchases, wills, etc., drawn up from the second half of the fifteenth century onwards. Plenty of such documents are preserved in their original form or as copies. They usually end with statements by witnesses, initially confirmed by seals and later also by signatures. In 1543, Jan Mysz-

teach people to act or behave in a certain way. This concept is discussed by M. MOSTERT, "New approaches to medieval communication?", in *New Approaches to Medieval Communication*, ed. M. MOSTERT,with an Introduction by M.T. CLANCHY (Turnhout, 1999), p. 26, and A.ADAMSKA, "Średniowiecze na nowo odczytane: O badaniach nad kulturą pisma", *Roczniki Historyczne* 65 (1999), p. 132.

[4] On the growing status of written word and literary skills in late medieval Poland see A. BARTOSZEWICZ, *Urban Literacy*, pp. 82-87.

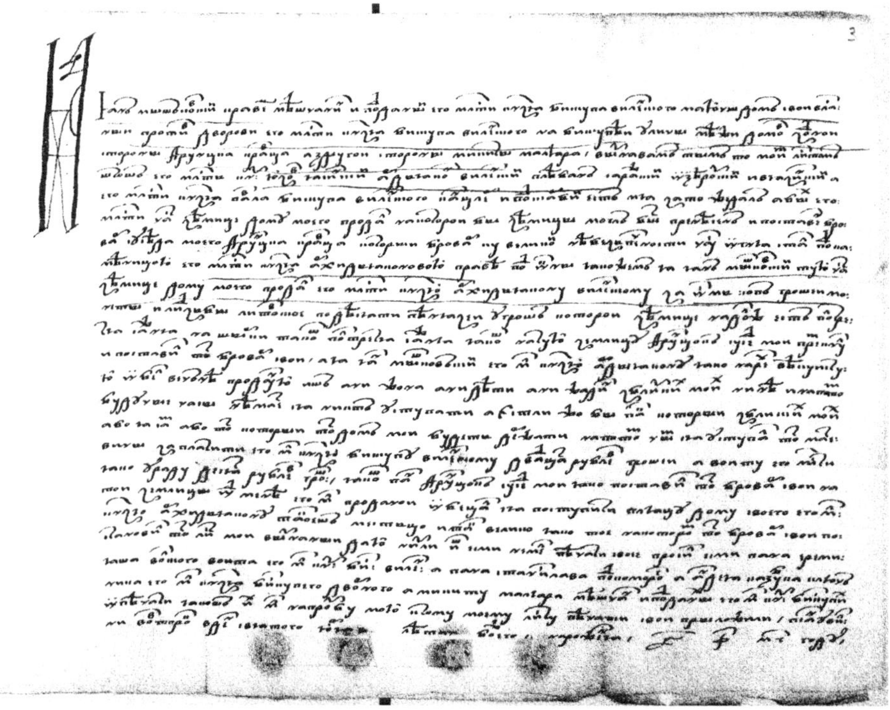

Fig. 18 Contract of selling a plot of land by a tailor Jan Myszkowski, an inhabitant of the bishop's *jurydyka*, 1543. MS Vilnius, VUB, F4-18345, f. 3r. Reproduced with the permission of VUB.

kowski, "tailor, burgher and a subject of His Grace the Bishop of Vilnius, who had his own house opposite the manor of His Grace the Bishop of Vilnius in Bishop Street between the house of the tailor Aruncok on one side and the house of the painter Mikita on the other" agreed to sell part of his plot to the archdeacon of Vilnius, Józef Jasiński. for 8 *kopas* of Lithuanian *grosz* (Fig. 18). The witnesses were mentioned at the bottom of a meticulous Ruthenian document written in *skoropis*, and four seals were stamped below. Jan Myszkowski, the document's issuer, himself confessed:

> because I did not have my own seal, I asked Mr Jeremiasz Wolski, the mayor of His Grace the Bishop of Vilnius, and Stanisław, the chamberlain, and Andrzej Kazubek, the butler of His Grace the Bishop's courtier, as well as the painter Miki-

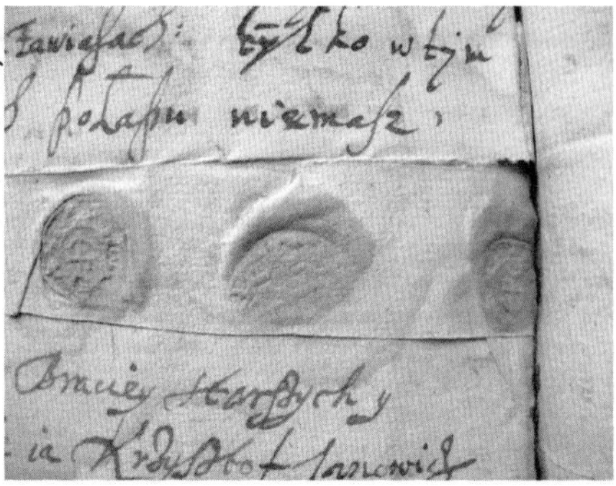

Fig. 19 Seals of the witnesses who confirmed the inventory of the house of Paweł Mydlarz and Mikołaj Mydlarz, 1621. MS Vilnius, LVIA, F22, ap. 1, nr 5344, f. 605v. Photo J. Niedźwiedź.

> ta, the townspeople and the Bishop's subjects to stamp their seals on my letter, which they did at my request.[5] (original in Ruthenian)

At that time, it was normal to validate such a transaction using documents written by scribes who specialised in producing them and confirm them with seals. Attaching seals to documents was a prolongation of a medieval practice. Although in the sixteenth century signatures also started to come into use in Lithuania, seals remained a common and trusted way of validating the documents. In this respect Jan Myszkowski had to rely on the help of his friends and neighbours, as he himself could not sign the document or press his signet on it. What is more, it can be assumed that, being a Polish-speaking Catholic, he had difficulties reading a document written in Ruthenian *skoropis* himself. Therefore, at each stage of the document's creation, both its production and its subsequent referencing, he had to use the competences of other people, equipped with better tools to either create or read its content.

Tailor Myszkowski belonged to the majority of Vilnius inhabitants, who, like him, had a limited ability to use texts, although it should be remembered that there were whole social groups operating on an even lower level of pragmatic literacy, even in the middle of the seventeenth century, when school attendance in the city had reached a high level.

On 8 December 1654, a lease agreement was signed: "the undersigned townspeople from the chamois-making trade" certify that they "leased from Mikołaj Kliczewski, the mayor of Vilnius" a two-wheeled mill and a fulling machine, for which they were to pay 30 *kopas* of *grosz* (that is 1800 Lithuanian *grosz*) annually. There would be nothing surprising about their signatures were

[5] MS VUB F4-18345, f. 3r

it not for the fact that the undersigned inhabitants of the city were not able to sign the document: "With this letter we confirm the above and since we cannot sign ourselves, we used the help of good people to put their signatures in the place of ours". The persons who signed beneath are as follows:

> Seal-bearer Stefan Dubowicz, the ayor of Vilnius, upon the request of the persons mentioned in this letter but not able to write. Orally asked by the persons named in this contract and not skilled in writing to sign, I signed it with my hand, Jan Minkiewicz, the mayor of Vilnius. Orally asked by the chamois-makers as a seal-bearer in this contract Mikołaj Richter *manu propria* [with my own hand].[6] (original in Polish)

The most pronounced factor that determined the level of competence in reading was gender. As a rule, women, regardless of their religious identity, had scarcely opportunities to go to school, so their possibilities to come into contact with texts was different from that of men. Some women could study at home, especially those of high social status. They were often supposed to lead family businesses, keeping their accounts and correspondence. Still, assigning women to a social role that consisted primarily of taking care of the household limited the range of texts they were supposed to read, which for men – especially those from the social elites – was, at least potentially, unrestricted.[7] The second most important factor was social class. It was the rule that economic and cultural capital were linked. Members of the nobility, clergy, and the merchant elites, that is classes in a privileged political and financial position, could and had to read much more than representatives of other social groups. In individual cases, women who belonged to these three elite social groups also gained greater skills in using texts. The third determinant of reading skills was religion. Christians were in a privileged position, with Catholics leading the way from the end of the fifteenth century. However, even the poorest non-Catholic citizens played a greater or lesser role in the circulation of texts in the city.

We may assume that at least from the end of the fourteenth century onwards every Vilnius inhabitant knew what writing was for and understood it as a way of representing speech. Such an understanding of the function of writing was popularised by religion. All confessions present in the capital city from the

[6] MS LVIA F23, ap. 1, no. 5096, f. 672r. Original in Polish.

[7] E. SNOOK, "Reading women", in: *The Cambridge Companion to Early Modern Women's Writing*, ed. L. LUNGER KNOPPERS (Cambridge, 2009), p. 40. See also chapter 4.

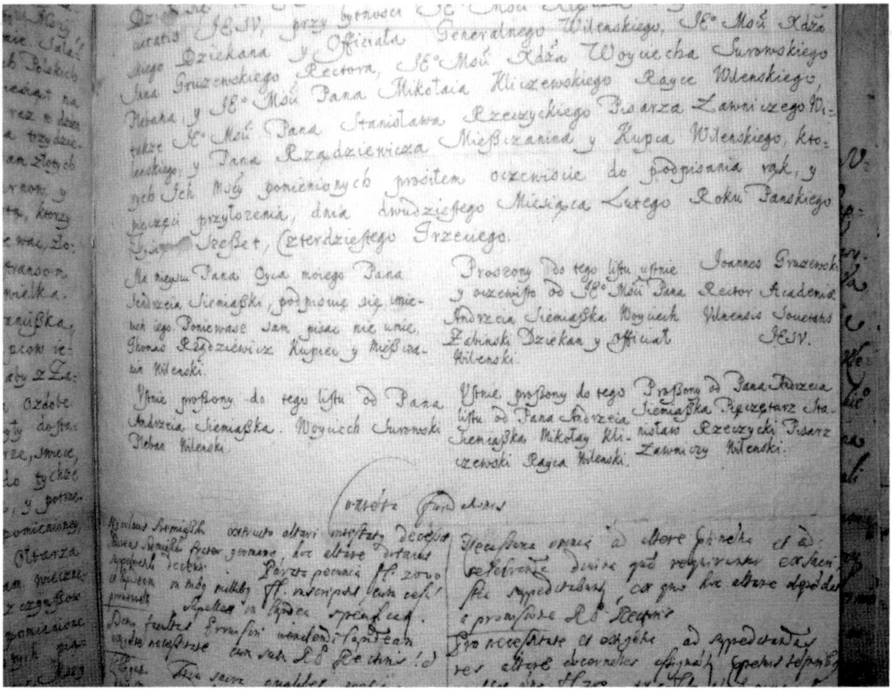

Fig. 20 Signature of Tomasz Rządziewicz in place of the signature of his semi-illiterate father: "I sign [this testament] in place of my father, Mr. Jędrzej Siemiaszko, who cannot write – Thomas Rządziewicz the merchant and citizen [*mieszczanin*] of Vilnius" (original in Polish). MS Vilnius, LVIA, F23, ap. 1, 5096, f. 212r. Photo J. Niedźwiedź.

end of the fourteenth century, that is Orthodox Christianity, Catholicism, Judaism and Islam, were religions of the Book, so the texts used by them, read aloud or sung during prayers, provided an idea of what writing was. Furthermore, writing was used to decorate sacral and other objects, so everyone could see it, whether in the form of Greek and Cyrillic inscriptions on icons, polychromes of sacred texts in the synagogue, or inscriptions on tombstones.

The same holds true for inscriptions on coins. In Vilnius, which was not only the political capital but also an economic centre, money naturally played a significant role, and from the mid-fifteenth century coins were regularly accompanied by a legend. Silver money, *półgrosz* (half *grosz*) and *grosz*, allowed the world of economics to interact with the world of politics, because in commercial transactions the circulation of coins became at the same time the circulation of the texts impressed on them. Even if someone could not assemble letters into words, they were able to identify the shape of the inscription "*Alexander rex Polonie, magnus dux Lituanie*", knowing what this stood for (see Figs. 27 and 28).

The level of reading competence of Vilnius town dwellers was steadily increasing, which means that the importance of writing in this society was rising. We can find an example illustrating this process in the formula closing the foundation charter for St. John's church from 20 February 1643: "In the place of my father, Mr. Jędrzej Siemiaszko, I sign this document with his name, because he is not able to write himself. Thomas Rządziewicz, merchant and burgher of Vilnius".[8] The founder was not literate, his son was.

Two things provide even stronger evidence of the spread of reading skills, that is the rapidly growing number of texts and the growing number of people involved into their production. With this I mean not only scribes, that is the direct producers of texts, but also those who commissioned them and their other users. An issue which cannot be resolved, at least for the time being, is the scope of the literate competences of the users of texts. The list of possible questions is long. Which types and levels of knowledge of writing can be determined among inhabitants of early modern Vilnius? How did the economy, politics, gender, education, religion, ethnicity, and social position determined literacy? How many people could read and how many could write? Who used which languages and types of script? What conditioned the choice of script and language? How many students attended the Vilnius schools, what was the quality and efficacy of these schools, and what was their influence on the literacy of the city's inhabitants?

The most difficult questions have to do with quantification. We will never be able to determine, for example, the exact numbers of students who actually passed through the cathedral school or the parish school of St. John's church in the first half of the sixteenth century, because we do not have the sources required to answer this question. Other quantitative questions are too general to be answered, for instance they question how many people could read in Ruthenian or Latin at the beginning of the sixteenth century.

As far as reading skills are concerned, the criteria determining whether or not someone had this ability are problematic. It is obvious that a *magister artium*, who opened a volume of Cicero's letters and made glosses in the margins, could read, but 'reading' could be different in the case of a Calvinist woman

[8] MS LVIA F23, ap. 1, no. 5096, f. 212r.

from the second half of the sixteenth century: she could accurately sing the Psalms printed in her hymn book, but would she able to understand the words of the Lithuanian Statute easily? And there were those who knew how to recognise individual words, for instance their names, but for whom that was the beginning and end of their reading skills.

The following example of a document, one of many similar documents that were issued at the time, is informative. An act of sale, drawn up in Vilnius on 16 September 1523, says that Jamaget Obdezakovych, Olikhno Osmanovych, and Yakhiata Girevych Geneshkovych renounce their patrimony for the benefit of the "mayors and councillors and the townsmen of Vilnius". The town gained part of a mountain and a mill, while the Geneshkovych family were compensated to the tune of 16 *kopas* of Lithuanian *grosz*.[9] The document was beautifully written by a professional scribe according to the standard form that was obligatory in such cases. We do not know if these three Tartar princes could read this Ruthenian document or sign it, let alone whether they would be able to create texts more complicated than signatures. It is important, however, that the Geneshkovychs knew what these lines written in careful *skoropis* meant and that, if necessary, they would be able to present the document, for instance in court. This somehow resolves the question of how many people were able to read Ruthenian texts, but at the same time raises other issues: how many people were in fact able to use such Ruthenian texts, and to what extent were such texts used?

A marble plaque from the tombstone of bishop Benedykt Woyna has survived to this day. Since it is located in the cathedral, most readers of the text must have been Catholics. An educated man, for instance a student of rhetoric at the Academy of Vilnius, could fully understand not only the whole Latin text, but also identify the literary genre (that of the eulogy) and assess its rhetorical qualities or even copy it into his personal rhetorical *silva rerum* (*sylwa*, a sort of commonplace book).[10] A large group of readers, especially women, did not know Latin but only Polish. Nonetheless, they were able to read the epitaph and understand individual words (for instance the name Benedictus Woyna) and recognise the language. Those even less competent in reading could understand whose tombstone it was, and that the inscription was in

[9] *Сборник палеографических снимков с древних грамот и актов хранившихся в виленском центральном архиве и виленской публичной библиотеке* (Vilnius, 1884), p. 8, No. 13.

[10] In manuscript *sylvas* we often encounter examples of the use of authentic epitaphs and other texts present in public space. Epitaphs are rewritten by seventeenth-century diarists, e.g. Stanisław Oświęcim, Maciej Vorbek-Lettow, or Albrycht Stanisław Radziwiłł.

praise of the deceased. And because the inscription was supposed to be primarily of a laudatory and commemorative nature, each of these three types of 'reading' evoked the associations required by its author, and thus the text functioned according to its assigned purpose. We should note that the second and third way of reading this text is used today by most visitors to Vilnius cathedral, mainly tourists who do not know Latin.

Reading and Power

From the end of the fifteenth century onwards, a very important group of texts, documents, became increasingly frequent in the lives of Vilnius' inhabitants, including those in non-privileged[11] social groups, for instance women, Jews, and the urban poor. Transactions, wills, waivers, donations, legacies, protestations, oblations, court sentences – all were of interest to people who possessed a large economical capital, that is who owned and had to manage some sort of property: the noblemen, burghers, and clergy. It became common practice to inscribe legal transactions in the registers of the municipal court, of the castle court, or of the Tribunal of the Grand Duchy of Lithuania and to obtain officially validated copies and confirmations from these institutions. This explains why the court registers are the main source of information about the affairs of the former inhabitants of Vilnius, and also why writing was so important to them. The names listed in a single document could run into several hundreds. This does not mean that all of these several hundred users of writing would be able to read the documents in Ruthenian, Latin or Polish fluently, let alone to copy them.

Here is one quite typical example of a situation that came about frequently in the sixteenth and seventeenth centuries. During the interrogation of witnesses and participants in the attack on the Calvinist church in 1611, people of different statuses and backgrounds testified before the Vilnius municipal court. One of the suspects was Andrzej Prochownik, a paver, who,

> having been arrested in the church, said that "I was going with a masonry hammer to the locksmith to commission him for a certain job, and passing the church on my way I was grabbed by the city watch who saw me holding the hammer, even though

[11] As a privileged social group (which possessed a significant social and economic capital), by which I mean wealthy male burgers, clergymen, noblemen, officials, etc.

> I was not guilty of anything. But I know nothing about the church".[12] (original in Latin)

His testimony, as in the case of the documents we discussed before, was written down by a scribe proficient in Latin (the protocol and the eschatocol of the document are in Latin). The suspect himself had no such competence, although he may have been able to read his own testimony. In any case, he certainly must have understood that the words he spoke under oath were recorded in writing and could be invoked if necessary.

The number of names of people such as that of Andrzej the paver, appearing in this huge and only partially preserved body of documents, reflects the scale of pragmatic literacy and the coexistence of the logosphere with the graphosphere. Urban authorities were aware of the affinity with the written word of the majority of the city's inhabitants and tried to take advantage of it in moments of crisis, at least from the second half of the sixteenth century onwards. In September 1581, as a result of the Jesuit Piotr Skarga's calls, anti-Calvinist riots broke out in Vilnius which resulted in the burning of books stolen from a Protestant bookseller. King Stephen Báthory, who at that time besieged the city of Pskov in western Muscovy, sent a letter to Jan Stanisławowicz Abramowicz, the governor of Vilnius, with the following annotation at the end:

> we therefore command that, as soon as you receive this letter, you openly announce it on the Market Square as well as in the streets of Vilnius, that people should behave peacefully and give no reasons for riots, in accordance with the old ways and customs that have survived from time immemorial to the days of my rule.[13] (original in Polish)

Almost sixty years later, in October 1639, another *voivode* of Vilnius, prince Krzysztof II Radziwiłł, tried to ease the anti-Calvinist mood in a similar way, having copies of his proclamations nailed to the castle gates, the city gates, and to the doors of Catholic and Orthodox churches. This action proved ineffective, not because the addressees did not understand the message, but because having understood it they tore the proclamations down during the night. This resulted in a fruitless investigation.[14]

[12] MS LNMB F93-1730.
[13] MS LNMB F93-1688.
[14] MS LNMB F93-1707.

The authorities also circulated texts about solemn and festive events, although in such cases their main audience were the elites, while those of lower economic and cultural capital may have understood them in part only. I am thinking of public ceremonies of accessions to office, the funerals of important public figures, or the ceremonial entries of rulers. An integral part of these ceremonial entries were speeches, declamations, para-theatrical performances, and the erecting of occasional architecture decorated with appropriate inscriptions. The translation of the remains of St. Casimir on 14 August 1636, for which examples of all the types of texts mentioned just now were prepared, was probably attended by all the inhabitants of the city, including non-Catholics and non-Christians, Tartars and Jews, with all paying homage to this deceased member of the grand duke's family.[15]

In the period under discussion, the ability to use texts was first of all a competence that involved the reader in the mechanisms of power, both judicial and administrative. In the game of power, texts were a tool for establishing and enforcing the rules, and the inhabitants of the city had to agree to these rules if they wanted to participate in the game. One of the preconditions was the ability to understand the meaning of the texts involved. The more wide-ranging this competence was, the greater the opportunities to the participant in the game were. That is why literary education was so important. The broader someone's literacy, the greater was the role he could play in a world regulated by the circulation of texts. At the beginning of the sixteenth century, when the Geneshkovych princes transferred their land to the city, the multi-level use of texts was mainly the domain of the elite. Several decades later, in the second half of the sixteenth century, all inhabitants of Vilnius were subject to the dictates of the written word, as the city and its functioning were increasingly dependent on texts and on the ability to use documents.

The use of texts that belonged to popular religious and secular literature was usually linked to the strengthening of the authority of those in power and of the institutions based on that authority, that is the Orthodox Church, the Catholic Church, the Protestant Churches, and the state administration. This tendency is hidden and more difficult in ordinary texts and than for instance in privileges or letters, where it manifested itself directly and openly.

[15] T. CHYNCZEWSKA-HENNEL, *Nuncjusz i król: Nuncjatura Maria Filonardiego w Rzeczypospolitej 1636-1643* (Warsaw, 2006), pp. 196-197.

Popular Reading and Elite Reading

There is no evidence of popular literature functioning in Vilnius before the sixteenth century. This is true both for pre-Christian Lithuanian literature and for the texts from the later period that were read by the Orthodox and Catholic inhabitants of the city. It is not until the beginning of the sixteenth century that some sources allow us to witness a change in this state of affairs. Popular reading often did not require personal contact with the text in its physical form, because its presence in society was most probably manifested through reading it aloud. This does not alter the fact, however, that the texts of prayers, songs, and rhyming legends about saints – in Polish, and probably also in Lithuanian – which were promoted with great success by the Vilnius Bernardines at the turn of the fifteenth and sixteenth centuries, originally had a written form. The oral character of this literature was therefore secondary only, as it was based on writing.[16]

In the second half of the sixteenth century, popular religious literature began to flourish, mainly due to the Reformation. Printed books in the vernacular languages became popular among the wealthier Protestant inhabitants of the city. Books in German were imported from Königsberg, Gdańsk, and from more distant Protestant cities for the Lutherans, who mostly spoke this language. The Calvinists, who mainly spoke Polish, printed their catechisms and hymnbooks in Lithuania itself, initially in Brest and Nyasvizh (for instance the *Kancjonał nieświeski*, or the Nyasvizh Hymnbook, 1563), and then in Vilnius (from 1594 onwards). They were intended both for private reading and singing at home, and for use during church services. The author of the preface to the Vilnius *Catechism* of 1594 recommended that the father of the family should teach the members of his family with the use of this booklet.

Catholics followed in the footsteps of Protestants. The songbook *Parthenomelica* was published by Walenty Bartoszewski in 1613 for the Catholic members of the city council, which annually celebrated solemn dawn Masses during Advent, although there is no doubt that the songs included in it were also performed in other parts of the liturgical year. Printed Orthodox prayer books for the Vilnius elite made an appearance even earlier; they included Skaryna's *Malaya podorozhnava knizhka* ('The Little Travel Book')

[16] J. Goody, *The Logic of Writing and the Organization of Society* (Cambridge, 1986), pp. 42-44.

from around 1522.[17] Catechisms and prayer books were published by the Mamonicz family and the printing house of the Orthodox Brotherhood. In inventories of property, which were compiled after somebody's death, we find much information about books intended for prayer in Polish and Ruthenian.

Popular religious texts also reached groups of a higher social status, including as they did sermons (published from the mid-sixteenth century), either in the form of postils or, in the case of funeral sermons and (less frequently) wedding sermons, individually. Postils, which were usually composed elsewhere, were expensive printed books, so they cannot even be found in the inventories left by the wealthy inhabitants of the city. Generally, people came into contact with these texts during church services, when the clergyman read them or created his own sermon based on them. In the first half of the seventeenth century, printing funeral sermons confirming the prestige of the deceased and his family became popular among the urban elites and the nobility living in Vilnius. They circulated among all Christian confessional groups present in the city and were usually published in Polish. Some of them have survived with annotations in the margins, although it is not known by whom these annotations were made. Usually, these are *nota bene*-marks in the more important places or general recommendations such as "worth reading" or "uplifting". Perhaps such sermons were read in private homes.

It seems unlikely that the *Lives of Saints* composed in Polish by the Jesuit Piotr Skarga were as popular as scholars suggest.[18] The first edition was published in Vilnius in 1579, but this does not necessarily mean that the work was widely available to inhabitants of the city. Because of its volume, it must have been an expensive book and, despite many reprints, it was surely difficult to obtain. It is neither mentioned in the catalogue of the largest urban book collection in Vilnius of the seventeenth century, which belonged to Stefan Lebiedzicz,[19] nor it can be found in other inventories of books owned by Vilnius towns dwellers. It appears mainly in the registers of libraries of churches and

[17] НЕМИРОВСКИЙ, *Франциск Скорина*, pp. 441-457; J. OCHMAŃSKI, "Najdawniejsze księgozbiory na Litwie od końca XIV do połowy XVI wieku", in: *Europe orientalis: Polska i jej wschodni sąsiedzi od Średniowiecza po współczesność: Studia i materiały ofiarowane Profesorowi Stanisławowi Alexandrowiczowi w 65 rocznicę urodzin*, ed. Z. KARPUS, T. KEMPA, and D. MICHALUK (Toruń, 1996), p. 82.

[18] H. BARYCZ, "Z dziejów jednej książki", in: ID., *Z epoki renesansu, reformacji i baroku: Prądy, idee, ludzie, książki* (Warsaw, 1971), pp. 656-660.

[19] MS LVIA F23, ap. 1, no. 5096, ff. 441r-441v; *AVAK*, vol. 9, p. 484; *Wilnianie*, pp. 185-186 and 189-192.

monasteries. However, private collections did contain shorter and more sensationally described Lives of individual Catholic and Orthodox saints.

Only a few Vilnius inhabitants read strictly literary texts or texts that we today consider belles-lettres because it required a significant cultural capital. They were mainly members of the political and religious elites and students of the Academy of Vilnius, the Orthodox Brotherhood's schools, St. John's parish school and the cathedral school, that is people who aspired to enter circles of the elites. We can certainly assume that poetry and rhetorical prose were available to professors and students (and this was not an insignificant group, as at the end of the sixteenth century it included up to about a thousand people), as well as to people that we know showed an interest in books, reading, and literature generally. These texts usually belonged to highly specialised clerks, such as Stanisław Koszutski, Łukasz Górnicki, Jakub Wujek, or Daniel Naborowski.[20] Others, although qualified to do so, did not necessarily read belles-lettres.

Many members of the Vilnius cathedral chapter had completed higher education and obtained academic degrees, so we would expect that this professional group was destined to devote some of their time to literature. However, on the basis of a dozen of last wills of Vilnius canons from the period *c.* 1550-1650, it can be concluded that they did not attach particular importance to books. A definitely more place in their testaments was taken by the enumeration of clothes, household equipment, and farm animals, and if they mentioned books at all, they were most often missals, breviaries, and postils, in short: professional literature. Relatively few of these men possessed larger book collections (we will discuss this below). Would this mean that the majority of the canons read nothing but official documents, bills, and texts related to the liturgy?

Canon Wojciech Grabowski, in his will from 1570, did not bequeath any book to anyone, but he marked the following at the beginning:

> I confess then that I leave this wretched world in the faith of the Roman Church, established by and sealed with the blood of Saints Peter and Paul. I have not let any heretic make me stray from this faith. I have always loathed their writings, which is why I have never wanted to read them. For with God's help I have ignored them and despised them.[21]

[20] Koszutski and Górnicki were secretaries of the king, Wujek was a Jesuit and a translator of the Bible into Polish (1599), Naborowski was a Calvinist activist and a judge. All of them were successful writers or poets.

[21] MS MAB F43-26618, ff. 1v-2r; see *Kościół zamkowy, czyli katedra wileńska*, 2, p. 118.

This remark of the canon testifies to his peculiarly motivated but very conscious choice of reading materials.

We may hypothesise that the canons of Vilnius (and probably the members of the lower secular clergy as well) had much contact with books relating to their spiritual vocation and profession. Nonetheless, their contact with the written word cannot have been limited only to the liturgy, even if their wills and the inventories of things left by them do not mention other texts directly. Identifying their reading habits more precisely requires further research.

Against the background of the whole population of Vilnius, the members of the chapter belonged to those people who used books very often. In the second half of the sixteenth century and in the seventeenth century, if the vast majority of the inhabitants of the capital had contact with books, it was with the prayer books, catechisms, and religious leaflet literature mentioned previously. This contact was often limited to listening to them being read aloud rather than including reading them for oneself. In sixteenth- and seventeenth-century Vilnius, texts were often present in people's everyday life, but they rarely performed functions referred to as *docere*, *permovere* and *delectare*.

The Production of Texts

It is no coincidence that the people with the most advanced literate skills maintained close ties with the authorities, both secular and clerical. By a high level of literacy I understand the ability to produce texts in the languages that had the greatest number of uses and the greatest influence in medieval and early modern Vilnius. People with such competence can be found in several groups. All of them were somehow connected to political, religious, and educational institutions, so we can talk about the institutional character of a large number of the texts written in Vilnius at the time.

First of all, we can distinguish the group of professional scribes, chancery clerks, and secretaries (which will be discussed later in detail). Initially, they were individual clergymen who worked for the grand dukes (up to the end of the fourteenth century). Later on, they appear in the capacity of employees in the grand duke's city, in the chancery of the chapter and the magnates' chanceries, as well as in the city, municipal, and *hospodar* (royal) courts and in the Tribunal of the Grand Duchy of Lithuania. In addition to professional clerks, there were also people in Vilnius who were not affiliated to these institutions, but who were more or less familiar with the drafting of documents and were professionally occupied with producing them for private individuals.

The second group includes the priests of the various rites. Up to the end of the fifteenth century they were the largest educated group with the best literate skills. Liturgical books were produced in Orthodox monasteries; Catholic monasteries, especially the Bernardines, brought together famous preachers and authors; and among the members of the cathedral chapter one could find many graduates of the University of Cracow. The role of the clergy in the production of texts increased in the sixteenth century, especially after the arrival of the Jesuits, and also after the reform of the Orthodox monasteries, but at that time a large number of texts was also created by lay people.

The majority of teachers active in the city came from the clergy (especially from the Jesuits). Their activity stimulated the formation of the third, very numerous group of producers and users of texts to write, that is pupils and students. The humanist model of education, which was introduced in Vilnius in the 1540s, was based on the study and creation of literature. The scale of school text production may be illustrated by some numbers. In the 1590s, the number of students of the Academy of Vilnius reached nine hundred,[22] and it was not the only school that operated in the city. The administrative and legal offices and the schools were the institutions that produced the largest numbers of texts. From the point of view of rhetorical discourse, it could be argued that the offices focused on two rhetorical genres, the judicial and political-administrative (the *genus iudiciale* and *genus deliberativum*), while the schools were mostly concerned with the epideictic genre (*genus demonstrativum*).

Printers, who often also doubled as booksellers, were specifically text producers. By the very nature of their profession, they had to be highly literate. Despite the promising beginnings of the Ruthenian printing industry initiated by Skaryna in 1524, it was not until the second half of the sixteenth century that printing houses were definitively established in Vilnius. Between 1574 and 1655, a total of fourteen publishing houses operated in the city,[23] publishing books mainly in Church Slavonic, Ruthenian, Latin, Polish, Lithuanian, and German. This small but highly qualified group of men of the pen (or rather the printing press) made Vilnius one of the most important centres of book production in the Polish-Lithuanian Commonwealth. Probably a significant part of their production was sold on the spot, to be used by the inhabitants of the city.

[22] PIECHNIK, *Początki Akademii Wileńskiej*, p. 113.

[23] *Drukarze dawnej Polski*, p. 5-6.

The ruling class should also be considered a separate group of text producers. To this group belonged the magnates who at the same time were high state officials, clergymen, and estate administrators, burgraves, mayors, and aldermen. Because of their functions, they had skilfully to use texts of all rhetorical genres in prose, and often also poetry. In the case of the higher-ranking clergy, the creation of texts was quite obvious, but from the end of the fifteenth century lay magnates also began to write and their involvement in the production of texts grew constantly. While we do not know much about King Casimir IV Jagiellon's competences in this area,[24] his sons, Alexander I Jagiellon and Sigismund I the Old, used texts freely.[25] The highest officials of the Grand Duchy of Lithuania who were their contemporaries in the first half of the sixteenth century, such as Olbracht Gasztołd (Albertas Goštautas), Mikołaj Mikołajewicz Radziwiłł, and Michał Gliński, were also proficient in the use of texts. Subsequent generations of magnates were not only limited to writing the texts demanded by their offices (especially letters), but expanded their writing interests to include poetry and artistic prose. This is clear, for example, from the work of Mikołaj Krzysztof Radziwiłł 'the Orphan'.

The prose and poetry written by these magnates would nowadays be referred to as court literature, which was cultivated mainly at the monarchic courts. In the fifteenth, sixteenth, and early seventeenth centuries, Vilnius was at times a place of residence for the courts of kings, queens and grand dukes, in particular those of Alexander I Jagiellon, Bona Sforza, Sigismund II Augustus, Stephen Báthory, Sigismundus III Vasa, and Władysław IV Vasa. It is also worth mentioning the many chanceries of magnates, who had their own palaces in Vilnius. Scribes who worked at royal and magnate courts and chanceries usually served as officials, secretaries, and chancery clerks, as mentioned above, so their legacy includes both official texts and those described as belles-lettres at the time.

All the texts from the domain of pragmatic literacy mentioned above formed part of a single system; separating or dealing with them separately, although useful for heuristic purposes, makes it impossible to arrive at an over-

[24] Urszula Borkowska pointed out that Casimir IV Jagiellon (1426-1492) and his older brother, the King of Poland and Hungary Władysław III Jagiellon (1424-1444), were educated in their childhood, which means King Casimir was a literate person. See U. BORKOWSKA, *Dynastia Jagiellonów w Polsce* (Warsaw, 2011), p. 366.

[25] E. POTKOWSKI, "Podpisy królów polskich", in: *Miscellanea historicoarchivistica*, 2, ed. E. POTKOWSKI (Warsaw, 1987), pp. 25-26. On the literacy skills of the rulers from the Jagiellon dynasty, see: A. ADAMSKA, "The Jagiellonians and the written word", pp. 153-169.

all picture of how written culture functioned in early modern Vilnius. A single person could create texts of quite different natures, and this cannot be treated as a coincidence. An official or a chancery clerk was proficient in drafting texts, and it is almost a rule that his ability to write manifested itself in a variety of fields. Duke Vytautas' secretary, Mikołaj Cebulka, apart from composing the duke's charters, was at the same time a skilful speaker who knew the rules of rhetoric, which he showed as a legate to Sigismund of Luxembourg. At the turn of the fifteenth and sixteenth centuries, Adam of Vilnius was an important person in the ducal chancery. Although we do not know his literary works (perhaps with the exception of one epigram), it cannot be ruled out that he wrote such texts as well, just like other professors of the University of Cracow who belonged to the Societas Litteraria Vistulana.[26] Slightly later, another humanist and the first printer in Vilnius, Francysk Skaryna, worked as the secretary and doctor of bishop John of the Dukes of Lithuania. To the statutes of the diocesan synod chaired by the same bishop (published in Cracow in 1528), the burgrave (*horodniczy*) of Vilnius castle, Ulrich Hosius (Hozjusz), added a rhymed dedication.[27]

Łukasz Górnicki, the secretary and librarian of King Sigismund II Augustus, who lived in Vilnius in the 1560s, wrote letters and documents in the royal chancery, and at the same time worked on the Polish-language version of *Il Cortegiano* by Baldassare Castiglione (published in Cracow under the title *Dworzanin polski* in 1566).[28] At the same time, his colleague Pedro Ruiz de Moros (Piotr Rojzjusz), also known as Doctor Spaniard,[29] and the parish priest of the main Vilnius catholic parish church of St. John the Baptist and St. John the Evangelist, wrote malicious Latin poems about the Lithuanians, for instance *Facies urbis Vilnae*. Another colleague from the court, Augustyn Rotundus, both secretary of the king and *Voigt* of Vilnius, in other words the royal administrator of the city, not only elaborated the text of the second Lithuanian

[26] KOSMAN, *Orzeł i Pogoń*, p. 32.

[27] J. FIJAŁEK, "Kościół rzymskokatolicki na Litwie", p. 294.

[28] The *Dworzanin polski* published in Cracow in 1566 was a Polish version of the famous dialogue by Baldassare Castiglione, *Il cortegiano* (1527).

[29] This is what he is called even in official documents, instead of using his name; in Polish: *Doktor Hiszpan*. In a document of 1568 from St. John's church its treasurer wrote as follows: "I, Krzysztof Bolimowski, the treasurer of Doctor Spaniard, the Vilnius archpriest, give evidence in the following writing". MS MAB F43-19347 (VKF1422). Doctor Spaniard is the main character of an epigram by Jan Kochanowski (I 79), the famous Renaissance Polish poet and his friend. See J. KOCHANOWSKI, "On a Spanish Doctor", in: J. KOCHANOWSKI, *Trifles, Songs, and Saint John's Eve Song*, ed. M. HANUSIEWICZ-LAVALLEE and trans. M.J. MIKOŚ (Lublin, 2018), p. 49.

statute (1566), but also *Rozmowa Polaka z Litwinem* (A Dialogue between a Pole and a Lithuanian; Cracow, 1564), in which he argued with Stanisław Orzechowski's opinions on the political system and independence of the Grand Duchy of Lithuania. Stanisław Koszutski, the secretary of Queen Barbara Radziwiłłówna as well as a colleague and predecessor of Górnicki in the position of royal librarian, was primarily responsible for the correspondence of the queen-to-be, but also undertook to defend her marriage to King Sigismund II Augustus in a Latin polemical epithalamium (1548). In the following century, Eliasz Pielgrzymowski, who held the office of notary of the Grand Duchy of Lithuania, composed a poem on the mission of Lew Sapieha to Muscovy (1601), while Daniel Naborowski, a municipal judge in Vilnius who drafted numerous legal documents, became famous as a leading representative of Polish Petrarchism. He is known as the author of poetic letters in Polish, addressed to the magnate Krzysztof II Radziwiłł, whom he served as a client and diplomat.

As has already been said, the community of active users of the written word was composed primarily of people in power, i.e. who had a large political, economic, social, and cultural capital. They produced the largest number of texts and most texts were produced for them. One may get the impression that this group formed to some extent a closed circle and that without its initiative the majority of texts would never have appeared. This is true to some degree, but we must remember that it is in fact difficult to talk about a single community consisting of dukes, bishops, the nobility, clergy, rich merchants, and the officials who were at their service. It was not a homogeneous group, and the circulation of texts among scribes was often either limited or non-existent. One should also take into account that the abovementioned classification of the groups that created or decided on the creation of texts reveals an ideal, and therefore a somewhat simplified image of the past. It assumes that these groups are were static and that the relationships between them durable. In fact, we deal more often with the isolation and discontinuity of phenomena in the textual culture of Vilnius than with some level at least of stability and continuity. This results in part from the processual nature and dynamics of these phenomena.

Certain groups of people producing the texts that are important to us (for instance cloistered religious institutions) communicated with the general population of Vilnius only to a small extent. Others, for instance the Jews or Tartars, due to their exclusiveness made their own texts available with difficulty only. Some other groups, seemingly coherent and quite uniform, changed with the passage of time, and this also determined the dynamics and quality of text production. For example, the textual culture at King Alexander's court was different from that at Sigismund II August's court. But even the circle of people connected to a single court was not immutable. Let us take a look at the 1560s and early 1570s, a period in which Vilnius experienced a particular flourishing of elite culture, and let us take into account the presence in the capital of the people who shaped its culture. The royal librarian Łukasz Górnicki, who resided here in the 1560s, often left Vilnius and finally settled in Tykocin. His colleague Pedro Ruiz de Moros died in 1570, and the parish of 'Doctor Spaniard' was taken over by the Jesuits, who had been brought here by bishop Protasewicz a year earlier and immediately started to organise a college on a big scale. King Sigismund II Augustus was accompanied by his chancery (in which Wacław Agryppa and Jan Kochanowski worked) would stay in the city for longer stretches of time. In such periods the cultural life of Vilnius became very intense not only thanks to the members of the court who resided in Vilnius, but also thanks to visiting guests and legates.[30] From July 1551 to March 1566, Sigismund August and his court stayed in Vilnius for sixty months without leaving.[31] On other occasions, however, the king did not come to the city for months or even years, and this resulted in the capital being less populated. Also magnates active as arts' patrons, such as Mikołaj Radziwiłł 'the Black', despite the fact that they had their palaces and conducted their business in Vilnius, spent most of their time in residences far from the city.

Trying to capture the people who wrote texts in Vilnius in past centuries 'red-handed', we encounter a difficulty similar to the one that prevented the physicist Heisenberg from characterising all properties of particles at the same time.[32] Seeking to describe the whole, we lose focus, while at the same time attempting to look more closely at a single text and its producers turns the story into an infinite sequence of microhistories.

Moreover, a whole series of texts created in Vilnius was intended not for the needs of the local market, but for export, as exemplified by *Dworzanin polski* (The Book of the Polish Courtier) by Górnicki or *Moscovia* by Possevi-

[30] L. GLEMŽA, "Vilniaus miesto ir pilies ryšiai XVI-XVIII a.", in: *Vilniaus Žemutinė pilis XIV a.-XIX a. pradžioje: 2005-2006 m. tyrimai*, ed. L. GLEMŽA (Vilnius, 2007), pp. 69-78.

[31] W. KOWALENKO, "Geneza udziału stołecznego miasta Wilna w sejmach Rzeczypospolitej", *Ateneum Wileńskie* 4.12 (1927), p. 89.

[32] On Heisenberg's uncertainty principle, see C. ROVELLI, *Seven Brief Lessons on Physics*, trans. S. CARNELL and E. SEGRE (London, 2015), Second Lesson.

no, both written in Vilnius, and the latter even being published here in 1583. And again, many texts intended especially for readers and users from Vilnius were created elsewhere, for instance liturgical books imported for the Vilnius chapter from Cracow, books produced by the cathedral scribes of Queen Hedwig[33] in a special scriptorium at St. Mary's church in Cracow – and later, at the end of the fifteenth century books from Gdańsk, already in printed form.

A similar issue is relevant to epistolography, which on the one hand can be treated as an important part of the textual culture of the city (letters were both written and received there), but since by their very nature letters function in a much wider space, they may concern the culture of the whole country or indeed even of Europe as a whole. Suffice it to say that from 1562 a permanent postal service connected Vilnius with Cracow and Venice.

Documents issued by the central administration functioned in a space that extended beyond the city as well. A privilege promulgated in Vilnius could relate to an estate located, for example, near Smolensk, Polatsk, or Tykocin, but it was recorded in the Lithuanian *Metrica* kept in Vilnius castle. All these phenomena constituted tension between the 'open' and 'closed' city.[34]

The incoherence, multi-layeredness and dynamics of the image of Vilnius writings would be even more visible if we knew more examples that did not fit directly into the 'official' circulation of texts of power and economy. I refer to the private correspondence of Vilnius inhabitants, notes kept for one's own needs, including annotations in the margins in books, perhaps diaries and miscellanies (*silvae rerum*). The private nature of these texts meant that they did not last. They did not need to be carefully stored or copied, as they did not serve, for example, to prove the legal status of a property. Therefore, it is difficult to assess today how many texts of these kinds were produced.

[33] E. Potkowski, "Katedralisi na dworze królowej Jadwigi: Z dziejów kultury książki w Polsce schyłku średniowiecza", in *Miscellanea historicoarchivistica*, 1, ed. E. Potkowski (Warsaw, 1985), pp. 237-238; id., "Monarsze dary książkowe w *polskim średniowieczu – pogrunwaldzkie dary Jagiełły*", in: *Ojczyzna bliższa i dalsza: Studia historyczne ofiarowane Feliksowi Kirykowi w sześćdziesiątą rocznicę urodzin*, ed. J. Chrobaczyński, A. Jureczko, and M. Śliwa (Cracow, 1993), p. 368.

[34] See the Introduction, p. 39, Chapter 5, p. 249, and Chapter 9, pp. 365-369.

Chapter 6

The Materiality of Texts

Texts of Vilnius

The most abundant group of texts from Vilnius that have survived to this day includes administrative and judicial documents relating to the functioning of the Grand Duchy of Lithuania, to the whole Polish-Lithuanian Commonwealth, to the diocese of Vilnius, and to the city itself: the Lithuanian *Metrica*;[1] the castle court registers (*księgi grodzkie*); the register of the cathedral chapter (*księgi kapitulne*); municipal books (registers; *księgi miejskie*); and the burgravate court registers (*księgi horodniczańskie*). Into these registers many documents were copied relating to the affairs of the residents of Vilnius, such as legal sentences, lawsuits, protestations, records of interrogations, certifications, privileges, legacies, exemptions, written copies of documents pre-

[1] The Lithuanian *Metrica* is a central archive of the Grand Duchy of Lithuania. It was kept since 1440s to the third partition in 1795 and consists of *c.* 600 volumes (books). In 1795 almost all the books were confiscated by Russians. Today they are kept in the Russian State Archive of Ancient Documents in Moscow <http://rgada.info/poisk/index.php?fund_number= 389&fund_name=&list_number=&list_name=&Sk=30&B1=+++%D0%9D%D0%B0%D0%B9%D1%82%D0%B8> (accessed 4.01.2021). Since 1987 the Polish, Lithuanian and Belarusian Academies of Sciences have been publishing *c.* 60 volumes of the Lithuanian *Metrica*. Cf. D. Antanavičius, "Originalių Lietuvos Metrikos XVI a. knygų sąrašas", *Istorijos šaltinių tyrimai*, 4 (2012), pp. 157-184; A. Zakrzewski, *Wielkie Ksiestwo Litewskie (XVI-XVIII w.): Prawo – ustrój – społeczeństwo* (Warsaw, 2013), p. 28; W. Krawczuk, "Metryka Koronna i Metryka Litewska", in: *Dyplomatyka staropolska*, ed. T. Jurek (Warszawa, 2015), pp. 206-212; A. Dubonis, D. Antanavičius, R. Ragauskienė, and R. Šmigelskytė-Stukienė, *Susigrąžinant praeitį: Lietuvos Metrikos istorija ir tyrimai* (Vilnius, 2016); I. Valikonytė, "Struktura i zasady kompletowania ksiąg sądowych Metryki Litewskiej Zygmunta Augusta", *Rocznik Lituanistyczny* 4 (2018), pp. 7-23.

sented orally in a chancery (Polish: *oblata*), transumpts, etc. Such registers also contained copies of economic and property documents, including accounts, inventories, debt records, purchase and sales transactions, wills, etc. Only a few of these documents have survived outside the official administration. We only know about the existence of some other documents from indirect accounts, for instance concerning the books of the Vilnius *qahal*[2] that have been destroyed.

A separate group of texts is the result of epistolography, the fundamental genre that functioned in the 'open' city. For the most part, letter writing left its trace somewhere between administrative and economic texts. The majority of the correspondence preserved is in Polish or Latin, and to a lesser extent in Ruthenian and German. We know about Tartar letters written in Duke Vytautas' chancery and we know also of Jewish letters, sent by members of the Vilnius community to their fellow believers in other cities of the Commonwealth. Only a few 'private' letters have survived on subjects other than political, administrative, and economic matters.

Texts in the public space were primarily inscriptions.[3] Most common were inscriptions on coins, epitaphs, icons, paintings, sculptures, and bells, as well as on stonework and the polychromes that decorated the Orthodox and Catholic churches or the synagogue. Inscriptions on secular buildings were less frequent. Written sources give information about seventeenth-century triumphal arches, usually raised on the occasion of the arrival of the ruler or religious ceremonies. It may be assumed that some Vilnius palaces also featured some texts. Most of the once existing inscriptions can no longer be found in Vilnius today, but the wording of some that were copied on paper have survived.

A last group of texts comprises books, both handwritten and printed. Until the mid-fifteenth century they were imported only. Later, they were also produced in Vilnius itself, in scriptoria, printing houses, offices, schools, monasteries, nunneries, and private homes. For the most part, these were books of with functional character, for instance liturgical or prayer books and hymn-

[2] Qahals were self-governing communities of Ashkenazi Jews in East Central Europe which existed until 1840. In the Polish-Lithuanian Commonwealth, the *qahals* usually gathered the Jewish inhabitants of a city or a town. The term *qahal* means also elected Jewish communal self-government. The *qahals* had juridical, educational, religious, and economic autonomy, which was guaranteed by the privileges of the Polish kings, the grand dukes of Lithuania, Parliament, and other authorities. Cf. *Gminy żydowskie w dawnej Rzeczypospolitej: Wybór tekstów źródłowych*, ed. and trans. A. MICHAŁOWSKA (Warsaw, 2003).

[3] Inscriptions will be discussed in Chapter 10, "Epideictic texts".

books, legal and scientific works, and textbooks. Against this background, literature that can be classified as a rhetorical epideictic genre (*genus demonstrativum*) or whose function can be described as *delectare* was definitely in the minority. Some such works also straddle the border between functional texts and belles-lettres, for instance sermons, epithalamia, panegyrics, and dedicatory letters.

In spite of wars and fires, so many of these texts have survived that it is both impossible and tedious to enumerate all of them. And there is no need to. To a greater extent than in the case of other cities they reveal Vilnius' dual nature as a city that was 'open' and 'closed' at the same time. An 'open' city is understood here as an economic and political space from and into which texts flow, connecting it with the outside world, while a 'closed' city is the space of everyday life in which texts flow as if in a closed circuit. The latter state in its pure form is rare, because a condition for the existence of every medieval and early modern city was the existence of an economic and political symbiosis with places and institutions that were outside its walls, such as villages, other cities, the ruler's court and religious institutions. Nevertheless, to a greater or lesser extent we can divide texts into those of the 'open' city and the 'closed' city.

An interesting problem emerges here. On the one hand, some of the texts of 'open Vilnius' were not intended for the city, while others, although written down in Vilnius, shaped its textual culture only to a small degree. The Slavonic Bible, edited by the humanist and printer Francysk Skaryna, although printed in Prague, is certainly a text that bears a close relationship with Vilnius. It began to circulate there shortly after it was printed in 1522. Skaryna sold it from here and copies of it were certainly used in Lithuania and probably in Vilnius.[4] On the other hand, it is clear that not every letter produced by the permanently moving chancery of King Stephen Báthory, when it stayed in Vilnius in 1581 and included the phrase "*datum Vilnae*" in its dating clause, had much to do with Vilnius. The selection of texts that make up the textual culture of the Lithuanian capital must therefore be arbitrary, and only common sense can decide on their selection. An attempt to separate the corpus of texts and define a selection of them as unambiguously Vilnian would result in the construction of 'scholastic' catalogues and categories, and those are not the aim of this book.

[4] Немировский, *Франциск Скорина*, pp. 308-310; A. Nagórko, "Franciszek Skoryna", in: *PSB*, 38, p. 292.

Materials for the Production of a Text

The materials used to produce texts in Vilnius were very similar to those used in other parts of Europe. I will discuss only those that were most common, keeping in mind less typical ones, such as metal, stone, wood, or canvas. Inscriptions were created by craftsmen working in Vilnius in the fifteenth and seventeenth centuries in various fields of art, such as medal art (inscriptions on medals and coins), goldsmithing, founding (inscriptions on monstrances, bells and cannons), painting, engraving, and sculpture, woodcarving, and stone masonry (inscriptions, for instance on icons, paintings, polychromes, tombstones, and architectural elements). Texts were also put on embroidered or woven fabrics. Parchment was rarely used, even in the fourteenth and fifteenth centuries, and then mainly for liturgical books and for the more important documents: paper was the basic writing material, on which one wrote with a quill.

Until the beginning of the sixteenth century, paper was imported from Kaffa, Novgorod, and Cracow. The first paper mill in Vilnius, and indeed in the whole of Lithuania, was established in 1524, proving the growing demand for this product. A document dated 16 November 1524, kept in the Lithuanian *Metrica* and issued by the burgrave of Vilnius castle (*horodniczy*) Ulryk Hozjusz, says that Carulus Bernart from Switzerland was granted the right to build a paper mill and a house upon the Vilnia River.[5] Therefore, in the first half of the sixteenth century two paper mills operated intermittently in the city.[6] In the last two decades of the sixteenth century the production of paper was monopolised by the Mamonicz family. Łukasz Mamonicz, the printer's brother, not only owned the existing mills in Vilnius but also founded a third one on the Vilnius estate called in Polish Powilno, in 1585.[7] This paper mill belonged to the Mamonicz family until about 1606, when prince Melchior

[5] НЕМИРОВСКИЙ, *Франциск Скорина*, pp. 416-417; ГРУША, *Белоруская кірылычна палеаграфія*, pp. 88-89. Both researchers question earlier hypotheses about the establishment of two paper mills in 1524. See also ŁOWMIAŃSKI, *Papiernie wileńskie XVI wieku*, p. 421; E. LAUCEVIČIUS, *Popierius Lietuvoje XV-XVIII a.* (Vilnius, 1967), p. 57.

[6] M.B. TOPOLSKA, *Czytelnik i książka w Wielkim Księstwie Litewskim w dobie Renesansu i Baroku* (Wrocław, 1984), p. 150; M. KOSMAN, *Orzeł i Pogoń: Z dziejów polsko-litewskich XIV-XX w.* (Warsaw, 1992), p. 135.

[7] In 1533 the city council bought the estate Lewoniszki. Since then it was called Powilno. Later, it was a suburb of Vilnius called in Polish Popławy, in Lithuanian Paplauja. See ŁOWMIAŃSKA, "Wilno przed najazdem moskiewskim", p. 295; BEDNARCZUK, "Nazwy Wilna i jego mieszkańców", p. 4.

Giedroyc took it into his possession, having previously married the widow of Łukasz Mamonicz.[8]

Demand for paper increased constantly. The records of the Vilnius cathedral chapter give us some idea of the amounts. Its administrator noted on 14 September 1578: "for the needs of the priests of the chapter, I sometimes bought 7 pounds (*libras*) of paper at 2,5 *grosz*, that is for 15,5 *grosz* in total",[9] and a year later: "for 8 pounds of paper for the needs of the chapter I paid 2,5 *grosz* per pound, that is 20 *grosz* in total".[10] This would mean that the scribes used up at least 200 sheets of paper a year to produce the capitular documentation (a pound, Polish *libra*, was twenty-four sheets). It was probably more, because some of the texts were entered into registers of the chapter that had been produced previously.

The chapter was only one of dozens institutions which together needed a huge amount of paper in the second half of the sixteenth century. Local paper production was not enough and Vilnius merchants still imported paper in large quantities from other cities, mainly from Cracow, where it was brought for instance from Głogów and Wrocław.[11] The register of the Vilnius cathedral chapter from 1550-1560 was kept on paper imported from Gdańsk.[12] The 1583 toll registers from Brest noted that in that year 603 *libras* of paper were imported into Lithuania, 513 of which for Vilnius.[13]

It is likely that Vilnius was an intermediary for trade in this material, where not only the inhabitants of the city but people from other places in the Grand Duchy of Lithuania could buy it as well. This is suggested by the large quantities of paper mentioned in the inventories of Vilnius merchants from the first half of the seventeenth century.

It is claimed that paper was not a cheap product, because even in the scribal offices of Lithuanian magnates in the seventeenth century secretaries had to use it sparingly.[14] However, on the basis of sporadic references and by way of analogy with other urban settlements we can determine exactly how expensive it was to write on. It proves to have been fairly cheap. In the register of the

[8] LAUCEVIČIUS, *Popierius Lietuvoje*, p. 59; TOPOLSKA, *Czytelnik i książka*, p. 150.

[9] *Regestr kapituły roku 1577 i roku 1578*, MS MAB F43-451, f. 22v;

[10] *Regestr kapituły roku 1579 i roku 1580*, MS MAB F43-452, f. 26r.

[11] R. RYBARSKI, *Handel i polityka handlowa Polski w XVI stuleciu*, 1, *Rozwój handlu i polityki handlowej* (Poznań, 1928), p. 189.

[12] MS MAB F43-211 (VKF445).

[13] ŁOWMIAŃSKA, "Wilno przed najazdem moskiewskim", p. 267.

[14] JARCZYKOWA, *"Papierowe materie" Piotra Kochlewskiego*, p. 95.

Vilnius chapter we have seen that in the years 1578-1580 a pound of paper cost 2.5 *grosz*.[15] Considering that the secretary who wrote on it earned 180 *grosz* per quarter, while the canon of Vilnius received a weekly wage of 88 *grosz*, it turns out that writing paper was not a particularly expensive commodity for those who used it for writing purposes.

In addition to paper, writing required quill pens, usually made of goose feathers, and ink. It was probably rather easy to obtain than the former. One could buy quills for a small price at the market, and in many houses geese were bred. Late medieval and early Renaissance quills had a wide tip, sharpened to the right or left. From the second half of the sixteenth century onwards, quills had an almost completely sharp tip, which entailed a change in writing technique.[16] It is difficult to determine exactly which ingredients went into the ink made in Vilnius. It was probably prepared from a mixture of iron sulphate, powdered *Cynips quercusfolii* larvae (that is, the larvae of the gall wasp), and a thickener.[17] The Tartars made their own ink following a similar recipe.[18] Since making it required some knowledge of chemistry, it can be assumed that it was sold by pharmacists. The quality of ink was sometimes low, and many of the preserved records have faded or changed their colour from black to rust, indicating a poorly prepared ink mixture, poor quality of the substrates used, or poor quality of paper.

Differences in the colour of ink, which became apparent over time, allow us to observe that many writers in the sixteenth and seventeenth centuries used personal writing sets. In the documents included in the municipal registers which have survived in the original, the main part of the document is written in one ink, while individual signatures are given in different inks.[19] It follows that those who wrote often carried their own pen and inkwell with them.

[15] *Regestr kapituły roku 1577 i roku 1578*, MS MAB F43-451, f. 22v; *Regestr kapituły roku 1579 i roku 1580*, MS MAB F43-452, f. 26r.

[16] J. SŁOWIŃSKI, *Rozwój pisma łacińskiego w Polsce XVI-XVIII wieku* (Lublin, 1992), pp. 44-48.

[17] A. GIEYSZTOR, *Zarys dziejów pisma łacińskiego* (Warsaw, 2009), p. 106.

[18] S. KRYCZYŃSKI, *Tatarzy litewscy: Próba monografii historyczno-etnograficznej* (Warsaw, 1938), p. 221.

[19] e.g. MS LVIA F23, ap. 1, no. 5096, f. 672r.

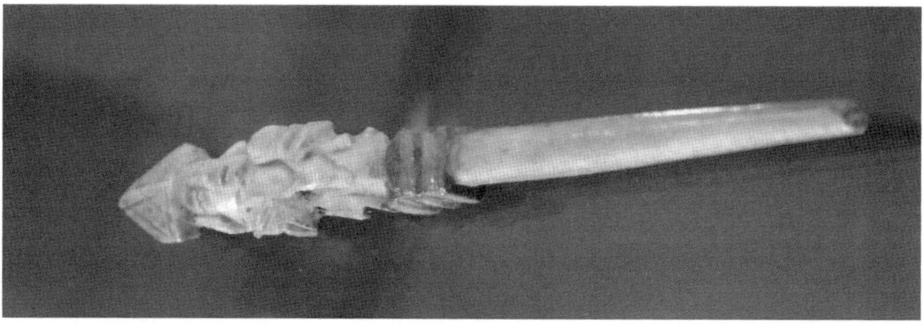

Fig. 21 Late medieval stylus excavated in the lower castle of Vilnius. Vilnius, LDKVR. Photo J. Niedźwiedź.

Parchment was used to produce the most important or most valuable texts, that is liturgical books (for instance the Torah) and some documents issued by the Lithuanian chancery. It was not a material frequently used in Vilnius. Paper played a much more important role.

In the fourteenth and fifteenth centuries, wooden tablets covered with wax (*cera*) were most probably used. In the Middle Ages, this was a typical material for making notes with a sharp stylus, usually made of steel or bronze. A Vilnius example of such a tool from the end of the fourteenth or fifteenth century was discovered during archaeological excavations in the lower castle (Fig. 21).[20] It is exceptionally decorative, made of bone, and its wider part is shaped in the figure of a bishop. Styluses must have been widely used in Vilnius, as in other cities of Poland, Livonia, and the Grand Duchy of Lithuania.[21] We know them from excavations conducted in Navahrudak (Nowogródek), Minsk, Vawkavysk (Wołkowysk), Polatsk, Slutsk, Braslav, and Pinsk. In Brest, archaeologists found not only a stylus but also a wax tablet (*cera*).[22] In the sixteenth century, with the spread of paper, wax tablets gradually became obsolete.

[20] This stylus was displayed at an exhibition of objects discovered during the excavations that preceded the reconstruction of the lower castle, entitled *Tarp kasdienybės ir prabangos. Restauruoti Lietuvos Didžiųjų Kunigaikščių rūmų archeologiniai radiniai* in 2011.

[21] K. Sołtan-Kościelecka, "Stilusy późnośredniowieczne z terenu obecny Polski", *Kwartalnik Kultury Materialnej* 50.2 (2002), pp. 123-132.

[22] M.B. Нікалаеў, *Гісторыя беларускай кнігі*, 1, *Кніжная культура Вялікага Княства Літоўскага* (Minsk, 2009), p. 22; Груша, *Белоруская кірылычна палеаграфія*, p. 66; J. Schaeken, *Voices on Birchbark: Everyday Communication in Medieval Russia* (Leiden and Boston, 2018), pp. 18-20.

It is possible that in the fourteenth and fifteenth centuries scrolls made of birchbark were used in Vilnius for writing in Ruthenian, like they were in the Ruthenian cities and towns which became part of the Grand Duchy of Lithuania, including Mstislavl, Viciebsk, Smolensk, and Kyiv,[23] where archaeologists discovered *gramotas*[24] with various contents. We also know that birchbark scrolls were used by the Lithuanian Tartars. However, if even birchbark was used in Vilnius, the role of this material was not as significant as in the Novgorod Republic, where birchbark documents were in common use in the Middle Ages.[25]

Towards the end of the sixteenth century, printing became the second most popular technique of producing texts after handwriting. Printers will be discussed below, but a few words should be devoted to type founders as manufacturers of the tools for the production of printed books: letters made of lead alloy with the addition of tin and antimony. Cyrillic type was mainly made in Vilnius, because it could be imported from very few places. It was made by two well-known printers, first by Francysk Skaryna and then by Piotr Mstislavets, who was active half a century later.[26] The fonts of Mstislavets were taken over by his early associates, the Mamonicz family, who successfully used their typeface throughout their many Cyrillic printed books. Fonts meant for Latin, Lithuanian, or Polish prints (the *Schwabacher*, *Fraktur*, or *Antiqua*) could be imported from other printing centres, but the growing number of printing houses and of books being produced required type founders to work *in situ* in Vilnius. One of them was Salomon Sultzer from Hungary.[27]

Spoken and Written Languages

A written record is the most fundamental representation of the past available to us and therefore, when considering the history of Vilnius from the four-

[23] Many discoveries of birchbark documents in the urban settlements of the Grand Duchy of Lithuania contradict a common opinion that this writing material is known almost exclusively from north-west Russia.

[24] *Gramota*: a Cyrillic document issued by a chancery (mainly charters or official letters).

[25] НІКАЛАЕЎ, *Гісторыя беларускай кнігі*, 1, p. 67; S. FRANKLIN, *Writing, Society and Culture in Early Modern Rus, c. 950-1300* (Cambridge, 2002), pp. 35-44; SCHAEKEN, *Voices on Birchbark*, p. 19.

[26] Z. JAROSZEWICZ-PIERESŁAWCEW, *Druki cyrylickie z officyn Wielki Duchy Litewski w XVI-XVIII wieku* (Olsztyn, 2003), pp. 59 and 208-209.

[27] J. NIEDŹWIEDŹ, "Sultzer Salomon", in: *PSB*, 45, p. 504

teenth to the seventeenth centuries, questions of language, script, and literacy are of key importance.

From the very beginning, Vilnius was a multilingual and consequently a multiscriptural city.[28] When Gediminas was building the town in the 1320s, its inhabitants spoke Ruthenian and Lithuanian. This reflected the linguistic situation in this part of the Grand Duchy of Lithuania. It was more or less here that the Lithuanian and Belarusian borderland began.[29] But apart from the Balts and Slavs, in fourteenth-century Vilnius one could hear German spoken by merchants who lived and did business here,[30] as well as two church languages, Church Slavonic, which was used in Orthodox churches and monasteries, and Latin, used in Catholic churches. In terms of language, the city was becoming ever more different from the region in which it was located. After the union with Poland and the granting of the Magdeburg law by King Jogaila (Władysław Jagiełło), Poles, speaking different varieties of Polish, as well as Tartars, whose immigration was supported by Duke Vytautas, began to settle in Vilnius.[31] Jews probably started to come in the fifteenth century, although for a long time they did not have their own organised community. The largest wave of Jews came to the city in the sixteenth century, and it was not until the beginning of the next century that the city became one of the most important Jewish centres in Lithuania.[32] In the sixteenth century and in the first half of the seventeenth century, when Vilnius flourished economically, politically, and cultur-

[28] J. NIEDŹWIEDŹ, "Multiscripturality in the Grand Duchy of Lithuania: New research approaches", trans. D.A. FRICK, *East European Politics and Societies and Cultures* 33 (2019), pp. 3-16.

[29] H. TURSKA, *O powstaniu polskich obszarów językowych na Wileńszczyźnie* (Vilnius, 1995), p. 13; L. BEDNARCZUK, *Języki Wielkiego Księstwa Litewskiego na tle porównawczym* (Vilnius, 1993), pp. 13-15.

[30] M. KOSMAN, "Wpływ unii jagiellońskiej na przemiany kulturalne w Wielkim Księstwie Litewskim w XV-XVI wieku", in: *Kultura i języki Wielkiego Kięstwa Litewskiego*, ed. M.T. LIZISOWA (Cracow, 2005), pp. 19-20.

[31] KRYCZYŃSKI, *Tatarzy litewscy*, pp. 5-15; С.В. ДУМИН, "Татарские князья в Великом княжестве литовском", *Acta Baltico-Slavica* 20 (1991), pp. 9-10; C. KUKLO, *Demografia Rzeczypospolitej przedrozbiorowej* (Warsaw, 2009), p. 223.

[32] I. COHEN, *History of the Jews in Vilnius* (Philadelphia, 1943), pp. 3-4; K. PIETKIEWICZ, *Wielkie Księstwo Litewskie pod rządami Aleksandra Jagiellończyka* (Poznań, 1995), p. 163; S. ALEXANDROWICZ, "Osadnictwo żydowskie na ziemiach litewskobiałoruskich od XV do XIX w. (Cechy szczególne)", in: *Świat nie pożegnany: Żydzi na dawnych ziemiach wschodnych Rzeczypospolitej w XVIII-XIX wieku*, ed. K. JASIEWICZ (Warszawa, 2004), p. 49; D. KATZ, *Lithuanian Jewish Culture* (Vilnius, 2004), p. 63; I. KLAUSNER, "Vilnius", in: *EJ*, 20, p. 528.

ally, among the city's inhabitants one could also encounter Italians, French, and even Scots.

The languages spoken by the city's inhabitants in the fourteenth century were therefore Lithuanian, Ruthenian, and German, and from the end of that century also Polish. During the fifteenth century the number of Lithuanian speakers decreased, although in the following centuries it was still large enough for sermons to be preached in their mother tongue. For example, in the privilege of 1527 issued by King Sigismund I the Old, there is a confirmation that in the main parish church of Vilnius, St. John's church, sermons were preached in both Polish and Lithuanian.[33] Lithuanian sermons were preached in the refectory of the Academy of Vilnius right up to 1634.[34] From the fifteenth century onwards, ever more Polish merchants and craftsmen came to Vilnius, and probably native Lithuanians learned Polish as well.[35] Hence, in the sixteenth and seventeenth centuries the (spoken) languages of everyday communication were Ruthenian (old-Belarusian), followed by Polish, Lithuanian, German, Yiddish, and Tartar. It is noteworthy that the Tartars underwent rapid linguistic assimilation, as at the beginning of the seventeenth century they only spoke Ruthenian and Polish.[36] Moreover, in the Christian liturgy Church Slavonic was used as well, while Hebrew was the language of Jewish worship as Arabic was the sacred language of Islam. The written Ruthenian language (called also *prosta mova*, 'simple speech') was widely used in state affairs.

The preserved texts only partially reflect this multilingual mosaic. The sources at our disposal are in languages different from those that the people used to speak to each other in Vilnius. Some spoken languages had a relatively adequate written form (for instance Polish), while written representations of others (for instance Lithuanian) are rare. We must remember, however, that even if a language had its own written version, there was a discrepancy between the written word and the spoken word. Relatively speaking, the smallest distance between spoken and written Polish appeared among educated people, especially in the seventeenth century. This was different in the case of Ruthenian, for instance. An example of the discrepancy between spoken and written language may be found in testimony given before the bishop's court: although witnesses testified in Polish or Ruthenian (and sometimes the border between

[33] *Zbiór praw i przywilejów*..., p. 42-43.

[34] H. WISNER, *Rzeczpospolita Wazów*, 3, *Sławne Państwo: Wielkie Księstwo Litewskie* (Warsaw, 2008), p. 264.

[35] TURSKA, *O powstaniu polskich obszarów językowych na Wileńszczyźnie*, p. 20.

[36] KRYCZYŃSKI, *Tatarzy litewscy*, pp. 228-229.

the two languages was fluid), faithful records of what was said have been preserved only in Latin.[37]

In the texts that survived we mainly encounter the following languages (that is, their grapholects):[38] Church Slavonic, Latin, Hebrew, Yiddish, Ruthenian, Polish, German, and sporadically Greek.

Latin, as well as Church Slavonic, can hardly be described as languages of everyday oral communication. Both were first and foremost languages of the liturgy (and therefore of Orthodox, Uniate, and Catholic liturgical books) and of the Bible. In their spoken version both these languages were based on how they were written down (they were 'secondarily oral'), so they were based on sets of strong rules. It is no coincidence that, unlike Polish and Ruthenian, Church Slavonic and Latin had codified grammars that were used in Vilnius schools from the 1570s-1580s. This strong prescriptivism aided formal and official discourses, such as in theology and law. The same prescriptivism, however, caused Latin and Church Slavonic to be inefficacious in everyday communication. Although Latin was the language of the Western European model of administration and had to fulfil still new functions, it functioned primarily as the language of writing used by the Church, the humanist elites, the schools and, in some part, by the administrative apparatus.

Polish and Ruthenian had a special status as languages of writing (grapholects) that were slowly replacing Latin and Church Slavonic. In the scholarly literature, Ruthenian is referred to as the "simple speech" or the "chancery language".[39] It is considered to be one of the literate languages used in Lithuania and the eastern areas of the Kingdom of Poland from the fourteenth century to the beginning of the nineteenth century. It was opposed on the one hand to Church Slavonic and on the other hand to the Belarusian and Ukrainian dialects, that is the living languages of oral communication. In this way its 'artificial' character is emphasised. Researchers dispute which Belarusian dialects formed its basis for it, but they agree that as early as the times of King Casimir IV Jagiellon (who ruled Lithuania from 1440) it was a fully developed and

[37] The differences in the function of spoken and written language are discussed by CLANCHY, *From Memory to Written Record*, pp. 206-211; and GOODY, *The Interface Between the Written and the Oral*, pp. 258-289.

[38] ONG, *Orality and Literacy*, pp. 102-107.

[39] Б.А. УСПЕНСКИЙ, *История русского литературного языка (XI-XVII вв.)* (Budapest, 1988), pp. 306-307; A. NAUMOW, "Domus divisa: *Studia nad literaturą ruską w i Rzeczypospolitej* (Cracow, 2002), p. 38.

homogeneous chancery language,[40] and was later also a language of literature. Additional components (adstrata) of Ruthenian, apart from living dialects, were Church Slavonic, and, depending on the types of text in which it was used (for instance chancery texts), also Latin and Polish. Until 1696, Ruthenian was a state language in the Grand Duchy of Lithuania, that is, it was used by most of the central and many local offices (land courts, castle courts, and magistrates' courts). This status was guaranteed by the provisions of the *Statute of the Grand Duchy of Lithuania*. It served not only the state, but also the Orthodox Church, and although it was used in secular matters, from the end of the sixteenth century it entered the sphere of *sacrum* ever more often, replacing Church Slavonic.[41] Some researchers note that the strong influence of Polish meant that in later times the Ruthenian literary language was heading towards a synthesis of two different language systems, East and West Slavonic, which is revealed in the lexical and syntactical calques taken from Polish.[42]

A number of prose forms developed in the Ruthenian language, including official and legal texts, letters, annals (*letopis, letopisets*), and sermons, and after the Brest Union some liturgical texts and short poems were written in Ruthenian as well,[43] but a number of ways of formulating thoughts existed only in genres cultivated in Latin and Polish. Among them one finds various epistolary forms, speeches, dialogues, Western European-style historiography, and finally most poetic genres.

We do not have many sources about the writing of German in Vilnius in its first centuries. The oldest known German texts are related to the Lutheran community in the late sixteenth century. In the Lutheran church there were two preachers, a German and a Polish one, and German was also taught in the Lutheran school.[44] However, it is highly probable that German had been a lan-

[40] *Ibid.*, p. 309. M.T. LIZISOWA, "O języku kancelarii Wielkiego Księstwa Litewskiego", in: *Wilno i kresy północnowschodnie: Materiały II Międzynarodowej Konferencji w Białymstoku 14-17 IX 1994 r. w czterech tomach*, 3, *Polszczyzna kresowa*, ed. E. FELIKSIAK and B. NOWOMIEJSKI (Białystok, 1996), pp. 68-73.

[41] УСПЕНСКИЙ, *История русского литературного языка*, pp. 319-322.

[42] LIZISOWA, "O języku kancelarii Wielkiego Księstwa Litewskiego", pp. 74-78.

[43] Short dedicatory poems or heraldic epigrams in Ruthenian were printed in Cyrillic books, e.g. in the first edition of the *Third Lithuanian Statute* (Vilnius, 1588) there is a *stemmat* and a dedicatory poem by Andrzej Rymsza dedicated to Lew Sapieha; Meletius Smotrycki preceded *Evangelie uchitielnoe* (Jewie, 1616) with an epigram on the Wołłowicz family's coat of arms; while an anonymous poet published *Na herb ich milostiey panow Maksymowiczow i Lomskykh z Lutshina* w *Biesiedach duchownych* (Vilnius, 1627). Longer poems and collections of songs in Ruthenian were mainly published in the Kyiv-Mohyla Collegium in Kyiv.

[44] Chapter 3, "Schools".

guage of written communication in Vilnius much earlier already, in the fourteenth and fifteenth centuries. In the fifteenth century, German was the mother tongue of many Vilnius merchants. They traded with merchants from German-speaking cities, for instance from Gdańsk.[45] In written communication they must have used German, as this was a common practice among the German elites of the cities and towns in Poland.[46] However, we do not have any traces of evidence that the *Voigt* of Vilnius or the city chancery used languages other than Latin, Ruthenian, and Polish.

Written Polish appeared in texts produced in Vilnius relatively late, probably not until the end of the fifteenth century, but it quickly became widely used. In the first half of the sixteenth century it was quite a well-developed code, with many genres, registers, rich stylistics and vocabulary. As it had been adapting Latin forms for a long time, it was becoming an increasingly efficient communication tool. At the same time, it had a fundamental advantage over Latin in that it was a Slavonic language. Hence it was easier to use in an environment dominated by spoken Ruthenian (old-Belarusian) or spoken Polish, as anyone who knew Ruthenian could understand Polish to a greater or lesser degree without the need to study it for a long time. For this reason, acquiring reading skills entailed mainly learning the alphabet and word formation. This was much more difficult with Latin, because in learning Latin knowing the alphabet was not enough. The Latin language could have been troublesome for Orthodox Christians, who did not have as good an access to Latin education as Catholics. *Latinitas* in its Polish version (*Latinitas Polonice*) was more accessible to them, provided of course that they were dealing with varieties of Polish that were not mixed with Latin, varieties which in the seventeenth century became very popular among the elites of the Commonwealth. It seems that from the second half of the sixteenth century onwards written Ruthenian became a less convenient and less universal code of communication for those who used writing than Polish.[47] However, when we take a closer look at the

[45] In the municipal archives of Gdańsk Anna Paulina Orłowska discovered several names of Vilnius merchants who traded there in the first half of the fifteenth century. I would like to express my gratitude to Dr Orłowska for sharing with me information about her discovery.

[46] BARTOSZEWICZ, *Urban Literacy in Late Medieval Poland*, pp. 64, 201.

[47] A. NAUMOW, "Domus divisa", pp. 45-48; D. FRICK, "The councilor and the baker's wife: Ruthenians and their language in seventeenth-century Vilnius", in: *Speculum Slaviae Orientalis: Muscovy, Ruthenia and Lithuania in the Late Middle Ages*, ed. V.V. IVANOV and J. VERKHOLANTSEV (Moscow, 2005), p. 57.

situation of the Polish language in Vilnius in comparison to other Slavonic languages, the matter will turn out to be more complicated.

The distinction between Polish and Ruthenian was sometimes fluid. Boris Uspenskiy noted that deciding that a text was in Ruthenian was sometimes based on the fact that it was written in Cyrillic script, which in fact might conceal a Polish text with only a few East Slavonic elements.[48] This approach assumes the existence of a uniform Polish language which was reflected in Polish texts written in the Latin alphabet. This uniform language would have an impact on texts written in Ruthenian. However, the living Polish language used in Vilnius in the sixteenth and seventeenth centuries did not need such standards and probably did not meet the standards imposed on it by the printed books produced by Karcan[49] or the Jesuits.

Standard Polish was for the most part established in the first half of the sixteenth century and consolidated over the next few decades, but there was no single colloquial norm, as individual dialects differed significantly from each other. This also applies to the Polish language in Lithuania. The spoken Polish language in Vilnius was influenced on all levels by Ruthenian and Lithuanian, mainly in the fields of lexis, phonetics and inflection.[50] When they needed to write in this language, educated people, often from Poland, exploited it in accordance with the rules established by the Cracow printers, almost 500 miles away. Perhaps this is the reason why the syntax of the written Polish language used in Vilnius does not differ from the syntax known from books printed in Poland.[51]

It was different with Ruthenian, which in Lithuania did not have fully established standards for writing.[52] Thus, written Ruthenian could combine elements of Church Slavonic and Polish (from the standard language) with the basis of the spoken language: Ruthenian, that is the old-Belarusian or 'local' language. This 'local' language was based on the Belarusian substrate with an admixture of the Polish superstrate and Lithuanian adstrate (or on the Polish

[48] УСПЕНСКИЙ, *История русского литературного языка*, pp. 319-322.

[49] Jan Karcan († 1611) was one of leading printers in Vilnius at the turn of the sixteenth and seventeenth centuries. Cf. Chapter 5.2.

[50] Z. KURZOWA, *Język polski Wileńszczyzny i kresów północnowschodnich XVI w.* (Warsaw, 1993), pp. 113-115, 206-209; EAD., *Ze studia nad polszczyzną kresową: Choice of Works* (Cracow, 2007), p. 189.

[51] KURZOWA, *Język polski*, p. 220.

[52] УСПЕНСКИЙ, *История русского литературного языка*, p. 309.

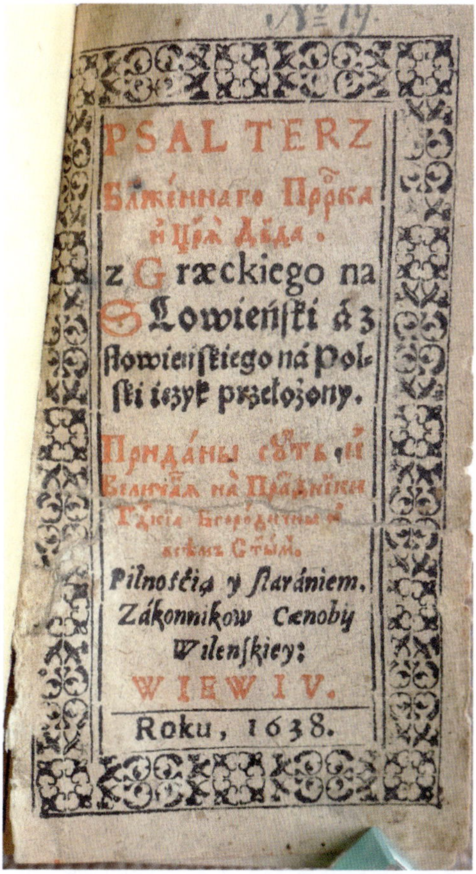

Fig.22 Orthodox prayer book published in 1638 in the printing house in Vievis (Jewie) for the Vilnian Orthodox Brotherhood. The title, in Polish and Ruthenian, says: "The Psalter of the Blessed Prophet and King David translated from Greek into Slavonic and from Slavonic into Polish". However, the Psalms in the prayer book were taken from the Polish Catholic translation of the Latin Vulgate, i.e. from the second (1575) or third (1577) edition of the so-called Leopolity): *Biblia to jest księgi Starego i Nowego Zakonu na polski język z pilnością według łacińskiej Biblijej od Kościoła krześijańskiego powszechnego nowo wyłożona* (Cracow, 1575). The editors of the prayer book were guilty of a dissimular to that of Smotrycki in his *Thrēnos*. Photo M. Nikalaeŭ.

substrate influenced by Belarusian and Lithuanian). In practice, this meant that the language of some Vilnius inhabitants was a hybrid language, for instance Polish with Belarusian phonetic characteristics, as well as with lexical and grammatical borrowings, or Ruthenian with Polish borrowings.

The linguistic identity and competence of Vilnius town dwellers depended on their place on the social ladder, their profession, and the environment in which they worked. Many of them were bilingual. This pertains not only to Orthodox Christians, Uniates, and Catholics, but also to Lutherans who spoke Polish and German.[53] Depending on the communicative situation, they could speak one or the other language, probably a language similar to the literary lan-

[53] FRICK, "The councilor and the baker's wife", pp. 56-57.

guage, but with strong regional influences. Only when it was written down, such a local spoken language had a chance to become distinct Ruthenian or Polish, defined by the choice of alphabet.

Scholars studying the languages in the eastern provinces of the Polish-Lithuanian Commonwealth draw attention to the diglossia and bilingualism of the literature produced there.[54] This is said to have relied on the opposition between Church Slavonic and Ruthenian (or 'simple speech') as two competing written languages. The relationship between both languages would have been similar to the situation in Poland, where Latin and Polish coexisted and competed with each other at the same time. In Vilnius, and probably also in other parts of Lithuania, this bipolar model seems to be too schematic, as the Ruthenian elite, which included the clergy from the monasteries of the Holy Trinity and the Holy Spirit, had at their disposal three or four literary languages, and in the case of those who knew Greek as many as five. Three Slavonic languages entered into particularly close and complex relationships because, as it happened, in the seventeenth century Church Slavonic began to compete with and complement not Ruthenian, but Polish.[55] An attempt to defend Church Slavonic at a relatively early stage prompted the Orthodox and Uniate leaders to react.[56]

When the Orthodox monk Meletius Smotrycki published his polemical treaty called *Thrēnos* in the printing house of the Vilnius Orthodox Brotherhood in 1610, he indicated on the title page that he had translated it from Ruthenian, even though the book was originally written in Polish.[57] Smotrycki's dissimulation was one of many actions of the Brotherhood which engaged rhetoric, texts, and language (Ruthenian, Church Slavonic, Polish and even Greek) in the defence of the independence of the Orthodox Church.

The Vilnius Orthodox Brotherhood was at that time the last bastion against the Catholic and Uniate attempts to sweep away the Orthodox faith from the city. Institutions of this type originated from Orthodox town brotherhoods, the so-called honey brotherhoods, which to some extent had the character of a guild. The first Orthodox confraternity had been founded in Vilnius around

[54] Успенский, *История русского литературного языка*, pp. 310-311.

[55] This question will be addressed in Chapter 9.4, "Prayer, song, and meditation".

[56] Naumow, "Domus divisa", pp. 40-43.

[57] M. Smotrycki, *ΘΡΕΝΟΣ, To jest lament jedynej św. powszechnej apostolskiej wschodniej Cerkwie… pierwej z greckiego na słowieński, a teraz z słowieńskiego na polski przełożony* (Vilnius, 1610). Cf. Frick, *Meletij Smotryc'kyj*, pp. 199-200.

1450.[58] At the beginning of the sixteenth century there were already several of them. These cooperatives were approved by a privilege of Stephen Báthory of March 1582, and in the years 1580-1597 there were four such communities: the brotherhood of magistrate members, of merchants and tanners, of furriers and the Ruthenian Brotherhood.[59] The new brotherhoods, not the honey-type ones, but those founded in the second half of the sixteenth century, set themselves new, more ambitious goals. First of all, they were an attempt to respond to the challenges that appeared with the spread of the Reformation and the Catholic Counter-Reformation in the form of the collegia run by the Society of Jesus. The Jesuits not only tried to prevent Calvinism, but also successively attracted the followers of the Orthodox Church to their side. This was the situation in Vilnius in the 1570s and 1580s. One of the Catholic programmatic works from that time aimed against the independence of the Orthodox Church was a study by Piotr Skarga, *O jedności Kościoła bożego* (On the unity of God's Church) from 1577. The purpose of the confraternities was to oppose such actions, mainly by improving the quality of religious life in the larger urban centres.[60] Their efforts focused on charitable work (giving loans without usury, supporting orphans and widows, maintaining hospitals, funding dowries, burying the dead, etc.) and strictly religious activities, such as praying and reading Holy Scripture together, organising schools, supervising the quality of services celebrated, and publishing Orthodox books in Church Slavonic, Polish, and Ruthenian.[61]

Although Ruthenian sermons began to appear in print at the beginning of the seventeenth century, as is shown by the example of Smotrycki's sermon preached at the funeral of Leonty Karpovych, the archimandrite of the Brotherhood's monastery in Vilnius (1620), it was more common to publish them in a

[58] MIRONOWICZ, *Bractwa cerkiewne*, p. 14.

[59] The statute from 1582 speaks of its headquarters located at Sawicz Street. The brotherhood had the character of a social club. Its purpose consisted in, among other things, charity work, the organisation of religious holidays, and helping each other. Cf. *AIZR*, 3, *1544-1587*, pp. 269-272; W. ŁUKASZ, 'W sprawie prawosławnych bractw miodowych w Wilnie', *Ateneum Wileńskie*, 13.2 (1938), pp. 288-290.

[60] In a letter to the Muscovite tsar in 1625, the Kyiv Brotherhood explained the objectives of its activities: "It is called a brotherhood and brings together Orthodox Christians who live among Lachs [Poles], Uniates, and the condemned heretics and wishes to be excluded from them and have nothing in common with them. They are only joined within the Orthodox community by love, they write their names down and call themselves brothers, and thus they are more suited to repelling dissenters", quoted in: J. BARDACH, "Bractwa cerkiewne na ziemiach ruskich Rzeczypospolitej w XVI i XVII wieku", *Kwartalnik Historyczny* 74.1 (1967), p. 77.

[61] MIRONOWICZ, *Bractwa cerkiewne*, pp. 18-19.

secondary Polish version. Abundant evidence is provided by the works of archimandrite Karpovych. In 1619, he issued a wedding sermon, the title page of which states that it was "translated from Ruthenian into Polish", and in the foreword we read an explanation of why the author chose Polish:

> Not only have I eagerly undertaken this small task (though the stake is the benefit of the Church and it is important), but I have also printed and presented to you the words I spoke during the wedding ceremony (translated into Polish, because this language is more suitable for many of you and your friends who arrived for this ceremony) to the immortal fame of this act and the enormously famous family of yours founded on the honour and glory of the glorious name of God.[62] (original in Polish)

The same happened with other types of texts, for instance correspondence. In the second half of the sixteenth century it was quite common to send messengers with an oral message.[63] In the cultural setting of the Grand Duchy of Lithuania, they could carry out their missions in Ruthenian, Lithuanian, Polish, etc. However, if someone decided to send a letter, it usually contained a text in Polish, less often in Latin. The *voivode* of Vilnius the chancellor of Lithuania Olbracht Gasztołd (Albertas Goštautas) wrote letters to Jerzy Radziwiłł, the castellan of Vilnius, in Polish,[64] although it is not obvious that they chose this language for face-to-face conversations. A bequest of Andrzej Dowgirdowicz (or rather Andriuška Dougirdovich) to the church in Łyntupy dated the Sunday before St. Prisca's Day (that is 14 January) in 1459, which was drafted by the canon of Vilnius Maciej[65] and was confirmed by a number of witnesses, is in Latin, although there is no doubt that the language in which the content of the document was discussed was Lithuanian or Ruthenian. Furthermore, when a copy of the document was made in 1627, it was translated into seventeenth-

[62] L. KARPOWICZ, *Przemowa i napomnienie do oblubieńców w stan św. małżeński wstępujących. Przy szlubie jego mości kniazia Samuela Ogińskiego, podkomorzyca trockiego… i jej mości panny Zofijej Billewiczówny, ciwunówny szandowskiej… Przy znamienitym zgromadzeniu tak niektórych ich mości panów senatorów, książąt, paniąt, urzędników ziemskich, jako i wielu innych zacnego szlacheckiego stanu osób czynione …* (Vilnius, 1619).

[63] W. TYGIELSKI, *Listy, ludzie, władza. Patronat Jana Zamoyskiego w świetle korespondencji* (Warsaw, 2007), pp. 31-32 and 35.

[64] MS LNMB F93-791.

[65] E.g. a letter from Vilnius of 12 March 1536, in: *Listy polskie XVI wieku*, 1, *Listy z lat 1525-1548 ze zbiorów Władysława Pociechy, Witolda Taszyckiego i Adama Turasiewicza*, ed. K. RYMUNT (Cracow, 1998), pp. 99-01.

century Polish. Andriuška Dougirdovich's bequest has therefore survived in languages that were not the ones he used on a daily basis.

In the first half of the seventeenth century, the Orthodox clergy noticed the problem of Ruthenian being gradually marginalised, so they tried to raise its status and experimented with ever newer kinds of texts in this language. Among their authors was Smotrycki, who translated *Evangelie uchitelnoe* (The Instructive Evangeliary) into Ruthenian.[66] In practice, however, Orthodox Christians in Vilnius, including Meletius Smotrycki, ever more often chose Polish and even Latin when writing about ecclesiastical affairs.

The factors that determined the choice of a specific language to prepare a specific text included the genre of the text, the time of its creation, the preferences of the author or the person who ordered it to be written, the competence of the scribe, the competence of the recipient, the credibility of a particular language and its official status, the purpose of rhetorical persuasion, etc. It is, however, necessary to stress that the choice of language meant not only that it was used, but that it also resulted in its adaptation or remodelling. When writing in Polish, Meletius Smotrycki carried out some 'language processing', making it 'more Orthodox' in terms of grammar, lexis, and phraseology.[67] The same phenomenon can be noticed in the translations of Orthodox prayers into Polish between the 1620s and 1650s (in prayer books printed in Vilnius). So the Polish language in Vilnius started to function not only as the second language of Latin culture (*Latinitas Polonice*),[68] but also as the second language of Orthodox culture (*Polonica Orthodoxe*), in some cases replacing Church Slavonic.

Without going too deeply into this problem, I would like to point out that, just as the languages of writing did not reflect the everyday speech of the inhabitants of Vilnius, so the texts as they have been preserved are not an accurate reflection of lives of those texts. They can at most reflect some aspects of those texts, although it might be more appropriate to say that they are intentional traces left behind by people who lived centuries ago and through writing attempted to function within their linguistic reality.[69]

[66] D. FRICK, "Introduction", in: M. SMOTRYCKI, *Rus' Restored: Selected Writings of Meletij Smotryc'kyj 1610-1630*, trans. D. FRICK (Cambridge, Mass., 2005), pp. XXX-XXXI.

[67] FRICK, *Meletij Smotryc'kyj*, pp. 191-192.

[68] J. NIEDŹWIEDŹ, "*Humanitas* na styku kultur: Kwestia dyskursów kolonialnych we wschodniej Europie, in: *Humanizm: Historie pojęcia*, ed. A. BOROWSKI (Warsaw, 2009), p. 245.

[69] Fortunately, within these intentional traces there are still other traces, which for a contemporary scribe were obvious and transparent, so he was unable to conceal or omit them.

The Shape of Script

The texts produced in Vilnius could be written not only in different languages but also using different types of script. The most important are the Cyrillic, Latin, Hebrew, and Arabic alphabets. An alphabet was sometimes assigned to a particular language, although there were numerous deviations from this rule. In Vilnius we find many examples of allography, that is a secondary adaptation of an alphabet to a language which was earlier expressed by another alphabet or did not have a written representation at all.[70]

The Cyrillic alphabet was used for the Church Slavonic, Ruthenian, and Tartar languages. The Latin alphabet in its several versions could serve Latin, Lithuanian, Polish, German, Italian, Latvian, Church Slavonic, and Ruthenian.[71] The Hebrew alphabet was used to write Hebrew and Yiddish texts as well as Karaim texts. Arabic script was used by the Tartars for writing their religious texts. Despite the fact that from the second half of the sixteenth century they translated the Quran, *kitabs*, *khamails,*[72] and other texts into Polish and Belarusian, they still used the Arabic alphabet supplemented with several new characters.[73]

This type of trace, not obvious to us, allows us to ask questions other than those that were written according to the rhetorical order of the text in force at the time of its creation.

[70] Such examples of allography can be find also in other parts of Europe and in the Polish-Lithuanian Commonwealth in the sixteenth-eighteenth centuries. Krzysztof Stopka wrote a valuable monograph about allography of Kipchak-Armenian and Polish-Armenian allography in the cities in the south-eastern part of the Polish Crown. Cf. K. STOPKA, *Języki oswajane pismem: Allografia kipczacko-ormiańska i polsko-ormiańska w kulturze dawnej Polski* (Cracow, 2013), pp. 9-51.

[71] Ruthenian and Church Slavonic were usually written in the Cyrillic alphabet. However, there are many early modern Ruthenian and Church Slavonic examples of Ruthenian texts annotated in the Latin alphabet (with Polish orthography), e.g. the Orthodox prayer books printed in Vilnius in 1624 and 1650 or Ruthenian songs written down in seventeenth-century books of miscellanies from contemporary Belarus and Ukraine. From the sixteenth century, Ruthenian documents were transcribed from Cyrillic into Latin alphabet for those native speakers of Polish language who could not read Cyrillic script but could understand another Slavonic language. From the second half of eighteenth century it was common the older Cyrillic documents were 'transliterated' from Cyrillic into Latin script, e.g. in the chancery the last King of Poland and Grand Duke of Lithuania Stanisław August Poniatowski (1764-1795).

[72] *Kitab* (Arabic 'book'): in the Grand Duchy of Lithuania, a collection of religious texts of various character (narrations from Quran and Hadith, religious rules, prayers, legends about the prophets, etc.). *Hamail* (Arabic 'things suspended' or 'amulet'): in the Grand Duchy of Lithuania, a small prayer book.

[73] The Arabic alphabet consists of 28 characters, while its Lithuanian version has 36 characters. KRYCZYŃSKI, *Tatarzy litewscy*, p. 239.

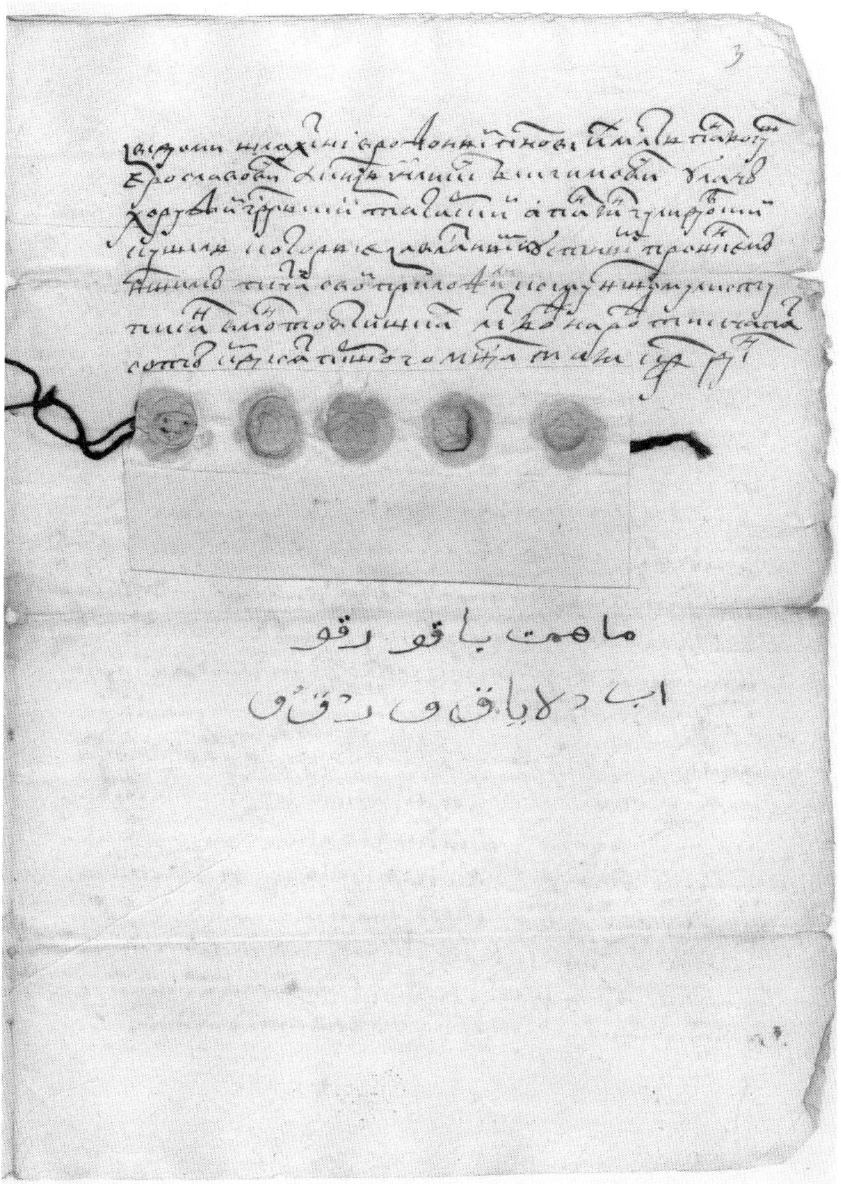

Fig. 23 Signatures in Arabic script of the warrant officer (*chorąży*) Mehmet Jakubowicz and Obdulach Jakubowicz under a Ruthenian document written in Montowtyszki (Lithuania) on 29 May 1571. Similar Arabic signatures must have been used by the Tartar inhabitants of Vilnius. MS Vilnius, MAB, F264-27, f. 3r. Reproduced with the permission of MAB.

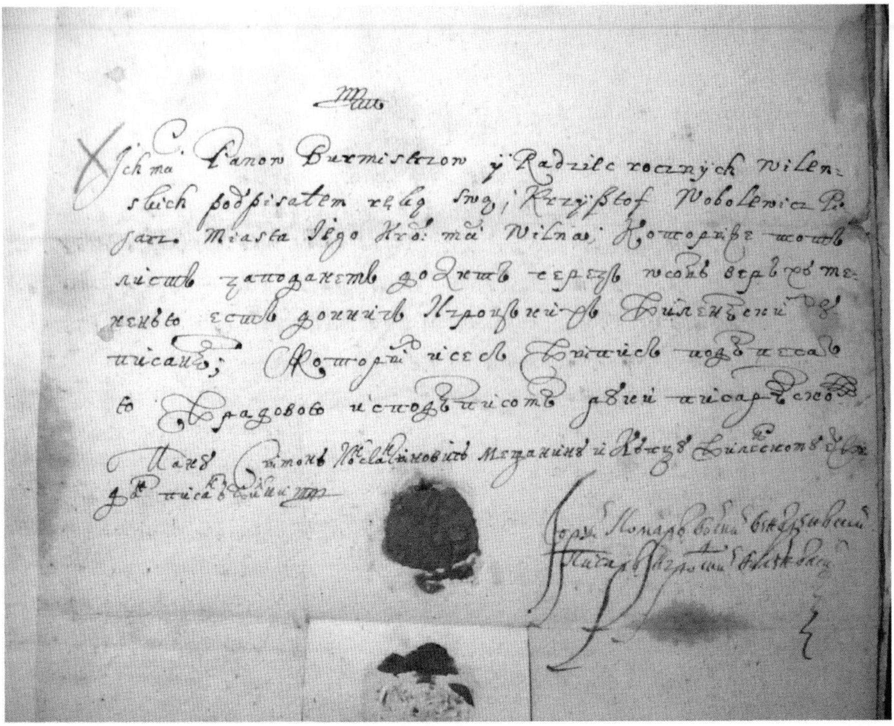

Fig 24 Polish *cancellaresca* script and Ruthenian *skoropis*. Document written by the Vilnius notary Krzysztof Wobolewicz, 1661. MS Vilnius, LVIA, F23, ap. 1, nr 5099, f. 28r. Photo J. Niedźwiedź.

Their attachment to this alphabet should be associated with their respect for the script in which the Quran had been written.[74] Unfortunately, it was not possible to find or identify any Tartar texts from Vilnius from before the mid-seventeenth century.

The Cyrillic script could be found in one of three varieties. The oldest one, which derived from Greek capitals, was *ustav*.[75] In the late Middle Ages, in the Grand Duchy of Lithuania this type of handwriting, which dates from the period of the Christianisation of the South Slavs by Cyril and Methodius in the ninth century, was mainly used in religious texts. It was used in Vilnius churches and monasteries, mainly in books imported from other parts of Ruthe-

[74] C. ŁAPICZ, "Trzy redakcje językowe muzułmańskiej legendy w piśmiennictwie Tatarów litewsko-polskich", *Acta Baltico-Slavica* 20 (1991), p. 156.

[75] ГРУША, *Белоруская кірылычна палеаграфія*, pp. 69-75 and 90.

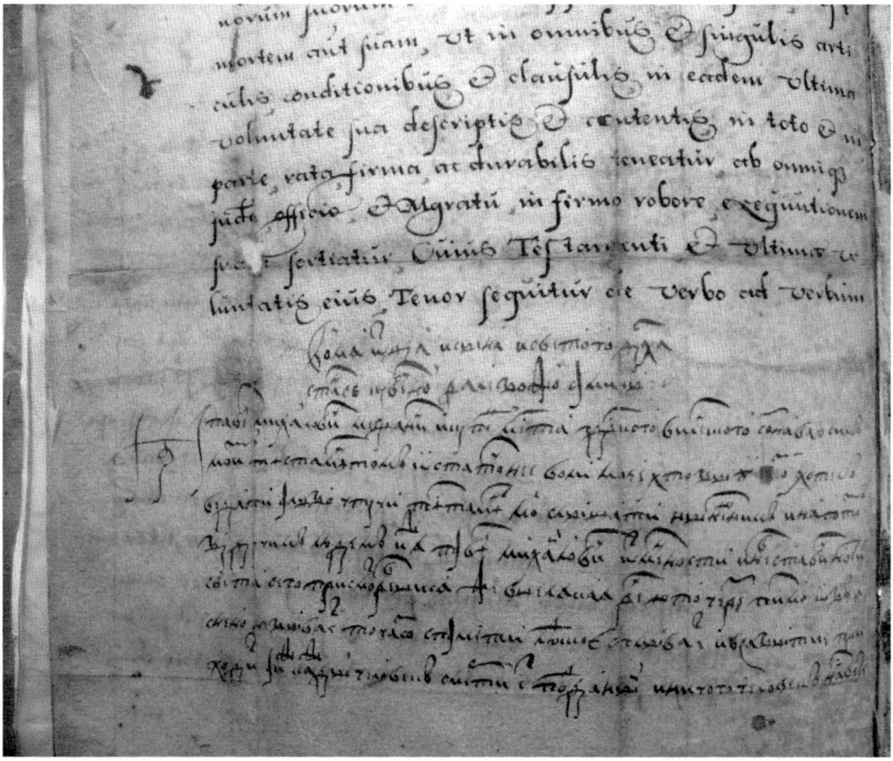

Fig. 25 Latin italic and Ruthenian *skoropis*. Testament of Paweł Michajłowicz Sznipka in the Vilniuis municipal registers, 1594. MS Vilnius, LVIA, F22, ap. 1, nr 5333, f. 90v. Photo J. Niedźwiedź.

nia, as well as in monumental painting and inscriptions on icons, which also featured Greek inscriptions.

During this period, a second type of Cyrillic script developed from *ustav* in the Balkans, called *semi-ustav*, which reached the Ruthenian lands in the last quarter of the fourteenth century.[76] It was a less careful script and quicker to use. We find it in Orthodox texts up to the seventeenth century, but also in late medieval documents and letters from the grand duke's chancery. A third type of Ruthenian Cyrillic script, *skoropis*, that is 'fast writing' or 'italic', was cre-

[76] B. HORODYSKI, *Podręcznik paleografii ruskiej* (Cracow, 1951), p. 27; M.H. ТИХОМИРОВ and A.B. МУРАВЬЕВ, *Русская палеография* (Moscow, 1966), p. 31; T. ROTT-ŻEBROWSKI, *Gramatyka historyczna języka białoruskiego* (Lublin, 1992), pp. 21-30; K. PIETKIEWICZ, *Cyrylica: Skrypt do nauki odczytywania pisma staroruskiego i rosyjskiego dla studentów archiwistyki* (Poznań, 1996), pp. 10-11.

Fig. 26 Gothic *textualis* script and a judge writing a sentence. Fragment of a monumental polychrome, showing the Passion of Christ on the north wall of the Franciscan Observant (Bernardine) church (St. Francis and St. Bernard's church) in Vilnius, *c.* 1530. Photo J. Niedźwiedź.

ated for the needs of the chancery.[77] It is believed that *skoropis* was developed in the third quarter of the fourteenth century under the influence of late Gothic-cursive.[78] This type of writing gained great popularity in the Ruthenian lands of the Polish Crown and in the Grand Duchy of Lithuania, where it was used in manifold variants until the eighteenth century. A large number of legal, political, and administrative texts, as well as privileges, wills, chronicles (*letopis*), etc. were written in *skoropis*. It was used by the Orthodox Church, despite the fact that liturgical books were still dominated by *semi-ustav* and *ustav*. The form of *skoropis* evolved, gradually assuming shapes similar to those of humanistic script (chancery hand). It is probable that in the second half of the sixteenth century and in the seventeenth century relatively many town dwellers

[77] Тихомиров and Муравьев, *Русская палеография*, p. 33; Груша, *Белоруская кірылычна палеаграфія*, pp. 90-92.

[78] Horodyski, *Podręcznik paleografii ruskiej*, pp. 27-28 and 48-55; Pietkiewicz, *Cyrylica*, pp. 10-11.

who were somehow involved in legal issues were able to read *skoropis*, as Ruthenian was the basic written language of the Vilnius institutions, such as the municipal court, the castle court, the Tribunal of the Grand Duchy of Lithuania, and various court commissions established on an *ad hoc* basis. This type of script was also used by the grand duke's chancery. Almost every document issued by these institutions was written in its entirety or in part in *skoropis*.

Cyrillic competed with Latin script and the Latin language. The beginnings of the city had been connected with the use of Latin script: Gediminas issued letters dated 25 January 1323 in Vilnius inviting merchants from Magdeburg, Bremen, Cologne, and other Hanseatic cities to settle here.[79] It was a new type of text and a new way of writing used by scribes who worked for the grand duke, and from the time of Vytautas it was used by the chancery he established. While only a few Latin texts from the times of Gediminas and his successors have survived, after the union with Poland the grand duke's chancery produced hundreds of documents and letters annually, and they were written using the documentary script and Gothic minuscule that were also used in documents in German. Official texts were dominated by Gothic minuscule, a cursive that had evolved from the fourteenth to the sixteenth century, and to a lesser extent by the *bastarda*.[80] Other types of blackletter, especially *textualis*, may have been present in religious books and in monumental painting.

Although no gravestones with Gothic inscriptions have been preserved in Vilnius, we have data that allow us to believe they once existed. For instance, princes and bishops buried in the cathedral were certainly commemorated with epitaphs. Moreover, Gothic script in the public sphere was well established through coins. From the second half of the fifteenth century onwards, the *półgrosz* of Casimir IV Jagiellon minted in Poland featured Latin inscriptions. In the 1490s, Alexander I Jagiellon founded a mint in Vilnius that operated for most of the period studied here. In Alexander's times, the basic coinage minted there was the Lithuanian *półgrosz* with the depiction of the coat of arms of Lithuania, Pogoń (Pahonia), and the Polish Eagle. These were the first Lithua-

[79] *Kodeks dyplomatyczny Litwy wydany z rękopismów w Archiwum Tajnem w Królewcu zachowanych*, ed. E. Raczyński (Wrocław, 1845), pp. 27-32; *Chartularium Lithuaniae*, *passim*.

[80] W. Semkowicz, *Paleografia łacińska* (Cracow, 2007), p. 361; A. Derolez, *The Palaeography of Gothic Manuscript Books: From the Twelfth to the Early Sixteenth Century* (Cambridge, 2006), pp. 123-134 and 142-157. R. Čapaitė published an extensive dissertation on the palaeography of the Latin scripts in the chancery of Duke Vytautas in R. Čapaitė, *Gotikinis kursyvas Lietuvos dzidžiojo kunigaikščio Vytauto raštinėje* (Vilnius, 2007).

Fig. 27 Gothic script on the *półgrosz* (half-grosch) of King Sigismund I the Old, minted at the Vilnius mint in *c.* 1512: "MONETA SIGISMUNDI IZ". Photo J. Niedźwiedź.

Fig. 28 Renaissance script on the *półgrosz* (half-grosch) of King Sigismund II Augustus, minted at the Vilnius mint in 1565: "MONETA MAG[NI] DUCAT[US] LITU[ANIAE]". Photo J. Niedźwiedź.

nian coins that had inscriptions. They imitated coins from other parts of Central Europe, but in Vilnius the use of a Latin text had a slightly different function from elsewhere. Silesian, Czech, Polish, and Prussian coins of that time could have contained inscriptions in Latin only. A Lithuanian coin, at least theoretically, could have been supplied with a Ruthenian inscription. The choice of blackletter was therefore a declaration of the ruler's attachment to the Latin, Western, and Catholic cultural model and was the most common carrier of the Western idea of power.[81] In Vilnius, for everybody using locally produced coins, be they an Orthodox Christian or a Jew, a Catholic or a Muslim, the official language of the ruler was Latin, which was identified with Catholicism, and its graphic representation was at first Gothic minuscule, and later *Antiqua*, that is a Renaissance script introduced in the second decade of the sixteenth century on the coins of King Sigismund I the Old.

[81] R. KIERSNOWSKI, "Funkcje dydaktyczne monet średniowiecznych", in: *Nauczanie w dawnych wiekach: Edukacja w średniowieczu i u progu ery nowożytnej: Polska na tle Europy*, ed. W. IWAŃCZAK and K. BRACHA (Kielce, 1997), pp. 228-229.

This was the beginning of the expansion of modern scripts, which had the function similar to that of monumental writing: it was exposed because it was used in public places.[82] Initially, such scripts were only used by the ducal court, that is they were used in the domain of authority. We have mentioned *Antiqua* in the legends of coins. Inscriptional capitals similar to this were used on the Renaissance tombstones of representatives of the ruling dynasty or high ranking Catholic hierarchies and magnates. The natural son of King Sigismund I the Old and bishop of Vilnius, John of the Dukes of Lithuania, was one of the first Vilnius inhabitants who, after their death, were honoured with a Renaissance epitaph.[83] Over the next few decades, inscriptions written in the new script became a fixed component of the local graphosphere, as the patterns of tombstone inscriptions were imitated by the magnates, nobles, clergy, and urban elites. Only a few of them have survived.

The fact that the Renaissance script was displayed in public spaces reflected its well-established position in the chanceries of the grand duke and the magnates. The royal secretaries, who were among the people who first came in contact with Renaissance culture, introduced new types of writing into chancery practice: humanist cursive, including various types of *cancellaresca*, 'italics' (both calligraphic and cursive italics), and the Italian humanist *bastarda*. These types of writing coexisted with blackletter and post-Gothic scripts,[84] which were gradually abandoned and eventually relinquished in the late sixteenth century.[85] Letters written in Polish in the first half of the sixteenth century were initially characterised by post-Gothic and mixed script, while at the beginning of the seventeenth century they were written almost exclusively in a humanist hand.

Ruthenian script was also influenced by Renaissance lettering. The printing house of Francysk Skaryna, who was active in Vilnius from 1524 to 1526, published books in Ruthenian, but their typeface, based on *semi-ustav*, had features of the Renaissance typefaces used at the beginning of the sixteenth

[82] Monumental writing in the early modern towns was thoroughly examined by Armando Petrucci in his important work A. PETRUCCI, *Public Lettering: Script, Power, and Culture*, trans. L. LAPPIN (Chicago and London, 1993), pp. 16-17.

[83] The lost tombstone was made for Vilnius cathedral by the Italian sculptor Giovanni Cini from Siena. The content of the epitaph is given by Sz. STAROWOLSKI, *Monumenta Sarmatarum, viam universae carnis ingressorum* (Cracow, 1655), p. 224.

[84] SŁOWIŃSKI, *Rozwój pisma łacińskiego w Polsce*, p. 52.

[85] SŁOWIŃSKI, *Rozwój pisma łacińskiego w Polsce*, p. 86-91; R. ČAPAITĖ, "XV-XVI amžiaus humanistinio kursyvo terminijos problemos", *Praeities pėdsakais* 52 (2007), pp. 83-99.

century in Prague, where Skaryna began his editorial work.[86] His successor, however, Piotr Mstislavets, who had learnt book printing in Moscow, was less inspired by Western typefaces and used the models of the printer Ivan Fedorov, who had based them on the calligraphy of liturgical books.[87] On the other hand, modern Western script had a strong influence on *skoropis*. This was probably due to the fact that it was mainly used by chancery clerks and scribes working for various institutions. Many of them had to produce both Cyrillic and Latin texts, so probably, in order to reduce the number of necessary quill movements, they assimilated the two scripts. Although most *skoropis* letters were still written separately, the hand became more fluid; there were ligatures and there was a tendency to write letters without lifting the quill from the paper. From the second half of the sixteenth century, in the titles of Ruthenian documents issued by the chancery of the grand duke one can see certain features taken from *Schwabacher* and *textualis*. This meticulous angular shape of letters was essentially based on *semi-ustav*.

It was not until the seventh and eighth decade of the sixteenth century that the newly established printing houses of Mikołaj Krzysztof Radziwiłł 'the Orphan' and Jan Karcan began to publish books in Polish and Latin[88] in which the best Cracow practices of printing were used: Latin texts were usually printed in humanist typefaces, while Polish texts were printed in *Schwabacher*. The latter, however, was not only the domain of the Polish language in Vilnius. It was also used for printing texts in German, Lithuanian, Latvian, and in the seventeenth century even in Ruthenian and Church Slavonic.[89] In principle, therefore, *Antiqua* and cursive were intended for Latin, while *Schwabacher* (with a few exceptions) was meant for the vernacular languages.[90]

We know relatively little about the Hebrew script in Vilnius before the middle of the seventeenth century, because most of its monuments were destroyed by the Nazis. There were many users of this script. As early as the middle of the sixteenth century a large Jewish community existed in Vilnius,

[86] Немировский, *Франциск Скорина*, pp. 359-363

[87] Jaroszewicz-Pieresławcew, *Druki cyrylickie*, pp. 208-209.

[88] *Drukarze dawnej Polski od XV do XVIII wieku, 5, Wielkie Księstwo Litewskie*, ed. A. Kawecka-Gryczowa, K. Korotajowa, and W. Krajewski (Wrocław, 1959), pp. 107-116, 205-210.

[89] M. Cubrzyńska-Leonarczyk, "O początkach drukarstwa w Supraślu", in: *Z badań nad dawną książką: Studia ofiarowane profesor Alodii Kaweckiej-Gryczowej w 85-lecie urodzin*, 1, ed. P. Buchwald-Pelcowa (Warsaw 1991), p. 173.

[90] M. Juda, *Pismo drukowane w Polsce XV-XVIII wieku* (Lublin, 2001), pp. 98, 152-154.

and in 1558 the King Sigismund II Augustus ordered them to pay taxes to the state treasury.[91] In the second half of the century a Jewish 'district' began to emerge in the area of Jatkowa, Szklanna and Żydowska Streets (today Mėsinių, Stiklių and Jewish Streets). The Jewish street was mentioned first in 1592. In 1573 the Great Synagogue of Vilnius was built. The *qahal* (the Jewish self-government administration) performed judicial and administrative functions and therefore the relevant books, called *pinkases* (*pinkas*, 'minute-book'), were kept there.[92] The *pinkases* were kept in Hebrew, although the sessions of the authorities were held in Yiddish.[93] This version of Hebrew is called chancery Ashkenazi Hebrew.[94] To some extent this bilingual Yiddish-Hebrew situation resembles the relationship between spoken Polish and written Latin or between spoken Ruthenian and written *prosta mova*. Probably also for the needs of the community, copies of the decisions of the Council (*Vaad*) of Four Lands and then the Council (*Vaad*) of the Land of Lithuania were made,[95] especially as,

[91] Д. Маггид, "Вильна", in: *JEBE*; Cohen, *History of the Jews in Vilnius*, p. 5; Katz, *Lithuanian Jewish Culture*, p. 63; D. Frick, "Jews and others in seventeenth-century Wilno: life in the neighborhood", *Jewish Studies Quarterly* 12.1 (2005), pp. 8-42.

[92] С. М. Дубнов, "Разговорный язык и народная литература польско-литовских евреев в XVI и первой половине XVII века", *Еврейская Старина* 1 (1909), pp. 10-11 and 14.

[93] M. Altbauer, "O języku dokumentów związanych z samorządem żydowskim w Polsce", in: *Żydzi dawnej Rzeczypospolitej: Materiały z konferencji "Autonomia Żydów w Rzeczypospolitej szlacheckiej"* (Wrocław, 1991), pp. 15-22.

[94] A. Michałowska-Mycielska, *Sejm żydów litewskich (1623-1764)* (Warsaw, 2014), p. 22.

[95] The Polish and Lithuanian *Vaads* were Jewish parliamentary institutions which decided about all aspects of religious, political, juridical, economic, educational, and social life in Jewish communities in the Polish-Lithuanian Commonwealth. The *Vaads* co-operated with the authorities of the state (the *Sejm* and Senate, and the central offices) and the local authorities. The Vaad was established in 1580 and in 1623 it was divided into a Polish (the *Vaad* of Four Lands) and Lithuanian one. Cf. Katz, *Lithuanian Jewish Culture*, pp. 73-84; M. Cieśla, "The other townsfolk: The legal status and social positions of the Jews in cities of the Grand Duchy of Lithuania in the seventeenth and eighteenth centuries", in: *Religion in the Mirror of Law Eastern European Perspectives from the Early Modern Period to 1939*, ed. Y. Kleinmann, S. Stach, and T.L. Wilson (Frankfurt am Main, 2016), pp. 307-328; M. Cieśla, "Żydzi a Rzeczpospolita", in: *Społeczeństwo nowożytnej Rzeczypospolitej wobec państwa*, ed. W. Kriegseisen (Warsaw, 2016), pp. 259-285. For the most recent publication about the history of the Lithuanian *Vaad* with a complete reference record, see Michałowska-Mycielska, *Sejm żydów litewskich (1623-1764)*; ead., "The council of Lithuanian Jews (1623-1764): Lithuania's central Jewish representation", *Biuletyn Polskiej Misji Historycznej – Bulletin der Polnischen Historischen Mission* 9 (2014), pp. 51-69. There were 34 sessions of the Lithuanian *Vaads* between 1623 and 1761. The Vaad issued its decrees in Hebrew. They were collected in a book called *pinkas*. Copies of the *pinkas* were preserved in the main Jewish settlements in Lithuania. Until the nineteenth century three copies were known. The Russian-Jewish historian Simon Dubnow (Семён Маркович Дубнов, 1880-1941) published the *pinkas* of the Lithuanian *Vaad* as an appendix to the journal *Еврейская*

from 1652 onwards, Vilnius used to send its representative to its gatherings. These books were imported from the cities of the Polish Kingdom (Lublin, Cracow) and from outside the Commonwealth.

All these institutions ensured the production and circulation of large numbers of texts. The shape of the script used for their production can be established only by analogy with the books and epigraphic monuments from other cities of the Grand Duchy of Lithuania that have survived. Religious books, for instance Torah scrolls, were calligraphied in a Gothic book hand. Books printed in Hebrew typefaces were also used. They were imported from the cities of the Polish Kingdom (Lublin, Cracow) and from outside the commonwealth.

Documents written in Ruthenian and Polish from the 1630s have been preserved in the Vilnius municipal registers. At the bottom of the page there are notes with signatures in Yiddish or Hebrew, in cursive or semi-cursive.[96] This allows us to assume that it was quite common to use Hebrew script in cases that involved Jewish and Christian parties, as was not an isolated phenomenon in Europe.[97]

On the other side of the river Neris there was a Jewish cemetery.[98] It may have been extant already in the late fifteenth century as, according to the tradition of the funeral fraternity, it was flooded by the river's waters as early as 1487, but researchers believe that it was not established until the end of the

старина with a Russian translation (*Областный пинкос еврейских общин Литвы (1623-1761)*, ed. S. Dubnow, trans. I. Tuvim, *Еврейская старина*, 1 (St. Petersburg, 1909), and 2 (St. Petersburg, 1912). In a new version it was republished by Dubnow in 1925 in Berlin. In 1924 Dubnow also published several documents issued by *Vaad* ("Дополнения к *Литовскому пинкосу*", ed. and trans. S. Dubnow, *Еврейская старина* 11 (1924), pp. I-XXXV). The history of the *pinkas* is discussed by Anna Michałowska-Mycielska, *op. cit*, pp. 18-23.

96 This is shown by a document from 20 September 1634 acknowledging the repayment of a debt, under which there is a validation by Vilnius Jewish merchants (MS LVIA F23, ap. 1, no. 5096, ff. 81r-81v), and by an entry (Polish: *oblata*) from 1670 in the registers of the Vilnius city council signed by representatives of the Jewish community, Cf. *Wilnianie: Żywoty siedemnastowieczne*, p. 323.

97 On the use of Hebrew in English documents written in Latin in the thirteenth century, see Clanchy, *From Memory to Written Record*, p. 202. Katalin Szende noticed the same phenomenon in medieval Hungary. Parts of the records of transactions between Christians and Jews were written in the Hebrew alphabet; see K. Szende, *Trust, Authority and the Written Word in the Royal Towns of Medieval Hungary* (Turnhout, 2018), pp. 249-286.

98 Маггид, *Вильна*; see S. Grzybowski, "Epitafia żydowskie w Polsce doby sarmatyzmu: Studium porównawcze", in: *Żydzi w Małopolsce: Studia z dziejów osadnictwa i życia społecznego*, ed. F. Kiryk (Przemyśl, 1991), p. 52.

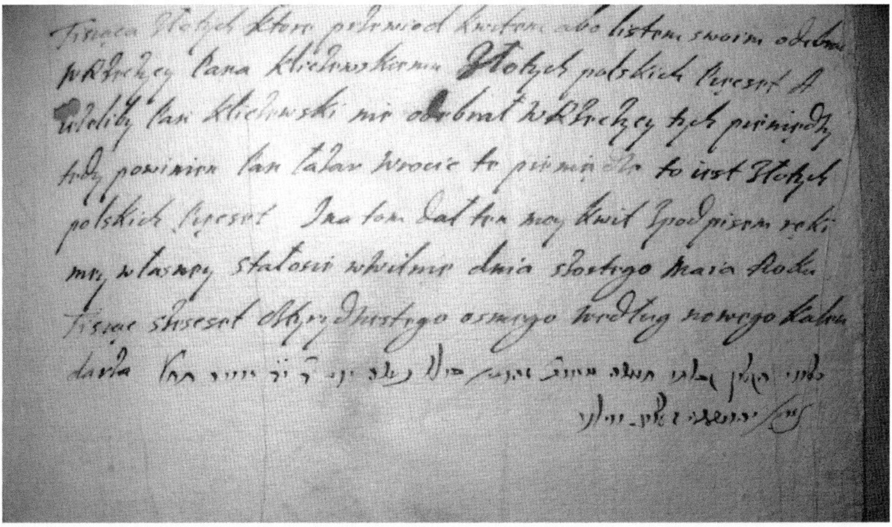

Fig. 29 The confirmation and signature of a Jew, Zelman Jakubowicz, in the Hebrew alphabet below a Polish-language document of lending money from 1648. MS Vilnius, LVIA, F23, ap. 1, nr 5096, f. 379r. Photo J. Niedźwiedź.

sixteenth century.[99] Probably, the tombstones were usually inscribed with concave Gothic or Gothic-Renaissance Ashkenazic script. This script was patterned after a book script, that was either written or drawn, and was present, for in stance, in the Hebrew liturgical books mentioned above.[100]

We have less trustworthy information about the texts of the Muslims living in Vilnius. The presence of Tartars in the city is corroborated both by written sources and by the name Tartar Street in the northern part of the city, in the suburb called Lukiškės, where they had a mosque.[101] Their script was mainly related to their religion. Certainly, Vilnius Tartars used the Quran and other books written in Arabic and Tartar, but from the sixteenth century, due to language assimilation, they wrote in Ruthenian and Polish, even if they still used the Arabic alphabet. Occasionally, Arabic signatures of Tartar witnesses appear in the documents of the castle court (*iuridicium castrense*; Polish: *sąd grodzki*) from the sixteenth and seventeenth centuries.[102] However, we know

[99] COHEN, *History of the Jews in Vilnius*, pp. 3, 124

[100] A. TRZCIŃSKI, *Hebrajskie inskrypcje na materiale kamiennym w Polsce w XIII-XX wieku: Studium paleograficzno-epigraficzne* (Lublin, 2007), pp. 128-131; A. TRZCIŃSKI and M. WODZIŃSKI, *Cmentarz żydowski w Lesku*, 1, *Wiek XVI i XVII* (Cracow, 2002), pp. 25-26.

[101] P. BORAWSKI, *Tatarzy w dawnej Rzeczypospolitej* (Warsaw, 1986), pp. 60-61.

[102] *AVAK*, 31, pp. 185-186, item 122.

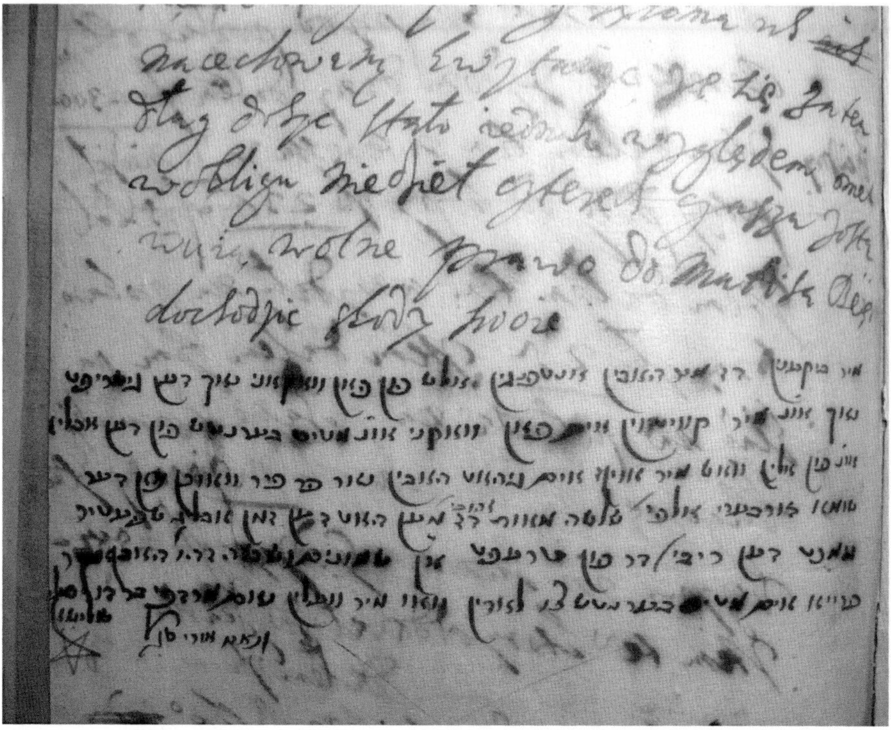

Fig. 30 A sloppy Polish *cancellaresca* script and Yiddish in Hebrew cursive. Confirmation of paying off a debt, 1634. MS Vilnius, LVIA, F23, ap. 1, nr 5096, f. 81v. Photo J. Niedźwiedź.

that in the first decades of the fifteenth century, Vytautas' chancery, which operated in Trakai and Vilnius, employed scribes who corresponded with the Crimean Khanate.[103] In the years 1496-1530, the Lithuanian chancery of Kings Alexander Jagiellon and Sigismund I the Old employed the Tartar prince Abrahim Tymirszyc.[104] However, documents written by Tartar chancery clerks have not survived.

This look at how the texts that formed the literary culture of early modern Vilnius were created allows us to draw several conclusions. As in many European cities, the texts of Vilnius are not only multilingual, but also multi-scriptural, and such an abundant diversity of scripts is rare elsewhere.[105] In Vilnius,

[103] KOSMAN, *Orzeł i Pogoń*, p. 104.

[104] PIETKIEWICZ, *Wielkie Księstwo Litewskie*, p. 27.

[105] Among the cities of the Commonwealth there is Lviv, while in southern Europe there is

people wrote in five alphabets: Cyrillic, Latin, Hebrew, Arabic, and occasionally Greek. These alphabets, depending on the circumstances, could take different forms. In total, more than twenty varieties of script could be distinguished. However, there were few readers (not to mention scribes) who used most of these scripts, because the scope of their use was strongly conditioned by social environment, chronological development, and the various functions of these texts. This is one of the reasons why it is impossible to create a 'model user' of texts or a single 'model' of the functioning of texts in the city.

A holistic view of the body of texts requires adopting many perspectives. One of them is that of treating the text, as far as is possible today, as an object in its material form, made of paper, stone or wood, ink, paints, and grooves, and suitable lettering. The way in which the object which is the text was made, does not only determine its reception. Above all it allows one to see the differences between the various traces of the past and to conceptualise their mutual relations. On this basis, we can talk about the users, manufacturers, and readers of these texts-as-objects, as well as about the ways in which they could be used.

Venice with probably some Dalmatian cities. The Latin, Arabic, and Hebrew alphabets were used in medieval Spain, while the Arabic and Latin alphabets coexisted in Sicily (e.g. in Palermo) before it came under Spanish rule.

Chapter 7

The Book

The Manuscript Book

Vilnius did not become a significant centre for the production of liturgical books until the mid-fifteenth century. That is to say, we do not know of any Orthodox or Catholic books that might have been produced there before that time. However, in the Grand Duchy of Lithuania, in the fourteenth and fifteenth centuries there were many Orthodox centres of manuscript book production. They certainly fulfilled the needs of the Orthodox inhabitants and churches of Vilnius.[1] References scattered across various sources speak of the copying of Orthodox books in Vilnius in the second half of the fifteenth century and the first years of the sixteenth century, which testify to the existence of scriptoria in those days.[2] It is believed that a scribe of the Lithuanian chancellor and *voivode* of Vilnius Mikołaj Radziwiłł (*c.* 1440-1509), named Vas'ka, worked in Vilnius and copied the encyclopaedic collection *Pritochnik* in 1483. From 1502 the scribe Matvei Desaty worked in Vilnius on the *Desatiglav* collection, which he completed at the monastery of Su-

[1] Нікалаеў, *Палата кнігопісаная*, pp. 126-131; id., *Гісторыя беларускай кнігі*, 1, pp. 33-76, 90-92; *Кириллические рукописные книги, хранящиеся в Вильнюсе: каталог*, ed. Н. Морозова (Vilnius, 2008). An example of such a manuscript may have been a collection of homilies by St. Isaac of Nineveh (Isaac the Syrian) with a panegyric of Grand Duke Vytautas, added ad the end of the book. It is probable that some copy of this panegyric was kept in Vilnius in the 1430s. See R. Cicėnienė, "Rankraštinė knyga – istorijos šaltinis: vieno LDK kodekso istorija", *Knygotyra* 63 (2014), p. 114.

[2] M. Bogucka, *Kazimierz Jagiellończyk i jego czasy* (Warsaw, 1981), p. 92.

praśl (today Poland) in 1507.[3] The monastery in Supraśl also received a manuscript of the Pentateuch and the historical books of the Bible compiled in Vilnius in 1514 by Fedor, the psalm singer [*diak*] of Metropolitan bishop Ivan Soltan, as well as a collection of the books of the Old Testament from 1517.[4] The first Catholic scriptorium was probably established at the end of the fifteenth century in the Bernardine convent. The leading figure there was the copyist and illuminator Ambroży of Kłodawa. The monastery was also the place where the monastic chronicle of Jan of Komorowo was written, as well as the *Summula aurea* by Jan Szklarek, a collection of prayers, regulations, and ascetic excerpts, a copy of which can be traced to the beginning of the seventeenth century.[5] The majority of liturgical books, however, were imported, as has already been discussed in the chapter on libraries.

The introduction of the technology of printing did not make the handwritten book redundant, and for a long time handwritten and printed books functioned in parallel and presumably were equally valid. In the sixteenth century the Cyrillic printing houses were not able to provide a sufficient number of liturgical books. For this reason, they had to be copied in the monastic scriptoria. Considering the rather weak cultural infrastructure of Lithuania, it was probably easier to continue the copying of manuscripts than to print books coming in large formats with beautiful decorations and in addition contained musical notation, such as Catholic graduals and antiphonaries or Orthodox chant books (*irmologions*), necessary for celebrating the communal liturgy in monasteries.[6]

The handwritten books kept by the various institutions included chancery registers, collections of documentary formulas, letter sheets, registers of various courts operating in the city, and parish registers. Systems of keeping docu-

[3] Manuscript of the Library of the Russian Academy of Sciences in St. Petersburg (Russia), shelf mark 24.4.28. The *Desatiglav* by Matvei Desatyi is discussed in Chapter 9, "Religious texts" and the "Introduction", note 154.

[4] НІКАЛАЕЎ, *Палата кнігопісаная*, pp. 73-74, 100-105; ID., *Гісторыя беларускай кнігі*, 1, pp. 67-68; A. PACEVIČIUS, *Biblioteki*, trans. B. KALĘBA, in: *Kultura Wielkiego Księstwa Litewskiego. Analizy i* obrazy, ed. V. ALIŠAUSKAS, L. JOVAIŠA, M. PAKNYS, R. PETRAUSKAS, and E. RAILA, trans. P. BUKOWIEC, B. KALĘBA and B. PIASECKA (Cracow, 2006), pp. 53-54; ГАЛЕЧАНКА, *Невядомыя и малавядомыя помнікі*, pp. 81-84 and 86-91.

[5] K. KANTAK, "Najważniejsze rękopisy franciszkańskie bibliotek wileńskich", *Ateneum Wileńskie* 5.14 (1928), p. 177.

[6] It is worth pointing out that antiphonaries were calligraphed in the Commonwealth as late as the first half of the eighteenth century. Copies of such manuscripts can be found, for example, in the nunnery of the Premonstratensians in Imbramowice near Cracow.

ments varied depending on the period and the office. Until the end of the fifteenth century, documents were usually stored loose or in bulks (*składki*), but in the next century they were either sewn into volumes or recorded in separate books prepared for this purpose.[7] The registers of the cathedral chapter, kept from 1502 on the initiative of provost (*praepositus*) Erazm Ciołek, and the books of the Lithuanian *Metrica* provide examples of this practice. We also notice that in sixteenth-century Vilnius economic books, which contained inventories, registers of incomes and expenses, etc., began to be kept first by institutions and, with time, also by wealthy town dwellers and nobles, creating a realm of small-scale personalised pragmatic literacy.[8] In the register of possessions left by mayor Lebiedzicz in 1649, apart from loose fascicules, there is a "blank [i.e. without any entries] register in green binding". Without any writing inside it was an object which was yet to become a register. There were many such private registers at the time, and they can be considered to be examples of the most commonly used variations of the manuscript book in early modern Vilnius.

A specific type of manuscript was created in the schools. It was a type of textbook which included notes of lectures, mostly in the fields of rhetoric, philosophy, and theology. All copies that have survived were created at the Academy of Vilnius. The oldest ones date from the 1580s, as for instance the volume of lectures entitled *Prologomena logicae*, dictated probably by Marcin Śmiglecki.[9] During lectures, students took notes and later copied them in leather-bound *in quarto* notebooks, which might contain between a few and several dozen pages. A separate group consisted of anthologies of *loci communes*, 'useful excerpts', also known as commonplace books, *eruditiones*, or rhetorical *silvae*.[10] They were usually ever-growing manuscripts, subject to a constant act of creation, with strongly personalised settings, in a way resem-

[7] This situation was common for chanceries and other offices both in the Kingdom of Poland and the Grand Duchy of Lithuania. See KRAWCZUK, *Metryka Koronna i Metryka Litewska*, s. 208; J. ŁOSOWSKI, "Akta sądów i urzędów szlacheckich w XIV-XVIII wieku", in: *Dyplomatyka staropolska*, ed. T. JUREK (Warsaw, 2015), p. 263.

[8] BARTOSZEWICZ, *Urban Literacy*, p. 6, 12, 350-358; J. TANDECKI, "Dokumenty i kancelarie miejskie", in: *Dyplomatyka staropolska*, pp. 442-445.

[9] MS VUB F3-2171.

[10] *Silva rerum* (Latin): 'a forest of things'. See J. Niedźwiedź, "Sylwa retoryczna: Reprezentacja kultury literackiej XVII i *XVIII w.*", in *Staropolskie kompendia wiedzy*, ed. I. DACKA-GÓRZYŃSKA and J. PARTYKA (Warsaw, 2009), p. 87-89; A. MOSS, *Printed Commonplace-Books and the Structuring of Renaissance Thought* (Oxford, 1996), pp. 134-185.

Fig. 31 Albert of Prussia (Albrecht Hohenzollern), *Księgi o rycerskich rzeczach a sprawach wojennych z pilnością zebrane a porządkiem dobrem spisane*, trans. M. Strubicz (Vilnius, 1561). MS Cracow, CZART., 1813 IV, f. 9r. Photo J. Niedźwiedź. Reproduced with the permission of MNK.

bling the hard drives of modern computers, at least when it comes to storing and organising information. Sometimes they included works authored by the owner of the rhetorical *silva*, such as elaborations, translations, and other exercises carried out in conjunction with classes in rhetoric and poetics.

Manuscript literary works from the second half of the sixteenth century and the first half of the seventeenth century can be considered as elite texts, of which only one or at most a few copies were produced, usually for the author's own use or meant as gifts for a significant person. A translation of the *Kriegsordnung* by Prince Albrecht of Prussia, *Księga o rycerskich rzeczach i sprawach* (The Book on Knightly Things and Affairs) was produced in 1561 for the library of King Sigismund Augustus. It was a richly decorated manuscript, translated and illuminated by Maciej Strubicz. In 1594, students of philosophy at the Academy of Vilnius presented a volume of poems to their teacher of philosophy, father Marcin Śmiglecki, on the occasion of his obtaining a doctorate in theology. It was a carefully calligraphied anthology in manuscript form, which at first glance resembled similar panegyrics printed at the Academy's printing house at that time. Manuscript books of this type were probably rare. Nonetheless, they were produced in Lithuania until the end of the seventeenth century, as is clear from the beautiful collection of handwritten emblemata from the Bernardine convent in Vilnius, the Orsha collegium, or the library of Katarzyna Radziwiłłowa née Sobieska.[11]

Printers

Initially printed books were imported, and the earliest trace of these imports to Vilnius is the *Agenda* of Konrad Baumgarten, published in Gdańsk by order of the Vilnius chapter in 1499.[12] However, at the beginning of the six-

[11] The reasons for and the circumstances surrounding the manuscript culture that flourished in the seventeenth and eighteenth centuries in Poland and Lithuania have aroused scholarly interest for several decades (see *Staropolska kultura rękopisu*, ed. H. DZIECHCIŃSKA (Warsaw, 1990)). Recently, this problem has been raised by Marek Prejs in M. PREJS, *Oralność i mnemonika: Późny barok w kulturze polskiej* (Warsaw, 2009) and by Rafał Wójcik in a review of this publication (R. WÓJCIK, "Uwagi na marginesie książki Marka Prejsa *Oralność i mnemonika: Późny barok w kulturze, Wydawnictwa Uniwersytetu Warszawskiego* (Warsaw, 2009)", *Terminus* 13.2 (2011), pp. 127-142).

[12] *Drukarze dawnej Polski od XV do XVIII wieku*, 4, *Pomorze*, ed. A. KAWECKA-GRYCZOWA and K. KOROTAJOWA (Wrocław, 1962), pp. 36-37; Z. NOWAK, *Początki sztuki drukarskiej na Pomorzu w XV wieku* (Gdańsk, 1976), pp. 154-155; ID., *Konrad Baumgart i początki sztuki dru-*

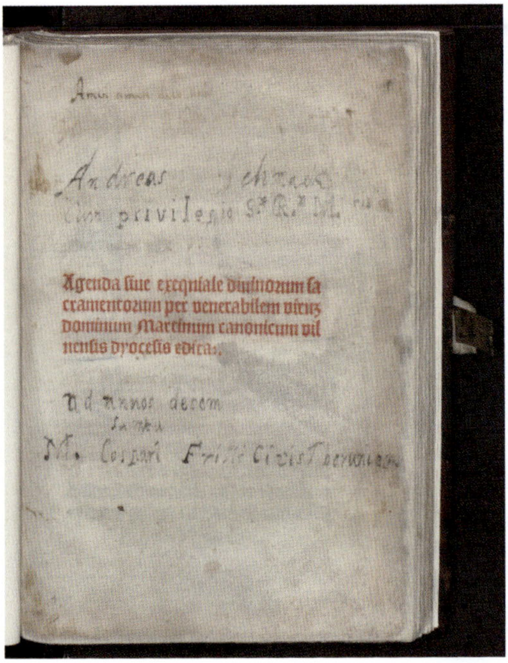

Fig. 32 *Agenda, sive exsequiale divinorum sacramentorum*, ed. Martinus canonicus Vilnensis (Gdansk, 1499). <https//polona.pl/item/agenda-sive-exsequiale-sacra mentorum-ed-martinus-canonicus-vilnensis,NDA3OTU0/3/#info:metadata> (accessed: 29.05.2022; public domain).

teenth century, users of Slavonic books showed a greater demand for texts than readers of Latin books. This resulted in the establishment of the first Lithuanian printing house in Vilnius, that of Francysk Skaryna.

Skaryna, a native of Polatsk, had studied at universities of Cracow and Padua, where he not only received a thorough education in the humanities, philosophy (master's degree), and medicine (doctorate), but also came into contact with the art of printing.[13] In 1517 he launched his own publishing house in Prague, where he published the famous Orthodox Bible, a volume undoubtedly intended mainly for Orthodox people who lived in the Grand Duchy of Lithuania. In 1522, his printing house was moved to Vilnius, where it probably operated until 1525. Here, Skaryna printed two books, *The Little Travel Book* (Malaya podorozhnaya knizhka, *c.* 1522)[14] and the *Apostle* (Apostol, 1525), which

karskiej w Gdańsku w XV wieku (Gdańsk, 1998), pp. 133-165; *Nad złoto droższe: Skarby Biblioteki Narodowej*, ed. H. Tchórzewska-Kabata and M. Dąbrowski (Warsaw, 2003), p. 133.

[13] Немировский, *Франциск Скорина*, pp. 200-216;

[14] *The Little Travel Book* is discussed in Chapter 9.

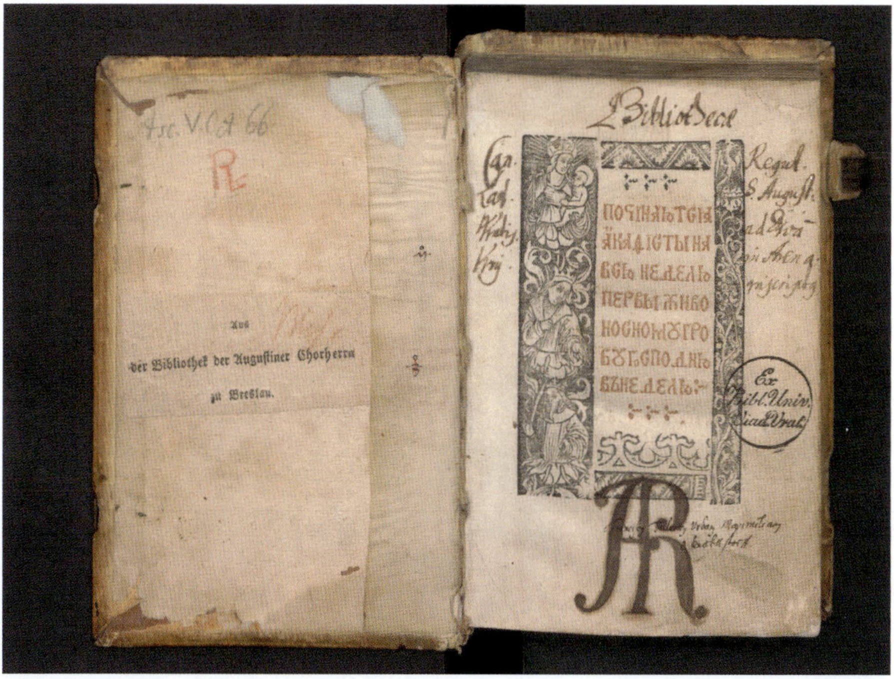

Fig. 33 F. Skaryna, *The Little Travel Book* (Vilnius, *c.* 1522). Wrocław, University Library. <https://www.bibliotekacyfrowa.pl/dlibra/> (accessed: 26.05.2022; public domain).

contained the Acts of the Apostles and the Apostolic Letters. He also kept selling the publications he had produced earlier in Prague. Skaryna's two-colour books, based on the best German and Venetian printed examples of the time, were elegantly designed and masterfully executed.

Skaryna's importance was not restricted to initiating printing in Vilnius. He also introduced the humanistic *philologia sacra* into the culture of Vilnius and the Grand Duchy of Lithuania. He personally prepared biblical texts, using their Church Slavonic version as well as the Czech Bible, and he translated some of hymns to the saints (*akathists*) directly from Greek in *The Little Travel Book*.[15] Into the language of these *akathists*, based on Church Slavonic, he introduced many borrowings used in his own contemporary Belarusian of the Polatsk region, which undoubtedly facilitated the reception of his texts by

[15] Немировский, *Франциск Скорина*, p. 351-359, 449, 452.

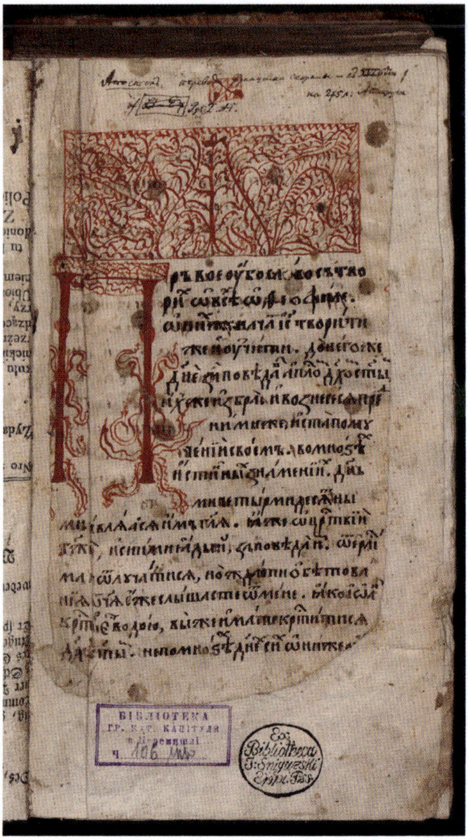

Fig. 34 Manuscript copy of the *Apostle* by F. Skaryna (Vilnius, 1525). The manuscript was made in the second half of the sixteenth or at the beginning of the seventeenth century for an unidentified Orthodox monastery of St. Michael the Archangel in the Ruthenian Voivodeship (*województwo ruskie*, part of the Kingdom of Poland). Warsaw (Poland), BN, MS 11907 III, p. 1r. <https://polona.pl/item-view/88c8bfab-9056-47ba-ad6d-9a306b8c8429? page =4> (accessed: 18.07.2022; public domain).

readers from the Grand Duchy of Lithuania. Some Orthodox townspeople from Vilnius showed a keen interest in Skaryna's publications. Among them were members of the Vilnius merchant elite such as Yakov Babich, Bogdan Onkov, and his brother Ivan, who were involved in the editorial work of the first Lithuanian printer.[16] The project was probably successful, as seems clear from the manuscript copies of Skaryna's books that were made as late as in the second decade of the seventeenth century.[17] However, Skaryna abandoned printing.

[16] Немировский, *Франциск Скорина*, pp. 417-418; A. Nagórko, *Franciszek Skoryna*, p. 291.

[17] Manuscript versions of the *Apostol* of Skaryna from the sixteenth century and 1619 are preserved in the National Library in Warsaw (shelf marks: Rps 11907 III; Rps. 11924 III). See A. Kaszlej, "Wpływ cerkiewnosłowiańskiej książki drukowanej na rękopiśmienną (na podstawie

This might have been a consequence of the negative reception of his publications by the Orthodox clergy, while in Vilnius itself perhaps a supply of printed books exceeding demand may have been an additional reason to stop. Skaryna's project had no direct followers either in the field of literature and philology, or in publishing. No more printing houses were established in Vilnius for the next half a century.

In fact, Vilnius did not become a printing centre until the 1570s, when it quickly became the leading printing hub in Lithuania and one of the most important ones in the Polish-Lithuanian Commonwealth. Alodia Kawecka-Gryczowa's study listed thirteen publishing companies that operated in Vilnius between 1574 and 1655. These belonged to the Mamonicz family (*c.* 1574-1624, in the first years in partnership with Piotr Mstislavets); Mikołaj Krzysztof Radziwiłł 'the Orphan' (1576-1586); Jan and Józef Karcan (1580-1620); Daniel of Łęczyca (1582-1589?, 1590-1600); Vasil Haraburda (1582); and the Jesuit academic printing house (1586-1805); the Calvinist Church's printing house (1592); Jakub Markowicz's printing house (1592-1607); the Orthodox printing house of the Brotherhood of the Holy Spirit (1595-1610 Vilnius; 1611-1646? Vievis; 1615-early eighteenth century Vilnius); the printing house of Salomon and Ulrich Sultzer (1596-1603); Melchior Pietkiewicz (1598); Piotr Blastus Kmita (1611-1612; later, until the mid-1650s, in Lubcz), and the Uniate Basilians' printing house (1628-1839).[18]

Initially, only Cyrillic books were published in Vilnius. It is assumed that in 1571 or 1572 Mstislavets printed *Czasloslovec* there.[19] The company founded a few years later by the Mamonicz family and Mstislavets also released printed books intended for the Orthodox Church.[20] The first printing house to produce Latin and later also Polish books was that owned by Radziwiłł 'the Orphan', which had been moved to Vilnius from Nyasvizh.

zbiorów Biblioteki Narodowej w Warszawie)", in: *Najstarsze druki cerkiewnosłowiańskie i ichstosunek do tradycji rękopiśmiennej: Materiały z sesji: Kraków 7-10 XI 1991*, ed. J. RUSEK, W. WITKOWSKI, and A. NAUMOW (Cracow, 1993), pp. 167-178.

[18] *Drukarze dawnej Polski od XV do XVIII wieku*, 5, *Wielkie Księstwo Litewskie*, pp. 5-6, 13-22, 40-43, 55-64, 70-86, 96-97, 107-118, 146-166, 175-180, 194-196, 205-210, 225-230, 235-236, 240-247, 264-265, 267.

[19] Z. JAROSZEWICZ-PIERESŁAWCEW, "Drukarstwo cyrylickie w Rzeczypospolitej", in: *Prawosławne oficyny wydawnicze*, p. 14.

[20] JAROSZEWICZ-PIERESŁAWCEW, *Druki cyrylickie*, pp. 63-66.

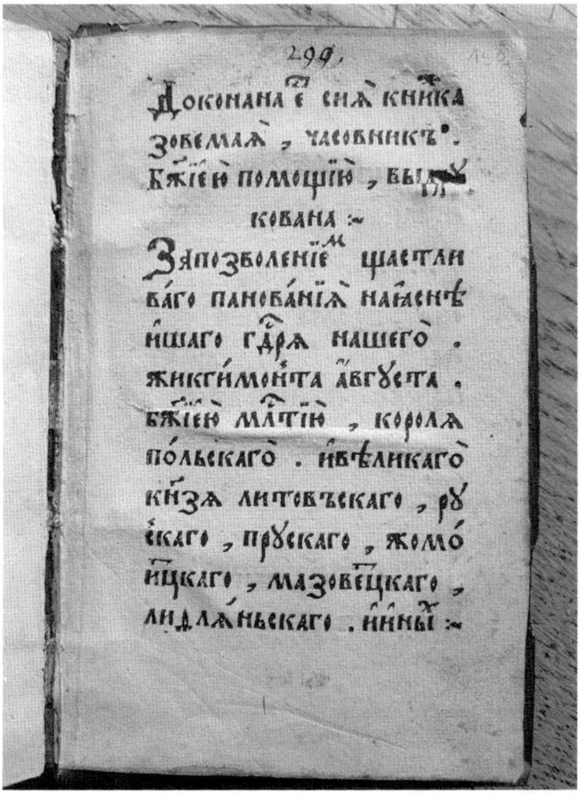
Доконана є сиѧ книга
зовемаѧ, часовникъ.
бжїею помощїю, вы[тис]
кована :~
Запозволенїемъ щастли
вого пакованїѧ наиаснѣ
йшаго гдрѧ нашего.
Жикгимонта Августа.
бжїею млтїю, королѧ
польскаго. и великаго
кнзѧ литовъскаго, ру
скаго, прускаго, жомо
йтскаго, мазовецкаго,
инфлѧньскаго. и иных :~

Fig. 35 Colophon of the *Chasoslovec* (*Chasovnyk*) printed by Mamonicz (Vilnius, 1572): "This book called *Chasovnyk* was printed with the help of God and with the permission of our Lord His Royal Majesty Sigismund Augustus, by the grace of the Lord King of Poland and Grand Duke of Lithuania, Ruthenia, Prussia, Samogitia, Masovia, Livonia, etc., with the blessing of Archbishop Ioan, by the grace of the Lord Metropolitan of Kyiv, Halych, and all Rus' in the famous city of Vilnius, in the house and with funds of Their Graces Mr Ivan and Mr Zenobii Zaretski" (original in Church Slavonic). Cracow, BJ, Cim. 1878. Public domain. Photo J. Niedźwiedź.

The prosperity of the publishing market in Vilnius coincided with the intensification of the city's economic and cultural life. Printers, along with other institutions, fuelled this development to a considerable extent. The previous chapters discussed the growing level of literacy among Vilnius residents and the rapidly increasing number of students. All of them needed books, and therefore the production of books began to be ever more financially rewarding. In addition, the increased demand from smaller Lithuanian cities affected the profitability of the printing industry. Thus, the book trade and book production became rooted in the economy and culture of Vilnius of the time.

The achievements of several of these printing houses deserve more careful attention. Kuźma Mamonicz ran a printing shop in a tenement house (*kamienica*) on the corner of Market Square and Szklanna Street (now Stiklių gatvė). At first, it specialised in Ruthenian printed books. With this experience Mstislavec founded another company and managed it in its first years. He brought in specialists from far and near.[21] From the very beginning he ensured high editorial standards for his books by providing clear printing on fine paper, large, carefully crafted woodcuts, and wide margins.[22] Presumably these advantages of his prints, as well as the high productivity of the Mamonicz' company, allowed them to obtain an order from chancellor Lew Sapieha to publish official publications such as the third *Statute of the Grand Duchy of Lithuania*, released for the first time in 1588.

The statute was later reissued several times in Ruthenian and Polish, also by Mamonicz's son, Leon, who inherited the printing house in 1607. Kuźma Mamonicz printed books for the Vilnius Brotherhood of the Holy Trinity, for instance grammar books for the Brotherhood's school,[23] but after joining the Uniate community he changed the target audience of his publications – at least partially – to Uniates and Catholics. Leon Mamonicz, however, published mainly in Polish. As many as 80% of his publications are in that language.[24] As a graduate of the Brotherhood's school, he received a humanist education, which is revealed in his poems and in the dedications to the books he published. After his death in 1624, the printing house was sold to the Uniate

[21] *Cracovia impressorum*, p. 384 (item 778, footnote); Iljaszewicz, *Drukarnia domu Mamoniczów w Wilnie* , pp. 68-69.

[22] See Шматаў, *Мастацтва беларускіх старадрукаў*, p. 61; В.Г. Пуцко, "Сюжетная гравюра в виленских изданиях Петра Тинофеева Мстиславца", in: *Беларуская кніга ў кантэксце сусветнай кніжнай культуры*, ed. М.А. Бяспалая *et al.* (Minsk, 2006), pp. 5-9.

[23] Jaroszewicz-Piereсławcew, *Druki cyrylickie*, pp. 74-75.

[24] Topolska, *Czytelnik i książka*, p. 110.

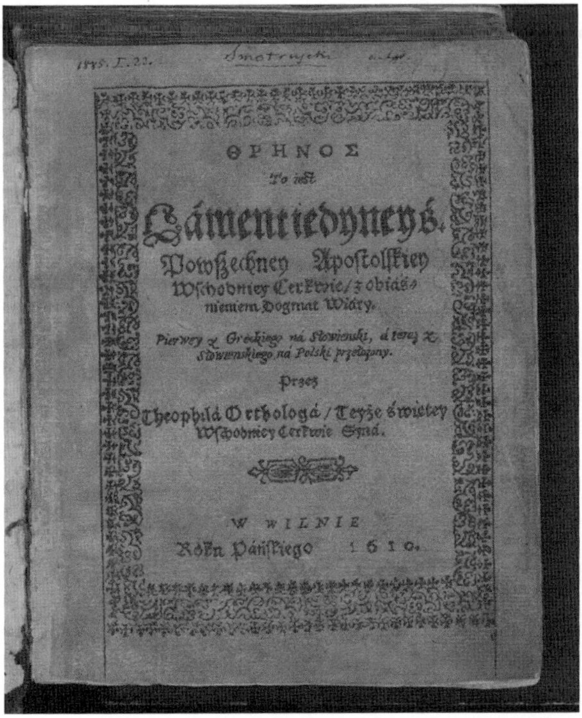

Fig. 36 M. Smotrycki, *Threnos* (*ΘΡΕΝΟΣ*), *to jest lament jedynej św. powszechnej apostolskiej wschodniej Cerkwie... pierwej z greckiego na słowieński, a teraz z słowieńskiego na polski przełożony* (Vilnius, 1610), title page. Cracow, BJ, I 40951 <http://neolatina.bj.uj.edu.pl/neolatina/page/show/id/10609.html> (accessed: 26.05.2022; public domain).

Basilians, who released their first publications in 1628. Similar to their predecessor, they continued to print mostly in Polish and, up to 1660, only a few publications out of more than fifty known today were in Cyrillic.[25] The output of the Basilian printing house included liturgical texts, catechisms, sermons, and polemical works, for instance *Obrona weryfikacyjej* (A Defence of a Verification) by Josef Velamin Rutski.

[25] Barbara Topolska states that there were four such prints (*ibid.*, p. 114); Zoja Jaroszewicz-Pieresławcew notes only one (JAROSZEWICZ-PIERESŁAWCEW, *Druki cyrylickie*, p. 121). See also PIDŁYPCZAK-MAJEROWICZ, *Bazylianie*, pp. 58-59.

It is assumed that the fact that Kuźma Mamonicz's started publishing for the Uniates in 1596 was the reason why the Orthodox Brotherhood decided to start its own printing house.[26] However, it had already been granted the privilege to create one, which would be tax-exempt, four years earlier, in 1592.[27] Its first publication, *Modlitwy* (Prayers), appeared in 1595,[28] and in the following year Stephan Zizany's grammar was published. This meant that the setting up the Brotherhood's printing house was well advanced long before Mamonicz became a Uniate. The Brotherhood's printing house began operating not as a result of Mamonicz' conversion, although perhaps Mamonicz changed faith out of the fear that, through being a member of the Orthodox Church, whose legal status was questioned at the time,[29] he might lose part of the publishing market, including that of the lucrative official publications.

Initially, the Brotherhood printing house operated at the monastery of the Holy Trinity. It did not publish much. From the years 1595-1610, we know only of twelve items, although they may have produced more. Even with such a modest number of books, the titles released by this printing house made it one of the main bastions of the persecuted Orthodox Church. One of the most famous polemical works in Vilnius was *Thrēnos* by Smotrycki, released in 1610, the publication of which resounded throughout the Polish-Lithuanian Commonwealth. In his publication, Smotrycki proved that the Orthodox could be successful opponents of the most prominent Catholic writers.[30] As a result, King Sigismund III Vasa, who was a supporter of the Union, issued an edict on 7 May 1610 ordering the closure of the Orthodox printing house. The editor Leonty Karpovich, who later became an archimandrite, was imprisoned for two years.[31]

In a way, the printing house continued its activity from 1611 in the Orthodox monastery in Vievis, which belonged to the Vilnius Brotherhood and was

[26] *Drukarze dawnej Polski od XV do XVIII wieku*, 5, *Wielkie Księstwo Litewskie*, pp. 59-62; TOPOLSKA, *Czytelnik i książka*, p. 110. JAROSZEWICZ-PIERESŁAWCEW, *Druki cyrylickie*, pp. 103-105; A. MIRONOWICZ, "Drukarnie bractw cerkiewnych", in: *Prawosławne oficyny wydawnicze*, pp. 56-58.

[27] *AVAK*, 9, pp. 144-153.

[28] TOPOLSKA, *Czytelnik i książka*, p. 110.

[29] T. KEMPA, "Prawosławie i unia w Polsce i na Litwie: sytuacja prawna, polityka władców i rola świeckich", in: *Między wschodem a zachodem. Prawosławie i unia*, ed. M. KUCZYŃSKA (Warsaw, 2017), pp. 41-46.

[30] FRICK, *Meletij Smotryc'kyj*, p. 184. The Orthodox-Uniate-Catholic polemic is discussed in Chapter 7.

[31] *Drukarze dawnej Polski*, p. 119.

located about 35 kilometres west of Vilnius. This printing house can be considered an autonomous branch of the Vilnius publishing house, which was restored in 1615 at the monastery of the Holy Spirit, the new seat of the Brotherhood. Both printing houses, in Vievis and Vilnius, were controlled by the Brotherhood, and some of their publications are identical, apart from amended title pages. Over the course of sixty-nine years the two printing houses released at least eighty-four publications.[32] In 1628 Smotrycki, then an Uniate who criticised his earlier views, mentioned that

> in its printing houses, the Vilnius Brotherhood [...] published writings full of errors and heresies that infect people's souls; and for thirty years now you have perniciously infected the Ruthenian nation.[33]

In this way, he confirmed the great effectiveness of the writings published there.

As far as the Protestants are concerned, originally their needs were met only by printing houses located outside Vilnius. In the last two decades of the sixteenth century, Calvinist books were published by Daniel of Łęczyca and Jan Karcan. The Protestant church's (*zbór*) printing house, established in 1592, was taken over by Jakub Markowicz in the same year. In spite of unfavourable conditions, over the course of fifteen years this enterprise published about twenty-five titles, mainly ones that served the Lithuanian Calvinist Church: catechisms, textbooks, and theological works. Later, after the church was burnt down in 1611, the main Calvinist printing houses were located far from Vilnius, mainly in Lubcz (where Piotr Blastus Kmita and his son Jan were active) and in the 1650s also in Kėdainiai (Kiejdany).[34] In 1615 it was noted in the registers of the Vilnius synod that a "Mr Pakosz promised a thousand *złoty* for a printing house and two *włoka* (*c.* 42,5 ha) of his land on which he wants to build a house for the printer. For which we would like to thank him and ask him to fulfil his promise".[35] Unfortunately, this project did not come to fruition.

A particularly important role in the production of books in Vilnius was played by the printing house of Mikołaj Krzysztof Radziwiłł 'the Orphan',

[32] TOPOLSKA, *Czytelnik i książka*, p. 112.
[33] SMOTRYCKI, *Paraenesis*, p. 12.
[34] *Drukarze dawnej Polski*, p. 123; TOPOLSKA, *Czytelnik i książka*, p. 99.
[35] *Akta synodów prowincjonalnych Jednoty Litewskiej 1611-1625*, p. 32.

which was handed over to the Academy of Vilnius in 1586.[36] From its very beginning, it had served the Jesuits, their religious and educational mission, and Counter-Reformation ideology. From as early as the 1570s it published the works of the priests and students of the Vilnius collegium, such as *The Lives of the Saints* by Piotr Skarga (1579), theological and polemical works, for instance the works Skarga directed against Andrzej Wolan and the Calvinists, and volumes of poetry, for instance the *Gratulatio* for Stephen Báthory (1579). After the acquisition of the printing house, the Jesuits tried to increase its production. This was not easy in the absence of well-trained printers and because of the rather strong competition from other publishers, primarily from the Karcan company. In a letter dated 2 January 1586, rector Garcia Alabiano reported these problems to the general of the congregation, pointing out the need to keep lay typographers in the collegium, "who are often heretics, drunkards, and badly behaved people".[37] The state of the printing house improved after it was taken over in 1592 by Daniel of Łęczyca, newly converted to Catholicism, who led it until his death in 1600.[38]

From the very beginning, similar to the members of other religious communities, the Jesuits treated publishing books as a form of defence of their faith, especially against Protestants. They were aware of the importance of printing to a greater degree than other Christians in Vilnius, and they broadened the missionary function of their printing house. One of their professors, Adam Brocus (Broke), who came from London, wrote on 13 June 1594 to general Aquaviva:

> For the common good of the Catholic Church and the students it is very desirable, Venerable Father, that you take care of the maintenance of typography in this collegium. For there is no Catholic printing house within 500 Italian miles, while in this city there are two heretic ones, one Calvinist and the other one Anabaptist, from where books that spread the plague are published every year. In turn, after they stopped us printing, Catholics have nowhere to print their books.[39]

The topos of the institution on the periphery of Catholicism, often used by the authorities of the Academy in relations with the Roman headquarters, forced

[36] *Drukarze dawnej Polski*, p. 15-16. *Vilnius akademijos spaustuvės šaltiniai*, pp. 64-66; PIECHNIK, *Rozkwit Akademii Wileńskiej*, pp. 194-195.

[37] *Vilniaus akademijos spaustuvės šaltiniai*, p. 64.

[38] H. BARYCZ, "Daniel z Łęczycy", in: *PSB*, 4, p. 406.

[39] *Vilniaus akademijos spaustuvės šaltiniai*, p. 67.

the English scholar to remain silent about the fact that until recently the Jesuits themselves had used the services of Protestants, namely of Daniel of Łęczyca, who issued for them for instance a Latvian translation of the catechism of Peter Canisius,[40] and Jan Karcan, who printed for them polemical works by Antonio Possevino and Andrzej Jurgiewicz.

From the letter written in 1586 by rector Garcia Alabiano, quoted above, we learn how the work in the printing house was organised. It is the only account of this type from Vilnius known today:

> In the first place, there should be at least two of our Jesuits employed: one priest familiar with literature who would supervise all the work, the other one an assistant-brother, who would take care of the printing house all day and help two external printers, two being the minimum number we must keep, one for arranging the text, the other for operating the press, and our brother for applying the printing ink. Then, the superior of the collegium himself, or through the head of the printing house, should take care to buy, at a certain time and place, supplies of paper and materials needed for printing ink, to prepare the powder for the lye, as well as machines that are often worn out; moreover, he should buy alloy and repair devices and other such things in order to cast and renew the fonts.[41]

In the first two decades of the seventeenth century, the academic printing house released relatively few publications, clearing the path for Józef Karcan. As he ran a prosperous printing house, the Jesuits did not develop production beyond their own needs. Their policy changed in 1619, when they received a privilege from King Sigismund III Vasa. On pain of a fine of a hundred *grzywnas*, it forbade other publishing houses from reprinting works issued by the academic printing house.[42] This privilege made it possible for the Jesuits to dominate the publishing market in Vilnius, all the easier because after the printing houses of Karcan and Mamonicz were closed down, they had practically no competition, neither from the Basilians nor from the Orthodox Brotherhood. From the 1620s, the Jesuits published about fifteen books a year. At least 640 titles were published by the Radziwiłł's printing house and later, in the years 1574-1655, by the Jesuit printing house. This accounted for half of all Vilnius publishing production by the middle of the seventeenth century.[43]

[40] K. Świerkowski, "Wilno kolebką drukarstwa łotewskiego", *Ateneum Wileńskie* 8 (1931-1932), pp. 184-204.

[41] *Ibid.*, p. 64.

[42] *Ibid.*, p. 23-24.

[43] Topolska, *Czytelnik i książka*, pp. 114-116.

Being the only Jesuit printing house in the region, the academic printing house served the needs of the university and other Lithuanian colleges, as well as the Catholic pastoral ministry in Lithuania. Among other publications, for the needs of the diocese of Samogitia it published Wujek's *Postylla* in Daukša's Lithuanian translation in 1599, and in 1606 one of the earlier translations of the *Mały katechizm* (Little Catechism) by Bellarmine entitled *Krótki zbiór nauki chrześcijańskiej* (A Short Collection of Christian Teachings).[44] It also published textbooks, theological books, poetry and occasional prose (for instance panegyrics written in collegia and sermons), dictionaries, and works on Lithuanian history. Academic works and some literary texts, including as for instance the first editions of *Lyrics* by Sarbiewski and *Praxis oratoria* by Zygmunt Lauksmin (Sigismund Lauxminus) were of broader than only local importance. Polish and Latin books from this publishing house can be found in all the major libraries of Central and Eastern Europe, and many copies of Latin works can be found all over Europe.

The biggest competitor of the academic printing house, both in terms of the number and rank of publications, was the publishing house of Jan and Józef Karcan, which released at least 140 titles over forty years.[45] Jan Karcan, originally from Wieliczka near Cracow in the Kingdom of Poland, was initially a Calvinist, and he issued a number of Protestant publications. Józef, his son, who took over the printing house in 1611, converted to Catholicism, and this was the profile of most of his publications. He himself gained the title of client [*servitor*] of the bishop of Vilnius.[46] The Karcans mostly published books in Polish, including translations (of Cicero, Titus Flavius Josephus, and Erasmus of Rotterdam), works by Protestant writers such as Andrzej Wolan, Stanisław Sudrowski, Bieniasz Budny, and Samuel Dambrowski, as well as writings of their Catholic opponents. Their publications were not only read by the inhabitants of the Grand Duchy of Lithuania. For example, the first edition of *Moscovia* by Antonio Possevino of 1586, which contained a remarkable bibliographical description, was a book intended for export: "*Vilnae, In Lithuania apud Ioannem Velicensem*". Usually it was not necessary to explain that Vilnius was

[44] Correspondence with Rome regarding its financing was conducted by Adamus Brocus, mentioned previously; see: *Vilniaus akademijos*, pp. 72-73. See also M. DAUKŠA, "Przedmowa do czytelnika łaskawego", in: J. WUJEK, *Postilla catholicka: Tai est izguldimas ewangeliu* (Vilnius, 1599; reprint: Vilnius, 2000), p. 42-45; J.Z. SŁOWIŃSKI, *Katechizmy katolickie w języku polskim od XVI do XVIII wieku* (Lublin, 2005), p. 134.

[45] TOPOLSKA, *Czytelnik i książka*, pp. 97-98.

[46] A. KAWECKA-GRYCZOWA, "Józef Karcan", in: *PSB*, 12, p. 25.

in Lithuania. Karcan provided the edition with a Latin introduction in which he pointed out that it was the first correct version of this text accepted by the author.

As has been already mentioned, Vilnius quickly grew to become the most important printing centre in Lithuania. According to Barbara Topolska, by the middle of the seventeenth century, 1,300 books had been published in the capital, accounting for 75% of all titles printed in Lithuania in the same period.[47] The studies and bibliographies available show that in the first half of the seventeenth century the number of publications grew steadily, and particularly dynamically by the turn of the sixteenth and seventeenth centuries and from the 1630s. The subject matter of the works published was broad, but religious literature dominated, both elite (theological works, polemics) and popular (prayer books and hymn books), while fiction, which was in demand in Cracow and Lesser Poland, is harder to find.

It is difficult to say anything about the production and sale of the most popular and cheapest prints, that is, romances, street literature, chapbook literature, and so-called folk literature. A small number of such items printed in Lithuania in the seventeenth century have survived. The only chapbooks were Jesuit pastiches that attacked Protestants, while prose narratives referred to the stories of miracles and hagiography: *Historyja o Janie Klemensie sędzim zamku possońskiego* (The History of John the Judge of Pozsony Castle) (Vilnius, after 1643), Samuel Dowgird,'s *Historyja o Zuzannie* (The History of Susanna) (Lubcz, 1624), *Historyja Barłaama i Josafata* (The History of Barłaam and Josaphat) (Kutein, 1638; in Ruthenian). Very few are typical romances, such as *Historyja muszyńska o Teagenesie i Charyklijej* (A Muszyna Story of Theagenes and Chariclea; Vilnius, J. Karcan, 1606).

Book historians note that popular chapbook narratives and books were very successful and easy to sell,[48] so their production was profitable and they assume that "having them [...] was as customary in Vilnius as in other cities of the Polish-Lithuanian Commonwealth".[49] Unfortunately, there are no bookshop catalogues or inventories of the Vilnius printing houses which could confirm the circulation of many romances in Vilnius before the middle of the seventeenth century. Neither do we know what kind of publications were traded by

[47] *Ibid.*, p. 119.

[48] "Karcan probably earned a lot from printing the sought-after market-stall literature and service books. His success in business is evidenced by the fact that in 1599 he bought a house, which Daniel of Łęczyca had to dispose of" (TOPOLSKA, *Czytelnik i książka*, p. 97).

[49] *Ibid.*, p. 169.

merchants who came here from Cracow or Lublin. Post-mortem inventories and some copies of cheap books that have survived are not helpful in this respect. They may have been worn out through being read or destroyed by fires, but the existing sources do not allow us to confirm either possibility.[50] If the range of books available in medium-sized Vilnius bookshops in the first half of the seventeenth century resembled those in Lublin, which contained 1,300-1,400 copies of about 100-200 titles,[51] around 15% would have been examples of popular narrative, satires, and romantic fiction. Unfortunately we do not have any data at our disposal for Vilnius.

Having said this, we should be cautious when making assumptions about how widespread the reading of romance and chapbook literature in Vilnius was. If we take into account the reading and writing skills of the inhabitants of the Lithuanian capital discussed in chapter five, which were probably less widespread than those of the inhabitants of Cracow, it may turn out that literature of this type, willingly purchased in Lesser Poland, cannot have been equally successful on the Lithuanian market. This does not mean that nobody in Vilnius or Lithuania read romances and popular stories, but perhaps what was commonly read in Lesser Poland might have had a more limited reception in the capital of Lithuania. For the time being, we can state that the books most frequently sold in Vilnius up to the middle of the seventeenth century included religious literature, mainly catechisms, prayer books, and meditation books, hymn books, psalters, textbooks, and editions of the ancient classics.[52] Other types of publications were used by the elite or by people who, by virtue of their profession, interacted with books, that is doctors, pharmacists, teachers, clerks, wealthier merchants, nobility, and the clergy. They probably knew narrative stories imported from Cracow as well.

[50] Religious books and stories about saints, e.g. *Żywot św. Władysława króla węgierskiego* (The Life of St. Vladislaus the King of Hungary) by Szymon Ugniewski (Vilnius, 1630) or *Nowy patron Polski* (The New Patron of Poland, the Blessed Stanisław Kostka) by Stanisław Tyszkiewicz, had a better chance of survival because, unlike secular romances, they found their way into institutional libraries, e.g. monastic ones, where whole book collections were kept. Most of the books from early modern Vilnius that have survived to this day come from the old monastic libraries. Popular publications may have shared the fate of textbooks and catechisms. Of large print runs, e.g. of primers, only single copies have survived to this day, and we can assume that of many editions no trace remains.

[51] E. Torój, *Inwentarze książek lubelskich introligatorów z pierwszej połowy XVII wieku*, (Lublin, 2000), p. 13.

[52] Religious and school literature accounts for nearly 70-80% of the Lublin bookbinder's inventory. See *ibid.*, pp. 17-18.

The most interesting stage in the development of printing in Vilnius was the half-century from the 1570s to the 1630s. During this period, all the main Christian communities used either their institutional printing houses (the academic, the Protestant, the Orthodox Brotherhood's and the Basilians' printing houses) or those run by the followers of a given confession. For instance, Piotr Mstislavec and Kuźma Mamonicz published Orthodox books in Church Slavonic, Daniel of Łęczyca, Jakub Markowicz, and Jan Karcan published mostly Calvinist books in Polish and Latin, while Salomon Sultzer printed Lutheran and Calvinist books in Latin and German.[53] However, a common practice, especially at the end of the sixteenth century and the beginning of the seventeenth, for Catholic printers was to publish books for Protestants, Orthodox books for Catholics and Protestants, and Protestant books for Catholics.

The multiplicity of confessions and printing houses created a cultural ferment in the city. The participants in the stages of the Catholic-Calvinist and Catholic-Uniate-Orthodox polemics, such as Skarga, Śmiglecki, Jurgiewicz, Wolan, Smotrycki, Bobrykowicz, Karpovych, and Kreuza Rzewuski, could expect their polemical and apologetical works to be printed quickly. This speeded up the writing and publication of new texts. Printing houses contributed to transforming Vilnius into a lens that focussed on rhetorical disputes going on in much wider territories of the Grand Duchy of Lithuania and the Polish Crown (as an 'open' city). To some extent, the agonistic function of Vilnius printing is a delayed reflection of the role played by the largest publishing houses of the sixteenth century in the West and South of Europe which were involved in the printing of Protestant-Catholic polemics.

By becoming a publishing centre for many confessional groups, Vilnius was becoming, on a microscopic scale, simultaneously Basel, Antwerp, Venice, and Rome from the times of the fiercest religious polemics. Yet, in this 'microscopic' publishing centre, the disputes were getting a more human size: Wolan and Skarga were acquaintances, while Smotrycki and Kreuza prayed in the same church of the Holy Trinity, perhaps using the same liturgical books. Thanks to printing, the discussions, originally conducted face to face, continued in books. It would be interesting to trace how the private sphere took on a public character, while at the same time preserving the personal dimension which is visible, for example, in Smotrycki's and Jurgiewicz's books.

[53] J. Niedźwiedź, "Sultzer Salomon", p. 504.

Bookbinding

Printing and bookbinding were two different crafts. A work that left the printing press in the form of quires was a semi-finished product only, and only bookbinders gave it the form of a book as we know it. Some volumes, however, were immediately bound at the request of the printing house.[54] Since binding was the last stage of production, it was natural that besides printers, bookbinders were also very often were involved in selling books. The privileges for the bookbinders' guild in Cracow from the times of King Sigismund III Vasa and John III Sobieski (respectively from the 1590s and 1670s) were written in such a way that bookbinders were always intermediaries between printers and booksellers or readers. For this reason, the Latin names of the profession, that is *introligator* and *compactor librorum* are used interchangeably with the term *bibliopola*, 'bookseller'. Booksellers were also called *librarius* or *venditor librorum*.[55] In Vilnius, the only bookbinding workshop that did not sell books was that of the Jesuits at the academic printing house. The authorities of the congregation, afraid of accusations of engaging in trade, forbade it.[56]

Thanks to the work of Edmundas Laucevičius, we know quite much about Vilnius bookbinders and we can also draw some conclusions about the sale of books. According to Laucevičius, the earliest sources speak of a bookbinder's workshop that operated at the scriptorium at the Orthodox cathedral of the Theotokos at the beginning of the sixteenth century. However, it may be assumed that bookbinders must already have worked in Vilnius earlier, as books were produced there from at least the middle of the fifteenth century. We know about a man known as Porfiry, who worked at the bookbinder's workshop at the Theotokos cathedral in the early sixteenth century.[57] The Russian National Library in St. Petersburg holds about twenty manuscripts associated with this workshop.[58] Someone, however, must also have bound the books of the Bernardines and the members of the Vilnius cathedral chapter during this period. This means that, at the beginning of the sixteenth century, also other bookbinders in the city must have been active, as the Catholic clergy would probably not have used the services of an Orthodox institution and its craftsmen in those days.

[54] TORÓJ, *Inwentarze książek lubelskich introligatorów*, p. 14.
[55] LAUCEVIČIUS, *Knygų įrišimai Lietuvos bibliotekose*, p. 11.
[56] PIECHNIK, *Rozkwit Akademii Wileńskiej*, p. 195.
[57] LAUCEVIČIUS, *Knygų įrišimai*, p. 42.
[58] TOPOLSKA, *Czytelnik i książka*, p. 160.

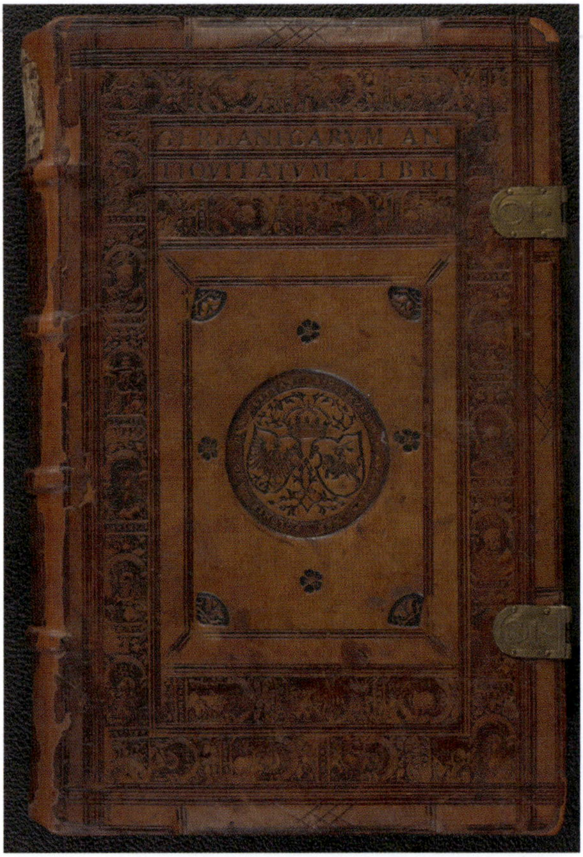

Fig. 37 The front cover of a book from the collection of King Sigismund Augustus with his supralibros made in Vilnius. Johannes Herold, *Originum ac Germanicarum antiquitatum libri* (…) (Basel, 1557). Warsaw, BN <https:/polona.pl/item-view/a311b15d-a76d-4ca0-a2dc-cf78e672c09f?page=0> (accessed: 15.07. 2023; public domain).

There is information from the 1540s on the binding of books purchased for the library of King Sigismund Augustus in Vilnius. Some of the bindings were produced with the use of fittings sent from Cracow in 1547, in order to assure that the covers of the royal books produced in Vilnius remained the same as

Fig. 38 The back cover of a book from the collection of King Sigismund Augustus with his supralibros made in Vilnius in 1560: "The monument of King of Poland Sigismund Augustus, 1560 AD". Francisco Alvares, *Historiale description de l'Ethiopie, contenant vraye relation des terres et pais du grand roy et emperor Prete Ian* (Antwerp, 1558). Warsaw, BN <https://polona.pl/item-view/af21318a-426b-48f2-ba6c-20fdc9997de0?page=0> (accessed: 15. 07.2023; public domain).

those manufactured in Cracow.[59] These fittings were used later that same year. The accounts of the Vilnius court, written down by Stanisław Włoszek, read as follows:

> For some books purchased for the library of His Majesty the King by the preacher Kuźma [Jan of Koźmin] according to the register provided by him sixty florins, eighteen *grosz*, 6 solid. For their binding ten florins, 21 *grosz*, 6 solid.[60]

The years 1557-1563 were marked by the intensive activity of an unidentified Vilnius bookbinder who worked for the king's library.[61] At that time, there was no guild of bookbinders in Vilnius, there were no printing houses, but the craftsmen who worked there knew their craft well.[62] The prices of the bindings varied greatly. A plain binding cost nine *grosz* then,[63] but in 1548 a protective casing for a Bible, a copy of the *Sachsenspiegel*, or a chronicle made of special chamois sheepskin cost as much as forty *grosz* per piece.[64]

That from 1492 onwards there was a mint in Vilnius, whose minters were able to produce the fittings necessary to decorate the bindings, aided the craft of bookbinding. The mint produced those fittings that were used to press the inscriptions onto the binding of the register of the mint's revenues, bound by an unknown bookbinder in 1551: "*Regestrum offitine monetarie Vilnensis per Martinum Conrat notarium eiusdem offitine facte a die 1 Januarii anno 1551 ad diem 31 Decembris 1551*" ("The Register of the Vilnius Mint Managed by Marcin Konrat, the Scribe of the Said Mint from 1 January to 31 December 1551").[65] On one of the pistons the inscription can be found used on Vilnius bindings from at least 1566: "*Frustra vivit qui nemini prodest*" ("He who was not helpful to anybody, lived in vain"). Tools with this inscription were pro

[59] M. KRYNICKA, "Oprawy książkowe z herbami ostatnich Jagiellonów w zbiorach Muzeum Narodowego w Krakowie", *Rozprawy i Sprawozdania Muzeum Narodowego w Krakowie* 12 (1980), p. 39.

[60] "Rachunki dworu Zygmunta Augusta spisane przez Stanisława Włoszka (1544-1548)", in: *Źródła do dziejów historyi sztuki i cywilizacyi w Polsce*, 1, ed. A. CHMIEL (Cracow, 1911), p. 241.

[61] KRYNICKA, "Oprawy książkowe z herbami ostatnich Jagiellonów ", p. 28.

[62] J. RODKIEWICZÓWNA, *Cech introligatorski w Wilnie: Zarys historyczny* (Vilnius, 1929), pp. 5-7, claims that the standard of sixteenth-century Vilnius bookbinding was low, which is refuted by the findings of Edmundas Laucevičius (E. LAUCEVIČIUS, *Knygų įrišimai*, p. 113) and M. Krynicka (KRYNICKA, "Oprawy książkowe z herbami ostatnich Jagiellonów", p. 28 and 38-40).

[63] *Encyclopedia wiedzy o książce*, column 1696.

[64] "Rachunki dworu Zygmunta Augusta", p. 278.

[65] LAUCEVIČIUS, *Knygų įrišimai*, p. 115.

Fig. 39 A binding of the book made probably in Vilnius after 1582: P. Skarga, *Artes duodecim sacramentariorum seu Zvingliocalvinistarum* (Vilnius, 1582), Cracow, MNK. Photo J. Niedźwiedź.

duced from 1577 by the moneyer P. Platinius, who produced tools for bookbinders from Lithuania and Poland, including Cracow, on a large scale. His pistons also bear the inscription "*Si Deus nobiscum quis contra nos*" ("If God is with us, who shall be against us?").

Many fittings used in the Vilnius mint were created to make supralibroses (coats of arms or monograms indicating ownership). One of them is the donative supralibros of Pedro Ruiz de Moros that adorns the cover of his *Decisiones* of 1563 and bears the inscriptions: "*Stemma Petri Royzii Maurei iuresconsulti regii*" and "*Discite monite iustitia*" ("Learn the law and obey it").[66] The supra-

[66] P. Rojzjusz, *Decisiones* [...] *de rebus in sacro auditorio [...] Lithuanico ex appellatione*

libros of Lew Sapieha comes from the Vilnius mint and its piston was made by the cutter and medallist Hanus Trilner (Trylner), who was its employee and later its manager in the years 1611-1627 and then again in 1652.[67]

Wealthy inhabitants, as well as institutions that operated in Vilnius, allocated considerable sums of money to bindings, as is shown not only by the inventories containing their descriptions, but also by the bills certifying such services. In 1578, the accountant of the Vilnius chapter noted a purchase of two missals for the Vilnius cathedral:

> for the second Roman missal for the same church I gave 2 *kopas*[68]
>
> for the redfish velvet for this missal I gave 1 *kopas* 28 *grosz* and for the binding 24 *grosz*
>
> I paid goldsmith Andriush 0 *kopas* and 55 *grosz* for nine *skojec [i.e. 1/24 grzywna* – J.N.) of silver to which he added old silver of one *skojec* for 10 *grosz* each
>
> for the red gold, with which he gilded this silver, each for 44 *grosz*, I gave 1 *kopas* 28 *grosz*, for a case from Sienicki for this missal I gave 30 *grosz*
>
> for bookmarks of silk for these missals I gave 0 *kopas* 24 *grosz*.[69]

As we can see, the binding of books could have been expensive, although if we take into account the cost of materials and the amount of work, it is not known whether it was a lucrative craft, after all.

There are mentions of fourteen bookbinders active in the city from the end of the sixteenth century and of twenty-three from the first half of the next century. However, their number could have been higher, as Laucevičius' calculations are based on the court registers of the cathedral chapter *jurydyka* from 1620-1650, which listed several booksellers and bookbinders, while the data from the municipal registers are very incomplete. One should also take into account that many printed books were taken to other Lithuanian towns for

iudicatus (Cracow, 1563); see K. PIEKARSKI, *Superexlibrisy polskie od XV do XVIII wieku*, 1, tabs. 1-40 (Cracow, 1929), tab. 25.

[67] M. GUMOWSKI, "Wileńska szkoła medalierska w XVI i XVII wieku", *Ateneum Wileńskie* 6.1-4 (1933-1934), pp. 80-81; LAUCEVIČIUS, *Knygų įrišimai*, p. 58 (item 197) and 62.

[68] *Kopa* ('three score', i.e. 'sixty'). In the Grand Duchy of Lithuania *kopa* was a monetary unit worth sixty *grosz*.

[69] *Regestr kapituły roku 1577 i roku 1578*, MS MAB F43-451, ff. 21v-22r.

binding, so there may well have been many more bookbinders who worked for the Vilnius market.[70]

The large number of these craftsmen allows the assumption of the existence of a guild. Laucevičius supposes that a guild operated as early as the late sixteenth century, but the documents do not confirm this. A more credible mention of the existence of the guild in 1633 was included in the Lithuanian *Metrica*. The guild is mentioned in the privilege of Władysław IV Vasa granted on 20 July 1633 to the Vilnius bookbinder Gothard Reck.[71]

The earliest known privilege for the bookbinding guild was issued by King John Casimir Vasa on 8 June 1664.[72] Four years later, on 29 January 1669, it was supplemented by a statute approved by the city council. To be accepted to the guild, one had to embark on a three-year working trip as a journeyman, and, after having returned and served a member of the guild for one year, one had to produce a masterpiece:

> And when the whole year passes after he declared he wanted to start his probation in the art, then he is given six additional weeks to make these books that are described in the main privilege, that is *Cosmographia mundi* of Münster *in folio* with edges spotted by many colours on a brown background, the leather lavishly gilded on both sides of the book, and twisted buckles; *Item Calepinus undecem linguarum* with edges made up in pig leather, boards with buckles on dry decorated firmly. *Item Missale Romanum in folio cum aeneis figuris*, Antverpiae, made in a large format with gilded edges and leather lavishly gilded everywhere, as well as firm buckle; *Item Breviarium Romanum in octavo* or other prayers *in octavo* in Polish made in a similar way; *Item Methodus grammaticus et Praeces minores*, gilded too in the same way, entire in red leather, with twisted buckles. The seniors of the guild are to take the *Missale Romanum* for needs of the guild. When the *Missale* is under preparation, they are to supervise the work.[73]

[70] "Since the Bibles will be bound in Dokudów, the lay senior members of the community as well as the servants of God shall take care to sell them and allocate the money for the needs and expenses of the church in Vilnius"; MS MAB F40-1136 (*Akta synodów litewskich prowincjonalnych 1638-1675*), p. 43.

[71] The privilege can be found in the book of the Lithuanian *Metrica* kept in the Central Archives of Historical Records in Moscow (CGDA, Lithuanian *Metrica*, F 389, b. 106, k. 560); Laucevičius provides only the Lithuanian translation (LAUCEVIČIUS, *Knygų įrišimai*, p. 118).

[72] *AVAK*, 10, pp. 66-73 and 83-86. The content of this document has been discussed in detail in the Polish, Lithuanian and Belarusian studies by Rodziewiczówna, Laucevičius, Topolska, and Nikolaeŭ.

[73] *AVAK*, 10, p. 69.

The statute of Vilnius bookbinders was modelled on the statute of the Cracow guild approved on 16 December 1603, fragments of which concerning the three-year working trip of the journeyman and the masterpiece were copied word for word: the Cracow journeyman, in the presence of the masters, should bind the *Cosmography* of Münster, Calepinus's dictionary, two formats of missal, a textbook of grammar and prayers, etc.[74]

In the 1640s and 1650s, even before the Muscovite invasion, the demand for books – and thus for binding as well – was much higher than in the 1660s, so more bookbinders must have been active. It is hard to imagine that in this professional circle there were no rules concerning the way of achieving the status of master. Perhaps the Cracow regulations mentioned above were already applied at that time.

The Book Trade

As has been already mentioned, from the middle of the sixteenth century the sale of books in Vilnius was mainly carried out by bookbinders. Their interests were secured by the privilege of John Casimir of 1664, mentioned above:

> There is major disorder in their craft, especially since the heretics and dissidents of other creeds or various sects introduce heretical books into our Vilnius, selling them in market stalls, while Jews bind Christian books and wrong bookbinders in many other ways, which must have detrimental consequences for the masters of the craft and be a harm to God [...] we grant this privilege so that no stall-keeper or Jew, nor any dissident shall dare to trade or sell books even though he was a member of the guild. The punishment will be confiscation of all the books [...].[75]

The problem of binding and selling books without the control of the guild became apparent as early as the end of the sixteenth century in Cracow, as can be seen in subsequent guild regulations. One may assume that craftsmen in Vilnius had similar problems. Unfortunately, sources on this subject from the

[74] *Prawa, przywileje i statuty miasta Krakowa (1507-1795)*, ed. F. PIEKOSIŃSKI and S. KRZYŻANOWSKI, 2, *1587-1696* (Cracow, 1909), p. 1313. The first version of the Cracow Statute was approved in 1592.

[75] *AVAK*, 10, p. 84.

period before the Muscovite invasion are lacking, so when it comes to the trade in books we can only propose working hypotheses.

The first problem concerns the scale of the book trade in Vilnius. Until the end of the fifteenth century books were still so exclusive that they were used mainly in the religious sphere, and only clergymen owned them privately. The book market was underdeveloped at that time, and most of the necessary books were imported. A certain change must have been brought about by the emergence of the Orthodox and Catholic scriptoria mentioned above, but although mass production of chancery records and growing demand for documents at the turn of the fifteenth and sixteenth centuries was unquestionable, book-copying services still were an exception. Printing would bring an improvement in the economic picture, and Skaryna's work only confirms this hypothesis. He was the first known bookseller in Vilnius, although his Vilnius contractors (among them maybe Yakov Babich) presumably sold books published by Skaryna while he was still in Prague.[76]

Probably already in the first half of the sixteenth century merchants brought ever more books from other cities of the Polish-Lithuanian Commonwealth to Vilnius, but significant changes did not occur until around the 1550s, when many humanists settled in Vilnius and increased demand for books. Some of the purchases for their libraries were probably made on the spot. It is no coincidence that during this period we can identify some bookbinding workshops working in Vilnius: where there were bookbinders, books were traded.

Although the Lithuanian capital could not compare with Cracow, the largest book-trading centre of the Commonwealth, it is justified to say that Vilnius served as the main bibliopolic hub in Lithuania. It was here that Protestant books, brought from Cracow, Gdańsk, and nearby Königsberg, were traded. Perhaps such printed books were the subject matter of the trade contacts made by Jan Katherle, a Vilnius town dweller, whom a Cracow publisher Maciej Wirzbięta (Wierzbięta) made his plenipotentiary in 1566.[77] During the anti-Protestant riots in September 1581, the Catholic crowd burned "the books of Evangelical doctrine confiscated by the order of the bishop of Vilnius in front of St. John's church".[78] In the polemic *Apologeticus*, the anonymous author

[76] НЕМИРОВСКИЙ, *Франциск Скорина* , p. 410; NAGÓRKO, *Franciszek Skoryna*, p. 291; M.B. TOPOLSKA, "Mecenasi i drukarze ruscy na pograniczu kulturowym XVI-XVII w.", in: *Prawosławne oficyny wydawnicze*, p. 35.

[77] *Cracovia impressorum*, p. 275 (item 600); M. JAGLARZ, *Księgarstwo krakowskie XVI wieku* (Cracow, 2004), p. 164.

[78] *Kopia listu króla Stefana do nieboszczyka pana wojewody smoleńskiego strony palenia*

mentions that these were not only books printed by Daniel of Łęczyca (attacked during the unrest) but probably also some imported ones. The pretext for this action were the resolutions of the Council of Trent, according to which a punishment should be inflicted on those

> [...] who would dare to bring to us books of a different religion, a vain effort! Nonetheless, [Catholics] hastened to burn such books overtly without the consent of His Majesty the King.[79]

Thanks to editions of sources and studies of the trade in books in Cracow in the sixteenth and seventeenth centuries, we have some knowledge about the contacts between Cracow and Vilnius. The documents that have survived suggest that the cooperation of the Cracow booksellers and printers was less active in the Vilnius book market than in other significant urban settlements in the Polish-Lithuanian Commonwealth such as Lviv, Warsaw, and even Lublin.[80] Jan Karcan was particularly active in the exchange of books between Vilnius and Cracow. In July 1586 he became the plenipotentiary of the eminent print master from Cracow Mikołaj Szarfenberger, and in February 1590 of Jakub Siebeneicher and Jan Szarfenberger. At first, their transactions involved an intermediary in the person of "*honestus Frölich, civis itidem et bibliopola Wilnensis*" and in the second case a bookseller from Vilnius, Stanisław Bogdan, was involved as well. In June 1590, Albertus Lampartowicz became the new plenipotentiary of Siebeneicher in Vilnius.[81] Karcan also came to Cracow at that time, as was recorded in the customs registers: "Jan Karczan from Vilnius [is taking] his books to his house".[82] Daniel of Łęczyca, associated with the Szarfenbergers during his time in Cracow, probably cooperated with this family.[83]

In the late sixteenth century the book market in Vilnius was probably well developed. The services of booksellers were used by the Jesuits, because they

ksiąg w Wilnie ewangelickich 1581 in septembre, MS LNMB F93-1688.

79 *Apologeticus, to jest obrona Konfederacyjej: Przy tym seditio albo bunt kapłański na ewanieliki w Wilnie z wolej a łaski miłego Boga przed harapem wynurzony*, ed. E. BURSCHE (Cracow, 1932), p. 75 (vv. 1597-1601).

80 R. ŻURKOWA, *Księgarstwo krakowskie w pierwszej połowie XVII wieku* (Cracow, 1992), pp. 144-171; JAGLARZ, *Księgarstwo krakowskie XVI wieku*, pp. 158-176.

81 *Cracovia impressorum*, pp. 357 and 371 (Nos. 732 and 758); see JAGLARZ, *Księgarstwo krakowskie XVI wieku*, p. 163.

82 JAGLARZ, *Księgarstwo krakowskie XVI wieku*, p. 163.

83 BARYCZ, *Daniel of Łęczyca*, p. 405.

themselves could not profit from trade. The lack of documentation regarding the academic printing house does not allow us to state unequivocally whether the Jesuits hired book traders, who exported books to other cities, or whether the network of contacts of the Society of Jesus was exploited. Future research in the Archivum Romanum may resolve this issue.

The increasing distribution of books from Vilnius is confirmed by their presence in the farthest corners of the Polish-Lithuanian Commonwealth and beyond its borders. For example, the second edition of the *Lyrics* by Sarbiewski (Vilnius, 1628) reached the collegium in Košice (Upper Hungary), as is shown by the provenance notes preserved in the book.[84] Part of this export probably travelled through Cracow, as is suggested by the archives of this city. As Renata Żurkowa has calculated, in the first half of the seventeenth century there is evidence of ten occasions of books being transported from Cracow to Vilnius.[85] The Vilnius booksellers are also mentioned in the archival documents, for instance Stanisław Stoiński, who in 1606 carried "books to his house", "Joseph the Vilnius bibliopole" in 1608, and, in 1618, Gotard Rek (Gothard Reck) from Vilnius, who transported three tied packages of unbound books on horseback.[86] Franciszek Jakub Mercenich, a book merchant from Cologne who was active in Cracow, did business with the booksellers of Vilnius. In his posthumous inventory the following entry can be found: "*sub litera C regestra et rationes bibliopolarum Viln[ensium]*". Several carts of books were sent to Vilnius by Cracow publishers, that is Andrzej Piotrkowczyk in 1624, 1629 and 1633, Krzysztof Schedel in 1643, and Łukasz Kupisz in 1649.[87]

Merchants from Cracow brought to Vilnius not only printed books produced by local workshops but also works imported from the fairs in Frankfurt and Leipzig. Whether the booksellers of Vilnius went to these cities in person is hard to say before further research has been done. Information about the trade in books with other cities of the Commonwealth is hardly more abundant, apart from the certainty that such trade certainly took place. It was certified for instance by the privilege granted on 30 June 1644 by King Władysław IV to Georg Förster, a printer from Gdańsk, allowing him to sell his printed books in Cracow, Vilnius, Poznań, Lviv, Lublin, and Warsaw.[88] Förster's business in

[84] "*Ex libris praefectis*" and "*Applicatus Collegio Cassaviensi 1686*". A copy is kept in the Slovak National Library in Martin.

[85] Żurkowa, *Księgarstwo krakowskie*, p. 173.

[86] *Ibid.*, p. 172.

[87] *Ibid.*, p. 173.

[88] *Privilegia typographica Polonorum*, p. 163 (item 128).

Vilnius was so successful that he undertook the task of editing the *Historiae Lithuaniae pars prior* (History of Lithuania part one) by Wojciech Wijuk Kojałowicz (Albertas Kojalavičius-Vijūkas), a professor of the Academy. Future research should focus on the role of relations not only with Gdańsk, but also with Warsaw, which in the seventeenth century play the role of intermediary in the exchange of books between Cracow and Western Europe.

Jewish merchants, both locals and visitors, were probably also involved in the importation of books to Vilnius. This was necessary, because in those days there were no Jewish printing houses in Lithuania.[89] From the second half of the sixteenth century, they brought Hebrew and Yiddish books mainly from Cracow and Lublin,[90] and probably also from other Jewish printing centres in Europe. The scale of this trade is difficult to estimate, but Vilnius slowly grew to become the largest urban Jewish centre in Lithuania, so demand must have been high. A similar situation can be seen in other parts of the Polish-Lithuanian Commonwealth.[91] Jewish books were sold at fairs, but both book merchants and bookbinders must also have been active in the city. The most popular titles included the Torah, the Prophets and the Psalter, the Talmud, rabbinical commentaries, for instance Szulchan Aruch,[92] moralising books like *Tseno Ureno* by Jacob ben Isaac Ashkenazi from Janów, and perhaps also fiction.[93]

Due to the lack of sources, it is difficult to say how the trade in books in the city, whether Christian or Jewish, was organised from a practical point of view. What the bookshops were selling could not have been different from what was sold in the other large urban centres of the Polish-Lithuanian Commonwealth. Trade in Christian books was concentrated near the Market Square (Rynek), where the Vilnius printers Karcan and Mamonicz had their tenement

[89] M. BAŁABAN, "Drukarstwo żydowskie w Polsce w XVI w.", in: *Pamiętnik Zjazdu Naukowego im. Jana Kochanowskiego w Krakowie 8 i 9 czerwca 1930* (Cracow, 1931), pp. 108-112.

[90] R. ŻURKOWA, "Udział Żydów krakowskich w handlu książką w pierwszej połowie XVII wieku", in: *Żydzi w Małopolsce*, p. 71.

[91] K. PILARCZYK, *Talmud i jego drukarze w pierwszej Rzeczypospolitej* (Cracow, 1998), p. 209.

[92] Krzysztof Pilarczyk estimates that between forty-eight and eighty thousand copies of Talmudic treatises were published in Cracow and Lublin in the sixteenth and seventeenth centuries. This figure illustrates the scale of demand for this type of books. It should be noted that imported books ought to be added to this number. See K. PILARCZYK, "Rozpowszechnianie Talmudu w Polsce w XVI i XVII w. a duchowość żydowska", in: *Duchowość żydowska w Polsce: Materiały z międzynarodowej konferencji dedykowanej pamięci profesora Chone Shmeruka: Kraków 26-28 kwietnia 1999*, ed. M. GALAS (Cracow, 2000), p. 53.

[93] ŻURKOWA, *Udział Żydów krakowskich*, pp. 77-78.

houses, and in Wielka and Zamkowa (Didžioji and Pilies) Streets. The list of lodgings planned for the royal court called *Rewizyja gospód* (Description of Lodgings) from 1633 mentions two "bookbinders's stalls" on this street, one of which was rented by the bookbinder Jakub Kruncius.[94] Many bookbinders lived and worked in the Vilnius chapter's *jurydyka*, so the trade in books could also take place in the northern part of the city. Books were sold not only by specialised booksellers, but they could also be bought at the general stalls on the Market Square, as mentioned in the fragment of the bookbinders' statute quoted above, as well as at large fairs or during sessions of the Lithuanian Tribunal.[95] In the second half of the sixteenth century and the first half of the seventeenth century, as many as a dozen or so booksellers could operate in the city at the same time.

Educational and religious institutions were also involved in the distribution of books. It is known that the Jesuits played a role in this using local booksellers. Reformed evangelists (Calvinists) sold books through Protestant churches [*zbór*]:

> The large number of apostasies is the consequence of the fact that many Evangelical books remain unused by students (because students do not know about them). Then on the basis of the authority of this sacred gathering we decide that in this Church of God every vicar present at this synod is to take as many copies of these books as he and the students in his congregation need. Then he is to pay their current possessor for them.[96]

The Price and Value of Books

Book prices in the sixteenth and seventeenth centuries in the Polish-Lithuanian Commonwealth, and not only those in Vilnius, have attracted the attention of researchers for many decades, but to this day no comprehensive study devoted to them has appeared.[97] Since no bookshop catalogues have survived (we

[94] *Rewizyja gospód dworu*, p. 212 (items 21 and 25).

[95] We encounter a similar situation in Lublin; see WNUK, *Mieszczanie lubelscy przełomu XVI/XVII wieku a książka*, p. 77.

[96] A canon of ten resolutions of the Vilnius Synod of 1631: *O rozprzedaniu ksiąg ewangelickich niektórych przy zborze wileńskim będących* (On the sale of certain Evangelical books kept at the Vilnius Evangelical church), MS MAB F40-1157 (Akta synodów litewskich prowincjonalnych 1611-1637), 130v.

[97] There is extensive research on book prices in early modern Europe. See R. HIRSCH,

do not even know if they ever existed),[98] this knowledge is based on post-mortem inventories and notes found in individual copies of books. This evidence is fragmentary and, with regard to Vilnius, residual.[99] The answer to the question as to how much a book cost in the city (that is, any specific title at a given time) must therefore await comprehensive study. The availability of books is even more difficult to determine.

Until the fourth quarter of the fifteenth century, book prices were so high that they could be afforded only by the institutions of the Church, and among private persons only by church and secular officials, the grand dukes and members of their families. Prices were expressed in high-value gold coins (in ducats, florins, and Hungarian *złoty*), and the most expensive manuscripts imported from Cracow in the fourteenth and fifteenth centuries cost as much as several dozen florins. In 1483, Marcin Gasztołd (Martynas Goštautas) paid at

Printing, Selling and Reading, 1450-1550 (Wiesbaden, 1974); A. NUOVO, *The Book Trade in the Italian Renaissance* (Leiden and Boston, 2013); *Selling and Collecting: Printed Book Sale Catalogues and Private Libraries in Early Modern Europe*, ed. G. GRANATA and A. NUOVO (Macerata, 2018). Regardless of the availability of sources, scholars in many countries encounter similar problems. In a recent publication, Andrzej T. Staniszewski examined the prices of books in the early modern agglomeration of Cracow. The researcher pointed out several difficulties in estimating the prices of books, such as the fragmentary character of the existing sources, a lack of information about the difference in price of bound and unbound books, inflation, and a lack of information about the prices of the cheapest books. Staniszewski writes that the price is no more important than the value of a book. This value can be estimated through relating the price of books to the economic and cultural capital of the inhabitants of the city. See STANISZEWSKI, *Historyje krakowskie*, pp. 170-174, 191-193.

[98] In the Polish-Lithuanian Commonwealth catalogues of books were published by booksellers from the cities of Royal Prussia, Gdańsk (Georg Förster, mid-seventeenth century), and Toruń (Johann Friedrich Hauenstein, Johann Christian Laurer, and Samuel Jansson Möller, the first half of the eighteenth century). See J. RUDNICKA, *Bibliografia katalogów księgarskich wydanych w Polsce do końca wieku XVIII* (Warsaw, 1975); I. IMAŃSKA, "Katalog toruńskiego księgarza Samuela Janssona Möllera z 1738 roku w zbiorach Biblioteki Katedralnej w Gnieźnie", *Archiwa, Biblioteki i Muzea Kościelne* 113 (2020), pp. 205-220. The lack early modern bookseller catalogues is one of main obstacles in carrying out research on the book market and book collecting in Vilnius. See I. IMAŃSKA, "Kilka uwag i spostrzeżeń o katalogach aukcyjnych jako źródle do badań księgozbiorów prywatnych", *Z Badań nad Książką i Księgozbiorami Historycznymi* 9 (2015), pp. 241-254; G. PROOT, "Prices in Robert Estienne's booksellers' catalogues (Paris 1541-1552): a statistical analysis", in: *Selling and Collecting*, pp. 171-210.

[99] An example is a register of the incunabula from the Wróblewski Library of the Lithuanian Academy of Sciences and Vilnius University Library. The incunabula contain some manuscript notes relating to the prices of the books. However, the notes were written at various times (sixteenth-seventeenth centuries) and places. Their usefulness for research on book prices in Vilnius is therefore limited. See V. VAITKEVIČIŪTĖ, "Inkunabulų sklaidos ir funkcionavimo ypatumai: Lietuvos atminties institucijų rinkinių atvejai", *Knygotyra* 74 (2020), pp. 17-18.

least thirty Hungarian florins for an antiphonary prepared by the scribes of Cracow cathedral.[100] An illuminated *in folio* Bible on parchment consisting of 1014 pages cost 100 florins in Cracow in 1415, while legal books bought by a professor of Cracow University, Jan Dąbrówka, in 1462 cost between ten and twenty Venetian ducats.[101] Paper manuscripts were cheaper, but the price of several *grosz* for a Bible at the beginning of the fifteenth century was a great deal of money. Usually the price of a paper manuscript (written in cursive, without decorations) started at one florin and could reach ten florins.[102] Vilnius prices were further increased by transport costs. The prices of illuminated Orthodox manuscripts were equally high. The *Kyiv Psalter* donated to St. Nicholas' church in 1518 cost at least a few dozen *kopas* of *grosz*, and only the richest people in Lithuania could afford such a donation.

Printing reduced the prices of books in general, also of those which were still handwritten for everyday use. At the beginning of the sixteenth century, a printed item cost from a few to several dozen *grosz*, depending on its size, which was still a considerable amount of money.[103] Later, the more popular printed books, such as textbooks, prayer books, and catechisms, could cost from one *grosz* to a few *złoty* in Lesser Poland. Specialist books were more expensive, and their price could reach up to several dozen *złoty*.[104]

The value of a book was strongly influenced by the quality of the binding, which, as we have seen, could account for a large part of its price. For example, the Roman missal bought for Vilnius cathedral in 1578 from Piotr Skarga cost two *kopas* (that is 180) of *grosz*, and its binding cost an additional twenty *grosz*.[105] The prices of the same title could vary much depending on the binding.[106]

[100] *Cracovia impressorum*, pp. 8-9 (item 20).

[101] W. SZELIŃSKA, *Biblioteki profesorów Uniwersytetu Krakowskiego w XV i początku XVI wieku* (Wrocław, 1966), p. 301.

[102] A. KOZŁOWSKA, "Ceny książek ręcznie pisanych", *Biuletyn Biblioteki Jagiellońskiej* 49 (1999), p. 49-52.

[103] SZELIŃSKA, *Biblioteki profesorów*, p. 303; W. URBAN, "Ceny książek w Polsce XVI-XVII w.", *Biuletyn Biblioteki Jagiellońskiej* 46 (1996), pp. 61-67.

[104] Prices of printed books from Lesser Poland are given by ŻURKOWA, *Księgarstwo krakowskie*, p. 40-42, and URBAN, *Ceny książek*, p. 61-67.

[105] *Regestr kapituły roku 1577 i roku 1578*, MS MAB F43-451, f. 21v; A year later the chapter registers note a slightly cheaper version of a similar kind of book: "When Wincenty was here, we paid four *złoty* worth twenty four *grosz*, that is one *kopa* and 36 *grosz*, for a bound Roman Missal handed over to Pozwole"; *Regestr kapituły za rok 1579 i za rok 1580*, MS MAB F43-452, f. 26r.

[106] TORÓJ, *Inwentarze książek lubelskich introligatorów*, p. 17.

Scholars investigating the history of bookselling and books in Cracow unanimously agree that books were expensive. They compare known book prices with the prices of basic commodities and average wages. Renata Żurkowa discusses the income of, among others, a maid, a nurse, a cook, bricklayer's and carpenter's journeymen, city officials, etc., trying to answer the question whether poor and moderately wealthy inhabitants of Cracow could afford books.[107] The question about the purchasing power of the city's inhabitants clearly implies another one, that is, how common the reading of books was in the seventeenth century (in this case in Cracow)?

We could subject data from Vilnius to a similar analysis. For example, in his last will from 27 April 1618, Szymon Lewonowicz mentioned the salary of his household servants: "For Józef the Brewer seven *kopas* (*shock*), for the merchant of salt Konrat six, the maid Helena for three years three *kopas* and *letnik* (a summer dress)".[108] If we take as a point of reference the valuation of the books of the scholar and book collector Salomon Rysiński from about the same period,[109] it follows that Helena, the maid, would have to work for a year and a half to save enough money to buy a Latin Bible in a small format (Rysiński valued it at three *złoty*), a year for *Wzorki białogłowskie* (Examples for Women; two *złoty*), and over six months for the Psalter in Maciej Rybiński's translation (one *złoty and* fifteen *grosz*). For his (probably annual) salary, the brewer Józef could buy fourteen copies of Plautus' comedies or the *Nicomachaean Ethics* by Aristotle in Greek (each volume for one *złoty*) and twenty-eight copies of Melanchthon's rhetoric or the poems of Statius (fifteen *grosz* each), or a large part of the edition of the *Obrona konfederacyi* (*The Defence of the Warsaw Confederation*) forty-two copies (at ten *grosz* each). On Szymonowic' *Sielanki* (*Bucolics*) the salt merchant Konrat would spend 1/30 of his yearly salary (twenty *grosz*), but for Ortelius' atlas (fifty *złoty*, or twenty-five *shocks* of *grosz*) he would probably have to work for more than four years without eating, heating his home, or buying any clothes.

[107] ŻURKOWA, *Księgarstwo krakowskie*, pp. 42-43.

[108] MS LVIA F22, ap. 1, no. 5344, f. 601r.

[109] Rysiński states that this valuation was based on the amounts he himself paid for each book: "It was calculated according to the old purchases, without transport, which I paid three times on the books, once on the books I bought in Nuremberg thirty-six *złoty*, the second time in Leipzig twenty-four *złoty*, and the third time in Basel fifty-four *złoty*. And I do not mention the 140 *złoty* I paid for seven years of lease and for books alone in the Słucki house"; MS NGAB Ф 694 оп. 1 ед. 450, f. 71r.

The second way to estimate the 'real' price of a book is to compare its value with the prices of other products. Among the items listed in 1663 and 1664 by Ludwik Bekier and Anna Desaus, members of the Vilnius merchant elite, two books by Martin Luther worth two and three *złoty* respectively and the Brest Bible worth eight *złoty* are mentioned.[110] The same registers list, among other things, white women's shirts (one *złoty* fifteen *grosz* each), canvas (fifteen *złoty*), an old amber mirror (six *złoty*), "a red dress with black lace" (twenty *złoty*), and a barrel of oats (five *złoty*). Animals cost, in turn: a hen (cock) fifteen *grosz*; a capon (castrated rooster) twenty five *grosz*; a laying hen fifteen *grosz*; a filly ten *złoty*; a calf ten *złoty*; and a nag (a small riding horse) thirty *złoty*.

The will of the mayor and merchant Stefan Dubowicz from 16 July 1657 (that is from the time of the Muscovite occupation) contains such items as books, tin, copper, brass – 1,200 *złoty*; a brick house on Szklanna Street – 2,500 *złoty*; a cloth stall near Fish End (at the end of Pilies Street) – 2,500 *złoty*; a string of pearls with beads – thirty *złoty*.[111] A year later, in 1658, the merchant Marcin Buchner gave his daughter a dowry that included long shirts for eight *złoty* each, ordinary dresses for thirty *złoty* each, and a satin black dress with lace for as much as 100 *złoty*.[112] At that time (1656), for 2,500 bricks one paid thirty-four *złoty*, and nine *złoty* for an iron grate.[113]

The prices provided here are quite random. They apply to the mid-seventeenth century and are very far from reflecting the cost of a market basket at the time.[114] However, from these examples (and from many others), we can gain some rather important insights into the availability of books in Vilnius. Above all, huge disparities in terms of income should be taken into consideration. There were people who had practically no assets and those who spent many times the annual income of the former on luxury goods. Therefore, for

[110] Registers date back to 1663 and 1664; MS LVIA F23, ap. 1, no. 5099, ff. 567v-571r.

[111] MS LVIA F22, ap. 1, no 5334, ff. 31r-37v.

[112] *Ibid.*, ff. 396v-398v.

[113] *Ibid.*, f. 625r.

[114] When studying prices in the past, one should always remember about inflation and the decline in the value of the most common coin, the *grosz*. A sudden collapse of the value of Polish and Lithuanian money happened in the 1660s, but its decrease in value was also observable earlier. Between 1550 and 1627, the thaler rose from thirty-four *grosz* to ninety *grosz*, while the silver content of the *grosz* decreased almost threefold (see W. ADAMCZYK, *Ceny w Warszawie w XVI i XVII wieku* (Lviv, 1938), pp. 4-5). For this reason alone, quoting the prices of goods (in this case books) without specifying the exact year of purchase is unreliable (see URBAN, *Ceny książek*, pp. 62-67, where in most cases we do not know the dates of the pricing of a book).

people from lower social classes, books were expensive both in terms of their earnings and as compared to other goods, for instance food. For the elite of craftsmen and merchants of Vilnius, purchasing a book was not a big problem; for one of the ordinary dresses of Miss Buchnerówna, whom we introduced before (the inventory also included much more expensive dresses for special occasions) one could buy ten or fifteen copies of Martin Luther's book or almost four copies of the Brest Bible. Theoretically, more wealthy town dwellers would be able to buy as many as a couple to several dozen books a year without any special burden to their budgets. Mayor Stefan Lebiedzicz's library of 1649 confirms this assumption. But it was an exception: the book collection even of very rich inhabitants of the city usually included only few items, as for instance the library of a merchant Ludwik Bekier. In other words, both those who could not afford them and those who had very high incomes bought few or no books. In this situation, asking whether books were cheap or expensive is largely academic. Neither the maid Helena, the brewer Józef, nor the merchant Buchner read the *Nicomachaean Ethics* in Greek, Melanchthon's rhetoric in Latin, or Szymonowic's *Sielanki* in Polish, because of their lack of cultural capital. They could at best read the Psalter, the Gospels, maybe the lives of the saints, and sermons (and they listened rather to the texts being read aloud than read them themselves).

Therefore the question of the availability of books, is, in fact, the question whether they were available to their most frequent users, that is church ministers, priests, monks and nuns, city scribes, municipal and other officials, teachers who were not clergy, doctors, and students.[115] All of them, except for students, were professionals of the written word and had a stable, greater or lesser income. Some priests put records in their wills that amounted to hundreds or thousands of *złoty*, so it is not surprising that their book collections (especially those of the members of the chapter) were among the largest.

Andrzej Strzałkowski, the scribe of the Vilnius chapter in 1554, not only received a house for use, but also a salary amounting to eight *kopas* of Lithuanian *grosz*.[116] This was quite an impressive income, which enabled him to buy

[115] This is confirmed by the testaments of the inhabitants of Wojnicz in Lesser Poland. Only three out of fifty-one wills from the years 1599-1676 mention books. Two of them are wills of collegiate priests (items 34 [1640] and 50 [1674]) and one is the will of Krzysztof Bliziński, a barber (1658). The latter owned twenty-one books, mainly herbals and medical works. Priests had slightly larger collections of books. See *Testamenty mieszczan wojnickich 1599-1809*, ed. P. Dymmel (Wojnicz, 1997), pp. 63, 75, 93.

[116] MS MAB F43-211 (VKF445: *Akta kapituły wileńskiej 1550-1560*), f. 80 (item 221),

books, the more so as over time it increased, so that in 1578 it amounted to twelve *kopas* per year.[117] We do not know how much other lower officials and teachers earned at that time, but their salaries were probably similar to those of Strzałkowski. Let us add that in those days the annual salary of a provincial teacher in Lesser Poland amounted to eight *złoty* a year, which is half as much.[118] In Lublin in the 1570s, a teacher earned ten *złoty*, and a city scribe thirty-two *złoty*. Similarly, in Warsaw in the 1580s, a mayor's scribe earned twenty *złoty* and the council's thirty-two *złoty*.[119]

If we assume that the prices of books in Vilnius at that time, despite the need to import them, were about as high as in Cracow, the scribe Strzałkowski could afford several books a year, even of the more expensive kinds, and could create a library similar to the one left by *Voigt* Feliks Langurga, *advocatus Vilnensis*, in 1551. According to the findings of Wacław Urban, classical works of literature, textbooks, and academic works could be purchased at a price of one to a dozen or so *grosz*.[120] At the beginning of the seventeenth century, the situation of the people who most often reached for books, that is teachers, did not deteriorate. In 1614, the rector of the Vilnius Calvinist school earned 150 *złoty* and the three other teachers seventy, sixty and fifty *złoty* respectively,[121] which meant that their financial potential allowed for the buying of books.

The financial capacity of students was rather different. As always, books were expensive for them, which probably contributed to the popularity of the manuscript copies created at the Academy of Vilnius even as late as the first half of the eighteenth century. Such manuscripts may have replaced many volumes, but students also needed printed textbooks, mainly of grammar, rhetoric, and poetics, as well as catechisms. These books must have been quite cheap, priced at a few *grosz*, printed in large editions, and often reprinted. Their production was launched by the academic printing house with the Acad-

14.04.1554.

[117] *Regestr kapituły roku 1577 i roku 1578*, MS MAB F43-451, f. 20v.

[118] W. URBAN, "Małopolskie szkoły parafialne w świetle akt sądowych krakowskiej kurii biskupiej z drugiej połowy XVI w.", *Przegląd Historyczno-Oświatowy*, 36.1-2 (1993), p. 6.

[119] ADAMCZYK, *Ceny w Lublinie od XVI do końca XVIII wieku*, pp. 103, 105; ID., *Ceny w Warszawie*, pp. 65, 108.

[120] URBAN, *Ceny książek*, pp. 64-65.

[121] *Akta synodów prowincjonalnych Jednoty Litewskiej 1611-1625*, p. 25.

emy's students in mind. In 1592, it issued two editions of Manuel Álvares's grammar.[122]

In a letter to general Aquaviva of 13 June 1594, Adam Brocus justified the need to keep the Jesuit printing house, citing mainly the need to reduce the price of books for students:

> students are forced to buy their books printed in Cracow which have to be brought here from a place more than a thousand miles away. At the same time, we can support them with low prices of both religious and secular books from our own printing house. Since we do not sell books here, we give them to the bookseller to trade them and pay ourselves what justice requires, so that the printing house has no losses.[123]

Brocus was right: books printed on the spot could have been cheaper, but if we take into account that the next textbook known to us that was often used in the Academy (the manual of rhetoric by Michał Radau) appeared in the academic printing house only in 1640,[124] then the argumentation of the English Jesuit raises a number of doubts. Even if we take into account that the copies of some editions may not have survived, it is clear that the Jesuits preferred to print panegyrics rather than textbooks.

In any case, the popular poetics of Jacobus Pontanus and Cypriano de Soarez's manual of rhetoric were mainly imported, while other textbooks from the turn of the sixteenth and seventeenth centuries were printed by the Karcans.[125] These books could be purchased cheaper if bought on the second-hand book market. There were probably many students who contributed to the development of the antiquarian book trade. This can be concluded from the provenance notes of seventeenth- and eighteenth-century volumes. However, rather little is known on this subject, mostly because the majority of textbooks that have survived come from institutional libraries, and only a few items that have survived belonged to private owners.

[122] Čepienė and Petrauskienė, *Vilniaus Akademijos spaustuvės leidiniai 1576-1805*, p. 12.

[123] *Vilniaus akademijos*, p. 67.

[124] Čepienė and Petrauskienė, *Vilniaus Akademijos spaustuvės leidiniai*, p. 121.

[125] Soarez was first published in Vilnius in 1680; see *ibid.*, p. 141; *XVII a. Lietuvos lotyniškų knygų sąrašas*, pp. 60, 109-110; Narbutienė, *Lietuvos Didžiosios Kunigaikštijos lotyniškoji knyga*, p. 139.

Chapter 8

Genus Deliberativum: Letters and Testaments

Preliminary Remarks

This chapter is devoted to texts which are associated with the rhetorical *genus deliberativum*. In the classical theory of rhetoric, this genre comprises for instance political speeches, in which orators convinced somebody to take (or not) certain political actions.[1] However, the *genus deliberativum* consists of a wide range of texts, which all refer to future events or actions. Their main quality is *utilitas* (utility).[2] These texts are to serve a community or its members in political and legal matters. Often, deliberative texts were entirely devoted to administrative matters.

The category of *utilitas* is the reason why I include into the *genus deliberativum* those written sources which helped the inhabitants of Vilnius in administrative and legal issues (an exception are texts relating to litigations and conflicts, which belong to the *genus iuidiciale*; they will be discussed in the next chapter). These sources provided a textual frame for the legal and political functioning of the city, and its institutions were anchored in them.[3]

We have to bear in mind, though, that Vilnius was not an urban settlement similar to most other towns, that is a centre of commerce, crafts, and local religious life. It was also the capital of the country, where the state institutions were located (among which the chancery and the Tribunal of the Grand Duchy of Lithuania). During the wars in the sixteenth and first half of the seventeenth

[1] LAUSBERG, *Handbook of Literary Rhetoric*, pp. 32-33, § 61.2.
[2] *Ibid.*, p. 72, § 173.
[3] The most important of them have been presented in Chapter 1.

century, the military staff operated out of Vilnius.[4] When the king stayed in the city, it became the capital of the entire Polish-Lithuanian federation. The Parliament of the Commonwealth and the parliamentary institutions (*konwokacja*) of the Grand Duchy of Lithuania gathered here,[5] and sometimes foreign missions resided in Vilnius as well. It was the capital of the voivodeship, the seat of many religious authorities (the Catholic bishopric, the Orthodox archbishopric, the capital of the provinces of the Jesuits, the Observant (Bernardine) Friars, the Dominicans and the Basilians, and the seat of the authorities of the Lithuanian Calvinists), and the university.

Such a concentration of functions in Vilnius (both as an 'open' and 'closed' city) gave rise to the production and use of huge numbers of various deliberative texts. Among them there are privileges, transumpts, charters, confirmations, sentences, and depositions of witnesses in legal proceedings, issued by the state, municipal, and church offices, chanceries, and courts. A slightly different group of deliberative texts includes collections of law, which were the city's 'legal settings'.[6] They provided the framework and basis, both legal and rhetorical, for a significant part of the documents referred to in this chapter.

These texts are rarely linked by literary criticism to belles-lettres since, according to the typology used by students of literature, they belong to applied literature (*literatura stosowana*),[7] but they were in fact of great importance for the literary culture of Vilnius as a whole, in terms both of its functioning and of the forms of specific works. They have a rhetorical structure derived from the tradition of Greco-Roman rhetoric, Roman law, and their medieval continuations. Their basis were collections of texts called in the Middle Ages *liber cancellariae*, *libri formularum*, *formulae*, etc.[8] They contained samples of

[4] In the spring and early summer of 1579, in Vilnius King Stephan Báthory planned his operations against Muscovy. See D. KUPISZ, *Połock 1579* (Warsaw, 2003), p. 93. During the campaigns of 1580-1582 Vilnius was also his base. Another example is the period 1609-1611, when Vilnius was the base of King Sigismund III Vasa.

[5] The informal parliamentary gathering of the Lithuanian nobility was called in Polish *konwokacja* (Latin *convocatio*). See K. ŁOPATECKI, "Konwokacja litewska 1615 roku: Z badań nad procedurą przyjmowania uchwał konwokacyjnych", *Krakowskie Studia z Historii Państwa i Prawa* 12.4 (2019), pp. 493-522; *Akta zjazdów stanów Wielkiego Księstwa Litewskiego*, 2, *Okresy panowań królów elekcyjnych XVI-XVII wiek*, ed. H. LULEWICZ (Warsaw, 2009).

[6] A. ADAMSKA and M. MOSTERT, "Introduction", in: *Writing and the Administration of Medieval Towns*, p. 4.

[7] Discussed in Chapter 1. See also SKWARCZYŃSKA, "O pojęcie literatury stosowanej", pp. 12-17. The texts of the *genus deliberativum* belong to the "the social-rhetoric group" within applied literature. *Ibid.*, pp. 17, 19.

[8] The literature on medieval and early modern formulae is vast. The Polish medieval

different types of documents, fictitious and authentic, which helped the notaries, scribes, *diaks* and so on to make the new documents.

Probably all inhabitants of Vilnius, who directly or indirectly came into contact with at least some of these texts, were to some degree able to recognise their rhetorical structures. Together with religious texts,[9] the genres belonging to the *genus deliberativum* played a decisive role in building an interpretative community[10] in late medieval and early modern Vilnius.

In this chapter I will discuss three types of deliberative texts of different characters. The first one are legal transactions, such as contracts of selling and buying, lending money, and registers of property. A particularly important type of written sources constituting the second group was epistolography, concerning in the first place political, financial, and administrative matters. And finally, last wills will be discussed, which can be placed at the crossroads between the public and private spheres. Legal transactions and last wills belong rather to the texts of the 'closed' city, while letters belong to the 'open' city.

These three genres do not make up the complete typology of the urban texts of the *genus deliberativum*. But, along with religious texts, they probably were the most often used texts in the city. Especially interesting here is that they render the modalities of applied literature quite well. Without any doubt letters were treated as a literary genre, and many historians of literature carried out studies about the literary features of this genre.[11] Last wills have not often been analysed as literary works. Still, there are several papers and other publications which have presented last wills from the point of view of literary criti-

formulae, which predominantly influenced Lithuanian chancery practice, were studied in several editions and studies, a.o. *Liber cancellariae Stanislai Ciolek: Ein Formelbuch der polnischen Königskanzlei aus der Zeit der Husitischen Bewegung*, ed. J. CARO, 2 vols. (Vienna, 1871-1872); *Liber formularum ad ius Polonicum necnon canonicum spectantium in codice Regiomontano asservatum*, ed. B. ULANOWSKI (Cracow, 1895); *Formularz Jerzego, pisarza grodzkiego krakowskego ok. 1399-1415*, ed. K. GÓRSKI (Toruń, 1950); G. WOJCIECH-MASŁOWSKA, "Dwa krakowskie libri formularum z XV wieku", *Studia Źródłoznawcze* 17 (1972), pp. 119-113; J. LUCIŃSKI, "Formularze czynności prawnych w Polsce w wiekach średnich: Przegląd badań", *Studia Źródłoznawcze* 18 (1973), pp. 149-179; G. KLIMECKA, *Z historii tworzenia języka dokumentu polskiego wieków średnich: Formularz ciechanowski* (Warsaw, 1997); T. MICHAŁOWSKA, *Średniowieczna teoria literatury w Polsce: Rekonesans* (Toruń, 2016), pp. 182-187.

9 Discussed in Chapter 11.

10 S. FISH, "Introduction", in: S. FISH, *Is There a Text in this Class?*, pp. 10-15.

11 SKWARCZYŃSKA, *Teoria listu*; JARCZYKOWA, "Papierowe materie"; *Epistolografia w dawnej Rzeczypospolitej*, ed. P. BOREK and M. OLMA (Cracow, 2014).

cism.[12] But financial contracts have as yet never been put into textbooks about the history of literature.

The three genres share at least two common features. The first one is obvious: they were all three written down and their materiality is comparable. The other is more significant: all three are derived from the rules of rhetoric as expressed in the medieval *ars dictandi*.[13] It is true that all medieval rhetorical genres have their roots in ancient rhetoric, but it was the *ars dictandi* that finally constituted the three genres discussed here.[14] Probably all public notaries, who prepared among other texts the contracts and testaments, were trained in the programme of the *trivium*: grammar, rhetoric, and dialectic. The *ars notaria* was taught as part of the *trivium*.[15] Knowledge of rhetorical genres and fluency in Latin formulary and phrases allowed them to compose these documents.[16]

Classicist literary criticism, which was launched in Italy in the times of Petrarch and lasted in Europe for the next three centuries, sought a clear distinction between texts which are literary and those which are not, and what distinguishes poetry from other kinds of textual production.[17] For example,

[12] Testaments were categorised as a literary genre, such as letter and sermon, by Małgorzata Borkowska (see BORKOWSKA, *Dekret w niebieskim ferowany testamencie*, p. 11), while its uniqueness and personal character is emphasised by Alicja Falniowska-Gradowska (A. FALNIOWSKA-GRADOWSKA, "Wstęp", in *Testamenty szlachty krakowskiej XVII-XVIII w. Wybór tekstów źródłowych z lat 1650-1799*, ed. A. FALNIOWSKA-GRADOWSKA (Cracow, 1997), p. X. Both researchers meticulously analyse the structure and *topoi* of wills. See also O. HEDEMANN, *Testamenty brasławsko-dziśnieńskie XVII-XVIII wieku jako źródło historyczne* (Vilnius, 1935), pp. 8-9.

[13] J.J. MURPHY, *Rhetoric in the Middle Ages: A History of Rhetorical Theory from Saint Augustine to the Renaissance* (Berkeley, Los Angeles, and London, 1974), pp. 194-268. On recent research on the *ars dictaminis*, see B. GRÉVIN, "Le dictamen dans tous ses états: Perspectives de recherchesorie et la pratique de l'ars dictaminis (XIe-XVe siècle)", in: *Le dictamen dans tous ses états: Perspectives de recherches sur la théorie et la pratique de l'ars dictaminis (XIe-XVe siècle)*, ed. B. GRÉVIN, and A.-M. TURCAN-VERKERK (Turnhout, 2015), pp. 9-25.

[14] D. WITT, "*Ars dictaminis*: Victim of *ars notarie*?", in: *Medieval Letters Between Fiction and Document*, ed. Ch. HØGEL and E. BARTOLI (Turnout, 2015), pp. 359-361.

[15] T. MICHAŁOWSKA, *Średniowieczna teoria literatury*, p. 184. Scholars dispute whether the *ars notaria* was a part of the *ars dictaminis* or that the *ars notaria*, which evolved from the *ars dictaminis*, dominated it in the thirteenth century. On this debate see: WITT, "*Ars dictaminis*: victim of *ars notarie*?", pp. 359-368. The Polish formulae from the fifteenth century confirm that in the notarial practice of the chanceries of Poland and Lithuania both *artes* were used simultaneously as one cluster.

[16] K. SKUPIEŃSKI, *Notariat publiczny w średniowiecznej Polsce* (Lublin, 1997), pp. 83-109; BARTOSZEWICZ, *Urban Literacy*, pp. 241-246.

[17] The discussion about the role of literature as a means of forming *humanitas* began among the Florentine humanists of the fifteenth century (Lorenzo Valla, Angelo Poliziano, and Giovanni Pico della Mirandola) and flourished in the next century. The dispute about *imitatio* and reception

since the fifteenth century humanist letters were strongly influenced by ancient epistolography (*imitatio*), and their authors put much effort into developing an aesthetic of elegance.[18] One of the side effects of this process of developing a new aesthetics for the *belles lettres* was the exclusion from them of many genres of the *ars dictandi*, such as last wills, contracts, privileges, ordinances, court sentences, etc.[19] However, the medieval rhetorical layers can still be distinguished in many early modern literary genres: for instance in letters, sermons, and historiography. In practice, the border between literature and other texts was still tenuous and blurred, especially considering prose genres, for instance the letters, last wills and contracts.

The structure of the texts belonging to these three genres reproduced – more or less – the structure of the formulary of medieval charters. They were written with the use of the rhetorical *topoi* of the rhetorical disposition (*dispositio*) of a text: *invocatio*, *arenga*, *intitulatio*, *promulgatio*, *salutatio*, *dispositio*, *clausulae*, *corroboratio*, and *subscriptio*.[20] Apart from the topoi of *dispositio* (that is construction), other *loci communes* or *formulae* were applied as well, especially in the arengas.[21] However, the *ars dictandi* cannot be re-

of the *Poetics* of Aristotle in the mid-sixteenth century (Francesco Robortello) belongs to the most important points in the process of building the early modern concept of literature. See FULIŃSKA, *Naśladowanie i twórczość*, p. 87-131.

[18] Many authors of manuals (e.g. Erasmus of Rotterdam) from the end of the fifteenth and the beginning of the sixteenth centuries showed what the *elegantiae linguae Latinae* were. In Cracow the problem was discussed, a.o. by Laurentius Corvinus, Ioannes Sommerfeld Aesticampianus, Conrad Celtis, Ioannes Ursinus and Paweł of Krosno (Paulus Crosnensis). See A. GORZKOWSKI, *Paweł z Krosna: Humanistyczne peregrynacje krakowskiego profesora* (Cracow, 2000), pp. 60-80.

[19] L. WINNICZUK, "Wstęp", in: Jan Ursyn z Krakowa, *Modus epistolandi cum epistolis exemplaribus et orationibus annexis: O sposobie pisania listów wraz z wzorami listów i mowami*, ed. L. WINNICZUK (Wrocław, 1957), pp. VII-X.

[20] K. MALECZYŃSKI, *Zarys dyplomatyki polskiej wieków średnich*, 1 (Wrocław, 1951), pp. 23-26; *Dyplomatyka wieków średnich*, ed. K. MALECZYŃSKI, M. BIELIŃSKA, and A. GĄSIOROWSKI (Warsaw, 1971), pp. 23-25; S. KĘTRZYŃSKI, *Zarys nauki o dokumencie polskim wieków średnich* (Poznań, 2008), pp. 59-60; SUŁKOWSKA-KURASIOWA, *Dokumenty królewskie i ich funkcja*, p. 51; B. WYROZUMSKA, *Kancelaria miasta Krakowa w średniowieczu* (Cracow, 1995), pp. 99-101; SKUPIEŃSKI, *Notariat publiczny*, pp. 149-151; A. ADAMSKA, *Arengi w dokumentach Władysława Łokietka: Formy i funkcje* (Cracow, 1999), pp. 35-41.

[21] ADAMSKA, *Arengi w dokumentach Władysława Łokietka*, pp. 43-127; EAD., "Treści religijne w preambułach polskich dokumentów średniowiecznych", *Studia Źródłoznawcze* 38 (2000), pp. 1-33, EAD., "Studying preambles today: A paradigm shift in diplomatic?", in: *Urkundenformeln im Kontext: Formen der Schriftkultur im Ostmitteleuropa des Mittelalters (13.-14. Jahrhundert)*, ed. S. ROSSIGNOL and A. ADAMSKA (Vienna, 2016), pp. 35-45; EAD., "Słowo władzy i władza słowa: Język polskich dokumentów monarszych doby średniowiecza", in: *Król w Polsce*

duced to the distinction of genres, *elocutio*, or structuralist analysis only. Reading, interpreting, and other rhetorical procedures should also be taken into account when we examine the rhetorical features of a text. The application of rhetorics in the aforementioned genres finally blurred the differences between literature and non-literary texts.

Documents were in constant circulation. Any text written according to the rules of juridical or deliberative rhetoric could be brought before the appropriate authority, its original was submitted and a certified extract from it was issued, or the original could be entered in the register and a copy of this entry could be requested. These entries and their copies reflect the ways the documents were used. They contain a date, a description of the circumstances of the entry (the office concerned, the official representing it, the persons who appeared, etc.), and an exposition (that is information on the submission of the document or testimony). These preliminary formulae were followed by the content: for instance a royal privilege, a will, a deed of sale, a protestation, an inventory, a purchase deed, etc. was quoted in Ruthenian, Latin, or Polish. At the end, there was a confirmation by the scribal office that the document had been entered into its registers, followed by the formulas of witnesses, seals, and, from the second half of the sixteenth century, signatures. Sometimes, there was added an annotation that a copy had been issued.

The languages and scripts of documents can be traces of their circulation. They reflect the complex linguistic situation of Vilnius. The initial and final formulas could appear in a language other than that of the main part of the document. Since the sixteenth century, often as many as three to four languages and three types of script met in a single document, for instance the initial formulas of an extract from the municipal books were written in the Cyrillic alphabet in Ruthenian; the content of the document was in Polish, but with excerpts in Latin; while the signatures could be put in Polish, Latin, Ruthenian and additionally in Yiddish in the Hebrew alphabet or in Tartar written in the Arabic alphabet. Usually, however, we encounter combinations of Ruthenian-Latin, Ruthenian-Polish, or Latin-Polish.[22]

XIV i XV wieku, ed. A. MARZEC and M. WILAMOWSKI (Cracow, 2007), pp. 57-88; EAD., "L'*Ars dictaminis* a-t-elle été possible en langue vernaculaire? Quelques sondages", in: *Le* Dictamen *dans tous ses états*, pp. 389-414.

[22] This phenomenon was discussed in Chapter 6, devoted to the graphosphere of late medieval and early modern Vilnius.

The forms of Latin, German, Ruthenian, and later Polish documents were introduced in Lithuania in the late Middle Ages.[23] In the fourteenth century, even before the formal location of Vilnius, some of its Catholic inhabitants, representatives of the Latin clergy and maybe some clerks who worked for the grand dukes, knew the formulae of the *ars dictandi*. In the 1380s the situation changed dramatically when the grand ducal chancery, the bishopric, and the town authorities were established. These institutions relied on the production, interpretation, and exchange of documents. In the times of Jogaila and Vytautas, that is at the turn of the fourteenth and fifteenth centuries, books with collections of formulae were imported from Cracow and came to Vilnius together with employees of the Polish chancery.

A similar process must have occurred also in the municipal chancery. The Magdeburg law required from the inhabitants that they validated their economic and social activities in writing. Thus, there had to be someone in the Vilnius town hall who could manage the bureaucracy. What is more, there had to be public notaries in the town, who could produce professional documents.

Some sources from the 1380s and 1390s confirm this supposition. In 1382 Hanul (Hans, Hannike) of Riga was a leader of the German community in Vilnius, who supported Grand Duke Jogaila.[24] Later on, Hanul became the *capitaneus Vilnensis*, a diplomat,[25] and, what is especially interesting for us, the secretary of Jogaila.[26] Hanul could compose letters and privileges in Latin and German[27] and was the first known Vilnius professional of pragmatic literacy (or applied literature). However, it is almost certain that such professionals had lived in Vilnius already earlier on.[28]

It is supposed that the first German inhabitants of Vilnius came from Livonia, and urban literacy in fourteenth-century Vilnius developed under the influ-

[23] I. SUŁKOWSKA-KURASIOWA, *Dokumenty królewskie i ich funkcja w państwie polskim za Andegawenów i pierwszych Jagiellonów 1370-1444* (Warsaw, 1977), p. 5; KOSMAN, *W kancelarii wielkiego księcia Witolda*, pp. 111-114.

[24] W. SEMKOWICZ, "Hanul, *namiestnik wileński* (1382-1387) i jego ród", *Ateneum Wileńskie* 7.1-4 (1930), p. 4; *Urzędnicy Wielkiego Księstwa Litewskiego. Spisy*, 1, *Województwo wileńskie*, p. 181.

[25] SEMKOWICZ, "Hanul, *namiestnik wileński*", pp. 7, 12.

[26] *Ibid.*, pp. 10.

[27] *Ibid.*, pp. 10-11.

[28] Władysław Semkowicz supposes that a certain Hennike, who was a translator, i.e. a Latin and German notary of Duke Gediminas, might have come from Riga and was Hanul's father. See *ibid.*, p. 6. This professional of pragmatic literacy might have lived in the German part of Vilnius and may have offer his writing proficiency not only for Gediminas, but to his neighbours as well.

ence of the city of Riga.[29] Only later on, strong relationships with Gdańsk and other Prussian cities came into being.[30] Although we do not know any documents issued or confirmed by the Vilnius authorities from before the mid-fifteenth century, we may suppose that they used formularies similar to those used in the other towns of the region. Until the beginning of the sixteenth century, probably most professionals of written word working in Vilnius were immigrants from Livonia, Masovia, Poland, Prussia, or Silesia.

During the times of the intensive reception of humanist culture, the external forms of documents and letters changed (the choice of script, spelling, *topoi*, etc.), but the basic structures of the texts were maintained. On the other hand, the number of varieties of genre increased. To facilitate their work, chancery clerks still used collections of *formulae*. From the sixteenth century onwards collections of *formulae* were put together locally, in Vilnius. An example of such a formulary is a manuscript created in the chancery of Sigismund II Augustus in the 1550s, which contained among other things copies of banishment sentences, plenipotentiary powers, and charters of ennoblement (for instance that of the eminent chronicler and bishop of Warmia Marcin Kromer).[31] In the seventeenth century, manuscripts of collections of letters were very popular among all social groups which need to write letters (especially the nobility, the clergy, and town dwellers).[32]

Since the main genres of text in late medieval and early modern Vilnius had common roots in classical rhetoric and the *ars dictandi*, we can discuss texts such as last wills and contracts, just as for instance elegies, from a rhetorical point of view. The cognitive functions of contracts, last wills, and elegies may vary, but the same is not necessarily true for their social functions. It is certain, however, that these three types of texts could have been subject to similar procedures of creation, interpretation, and use.

29 *Ibid.*, pp. 16-17.

30 ROWELL, "Vilniaus pirklių partnerių tinklas XV a. viduryje. Šaltiniotyrinis aspektas", pp. 19-28; ORŁOWSKA, "Kontakty handlowe Gdańska i Wilna", pp. 59-91.

31 MS LVIA F1135, ap. 2, no. 24.

32 M. TRĘBSKA, "Oskarżenia i apologie w staropolskich wzorach korespondencji z synami marnotrawnymi i ich dyrektorami", in: *Epistolografia w dawnej Rzeczypospolitej, 5 (stulecia XVI-XIX): Nowa perspektywa historycznoliteracka*, ed. P. BOREK, and M. OLMA (Cracow, 2015), pp. 173-191.

Legal Contracts: Transactions and Donations

In premodern times writing contracts was a daily practice among the inhabitants of Vilnius. In this respect Vilnius did not differ from other European cities. However, we have to bear in mind that written contracts were made only in specific cases. We find them usually when somebody bought land or a building, merchants sold commodities wholesale, an artisan executed an expensive and complex work, a banker or usurer lent large sums of money, and, finally, when pious Christians donated expensive properties to the Church. When somebody bought for instance a horse, shoes, or a *libra* of paper, or had a book bound, he or she made only an oral agreement with a seller or artisan.

Written agreements probably came to Vilnius with its first German inhabitants. As we remember, in the fourteenth century the city consisted of two separate Christian settlements, the Ruthenian town[33] between present-day Pilies (Castle) Street and the Vilnia River, and the German town between present-day Vokiečių (German) Street and St. Nicolas' church.[34] We do not know anything about the use of documents in the Ruthenian town; supposedly Ruthenian law was used there.[35] The Germans, who came to Vilnius mainly from Riga and other Livonian towns,[36] certainly introduced writing into the organisation of their commerce. In the last decades of the fourteenth century, the earliest written sources confirm that they used different types of documents.[37] Magdeburg law, granted to Vilnius by the privilege of King Jogaila in 1387, required from its inhabitants, both German and Ruthenian, to use written agreements in many cases. The sources from the next decades inform us that the use of writing in financial matters was a standard procedure.

In the first half of the fifteenth century Vilnius merchants exported to Gdańsk and other places furs and wax and imported Flemish and English cloth and iron.[38] They had to draw up written contracts relative to trade, settlements,

[33] In his chronicle (1394), Wigand of Marburg mentioned the "*civitas Ruthenica*" under the year 1383, when the Ruthenian town was burnt down by the Teutonic Knights. See Wigand von Marburg, *Nowa kronika pruska*, ed. S. ZONENBERG, and K. KWIATKOWSKI (Toruń, 2017), pp. 500-504; SEMKOWICZ, "Hanul, namiestnik wileński", p. 4; J. OCHMAŃSKI, "Krzywy Gród wileński: Próba lokalizacji", in: ID., *Dawna Litwa*, pp. 89-90.

[34] OCHMAŃSKI, "Krzywy Gród wileński. Próba lokalizacji", p. 89.

[35] J. OCHMAŃSKI, "Ruskie wzory organizacyjne w państwie litewskim XIV-XV wieku", in: ID., *Dawna Litwa*, p. 76.

[36] SEMKOWICZ, "Hanul, namiestnik wileński", pp. 7-9.

[37] *Ibid.*, pp. 10-11.

[38] ORŁOWSKA, "Kontakty handlowe Gdańska i Wilna", p. 65.

and credit.[39] Valuable sources confirming the use of the written word in financial matters can be found in the episcopal archives. For example, on 16 July 1422 Martinus Wołoch and his wife Dorota donated a meadow to the Vilnius Franciscans. Witnesses were Petrus, a "*civis Vilnensis*", goldsmith Marcus, and Mr Laurinus.[40] And in 1440 this donation of the Muntholt family to the Vilnius Franciscans took effect.[41]

In the second half of the century, written contracts and donations grew in number. Documents became ever more widely used, which reflected social changes occurring in the Grand Duchy of Lithuania. During the fifteenth century, the number of people who were literate and used writing grew.[42] The Lithuanian *Metrica*, established in the 1440s, confirm this, as many private documents were put into its books. Mindaugas Klovas has established that the majority of private documents (contracts, donations, last wills) written in the Grand Duchy of Lithuania were issued in Vilnius: mainly in Latin but also in Ruthenian.[43] We have to bear in mind, however, that often documents issued in Vilnius belonged to the 'open' city: people came to Vilnius to have their documents written.

The growing demand for documents in Lithuania was probably one of the reasons why so many Vilnians studied at the University of Cracow at the time.[44] After returning to their home city they could get a good job in one of the offices located there. It was also a reason why so many Polish, Prussian, and Silesian professionals of the written word migrated to Lithuania in the fifteenth and sixteenth centuries. They were hired in institutions of the state (such as Adam Jakubowicz of Kotra) and of the urban settlements, for instance as the notaries of the Vilnius magistrate (such as Cyryl of Głubczyce).[45]

As all the registers of the city council and the aldermen's court were lost in 1655,[46] it is difficult to establish how many people had written contracts drawn up in Vilnius in the fifteenth century. Probably Vilnius, with a few other Lithuanian towns, was a leading centre of this kind of using documents.[47]

[39] *Ibid.*, pp. 74-77.

[40] *Kodeks dyplomatyczny diecezji wileńskiej*, 1, pp. 112-113.

[41] *Ibid.*, 1, p. 190.

[42] ГРУША, *Документальная письменность*, pp. 174-242.

[43] KLOVAS, *Privačių dokumentų atsiradimas ir raida*, p. 76.

[44] See Chapter 3.

[45] BARTOSZEWICZ, *Urban Literacy*, p. 276.

[46] See Chapter 2. See also *Zbiór praw i przywilejów*, p. 229-230; RAGAUSKAS, "1650 m. kovo 30 d. Vilniaus suolininkų teismo įrašų knygų aprašas", pp. 262, 264-265.

[47] Vilnius and Kaunas are the first Lithuanian towns in which city registers were introduced

There is a register in which some remnants of the former city archive have survived, containing as it does a few seventeenth-century copies of documents issued by the aldermen's court in the 1490s. The register was kept in Latin and contains transactions of the buying and selling of properties situated outside Vilnius by the city's inhabitants. The table of contents put at the beginning of this register reflects the character of these transactions:

> 1491
> Venditio agri in Antocole per honestum Hanko Macewicz domino Petro Aurifabro _ _ _ 1. Antokol
>
> 1492
> Id. Janko Maćkowicz curiam suam in Antocole eidem Dobro Petro Aurifabro vendit _ _ _ 1. Antokol
>
> 1495
> Venditio agri in Porudomina per Matheum Bucher provido Dyonisio Kuzmin _ _ _2. Porudomina
> Eodem
> Venditio agri Coryst dictum per famatum dominum Jachno Advocatus Vilnensi Provido Petro Janowicz seu Waznikowicz _ _ _ 2.
>
> Eodem
> Venditio agri Koncowicz dicti per Julianam Jarmołowa Famoso Andreae Demeszkowi _ _ _3.
>
> Eodem
> Venditio agri in Antocole per Lucam Jakowicz provido Joachimo Krolang _ _ _3. Antokol
>
> Eodem
> Venditio prati inter Montes per Petrum Tolsorykowicz Famoso domino Nicolao Deszczko _ _ _3.
>
> Eodem
> Ven[di]tio agri in Corusa per Elisabetham Łysznanka domino Petro Wazniakowicz _ _ _4. xx Korusa
>
> [...]

in the 1480s. See Груша, *Документальная письменность*, p. 281-282.

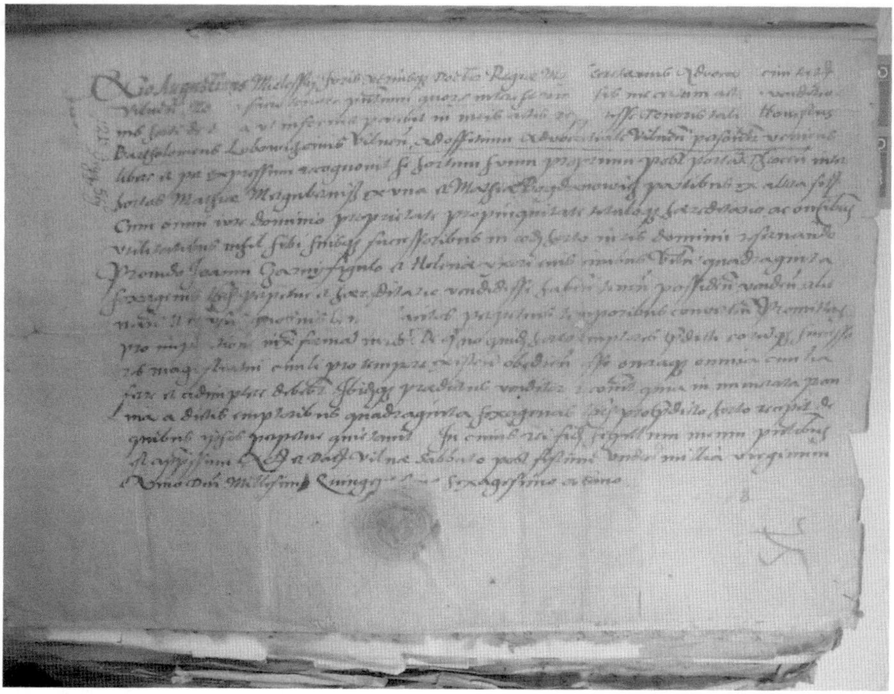

Fig. 40 Document of selling a garden confirmed by *Voigt* Augustyn Rotundus. MS Vilnius, LVIA, F22, ap. 1, nr 5333, f. 75r. Photo J. Niedźwiedź.

Eodem
Venditio villae Na Peczusy per famosum dominum Joannem Filipowicz Famoso Andreae Mikołajewicz____4. Peteszach[48]

We may suppose that the names listed in these documents represent the three main ethnic groups in Vilnius: Ruthenians (Julianna Jarmołowa), Poles (Elisabetha Łysznanka) and Germans (Matheus Bucher). This means that at the time the contracts were drawn up, the form of the Latin contract was well known to all ethnic groups in Vilnius. Later on we also encounter documents of seals in Ruthenian; however, the introductory and closing formulas in the aldermen's registers were in Latin. For instance, in 1565 Maria Ondreevna Ivanovicha Princess Izheritskaya, wife of Paweł Ostrowicki, the Vilnius land judge, confirmed a plenipotentiary and selling contract in Ruthenian.[49]

[48] LVIA F. 22, Ap. 1 b. 1, nr 5333, fol. 1.
[49] LVIA F22, Ap. 1 b. 1, nr 5333, fol. 58-63.

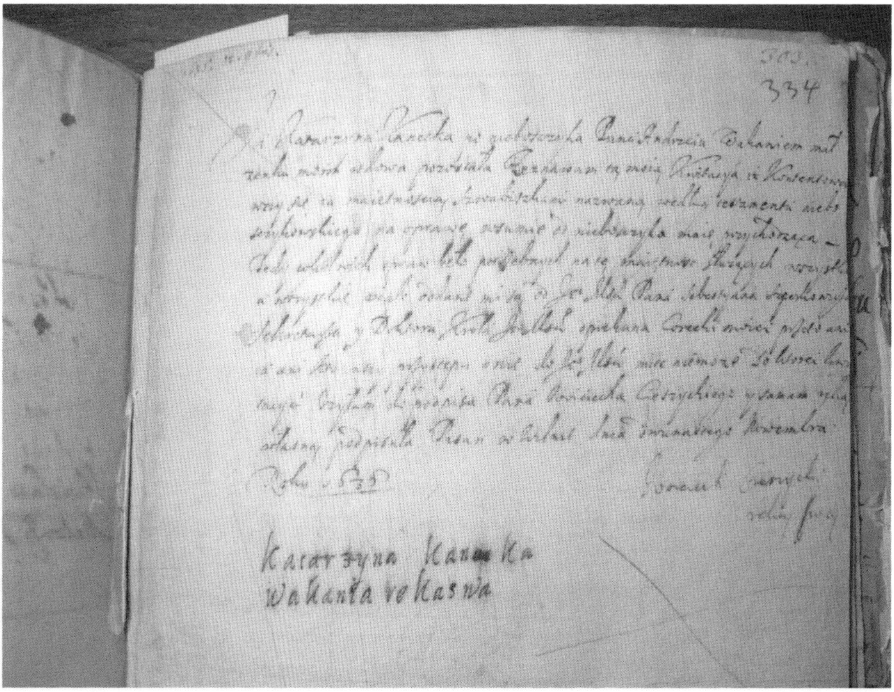

Fig. 41 Receipt in Polish, in which Katarzyna Kanecka Wakania renounces any money from a royal secretary and doctor Sebastian Szperkowicz, Vilnius, 12 November 1636. MS Vilnius, LVIA, F23, ap. 1, nr 5096, f. 334. Photo J. Niedźwiedź.

There is nothing unexpected in most of the contracts and donations: their structure, rhetoric, vocabulary, etc. did not differ from those written in other urban settlements in the Polish-Lithuanian state. Latin, Ruthenian, and, later, Polish contracts of selling and buying, lending money, donations, etc. were used in much the same way elsewhere. Vilnius was part of a pan-European economic community, which was based among other things on writing. In the sixteenth and seventeenth centuries, nobody treated these documents as literature. Different from letter writing, the ability to draw up contracts was by no means treated as an art. A contract should nevertheless be written properly, according to the required rules, or it could be questioned and considered invalid. Documents meant money and probably thousands of such documents circulated among the inhabitants of Vilnius in the sixteenth and seventeenth centuries. Some post-mortem inventories from the seventeenth century reveal that their possessors kept the agreements in their micro-scale home archives, that is in the chests which also were used to keep their money and financial registers.[50]

Usually the contracts or their authenticated copies were written on paper, but in case of particularly important agreements parchment was used, even in the late sixteenth and seventeenth centuries. For instance, on 7 June 1590, in Vilnius Piotr Stabrowski, the *ciwun* (a Samogitian official of the grand duke) of Wiekszwiany, sold his home in Vilnius called *Kamienica Wirszyłowska* to the Vilnius Protestant Reformed (Calvinist) community for 2000 *kopas* of Lithuanian *grosz*.[51] Since the document was validated in the Tribunal of the Grand Duchy of Lithuania, it was written in Ruthenian. The solemn copy (*wypis*) of the charter issued on 3 July 1590 was neatly calligraphed on parchment and beautifully decorated. It was sealed with the seal of the Tribunal and signed by twelve witnesses in Polish.

Early modern documents of special importance, like this one, used a centuries-old form, derived from that of medieval charters. Their sumptuous lettering and illuminations made them also beautiful objects of applied art. The illumination usually exceeded its decorative function, however. Decoration usually transmitted a complex message, which to some users was no less important than the contents of the text.[52] In the sixteenth and seventeenth centu-

[50] Certainly, many of the merchants and artisans kept their financial records of incomes and expenses, which was a common practice among the inhabitants of the European towns since the thirteenth century. In my research I did not find any such book from Vilnius, but the other sources confirm they existed. Only some financial records from early modern Vilnius survived; see LVIA F458, Ap. 1 b. 2. Some books of the expenses of royal court and the magnate courts, which operated in Vilnius, have survived, but these are another type of sources than the registers of the merchants. See the *Regestrum illustrissimi domini Alexandri magni Litvanie principis per manus magistri Erasmi sue celsitudinis secretarii transierunt*, 1494-1500, AGAD, Archiwum Skarbu Koronnego, MS 1/7/0/1/23 <https://www.szukajwarchiwach.gov.pl/jednostka/-/jednostka/17711133> (accesssed: 01.03.2022). See MS LVIA F23, ap. 1, no. 5096, ff. 441r-441v; *AVAK*, vol. 9, p. 483; *Wilnianie*, p. 194.

[51] MS LNMB F101-41. <http://pergamentai.mch.mii.lt/IstoriniaiLietDok/istoriniailietdok_5lt.pl.htm> (access: 15.02.2022). See R. DIRSYTĖ, "Kolekcja pergaminów ze zbiorów Litewskiej Biblioteki Narodowej im. Marynasa Mažvydasa", *Bibliotheca Nostra: Śląski Kwartalnik Naukowy* 41.3 (2015), p. 26; A. ROPA and E. ROPS, "The functions of illuminated charters from Latvian and Lithuanian archives in a European context", in: *Illuminierte Urkunden: Beiträge aus Diplomatik, Kunstgeschichte und Digital Humanities – Illuminated Charters: Essays from Diplomatic, Art History and Digital Humanities*, ed. G. BARTZ and M. GNEIß (Cologne, 2019), pp. 442-443.

[52] A good example are the ennoblement charters issued in the sixteenth and seventeenth centuries by the royal chancery, e.g. the ennoblement acts of Andrzej Czarnecki (Smolensk, 25 June 1611, CZART. MS 1063) or Jan Januszowski (Cracow, 24 January 1588, The National Muse-

ries, illuminated documents were associated with medieval traditions of making charters, but no less important was the context of early modern emblems. Certain charters, like the 1590 Vilnius contract, were situated in a borderland between pragmatic literacy and new types of literature, not defined by classicist poetics.

The Rhetoric and Use of Letters

Letters belong to the earliest examples of the use of writing in Vilnius. Probably some medieval epistolographic *formulae* were used in Vilnius as early as the fourteenth century. These formulas instructed authors how to write a letter. In the last decades of the fourteenth century, the German merchants in Vilnius corresponded with their business partners. For instance, in the 1380s Hanul, the aforementioned leader of the German community, wrote a letter to the councillors of Toruń in which he demanded that a certain Nicolas, a citizen of Toruń, pay his debt.[53] Some of the Catholic inhabitants of Vilnius had studied the arts of the *trivium* and possessed a basic knowledge of how to manage their correspondence. In this respect Vilnius was similar to other urban settlements of Poland, Prussia, and Livonia, where merchants conducted their businesses among other things by means of letters.[54] They usually wrote about money, legal matters, and sometimes they mentioned job applications or even gave culinary recipes.[55] Problems of travelling safely, losing money, thefts, robberies, frauds, the merchants being imprisoned, etc. were often handled by the chanceries of the late medieval towns. Municipal notaries had to know how to write different types of letters, and this is why in the urban chanceries epis-

um in Warsaw, MS 1793). See J. KILIAŃCZYK-ZIĘBA, "On the diploma of nobility of Jan Januszowski and a portrait of a renaissance printer", *Terminus: Special Issue* 1 (2019), pp. 81-105. For methodological issues of research on the decoration of different types of medieval charters, see: E. DANBURY, "The study of illuminated charters, past, present and future: Some thoughts from England", in: *Illuminierte Urkunden*, pp. 259-280. This study may be instructive also for research on the decoration of documents in early modern times.

[53] SEMKOWICZ, "Hanul, *namiestnik wileński*", p. 10-11.

[54] BARTOSZEWICZ, *Urban Literacy*, pp. 104-105.

[55] *Ibid.*, pp. 360-362.

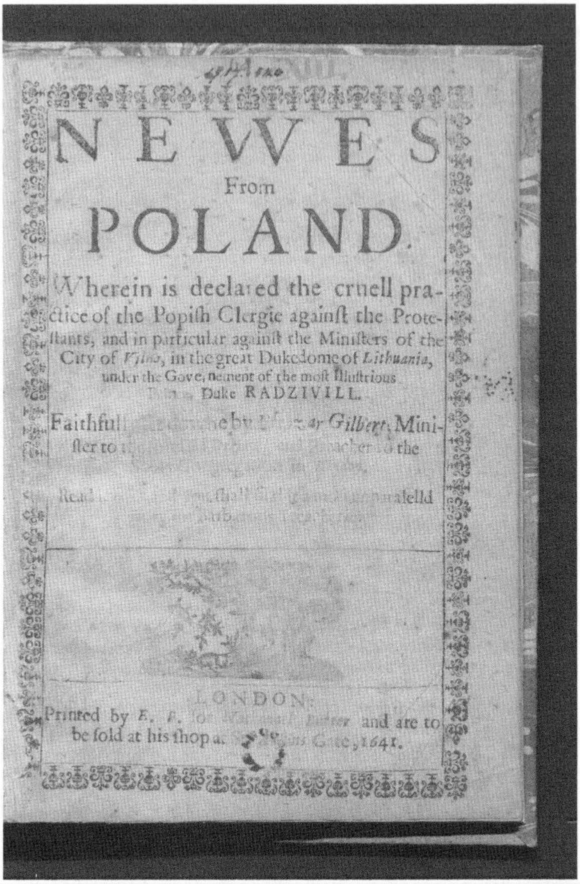

NEWES
From
POLAND.
Wherein is declared the cruell practice of the Popish Clergie against the Protestants, and in particular against the Ministers of the
City of Vilna, in the great Dukedome of Lithuania,
under the Governement of the most Illustrious
[illegible] Duke RADZIVILL.
Faithfull[illegible] by [illegible] Gilbert, Minister to [illegible] the
[illegible]
LONDON:
Printed by E. [illegible] and are to
be sold at his shop [illegible] Gate, 1641.

Fig. 42 Example of a text of the 'open' city and of spreading news in letters. An English paper informing about anti-Calvinist riots in Vilnius in 1640, based on letters sent from Vilnius by the Radziwiłłs (see Chapter 9): Eleazar Gilbert, *Newes from Poland, wherein is declared the cruell practice of the Popish clergie against the Protestants and in particular against the ministers of the city of Vilna* (London, 1641). MS Warsaw, BN <https://polona.pl/preview/437b35b6-e0d9-481a-bbf1-0f95c44abf03> (accessed: 31.05.2023; public domain).

tolographic *formulae* were used.[56] We do not have any letters actually issued by the Vilnius authorities in the fifteenth century, but judging from the textual practices of the chanceries of similar towns of the region[57] we can make an educated guess that Vilnius was not an exception.

In the sixteenth and seventeenth centuries, the urban authorities, that is the *Voigt*, the aldermen's court, the city council, and the mayors produced a great number of letters. They concerned not only the private businesses of particular merchants, but also matters concerning the whole urban community and its constituant parts, such as the guilds. To some degree the city authorities meddled in the politics of the State, for instance by sending representatives to the session of the Parliament in Warsaw.[58] This is why many sixteenth- and seventeenth-century letters produced by city notaries were sent to the king or other important Lithuanian and Polish politicians.

Due to its character as the capital city, Vilnius was an important space where information was exchanged by letter. As a centre of power, the city gained the function of a postal station, a place where information was exchanged, processed, and sent on.[59] On 18 October 1558 King Sigismund Augustus issued an ordinance which set up a regular postal service between Cracow and Venice.[60] There was already a network of connections between Cracow, Vilnius and other parts of the Polish-Lithuanian Commonwealth, but this was deemed insufficient for the needs of the king. Because of the growing status of Vilnius as a capital, on 11 July 1562 the royal chancery issued a new ordnance in Vilnius, which extended the regular postal service, which now was

[56] *Ibid.*, pp. 150, 354, 389. The formularies used in Vilnius in the fifteenth century may have been imported from Cracow, which was an influential place in formulae production at the time. See K. GÓRSKI, "Wstęp", in: *Formularz Jerzego*, pp. XVII-XIX.

[57] BARTOSZEWICZ, *Urban Literacy*, pp. 107-108.

[58] From 1569 Vilnius, as a capital city, had the privileges of the nobility (just as Cracow). This meant that its representatives could attend the sessions of the *Sejm* and take part in the election and coronation of the king. See BOGUCKA and SAMSONOWICZ, *Dzieje miast i mieszczaństwa*, pp. 322-323.

[59] J. PTAŚNIK, *Z dziejów kultury włoskiego Krakowa* (Cracow, 1906), pp. 43-44, 48.

[60] *Ordinatio postae Cracoviae Venetias... proficitur*, AGAD, Metryka Koronna MS 91, ff. 402v.-403v. <http://agadd2.home.net.pl/metrykalia/MK/0091/> (access: 23.02.2022). See D. QUIRINI-POPŁAWSKA, "Sebastiano Montelupi, toscano, mercante e maestro della posta reale di Cracovia: Saggio sulle comunicazioni Polonia Italia nel '500", trans. M. OLSZAŃSKA and S. ESPOSITO, *Quaderni di Storia Postale* 13 (1989), pp. 43, 45.

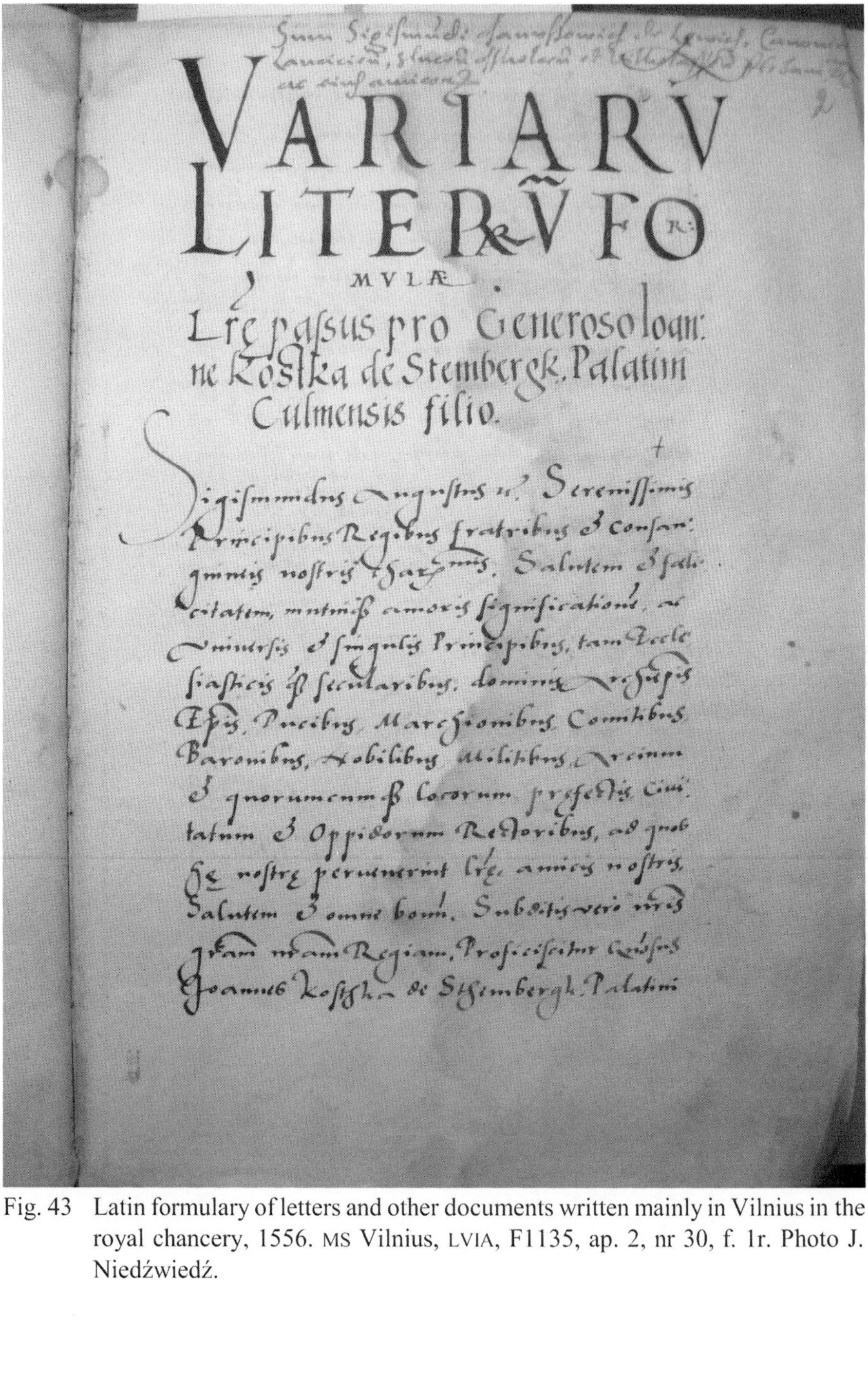

Fig. 43 Latin formulary of letters and other documents written mainly in Vilnius in the royal chancery, 1556. MS Vilnius, LVIA, F1135, ap. 2, nr 30, f. 1r. Photo J. Niedźwiedź.

to connect Vilnius with Cracow, Vienna, and Venice.[61] The first operator of the extended postal service was Cristoforo de Taxis. Couriers were to cover the distance between Venice and Cracow in ten days, and when the court stayed in Vilnius, they were to reach that city within a further five days.[62] Since this solution did not work and the postal service to Vilnius did not work well, a new operator was appointed in 1564, Pietro Maffon of Brescia.[63] Finally, in 1568, the service was put into the hands of Sebastiano de Montelupi, a Florentine nobleman, Cracow merchant, and banker.[64] The Montelupi family ran the postal services for almost a century.[65]

Sometimes, for instance during war, postal transport took even less time than was required by the norms of the royal privileges. The Livonian War of 1579-1582 provides an interesting example of the intermediary function of Vilnius as a conduit for huge amounts of information.[66] On 30 August 1579 King Stephen Báthory recaptured Polatsk from the Moscovites. At that time, the Bishop of Włocławek, one of king's diplomats, was staying in Vilnius. In a letter to Marcin Kromer, written probably between 11 and 18 September, the bishop stated that he was sending Kromer a copy of the king's edict.[67] This was a Latin narration about the siege written by a royal secretary and printed in the Polish camp in Polatsk just after the town was taken. This means that the letters and the printed report of the success of Báthory's troops reached Rozdrażewski within a week. The bishop immediately forwarded the 'edict' further south and west. Within a couple of months the edict was reprinted in Warsaw (1579), Cologne (1580, twice), Prague (in a Czech translation, 1580), and London (in an English translation), and in 1579 it reached Vienna, Venice, and Rome (where was translated into Italian and was printed in 1582).[68]

[61] *Constitutio postae cursusque publici*, AGAD, Metryka Koronna MS 96, ff. 32r.-34r. <http://agadd2.home.net.pl/metrykalia/MK/0096/> (accessed: 23.02.2022). See K.J. PIOTROWSKI, *Studia nad dziejami poczt w Polsce XVI-XVIII w.* (Łódź, 1962), pp. 23-27 <http://hdl.handle.net/11089/17158> (accessed: 27.02.2022); QUIRINI-POPŁAWSKA, "Sebastiano Montelupi", pp. 44-46.

[62] *Ibid.*, p. 46.

[63] PIOTROWSKI, *Studia nad dziejami poczt*, p. 27.

[64] *Ibid.*, p. 29; QUIRINI-POPŁAWSKA, "Sebastiano Montelupi", p. 46.

[65] PIOTROWSKI, *Studia nad dziejami poczt*, p. 79.

[66] J. NIEDŹWIEDŹ, "Polska szesnastowieczna propaganda wojenna w działaniu: przypadek Atlasu Księstwa Połockiego (1580)", *Terminus* 19.2 (2017), p. 480.

[67] See *Korespondencja Hieronima Rozrażewskiego*, 1, *1567-2 VII 1582*, ed. P. CZEPLEWSKI (Toruń, 1937), p. 297 (item 227); NIEDŹWIEDŹ, "Polska szesnastowieczna propaganda wojenna", p. 480.

[68] *Ibid.*, pp. 490-492.

The exchange of information between north and south was not only important for politics and the economy, but also for cultural exchange in general. Literary texts also moved along this route, and through their circulation reading tastes were shaped.

In the development of fifteenth- and sixteenth-century epistolography a significant role was played by the royal and ducal chanceries, especially that of Duke Vytautas (although most of his letters were sent from his residences in Trakai[69] and from other places in the Grand Duchy of Lithuania), and, later, the scribal offices of Grand Duke Švitrigaila, King Alexander I Jagiellon,[70] and Sigismund II Augustus. The Vilnius cathedral chapter also played a role. One of the main tasks of chancery clerks and secretaries was to conduct correspondence, mainly in Latin, and from the sixteenth century in Polish as well (although some letters were written in Ruthenian and, less frequently, in other languages). Epistolographic *formulae*, so popular at the turn of the fifteenth and sixteenth centuries, either printed or in manuscript,[71] were helpful in this respect. In the Library of Vilnius University a volume including several manuals of epistolography from this time has survived. They had been mostly printed in Central Europe, for instance by Paulus Niavis and Jan Sommerfeld (Aesticampianus) the Elder. It is hard to say when this collection arrived in Vilnius, but it is quite possible that this happened already in the first half of the sixteenth century. A manuscript collection of models of letters under the title *Variarum litterarum formulae*, containing several hundred letters in Latin and one letter in Polish,[72] was put together in the royal chancery in Vilnius in the

[69] Trakai (Polish: Troki) is a town *c.* 25 km west of Vilnius. It was the capital of the Trakai voivodeship and in the Middle Ages one of the main residences of the grand dukes of Lithuania.

[70] *Codex epistolaris Vitoldi magni ducis Lithuaniae 1376-1430*, ed. A. PROCHASKA (Cracow, 1882); *Monumenta Medii Aevi Historica res gestas Poloniae illustrantia*, 2, *Codex epistolaris saeculi decimi quinti 1384-1492*, ed. A. SOKOŁOWSKI and J. SZUJSKI (Cracow, 1876), pp. 76-77; *Akta Aleksandra króla polskiego*. Many of Alexander's Latin letters were written in Vilnius, as the ruler often stayed in the capital.

[71] E.J. POLAK, *Medieval and Renaissance Letter Treatises and Form Letters*, 1, *A Census of Manuscripts Found in Eastern Europe and the Former USSR* (Leiden, 1993); KOROLKO, *Seminarium*, p. 121.

[72] The addressee of the only Polish letter was the Queen of Hungary, Isabella Jagiellon (1519-1559); it was written in Vilnius on 26 December 1557. See MS LVIA F1135, ap. 2, no. 30, f. 166r-167v. Sigismund Augustus and his sisters Isabella, Sophia, Anna, and Catherine exchanged their correspondence in Polish and sometimes in Italian. On the Italian letters of Isabella Jagiellon, see M.F. MOLNÁR, "Isabella and her Italian connections", in: *Isabella Jagiellon, Queen of Hungary (1539-1559): Studies*, ed. Á. MÁTÉ and T. OBORNI (Budapest, 2020), pp. 168-169.

1550s.[73] It contained copies of authentic letters written on behalf of Sigismund II Augustus, mostly concerning public matters. The volume opens with a document called *salvus conductus* (safe conduct) issued in Vilnius on 26 December 1552 for the Chełm *voivode* Jan Kostka, who was going to study in Germany.[74]

Being able to conduct a correspondence opened the doors to a career for graduates of universities and later also of the humanist *gymnasia* or even of parish schools, as we conclude from the analysis of the biographies of many Lithuanian and Polish humanists. Writing letters was not a simple matter: the collections of model letters mentioned above show how extensive this area was.

The construction of the late medieval letters produced by the monarchic chanceries residing in Vilnius was similar in their scheme to that of charters. Letters followed the rules of the medieval *ars epistolandi*.[75] The medieval letter had a fixed structure, which consisted of five parts.[76] At the beginning of the letter, there was often a superscription, followed by a salutation (*salutatio*) or a courteous form of address with *captatio benevolentiae* formulas (requesting the addressee's kindness), which replaced the notification present in other documents. The second part was the *exordium*. It was followed by the content of the letter: the *narratio* and *petitio*. The letter ended with a *conclusio* and sometimes with *ad relationem* formulas.[77] The humanist letter largely inherited the medieval epistolographic forms, but it was enriched by rhetoric and styles derived from Roman epistolography.[78]

[73] The only provenance note from the sixteenth century that has survived states that the book belonged to Zygmunt Januszowicz from Łowicz, a canon of Łęczyca and, among others, the parson of Slutsk "*ac eius amicorum*". MS LVIA F1135, ap. 2, no. 30, f. 2r.

[74] MS LVIA F1135, ap. 2, no. 30, f. 2r-3r.

[75] C.B. FAULHABER, "The letter-writer's rhetoric: The *summa dictaminis* of Guido Faba", in: *Medieval Eloquence: Studies in the Theory and Practice of Medieval Rhetoric*, ed. J.J. MURPHY (Berkeley, Los Angeles, and London, 1978) , p. 86; P. CAMMAROSANO, "L'éloquence laïque dans l'Italie communale (fin du XIIe-XIVe siècle)", *Bibliothèque de l'école des chartes*, 158.2 (2000), pp. 435-436; T. MICHAŁOWSKA, "Epistola", in: EAD., *Literatura polskiego średniowiecza* (Warsaw, 2011), pp. 227-230; M. CAMARGO, "Epistolary declamation: Performing model letters in medieval English classrooms", *Huntington Library Quarterly* 79.3 (2016), pp. 348-351.

[76] MURPHY, *Rhetoric in the Middle Ages*, pp. 222-226, 228-236.

[77] MICHAŁOWSKA, "Epistola", p. 228; SUŁKOWSKA-KURASIOWA, *Dokumenty królewskie i ich funkcja*, pp. 57-58.

[78] From the second half of the fourteenth century early humanists tried to imitate the literary forms of Roman epistolography (see Petrarch, *Epistulae familiares*). In the next century the modified models of rhetoric and epistolography was introduced by Italian writers. See M. CAMARGO, *Ars Dictaminis, Ars Dictandi* (Turnhout, 1991), p. 49; P. MACK, "Humanist rhetoric and dialectic", in: *The Cambridge Companion to Renaissance Humanism*, ed. J. KRAYE (Cambridge, 2010),

Vilnius letters did not differ in their rhetoric from the letters written throughout Europe from the end of the fifteenth century. They contain a salutation, exposition (*narration*), petition, and complimentary formulas. See, for instance, a letter in which the Vilnius city council assure a Calvinist prince and *voivode* of Vilnius, Krzysztof II Radziwiłł that they had done everything in their power to prevent anti-Calvinist riots:

> [*salutatio:*] Your Grace!
>
> [*captatio benevolentiae:*] We extend our great thanks for Your Grace's warning, [*narratio:*] since due to our duty and official oath we often admonish and encourage the commonalty to remain calm and to let us know about any wanton ideas they should hear of. But by God's grace we have not heard to date of anything Your Grace wrote to us about. The mayor, elected annually, visited the [Jesuit] Collegium and talked with its authorities. They confirmed that they did not know anything about the plans [of students supposedly preparing the riot]. Still, they take care so that no actions infringe their honour or the honour of their students. [*petitio:*] We remain at the disposal of Your Grace, our Graceful Lord. Written in Vilnius on 5 September 1619.
>
> [*complimentary clauses:*] The humble servants of Your Majesty and our Merciful Lord,
>
> Burghers and Councillors of
> the Royal City of
> Vilnius.[79]

The skill of composing letters required not only a general knowledge of the scheme, however, but also the ability to apply it to various genres of epistolography. At the beginning of the sixteenth century, textbooks on epistolography listed at least a dozen letter types, for instance the *epistola salutatoria*, the

p. 84; P. FINDLEN, "Introduction: With a letter in hand-writing, communication, and representation in Renaissance Italy", in: *The Renaissance of Letters: Knowledge and Community in Italy, 1300-1650*, ed. P. FINDLEN and S. SUTHERLAND (London and New York, 2020), pp. 1-20. In fifteenth-century Poland and Lithuania these new forms coexisted with the medieval *ars epistolandi*. Both forms can occur in letters of the same author sent to different recipients, e.g. in the correspondence of cardinal Zbigniew Oleśnicki (1389-1455). See J. NIEDŹWIEDŹ, "Zbigniew Oleśnicki i jego listy do humanistów", *Terminus* 1.1 (1999), pp. 188-189.

[79] MS LNMB F93-1691.

gratiarum actoria, and the *offensiva*.[80] This knowledge was based on the immense and rich tradition of medieval epistolography.[81] Many of the aforementioned genres were invented within the frame of the *ars dictandi* in the eleventh to fourteenth centuries.[82] Every student of the cathedral school in the fifteenth century and in St. John's parish school from the beginning of the sixteenth century who studied the programme of the *trivium* obtained the essential knowledge and skills needed to compose letters.[83]

There were in fact many more genres of letters, although not all of them were described at the time. Their variety is confirmed by the collection of model letters originating in the chancery of Sigismund II Augustus, mentioned before. A secretary had to be able to use all of them, adapting the rhetorics to the differing aims of the letters he had to write.

Humanist schooling in Vilnius placed special emphasis on teaching epistolography. At the Academy of Vilnius, students learned to write letters in Polish in the lower grammar classes by reading and interpreting letters of ancient authors, while the theory and practice of epistolography were mostly taught in the poetics class. Manuscript textbooks from the second half of the seventeenth century and the first half of the eighteenth century show how much time and effort was devoted to this issue. Letter genres were discussed because of their purpose and subject matter, as well as for their style. A large number of examples were also dictated, on which students then modelled their own letters.[84]

[80] J. URSINUS, *Modus epistolandi cum epistolis exemplaribus et orationibus annexis* (*O sposobie pisania listów wraz z wzorami listów i mowami*), ed. and trans. L. WINNICZUK (Wrocław, 1957), pp. 17-29.

[81] R. WITT, "Medieval 'ars dictaminis' and the beginnings of humanism: A new construction of the problem," *Renaissance Quarterly* 35.1 (1982), pp. 1-35.

[82] WITT, "*Ars dictaminis*: Victim of *ars notarie*?", pp. 361-362, 366-367; F. DELLE DONNE, "Dalle lettere cancelleresche ai dictamina: Processi di finzionalizzazione e tradizione testuale", in: *Medieval Letters Between Fiction and Document*, pp. 393-405; MICHAŁOWSKA, "Epistola", p. 231; EAD., "Epistola dedicatoria", in: EAD., *Literatura polskiego średniowiecza*, pp. 239-243; R. KÖHN, "Correspondence", in: *Brill's Encyclopedia of the Middle Ages* (2016) <http://dx-1doi-1org-1lk0ibnmn0110.hps.bj.uj.edu.pl/10.1163/2213-2139_bema_SIM_033808> (accessed: 27.02.2022).

[83] MACK, "Humanist rhetoric and dialectic", p. 91.

[84] E.g. *Quincunx rhetoricus in libros quattuor ad Caium Herennium, Marci Tulii Ciceronis, Aristotelis, Quintiliani et aliorum doctrinis illustratus*, MS MAB F41-612, f. 96r; *Tyrocinium eloquentiae*, MS VUB F3-1067, f. 39r; [*Rhetorica*], MS VUB F3-2199, f. 7v; *Regni rhetorici leges*, MS VUB F3-1067, f. 214r; *De legibus Tullianae Reipublicae Heliconium consilium concernentibus*, MS VUB F3-1375, f. 23r; [*Rhetorica*], MS VUB F3-1395, f. 2r; [*Rhetorica*], MS VUB F3-1427, f. 4v; [*Rhetorica*], MS MAB F264-1381, f. 112r.

Those who mastered the principles of this art could count on employment not only in the state chancery, but also at the courts, as well as in the scribal offices working for the members of the lay and ecclesiastical elite. Marcin Kromer, who wrote in his *Polonia*, a description of Polish lands, about the tasks of the queen's secretary, stressing that "his duties include writing letters in the name of the queen, sealing them, reading letters addressed to the queen, and responding to them".[85] Thanks to such secretaries, in the sixteenth and seventeenth centuries ever more letters were written at the courts of bishops John of the Dukes of Lithuania and Paweł Holszański, as well as at the chanceries of the Gasztołd, Radziwiłł, Sanguszko, and Sapieha families.[86]

High literary competence is visible, for instance, in a letter dated 7 July 1531 in Vilnius. The *voivode* of Vilnius and Lithuanian chancellor Olbracht Gasztołd (Albertas Goštautas) asked Mikołaj Nipszyc, the royal secretary, to send a marten-skin coat and 100 *złoty* to Ioannes Dantiscus (Jan Dantyszek), who received from the emperor the title of count for Gasztołd (Nipszyc himself received a gift in the form of two lynx skins).[87] The author of the letter, the chancellor's secretary, demonstrated not only his knowledge of the epistolary art, but also his skills in using written Polish. Although from the beginning of the fifteenth century the Polish language was mainly standardised[88] and was commonly used in writing (in law, administration, religious texts, poetry, etc.),[89] it was still more problematic to use than Latin. The problem was spelling, punctuation, and a lack of vocabulary in some areas. This situation was changing only over the first half of the sixteenth century.[90]

In the first three decades of the sixteenth century, the Polish language began to play an increasingly important role in the royal chancery, among other

[85] KROMER, *Polonia*, p. 147. See also: TYGIELSKI, *Listy, ludzie, władza*, p. 25-33.

[86] Mariola Jarczykowa in her valuable study about carrying correspondence by Piotr Kochlewski († 1646), a secretary of Prince Krzysztof II Radziwiłł, showed deep insights into this activity in the first half of the seventeenth century. See JARCZYKOWA, *"Papierowe materie"*, pp. 18-20, 92-140.

[87] *Listy polskie XVI wieku: Listy z lat 1525-1548 ze zbiorów Władysława Pociechy, Witolda Taszyckiego i Adama Turasiewicza*, 1, ed. K. RYMUT (Cracow, 1998), p. 15.

[88] S. URBAŃCZYK, "W sprawie polskiego języka literackiego", in: ID., *Prace z dziejów języka polskiego* (Wrocław, 1979), pp. 169-170, 185.

[89] On the heyday of the Polish medieval literature in the fifteenth and the first decades of the sixteenth centuries, see T. MICHAŁOWSKA, *Średniowiecze* (Warsaw, 1995), pp. 329-657, and M. WŁODARSKI, "Wstęp", in: *Polska poezja świecka XV wieku*, ed. M. WŁODARSKI (Wrocław, 1997), pp. I-CXVIII.

[90] Z. KLEMENSIEWICZ, *Historia języka polskiego* (Warsaw, 1976), pp. 216, 219, 243-244, 251-261.

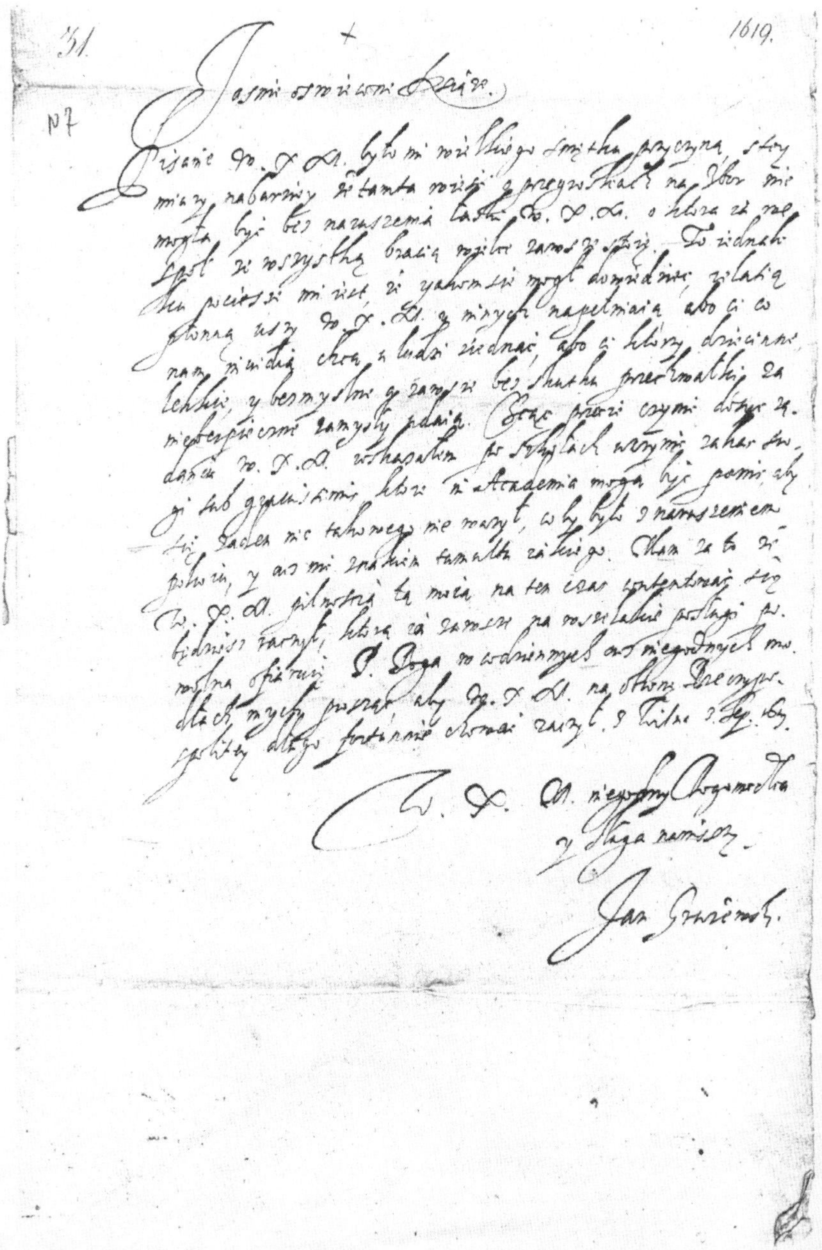

Fig. 44 Letter of the rector of the Academy of Vilnius, Jan Grużewski, to Prince Krzysztof II Radziwiłł, Vilnius, 3 September 1619. MS Vilnius, LNMB, F93-1690, f. 1. Reproduced with the permission of the LNMB.

things as a complementary language of epistolography.[91] The same process is clearly visible in the towns and manor houses in Poland and Lithuania, where Polish became ever more widespread in documents.[92] In the chanceries of the magnates, Polish gradually became the main domestic language, while in international affairs Latin still dominated. This process can be seen in the 1540s, for instance in the correspondence among members of the Radziwiłł family, especially Mikołaj 'the Black', Mikołaj 'the Red', and his sister Queen Barbara. These magnates and Sigismund II Augustus might have exchanged letters in Latin or Ruthenian, but they chose Polish as a more direct and convenient language of contact. Queen Barbara Radziwiłłówna did not know Latin, so the king or his secretary sent her letters in Polish and she answered in the same language, usually helped by her personal secretary Stanisław Koszutski.[93]

Letters written in Vilnius were usually of a political, administrative, or economic nature. Modern, centralised management, introduced gradually in Lithuania in the first half of the sixteenth century thanks to Queen Bona Sforza, who possessed significant properties in Lithuania, required efficient bookkeeping and reporting. In the archives of the Radziwiłł family hundreds of letters from the sixteenth and seventeenth centuries regarding the administration of their lands have survived. Their authors either wrote them in Vilnius, sent them to Vilnius, or mentioned Radziwiłł's dealings in the city. For example, in his letter from 17 August 1626 Olbrycht Karmanowski (*c.* 1580-after 1635), a client of Prince Krzysztof II Radziwiłł, informed his patron about economic matters of the village Jašiūnai (Jaszuny): the revision of the property, a delimitation between the property of the prince and the Jesuits, the buying out of pledged peasants, a funeral in Vilnius, and the building of a wood tar

[91] B. KACZMARCZYK, *Język polski w kancelarii królewskiej w pierwszej połowie XVI wieku* (Wrocław, 2003), pp. 47-48.

[92] In the Grand Duchy of Lithuania, until the end of the fifteenth century the main languages of private documents were Latin and Ruthenian. However, in the first decades of the sixteenth century Polish was introduced. See KLOVAS, *Privačių dokumentų atsiradimas ir raida*, pp. 320-322. In the seventeenth century, Polish became the main language of private documents. At the turn of the seventeenth and eighteenth centuries Ruthenian was almost entirely supplanted by Polish.

[93] See Chapter 4. See also PRZEŹDZIECKI, *Jagiellonki polskie w XVI wieku*, 1, pp. 301-344; *Listy polskie XVI wieku: Listy z lat 1525-1548*, pp. 90-3, 431-434, 442-443, 453-459, 490-491; RAGAUSKIENĖ and RAGAUSKAS, *Barboros Radvilaitės laiškai*, pp. 137-145; BORKOWSKA, *Dynastia Jagiellonów*, p. 196.

furnace.[94] Karmanowski wrote that he sent the message through a Tartar, probably a servant of the prince.[95]

From the end of the sixteenth century, the most expanded use of letters as tools of communication, especially on the international level, was associated not with chanceries of the monarchs and local politicians, but rather with the Jesuits. All institutions of the Lithuanian province of the Society of Jesus, to begin with the Academy of Vilnius, functioned on the basis of an ongoing circulation of correspondence. The Archivum Romanum Societatis Iesu stores a large number of letters and other documents sent to its headquarters by the provincials, rectors, professors, and other members of the society who resided in Vilnius. They concern all aspects of the functioning of the Vilnius Jesuit institutions.

Under these circumstances, it is difficult to talk about wholly private letters written in Vilnius. Since ancient times, letters were divided into public (*littere publicae*) and private (*litterae privatae*),[96] and this division was maintained by the medieval *ars dictandi* and Renaissance rhetoric. There were several conditions which decided about letters' privacy: they were considered private when they had quite a narrow group of addressees, non-public content, and by their style. Sometimes the authors of letters, especially of political ones, tried to hide sensitive information in their correspondence.[97] Information put in a private letter, however, was private only to a certain degree, and a written letter was almost always considered to belong to the public sphere. Research on the correspondence of the Lithuanian magnates and their clients in the first half of the seventeenth century confirms this.[98] Private letters were read by outsiders, were copied, and were sometimes stolen and used in a political struggle.[99]

We know of only a few examples of 'private' correspondence from Vilnius from the period before the mid-seventeenth century. At best, a couple of letters containing information on private matters could be enumerated, such as

[94] O. KARMANOWSKI, *Wiersze i listy*, ed. R. GRZEŚKOWIAK (Warsaw, 2010), pp. 77-78.

[95] *Ibid.*, p. 78.

[96] This division was presented by Cicero in his *Epistulae ad familiares* (II 4.1). See M.T. Cicero, *The Letters to His Friends*, trans. W.G. Williams, 1 (London and Cambridge, Mass., 1928), pp. 100-103.

[97] JARCZYKOWA, *"Papierowe materie" Piotra Kochlewskiego*, pp. 109-116.

[98] M. JARCZYKOWA, "Listy z XVI i XVII wieku w obiegu czytelniczym", in: EAD., *Korespondencja i literatura okolicznościowa w kręgu magnaterii Wielkiego Księstwa Litewskiego* (Katowice, 2019), pp. 34, 39-40.

[99] *Ibid.*, pp. 35-49.

the letters of Queen Barbara Radziwiłłówna to King Sigismund Augustus.[100] However, as was shown there, these letters were scrutinised by the queen's brother, Mikołaj Radziwiłł 'the Red', and other people.

The most personal letters would probably be those exchanged between humanists, but their personal nature was determined by their individual style rather than by their subject matter. Nevertheless, the humanist letter quite often took the form of the literary letter, which belonged to the epideictic genre (*epistola generis demonstrativi*), such as the letter addressed to Prince Janusz Radziwiłł by the Jesuit lecturer Maciej Kazimierz Sarbiewski:

> In my school, I am raising for you ninety noble young men, all in the prime of their lives, all Arcadians, some of whom will in the future serve your pen, and others your sword. If not at school now, you will one day be a speaker in court and a commander in array for them. Keep well, my friend, the comfort of your Father, the jewel of your homeland, and the gem of the Radziwiłłs, and read this letter, which I wrote and sent at the request of His Grace, your Father. In Vilnius, on the first of November, 1627.[101] (original in Polish)

Even letters exchanged between friends and acquaintances which concerned rather intimate matters bore the clear imprint of rhetorical formalities. The letters of Sarbiewski to his friend the bishop of Płock, Stanisław Łubieński, may serve as an example of this tendency.[102] The letter shows the requested structure, but all kinds of formulas and its restrained character, almost a kind of self-censorship, result from the fact that each letter could be used as a text distributed among a wider audience. One may assume that in the period under discussion, in Vilnius all texts, including letters, belonged, at least potentially, to the public sphere. The double foil of creating texts (making direct contact and showing self-restraint) can be seen both in Halszka Milewska's letter to abbess Kuczkowska of March 1627,[103] on women's participation in written culture, as well as in Adam Talwosz's letter to Paweł Pogorzelski, a preacher of the Vilnius Calvinist congregation, in which he warned his colleague that the Jesuit students planned an attack on the Calvinist church in Vilnius:

[100] Discussed in Chapter 4.

[101] *Kopie listów jezuity Sarbiewskiego oraz księcia Janusza Radziwiłła (1612-1655)*, ed. M. Jarczykowa and trans. A. Golik-Prus, *Terminus* 12.1 (2010), p. 238.

[102] *Korespondencja Macieja Kazimierza Sarbiewskiego ze Stanisławem Łubieńskim*, ed. and trans. J. Starnawski (Warsaw, 1986); J. Starnawski, "O korespondencji poety z biskupem Stanisławem Łubieńskim", in: id., *W świecie barokowym* (Łódź, 1992), pp. 24-30.

[103] Quoted in Chapter 4.

My Dear Mr Preacher!

Shortly before my departure yesterday, one *adversae religionis homo* [a person of the opposite faith] told me that he heard from students who were discussing when they could effectuate their idea to attack the church [*zbór*], *conclusum inter illos* [decided among them] that they wish to do so upon their arrival from Trakai on the 7 *die Septembris* [of September]. I did not have time to see you because it was too late, but I immediately went to the gracious Mr Treasurer and I told him about that, asking that *tanquam senator, prospiciat securitati* [as a senator he would see to precautions]; he promised today to talk both with the suffragan and with the rector, and seriously exhort the students not to burn down the church. He also added that there are *decreta scientia*, according to which His Grace the bishop, when departing, severely forbade them not to do anything that would cause a commotion. Furthermore, he said as well that he had declared to the *voivode* of Vilnius that he would not respect any of those who start a tumult, but even though the bishop and the *voivode* forbid the students severely from pursuing any such actions, one should not rely solely on their words, and on the appointed day we should be more vigilant so that the church was closed and that the inhabitants of the Protestant quarter do not walk in the streets. Please be so kind as to show this letter of mine to those concerned. I wanted to write this to the suffragan but I do not know where he left Vilnius for; if I knew where to send the letter, I would write to him; if he returns to Vilnius, please let me know. Asking the Lord to be the defender of his faithful and to bring to naught the perverse plans [of the perpetrators], I crave your grace and pious prayer.

Datum in Rykantai *die 29 Augusti anno 1619*
Always supporting you and
in everything ready to serve you
Adam Talwosz
with my own hand[104] (original in Polish)

From the second half of the sixteenth century onwards, several dozen institutions were active in the city, such as courts, state and municipal offices, and religious institutions, which maintained an abundant correspondence in Latin, Polish, Ruthenian, and German, and probably also in Hebrew and Yiddish. Letters were of considerable importance for the functioning not only of the administration, but also for the economy of the city and the State, and therefore significant amounts of money were spent on sending them. In the records of the expenses of the Vilnius chapter, the administrator noted in 1579: "to His Grace

[104] MS LNMB F93-1689.

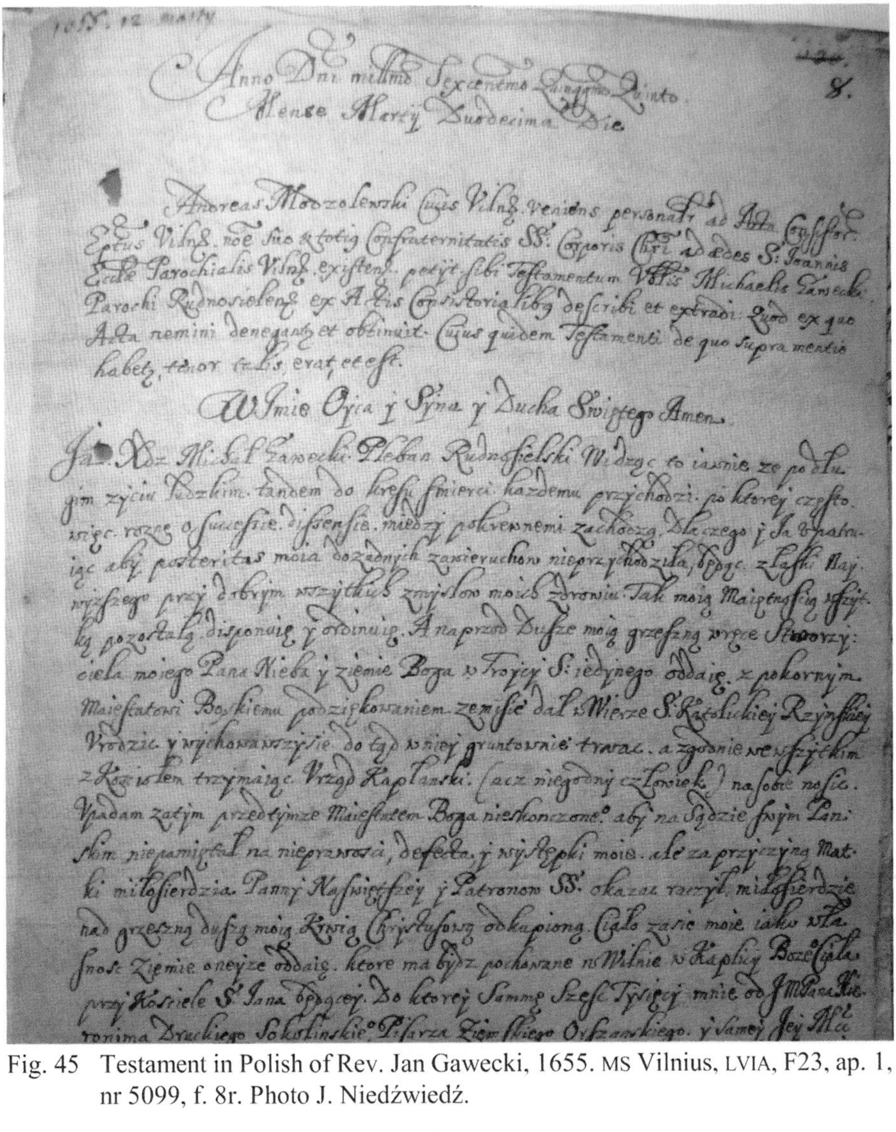
Anno Dni millmo Sexcentmo Quinquagmo Quinto Mense Marty Duodecima Die

W Imie Oyca y Syna y Ducha Swietego Amen.

Fig. 45 Testament in Polish of Rev. Jan Gawecki, 1655. MS Vilnius, LVIA, F23, ap. 1, nr 5099, f. 8r. Photo J. Niedźwiedź.

Father Suchodolski for the expedition of the Viciebsk letters from the chancery in Warsaw, by order of Their Graces I gave 10 thalers, that is 40 *kopa* 40 *grosz*".[105]

[105] *Regestr kapituły za rok 1579 i za rok 1580*, MS MAB F43-452, f. 20v.

This mass production of letters sent from and to Vilnius made it an 'open' city, involving it in a much wider circulation of the written word. Letters functioned in a way slightly similar to the books and documentation discussed earlier. Although the functions of documents, books, and letters were different, it is possible to point out their common features. One of them is their intensified production and exchange, as well as their preservation in archives and libraries. Even more important is the fact that all these types of text were based on a similar internal arrangement, which assumed the use of a common structure, topoi, and style, which are part of the ways of looking at and interpreting the world shared by many of the sixteenth- and seventeenth-century inhabitants of Vilnius. This facilitated their navigation through the world of the various texts that belonged to the same rhetorical system.

The Rhetoric of a Private Document: The Will

The making of a last will and testament became a widely spread practice in Vilnius only in the second half of the fifteenth century, although the oldest known Vilnius testaments had already been written by the end of the fourteenth century. We know one of them. On 27 October 1398 a certain Nicolas of Cracow wrote and signed the last will of the bishop of Vilnius, Andrzej: "*Nicolaus Nicolai de Cracovia clericus publicus [...] manu propria scribens, signo*".[106] Nicolas of Cracow is the first known public notary of Vilnius. On the basis of this testament we can formulate a hypothesis regarding the last wills and possibly even the vast part of pragmatic literacy in fifteenth-century Vilnius. Starting from the location of the city, professionals of the written word from Cracow and other towns of the Kingdom of Poland settled in Vilnius and introduced new variants of the Latin *formulae*, which were common in Poland, in the city. Earlier on, Vilnius literacy had been influenced by Riga and maybe also by Prussia. Probably at the turn of the fourteenth and fifteenth centuries the 'Riga / Livonian' and 'Cracow / Polish' *formulae* and literary customs coexisted in the city for some time. Further investigation might shed some light on this problem. The main obstacle may prove to be an insufficient number of sources.

Most of the last wills from Vilnius we know date from the sixteenth and seventeenth centuries; however, what is left is only a fraction of the former

[106] *Kodeks dyplomatyczny diecezji wileńskiej*, pp. 54-59.

collections of the testaments. In the remnants of the municipal registers, only 38 last wills composed between 1546 and 1655 survive,[107] and only seven of them date from the sixteenth century.[108] The number of extant testaments can be increased by those which were put in other registers, however: the Lithuanian *Metrica*, the archives of the consistory, of the Vilnius chapter, and of the Calvinist and Lutheran churches. Some testaments whose originals are unknown today were printed in the nineteenth century. Probably *c.* 80 last wills written up to 1655 have survived, which may be less than 15% of their original number. We can estimate that only in the first half of the seventeenth century the inhabitants of Vilnius must have registered in the books of the aldermen's court no less than 500 last wills.[109] However, we can also make a comparison

[107] *Testamenty w księgach miejskich wileńskich*, pp. 17-28.

[108] We know about 1430 last wills from Cracow which were registered in the city books between 1307 and 1550. See *Katalog testamentów z krakowskich ksiąg miejskich do 1550 roku*, ed. J. Wysmułek (Warsaw, 2017). In the late Middle Ages, Cracow was bigger, had a much more developed municipal chancery, but the level of literacy of its inhabitants was by no means higher than of the Vilnians. However, if we take into account this disproportion, before 1550 in Vilnius there must have been written a couple of hundreds testaments. At that time the inhabitants of Polish, Transylvanian, Masovian, Prussian, and Upper-Hungarian towns towns of a similar size similar to Vilnius (or even smaller) ones, widely used the last wills. The number of existing documents varies from a dozen to a couple of hundreds. See J. Majorossy, "Archives of the dead: Administration of last wills in medieval Hungarian towns", in: *The Public (in) Urban Space: Papers from the Daily Life-Strand at the International Medieval Congress (Leeds, July 2003)*, ed. J. Rasson and G. Jaritz (Krems, 2003), pp. 21-27; *Das Pressburger Protocollum Testamentorum 1410 (1427)-1487*, ed. J. Majorossy and K. Szende, 1, *1410-1487*, and 2, *1467-1529* (Vienna, 2010-2014); *Testamenty mieszczan warszawskich od XV do końca XVII wieku: Katalog*, ed. A. Bartoszewicz, A. Karpiński, and K. Warda (Warsaw, 2017); M. Lupesku Makó, "Spoken and written words in testaments: Orality and literacy in last wills of medieval Transylvanian burghers", in: *Uses of the Written Word in Medieval Towns*, pp. 273-286; K. Justyniarska-Chojak, *Testamenty i inwentarze pośmiertne z ksiąg miejskich województwa sandomierskiego* (Kielce, 2010); Bartoszewicz, *Urban Literacy*, pp. 17-18, 193-196, 362-366; *Testamenty z ksiąg sądowych małych miast polskich do 1525 roku*, ed. A. Bartoszewicz, K. Mrozowski, M. Radomski, and K. Warda (Warsaw, 2017); R. Kubicki, *Testamenty elbląskie: Studium z dziejów miasta i jego mieszkańców w późnym średniowieczu* (Gdańsk and Sopot, 2020); M. Sumowski, "Duchowni w testamentach mieszczańskich: Mieszczanie w testamentach duchownych: Zapisy ostatniej woli jako źródła do badania powiązań (Prusy, XV-początek XVI wieku)", *Kwartalnik Historii Kultury Materialnej* 68.3 (2020), pp. 315-334.

[109] The catalogue of the last wills in the books of the Vilnius aldermen's court lists 248 testaments: 31 from the first half of the seventeenth century and 210 from the second half of the seventeenth century. The aldermen court books from 1661-1700 are rather complete, while the previous ones were almost entirely destroyed. However, it is likely that in the first half of the seventeenth century the number of the testaments was even higher than after the Muscovite invasion. It is estimated that after 1655 Vilnius lost at least 50% of its population which inevitably affected the text production (see

with other, similar-sized towns in the Kingdom of Poland, Poznań, Lublin, and Lviv, whose aldermen books are much better preserved than those from Vilnius. Between 1550 and 1655, in Poznań 1478 testaments were registered,[110] and in Lviv 1316.[111] In Lublin, between 1590 and 1655 the municipal books list 376 last wills and 200 post mortem inventories.[112] This means that in a similar period (1550-1655) in Vilnius there could have been written at least 500-1500 last wills and testaments. As far as we know, Vilnius did not keep special registers of testaments (*libri testamentorum*), like Cracow, Lviv, Poznań, Warsaw (Stara Warszawa) and other towns.[113]

The inhabitants of Vilnius knew well that a last will in written form was necessary, especially when there was a need to divide a large fortune after the death of its owner. There were hundreds of properties liable to be divided, so inheritances, sometimes very complicated, were plentiful. In 1639, Zuzanna Litaworówna Chreptowiczówna Aleksandrowa Połubińska expressed her desire to prevent problems with the division of her estate, pointing out that she was preparing a testament

> [...] in order to prevent any discords and dissension that might arise between my husband, or the Navahrudak *voivode*, my father, my brothers and other relatives after my death over my possessions, both chattels and property, which the supreme Lord gave me with his generous hand for my earthly journey, God save me, and hence I wish to leave concord and love and peace.[114] (original in Polish)

ŁOWMIAŃSKA, *Wilno przed najazdem moskiewskim*, p. 221). Taking into account a high level of pragmatic literacy in the city before the Muscovite occupation, we can cautiously estimate that in the first half of the seventeenth century no less than 500 last wills could be recorded in the aldermen's court books.

[110] *Katalog testamentów poznańskich z drugiej połowy XVI i z XVII wieku*, ed. A. KARPIŃSKI and U. AUGUSTYNIAK (Warsaw, 2017), pp. 19-299.

[111] *Testamenty mieszkańców lwowskich z drugiej połowy XVI i z XVII wieku: Katalog*, ed. O. WINNYCZENKO (Warsaw, 2017), pp. 19-245.

[112] A. WNUK, "Szlachta w testamentach i inwentarzach mieszczan lubelskich z końca XVI i pierwszej połowy XVII wieku", *Klio* 42.3 (2017), p. 131.

[113] WYSMUŁEK, *Testamenty mieszczan krakowskich*, pp. 107-112; BARTOSZEWICZ, *Urban Literacy*, pp. 215, 240; B. PETRYSZAK, "Sporządzanie testamentów we Lwowie w późnym średniowieczu – pisarze, ceny, okoliczności", *Kwartalnik Historii Kultury Materialnej* 62.3 (2014), p. 332; Z. GÓRSKI, "Organizacja kancelarii miejskiej Starej Warszawy i system pracy pisarzy miejskich", *Acta Universitatis Nicolai Copernici: Historia* 69.147 (1984), pp. 118-119, 121-122; I. GRZELCZAK-MIŁOŚ, *Mieszczaństwo poznańskie w świetle Libri testamentorum* (Poznań, 2011), pp. 47-49 <https://repozytorium.amu.edu.pl/handle/10593/990?mode=full> (accessed: 26.02. 2022).

[114] *Testament Zuzanny Chreptowiczówny Połubińskiej z 1639*; an excerpt from Vilnius

Last wills issued by the inhabitants of the city were subject to written law. In the Magdeburg law there were some regulations about making testaments.[115] These rules were translated into Polish and commented on by two sixteenth-century Polish jurists, Bartłomiej Groicki and Paweł Szczerbic.[116] In medieval and early modern Poland and Lithuania there were also other juridical regulations that decided about particularities of urban last wills and dispositions of a deceased person's property.[117] The first statutes regarding last wills were issued in the fourteenth century.[118] In the first half of the sixteenth century there occurred a wave of legal reforms in the Polish-Lithuanian monarchy. Among other things, new regulations related to the use of last wills appeared. For example, in 1530 King Sigismund the Old confirmed the new version of the relevant by-law (*wilkierz*) of Cracow.[119] In the case of Vilnius, the rules regarding testaments were discussed in the privileges of King Sigismund the Old from 1543[120] and in the Statute of the Grand Duchy of Lithuania from 1529 (as we remember, the authorities of some *jurydykas* used the Statute rather than the Magdeburg law).[121]

At the request of the city authorities, the legal frame of the testamentary practices of Vilnius inhabitants was regulated by King Sigismund I the Old in a privilege issued in Cracow on 18 January 1543. He ordered that all wills must be officially validated in the municipal registers according to the Magdeburg

municipal books, MS MAB F43-26666, f. 2r.

[115] M. MIKUŁA, *Municipal Magdeburg Law (Ius municipale Magdeburgense) in Late Medieval Poland: A Study on the Evolution and Adaptation of Law*, trans. A. BRANNY (Leiden and Boston, 2021), p. 180.

[116] B. GROICKI, *Tytuły prawa majdeburskiego*, ed. K. KORANYI (Warsaw, 1953), pp. 177-194; P. SZCZERBIC, *Ius municipale to jest prawo miejskie majdeburskie, nowo z łacińskiego i z niemieckiego na polski język z pilnością i wiernie przełożone*, ed. G.M. KOWALSKI (Cracow, 2011), pp. 214-217; ID., *Speculum Saxonum, albo prawo saskie i majdeburskie porządkiem obiecadła z łacińskich i niemieckich egzemplarzów zebrane, a na polski język z pilnością i wiernie przełożone*, 2, ed. G.M. KOWALSKI (Cracow, 2016), pp. 503-505.

[117] M. MIKUŁA, "Statuty prawa spadkowego w miastach polskich prawa magdeburskiego (do końca XVI wieku", *Z Dziejów Prawa* 7 (2015), p. 33; ID., "Tradycje prawne w regulacjach testamentowych w miastach Królestwa Polskiego XIV-XVI wieku: prawo sasko-magdeburskie, prawo kanoniczne i rzymskie oraz prawodawstwo lokalne", *Kwartalnik Historii Kultury Materialnej* 68.2 (2020), pp. 131-158.

[118] MIKUŁA, *Municipal Magdeburg Law*, pp. 180-181.

[119] WYROZUMSKA, *Kancelaria miasta Krakowa*, p. 91.

[120] *Zbiór praw i przywilejów*, pp. 75-76.

[121] The general rules of the last wills were present in all versions of the statute. A question of wills in non-privileged cities was regulated by the third *Statute of the Grand Duchy of Lithuania* from 1588; see *Statut*, p. 237, Chapter 8, art. 9.

law, except for those written down before the privilege had been granted. In accordance with previous common practice, wills were drawn up "in the presence of special persons, good people worthy of trust".[122]

The fees for registering testaments in the municipal books were fixed in the city statute in 1552:

How Much Should Be Paid for the Last Wills

> For each testament the *Voigt* should be given 15 *grosz*, the notary 12 and each alderman 6. If the *Voigt* sends the aldermen and the notary to make any other deeds, the *Voigt* will be given 6 *grosz*, the notary also 6 and each alderman 3.[123]

As we can see, the fees for making last wills were relatively high. On the other hand, the statute regulated the prices and prevented the authorities from inflating the fees and from other financial abuses. In the long run, the clear procedures and fixed fees facilitated more people to make their last wills in the office.

Vilnius wills, like all wills produced in the region, are valuable for being the only documents of their kind that allow the past to be interpreted from many perspectives.[124] On the one hand, they provide descriptions, sometimes very detailed, of the world of things left behind by the inhabitants of the city. They are testimonies to the mentality or *episteme* of the people who drafted them: their religious beliefs, the exercise of power by the authorities, legal issues, pious deeds, relationships within the families and with people outside it, self-fashioning, etc.[125] On the other hand, the testament was an important

[122] *Zbiór praw i przywilejów*, p. 75; *Собраніе древнихъ грамотъ и актов городовъ*, 1, pp. 77-78.

[123] *Zbiór praw i przywilejów*, p. 100.

[124] The various interpretations of medieval testaments in the East Central Europe are presented in the special issue of *Kwartalnik Historii Kultury Materialnej* 61.2 (2013).

[125] On the value of wills as a source for religious and cultural history, see the scholarly discussion presented by A. ADAMSKA, "Stąd do wieczności", pp. 185-200. See also: U. AUGUSTYNIAK, "Wizerunek Krzysztofa II Radziwiłła jako magnata-ewangelika w świetle jego testamentów", *Przegląd Historyczny* 81.3-4 (1990), pp. 461-477; L. KARALIUS, "Testamentai", in: *Lietuvos Didžiosios Kunigaikštijos kultūra: Tyrinėjimai ir vaizdai*, ed. V. ALIŠAUSKAS *et al.* (Vilnius, 2001), pp. 714-723; B. POPIOŁEK, *Woli mojej ostatniej testament ten ... Testamenty staropolskie jako źródło do historii mentalności XVII i XVIII wieku* (Cracow, 2009); L. TYMIAKIN, "Religijność siedemnastowiecznych przemyślan w świetle leksyki testamentowej" *Rocznik Przemyski* 42.3 (2006), pp. 95-112; FRICK, *Kith, Kin, and Neighbors*, pp. 359-364; *Тастаменты шляхты і мяшчан Беларусі другой паловы XVI ст. (з актавых кніг Нацыянальнага гістарычнага*

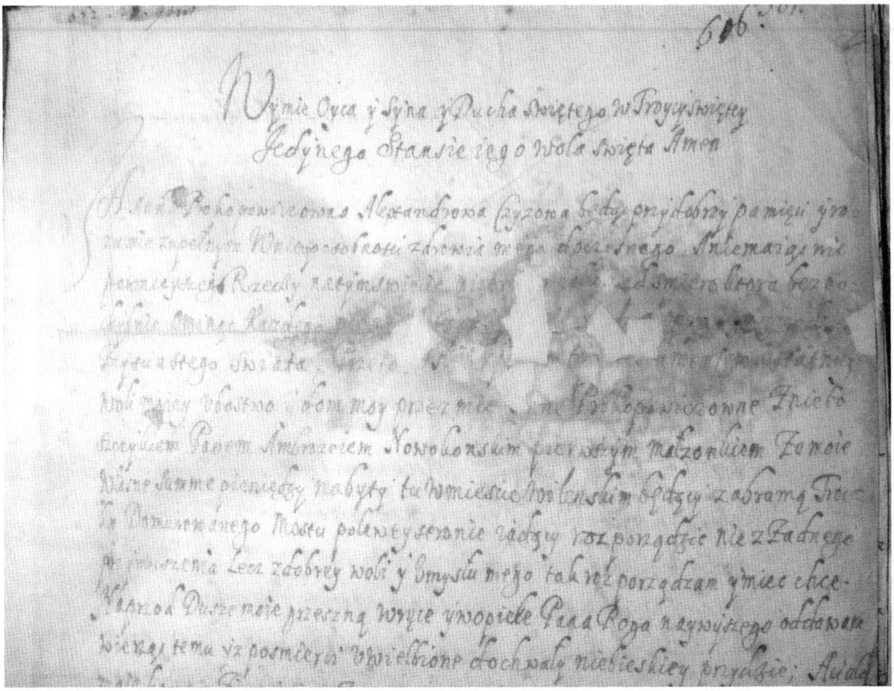

Fig. 46 The beginning of the testament of Mrs. Anna Czyżowa, 1652, in Polish. Vilnius, LVIA, MS F23, ap. 1, nr 5096, p. 606r. Photo J. Niedźwiedź.

form of the social communication. This second aspect interests us more here, in which a rhetorised text formed the basis for a rhetorical act. A will was an extremely performative text. Few texts had such impact on the lives of those who succumbed to their persuasive power. Its uniqueness also lies in the fact that hardly any literary genre from past centuries can be so individualised, paradoxically in spite of its schematised rhetoric.[126]

архіва Беларусі), ed. А.Ф. Аляксандрава, В.У. Бабкова, and І.М. Бобер (Мінск, 2012); U. Zachara-Związek, "Legaty testamentowe mieszczan krakowskich na rzecz kościoła i klasztoru bernardynów na Stradomiu w drugiej połowie XV wieku", *Kwartalnik Historii Kultury Materialnej* 63.1 (2015), pp. 29-40; Н. Білоус, "Вызнаваю сим моим тастаменътом и ѡстатнею волею своею. Тестаменти волинських міщанок кінця XVI-XVII ст.", *Соціум: Альманах соціальної історії* 13-14 (2017), pp. 127-160; Wnuk, "Szlachta w testamentach i inwentarzach mieszczan lubelskich", pp. 129-157.

[126] On the tension between the individual and formal character of the last will, see Adamska, "Stąd do wieczności", pp. 194-196.

For wills are no less schematic than privileges.[127] The *formulae* of the Vilnius testaments did not differ from the thousands of testaments written in other parts of the Polish-Lithuanian federation in the sixteenth and the seventeenth centuries.[128] A comparison reveals that in the entire state early modern testaments were made in a very similar way; irrespective of whether it was drafted in Polish (the most common language of a last will), Ruthenian, or Latin. The form of the Orthodox testaments from Kyiv, written in Ruthenian in the last decades of the sixteenth and in the first half of the seventeenth century, did not differ significantly from the Polish testaments of the Catholic town dwellers from the Sandomierz voivodeship, those of the Lithuanian Calvinist magnates, of the Ruthenian testaments of the Tartars from Minsk or those of the peasants from the Cracow voivodeship.[129]

The scheme was based both on local practice and on the samples of wills given in the *formulae*. For example, in his popular commentary on the Magdeburg law of 1567, Bartłomiej Grodzicki included four sample testaments, three in Polish and one in Latin.[130] A typical testament was built from the preliminary formulae (*invocatio*, *superscriptio, arenga*), followed by the main part or disposition (*dispositio*), in which the testator expressed his or her will, and the final *formulae*: the list of the witnesses and executors, sanctions, signatures, information about the notary, etc.[131] Usually the testament was sealed by the witnesses.

Here is an example of a heavily formalised will from the registers of Vilnius' cathedral chapter. Its form is similar to thousands of last wills which were

[127] Privileges have been discussed in Chapter 1.

[128] One of the oldest Polish testament formulae was written in Cracow in 1485. See J. WYSMUŁEK, *Testamenty mieszczan krakowskich*, pp. 103-107. On the formulae of the last wills see G. JAWOR, "Stałe formuły w testamentach polskich", *Rozprawy Komisji Językowej: Wrocławskie Towarzystwo Naukowe*, 12 (1981), pp. 217-233; L. TYMIAKIN, "O formułach w XVII-wiecznym testamencie przemyskim" *Rocznik Przemyski* 27 (1990), pp. 141-145; A. FALNIOWSKA-GRADOWSKA, "Wstęp", in: *Testamenty szlachty krakowskiej XVII-XVIII w. Wybór tekstów źródłowych z lat 1650-1799*, ed. A. FALNIOWSKA-GRADOWSKA (Cracow, 1997), pp. XVI-XIX; JUSTYNIARSKA-CHOJAK, *Testamenty i inwentarze pośmiertne*, p. 32-72.

[129] Н. БІЛОУС, *Тестаменти киян середини XVI – першої половини XVII ст.* (Київ, 2011); *AVAK*, 31 (Vilnius, 1906), p. 282; JUSTYNIARSKA-CHOJAK, *Testamenty i inwentarze pośmiertne*; *Testamenty chłopów polskich od drugiej połowy XVI do XVIII wieku*, ed. J. ŁOSOWSKI (Lublin, 2016).

[130] GROICKI, *Artykuły prawa majdeburskiego*, pp. 190-194.

[131] JUSTYNIARSKA-CHOJAK, *Testamenty i inwentarze pośmiertne*, pp. 33-63; БІЛОУС, *Тестаменти киян*, pp. 62-88; A. FALNIOWSKA-GRADOWSKA, "Wstęp", pp. XIV-XIX.

written in Vilnius and other Polish-Lithuanian towns, but the arenga was heavily reduced:

> In the year 1654 on the twenty-first day of February, father Stanisław Pacewicz *Societatis Iesu*, standing before an official clerk, submitted the will of Dorota Paszkowska, which is hereby properly registered: [*invocatio:*] In the name of the Father, the Son, and the Holy Spirit. Amen. [*superscriptio:*] I, Dorota Paszkowska [*promulgatio:*] announce in this written will of mine that, being close to death, I undertake certain decisions concerning my movable and immovable property. [*dispositio:*] Firstly, I bequeath my little house to the chapter's *jurydyka*; all the money is donated for [the chapel of] Holy Mary of Loreto at St. John's, with the exception of 50 *złoty*, which is to be given to my sister Paszkowska Anna, and 150 *złoty* for my brother Krzysztof Paszkowski; one bond of the amount of 100 *kopas* issued to Tobiasz, the tailor in Skopówka. The second bond amounting to 150 *złoty* issued to Wojciech, the son-in-law of that tailor. The third bond of 200 *złoty* issued to Marcin, the soap maker, who lived in a noble's bricked house in Horse Street. The fourth bond for thirty *kopas* issued to the trumpeter Maleczka. I wish to donate all of these sums to the Holy Mary of Loreto at St. John's. I bequeath all my movable property to the same Holy Mary. I bequeath my patterned azure cloth coat to my sister with a chest that contains the things mentioned, deposited with Ludwik the painter in Bernardyńska Street.
>
> This will is signed by hand with the following words: [*signature:*] Dorota Paszkowska.[132] (original in Latin and Polish)

Although Dorota Paszkowska was able to put her signature on the will, this indigent Vilnius townswoman is not likely to have drafted her own will herself and so she probably used the services of a male expert in drawing up such texts, perhaps father Stanisław Pacewicz, mentioned in the protocol of the will, or a public notary. However, the wealthier inhabitants of the city also supposedly called on specialists in the drafting of wills at this particular moment of their lives.[133] The last will and testament of canon Stanisław Górecki of 1584 was evidently not prepared by himself, because his old-age signature reveals a completely different handwriting from that in which the whole document was written. It was a common practice in this part of Europe, that the testator dele-

[132] *Protokól spraw potocznych przy sądu wielebnej kapituły wileńskiej za urzędu jego mości księdza Wawrzyńca Mocarskiego kanonika wileńskiego, prokuratora kapitulnego roku 1648 miesiąca Octobra sprawiony*, 1648-1662, MS MAB F43-590, ff. 48v-49r.

[133] HEDEMANN, *Testamenty brasławsko-dziśnieńskie*, p. 12.

gated the writing of the last will to a person well versed in legal matters, which guaranteed the legal and social validity of the testament.[134] This fact raises an issue: who was the author of the last will? The testator or the scribe?[135] In case of most wills the answer is: both.

For example, the will of the archdeacon of Vilnius, Grzegorz Święcicki, from 1617, retains all the formal features that characterised Mrs Paszkowska's will, but its content is much more extensive, and not only because the inventory of goods was longer. The disposition is extremely detailed and father Święcicki would supervise his funeral from beyond the grave, including the menu at the wake:

> I have at Sir Mikołaj Kiszka's home twelve hundred Polish *złoty*, of which I allocate two hundred for the funeral to cover the costs of the chasuble, the chalice, the fine London cloth, the shroud, the coffin, the charge for ringing bells [during the liturgy, the funeral itself, etc.], the psalters, the processions of monks and secular priests, lunch served according to the opinion of the priest at the castle [meaning the canons), as well as other church rituals. For the banquet [after the funeral], fudge and all kinds of necessities, and fish from the Rukonys (Rukony) manor farm and from houses are to be served.[136]

It is obvious that the will of the archdeacon was drafted in accordance with legal rhetoric. However, a closer look reveals two other genres: those of description and narration, which were two progymnasmatic exercises.[137] School rhetoric deeply influenced seventeenth-century last wills. The testators, especially those who had received some literary education, not only took care of the accuracy of their last wills, but also of their rhetorical shape. They required

[134] ADAMSKA, "Stąd do wieczności", pp. 192-193, 196.

[135] Ł. GOŁASZEWSKI, "Knyszyńskie testamenty składane ustnie wobec władz miejskich na przełomie XVII i XVIII wieku: Teksty autorstwa umierających, czy też pisarzy miejskich?", *Kwartalnik Historii Kultury Materialnej* 62.3 (2014), pp. 345-366.

[136] *The testament of archdeacon of Vilnius Grzegorz Święcicki from 1617*, MS MAB F43-26717, f. 1r.

[137] M. KRAUS, "Aphthonius and the progymnasmata in rhetorical theory and practice", in: *Sizing Up Rhetoric*, ed. D. ZAREFSKY and E. BENACKA (Long Grove, Illinois, 2008), pp. 52-67; B.B. AWIANOWICZ, *Progymnasmata w teorii i praktyce szkoły humanistycznej od końca XV do połowy XVIII wieku: Dzieje nowożytnej recepcji Aftoniosa od Rudolfa Agricoli do Johanna Christopha Gottscheda* (Toruń, 2008), pp. 129-133; MACK, "Humanist rhetoric and dialectic", pp. 90-91; J. LOVERIDGE, "The practice of the progymnasmata in the Middle Ages: Ancestry and probability in Alan of Lille's Anticlaudianus", in: *Les progymnasmata en pratique, de l'Antiquité à nos jours*, ed. P. CHIRON and B. SANS (Paris, 2020), p. 217.

from the notaries that they applied an extended apparatus of *elocutio*. Rhetorical displays were most visible in the preamble (*arenga*).[138] Early modern preambles were rooted in the medieval *ars dictandi* tradition. One such rather popular Latin preamble derived from the thirteenth- and fourteenth-century preambles of the *oblivio-memoria* type,[139] often translated into Polish. It can be found in the Latin will drafted in 1572 of Anna, the wife of a Vilnius goldsmith, Jan Stor. Anna Stor,

> often considering in her soul the human condition, which is similar to wild flowers that are growing today, while tomorrow – according to the words of our Saviour – they will end up in the furnace, and since no mortal can be more sure of anything than of death, but less sure of anything than the hour of death that carries us away from the catastrophe of our present life,[140] (original in Polish)

managed her estate in such a way that there would be no dissensions between those still alive, just as Mrs Połubińska was to do half a century later. The need to write down the will of mayor Maciej Rudomina in 1586 was substantiated by the notary in a different way. The preamble that precedes this Polish document reads as follows:

> contemplating and considering this miserable life and the present earthly secular journey, [we note that] there is no one who has an eternal home here or the power to live the years of Nestor, and nothing has been invented to escape the snares of earthly death.[141]

Similar preambles can also be found in testaments written in Ruthenian. These Vilnius wills differ from many wills in the Ruthenian language and written in Cyrillic script issued by the grand duke's chancery, which do with-

[138] K. Justyniarska-Chojak discussed the most common topoi in the arengas from the early modern urban testaments from the Sandomierskie Voivodeship; see JUSTYNIARSKA-CHOJAK, *Testamenty i inwentarze pośmiertne*, pp. 48-53.

[139] ADAMSKA, *Arengi w dokumentach Władysława Łokietka*, pp. 44-45.

[140] "*(...) animadvertens ac saepissime in animo praemeditans statum vitae humanae floribus campi similem, quae hodie crescunt, cras vero iuxta dicta Salvatoris nostri in clibanum mittuntur et quod unicuique mortalium nihil certius morte, hora porro mortis quae ex hoc naufragio vitae praesentis migrandum sit nihil incertius*" (MS LVIA F22, ap. 1, no. 5333, f. 77r).

[141] "*(...) praemeditans et considerans hac in miserrima vita et in praesenti temporali peregrinatione seculari, neminem estae, qui perpetuam hic haberet mansionem, ut quam vis etiam Nestoreos pervixisset annos, nullum esse repertum, qui mortis temporalis laqueos evadere posset*" (MS LVIA F22, ap. 1, no. 5333, f. 83r).

out preambles, but certain formulas (for instance "whoever sees it or hears it read") come directly from the collections of *formulae* used by this chancery:

> In the name of the Father and of the Son and of the Holy Spirit, let it happen for the eternal glory of God. Amen.
>
> I, Pavel Mikhailovich, burgher and merchant of the grand-ducal city of Vilnius, testify with my last will and testament for those who would like to know or hear about it when it is read, people in the present and in the future, that I, Pavel Mikhailovich, seeing the changeability and uncertainty of this world and that every thing that has not been explained in writing after some time escapes from human memory into oblivion; and whereas every person is subject to death and nothing in the world is less sure than the time of death, therefore, although my body is ill, my mind remains in good health, first and foremost, I entrust my sinful soul to the power and defence of the Triune God, while having made up my mind I decide that after my death all my impecunious property, both movable and immovable, is handed over to my nephew, Khotei Kurylovych, who is with me at the present moment, so that no contention arises over it after my departure.[142] (original in Ruthenian)

The preamble exhibits a longstanding process of transition from the Latin and Polish Catholic formulary to the Ruthenian documents written for the Orthodox. For example, it contains formulas that emphasise the importance of writing so that memory can be stored and it has a reference to the Holy Trinity. These formulas appeared earlier in innumerable Latin and Polish documents and belong to the group of *memoria-oblivio* religious arengas.[143]

In Pavel Mikhailovich's will of 1594 there are many phrases and words taken from the Polish language (for instance *mieshchanin, maientnost', ostatniaya volya*), and this shows how strong the influence of Polish texts on Ruthenian ones was. We find a very similar preamble in Helena Łukomska's will of 1650, registered in the city books of Orsha the following year.[144] Not much later, Polish completely dominated wills, and in the first half of the seventeenth century most wills recorded in Vilnius city registers were written in this language. Latin was sometimes used to prepare the wills of Catholic cler-

[142] MS LVIA F22, ap. 1, no. 5333, ff. 90v-91r.

[143] ADAMSKA, *Arengi w dokumentach Władysława Łokietka*, pp. 43-48; EAD., "Treści religijne w preambułach polskich dokumentów średniowiecznych", pp. 3-4.

[144] BORKOWSKA, *Dekret w niebieskim ferowany testamencie*, pp. 60-61.

gymen, for instance that of bishop Walerian Protasewicz,[145] and some other people, such as foreigners and magnates.

Ruthenian and Polish were probably the main languages of the testaments of the Vilnius Tartars, who lived on Šnipiškės. Making testaments was a common practice in the Tartar communities in the Grand Duchy of Lithuania,[146] and Vilnius was no exception. They were literate in ways similar to the other inhabitants of the city, which is confirmed by many documents from the municipal and other courts. A few Tartar last wills are known from the Vilnius castle court registers, among them the will of a woman called Abrahimowa (1598) and of Islam Abszamiecirowicz (1643).[147] Abrahimowa used a standard preamble: "in this world there is nothing more certain for every man than death, for the healthy person must expect sickness, and the sick awaits death".[148]

Unfortunately, we have no knowledge whatsoever about Jewish testaments in Yiddish, as they were entered in the registers of the *qahal* and were probably lost as early as the eighteenth century.

Last wills of Christian testators often included detailed regulations concerning their funeral, which was a general mark of early modern wills.[149] Although the main aim of the funeral ceremony was to lead the deceased to the other world, its staging was supposed to be attractive to the mourners and to display the status of the deceased. It was no different with wills, which took on the characteristics of epideictic texts especially in the seventeenth century.[150] The authors of the introductions to wills, that is their *publicatio*, preamble (*arenga*), and *narratio*, reached for well-established topoi required by the rhetoric of this literary genre, such as the inevitability of death and its unknown time, the vanity and shortness of human life and the vanity of the world, the desire to prevent disputes over the property left behind, and the topoi of *humili-*

[145] D. Antanavičius, "Vilniaus vyskupo Valerijono Protasevičiaus 1579 m. kovo testamentas", *Lietuvos istorijos metraštis* 1 (2006), pp. 123-144.

[146] O. Winnyczenko, "Dwa tatarskie testamenty wojskowych z pierwszej połowy XVIII wieku", *Rocznik Lituanistyczny* 3 (2017), pp. 261-262.

[147] Frick, *Kith, Kin, and Neighbors*, pp. 363-364. More Tartar last wills are known from the Trakai castle court registers, where since the end of the fourteenth century a community of Tartars have lived. Their last wills from the first half of the seventeenth century were written mainly in Polish and some in Ruthenian. See *AVAK*, 31 (Vilnius, 1906), pp. 317-318 (1643, Polish), 319-321 (1644, Ruthenian), 323-325 (1645, Polish), 335-336 (1646, Polish).

[148] Quoted after Frick, *Kith, Kin, and Neighbors*, p. 363.

[149] The instructions about the funeral we find in numerous testaments from all parts of the Polish-Lithuanian Commonwealth. See Falniowska-Gradowska, "Wstęp", pp. XIV-XVI; Justyniarska-Chojak, *Testamenty i inwentarze pośmiertne*, pp. 61-63.

[150] See Chapter 10, on the *genus demonstrativum*.

tas. The most pompous wills, often prepared for the city elites and the nobility, were marked by the use of the rhetorical period, elaborate vanitative topoi and concepts, and above all by modifications of the formulas we have encountered so far:

> In the name of the Father, and of the Son, and of the Holy Spirit. Amen.
>
> Since all things in this miserable world, no matter their variety, are subject to condemnation, and men must take pride in this right to be subordinate to death, over which nothing is more sure, although its time and manner, that is when and where it should happen, are uncertain, therefore I, Marta Janowiczówna Marcinowa Kiewliczowa, remembering the teaching and admonitions of our Saviour, who told us to be alert and ready no matter the time, since we know neither the day nor the hour of our departure from this world, as well as taking great care to prevent any squabbles, discord, or legal altercations between my relatives, kinsmen, and my husband after my death, since I know that fickleness and inconstancy are often observed in this world, being sane and clear-headed (although stricken by God with illness), I manage and dispense my property in the following way.[151] (original in Polish)
>
> In the name of the Holiest Trinity, Father, Son, and the Holy Spirit, become effective for the eternal glory of the Lord.
>
> Although every Christian needs to be alert in their condemned body as in a watchtower, which was entrusted to them but for a short time, because venomous Death can shoot at any time of one's life, one should be even more watchful when a disease, as God's scourge, comes and exposes one like an unmissable target.[152]

Personified Death, which directed "the arrow that cuts the close connection between the body and the soul" at Matys Zawistowski, a Vilnius town dweller, probably made its way into his will recorded in the municipal registers in 1642 from funeral sermons, epicedial poetry, painting, and tomb sculpture. The seventeenth-century testament thus became part of the extensive *theatrum Mortis* in which the inhabitants of Vilnius often participated.

[151] *The Testament of Marta Kiewliczowa from 1634*, MS LVIA F22, ap. 1, no. 5333, ff. 172r-172v.
[152] *The Testament of Matys Zawistowski from 1642*, MS LVIA F22, ap. 1, no. 5333, f. 214r.

Chapter 9

Texts in a Dispute

Few phenomena are as conducive to the creation of texts as disputes. The more discord and contention, the more we know about the past. Conflicts resulted in the production of documents because they forced people to describe and record events, as "all human matters, not explained and not described, in the future become forgotten".[1] Describing a dispute is a way of conducting it, and a text can be a more effective weapon in combat than a harquebus. To a large extent, therefore, we get to know the life of a city through the accounts of conflicts waged there. It should be remembered, however, that by relying on such texts we may be creating a one-sided image of the past.[2]

The 'Open' City vs. the 'Closed' City

When we consider 'the city in a state of discord', the question arises as to how or to what extent this category can be applied to Vilnius. This is not a simple matter, because the political and religious debates that took place there concerned not only the city itself, but the whole of the Grand Duchy of Lithuania, the Polish-Lithuanian Commonwealth, and sometimes even the whole of European Christianity or the Jewish interpretation of Halakha. How should one treat, for example, Marcin Śmiglecki's book, published at the end of the six-

[1] *Testament Jakuba II Dessausa, mieszczanina wileńskiego z 13 listopada 1675 roku*, rkps LVIA SA 5337, ff. 107-108, as cited in *Wilnianie*, p. 29.

[2] FRICK, "*Słowa uszczypliwe*", pp. 16-17; ID., *Wstęp*, in: *Wilnianie*, pp. XXVIII-XXX.

teenth century by the Jesuit printing house in Vilnius, aimed at the leader of the Polish Brethren (Arians) from Lesser Poland, Fausto Sozzini (Faust Socyn)?[3] This work had more to do with the events that took place in Lesser Poland at that time than with the disputes in which the residents of Vilnius took part. Should it be taken into account in this discussion of the literate culture of Vilnius? Is the fact that Śmiglecki lived and published his book in Vilnius not an accidental event? A few years later, the provincial authorities moved Śmiglecki to Poznań and Cracow, where he published similar polemical works. Therefore, he might just as well have published in Ingolstadt[4] or Rome, provided that his books were later distributed in the Polish-Lithuanian Commonwealth. Should this publication of a work against Sozzini then be regarded as marginal to the textual culture of the city? After all, only a small group of inhabitants was involved in the Arian dispute, to wit the author, a dozen or so Jesuits, printers, and a few booksellers. However, this dispute was to some extent rooted in the reality of sixteenth-century Vilnius because, after all, Śmiglecki lived here. In fact, it also happened sometimes that a book representing a stance in a dispute was printed in Vilnius, even though neither its author nor its subject matter was connected with the city. How should one regard Antonio Possevino's *Moscovia*, the first edition of which was published in Vilnius in 1586,[5] and which was, among other things, a voice in the discussion on the union of the Catholic Church with the Orthodox Church?

Publishing in Vilnius was easier than in other places in the Grand Duchy of Lithuania, and this is why the authors and their patrons so often chose Vilnius. They also could think about increasing the range of their intended audience. Vilnius was a great trade centre, which facilitated the distribution of polemical books both in the city and in distant regions. An example of the "printed polemic of 1594" between the Catholics and the Polish Brethren (the Arians) is very instructive and helps us to understand the role of Vilnius in conflicts distant and close.

In January 1594, Marcin Śmiglecki, whom we already know, despite the hardships of the winter journey, travelled from Vilnius all the way to Novahrudak, a town more than 180 kilometres away, to face an Arian minister of the

[3] M. Śmiglecki, *Zachariae prophetae pro Christi divinitate illustre testimonium adversus Fausti Socini anabaptistae cavillationes propugnatum* (Vilnius, 1596).

[4] The college in Ingolstadt, founded in 1556, was an important Jesuit educational and scientific institution in Europe and the Jesuit headquarters in Germany. Its prolific printing house published works of the most influential Catholic writers and scholars of the time.

[5] A. Possevino, *Moscovia* (Vilnius, 1586).

local church, Jan Licyniusz Namysłowski, a well-known polemicist, writer, and theologian, in a dispute. This famous dispute lasted two days, 24 and 25 January. As expected, neither of the speakers was convinced by his opponent's arguments, nor did either of them delude himself as to the result of the confrontation.[6] Soon afterwards, an account of the event was published in Vilnius under the name of Wojciech Zajączkowski, although it was most probably written by Śmiglecki himself.[7] A year later, Śmiglecki published his book *O bóstwie przedwiecznym Syna Bożego* (On the Eternal Divinity of the Son of God),[8] which was certainly inspired by that disputation, and which was also a response to the accusations of a certain 'Refuter', behind which pseudonym hid none other than Fausto Sozzini himself.[9]

The example of Śmiglecki's anti-Arian polemic inspires the question as to how Vilnius, where this Jesuit scholar lived, opened up to the outside world. The dispute did not take place in the city. Only a small part of it happened within the city walls. However, going beyond the city in the physical sense is not equivalent of going beyond the textual culture of the city. Quite the contrary. The perspective changes: we are looking at a city entangled in an external conflict, in which it was the hallmark of one of the parties. Thus, space acquires a symbolic meaning. In the case of Śmiglecki and Sozzini, space was

[6] Daniel Mikołajewski expressed this conviction directly in his description of the later disputation with Śmiglecki: "It is, however, hard to prevent people from having opinions that are not well thought through, or to put prejudice out of the mind of our enemies, or even to assess the benefit of that disputation when its results are evaluated so differently. For some people said that everyone returns home with his or her own view as no matter or truth has ever been understood in the same way by all people" (D. Mikołajewski, *Dysputacyja wileńska, którą miał ks. Marcin Śmiglecki Societatis Iesu z ks. Danielem Mikołajewskim, sługą Słowa Bożego, de primatu Petri, a o jednej widomej głowie Kościoła Bożego dnia 2 czerwca w roku 1599: Od samego autora cale i szczyrze wydana. Nie zaniechały się i przysadki ks. Śmigleckiego z odpowiedzią na nie tegoż ks. Daniela Mikołajewskiego* (Toruń, 1599), f. A4r).

[7] W. Zajączkowski (M. Śmiglecki?), *Opisanie dysputacyjej nowogródzkiej, którą miał ks. Marcin Śmiglecki Societatis Iesu z Janem Licyniuszem, ministrem nowokrzczeńskim o przedwiecznym bóstwie Syna Bożego. 24 i 25 Ianuarii w roku 1594, wydane przez ks. Wojciecha Zajączkowskiego* (Vilnius, 1594); see Natoński, *Humanizm jezuicki*, p. 80.

[8] M. Śmiglecki, *O bóstwie przedwiecznym Syna Bożego: Świadectwa Pisma świętego do trzech przedniejszych artykułów zebrane: Przeciwko wszystkim Pana Jezusa Chrystusa nieprzyjacielom: Gdzie się też odpowiada na refutacją od Refutarza jakiegoś nowokrzczeńca przeciw ks. d. Jakubowi Wujkowi wydaną* (Vilnius, 1595); id., *Zachariae Prophetae pro Christi Divinitate illustre testimonium ...*

[9] F. Sozzini, *Refutatio libelli quem Jacobus Vuiekus Iesuita anno 1590 Polonice edidit de divinitate Filii Dei et Spiritus Sancti* (s.l., 1593); and the Polish translation *Refutacyja książek* (s.l., 1593).

marked with names: Vilnius, Cracow, Raków, and Novahrudak, as the dispute took place at least in these four places, and at the same time.

In order to fully understand this issue, we shall use the concepts of 'closed' city and 'open' city, which I defined in the Introduction. These concepts prove useful when considering Vilnius as the administrative and political centre of the Grand Duchy of Lithuania, but also when thinking about disputes that concerned the city itself, for instance polemics between its Orthodox Christians and Uniates, whose seats were positioned symmetrically on either side of Ostra Street (Aušros Vartų Street). A struggle with words and books between the archimandrites of the Uniate monastery of the Holy Trinity and of the Orthodox monastery of the Holy Spirit seems to have taken place in the city: it was here that the participants in the dispute and their supporters lived; it was also here that books about the union of the Churches were written and published. Therefore, this contention can be seen from the perspective of a 'closed' city: the archimandrite of the monastery of the Holy Trinity, Leon Kreuza Rzewuski, attacked the Orthodox Christians from the monastery on the opposite side of the street, to which the Orthodox archimandrite Meletius Smotrycki responded with accusations against the Uniates. Both adversaries wanted to gain several thousand believers of the Eastern rite who lived in Vilnius at the time. From the perspective of the 'open' city, this dispute was part of a wider conflict that involved all members of the Orthodox and Uniate Churches in the Polish-Lithuanian Commonwealth. The struggle in Vilnius between supporters of both sides resonated widely in Kyiv, Ostroh, Lviv, and Cracow.

The opening up of the city also worked the other way round. The writings and statements of the members of both parties which were not connected with Vilnius, had a direct impact on what was happening in the city and in the texts that were written there. In 1597, Grzegorz of Żarnowiec, a Calvinist from Lesser Poland, published in Vilnius the second, amended edition of his postil, as well as the second edition of his *Obrona Postylle* (The Defense of the Postil) of 1591, in which he responded to the charges of Jakub Wujek, a well-known translator of Holy Scripture and Catholic polemicist.[10] The same applies to earlier political disputes in the 1540s between Queen Bona and chancellor Gasztołd or between Sigismund II August and the opponents of his marriage

[10] R. Czyż, *Obrona wiary w edycjach postylli Grzegorza z Żarnowca* (Warsaw, 2008), pp. 16-33. A dispute arose in connection with the *Defense of the Postil*, in which, apart from Wujek, another Jesuit, Stanisław Grodzicki, also participated; see D. Frick, *Polish Sacred Philology in the Reformation and the Counter-Reformation. Chapters in the History of the Controversies (1551-1632)* (Berkeley, 1989), pp. 169-175.

with Barbara Radziwiłłówna. The marriage was attacked, among others, by a *Ruthenus* from the Kingdom of Poland, Stanisław Orzechowski, and by Andrzej Trzecieski the Younger, who came from Greater Poland. They were opposed by Queen Barbara's secretary, Stanisław Koszutski (who also originated from Greater Poland), in a Latin apologetic epithalamium.[11] Vilnius featured only as a background to these events and texts.

Agonistic Culture

Humanist rhetorical thinking and the Jesuit education based on it stemmed from a culture of dispute, an agonistic culture. Even the Catholic theology of the time referred to the struggle of the forces of darkness against God. A Christian of the post-Tridentine Era was therefore obliged to wage war with Satan, the sinful world, and his or her own carnality. Its essential element was the defense of the Church against its enemies, that is, the unfaithful, schismatics, and heretics. The provision of tools to deal with these opponents must have played a significant role in Catholic education. One of these tools was Jesuit spirituality, in which the element of self-exercise, overcoming and perfecting oneself, is constantly present. A second tool was the system of education developed by the Jesuits. The main components of agonistic culture in this system were firstly to show rhetoric as the basis of culture, and secondly to show rhetoric as a way of acting in the world, especially in overcoming difficulties and fighting opponents (the *genus iudiciale* and the *genus deliberativum*) and in modelling the image of the world (*genus demonstrativum*). This culture included student competitions as part of rhetorical performances given on holidays. Marcin Śmiglecki, who debated with Protestants in public, organised disputations for his philosophy students several times a year.[12] These disputations also included the defence of master's and doctoral theses, the publication of academic work in which controversial issues were raised, the rejection of accusations against the Jesuits by the lay Catholics and by members of the diocesan clergy, and finally public religious disputes with dissenters. Some-

[11] Chapter 4.2; J. Niedźwiedź, "Szesnastowieczne epitalamia łacińskie w Polsce", in: *Szesnastowieczne epitalamia łacińskie w Polsce*, ed. J. Niedźwiedź and trans. M. Brożek (Cracow, 1999), pp. 44-46.

[12] K. Drzymała, "Lata szkolne i profesorskie ks. Marcina Śmigleckiego T.J.", in: *Sprawozdanie Dyrekcji Zakładu Naukowo-Wychowawczego OO. Jezuitów w Bąkowicach pod Chyrowem za rok szkolny 1937/38* (Bąkowice 1938), pp. 37-38.

times Jesuits from Vilnius engaged in political disputes, but for them this last form of activity was rather exceptional.

This structure of education required constant referring to rhetorical categories in higher education as well, for example in treatises that performed persuasive functions: the reader had to be convinced of the theses put forward not only through logic, but also on the basis of rhetorical evidence. A clear example of this is provided by works of polemical theology, which on the one hand had the qualities of an academic treatise, but on the other hand strove to use rhetorical proof as one of their basic means of persuasion. And it was not only in religious polemics that we can see such rhetoricity.

Although in the Polish-Lithuanian Commonwealth, just as in other European countries in the sixteenth and seventeenth centuries, religious differences led to social and political tensions and violence, there was also room for dialogue. Until the mid-seventeenth century, in the Polish-Lithuanian Commonwealth a kind of fragile *convivencia* can be observed.[13] It is an open question to what extent this coexistence between different religious, ethnic, and cultural communities was born from necessity, choice, or the result of a temporary weakness of the Catholic authorities of the State. Nevertheless, physical violence and religious warfare were not the only resorts of convincing opponents, and very often religious conflicts were discussed in 'wars of books' (*bibliomachia*) and oral polemics. Theological and rhetorical studies were largely aimed at preparing students to conduct such disputes. However, we should not forget the other aims and results of teaching in Jesuit colleges, especially the preparation of lay students to engage in public affairs after they left school. At this point, however, we will focus on the rhetorical and agonistic part of their education.

The Methodology of a Dispute: Jesuit Polemical Theology

The principles of polemical theology (also known as 'controversial' from *controversiae*, or 'positive theology') were laid out in Ignatius of Loyola's

[13] The Spanish term *convivencia*, describing a peaceful and fruitful cultural, social, and economic exchange between the Muslim, Christian, and Jewish communities on the Iberian Peninsula in the Middle Ages, is challenged by many researchers. See L.M. ALVAREZ, "Convivencia", in: *The Oxford Dictionary of the Middle Ages*, ed. R.E. BJORK (Oxford, 2010) (<https://www.oxfordreference.com/view/10.1093/acref/9780198662624.001.0001/acref-9780198662624>, accessed 14.03.2021).

instruction *Some Recommendations for the Promotion of the True Faith, Especially in Germany and France.*[14] St. Ignatius recommended the use of methods in the struggle with Protestants that were similar to those they used themselves. He therefore called for the practice not only of 'perfect' theology, also referred to as 'scholastic', based on solid philosophical preparation, but also of 'concise theology', limited to the most important dogmatic issues and to conducting polemics with dissenters.[15] Its main aim was to defend the teachings of the Catholic Church and, if necessary, to overturn the accusations made by its opponents. This way of practising theology was intended for a wider group of people who studied at Jesuit universities, and was to be explored, among others, by students of the rhetoric class. Unlike 'perfect' theology, 'concise' theology was to be more easily assimilated both by students and by large numbers of believers. This is why Ignatius of Loyola did not recommend a thorough philosophical grounding in the case of this subject. Argumentation would be based on references to *loci communes*, dogmas, and the teachings of the Church in general, while syllogisms would replace dialectic reasoning.[16]

Polemical theology thus became well established in Jesuit schools, and so it is no wonder that when the *Ratio Studiorum* was being developed,[17] much attention was devoted to this subject, above all by considering its position in the teaching process. The authors of the first version of this document suggested that *controversiae* were more suitable for listeners from the northern part of Europe, the so-called northern countries, where Protestants had achieved significant successes in spreading their teachings. The Polish-Lithuanian Commonwealth was also included in this list. Scholastic theology was mainly intended for people from Spain and Italy, especially since students from these countries were supposed to be more capable and better able to assimilate the subtleties of the reasoning of St. Thomas Aquinas, which could not be said of students from the north. The Jesuits from Lithuania and Bavaria, among others, protested against such a stance so effectively that in the final version of the *Ratio Studiorum* controversial theology was considered to be part of a general theological education based on Thomistic enquiry.[18]

[14] NATOŃSKI, *Humanizm jezuicki*, p. 10.

[15] On the authority of St. Ignatius as a theologian and writer, see P.-A. FABRE, "The writings of Ignatius of Loyola as seminal text", in: *A Companion to Ignatius of Loyola: Life, Writings, Spirituality, Influence*, ed. R.A. MARYKS (Leiden, 2014), pp. 103-122.

[16] *Ibid.*, p. 12.

[17] See Chapter 3.

[18] NATOŃSKI, *Humanizm jezuicki*, pp. 26-35.

As a result, for the next two centuries the Academy of Vilnius offered lectures in this field, often given by eminent scholars, such as Maciej Kazimierz Sarbiewski, who, by the way, received his doctorate in theology here. Some manuscripts that are transcripts of their lectures have survived.

Robert Bellarmine played a major role in the formation of positive-controversial (polemical) theology. He gave the discipline its final form in the *Collegium Romanum* between 1576 and 1587. This was of considerable importance for the university in the capital of the Grand Duchy of Lithuania. He supervised the course of studies of the future professors of theology at the Academy, for instance Marcin Śmiglecki, Emmanuel de Vega, and Jan Brandt. The Vilnius Faculty of Theology was based on the Bellarminian models known from the Collegim Romanum. In addition to polemical theology, chairs of moral and scholastic theology as well as of Holy Scripture were established. In a short time, Vilnius became one of the most important centres of Jesuit theology in the Commonwealth, next to Poznań. However, as Bronisław Natoński has shown, the majority of students who chose the theology course restricted their studies primarily to exploring controversies and to moral theology, while relatively few decided to take a full course in scholastic theology.[19] It should therefore come as no surprise that the general level of theological education of priests did not go beyond a collection of basic pieces of information in this field. This did not prevent the publication of numerous polemical works and the conduct of disputations at a respectable level. Knowledge of both rhetoric and logic, the teaching of which flourished at the Academy of Vilnius at the turn of the sixteenth and seventeenth centuries, was helpful in this regard.

Polyphonic Texts of Dispute (the 'Closed' City)

The settlement of disputes in a civilised manner usually took place in the courts. It seems that the inhabitants of Vilnius used their services on a regular basis, especially since in this city of no more than 20,000 inhabitants there were several courts, for instance the municipal, the land, the burgrave's, and the bishop's courts, the Lithuanian Tribunal, etc. These courts had different competences and their choice was determined by the legal matter to be dealt with. The inhabitants of Vilnius were accustomed to deal with their legal mat-

[19] NATOŃSKI, *Humanizm jezuicki*, p. 18; PIECHNIK, *Początki Akademii Wileńskiej*, pp. 51, 140.

ters in front of an appropriate court and by using written documents. In other words, the members of Vilnius society in the fifteenth-seventeenth centuries, just as in other early modern towns, were literate or highly literate when it came to litigation in a court of law. The registers of the juridical institutions provide much information about the affairs of Vilnius residents in the early modern period, and we can reconstruct the microhistories of people who would probably not be in our field of interest, were it not for their legal contentions.[20]

Usually, court narratives are simple and formalised. The main voices in these documents belonged to the language of juridical genres and forms required by the legal system and to the scribe. However, the languages of the people who came to the court often emerge below (and sometimes together with) the language of the legal procedures itself.[21] Thanks to the depositions of witnesses we have access to traces of the everyday language spoken by the inhabitants of sixteenth- and seventeenth-century Vilnius. Before the mid-sixteenth century, the languages of court litigations were almost entirely Latin and Ruthenian; afterwards, other languages also came in use, mainly Polish in all the Christian courts, and Yiddish in the Jewish court. Latin depositions were in the form of *oratio obliqua* and *oratio recta*. They were translated from the vernacular into Latin. Since the second half of the sixteenth century, *oratio recta* was also common in registers kept in several languages: the *formulae* were in an official language (usually Latin), depositions in the vernacular. Polish and Ruthenian registers often did not make any difference between *oratio recta* and *obliqua*. Syntactic constructions such as: "then the witness

[20] Scholars have for a long time studied the language of court texts of late medieval and early modern Polish; see W. URBAN and A. ZAJDA, "Wstęp wydawców", in: *1543: Zapisy polskojęzyczne w księgach sądów szlacheckich województwa krakowskiego*, ed. W. URBAN and A. ZAJDA (Cracow, 2004), pp. 7-28; U. ZACHARA-ZWIĄZEK, *Łacina późnośredniowiecznych ksiąg ławniczych Starej Warszawy* (Warsaw, 2019). David Frick analysed Vilnius court books as historical sources, on the one hand, and as rhetorised genres of text on the other, see D. FRICK, "Wstęp", in: *Wilnianie*, p. XXIX-XXX; ID., "Słowa uszczypliwe", pp. 16-17.

[21] One of the most efficient attempts of examining early modern court narrations is the classic monograph by Carlo Ginzburg (C. GINZBURG, *The Cheese and the Worms: The Cosmos of a Sixteenth-Century Miller*, trans. J. TEDESCHI and A. TEDESCHI (Baltimore, 1980)). Vilnius court texts were scrutinised by David A. Frick, which resulted in a series of his publications about different aspects of life in Vilnius in the seventeenth century. He also examined the linguistic form of the depositions of the witnesses. See FRICK, *Kith, Kin, and Neighbors*, pp. 109-110, 274-289. The Polish legal texts from early modern Vilnius, among them the court records, were examined by Z. KURZOWA, "Z badań and polszczyzną północnokresową XVII i XVIII w. (Uwarunkowania historyczne: Opis system fonetyczno-fonologicznego: Perspektywy rozwojowe)", in: EAD., *Ze studiów nad polszczyzną kresową: Wybór prac* (Cracow, 2007), pp. 206-207.

complained that 'he threatened me'" – incorrect from the point of view of normative grammar – occurred permanently in the court registers and became the norm. In the seventeenth century the Vilnius scribes tried to record depositions close to the spoken language, which sometimes resulted in fascinating linguistic inventions.

Probably in each of these texts one can discern several voices: the voice of the scribe, those of the parties in the litigation, and that of the community (or society) they belonged to. This is manifested by the pattern of languages they used.

For example, a trial that took place in 1556 between Isaac ben Yakub and Jonah ben Isaac concerning the settlement of a joint lease of Polatsk customs collection was recorded in the files of the Vilnius *qahal* court (*beth din*). As no agreement was reached, the parties appealed to a higher court, namely to Salomon Luria, the rabbi of Ostroh. Written testimonies of both Jews were presented in Yiddish with the addition of single Talmudic phrases and one technical term, *arenda* ('tenancy'), borrowed from Polish. A number of similar testimonies can be found in the books of the rabbinical court in Vilnius from the years 1593-1597. They are valuable sources for historians of the early modern language of the Jewish community in the Grand Duchy of Lithuania.[22] They also enable approaching some of the everyday problems encountered by the inhabitants of early modern Vilnius.

Similar micro-stories, partly told by the participants in the events themselves, are quite frequent in the documentation of Christian courts; they concerned both financial and criminal cases. Most frequently they contain complaints about 'boasting' (that is threats), invectives, fisticuffs, theft, wrong accusations, failure to pay back a debt, or failure to appear for an agreed job, as in the court registers of the Vilnius chapter written in Polish:

On 10 October 1652

> Ms Cecylia Ibińska, who was under the juridical authority of the chapter of Vilnius, sued her neighbour, Sebastian, a cartwright, due to the fact that having lived in her house past the lease term (where he leased a flat until an agreed date), he tenaciously stayed at the place. In order to have the matter settled by the court, Ms Ibińska described the events, which were recorded in the books.

[22] Дубнов, *Разговорный язык*, pp. 10-12. In the first half of the seventeenth century, Rabbi Sabatai ben Meir ha-Kohen was the judge (*dayan*).

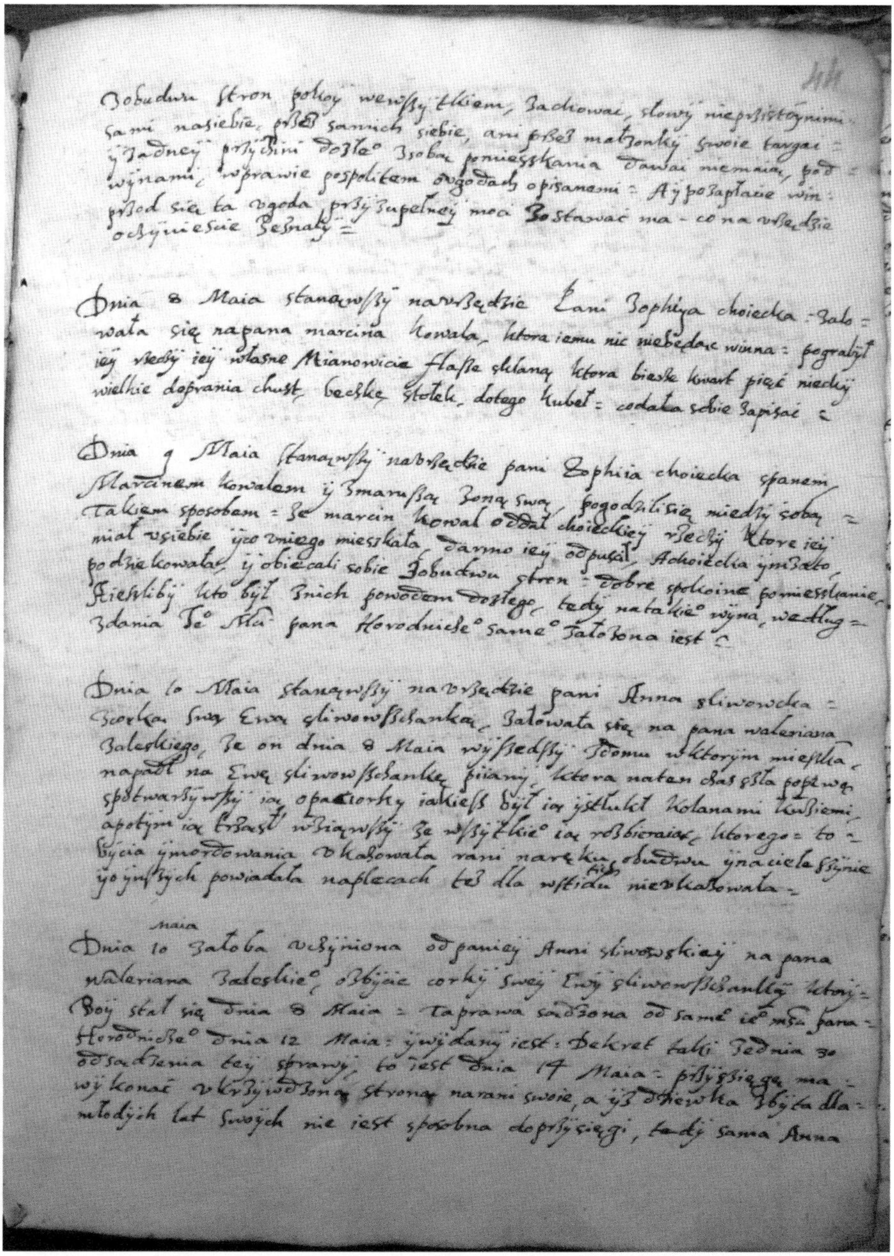

Fig. 47 A page from the court register of the Vilnius burgrave (the *horodniczańska* or burgrave's *jurydyka*), 1620. Vilnius, LVIA, MS F20, ap. 1, nr 4563, f. 44r. Photo J. Niedźwiedź.

On 11 October 1652

Summoned due to Ms Ibińska's plaint, Sebastian, the cartwright, appeared before the court to excuse himself and said that Ms Ibińska owed him 10 Polish *złoty* for various jobs concerning knives, "upon the payment of which I will vacate her house", but he did not present any document confirming the debt nor did he want to swear the required oath. Therefore, having found the said Sebastian's explanation to be insubstantial, the prosecutor's court ordered him to leave the house of Ms Ibińska, giving him, however, one week to do so.[23]

Similar cases were brought before Piotr Nonhart in 1619 and Wawrzyniec Skrzetuski in 1620, the Vilnius burgraves (*horodniczy*), by inhabitants of Vilnius who lived under the jurisdiction of the *jurydyka* of the burgrave (*horodnictwo*). As in the case of the chapter's *jurydyka* court, they were mostly brought by non-elite townsmen or the representatives of the populace. A few examples selected from hundreds of Polish entries in the registers of the *horodnictwo* give us an idea of the nature of these cases, and at the same time allow us to enter the world of disputes of the inhabitants of the burgrave's *jurydyka*:

On 22 April [1619]. Jan Pilnik and his wife sued and gave testimony against Bartosz the tailor who beat and assaulted Pilnik's wife, signs of abrasions on her face and hair torn from her head, and threatened him, which was recorded in the files.

On 29 July [1619]. Having come to the court, Mr Jan Chojecki, in the absence of his father Jerzy Chojecki, filed a petition against his stepmother, Zofija Ostrowska, according to which on 25 July she stole 200 *złoty* from her husband Jerzy Chojecki and the said Jan Chojecki, her stepson, bought a chest and left the house taking all the documents confirming the ownership of the property. Apart from that, she also threatens her husband and stepson.

On 1 August [1619]. Having come to the court, Wojciech the blacksmith said that a flunkey [NN], a servant of [NN], left him a horse that had a sickness in its legs to be treated. The blacksmith began to treat this ailment successfully, but as the horse also suffered from another recondite disease and did not want to eat, it died. The office saw that the condition of the horse's legs improved significantly.

[23] *Protokół spraw potocznych przy sądu wielebnej kapituły wileńskiej za urzędu jego mości księdza Wawrzyńca Mocarskiego kanonika wileńskiego, prokuratora kapitulnego roku 1648 miesiąca Octobra sprawiony*, MS MAB F43-590, f. 36r.

On 11 May [1620]. Having presented herself before the court, the honest Ms Dorota Mistakowska, a tailor, complained in tears about Mrs Marcinowa, a tailor, first name Połonia, who stirs conflicts between the said Dorota Mistakowska and her husband, slandering her and telling people for instance Mrs Kłodziewska, the wife of the usher, rumours about her, according to which Ms Mistakowska behaves dishonestly and cohabits with other [male] tailors, which Ms Mistakowska repudiates and wishes herself to be cleared of any such allegations, which is why she gave her testimony for the protocol and wants to have the case decided by the court.

On 31 May [1620]. Mr Tomasz Szczawieński sued Ms Zofija Chojecka for stealing, in an unknown way, an Italian cock and a laying hen. Mr Szczawieński, having recognised the hen, bought it back for 6 Lithuanian *grosz* from the apothecary Balcerowa in Užupis, who in turn purchased it from Ms Chojecka. He has not recovered the cock, but he said that the cock was found together with the hen.

On 31 May [1620]. Having stood before the court, Walenty the carpenter complained about Ms Zofija Chojecka for stealing a hen on 26 May. Walenty the carpenter blames no one else but the said Chojecka. Three other laying hens went missing previously for ten weeks.

On 1 June [1620]. Mrs Marcinowa, a neighbour of Ms Chojecka, gave her personal testimony in the court that she carried that laying hen from Chojecka's hand to Mrs Balcerowa the apothecary to Užupis. Mrs Chojecka's reply is to be given tomorrow.[24]

Conflicts between townspeople, similar to those quoted above, were mentioned by an anonymous Jesuit poet in a pamphlet from 1624 aimed at the Evangelical priest Samuel Dambrowski, but for persuasive purposes the only wrongdoers mentioned in it are Lutherans from German (Nemiecka) Street:

Some people confess only their lesser sins,
    Hiding those that stink worse.
"I am in conflict with my neighbour and I am still angry with him
    Which is why I never invite him".
But what about theft and fraud,
    Or cheap materials sold too dearly?
Cheating on pounds and quarts, usury and theft

[24] *Księgi sądowe jurysdykcyjej horodnictwa wileńskiego roku 1619 od dnia 2 marca roku mienionego*, MS LVIA F20, ap. 1, nr. 4563. The socio-topographical analysis of this source in: FREJLICH, *Pod przysądem horodnictwa wileńskiego*, pp. 155-228.

Or deceiving one's neighbour!
Mephitic lusts, ugly lechery
Be it by the will, or by the deed – who will count them all?[25]

These were mostly cases concerning individuals. The brawl between the members of two guilds who fought for priority during the ceremonial entry of King Władysław IV Vasa in 1648 reverberated more widely in the town. Let us have a look at a version of the guild of furriers in the form of a protestation (*protestacja*) lodged in the municipal court against the locksmiths and knife smith

> who, during the happy arrival of His Majesty in Vilnius, despite the noble magistrate's exhortation to behave as honestly as possible, when the plaintiffs were passing with their flag and in the prescribed order through the Gate of Dawn to meet the king in the city fields, the defendants, obstructing their departure, attacked them there with weapons and beat, cut, and fatally injured them, while other people dispersed; they even deprived Mr Jerzy Pizylewicz of an eye shooting him from a musket (*bombardae*), as evidenced by the hearing of the injured parties and the witnesses conducted by the city's lay judges on 20 March of this year. Furthermore, we demand punishment for those guilty of the public unrest and the insult to the king's presence. The case was heard and the defendants were summoned.[26]

The narratives from court registers are marked by a multitude of perspectives.[27] The rhetoric used in these texts can be analysed at at least two levels as we hear the objective voice of the office, that is the voice of the legal procedure, and the voice of the defendant, and if there are more parties or witnesses, they become even polyphonic. Since most of the cases registered in the court books were quite simple, this polyphonic rhetoric is not very complicated. The voice of the legal formulary arranged the narrative and to some extent made it more consistent in style and essence, quoting, for example, the final verdict, if this was arrived at (many cases ended in a settlement). However, even in spite

[25] *Tajemna rada abo exorbitantiae niektóre Samuela Dambrowskiego supersuspendenta konfusyi szachskiej od pewnych osób tejże sekty do pospólstwa luterskiego we zborze miane i od nichże naganione*, in: Z. NOWAK, *Kontrreformacyjna satyra obyczajowa w Polsce XVII wieku* (Gdańsk, 1968), p. 272.

[26] MS BJ 2926, pp. 270-277.

[27] J. NIEDŹWIEDŹ, "Strzała w nodze świętego Michała: Daniel Naborowski i wileńskie narracje sądowe z XVII w.", in: *Daniel Naborowski. Krakowianin – Litwin – Europejczyk*, ed. K. GAJDKA and K. FOLLPRECHT (Katowice and Cracow, 2008), pp. 83-101.

of this organising of the texts, they still speak with various voices, which is revealed, for instance, in the change of grammatical person observable in verbs and in borrowings from colloquial language, as I mentioned above.

Against this background, one would perceive differently the narratives about conflicts which were settled from those in which one 'orator' finally gave way, or at least tried to, the events being presented to from one point of view and with one rhetorical strategy. This does not mean that other voices do not emerge from behind the main façade. However, a skilful orator was able effectively to hide them or even use them. The dispute itself was then levelled out, because the arguments of the opposing side were disarmed, deprived of their strength, and subordinated to a different rhetorical strategy. Thus texts which are not narratives from the court seek to reduce the polyphony to a monologue, as is the case in most agonistic books, for instance in accounts of disputations, or in polemical treatises, such as *About the Unity of the Church of God Under the One Shepherd and About Greek Apostasy* by Piotr Skarga.[28]

This technique was not only used in the great religious debates of the 'open' city. A text of Jesuit provenance that presents an interesting example in this respect, will be discussed here in some detail.

The Jesuits' presence in Vilnius began not with a contention of Protestants or Orthodox Christians, but of Pedro Ruiz de Moros, a Catholic, and, moreover, a clergyman, known as Doctor Spaniard.[29] From the turn of 1566-1567, he was the archpriest of the parish church of St. John the Baptist and St. John the Evangelist, a most important church because it was the second-largest and best equipped Catholic church in the city after the cathedral. It was this church that the Jesuits began to zealously strive to take over, and their efforts were supported by bishop Protasewicz. According to the fathers from the newly established collegium, other, equally profitable prebends were offered to Ruiz de Moros, but he was stubborn because he was ill disposed towards the Order. And since the parish's collator was none other than the king himself, whom Doctor Spaniard had served for decades as a distinguished secretary and lawyer, the Jesuits and Protasewicz could not do much to achieve their goal.[30] There are only few documents revealing the course of the dispute. If we had court records and correspondence between the parties at our disposal, different

[28] P. Skarga, *O jedności Kościoła Bożego pod jednym Pasterzem i o greckim od tej jedności odstąpieniu* (Vilnius, 1577).

[29] As was already mentioned in Chapter 5.

[30] S. Rostowski, *Lituanicarum Societas Jesu historiarum libri decem*, ed. J. Martynov (Paris, 1877), p. 42; Tazbir, "Roizjusz Piotr", p. 502.

types of narrative and rhetoric could be compared. Unfortunately, we have only the accounts of the Jesuits, who tried to present the whole situation not so much as a dispute, but rather as a parable of patience rewarded by God:

> Since in 1571 our people did not have a church, nor could they celebrate [services] in the parish church of St. John adjacent to our collegium, which Roisius the Spaniard [i.e. Ruiz de Moros] did not want to allow for no reason, and since there was no other convenient place nearby to build a church, father rector, entrusting the matter to God, thanks to the letters given to the apostolic nuncio Vincenzo dal Portico and the king's minor sister, in which he asked the king to join the church and the collegium, as well as to donate Roisius' house, through which there was a passage to the church, received an exceptionally generous privilege from King Sigismund II Augustus. However, our people did not want to exercise this right during the lifetime of Roisius, believing that we should wait for a more favourable opportunity to complete this case, because of which he was outraged at us, being seriously angry with the envy of the elder [man] and he was determined in his pretence that he did not want to accept any of the much more favourable benefits offered to him by the [bishop] of Vilnius.[31]

The dispute would probably have lasted much longer than two years if "Doctor Spaniard", who successfully opposed the Jesuits, had not died in 1571. The Jesuits, to whom the bishop had promised the property, immediately took over the parish buildings and placed a school in Ruiz de Moros' house.[32]

> But soon God freed us from all difficulties and the need to wait long, taking Roisius less than one month after this royal privilege was issued. So this parish church of St. John the Baptist, which is the most spacious and magnificent in this city, is subject to our supervision,[33]

concludes the author with satisfaction. Soon, new buildings were to be erected around the church. This was the beginning of an impressive university complex. The conflict between the Jesuits and Doctor Spaniard was like a prelude to the future undertakings of the Jesuits in the Lithuanian capital and to the large number of texts that were written over the years to come.

[31] *Historia seu succincta narratio de origine ac fundatione Collegii Vilnensis Societatis Jesu ab Anno 1569 usque ad annum 1611 in Julio*, ARSI Lit. 38f., p. 8.
[32] J. Fijałek, "Kościół rzymskokatolicki na Litwie", p. 740.
[33] *Historia seu succincta narratio*, p. 8.

In the narrative analysed here, Ruiz de Moros' voice was suppressed by reducing his claims to the grumblings of an old, batty, and malicious man.[34] In this way the claims of the Jesuits , additionally supported by the king and the local bishop, were presented as fully justified. In fact, we do not know the position of Roisius, because the author of the chronicle did not call on any of the arguments voiced by him. However, knowing about his level of experience as a lawyer, it is hard to imagine that he would base his claims only on his own caprice and stubbornness, as the Jesuits wished to present them.

Trying to turn off one's opponent's voice is a mark not only of Jesuit agonistic rhetoric. All parties in a dispute sought to monologise the narrative. Such efforts are visible in the majority of works featuring as voices in polemics between members of all Christian communities present in the city at the turn of the sixteenth and seventeenth centuries.

The Texts of Religious Polemics (the 'Open' City)

The sixty years from 1570 and to 1630 were marked in Vilnius by constant polemics between Calvinists, Lutherans, Polish Brethren (Arians), Catholics, Uniates, and Orthodox Christians. And separate mention should be made of the polemic concerning a commentary on *Yore de'a* among Jewish scholars of the 1540s. We will say more on this issue in the further part of this chapter. In the middle of the seventeenth century, the temperature of interconfessional disputes somehow lowered, and the battlefield moved to other regions of the state and to other cities. Therefore, at the end of the sixteenth and in the first half of the seventeenth century, when the actions of Jesuits gradually led to the dominance of the Catholics (including the Uniates) in the capital of the Grand Duchy, religious disputes in the city reached their climax. The torrent of polemics and disputes decreased in the third decade of the seventeenth century, when a state of equilibrium was reached in the city. The Jesuits could afford to stop both provoking Lithuanian Protestants forced on to the defensive and harassing Orthodox Christians, who desperately defended their confession

[34] The malicious Jesuit author forgot to mention that Ruiz de Moros had a squint (which was commonly known) to present Doctor Spaniard as a totally ridiculous person. See "Although Roisius the Spaniard, has a squint ("*krzywe oczy*"), // His wisdom always goes on the right paths". M. Rej, *Źwierzyniec, w którym rozmaitych stanów ludzi, źwirząt i ptaków kształty, przypadki i obyczaje są właśnie wypisane: A zwłaszcza ku czasom dzisiejszym naszym niejako przypadające* (Cracow, 1562), p. 76r.

against the increasingly strong Vilnius Uniates. This does not mean, however, that Catholics stopped their persecutions altogether.

In principle, religious polemics were fought between the four camps, that is between the Catholics and the Protestants, and, on the other hand, between the Orthodox and the Uniates. However, there were also other configurations. Although the Augsburg Evangelicals (Lutherans) and Reformed Evangelicals (Calvinists) were essentially found in the same camp, there were nevertheless controversies and disputes between them, mainly of a dogmatic nature. We also know of rabbinical discussions on the interpretation of Joseph Karo's treatise, which will be discussed later.

The Jesuits were the main animators in the heated disputes between 1580 and 1632. Among them, a special role was played by Piotr Skarga, who worked in Vilnius from 1573.[35] Some other Jesuits were particularly active in the struggle against the Calvinists, such as Marcin Śmiglecki, mentioned above, Jakub Wujek, Stanisław Warszewicki, and Stanisław Grodzicki, as well as a graduate of the Academy and member of the cathedral chapter, canon Andrzej Jurgiewicz. The main Protestant opponents of the Vilnius Catholics included the Arian Fausto Sozzini, who lived not in Vilnius but in the Cracow voivodeship, and Vilnius Calvinist activists, the most vociferous of them being Andrzej Wolan.

The Jesuits carried out their mission on two fronts, against their Protestant and Orthodox adversaries, although in their struggle against Orthodoxy they were replaced after 1596 by polemicists who supported the Union. Apart from the Jesuits Piotr Skarga and Stanisław Grodzicki, to this group belonged clergymen connected to the Uniate monastery of the Holy Trinity: Hypacy Pociej, Jozafat Kuncewicz, Josyf Veliamyn Rutsky, and Leon Kreuza Rzewuski. On the Orthodox side, they were opposed by the archimandrites of the Holy Spirit monastery: Leontyi Karpovych, Meletius Smotrycki, and Józef Bobrykowicz, as well as by Orthodox polemicists from outside Vilnius, including Hiob Borecki and Zachariasz Kopysteński, and a member of the community of the Czech Brethren, Marcin Broniewski, who supported them with his pen.

[35] The role of the Jesuits in the initiation of the Counter-Reformation campaign in Vilnius was pointed out by father Stanisław Załęski: "In St. John's church, [Warszewicki and Skarga] began a series of sermons on the Most Blessed Sacrament, refuting the false teachings of Calvin; they took over the pulpits in the cathedral and other churches because, apart from a few Dominicans, there were no other suitable preachers in Vilnius" (S. ZAŁĘSKI, *Jezuici w Polsce*, 1, *Walka z różnowierstwem 1555-1608*, 1, *1555-1586* (Lviv, 1900), p. 190).

The Lithuanian Calvinists also undertook various measures against the Polish Brethren, who are often mentioned in the provisions of their provincial synods. Already in 1592, Andrzej Wolan published in the church's printing house three letters rebutting the Arian doctrine which negated, for instance, the deity of Jesus. Two of these letters were addressed to minister Jan Licyniusz Namysłowski, whom we have meant before. Wolan mentioned that they had previously conducted an oral debate. The tone of the text brings to mind an exhortation letter (*epistola monitoria*). Apparently, Wolan did not want to spoil his relations with Namysłowski with an offensive letter (*epistola offensiva*), with which he would undoubtedly have satisfied the Jesuits.[36] Later, the rhetoric of the Vilnius Calvinists became more fierce, which can be seen in a publication by Wojciech Salinarius entitled *Cenzura albo rozsądku na konfessyją ludzi tych, którzy pospolitym nazwiskiem rzeczeni bywają arriany, a w rzeczy samej są socynistami ... księgi ...* (Censorship or the Reason for the Faith of People Who Use Their Common Name to Refer to Arians, But Are in Fact Socynians ... Books ...), published in 1615 thanks to the efforts of the synod.[37] The fifth canon of the provisions of the Vilnius synod held in 1626 in its turn addressed the issue of publishing anti-Trinitarian texts: "We submitted *Scripta antisociniana* [anti-Socinian texts] by the late father Doctor Krośniewicz of blessed memory *sub censuram* [to the censorship] of father Adam Raszewski".[38] The Lithuanian catechisms published by the Calvinists also had an anti-Trinitarian undertone, which is particularly evident in the prefaces that precede them.[39] These texts, like the anti-Arian works of the Jesuits, were important not only locally: their reception went far beyond Vilnius and Lithuania. The same can be said about the disputations held in the city.

The polemic between the Jewish scholars about Joseph Karo's (1488-1575) treatise mentioned above was of supra-regional importance.[40] In 1646, two separate commentaries on the famous halakhic treatise of Joseph Karo

[36] A. Wolan, *Epistolae Aliquot Ad Refellendum Doctrinae Samosatenianae errorem, ad astruendam Orthodoxam de Divina Trinitate sententiam, hoc tempore lectu non inutiles. Ab Andrea Volano scriptae* (Vilnius, 1592).

[37] D. Chemperek, "Środowisko literackie protestantów w Wilnie pierwszej połowy xvii wieku: Krąg pisarzy zborowych", *Wschodni Rocznik Humanistyczny* 4 (2007), p. 48.

[38] *Akta synodów litewskich prowincjonalnych z lat 1611-1637*, ms mab F40-1157, f. 95r. See E. Hłasko, "Stosunek jednoty litewskiej do arian w świetle kanonów wieku xvii", *Ateneum Wileńskie* 11 (1936), pp. 283-290.

[39] M. Malicki, "Nieznany dotychczas polski katechizm kalwiński ze zbiorów Biblioteki Księcia Augusta w Wolfenbüttel", *Biuletyn Biblioteki Jagiellońskiej* 43.1-2 (1993), p. 59.

[40] L.I. Rabinowitz, *Shlulhan Arukh*, ej, vol. 18, p. 530.

Shulchan Aruch were published independently of each other. They particularly concerned the part of the work entitled *Yore de'a*, which deals with, among other things, ritual slaughter, kosherness, purity, conversion, and mourning. The author of the first commentary, entitled *Turei Zahav*, was David ha-Levi Segal, rabbi of Ostroh.[41] The second, *Siftei Kohen*, known as *Shakh*, was published by the Vilnius scholar Shabbatai ben Meir HaKohen (1621-1662).[42] Shabbatai, who disagreed with the solutions proposed by David, wrote the polemical work *Nekuddot haKesef*. Although this text appeared in print only in 1677 after the death of both these men, it had probably been known in manuscript copies, since David responded to it in *Daf Aharon* (Last Page), added at the end of his treatise. Shabbatai was not to be outdone and wrote *Kunteres Aharon* (Last Supplement), also published in 1677.[43]

Disputations in Vilnius: Between Rhetorical Action and Dialogue

There are two meanings of the word 'disputation' which will be used here. The first one means a public encounter of at least two opponents who try to convince each other by their arguments. The other meaning is a manuscript or printed relation of such an encounter. It can be considered a literary genre.[44] The relationship between the two forms of disputations resembled the *à rebours* relationship between script and performance. First, a performance took place on the basis of which later the 'play' was written and distributed in print or in manuscript. Disputation understood as a literary genre combines the qualities of a dialogue and a polemical sermon, of a theological and a polemical treatise, of drama and speech, in which the latter belongs to the rhetorical judicial genre (*genus iudiciale*), although sometimes even more to the epideictic genre (*genus demonstrativum*). Disputation-dialogues were also supposed to play the role of reports from the ideological battle field, as well as manuals on how to debate with people of a different faith and effectively reject their arguments.

[41] M. BAŁABAN, "Dawid ben Samuel haLewi", in: *PSB*, 4, p. 461.

[42] COHEN, *History of the Jews in Vilnius*, pp. 196-197; T. POLAŃSKI, "Sabbataj ben Meir ha-Kohen", in: *PSB*, 34, p. 241.

[43] Sh. EIDELBERG, "Shabbetai ben Meir haKohen", in: *EJ*, 18, pp. 338-339.

[44] Disputation as a literary genre was recently discussed by M. RYSZKA-KURCZAB, "May every lover of truth find it through reading": Manners of authenticating the message in sixteenth-century accounts of Polish religious disputations, *Terminus* 20 (2018), Special Issue, pp. 113-144.

The first disputation is said to have taken place as early as 1570. According to the Jesuits, the Calvinists led by Andrzej Wolan, "*homo cerebrosus, pugnax, sectator Calvini perditus*" ("a deranged and belligerent man, and wicked supporter of Calvin"),[45] as a later Jesuit historian described him, gathered under the walls of the collegium and provoked the Catholics. A discussion arose because the Jesuits answered from the windows. A few days later this resulted in a public disputation that lasted three days. It was attended by many inhabitants of the city and therefore one of its main goals, strengthening the faithful Catholics, could be achieved.[46]

Another known public disputation, this time between Jesuits, was conducted on 15 August 1574 at the beginning of the new academic year. The participants were the Spaniard Pedro Viana (1549-1609), professor of polemical theology, and the Scotsman John Hay (1546-1608), professor of philosophy.[47] The course of the debate is unknown, but on the basis of the theses printed in Cracow[48] we can guess that it had the character of a dialectic display. The disputation between Hay and Viana was not only an academic show. The two scholars represented two different attitudes towards Aristotelism: Hay based himself on some ideas of Duns Scotus while Viana was a follower of orthodox Thomism.[49] The academic and personal conflict between them increased. In the end, provincial Francisco Sunyer (also a Spaniard) moved Hay to Cracow and Viana replaced his Scottish colleague on the chair of philosophy.[50] Public disputations between Jesuit students took place in the following years.[51]

In Vilnius, the next public discussions between Catholics and Protestants did not take place until the 1590s. Earlier on, however, a high-profile international theological disputation was held there between Calvinists and Lutherans. It took place on 14 June 1585 and had the Eucharist as its subject; it was a

[45] ROSTOWSKI, *Lituanicarum Societas Jesu historiarum libri decem*, p. 43.

[46] *Ibid.*, pp. 43-44.

[47] R. DAROWSKI, "First Aristotelians of Vilnius", *Organon* 15 (1979), p. 74. PIECHNIK, *Początki Akademii Wileńskiej*, p. 124; R. DAROWSKI, "Pedro Viana SJ (1549-1609) et son activité de philosophie en Lituanie", *Forum Philosophicum* 3 (1998), pp. 199-201.

[48] *Assertiones theologicae et philosophicae, in Collegio Vilnensi Societatis Iesu, sub renovationem autumnalem deiendendae anno Domini 1574* (Cracow, 1574).

[49] DAROWSKI, "First Aristotelians of Vilnius", p. 74; PIECHNIK, *Początki Akademii Wileńskiej*, p. 124.

[50] Roman Darowski remembered the fact that Viana was keen to intrigue against his opponents. He was suspected of political machinations against King Stephen Bathory, which resulted in removing the Jesuit from the Vilnius college in 1578. See DAROWSKI, "Pedro Viana SJ (1549-1609) et son activité", pp. 200-201.

[51] DAROWSKI, "Pedro Viana SJ (1549-1609) et son activité", p. 201.

result of controversies which had arisen after the proclamation of the Sandomierz Agreement in 1570, that is the promise of mutual respect and future collaboration signed between the Lutherans, Calvinists, and Czech Brethren living in the Polish-Lithuanian Commonwealth.[52] The report, written in Latin, informs us in detail about the course of the debate.[53] It was held in the palace of the Radziwiłłs of Biržai on Vilnius Street, and the patron and moderator of the meeting was the governor of Vilnius, Krzysztof Radziwiłł 'The Thunderbolt'. The main disputant on the Calvinist (Helvetian) side was the representative of the Vilnius church [*zbór*], Dr Andrzej Wolan "*politicus et secretarius Regius*" ("a statesman and a royal secretary"), while his Lutheran opponent was Paul Weiss, "*Academiae in Monte Regio theologiae professor secundarius*" ("the assistant Professor of Theology at the University of Königsberg") and the envoy of the Prussian regent George Frederick of Brandenburg-Ansbach. Several high officials of the Reformed Evangelical Church of Lithuania, as well as representatives of both Protestant churches [*zbory*] from Prussia, Lithuania, and Poland took part in the dispute.

The manuscript report of the debate, preserved in the library of Wolfenbüttel, is an example of a theological dialogue based on the sixteenth-century culture of disputation. In a sense, its form resembles a sermon from a popular postil, with a distinctive dialogic element.[54] Unlike the later disputations with the Jesuit Śmiglecki and the Arian Namysłowski on one side and the Calvinist Mikołajewski on the other, the gathering of 1585 was held in international Latin (although Wolan used Polish when responding to Krzysztof Radziwiłł). The remaining elements of the colloquium, both as rhetorical action and a text, were analogous to those conducted in Polish, but the spirit of the text is different from that of works interpreting clashes between Catholics and Protestants.

There were two rounds, one in the morning and one in the afternoon. Wolan, in his role as respondent, put forward four theses that formed the basis for

[52] D. Petkūnas, "1585 metų Vilniaus kolokviumas – kunigaikščio Kristupo Radvilo Perkūno pastangos išsaugoti ekleziastinę bendrystę tarp LDK Liuteronų ir Reformatų bažnyčių", in: *Colloquium habitum Vilnae die 14 Iunii, anno 1585 super articulo de Caena Domini*, ed. J. Gelumbeckaitė and S. Narbutas (Vilnius, 2006), pp. 181-183; id., "Wilno 1585 Colloquium: Lutheran and Reformed discord over sacramental theology in Lithuania", *Odrodzenie i Reformacja w Polsce* 49 (2005), pp. 17-34.

[53] For critical edition of the text with images and translations into Lithuanian and German, see: *Colloquium habitum Vilnae die 14 Iunii*.

[54] L. Przymuszała, *Struktura i pragmatyka* Postylli *Samuela Dambrowskiego* (Opole, 2003), pp. 57-70.

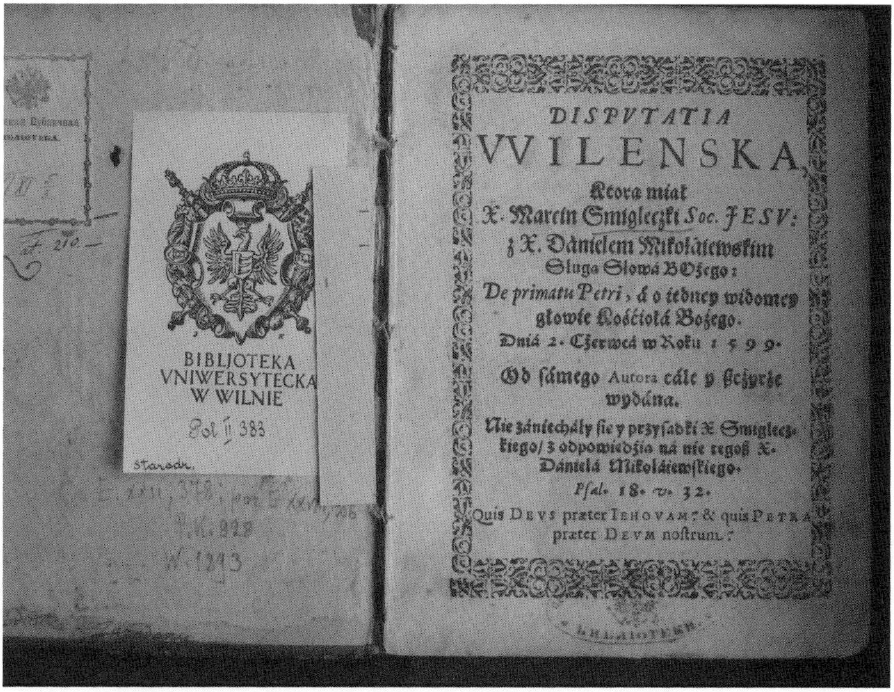

Fig. 48 D. Mikołajewski, *The Vilnan Disputation* (Vilnius, 1599). <https:// dbc.wroc.pl/dlibra/publication/13385/edition/11901> (accessed: 31.05.2022, public domain).

the discussion with Weiss as the opponent. The other participants were moderators. The report kept in Wolfenbüttel was prepared by one of the Augsburg Evangelicals and was later authorised by Weiss. It is factual and meticulously reflects the arguments of both sides. It is also characterised by a rather frugal interpretation of the issues raised. This last quality distinguishes the dialogue of 1585 from other texts of this type published in the next decade by the Jesuits and Calvinists. Apparently, during the colloquium, the Calvinists and Lutherans were guided by the ideas of the Sandomierz Agreement (*Consensus Sandomiriensis*). This 1570 agreement provided for political co-operation of the Reformed communities in the Polish-Lithuanian Commonwealth, mutual acknowledgment of their sacraments, and joined synods. One of the results of the co-operation was the publication of a new Protestant translation of the Bible into Polish by Daniel Mikołajewski (the so-called the Gdańsk Bible, published in 1632).

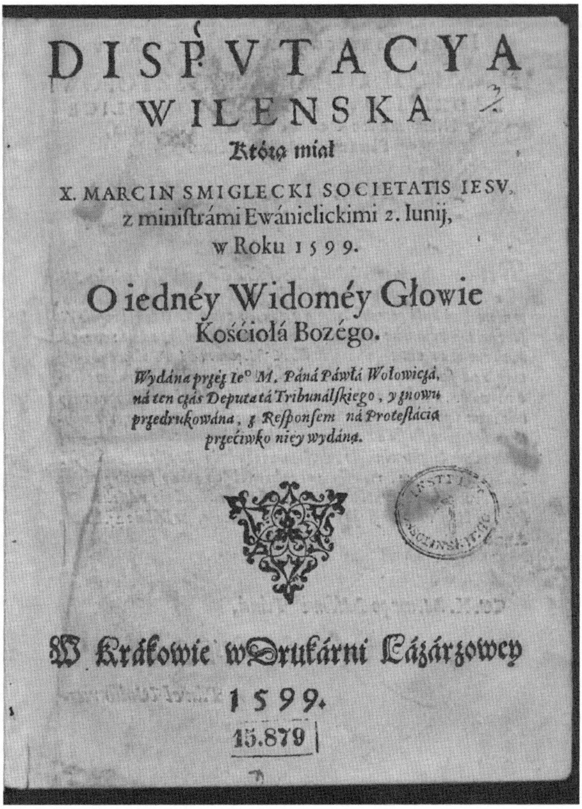

DISPVTACYA
WILENSKA
Ktorą miał
X. MARCIN SMIGLECKI SOCIETATIS IESV,
z miniſtrámi Ewánielickimi 2. Iunij,
w Roku 1599.
O iednéy Widoméy Głowie
Kośćiołá Bożégo.
Wydána przez Ie° M. Páná Páwłá Wołowicżá, ná ten czás Deputatá Tribunálſkiego, y znowu przedrukowána, z Reſponſem ná Proteſtácią przećiwko niey wydáną.
W Krákowie w Drukárni Łázárzowey
1599.

Fig. 49 M. Śmiglecki, *The Vilnan Disputation* (Cracow, 1599). <https://dbc.wroc.pl/dlibra/publication/4958/edition/4779> (accessed: 31.05.2022, public domain).

The counterpoint to the Vilnius inter-Protestant debate is a published record of the disputation held on 2 June 1599 concerning the one and only head of the Church. It took place shortly after the end of the synod of the Unitas Lithuaniae, during which many Protestants from Lithuania and the Crown signed a broadly discussed agreement with representatives of the Orthodox elite.[55] The respondent was the Jesuit priest, theologian, and professor of the

[55] *Unia ichmościów panów senatorów stanu rycerskiego greckiego i ewangelickiego nabożeństwa Obojga Narodów Korony Polskiej i Wielkiego Księstwa Litewskiego przy prawie i wolnościach in casu religionis oponujących się w Wilnie zawarta anno 1599*, MS MAB F40-833, ff. 2r-3v.

Academy of Vilnius Marcin Śmiglecki; the opponent was the priest Daniel Mikołajewski, the aforementioned translator of the Bible (the Gdańsk Bible). Interestingly, accounts authorised by both disputants have survived. Thanks to them we know that at the beginning of September the reverend Mikołajewski responded to Śmiglecki's publication, which had been printed a few weeks earlier in Vilnius. In addition, at the end July and in the beginning of August, Marcin Gracjan Gertich, the superintendent of the Czech Brethren, at the request of the authorities of the Lithuanian Calvinist Unity, published a book in Vilnius rebutting the charges made by father Śmiglecki.[56] We will be more interested in the Jesuit version, because it shows better the mechanisms of such texts. However, we will also look to the Protestant narration of the events.

The Jesuit text is preceded by a letter of dedication from Paweł Wołłowicz addressed to the Catholic magnate Mikołaj Krzysztof Radziwiłł 'the Orphan', in which the circumstances of the dispute are presented. The author was surprised that the meeting could take place only then, although both Catholics and Calvinists had long been looking for opportunities to hold it. According to him, the guilty ones were, of course, the Protestants, who were obstructive, for instance at first "they wished to conduct the disputation in writing, which is unreasonable *inter praesentes* [in the presence of the participants]" and "impeded the matter with various conditions pertaining particularly to the venue and time".[57] Among other things, they did not want the dispute to take place in the buildings of the Academy. Finally, the place designated by the Protestants was agreed. The Calvinists demanded this, because they were the ones who asked the questions, to which the Jesuits humbly agreed and "listed four articles about which they were to discuss".[58]

[56] M.G. Gertich, *Protestacyja przeciwko niesłusznej chlubie tych, co za przyczyną distputacji ks. Marcina Śmigleckiego z ks. Danielem Mikołajewskim ministrem Ewangelii P.N.J. Krystusa o widzialnej głowie Kościoła Bożego etc. przed zwycięstwem triumfują* (Vilnius, 1599). Śmiglecki refuted father Gertich's accusations in the second Cracow edition of the disputation, quoted here. See Estreicher, *Bibliografia polska*, 28, pp. 307-308; Natoński, *Humanizm jezuicki*, pp. 102-107.

[57] M. Śmiglecki, *Dysputacyja wileńska, którą miał ks. Marcin Śmiglecki Societatis Iesu z ministrami ewanjelickiemi 2 Iunii w r. 1599 o jednej widomej głowie Kościoła Bożego*, published by Mr Paweł Wołowicz, a judge of the Lithuanian Tribunal, and reprinted with a reply to the protest (*protestacja*) against (the first edition) of this book, 1599, f. A2r. In the "Foreword to the Reader" ("*Przedmowa do Czytelnika*"), Mikołajewski rejected the allegations made by Śmiglecki, presenting in detail the circumstances of setting the date of the debate and blaming the Catholic side. D. Mikołajewski, *Dysputacyja wileńska*, ff. B2v-B3v.

[58] *Ibid.*, f. A2v.

On the agreed day, the moderators sat down to hear the disputation: the Lithuanian chancellor Lew Sapieha on the Catholic side, and the marshal of the Grand Duchy of Lithuania, Jerzy Radziwiłł (1578-1613), representing the Protestants. Those present were reminded of the five conditions of the colloquium:

1. Only two speakers were to talk, if someone else wanted to join in, it was only with the consent of the moderators.
2. Only ministers of the Churches were supposed to argue, without resorting to the help of any third parties.
3. Prefaces, acclamations, sermons, and all kinds of long speeches were forbidden.
4. "The evidence was to be derived from Scripture", and if the ministers wanted to invoke the Church Fathers, they would allow the Catholics to do the same.
5. The Protestants were supposed to keep to the subject.

And so the disputation was conducted for six hours according to these rules in such peace and humility that there were no offensive words, no mocking, no shouting, except for one laugh when the honourable minister argued that *Petrus* and *Petra* mean different things because *Petrus est masculinum, petra foemininum*, as if *synonima* could not be *diversis generis*, which is known even to the pupils in the Donatus class. However, this laughter soon ceased by order of the moderators.[59]

The report, printed a few weeks after the event, was based on "a few sufficient minutes written during [the disputation], immediately gathered and given to all those present to authorise".[60] Wołłowicz emphasised that this was a faithful account of the discussion, and that the aim of the publication was primarily to prove that "there is, and can be, no evidence against the Catholic truth, which has already lasted for one and a half thousand years and will last until the end of the world".[61] Secondly, the point was that "the victorious claimed

[59] *Ibid.*, f. A2v-A3r.
[60] *Ibid.*, f. A3r.
[61] *Ibid.*, f. A3r.

victory for themselves",[62] so the public had to be provided with evidence of the truth, that is the true, Catholic, victory had to be described.

At the end of the book, Śmiglecki added an extract in which he summarised the arguments with which the statements of the Protestants could be refuted: "Also, learn how to answer an evangelical if someone asks you how a Jesuit was defeated by a church minister".[63] This last fragment explains the meaning of the publication of *Dysputacyja wileńska* (Vilnius Disputation) and why the debate was initiated at all. The version of it written from Śmiglecki's perspective is to be, on the one hand, a set of model instructions on how to deal with the accusations made by the Calvinists, and on the other hand – and this seems to be much more important – physical proof of the superiority of Catholic arguments over evangelical ones. In other words, the Jesuits are more concerned with the propaganda overtones of their victory than with the substantive importance of the disputation, "Finally, if you ask me who won this disputation, I will briefly say that you can work it out for yourself by reading this without my help. And if any man denies it boldly, reply to him with confidence: *Nego, proba quod dicis* [I deny, prove what you say]".[64]

The propagandistic significance of this kind of event must have been very clear to public opinion, as the dispute took place "in the presence of a great many princes, senators (including five *voivodes* [...]), judges of the Tribunal, knights, and ordinary people of the Roman, Greek and evangelical rites",[65] The extent of its influence was strengthened by the publications mentioned above. Victory was to be confirmed by the audience, as it was also, for example, after the disputation in Novahrudak of 1594, when "one of the greater men of them admitted before one of our moderators that Licyniusz did not stand up to the Jesuit".[66]

[62] "One of those victors that I know well, who recently came to the court, claimed obstinately before a high official of the king and other people that his people had won. As the others did not believe him and quarrelled with him, he swore that he should die before matins if he is wrong, adding some blasphemies against the Mass, the Blessed Sacrament and Holy Mary. Suddenly, his health failed and he did not live to see not only the next day (Lord have mercy on him as he was known to me and to many others) but also the evening. Thus the Lord punishes blasphemies immediately" (*ibid.*, ff. A4r-A4 v.).

[63] *Ibid.*, f. H4r.

[64] *Ibid.*

[65] Mikołajewski, *Dysputacyja wileńska*, f. C1v. The author of *Summa dysputacyjej wileńskiej* writes that "several thousand people witnessed this". *Ibid.*, f. S4r.

[66] Zajączkowski, *Opisanie dysputacyjej nowogródzkiej*, p. 54.

Thus, Śmiglecki's action was, first of all, a rhetorical act or, as Mikołajewski wished, an eristic one. The argument would be based on the fourteenth principle formulated later by Arthur Schopenhauer, according to which one should triumphantly announce one's victory, even if in fact one did not prove one was right.[67] Mikołajewski writes:

> The ultimate aim of father Śmiglecki's *Foreword* to the *Vilnius Disputation* is to credit himself with the victory and present us as defeated and convinced, so in his letter to the Vilnius bailiff he had boasted that he won the disputation even before it took place![68]

However, the Protestants themselves strove no less to prove their victory and resorted to tricks similar to those used by the Jesuits. The poem published at the end of Śmiglecki's book, *Summa dysputacyjej wileńskiej* (The Summary of the Vilnius Disputation), signed with the initials A.P., quoted the words of "the most excellent disciples of father Śmiglecki", who indirectly acknowledged Mikołajewski's superiority.

> After the disputation, they reportedly said: "Mikołajewski
> should be sent to Cracow and given a penny for board,
> to dispute with those learned there
> and see if he can win". "But do we not have a good school here?"
> they said. "Yes, but there he would lose completely".[69]

Śmiglecki also drew attention to the eristic character of this type of publication in the record of the Novahrudak disputation of 1594. He warned Catholic readers of the dishonest devices of heretics who never respond directly to accurate arguments, and when they are shown a text that undermines their argument, they "jump to another text, which speaks of a different matter and so its words should be understood differently".[70] According to Śmiglecki, examples of such conduct could be found in previous disputations: of Jan Krotowicjusz with Jesuits in Poznań; Marcin Czechowic, Jan Niemojewski, and Piotr Statorius in

[67] A. SCHOPENHAUER, *Die Kunst, Recht zu behalten*, ed. F. VOLPI (Frankfurt am Main and Leipzig, 1995), p. 51, *Kunstgriff 14*; the German text with an English translation: <http://coolhaus.de/art-of-controversy/>, access 7.06.2021).

[68] MIKOŁAJEWSKI, *Dysputacyja wileńska*, f. A4r.

[69] *Ibid.*, f. S4r.

[70] ZAJĄCZKOWSKI, *Opisanie dysputacyjej nowogródzkiej (Do Czytelnika)*.

Lublin; and Szymon Budny's colloquium with the bishop of Samogitia, Jan Domanowski, in Polatsk.

Similar accusations were made by Mikołajewski against Śmiglecki, mainly concerning the unreliable quotation of arguments. Mikołajewski mentioned two eristic techniques, described later by Schopenhauer, that is, *mutatio controversiae* and the *relative-absolute* confusion.[71]

> For in the printed edition of this disputation he used a great strategy and art to defeat his opponent: Śmiglecki omitted in silence many of my arguments, putting into my mouth other, trifling ones, while blunting some of those that I had actually used or ascribing them to himself. He left out many of the quotations and replies I gave to his utterances (for example, he maintained that I stated that St. Matthew wrote his Gospel in Greek and he deemed this my argument), while he presented the arguments I used with regard to particular fragments [of Scripture] and their interpretation as general opinions.[72]

Daniel Mikołajewski solemnly declared in his dedication to Andrzej Leszczyński that his wish is for "people to be provided with a true and sufficient account of this disputation",[73] but it is hard to resist the impression that through their publications both adversaries intended, above all, to prove that they were right. Their exchange of ideas was only an apparent dialogue and resembled a dialectical game of chess rather than a search for truth. The dialectical rules imposed on their dialogue forced them to play from different angles and come up with intricate, freshly thought-up arguments.[74] Their aim was to prove their victory and to this end in their texts they quite consciously and skilfully used the art of persuasion and the art of conducting disputes. Therefore, neither of the narrators depicted the Vilnius rhetorical performance faithfully, but they constructed two dialogues on the basis of it (understood as a genre of prose, such as Castiglione's *Il libro del cortegiano*), in which Marcin Śmiglecki and Daniel Mikołajewski were supposed to be the better or worse theologians and logicians. In fact, each of these theologians became a literary figure of himself, and the world seemed to be magically turned into a text, and into a text whose

[71] SCHOPENHAUER, *Die Kunst, Recht zu behalten*, pp. 43-44, 53, 59 (*Kunstgriffe* 3, 18, 29).

[72] MIKOŁAJEWSKI, *Dysputacyja wileńska*, f. A4v.

[73] *Ibid.*, f. A2v.

[74] Methods of dialectical argumentation employed in the Protestant-Catholic colloquia are discussed by Magdalena Ryszka-Kurczab, using the example of a disputation between Hieronim Powodowski and Jan Krotowicjusz, as well as Mikołajewski and Śmiglecki. RYSZKA-KURCZAB, "May every lover of truth find it through reading", pp. 189-207.

rhetoric forces, or at least valiantly attempts to persuade, the reader to adopt an attitude sympathetic to the orator's views. Juxtaposing Śmiglecki and Mikołajewski's texts shows the violence of a dispute's rhetoric, of an aggressive interpretation that makes it very difficult, if not impossible, to actually uncover the past. For although Mikołajewski's account seems to be more accurate and the two texts complement each other, the reader who had not been in Vilnius on 2 June 1599 would never find out what actually happened during this famous gathering.

Polemical Treatises: Between Tumults and Disputations

Let us move for a moment to Lesser Poland at the end of the 1540s. In a manuscript containing the chronology of the reign of King Władysław IV Vasa, the anonymous author, undoubtedly a Catholic, wrote:

> 1640: <On> Maundy Thursday <in> Vilnius, the Lutherans repeatedly disrespected the Catholics and monks, and academics, showing contempt for our holy Catholic faith, for which they were accused and summoned before the lower chamber of the Parliament [*Sejm*] and rightly punished, and one church [*zbór*] was ordered to be demolished, what students immediately brought into effect.[75]

This short note, despite containing about as many inaccuracies as words, is a kind of epilogue to the conflict that had lasted in Vilnius for seventy years and which put its mark on the topography of the city. In 1640, in accordance with the decision of King Władysław IV Vasa, the Calvinist church (not the Lutheran one, as the anonymous Catholic writer states) was removed from Zborowa Street and rebuilt in the Evangelical cemetery beyond the city walls, where it still is today, in Pylimo gatvė.[76] The destruction of the *zbór* in urban space did not resolve all conflicts in Vilnius, since six years later the king had to guarantee again the freedom of religion of the Calvinists. The municipal authorities, dominated by Catholics and Uniates, confirmed this freedom in the following letter:

[75] MS CZART. 1320 IV, f. 278.

[76] A.S. RADZIWIŁŁ, *Pamiętnik o historii w Polsce*, 2, *1637-1646*, ed. and trans. A. PRZYBOŚ and R. ŻELEWSKI, (Warsaw, 1980), p. 210.

Mr Rosochacki

Our dear Lord and Friend

We have acknowledged with great respect and, to satisfy His Majesty's will, we have ordered that the universal of His Majesty be registered in the municipal registers, or rather His *literas monitorias* [exhorting letter] addressed to all the municipal authorities to the effect that *dissidentes relligione* [religious dissidents] should suffer no *praeiudicia et oppressiones* [prejudice and persecutions] in celebrating their services. However, we need to keep the original copy of it as stronger proof for those wanton people, should any appear after [the receipt of this document]. We are willing to issue to you, Dear Lord, *extractem* [an extract], remaining at your disposal in the future.

From Vilnius, 12 April 1647.

The Humble Servants and Friends of
Our Dear Lord
Mayors and Councillors of Vilnius
the City of His Majesty[77] (original in Polish)

In a similar letter, the king also admonished bishop Abraham Woyna. He commanded that the bishop should prevent people subordinate to him from "disturbing services". First of all, they would not "interrupt their rites or initiate anything" that might lead to a violation of "security and the common peace".[78]

The universal royal letter is one of the genres of text that became a permanent element of the city's textual culture. Almost seventy years earlier, King Stephen I Báthory, staying near Pskov during the Livonian War, had admonished the authorities of Vilnius with the following words:

Should anyone persistently violate the common peace and maliciously initiate civil commotion, you are to detain each such person subordinate to your jurisdiction in accordance with the obligations of our office towards our teaching, and having detained them, you are to inform us about it as acting otherwise you will be disgraced in our eyes.[79] (original in Polish)

[77] MS LNMB F93-1716.

[78] *List upominalny Władysława IV, króla polskiego do ks. Woyny, biskupa wileńskiego o prześladowanie ewangelików w Wilnie: Niecały, na pół przedarty* z grudnia 1646, excerpt from the books of the Vilnius voivodeship from 7 February 1647, MS LNMB F93-1715.

[79] *Kopia listu króla Stefana do nieboszczyka pana wojewody smoleńskiego strony palenia*

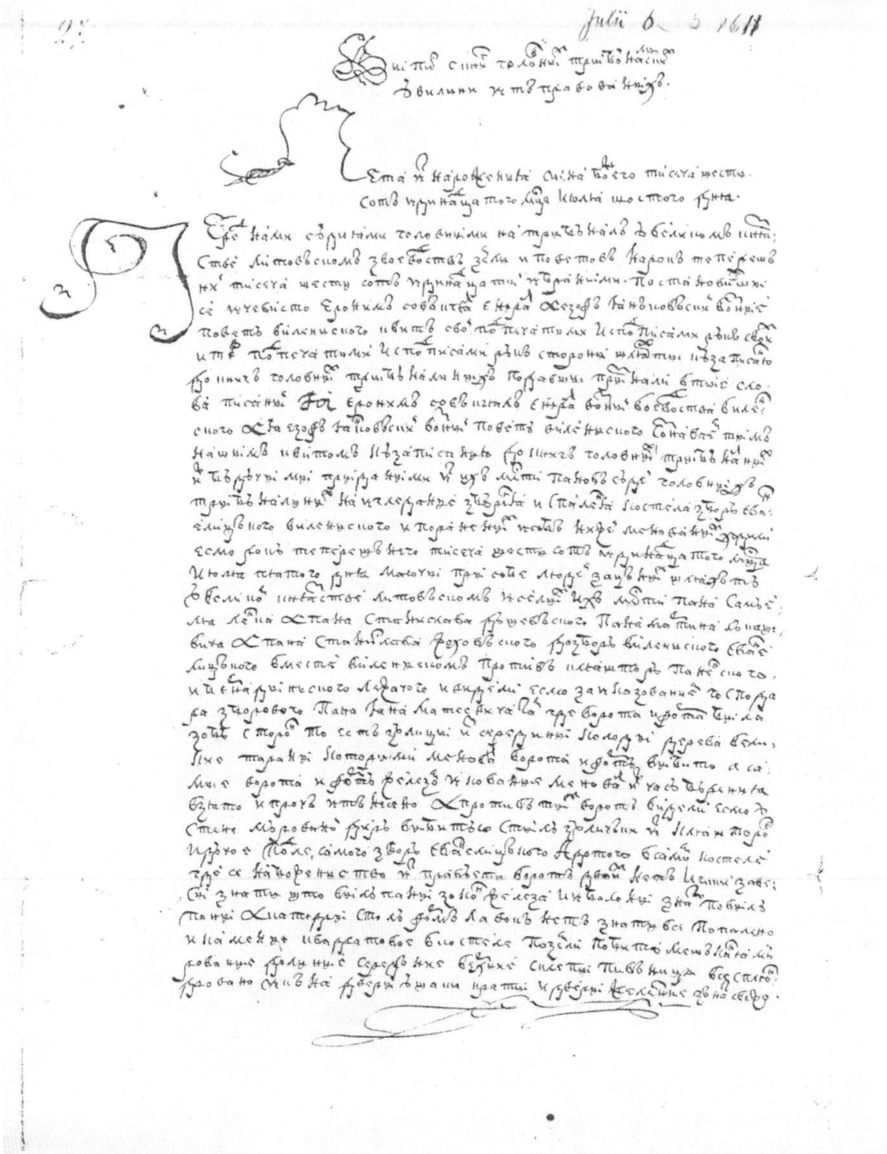

Fig. 50 An excerpt from the registers of the Tribunal of the Grand Duchy of Lithuania. A Ruthenian document related to the trial concerning anti-Calvinist riots, Vilnius, 6 June 1611. Vilnius, LNMB, MS F93-1732, p. 1. Reproduced with the permission of the LNMB.

ksiąg w Wilnie ewangelickich 1581 in Septembre, MS LNMB F93-1688.

Sometimes, the church authorities joined in the action of bringing peace to the city. Bishop Abraham Woyna ordered in October 1639, that is during a very turbulent period in Vilnius, that a call to maintain order be announced from church pulpits and that tumults should be avoided. His elegant letter, written in humanist Latin, was entered into the municipal register and has thus survived.[80]

Anti-Protestant, or in fact anti-Calvinist riots took place periodically. Attempts undertaken by the rulers and by the secular and clerical authorities to prevent them were sporadic and rarely effective. More serious civil strife took place in 1581, then in 1591, when a Calvinist church (*zbór)* was burnt for the first time. In consequence, a parliamentary committee was established to investigate the events in Vilnius.[81] At the beginning of July 1611, the *zbór* was reduced to ashes again. In 1623, there was new unrest, and finally, in the autumn of 1639 and spring of 1640, riots with firearms broke out. This, as we have already seen, resulted in the definitive destruction of the Calvinist church within the city walls. In addition, there were smaller-scale excesses, for example Protestant funeral processions were pelted with stones as they passed by St. John's church from the *zbór* to the cemetery located outside the city walls.

The second hotspot in the city was the Jewish 'quarter'.[82] The Jewish community in Vilnius increased in the second half of the sixteenth century.[83] Like in other urban settlements of the region, the growing economical position of the Jewish communities caused or contributed to the attacks by the Christian inhabitants of the city on the Jews. Since the end of the century, anti-Jewish riots broke out several times. This happened for the first time on 7 May 1592. The Jews were robbed by the crowd, whose enthusiasm was aroused because the Catholics celebrated that day the feast of the Ascension.[84] The king, the state, and the noble courts came to Jewish community's defence, but the riots were repeated. Another series of anti-Jewish riots took place in March 1634[85] and on 4-6 March 1635. The last one was one of the most serious: two Jews were wounded, the Jewish cemetery was devastated, the Jewish school and

[80] MS LNMB F93-1699.

[81] *Zbiór pomników reformacji Kościoła polskiego i litewskiego: Zabytki z wieku XVI* (Vilnius, 1925), pp. 60-91.

[82] *Wilnianie: Żywoty siedemnastowieczne*, pp. 269-270; D.A. FRICK, "Jews and others in seventeenth-century Wilno: Life in the neighborhood", *Jewish Studies Quarterly* 12 (2005), pp. 8-42.

[83] COHEN, *Vilna*, p. 24; KEMPA, *Konflikty wyznaniowe*, pp. 525-526.

[84] KEMPA, *Konflikty wyznaniowe*, p. 528.

[85] *AVAK*, 28 (Vilnius, 1901), pp. 136-139; See KEMPA, *Konflikty wyznaniowe*, p. 535.

synagogue were attacked, and several Jewish houses were robbed. Similar attacks were repeated in 1640 and 1641.[86] All these events caused a number of lawsuits and trials, and consequently produced a huge amount of court documents (protests, forensic examinations, verdicts, etc.).[87]

Finally, controversy around the Brest Union caused a number of polemics and violent conflicts. In the first half of 1596, before the agreement between the Catholic and the Orthodox Churches was reached, the Brotherhood of the Holy Trinity and the Orthodox town dwellers had actively opposed it. The situation in the city was still tense, because most Orthodox inhabitants of Vilnius and the clergy did not want to join the union. For this reason, in 1607 the Orthodox community did not allow the Uniate Metropolitan to enter the urban space and expelled all Uniates from the city.[88] The riots mainly broke out in the area of the monastery of the Holy Trinity, about the affiliation of which the Orthodox Brotherhood and the supporters of the union argued between 1605 and 1609. The most dramatic events took place in 1609. On 2 January, the soldiers of Mikołaj Krzysztof Radziwiłł 'the Orphan', introducing by force the decisions of the Brest Union and additionally supported by royal decrees of King Sigismund III Vasa, seized most Orthodox churches and monasteries, to start with the monastery of the Holy Trinity. The Orthodox Brotherhood moved to the monastery of the Holy Spirit at Ostra Street, which took a new name from this monastery (i.e. the Brotherhood of the Holy Spirit), and the conflict continued. During the spring session of the Parliament (*Sejm*), the Orthodox Christians tried to reclaim these places. At the same time, similar attempts were made by monks and members of the Brotherhood of the Holy Spirit under the leadership of Samuel Sienczyłło, the leader of the Orthodox Church and the former archimandrite of Holy Trinity church. Riots broke out on 9 March 1609.[89] The decision of the parliamentary tribunal announced that summer, that the Orthodox churches should be left to the Uniates, outraged the Vilnius Orthodox community. On 12 August, one of them carried out an unsuccessful attack on archbishop Hipacy Pociej.[90] The Metropolitan bishop, who was then

[86] FRICK, *Kith, Kin, and Neighbors*, pp. 400-407; KEMPA, *Konflikty wyznaniowe*, pp. 535-536.

[87] Some of them were published in *AVAK*, 28 (Vilnius, 1901), pp. 133-156.

[88] A. MIRONOWICZ, "Kościół prawosławny i unicki w Rzeczypospolitej w latach 1596-1648", *Беларускі Гістарычны Зборнік – Białoruskie Zeszyty Historyczne* 5 (1995); ID., *Józef Bobrykowicz*, p. 43.

[89] SZEGDA, "Metropolita Józef Welamin Rutski (1613-1637)", p. 298.

[90] I. STEBELSKI, *Chronologia albo porządne według lat zebranie znaczniejszych w Koronie*

heading for an audience with King Sigismund III in Vilnius, lost three fingers, which his colleague Rutski arranged to be placed solemnly on the altar of the Orthodox church of the Holy Trinity. This case, publicised by the Uniates, only strengthened their position. In the following year, as a result of the publication of Smotrycki's *Thrēnos*, the Brotherhood was ordered to close its printing house.[91] Despite constant pressure and subsequent anti-Orthodox activity in the early 1620s, for the next two decades the monastery of the Holy Spirit remained one of the main bulwarks of Orthodoxy in the Commonwealth.[92]

All these events left traces in the form of texts, but not all of these traces have survived. They include universals and special letters of the kings and bishops, mentioned previously, but most extensive is the legal documentation. The authority of these texts inspired their relatively careful preservation and longevity. Private manuscripts or even publications in print were less lucky, as not only were there fewer of them, but the following generations also took less care of them.

There are no sources concerning religious turmoil before the arrival of the Jesuits. The conflict was incandescent, as Lutherans or Calvinists were certainly not welcomed by the municipal and religious authorities, but apart from the removal of Kulvietis' school[93] and King Sigismund I the Old's anti-Lutheran edicts (1522 and 1535),[94] no more serious anti-Protestant actions were undertaken in Vilnius. The arrival of the Jesuits completely changed the situation.

The struggle took place on several levels and its intensity varied. Of course, the temperature of disputes still depended on who was speaking out against whom. By their nature, Arian-Catholic polemics were less fierce, because they did not directly concern the city and were conducted remotely, by means of the printed word. There were few Polish Brethren in Vilnius, as their communities were spread in other parts of the Grand Duchy, and mostly

Polskiej i w Wielkim Księstwie Litewskim, a mianowicie na Białej Rusi w Połocku dziejów i rewolucyi, zwłaszcza tych, które się tyczą tak starodawnego Monastyru Św. Spasa za Połockiem, niegdyś przez św. Panny i Matki Ewfrozynę i Parascewię Hegumenie rządzonego, jako też teraźniejszego klasztoru na Zamku Połockim założonego (Vilnius, 1782), pp. 179-180; J. STRADOMSKI, *Spory o "wiarę grecką" w dawnej Rzeczypospolitej* (Cracow, 2003), p. 37, n. 48.

[91] See Chapter 7.

[92] STRUMIŃSKI, *Przedmowa*, p. XIII.

[93] See Chapter 3.

[94] P. KRAS, "Od represji do kompromisu: Edykty antyprotestanckie Zygmunta I i Zygmunta II Augusta", in: *Jagiellonowie i ich świat*, ed. B. CZWOJDRAK, J. SPERKA, and P. WĘCOWSKI (Cracow, 2015), pp. 361-367.

through the Polish Crown. The Lutherans' position was different. Despite their large number in Vilnius, they were placed in the margin of local religious conflicts. Definitely more heated were arguments between the Calvinists and the Catholics on the one hand, and between Orthodox, Uniates and Catholics on the other. They are far more interesting for us, because they tell us more about social and confessional relationships at the time. The Jesuits perceived the Reformed Protestants as the greatest threat, more serious even than the Orthodox Church. Although there were relatively few Reformed Protestants in Vilnius, they constituted a significant political and intellectual force. Their compact community was located near Zborowa Street, and the most eminent of them belonged to the nobility and the magnates.

Polemics, although this term sometimes sounds too euphemistic, involved not only eloquent humanists and clergymen of all confessions. Sometimes they took the form of the disputations discussed earlier, but in Vilnius such colloquia occurred only sporadically. They were more frequent in the provinces, as in the case of the Novahrudak disputation. The publication of books, which are still the main sources of knowledge about the contentions of the late sixteenth and early seventeenth centuries, was more common. These polemical books, although addressed to a wider audience, possessed an elite character, especially if a work was written in Latin. Attempts to exert influence on a broader scale were made by giving anti-Catholic or anti-Protestant sermons, mainly anti-Calvinist ones, as well as anti-Uniate and anti-Orthodox ones. They were preached in Vilnius churches and were often published. As a result of this practice, Vilnius residents' awareness of their own faith was deepened, wider circles of Catholics, Protestants, Orthodox Christians, and Uniates joined in the polemics, and they now presented their beliefs not only orally. This exchange of views resulted in a specific group of texts, often of a narrative nature, of high informational value for modern scholarship: depositions of witnesses before the courts dealing with the riots. Their authors and frequently their protagonists talked about the burning of the Protestant church (*zbór*), the theft of goods, attacks on funeral processions, and other violations of public order, and also about shot wounds and other bodily injuries, such as those caused by throwing stones. These texts were recorded in the municipal court registers of Vilnius, Trakai, and Hrodna, as well as in the books of the Lithuanian *Metrica*.

The riots usually took place around the district inhabited by the Calvinists, that is in the area of Zborowa Street (today between Literatų gatvė and Šv.

Mykolo gatvė).[95] After subsequent uproars, the whole district became a fortified complex of bricked-up houses, a kind of fortress in the city. These fortifications were also useful in 1639, when violent riots broke out once more and the Calvinists proved able to defend themselves in their district. The Calvinist district was located between two Catholic bastions in the city: the Academy of Vilnius with St. John's church in the northern part and the convent complex of the Bernardine friars (later also the Bernardine nuns), with the three churches of St. Michael, St. Francis, and St. Bernard, as well as the church of St. Anne in the south. Next to the Calvinist houses there was a *zbór* with a hospital, a school, and ministerial houses.[96]

I will not present the history of the Evangelical-Catholic clash, which lasted almost seventy years, because it has been thoroughly investigated by twentieth- and twenty-first-century historians.[97] Instead, I will focus on the traces these events left in the texts of the 'city in a state of conflict'.

We can only guess what the Jesuit Piotr Skarga used to say in the sermons he delivered at St. John's church, as written versions of them, even though some copies of them circulated at the time, have not survived. However, his later postil, in which he probably reused homilies written in Vilnius, was published several times. One thing is certain: they must have been anti-Calvinist in character. Skarga intensified his attacks on the Calvinists shortly after he became the rector of the Academy in 1579.[98] These attacks reached their climax in the second half of September 1581, when the king was abroad, involved in war against Muscovy and staying at a camp near Pskov.

After a series of harassing sermons had been delivered by Skarga, on the order of Mikołaj Krzysztof Radziwiłł 'the Orphan' the Catholics confiscated

[95] *Wilnianie*, pp. 465-469.

[96] *Ibid.*

[97] H. MERCZYNG, "Czterokrotne zburzenie zboru ewangelickiego w Wilnie", in: W.G. STUDNICKI, *Zarys historyczny wileńskiego kościoła ewangelicko-reformowanego i jego biblioteki* (Vilnius, 1932); B. ZWOLSKI, *Sprawa zboru ewangelicko-reformowanego*; ID., "Zburzenie zboru ewangelicko-reformowanego w Wilnie w 1682 r.", *Ateneum Wileńskie*, 12 (1937), pp. 482-514; J. TAZBIR, *Szlachta i teologowie: Studia z dziejów polskiej kontrreformacji* (Warsaw, 1987), pp. 165-166; H. WISNER, "Likwidacja zboru ewangelickiego w Wilnie (1639-1646): Z dziejów walki z inaczej wierzącymi", *Odrodzenie i Reformacja w Polsce* 37 (1993), pp. 89-102; ID., *Rzeczpospolita Wazów*, 3, pp. 276-277; *Wilnianie*, pp. 472-489; J. NIEDŹWIEDŹ, "Strzała w nodze świętego Michała: Daniel Naborowski i wileńskie narracje sądowe z XVII w.", in: *Daniel Naborowski: Krakowianin – Litwin – Europejczyk*, ed. K. FOLLPRECHT and K. GAJDKA (Katowice, 2008), pp. 83-101; KEMPA, *Konflikty wyznaniowe*, 97-180, 299-339, 404-439, 488-523.

[98] L. GRZEBIEŃ, "Chronologia pobytu i działalności Piotra Skargi w Wilnie (1573-1584)", *Senoji Lietuvos Literatūra* 35-36 (2013), p. 27.

Protestant books kept by the printer Daniel of Łęczyca and burnt them in front of St. John's church. The Calvinists complained that the Catholics were obstructing Protestant funeral processions along Św. Jana Street (Šv. Jono gatvė) and forbade them to sing funeral songs. Often, students of the Academy threw stones at funerals, almost killing several people. Last but not least, they uttered threats against the Protestants.[99] After being informed about the riots, the king immediately sent the pacification edict of 30 September, in which he drew attention to the obligation to preserve religious peace:

> But since God foreboded that in the final days of this earthly world things will worsen, we will not force anybody violently to believe but according to the oath we swore during our coronation to all the estates of the Kingdom of Poland and the Grand Duchy of Lithuania that we will maintain and defend the peace among people of different faiths. We want to fulfil this obligation of ours and remember it always, trusting in God's judgement, for he is to judge people's consciousness. [And we decide to do so] not only because we were obliged by all the estates of the two countries to defend and maintain religious peace but also because it is the ancient custom of this country to tolerate people of different faiths.[100] (original in Polish with Latin phrases)

After royal intervention, peace prevailed in the city for a long time. However, this did not mean that religious controversy ceased. It was conducted among other means through publications and other polemical writings. Apart from typical polemics in the form of dialogues or treatises, a very interesting work has survived in which the Calvinists presented their version of this stage of the drawn-out dispute. An anonymous work of over 1,800 lines[101] entitled

[99] E. BURSCHE, "Nieznany poemat wileński o konfederacji warszawskiej", *Reformacja w Polsce* 3 (1924), pp. 271-291.

[100] *Kopia listu króla Stefana do nieboszczyka*, MS LNMB F93-1688. It is worth to add that the edicts, both in manuscript and printed form were exhibited in the public places; they were usual forms of managing the order in Vilnius at that time. After the death of King Stephen Báthory in 1586, the *voivode* of Vilnius, Krzysztof Radziwiłł "The Thunderbolt", ordered to issue *The Articles about Maintaining the Common Peace after the Death of King Stephen*, which were to be "publicly declared and nailed to the gates of the castle and the city, to inform everybody who arrives to the city". *Artykuły zastanowienia pokoju pospolitego po zejściu króla Stefana* (Vilnius, 1586), title page. See M. CYTOWSKA, *Bibliografia druków urzędowych XVI wieku* (Wrocław, 1961), pp. 153-154.

[101] The question of the authorship of this poem remains unresolved. Wacław Agryppa or Stanisław Niniński were indicated as possible authors; see BURSCHE, *Nieznany poemat*, p. 271; ID., "W sprawie autorstwa "Apologeticusa"", *Reformacja w Polsce*, 7-8.25-32 (1935-1936); H. BARYCZ, "Agryppa czy Niniński", *Reformacja w Polsce*, 7-8.25-32 (1935-1936), pp. 426-437.

Apologeticus, or the Defence of the Confederation, as Well as Seditio *or the Tumults of Priests against Evangelicals in Vilnius, as God Permitted, Published in the Defence against the Whip*, was published in 1582.[102] The author carefully chose its literary form by employing Polish alexandrines (*trzynastozgłoskowiec*) and giving it an epic character.[103] The *Apologeticus* (with a title clearly taken from the works of Tertullian) is an account that contains a number of poetic paraphrases of different sources and accounts of non-specified witnesses, and therefore belongs to a large number of similar pieces of narrative poetry (including *Jezda do Moskwy* (The Raid on Muscovy) by Kochanowski),[104] which were written in Lithuania and the Crown concerning current political events. The difference, however, lies in the fact that these compositions were mainly about deeds in war, whereas religious conflicts were usually described in prose, particularly in the forms of a treatise or an account of a dispute. The choice of form reveals the idea of subordinating the stylistic format of the text to its function: a story of events should be told in epic form, whereas a polemical work, which used syllogisms and logic-based argumentation, usually took the format of a treatise. The polemical narrative *Apologeticus* refers to many literary genres: epic poetry (epos and satire), religious polemical writings, and court documents. The *Apologeticus* is an example of a non-classicist attitude towards narrative poetry and prose. However, the tradition of writing such multi-layered literary forms, called *sylvae*, harkens back to Antiquity.

The narrative poetry about politics and war written at the time in Vilnius and throughout the Polish-Lithuanian Commonwealth was mostly of the *sylvae*-type, in which the rhymed narrative blended in documents of various kinds. It may be assumed that Latin-language poems were more unified, mainly due to the fact that they imitated Virgil and other Latin authors who provided ready-made structural and stylistic solutions. An account in the form of a poem was therefore placed within the scheme of the already existing topos (of *inventio*, *dispositio*, and *elocutio*), thanks to which the poem became more fluent. The Polish-language epic was only just being created, so it was more difficult to apply such procedures to it. It required taking over topoi from the Latin epic and adapting them to the requirements of the Polish language. Most authors did

[102] *Apologeticus to jest obrona Konfederacyjej: Przy tym seditio albo bunt kapłański na ewanieliki w Wilnie z wolej a łaski miłego Boga przed harapem wynurzony*, ed. E. BURSCHE (Cracow, 1932).

[103] *Apologeticus*.

[104] J. NIEDŹWIEDŹ, "Mercator's Lithuanian-Russian borderlands: *Russiae pars amplificata* (1595) and its Polish Sources", *Imago Mundi* 2 (2019), pp. 151-172.

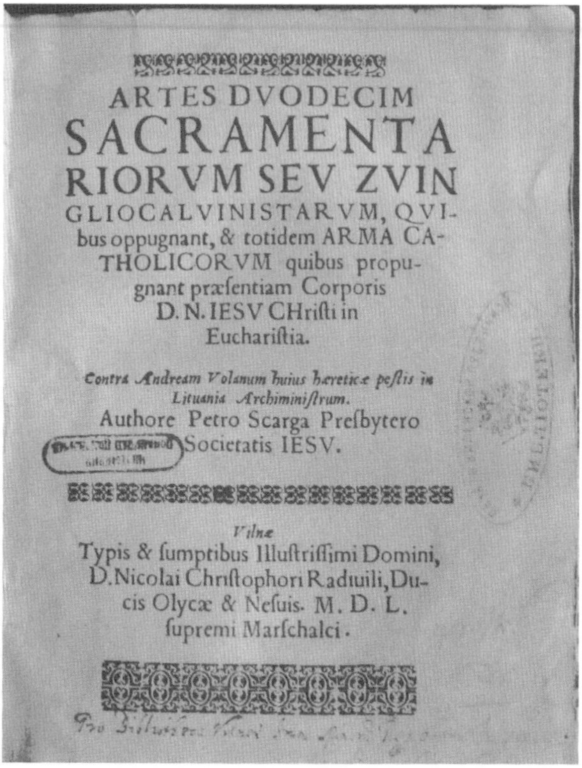
ARTES DVODECIM
SACRAMENTA
RIORVM SEV ZVIN
GLIOCALVINISTARVM, QVI-
bus oppugnant, & totidem ARMA CA-
THOLICORVM quibus propu-
gnant præſentiam Corporis
D. N. IESV CHriſti in
Euchariſtia.

Contra Andream Volanum huius hæreticæ peſtis in
Lituania Archiminiſtrum.
Authore Petro Scarga Preſbytero
Societatis IESV.

Vilnæ
Typis & ſumptibus Illuſtriſſimi Domini,
D.Nicolai Chriſtophori Radiuili,Du-
cis Olycæ & Neſuis. M. D. L.
ſupremi Marſchalci.

Fig. 51 Title page of an anti-Calvinist book in which the Jesuit Piotr Skarga attacked the Calvinist Andrzej Wolan as "the arch-minister of this heretic plague". P. Skarga, *Artes duodecim sacramentariorum seu Zvingliocalvinistarum, quibus oppugnant et totidem arma Catholicorum quibus propugnant praesentiam corporis Domini nostri Iesu Christi in Eucharistia contra Andream Volanum, huius hereticae pestis in Lituania archiministrum* (Vilnius, 1582). Photo J. Niedźwiedź.

not manage to achieve an impression of harmony and uniformity in their text, and it seems they probably did not really strive for it, because they aimed at making a different impression: of objectivity and authenticity. The sources (Holy Scripture, the Fathers of the Church, canon law, a transcript of a sermon by Skarga, the court's *protestacje*, or depositions by the witnesses) they in-

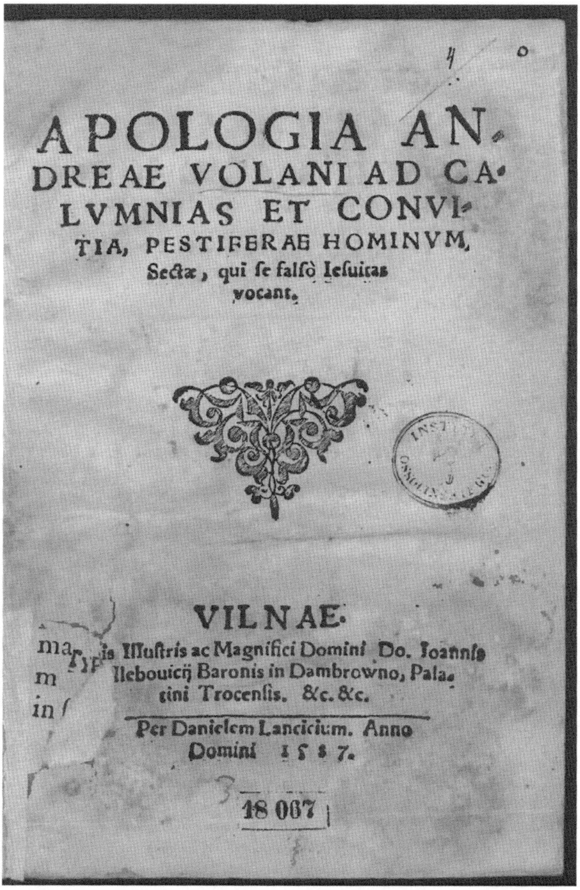

Fig. 52 Andrzej Wolan's response to the Catholic attacks: *Apologia Andree Volani* (Vilnius, 1587). Wrocław, OSSOL. XVI.Qu.2214 <https://www.dbc. wroc.pl/dlibra/doccontent?id=4172> (accessed: 31.05.2022, public domain).

cluded in the poem are best distinguished in terms of their style, although it is sometimes difficult or impossible to identify their original versions.[105]

The author of *Apologeticus* was faced with the task of creating a collage of texts written in Vilnius during the stormy September month of 1581. These

[105] The editor of the *Apologeticus* identified many sources of the author of this work. See E. BURSCHE, "Wstęp", in: *Apologeticus*, pp. XLVIII-LIX.

could be diaries, letters, excerpts from court books, handwritten and printed leaflets, and finally, most ephemeral of all, oral accounts. It is difficult to discern the sylvan character and merging of these different testimonies in *Apologeticus*, because it is impossible to indicate the texts on which they are based. The only exception is the letter of King Stephen Báthory (1581). The author's erudition, his knowledge of theology and Holy Scripture, and references to the work of Jan Kochanowski are easier to establish.

The *Apologeticus* was not a work primarily addressed to Catholics. The main target audience was that of the author's co-religionists, as was the case with most polemical works published at the time in Vilnius.[106] On the basis of stylistics and persuasive procedures, it is possible to point out the several functions of this text. In the first place, it had to provide the Calvinist version of the events, which, incidentally, was largely confirmed by other sources. The fact that it was written in Polish alexandrines and not in Latin hexameters means that its target readers were to be, first and foremost, inhabitants of the Commonwealth and, secondly, average members of the Protestant Church who did not necessarily know Latin. The publication was supposed to strengthen the community of Vilnius Calvinists, to testify to cases where they were persecuted, but also to provide members of the Protestant Church outside Vilnius with arguments against their religious antagonists.

Polemical Discourses 1 (Protestants vs. Catholics): Between a Treatise and a Pasquil

In the late sixteenth century, it was to be expected that sooner or later a more serious Protestant-Catholic dispute would take place in Vilnius. Both sides had been anticipating such a confrontation for many years. The arrival of the Jesuits in the city and the foundation of Protestant and Catholic printing houses only accelerated it. The chain of polemical texts began in 1574 with a dispute between Andrzej Wolan and Piotr Skarga, who had arrived in Vilnius

[106] In the conclusion of an anti-Protestant paper published a few years earlier, Śmiglecki wrote "to [Lutheran and Calvinist] ministers" that not only Protestants, but also "Catholics [should be the addressees of the pamphlet], so that they would know you as coins of diminished value and would not care for your voices" (M. ŚMIGLECKI, *Absurda synodu toruńskiego, który mieli ewangelicy w Toruniu roku pańskiego 1595 mense Augusto i teraz do druku podali* (Vilnius, 1596), p. 41). It is hard to imagine that Śmiglecki was able to win his enemies' favour using offensive rhetoric. It therefore follows that the text was mainly aimed at Catholics.

a few months earlier. Both humanists probably met in the house of their mutual friend Augustyn Rotundus, an important meeting place of intellectuals.[107] This meeting resulted in a private letter sent by Skarga to Wolan,[108] to which the Protestant responded with a pamphlet, *Vera et orthodoxa veteris ecclesiae sententia de Coena Domini ad Petrum Skarga* (The True and Orthodox Sentence of the Ancient Church about the Lord's Supper to Piotr Skarga), published in Łosk.[109] This triggered a response from the Jesuit Francisco Torres, who had published two texts in Florence and Rome.[110] Skarga himself probably struggled with an immediate response, but thanks to the support of the Vilnius chapter, in 1576 he published the treatise *Pro Sacratissima Eucharistia contra haeresim Zvinglianum ad Andream Volanum* (For the Most Sacred Eucharist Against the Heresy of Zwingli and Andrzej Wolan).[111] The two publications by Wolan and Skarga triggered a wave of texts and, at the same time, a war fought with texts for a quarter of the century: the Vilnius 'bibliomachy' (1574-1599).[112] The debate focussed on the same subject that the Calvinists and Lutherans had discussed during the Vilnius Colloquium of 1585, that is, the Eucharistic sacrifice. The second important topic discussed in their writings was the Catholic and Orthodox cult of images.

These disputes generated the publication of about thirty books (not all of which are still extant today), most of them published in Latin in Vilnius. Initially, the main participants were Skarga and Wolan. Later the Jesuit was replaced by an alumnus of the Vilnius Academy and canon of the Vilnius chapter, father Andrzej Jurgiewicz. Between 1586 and 1599 he published a total of nine books directed at Wolan. His polemical talent was so brilliant that some of his works were reprinted abroad or were translated into Polish, French, Czech, and German. Wolan responded to Jurgiewicz' attacks quite modestly. We only know of three writings of this type by him. Other speakers in the debate included Torres, Antonio Possevino, Emmanuel de Vega, Wojciech Rościszew-

[107] Rotundus wrote, among other things, the afterword to Wolan's treatise *De libertate politica sive civili*; see MAZURKIEWICZ, "Wstęp", pp. 31-33.

[108] ESTREICHER, *Bibliografia polska*, 33, p. 242.

[109] A. WOLAN, *Vera et orthodoxa veteris ecclesiae sententia de Coena Domini ad Petrum Skarga* (Łosk, 1574). There are no existing copies of this edition'; see *Drukarze dawnej Polski od XV do XVIII wieku*, 5, *Wielkie Księstwo Litewskie*, p. 124.

[110] NATOŃSKI, *Humanizm jezuicki*, p. 115.

[111] P. SKARGA, *Pro Sacratissima Eucharistia contra haeresim Zvinglianum ad Andream Volanum praesentiam corporis Domini nostri Iesu Christi ex eodem sacramento auferentem libri tres* (Vilnius, 1576).

[112] *Ibid.*, pp. 114-123.

ski, Federicus Borussus, students of the Academy (for instance the young Abraham Woyna and Jan Sapieha), to name only the most eminent voices. Wolan's supporters included Stanisław Sudrowski, Jan Łasicki, Jan Radwan, and Jan Tostius.

Piotr Skarga was initially the main religious polemicist of Vilnius, but not the only one. After his departure from Vilnius, the most important writers fighting heresy and schism were Marcin Śmiglecki and Stanisław Grodzicki. Since Jurgiewicz took on the burden of the polemics against Wolan, they could devote their pens against other Calvinists and the Polish Brethren. The rhetorical methods of refuting one's opponent's views were quite clearly displayed by them.

In his previously mentioned reply of 1595 to the Arian *Refutacja* (*Refutation*), Śmiglecki revealed his method of argumentation: "I undertook to prove, using this letter of St. Paul, that Christ was tempted in the wilderness".[113] The Jesuit wanted to demonstrate that the Jews put Jesus' patience to the test as early as Moses' times, which was supposed to prove Jesus' existence even then. First, he gave his two most extensive arguments, then he quoted each of the three accusations of his Opponent (Fausto Sozzini), and he refuted them one by one.

Śmiglecki searched for explanations of the passage about Moses and the copper snake throughout the Bible, demonstrating his perfect biblical knowledge. In this polemic, he rebutted individual fragments of his Opponent's accusations by means of a philological deconstruction and semantic analysis of the words. He also pondered what should be interpreted figuratively and what should literally and, obviously, he accused his opponent of misinterpreting and distorting the biblical text. According to him, his Opponent used "unfair scolding" and "insincerity",[114] and he suggests that his second lecture might prove even more dull-witted than the first one. He rhetorically asks whether "anyone has heard such nonsense since the beginning of the Gospel",[115] and says that Czechowic "explains this place in the Holy Scripture with boldness and overinterpretation" and "is not faithful to its true meaning".[116]

In a Latin polemical work, *Zachariae Prophetae pro Christi Divinitate illustre testimonium* (The Illustrious Testimony of the Prophet Zechariah about the Divinity of Christ), published in Vilnius in 1596, father Śmiglecki referred

[113] Śmiglecki, *O bóstwie przedwiecznym Syna Bożego*, p. 222.
[114] *Ibid.*, p. 224.
[115] *Ibid.*, p. 226.
[116] *Ibid.*, p. 224.

to fragments of a polemical work by Fausto Sozzini from 1590 and carefully refuted his theses. Technically speaking, Sozzini's text was placed in square brackets, for instance it could be an excerpt of Sozzini's work about Jakub Wujek's method of interpreting the Hebrew text of the Bible.[117] Sozzini demanded that Wujek seek meaning rather than grammatical relationships between individual words and suggested that this way of reading the Bible led Wujek to absurdities ("*eum in infinita absurda deventurum*").[118] Before Śmiglecki started to present counter-arguments, he set him a limit: "So much for Sozzini. What could he say that would be more bold and arrogant?"[119] The logic of the argumentation did not require this sentence to take such a form, because Śmiglecki could have simply written: "So much for Sozzini. The author is wrong because ..." or "he writes absurd things because ...". He replaced the affirmative sentence with a rhetorical question, used metonymy (instead of 'he is wrong' he writes "bold"), added an example of synonymy, and repeated that the words of his opponent are "bold and arrogant", suggesting that Sozzini is the same as his words.

In a letter to the reader at the end of this work, Śmiglecki used other figures, for instance in the sentence "Dignified Reader, thanks to Fausto Sozzini alone, learn about the pitiful habits of the Anabaptists, who only want to remove from human hearts faith in the true God and His true Son".[120] The name of the Arian writer, Faustus, was associated with the adjective *infaustus* ('ominous, sinister') via a pseudo-etymological figure. He also ascribed evil intentions and ill will to the Polish Brethren. "I know that the mouths of no other heretics are fuller with repetitions of the Holy Scripture", the Jesuit wrote, and immediately explained that this was only because they wanted to appear religious, since the views of the Arians are "extremely contagious" and "deceitful", because they are based

[117] The Jesuit Jakub Wujek translated the Bible into Polish. The New Testament was published in 1593, the Psalter in 1594. Accepted by the Jesuit authorities, the ultimate version appeared in Cracow in 1599, two years after the death of the translator.

[118] F. SOZZINI (SOCINIUS), *Responsio ad libellum J. Wuieki Iesuitae Polonice editum De divinitate Filii Dei et Spiritus Sancti ubi ead. opera refellitur quicquid Robertus Bellarminus itidem Iesuita disputationum suarum tomo primo, secundae controversiae generalis libro primo de eadem re scripsit* (Raków, 1624), p. 179.

[119] "*Haec Socinus. Quid audacius et insolentius dici potuit?*" (ŚMIGLECKI, *Zachariae Prophetae pro Christi Divinitate illustre testimonium*, p. 1).

[120] "*Disce candide Lector ex uno Fausto Socino, infaustos Anabaptistarum mores: quibus id unum propositum est, ut veri Dei et veri Filii eius fidem ex hominum pectoribus tollant*" (*ibid.*, p. 35). See S. RADOŃ, *Z dziejów polemiki atyariańskiej w Polsce XVI-XVII wieku* (Cracow, 1993), p. 69.

on "a corruption and an obstinate twisting of Scripture" or "betrayal and rape of the divine text".[121] The final argument discrediting Sozzini is the last sentence of the letter and of the whole piece: "*eiusque tum scripta, tum nomen tanquam anathema execrentur. Vale*" ["both his scriptures and his name be cursed. Be well"].[122]

Careful argumentation, providing logical and philological evidence, and showing contradictions in one's opponent's argumentation prove to be secondary to the ultimate goal of the polemicist, which is to convince the reader. This persuasion was based not so much on a logical approach and on scientific evidence as on the application of a whole arsenal of rhetorical measures. Thus, logical argumentation was to a large extent subordinated to rhetorical argumentation. The author presented many arguments based on philological and theological enquiry in order to reach the conclusion formulated at the very beginning of his work:

> Only Sozzini can show us how great the pride or recklessness is that prompts someone to corrupt Holy Scripture and erase its meaning. He: a man particularly arrogant, incomparable in his frivolous interpretation to anyone.[123]

However, Śmiglecki lagged far behind priest Jurgiewicz, mentioned previously, the 'hammer of Wolan' (to paraphrase the title of the famous fifteenth-century treaty on witchcraft)[124] when it comes to both the use of rhetorical and eristic arguments and 'negative campaigning'. In his first text from 1586, published when he was a student of the Academy of Vilnius, Jurgiewicz defended the Catholic cult of images, drawing mainly on arguments similar to those used by Śmiglecki and refuting, point by point, the thesis of Wolan.[125] His later

[121] "*Pestilentissimus*", "*mendus*", "*Scripturarum corruptio et violenta contorsio*", "*perfidia et divinarum literarum violatio*. ŚMIGLECKI, *Zachariae Prophetae pro Christi Divinitate illustre testimonium*, pp. 35-36.

[122] *Ibid*., p. 36.

[123] "*Quanta sit Anabaptistarum in corrumpendis sacris Scripturis and ad quovis sensus detergendis, vel insolentia, vel temeritas, unus Socinus docere potest, homo in hoc genere audacissimus and cui in hac interpreandi licentia parem haud facile* invenias. *Ibid*., p. 1.

[124] H. INSTITORIS and J. SPRENGER, *Malleus maleficarum*, ed. Ch.S. MACKAY (Cambridge, 2006).

[125] A. JURGIEWICZ, *De pio et in sancta Ecclesia iam inde ab apostolis receptissimo sacrarum imaginum usu, deque sacrilega novorum Iconoclastarum in exterminandis illis per summam Christi contumeliam, immanitate: Itemque de sanctorum veneratione et invocatione theses in Academia Vilnensi disputandae, adversus impium et famosum libellum a Volano quodam recenti Iconomachorum Archiministro editum: Propugnatore Andrea Iurgevicio, sancte theologiae can-*

books include, apart from substantive issues, eristic tricks that were not very tasteful. He began the letter of dedication of the polemic of 1590 with a humanist greeting: "*Andreae Volano saniorem mentem*" ("I wish Andrzej Wolan sanity of mind").

In the main part of his treatise, Jurgiewicz asked Wolan seventy-four questions in which he referred to texts published by Calvinists, Lutherans, and the Polish Brethren, showing solid knowledge of them. However, he did not try to understand the ideas of his opponents, but merely to show up their inconsistencies and absurdities. He often takes sentences out of context and makes accusations based on them:

> Number 32. Why do you create and worship many gods like pagans? Namely, the eternal one, who created heaven and earth, and the other one, a pure creature, which was created over time in the womb of the Blessed Virgin Mary? Sozzini in the quoted book, Czechowic, your Niemojewski, and others.
>
> Number 33. Why do you teach that Christ is a thief, cheater, adulterer, and murderer? This is what Luther writes in his fourth Latin book, published in Jena in 1558, on page 89. All the inspired prophets, he says, saw that Christ who was to come would be the greatest thief, murderer, adulterer, thief, perpetrator of sacrilege, and blasphemer, who is second to no one in the whole world. Is this how you sing the glory of Christ, famed Luther?[126] (original in Polish)

Such argumentation is extremely rhetorical, but father Jurgiewicz often crossed the thin line dividing rhetoric from eristic, using for instance the *argumentum ad personam* and accusing Wolan of stupidity, dishonesty, drunkenness, ignorance, poor knowledge of Latin, bad will, and low origin:

> On page twenty-one Wolan tells us a long story about his parents, but does not mention the most troublesome point. Our question is, whether his parents were brewers in Lwówek? I say they were and he himself does not prove otherwise. If he asks me how I know this, I will answer. Here, a good man wrote a letter to a friend

didato et artium liberalium et philosophiae magistro, praeside R.P. Emanuele a Vega in ead. Academia sanctissimae theologiae professore ordinario ([Vilnius], 1586).

[126] A. JURGIEWICZ, *Quaestiones de haeresibus nostri temporis Andreae Volano et Lithuaniae Ministris: Per Andream Ivrgielevicivm Canonicvm Vilnensem propositae. Iussu et Authoritae Illustrissimi et Reuerendissimi in Christo Patris et Domini D. Georgii D.M. Tituli S. Sixti, S.R.E. Praesbiteri Cardinalis Radziwił nuncupati, Episcopatus Vilnensis perpetui administratoris etc. in lucem editae* (Vilnius, 1590), p. 21.

> of mine from Greater Poland on the last day of April 1588, which reads as follows: "I found out that Wolan's father was a Catholic and not a nobleman but a brewer, devoted to entertainment, and several times a councillor".[127] (original in Polish)

The *ad personam* and *ad hominem* arguments used in prose are, however, quite mild when compared to those used in polemical poetry.

Polemical Verses: Between Pasquils and Riots

Andrzej Wolan made similar accusations of undesirable origin against Jurgiewicz already in his early texts, for instance in the epigrams preceding the treatise *Na błazeńską i osławioną książeczkę jezuickiej szkoły wileńskiej i możnego oszczerczego bluźniercy Andrzeja Jurgiewicza, księżyny i kanonika wileńskiego* (On the Buffoonish and Ill-famed Book from the Jesuit Vilnius School and Mighty Slanderous Blasphemer Andrzej Jurgiewicz, A Black Coat and Canon of Vilnius).[128] These malicious poems were created by the German poet Johann Tostius, who referred to the quite common practice of supplementing a treatise with a lampoon. "If you think that I will ignore the conversations that [Tostius] had with you in Vilnius about these poems and about his other (not very evangelical) fabrications, you are very mistaken", Jurgiewicz threatened.[129] Poems of this kind were written by both students (in Jurgiewicz' works appearing under pseudonyms) and by renowned poets. The treatise of 1586, in which Wolan replied to a professor of the Academy of Vilnius, Emmanuel de

[127] "*Narrat nobis Volanus pag. 21 de suis parentibus longam historiam, sed punctum difficultatis non tangit omnino. Quaestio nostra est: an eius parentes fuerint coctores cervisiae Lwowcovii? Ego asserui fuisse; ipse non probat contrarium. Si petat a me unde it habeam, dicam. Vir quidam bonus literas huc scripsit, ad quendam amicum meum ex Polonia maiori, ultima Aprilis, anno 1588, ubi haec verba habentur: 'De Volano haec accepi, parentem eius fuisse catholicum, nullo modo nobilem, sed braxatorem, iocis deditum, aliquoties consulem*". A. Jurgiewicz, *Anatomia libelli famosi et scurrilis Andreae Volani Lwowcoviensis apostate et prafecti Synagogae Calvinisticae Vilnensis, per Andream Iurgevicium canonicum Vilnensem*, ([Vilnius,] 1591), f. B2v.

[128] A. Wolan, *Ad scurillem et famosum libellum Iesuiticae Scholae Vilnensis et potissimum maledici conviciatoris Andreae Iurgevitii, sacrificuli et canonici Vilnensis* (Vilnius, 1589).

[129] A. Jurgiewicz, *Mendacia et convitia evangelica Andreae Volani Lwowkoviensis, secretarii, si diis placet, Magni Ducatus Lituaniae, ex ipsius scriptis fideliter collecta et breviter refutata: per Andream Iurgeuicium Canonicum Vilnensem: Additi sunt in fine turpissimi errores eiusdem Volani in grammatica* (Vilnius, 1588), p. 2.

Vega,[130] included, among other things, a poem by Jan Radwan, later the author of the excellent poem *Radivilias*. In this war, however, the Jesuits had more scope to show off their epigrams. They accused him of drunkenness in one of the first anti-Wolan texts.

Łukasz Krasnodomski
On Wolan's Wolanberg

We read that excellent men often named
Famous cities after themselves.
Witnesses include Romulus, the founder of Rome,
As well as Alexander and Antiochus.
From the name of Wolan Wolanberg was created:
But the village should rather be called *Beerberg*.[131] (original in Polish)

It is difficult to answer the question why Andrzej Wolan's texts aroused such aggression among the Catholic clergy, if one compares them the attacks on his friends Grzegorz of Żarnowiec and Daniel Mikołajewski.[132] Probably three of these texts were exceptionally accurate: a treatise on the presence of Christ in the Eucharist; five books of polemics with Skarga; and a work criticising the cult of images.[133] As a matter of fact, Wolan often used means similar to those

[130] A. Wolan, *Assertionum de Eucharistia falsarum cum doctrina apostolica et sententia veteris Ecclesiae pugnantium ab Immanuele Vega Vilnensi Iesuita publicatum confutatio* (s.l., [1586]). Radwan's work was published in: J. Radvanas, *Raštai – Opera*, ed. and trans. S. Narbutas (Vilnius, 2009), pp. 23-24.

[131] The work was included in an anthology of fourteen epigrams written by students of the Pontifical Alumnat, to be found at the end of the polemic of Wojciech Rościszewski, *Ad orationem Andreae Volani, qua et errores in Ecclesia Romana si diis placet reprehendit et Pontificem ad deserendum pontificatum adhortatur Ioannis Bobola, in Academia Vilnensi Societatis Iesu studiosi responsio* [Vilnius, 1587?].

[132] He donated to the latter a copy of *Meditatio in Epistolam divi Pauli ad Ephesios* (Vilnius, 1592). See Estreicher, *Bibliografia polska*, 33, p. 249.

[133] A. Wolan, *Defensio verae orthodoxae veterisque in Ecclesia sententiae de Sacramento Corporis et Sanguinis Domini nostri Iesu Christi, veraque eius in Coena sua praesentia contra novum et commentitium Transubstantionis dogma, aliosque errores ex illo natos ad Petrum Scargam Iesuitam Vilnensem, vanissimi huius commenti propugnatorem* [...]*: Respondentur quoque obiter Francisco Turriano ex* ead. *factione monacho, qui duobus libris, altero Florentiae, altero Romae publicatis, Scargam sibi suscepit contra Volanum defenendum* (Łosk, 1579); id., *Idololatriae Loiolitarum Vilnensium oppugnatio. Itemque ad nova illorum obiecta responsio, nunc primum in lucem edita* (Vilnius, 1583); *id.*, *Libri quinque contra Scargae Iesuitae Vilnensis Septem missae sacrificiique eius columnas et librum 12 artium Zwingliocalvinistarum, quibus is, veritatem doctrinae apostolicae et sanctae veteris Ecclesiae de sacramento Coene Domini evertere*

of his Jesuit adversaries in these publication, resorting to eristic tricks, puns, insinuations, and malice, for instance accusing Jesuits of using their order's name without grounds and often calling them "a sect" and "Loyolitans".[134] Perhaps the Jesuits and Jurgiewicz who attacked Wolan appreciated his literary and polemical talent in this paradoxical way, but also his knowledge of theology and the humanities:

> The wicked people of the mendicant order founded around 1212, who abused the ignorance of people, dealing with paintings, trumpery, and all unmanly ornaments, tricked wretched people into following a false religion, and filled the whole world with imaginary works on worship and reverence of the saints. Among these authors, there are other strange things consisting of the history of the saints and their miracles, among which the most famous are the *History of the Lombards* and the *Golden Legend*.[135] (original in Latin)

The reason for the Jesuit attacks on another member of the Vilnius Protestant elites, father Samuel Dambrowski, the highly respected author of the *Postylla*, was similar. Less than a year after the anti-Calvinist riots in the spring of 1624, two anti-Lutheran texts against Dambrowski were published in Vilnius: the anonymous *Tajemna rada* (Secret Council) and *Relacyja a oraz suplika zboru wileńskiego* (*The Guilt and Supplication of the Protestant Community in Vilnius*), which were probably written by the Jesuit Jan Chądzyński.[136] Both works are marked by the poetics of street literature, but considering their Jesuit origin one can speak rather of a pastiche, a practice quite common in the third and fourth decades of the seventeenth century, consisting of the use of popular literature to discredit Protestants.[137] The first text refers to a secret 'synod' of Vilnius Lutherans, mainly craftsmen, women, and other allegedly unreliable people who criticise Dambrowski's irenic views.[138] Chądzyński's work is a

studet: Adiectae est tam Volani, quam purae religionis sectatorumque eius adversus Antonium Possevinum Iesuitam Romanum defensio, ubi Roma Babylon esse ostenditur, auctore Iohanne Lasicio Polono ad Medicinae Docorem Hieroninum Filipowski (Vilnius, 1584).

[134] A. WOLAN, *Apologia Andreae Volani ad calumnias et convitia pestiferae hominum sectae, qui se falso Iesuitas vocant* (Vilnius, 1587), p. Cr.

[135] A. WOLAN, *Idololatriae Loiolitarum Vilnensium oppugnatio*, in: A. VOLANAS (A. WOLAN), *Rinktiniai raštai*, ed. I. LUKŠAITĖ and M. ROČKA (Vilnius, 1996), p. 209.

[136] Both these rare texts were discussed and published by Zbigniew Nowak in the valuable treatise NOWAK, *Kontrreformacyjna satyra*, pp. 70-87, 269-305.

[137] Z. NOWAK, "Literatura sowiźrzalska wobec reformacji", *Pamiętnik Literacki* 66.3 (1965), pp. 17-32.

[138] NOWAK, *Kontrreformacyjna satyra*, p. 72, 76-77.

cycle of three fictional letters and several epigrams. This text was inspired by a fatal accident of the preacher of the church in Vilnius, Mikołaj Burchard, who died following a fall from a ladder:

Apostrophe to the city of Vilnius

O unhappy city! O the city that is an
Apparent decoration of the Grand Duchy of Lithuania!
Other Protestants are driven out of the city,
And these have safe homes in thee.
But on the other hand I will say that you are happy,
For you punish the false prophets more severely.
In other cities, Protestants are driven away
While in you [= in Vilnius] mischief-makers break each other's necks.[139]

In his Polish-language pasquil, written according to the rules of the *ars poetica*, Chądzyński ridiculed not just their ministers of the Church, but the whole milieu of the Vilnius Protestants. Among the ridiculed persons was for instance Maciej Vorbek Lettow, a diarist and the later doctor of King Władysław IV Vasa.

Disputes between the old church minister Dawid Krusius and the young Adam Reks, which ended in a fight between their followers in the Lutheran Evangelical-Augsburg church in Vilnius on 16 June 1641, gave Catholics reasons for further attacks on Lutherans.[140] In the Basilian printing house, they probably published two works in 1641: *Bitwa ministrów saskich wileńskich* (The Fight of the Saxon Vilnius Ministers), which referred to the tradition of the mock-heroic poem *Nowiny ponowione* (*The Latest News*). The third anti-Lutheran poem published in the same printing house in 1642 is entitled *Witanie na pierwszy wjazd z Królewca do Kadłubka Saskiego Wileńskiego Iksa hern Lutermarchra* (The Salutation on the First Entry From Königsberg of the Lutheran Vilnius Cripple Minister Herr Lutermarcher).[141]

[139] J. CHĄDZYŃSKI, *Relacyja a oraz suplika zboru wileńskiego saskiego do hern Martyna Lutra za predykantem Burchardym ministrem swoim, który roku 1623, dnia 14 Octobra, w sobotę, dla traktamentu gości, miłych swoich protestantów, po kury łażąc, z drabiny spadł i szyję szczęśliwie złamać raczył, od wiernych owieczek na piersiach onemu w trunnie położona* (Vilnius, 1624), in: NOWAK, *Kontrreformacyjna satyra*, p. 291.

[140] NOWAK, *Kontrreformacyjna satyra*, p. 89.

[141] *Witanie na pierwszy wjazd z Królewca do Kadłubka Saskiego Wileńskiego Iksa hern Lutermarchra: Drukowano w Witembergu roku 1642 dnia wczorajszego* (Vilnius, 1642). The only

Aside from its ideological flavour, this publication can be considered as one of the most interesting literary texts of early modern Vilnius.[142] Like most works described as street literature, the text is a parody on recognised and frequently used literary forms and genres. In this case, the author parodies panegyrical Jesuit publications issued by the Academy on the occasion of the ceremonial entries of the rulers of the Commonwealth into the capital. It was provided with an appropriately designed title page, a dedication letter, and an anthology of texts in notable genres, such as stemma, epigram, song, eucharistikon,[143] and poetic dialogue. In the original anthologies, the authors introduced the citizens of Vilnius who welcomed the king, for instance representatives of the clergy, the city council, the wealthiest town dwellers, the nobility, and the community of the Academy of Vilnius. Such anthologies were marked by the presence of works in many languages, which reflected the multi-ethnicity and multilingualism of both the university and the city, as can be seen in the anthology commemorating the entry of king Sigismund III Vasa of 1589.[144]

The author of *The Salutation on the First Entry* employed both measures in his text. However, the Evangelical minister (according to the chapbook fashion called *świnister*, which is a play on words using *minister* and *świnia*, 'swine') is greeted in Vilnius not by notable dignitaries but by those who were considered the worst in Catholic (and male) eyes, that is a Lutheran woman, the Orthodox town dweller Sieńko Nalewajko (an aptronym from *nalewać*, 'to pour' in Polish), and two Jews, Leib Szkolnik (Leo the Teacher) and Łachman Rabin (another aptronym: *łachman* means 'a rag' in Polish). They all speak their own languages: Nalewajko speaks Ruthenian, the women Polish with words of Ger-

copy of this pasquil is preserved in the University Library in Warsaw.

[142] A. BRÜCKNER, "Z literatury sowizdrzalskiej", *Pamiętnik Literacki* 12 (1913), pp. 100-102.

[143] *Eucharistikon* (*poema gratiarum actoria*) was a poem in which poet expressed his gratitude to somebody. It is also the name of a literary genre which belongs to the category of *silvae*. Eucharistical poesis was practiced in the Jesuit colleges and is mentioned by Sarbiewski in his manual of poetry. See M.K. SARBIEWSKI, *O poezji doskonałej, czyli Wergiliusz i Homer* (*De perfecta poesi, sive Vergilius et Homerus*), ed. S. SKIMINA and trans. M. PLEZIA (Wrocław, 1954), pp. 492-493 (246).

[144] Texts of this kind will be discussed in the next chapter. See *Gratulationes serenissimo ac potentissimo principi Sigismundo III D. G. regi Poloniae magnoque duci Lithuaniae etc. etc. in optatissimo et felicissimo S. R. M. suae Vilnam adventu factae ab Academia Vilnensi Societatis Iesu* (Vilnius, 1589), in: *Kalbų varžybos: Lietuvos Didžiosios Kunigaikštystės valdovų ir didikų sveikinimai: Competition of Languages – The Ceremonial Greetings of the Grand Duchy of Lithuania's Rulers and Nobles – Koncert języków: Pozdrowienia władców i magnatów Wielkiego Księstwa Litewskiego*, ed. and trans. E. ULČINAITĖ (Vilnius, 2010), pp. 206-215.

man origin, while the Jews speak a mix of Polish and Yiddish. Instead of an anthology of multilingual congratulatory works, there is one, but in six languages:

> *Kaip ad nos il tes Hencher licha duszka minister?*
> *Ar tanis bolsz alloon ewona litewska gut est?*
> *Od galgen pryszodl, lecz entade sydera weyzdy,*
> *Su dich przyniosleś hreckoje gamma tibi.*
> *Du kanst greckie logos kadu tua burna hłaholi,*
> *Os nori, francie, sasów ducere flux na hlaholi.*[145]

There were other, similarly anti-Lutheran works. One of them was *Kolenda paniom saskim* (Christmas Wishes for Lutheran Ladies) from 1620-1622, of which only copies of excerpts have survived.[146]

Polemical texts, published with a great deal of effort, did not usually reach the ordinary inhabitants of the city directly, as they were written in Latin, just as the Latin epigrams in Andrzej Wolan's book. It can be assumed, however, that the poems in Polish were widely known among the Catholic inhabitants of the city, all the more so as they spoke of widely known people. Together with polemical treatises, these works certainly contributed to the polarisation of religious attitudes and, together with other texts still to be discussed, were a catalyst for the Catholic-Protestant riots.

Polemical Discourses II (Orthodox Christians vs. Catholics and Uniates)

The pioneer of the Vilnius Orthodox-Catholic (and later also Uniate) disputes was Piotr Skarga. Exactly at the time when his polemic with Andrzej Wolan began, he was preparing a publication devoted to the union of the Orthodox and Catholic Churches, or rather to the subordination of the Orthodox Church to the power of Rome. In this case as well, one of Skarga's speeches initiated a long-lasting controversy and polemic, although this time the influence of his activity was to be felt twenty years later, when the union had already taken shape.

[145] *Witanie na pierwszy wjazd z Królewca do Kadłubka Saskiego Wileńskiego*, p. A2r. See NOWAK, *Kontrreformacyjna satyra*, p. 326.

[146] K. BADECKI, *Literatura mieszczańska w Polsce XVII wieku: Monografia bibliograficzna* (Lviv, 1925), p. 157; NOWAK, *Kontrreformacyjna satyra*, pp. 105-106.

His treatise *O jedności Kościoła Bożego* (On the Unity of the Church of God) had been written already in 1574, was published in the Radziwiłł printing house three years later, and was reprinted twice during author's lifetime. In the first part, Skarga argued that the Pope is the head of the Church. In the second part, he presented the history of the separation of the Greek Orthodox Church from the Roman Church and of the attempts to reunite them. The most interesting is the third part, in which the author presented a proposal for the union of the Orthodox Ruthenians living in the Polish-Lithuanian Commonwealth with the Latin Church. Skarga did not discuss the issue of the salvation of the Ruthenians, but he argued that the Polish-Lithuanian Commonwealth, united under one Catholic ruler, would benefit from such an agreement, and that Ruthenians could easily communicate with Polish Catholics in a Slavonic language. Examining from Vilnius the condition of the Orthodox Church, which was in a state of crisis at the time, such a solution seemed reasonable, beneficial, and salutary. Looking more closely, one senses in Skarga's words a kind of condescension and a sense of civilisational (and humanist) superiority of the Catholic faith over Orthodoxy. Father Stanisław Grodzicki (1541-1613), a colleague of Skarga, expressed his views in the same spirit in his sermons on the reform of the calendar, delivered in St. John's church in the spring of 1587.[147]

These sermons were concerned particularly with the dates of the celebration of Easter, and his other main opponents were actually the Protestants (see "*Lutrowa fantazyja o Wielkiejnocy*" – "Luther's fantasy on Easter").[148] However, father Grodzicki first of all criticised Orthodox Christians. In the 1580s the hierarchs of the Orthodox Church rejected the Gregorian calendar, introduced by Pope Gregory XIII in 1582.[149] The accusations Grodzicki levelled at them concerned not only theological matters, they referred also to everyday experience: "The slavery of the Greek Church under the Turkish tyranny is a clear sign of God's wrath and hard punishment. 3. Exod. I. The Greek Church is dying and the Roman Church is expanding".[150] He openly pointed out the

[147] S. GRODZICKI, *O poprawie kalendarza: Kazanie dwoje ks. Stanisława Grodzickiego Doktora i Professora w Akademiej Wileńskiej Societatis Iesv* (Vilnius, 1589). The first one was preached on White Sunday (the first Sunday after Easter), and the second one on the second Sunday after Easter in St. John's church; they were joined in one collection by Stanisław Młodecki and republished by him. The book was a bestseller: it was published three times, twice in 1587 and once in 1589.

[148] *Ibid.*, p. 12.

[149] M. MELNYK, *Pre-ekumenizm i konfesjonalizm: Prawosławne dążenia zjednoczeniowe w Pierwszej Rzeczypospolitej (1590-1596)* (Cracow, 2018), pp. 91-97.

[150] *Ibid.*, p. 33.

Ruthenians' ignorance and naivety in explaining the Gospel. For example, Orthodox priests allegedly explained to their believers that Orthodox Easter rightly takes place later, because the Catholic Easter often falls in winter, and yet it is known that Passover in the times of Jesus was supposed to take place in spring. With the sense of superiority of one that used to travel the world, Grodzicki wrote:

> The Ruthenians point out our present cold weather and threaten a simple man with it. They are simpletons to a much greater extent in these matters and not only because they themselves do not know what happens in their calendars, because six years ago (as it occurs every few years) their Easter was only one day later than ours, but a bit before that it was three days later. It must have been extremely cold then! But far more so because what they reproach us with beats their own noses. For sometimes they believe that elsewhere, and especially where Christ the Lord lived, it was warmer in those days than it is here in our times, and at other times they say it was colder. If they do not believe it, they should ask those who have been there, or they should travel closer, to Italy or to Spain, and they will see that not only the fields but also the trees are already green. And if they believe that elsewhere it is far warmer, why do they determine the beginning of the spring on the basis of warm weather in Lithuania? [...] But lovely Ruthenians do not care about this and it may be expected that soon they will determine the date of Pascha in accordance with Muscovite or Lappish frosts.[151] (original in Polish)

This low intellectual evaluation of the 'schismatic' clergy was a consequence of the strong anti-Orthodox attitude among the Vilnius Jesuits in the 1570s and 1580s, which is noticeable, for example, in the handbook of moral theology from the years 1578-1580.[152] Orthodox Christians, especially those from Vilnius, could not be treated as equal partners by them.

This must have changed soon. It was in the 1580s and 1590s that the Orthodox community made an effort to raise the prestige of the Orthodox Church.[153] On the eve of the Brest Union of 1596, these circles, both Orthodox and Uniate, were ready to engage in polemics. A large number of the texts important for our investigation were connected with Vilnius: here they were written, printed,

[151] *Ibid.*, p. 12.

[152] "*Sicut olim Noiraliani et Donatistes, et nunc Graeci, Russeni, Boemi et Luterani, et praecipue Henricus Octavus Angliae rex*"; MS BJ 2047 (note at the end: *Laus Deo et Beatissimae Virgini Mariae* A.D. *1580 18 Iulii die in celebri Collegio Vilnensi Societatis Iesu. D. Nicolaus Dicius Posn<aniensis>*).

[153] See Chapter 3.

read, and referred to in numerous polemics. As in the case of the Catholic--Protestant disputations, printing and the opportunity to distribute a large number of polemical texts was of great importance.[154]

One of the first such publications was *Kazanie św. Kiriła, patryjarchy jerozolimskiego o Antychryście i znakach jego* (The Sermon of St. Cyril, the Jerusalem Patriarch, on Antichrist and His Signs) by Stefan Zizani, issued on the eve of the Union (and undoubtedly connected with the riots at the beginning of 1596).[155] However, books that caused much greater commotion were published in Vilnius after the announcement of the Union, including, from the Catholic perspective, one by Piotr Skarga (*Synod Brzeski*), Uniate ones by Hipacy Pociej (*Synopsis* and *Antirresis*) and an Orthodox one, although written by the Protestant Marcin Broniewski (*Apokrisis*).[156] All these texts found their continuation in the polemic's collection, which consisted of dozens of similar works.

Most of these works were published in Polish, while Protestant-Catholic polemics were published almost exclusively in humanist Latin. Writing in Polish was unusual, and when the Jesuit Piotr Skarga published his work under the title *Siedem filarów* (Seven Pillars) in 1582, aimed at the opinions of the Calvinist Andrzej Wolan about the nature of the Eucharist, he explained the choice of the language in the subtitle of the work: "for the understanding of the common people".[157] Wolan criticised Skarga for writing it in Polish in his treatise *Five*

[154] J. STRADOMSKI, *Polemika religijna okresu unii brzeskiej a rozwój drukarstwa prawosławnego w Rzeczypospolitej*, in *Prawosławne oficyny wydawnicze*, pp. 70-71.

[155] The earlier *Katechezis* by Zizani was replied to in a work entitled *Kąkol* (Cockle) written by a graduate of the Academy of Vilnius and published by the Academic printing house.

[156] P. SKARGA, *Synod brzeski* (Cracow, 1597); H. POCIEJ, *Synopsis zawierający w sobie opisanie synodu brzeskiego* [1596, today unknown] *abo apologija przeciwko Krzysztofowi Philaletowi, który niedawno wydał książki imieniem starożytnej Rusi, religiej greckiej, przeciw książkom o synodzie brzeskim, napisanym w roku Pańskim 1597* (Vilnius, 1600); M. BRONIEWSKI, *АПОКРIΣIΣ abo odpowiedź na książki o synodzie brzeskim imieiem ludzi starożytnej religijej greckiej* (Raków, 1597). The first edition or the work by Broniewski was published in the Arian printing house in Raków (Poland) in 1597 under the pseudonym Christophor Philalet, but two more, in Ruthenian and Polish, were published in Vilnius in the same year. See K. ZECHENTER, "Dzieło Hipacego Pocieja o Unii Brzeskiej|", *Analecta Cracoviensia* 20 (1988), pp. 501-516; MELNYK, *Pre-ekumenizm*, pp. 78-88, 340.

[157] P. SKARGA, *Siedm filarów, na których stoi katolicka nauka o Przenaświętszym Sakramencie Ołtarza, postawione przeciw nauce zwingliańskiej, kalwińskiej Jędrzeja Wolana i przeciw pedagogijej teraz po polsku wydanej jednego ciemnego ministra z ciemnej drukarnijej, przez księdza Piotra Skargę, kapłana Societatis Iesu, który to, co po łacinie przeciw temuż Wolanowi dwakroć pisał, dla pojęcia pospolitego po polsku zebrał* (Vilnius, 1582); see D. CHEMPEREK, "Siedm filarów Piotra Skargi. Geneza i aspekt retoryczny", *Ruch Literacki* 54.4-5 (2013), p. 429.

books against Seven pillars of a Vilnius Jesuit Skarga. He accused Skarga of not being a serious theologian but rather a ridiculous jester ("*facetus histrio*"), whose purpose was to entertain the crowd. His later polemical texts against Wolan were written by Skarga in Latin.[158] The Latin language opened the city to the whole of Latin Europe. In the case of union-related polemics, Vilnius was a city open primarily to the Polish-Lithuanian Commonwealth, and possibly also to other areas where a Slavonic language was spoken (for instance Muscovy, where the writings of Smotrycki and Zachariasz Kopysteński were known). Although individual texts were written in Ruthenian or partly in Latin (for instance dedication letters), most of them were in Polish. In the Calvinist-Arian-Catholic disputes this language would have functions similar to those of Latin. In such cases it became the second language of *Latinitas*.

Polish was used more commonly in literature, and it was easier to write in that language than in Ruthenian. During the sixteenth century, Polish emancipated itself from Latin as a written language, so that it was able to carry the weight of theological debates, and especially of political disputes. Translations from other languages, mainly from Latin, Greek, and Italian, played an extremely important role when it was necessary to create a terminology and syntax already developed in these languages. In Vilnius, this practice also guaranteed that texts would be more accessible, especially when they were read aloud, and they could have found a far wider audience than Latin texts.

The participants in the dispute over the union did not sign their works. The preference for anonymous authorship distinguished them from earlier Catholic and Protestant polemicists, who most often appeared in Vilnius publications with an open visor.[159] Representatives of both the Orthodox and Uniate communities either published anonymously or used pseudonyms. Broniewski appeared as Christopher Philalet and Smotrycki as Theophile Ortholog.

[158] A. Wolan, *Libri quinque contra Scargae Iesuitae Vilnensis septem, missae, sacrificiique eius columnas: et Librum 12 artium Zuinglio-calvinistarum: Quibus is, veritatem doctrinae apostolicae, et Sanctae veteris Ecclesiae, de Sacramento Coenae Domini evertere studet* (Vilnius, 1584), p. 2. Wolan not openly expressed his concern about Skarga's provoking the crowd against the Protestants, just as on the occasion in September 1581 which was discussed earlier in this chapter. See M. Baliński, "Andrzej Wolan: Jego życie uczone i publiczne", in: id., *Pisma historyczne*, 3 (Warsaw, 1843) p. 69-70; Chemperek, "Siedm filarów Piotra Skargi", p. 429.

[159] Smotrycki did not like this anonymity: "This is clearly evidenced by the present deed of the anonymous authors who have recently published *scripta*, full of weird and unheard of immodesty entitled *Niejaki Nalewajo*" (M. Smotrycki, *ΘΡΕΝΟΣ*, p. ()()()() II^{v}). Smotrycki also hid his name.

Many Orthodox and Uniate polemicists referred to the Greek literary tradition not only through their pseudonyms, derived from the Greek language, but also through titles whose first part was in Greek, sometimes written in the Greek alphabet, such as *Apokrisis* by Broniewski, *Synopsis* and *Antirresis* (*ΑΝΤΙΡΡΕΣΙΣ*) by Pociej, *Antigraph*, sometimes attributed to Smotrycki,[160] and *Paregoria* (*ΠΑΡΗΓΟΡΙΑ*) by Joachim Eliasz Morochowski.[161] Smotrycki graecisised his texts as far as possible, writing on the title page of his *Thrēnos* (*ΘΡΕΝΟΣ*) that it was translated from Greek into Ruthenian, and from Ruthenian into Polish. Today we know that that was a hoax, which was, incidentally, characteristic of Protestant literature.[162]

The use of the Polish language in Uniate-Orthodox polemics made possible the use of the rhetorical procedures which earlier had been employed by Catholics and Protestants. In his *Antirresis*, published in 1597,[163] Pociej responded to Broniewski's *Apokrisis* in a way similar to the way in which Jurgiewicz and Skarga had dealt with Wolan's publications: he quoted fragments of Broniewski's text and commented on them extensively. In his comments, he often used a rhetorical quotation, that is he recalled various original sources such as letters, documents, and fragments of books, selected in such a way as to give the reader an impression of providing reliable arguments. In this way, he achieved a highly persuasive effect of objectivity, which probably all participants in sixteenth-century religious disputes were striving for.

The effect of objectivity was always supported by additional rhetorical devices, such as prosopopoeia, rhetorical images (*imagines*), and topoi. Here,

[160] *Antigraph albo odpowiedź na skrypt uszczypliwy, przeciwko ludziom starożytnej religijej greckiej od apostatów Cerkwie wschodniej wydany, któremu tytuł: "Heresiae. ignoranciae i politika popów i mieszczan Bractwa Wileńskiego", tak też i na książkę rychło potym ku objaśnieniu tegoż skryptu wydaną nazwiskiem "Harmoniją": Przez jednego brata Bractwa Cerkiewnego Wileńskiego religijej greckiej w porywczą dana* (Vilnius, 1608). Teresa Chynczewska-Hennel threw doubt on Smotrycki's authorship of this work. See T. CHYNCZEWSKA-HENNEL, "'Ruś zostawić w Rusi': W odpowiedzi Sławomirowi Gawlasowi i Hieronimowi Grali", *Przegląd Historyczny* 78.3 (1987), pp. 538-539.

[161] J.A. MOROCHOWSKI, *ΠΑΡΗΓΟΡΙΑ abo kamień z procy prawdy Cerkwie święterj prawosławnej ruskiej na skruszenie fałecznociemnej Perspektywy albo raczej paszkwilu od Kassjana Sakowicza* (Kyiv, 1644).

[162] FRICK, *Meletij Smotryc'kyj*, p. 184; ID., *Polonica Orthodoxe*, p. 18; K. MELLER, *"Noc przeszła, a dzień się przybliżył", in: Studia o polskim pisnnictwie reformacyjnym XVI wieku*, (Poznań, 2004), pp. 142-162.

[163] H. POCIEJ, *Antirresis abo apologija przeciwko Krzysztofowi Philaletowi, który niedawno wydał książki imieniem starożytnej Rusi, religiej greckiej, przeciw książkom o synodzie brzeskim, napisanym w Roku Pańskim 1597*, ed. J. BYLIŃSKI and J. DŁUGOSZ (Wrocław, 1997).

too, Orthodox and Uniate authors used well-known and tested solutions. In addition to efficient argumentation supported by wide-ranging knowledge and reading, this rhetorical shape of the text ensured the great success of Meletius Smotrycki's *Thrēnos* of 1610. The prosopopoeia used by him, in which the Orthodox Mother-Church addresses her congregation,[164] was much earlier employed in religious and apologetic literature, but it is difficult to resist the impression of the similarity of Smotrycki's text to Skarga's *On the Unity of God's Church*, especially since he directly refers to this work.

Skarga quoted the words of Pope Leo IX addressed to the patriarch of Constantinople:

> You close the kingdom of heaven to mankind, you do not enter it yourself, and you do not let others in, and yes, you close it to them when you spit in the face of your Mother [the Roman Church] and dishonour and disgrace her, and separate her lambs from her, and curse and whip them, forbidding them to listen to their Mother's voice.[165] (original in Polish)

In Smotrycki's text, the Orthodox Mother-Church herself turns to her sons but in a style very much reminiscent of Jesuit lyrics:

> Son, I will show you me, your Mother with all God's blessings; I stand before you, and with humility I ask you for your consent to a gentle conversation with you. Lift your reverend head, and look at your Mother with a cheerful eye, look, my son, and recognise me, show humanity and humility appropriate for children, let me approach you, and after pulling down your hands receive me, let not your heart be hardened; raise your eyes to your aching Mother with your gracious gaze, let me once again speak calmly to you, for I did not come to you to taunt you, but to teach you; I did not come to excite you in the fervour of anger, but to make you willing and humble; I did not come to break a son's love for his Mother, but rather, for reconciliation. Be amazed, son, looking at your Mother's unheard of obsequiousness![166] (original in Polish)

[164] L. STEFANOWSKA, "Thrēnos Meletija Smotryckiego: Funkcja retoryki w teście polemicznym", in: *Ukraina: Teksty i konteksty: Księga jubileuszowa dedykowana profesorowi Stefanowi Kozakowi w siedemdziesiątą rocznicę urodzin*, ed. B. NAZARUK, W. SOBOL, and W. ALEKSANDROWYCZ (Warsaw, 2007), pp. 143-144.

[165] P. SKARGA, *O jedności Kościoła bożego pod jednym pasterzu i ruskiem od tej jedności odstąpieniu: Synod brzeski i Obrona synodu brzeskiego*, ed. S. ZAŁĘSKI (Cracow, 1885), p. 206.

[166] SMOTRYCKI, *ΘΡΕΝΟΣ*, p. 22.

Just like Skarga, Smotrycki also used the topos of the welfare of the Commonwealth and the king, although for completely different purposes. Skarga admonished Orthodox Ruthenia: "God gave you one Lord and one Commonwealth together with Catholics and the Latin Church because he wanted to draw you to one Church and one faith, in which one needs to strive for concord to earn salvation".[167] Smotrycki, on the other hand, considered attacks on the Orthodox Church to be detrimental to the common good:

> And the worst thing is that the inimical enemies of the Commonwealth, our homeland, and our gracious king, let their tongues run riot slandering the honour built with the virtuous deeds of Christ's blameless sheep. Doing so, [the author] follows his own words: "*Omne verbum malum*" ["Every word is bad"]. "In the name of God does he speak false and malicious words against them". Even he and the father of all lies, the enemy of the soul [= Satan] could not invent worse calumnies on innocent people, than this tool [of Satan] that in its raving head plotted lies to denigrate and calumniate God's faithful.[168] (original in Polish)

Invectives and insults (*calumniae*), often appearing as variations on *ad personam* and *ad hominem* arguments, belonged to the permanent repertoire of polemical devices used so far, which we have already encountered in canon Jurgiewicz's texts. Efficient use of them, which cannot be denied in the case of Smotrycki, was one of the basic conditions for an effectively conducted dispute. They can be treated as an effusion of the author's emotions, but for experienced orators it was yet another way of influencing the emotions of readers and listeners according to the rhetorical theory of affects.

However, referring to affects was most effective not in polemical treatises, but in sermons. Smotrycki himself was an esteemed and experienced orator, and so he gave many polemical sermons, but, as in the case of almost all humanists that participated in the Vilnius Catholic-Orthodox-Arian-Uniate-Calvinist disputes, no examples of his texts of this type have survived.

Polemical Sermons: Between Positive-Controversial Theology and Riots

A polemical sermon transferred a religious dispute from the pages of treatises to the level of rhetorical action. Therefore, it was a performative act,

[167] P. SKARGA, *O jedności Kościoła bożego*, p. 208.
[168] M. SMOTRYCKI, *ΘΡΕΝΟΣ* (Foreword to the reader).

whose effects we know for example from *Apologeticus*. In the last decades of the sixteenth and the early seventeenth centuries, such texts were delivered in all Christian churches in Vilnius. Usually they were not written down, but were often improvised on the basis of postils or the polemical works discussed above. Therefore, a sermon was both a link with scholarly disputations and treatises and a form of the popularisation of the ideas formulated in them.

Sometimes the most prominent authors made attempts to enclose a rhetorical action into published works which imitated the oral character of a speech. Such literary activities were known from ancient times: all of Cicero's speeches are written texts imitating rhetorical actions, either real or sometimes fictional (for instance *In Verrem actio secunda*). Early modern humanists – trained on Cicero's works – did the same.[169]

The cycle of polemical sermons of Stanisław Grodzicki sheds some light on this issue. In 1589, he published a series of six eucharistic sermons in which he severely attacked Protestants. This book initiated the publication of similar Polish anti-Protestant cycles of fictitious sermons, the most important of which are *Kazania sejmowe* (The Eight Sermons Before the *Sejm*) by Piotr Skarga (1597), whose construction as a literary cycle has been discussed several times.[170] Cycles of polemical sermons to some extent developed a medieval tradition of postils but generally they were a new literary genre.[171]

In his publication, Grodzicki joined the polemic of Skarga, Jurgiewicz, and Wolan, which had been going on for several years.[172] His next polemical sermon was published as well; it was combined with a sermon delivered at the

[169] E.g. the well-known Polish humanist Andrzej Frycz Modrzewski (*c.* 1503-1572) wrote a series of four fictitious speeches (1543-1546) about the necessity of reforming the law of punishing homicides. See A. FRYCZ MODRZEWSKI, *Mowy*, ed. Ł. KURDYBACHA and K. KORANYI, and trans. E. JĘDRKIEWICZ (Warszawa, 1954).

[170] Skarga's *Eight Sejm Sermons* were added to his collection of written sermons (postilla), *Kazania na niedziele i święta* (Cracow, 1597). This work was reinterpreted by the enlightenment intellectuals in the second half of the eighteenth century, and from then it was established as one of the canonical texts of Polish literature. See Cz. HERNAS, *Barok* (Warsaw, 1976), pp. 164-168; J. ZIOMEK, *Renesans* (Warsaw, 1977), pp. 399-402; J. TAZBIR, *Piotr Skarga: Szermierz kontrreformacji* (Warsaw, 1978); M. KLIMOWICZ, *Oświecenie* (Warsaw, 1998), p. 129.

[171] There are several differences between the postil and the cycle of polemical sermons. The polemical cycle was shorter than a postil (a couple of texts only), based on classical rhetoric, organised in a cycle (i.e. the composition of the texts and their internal relations were important), and was designed for a more general public than the clergy only. Sometimes cycles of polemical sermons had a hidden political agenda, such as Skarga's *Eight Sejm Sermons*.

[172] S. GRODZICKI, *O jednej osobie w używaniu Sakramentu Ciała Pańskiego w Kościele Bożym zwyczajnej: Kazań sześć* (Vilnius, 1589).

funeral of Katarzyna Radziwiłłowa née Tęczyńska in 1592 in Vilnius cathedral. Father Grodzicki polemicised with the anonymous sermon *Trutina Psychotropii* (Considerations on the Transmigration of Souls) which had criticised the Catholic doctrine of Purgatory. The polemical part begins with malice and invectives:

> In the name of God, let us begin with the title and analyse the main word recently imported from the Greek together with its explanation. *Psychotropia abo czyściec* (*The Transmigration of Souls Or Purgatory*). The title reflects the faith and books. New faith, new inscription. Stupid books, stupid title. So that judging by the door you know what you can expect in this empty barn.[173] (original in Polish)

The defence of the concept of Purgatory was undertaken once more in another funeral sermon given by Grodzicki in St. John's church a year later, during the funeral of another member of the Radziwiłł family.[174]

Probably, two Calvinist activists, Jan Łasicki and Hieronim Filipowski, listened to a similar sermon in the cathedral, as is mentioned by Łasicki in a dedication letter of 10 May 1584, which preceded his apology against Antonio Possevino.[175] We have interesting testimony to the reception of a similar sermon by supporters and opponents of Jesuit rhetoric.

The central part of the Protestant anti-Jesuit poem *Apologeticus*, mentioned above, is "*Summa kazania jezuity Skargi*" ("The Summa of the Sermon of Skarga, a Jesuit"), that is, using modern terminology, a summary and paraphrase, but above all a parody of the homily delivered on 27 September 1581 in St. John's church. In order to make the text more persuasive, the author aptly imitated figures characteristic of Skarga's style, such as anadiplosis, litotes, aetiology, apostrophes, and exclamations:

[173] S. GRODZICKI, *Kazanie na pogrzebie Oświeconej Księżny J.M. Paniej P. Katarzyny z Tęczyna Radziwiłowej, wojewodzinej wileńskiej etc. etc. miane w kościele tumskim wileńskim dnia 20. Julii roku Pańskiego 1592*, by father D. Stanisław Grodzicki, a theologian from the Society of Jesus. Together with *Trutina Psychotropii*, published against this sermon written by the court Protestant priest it was published in Vilnius, by the Society of Jesus' Academic printing house in 1592 (quotation from p. 45).

[174] S. GRODZICKI, *O czyścu kazanie wtóre ks. d. Stanisława Grodzickiego, theologa Societatis Iesu 26 dnia stycznia miane w kościele ś. Jana: Przy pogrzebie Jego Ks. M. Pana Pana Olbrichta Radziwiła na Ołyce i Nieświeżu W. Ks. Litewskiego wielkiego marszałka, starosty rowieńskiego, samborskiego etc. etc.* (Vilnius, 1593).

[175] J. ŁASICKI, *Pro Volano et puriore religione defensoribusque eius adversus Antonium Possevinum socium Iesu scriptum apologeticum*, in: WOLAN, *Libri quinque contra Scargae Iesuitae Vilnensis Septem missae.*

O Catholics, you have waited so long,
Why are you afraid to attack the heretics?
There's nothing to be afraid of, these walls are new,
Only gather there and they will soon be littered with holes.
I will lead you with a crucifix,
Having the Pope's blessing to do so.
I will scare them with holy water,
Especially as I see your indolence and bashfulness,
Yours, Catholics, who have your bishop with you
but no courage to do anything.[176] (original in Polish)

Despite imitating Skarga's style, the anonymous author apparently tried to refute Skarga's statement by emphasising the non-Christian aggressiveness of Catholics and especially of the Jesuits, which was a popular topos in polemical Protestant literature:

They are unworthy traitors and this is how we should deal with them:
Kill them all even if means offending
God. [But] He will regard it a beautiful favour.
Promises a mortal and eternal reward
For your knighthood, if you prove it,
When you will not stand the wrongful heretics.

(ll. 1735-1740; original in Polish)

There is a contradiction in this poetic sermon composed in Skarga's style. On the one hand, the author tried to achieve the effect of objectivity by using a rhetorical para-quotation, and on the other, in imitating Skarga he clearly discredited him, for instance by putting an ironic and disrespectful description of the Pope in the mouth of his model, the preacher. The Jesuit himself was treated no better. In order to make sure that the reader had no doubts about what a contemptible person he was, and that one should not believe his arguments to any extent, appropriate comments were placed in the margin: "Skarga, the hetman of the Vilnius War. God forbid", and below a paraphrase of a widely known invective: "The son of the devil is lying".[177]

[176] Incidentally, a significant remark: "In the year 1581 27 *Septembris* on the day of St. Stanislaus". The author cannot cope with the traditional way of marking time using the names of saints. *Apologeticus*, pp. 80-81.

[177] *Apologeticus*, p. 80.

The anonymous poet had to find a balance between creating the impression that he was quoting someone else's words reliably and persuasion aimed at discrediting the ethical and theological value of the text that had been 'quoted'. To put it differently, Skarga's should sound genuinely false, according to the evangelical guidelines for interpretation "you will know them by their fruits". However, we must still remember that a polemical sermon was a performative act, not only a play on words. In September 1581, the rhetoric of the dispute, which we observed in the records of disputations, trials, and polemical sermons, moved on to the streets of the city. And that was not the end of it. In the subsequent decades, just like in 1581, the rhetorical action turned into riots:

> And when the dawn came, they made a fire under the roof and lit it [i.e. the Calvinist church]. Seeing such a tumult, I had no courage and I did not have anyone to accompany me. During the day, I sent messages to the mayors and all the townsmen from whom I could not obtain help in time. Next, I myself went to the vice-chancellor but I was not given even a single man. [...] Since the tumult did not cease until 5 p.m., as I have written before, they burnt every wooden thing in the church [*zbór*], they robbed rooms they knew about and did not spare the church hospital, which was nearby. I, although injured, managed to get to the senators in a caleche, and other townsmen came there as well asking for advice and help, but we received neither. Now, for the night ahead, the city gathers guilds, fearing more danger to come.[178]

This excerpt from the letter dated on 3 July 1611 by the vice-*voivode* Jan Siesicki was no longer a polemical letter, but a factual report for the Catholic *voivode* of Vilnius, Mikołaj Krzysztof Radziwiłł. It is a valuable source of information about the details of the anti-Calvinist riots provided by an eyewitness. However, a copy of this letter, found in the archives of the Lithuanian Calvinists, was part of the documentation of the Vilnius Commission, which in 1611 tried to explain the events and to find and punish the perpetrators.[179] The fact that the letter was put in such a place makes it a rhetorical and intertextual quotation and yet another text of the city in dispute.[180]

[178] *Z listu pana Siesickiego, podwojewodzego mego wileńskiego de data z Wilna 3 Julii 1611*, MS LNMB F93-1729.

[179] TAZBIR, *Szlachta i teologowie*, p. 177.

[180] Siecicki's letter as such is not a polemical text. However, in the context of the entire documentation it is opalescent. It is still a letter (actually, a rhetorical *narratio* which is part of the letter) and simultaneously, as a part of the trial documentation it is a polemical text. The polemical potential of the letter lies in its use and intertextual nature of the trial documentation.

Chapter 10

Epideictic Texts

The Epideictic Art

At a first glance, epideictic texts seem to be less important in comparison with the two types of texts that have been discussed in the previous chapters: deliberative (administrative) and juridical texts. Epideictic or demonstrative cultural texts belong to the third genre of the classical theory of rhetoric, the *genus demonstrativum*.[1] The theory behind it describes the rules for creating texts of praise (panegyric, *laudatio*) and reprimand (*vituperatio*), as well as the functions of this branch of oratory. The most important of these rules are that these texts should provide pleasure, honour and commemorate important events or people, highlight the positive or negative aspects of reality, and, above all, maintain *decorum*. The decisive role in this genre is played by the public, whose task is to decide whether the orator (or author) mastered his job of producing and presenting the *opus*. Epideictic art is seemingly extravagant and superfluous, because at a first glance it does not perform functions as important as those of the *genus deliberativum* or *iudiciale*: it has no direct connection with law, politics, or economics. Thus one can challenge the practicality or even utility of the *genus demonstrativum* and the praises or reprimands that belong to this genre.

On the social level, however, its role is not less important than the two other rhetorical genres, as it allows a community to elaborate forms of coexis-

[1] Aristotle, *On Rhetoric*, pp. 75-83; Lausberg, *Handbook of Literary Rhetoric*, pp. 33-34; J. Niedźwiedź, *Nieśmiertelne teatra sławy. Teoria i praktyka twórczości panegirycznej na Litwie w XVII i XVIII w.* (Cracow, 2003), pp. 26-28.

tence in official situations, including religious and political occasions. Political propaganda, public relations, and ideologies of power and religion could not have developed without the *genus demonstrativum*. In other words, the epideictic art and epideictic texts play a crucial role both in constructing social relations and relations of power, and in constructing and maintaining the collective memory of, for instance, late medieval and early modern towns.

Epideictic art, based on the principles of epideictic rhetoric, is usually addressed to a large audience, so it plays an important role in bonding different people and social strata, whether horizontally (within the same social stratum) or vertically (allying different layers of society). Consider, for instance, the ideas of the unity of the Polish-Lithuanian Commonwealth as expressed in the triumphal arch built on Zamkowa (Pilies) Street on the occasion of the arrival of King Sigismund III (1611), which were addressed both to the high-ranking clergy and magnates and to the common people of Vilnius, including the Jews.

Attention should be paid to five points that are crucial for the epideictic genre. The first is the idea of 'immortality' and fame. Epideictic art is intended to preserve the memory of people or events, to create and maintain the impression of continuity and historical awareness of a given society. It is no coincidence that in the past the division line between historiography and panegyrics (and poetry as such) was not always very clear.[2] Panegyrical art preserved images of facts from the present time in the collective memory, referring to the functions of ancient panegyrical literature. This rhetorical permanence and continuity are essential for the legitimisation of power. That is why Kings Sigismund III and Władysław IV Vasa set in motion an epideictic machine designed to emphasise their relationship with St. Casimir, that is with the Jagiellonian dynasty, presented as 'at home' in Vilnius.

A second aspect of epideictic art is the affirmation of reality. Even when entering the field of religion, the *genus demonstrativum* models earthly reality, the reality of this world. A panegyric in honour of the Virgin Mary used all available means to visualise her glory and thus make it topical for the here and now, for our use. In such circumstances, the main aesthetic category is splendour. In a panegyrical text, even in the case of epicedia (funeral odes), evanescence and misfortune are removed from the field of vision – at least for a moment. This sublimation is achieved using means that affect our senses and

[2] J. C. SCALIGER, *Poetices libri septem* (Lyons, 1561), p. 3. L. ŚLĘKOWA, "Przeszłych wieków sprawy jako przedmiot poetyckiego przedstawienia w literaturze XVI w.", in: *Dawna świadomość historyczna w Polsce, Czechach i Słowacji*, ed. R. HECK (Wrocław, 1978), p. 84.

intellect. They include elaborate metaphors and sentence rhythms, costumes made of expensive fabrics, loud fireworks, or the heavenly harmony of cornets and violins resounding from the minstrels' gallery of Vilnius' St. John's church. The world is admirable.

This admiration gives rise to the third function of epideictic art, that is *voluptas*, the pleasure of listening to, watching, or reading a text or a theatrical or musical performance. This area of art is governed by the ludic aspect and the aesthetic experience, which paradoxically determine the transience of works that are to last forever. The five-hour *dramma per musica* performed at Vilnius' castle before the members of the court and the guests of King Władysław IV was an incredibly attractive and enjoyable spectacle.[3] Today, it is difficult to adapt to the tastes of people from the seventeenth century, and if we ever manage to reconstruct such a spectacle as it was presented in Vilnius castle with fidelity to all historical details, it might turn out to be deadly boring. Already in the eighteenth century, works from the previous century lost their status as entertainments. But whenever any text is read or performed, pleasure is, or at least should be, its strongest asset. It should strongly influence the emotions and draw the reader or participant into its world. The experience of epideictic art, whether intellectually or emotionally, is therefore temporary and transient.

The fourth dimension of epideictic art, that is paraenesis, determines the place of individuals in society and reminds them of its hierarchy: everyone has his or her place in a procession or festive entry, be it bishop, nobleman, or beggar. Although members of the social elite have the opportunity to experience more fully the values of panegyrical works, such texts were addressed also to the lower social strata. A printed panegyric could be read by a magnate, a nobleman, but also by a student of plebeian origin, although each of them would read it in a different way. Similarly, a bishop and a shoemaker would take part in an inauguration of office in a different manner. A *castrum doloris* built in a church was admired by everyone, although many funeral participants

[3] King Władysław IV Vasa was an enthusiast of theatre, music, and opera. At the Warsaw royal castle *dramma per musica* performances were performed (for the first time in 1628). During his long stays in Vilnius, three operas were staged, in 1636, 1644 and 1648. Apart from that, a number of other theatrical events took place there. E.g. Queen Cecilia Renata of Austria (1611-1644), the wife of King Władysław, directed many ballet performances performed in Vilnius castle in 1639, 1642, and 1644. See A. SZWEYKOWSKA, "Imprezy baletowe na dworze Władysława IV", *Muzyka* 45.2 (1967), p. 21.

did not understand the Latin inscriptions and allegories written and depicted on the monument.

A panegyrical work was usually a projection of society's ideals. A printed panegyric petrified a role model, determining the place of the protagonist of such a work in the surrounding world. St. Casimir was a patron saint to the Catholics and a respected member of the Jagiellonian dynasty to Jews. King Władysław IV, who was related to the saint, was a loving ruler for all those who came into contact with him, seeing him in his majestic robes[4] or admiring his literary image, expressed in the pages of the panegyric *Ver Lukiskanum*, written by the Vilnius Jesuits in eighteen languages.[5]

The last, fifth component of epideictic art was reprimand or *vituperatio*. It is the component of an epideictic speech that was used to fight enemies. It could be used both in political struggle and in religious polemics, but it employed the same topoi, as Aphthonius of Antioch, Quintilian, Hermogenes of Tarsus, and Priscianus Caesariensis had pointed out in their manuals of rhetoric.[6] The vituperative variety of panegyrical art consisted in the 'affirmation of a topsy-turvy world'; it presents a panegyric with a minus sign, which, however, assumes the existence of a positive side to the reality being criticised. When, following the Polish-Lithuanian victories at Smolensk in 1611 and 1634, the depreciation of Muscovy in panegyrics reached its peak, panegyrics also functioned as a lever that raised the glory of the Commonwealth and its ruler.[7]

[4] On the role and meaning of clothes in the royal court of the Polish-Lithuanian state, see M. MOLENDA, *Splendide vestitus: O znaczeniu ubiorów na królewskim dworze Jagiellonów w latach 1447-1572* (Cracow, 2012), pp. 236-241.

[5] *Ver Lukiskanum ad serenissimarum maiestatum præsentiam efflorescens, publicæ felicitatis amaenitatem et minimae Societatis Jesu venerabundam hilaritatem iisdem serenissimis Vladislao IV, et Ludovicæ Marae Poloniarum maiestatibus typo exibet* (Vilnius, 1648). A modern reprint with Lithuanian translation in: *Kalbų varžybos: Lietuvos Didžiosios Kunigaikštystės valdovų ir didikų sveikinimai – Competition of Languages: The Ceremonial Greetings of the Grand Duchy of Lithuania's Rulers and Nobles – Koncert języków: Pozdrowienia władców i magnatów Wielkiego Księstwa Litewskiego*, ed. and trans. E. ULČINAITĖ (Vilnius, 2010), pp. 230-253. See J. NOWAK-DŁUŻEWSKI, *Okolicznościowa poezja polityczna w dawnej Polsce: Dwaj młodsi Wazowie* (Warsaw, 1972), pp. 47-49; E. ULČINAITĖ, "Baroko literatūra", in: E. ULČINAITĖ and A. JOVAIŠAS, *Lietuvių literatūros istorija. XIII-XVIII amžiai* (Vilnius, 2003), p. 255.

[6] LAUSBERG, *Handbook of Literary Rhetoric*, pp. 105-109, 175-176; Priscianus Caesariensis, *Praeexercitamina: Retoryczne ćwiczenia wstępne*, trans. J. NIEDŹWIEDŹ, with an introduction by A. GORZKOWSKI, *Terminus* 2.1-2 (2000), p. 208-209.

[7] K. OBREMSKI, *Panegiryczna sztuka postaciowania: August II Mocny (J. K. Rubinkowski, Promienie cnót królewskich ...)* (Toruń, 2003), pp. 100-111.

Our knowledge of epideictic art in Vilnius before the end of the fifteenth century is limited. In the sources, its presence was only remarked on from the first half of the sixteenth century onwards. Initially, it was connected exclusively with the Church, the royal court, and, to a lesser extent, with the courts of magnates. It became popular in the last thirty years of the sixteenth century, mainly due to the Jesuits, and reached its apogee in the seventeenth century. It formed an element of the various forms of public life, chiefly religious celebrations (for instance processions) and political events (for instance accessionsas to offices and reunions of the Lithuanian nobility (*konwokacja*)). Over time, however, it began to expand uncontrollably. From the late sixteenth century, the panegyrical element gained the upper hand over other functions of rhetoric. Rhetorical ornamentation and splendour came to the fore, and every cultural text had to impress with its demonstrativeness.

There are hardly any descriptions of the *theatrum ceremoniale* performed in Vilnius by members of the Jagiellonian dynasty (that is, until 1572).[8] However, we do have sources from the Kingdom of Poland,[9] and we can hazard a guess about similar ceremonies and rituals in the Grand Duchy of Lithuania, including in Vilnius. There must have been ceremonial entries of Kings Alexander Jagiellon, Sigismund the Old, and Sigismund II Augustus into Vilnius, even if none of their descriptions have survived. Several members of the royal family were buried in Vilnius cathedral (for instance King Alexander in 1506 and Queen Elisabeth of Austria in 1545), even if there are only succinct mentions about the fact that these funerals took place.

In the second half of the sixteenth century the situation changed. The Jesuits wrote many relations about the triumphal entries of King Stephen Báthory

[8] Among them are relations concerning the treaty of the first Duke of Courland Gotthard Kettler with King Sigismund August, signed in the Vilnius castle on 28 November 1561, and the wedding of Catherina Jagiellon and Duke John of Finland in 1562, which will be discussed later. There might be three combined reasons which caused such relations to be so rare. Firstly, by the end of the fifteenth century it was Cracow where the coronations, royal burials, and marriages took place. This started to change only during the reign of the Grand Duke and later King Alexander Jagiellon. Secondly, more sources from the sixteenth century than from earlier times have survived. Thirdly, it seems that in the mid-sixteenth century authors described state ceremonies more often than in previous centuries. This increased interest in descriptions of state occasions may be attributed to the interest of the sixteenth-century literary audience. It was not only information but also a form of entertainment of the readers of chronicles, letters, and printed and manuscript news (*avvisi*).

[9] U. BORKOWSKA, "*Theatrum Ceremoniale* at the Polish court as a system of social and political communication", in: *The Development of Literate Mentalities in East Central Europe*, ed. A. ADAMSKA and M. MOSTERT (Turnhout, 2004), pp. 431-450.

in 1579 and in the 1580s.[10] The academics built a triumphal arch and the mayor greeted the king at the gates of the city with a Ciceronian speech.[11] The most splendid performances in Vilnius took place during the reign of the two kings from the Vasa dynasty, Sigismund III and his son Władysław IV. Their arrivals (for instance those in 1611, 1634, 1643, and 1647) were great theatrical performances that involved almost all inhabitants of the capital. They were colourful, permeated with the symbolic gestures, images, music, and architectural shapes, with an arranged sequence of events and dramaturgy. The mourning ceremonies after the deaths of King Sigismund III and his wife Queen Constance or Władysław IV were also great performances.

However, we do not need to resort to such spectacular forms as great paratheatrical spectacles. A funeral of someone of lesser rank than a queen, apart from its function of sending the deceased to the other world and finally saying farewell to him or her, became an opportunity to set the panegyrical machine in motion. From the extant lists of expenses for mourning ceremonies following the death of mayor Marcin Kiewlicz, which took place at the turn of February and March 1645, we learn that a tailor was paid four *złoty* for the pall, "tailors who sewed all the grave cloths were paid twenty-five *złoty*", "for painting coats of arms: sixteen *złoty*", "the city watch, who carried the body: three *złoty*", and ringing the bells for five days in ten Catholic and Orthodox churches together with processions in eight churches cost the tidy sum of 268 *złoty*. On the occasion of the funeral, an epideictic publication or a funeral sermon was printed ("For books published on the occasion of the funeral: fifty-two *złoty*"). All funeral expenses, together with a lavish fast-day wake, at which tench, pike and crucian carp as well as wine (for 120 *złoty*) were served, amounted to no less than 2454 *złoty*.[12] Concern for the soul of the deceased or dealing with the trauma of death were undoubtedly the primary motivations for these funeral arrangements, but their epideictic dimension seems to be no less important. It is visible in the creation and maintenance of the appropriate *decorum*, that is in adapting the ceremonies that accompanied Marcin Kiewlicz's burial to his social status.

[10] PIECHNIK, *Początki Akademii Wileńskiej*, p. 56, 91.

[11] E. BUSZEWICZ and J. NIEDŹWIEDŹ, "Wstęp", in: J. KAL, "Religionis, Reipublicae, Vilnae, Collegii et omnium ordinum gratulatio: Radość i powinszowania Religii, Rzeczypospolitej, Wilna, Kolegium oraz wszystkich stanów", in: *"Umysł stateczny i w contach gruntowny": Prace edytorskie pamięci Profesora Adama Karpińskiego*, ed. R. GRZEŚKOWIAK, R. KRZYWY, and A. MASŁOWSKA-NOWAK (Warsaw, 2012), p. 19.

[12] MS LVIA F694, ap. 1, no. 3338, ff. 14r-17r.

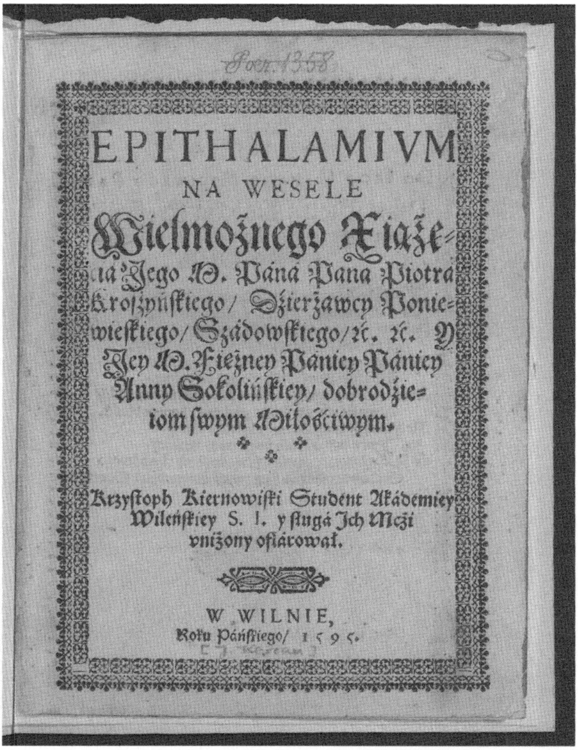
EPITHALAMIVM
NA WESELE
Wielmożnego Xiąże-
cia Jego M. Pána Pana Piotra
Kroszyńskiego / Dzierżawcy Ponie-
wieskiego / Szádowskiego / etc. etc. Y
Jey M. Księżney Pániey Pániey
Anny Sokolińskiey / dobrodzie-
iom swym Miłościwym.
Krzystoph Kiernowiski Student Akádemiey
Wileńskiey S. I. y sługá Ich Mczi
vniżony ofiárowal.
W WILNIE,
Roku Páńskiego / 1595.

Fig. 53 Example of an epideictic print from the end of the sixteenth century. A Polish epithalamy written on the wedding of Piotr Kroszyński and Anna Sokolińska. The author was a certain Krzysztof Kiernowiski, a student of the Academy of Vilnius and client of the newly-weds. Dozens of similar books were printed in Vilnius at the time. K. Kiernowiski, *Epithalamium na wesele wielmożnego książęcia jego mości pana pana Piotra Kroszyńskiego, dzierżawcy poniewieskiego, szadowskiego etc. i jej mości księżnej paniej paniej Anny Sokolińskiej, dobrodziejom swym miłościwym* (Vilnius, 1595). BJ <https://jbc.bj.uj.edu.pl/dlibra/-publication/709734/edition/671874> (accessed: 31.05.2022, public domain).

Similar activities supported by the rhetorical genre of epideictic could be encountered in composing last wills (especially in their preambles), preaching (for instance in funeral sermons), wedding speeches (and publishing them), applying rhetorical periods to court narratives, financing baroque altars, and reconstructing places of worship (for instance the synagogue in 1642), as well as in the practice of belles-lettres in Vilnius' humanist schools. Seventeenth-century Vilnius was dominated by epideictic art. It was used on special occasions, such as in the aforementioned state and religious ceremonies or rituals relative to the life and death of the elite of the state and city. It also had a strong influence on the material form of the city that is (to some extent) still visible today. The city and many of its buildings (gates, squares, major streets, churches, the royal castle, etc.) were the settings of epideictic performances. Some of them were also monuments of epideictic art, and as such played an important role in shaping and keeping the cultural memory alive of the inhabitants of Vilnius and the Grand Duchy of Lithuania.

Demonstrative Texts in the 'Closed' City: Literature on Display

One of the most common forms of the epideictic texts contributing towards building the cultural memory of late medieval and early modern Vilnius (and of other places as well) is that of the epigraph. Because of epigraphs and other inscriptions in public places, the city and its single buildings of could be read like a book carved in stone.[13] However, epigraphs cannot be understood only as the inscriptions put on hard materials, such as stone, metal, or wood.[14] The emphasis should not be on the material of the inscription but rather on its communicative role.[15]

[13] PETRUCCI, *Public Lettering*, p. 13-14.

[14] In recent thirty years, researchers challenged traditional definitions of epigraphy and the epigraph. See R. FAVREAU, *Épigraphie médiévale* (Turnhout, 1997), p. 5-31; A. ZAJIC, "Aufgaben und Stand der mittelalterlichen und frühneuzeitlichen epigraphischen Forschung in Österreich: Mit einem Schwerpunkt auf inschriftenpaläographischen Fragestellungen", in: *The History of Written Culture in the "Carpatho-Danubian" Region I. (Latin Paleography Network – Central and Central East Europe)*, ed. H. PÁTKOVÁ, P. SPUNAR, and J. ŠEDIVÝ (Bratislava and Prague, 2003), pp. 79-90; M.A. JANICKI, "Inskrypcja w przestrzeni publicznej – przykład Krakowa i Małopolski w XIV-XV wieku", in: *Historia społeczna późnego średniowiecza*, ed. S. GAWLAS (Warsaw, 2011), 245-273; ZAJIC, "Texts on public display", pp. 389-426.

[15] E. SKBIŃSKI and P. STRÓŻYK, "Epigrafika jako problem badawczy: Tezy metodyczne",

Inscriptions were addressed to a large audience and their exhibition in public space can be compared to publication of a book. However, they work not only as books to be read but also as public books to be watched. This kind of texts can be called literature on display. They are usually inscriptions which were specifically designed for epideictic purposes. People watched them and recognised a literary text in them before they read them. This was possible because the members of the public belonged to an interpretative community. They were accustomed to recognise these literary texts and knew (or knew of) the procedures of interpreting them.[16] In case of a text belonging to this literature on display, interpretation was based on the fact that the members of the interpretative community sometimes had no intention, need, or possibility to read it. They only had to recognise it as an inscription and could guess its function in this particular space.

Not everybody had the same possibilities to come into contact with an inscription. Firstly, access to many areas in the city where inscriptions were displayed (which we understand today as public spaces[17]) was limited to certain groups of people. For instance, the Jews did not enter the Christian churches, and the Christians did not enter the synagogue; women could not enter the male part of the synagogue or the presbytery of the Orthodox churches; common people could not visit the ceremonial rooms of Vilnius castle or even its courtyard; not everybody was allowed to the cloisters in a monastery or nunnery, etc.

Secondly, the members of the audience belonged not only to different social strata but also to different reading communities. As the result, they possessed different levels of literacy (or literacies)[18] and their perception and understanding of an inscription could have many different levels and dimensions. For instance a magnate, who *read* a Latin inscription on the triumphal arc during the solemn procession on the occasion of the canonisation celebrations of St. Casimir in 1604, certainly perceived and understood it in a different way

Studia Epigraficzne 1 (2014), pp. 21-27; M.A. Janicki, "Inskrypcja w przestrzeni publicznej", p. 49.

[16] S. Fish, "How to recognize a poem when you see one", in: S. Fish, *Is There a Text in This Class? The Authority of Interpretive Communities* (Cambridge, Mass., 1980), pp. 322-337.

[17] Andreas Zajic. in his paper "Texts on public display" (p. 393), explains that public space in early modern towns had a different meaning and function than in a contemporary city. In early modern Vilnius accessibility and meaning of public space was even more complicated, mainly because of the multi-confessional character of the city.

[18] See Chapter 1.

from a Jewish merchant who *saw* the same inscription in passing by, or the wife of a Ruthenian citizen of Vilnius who could both *see* the inscription and *listen to* its translation made for her, for instance by her husband or son. Nevertheless, the 'patrons' and 'authors' of an inscription must have assumed many levels in its perception: seeing, silent reading and reading, translation, and even copying.[19] All readers, listeners, and viewers were also assumed to experience emotions (*affectus*), such as love, pleasure, delight, curiosity, surprise, or even envy.[20]

Probably an inscription was perceived as a literary genre even by those who did not receive any formal education. It was one of the basic epigraphic forms in late ancient, medieval, and early modern culture. In the form of an adage (*sententia, gnome*) it was commonly used in education, including in mnemonic exercises, and as one of the initial rhetorical exercises called *progymnasmata* (or *praeexercitamina*).[21] In Renaissance literature and art, inscription became a literary genre in its own right.[22] Everywhere in early modern Europe, inscription became a crucial part of demonstrative art and an important element in the discourse of power.[23]

[19] The inscriptions from the triumphal arcs have been copied and published by Kwiryn Knogler, and they will be discussed *infra*. See Q. CNOGLERUS, "Pompa Casimiriana sive de labaro d. Casimiri, Casimiri Regis Poloniae et F. Iagellonis N.M.D. Lithuaniae principis etc. a Leone X pontifice maximo in divos relati, ex urbe transmisso et Vilnam Lithuaniae metropolim solenni pompa ad 6 Idus Maii anno MDCIV illato Quirini Cnogleri Austrii sermo panegyricus", in: G. ŚWIĘCICKI, *Theatrum s. Casimiri, in quo ipsius prosapia, vita, miracula et illustris pompa in solemni eiusdem apotheoseos instauratione, Vilnae Lithuaniae metropoli, VI Idus Maii anno Domini MDCIV instituta graphice proponuntur* (Vilnius, 1604), pp. 83-88.

[20] In seventeenth-century manuals of rhetoric the affections (*affectus*) were widely discussed. Literature was to affect the feelings of readers and listeners, and catalogues of rhetorical styles corresponding to individual *affectus* were produced. Learning about the affections came from classical rhetoric and later (also from the medieval) reception of Aristotle. See N. CAUSSINUS, *De eloquentia sacra et humana libri XVI* (Paris, 1643), pp. 439-555, 694-697; G. VOSSIUS, *Rhetorices contractae, sive partitionum oratoriarum libri V* (Amsterdam, 1655), pp. 24-27; Z. RYNDUCH, *Nauka o stylach*, pp. 97-85; ULČINAITĖ, *Teoria retoryczna*, pp. 136-137; J. NIEDŹWIEDŹ, *Nieśmiertelne teatra sławy*, p. 85-86.

[21] Priscianus, *Praeexercitamina*, pp. 204-206; B.B. AWIANOWICZ, *Progymnasmata w teorii i praktyce szkoły humanistycznej od końca XV do połowy XVIII wieku: Dzieje nowożytnej recepcji Aftoniosa od Rudolfa Agricoli do Johanna Christopha Gottscheda* (Toruń, 2008), pp. 129-133.

[22] M. FUMAROLI, "Sur le seuil des livres: Les frontispices gravés des traités d'éloquence (1594-1641)", in: ID., *L'École du silence: Le sentiment des images au XVIIe siècle* (Paris, 1998), p. 422.

[23] The high status of inscriptions among the cultural texts in early modern Europe confirms the fact that the Académie royale des Inscriptions et Médailles (today the Académie des inscriptions et belles-lettres, a part of the Institute de France) was established in Paris in 1663, with the

Fig. 54 Latin commemorative inscription on the outer wall of the chapel of St. Casimir in Vilnius cathedral, 1636. Photo J. Niedźwiedź.

It was also one of several genres of epigraphic writings in the medieval and early modern city.[24] The inscription could evolve into longer literary forms, such as the elogium. The epitaph also came from simple inscriptions, but in the

main purpose of designing inscriptions for buildings and medals founded by King Louis XIV. See "Royal Academy of Inscriptions and Literature", in: *The Encyclopedia of Diderot and d'Alembert Collaborative Translation Project*, trans. R. Benhamou (Ann Arbor, 2003) <http://hdl.handle.net/2027/spo.did2222.0000.217> (accessed 8.04.2021)

[24] Zajic, "Texts on public display", p. 425.

Middle Ages and early modern times it developed into a separate literary genre.

In Vilnius, only a few early modern inscriptions with functions different from funerary, pious, or parenetic (adhortatory) functions have survived. They are carved on slabs, remembering the building of Catholic churches. We do not know if there were any inscriptions (sometimes in form of epitaphs) marking historical events or the foundation of non-ecclesiastical buildings. Such monuments are in fact known from the towns in Poland and other Central-European countries,[25] so it is probable they could have been present also in Vilnius, for instance on the city gates, the walls of the town hall, the university or the castle.

Usually the purpose of making an inscription was to express someone's piety or adherence to a confession, to build or announce someone's prestige or ethos.[26] Inscriptions also played an important role in the construction of the collective memory of the urban society or of certain social groups living in Vilnius. Although the authors of inscriptions were taught in school that literature is "*aere perennius*" ("lasting more than bronze", as Horace had considered his own poetry), they nevertheless protected their literary works by having them carved in durable materials such as stone or metal. In doing so, they showed their trust in the durable and eternal nature of the memory which they forged in durable and (hopefully) eternal inscriptions.

Epitaphs

The epitaph was the most common genre of literature on display in early modern Vilnius. However, the city lost most such texts, mainly in the nineteenth and twentieth centuries, as during the time of the partitions of the Polish-Lithuanian Commonwealth and later, during the Soviet occupation, practically all tombstones in Orthodox churches were removed.[27] We know that

[25] In the main parish churches of Gdańsk (the state of the Teutonic Order), Cracow (Poland), and Vienna (Austria), fifteenth-century epitaphs recorded the memory of the burghers who took part in political conflicts and fell victim to prosecutions. In each case, the epitaphs not only commemorated the innocent victims but also recorded the historical events. See ZAJIC, "Texts on public display", p. 413.

[26] JANICKI, "Inskrypcja w przestrzeni publicznej", p. 264.

[27] From the first partition of the Polish-Lithuanian Commonwealth (1773), the Russian authorities began the destruction of the Uniate Church on the occupied territories. Until 1795, the

Paweł of Kodeń Sapieha, the marshal of the *hospodar* (the grand duke) and *voivode* of Navahrudak, was buried in the church of the Holy Trinity in 1579, but his epitaph – and it is unlikely that such an important person would not be honoured with a tombstone – does no longer exist. From this large Gothic church, where dozens, if not hundreds of important people were buried, only three epitaphs have survived. The same is true of St. John's parish church. In vain we look for the tombstone of Krzysztof Rozdrażowski, who died "during the siege of Zavoloche for the king and homeland"[28] in 1580 and was buried here. However, this tombstone had existed, and its inscription had been recorded for posterity by Szymon Starowolski, a seventeenth-century Polish scholar and writer. There had also been an inscription on the iron door that led to the Great Synagogue, which read "Offered by the guild of tailors for the eternal memory of God's glory, 5663 [1638]", the only trace of which is a photograph from the beginning of the twentieth century.[29]

The fate of the inscriptions in the church of the Holy Spirit and the cathedral of the Theotokos was even worse, where not a single old epitaph or inscription has survived, as in the past there has been no historian to record them for us. The nineteenth-century historian Teodor Narbutt mentioned numerous coffins floating in the latter church's flooded crypts, as well as a grave in which a golden plaque with a Ruthenian text was found. He assumed that this may have been the grave of Princess Uliana of Tver or Queen Helena. Unfortu-

Russian Orthodox Church took over 2500 Uniate churches and monasteries. See M. RADWAN, *Carat wobec Kościoła greckokatolickiego w zaborze rosyjskim 1796-1839* (Lublin, 2004), pp. 27-29. After the end of the November Uprising against Russia (1830-1831), Russian prosecutions led to abolishing the Uniate Church. From the second half of the nineteenth century, the vast majority of non-Orthodox places of memory was destroyed as a result of Russification and Russian politics of memory. The Soviet authorities continued the imperial policy against the memory of the Grand Duchy of Lithuania. Thousands of historic monuments (churches, castles, manor houses, cemeteries, epitaphs, etc.) were destroyed before 1991, when Belarus and Lithuania regained their independence.

[28] "*in oppugnatione Zawolociae pro rege suo et patria rem fortiter gerens in necessario arcis capiendae conatu, globo in fronte immerso anno Domini 1583 die 10 Octobris, aetatis suae 33 animose occubiuit*" ("during the siege of Zavoloche for the king and homeland in the brave and necessary attempt of taking the castle he was hit with a bullet in his forehead and courageously died on 10 October 1583 at the age of 33"). STAROWOLSKI, *Monumenta Sarmatarum*, pp. 229-230. Actually, the Muscovite stronghold of Zavoloche (near Pskov in North-West Russia) was besieged by the Polish-Lithuanians from 5 October 1580 and was taken on 23 October. The author of the inscription (or Starowolski) made a mistake in the year. A sixteenth-century Polish historian, Joachim Bielski, confirms Rozdrażewski's death in 1580; see M. BIELSKI, and J. BIELSKI, *Kronika polska* (Cracow, 1597), p. 776. See also KRASZEWSKI, *Wilno*, 2, pp. 443, 466.

[29] МАГГИД, *Вильна*.

nately, nobody copied the inscription.[30] It is not known to what extent what Narbutt remembered (he was known for his practice of fabricating his sources) can be accepted at face value, but it is certain that from the fifteenth century the dead were honoured in Vilnius with commemorative texts. Starowolski's *Monumenta Sarmatarum*, published in Cracow in 1655, provide a selection of them from the cathedral and the churches of St. John, St. Casimir, the Franciscans and St. Michael, but these are only Catholic epitaphs written in honour of people who belonged to the political elite or the high clergy. In Starowoski's work, almost exclusively men appear, though epitaphs of women were also present in the churches he visited.[31]

The tombstones that have survived seem to confirm the assumption that writing and making epitaphs public was an art intended for the more important inhabitants of Vilnius, as it was in the whole of Lithuania. These tombstones covered the graves of the nobility and clergy, while inscriptions dedicated to ordinary town dwellers are extremely rare. Were epitaphs in Vilnius also quite rare in centuries past? Their modern edition, *Inscriptiones ecclesiarum Vilnensium*,[32] notes relatively few inscriptions from before 1655, and even if we extend the list with epigraphs recorded by Starowolski, Vilnius was not equal to Cracow, Lviv, or Poznań.

If this was indeed the case, the capital of Lithuania would have been an exception in comparison with the other large urban centres of the Polish-Lithuanian Commonwealth and of Europe generally.[33] However, it was not. In the sixteenth and seventeenth centuries, the members of the family of the deceased were obliged to fund an epitaph if they could afford one. The inscription reminded surviving relatives of the need to pray for the deceased and ensured

[30] T. NARBUTT, *Pomniejsze pisma historyczne szczególnie do Litwy odnoszące się* (Vilnius, 1856), pp. 83-84.

[31] The only female epitaphs Starowolski mentioned belonged to queens and saints. The *Monumenta Sarmatarum* is a good example of the genderisation of early modern historiography, in which female characters were marginalised. It is worth adding that the masculinisation of the past is only one of several filters applied by Starowolski. He recorded only Latin epitaphs from the Catholic churches. This attitude heralded the main line of the Polish historiography up to the twentieth century (as a history of a nation of Catholic noblemen).

[32] *Inscriptiones ecclesiarum Vilnensium: Inskrypcje z wileńskich kościołów: Vilniaus bažnyčių įrašai*, 1, ed. W. APPEL and E. ULČINAITĖ (Vilnius, 2005).

[33] For the history of epitaphs in late medieval and early modern Western Europe (especially France), see Ph. ARIÈS, *The Hour of Our Death: The Classic History of Western Attitudes Toward Death over the Last One Thousand Years*, trans. H. WEAVER (New York, 2013), pp. 235-258.

that they would be remembered: stone and text had for centuries been topoi in the maintaining the memory of the dead.

The efforts in constructing the memory of the dead could have two forms, performative and material. To the first group belong funeral ceremonies such as keeping a vigil over the body, having a Mass said, and offering a funeral reception (*stypa*), prayers for the dead (especially annual exequies, in the Catholic Church); to the second group belong funeral sermons, panegyrics, epitaphs, mausolea (chapels) in the churches, etc. All these forms of commemoration of the dead significantly contributed to building a collective memory. Collective memory relies on *memoria*, on different forms of remembering the dead.[34] The purpose of *memoria* was helped by making symbolic ties between present and past members of a community.

From Roman times onwards, epitaphs played a special role in celebrating the memory of the dead.[35] The epitaph makes the dead present, mainly through of its textual nature. This is caused by a textual procedure, common in Western literature, which is called a 'manifestation' or 'making present' (Polish: *uobecnienie*[36]).

Founding an epitaph was a complex task. It required different forms of capital: economical, social, and cultural. The founders had to make considerable financial efforts to have a tombstone made and to put an epitaph in a privileged place in a church. In every medieval and early modern town the inhabitants negotiated or even struggled for a place (which was usually limited)

[34] The concept of *memoria* was introduced by the German historian Otto Gerhard Oexle; see O.G. OEXLE, "Die Gegenwart der Lebenden und der Toten", pp. 74-107; ID., "Memoria als Kultur", in: *Memoria als Kultur*, ed. O.G. OEXLE (Göttingen, 1995), pp. 9-78.

[35] ARIÈS, *The Hour of Our Death*, p. 312.

[36] According to the philosopher Juliusz Domański, manifestation (*uobecnienie*) is one of the major qualities of a written text. Domański examined a.o. the role of manifestation in the writings of early Renaissance writers (Petrarch, E.S. Piccolomini, Zbigniew Oleśnicki, Marsilio Ficino, and Thomas à Kempis), especially in relation to epistolography and the dialogue between absent people. J. DOMAŃSKI, *Tekst jako uobecnienie: Szkic z dziejów myśli o piśmie i książce* (Warsaw, 1992), pp. 100-125. Domański's concept of the manifestation in the text can be also used in a wider discussion about beliefs of the presence of the dead in past societies. It seems that manifestation is an indispensable component of *memoria*; understanding how manifestation in a (literary) text works can explain how the dead are present in and through literary genres (such as the epitaph, threnody, funeral sermon, epicedion, last will, funeral oration, panegyric, epos, *silva*, etc.).

Fig. 55 Latin cenotaph of bishop Benedykt Woyna in Vilnius cathedral, 1615. Photo J. Niedźwiedź.

where their epitaphs could be placed.[37] The lack of space on the walls of early modern churches in the Polish-Lithuanian Commonwealth is confirmed by the sources.[38]

[37] About the common practice of negotiating the most visible place in the public space in medieval Austrian towns ,see ZAJIC, "Texts on public display", p. 397.

[38] Adam Jarzębski († 1648 or 1649), a composer, musician, and poet (who visited Vilnius with his patron, King Władysław IV), provides us with a good example from another city of the Polish-Lithuanian commonwealth, i.e. Warsaw. He expressed directly the deficiency of space for epitaphs in the main church of Warsaw. In his rhymed guide (1643) Jarzębski mentioned the epitaphs in the church: "The poisoned German (!) Masovian dukes lie there. There are many epitaphs, it is difficult to find clear space [on the wall]" ("*Tam ci leżą mazowieckie | Książęta strute, niemieckie. | Epitafij wiele różnych, | Trudno znaleźć miejsc a próżnych*"). See A. JARZĘBSKI, *Gościniec abo krótkie opisanie Warszawy* (Warsaw, 1900), p. 26, lines 641-644. Probably Jarzębski did know Latin and the phrase "*germani fratres*" from the Latin epitaph of the

And then, the epitaph was supposed to be not only an object as part of the *memoria* of the deceased, but also a sign of prestige: it was often a monument to the family and, like funeral ceremonies, was intended to determine the deceased's place in the social hierarchy of the city and, sometimes, the entire country.

All these circumstances, that is the memory of the dead as well as the wealth and prestige of Vilnius residents, encourage us to believe that they probably ordered many epitaphs. This hypothesis, however, needs to be confirmed by sources more certain than mere assumptions.

In the right nave of the Bernardine church, there is a plaque commemorating Paweł Janowicz of Nosek, who died in 1625, and his wife Katarzyna, who commissioned the plaque. Under the crucifix, the spouses kneel, followed on both sides by their sons and daughters, ever smaller in reverse order of age. Below the image there is an inscription.[39] Such a graphic-textual epitaph structure was typical and frequent in sixteenth- and seventeenth-century sepulchral sculpture, and resembles the tombstones of, for instance, Cracow or Gdańsk. Janowicz' gravestone shows that the Vilnius stonemasons were also familiar with it. However, how often were such characteristic solutions employed, and how willingly were such texts commemorating the deceased used?

The answer to these questions can be found in three seventeenth-century texts, an Orthodox one, a Catholic-Uniate one, and an Evangelical-Augsburg (Lutheran) one. In the will of Akwilina Stryludzianka, the wife of Paweł Dorofiejewicz, dated 1651, we read that she ordered to be buried in the graveyard of the Orthodox church of the Holy Spirit. She also asked that "an image of the Blessed Virgin painted on wood, framed in silver, which she loved very much, be handsomely framed and put up in a decent (*dogodny*) place instead of her epitaph".[40] In the Orthodox tradition, the icon plays a more important role than in western Christianity (even a more important role than in the Catholic Church). It is considered to be sacred, a window and mediation between two

brothers Stanisław and Janusz, the last Piast rulers of Masovia, were understood as "*niemieccy bracia*" instead of "*rodzeni bracia*".

[39] "*D.T.O.M. In this grave lies the body of the honest Mr Paweł Janowicz of Nosek, a burgher and merchant of the city of Vilnius. He lived in this world for forty-seven years, died in 1625, on 4 April, and his wife, Mrs Katarzyna Janowna, commemorated his memory with this plaque. Lord, have mercy on his soul*" (after a transcription from the tombstone in the Bernardine church in Vilnius, made by the author).

[40] MS BJ 2926, p. 43.

spheres, the human and the divine.[41] Mrs Dorofiejewiczowa's icon was first of all a holy object. However, in this case the icon's purpose was also to keep her memory alive and was a substitute for a funerary inscription and a memorial picture (or picture of memory).[42] The Orthodox or Uniate icon could not represent her directly, because since the iconoclasm movement (of the eighth and ninth centuries) eastern Christian art has been very strict with the canons, and unlike Catholic or Protestant art forbade representations of persons that were not sacred, such as the founders. Mrs Dofofiejewiczowa could not act like her Catholic neighbours who (if they were rich enough) had every possibility to exhibit their portraits in the church, even on the holy pictures on the altars. She chose another way to visually commemorate herself in the holy space of an Orthodox church. Even though her icon did not render her in by way of a portrait, it played the role of a memorial picture. The members of her community who prayed and lit the candles before the picture simultaneously recalled Mrs Dorofiejewiczowa and confirmed the *memoria* related to her.[43] This recollection was facilitated by the fact that in her will she directly expressed her strategy of making the icon-epitaph well visible. We must remember that not everybody could put their icon in a church, and Mrs Dorofiejewiczowa's high social status (her social and economic capital) must have helped to have this instruction of her last will obeyed.

Her efforts were not exceptional. Not much earlier, in 1649, bishop Abraham Woyna had written in his will:

> To the church of the Holy Trinity in Vilnius, where my father's body lies and which immediately after his death I presented with a silver cross and a chalice and vestments [...] I bequeath a thousand *zloty* and a reddish marble table from my

[41] Grigorij (Gregory) KRUG, *Myśli o ikonie*, trans. R. MAZURKIEWICZ (Białystok, 1991).

[42] According to Otto Gerhard Oexle, a memorial picture (*Memorialbild*) is basically a portrait of the dead. It was very often part of a tombstone. Such a picture is one of many acts of constructing a person's *memoria*. See O.G. OEXLE, "Memoria und Memorialbild", in: Memoria: *Der geschichtliche Zeugniswert des liturgischen Gedenkens im Mittelalter*, ed. K. SCHMID and J. WOLLASCH (Munich, 1984), pp. 384-440.

[43] The form of an individual Orthodox prayer in a church differs from those of Catholic or Protestant prayers. The icons are located in the iconostasis, on the walls, and on the pillars of the Orthodox church. Persons who visit the church light a candle before an icon, cross themselves, bow before it, and sometimes kiss it. Next, they move to another icon and repeat the procedure. So Mrs Dorofiejewiczowa's icon had a good chance to be venerated in the church of the Holy Spirit.

> Vilnius court, for an epitaph, so that [the monks] pray to God for my father's soul and mine.[44]

This record is interesting not only because it talks about the functions of the epitaph and its meaning, but also because it informs us about how the material for the gravestone plaque was obtained. In Lithuania, there were no quarries from which to extract stones suitable for carving inscriptions, so the raw materials had to be brought from places hundreds of kilometres away. Probably the majority of Vilnius tombstones were made of imported stone. In this respect, the residents of Vilnius had fewer options than the inhabitants of Cracow, who, within a radius of one hundred kilometres, had different types of stone at their disposal.[45] Bishop Woyna ordered to recycle a precious piece of his furniture, because red marble was extremely rare in Vilnius churches. In the economy of memory the epitaph of Woyna's father seems to have been a good investment: it must have stood out from other such monuments in the Uniate church of the Holy Trinity.

The third text, and the most interesting one, comes from the diary of Doctor Maciej Vorbek-Lettow, physician to the king. It explains why, a quarter of a century later, bishop Woyna thought so carefully about the making of his tombstone. In 1624, Lettow's father, Mateusz, died. As the diarist writes, "the right honourable gentleman, Mr Daniel Naborowski, the castle judge in Vilnius, a good and trustworthy friend of the deceased and mine, wrote an epitaph for the deceased and gave it to me".[46] The doctor quoted two texts, a Latin eulogy and a Polish poem. Some time later, another epitaph, in the author's opinion superior to Naborowski's text, was written by a distant cousin of the Lettows, the proconsul of the town of Malbork (Marienburg) in Royal Prussia, Jerzy Fenig. This text was given to "the stonemason of his royal majesty" Antoni Włoch (Anthony the Italian)[47] to be engraved. However, as "his chil-

[44] MS MAB F43-26739, f. 2v. The epitaph of bishop Woyna's father did not survive. Almost all monuments with Latin and Polish inscriptions were destroyed in the nineteenth century, when the Holy Trinity Uniate church was taken over by Orthodox monks.

[45] J. RAJCHEL, *Kamienny Kraków*, 2nd, corrected edn. (Cracow, 2005), pp. 13-14.

[46] VORBEK-LETTOW, *Skarbnica pamięci*, pp. 241-242.

[47] *Włoch* (Pol. 'Italian') was probably the stonemason's nickname. He must have been one of dozens Italian artisans and artists who took part in building the royal castle in Vilnius from the first half of the sixteenth century. On the Italian immigrants working in the Polish-Lithuanian state in the fifteenth-eighteenth centuries, see J. POMORSKA, *Artyści włoscy w Polsce* (Warsaw, 2004).

dren tore the paper with the text into small pieces while playing", it was necessary to return to the original versions.

> This task was long incomplete, not because I wanted to abandon it, but as I currently live with my wife and children in Warsaw at His Majesty's court there was not way to hasten the indolent. However, leaving my duties behind, I came to Vilnius. Drawing from these two epitaphs, I composed another one and had it engraved on the red marble plate. The epitaph was embedded in the crypt where my parents are buried.[48]

The crypt of the Vorbek-Lettows was located in the Evangelical-Augsburg (Lutheran) church on Niemiecka street (today Vokiečių gatvė). After Dr Maciej Vorbek-Lettow's death (on 7 June 1663) he was buried in a new family chapel in the Lutheran cemetery, located outside the city walls near Ludwisarska street.[49] The epitaphs of his ancestors were also transferred there, among them the oldest one from 1556. It formed a kind of family mausoleum,[50] one of many such places in early modern Vilnius and the Polish-Lithuanian Commonwealth.

Neither Mrs Stryludzianka's icon, nor the epitaphs in the church of the Holy Trinity and in the Evangelical-Augsburg church have survived. However, the three testimonies quoted above speak of the universality of this commemorative form. It follows that not only Catholics but members of all Christian churches were accustomed to making epitaphs. This common form of remem-

[48] *Ibid.*, p. 66.

[49] W. WOŁKANOWSKI, "Pamięć ludzka jest krucha ... Dawne cmentarze ewangelickie w Wilnie", *Przegląd Bałtycki* 8.11.2017 <https://przegladbaltycki.pl/6256,pamiec-ludzka-krucha-dawne-cmentarze-ewangelickie-wilnie.html> (accessed 16.04.2021)

[50] At the beginning of the nineteenth century, a new Lutheran cemetery in Vilnius was established on Buffałowa Hill (today Pamėnkalnis). Epitaphs of the Vorbek-Lettows were transferred there from the old cemetery. See A.H. KIRKOR, *Wilno i koleje żelazne z Wilna do Petersburga i Rygi oraz do granic na Kowno i Warszawę: Przewodnik z planem, widokami Wilna i mappą kolei żelaznych* (Vilnius, 1862), p. 193. The Lutheran necropole in the form of a romantic park was closed by the Soviet authorities in 1956. Until 1964 all monuments, sculptures, and the neo-classical chapel were demolished, and the Palace of the Weddings was built in their place in 1974. The epitaphs of the Vorbek-Lettows and other historical tombstones were probably used as building materials (just like thousands of matzevahs from the biggest Jewish cemetery in Vilnius on Holendernia Street, today Olandų gatvė). See WOŁKANOWSKI, "Pamięć ludzka jest krucha"; ŚNIEŻKO, *Cmentarz ewangelicki w Wilnie 1806-1956*; KASPERAVIČIENĖ, *Evangelikų liuteronų ir evangelikų reformatų kapinės*. Only a few photographs of early modern tombstones from the Lutheran cemetery in Vilnius survive. Some of them are available on the website of the Lithuanian Archives: <http://virtualios-parodos.archyvai.lt/lt/> (accessed: 4.06.2023).

bering the death was possible because the Christian inhabitants of Vilnius belonged to the same emotional communities.[51] Therefore, most probably Vilnius did not differ much from Polish cities in terms of the number of monuments. Catholic, Orthodox, and Protestant churches in Vilnius had to be full of inscriptions in verse and prose dedicated to the dead. And in Vilnius tombstones were multi-confessional.

Not only Christians commemorated their deceased by means of texts. As we mentioned before,[52] according to the tradition of the Jewish Funeral Brotherhood, the Jewish Old Cemetery[53] had been established as early as 1487.[54] It surely existed in the late sixteenth century, because the Jews lived in the city in 1593 and the cemetery was mentioned in the privilege granted by King Sigismund III Vasa for the Vilnius Jews in 1629.[55] Archaeological excavations confirmed that there were Jewish burials in the second half of the sixteenth century.[56] The Jewish cemetery was located on the other side of the Neris River, more or less opposite the lower castle. Since 1642, Jewish funeral processions were allowed to cross the Stone Bridge (Most Kamienny) without having to pay toll.[57] The cemetery was used for about three hundred years, until the nineteenth century, and was well preserved until the first half of the twenti-

[51] Barbara H. Rosenwein examined epitaphs from late Roman and early medieval towns in Gaul. She traced their forms and observed that the epitaphs in particular towns shared a vocabulary which differed from vocabularies used in the epitaphs in other towns. Rosenwein made an assumption that the particular vocabulary used in the Gallic epitaphs can be a manifestation of an emotional community in a town. See B.H. ROSENWEIN, *Emotional Communities in the Early Middle Ages* (Ithaca and London, 2006), pp. 57-78. In early modern Vilnius, the fact that the inhabitants tended to build their *memoria* in the form of an epitaph can be treated as a manifestation of an emotional community (or communities). However, unlike in Roman and early medieval Gaul, the forms of epitaphs in the sixteenth and seventeenth century were much richer and diversified, and analyses similar to those made by Rosenwein would prove to be more complex (if they were possible at all).

[52] Chapter 16.

[53] The New Cemetery was established in the nineteenth century and was located on Holendernia street, today Olandų gatvė.

[54] COHEN, *History of the Jews in Vilnius*, p. 124; МАГГИД, *Вильна*. In both publications there are photographs of the cemetery. Elmantas Meilus pointed out that there are no substantial sources confirming the year; see E. MEILUS, "The history of Vilnius Old Jewish Cemetery at Šnipiškės in the period of the Grand Duchy of Lithuania" *Lithuanian Historical Studies* 12 (2007), pp. 64. Meilus based his valuable study on the works Jewish historians: I. KLAUSNER, *History of the Old Jewish Cemetery in Vilnius* (Vilnius, 1935) and D. FISHMAN, *Historical Overview of the Jewish Cemetery in Shnipishok* (unpublished).

[55] MEILUS, "The history of Vilnius Old Jewish Cemetery", p. 68.

[56] *Ibid.*, p. 68.

[57] *Ibid.*, p. 70.

eth century, when several hundred tombstones (*matzevahs*) must have been there. However, as after its destruction by the Nazis and in Soviet times a sports hall was built in its place,[58] we do not know anything about the *matzevahs* from this necropolis.[59] Unlike Christians, of whom only the richest could afford a gravestone, most Jews had permanent graves, initially of wood and then of stone, with Hebrew inscriptions. The court documents from the first half of the seventeenth century inform us that both types of funeral monuments were present at the Old Cemetery. In 1635 the Jewish cemetery was destroyed during an anti-Jewish riot:

> The violent and armed crowd of several hundred people came to the enclosure (*ogród*) of the Jews, which is in the suburb of Vilnius on the other side of the Neris River, in which place they bury the late Jews. The attackers trespassed this enclosure and smashed and scattered thirteen wooden and stone tombs. They also destroyed thirteen tablets with inscriptions in Jewish letters, which were placed over the tombs. We saw on the snow the upper parts of these tablets knocked down and smashed on pieces.[60]

The fact that some of the tombs were made of wood confirms the problem which the Christian inhabitants of Vilnius encountered as well: the lack of stone suitable for making epitaphs. Only opulent Jews could afford stone epitaphs. However, even Jews of modest income remembered the late members of their families by a funeral inscription, even if it was to be put on a wooden tablet only. The scale of the use of inscriptions reflects the level and status of literacy among this group of Vilnius residents. Every pious Jew had to be able to read in order to study the Scriptures, so practically every man was able to read inscriptions on *matzevahs*.

The oldest known tombstone in the Old Vilnius cemetery was dated 1636 (5396); it belonged to rabbi Menahem Manish, son of Yitzhak Hayes.[61] Jewish

[58] The new luxurious buildings were built on the last parts of the Jewish cemetery (without the tombstones) in 2007. The international Jewish community protested against the decisions of the Lithuanian authorities, but without success. See N. ADOMAITIS, "Jews protest to Lithuania over ancient cemetery", *Reuters*, August 22, 2007, 4:12 PM <https://www.reuters.com/article/us-lithuania-jews-idUSL2183316620070822> (accessed: 12.05.2021).

[59] S. GRZYBOWSKI, *Epitafia żydowskie w Polsce doby sarmatyzmu*, p. 50.

[60] *AVAK*, 28 (Vilnius 1901), pp. 155-156; MEILUS, "The history of Vilnius Old Jewish Cemetery", p. 70.

[61] KLAUSNER, *History of the Old Jewish Cemetery in Vilnius*; MEILUS, "The history of Vilnius Old Jewish Cemetery", p. 68; "Wilno" in: *Wirtualny Sztetl* <https://sztetl.org.pl/pl/

inscriptions most probably did not differ much in their content from the forms commonly used in Hebrew epigraphy in this part of Europe.[62] We can draw this conclusion from monographs by H.N. Maggid (1829-1903)[63] and I. Klausner.[64]

A Hebrew epitaph was structured according to certain rules and was divided into four parts: a preliminary formula, the body of laudation or praise with elements of lamentation, an informative part, and closing formulae.[65] Fixed elements included the name of the deceased at the beginning, his or her age, usually provided in a descriptive way, and the date of death. Praise was supposed to constitute the most extensive part. It began with fixed formulae: "perfect and righteous man" ("איש תם וישר") or "honourable and modest woman" ("אשה חשובה וצנועה").[66] The final formula almost always had the following form: "May his / her soul be bound up in the bond of eternal life" ("תנצב"ה").[67] The laudatory elements and titles could be particularly elaborate and varied. This is indicated by the material from other cities of the Polish-Lithuanian Commonwealth with which these tombstones can be compared.[68]

Vilnius tombstones from the seventeenth century, as well as *matzevahs* from Lublin and other towns of Lesser Poland, were devoid of any decorations

miejscowosci/w/1044-wilno/114-cmentarze/38803-cmentarz-zydowski-na-pioromoncie-w-wilnie-juozapaviciaus-g> (accessed: 12.05.2021).

[62] Hebrew sepulchral epigraphy in medieval and early modern Poland was examined by Leszek Hońdo in his fundamental work *Hebrajska epigrafika nagrobna w Polsce* (Cracow, 2014). The content of the inscriptions is meticulously examined in chapter 4, "The structure of formulaic forms and the typical content of their elements", pp. 131-215.

[63] Х.Н. Маггид (Hillel Noah Maggid-Steinschneider), אנליוו ריע *Матеріалы къ исторіи Виленской еврейской общины въ краткихъ біографическихъ очеркахъ ея дѣятелей с разными генеалогическими и біографическими заметками* (Vilnius, 1900). The book commemorates the most notable members in the history of the Vilnius Jewish community. In the first volume of this work (and the only one published) Maggid wrote *c.* 300 short biographies, many of which were based on the epitaphs. The author quoted fragments of some of them.

[64] Klausner, *History of the Old Jewish Cemetery.*

[65] *Ibid.*, pp. 52-57. Trzciński and Wodziński, *Cmentarz żydowski w Lesku*, pp. 29-35; M. Wodziński, *Hebrajskie inskrypcje na Śląsku XIII-XVIII wieku* (Wrocław, 2003), pp. 82-159; A.M. Bogdańska, "Studium cmentarza żydowskiego Galicji Wschodniej na przykładzie kirkutu w Lutowiskach", in: *Pogranicza Galicji: Studia*, ed. T. Bujnicki and J. Niedźwiedź (Bielsko-Biała, 2005), p. 19.

[66] Wodziński, *Hebrajskie inskrypcje na Śląsku XIII-XVIII wieku*, pp. 152-153.

[67] *Ibid.*, pp. 134-135.

[68] L. Hońdo, "Tytuły osobowe na nagrobkach na przykładzie starego cmentarza żydowskiego w Krakowie", in: *Żydzi i judaizm we współczesnych badaniach polskich*, 2, *Materiały z konferencji, Kraków 24-26 XI 1998*, ed. K. Pilarczyk ands S. Gąsiorowski (Cracow, 2000), pp. 161-177.

and consisted only of concave lettering.[69] It was not until the beginning of the seventeenth century that architectural elements, such as embedded columns, began to be added.[70] Thus, as in the case of the majority of Christian gravestones, the dominant element consisted of letters carved in stone.

The Style of Christian Funerary Inscriptions

Let us return to the Christian funeral epigraphy. Groups of Catholic epitaphs, relatively large for Vilnius standards, have survived in the cathedral, in the Bernardine church and in St. Michael's church (of the Bernardine Sisters). The oldest ones come from the first half of the sixteenth century. They were made by Italian artists who worked in Vilnius and rebuilt the lower castle and the cathedral. Among these Italians was Giovanni Cini, who produced the monuments of Albertas Goštautas and bishop Holszański. It is worth noting that stonemasons and sculptors from Italy also worked in the city in the next century, as has been unambiguously mentioned by Lettow.

Inscriptions were a major part of each gravestone. Older inscriptions from the sixteenth and early seventeenth centuries took the form of a prose text, sometimes quite simple, such as the epitaph of Grand Duke Vytautas of 1535,[71] Barbara Zawiszanka of 1603, and the epitaph of Paweł Holszański mentioned above:

> *Illustrissimus ac Reverendissimus Dominus D. Paulus Dux Olsenensis Dei Gratia Episcopus Vilnensis, ex Episcopatu Luceoriensi, assumptus ad Episcopatum Vilnensem anno Domini 1536. Mortuus 1555.*[72]

Some of them may have been written in elegiac distichs, such as the now lost tombstone of Barbara Radziwiłłówna of around 1551, perhaps by Stanisław Koszutski:

[69] TRZCIŃSKI, *Hebrajskie inskrypcje na materiale kamiennym*, p. 147.

[70] Ш.В. КИСЕНБАУМ, *Еврейские надгробные памятники города Люблина (XVI-XIX в). Приложение к "Еврейской Старине"* (Санкт-Петербург, 1913), tables 4-9.

[71] M.A. JANICKI, "Grób i komemoracja wielkiego księcia Aleksandra Witolda w katedrze wileńskiej w kontekście upamiętnienia Władysława Jagiełły w katedrze krakowskiej i propagandy jagiellońskiej XIV-XVI w.", *Przegląd Historyczny* 111.4 (2020), pp. 770-771, 789-792.

[72] STAROWOLSKI, *Monumenta Sarmatarum*, p. 222.

Barbara, quae tegitur tumulo regina sub isto,
Augusti coniunx altera regis erat.
Commoda multa tulit multis, incommoda nulli,
A qua se laesum dicere nemo potest.
Immatura obiit decima trieteridi capta,
Bis viduos fatis linquere iussa toros.
Occidit ante diem, et quamvis anus illa fuisset,
Diceret Augustus, occidit ante diem.

Coronata 7. Decembr. Anno 1550. Obiit 8. Maii.[73]

Queen Barbara, buried in this grave, was the second wife of King Augustus. She brought happiness to many people, misery to none, and nobody can say that she offended them with anything. She passed away prematurely in her third decade, forced by fate to leave her bed widowed for the second time. She had died before the day came. And though Augustus might say that she should have died as an old woman, she had died before the day came.

Crowned on 7 December 1550. She died on 8 May.

Pedro Ruiz de Moros (Doctor Spaniard) also wrote a cycle of nine epitaphs devoted to Queen Barbara.[74] In epigram 2, Doctor Spaniard makes an interesting parallel between two capitals, Cracow and Vilnius:

Barbara, Sauromatum cubat hic regina, potenti
De Radivilorum nobilis orta domo.
Dat mortem, quae sceptra dedit, Cracovia; regis
Quae dederat thalamum, Vilna dedit tumulum.

Here lies the Queen of the Sarmatians Barbara, who descended from the potent house of the Radziwiłłs. Cracow, which gave her the sceptre (power), gave her also her death; Vilnius, which gave her the matrimonial bed, gave her also her tomb.

Ruiz de Moros, who was a naturalised Lithuanian, in a way similar to that of his friend, the *Voigt* of Vilnius Augustyn Rotundus,[75] defended the equal rights of the Grand Duchy of Lithuania and the Kingdom of Poland. In his epigram,

[73] STAROWOLSKI, *Monumenta Sarmatarum*, p. 217-218.
[74] P. RUIZ DE MOROS (Petrus Royzius), *Petri Royzii Maurei Alcagnicensis Carmina: Pars II*, pp. 34-36.
[75] The polemic between Rotundus and Orzechowski has been discussed in Chapter 7.

Fig. 56 The monument of Barbara Tyszkiewiczowa (née Naruszewicz) in her mausoleum in the Holy Trinity Uniate church in Vilnius, *c.* 1627. The project by the royal architect Matteo Castello. Photo J. Niedźwiedź.

gram, Doctor Spaniard not only bewailed the late queen but also suggests that Vilnius cathedral, as the burial place of the ruling dynasty, is as important as Cracow cathedral, the place of the coronation (and a burial place as well).

Koszutski's and Ruiz de Mors' epitaphs were written in elegiac distichs, the most common form used in Latin epitaphs in the sixteenth century. From the beginning of the seventeenth century onwards, elogia and stemmata became ever more popular.[76] One of the oldest elogia is a partially preserved plaque commemorating Cardinal Jerzy Radziwiłł from 1600 and a cenotaph made for bishop Benedyct Woyna on red marble from 1615.[77] Sometimes the addition of

[76] On the career of the elogium in the literature of the seventeenth and eighteenth centuries, see B. OTWINOWSKA, "Elogium – *flos floris, anima et essentia* poetyki siedemnastowiecznego panegiryzmu", in: *Studia z teorii i historii poezji*, series 1, ed. M. GŁOWIŃSKI (Wrocław, 1967), *passim*.

[77] *Inscriptiones ecclesiarum Vilnensium*, pp. 68-70, 108-111.

Fig. 57 Tombstone of the mayor of Vilnius, Atanazy Braga, and his son Antoni Braga, after 1580 (?), Holy Trinity Uniate church in Vilnius. Photo J. Niedźwiedź.

an image of the deceased transformed a tombstone into a complex structure combining architecture, heraldry, and portrait sculpture. A rather modest, yet elegant example of this type is the tombstone of Samuel Pac of 1627 in the cathedral, probably the work of Matteo Castello or his nephew Costante Tencalla.[78] A group of the richest compositions of this type has survived in the Sapieha family mausoleum in St. Michael's church, which will be discussed later.

The dominance of word over image can be seen in the tombstone of Barbara Tyszkiewiczowa (née Naruszewicz), the wife of the *voivode* of Trakai, who died in 1627. The monument was designed and executed by the royal architect Matteo Castello.[79] It is located by the northern wall of her funerary chapel-mausoleum, which was added to the Uniate church of the Holy Trinity.[80] The decoration of the monument is simple: the architectural shape (framing, volute)

[78] M. KARPOWICZ, *Matteo Castello: Architekt wczesnego baroku* (Warsaw, 1990), pp. 78-79, picture 86.

[79] KARPOWICZ, *Matteo Castello*, pp. 77-78, picture 83.

[80] Józef Ignacy Kraszewski mentioned that there were other monuments of the Tyszkiewicz family, built in the first half of the seventeenth century. See J.I. KRASZEWSKI, *Wilno*, 3, p. 72.

and the combination of brown, black, and white marble are characteristic of the 'Vasa Baroque'.[81] It is complemented by a four-field coat of arms and a graphic shape, but its main part is a piece of literature on display: a long elogium, in which an unknown poet praises the virtues of a Christian woman, wife and mother.

The epitaph of Atanazy Braga and his son Antoni, located in the same church right at the entrance to the seventeenth-century grave chapel of the Tyszkiewicz family, has a similar textual and aesthetic character. It is the only Orthodox tombstone memorial in Vilnius from the sixteenth century known today. It consists of two parts: on the left, one can see the coat of arms of the Bragas while on the right is featured a Church Slavonic (Cyrillic) inscription: "Here rests God's servant Atanazy Fiedorowicz Braga, mayor of Vilnius, who died in the 1576th year since the birth of our Saviour on the fifteenth day of October. And he lived in this world fifty-seven years. His son Antoni lies here too. He died in the year 1580 on the third of October".[82] The whole composition is surrounded by a border in the Renaissance style. The uniqueness of this monument lies in the transposition of monumental Latin writing[83] into Orthodox art. The function of the capital letters is taken over by decorative *semiustav* modelled on fonts used in printing.

Epitaphs were a well-known textual / literary form not only because the inhabitants of Vilnius lived surrounded by them, but also because they (by which I mean almost exclusively men) wrote such texts themselves. Daniel Naborowski, the creator of tombstone inscriptions mentioned above, was an outstanding poet, but then, all students who completed several years at a humanist school had learnt to write epitaphs. In the second half of the sixteenth century and the first half of the seventeenth century, practically all of them would have been able to write an epitaph, for better or worse, as this was taught at school. Jacobus Pontanus' manual of poetics, used at the Academy of Vilnius, provided the rules for composing an epitaph, and we can also find them in manu-

[81] Mariusz Karpowicz supposes the monument was partially rebuilt and destroyed in the nineteenth century. See KARPOWICZ, *Matteo Castello*, p. 77.

[82] "ТУТ ЛЕЖИТ РАБ БОЖІИ ΩΘЯНА | СЕІ ФЕДОРОВИЧ БРАГА БУРМИ | СТР МЕСТА ВИЛЕНСОГО А ПРЕ | ВСТАВИШСЯ В ЛЕТО ОТ ВОПЛО | ЩЕНІЯ СП<А>СА НАШЕГ$_{\text{О}}$ АФОΣ | МѢСЕЦА ΩКТ$_{\text{Е}}$БРА КΣ ДНЯ | А ЖИЛ НА СВЕТ$_{\text{Е}}$ ЛѢТ НЗ. ТУТ | ЖЕ ЛЕЖИТ І СЫН ЕГО АНТО | НІИ ΩН ЖЕ ПРЕВСТАВИШСЯ | В ЛЕТО АФП М<ѢСЕ>ЦА ΩК | ТЕБРА Г ДНЯ", the epitaph of Atanazy and Antoni Braga in the Holy Trinity Uniate church in Vilnius. Transcription made by the author. See KRASZEWSKI, *Wilno*, 3, pp. 72-73.

[83] PETRUCCI, *Public Lettering*, pp. 13, 19-28.

script treatises on poetry from the second half of the seventeenth century, obligatorily with a large number of examples.[84] This was a practical skill to be applied in everyday life (if one can put it this way): with the high mortality rates of the time, it was always to be expected that such a text would have to be drafted for a wife, children, parents, friends, or neighbours. Therefore, the epitaph belonged to the most 'interactive' textual genres, and its status was quite high – in spite of the fact that it was low in the hierarchy of poetic genres – because an inscription carved in stone was supposed to commemorate someone forever.

Mausolea

In early modern Vilnius architectural and textual form appeared with the mausoleum. This was a building (or part of a building) whose purpose was religious but was also meant to remember the dead. The early modern mausoleum in the form of a chapel of a church was a continuation of a medieval tradition with some inspirations from Roman funerary art.

The first such place of this kind in Vilnius was the cathedral. Since the end of the fourteenth century it became the burial place of the grand dukes of Lithuania, their wives, and other members of their families.[85] Grand Duke Vytautas was buried there in 1430. In 1535 he was commemorated with a new Renaissance monument founded by Queen Bona Sforza.[86]

In 1484 King Casimir Jagiellon built a chapel in which the members of the royal family were to be buried, among them his sons, Prince Casimir Jagiellon († 1484) and King Alexander Jagiellon († 1506). The chapel was called the Royal Chapel.[87] In the 1620s King Sigismund III Vasa commissioned the Swiss architect Matteo Castelli to design a new royal mausoleum.[88] The chapel, called the Royal Chapel or the Chapel of St. Casimir (Jagiellon) was completed

[84] NIEDŹWIEDŹ, *Nieśmiertelne teatra sławy*, pp. 74-76, 98, 180.

[85] JANICKI, "Grób i komemoracja wielkiego księcia Aleksandra Witolda", pp. 776-777, 779-781.

[86] *Ibid.*, pp. 770-771, 788-792.

[87] RKPS VUB, F4-35808 (A-2472), p. 94. This medieval chapel was demolished in 1631 and was replaced by the new Wołłowicz's Chapel.

[88] Mariusz Karpowicz discussed the history of building of the chapel and the novelty of the architectural solutions introduced by Castello. See KARPOWICZ, *Matteo Castello*, p. 73-79, pictures 74, 77-82, 84-85, 87-89.

in 1636 by Costant Tencalla.[89] Epitaphs and other inscriptions on the walls, carved in multi-coloured stones imported from Cracow (some 700 km. away), remembered the members of the Jagiellons and the Polish Vasas. The Royal Chapel was not only a building, but also a literary message on display. The mausoleum was a complex text, designed to be read and interpreted on several levels: as a hagiographical text, as a manifestation of Counter-Reformation ideas, and as a historical account of the continuity of royal power in the country. The Vasas, who were the founders of the chapel, copied from similar monuments in Poland, in particular from the Sigismund Chapel, a Renaissance mausoleum built by King Sigismund the Old in 1536.[90]

The Sigismund Chapel introduced to Poland and Lithuania the trend of commemorating noble families in mausolea attached to a church as semi-independent buildings. In sixteenth- and seventeenth-century Poland and Lithuania hundreds of these chapels-mausolea were built.[91] In Vilnius cathedral were founded, among others. the mausolea of the Gasztołds (from the first half of the sixteenth century) and the Wołłowicz family (built in 1631). The chapel of Barbara Tyszkiewiczowa (of 1627) in the Holy Trinity Uniate church has a form whose distant model was the Sigismund Chapel.

Chancellor Lew Sapieha (1557-1633) chose yet another form of commemorating him and his family: their mausoleum was located in a nunnery. This form was well established in Christian tradition and was known from the early Middle Ages onwards. In the last years of the sixteenth century Sapieha commissioned the church of St. Michael, which was built in 1629. It was designed as the family mausoleum where the Sapiehas were to be buried. The nunnery of Bernardine Sisters was founded together with the church. One of the sisters' tasks was keeping the memory of their patrons. The chronicle of the nunnery confirms the close relationships between the sisters and the Sapiehas.[92] At the south wall of the church, an impressive Renaissance monument of chancellor Lew Sapieha († 1633) and his two wives Dorota (*de domo* Firlej, † 1591, see Fig. 16) and Elżbieta (*de domo* Radziwiłł, † 1611) was built.[93] Other monuments in the church served the memory of their sons, Krzysztof Mikołaj († 1631) and Jan Stanisław († 1635), and that of Teodora Krystyna Sapieha (*de*

[89] M. KARPOWICZ, *Baroque in Poland* (Warsaw, 1991), pp. 32, 296-297, pictures 75, 76.

[90] H. KOZAKIEWICZ and S. KOZAKIEWICZ, *The Renaissance in Poland* (Warsaw, 1976), pp. 28-32,

[91] *Ibid.*, pp. 202-203, 220-223, 228-229, pictures 188, 197-201, 227, 228, 232.

[92] *Kronika bernardynek świętomichalskich w Wilnie*, p. 338. See also Chapter 4 (pp. 213, 217).

[93] *Ibid.*, pp. 243-253.

domo Tarnowska, wife of Kazimierz Lew Sapieha, † 1652). The memorial monuments in St. Michael's church have chiefly drawn the interest of art historians, primarily due to their (for Lithuania) unique iconographic and ideological programme, as well as for their artistic value.[94] However, the bust of Krzysztof Sapieha is not only an example of excellent early baroque portraiture sculpture,[95] it is also a sophisticated literary text.[96] The majuscule letters, filled with yellow gold forged in black 'marble' from Dębnik,[97] had an ornamental and aesthetic value, but first of all they presented an elogium, which belonged to the *genus demonstrativum*. The seventeenth-century viewer would probably start reading the tombstone from the epitaph, the main element of the composition. Although it cannot be ruled out that the aforementioned Szymon Starowolski may have admired the marble bust of Krzysztof Sapieha, in his work he reduced the *monumentum* simply to text. For him, "*Monumenta Sarmatarum*" were primarily literary, while sculpture and other visual arts were merely derivatives of the rhetorised word.

Votive Offerings

A group of commemorative texts somewhat similar to epitaphs are inscriptions on votive offerings (ex-votos). A Catholic ex-voto could be any object placed in a church which reminded one about a miracle done by God, especially if the miracle came about with the help of a saint. Since the Middle Ages such votive offerings were accompanied by inscriptions. The use of script testifies that ex-votos were made not only for God (who knows everything and did not need to be informed about His miracles) but also for those people who could read. Votive offerings had primarily an educational function, but they also kept the memory of people and events alive.[98]

[94] M. MATUŠAKAITĖ, *Išėjusiems atminti. Laidosena ir kapų ženklinimas LDK* (Vilnius, 2009), pp. 144-162, 184-191.

[95] It was executed by Sebastian Sala (after 1587-1653), an Italian artist who lived in Cracow from *c.* 1623. See KARPOWICZ, *Baroque in Poland*, pp. 43, 301, picture 105.

[96] STAROWOLSKI, *Monumenta Sarmatarum*, pp. 238-239; *Inscriptiones ecclesiarum Vilnensium*, pp. 258-261; MATUŠAKAITĖ, *Išėjusiems atminti*, pp. 174-180.

[97] Dębnik is a village *c.* 30 km northwest from Cracow (Poland). At the beginning of the seventeenth century a quarry of black limestone (similar to marble) was established there. The so-called 'Dębniki marble' was widely used in architecture in the entire Polish-Lithuanian Commonwealth in the seventeenth and eighteenth centuries.

[98] For Philippe Ariès *ex-votos* are representations of cured body parts, pictures etc. The

Although votive offerings did not fit into any normative poetics, their role in maintaining memory was similar to (and as important as) that of epitaphs. Their purpose was not to recall the memory of the dead, but they also, like epitaphs, contributed to building the collective memory of their Catholic community. They were kept in many churches where relics or holy pictures were preserved. Together with books of miracles,[99] they confirmed the power of the relics and holy pictures and proved that prayers said in this particular place were effective.

They were made mainly by Catholics, who hung silver symbols of miracles performed in a church thanks to the mediation of its holy pictures and relics. The largest collection of them was kept in the St. Casimir's or the Royal Chapel. At the end of the fifteenth century, the cult of Prince Casimir Jagiellon, buried in Vilnius cathedral, had started. It was reinforced when King Sigmund the Old made attempts to have his older brother canonised. In 1513 Andrzej Krzycki (1482-1537), a Polish neo-Latin poet and secretary of Queen Barbara Zápolya (Szapolyai), mentioned that wax offerings were placed near the tomb of Prince Casimir Jagiellon. Even though the canonisation process was interrupted for more than 80 years, the cult lasted.

French scholar does not notice that in the seventeenth century they could also come in the form of written texts. See Ph. ARIÈS, *The Hour of Our Death*, pp. 305-307. Ariès associates the votive offering with the "popular piety" (p. 305) i.e. with the piety of common people. If so, writing about miracles on the votive offerings can be regarded as yet another testimony to the growing trust in the written word and the growth of a literate mentality in medieval and early modern Europe (see ADAMSKA and MOSTERT, "Introduction", p. 1). Even those people who could not write, must have commissioned an occasional scribe and an artisan to execute an inscription.

[99] Books of miracles have been kept in many Catholic and Uniate churches, monasteries, and nunneries in Poland and other countries in East Central Europe (e.g. *Liber miraculorum Beatae Virginis Monasterii Czenstochoviensis*, kept from 1593 in one the most famous Catholic sanctuaries in Europe, the Pauline monastery of Jasna Góra in Częstochowa (Poland)). They are a valuable source for historians of medieval and early modern societies (see M. DELIMATA-PROCH, "Choroby w świetle księgi cudów i łask Matki Bożej Świętogórskiej (XVI-XVIII w.)", *Kwartalnik Historii Kultury Materialnej* 66.3 (2018), pp. 271-287). Vilnius became an important place of pilgrimage only in the seventeenth century, after the canonisation of St. Casimir and, later in the second half of the seventeenth century, when the chapel of Our Lady of the High Gate (Our Lady of the Gate of Dawn, *Matka Boska Ostrobramska*) was built. Stories about miracles of the holy pictures of Our Lady in Vilnius and in other places in the Grand Duchy of Lithuania were printed by the Basilian (Uniate) printing house in Supraśl. See M. CUBRZYŃSKA-LEONARCZYK, *Oficyna supraska 1695-1803: Dzieje i publikacje unickiej drukarni ojców bazylianów* (Warsaw, 1993), pp. 144-147; see also A. MIRONOWICZ, "O parafii kornińskiej, ikonie łaskami słynącej i księdze cudów", in: *Księga cudów przed ikoną Matki Bożej w Starym Korninie dokonanych*, ed. A. MIRONOWICZ (Białystok, 1997), pp. 5-17.

Several hundreds of ex-votos are listed in *Spisanie srebra w Kaplicy Królewskiej przy grobie św. Kazimierza od różnych osób* ex voto *zawieszonych od roku Pańskiego 1603* [*do 1627*] (Catalogued Silvers From the Royal Chapel At the Grave of St. Casimir Given by Various People *Ex Voto* and Hung There Since the Year of Our Lord 1603 [Until 1627]). These brief mentions are the opposite of the registers of the burgrave's court (*sąd horodniczański*) or the Vilnius chapter discussed in the previous chapter. They commemorated people who would not appear in any other text with a memorial function. Unlike court records, these notes carry a positive message, for instance that someone has recovered from illness and did not die from it, that a wound had been healed and was not infected. Most often, these small silver plates with inscriptions were given by women, noblewomen and burghers, maids and married women:

12. A plaque hung on a silk cord, the Passion on one side, an image of Our Lady with the Child engraved on the other side with the inscription *Sub tuum praesidium confugimus sancta Dei genitrix*.
13. A plaque hung on a silk cord, featuring the Passion, on the other side the image of the Virgin Mary with the Child engraved without an inscription.
    [...]
25. A silver plaque with the image of St. Casimir and the name of Katarzyna Krzeczonowiczówna.
    [...]
28. A silver plaque with the image of St. Casimir and a text in Polish. 1604.
    [...]
31. A silver plaque with the image of St. Casimir with a female kneeling, with an inscription in Polish "St. Casimir, be so kind as to ask God for bodily health and eternal life after death for us".
32. A silver plaque with the image of St. Casimir in the clouds, under him a female kneeling and holding a child, with a text in Polish "In 1603 on 14 November Anna Ciołkówna Piasecka, wife of the *starosta* of Giełwany [Gelvonai]".
    [...]
36. A silver plaque with the image of St. Casimir and the name "Wojciech Mafon".
    [...]
48. A silver plaque and an image of St. Casimir, below a female kneeling, with a text: It was offered in thanks to God that he showed the grace to save me from illness through the intermediary of St. Casimir. Anno Domini 1605.
49. A silver plaque hung on three silver chains, on which there is the Passion and a female kneeling, a baby in swaddling clothes lying in front of her, on the other side there is a Latin inscription: *Generosa matrona Polonia Jasińska*

coniunx Alexandri Mosalski de Sapieżyszki compos. voti sancto Domino Casimiro suplex obtulit Anno 1605 die 8 Junii.

50. A silver plaque and image of St. Casimir. Below, a young man kneeling.
51. A little plaque of silver and the Passion; below it, St. Casimir's image and a kneeling maiden. On the other side there is a Polish inscription: "I, Barbara Maksentówna, am delighted with the fact that I was granted Saint Casimir's grace".

[...]

117. On 19 August, a silver plaque hung on a string of red silk was presented. On it, the Blessed Virgin Mary on the moon holds the Infant, and under her, St. Casimir, holding a lily in his right hand and he has his left hand on the head of a kneeling boy. The sun near to one edge, the moon near the other one, and on the other side there is a Latin inscription: *Elisabeth infans Hieronimi Japlko civis Vilnensis.*[100]

Similar collections must have hung in other Catholic churches and chapels, for instance in the chapel over the Sharp Gate (the Dawn Gate, Lithuanian: Aušros vartai; Polish: Ostra Brama, Belarusian: Вострая Брама), built in the second half or the seventeenth century. Almost all the votive plaques from early modern Vilnius churches got lost as the result ot the Muscovite occupation in the mid-seventeenth century, later wars, and the Russian and Soviet occupation of Lithuania in the nineteenth and twentieth centuries.

Other Inscriptions: Foundation, Pious, and Parenetic Inscriptions

A separate group of inscriptions in the urban space were those placed on buildings and all kinds of objects, also those for daily use, most often in the form of dicta. This type of epigraphic monuments include inscriptions on bells, cannons, coins, medals, everyday objects such as spoons, and buildings. Only a few of the latter have survived, some of them only indirectly. These include for instance the inscriptions in the Royal Chapel dedicated to the rulers buried there. They were recorded by the aforementioned Starowolski in his *Monumenta Sarmatarum*.

Medieval inscriptions must have been placed in many churches, such as the fifteenth-century parish churches of St. John or St. Nicolas and the cathedral,

[100] *Spisanie srebra w Kaplicy Królewskiej przy grobie św. Kazimierza od różnych osób ex voto zawieszonych od roku Pańskiego 1603 [do 1627]*, MS VUB F4-35808 (A2472), pp. 94-118.

but none of them survived.[101] A number of Gothic-minuscule inscriptions, part of late Gothic wall-paintings was discovered in the 1980s in the Bernardine church. Later texts painted or carved on the walls are more frequent. An interesting set of seventeenth-century painted inscriptions was discovered in 1991 in the crypt of the Jesuit St. Casimir church, and in the 2000s in the cells and cloister of the Bernardine convent. All these fragments inform us that the Catholic churches in Vilnius were covered with dozens (or even hundreds) inscriptions, and that their users were literally surrounded by different genres of texts. Literate people tended to be in constant contact with religious or moral admonitions.[102]

Texts of a moral character existed not only in sacral spaces. A large complex of inscriptions was located at the bishop's estate in Verkiai near Vilnius. Bishop Eustachy Wołłowicz (1616-1630) ordered that the fireplace, lintels, walls, and ceiling beams be decorated with inscriptions, which not only constituted an ideological programme that reflected his philosophical interests, but also turned the house into a book. They have not survived, but we know them thanks to anonymous copyists for whom such inscriptions were an extremely interesting subject.[103] It is likely that other buildings, such as the Renaissance lower castle, were also decorated in this way, but there are no traces that confirm this hypothesis.

To these monuments foundational inscriptions should be added, for instance on the Brothers Hospitallers' church from 1543, in St. Michael's church from 1625, on the outside of St. Casimir's chapel from 1636, and on some smaller buildings, such as the chapel of St. Florian in the Bernardine church: "*Capella Sancti Floriani Martiris et Patroni Regni Poloniae. Erecta* A.D. *1632*".

[101] In a medieval crypt in the cathedral, a Byzantine fresco representing the crucifixion was discovered. It was certainly provided with some inscriptions, now lost. The Byzantine frescoes in Trakai (in the castle on the island and in the parish church) from the 1420s bear traces of inscriptions. See G. MICKŪNAITĖ, "Word for images: On perceptions of 'Greek manner' in Lithuania and Poland", in: *The Polish-Lithuanian Commonwealth: History, Memory, Legacy*, ed. A. CHWALBA and K. ZAMORSKI (New York, 2021), pp. 63-68, 70.

[102] A. ZAJIC, "Texts on public display", pp. 414 -418

[103] The copyist noticed "Sentences which are written down at Werki near Vilnius, at the episcopal court, in chambers, in the table room and in the hallways" ("*Sententie, które są pisane w Werkach nad Wilnem we dworze biskupim w pokojach, w stołowej izbie i w sieniach*"), MS CZART. 1662 IV, pp. 420-424. The Inscriptions were published by Marek Janicki on the basis of another source from the Library of the Zamoyski Ordinances, MS BN 1291; see M.A. JANICKI, "Willa Eustachego Wołłowicza w Werkach pod Wilnem i jej epigraficzny program ideowy", *Barok* 4.2 (1998), pp. 139-149.

It is possible that the Vilnius synagogue (the Great Synagogue of Vilna), built in the 1630s, was also decorated with foundational and other inscriptions. It was a common practice to paint large Hebrew inscriptions on the inside walls of synagogues in the Polish-Lithuanian Commonwealth. Some of them have survived in the Isaac synagogue in Cracow (mid-seventeenth century) and in the synagogue in Tykocin (now in Poland, before the partitions in the Grand Duchy of Lithuania; seventeenth-nineteenth centuries). It is almost certain that the Vilnius synagogue was not an exception but that all its wall inscriptions perished in the fires of 1655 and 1748. There are known only two pairs of iron doors with Hebrew inscriptions, which state that they were funded by the societies of tailors in 1640 and the that of the Psalm reciters in 1642.[104]

Inscriptions of a similar function must have been put in all places where inhabitants of Vilnius used to pray: in the synagogue, the mosque, and the churches. Among the inscribed objects were also bells, used in Vilnius churches. There must have been several dozen of them in the city. Most of them were covered with longer or shorter inscriptions, in Church Slavonic or Latin, depending on the rite. The oldest ones, including the big bell called Half-Sigismund, were melted in a fire in 1610, while others were taken or destroyed by the Muscovites. A trace of them has remained in later notes: "the other bell, cracked, with a superscription: "*Divino auxilio me fecit Breutelt S*[*acrae*] *R*[*egiae*] *M*[*aiestatis*] *Fusor Wilnae* 1643" ("I was made with God's help by Breutert, the bell-founder of His Majesty in Vilnius 1643"), says the nineteenth-century chronicle of the parish church in Kurland Goldingen (today Kuldīga in Latvia).[105] The first bells were imported, but since the first half of the sixteenth century there was the Foundry (*Puszkarnia*) near the castle. It was

[104] Both inscriptions are mentioned by Lucy S. Dawidowicz who remembered them from when she stayed in Vilnius in 1938. See L.S. Dawidowicz, *From That Place and Time: A Memoir, 1938-1947* (New York, 1989), p. 38. During archaeological excavations in 2019, a memorial inscription from 1796 was discovered which recorded the foundation of a Torah reading table. See J. Seligman, "Between Yerushalayim De Lita and Jerusalem – The memorial inscription from the bimah of the Great Synagogue of Vilna", *Arts* 9.2 (2020), pp. 1-18. The results of the excavations are documented at the web site *The Great Synagogue and Shulhoyf of Vilna (Vilnius): A Research, Excavation, Preservation and Memorial Project*: <http://www.seligman.org.il/vilna_synagogue_home.html> (accessed: 2.06.2021).

[105] *Kronika Kościoła Parafialnego w Goldingen, położonego w Diecezyi Wileńskiej, Gubernii Kurlandskiej, Powiecie Goldyngskim, Dekanacie Kurlandzkim 1849*, MS VUB F4-2624. Michael Breutelt came from Lorraine and was active in Vilnius from *c.* 1630. He specialised in making cannons and bells. See M. Brensztejn, *Zarys dziejów ludwisarstwa na ziemiach b. Wielkiego Księstwa Litewskiego* (Vilnius, 1924), pp. 43-47.

established because of the need of producing artillery for the wars against Muscovy.

In the sixteenth and seventeenth centuries the Vilnius foundries produced a huge number of cannons.[106] Research carried out by Tadeusz Marian Nowak revealed that up to 20% of the early modern cannons in the Polish-Lithuanian Commonwealth had inscriptions.[107] A detailed list of weapons from 1565 confirms that 180 cannons were made in Vilnius, 28 of which had longer inscriptions.[108] They usually carried a moral or propaganda message related to the name of the gun.[109] For example, in 1551 King Sigismund Augustus commissioned a large number of guns in the Foundry, some of which had the names of the Polish and Lithuanian rulers. On the cannon called Vitoldus (Vytautas) an epigram was placed:

Sum Vitoldus ego, Vitoldi ex nomine dictus.
Concutio turres, moenia sterno. Cave!

I am Vytautas and I took my name after Vytautas.
I overturn towers and destroy walls. Be careful![110]

This erudite elegiac distich brings to mind Grand Duke Vytautas († 1430), famous in the sixteenth century for his military achievements in the wars against Muscovy, the Teutonic Order, and the Tartars. The epigram recalls historical events but also contributes to building an official narration about the past of the Grand Duchy of Lithuania.[111] It also updates history: Sigismund Augustus (just like his cousin Vytautas a century and a half earlier) had to deal

[106] *Ibid.*, pp. 21-26.

[107] In a series of publications Tadeusz Marian Nowak presented the results of his long research on the technical aspects of early modern artillery in the Polish-Lithuanian Commonwealth. He noted 558 bronze cannon barrels from the sixteenth-eighteenth centuries, 99 of which bear long inscriptions. See T.M. NOWAK, "O 'mówiących działach' artylerii polskiej XVI-XVIII wieku", *Napis* 12 (2006), p. 380.

[108] *Strzelba i municyja własnym nakładem jego królewskiej mości sprawiona MDLXV w Wilnie i na zamki pograniczne rozesłana*, CZART. 1814. T.M. NOWAK, "Sprzęt artylerii polskiej XVI wieku w świetle inwentarza z lat 1551-1565", *Studia i Materiały do Historii Wojskowości*, 9.2 (1963), pp. 281-302; BRENSZTEJN, *Zarys dziejów ludwisarstwa*, p. 27.

[109] The ideological dimensions of the guns cast in the Polish-Lithuanian Commonwealth is discussed by K. ŁOPATECKI, "Ideowa wymowa ozdób armatnich z przełomu XVI i XVII wieku", in: *Nad społeczeństwem staropolskim*, 1, *Kultura – instytucje – gospodarka w XVI-XVIII stuleciu*, ed. K. ŁOPATECKI and W. WALCZAK (Białystok, 2007), pp. 249-270.

[110] NOWAK, "O 'mówiących działach'", p. 381.

[111] See the subchapter: 'The building of Lithuanian identity'.

Fig. 58 Muslin cover made by Helena Wiekowicz, wife of Dawid Blinstrub, 1647. *Album zabytków ewangelickich w Wilnie wydany przez Towarzystwo Miłośników Reformacji Polskiej im Jana Łaskiego* (Vilnius, 1929), picture XXII.

with threats from Muscovy and the Tartars. It is highly probable that this one and many other poems were composed by humanists from the royal chancery.[112] Maybe the king as a commissioner also took part in choosing the topics. One cannon cast in 1551 recalls his father Sigismund the Old; three others bear the name of Sigismund Augustus.[113] An inscription on a cannon cast by Breutelt seven decades later brings an even more sophisticated propaganda message: "*Materiam Sigismundus, formam omine fausto rex Vladislaus regno ineunte dedit. Anno Domini* MDCXXXIII, *Vladislai Quarti primo*" ("King Sigismund [III Vasa] gave me [my] material, King Władysław [my] form as a lucky omen when he entered upon his reign. In 1633, the first year of Władysław the Fourth").[114] Even such a short inscription as this one could be a gem of seventeenth-century conceit literature. The anonymous author of this text

[112] The list of potential authors of 34 inscriptions composed in hexameter and elegiac distich in 1551 (and a bit later) is short. It may be supposed that their author was Stanisław Koszutski, the royal librarian and neo-Latin poet who lived in Vilnius at that time.

[113] *Ibid.*, pp. 381-382.

[114] Quoted after BRENSZTEJN, *Zarys dziejów ludwisarstwa*, p. 44.

played with the philosophical terms of *materia* and *forma*[115] and the ordinal numbers 'fourth' and 'first'.

To the public graphosphere of medieval and early modern cities like Vilnius also belonged smaller objects with religious purposes. Among them were liturgical chalices, cloths (for instance tablecloths), monstrances, etc. Before the Second World War an interesting collection of such objects belonged to the Evangelical Reformed (Calvinist) Council (or Synod) in Vilnius. A silver can was donated in 1629 to the Vilnius Calvinist church by Maria Radzimińska Talwoszowa, wife of the aforementioned Adam Talwosz, castellan of Samogitia, bearing an inscription "[The can] purposely made for the Table of the Lord".[116] Interesting inscriptions were put on the covers meant for the liturgical chalices. They were lavishly embroidered and some of them carried inscriptions made by women. The known covers belonged to provincial churches but similar cloths must have been used in Vilnius as well.

For example, a muslin cover made in 1647 was decorated with an inscription in capital letters: "*Verbum Dei manet in aeternum*" ("The Word of God will last forever") and colourful flower ornament. Its author embroidered her name around the cloth: "Helena Wiekowicz, wife of Dawid Blinstrub, 1647" (Fig. 58).[117] This example of a funding inscription is very interesting. Usually the donors hired artisans to make inscriptions for them. The artisan often added their name, just like Breutelt did on his bells or cannons. However, in the case of the embroidered cover a noblewoman, Helena Blinstrub,[118] put her signature both as the donor and as the maker. She expressed not only her position but also literacy skills in a way available only to the women of the social class she belonged to.

[115] M.A. Krąpiec, "Materia i forma: Ich różne rozumienie w historii filozofii", *Roczniki Filozoficzne* 16.1 (1968), pp. 55-65.

[116] *Album zabytków ewangelickich w Wilnie wydany przez Towarzystwo Miłośników Reformacji Polskiej im Jana Łaskiego* (Vilnius, 1929), picture xv.

[117] "Helena Wiekowiczówna Dawidowa Blinstrubowa roku 1647". *Ibid.*, picture xxii. The cover was a gift to the Calvinist church in Astrashyna (Ostraszyn, Belarus). See M. Jackiewicz, "Blinstrubowie i Janczewscy z Blinstrubiszek", *Przegląd Wschodni* 13.4 (2014), p. 1134. Probably Helena Blinstrubowa made the cover when she visited her widowed mother-in-law (also called Helena) in Ostraszyn. The mother-in-law belonged to the Szwykowski family, the owners of Ostraszyn and the patrons of the church.

[118] Helena Blinstrubowa belonged to the Samogitian family Wiekowicz (coat of arms Pobóg). Her husband, Dawid the younger, was a descendant of an important Calvinist family, the Blinstrub of Blinstrubiszki (Blinstrubiškiai, Lithuania). See K. Niesiecki, *Herbarz polski*, ed. J.N. Bobrowicz, 9 (Leipzig, 1842), p. 293; *Akta synodów prowincjonalnych jednoty litewskiej 1626-1637*, p. 176.

Epigraphic Ephemera

The question what is an ephemeral inscription and what is not might cause a long debate (just as the question: what is an inscription?). Any inscription which survived should not be treated as ephemeral, because it survived several hundred years. However, in this study the function of an inscription has a decisive role in determining whether it belongs to this class of texts. As epigraphic ephemera I understand inscriptions of temporary use in Vilnius, often written, painted, or carved on perishable materials such as paper or wood.[119] Among them there are graffiti, public announcements, inscriptions on banners, texts put on occasional buildings, such as *castra doloris* or triumphal arches, etc. Among epigraphic ephemera I also number coins and medals. They are highly 'movable' and may belong to one place only for a very short time.

We do not know much about medieval or early modern graffiti in Vilnius, but it is almost certain that this genre of inscription must have existed in the city. In other cities, towns, and villages in the Polish-Lithuanian Commonwealth it was a common practice for people to carve their names and dates on the church walls.[120] In 2022 the only known example of early modern graffiti in Vilnius were found. They are on the bricks of the southern outer wall of St. Anne church, a.o. an inscription: "TOMASZEWSKI 1669 D[ie] 18 S[eptembris]".

An example of epigraphic ephemera was the royal letter of King Stephen Báthory from 1581, presented in the previous chapter. The king ordered copies of the letter to be publicly exhibited and read aloud: "when you get this letter we order to put it immediately on public display (*jawnie*) in the Market Square and to announce it on the streets of our city of Vilnius".[121] One can suppose that this example of exhibiting an ephemeral text was not a unique instance. Probably it was the custom that the municipal, ecclesiastical, or state authorities published some of their decisions in such a way.

Inscriptions on occasional architecture had a completely different purpose than royal or municipal documents displayed in the Market Square, but all of them shared in the same ephemeral nature. In the sixteenth and seventeenth

[119] In the older tradition of research on epigraphy, the epigraphical nature of such written texts was questioned. See JANICKI, "Inskrypcja w przestrzeni publicznej", p. 246-247.

[120] The author of this book examined early modern graffiti on walls of churches in Lesser Poland (Cracow, Dorowoda, Lublin, Opatów, Sienno, and Włoszczowa), where such texts survived. The results of this research will be published in the future.

[121] *Kopia listu króla Stefana do nieboszczyka pana wojewody smoleńskiego strony palenia ksiąg w Wilnie ewangelickich 1581 in Septembre*, MS LNMB F93-1688.

Fig. 59 Silver coin minted after the recapturing of Polatsk and Livonia by King Stefan Bátory in 1579: "Livonia and Polatsk recuperated". Probably such coins were disseminated among the viewers of the triumphal entrance to Vilnius and other cities in Lithuania and Poland. Cracow, MNK. Photo J. Niedźwiedź.

centuries, a huge number of such texts was written, carved, or painted and displayed in Vilnius. For example, the account of the solemn entrance to the city on 24 July 1611 by King Sigismund III Vasa contains detailed descriptions of the triumphal arches and of Latin texts put on them.[122] From the last decades of the sixteenth century onward royal entries, Catholic processions, etc. were always marked by diverse forms of inscriptions, and not only on ephemeral architecture. They appeared on the banners of military units and of the guilds,[123] or on the occasional silver coins or rather medals minted for that day and thrown into the crowd. Such coins with the inscription *Polotia recepta* were minted (maybe in the Vilnius mint) on the occasion of the triumphal entries of King Stephen Báthory into the Polish and Lithuanian towns after

[122] *Triumfo diena: 1611 m. birželio 13 d. Smolensko pergalė ir iškilmingas Zigmanto Vazos sutikimas Vilniuje 1611 m. liepos 24 d – Dies Triumphi: Victoria Sigismundi III die XIII Junti A.D. MDCXI Smolensco expugnato et triumphalis ingressus Vilnom die XXIV Julii A.D. MDCXI celebratus – Day of Triumph: The victory at Smolensk on June 13, 1611 and the ceremonial reception of Sigismund Vasa in Vilnius on July 24,1611*, ed. E. Ulčinaitė and E. Saviščevas (Vilnius, 2011), pp. 154-210; J. Kiaupienė, "Theatrum ceremoniale w barokowym Wilnie", in: *Wokół Wielkiego Księstwa Litewskiego i jego tradycji*, ed. B. Manyś and M. Zwierzykowski (Poznań, 2016), p. 107.

[123] Such banners are visible on the Stockholm Scroll. This is a visual account of the entrance of Queen Constance of Austria into Cracow on 4 December 1605. The scroll is 16 metres long and shows in detail all the participants of this event and the splendour of the spectacle of power. The triumph in Vilnius six years later (which will be discussed below) probably had a similar character. See M. Zdańkowska, *Rolka sztokholmska: Skarb Zamku Królewskiego w Warszawie – The Stockholm Scroll: A Treasure of the Royal Castle in Warsaw* (Warsaw, 2019).

conquering Polatsk (30 August 1579) during the Livonian War.[124] There were also medals minted on the occasion of the triumph of King Sigismund III, coined by Hanus Trilner in 1611, one representing the king and queen and another one with the map of Smolensk and the portrait of the king.[125]

Another epigraphic ephemerum was the long votive poem written in 1513 by the previously mentioned poet Andrzej Krzycki.[126] Probably it was written on a parchment card or wooden board and placed in the royal chapel in the cathedral.[127] At that time, in the same chapel the medieval hymn *Omni die dic Marie* was displayed. Its manuscript copy was discovered in the coffin of Prince Casimir Jagiellon in 1498 and it was believed that its author was the prince.[128] This last ephemerum was known as late as in the first decade of the seventeenth century.[129]

Inscriptions: Memory and Competition

The inscriptions of the late medieval and early modern city played a crucial role in two areas of the literary field. Firstly, they contributed to building urban memory. Secondly, they were important in the competition between different social groups and individuals. In the case of Vilnius, both areas were important for the 'closed' and 'open' city.

Most of the epitaphs in Vilnius built *memoria*: the memory of the dead and the ties between the members of the local community. However, Vilnius was the capital of the country and epitaphs, mainly those in the Catholic, Uniate, and Orthodox churches, also recorded the memory of grand dukes, national saints (Stanislaus, later Casimir), and key members of the Lithuanian elites. Many epigraphic ephemera, such as inscriptions on triumphal arches, or in-

[124] G. FRANCZAK, "*Polotia recepta*: Mapa Księstwa Połockiego – teksty i preteksty sporu o władzę", *Terminus* 23.2 (2021), pp. 97-133.

[125] M. GUMOWSKI, "Wileńska szkoła medalierska", p. 83; *Lietuva medaliuose XVI a.-XX a. pradžia – Lithuania in Medals: Sixteenth-Early Twentieth*, ed. V. RUZAS (Vilnius, 1998), pp. 18, 82-83, pictures 22-23, 178-179.

[126] A. KRZYCKI (Andreas Cricius) "*Ad tumulum divi Casimiri, fratris regii, salutatio in primo adventu Vilnam Andreae Cricii inclitae Barbarae reginae Poloniae cancellarii*", in: ID., *Carmina*, ed. K. MORAWSKI (Cracow, 1888) p. 53-56; J. FIJAŁEK, "Opisy Wilna aż do połowy wieku XVII-go" [part 2], *Ateneum Wileńskie* 2.5-6 (1924), pp. 132-133.

[127] JANICKI, "Grób i komemoracja", p. 786.

[128] ŚWIĘCICKI, *Theatrum s. Casimiri*, p. 54.

[129] *Ibid.* See also Chapter 9.

scriptions on cannons, were vehicles of the historical memory of the country as a whole as well.

Vilnius inscriptions could also bear a political message, especially those designed for the 'open' city and the 'capital'. Texts and single words presented values important for the country (for instance *respublica*, *patria*, *virtus*, *Lithuania*, *pietas*, *cives*, *religio*, *sacra regia maiestas*, etc.). However, politics were also important in the 'closed' city. In most European medieval and early modern urban settlements inscriptions could represent the rivalry between the representatives of the city's elites, the city's quarters (*contrade*) in the Italian cities, or between the nobility and burghers in the Austrian towns.[130] In the case of Vilnius inscriptions rendered the interconfessional tensions in the city. On the one hand, they counterbalanced messages put in the inscriptions of the opponents (such as the Orthodox and Catholic inscriptions exhibited during the triumph of King Sigismund III in 1611, which will be discussed later); on the other hand, their purpose was to strengthen the identity of one or another religious community. In such cases, the inscriptions were usually put inside the churches or the synagogue.

Texts put on buildings, monuments, tombstones, bells, cannons, smaller objects, etc. made the city a script-accumulating place. They were everywhere and they literally made a city a place to be read and interpreted. They also contributed to constructing Vilnius as a symbol – a religious, state, and national symbol.

Inscriptions were supposed to be eternal, public 'texts of memory', and for this reason were fixed in materials resistant to the ravages of time. Paradoxically, most of the texts referred to in this chapter have been preserved thanks to these epigraphic sources being recorded on paper.

Panegyrics in Vilnius: The Creation of Memory and Prestige

As we may remember, the books for the funeral of mayor Marcin Kiewlicz, who died in February 1645, cost the substantial sum of fifty-two *złoty*. Most probably they contained a printed funeral sermon or an epicedium, a funeral ode. In any case, the text was most likely written in the Jesuit environment. The printed text in honour of Kiewlicz was an important complement to the funeral ceremonies, because in the future, apart from requiem masses and an

[130] ZAJIC, "Texts on public display", pp. 404-406, 410, 412.

epitaph, it was to shape and maintain the memory of the deceased. Apart from its commemorative function, however, the text also played another role, that is, it also promoted the glory of the deceased, and especially of the family surviving the deceased.

The same was true of most of Vilnius' panegyrical publications, which combined the two functions of commemoration and building prestige. Both were based on a conscious and expressive modelling of an image of reality. Scaliger wrote about this at the beginning of his poetics, granting the poet divine powers in creating the world.[131] This kind of rhetorical action is useful for creating texts that are not aimed at an objective relationship, but at persuasion. The point of a panegyric was that it was an affirmative or depreciating evaluation of the person or thing being described.[132] All stages of the protagonist's existence had to be shaped in such a way as to testify to his virtue, goodness, piety – everything that determined that he or she should be immortalised in a speech or poem.

In the eyes of ancient, medieval, and early modern authors, when it was fitted into a written text, the image that had been created gained an important feature. Writing it down meant that, once it had been formed, a memory could remain relatively unchanged, avoiding distortion or blurring.[133] This picture could of course be challenged by political opponents or by later authors. Still, the starting point was the belief that the written word could have a fixed, unchangeable meaning and could form an everlasting memory about a person. This belief was based on the assumption, that the author had the ability and power to create the meaning of a message.[134]

The affirmative portrait in a panegyric thus was to be an inflexible interpretation, which constantly reduced the person or event described to a message

[131] J.C. SCALIGER, *Poetices libri septem* (Lyons, 1561), pp. 3-6.

[132] Aristotle, *Dzieła wszystkie*, p. 313.

[133] GOODY, *The Logic of Writing*, pp. 20-22.

[134] This essentialist approach stressed the role of the author in the creation of the meaning of a text. The poet "*quasi alter Deus*" (SCALIGER, *Poetices libri septem*, p. 3) created a fixed meaning of his work and the reader's task was to decipher the message and properly interpret it. In the second half of the twentieth century, philosophers and literary critics completely changed the notion about what makes the meaning of a text. They insisted that, more important than the author's intention, is the act of interpretation. See U. ECO, *The Role of the Reader: Explorations in the Semiotics of Texts* (Bloomington, 1979), pp. 200-260; R. RORTY, "The pragmatist's progress", in: U. ECO, R. RORTY, J. CULLER, and Ch. BROOK-ROSE, *Interpretation and Overinterpretation*, ed. S. COLLINI (Cambridge, 1992), pp. 89-108; S. FISH, "How to recognize a poem when you see one", pp. 322-337.

that had been formulated once and for all. This helped organise the existing social hierarchy, which was confirmed by texts such as panegyrics or historiography. Of course, the consolidation of the social hierarchy was in the interest of the people ranked highest in it. Their interest and willingness to pay the poets and prose writers who praised them was the reason for the high position of the rhetorical *genus demonstrativum*. Epideicticity was in fact supposed to create and consolidate the image of the world created by the text.

In the Lithuanian capital, a complex game of panegyrical texts was played continuously from the mid-sixteenth century onwards. The object of this game was to constantly redefine and re-establish the social hierarchy. Panegyrics were paid for by kings, magnates, and members of the urban elite. By 'payment' one should understand a complex network of interrelations between patrons and clients.[135] Remuneration did not necessarily mean spending fifty-two *złoty* (which was the sum paid for printing the funerary sermon devoted to the late mayor Kiewlicz), it could also mean political support, patronage, or admission to the table. Just as the client had to seek the support of a patron who provided him with care or payment, the patron himself had to take care of his image and use the services of the authors and artists who shaped it.

Apart from religious texts, panegyrics constitute the most numerous group of books published in Vilnius.[136] The heyday of epideictic literature was the seventeenth century, but it was initiated by the Jesuits already in the 1570s. Panegyrical literature was then the domain of the 'open' city, but over time it also spread into the 'closed' city. Magnates and the nobility from outside the capital, as well as wealthy town dwellers, that is the Lithuanian political and financial elites, resorted to this kind of text. Not only individual authors, but to a greater extent institutions and corporations that brought together the intellectual elite, such as the Academy of Vilnius, the Orthodox Brotherhood, the

[135] A.F. MAROTTI, "Patronage, poetry, and print", *The Yearbook of English Studies* 21 (1991): *Politics, Patronage and Literature in England 1558-1658: Special Number*, pp. 1-26; S. KETTERING, "Patronage in early modern France", *French Historical Studies* 4.17 (1992), pp. 839-850; A. MĄCZAK, *Klientela: Nieformalne systemy władzy w Polsce i Europie XVI-XVIII w.* (Warsaw, 1994), pp. 16-17; K.M. DMITRUK, "Wokół teorii i *historii mecenatu*", in: *Z dziejów mecenatu kulturalnego w Polsce*, ed. J. KOSTECKI (Warsaw, 1999), pp. 17-18; J. COLE, "Cultural clientelism and brokerage networks in early modern Florence and Rome: New correspondence between the Barberini and Michelangelo Buonarroti the Younger", *Renaissance Quarterly* 60 (2007), pp. 730-731.

[136] According to Maria Barbara Topolska's calculations, panegyrical literature made up one third of the printed books in the Grand Duchy of Lithuania in the sixteenth and seventeenth centuries; see TOPOLSKA, *Czytelnik i książka*, p. 125.

Protestant Churches, the Basilians, and the Catholic Orders, also benefitted from their patronage. Individual authors usually acted on behalf of these groups and institutions.

The Jesuit Respublica Litteraria *in Vilnius At the Turn of the Sixteenth and Seventeenth Centuries*

At the turn of the sixteenth and seventeenth centuries, Vilnius panegyrics were dominated by works published by the Jesuit community. They usually included poetic anthologies written by their most talented students, supported by their professors. Apart from volumes addressed to rulers, such publications included funeral texts dedicated to magnates, for instance to Katarzyna Radziwiłłowa (1592),[137] or panegyrics for the living, for instance on the occasion of Mikołaj Krzysztof Radziwiłł 'the Orphan's' (1604) entering the Vilnius *voivodeship.*[138]

At the same time, the custom of honouring people who belonged to the academic community with panegyrics became widespread. Some of these texts have survived. These are either funeral or congratulatory texts commemorating the acquisition of an academic title. With two funeral poems, both from 1595, students honoured their fellow students Jerzy Chodkiewicz and Jan Barszcz.[139] Students of the elite and international papal seminary specialised in congratulatory texts. For example, in 1593 and 1595 they prepared anthologies of poems for their fellow students Franciszek Sucholewski, Mateusz Newe, and Fryderyk Kostka on the occasion of the first Mass of the former and the latter two being awarded their master's degrees.[140]

[137] *Threni in exequias illustrissimae Catharinae Radivilae de Tenczyn ducis in Byrże et Dubingi, palatinae Vilnensis etc. etc. nomine Parthenicae Sodalitatis in Academia Vilnensi Societatis IESV institutae, a praecipua iuventute eiusem Sodalitatis conscripti* (Vilnius,1592).

[138] *Panegyrica ... Nicolao Christophoro Radzivilo ... post Auspicatissimum initium Vilnae Palatinatum, ab ... Nicolao Christophoro, Ioanne Alberto, Alberto Stanislao Radzivilis, & quibusdam aliis bonarum artium cultoribus, nomine totius Academiae Vilnensis Societatis Iesu, summa fide & observantia* (Vilnius, 1604).

[139] *Parentalia in obitum illustris et magnifici domini d. Georgii Chodkievicii, generalis capitanei Samogitiae etc. etc. a sodalibus Congregationis Parthenicae Academiae Vilnensis Societatis Iesu mortem sodalis sui et moderatoris quondam vigilantissimi deflentibus conscripta* (Vilnius, 1595); *Funebris laudatio et threnodiae in exequias ornatissimi et lectissimi adolescentis Ioannis Barscii a studiosa iuventute conscriptae in Academia Vilnensi Societatis Iesu* (Vilnius, 1595).

[140] *Daphnogenetica praeclaris et nobili genere natis iuvenibus d. Matthaeo Newe, d. Frideri-*

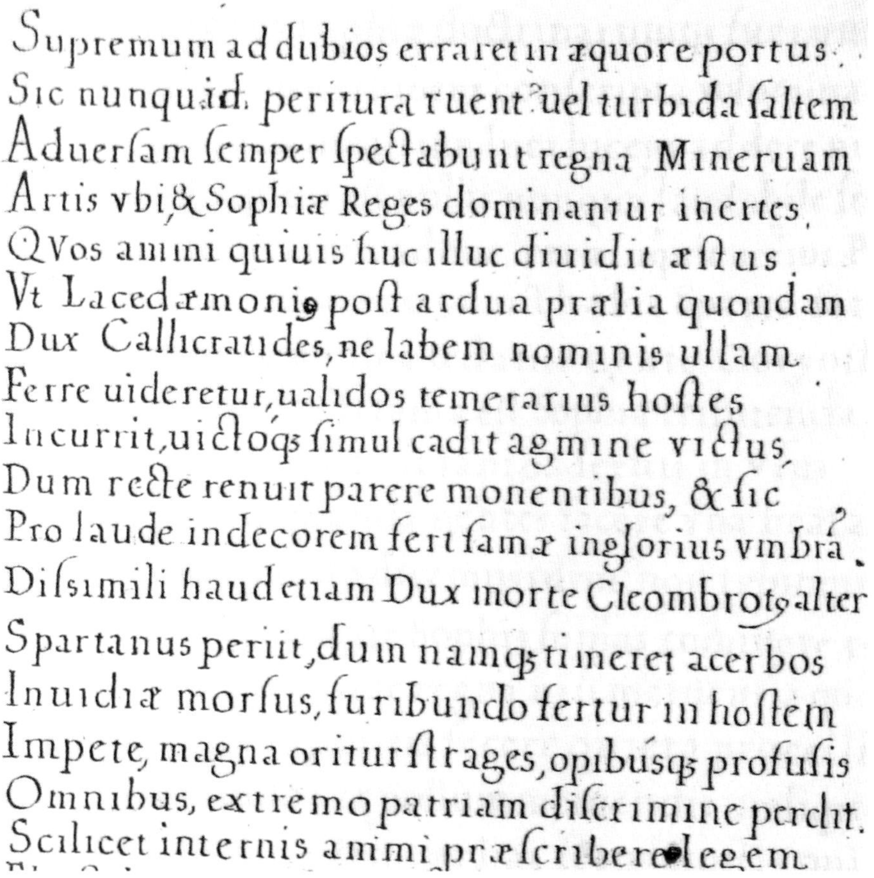
Supremum ad dubios erraret in æquore portus.
Sic nunquid, peritura ruent? uel turbida ſaltem
Aduerſam ſemper ſpectabunt regna Mineruam
Artis vbi, & Sophiæ Reges dominantur inertes.
QVos animi quiuis huc illuc diuidit æſtus.
Vt Lacedæmonius poſt ardua prælia quondam
Dux Callicratides, ne labem nominis ullam
Ferre uideretur, ualidos temerarius hoſtes
Incurrit, uictoq; ſimul cadit agmine victus,
Dum recte renuit parere monentibus, & ſic
Pro laude indecorem fert ſamæ inglorius vmbrã.
Diſsimili haud etiam Dux morte Cleombrotus alter
Spartanus periit, dum namq; timeret acerbos
Inuidiæ morſus, furibundo fertur in hoſtem
Impete, magna oritur ſtrages, opibúsq; profuſis
Omnibus, extremo patriam diſcrimine perdit.
Scilicet internis animi præſcribere legem

Fig. 60 Panegyric for Marcin Śmiglecki, written by his students in 1594. *Gratulationes in promotione doctissimi et eruditissimi R.D. Martini Smiglecii Societatis Iesu artium et philosophiae magistri a studiosis Philosophiae amoris ergo et officii in amantissimum Praeceptorem conscriptae* (Vilnius, 1594). Uppsala, CR, Carmina Latina et Graeca gratulat. IV. Script. lat. rec., nr 2; 59:42. Public domain.

co Kostkae a Skothow, Prutenis, Quo die in alma, quae Vilnae est, Societatis IESV Academia, liberalium Artium ac Philosophiae Magisterij insignibus supremaque solenniter laurea sunt adornati: Amici et in Seminario Pontificio contubernales gratulabundi dd VII *Idus Octobris anno Domini 1595* (Vilnius, [1595]); *Gratulationes neomysticae reverendo ac erudito viro d. Francisco Sucholewski Pontificis Maximi alumno, s. theologiae in Academia Vilnensi S. I. auditori, sacri primum operanti. A nonnullis eiusdem Academiae studiosis amoris et observantiae ergo oblatae*, [Vilnius, 1593].

The authors of the poems who signed them were Swedes, Lithuanians, or Poles and German inhabitants of Prussia or Livonia. Incidentally, the same authors published the cycle of epigrams against Andrzej Wolan discussed above.[141]

A congratulatory piece written in 1594 by several students of Marcin Śmiglecki from the Academy, on the occasion of Śmiglecki receiving his doctorate, is a unique text that illustrates the penetration of the epideictic genre into friendly personal relations.[142] In the *Gratulationes* for Śmiglecki, the personified Seven Liberal Arts proclaim the glory of philosophy and the new doctor. What makes the work exceptional is the fact that it is an extremely carefully calligraphed manuscript that imitates a print. Even if there were more manuscript copies of this anthology, it was used by a narrow circle of students and a lecturer who was only a little older than them. For Śmiglecki it must have been a valuable souvenir. He probably took it along with him to Poznań and Kalisz, and after his death it ended up in the library of the one of the local colleges, with which it was robbed and transported to Uppsala during the Swedish occupation in 1655.

The publication of an extensive collection of poems on the occasion of bishop Benedyct Woyna's episcopal inauguration in Vilnius cathedral in 1600, published by the academic Sodality of the Blessed Virgin Mary,[143] was somewhat similar, although certainly much more public in character. Among the authors we find both members of the fraternity and people who were no members. The works published were the fruits of the literary creativity of the sons of acquaintances, but also of friends and members of the bishop's family, both those who had poetic talent and those who had other skills: Stanisław Woyna,

[141] Gregorius Koch, Olaus Laurentius Gothus, Ioannes Bobola, Nicolaus Korycki, Udalricus Mylonius (on behalf of Sodality of the Blessed Virgin Mary), Raphael Wasilewicz, Ioannes Florentius Stockholmiensis. See also Chapter 9.

[142] *Gratulationes in promotione doctissimi et eruditissimi R.D. Martini Smiglecii Societatis Iesu artium et philosophiae magistri a studiosis Philosophiae amoris ergo et officii in amantissimum Praeceptorem conscriptae* [Vilnius, 1594], MS CR Carmina Latina et Graeca gratulat. IV. Script. lat. rec., no. 2 (CR 59:42). This work was pasted into a volume that contained six printed texts published at that time in Braniewo and apparently does not differ from them in terms of typography. The poems were authored by Wawrzyniec Koch, Jan Przeciszowski, Stanisław Przeciszowski, and Sebastian Rozmusewicz from Lviv.

[143] *Gratulatio illustrissimo ac reverendissimo D.D. Benedicto Woynae episcopos Vilnensi a Sodalitate B.V. Mariae Annunciatae S. I. Academica Vilnensi* ([Vilnius], 1600). In addition, the Academy of Vilnius released a series of emblems composed by the sons of magnates Stanisław and Jan Kiszek: *In auspicatum illustrissimi ac reverendissimi Domini D. Benedicti Woynae D.G. Episcopi Vilnensis ad suam sedem ingressum Gratulatio a Stanislao et Ioanne Kiszka fratribus, in Academia Vilnensi Societatis Jesu studiosis, oblata* ([Vilnius], 1600).

Jan Eysmont, Mikołaj Kuklicki, Piotr Grącki, Ioannes Udbynaeus Dana, Stanisław Kurkleczyński, Jan Sapieha, Mikołaj Krzysztof Radziwiłł 'the Orphan', Aleksander Sapieha, Krzysztof Chalecki, Krzysztof Sapieha, Jerzy Kroszyński, Mikołaj Kroszyński, Marcin Wierciński, and many others. The printer also left his mark. Instead of errata, at the end he attached the *Licentiae Typographi*, in which he jokingly explains that, since poets can change the shape of words for the sake of rhythm, he should also be allowed to twist some phrases.[144]

The work opens with an ornamental title page that features the symbol of the Annunciation, with the stemma of the Woyna family on the reverse, followed by a letter of dedication from the prefect of the sodality, Jan Burba. This is followed by a series of works, first those written by the members of the sodality (*Sodalium in officio donarium*, f. Br), and then by other persons (*Donaria aliorum*, p. C2), at least twice as many. At the end (ff. Gv.-G2v.), the prefect of the sodality appears again, this time as the author of a prayer to Our Lady for the bishop, written in Sapphic stanzas. The texts by Burba, who perhaps was the editor of the volume, provide the framework for the whole volume. The book is very diverse in terms of content: the editor paid special attention to its *varietas*, for instance poems by poets from the same family are not adjacent to each other, the genres are also mixed and included stemmata, eteostikons, anagrams, onomastikons, emblems, acrostics, and elogia. The metre is not so varied, as the authors used mainly the elegiac distich, hexameter, hendecasyllabic verse and the Sapphic stanza.

The *Gratulatio* was, apparently, a social event: a text that repeated on a wider scale the 'social' publications, mentioned previously, created within the walls of the university. We will never find out about the circumstances in which it was produced, that is who came up with the idea for the Festschrift and who its editor was, what difficulties were encountered, whether the authors sent the texts in a timely manner, which of them required the greatest amount of editorial intervention, who financed the printing, how many copies were produced, what were the relations of the editor with the protagonist and addressee, to what extent *Gratulatio* was inscribed in the client-patron relations of the time and whether the authors could be described as clients, in what cir-

[144] "*Errata non scriberemus, vetuit Typographus sibi itidem dictitans ut Poetis suas esse licentias. Utrisque ignosces si nimia licentia. Nam aliorum auctoritate sese defendunt Poetae, aliorum consuetudine sese Typographus tuetur*" (*Gratulatio illustrissimo ac reverendissimo D. D. Benedicto Woynae*, f. G2v.

cumstances the bishop was given the panegyric, and what the consequences of this ceremony were the following day. However, on the basis of this book we can talk about the ambition and tastes, talent and intelligence of the authors, the editor's concept, and the diligence of the printer.

There is no doubt that these works, created under the aegis of the Vilnius Academy, belong to an epideictic culture aimed at a relatively large audience. However, beneath the surface of official epideictic literature there is something else, namely the personal and close relations between friends from the Academy who were at the same time members of Vilnius's *respublica litteraria*.[145] For the poets who belonged to this community, panegyric became not only a means of commemorating an event and enhancing the prestige of its hero, but also a way of expressing friendship through text, perhaps the only way available to them.

Panegyrical Sermons in the First Half of the Seventeenth Century

In the first half of the seventeenth century, especially in the 1630s and 1640s, occasional sermons became a very popular panegyrical form. Depending on the year, they accounted for between one third and half of epideictic texts published.[146] Although Jakub Olszewski, the main Jesuit preacher in those days, denied that the sermon he delivered after the Polish-Lithuanian victory over Moscovites at Smolensk in 1634 was supposed to be "a panegyric, for is a church a place for the praise of man rather than God?",[147] the listeners, remembering the ethical and evangelical aims of sermons, expected epideictic texts.[148] Funeral or wedding sermons gained the status of panegyric mainly

[145] On the concept of the 'republic of letters' and its metamorphoses in the early modern and contemporary world, see a splendid study by Barbara Kaszowska-Wandor, B. KASZOWSKA-WANDOR, *Res publica [post] litteraria. Od poetyki wspólnoty do postliteratury* (Cracow, 2020).

[146] J. DROB, "Drukowane kazania franciszkańskie w XVI-XVII wieku", in: *Franciszkanie w Polsce XVI-XVIII wieku*, 1, ed. H. GAPSKI and C.S. NAPIÓRKOWSKI (Niepokalanów, 1998), p. 329; NIEDŹWIEDŹ, *Nieśmiertelne teatra sławy*, p. 103.

[147] J. OLSZEWSKI, *Tryumf przezacnej konwokacyjej wileńskiej ich mościów panów senatorów i posłów Wielkiego Księstwa Litewskiego po zwycięstwie otrzymanym od ... Władysława IV ..., kiedy 24 dnia lutego roku tego zwyciężywszy potężne wojsko z wielu narodów zacnych zebrane pod Smoleńskiem obóz nieprzyjacielski z armatą wzięli: Kazaniem przy podziękowaniu Panu Bogu stawiamy per Jacobum Olszewski ... w kościele katedralnym wileńskim 7 dnia marca* (Vilnius, 1634), f. A2 v.

[148] NIEDŹWIEDŹ, *Nieśmiertelne teatra sławy*, pp. 254-261.

through publication, as in appearing in print their epideictic function was strengthened. Just like epitaphs, they were material testimonies to the virtue of the deceased, but they also included praise of the living, especially in stemmata and letters of dedication.

Therefore, the family members left behind paid special attention to this part of the funeral and ordered sermons from priests who were sure to do their job well. "The gracious lady wished that the glory of the deceased would last. Therefore, according to her will, the sermon was printed, so that many people could read it. This sermon I present to you", wrote the archimandrite of the Holy Trinity church, Aleksy Dubowicz, in a Polish dedicatory letter to the widow Izabella Lacka Tryznina in 1645.[149]

Regardless of the confession, funeral sermons published in Vilnius were mostly in Polish, even if they were given in the church in Ruthenian or in another language. Only a few sermons from the academic community were printed in Latin or translated into Latin, for instance Maciej Kazimierz Sarbiewski's *Laska Marszałkowska albo kazanie na pogrzebie Jana Stanisława Sapiehy* (The Mace or a Sermon at the Funeral of Jan Stanisław Sapieha) of 1635.[150] The use of the Polish language made the sermons a rather universal medium that propagated values approved by the Church and the social elites.

Since the 1570s, the Jesuits dominated Catholic oratory in Vilnius, not only because their congregation was the largest one in the city, but also because they had their own printing house, where they could easily reproduce their sermons. For this reason, they win in the league table of the most popular seventeenth-century preachers in Vilnius. But we must remember that our knowledge of preachers' activity is based on publications, and that the sermons of many esteemed preachers were not always printed. Nevertheless, those whose sermons were published were certainly among the preachers most willingly listened to.

In the second half of the sixteenth century, the oratorical skills of Piotr Skarga and Stanisław Grodzicki, particularly active in the 1590s, were highly valued. In the next century, among the outstanding Jesuit preachers who were

[149] A. DUBOWICZ, *Kazanie na pogrzebie jaśnie wielmożnego pana p. Teofila Tryzny wojewody brzeskiego, wołkowyskiego, błudnieńskiego etc. starosty, miane w cerkwi byteńskiej zakonu św. Bazylego dnia Februarii roku 1645 przez ks. Aleksego Dubowicza, archimandrytę wileńskiego zakonu św. Bazylego* [Vilnius, 1645].

[150] M.K. SARBIEWSKI, *Laska Marszałkowska albo kazanie na pogrzebie Jana Stanisława Sapiehy* (Vilnius, 1635). See K. STAWECKA, "Maciej Kazimierz Sarbiewski jako prozaik", *Roczniki Humanistyczne* 31.3 (1983), pp. 101-106.

commissioned to preach panegyrical sermons were, among others, Jan Aland, Mateusz Bembus, Jakub Hasjusz, Kazimierz Wijuk Kojałowicz (Kojalavičius-Vijūkas), Sigismundus Lauxminus (Zygmunt Lauksmin), Jakub Olszewski, Maciej Kazimierz Sarbiewski, and Jan Widziewicz. Among those mentioned above, father Olszewski was particularly prolific and valued. His occasional sermons were those most often published in Lithuania in the seventeenth century.[151] The Bernardines and Dominicans tried to compete with the Jesuits, for instance in 1649 it was a Bernardine priest, Augustyn Wituński, who preached at the funeral of bishop Abraham Woyna, not a Jesuit.[152] In 1650, Rajmund Zajączkowski, a Dominican, delivered from the pulpit a panegyric "forged on the necks of foes to open the treasury of eternal [...] glory" of the captain and colonel Adam Łukijański Pawłowicz.[153] Interestingly, the friars (or their patrons) preferred to publish not at the Jesuit printing house, but in that of the Basilians, as is shown by their other sermons.[154] It is possible that the Basilians' services were cheaper, but it is not impossible that the choice of the printing house was determined by competition.[155]

[151] J. NIEDŹWIEDŹ, "Wstęp", in: *Dwa kazania wygłoszone po śmierci Katarzyny Habsburżanki i Zygmunta III Wazy*, ed. J. NIEDŹWIEDŹ (Warsaw, 2017), p. 8.

[152] A. WITUŃSKI, *Przywilej nieśmiertelności jaśnie wielmożnego i przewielebnego jego mości ks. Abrahama Woyny, biskupa wileńskiego w kościele katedralnym wileńskim w dzień pogrzebu ciała jego tłumaczony przez ks. Augustyna Wituńskiego zakonu Franciszka świętego bernardynów mianowanego prowincyi polskiej ojca i kaznodzieje wileńskiego: Dnia 14 maja roku 1649*, (Vilnius, [1649]).

[153] R. ZAJĄCZKOWSKI, *Klucz herbowy w domu Pawłowiczowskim marsowa buława z serca żelaznego jego mości pana pana Adama Łukijańskiego Pawłowicza, rotmistrza i pułkownika odważnego, na karkach nieprzyjacielskich ukowany, a na otwarcie skarbnice wiekuistej tego męża chwały: Na wyprowadzeniu ciała jego z kościoła ojców dominikanów w Wilnie ogłoszony dnia 28 Junii roku Pańskiego 1650 przez ks. Rajmunda Zajączkowskiego dominikona, świętej teologiej stud. fr. et decan* (Vilnius, [1650]).

[154] E.g. A. WITUSKI, *Okowy nieśmiertelnej sławy i chwały jego mości pana p. Jerzego Deszpota Zienowicza, starosty opiskiego, pułkownika mężnego i sławnego w dzień pogrzebu ciała jego w kościele wileńskim Franciszka świętego ojców bernadynów praesentowane przez ks. Augustyna Wituńskiego tegoż zakonu i kościoła lektora i kaznodzieje, ojca prowincyi polskiej, dnia 15 Martii 1649* (Vilnius, [1649]).

[155] Nevertheless, it happened after all that both the Bernardines and Dominicans, e.g. Wituski and father Petroniusz Kamieński OP, published at the Jesuits' printing house. In the second half of the seventeenth century, the Dominicans in Vilnius matched the Jesuits in the field of funeral

The Basilians, of course, did their own printing. The main panegyrical speaker of this order was the archimandrite of the monastery of the Holy Trinity, father Aleksy Dubowicz, whom we already know because of his sermon in praise of the author Jan Kolenda (see Chapter 1). He was also the author of three other printed laudatory sermons. The Basilians of Vilnius also published a sermon by Jan Dubowicz, the archimandrite of the monastery in Derman, written on the occasion of the funeral of aforementioned Barbara Tyszkiewiczowa. This was a variant of the panegyric on her epitaph, which was discussed above.[156]

The Orthodox Brotherhood's printing house released at least several funeral and wedding sermons of the renowned Orthodox preachers Leonty Karpovych and Meletius Smotrycki,[157] but many more such texts must have been prepared and delivered. Smotrycki's sermon, delivered during the funeral of Karpovych in November 1620, was published in two languages, Ruthenian and Polish. As these were times of acute Catholic-Uniate-Orthodox conflict, the work combines features of epideictic and judicial speech. The author used a device similar to that used in *Thrēnos*: Mother Church spoke to her Orthodox children.[158]

The most distinguished of the Protestant orators were the Lutheran ministers Krzysztof Bittner and Andrzej (Jędrzej) Schönflissius, as well as Samuel Dambrowski.[159] Since at that time only Catholic, Uniate, and Orthodox printing houses operated in Vilnius, the Protestants had to publish their Vilnius sermons in Lubcz or Königsberg, such as reverend Schönflissius's sermon of 1637 in memory of mayor Jakub Gibel.[160]

preaching, especially thanks to the work of the provincial and renowned orator Michał Woyniłłowicz.

[156] J. DUBOWICZ, *Kazanie na pogrzebie jaśnie wielmożnej paniej jej mości paniej Barbary Naruszewiczowej Januszowej Skuminowej Tyszkiewiczowej, wojewodzinej trockiej, jurborskiej, nowowolskiej etc. etc. starościny, miane w cerkwi wileńskiej Trójce Przenaświętszej 2 dnia września roku Pańskiego 1627 przez o. Jana Dubowicza Ordinis S. Basilii* [Vilnius, 1627].

[157] M. PIDŁYPCZAK-MAJEROWICZ, "Język ksiąg religijnych Kościoła unickiego", in: *Kultura i języki Wielkiego Księstwa Litewskiego*, p. 220.

[158] D. FRICK, "Introduction", in: *Rus' Restored: Selected Writings of Meletij Smotryc'kyj 1610-1630*, ed. and trans. D. FRICK (Cambridge, Mass., 2005), pp. XXXIII-XXXIV.

[159] Today, we know of 37 such sermons by Dambrowski. See M. PAWELEC, "Kazania funeralne Samuela Dambrowskiego: Z dziejów protestanckiego kaznodziejstwa XVII w.", in: *Kultura funeralna ziemi wschowskiej*, ed. P. KLINT, M. MAŁKUS, and K. SZYMAŃSKA (Wschowa, 2010), pp. 55-58.

[160] J. SCHÖNFLISSIUS, *Antidotum spirituale to jest lekarstwo duchowne na truciznę* srogiej śmierci przy obchodzie pogrzebu niegdy pobożnego i szlachetnego męża jego mości pana Jakuba

When they talked about the protagonists of their sermons, both living and dead, all preachers, regardless of their religion, drew from a common pool of rhetorical tricks that were used to form a hortatory (parenetic) image.[161] At the same time, such an image, striving to be in each case a 'hypermodel' (because the protagonist was supposed to stand out above the standard model), triggered the mechanism of panegyrical exaltation. Praised in panegyrical sermons, the protagonists were expected to meet the ideals postulated by the community, indeed, to exceed them considerably. Therefore, if we could hear the sermon delivered over Marcin Kiewlicz's coffin, we would certainly hear that he was an absolutely exceptional citizen of Vilnius, and also – even though he was a sinner (for who is without sin?) – a Christian who stood out far above the norm. All this would be served according to the principles of epideictic art, that is including *comploratio*, *laudatio*, and *consolatio*, with a particularly well developed laudatory part.

Not only in praise, but also as a means of forming images did the speakers reach for topoi which then were commonly used. Here we include two examples of sermons written in Polish, one Lutheran and the other Orthodox. Both images could be found in any religious text, in any country in Europe or colonised by Europeans. During the funeral service in honour of King Sigismund III and Queen Constance of Austria, reverend Schönflissius used topoi known from many poetic texts:

> We also experienced this now (how regrettably!). For cruel *Death* has taken the brightest Constance, Queen of Poland. And then she attacked His Majesty Sigismund III, the King of Poland and Sweden, etc. who reigned happily for forty-five years. Oh, cruel Death, you lioness, are you so covetous that you devoured both royal bodies and swallowed them within a year? And could you not stop at the first hunting, so you were bold and cruel enough to lay your violent hands on the other one? You planted your sharp scythe, with which you cut in the courtyard of our homeland two large flowers, the fragrance of which was spreading all over the Polish Kingdom and the Grand Duchy of Lithuania. You, Death, deserve significant scolding because you defaced our homeland with your cruelty. Then we can

Gibla burmistrza wileńskiego: W Wilnie na cmyntarzu saskim anno 1637. 2. Decemb. pokazane przez ks. Jędrzeja Schönflissiusa kaznodzieję polskiego Confess<ionis> August<anae> (Königsberg, 1638).

[161] J. Sarcevičienė, "*Bene vixit ideo bene mortua est:* Śmierć kobiety w kazaniach pogrzebowych Wielkiego Księstwa Litewskiego pierwszej połowy XVII wieku", *Barok* 13.1 (25) (2006), pp. 79-93; D. Platt, *Kazania pogrzebowe z przełomu XVI i XVII wieku: Z dziejów prozy staropolskiej* (Wrocław, 1992), pp. 81-93.

say with Jeremiah the prophet: "Death has climbed in through our windows and has entered our fortresses", which, fencing with its sharp sword, injured two royal heads, and injured them fatally and laid them down evenly on the ground. "Alas, sword of the Lord, how long till you rest? Return to your sheath; cease and be still", says Jeremiah (Jer. 47:6).[162]

In his turn, father Leonty Karpovych, the archimandrite in the church of the Holy Spirit, displayed before his listeners a vision of happiness in paradise, which would be enjoyed by the newlyweds of 1619, Prince Samuel Ogiński and Zofia Billewiczówna, after the end of their lives:

> Oh, how delicious are the dishes at this banquet! How sweet is the wine from the heavenly cellar! How melodious is the music of grateful angelic choirs! How enjoyable is the bean-feast with them (and with so many adored sons and daughters of Adam)! How cheerful are the spiritual dances, games, and exclamations! How amazing and how delightful the views and *spectacula* that appear there![163]

Laudatory sermons significantly contributed to the dissemination and consolidation of rhetorical intuition, that is the recognition of the internal structure of an epideictic text. In Vilnius, in the first half of the seventeenth century, there were probably very few Christians who would not have recognised, to a greater or lesser degree, the devices used in laudatory rhetoric, even if most of them were rather modestly literate. This is confirmed by the large number of epideictic devices used in the testaments of the nobility and town dwellers of Vilnius we have looked at. Epideictic rhetoric provided a language for categorising and valuing the social system in which the inhabitants of Vilnius lived, as well as for describing (or telling stories about), more or less skilfully, their place in the social hierarchy. Those who had great political or economic influence negotiated, with the aid of poetry and panegyrical prose among other means, their position in this hierarchy; those who did not have money or power could, at most, identify their place in this structure. In both cases, epideictic culture forced self-determination and contributed to the shaping of the identity of the groups and individuals who lived in seventeenth century Vilnius.

[162] J. SCHÖNFLISSIUS, "Kazanie pogrzebne królewskie", in: *Dwa kazania wygłoszone po śmierci Katarzyny Habsburżanki*, pp. 156-157.

[163] KARPOWICZ, *Przemowa i napomnienie*, f. C2v.

Religious Theatre and the Theatre of Power

The Art of Epideictic Art in the City

The *genus demonstrativum* serves laudation. But laudation of whom or what? Priscianus Caesariensis wrote that one can praise people, cities, trees, and even mute animals (*muta animalia*).[164] Seventeenth-century rhetoricians from Vilnius would have clarified Priscianus's definition, adding that it is mainly a matter of praise for people who deserve it, such as kings, lay and ecclesiastical princes, magnates, and high officials – in short, people in power. At this point, the epideictic genre can be easily associated with political propaganda, which was nothing more than a kind of praise for rulers.

Epideictic texts understood demonstrativeness as considered by rhetoric and classical literature as a tool of power and a way of showing its strength[165] – or, on the contrary, a field of hidden rivalry. Rivalry played a role, for instance in conducting the funerals of magnates and the wealthiest town dwellers, or in assuming offices. The features of the persons being praised were described with superlatives, calling them the wealthiest, the most pious, the most virtuous, etc., but there was always a latent context in which similar characteristics were attributed to their competitors. Usually they were not mentioned, and the only exception to this rule were the ancestors, who had to be matched in their greatness. The competition of potential and actual rivals determined the use of any propaganda measures to neutralise them rhetorically or balance their position. Therefore, an entry into the city or a funeral was supposed to be breathtaking and lavish.

Representations of power, although they employed symbols, took on concrete forms. Abstraction was avoided, and each element had a specific meaning. In the colour and costliness value of the ruler's robes, in the epithets used in an inscription of praise on the triumphal arch, in the gesture of throwing coins with the ruler's image into the crowd, and even in the colour of the coat of the horse he rode – everywhere a message was encoded. This strongly influenced the senses and, through them, the emotions. What in the twentieth century was called baroque art was often just specific, functionalised, and attractive political propaganda such as this. In order for the viewers to submit volun-

[164] Priscianus of Caesariensis, *Praeexercitamina*, p. 208.

[165] CURTIUS, *European Literature and the Latin Middle Ages* (Princeton and Oxford, 2013), pp. 167-178. OBREMSKI, *Panegiryczna sztuka postaciowania*, p. 113.

tarily to the imposed order of the authorities and adopt an attitude of readiness to be convinced, which is the foundation of the art of rhetoric, they needed to join in the rituals of the theatre of power.

Theatre and Drama

The public theatre of power was probably the most common type of performance art in early modern Vilnius. The 'regular' theatre, with its stage, actors, and a script written beforehand, was more a niche form limited to two environments, that is the royal court and the Jesuit school, perhaps with the addition of other humanist schools that operated in the city, to wit the Orthodox, Calvinist, and Lutheran schools. There are no written sources that mention the presence of wandering troupes of actors, although it is possible that from the middle of the sixteenth century onwards, they came to the capital during large fairs. Perhaps the Bernardines organised mystery plays or other religious performances at the beginning of that century. While we can speak of a developed musical culture in Vilnius in the sixteenth and seventeenth centuries, it is probably not possible to say the same about the theatre, which remained an artistic field enjoyed by the political and intellectual elites. Both groups maintained close and frequent relations.

Theatrical performances were probably staged at the Jagiellonian court in Vilnius as early as the first half of the sixteenth century. Both Bona Sforza and her son were interested in theatre, as is shown by the staging of *Iudicium Paridis*, which was seen by the young queen during the carnival of 1522 in the Wawel castle in Cracow.[166] However, the lack of sources makes it impossible to say something more concrete about early humanist theatre in Vilnius.

In the second half of the sixteenth century, important events were probably accompanied by allegorical performances, similar to those presented on the Market Square in Cracow on the occasion of chancellor Jan Zamoyski's wedding to a king's niece Griselda Báthory (Gryzelda Batorówna) in June 1583.[167]

[166] B. Król, S. Mrozińska, and Z. Raszewski, "Inscenizacja '*Iudicium Paridis*' na Wawelu w r. 1522", *Pamiętnik Teatralny* 3.1 (1954), pp. 3-22; W. Roszkowska, "Od 'Iudicium Paridis' (1502) do 'Sądu Parysa' (1542): Golsa do dziejów staropolskiej kultury teatralnej", in: *Literatura staropolska i jej związki europejskie: Prace poświęcone XVII Międzynarodowemu Kongresowi Slawistów w Warszawie w roku 1973*, ed. J. Pelc (Wrocław, 1973), pp. 175-176; J. Ziomek, *Renesans* (Warsaw, 1977), p. 98.

[167] M. Bielski and J. Bielski, *Kronika polska*, pp. 793-794; S. Leśniewski, *Jan Zamoyski:*

With time, such shows were monopolised in Vilnius by the Jesuit Academy. However, the sources remain silent about regular theatrical performances at court until the rule of King Władysław IV Vasa (1632-1648).

The king stayed in Vilnius five times during his fourteen-year reign. Each of his stays was long and was accompanied by lavish performances organised even during Lent, which astonished the more zealous Catholics. During his journey across Europe in 1624-1625, Władysław had become a great lover of the Italian theatre, especially of *dramma per musica* and ballet, which he began to inject into his court in Warsaw soon after his return to Poland. Władysław's first wife, Queen Cecilia Renata of Austria, shared these passions. Whenever the king or queen stayed at the grand ducal palace at the lower castle, opera or ballet performances and masquerades took place there. The queen and her court also participated in the latter, for instance during the carnival of 1639, about which the Lithuanian chancellor Albrycht Stanisław Radziwiłł wrote in his diary with a certain distance:

> 6 March. At night, dances took place in the castle, at which the queen and the princess appeared with the women of the court in magnificent masks. The king's house celebrated the Bacchic holiday with dancing for the whole three days, until the dawn of Wednesday [Ash Wednesday] ended the party. I, suffering from benign gout, was happy to lie at home.[168]

King Władysław IV initiated opera at Vilnius. Three *drammi per musica* performances were staged for the first time in Vilnius castle: *Il ratto di Helena* (4 September 1636), *L'Andromeda* (6 March 1644), and *Circe delusa* (16 April 1648).[169] These performances were among the most ambitious of their kind in

Hetman i polityk (Warsaw, 2008), pp. 80-81; D. KOSIŃSKI, *Teatra polskie: Historie* (Warsaw, 2010), p. 298; FRANCZAK, "*Polotia recepta*", pp. 121-123.

168 RADZIWIŁŁ, *Pamiętnik o historii w Polsce*, 2, *1637-1646*, p. 123. Similar masquerade balls were arranged during Shrovetide 1644; *ibid.*, p. 389. See SZWEYKOWSKA, "Imprezy baletowe na dworze Władysława IV", p. 21; J. ŻUKOWSKI, *Balety królowej Cecylii Renaty*, in: *Silva Rerum*, <https://www.wilanow-palac.pl/balety_krolowej_cecylii_renaty.html> (accessed 01.07. 2023).

169 K. TARGOSZ-KRETOWA, *Teatr dworski Władysława IV (1635-1648)* (Warsaw, 1965), pp. 306-307; J. TRILUPATIENĖ, "Dramma per musica in early seventeenth-century Vilnius", trans. V. AGLINSKAS and R. KONDRATAS, in: *Opera Lietuvos didžiųjų kunigaikščių rūmuose* (Vilnius, 2010), pp. 120-129. Editions of texts: [*Sumariusz polski*] *Idyllum albo akt o porwaniu Heleny*, in: *Dramaty staropolskie. Antologia*, ed. J. LEWAŃSKI, 5 (Warsaw, 1963), pp. 49-57; *Opera Lietuvos didžiųjų kunigaikščių rūmuose* (reproductions of the editions of three texts and their translation by Dainius Būrė into Lithuanian).

Europe at that time.[170] The librettos for the operas were written by Virgilio Puccitelli, but the composers remain unknown. The score for *Il ratto di Helena* was probably composed by Marco Scacchi, the kapellmeister of the royal ensemble. Agostino Locci was responsible for special effects and the theatrical machinery. The operas were performed by musicians who belonged to the royal musical ensemble, mostly Italians and Poles.

Operas were usually staged to mark important events, such as the arrival of Queen Marie Louise Gonzaga in Vilnius in 1648. Their audience consisted of the royal court, the highest state officials, and, quite often, foreign guests. The performances were long, about five hours, with the individual acts being separated by ballet interludes. The audience, especially people more familiar with music and theatre, were delighted with the high quality of the performances, both in terms of music and staging. The papal nuncio Mario Filonardi, who was very impressed by the special effects used in the performance about the abduction of Helena, described them in his reports to Rome.[171]

Performances organised at the Academy of Vilnius had a wider audience than the elite court spectacles. From the foundation of the university, public recitations and performances were held several times every year. According to the *Ratio Studiorum* of 1599, closed declamations, that is recitation demonstrations by students who presented their own compositions, were organised every Sunday.[172] Open declamations or theatrical performances were held on the occasion of major holidays and other celebrations, such as a visit of a bishop, patron, or ruler. The walls of the cloisters were then decorated with works written by students, including sentences, symbols, elogia, and emblems.[173] The texts most often recited during the declamations included Latin speeches, dialogues, odes, elegies, and epigrams. According to the recommendations of the order's authorities, theatrical performances were supposed to take place less frequently, preferably once at the end of the school year (in July), so that the rehearsals did not distract students from more important activities.

Parents, founders, bishops, and other dignitaries were invited to the performances, while the students and professors of course participated in them, but it was not uncommon for the inhabitants of Vilnius to attend them as well. The first performance of this kind in Vilnius, the tragedy *Hercules*, probably by the

[170] TARGOSZ-KRETOWA, *Teatr dworski*, pp. 158-159.

[171] T. CHYNCZEWSKA-HENNEL, *Nuncjusz i król: Nuncjatura Maria Filonardiego w Rzeczypospolitej 1636-1643* (Warsaw, 2006), pp. 213-215.

[172] *Ratio atque institutio studiorum* SJ, *czyli Ustawa*, pp. 93-94, 98, 120.

[173] They were referred to as *affixiones*; see Chapter 3, "Schools".

Italian Jesuit Stefano Tuccio, was open to the public. It was staged on the occasion of the inauguration of the college in 1570, and its text was brought from Rome.[174] Subsequent dramas were performed in the years 1574 (*Jephte*), 1581 (*Jehu*), 1584 (*De Angelorum cura*) and 1597 (*Saul et Davidis comoedia*).[175] Later, they were also written in Vilnius. These were usually shorter pieces, poems in Latin or Greek, or shows whose genre was difficult to define. Accounts of extended performances have survived in the Jesuit Archivum Romanum.[176] They describe performances that celebrated the welcoming of King Stephen Báthory in 1579 and 1582 (which will be discussed later), cardinals Radziwiłł and Bolognetti in 1584, and King Sigismund III in 1589. In addition, dialogues were performed at Easter, Shrovetide, Christmas, or on St. Catherine's Day. Outstanding texts of this type were written by Kasper Pętkowski, whose allegorical dialogue was performed before King Stephen Báthory.[177]

Much information on drama and academic theatre in Vilnius is provided by the so-called Uppsala Codex (*Codex Upsaliensis*), which contains several texts from the turn of the sixteenth and seventeenth centuries, including two plays by the Jesuit and subsequently famous lexicographer Grzegorz Knapiusz (Cnapius), that is the comic tragedy *Philopater seu pietas* of 1596 and the tragedy *Faelicitas* of 1597.[178] It was noted that both dramas were staged in Vilnius, for instance beneath the Polish Epilogue of *Faelicitas* there is an annotation: "Written in Vilnius in 1597 and staged there. It was performed in Poznań in July 1599".[179] Because it was a custom to exchange texts, it can be assumed

174 POPLATEK, *Studia z dziejów jezuickiego teatru*, p. 167; PIECHNIK, *Początki Akademii Wileńskiej*, p. 49. E. ULČINAITĖ, "Mokyklinė Baroko drama: Antikinės dramos tradicijos ir aktualijų atspindžiai", in: *Lietuvos jėzuitų teatras: XVI-XVIII amžiaus dramų rinktinė*, ed. and trans. E. ULČINAITĖ (Vilnius, 2008), p. 12. The figure of Hercules was quite popular in Jesuit playwriting in the sixteenth century. In the Bibliothèque d'Étude et du Patrimoine de Toulouse, shelf number 840, there is a 1743-verse Jesuit drama *Hercules coelifer: Tragicomoedia* in five acts, written in iambic verse, which tells the story of the release of Prometheus.

175 PIECHNIK, *Początki Akademii Wileńskiej*, p. 99.

176 *Ibid.*, pp. 99-100.

177 POPLATEK, *Studia z dziejów jezuickiego teatru*, pp. 138-140; ULČINAITĖ, "Mokyklinė Baroko drama", pp. 25-27; EAD., "Utwory powitalne na cześć władców i magnatów w literaturze Wielkiego Księstwa Litewskiego XVI-XVIII wieku: Tradycje a specyfika lokalna", trans. B. PIASECKA, in: *Kalbų varžybos*, pp. 41-45.

178 MS CR R 380. These works were published in Latin (G. KNAPIUSZ, *Tragoediae: Philopater, Faelicita, Eutropius*, ed. L. WINNICZUK (Wrocław, 1965)), and translations of them into Lithuanian by Eugenia Ulčinaitė (ULČINAITĖ, *Lietuvos jėzuitų teatras*, pp. 57-191) have been published recently.

179 "*Facta Vilnae 1597 et ibid. exhibita est. Posnaniae vero spectata 1599 in Iulio*". MS cr

that other dramas from the Uppsala Codex (or some similar to them) may have also been performed at the Academy of Vilnius.

Dialogues, such as those by Pętkowski, had a simple structure: they were short, had between one and three acts, and featured several characters.[180] Regular dramas, such as those from Uppsala, were long, with five acts in Latin separated by Polish or Latin interludes. In order to make it easier for viewers to find their way around the content of the plays, they were preceded by a speech by the personified Prologus, who summarised and explained their meaning in Polish. Probably the same actor performed the Epilogus, once again emphasising moral teachings that followed from the play, as those at the end of the comedy *Odostratocles* from the Uppsala manuscript. Interludes, on the other hand, had a lighter character and were mainly supposed to entertain the audience. Within the comedy mentioned before, the author interspersed three one-act plays: *Dąb* (Oak), *Słowik* (Nightingale), and *Wyprawa na brody* (The Expedition to the Beards).

Each time, staging a drama was an important event in the life of the university. It usually took place to mark the beginning of a new semester, at the end of a year, or on the occasion of the visit of a significant person. The cast consisted of perhaps up to sixty people. The performances lasted several hours, gathered a large audience, and for the latter reason it is likely that they were initially performed in the university courtyard. From at least 1616, there was a public performance hall in the Academy buildings. A "hall for public performances" on the first floor, in the wing located on the St. John's Street side, was marked on the plan of the college from 1642/1643.[181] Decorations, costumes, and props were used, perhaps even simple theatrical machines, as they are mentioned by Maciej Kazimierz Sarbiewski in his lectures on poetics.[182]

If we assume that the Jesuits organised performances every year, it will turn out that as many as between seventy and eighty different dramas could have been staged in the period under discussion; unfortunately, most of them are unknown today. The average student who reached the poetics and rhetoric class was therefore well acquainted with theatre and theatrical techniques, both

R 380, f. 90v. Below is the information that the text is a holograph by Grzegorz Knapiusz. A similar note is written below *Philopater*.

[180] A. Soczewka, "Wstęp", in: *Łacińskie dialogi Kaspra Pętkowskiego*, ed. A. Soczewka (Niepokalanów, 1978), p. 74.

[181] J. Okoń, *Dramat i teatr szkolny: Sceny jezuickie XVII wieku* (Wrocław, 1970), p. 252.

[182] B.B. Awianowicz, "Co faktycznie przedstawiają ilustracje w IX księdze *De perfecta poesi* Macieja Kazimierza Sarbiewskiego?", *Barok* 12.1 (23) (2006), pp. 129-142.

theoretically (from lectures or as a spectator), and practically, as everyone had to take part in oratorial activities and declamations, and some in performances as well. Thus, the Jesuit school prepared future actors on the stage of the Polish-Lithuanian Commonwealth, while at the same time promoting the topos of the world as theatre.

The aim of both the Jesuit dramas and the sophisticated operas staged at the royal castle was primarily to provide the audience with entertainment, referring in this way to the rhetorical category of *delectare*. In the case of Jesuit theatre, it was also aimed at shaping the moral attitudes of the students of the Academy, as well as giving them occasions to practise declamation, which, as such, was another rhetorical category, namely *docere*. The two theatres, the one of the royal court and that of the Jesuits, differed widely from each other because of the professional character of the court stage and the amateur nature of the Jesuit stage, the languages of the performances (Italian and Latin with Polish, respectively), the artistic means used, innovative experiments and scholastic conservatism strengthened by being subordinate to the rules of the Jesuit order, as well as dissimilar audiences.[183] But there was one important common element, which we will present later. It was realised through including both theatres into the rituals of the State and the Catholic Church. In the sixteenth and seventeenth centuries, in the urban space of Vilnius, the theatre became an exceptionally politicised and ideologised artistic form, acquiring functions different from those in other large cities of the Polish-Lithuanian Commonwealth.

The Theatricalisation of Religion and Power

Theatrical and para-theatrical performances, religious as well as secular, entered into close relations with each other. The *sacrum* sanctified the secularity of power and, conversely, the authority of power strengthened the *sacrum*. Due to the officially Catholic character of the state, this relationship between secular and ecclesiastical power had a clearly Catholic, post-Tridentine features. Most of the great para-theatrical celebrations in the city were strongly supported by the hegemony of the Roman Church. However, other Christian confessions, those of the Orthodox and Protestant Churches, also sought to be

[183] POPLATEK, *Studia z dziejów jezuickiego teatru*, pp. 42-44; SOCZEWKA, "Wstęp", pp. 80-81.

identified with power, especially when individual state officials were members of the Churches not identified with the State, as in the case of the Calvinist Radziwiłł clan. In such circumstances, Vilnius epideictic art, next to open polemics, was a field of more discreet but equally important inter-denominational rivalry, especially in the first decades of the seventeenth century. This is visible, for instance, in the account of the entry of King Sigismund III Vasa into Vilnius in 1611, which will be discussed later.

The Vasa dynasty ruled during a period when particular importance was attached to a type of celebration of power that involved the synthesis of many arts, including theatre, literature, architecture, sculpture, painting, and music. During the times of Kings Sigismund III and Władysław IV (i.e. 1588-1648), the inhabitants of Vilnius had the opportunity to participate in several dozen spectacular performances. The city served as the stage for this theatre.

The theatricalisation of public life at that time was common and had a long tradition. From ancient times, the theatre of power took over the form of the triumphal procession.[184] The events were carefully directed and the participants were given specific roles to play in accordance with the planned scenario. The gestures, movements, time of action, and decorations were all important in such a spectacle, as well as appropriate places for the extras, that is all residents of the city. Vilnius was designed haphazardly, so its space had to be re-adapted for the purposes of these shows, unlike Nyasvizh (Nieśwież, in today's Belarus), which was designed in the 1580s in such a way that the street network facilitated the organisation of religious theatrical performances of power.[185] Attempts to adapt Vilnius to the function of a theatrical space in the

[184] A. FOWLER, *Triumphal Forms: Structural Patterns in Elisabethan Poetry* (Cambridge, 1970), pp. 27-29; CHROŚCICKI, *Sztuka i polityka*, p. 77; L. ŚLĘK, "Wiersze Samuela Twardowskiego pod wjazd pisane", in: *Wielkopolski Maro: Samuel ze Skrzypny Twardowski w wielkiej i małej Ojczyźnie*, ed. K. MELLER and J. KOWALSKI (Poznań, 2002), pp. 76-78; NIEDŹWIEDŹ, *Nieśmiertelne teatra sławy*, pp. 110-111; KOSIŃSKI, *Teatra polskie*, pp. 293-300; D. ZUPKA, *Ritual and Symbolic Communication in Medieval Hungary under the Árpád Dynasty (1000-1301)* (Leiden, 2016), pp. 117-138.

[185] Nyasvizh was designed by the Jesuit architect Giovanni Maria Bernardoni on the demand of Prince Mikołaj Krzysztof Radziwiłł "The Orphan" as a new type of the Renaissance *città*. The plan of the town is based on an Italian conception of the polycentric and labyrinthine city. In Nyasvizh, the plan of the town was to make the Catholic churches stand out. Radziwiłł, who was raised by his father Mikołaj "the Black" as a Calvinist, converted to Catholicism in 1567. His many foundations, among them churches in Nyasvizh, supported the Counter-Reformation activities of the Catholic Church in the Grand Duchy of Lithuania. See T. BERNATOWICZ, *Miles christianus et peregrinus: Fundacje Mikołaja Radziwiłła "Sierotki" w ordynacji nieświeskiej* (Warsaw, 1998), pp. 20-29.

seventeenth century can be seen in the construction of new churches and the transformation of existing ones together with their surroundings, and probably in the positioning of monumental epigraphs as well. This tendency was common at the time in all major cities of Europe, including the Polish-Lithuanian Commonwealth.[186]

Descriptions of some of these events have survived; unfortunately, most of them are not very detailed. They included processions, funerals of significant persons, triumphal entries after victories, greetings of the king, weddings of magnates, inaugurations of the sessions of Parliament, regional councils and convocations, anniversaries, consecrations of churches and chapels (for instance that of St. Casimir in 1636), and above all solemn entries of dignitaries who assumed their offices, for instance that of *voivode* Janusz Radziwiłł in 1653, archbishop of Polatsk Melecjusz Smotrycki in 1621, or bishops Abraham Woyna and Jerzy Tyszkiewicz in 1631 and 1650.[187] Some other celebrations were closed, accessible to a small group of members of some corporations. These included feasts of religious brotherhoods, priestly ordination or the conferment of master's and doctoral degrees at the Academy of Vilnius. All of them, however, had their own rituals and were carefully choreographed.

Public city shows were organised in Vilnius already in the late Middle Ages. Most of them were related to the 'open' city and its role as the capital of the country. Among these events were receptions of foreign envoys and celebrations of the births, marriages, and burials of the members of the ruling dynasty. In the fifteenth and sixteenth centuries great importance was attached to reception ceremonies for the Muscovite legations. When celebrating solemn entries into the city, the prestige of the two rival powers counted much.[188] A detailed rhymed description of the reception of the Muscovites in Vilnius on 6 January 1602 was written by Eliasz Pielgrzymowski, the notary of the Grand Duchy of Lithuania.[189]

[186] L. BENEVOLO, *The European City*, trans. C. IPSEN (Oxford andCambridge, Mass., 1993), pp. 126-132; CHROŚCICKI, *Sztuka i polityka*, pp. 50-57; PETRUCCI, *Public Lettering*, pp. 43-51.

[187] H. WISNER, *Janusz Radziwiłł, 1612-1655: Wojewoda wileński, hetman wielki litewski* (Warsaw, 2000), p. 157; FRICK, *Meletij Smotryc'kyj*, p. 78; G. ZUJIENĖ, "Ceremoniał ingresu biskupów wileńskich w XVII-XVIII wieku", *Barok* 13.1 (25) (2006), pp. 59-71.

[188] M. SIRUTAVIČIUS, *Maskvos pasiuntinių priėmimo ceremonialas lietuvos valvodo dvare Vilniuje XV a. pabaigoje – XVI a. viduryje*, in *Vilniaus Žemutinė pilis XIV a.- XIX a. pradžioje 2005-2006 m. tyrimai*, ed. L. GLEMŽA (Vilnius, 2007), pp. 8-32.

[189] E. PIELGRZYMOWSKI, *Poselstwo i krótkie spisanie rozprawy z Moskwą: Poselstwo do Zygmunta Trzeciego*, ed. R. KRZYWY (Warsaw, 2010), pp. 215-216.

The oldest descriptions of the royal ceremonies in Vilnius must have existed as early as the late fifteenth century. They were related to the reign of Alexander I Jagiellon, the Grand Duke and since 1501 also the King of Poland, who lived in Vilnius for long periods. In his chancery worked humanists who were competent to record the most important events. One such event was the funeral of the king in 1506. We have only an abstract from the later historical work of Marcin Kromer (1555): "the royal funeral [of Alexander I Jagiellon] was conducted with wonderful pomp and [the king was] then properly buried in the chapel of the Vilnius basilica next to [Prince] Casimir's body".[190] The funeral must have been similar to those organised in Cracow after the deaths of Casimir IV Jagiellon (1492) and John I Albert (1501).[191] We can only speculate if there any funeral poems were performed, remembering the late king.[192]

The first surviving references to other ceremonies date from the times of Sigismund II Augustus. The renowned author and the royal secretary Łukasz Górnicki mentions in his *History of the Polish Crown between 1527 and 1572* (written in 1595-1603 and published in 1637) for example performances and fireworks held in mid-July 1540 on the occasion of the birth of the son of the king's daughter Isabella Jagiellon and her Hungarian consort John Zápolya, as well as the ceremonial reception of John, Duke of Finland (the future king of

[190] M. KROMER, *De origine et rebus gestis Polonorum libri XXX* (Basel, 1555), p. 671. King Alexander's is the only royal body buried in Vilnius cathedral. The main burial place of the rulers of the Polish-Lithuanian state remained the Wawel cathedral in Cracow. King Alexander also wanted to be buried in Cracow with his predecessors, but his wish was not fulfilled (see M. KROMER, *Kronika, to jest historyja świata*, ed. D. ŚNIEŻKO, D. KOZARYN, and E. KARCZEWSKA, 3 (Szczecin, 2019), p. 238). However, since the funeral of Alexander Jagiellon the role of Vilnius cathedral rose and it became the second royal necropole in the Polish-Lithuanian state. As mentioned above, three queens were buried there. In 1648 the heart and entrails (*cor et viscera*) of King Władysław IV Vasa were deposed in the royal chapel vault in Vilnius, while his embalmed body was transported to Cracow. See H. WISNER, *Władysław IV Waza* (Wrocław, 2009), pp. 176-177; J. PIETRZAK, "*Ciało umarłe większego wymaga opatrzenia* – sekcja zwłok polskich królów i królowych od XVI do XVIII wieku w kontekście przygotowań do ceremonii pogrzebowej", in: *Śmierć, pogrzeb i upamiętnianie władców w dawnej Polsce*, ed. H. RAJFURA, P. SZWEDO, B. ŚWIADEK, M. WALCZAK, and P. WĘCOWSKI (Warsaw, 2020), pp. 159, 165.

[191] M. STARZYŃSKI, "Last tribute to the king: The funeral ceremony of the Polish King Kazimierz the Jagiellon (1492) in the light of an unknown description", *Viator* 45.2 (2014), pp. 289-302.

[192] The other members of the Jagiellonian dynasty were recorded in epicedia (King Casimir IV Jagiellon and Cardinal Frederic Jagiellon); see R. GANSINIEC, "*Sbigneis* Mikołaj Kotwicza", *Pamiętnik Literacki* 48.1 (1957), pp. 123-125; M. STARZYŃSKI, "Wiersze na śmierc króla w późnośredniowiecznej Polsce", in: *Śmierć, pogrzeb i upamiętnianie władców*, pp. 77-87.

Sweden John III) and his wedding to Catherine Jagiellon on 4 October 1562.[193] More detailed descriptions of entries into the city were provided by the Jesuits, but not until they welcomed King Stephen Báthory in the spring and summer of 1579.[194]

State ceremonies such as weddings, ceremonial entries, and funerals in Vilnius happened sporadically. Religious feasts took place every year. At least from the fifteenth century onwards, Vilnius hosted processions to mark the feast of Corpus Christi.[195] In the last decades of the sixteenth century (from 1586 or 1587) these processions changed into lavish para-theatrical performances.[196] Their basis was still the earlier, medieval procession, whose rules were prescribed in the synodal statutes. However, after the Council of Trent (1545-1563), their character changed dramatically. One can observe a strong influence of humanist literature, theatre, and art on the Corpus Christi procession. They gradually exceeded its liturgical purpose and gained the character of Counter-Reformation theatrical performances, which engaged the arts of rhetoric, poetry, painting, sculpture, and music.[197]

The pomposity which characterised such performances in the first half of the seventeenth century was discussed by Walenty Bartoszewski (the literary pseudonym of Jan Bartoszewicz, *c.* 1573-1645), a Jesuit poet and panegyrist,[198] in his account of the Corpus Christi celebrations of 1614.[199] On this occasion,

[193] Ł. GÓRNICKI, *Dzieje w Koronie Polskiej*, ed. H. BARYCZ (Wrocław, 2003), p. 15, 148-157. On the wedding of Catherina Jagiellon and John of Finland, see PRZEŹDZIECKI, *Jagiellonki polskie*, 3, p. 40; RAGAUSKIENĖ, "The marriage of Catherine Jagiellon and John III Vasa in Vilnius (1562)", pp. 102-106.

[194] ULČINAITĖ, *Utwory powitalne*, pp. 31-41; BUSZEWICZ and NIEDŹWIEDŹ, "Wstęp", p. 17-21.

[195] In 1320 the Corpus Christi feast was introduced in the diocese of Cracow and later in other dioceses of the Gniezno archdiocese. See H. ZAREMSKA, "Procesje Bożego Ciała w Krakowie w XIV-XVI wieku", in: *Kultura elitarna a kultura masowa w Polsce późnego średniowiecza*, ed. B. GEREMEK (Wrocław, 1978), p. 26.

[196] I am quoting after OKOŃ, *Dramat i teatr szkolny*, p. 84; ID., "Wstęp", in: *Dramaty eucharystyczne jezuitów. XVII wiek* (Warsaw, 1992), pp. 6-7.

[197] M. PASEK, "Słowo – obraz – spektakl: Korespondencja sztuk w opisach wileńskich procesji na Boże Ciało autorstwa Walentego Bartoszewskiego", *Zeszyty Naukowe Towarzystwa Doktorantów UJ Nauki Społeczne* 14.3 (2016), pp. 70-71.

[198] *Encyklopedia wiedzy o jezuitach*, p. 29; M. PASEK, "Bezoar z łez ludzkich czasu powietrza morowego by Walenty Bartoszewski as an example of 'A prescription for the soul and the body' at the time of the Plague' na czas zarazy", *Tematy i Konteksty* 1 (2020: special issue in English), pp. 122-124.

[199] Jan Okoń (OKOŃ, *Dramat i teatr szkolny*, p. 82) associates the performances of Corpus Christi staged in Vilnius with the Jesuit theatre, but it should be remembered that the Vilnius

the city and the Jesuit Academy built "altars, predominantly in the market squares", at which "ornamental turrets" and "splendid-looking high towers" were erected, decorated with "golden candlesticks", "golden chains with diamonds, *roztruchan* [a silver goblet in the shape of an animal], and trays", as well as cloth of gold. The streets were adorned with trees and garlands and sprinkled with flowers. Houses made of bricks were upholstered with expensive materials, and painted portraits were displayed in the windows. Cannons and arquebuses were taken out of the arsenal and were shot into the air. All participants in the procession, the guilds, the army, and the students of the Academy of Vilnius, turned up in festive costumes.[200]

The spectacle described by Bartoszewski resembled to some extent Spanish *autos sacramentales*; it was supposed to express Catholic truths regarding faith and dogmas through visualised allegories. Various images, figures, and props were carried on eight carts. The first one presented the Warring Church surrounded by angels, preceded by a rider who personified the Christian Knight. The following carts displayed Faith, Hope, Love, Old Testament heroes, and the Ark of the Covenant, all in the company of their own retinues.

The second figure

On the golden wagon goes dressed up as Faith,
    Surrounded by the four eminent virtues.
Four Evangelists walk carrying books
    And four Doctors dressed in purple.
St. Paul strides with the name of Jesus,
    To which the angel turns his eyes.
Beautiful Truth on horseback leads them all,
    The pyramid of Faith shows the following inscription to all:
THERE IS ONE GOD, ONE BAPTISM, AND ONE FAITH,
    Let not the hellish monster boast of another.
A virginal with violins is next to this figure,

chapter and the city council also had a great say in their organisation. The extant sources say that the canons organised processions to mark the canonisation of St. Casimir in 1604 and the translation of his body into a newly-built chapel in 1636. Probably they based on their experiences in organising the theatre-like processions on the Corpus Christi performances.

[200] W. BARTOSZEWSKI, *Pobudka na obchodzenie świątości rocznej tryumfu i pompy Ciała Bożego dana a jaśnie oświeconemu i najwielebniejszemu w Panu Chryście ojcowi i panu, panu Benedyktowi Woynie z łaski bożej biskupowi wileńskiemu ofiarowana* (Vilnius, 1614), pp. A2r-A2v. See J. PELC, *Słowo i obraz na pograniczu literatury i sztuk plastycznych* (Cracow, 2002), pp. 158-159.

Praising the Lord in this sacrament with trombones.[201]

Performances such as the one on 29 May 1614[202] were not merely examples of panegyrical theatre, as, with their splendour, they went beyond the simple ways in which epideictic texts were supposed to impress the audience. As Bartoszewski makes clear, the script of such a spectacle was so sophisticated and complex that it must be assumed that such a celebration of the Blessed Sacrament, apart from its ritual and panegyrical dimensions, also played a missionary role, as well as having a polemical, anti-Protestant meaning. This educational value of the procession on the occasion of Corpus Christi is mentioned in seventeenth-century ecclesiastical regulations.[203] This catechisation was conducted through art, or rather through the arts.

The pyramid of Faith, which is a simple emblematic construct, was complemented by additional text, theatrical action, and music, the smell of incense and flowers, by costumes and gestures, and by the symbolism of numbers. Thanks to this abundance of artistic means, the congregation could experience the spectacle that took place before their eyes, participating in it both through the senses and intellectually. In the post-Tridentine period this influence on the spectator's mind was motivated by philosophical theories of the time, developed by the Jesuits, who spoke of the ways art was perceived. It was supposed to rely on the activity of the inner sense (*fantaisie*, *esprit*), which consisted of five functions that enabled the image provided by the external senses to be processed and understood.[204] This theory contributed to the flourishing of intersemiotic forms of persuasion, which involved the external senses, that is sight, hearing, smell, touch, and taste. It influenced the development of

[201] BARTOSZEWSKI, *Pobudka*, pp. A2v-A3r.

[202] In 1615, Bartoszewski wrote another description of the Corpus Christ performance: W. BARTOSZEWSKI, *Dowody procesyjej nabożnej i poważnego tryumfu w dzień roczny przenaświętszego Ciała Bożego jaśnie wielmożnemu panu jego mości panu Chrisztofowi Słuszcze wojewodzie wendeńskiemu na ten czas marszałkowi trybunalskiemu wileńskiemu ofiarowane* (Vilnius, 1615). Summaries of similar performances in Vilnius from 1625, 1631 and 1633 have survived; see OKOŃ, *Dramat i teatr szkolny*, pp. 95-97.

[203] J. SMOSARSKI, "Religijne widowiska parateatralne w Polsce XVII wieku: Kilka przykładów", in: *Dramat i teatr sakralny*, ed. I. SŁAWIŃSKA *et al.* (Lublin, 1988), pp. 122-126.

[204] J. LOACH, "The teaching of emblematics and other symbolic imagery by Jesuits within town colleges in seventeenth and eighteenth century France", in: *The Jesuits and the Emblem Tradition: Selected Papers of the Leuven International Emblem Conference 18-23 August, 1996*, ed. J. MANNING and M. VAN VAECK (Turnhout, 1999: *Imago Figurata* 1a), pp. 169-170.

emblematics in the seventeenth century, but, as we can see, it was used also in urban religious theatre.

The increasing importance of the *theatrum ceremoniale* in the first half of the seventeenth century is shown by the fact that in 1651, one year after the Vilnius bishopric was entrusted to bishop Jerzy Tyszkiewicz, he established the office of master of ceremonies at the cathedral.[205] He entrusted it to Jan Krąpnicki, canon of Piltene (now Latvia) and chaplain of Kiszkas's chapel. His main task was to direct processions with relics, the Corpus Christi processions, the Easter celebrations, etc. All canons, ministers, and clerics were subordinate to him, and the dean and the vice-verger of the cathedral were to be his helpers. Particular emphasis was placed on cooperation with a municipal official appointed to take care of the celebrations, which meant that the magistrate also had its own master of ceremonies. In advance, father Krąpnicki was obliged to determine the route of the procession and walk it. He also designated people to carry a canopy and keep the order of the ceremony. During the service in the cathedral, he was supposed to stand "in the presbytery and accompany the bishop, supervising everything". His duties also included organising ceremonial funerals and funeral services in accordance with the Roman missal and with diocesan regulations.[206]

Bishop Tyszkiewicz's document codified a practice that had been in place for decades, as even before it was promulgated someone had to organise such celebrations as the great procession with the relics of St. Casimir on 14 August 1636, described by Nuncio Filonardi and Albrycht Stanisław Radziwiłł,[207] or the Corpus Christi celebrations recorded by Bartoszewski. The repetitiveness of such events was to some extent helpful for their directors.

Seventeenth-century processions on Corpus Christi led to four altars, in the portico of the cathedral, in St. John's parish church, on the Market Square near Trybunalski (or Poznański) House, and in the Brothers Hospitallers' church in front of Żagiel's House.[208] Royal entries usually began at St. Stephen's church, and then the procession entered the city through the Rūdninkų Gate, continued along Rudnicka (Rūdninkų) Street, and reached the Market Square, from where

[205] *Ordinatio Magistri Ceremoniarum Ecclesiae Cathedralis Vilnensis* (1651), MS MAB F43-19455.

[206] "*Si quando funeralia seu exequia solenni ritu erunt celebrandae, provideat omnia, curetque singula opportuno tempore praeparari, iuxta praescriptum in Pontificali Romano et nostras Synodales Constitutiones*"; *ibid.*

[207] CHYNCZEWSKA-HENNEL, *Nuncjusz i król*, pp. 191-196.

[208] *Biskupstwo wileńskie*, p. 163.

it reached the lower castle via Zamkowa (Pilies) Street.[209] A similar path was followed by other dignitaries during their entries, including *voivodes*, bishops, and foreign legations.[210] Only the route of the entries of Orthodox and Uniate bishops must have been shorter, because their churches were located near the Gate of Dawn (the Miedniki Gate or Ostra Brama) and the Rudnicka Gate (the Rūdninkų Gate), but this does not mean that they were less ceremonial. In the spring of 1621, Meletius Smotrycki, the newly ordained archbishop of Polatsk, made a grand entry, which was also a political statement similar to the one that the Orthodox Church organised during the ceremonial entry of King Sigismund III in 1611.

The Royal Entry Into Vilnius of 24 July 1611

The details of ceremonial entries and of the texts written on these occasions in the second half of the sixteenth century and in the seventeenth century are provided by accounts of such events. One of them is the Latin narrative entitled *Dies triumphi* (or *Triumphus et ingressus regis Vilnam die 24 Iulii 1611 anno*),[211] which describes the triumphal entry of King Sigismund III Vasa that took place on 24 July 1611 after the capture of Smolensk.[212] The account was an official narrative, which was probably copied several times and distributed in the country and abroad, as this was a standard procedure after any significant event. One of its two existing copies is a luxurious manuscript currently held in the Saxon State Library in Dresden (Germany), the other is an

[209] ULČINAITĖ, *Utwory powitalne*, pp. 22-23.

[210] ZUJIENĖ, "Ceremoniał ingresu biskupów wileńskich w XVII-XVIII wieku", pp. 66-77.

[211] *Triumphs et ingressus Regis Vilnam die 24 Iulii 1611 anno*, MS CZART. 1577 IV, pp. 478-486, and *Dies triumphi in faustissmum reditum serenissimi ac invictissimi domini, domini Sigismundi Tertii Poloniae et Sveciae Regis de Smolensko ab ipsius maiestate expunato Vilnae XXIV Iulii celebrata anno Domini 1611*, Saxon State Library in Dresden (Germany), Msc G 258. A facsimile of the latter was published in: *Triumfo diena: 1611 m. birželio 13 d. Smolensko pergalė ir iškilmingas Zigmanto Vazos sutikimas Vilniuje 1611 m. liepos 24 d.*, ed. E. ULČINAITĖ and E. SAVIŠČEVAS (Vilnius, 2011), pp. 93-324. See ALSO CHROŚCICKI, *Sztuka i polityka*, p. 73; H. WISNER, *Zygmunt III Waza* (Wrocław, 2006), p. 150.

[212] Smolensk (now Russia) was one of the most important centres of Kyivan Rus' (ninth-twelfth centuries) and later was the capital of an independent principality. At the turn of the fourteenth and fifteenth centuries, Grand Duke Vytautas incorporated it into the Grand Duchy of Lithuania. In 1514 the city was captured by Muscovite army. The Lithuanians several times made attempts to regain Smolensk and eventually succeeded in 1611, after a siege which lasted twenty months.

Fig. 61 Polish and foreign officials during the ceremony of the entry of Queen Constance of Austria into Cracow on 4 December 1605. In the front, Bartłomiej Nowodworski in a coat with the Maltese Cross. Probably he was dressed in a similar way at the entry into Vilnius, six years later. A fragment of the *Stockholm Scroll*, 1605. Warsaw, The Royal Castle Museum. <https://www.zamek-krolewski.pl/ strona/wizyta-archiwum-wystaw-czasowych/894-krol-sie-zeni-rolka-sztokholmska-skarb-zamku> (accessed: 31.05.2022; public domain).

eighteenth-century copy kept in the Czartoryski Library in Cracow (Poland).[213] The source gives two types of information about using texts in early modern Vilnius. Firstly, it is itself an example of the written accounts which followed state feasts. Secondly, it recorded other texts (inscriptions, songs, and plays) which were written on this particular occasion. The *Dies triumphi* is divided into two parts. In the first part the anonymous author presents the event; in the second the poetical and prose texts, the score of the songs and a detailed des-

[213] There are some differences between them. The Cracow version was probably based on a seventeenth-century copy which differed from the Dresden one.

Fig. 62 Royal standard bearer (*chorąży*) Sebastian Sobieski during the ceremony of the entry of Queen Constance of Austria into Cracow on 4 December 1605. A fragment of the *Stockholm Scroll*, 1605. Warsaw, The Royal Castle Museum. <https://www.zamek-krolewski.pl/strona/wizyta-archiwum-wystaw-czasowych/894-krol-sie-zeni-rolka-sztokholmska-skarb-zamku> (accessed: 31.05.2022; public domain).

ription of the triumphal arches is recorded.[214] These descriptions were delivered to another anonymous author, who edited them.[215]

The ceremony lasted from morning till evening, was attended by the King and Queen Constance of Austria, Prince Władysław Vasa of Sweden, Princess Anna Vasa (a younger sister of the king), a large number of Lithuanian and Polish officials and dignitaries, city authorities, clergy, and townsmen, probably almost all inhabitants of the city and its suburbs. At dawn, the queen, who was staying in the lower castle, left for a villa three miles from the city, where the king had stayed overnight and where the day before he had been greeted by Prince Władysław. The queen was accompanied by 400 nobles, merchants, and inhabitants of Vilnius, and was preceded by 40 banners. Two miles outside the city, four expensive Persian tents were put up. In them, a Mass was said and

[214] E. Ulčinaitė, "The triumph of Sigimund Vasa in the context of ceremonial greetings offered to other rulers of the Grand Duchy of Lithuania", in: *Triumfo diena*, p. 75.

[215] This multi-authority of the second part confirms a description of the triumphal arch commissioned by the queen. The designer of this monument, Ruggiero Solomone, put its description in the first person. He also added extended explanations of the inscriptions put on the arch. See *Triumpho diena*, pp. 154-175.

the royal retinue was awaited. Meanwhile, spectators gathered along the entry route to the city.

At the head of the retinue, which to the anonymous author was reminiscent of a long snake, was the coach of Anna Vasa, followed by Prince Władysław, and then by the papal nuncio, the bishop of Vilnius, senators, the highest Polish and Lithuanian officials, noble matrons, ladies, and maids. They were followed by a colourful cavalcade that consisted of 200 Tartars, 100 light Cossack cavaliers, 100 armed German cavaliers (*Reiter*) commanded by the Maltese Knight Bartłomiej Nowodworski (see Fig. 61), and next by units of 100 court halberdiers and 300 foot guards. They were followed by 30 Lithuanian officials who were to attend a session of the Lithuanian Tribunal, royal courtiers, and riders dressed in Persian costumes. The king was preceded by chancellor Lew Sapieha and marshal Krzysztof Dorohostajski, Polish chancellor Feliks Kryski, and Prince Krzysztof Zbaraski.

Sigismund III himself was dressed in a purple robe with a red sash, which, according to the anonymous author of the account, referred to ancient "septentrional" triumphs, and he was riding a pinto horse with a valuable harness. The ruler was followed by chamberlain Andrzej Bobola and standard-bearer (*chorąży*) Sebastian Sobieski,[216] who led a large Hungarian infantry unit (see Fig. 62). He guarded the prisoners of war, including two Muscovite *voivodes*.

The retinue stopped at the tents, where the king was solemnly greeted by the queen, senators, church dignitaries, Lithuanian ladies, and court ladies. Speeches were made by those welcoming the king, to which Sigismund politely responded. And although some spoke briefly, like nuncio Francesco Simonetta, who gave a "short and solemn speech", bishop Benedykt Woyna perorated on behalf of himself, the senators of Lithuania, and the Grand Duchy of Lithuania "for almost an hour".[217]

It must have already been the afternoon of the hot summer's day when the procession with the sounds of timpani and trumpets moved off towards the city. The hills before the city (presumably the Rossa Hill) were filled with crowds of Vilnius inhabitants. In front of the Gate of Dawn (the Miednicka Gate) the king was greeted by 400 burghers on horseback and on foot, as well

[216] In the Dresden copy there is a mistake: "*Marcus Sobieski, Vexillifer Regni*". See *Triumfo diena*, p. 125.

[217] "*Antistes Vilnensis exorsus salutatoriam orationem laudisque sacrae regiae maiestati exagenans et debitum observantiae cultum cum gratulatione coniugens integra fere hora peroravit; non minus perbenigne et clementer quam diserte et eleganter ab ipsamet sacra regia maiestate eidem responsum*" (*Triumphus et ingressus*, f. 182r.; *Triumfo diena*, p. 134).

as by the city council, whose representative gave a solemn speech. In the sixteenth and seventeenth centuries the municipal authorities of the royal cities (Gdańsk, Cracow, Toruń, etc.) made every attempt to stress the fact that they were also the members of the Commonwealth (*respublica*).[218] It was the same in Vilnius, especially when the king arrived in the city.

The gate itself was turned into a stemmatic construct:

> When they entered the gate, as we read in the account, an eagle made by a craftsman waved its wings, turned its neck, lifted its beak and head, and gave a greeting with the words that were hung above the gate with the coats of arms of his royal majesty.[219]

Just behind the Gate of Dawn (the Miednicka Gate) there was a *theatrum*, presumably a kind of stage from which students of the Academy of Vilnius gave their declamations. The king was greeted yet again next to the Orthodox church of the Holy Spirit and the Uniate church of the Holy Trinity with the music of church bells and singing. The students of the Orthodox Brotherhood school greeted the king and "all hailed the king with Greek [that is Orthodox] poems and music from an ornate and costly-built stage".[220] The Uniates also greeted the king with music. At the end of the account, its anonymous author quoted the song of the Uniates and the poems declaimed by the Orthodox students.[221]

[218] FRIEDRICH, "Royal entries into Cracow, Warsaw and Danzig", pp. 386-387. This valuable publication is accompanied by English translations of sources describing public festivals in the Polish Crown (with Royal Prussia) in the sixteenth-eighteenth centuries.

[219] *Ibid.*, f. 182v. Similar mechanical eagles were built in Cracow. One of them has survived to this day on the organ of St. Mary's church in Cracow, see K. TARGOSZ, "Oprawa artystyczno-ideowa wjazdów weselnych trzech sióstr Habsburżanek (Kraków 1592 i 1605, Florencja 1608)", in: *Theatrum ceremoniale na dworze książąt i królów polskich. Materiały konferencji naukowej zorganizowanej przez Zamek Królewski na Wawelu i Instytut Historii Uniwersytetu Jagiellońskiego w dniach 23-25 marca 1998*, ed. M. MARKIEWICZ and R. SKOWRON (Cracow, 1999), p. 211.

[220] "*Quando haec cessant, iuventus schismaticorum in theatro opposito ornate et sumptuose extructo carmina Graeca harmoniae musicis iungit serenissimumque salutat, qui ulterius aggrediens ab arcu triumphali a civibus et mercatoribus sumptuose artificioseque erecto (cuius est ad finem narrationis description) sistitur*" (*Triumphs et ingressus*, f. 182v., *Triumfo diena*, pp. 144-145).

[221] Three Orthodox poems were written in Latin in elegiac distichs. The Uniate songs were fragments of the Psalms in Church Slavonic. The anonymous author wrote them not in Cyrillic script but in Latin script, with Polish orthography. On the margins Latin versions of the Psalms were added (see *Triumfo diena*, pp. 308-324). Musical notation was added, which was unusual

Two triumphal arches were erected in the city centre, one financed by the townsmen at the intersection of Ostra Street and the Market Square, and the other one "at a significant cost" by the Jesuits on Zamkowa (Pilies) Street, between St. John's church and the Radziwiłłs' palace. A third arch was built near the castle. It was commissioned by the queen and designed by the king's chaplain Ruggiero Solomonio. The arches were decorated "*emblematibus ac schematibus*".[222] Speeches were given at the first two arches, but especially sophisticated declamations could be heard at the Jesuit arch. The anonymous author of the account quotes the texts, among them chants and poems performed by Jesuit students.[223] The arches are meticulously described.

The Mass, at which the *Te Deum* was sung solemnly, took place at the Bernardines, because the cathedral was still in ruins after the previous year's fire. In front of the church the chapter and the Orthodox clergy welcomed the king. Of course, all these events were accompanied by speeches. Towards the evening, the king and his retinue went to the palace at the lower castle. The third triumphal arch was erected here, in front of the gate, next to which the royal ensemble played. The arch closed the route through the city like a clasp, as it was decorated with a stemma with the Pogoń, analogous to the Polish White Eagle at the Gate of Dawn. Their entrance into the palace was accompanied by salutes fired from cannons in both castles, and by the sound of timpani and trumpets.

Similar entries like the one in 1611 took place both earlier and later. Stephen Báthory, for instance, was greeted splendidly in March 1579 and February 1582, and Sigismund III's first entry took place in 1589, when he was heading to Sweden. The greatest celebrations of this type were held on 24 June 1634 during the triumphal entry of Władysław IV Vasa following his victory at Smolensk[224] and on 19 March 1648, when Queen Marie Louise Gonzaga was received for the first time, and "Vilnius surpassed in terms of organisation and splendour seen [...] the coronation of the queen in Cracow".[225] The account entitled *Triumphus et ingressus* allows us to see how many texts were written in connection with this event. Panegyrical speeches were mentioned as *oratio gratulatoria*, *salutatoria*, and *eucharistica* (congratulatory, greeting, and

in such publications. See A. PISTER, "Uniate chants glorifying Sigismund Vasa's triumph: Features of musical structure and notation", in: *Triumfo diena*, pp. 85-89.

[222] *Triumphs et ingressus*, f. 182v., *Triumfo diena*, p. 146.

[223] *Triumfo diena*, pp. 180-182, 210-216.

[224] RADZIWIŁŁ, *Pamiętnik o historii w Polsce*, vol. 1, *1632-1636*, p. 380.

[225] RADZIWIŁŁ, *Pamiętnik o historii w Polsce*, vol. 3, *1647-1656*, p. 70.

thanksgiving speeches). Many examples of these have been preserved in seventeenth-century manuscripts.[226] They include a speech given by Maciej Kazimierz Sarbiewski on behalf of the Academy on the occasion of Władysław IV's arrival in Vilnius in 1636, recorded as a model in a textbook of rhetoric, and another printed speech by this author was delivered after the ceremonial translation of the remains of St. Casimir.[227] A number of printed publications accompanied the most important events. For example, in 1611 the triumph of King Sigismund III was accompanied by two panegyrics printed in Vilnius at that time.[228]

Since such events were a theatre of both religious and secular power, their culmination had to be a solemn Mass during which a sermon specially written for the occasion was delivered. In the 1630s, father Jakub Olszewski, a professor of the Academy of Vilnius, specialised in this type of official occasional sermon. He spoke twice on behalf of the Jesuits, for instance after the Smolensk victory of 1634, and both sermons, which glorified the Vasa family, Lithuania, and the Catholic Church, were published by the Academic printing house.[229]

[226] *Na wjazd jego mości pana Chodkiewicza wojewody wileńskiego witanie*, MS CZART. 1320 IV, ff. 44v-45v.

[227] M.K. SARBIEWSKI, *Oratio panegyrica habita in praesentia serenissimi ac invictissimi Vladislai IV Poloniae et Sueciae Regis a r. p. Matthia Casimiro Sarbiewski Societatis Iesu s. theologiae doctore et sacrae regiae maiestatis concionatore in solenni corporis C. Casimiri translatione, priusquam publica processione per urbis Vilnae plateas in regium cathedralis templi sacellum deferretur anno 1636 14 Augusti* (Vilnius, 1636). Sarbiewski's two speeches from the 1630s were given as examples in Vilnius rhetoric manuals from the first half of the seventeenth century: *Quincunx rhetoricus in libros quattuor ad Caium Herennium, Marci Tulii Ciceronis, Aristotelis, Quintiliani et aliorum doctrinis illustratus*; the first is a salutation for bishop Benedykt Woyna, the second a speech of thanks to Władysław IV, who participated in Sarbiewski's doctoral defence on 5 July 1636. Soon afterwards Sarbiewski was appointed royal preacher. See MS MAB F41-612, pp. 261, 264. A copy of the salutation for bishop Woyna is also included in MS CZART. 1659 IV, pp. 379-380.

[228] G. BORASTA (Gregorius Laurentius Borastius), *Panegyricus Sigismundo III, Poloniae et Sveciae regi etc. etc. invictissimo* (Vilnius, 1611); Cesare Baroffi, *In triumpho serenissimi ac potentissimi principis Sigismundi III Poloniae et Sveciae Regis etc. etc. e Moscovia post insignes gloriosae partas victorias feliciter redenuntis oratio* (Vilnius, 1611). See A. PERZANOWSKA, *Najjaśniejszym: Panegiryki i utwory pochwalne poświęcone królom i krolowym polskim w zbiorze starych druków Muzeum Narodowego w Krakowie* (Cracow, 2018), pp. 44-45, 47-48.

[229] J. OLSZEWSKI, *Tryumf przezacnej konwokacyjej wileńskiej ...*; ID., *Tryumf przesławnej Akademii Wileńskiej S.I. po zwycięstwie otrzymanym od Władysława IV króla polskiego, wielkiego książęcia litewskiego, kiedy 24 dnia lutego roku tego zwyciężywszy wojsko moskiewskie pod Smoleńskiem obóz nieprzyjacielski z armatą wzięli. Kazaniem przy podziękowaniu Panu Bogu wystawiony: Per eundem Jacobum Olszewski S.I., sanctae theologiae doctorem, almae Academiae Vil-*

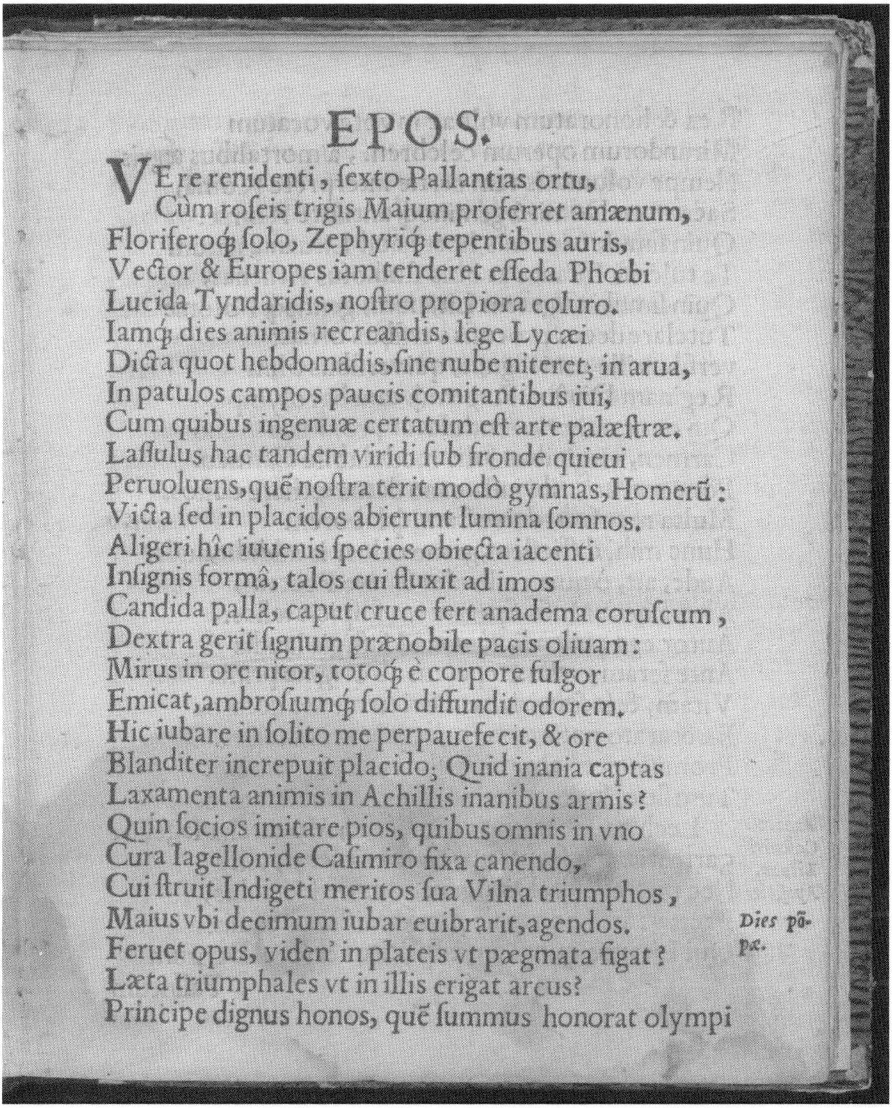
EPOS.

VEre renidenti, ſexto Pallantias ortu,
Cùm roſeis trigis Maium proferret amænum,
Floriferoq; ſolo, Zephyriq; tepentibus auris,
Vector & Europes iam tenderet eſſeda Phœbi
Lucida Tyndaridis, noſtro propiora coluro.
Iamq; dies animis recreandis, lege Lycæi
Dicta quot hebdomadis, ſine nube niteret; in arua,
In patulos campos paucis comitantibus iui,
Cum quibus ingenuæ certatum eſt arte palæſtræ.
Laſſulus hac tandem viridi ſub fronde quieui
Peruoluens, quẽ noſtra terit modò gymnas, Homerũ:
Victa ſed in placidos abierunt lumina ſomnos.
Aligeri hîc iuuenis ſpecies obiecta iacenti
Inſignis formâ, talos cui fluxit ad imos
Candida palla, caput cruce fert anadema coruſcum,
Dextra gerit ſignum prænobile pacis oliuam:
Mirus in ore nitor, totoq; è corpore fulgor
Emicat, ambroſiumq; ſolo diffundit odorem.
Hic iubare inſolito me perpauefecit, & ore
Blanditer increpuit placido; Quid inania captas
Laxamenta animis in Achillis inanibus armis?
Quin ſocios imitare pios, quibus omnis in vno
Cura Iagellonide Caſimiro fixa canendo,
Cui ſtruit Indigeti meritos ſua Vilna triumphos,
Maius vbi decimum iubar euibrarit, agendos. *Dies põpæ.*
Feruet opus, viden' in plateis vt pægmata figat?
Læta triumphales vt in illis erigat arcus?
Principe dignus honos, quẽ ſummus honorat olympi

Fig. 63 Latin epos commemorating the canonisation of St. Casimir in 1604. Jan Krajkowski, *Epos de S. Casimioro Iagellonide Poloniae ac Lituaniae principe et patrono* (Vilnius, 1604), f. A3r. Warsaw, BN. <https://polona.pl/preview/493caa51-8467-4446-b353-700f1ac4508> (accessed: 06.06.2023; public domain).

nensis procancellarium et ordinarium ecclesiae parochialis Vilnensis concionatorem w kościele farskim św. Jana wileńskim 12 dnia marca (Vilnius, 1634).

Triumphal arches were texts which offered exceptional opportunities for combining multiple forms of messages. Such constructions consisted of a combination of architecture, sculpture, and painting, and they formed the background for the rhetorical performance that they presented, being at the same time an emblem and theatrical decoration themselves. Unfortunately, we do not know what the examples of occasional architecture listed in the *Triumphus et ingressus* looked like. We can only suppose that they resembled those raised for the Vasas in Gdańsk and Cracow.[230] Detailed descriptions of the arches and street decorations put up on the occasion of the canonisation celebrations of St. Casimir have survived. The event was held in Vilnius on 10 May 1604.[231] These temporary buildings stood in the same places as seven years later during the entry of Sigismund: the burgher's arch was erected by the Market Square, the Jesuit one was by St. John's church, and the capitular one in front of the castle.

In 1604, the academic arch was about sixteen metres high and eight metres wide, and fifteen people could pass through its gate at the same time. White and blue flags hung on both sides. The portal of the gate featured Chastity on the right-hand side and Piety on the left, with subscriptions. Above the portal were the coloured coats of arms of bishop Woyna and the Jesuits. In the centre of the arch was placed the image of St. Casimir. Above it, two angels emerged from the clouds, placing a golden wreath on the saint's temples. He was surrounded by the patrons of Vilnius parish church, St. John the Evangelist with a rose and lilies and St. John the Baptist with a green sprig. Each figure was provided with an epigram, which together constituted an 'emblem'. On the sides there were two balconies on which musicians sat. Above it, the two-metre high statues of St. Adalbert, the patron saint of Poland, and St. Nicolas, the patron saint of Lithuania, and the Pogoń at the very top. On the lower sides of the arch (under which wicket gates were probably located) were the patron saints of the Lithuanian nobility, Saints George and Martin riding horses. "The hanging hind legs of horses", writes the author of the report, Kwiryn Knogler (Quirinus Cnoglerus), "were masterfully carved and even more elaborately painted".[232] In these places there were epigraphs, quotations from Holy Scrip-

[230] CHROŚCICKI, *Sztuka i polityka*, p. 43; TARGOSZ, *Oprawa artystyczno-ideowa*, pp. 241-242; B. FABIANI, *Życie codzienne na Zamku Kólewskim w epoce Wazów* (Warsaw, 1996), pp. 163-164; ULČINAITĖ, *Utwory powitalne*, p. 55.

[231] CNOGLERUS, "Pompa Casimiriana", pp. 83-88, 110-113.

[232] *Ibid.*, p. 111.

ture. In addition to these images, other historical and allegorical representations were painted on the arch.

In 1604, performances in Polish, Greek, and Latin were given at each of the arches; their content was quoted by Knogler.[233] The central element of these buildings was the word, and therefore literary texts may be one of the keys to unravelling the depictions featured on these objects. Thanks to the Jesuit anthologies of texts published to mark solemn entries, we can decipher the ideological programme of these temporary buildings. The printed panegyrics were analogues, or literary equivalents of the urban space in which the spectacle of power took place.[234]

Poems published in these anthologies were authored by students of the Academy. They were mostly written in Latin, although some of these collections contained cycles of poems in various languages. An exceptionally high number of such poems is to be found in the *Certamen linguarum* cycle, attached to the anthology *Ver Lukiskanum* presented by the Jesuits to King Władysław IV and Queen Marie Louise Gonzaga, who stayed in their residence in Lukiškės near Vilnius in 1648.[235] This publication contains, among other things, epigrams written in no fewer than eighteen languages.[236] The custom of publishing and presenting such works, however, began much earlier, with the collection *Gratulationes* of 1579, which consists of twenty-two works and cycles for King Stephen Báthory.[237]

[233] CNOGLERUS, *Pompa Casimiriana sive de labaro d. Casimiri*, pp. 101-111.

[234] E.J. PETERS, "Printing ritual: The performance of community in Christopher Plantin's La Joyeuse et Magnifique Entrée de Monseigneur Francoys ... d'Anjou", *Renaissance Quarterly* 61 (2008), p. 373.

[235] ULČINAITĖ, *Utwory powitalne*, p. 57.

[236] Two epigrams are written *Anglicae* and *Scoticae*. In fact, both of them are in English:

Anglicae

Into its own tears turned Lukiscos snow
Weathred the bed where Aprilis lillies grow.

Scoticae

Bony Lukisos, whose beauty in the Spring
The Queen delights and recreates the King.

Ver lukiskanum, p. C2v.

[237] *Ibid.*, pp. 37-39. BUSZEWICZ and NIEDŹWIEDŹ, *Wprowadzenie do lektury*.

The poems included in these anthologies were recited by students of the Academy, usually dressed up as allegorical figures, such as Religio, Respublica Litteraria, and Respublica Polona. The performances took place during the entries themselves (in 1611 by the Gate of Dawn and the triumphal arch), during rulers' visits to the university, or during performances in the royal castle. In 1579, the Jesuits reported that during a performance staged in the lower castle, students were to play the representatives of ten provinces of the Polish-Lithuanian Commonwealth and recite panegyrical poems and multilingual speeches, dressed in corresponding regional costumes. King Báthory was gifted a stemmatic composition that consisted of works written by students and received a "volume of poetry printed on the occasion of his arrival".[238] This was probably the *Gratulationes* mentioned above. An account of the performance of Kacper Pętkowski's dialogue of February 1582, also performed for Stephen Báthory, has survived.[239]

Apart from the Jesuit anthologies that accompanied state ceremonies, such as the entries of monarchs and other important persons (for instance the Muscovite legates on 5 January 1602, as described by Eliasz Pielgrzymowski[240]), homages (for instance of the duke of Courland in 1639), weddings, or funeral services (for instance following the death of Queen Constance of Austria in 1631[241]), in the first half of the seventeenth century other panegyrics were also published, usually in the form of speeches or occasional sermons, rarely in various forms of poetry, such as elogia or songs. The largest number of such texts was published after the Smolensk victory in 1634: at least ten were published in Vilnius alone.[242] The operas staged at the lower castle also conveyed

[238] A letter by Krzysztof Warszewicki to Francisco Sunyer dated 14 January 1578, as quoted in: PIECHNIK, *Początki Akademii Wileńskiej*, p. 56; see J. POPLATEK, *Studia z dziejów jezuickiego teatru szkolnego w Polsce* (Wrocław, 1957), p. 138; ULČINAITĖ, *Utwory powitale*, p. 39.

[239] K. PĘTKOWSKI, *Dialog o pokoju dla króla Stefana*, trans. H. SZCZERKOWSKA, in: *Dramaty staropolskie: Antologia*, ed. J. LEWAŃSKI, 4 (Warsaw, 1961), p. 365-418; K. PĘTKOWSKI, "*Περί τής Είρήνης πρός τόν Βασιλέα Στέφανον διαλογέ*", in: *Łacińskie dialogi*, pp. 125-149; ULČINAITĖ, *Utwory powitalne*, p. 43.

[240] PIELGRZYMOWSKI, *Poselstwo*, pp. 215-216.

[241] The funeral celebrations are mentioned by Jakub Olszewski in the foreword to the funeral sermon *Żałoba po śmierci najjaśniejszej Konstancjej królowej polskiej, księżny litewskiej etc., arcyksiężny rakuskiej w kościele katedralnym wileńskim 19 iulii 1631 wystawiona przez ks. Jakuba Olszewskiego Soc<ietatis> Iesu doctora i dziekana św. teologijej, kościoła farskiego wileńskiego kaznodzieje* (Vilnius, 1631).

[242] These were works signed with the names of Mikołaj Grodziński, Zygmunt Lauksmin, Stanisław Florian Obryński, Jakub Olszewski, Benedykt Piotrowicz, Aleksander Radoński, Jan Rywocki, Mikołaj Sapieha, and Aleksander Walerian Wysocki. See NOWAK-DŁUŻEWSKI, *Okolicz-*

a panegyrical and propaganda message.[243] Most of these panegyrics and two opera libretti were printed by the Jesuit printing house, which testifies to the symbiosis of the monarchy and the Society of Jesus with respect to the formation of literature and official art.

The latter aspect can also be seen quite clearly in the account of 1611. The triumph of Sigismund III Vasa was organised in such a way that its undertone was clearly Catholic and monarchical. Probably such an ideological message was dictated by the king's propaganda services, led by Polish vice-chancellor Feliks Kryski.[244] As far as possible, nuances that could destroy the uniform rhetorical image of the 'Catholic' capital of Lithuania were overshadowed. However, cracks and scratches are discernible in this image. For instance, the first place of worship the king had to pass was the 'schismatic' church of the Holy Spirit. Worse still, the teachers and students of the Orthodox Brotherhood's school (it is not known whether it was still managed by Melecjusz Smotrycki) staged a performance and, like the Jesuits, organised declamations in honour of the ruler. Considering the fact that the Orthodox Church was persecuted at that time and less than a year earlier scandalous events connected with the publication of the *Thrēnos* took place,[245] the rhetorical action of the Brotherhood turned out to be a manifestation of the presence of the Orthodox Church in the city. However, in order to somewhat weaken its force, the organisers of the king's entry set up a stage just behind the Gate of Dawn, where Jesuit students performed, thanks to which Vilnius welcomed the king as a Catholic city. In order to avoid similar inconveniences, several years later, precisely at the place of the Jesuit performance, the Carmelite monastery was built, to which, in the times of King Władysław IV (1632-1648), the early baroque church of St. Teresa was added. Although founded by chancellor Stefan Pac, it was decorated with the Swedish marble and the coat of arms of the Vasa's Sheaf (*Snopek*) above the main portal.[246]

nościowa poezja polityczna w dawnej Polsce: Dwaj młodsi Wazowie, p. 319.

[243] TARGOSZ-KRETOWA, *Teatr dworski*, pp. 98-103; RASZEWSKI, *Krótka historia teatru polskiego* (Warsaw, 1978), p. 31.

[244] U. AUGUSTYNIAK, *Informacja i propaganda w Polsce za Zygmunta III* (Warsaw, 1981); G. FRANCZAK, "Faex gentium: Polacy w Moskwie wobec rosyjskiej "mniejszości" (1606-1612)", in: *Etniczność, tożsamość, literatura: Zbiór studiów*, ed. P. BUKOWIEC and D. SIWOR (Cracow, 2010), pp. 48-49.

[245] See Chapter 9.

[246] In 1587 Prince Sigismund Vasa, son of Swedish King John III of Sweden and Queen Catherina Jagiellon, was elected King of Poland and Grand Duke of Lithuania. He initiated the Polish-Lithuanian branch of the Vasa dynasty which ruled until 1668.

While it was not possible to ignore Orthodox Christians at the time of the king's entry in 1611, not a single word was said about other confessions, even Protestants. As we will remember, three weeks before the triumph a tumult found place in the city, during which the Calvinist church [*zbór*] was burnt down. Although the author of the *Triumphus et ingressus* mentioned the officials who came to the session of the Lithuanian Tribunal, he did not even allude to the main court case to be settled in the near future, that is the finding and punishing of those guilty of the tumult. The king's route ran near the devastated church, but the story was drowned out by shooting from cannons and joyful trumpet fanfares.

This official ideological unity reached its climax during the reign of Władysław IV. The procession that accompanied the translation of the remains of St. Casimir on 14 August 1636 to the newly built chapel in the cathedral was a great propaganda spectacle, in which not only Catholics and other Christians, but also Jews and Muslims participated. According to Albrycht Stanisław Radziwiłł, they paid homage to a member of the ruling dynasty.[247] The personification of unity was the king himself:

> Today, we all sing Alleluia following the king's example, we all worship God and thank his majesty because he gave the widowed homeland a spouse, presented the Commonwealth with a skilful governor, a faithful guardian of our rights and freedoms, a zealous patron of churches and all clergy, a softhearted maecenas of the Academy, a merciful carer for the infirm, as well as a master and father of all the people.[248]

A visible sign of the continuity between the Jagiellonian and Vasa dynasties was the chapel of St. Casimir, whom the Vasas, in an elogium carved on the wall of the building, called their relative, while their own family was described as the 'Jagiellonids' (see Fig. 54). This inscription resonates with a panegyrical speech delivered by Maciej Kazimierz Sarbiewski and the ode composed four years earlier on the occasion of the election of Władysław IV, which closes his *Lyricorum libri IV*: "May the first descendant of the last Sigismund and the closest offspring of the ancient Jagiellons reign".[249]

[247] CHYNCZEWSKA-HENNEL, *Nuncjusz i król*, pp. 195-196.

[248] OLSZEWSKI, *Triumf przezacnej Akademii Wileńskiej*, f. A3v.

[249] In his speech, Sarbiewski mentioned all the Jagiellonian rulers who were in heaven (as everyone, according to the speakers, deems), presenting Sigismund III Vasa and Władysław IV Vasa as their arch-Christian successors. M.K. SARBIEWSKI, *Oratio panegyrica*, pp. 13-14. M.K.

In the seventeenth century, grand entries and other state ceremonies provided occasions to bring history up to date and contextualise it anew. Each time, the organisers used new works (for instance a triumphal arch, Sarbiewski's speech, poetic cycles), which reminded one of the legitimacy of Sigismund or Władysław's rule over Vilnius. In such moments, the city was becoming more than an everyday capital of the Grand Duchy of Lithuania, a monument to its identity and a place of memory.

The Other Side of the Coin, or Bills

The author of the account called *Triumphus et ingressus* mentions several times that Persian tents were expensive, that the Jesuits built their triumphal arch at considerable cost, and that the king's robes were made of a valuable material. The show had its price, but for obvious reasons the narrative omits financial questions. This does not alter the fact that someone had to pay and document the expenses. Although the bills and documents from July 1611 have not survived, we can guess that the amount of paper used to make them may have been equal to the number of sheets needed to print the panegyrics for the king.

The organisation of any celebration in the city required fairly complicated logistics. Even a poor widow's ordering a requiem mass was reflected in church documentation.[250] The funeral of mayor Kiewlicz required far more complicated bookkeeping (as already mentioned), not to mention royal entries, processions, or enthronements of bishops. When it comes to Vilnius epideictic texts, we must not forget the texts that constituted their economic infrastructure. The most valuable documents of this type are lists of lodgings suitable for the stay of the royal court when Władysław IV visited the city in 1636 and 1639. The quartermaster (*stanowniczy*), a court clerk responsible for accommodation, walked from house to house along all the streets of Vilnius and drew up

Sarbiewski, Ode IV 38 *Ad Libertatem: Cum Vladislaus IV maximis ad Vistulam comitiis rex Poloniae renuntiaretur*, in: ID., *Liryki oraz Droga rzymska i fragment Lechiady*, ed. M. KOROLKO and J. OKOŃ, trans. T. KARYŁOWSKI (Warsaw, 1980), p. 434. See NOWAK-DŁUŻEWSKI, *Okolicznościowa poezja polityczna w Polsce: Dwaj młodsi Wazowie*, p. 15.

[250] E.g. the list of mass intentions of the Lithuanian Jesuits from 1583-1634: *Anno Domini 1583 Iussu R.P. Provincialis Suffragia scripta Vilnae 1 Februarii*, MS BJ 185.

a detailed register of the majority of buildings in the Lithuanian capital.[251] This is only one of the economic records relating to the practical organisation of royal stays in Vilnius and the accompanying celebrations. Since the expenditure books of Vilnius city hall, the Academy of Vilnius, and the castle have been lost, we will probably never find out about the expenses relating to the publication of panegyrics, the organisation of entries, balls, fireworks, or operas staged in the royal castle.

Is A Scholarly Text Demonstrative?

Using the traditional rhetorical categories, it is difficult unambiguously to assign a function to scholarly texts based on a traditional rhetorical schema. In principle, one should speak of instruction (*docere*) or, using a more modern term, information. At the same time, however, we must not forget about the persuasion and creativity of academic texts, which is what contemporary theorists of science draw attention to.[252] Following these assumptions, Stanley Fish emphasises the rhetorical aspect of science,[253] but ignores some of the implications of such approach. In the case of scholarly literature created in Vilnius before the mid-seventeenth century, its rhetoricity cannot be reduced to persuasion and the creation of meaning alone, as a scholarly text of the time may have been an example of each of the three types of rhetoric. First of all, it informed and convinced the reader of a certain stance, using logical and rhetorical argumentation. Secondly, it opposed, overtly or covertly, an existing understanding of an issue. Thirdly, it used certain aesthetic rules. Even if it was a formalised argument, the author must pay attention to aesthetics and linguistic correctness, if only for the language to be communicative and for the argument to be orderly. In other words, a sixteenth- and seventeenth-century researcher must use art: *ars*.[254]

[251] *Rewizyja gospód dworu jego królewskiego mości w mieście Wilnie*; PAKNYS, *Vilniaus miestas ir miestiečiai 1636 m.*

[252] T.S. KUHN, *The Structure of Scientific Revolutions* (Chicago and London, 1996), pp. 176-187.

[253] S. FISH, "Demonstration vs. persuasion: Two models of critical cctivity", in: ID., *Is There a Text in this Class?*, pp. 356-372; ID., "Rhetoric", in: ID., *Doing What Comes Naturally: Change, Rhetoric, and the Practice of Theory in Literary and Legal Studies* (Durham and London, 1989), pp. 485-494.

[254] K. TARGOSZ, "Jedność nauki i sztuki w dziele dzieła Jana Heweliusza", *Quarterly of the History of Science and Technology* 21.4 (1976), pp. 634-640.

Many Vilnius scholarly texts were by their nature examples of epideictic literature. This was true particularly of historical works, which at that time were treated as a branch of oratory, for instance *Moscovia* by Antonio Possevino, published in Vilnius in 1586, or *Historia Lituana* by Wojciech Wijuk Kojałowicz (Albertas Kojalavičius-Vijūkas) (its first part appeared in Gdańsk in 1650, while part two appeared in Antwerp in 1669). One of the main goals set by Kojałowicz was to present the history of the Grand Duchy of Lithuania in elegant, humanist Latin. This work, which today inspires ever more vivid scholarly interest, is one of the most important historical narratives on seventeenth-century Lithuania. Kojałowicz relied greatly on the chronicle of the Grand Duchy of Lithuania by Maciej Stryjkowski (1582), complemented it with events from the following decades, rewrote it, and also gave it a new literary shape. In Kojałowicz's version Stryjkowski's text, which had been polyphonic, multi-styled, and had combined narrative prose with Virgilian stylistics adapted to the Polish alexandrine, was replaced by an imitation of Roman historiography. Following Livy's example, he introduced speeches and even dialogues into the text.[255]

The epideictic component is even more clearly visible in Kojałowicz's minor historical texts, devoted to the genealogy of the Radziwiłł family and the Cossack uprising between 1648 and 1649.[256] All these works also had other functions, especially instructive ones (*docere*), but even a superficial analysis of the text allows us to relate them to the culture of rhetorical praise. This culture is reflected in particular in popular historical accounts such as the works of Samuel Dowgird, a courtier of the *voivode* of Vilnius Krzysztof II Radziwiłł, who wrote biographies of rulers of the Grand Duchy of Lithuania.[257]

[255] D. Dilytė, "Alberto Vijūko-Kojalavičiaus Lietuvos istorijos kalbos", *Senoji Lietuvos literatūra*, 27 (2009): *Albertas Vijūkas-Kojalavičius iš 400 metų perspektyvos*, pp. 118-119, 130-133.

[256] A. Kojalavičius-Vijūkas, *Fasti Radiviliani gesta illustrissimae domus ducum Radziwił compendio continentes* (Vilnius, 1653); id., *Copiarum Magni Ducatus Lituaniae adversus Zaporowianos Cozacos anno 1648 et 1649 gesta compendiario narrata* (Vilnius, 1651). Reprints of both works have been published together with their Lithuanian translation: A. Vijūkas-Kojalavičius (W. Wijuk Kojałowicz), *Lietuvos istorijos įvairenybės*, 1, ed. D. Kuolys, trans. D. Antanavičius and S. Narbutas (Vilnius, 2003).

[257] S. Dowgird, *Genealogia albo krótkie opisanie wielkich książąt litewskich i ich wielkich a mężnych spraw wojennych uczynione niegdy przez Matysa Strykowskiego, teraz odnowione i znowu na świat wydane przez Samuela Dougirda z Pogowia* (Lubcz, 1626); edition with a Lithuanian translation: S. Daugirdas, *Genealogija, arba Trumpas didžiųjų Lietuvos kunigaikščių ir jų didžių bei narsių žygių aprašymas, kadaise Motiejaus Strijkovskio sukurtas, o dabar atnaujintas ir vėl išleistas Samuelio Daugirdo iš Pagaujo*, ed. and trans. R. Koženiauskienė, *with* comments

At the other end of the spectrum are diarists and sylvic diaries, such as Maciej Vorbek-Lettow's, that were less based on the *ars* and were therefore valued as working collections of information on historical events.

Other scholarly works written in Vilnius had to have, even if for formal reasons only, the structure of a treatise but were subject to many rules of a rhetorical epideictic kind. These were studies in the field of rhetoric by Kazimierz Jan Wojsznarowicz and the Jesuits Kazimierz Wijuk Kojałowicz (Kazimieras Kojalavičius-Vijūkas) and Zygmunt Lauksmin,[258] the latter's being studies in the field of music theory, and Marcin Śmiglecki's treatise on usury. Although we should not claim too categorically that all scholarly literature of the sixteenth century and the first half of the seventeenth century was exclusively rhetorical,[259] we can put forward a hypothesis that the discourse in the works of scholars who worked in Lithuania in that period was partially epideictic in nature.

Early modern scholars, who believed that truth can be attained through rationalist study of the phenomena surrounding them, described those phenomena using rhetorised language, that is language criticised for its figurativeness, imprecision, and 'non-scholarly character' over the following centuries. Like a poet, an orator can use dangerous tricks to seduce listeners, to present them with an image of reality he wants to convey to them rather thanan image of what is 'real'. This was Plato's basic accusation against the sophists,[260] and similar objections against rhetoric were put forward by his successors.[261] At the opposite pole of the rhetorical model of language, there was a scientific language of description, free from any manipulation, strict, like the language of St. Thomas Aquinas and the Thomists, among whom the Jesuits acquired a promi-

by K. GUDMANTAS (Vilnius, 2001).

[258] K. WOJSZNAROWICZ, *Orator polityczny różnym aktom pogrzebowym służący, nowo na świat w roku 1644 wydany* ([Vilnius] 1644); K. WIJUK KOJAŁOWICZ, *Institutionum rhetoricarum pars I-II* (Vilnius, 1654); Z. LAUXMIN, *Praxis oratoria sive praecepta artis rhetoricae, quae ad comparandum orationem necessaria sunt* (Frankfurt am Main, 1665), there is a reprint edition with Lithuanian translation by Eugenija Ulčinaitė in: Ž. LIAUKSMINAS (Z. Lauxmin), *Rinktiniai raštai: Opera selecta*, ed. B. GENZELIS (Vilnius, 2004).

[259] E. Buszewicz wrote a paper on the rhetorical nature of M.K. Sarbiewski's treatise *De acuto ac arguto / O poincie i dowcipie*, in: *Lektury polonistyczne: Retoryka a tekst literacki*, 1, ed. M. HANCZAKOWSKI and J. NIEDŹWIEDŹ (Cracow, 2003), pp. 23-52. The relations between rhetoric and dialectical argumentation were also studied by K. KOEHLER, *Stanisław Orzechowski i dylematy humanizmu renesansowego* (Cracow, 2004), pp. 37-51.

[260] Platon, *Gorgiasz*, in ID., *Gorgiasz: Menon*, trans. W. WITWICKI (Kęty, 2002), pp. 23-24.

[261] FISH, "Rhetoric", pp. 471-477.

nent place. Meanwhile, in many sixteenth- and seventeenth-century scholarly works it was normal to use techniques specific to the *ars bene dicendi*.

In the last two decades of the sixteenth century, even the lecturers of the Academy of Vilnius who taught philosophy, or more precisely logic, attached importance to more than just correctness when it came to constructing logical sentences. In the treatise called *Prologomena logica*, which perhaps dates from the early 1580s, an "*exemplum thematis coniuncti singularis*" can be found. The author of this lecture on fourteen topics considers the following issue: "*An ministri Vilnenses iure sint vulnerati*" ("Were the Vilnius ministers [probably Calvinists] rightly injured?").[262] Of course, the logical argumentation should be reducible to the correctness of the conclusions, and only this aspect should be important for a professor and his students. However, the whole logical structure was subordinate to a wider sphere, namely that of rhetoric. Logical reasoning was subject to rhetorical argumentation, and its value depended not only on the correctness of the argument, but also on its persuasive power.

In the polemical parts of scholarly works, we often encounter persuasion characteristic of *genus iudiciale* and strictly rhetorical devices (for instance *argumentatio ad personam*), for instance in the polemical treatise of the Jesuit Stanisław Grodzicki on sacred philology, devoted to the translation of the Bible into the Polish language:

> Let us, then, show both in the Brest and Nyasvizh Bibles no less cunning falsifications than those of Luther. And in order for this treatise to be more complete, we will start with their daddy, Calvin, and finish with Grzegorz of Żarnowiec, providing no more than one example of falsification for each of them, leaving many more for another occasion.[263]

In the light of what has been said above, a scholar, in this case a theologian, who believed that he was right and that his theory, for instance about the primacy of papal power, was true, acted in such a way as to convince as many

[262] *Prologomena logica* (1580s?), MS VUB F3-2171, ff. 217r-219r. On the following pages there is another example, probably referring to the wars fought by Stephen Báthory (1579-1582): *Exemplum thematis coniuncti comparati. An bellum Moschoviticum sit relinquendum an vero continuatum?*, *Ibid.*, ff. 221v-223r.

[263] S. GRODZICKI, *Prawidło wiary haeretyckiej: To jest okazanie, iż wodzowie kacerscy nie Pismo św. ale własny mózg swój za regułę albo prawidło wiary sobie mają: A przy tym pierwsza centuria albo sto jawnych fałszerstwa w wierze z obrony Postylle kacerskiej od fałecznego proroka Grzegorza Żarnowca wydanej zebranych* (Vilnius, 1592), p. 39. FRICK, *Polish Sacred Philology*, pp. 169-175.

supporters of a different theory as possible. The same was done by his opponents, who not only believed that the Pope was not the head of Christians and humanity, but also that he acted as Satan's tool. In this altercation between scholars, a great deal of evidence, witnesses, and testimonies were cited, but the weapon that determined success was rhetorical persuasion.

Philosophical and theological treatises should be treated separately. Where discussion concerns matter itself and where no controversial issues are strongly emphasised, dialectical argumentation usually comes to the fore. One of the oldest such treatises based mainly on logical persuasion is a manuscript manual on moral theology according to St. Thomas Aquinas *De caritate*, written between 1578 and 1580.[264] Several years later, Marcin Śmiglecki released a well-known study on logic, the first version written for the use of students of philosophy in Vilnius, which after publication also enjoyed popularity at the University of Oxford.[265]

The poetic treatises of Maciej Kazimierz Sarbiewski, including the *Praecepta poetica*, *De perfecta poesi* and *Dii gentium*, written for the needs of the college in Polatsk and the Academy of Vilnius, are based on a similar dialectic method of argumentation, although the argument is related to the rhetorical aspect to such an extent that it is difficult to separate these two layers. As recent research has shown, Sarbiewski used the concepts and methodology of St. Thomas Aquinas in his treatise *De acuto et arguto*, for instance in the manner he formulated his definitions.[266] Sarbiewski, known today mainly for his poetry, was first of all a philosopher and theologian, who studied, among other things, the *Summa theologiae* by Aquinas.

The rhetorical and epideictic aspect of many of the treatises by Sarbiewski, Lauksmin, Kojałowicz, and Śmiglecki mentioned above had one more dimension, that is performativity. These texts are lectures in written form, so the rhetorical *actio* must have been an essential, although not their ultimate, component. A scholar went through all the stages of the rhetorical preparation of

[264] MS BJ 2047.

[265] M. ŚMIGLECKI, *Logica ... selectis disputationibus et quaestionibus illustrata* (Igolstadt, 1618); see RYSZKA-KURCZAb, *op. cit.*, p. 203.

[266] This problem is discussed by Aleksandra Krogulska in an unpublished paper (A. KROGULSKA, "Chwyty dialektyczne w traktatach teoretycznoliterackich M. K. Sarbiewksiego na przykładzie rozprawy *De acuto et arguto*"); see A. KOŁOS, "Poetyka konceptu Macieja Kazimierza Sarbiewskiego w kręgu historii idei", *Forum Poetyki* (2017),1, pp. 6-17; H. SZABELSKA, "Między tęczą a kryształem: Echo u Macieja Kazimierza Sarbiewskiego jako gatunek odbicia w świetle jego komentarza do Summy teologicznej Akwinaty", *Terminus* 23.1 (2021), pp. 25-53.

the text, that is *inventio*, *dispositio*, and *elocutio*, he mastered the text by heart and delivered it, and then he returned to *elocutio* when he edited the texts written by his students. Somewhere along the way, the rhetorical power of the living word was revealed and captivated the students of Marcin Śmiglecki – amantissimi praeceptoris or of Jan Grużewski and Adam Rassius.[267] Performativity was constantly present in the life of Vilnius scholars, both during lectures, religious disputations, and during the defence of doctoral theses and other examinations.

The activities of the Academy, which were essentially conducted within its walls, were to a considerable extent directed towards the outside world, that is the city. Some of the scholarly texts produced in the Academy, such as rhetorical or philosophical treatises, in manuscript, were mainly intended for students of the collegium as teaching aids. Sometimes they left the Academy and wandered with them to distant places. On such occasions Vilnius once again was becoming an 'open' city. Printed texts, such as the dictionaries of Konstantinas Sirvydas (Konstanty Szyrwid), Grzegorz Knapiusz (Cnapius), and Salomon Rysiński, were mainly intended for external reception. The Academy turned out to be the place where the exchange and dialogue of texts between the city and the outside world took place. In literary culture (the literary field), it performed similar functions to the city seen as an area of economic exchange (in the economic field), that is it was an intermediary between the 'closed' city and the 'open' city.

The Building of Lithuanian Identity (The Panegyrical Art of the 'Open' City)

A Panegyrical History

As was mentioned above, the state ceremonies that were organised in the city used to make references to history. It was possible to invoke history, because during the sixteenth century Vilnius became the main centre for the production and presentation of historical texts intended to preserve the official version of the past of the Lithuanian state. Texts written and published in Vilnius contributed to the shaping of the identity of the Lithuanian nation and became an integral part of it. Although the beginnings of this process can be

[267] VORBEK-LETTOW, *Skarbnica pamięci*, pp. 14, 31.

traced back to the times of Alexander I Jagiellon (that is to the very end of the fifteenth century), it reached its culmination at the turn of the seventeenth and eighteenth centuries.

The triumphal arches raised to celebrate Władysław IV's entries into various cities of the Polish-Lithuanian Commonwealth – certainly including Vilnius – featured figures of rulers from the Jagiellonian dynasty, usually accompanied by an epigrammatic commentary.[268] In the Lithuanian capital the memory of this dynasty was 'reactivated' for the purposes of architectural panegyric not only because it was 'local', but also because according to the propaganda of the time the Vasa dynasty was descended from the Jogaila and Gediminas dynasties.[269] This suited both the Vasa family and the Lithuanian elites, that is the city authorities, officials, and the Jesuits. They financed the triumphal arches,[270] so they also approved of the ideological programme of the monuments. One of the few surviving texts of the city in which one can still read the epideictic game with history, is St. Casimir's chapel, completed in 1636. It is a Jagiellonian-Vasovian mausoleum, which makes reference to the architecture of Sigismund's chapel in Cracow cathedral. A similar project is the Vasa chapel erected thirty years later (in 1664-1666 and 1679) in the Wawel cathedral in Cracow.[271]

However, it seems that not only the propaganda of the royal court, which generally remained outside Lithuania, helped to strengthen the official interpretation of the state's history, but that it was also consolidated by the joint actions of the Lithuanian magnates and nobility, together with the humanists who were their clients. The works of the Jesuit poet, speaker, and theoretician of elocution Kazimierz Wijuk Kojałowicz, who in the 1660s was rector of the

[268] P.P. PIASECKI, *Kronika* (Cracow, 1870), pp. 80-81; CHROŚCICKI, *Sztuka i polityka*, pp. 35-45.

[269] The members of the Polish-Lithuanian branch of the Swedish Vasa dynasty, who ruled the Polish Lithuanian-Commonwealth between 1587 and 1668, were descendants of the Jagiellons. King Sigismund III Vasa (1566-1632) was the son of the Queen of Sweden, Catherina Jagiellon (1526-1583), and a grandson of King Sigismund I the Old. In their propaganda the Vasas stressed their Jagiellonian origins. The relationships between Vasas and Jagiellonians were expressed in many works of art and monuments founded by Sigismund III, Władysław IV, and John Casimir Vasa, e.g. the Sigismund Column in Warsaw (1644) and the Vasa chapel in the Wawel cathedral in Cracow (1666). See CHROŚCICKI, *Sztuka i polityka*, pp. 35-45.

[270] A.S. Radziwiłł wrote: "On the fifteenth day of that month [January 1639] an entry to Vilnius [took place]. The city spent a lot to welcome the new queen, who came here for the first time" (A.S. RADZIWIŁŁ, *Pamiętnik o historii w Polsce*, 3, *1637-1646*, pp. 117-118).

[271] KARPOWICZ, *Baroque in Poland*, p. 306, picture 143. In this chapel most of the members of the Polish-Lithuanian branch of the Vasa dynasty are buried.

Academy of Vilnius, are quite exemplary in this regard. He was repeatedly asked to write panegyrics dedicated to the patrons of the congregation, including King Władysław IV, bishop Walerian Protasewicz, Jerzy Tyszkiewicz, and the Lithuanian chancellor Albrycht Stanisław Radziwiłł. Since a panegyric was a story about the deeds of heroes, the history of their ancestors had to become an inseparable part of it, and their background was always the history of the Grand Duchy of Lithuania, including its mythical history. Kojałowicz and other panegyrists consolidated the legends that had already been instilled in this way, for instance the ethnogenetic myth about the arrival of Palemon and his Roman companions in Lithuania, the legend of the founding of the capital, or symbolic events such as the battles of Grunwald (1410) and Orsha (1514), and finally the figures of legendary and historical national heroes. A panegyric from 1644 in honour of Prince Charles Ferdinand Vasa, who had just become the bishop of Płock, consists of five prosopopoeiae, delivered by the prince's personified coats of arms. The rider depicted on the Lithuanian coat of arms, Pogoń, talked about the images of Lithuanian rulers in the following manner:

> This painting shows the excellent triumphant Gediminas. It features the frightening Algidras, who threatens the Muscovite power. Additionally, the vanquisher of the Teutonic Knights and Asians, Vytautas. Moreover, the eternal decoration of the world, the fear of enemies, the phenomenon of his times and yours, Prince Charles, great relative, Władysław Jagiełło (Jogaila).[272] (original in Latin)

The same figures and events were presented in another form by Jan Radwan several decades earlier, in the epic *Radivilias* from 1592, which praises Mikołaj Radziwiłł 'the Red'.[273] The shield of the Radziwiłłs' coat of arms presented in the third book of the poem, equivalent to the shield of Aeneas, depicts the history of Lithuania from the arrival of Palemon, a legendary relative to the emperor Nero, to the present day of the author. It features the same figures

[272] K. WIJUK-KOJAŁOWICZ (Kojalavičius-Vijūkas), *Panegyricus in laudem serenissimi Poloniae et Sueciae principis Caroli Ferdinandi in ingressu ad episcopatum Plocensem sub titulo Via regia, per allusionem ad stemmata eiusdem nomine Domus Professae Vilnensis. 1644*, in: ID., *Panegyrici heroum varia antehac manu sparsi nunc ab auctore proprio p. Casimiro Wijuk Kojałowicz Societatis Iesu, sanctae theologiae doctoris in gratiam iuventutis studiosae in unum collecti* (Vilnius, 1668), p. 99.

[273] Ž. NEKRAŠEVIČ-KAROTKAJA, "Latin epic poetry and its evolution as a factor of cultural identity in Central an Eastern Europe in the sixteenth and seventeenth centuries", in: Latinitas *in the Polish Crown and the Grand Duchy of Lithuania: Its Impact on the Development of Identities*, ed. G. SIEDINA and M. GARZANITI (Florence, 2014), p. 26.

mentioned by Kojałowicz in a panegyric for the newly-enthroned bishop of Płock. There are more works that tell history in a manner similar to the texts of Kojałowicz and Radwan,[274] but these two texts show quite well the practical application of poetry and history in the discourse of politics and identity.

The relations between the two arts, poetry and history, were discussed from a theoretical perspective in the 1620s by Maciej Kazimierz Sarbiewski, who referred to the poetics of Aristotle and Julius Caesar Scaliger. He clearly separated historical literature from poetry because, according to him, historiography tells one only about what was or is, while poetry has a more universal dimension and speaks of things that could happen.[275] Following Sarbiewski's thought one could say that epideictic texts written in Vilnius would therefore straddle the borderline between poetry and history, because writing historical narrative required the employment of devices reserved for poetry, for instance the character of the speaking heraldic Pogoń from Kojałowicz's piece, or allegories performed by Jesuit students in triumphal arches next to St. John's church. Therefore, Radwan's poem would be treated by Sarbiewski as a *sylva* (a common-place book) that contains only some of the elements that characterise poetry.[276]

Sarbiewski's own poetry, his odes, are also full of allusions to political events, heavily marked by republican, Sarmatian-Palemonic,[277] and Catholic ideology.[278] The poet recalled, among other things, the military successes of

[274] Four epic poems published in Vilnius are worth mentioning: F. GRADOWSKI, *Hodoeporicon Moschicum* (1581); A. RYMSZA, *Deketeros akroama* (1585); E. PIELGRZYMOWSKI, *Poselstwo i krótkie spisanie rozprawy z Moskwą* (1601); L. BOIERUS (W. Bojer), *Carolomachia* (1606). See J. NIEDŹWIEDŹ, "How did Virgil help forge Lithuanian identity in the sixteenth century?", in: Latinitas *in the Polish Crown and the Grand Duchy of Lithuania*, pp. 35-47

[275] SARBIEWSKI, *O poezji doskonałej, czyli Wergiliusz i Homer*, pp. 5-21.

[276] Sarbiewski was also the author of such a sylvic poem dedicated to Jan K. Chodkiewicz *Obsequium gratitudinis*; see M.K. SARBIEWSKI, *Obsequium gratitudinis*, in: ID., *Lemties žaidimai: Poezjijos rintkinė: Ludi Fortunae: Lyrica selecta*, ed. and trans. E. ULČINAITĖ (Vilnius, 1995), pp. 541-575.

[277] In the sixteenth century, the Polish and Lithuanian nobility invented legends about their mythical origins (ethnogenetic myths). The Polish nobility claimed their ancestors were the ancient Sarmatians, while the Lithuanians believed they were descendants of the refugees from ancient Rome, whose commander was legendary Publius Libo Palemon. See ZACHARA-WAWRZYŃCZAK, "Geneza legendy o rzymskim pochodzeniu Litwinów", pp. 5-35; NIENDORF, *Das Großfürstentum Litauen 1569-1795*, pp. 59-63; NIEDŹWIEDŹ, "How did Virgil help forge Lithuanian identity", pp. 36-37.

[278] D. KUOLYS, "Motiejus Kazimieras Sarbievijus politiniame Lietuvos Didžiosios Kunigaikštystės teatre", in: *Motiejus Kazimieras Sarbievijus lietuvos, lenkijos, europos kultūroje*, pp. 318-326.

Sigismund III and Władysław IV within the broad perspective of general history and the mission of the Church.[279] However, even if Sarbiewski referred to politics and to military and historical events, he did so differently from the authors mentioned above, and probably thanks to the poetic generalisation of the topics he tackled, his texts, and not the panegyrics of Kazimierz Wijuk Kojałowicz, were highly appreciated by his contemporaries.

Historiography in Vilnius

Both Sarbiewski and the authors of the laudatory *sylvae* (commonplace books) relied on the works of historians. The prime achievement in this field was the history of Lithuania by Wojciech Wijuk Kojałowicz, Kazimierz's older brother. Thanks to the use of Latin language, this work became an official version of the history of the Grand Duchy of Lithuania, especially for Western European readers. It is no coincidence that the first volume was published in Gdańsk and the second in Antwerp. When Kojałowicz was working on his text, the history of the Lithuanian state was already well established and widespread in Lithuania itself, as is shown by seventeenth-century panegyrics. The aim of these works was not so much to teach readers and listeners about history. Rather, it drew on already common historical knowledge as ready-made materials for the purposes of political propaganda. This knowledge had been established and negotiated from the beginning of the sixteenth century.

The foundation of this historiography were Ruthenian chronicles (*latopisy*) and foreign chronicles, including the chronicle of Jan Długosz (1480). On their basis, new versions of chronicles in Ruthenian were created, bringing together and organising the history of the Grand Duchy of Lithuania, its ruling dynasty, and the other aristocratic families. Three versions of the chronicle [*latopis*] from the 1520s and 1530s (including the *Chronicle of Bychowiec*) attribute a special role to the Gasztołd family, and for this reason it is assumed that their creation was inspired by Wojciech Gasztołd (Albertas Goštautas), the *voivode* and chancellor of the Grand Duchy of Lithuania from 1522 to 1539.[280] Soon afterwards, genealogies of the Ruthenian and Lithuanian princes written in

[279] E. BUSZEWICZ, *Sarmacki Horacy i jego liryka: Imitacja – Gatunek – Styl: Rzecz o poezji Macieja Kazimierza Sarbiewskiego* (Cracow, 2006), p. 278.

[280] O. ŁATYSZONEK, "Polityczne aspekty przedstawienia średniowiecznych dziejów ziem białoruskich w historiografii Wielkiego Księstwa Litewskiego XV-XVI w.", *Białoruskie Zeszyty Historyczne – Беларускі гістарычны зборнік* 25 (2006), pp. 22, 32-35.

Ruthenian began to be compiled.[281] They were used by later historians to compose the modern biographical compendia then popular in Europe,[282] for instance *Genealogy of the Grand Dukes of Lithuania* by Samuel Dowgird, studies on the Radziwiłłs by Andrzej Wargocki and Wojciech Wijuk Kojałowicz[283] and the biographical compendium on the Jagiellons attributed to Tomasz Porzecki (*Aeternitas serenissimorum stirpis Jagellonicum regum*, 1639).[284] Catalogues of Lithuanian rulers were a response to similar catalogues of Polish rulers created from the 1640s.[285]

The history of the State was of great interest to the milieu of Vilnius humanists in the 1560s and 1570s, because it had a practical application in political discourse. Augustyn Rotundus, a friend of Maciej Stryjkowski who has been mentioned several times in this book, was the author of an outline of Lithuanian history (which unfortunately has not survived), that he sent to Mikołaj Radziwiłł 'the Black' in the days preceding the Lublin Union of 1569. Historical erudition was useful for the *Voigt* of Vilnius when he was putting together his arguments in the dialogue *Rozmowa Polaka z Litwinem* (A Dialogue between a Pole and a Lithuanian), meant as a polemic with Stanisław Orzechowski's dialogue entitled *Quincunx* (both published in Cracow in 1564).[286] Referring to historical factography, Rotundus demonstrated that the Grand Duchy of Lithuania was politically equal to the Kingdom of Poland, and, above all, he proved that it had its own long and glorious history. Similar ideas of political independence of the Lithuanian Commonwealth (or Republic, (in the original sources: *Rzeczpospolita Litewska*) guided both Stryjkowski

[281] One example is the seventeenth-century transcription of an older manuscript that contains biographies of the Rurikids and Gediminids, MS CZART. 2211 IV; here, inter alia *Rod wielkich kniaziej ruskich otkol rodiszasja* and *Rod litowskich kniaziej.*

[282] R. KRZYWY, "*'Reges et principes Regni Poloniae': Adriana Kochana Wolskiego jako przykład wierszowanego katalogu władców*", *Acta Sueco-Polonica* 10-11 (2001-2002), pp. 95-104.

[283] DOWGIRD, *Genealogia albo krótkie opisanie wielkich książąt litewskich*; A. WARGOCKI, *Dom oświeconych książąt na Bierżach i Dubinkach opisany anno Domini 1621*, MS NGAB Ф 694 оп. 1 ед. 1, ff. 1r-14v; A. KOJALAVIČIUS-VIJŪKAS, *Fasti Radiviliani*, *passim*.

[284] E. ULČINAITĖ, "Szkoła poetycka Sarbiewskiego na Litwie w XVII-XVIII wieku", in: *Corona scientiarum: Studia z historii literatury i kultury nowożytnej ofiarowane profesorowi Januszowi Pelcowi*, ed. J.A. CHROŚCICKI *et al.* (Warsaw, 2004), pp. 374-375.

[285] See H.-J. BÖMELBURG, *Polska myśl historyczna a humanistyczna historia narodowa (1500-1700)*, trans. Z. OWCZAREK, with an introduction by A. LAWATA (Cracow, 2011), pp. 415-430.

[286] Both dialogues are published in: *Stanisława Orzechowskiego i Augustyna Rotundusa debata o Rzeczypospolitej*, ed. K. KOEHLER (Cracow, 2009).

and, several decades later, Kojałowicz.[287] These catalogues of Lithuanian rulers and other historical works can to some extent be described as polemical historiography.

As I have already mentioned, because of its function as a capital city, Vilnius was the place within the Grand Duchy of Lithuania where the process of the conception and codification of Lithuanian history developed to a large extent. Equally important, however, was to make it broadly known. This took place in several ways. Firstly, through books printed and sold by Vilnius booksellers, who distributed Stryjkowski's *Kronika* and Dowgird's *Genealogia*. Secondly, and this seems to be of much greater importance, thanks to humanist education, which, within the framework of rhetorical classes, disseminated knowledge of local history.[288] Seventeenth-century manuscript commonplace books contain a large number of historical notes, which could be used in panegyrical texts. These include for instance catalogues of the grand dukes of Lithuania or Vilnius bishops, or short notes, for instance *Jakie jest pochodzenie Litwinów* (What is the Origin of the Lithuanians).[289] Although history was not a separate subject in the Jesuit curriculum, the Academy of Vilnius played an important role in promoting the history of the homeland, drifting away from the requirements of the *Ratio studiorum*.[290] In the 1604 declamation, the personified Art of History, similar to Theology and Rhetoric, praised St. Casimir.[291] History was certainly also taught in other schools in Vilnius. Indirect evidence for this is provided by the library of Stefan Lebiedzicz,[292] which contained a large collection of publications in the field of historiography. His interest in history was probably inspired at the Orthodox Brotherhood's school.

Popular historiography became strongly rooted in the landscape of seventeenth-century Vilnius, both metaphorically and literally. Both on a daily basis and during religious holidays, the inhabitants of the city, regardless of

[287] D. Kuolys, "Alberto Vijūko-Kojalavičiaus istorinis pasakojimas: Respublikos kūrimas", in: A. Vijūkas-Kojalavičius (W. Wijuk Kojałowicz), *Lietuvos istorijos įvairenybės*, 2, ed. D. Kuolys, trans. R. Jurgelėnaitė (Vilnius, 2004), pp. 391-397.

[288] M. Janik, "Wśród form popularyzacji historii w xvii wieku", in: *Staropolskie kompendia wiedzy*, ed. I.M. Dacka-Górzyńska and J. Partyka (Warsaw, 2009), pp. 203-224; K. Puchowski, *Edukacja historyczna w jezuickich kolegiach Rzeczypospolitej 1565-1773* (Gdańsk, 1999), p. 39.

[289] *Catalogus episcoporum Vilnensium: Unde sit origo Lituanorum?*, ms Czart. 1662 iv, ff. 413r-414r; 450r-457r; see Stoberski, *Między dawnymi i młodszymi laty*, p. 62.

[290] Puchowski, *Edukacja historyczna w jezuickich kolegiach Rzeczypospolitej*, p. 50.

[291] Q. Cnoglerus, *Pompa Casimiriana*, p. 107.

[292] See Chapter 3.

their level of education, encountered visible signs of official history, such as tombstones, chapels, triumphal arches, *castra doloris*, houses of prayer with inscriptions, or heraldic representations. Above all, however, the city itself became a symbol of Lithuania and a sign of its past, a place of memory both for its inhabitants and for all Europeans:

> The Grand Duchy of Lithuania is now divided into ten voivodeships, that is provinces, whose main city and capital is now Vilnius, called [*miasto*] *wileńskie* in the local language, and in German *die Wilde*, which was founded at the confluence of the Neris and the Vilnia in 1305 by Duke Gediminas. Today, it is the seat of the *voivode*, the first among Lithuanians, and the bishop of the Roman rite, subordinate to the archbishop of Lviv, as well as the Ruthenian Metropolitan, who has seven bishops of the Greek rite under him.[293] (original in Latin)

[293] G. MERCATOR, *Atlas minor Gerardi Mercatoris a Iudoco Hondio plurimis aeneis tabulis auctus atque illustratus* (Amsterdam, 1610), p. 142.

Chapter 11

Religious Texts

The Religious Identity of Vilnius

Probably most medieval and early modern urban settlements in Europe had their own religious identity. The town gained this identity thanks to the number and dedication of its churches, the veneration of a local saint, unique church fairs, the residence of the church authorities or important religious institutions, etc. It was also defined by the number and set of different religions that operated in the town and the respective numbers of their followers. A crucial role must be acknowledged for the texts produced for any particular town and its inhabitants. Vilnius was not an exception in this respect. The main goal of this chapter is to present the process of building the textual religious identity of Vilnius. Another issue is the function of religious texts in the life of the city's inhabitants.

The beginnings of religious texts in Vilnius were humble. Pre-Christian Lithuanian rulers used writing, but only for political matters. Before 1385, when Grand Duke Jogaila (Władysław Jagiełło) was baptised, the dukes of Lithuania cultivated their primordial polytheistic religion,[1] which did not rely on writing at all.[2] The only medieval sources related to its gods and rites were

[1] I do not use the terms 'pagan' and 'paganism', traditionally associated with pre-Christian religion in Lithuania. Firstly, the term, coined and used by Christians, deprecates non-Christian religions (just like 'heretics' for the Protestants and 'schismatics' for the Orthodox). Secondly, in the fourteenth and fifteenth centuries, in Lithuania the noun *paganus* was ambiguous. The Catholics called both the Muslim Tartars and pre-Christian Lithuanians 'pagans'.

[2] M. Kosman, *Zmierzch Perkuna, czyli ostatni poganie nad Bałtykiem* (Warsaw, 1981); D. Baronas, "Christians in late pagan, and pagans in early Christian Lithuania: The fourteenth

written by Christian authors (Poles, Ruthenians, and the Teutonic Knights). After the formal introduction of Catholicism into the Grand Duchy of Lithuania, practising the old religion ceased in Vilnius. Jogaila ordered the holy places to be destroyed and built a Catholic cathedral on their spot.[3]

When Jogaila introduced Roman Christianity into Lithuania, religions based on holy texts were not a complete novelty in Vilnius. Although he eventually chose Catholicism, he was brought up in the Orthodox religious culture and spirituality,[4] and his experience with written culture had Ruthenian-Orthodox roots. Many members of the Lithuanian elites in the late fourteenth century had a strong relationships with Ruthenian Orthodox culture. On the other hand, some Catholic merchants, artisans, and clergy also settled in the town. The presence of the Christian community in Vilnius dates back at the latest to 1323, that is the year in which Duke Gediminas issued letters in which Western merchants and artisans were invited to settle in the town. It is certain that Catholics employed by Gediminas wrote these letters.

In the next decades, the first churches were built. Catholic clergy, presumably mendicants, organised a parish in the 'Latin' part or the town, called later The Big Quarter or The Polish Quarter, inhabited by Catholics.[5] Meanwhile, for a long time in the Ruthenian part of the town, called Okole, Ruski Koniec (the 'Ruthenian End'), or *Civitas Ruthenica* on the Vilnia River,[6] there were at least two Orthodox churches (among them the church of the Dormition, later the cathedral of the Dormition, built in the 1340s) with quite a large number of followers.[7] For this reason, the ways of self-government of the inhabitants of both Vilnius settlements, subject to the power of writing and texts, were soon to spread throughout the area where the newly established city was growing.

and fifteenth centuries", *Lithuanian Historical Studies* 22 (2018), pp. 161-169; R. Balsys, *Paganism of Lithuanians and Prussians*, 1 (Klaipeda, 2020).

3 Although the old religion was not professed in the city any longer, it survived much longer in the rural parts of ethnic Lithuanian regions. The inhabitants of these territories were formally baptized, but they still cultivated many old beliefs at least until the seventeenth century. Still, it was a religion without script. See V. Kamuntavičienė, "The religious faiths of Ruthenians and Old Lithuanians in the seventeenth century according to the records of the Catholic Church visitations of the Vilnius diocese", *Journal of Baltic Studies* 46.2 (2015), pp. 157-170.

4 Jogaila's mother was an Orthodox princess, Uliana of Tver (†1391). See A. Naumow, "Jagiełło wobec prawosławia", in: id., *Domus divisa*, p. 175.

5 Тимошенко, *Руська релігійна культура Вільна*, p. 6.

6 *Ibid.*

7 Katalynas, *Vilnaius plėtra*, p. 57.

Shortly after the 'baptism of Lithuania' in 1387,[8] Vilnius was inhabited only by followers of religions of the Book: Orthodox Christians, Catholics, and Muslim Tartars. As we indicated earlier in this book, during the next century this blend of religious communities was to be enriched by Jews, Augsburg Evangelicals (Lutherans), Reformed Evangelicals (Calvinists), Polish Brethren, and finally, in the last years of the sixteenth century, Uniates. All these faiths are characterised by the fact that they are universal religions, based on the written word. This means that their followers obey laws written in books, especially in the Holy Book, which is their basic point of reference.

The use of texts, including religious ones, and the introduction of a group of religious 'functionaries' (the clergy), who guarded the texts' interpretation, stabilised the principles according to which society functioned.[9] The written word was – or at least was meant to be – a guarantee of the orthodoxy of a religious set of beliefs.

Although the religions present in Vilnius differed in many points, their attitude towards the written word was in many respects similar. Firstly, because all of them came from the same Middle Eastern and Mediterranean roots; secondly, because for a long time they had coexisted in Europe and had shared many textual practices, for instance in the processes of book production (both in manuscript and printed forms),[10] the ways in which the holy books were kept, commenting on the holy texts, public preaching, etc.

All Vilnius confessions produced many texts, which formed similar classes. Their similar functions are the main reason why in this chapter the religious texts of Christianity, Islam, and Judaism are presented together, and why a particular emphasis is placed on their similarities rather than on differences.

It may be supposed that more copies of religious texts circulated in the city than of texts belonging to other segments of the written culture. This can be confirmed by the post-mortem inventories of early modern booksellers. Al-

[8] The 'baptism' of Lithuania should be understood in the first place as the conversion of the ruling house and the non-Orthodox Lithuanian elites to Catholicism. With time, the official discourse of the Catholic Church and of many Catholic historians gladly omitted the presence of the large Orthodox community in the Grand Duchy of Lithuania in the late fourteenth century.

[9] GOODY, *The Logic of Writing and the Organization of Society*, pp. 20-22.

[10] In early modern Vilnius probably the only religious text in the form of a scroll was the Torah used in the liturgy in the synagogue. Other books, even Jewish ones, had the form of a codex. The European Jewish community adapted codices for study purposes in the early Middle Ages. I.M. RESNICK, "The codex in early Jewish and Christian communities", *The Journal of Religious History* 17.1 (1992), pp. 10-11.

though we do not have such inventories from Vilnius,[11] we may take it that the repertoire of Vilnius merchants specialised in the book trade and bookbinders did not differ from for that of their colleagues in, say Lublin.[12] No less than half of the books sold in the Polish-Lithuanian Commonwealth in the sixteenth and seventeenth centuries were catechisms, prayer books, psalters, and missals. The vast majority of the books production in Vilnius also had a religious character. This huge number of religious texts was caused by the fact that worship was at the very centre of the organisation of premodern societies.

Many of these texts have already been mentioned in the previous chapters about literacy, the use of texts by women, book production, religious polemics, inscriptions, etc. This is due to the fact that many of these texts had several functions, not exclusively religious ones. From the point of view of their purposes in worship they can be divided into three main groups. The first one is that of the Holy Books (Holy Scripture and the Quran), their translations and interpretations: theological treatises, midrashes, tefsirs, etc. The texts of personal prayers and liturgical rites belong to the second group: prayer books, texts of chants and songs, agendas, breviaries, psalters, missals, Evangelia, Apostols, sacramentaries, lectionaries, and other books used in in the liturgy. Manuals of meditation also belong to this group. Apart from that, there were also liturgical regulations and manuals, printed and handwritten, which helped in celebrating church services or saying prayers (for instance manuals for the confessors). The last group consists of texts that taught religion on a basic or advanced level. These texts might also have also an admonishing function, such as catechisms and sermons. To this group belonged also texts that strengthen personal piety or gave pious entertainment, such as lives of saints, epic poems about saints, and literary paraphrases of the Bible.

The vast majority of the kind of texts concerning religion in late medieval and early modern Vilnius was also created and used in other parts of Europe. Among them there were for instance the *Pater noster*, Canisius' and Luther's catechisms, the Torah, the oktoechos, psalms, horologia, etc. In this respect Vilnius did not differ from other urban settlements: probably in all smaller and bigger European towns religious texts were used more or less in the same way. It was not the texts themselves but the Vilnius cultural context which decided about differences meaning, that is about the way in which they functioned. Firstly, the range of these texts in Vilnius was remarkably wide. Secondly, the

[11] See Chapter 7.

[12] Toruj, *Inwentarze książek lubelskich introligatorów*.

multi-religious and multi-confessional character of the city differed from most other European towns. Many travellers from Western Europe noticed this variety, for instance the nuncio Jacobus Piso in 1514 and Zacharias Ferreri in 1521.[13] Thirdly, as the capital city of the country and the seat of an Orthodox archbishopric and a Catholic bishopric, Vilnius played a special role in the religious life of the Orthodox and Catholic communities. Later on, it also became an important religious centre for the Lithuanian Protestants and Jews.

Introducing the Reformation into the city increased the accessibility of the inhabitants of Vilnius to religious texts of a different character.[14] While the clergy began to lose its monopole on the use of the written word, lay members of the Churches gained great influence on the production, interpretation, distribution, and use of religious texts throughout the period we are interested in. In the case of some texts, such as liturgical books or the entire Bible, the Catholic and Orthodox clergy remained their main users. Other genres, such as prayers and catechisms, could – and indeed they supposed to – be shared.

By the end of the sixteenth century the clergy of all Vilnius confessions had to offer their flocks texts which facilitated both their auto-identification with a Church and their response to the texts of their religious competitors. This situation mirrored processes which went on in other places in Europe at the time, but which in Vilnius were even more complex.

The use of the religious texts mentioned above depended on many factors: age, gender, profession, confession, social status, and possession of different forms of capital, especially of economic and cultural capital. For example, the Holy Books were used mainly by professionals of the written word: by clergy and scholars who studied them. However, some religions were more open in this respect than others. Jews, Tartars, and Protestant laymen relatively frequently came into contact with sacred texts, because their liturgies required them to read the Torah, the Quran, and the Bible. It was different with the three dominant confessions in Vilnius the Catholic and the Orthodox Churches, and later also the Uniate Church, which restricted access to the Bible. Reading the Bible was also genderised. In all religions, male believers had better access to the Word of God than female ones. This does not mean that women did not have any contact with the holy texts at all. Such contact was determined by several factors. Protestant women were privileged, because they were required to read the Bible (usually in translations in vernacular languages), while lay

[13] Fijałek, "Opisy Wilna" (part II), pp. 135-137, 149-150.

[14] See Chapter 3 on schools and schooling.

Catholic or Orthodox women were not subject to any such requirement. Yet we have to bear in mind that fragments from the Holy Books were read aloud in the churches, the synagogue, and the mosque, and virtually all inhabitants of Vilnius had a possibility to listen them – usually in the liturgical languages: Latin, Church Slavonic, Hebrew, and Arabic.

Catechisms can serve as another example of the differentiation of readers of religious texts. In this case the main factor of their use was age: catechisms were provided for schoolboys. Except teachers of religion, adults probably rarely read such books. Incidentally, it may be supposed that not only boys came into contact with catechisms. They were often treated as primers and published as a set. Those girls who acquired their reading skills at home probably came into contact with the same catechisms their brothers read in school. Nevertheless, girls' access to them used to be more limited.

Religious texts impacted on everyday life in Vilnius both directly and indirectly. Measuring time, daily and holiday prayers, discourse about sins and virtues, and the way money was to be spent, were regulated by instructions, orders, and hints present in the different types of religious texts available. These texts were not less important than the law, which by the way was linked to religious regulations as well.

Holy Texts and Their Interpretations

Holy Books

During the fifteenth and sixteenth centuries, the demand for the Bible (the entire text and its singular books) among all Christian communities in Vilnius grew steadily. All of them needed copies of the Bible, clergymen, monks, nuns, and lay people. Among the separate books, the Book of Psalms was especially important. Bibles were also had an obligatory place in ecclesiastical libraries. The majority of bible manuscripts was imported, especially in the first centuries of Vilnius' history.

In the fourteenth century, Vilnius Catholic priests had to possess the whole Latin Bible either entire or in a collection of all its parts. Bibles were kept in the churches: in St. Nicolas church, the Franciscan church, the cathedral, and in St. John's church. In the fifteenth century, copies of the Holy Books were produced for the Vilnius book market, with the needs of the local clergy in mind. Good examples of this are copies of the Bible made in the second half of the fifteenth century for Vilnius' churches by professional scribes in Cracow (*kathedrales*[15]). Probably since the end of the fifteenth century onwards, its Latin versions were imported. This situation did not change until the eighteenth century: the Lithuanian printing houses did not publish Catholic Bibles, neither in Latin or in Polish. We encounter only some psalms printed in prayer books, hymn books, and catechisms, or pericopes from the Gospels.

However, many copies of the Catholic Bible and its parts circulated, which were published elsewhere. The spread of the Reformation and the Counter Reformation accelerated this process. From the end of the sixteenth century, among Catholics the obligatory version was the Clementine Vulgate, published for the first time in 1592.[16] Copies were imported into Lithuania as well.[17]

Since the 1560s, in the Polish-Lithuanian Commonwealth an impressive number of translations of the Bible in Polish were printed, among them two Catholic versions.[18] In 1561 Cracow saw the first edition of the Bible of Jan Leopolita, and in the 1590s a new translation was prepared by the Jesuit Jakub Wujek. In Cracow the gospels (1593), the Psalter (1594), and posthumously the entire bible (1599) appeared in his translation. This version, many times reprinted, became the standard Polish version of the Catholic Scripture, which was used also in the Grand Duchy of Lithuania. In 1647, the Jesuit Jan Jachnowicz published the *Ewangelie polskie i litewskie* (Polish and Lithuanian Gospels). There were pericopes of the Gospel for Sundays and holidays which contained Wujek's version of the text or Jachnowicz' Lithuanian translation.[19] The book was very popular in Lithuania, as it is shown by its many reprints.

The Orthodox Church also made every effort to get volumes of Scripture. From 1502, scribe Matvei Desaty worked in Vilnius on a copy of the Church

[15] See Chapter 7.

[16] The Clementine Vulgate was to some extent read by the Uniates, who primarily used the Church Slavonic translation. They also consulted the Polish Bible of Wujek.

[17] Several copies of the Clementine Vulgate from Vilnius Catholic churches are preserved in the LNMB. They were published in Antwerp, Leiden, and Cologne, e.g. *Biblia sacra vulgatae editionis Sixti Quinti pontificis maximi iussu recognita atque edita* (Antwerp, 1618), from the papal seminary in Vilnius <https://ibiblioteka.lt/metis/publication/LIBIS000000016734?q=952fb510d> (accessed: 6.06.2023).

[18] On the history of translations of the Bible into Polish in the sixteenth and seventeenth century, see D.A. Frick, *Polish Sacred Philology in the Reformation and the Counter-Reformation: Chapters in the History of Controversies (1551-1632)* (Berkeley, 1989).

[19] *Ewangelie polskie i litewskie tak niedzielne, jako i wszytkich świąt, które w Kościele katolickim według rzymskiego porządku przez cały rok czytają* (Vilnius, 1647).

Slavonic translations of the books of the Bible entitled *Desatiglav* (called also the Supraśl Manuscript), which he finally completed in Supraśl in 1507.[20] The *Desatiglav* is a richly illuminated parchment manuscript of 550 leaves. It contains the books of Prophets, Job, Proverbs, Kings, Ecclesiastes, Song of Songs, *Sentences* by Menander, Sirach, Psalms, Gospels, Apocalypse, *Apostol* (that is the Acts of the Apostles, the seven Catholic Epistles and the Pauline Epistles) and the *typikon* with the autobiography of Matvei. The manuscript shows the potential of the Orthodox monastic scriptoria in the Grand Duchy of Lithuania. We may suppose that *Desatiglav* was not the only example of rich and beautiful Bible manuscripts.

It may be assumed that the demand for books of the Bible contributed to the development of Cyrillic print culture. Ten years after Matvei finished the *Desatiglav*, Francysk Skaryna completed printing the Orthodox Bible in Prague (1517[21]). Skaryna's Bible heralded an enormous movement in the field of bible printing and in Slavonic sacred philology (especially in Polish and Ruthenian) in the next decades.

In principle, in the sixteenth century the Orthodox used Church Slavonic manuscript Bibles. The situation changed in 1581, when for the first time the entire Church Slavonic Bible was published in Ostroh.[22] The publication of the Ostroh (Ostrog) Bible was an enormous success: copies of this edition were widely used in the Polish-Lithuanian Commonwealth, Muscovy, Moldova, and on the Balkan Peninsula under Ottoman occupation.[23] Copies of the Ostroh

[20] From 1910, the manuscript is held in the Library of the Russian Academy of Sciences in St. Petersburg (Russia), shelf mark 24.4.28). See С.Ю. Темчин, "Роль Матвея Десятого в православной культуре Великого княжества Литовского", in: *Latopisy Akademii Supraskiej*, 1, *Prawosławni w dziejach Rzeczypospolitej*, ed. U. Pawluczuk (Białystok, 2010), pp. 27-35; М.В. Нікалаеў, *Гісторыя беларускай кнігі*, 1, pp. 105, 348-351; facsimile: *Библия Матфея Десятого 1507 года. Из собрания Библиотеки Российской академии наук*, 2 vols. (Санкт-Петербург, 2020). <https://www.postkomsg.com/reading_room/227714/?fbclid=IwAR1BpDrq5H5X5V5a7K4SPNjsSfAvfjgzCFuvS7TE0iVAYsX1Aq7t0CoKdIE> (accessed: 6.06.2023).

[21] This has been discussed in detail in Chapter 5.

[22] Ostroh (Острог) is a town in Volhynia in western Ukraine. Until the Union of Lublin in 1569 it belonged to the Grand Duchy of Lithuania, later to the Kingdom of Poland. The town was owned by Prince Konstanty Wasyl Ostrogski (Kostiantyn Vasyl Ostrozkyi, 1526-1608), a patron of the Orthodox Church. In the second half of the sixteenth century the town was one of major centres of Orthodox culture in the Polish-Lithuanian Commonwealth.

[23] The publication of the Ostroh (Ostrog) Bible was one of the major achievements of early modern Orthodox sacred philology. The Orthodox humanists who worked at the Ostroh Academy (founded *c.* 1577), prepared a critical edition of the Bible, which was printed by the printer Ivan Fedorov. Its editors consulted the Church Slavonic manuscripts of Gennady's Bible (from the 1490s) with the Aldine Septuaginta (1518), the Vulgate, and several other editions. See A.A.

Bible were not only brought to Vilnius, the text was also edited there. There are copies known of the Ostroh Bible with so-called 'Vilnius pages'.[24] In the 1590s someone of the Mamonicz printing house in Vilnius became the owner some printed sheets of the Ostroh Bible. Mamoniczs decided to print the lacking parts of the Old Testament and put into circulation copies of the Ostroh Bible.[25] Their primary market was Vilnius and the Grand Duchy of Lithuania with its large Orthodox population. Since the 1580s the Ostroh Bible became the standard Church Slavonic version used by the Orthodox and Uniates in Vilnius.

The Mamoniczs, the printing house of the Orthodox Brotherhood, and the Basilians published also individual books of the Bible, for instance psalters and apostols.[26] In polemics conducted in Polish, members of these communities used various Polish translations, but the Orthodox Church showed great reserve towards the Catholic versions, checking quotations from Wujek's Bible translation against the Septuagint.[27] The Uniates could use the Church Slavonic and Vulgate versions as well as that by Wujek.

Гусева, *Издания кирилловского шрифта второй половины XVI в.: Сводный каталог*, 1 (Moscow, 2003), pp. 588-590; Е.Л. Немировский, "Острожская Библия: Как находили и вводили в оборот самое знаменитое издание Ивана Федорова", in: *Федоровские чтения 2005* (Moscow, 2005) pp. 89-166; П. Кралюк, "Острозька Біблія та філософська й богословська думка в Острозькій академії", *Наукові записки: Серія "Філософія"* 4 (2008), pp. 11-12 (with a large bibliography on the Ostroh Bible). Е.Л. Немировский, *Славянские издания кирилловского (церковнославянского) шрифта*, 2.2, *1593-1600* (Moscow, 2011), pp. 78-79.

[24] Н.П. Бондар, "Острожская Библия с 'виленскими листами' из собрания НБУВ", in: *Книга и мировая цивилизация: Материалы 11 Международной книговедческой научной конференции по проблемам книговедения, (Москва, 20-21 апреля 2004 г.)*, 2 (Moscow, 2004), pp. 355-359.

[25] There are seven known copies of the Ostroh Bible with the "Vilnius pages"; see A.A. Гусева, *Издания кирилловского шрифта второй половины XVI в.: Сводный каталог*, 2 (Moscow, 2003), p. 999; Н.П. Бондар, "До історії друкування 'вільнюських аркушів' 1595 р.: філігранологічний аналіз примірників Наукові праці Національної бібліотеки України імені В.І.Вернадського, 31 (2011). pp. 203-213 ; Ead., "Экземпляры кириллических изданий вильнюсских типографий из фондов Национальной библиотеки Украины имени В.И. Вернадского как источник историко-книговедческих и филигранологических исследований", *Vilniaus universiteto bibliotekos metraštis* (2015), pp. 415-416.

[26] The number of editions and manuscripts of Cyrillic biblical books used in Lithuania is so large that a comprehensive list of them has not been compiled to this day; see Нікалаеў, *Гісторыя беларускай кнігі*, 1, pp. 105-122.

[27] Frick, *Meletij Smotryc'kyj*, pp. 200-205.

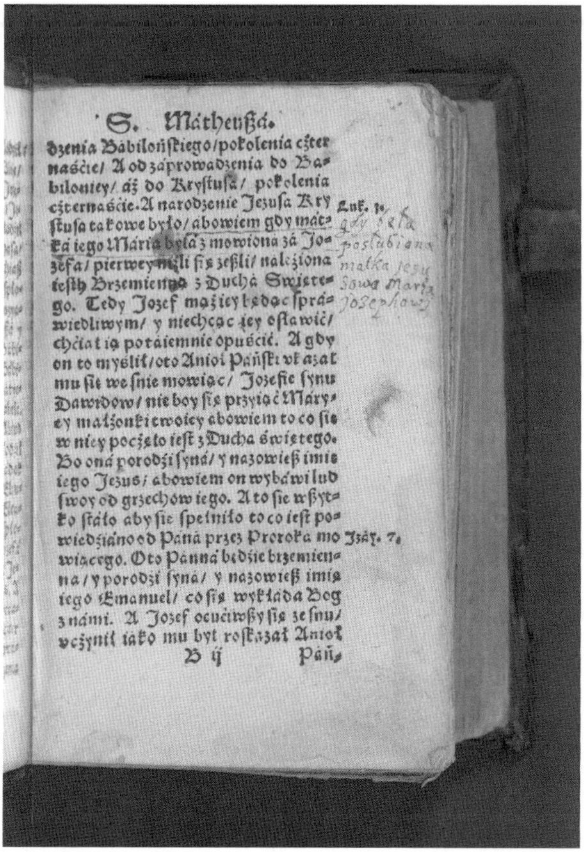
S. Máthewſzá.
dzenia Bábilońſkiego/pokolenia cztér
náśćie/ A od záprowadzenia do Ba-
biloniey/ áż do Kryſtuſá/ pokolenia
czternaśćie. A narodzenie Jezuſá Kry Luk. 1.
ſtuſá takowe było/ abowiem gdy mátk-
ká iego Máriá byłá zmowiona zá Jo-
zefá/ pierwey niżli ſię zeſzli/ nalezioná
ieſth brzemienna z Duchá Swięte-
go. Tedy Jozef mąż iey będąc ſprá-
wiedliwym/ y niechcąc iey oſławić/
chćiał ią potáiemnie opuśćić. A gdy
on to myślił/ oto Anioł Páńſki vkazał
mu ſię we śnie mowiąc/ Jozefie ſynu
Dawidow/ nie boy ſię przyiąć Máry-
ey małżonki twoiey abowiem to co ſię
w niey poczęło ieſt z Duchá świętego.
Bo oná porodźi ſyná/ y nazowieſz imię
iego Jezus/ abowiem on wybáwi lud
ſwoy od grzechow iego. A to ſię wſzyt-
ko ſtáło áby ſię ſpełniło to co ieſt po-
wiedziáno od Páná przez Proroká mo- Izáy. 7.
wiącego. Oto Panná będźie brzemien-
na/ y porodzi ſyná/ y nazowieſz imię
iego Emanuel/ co ſię wykłáda Bog
z námi. A Jozef ocućiwſzy ſię ze ſnu/
vczynił iáko mu był roſkazał Anioł
B ij Páń-

gdy była
poslubiona
matka jesu
sowa Marja
Josephowi

Fig. 64 Marginal note of a reader of the Protestant New Testament (a fragment of the Radziwiłł Bible) published in Vilnius in 1580 by Jan Karcan. Warsaw, BN, 996 I Cim <https://polona.pl/preview/db0a90aa-33db-4abb-ba6e-90a7d62776e2> (accessed: 26.06.2023; public domain).

Although the main Orthodox version was the Church Slavonic one, there were also some attempts to translate some fragments of the Bible into vernacular Ruthenian. The Orthodox were provided with a set of pericopes in this language in a postil edited by Meletius Smotrycki, *Evangelie uchitelnoe* (Instructive Evangeliary) from 1616.[28]

The Protestants in the Polish-Lithuanian Commonwealth sought to use the vernacular Bible, that is in Polish or German. Work on the Polish translation begun in the 1550s in the town of Pińczów (Poland), the centre of the Polish Reformation. The patron of this endeavour was the *voivode* of Vilnius, Mikołaj Radziwiłł 'the Black'. In 1563, in Brest, this famous version (called the Brest, Pińczów, or the Radziwiłł Bible) was published. It was in Vilnius that many copies of the 'Brest Bible' were stored in the palace of Radziwiłł 'the Black' on Zamkowa (Castle) Street. This version was also used by the Polish-speaking Lutherans. German members of the Vilnius Lutheran community read Luther's translation into German.

In 1572, in Nyasvizh (today Belarus), the next Polish Protestant translation, made by Szymon Budny, appeared.[29] This version, called the Nyasvizh Bible, was published for the Polish Brethren. Those supporters or members of this community who lived in Vilnius (for instance Mikołaj Radziwiłł 'the Black') certainly possessed and read Budny's translation.

The final Protestant Polish translation, made for the Calvinists and Lutherans in the Polish-Lithuanian Commonwealth, was the Gdańsk Bible, translated by Daniel Mikołajewski and printed in 1632. It became the standard Polish Protestant version until the twentieth century. The Lithuanian Calvinists were actively involved in the publication of the Gdańsk Bible, which is confirmed by the protocols of the annual synods of the Lithuanian Calvinist community in Vilnius of 1629 and 1634.[30]

Apart from translations of the entire Bible, parts of it were also read in Vilnius. The Vilnius and other Lithuanian and Polish printing houses produced a huge number of Polish gospels, psalters, or collections for liturgical use (such as the Orthodox *Apostol*). The gospels from the Radziwiłł Bible were several times reprinted in Lithuania (twice in Vilnius, in 1580 and 1593). In the seventeenth century the Calvinist community in Vilnius widely used poetic translations of the Psalter by Maciej Rybiński (1566-1612), which in the Polish-Lithuanian Commonwealth had at least fifteen editions in 1605-1641.[31] In 1619 the

[28] D. FRICK, "Introduction", in: SMOTRYCKI, *Rus' Restored*, pp. XXIX-XXX.

[29] The patron of the publication of the Brest Bible and the Nyasvizh Bible was Mikołaj Radziwiłł "the Black".

[30] *1. O wydaniu Biblii św. consens*, and, of 1634, *9. O Biblii gdańskiej editii*; see *Akta synodów litewskich prowincjonalnych 1611-1637*, MS MAB F40-1157, pp. 113r, 146r.

[31] First edition: *Psalmy Dawidowe*, trans. M. RYBIŃSKI (Raków, 1605). See ESTREICHER,

synod of the Lithuanian Calvinists appointed Salomon Rysiński to choose psalms for the new Polish edition of the Heidelberg catechism. Canon 1 of the protocols stated:

> If there is a lack of some psalms [in the earlier editions], they should be supplemented by translations of Rybiński, Kochanowski, or Mr. Rysiński and Naborowski. The melody for the songs and psalms should be the same as earlier. For the new psalms the melody should be based on the *Methodus* of Lobwaser.[32] (original in Polish)

In the catalogue of his library, Salomon Rysiński mentioned Rybiński's Psalter.[33] The number of copies showed that the orders of the church authorities that obliged members of the Protestant communities to read the Bible constantly were obeyed. In early modern Vilnius, one could probably find copies of all publications listed above.

The Holy Books of the Jews, the Torah and the entire Hebrew Bible (the Tanakh) were imported into the city from other Jewish centres, but it can be assumed that they were also copied in Vilnius from the beginning of the seventeenth century. From the end of the sixteenth century onwards, Vilnius became one of the main centres of Jewish settlement in Lithuania: the economic, religious, and intellectual hub of a quickly growing Jewish community.[34] Since it was always the duty of a pious Jew to study the scriptures, and since the literacy rate of the Jewish community was high, there must have been many copies available, especially in the first half of the seventeenth century.[35] Biblical texts were necessary for instance for saying prayers in the Great Synagogue. In everyday religious practices and study, translations of the Bible and of its individual books into Yiddish, which had been published in Cracow since at least the early 1570s, were certainly used.[36] In Jewish Vilnius, copies of the Midrash, the Talmud (the Mishnah and Gemara), as well as other texts were used for worship and study, but we do not have any information about the scriptoria in which at least some of these books were calligraphed. Religious rules for copy-

Bibliografia Polska, 15 (1897), pp. 74-76.

32 *Akta synodów prowincjonalnych jednoty litewskiej 1611-1625*, p. 50.

33 MS NGAB Ф 694 оп. 1 ед. 450, f. 60r.

34 Маггид, *Вильна*.

35 M. Bałaban, *Historia Żydów w Krakowie i na Kazimierzu* (Cracow, 1931), p. 433.

36 I. Schiper, "Język potoczny Żydów polskich i ich literatura w dawnej Rzeczypospolitej", in: *Żydzi w Polsce odrodzonej*, 1, ed. I. Schiper, A. Tartakower, and A. Hafftka (Warsaw, 1932), pp. 229-230.

ing the Torah were very strict, so these scriptoria were highly specialised institutions. From ancient times the Torah intended for liturgy had to be in form of a manuscript scroll,[37] first in papyrus and since the Middle Agnes on parchment. Over time, a Torah for study could also be in the form of a parchment manuscript codex,[38] and later it could also be printed on paper. Such books were probably present in many Jewish homes in Vilnius. They must have been imported from Cracow or Lublin, or from beyond the borders of the Polish-Lithuanian Commonwealth (Amsterdam, Venice).[39]

The Vilnius Tartars used their Holy Book, the Quran, in a slightly different manner than the other religious communities in Vilnius. A significant number of Tartars lived in the suburban Lukiškės (Łukiszki), where a wooden mosque was built on the bank of the Neris, similar to those preserved until today in Bohoniki in the north-east of Poland or Raižiai in Lithuania. In the sixteenth century the Muslim clergy that led the Vilnius community could read Arabic, so they could use the original text of the Quran or the *sufras* (containing the thirtieth part of the Quran). An anonymous Pole, who visited the mosque in 1581, wrote that he saw "the Alcoran written in the Arabic script".[40] The author of this letter wanted to buy for David Chytraeus a copy of the Quran or any other Arabic book, but the local Muslims did not have such books for sale.[41]

In the second half of the sixteenth century the Tartars began to adopt the Ruthenian and Polish languages, which made it necessary to translate the Quran into these languages.[42] These translations were found in commentaries to the Holy Quran called tafsirs. In Lithuania, this was an interlinear translation of the Quran in a Belarusian or Polish version, where the Polish or Belarusian text was written in a cursive hand in the Arabic alphabet. This practice of

[37] Resnick, "The codex in early Jewish and Christian communities", pp. 1-17.

[38] J. del Barco, "From scroll to codex: Dynamics of text layout transformation in the Hebrew Bible", in: *From Scrolls to Scrolling: Sacred Texts, Materiality, and Dynamic Media Cultures*, ed. B.A. Anderson (Boston, 2012), pp. 91-118.

[39] Żurkowa, *Udział Żydów krakowskich*, pp. 60-61, 71.

[40] *"Ex epistola a Polono ad Davidem Chytraeum scripta anno 1581"*, p. 322.

[41] *"Si Alcoranum vel alium quemvis librum typis editum hic videre licuisset, eum certe, magno vel pretioso compratum, ad te misissem. In tanto autem librorum defectu nihil se vendere posse dicebant", ibid.*

[42] H.S. Szapszał, "O zatraceniu języka ojczystego przez Tatarów w Polsce", *Rocznik Tatarski* 1 (1932), pp. 34-48; P. Borawski and A. Dubiński, *Tatarzy polscy: Dzieje, obrzędy, legendy, tradycje* (Warsaw, 1986), pp. 255-256.

transliteration required some modifications to the script.[43] Presumably, it was developed in the late sixteenth century for translations directly from Arabic. The oldest known translation of fragments of the Quran into Polish dates from the sixteenth century.[44] The oldest complete example of such an interlinear translation is the Minsk Tefsir from 1686.[45] Linguistic analysis revealed that the original translation was made in the sixteenth century.[46]

Sacred texts in Vilnius were mostly accessed by the clergy, which usually meant men.[47] They usually possessed a suitable education or social origin, and often a combination of these. Lay inhabitants of Vilnius also read the Holy Books. However, the regulations and customs of religious communities on lay access differed significantly. Psalters were used to teach reading and for individual prayer among all Christians and Jews. Small fragments of the Bible were also available in prayer books, catechisms, and primers, but it is doubtful whether entire books of the Bible were read aloud in Catholic houses, as was the case in Calvinist ones. An Orthodox merchant was probably not used to studying the book of Genesis on Sundays, which many Jewish merchants had undoubtedly done the day before.

[43] KRYCZYŃSKI, *Tatarzy litewscy*, pp. 239-240; CZ. ŁAPICZ, "Zawartość treściowa kitabu Tatarów litewskopolskich", *Acta Baltico-Slavica* 20 (1991), p. 190; G. MIŠKINIENĖ, *Seniausi lietuvos totoriu rankraščiai. Grafika, transliteracija, vertimas, tekstu struktura ir turinys* (Vilnius, 2001), pp. 14-15; KONOPACKI, *Życie religijne Tatarów na ziemiach Wielkiego Księstwa Litewskiego*, p. 138; НІКОЛАЕЎ, *Палата кнігопісаная*, p. 59, 61.

[44] KONOPACKI, *Życie religijne Tatarów na ziemiach Wielkiego Księstwa Litewskiego*, p. 135.

[45] The manuscript is preserved in the Central Library of the National Academy of Sciences of Belarus in Minsk. At the Nicolaus Copernicus University in Toruń (Poland) a project on Tatars tefsirs from the sixteenth-nineteenth centuries is carried out. See: *Projekt "Tefsir"* <http://www.tefsir.umk.pl/o,1,o-projekcie.html>. A result of the project is a publication *Tefsir Tatarów Wielkiego Księstwa Litewskiego: Teoria i praktyka badawcza – Тафсир Татар Великого княжества Литовского: Теория и практика исследования – The Tafsir of the Tatars of the Grand Duchy of Lithuania: Theory and Research*, ed. J. KULWICKA-KAMIŃSKA and CZ. ŁAPICZ (Toruń, 2015).

[46] J. KULWICKA-KAMIŃSKA, "Projekt Tefsir – Wydanie krytyczne XVI-wiecznego przekładu Koranu na język polski / The Tefsir Project – Critical edition of the sixteenth century Polish translation of Koran", *Nurt SVD* 2 (2017) pp. 211-212; EAD, *Dialogue of Scriptures: The Tatar Tefsir in the Context of Biblical and Qur'anic Interpretations* (Berlin, 2019).

[47] See Chapter 4.

Explaining Holy Books

A common feature of all religions of the Book represented in Vilnius was that the interpretation of holy texts was entrusted to well-educated experts. In principle, two types or two levels of exegesis can be distinguished. The first was to study the Scriptures and the commentaries on them written by the authorities in order to better understand God and his message. Studies, conducted not only in Vilnius,[48] allowed scholars to transpose the Word of God into a practical system of duties, commandments, prohibitions, etc. used in the everyday life of society. The second level of interpretation resulted from the first one. It explained to the faithful the teaching derived from the Scriptures. This had a greater catechetical dimension. The basic literary form used in this method of exegesis was the sermon.

In the second half of the sixteenth century, Vilnius became a major centre of theological studies, especially of Catholic theological studies. Saying this, we must remember, that theological studies were anchored in all three religions of the Book and that they were limited by religious dogmas. At that time one notices a kind of petrification of the doctrine of all Christian Churches (maybe with the exception of that of the Polish Brethren, who were absent from Vilnius), which is an aspect of confessionalisation processes. Consequently, Vilnius theologians carried out their studies in a space framed by the interpretations of religious doctrine established by their predecessors. Probably all scholars engaged in theological studies in Vilnius were members of religious institutions. They were usually priests and teachers in the Jesuit Academy of Vilnius, in the Protestant and Muslim schools, members of the Vilnius chapter, of the Jewish *qahal* court, Catholic and Orthodox monks, and rabbis of the Great Synagogue. Theology was a part of their profession that did not favour any trespassing into unorthodoxy.

The Christian confessions had at their disposal resilient institutions whose purpose was precisely to study the Holy Scriptures and to promote theological education. In the Catholic Church, religious orders and male congregations specialised in both these areas. At the beginning of the sixteenth century, theological studies were taught by the Bernardines and Dominicans (in their Studium Generale), later joined by the Carmelites, but above all by the Jesuits.

[48] M.A. SHULVASS, "The story of Torah study in Eastern Europe," in: ID., *Between the Rhine and the Bosporus: Studies and Essays in European Jewish History* (Chicago, 1964), pp. 70-128.

Jesuit documentation informs us about the teaching of theology in the papal seminary and the Academy of Vilnius. Studies were divided into several branches: dogmatic, polemical, and moral theology. The Faculty of Theology was established in 1579, though theological studies had been carried out since 1571.[49] Courses of dogmatic theology were conducted by outstanding theologians of the time, among them Antonio Arcias, Baltazar Hostounský, Stanisław Grodzicki, Marcin Śmiglecki (who in 1594 got the degree of *magister theologiae* in Vilnius), Jacobus Ortiz, Mateusz Bembus, and Maciej Kazimierz Sarbiewski.[50] The level of the lectures is shown by the extant notebooks and printed works. The lists of courses and manuscript course books inform as about the topics of the Jesuit lectures on theology. The course was based on works by St. Thomas Aquinas. We have, for instance, the manuscript records of lectures given by Maciej Kazimierz Sarbiewski in two terms of the academic years 1631-1632 and 1632-1633. Sarbiewski commented on the *Summa theologica* by St. Thomas.[51] Lecturers of dogmatic theology applied a scholastic approach to interpreting dogma.[52] A part of theological studies consisted of interpreting Holy Scripture, also in Greek and Hebrew.

An important feature of a Catholic theology at that time was its polemical character. Even the students of the lower (rhetorical) classes learned some elements of Catholic polemical theology. They were expected to gain basic knowledge about how to respond to the Protestant interpretation of the Holy Scriptures and the Christian faith.[53]

Those students who chose an ecclesiastic career had to listen to (at least some) lectures in advanced theology. Some of them continued their theological

[49] PIECHNIK, *Początki Akademii Wileńskiej*, pp. 51-52.

[50] *Ibid.*, pp. 145-162; L. PIECHNIK, *Rozkwit Akademii Wileńskiej*, pp. 133-135, 148.

[51] M.K. SARBIEWSKI, *In primam partem Summae Theologicae divi Tomae Aquinatis doctoris Angelici Commentarius in certos de Deo uno, et trino tractatus distributes* and *Commentarius in reliquam primam D. Thomae Aquinatis Summae Theologicae a questione L. Partem de angelis* (MS VUB F3-2037). Since Sarbiewski enjoyed considerable esteem at that time, an anonymous scribe did not omit to mark on the title pages that the "Sarmatian Horace" was the author of these lectures: "*In Academia Vilnensi Societatis Jesu sub professore Reverendissimo Patre Matthia Casimiro Sarbiewski Anno 1631 Horis Matutinis*"; "*In Academia Vilnensi sub Professore Reverendissimo Patre Matthia Casimiro Sarbiewski Anno 1632 Horis pomeridianis*". See J. OKOŃ, "Un commentaire inconnu de Sarbiewski de la Somme de Saint Thomas d'Aquin", *Humanitas* 1 (1930), pp. 15-32; J. ZDANOWICZ, *Sarbiewski na tle kontrowersyj teologicznych swojego wieku* (Vilnius, 1932).

[52] PIECHNIK, *Rozkwit Akademii Wileńskiej*, pp. 125-132.

[53] NATOŃSKI, *Humanizm jezuicki*, pp. 26-35. Positive-controversial theology has been discussed in Chapter 9.

research. In the period between 1550 and 1655, all members of the clergy were involved to some extent in theology. As a result, Catholic theological and ascetic literature, which was collected or written by Vilnius clergymen (and examples of which have already been mentioned many times), constituted a very important part of the corpus of locally produced texts. The manuscript created by the Franciscan Observant (Bernardine) brother Andrew of Vilnius (from the 1590s), testifies to his interest in various aspects of theology and philosophy. In addition to his rough notes, brother Andrew included into them notes on three treatises, including a record of Hannibal Rosselli's lectures on Aristotle's third book *On the Soul* (1583) and a treatise on the methods of practising exegesis of the scriptures (1588).[54] The third text was a treatise on usury by Śmiglecki. This treatise was published in Vilnius twice in 1596, and one of these editions was the base from which brother Andrew worked. On the copied title page the owner noted:

> I started to write this in the year 1596 on *26 Aprilis. Frater Andreas Vilnensis sacerdos Ordinis Minorum et Observantum* by order of the Reverend Father Master Benedict Anzelmus of Lviv. Loaning, expecting nothing in exchange, the sum of 6 *złoty* 36 [*grosz*] in Kaunas. (original in Polish)

It is clear that brother Andrew was up to date with the latest literature published by the Jesuits.

The Orthodox Church in the Polish-Lithuanian Commonwealth was the last of the Christian Churches to build its own confessional identity. The process started in the 1570s and accelerated in the 1590s, when the Union of Brest took place (1596). Vilnius, together with Kyiv, Lviv, and Ostroh, was the major centre in this process. Theological works by Orthodox authors were usually polemical, like the writings of Meletius Smotrycki and Józef Bobrykowicz (Josif Bobrikovich). The basics of theology were taught in the Vilnius Brotherhood school, which also contributed to increasing the level of theological knowledge among the Orthodox inhabitants of Vilnius.

[54] *Explicationes in Librum Tertium de Anima inceptae ad scribendum per me fratrem Andream Vilnensem sub reverendo patre Anibalo Roselo de Calabria lectore generali Crac<oviensi> anno Domini 1583* XI *Julii Hor. Oct.*; *Metamorphoseos conceptum super universis sensibus divinae scripturae, quorum primi sunt: historia sive litera; tropologia et mysticus sive spiritualis. Hic vero duplex allegoricus nimirum et anagogicus datur. Ex quibus tanquam fontibus hace transformatio haurietur. Vilnae diei prima Ianuarii anno salutis 1588*, MS CZART. 3681 I.

As early as the 1620s, the Uniates, who competed with the Orthodox in the city, established their own Basilian monastery, where theological studies were carried out by Leon Kreuza Rzewuski, among others.

The Protestants of Vilnius had already earlier accepted a similar attitude towards theology. The Calvinist and Lutheran theologians did not write huge treatises but rather lectured or disseminated popular theological knowledge in the form of sermons and postils. An example of such work is a sermon by Andrzej Schönflissius, written to commemorate the coronation of King Władysław IV Vasa in 1632.[55] The author analysed the role of the king in the state, but did so from a theological standpoint.[56]

The task of the Protestant theologians in Vilnius was to explain the ways of interpretating the Bible and of disputing them in the frame of the commonly accepted Protestant principles of the faith. In his memoirs, Maciej Vorbek-Lettow gave an insight into the way of theological discussions between the teacher and his pupils in the Lutheran community in Vilnius.[57]

In the first half of the seventeenth century, Jewish scholars carried out their research upon the Holy Texts. Their studies mostly concerned the interpretation of Jewish law, that is Halakha. In the last years before the Muscovite invasion, Vilnius was home to many eminent and highly-regarded experts on the law and the Talmud. In the 1640s, Shabbatai ben Meir HaKohen returned to the city. Moses ben Isaac Judah Lima, who became a rabbi in 1655, and Aaron Samuel ben Israel Kaidanover,[58] who escaped the Cossack massacres, lived there from 1650 onwards. Another well-known author of commentaries on the Talmud was the pupil of Lima, Ephraim ben Jacob HaKohen.[59] All these scholars enjoyed great respect, most of them were members of the court of the Vil-

[55] A. SCHÖNFLISSIUS, *Korona na szczęśliwą koronacyją najaśniejszego Władysława IV* (Lubcz, 1633).

[56] Schönflissius was not the only preacher in the Polish-Lithuanian Commonwealth who practised an early modern 'political theology'. Among the Catholics the Jesuit Piotr Skarga and Fabian Birkowski, a Dominican from Cracow, were known because of their political homiletic activity.

[57] VORBEK-LETTOW, *Skarbnica pamięci*, p. 241-242; and see Chapter 3 of this book.

[58] COHEN, *History of the Jews in Vilnius*, pp. 187-188; M. BERSOHN, *Słownik biograficzny uczonych Żydów polskich XVI, XVII i XVIII wieku* (Warsaw, 1906), pp. 46-47.

[59] J. FRENKEL, "Literatura rabiniczna Żydów w dawnej Rzeczypospolitej", in: *Żydzi w Polsce odrodzonej*, 1, p. 222; EIDELBERG, *Shabbetai ben Meir ha-Kohen*, pp. 338-339; I.M. TA-SHMA, "Moses ben Isaac Judah", *EJ*, 13, pp. 22-23; A. FUERST, "Ephraim ben Jacob haKohen", *EJ*, vol. 13, p. 459.

nius *qahal* (*bet din*), but all of them conducted research, which in the second half of the century was to make them widely known across Europe.

Particularly popular was Shabatai's treatise *Siftei Kohen* (or *Shakh*, ש״ך), published in Cracow in 1646. This is a commentary on the *Yoreh De'ah*, part of the famous work *Shulchan Aruch* (1565) by Rabbi Joseph Karo.[60] Shabatai's treatise commented on several halakhic rules regarding laws of kashrut (dietary laws). He adjusted them to the life of Ashkenazy Jews in the Grand Duchy of Lithuania. The treatise was widely respected and has been reprinted in each edition of the *Yoreh De'ah* published after 1674.[61] Lima also wrote a commentary on *Shulchan Aruch*, specifically on the part *Ewen Haezer*, published by one of his three sons in Cracow in 1670 under the title *Helkat Mehokek*. Ephraim ben Jacob HaKohen studied both the mystic dimension of the law and the Talmud. Research on the Talmud was carried out at that time by Joshua Heschel Zoref and Abraham Joshua ben Jacob Heschel,[62] as well as by Moses ben Naphtali Hirsch Rivkes. In the introduction to the Amsterdam commentary on *Shulchan Aruch* Rivkes deplored that in August 1655 (during the Muscovite invasion) he had lost his commentary on the treatises entitled *Zebahim* and *Menahot*, on which he had worked for a long time.[63]

During this period, most works of Jewish scholars remained in manuscript. Those that were not destroyed during the fire in the Jewish quarter started by the Muscovite soldiers on 8 August 1655, did not appear in print until the second half of the century. In addition, responses written by Vilnius rabbis, published in various collections, for instance the one by Moses ben Isaac Judah, have survived in fragmentary form.

We know much less about the texts of the Vilnius Tartars. Like all Tartar literature from the past, they had a religious character.[64] Few manuscripts were

[60] Joseph Karo (1488-1575) based his work on the thirteenth-century treatise by rabbi Jacob ben Asher (*c.* 1270-1340). The *Shulchan Aruch* (שֻׁלְחָן עָרוּךְ) by Karo was a comprehensive study of all aspects of Jewish law and since the sixteenth century has been one of the most influential rabbinic texts. See J.R. BERKOVITZ, "Rabbinic culture and halakhah", in: *The Cambridge History of Judaism*, 7, pp. 359-360.

[61] Shabbatai ben Meir HaKohen, *שפתי כהן* (Cracow, 1646) See COHEN, *History of the Jews in Vilnius*, p. 196; EIDELBERG, *Shabbetai ben Meir haKohen*, p. 338; BERKOVITZ, "Rabbinic culture and halakhah", p. 360. After emigration to Holešov in Moravia, Sabatai published a commentary on another part of the *Shulchan Aruch*, devoted to civil and criminal law. It was published in Amsterdam in 1661 under the title *Choshen Mishpat*.

[62] J. OCHMAN, *Peryferie filozofii żydowskiej* (Cracow, 1997), pp. 118, 125-126, 129, 259.

[63] COHEN, *History of the Jews in Vilnius*, p. 42.

[64] J. SZYNKIEWICZ, "Literatura religijna Tatarów litewskich i jej pochodzenie", *Rocznik Tatarski* 2 (1932), p. 139; KRYCZYŃSKI, *Tatarzy litewscy*, p. 217; ŁAPICZ, *Trzy redakcje*, p. 155.

produced by Lithuanian Muslims in the seventeenth century. Most of them are anonymous and their place of origin is unknown, so we can only make assumptions about their contents and use. The possibility that they may also have been created in Vilnius results from the large size of the local community that lived in Lukiškės from the fifteenth century onwards.

One of the main books used by the Muslim clergy were the tafsirs, mentioned above, that is commentaries on the Quran containing interlinear translations of the holy text, written above the Arabic original. They belonged to the equipment of every mosque, and the whole community funded them, as they were expensive.

Another interesting textual form was the *kitab* or half-*kitab*, books used by clergy and lay people alike.[65] They contained stories about the prophet, the life of Muhammad, translations of prayers, and legends from the Middle East, for instance *Seven Sleepers*, *King Solomon's Ring*, or *Alexander the Great*,[66] and they explained religious rites.[67] The oldest of these books, from the middle of the seventeenth century, contains among other things *Disput musulmanina s judiejem* (A Dispute between a Muslim and a Jew), *Dialog Muhammada s Satanom* (Muhammad's Dialogue with Satan), and *Powiest' o napisanii sury "Al Chamda"* (The Tale of the Writing of the "Al Chamda" Sura).[68]

Tartar writers were particularly active in the period of religious disputes at the beginning of the seventeenth century. It is assumed that at that time short theological texts aimed at proving the truth of Muhammad's teachings were written, for instance dialogues on the superiority of Islam over Judaism, which were included in the translations of the *kitabs*. Probably, for apologetic purposes Muslim clerics also used the Bible. In the library of the University of Warsaw is a copy of the Nyasvizh Bible (translated into Polish by Szymon Budny and printed in 1572), with Muslim glosses in Arabic and Polish.[69]

If, in seventeenth-century Vilnius, Muslims used texts in the way assumed here – which is quite probable – this would mean that all religions of the Book produced and used 'secondary' theological texts. These actions did not necessarily result from the need to conduct the disputes which were the essence of

[65] KRYCZYŃSKI, *Tatarzy litewscy*, p. 218; ŁAPICZ, *Zawartość treściowa kitabu*, pp. 169-191.

[66] MIŠKINIENĖ, *Seniausi lietuvos totoriu rankraščiai*, p. 16.

[67] SZYNKIEWICZ, "Literatura religijna Tatarów litewskich i jej pochodzenie", p. 139.

[68] The historical sources stored in Kazan and St. Petersburg were edited by MIŠKINIENĖ, *Seniausi lietuvos totoriu rankraščiai*, p. 144, 146, 184-186.

[69] *Ibid.*, p. 55. KONOPACKI, *Życie religijne Tatarów na ziemiach Wielkiego Księstwa Litewskiego*, p. 155.

the dominant agonistic culture; they were also a response to a climate favourable to theological studies and to the increasing opportunities of disseminating texts. Thanks to the development of education, printing, and greater access to writing materials and books, more clerics and lay people were able to deepen their interest in religion.

Prayers

Everyday and Festive Prayers and Songs

Prayers were texts known to everyone, because every follower of a religion of the Book was obliged to pray daily either using Christian prayers such as the Lord's Prayer or Hail Mary, the Muslim Salah, the Hebrew Shema Yisrael or Amidah. The Vilnians knew their prayers by heart and usually learned them in their early childhood. The requirements regarding every day prayers were put in every Christian catechism and in many primers.

The texts of the prayers were codified and fixed. Improvised prayer of one's own authorship was a rarity. Although many people in Vilnius could not read, especially in the first century after the foundation of the city, they recited prayers as internalised written texts recorded in their memory. The orality of prayers was secondary and was always a derivative of the model written form. As in the case of the Holy Books, it was the written version that determined the unchangeability and dogmatic correctness of the prayers uttered. A prayer could not differ from the written version of the religious laws, which demanded that it be reproduced correctly, even if it was said in one's mind only and was not articulated.

However, in addition to the basic, usually quite short texts of prayers, there were many other prayers, longer, more specialised and sophisticated ones, often intended for special occasions. Some of them may have been texts for both private use and for use in the liturgy, for instance psalms, Kaddishim, litanies, hymns, hours, etc. All confessions valued prayer highly and encouraged its constant practice. This is the anonymous author of the preface to an Orthodox prayer book:

> A truthful prayer chases away devils, calls to the angels for help, is a shield in the case of night fears, during the day it is a rest from work, a defence for youths, defervescence for the elderly, the pilgrims' companion, joy for the troubled, an

i wmodlitwach moich : i od
ſſkod przyſſłych raczy mie
obronicz : Ktory z bogiem
oiczem i z duchem ſwiatym
zyieſſ na vieki : A :
Modlitwa . Za Miaſto :
Vyſluchai pa
nie modlitwy
naſſe : a mia
ſto naſſe vez
mi w moc
i w opatrznoſcz ſwa : ze by
aniolowie twoi ſtrzegli mu
row iego : Vyſluchai pa

Fig. 65 *Prayer for The Town* in a prayer book belonging to the Lithuanian chancellor Olbracht Gasztołd, *The Shield of the Soul* (*Szczyt duszny* or *Clypeus spiritualis*), p. 82. Munich, Universitätsbibliothek der Ludwig-Maximilians-Universität, Cim. 89, <https://epub. ub.uni-muenchen.de/11772/> (accessed: 07.06.2023, public domain).

escape for orphans and widows, and, as St. Chrysostom says: "There is nothing more powerful than a man praying".[70] (original in Polish)

[70] *Wykład liturgiej świętej i modlitwy z doktorów św. według św. wschodniej i apostolskiej Cerkwie zebrane i na wielu miejscach z pilnością poprawione: Przydane są do tego i inne modlitwy na kożdy dzień św. ojca naszego Cyrilla i kalendarz dni przez rok idących z Paschalią* (Vilnius, 1624), f. A3v. The only known copy in CR, Teol. Asket.

As early as at the beginning of the sixteenth century, in Vilnius a growing demand for Catholic prayer books among lay people can be noticed. Firstly, they were the members of the social elite who could afford such books. One of them that has survived is a lavishly illuminated prayer book made for chancellor Olbracht Gasztołd in Cracow in 1528, in the workshop of the painter Stanisław Samostrzelnik.[71] This is a Polish translation of popular Latin prayers: *Szczyt duszny* or *Clypeus spiritualis* (The Shield of the Soul), *Godziny o Pannie Maryjej* (The Hours of the Holy Virgin), and prayers to saints: to Nicolas, George, Anne, Barbara, Catherine of Alexandria, and Christopher.[72] The book contains a set of prayers recorded in other prayer books from the end of the fifteenth and the first decades of the sixteenth century; for instance, the prayers to the saints from the last part of the book were printed in Cracow in 1513 in the *Hortulus animae Polonice* of Bernard (Biernat) of Lublin.[73] The luxurious book was designed especially for Gasztołd, and probably he himself (at least to some extent) decided about its content. The reader can find here *The Prayer for The Town*:

> Lord, hear our prayers and take our town in your mighty protection to make the angels protect its walls. Hear, Lord, your people, and let your mercy approach and move away the fire of your wrath from your people and this town. We have heard the sorrow of this town, Lord, be merciful. Hear, Lord, the prayer of your servants. Bless and consecrate this town, o Dear Lord. Protect the peace and mercy of your servants who stand before you with their pure hearts forever and ever, God of Israel![74] (original in Polish)

For Gasztołd, who took special care for the development of the capital in the first decades of the sixteenth century, this prayer could be especially useful.

It is probable that other Catholic members of the Lithuanian elite could also have manuscript or printed versions of prayer books. This may have be-

[71] The original is preserved in the Universitätsbibliothek der Ludwig-Maximilians-Universität in Munich (shelf mark Cim. 89 or 4° Cod. MS. 1097). A facsimile of the book was printed in 2015: *Modlitewnik Olbrachta Gasztołda, kanclerza wielkiego litewskiego 1528 r. Facsimile*, ed. W. WYDRA (Poznań, 2015).

[72] The unknown translator of the prayer book came from Little Poland. See M. OSIEWICZ, "Cechy dialektyczne *Szczytu dusznego* z 1528 r. (modlitewnik Olbrachta Gasztołda)", *LingVaria* 15.1 (2020), pp. 163-164, with an up-to-date bibliography of Gasztołd's prayer book.

[73] The *Hortulus animae Polonice* (*Raj duszny*) is one of the oldest books printed in Polish. It was a translation of the humanist Bernard of Lublin of a Latin work, *Antidotarius animae*.

[74] "Modlitewnik Obrachta Gasztołda", in: *Chrestomatia staropolska*, p. 42.

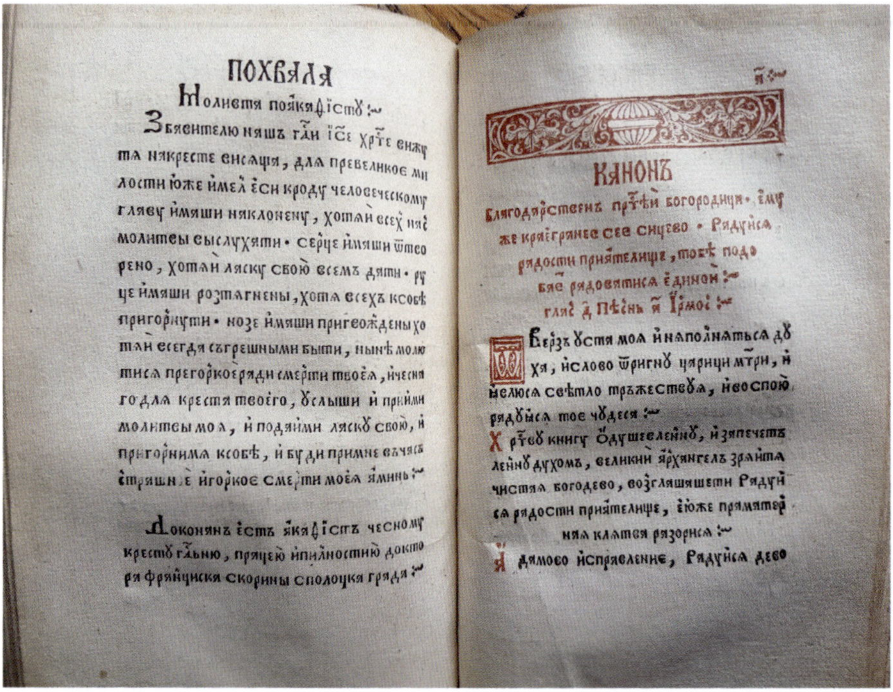

Fig. 66 F. Skaryna, *The Little Travel Book* (Vilnius, *c.* 1522). On the inferior margin of the left page the colophon of the printer; on the right, the start of the Canon of the Virgin Mary. Cracow, BJ, Cim 561. Public domain. Photo J. Niedźwiedź.

come fashionable in Lithuania and Vilnius because Polish magnates and the members of the ruling house possessed such books in Latin and Polish, among them Queen Bona and King Sigismund the Old.[75]

We do not have any information about the import of Catholic prayer books from Cracow and other cities to Vilnius in the early sixteenth century, but we may suppose that market was ready for such books. First of all, the parish school of St. John operated from 1513. As was explained in Chapter 3, the patrons of the school were both the parish priest and the Catholic members of the city council. This means that a group of potential users of prayer books existed. Secondly, the city elite had many contacts with those urban settlements in Poland and Royal Prussia (especially Cracow and Gdańsk) where the use of prayer books in Latin, Polish, and German was common at the turn of the fifteenth and sixteenth centuries. Thirdly, the publication of *The Little Travel*

[75] W. WYDRA, "Wstęp", in: *Modlitewnik Olbrachta Gasztołda*, pp. 10-11.

Book by Skaryna (*c.* 1522) was an attempt to introduce a prayer book addressed not only to the Orthodox clergy but to the Orthodox lay elite of the city and the State as well. He may have published his books in Church Slavonic and Ruthenian rather than in Latin or Polish because he may have been afraid that the import of Polish and Latin prayer books and liturgical books would make publishing them in the Grand Duchy of Lithuania unprofitable.

Most of the Catholic prayers recited in Vilnius belonged to the general and universally used corpus of texts of this type, so we encounter them in other places in the Christian, Muslim, and Jewish world as well. Their specificity lies in their use at a particular time and place. For example, the songbook *Parthenomelica* published in 1613 by Walenty Bartoszewski, apart from many popular songs which "the respected senate of the city of Vilnius [...] performs handsomely every year during dawn Masses at the time of the desired Advent of the Lord", contains *Pienie X* as the *Song of St. Adalbert*: "*Boga Rodzica dziewica, Bogiem wsławiona Maryja ...*" ("The Virgin Mother of God, God-famed Mary").[76] It is quite surprising that this medieval trope, not entirely understandable in the seventeenth century, was sung in St. John's church in Vilnius.[77] The way in which Szymon Budny's translation of the 'Arian' Bible (1572)[78] was employed, adapted into Ruthenian on the one hand, by Meletius Smotrycki and, on the other hand, by the Tartars in seventeenth-century *kitabs*, may seem even more unusual.[79]

[76] W. BARTOSZEWSKI, *Parthenomelica albo Pienia nabożne o Pannie Naświętszej, które poważny Senat miasta wileńskiego spólnym a porządnym obywatelów swoich i innej młodzi nabożeństwem i kosztownym apparatem, czasu pożądanego adwentu Pańskiego, na roraciech przystojnie co rok odprawuje. Niektóre poprawione, niektóre z łacińskiego na polskie przełożone, niektóre nowo teraz złożone. Na cześć i chwałę wcielenia Pańskiego i na wielbienie Bogarodzicy* (Vilnius, 1613), pp. B4r-C2r.

[77] The *Bogurodzica* is the oldest known song composed in Polish, probably dating from the thirteenth century. In the fifteenth century it was known as the *carmen patrium* (the 'song of the fathers') and was performed by Polish knights before battles (e.g. before the Battle of Grunwald in 1410). It was published for the first time in 1505 in the *Statuta Regni Poloniae* by chancellor Jan Łaski. Publication of the *Bogurodzica* in 1613 may be proof that the song was still popular, or at least was revitalised in the Polish Catholic liturgy after Council of Trent. For a recent recapitulation of two hundred years of research on the *Bogurodzica*, see E. RANOCCHI, "In search of origins: *Bogurodzica*", in: *The Routledge World Companion to Polish Literature*, ed. M. POPIEL, T. BILCZEWSKI, and S. BILL (Abingdon-on-Thames, 2022), pp. 1-11.

[78] The humanist Szymon Budny (1530-1593) translated into Polish and published his version of the Bible for the Polish Brethren (called the "Arians"): *Biblia to jest księgi Starego i Nowego przymierza znowu z języka hebrayskiego, greckiego i łacińskiego na polski przełożone* (Zaslawye, 1572).

[79] FRICK, "Introduction", in: SMOTRYCKI, *Rus' Restored*, pp. XXIX-XXX; Г. МИШКИНЕНЕ,

The late medieval hymn *Omni die dic Mariae* became very popular through the intermediary of Vilnius. It was the favourite prayer of St. Casimir, who, until the ninetheenth century, was considered to be the author of the text. "This prayer", as canon Grzegorz Święcicki wrote in 1604. "was discovered in the year of Our Lord 1498 in the handwritten book owned by St. Casimir by brother Krzysztof Złotkowski and put on public view, near the grave, which the brother himself testifies to".[80] Święcicki found a copy of the text at the head of the saint's bed when inspecting his relics in August 1604 and described it as his "daily prayer composed by himself". Although today we know that St. Casimir did not author this text, which was actually a late mediaeval cento,[81] it gained great popularity throughout the Polish-Lithuanian Commonwealth.

From the end of the sixteenth century, in Vilnius the sublimation of the spiritual life in the form of personal prayer became ever more common among all Christian confessions present in the city. This was not only due to the catechesis practised in Vilnius schools, but also to the Orthodox Brotherhood and the Catholic religious confraternities, which became much more active during this period. Apart from the existing confraternity of St. Martin (gathering inhabitants of German origin) and the Archconfraternity of St. Anne, the confraternity of St. John the Baptist, the archconfraternity of Corpus Christi, and the archconfraternity of Mercy in St. John's church emerged in 1573, as well as the confraternity of the Name of God founded in 1590 at the Dominican church of the Holy Spirit.[82] These institutions introduced new forms of public services and private prayers, including meditation. This was also due to the elite Sodality of the Blessed Virgin Mary, which was active at the Academy of Vilnius, and whose members knew the Jesuit way of performing spiritual exercises. Another important institution which popularised new forms of collective prayers was the Brotherhood of the Holy Rosary. In 1627 a spiritual guidebook provided for the Lithuanian Congregation of the Rosary was published in Cracow by the Vilnius Dominican father Walerian Andrzejowicz under the title *The Garden of the Roses*. The author meticulously explained the spiritual

"Полемика между мусулманами и иудеями (на материале арабскалфавитных рукописей литовских татар середины XVII в.)", *Krakowsko-wileńskie studia slawistyczne*, 4, ed. M. Kuczyńska, W. Stępniak-Minczewa, and J. Stradomski (Cracow, 2009), pp. 239-241.

80 Święcicki, *Theatrum S. Casimiri*, p. 59.

81 R. Mazurkiewicz, "Zapomniane polonicum w zbiorach Biblioteki Watykańskiej", *Terminus* 3.1-2 (2001), pp. 172-174.

82 In 1594, a prayer book was published for this brotherhood by Krzysztof Warecki; see *Vilnius Akademijos spaustuvės*, p. 27.

meanings of the rosary and added a whole cycle of contemplations on the parts of the rosary prayer. The patron of the second edition of the book (1646) was Zofia Chodkiewiczowa (née Drucka Horska, †1657), the wife of the *voivode* of Vilnius, Krzysztof Chodkiewicz.[83] These prayer books were designed for the members of the local confraternities.

The Jesuits and Carmelites practised meditation as an important part of their spiritual development. In the last decades of the sixteenth century elements of Ignatian and Carmelite meditation also influenced the religious life of lay people.

For religious activities one needed books, in particular spiritual guides that led Catholics through the successive stages of prayer. Meditative books in Polish reached Vilnius relatively early, because as early as 1588 the Jesuit Szymon Wysocki published a volume with a long Polish title:

> *The Gate of Paradise, that is the Brave Exercises of the Spiritual Life. The Person, Who Practices Them, Easily Will Gain the Christian Perfection. This Book Was Composed and Practised by Some Nun in Italy and at the Beginning It Was Written in Italian on the Order of the Bishop of Cremona; Later It Was Translated into Several Other Languages, Because it Was Very Beneficial For the People; Finally It Was Translated into Polish by Some Jesuit Father, With the Permission of the Authorities. Some Pious Exercises Were Added, Especially Those about the Passion of Our Lord, to be Practised for the Entire Week.*[84]

This new type of prayers was primarily popular among the social elites. Female readers were especially welcome to use them. The translator of *The Gate of Paradise* dedicated it to Princess Katarzyna of Tęczyn Radziwiłłowa (1544-

[83] W. ANDRZEJOWICZ, *Ogród różany abo opisanie porządne dwu szczepów wonnej róży hierychuntskiej, to jest o dwu świętych różańcach dwojga bractw Błogosławionej Panny Maryjej i Naświętszego Imienia Pana Jezusowego w Zakonie Kaznodziejskim szczepionych k woli braciej i promotorom obojga bractw świętych przez wielebnego ojca brata Waleryjana Lithuanidesa, prezydenta bractw pomienionych tegoż zakonu* (Cracow, 1627). The edition from 1646 was edited by Hilary Mackiewicz. Estreicher noted also an edition from 1612. See ESTREICHER, *Bibliographia Polska*, 12 (1891), p. 152 and 23 (1910), p. 301.

[84] *Fortka niebieska, to jest dzielne ćwiczenia żywota duchownego, w których kto się będzie chciał ćwiczyć, doskonałości chrześcijańskiej snadnie może dostąpić. Te złożyła i w nich się ćwiczyła panna niektóra zakonna we Włoszech, które naprzód językiem włoskim z rozkazania biskupa kremońskiego napisano, po tym w rozmaite języki dla pożytków ich, które w ludziach czyniły przełożono, na ostatek i na polskie przez jednego kapłana Societatis Iesu przetłomaczono z dozwoleniem starszych. Przydano niektóre nabożne ćwiczenia, a osobliwie przez cały tydzień o męce Pańskiej rozmyślania*, ed. and trans. Sz. WYSOCKI (Vilnius, 1588).

Fig. 67 The title page of the emblemata collection of H. Bildziukiewicz, *Divi Tutelaris Patrii Casimiri insigne virtutum hieroglyphicis emblematum figuris adumbratum. Poloniarum Reginae Constantiae … deusta observantia humiliter oblata* (Vilnius, 1610). CZART. (MNK) 28066 II <https://cyfrowe.mnk.pl/dlibra/publication/9670/edition/9494/content> (accessed: 07.06.2023, public domain).

1592), the wife of the *voivode* of Vilnius Mikołaj Krzysztof Radziwiłł 'the Orphan'. Wysocki stressed his opinion that a useful spiritual guide, even if written for use of the clergy, should not be sent to the nunneries or hermitages, but rather be read by lay people.[85] This declaration and its practice were not rare at that time. The popularity of *The Gate of Paradise*, which was reprinted

[85] *Ibid.*, pp. †2r-†2v.

several times reprinted in Poland, proves that the lay members of the Catholic Church were interested in adapting and practising some prayers or meditations provided primarily for priests, monks, and nuns. The seventeenth century was the heyday of spiritual guides and meditative texts.[86] A large amount of such literature, mostly imported from the Kingdom of Poland, is recorded in the inventories of private and church libraries from that period.

At the time, a new and fashionable type of pious reading was that of emblems. A person who used them, engaged his or her reading skills but also the sense of sight and memory. Contemplation or meditation of an emblem was usually a private act of reading, often in silence. It required some quiet space (for instance a chapel in a church) and knowledge about ways of meditating. The reader of an emblem should show some interpretative skills to understand allegory and complex relationships between a picture (*icon*) and the accompanying text (*subscription*). One of the finest examples of such a book is a collection of emblems *The Splendid Depiction in Emblems and Hieroglyphics of the Virtues of Our Home Protector Saint Casimir*, published in the first half of 1610 by a student of the philosophy in the Academy of Vilnius, Hieronim Bildziukiewicz.[87] The book was dedicated to Queen Constance of Austria, who was staying in Vilnius castle for several months, awaiting the return of the king from an expedition against Muscovy.

It might appear that only the social elites could afford to meditate on emblems, but this was not necessarily true. It is true that the magnates bought or commissioned emblem books, but in the seventeenth century even the common inhabitants of Vilnius could buy singular emblem prints in the bookshops or on the Market Square.[88] They could also gain basic competences to pray with an

[86] On the widespread use of meditation practices and texts, see L. MARTZ, *The Poetry of Meditation: A Study in English Religious Literature of the Seventeenth Century* (New Haven, 1954), pp. 1-20; E. POPRAWA-KACZYŃSKA, "Ignacjański 'modus meditandi' w kulturze religijnej późnego baroku: Rekonesans", in: *Religijność literatury polskiego baroku*, ed. Cz. HERNAS and M. HANUSIEWICZ (Lublin, 1995), pp. 259-270; GRZEŚKOWIAK, and NIEDŹWIEDŹ, "Wstęp", pp. 64-69.

[87] H. Bildziukiewicz, *Divi Tutelaris Patrii Casimiri insigne virtutum hieroglyphicis emblematum figuris adumbratum. Poloniarum Riginae Constantiae... deusta observantia humiliter oblata* (Vilnius, 1610). The icons of the emblems were executed by Tomasz Makowski. See PELC, *Słowo i obraz*, pp. 157-158; S. MASLAUSKAITĖ-MAŽYLIENĖ, *Dzieje wizerunku św. Kazimierza od XVI do XVIII wieku: Między ikonografiją a tekstem* (Vilnius, 2013), pp. 140-146. The author was probably a brother of Tomasz Bildziukiewicz, a royal secretary and the *Voigt* (*wójt*) of Vilnius in 1621-1649.

[88] Single prints of holy pictures, usually copper plates imported from the Netherlands, were popular Christmas gifts among Catholics in the seventeenth and eighteenth centuries. See R.

emblem, because some Catholic institutions, such as the confraternities, promoted new forms of piety. Some pious books also contained simple instruction manuals for praying. All this enriched the religious culture of Vilnius in the last decades before the Muscovite invasion and played an important role in shifting the modes of using the written word.

Orthodox prayer practices did not differ significantly from the Catholic ones. Every member of the Orthodox community was required to memorise the words of prayers and repeat them every day. In a primer from 1633 there are among others morning and evening prayers and admonitions such as: "When you go to bed, make the sign of the cross on yourself and say: In the name of the Father, Lord Jesus Christ, have mercy upon us".[89]

From the beginning of the sixteenth century, there was a large group of Orthodox who used a book as a manual of proper praying. *The Little Travel Book* of Skaryna (1522) was a novelty among the Orthodox inhabitants of Vilnius. It was a small book (in 8°), which could be especially useful on the road. Skaryna printed his book in two colours, red and black, which was also a rarity in this part of Europe, and added many woodcuts and initials. It contained a number of liturgical texts, which could serve both lay people and clergy. Actually, this luxurious publication is not one book but a set of 21 smaller entities: psalter, *horologion*, seventeen canons and *akathists*, *hexameron*, and the order of the service in the church (that is menologion and calendar (Пасхалии)).[90] Each of them had its own colophon (see Fig. 66), which usually took a form similar to this one:

> The end of the *akathist* in honour of God in the Holy Trinity and of the Prophet of God St. John the Baptist. By the work and diligence of doctor of medical sciences Francysk Skaryna from the famous city of Polatsk.[91] (original in Polish)

GRZEŚKOWIAK and J. NIEDŹWIEDŹ, "Nieznane polskie subskrypcje do emblematów Ottona van Veen i Hermana Hugona: Przyczynek do funkcjonowania zachodniej grafiki religijnej w kulturze staropolskiej", *Terminus* 14.25 (2012), pp. 54-62.

[89] *Dla dziatek nauka czytania*, p. C4v.

[90] Until today there are 171 known booklets which have been included in 23 volumes of *The Little Travel Book*; see Е.Л. НЕМИРОВСКИЙ, *Франциск Скорина*, pp. 430-467; Id., *Славянские издания кирилловского (церковнославянского) шрифта: 1491-2000, Инвентарь сохранившихся экземпляров и указатель литературы*, 1, *1491-1550* (Moscow, 2009), p. 130.

[91] Ф. СКАРЫНА, *Малая подорожная кнiжка* (Vilnius, 1522?), p. 60v. A copy in the Jagiellonian Library (Cracow), shelfmark: Cim. 561.

Placing the colophon after each booklet meant that these small booklets were designed to be sold separately, and in this way they became affordable to a wider audience. It is probable that some Orthodox inhabitants of Vilnius could buy only part of *The Little Travel Book* (for instance one *akathist* or the psalter) and use it in church, at home, or on their travels without any solid binding.[92] Later some of these booklets could be put together in different combinations.[93] From the very beginning it was a 'plastic' volume, and there are no two identical copies of the book. Among the 23 copies of *The Little Travel Book* known today there is not one with all the booklets printed by Skaryna.[94] Each copy answered the needs of an individual reader. Its final shape was rather the matter of its binding than by Skaryna's designing the final version of the book. The books produced by Skaryna were an experiment. We do not know to what extent it was a successful financial enterprise, but it certainly influenced the literary and religious culture of the Grand Duchy of Lithuania.[95]

Some of the prayers and songs printed by Skaryna had been originally written in Vilnius. These included the hymns of Francysk Skaryna, who was the first to write vernacular poems in Vilnius in the Church Slavonic-Ruthenian language, following the pattern of Western European Latin poetry, using rhyme and acrostics (*c.* 1522).[96] Skaryna initiated and encouraged the Orthodox inhabitants of Vilnius to use printed prayer books. In the next decades and in the seventeenth century it became a custom among the city elite (and probably not only among elite) to acquire such books. They were imported and, later, after

[92] We conjecture that Skaryna may have designed his publication as a collection or a series in the modern sense. He could publish the parts of *The Little Travel Book* over a longer time (2-3 years). At least some buyers collected them in a small library, and ultimately had them bound together. Taking into account Skaryna's ingenuity and creativity, this supposition seems to be plausible.

[93] НЕМИРОВСКИЙ, *Франциск Скорина*, pp. 441-448; А. ВОЗНЕСЕНСКИЙ, "Сведения и заметки о кириллических печатных книгах, 1, Малая подорожная книжка Франциска Скорины" in: *Труды Отдела древнерусской литературы* 51 (St. Petersburg, 1999), pp. 338-339.

[94] The last copy was discovered in 2004 in Moscow. See Е.Л. НЕМИРОВСКИЙ, "Заметки о старопечатных изданиях", *Україна: культурна спадщина, національна свідомість, державність* 15 (2006-2007), p. 186.

[95] A. NAUMOW, "Biblia i liturgia w systemie wartości kultury ruskiej", in: *Między Wschodem i Zachodem*, pp. 134-135; ТИМОШЕНКО, *Руська релігійна культура Вільна*, pp. 208, 573.

[96] "Akathist of St. Nicolas" and "Akathist of St. Peter and Paul" in: СКАРЫНА, *Малая подорожная книжка*. See НЕМИРОВСКИЙ, *Франциск Скорина*, pp. 450-452; A. NAUMOW, "Wiara i historia: Z dziejów literatury cerkiewno-słowiańskiej na ziemiach polsko-litewskich", in: *Studia slawistyczne krakowsko-wileńskie* 1 (Cracow, 1996), pp. 20, 83; ID., "Biblia i liturgia w systemie wartości kultury ruskiej", pp. 134-135.

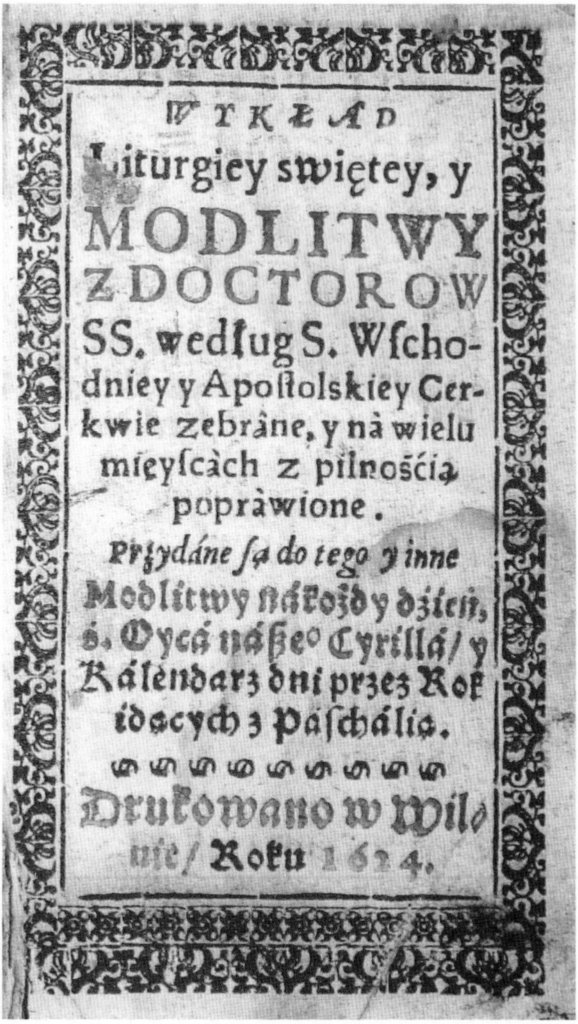
WYKŁAD
Liturgiey świętey, y
MODLITWY
Z DOCTOROW
SS. według S. Wschodniey y Apostolskiey Cerkwie zebrâne, y nà wielu mieyscàch z pilnośćią poprâwione.
Przydáne są do tego y inne Modlitwy nákożdy dźień, ś. Oycá nászeo Cyrillá, y Kálendarz dni przez Rok idących z Páschália.
Drukowano w Wilnie / Roku 1624.

Fig. 68 Orthodox prayer book in Polish and Church Slavonic: *Wykład liturgiej świętej i modlitwy z doktorów świętych według Świętej Wschodniej i Apostolskiej Cerkwie zebrane i na wielu miejscach z pilnością poprawione* (Vilnius, 1624). CR. Public domain.

the establishment of the Mamonicz' printing house in the 1570s, they were published also in Vilnius. High supply and demand (the demand especially thanks both to the development of the art of printing in Lithuania and to imports from Cracow) made prayer books one of the most popular types of printed books.

The Orthodox prayer books from the first half of the seventeenth century were published by the Brotherhood's printing house. They contained liturgical texts, commentaries on them, and explanations on how to participate in the service. The Vilnius booksellers and bookbinders offered both prayer books printed by the Brotherhood's printing house and imported ones. Among the most popular were the Orthodox books of hours (*chasoslov*) and psalters. An especially popular book was *Everyday prayers*, reprinted by the Brotherhood several times.[97] All of them were in Church Slavonic. Interestingly, these texts were printed in both *Schwabacher* (Latin) script and italics.

> MAGNIFICAT or the Song of Holy Virgin, *Luc. 1, 4 et sec.* Which the choirs sing or speak *alternatim* verse by verse. And after every verse there follows *Chestniejszuj Cheruvi, etc.*:
>
> "Weliczyt dusza moja Hospoda i wozradowasia duch moj o Bożie Spase mojem.
>
> *Czestniejszuju Cheruwim i sławneijszuju wojsinnu Serafim bez isilinia Boha sława rozdszuju suszczuju Bohorodicu tia wieliczajem*". (original in Polish and Church Slavonic in Latin alphabet)[98]

Explanations of the liturgy were written in Polish. The use of the 'Polish' font and Polish language and orthography may be evidence of the Polonisation of the Orthodox elites of Vilnius, who were among the potential users of this book.

The members of the Vilnius Protestant communities probably used prayer books more often than in the Catholics or Orthodox. The obligation of prayers was repeated several times in documents issues by the Vilnius Protestant authorities, which took special care to instil a sense of this duty in children. The Calvinist synod stated in 1629:

[97] *Молитви повседневні* (Vilnius, 1595, 1596, 1601).

[98] *Modlitwy z doktorów św. według św. wschodniej Cerkwie obrane, do których Akafist Panu Jezusowi i Kanon do Przenaświętszego Ducha Boga i Akafist Naświętszej Pannie Maryjej i inne wielce nabożne prośby teraz nowo przyłożone i na świat wydane* (Vilnius, 1650), pp. 66-67.

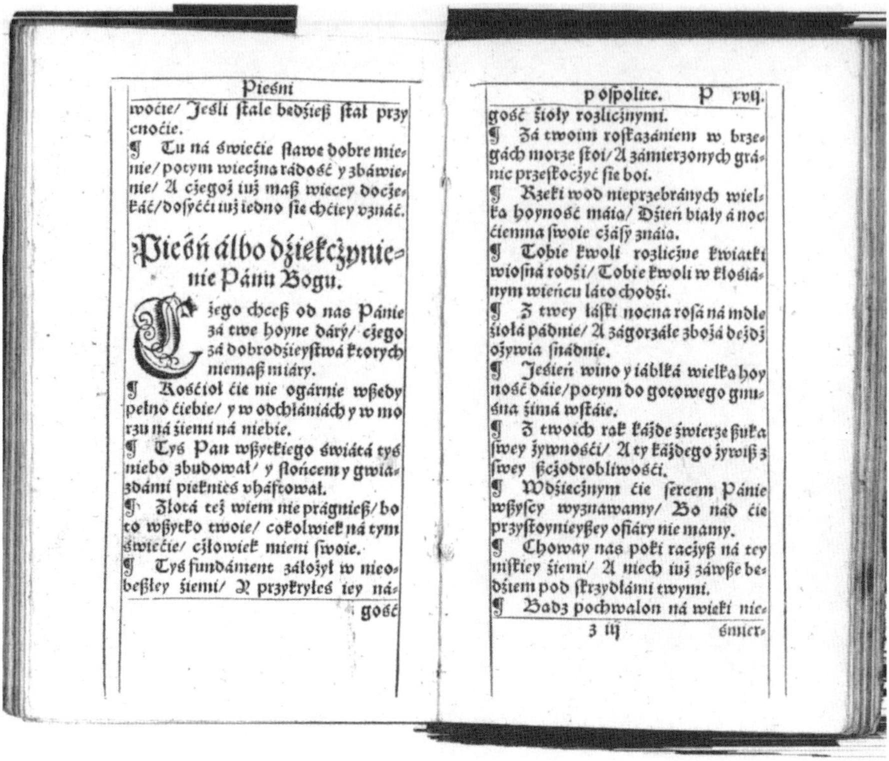
Pieśni

woćie/ Jeśli ſtale bedźieß ſtał przy
cnoćie.
¶ Tu ná świećie ſławe dobre mie-
nie/ potym wiecżna rádość y zbáwie-
nie/ A cżegoż iuż maß wiecey docże-
káć/ doſyćći iuż iedno ſie chćiey vznáć.

Pieśń álbo dźiekcżynie-
nie Pánu Bogu.

Cżego chceß od nas Pánie
zá twe hoyne dáry/ cżego
zá dobrodźieyſtwá ktorych
niemaß miáry.
¶ Kośćiol ćie nie ogárnie wßedy
pełno ćiebie/ y w odchłániách y w mo
rzu ná źiemi ná niebie.
¶ Tyś Pan wßytkiego świátá tyś
niebo zbudował/ y słońcem y gwia-
zdámi pieknieś vháftował.
¶ Złotá też wiem nie prágnieß/ bo
to wßytko twoie/ cokolwiek ná tym
świećie/ cżłowiek mieni ſwoie.
¶ Tyś fundáment záłożył w nieo-
beßłey źiemi/ A przykryłeś iey ná-
gość

pospolite. P xvij.

gość źioły rozlicżnymi.
¶ Zá twoim roſkazániem w brze-
gách morze ſtoi/ A zámierzonych grá-
nic przeſkocżyć ſie boi.
¶ Rzeki wod nieprzebránych wielka hoyność máia/ Dźień biały á noc
ćiemna ſwoie cżáſy znáia.
¶ Tobie kwoli rozlicżne kwiatki
wioſná rodźi/ Tobie kwoli w kłoſiá-
nym wieńcu láto chodźi.
¶ Z twey láſki nocna roſá ná mdłe
źiołá pádnie/ A zágorzáłe zbożá deżdż
ożywia ſnádnie.
¶ Jeśień wino y iáblká wielka hoy
ność dáie/ potym do gotowego gnu-
śna źimá wſtáie.
¶ Z twoich rąk káżde źwierze ßuka
ſwey żywnośći/ A ty káżdego żywiß z
ſwey ßcżodrobliwośći.
¶ Wdźięcżnym ćie ſercem Pánie
wßyſcy wyznawamy/ Bo nád ćie
przyſtoynieyßey ofiáry nie mamy.
¶ Chowáy nas poki racżyß ná tey
niſkiey źiemi/ A niech iuż záwße be-
dźiem pod ſkrzydłámi twymi.
¶ Bądź pochwalon ná wieki nie-
Z iij śmierć-

Fig. 69 J. Kochanowski, Hymn *What Do You Want from Us, Lord, for Your Generous Gifts* (*Czego chcesz od nas, Panie*) in the Polish Calvinist *Katechizm* (Vilnius, 1594). Uppsala (Sweden), CR. Public domain.

> The rector and his colleagues [that is other teachers from the Vilnius Calvinist college] *per custodes* should make sure that the Christian children [i.e. the students], who live in the lodgings, pray to God every morning and evening, also at dinner and supper; during the meal every student should recite an adage three times or repeat something from the class of that day.[99] (original in Polish)

From the 1540s, Protestant prayer books and songbooks (prayer was often sung) were combined with catechisms in one volume. In the second half of the sixteenth century the Vilnius Calvinists had at their disposal song books printed in Königsberg, Cracow, and Nyasvizh. Among them, there were three editions of the songbook by Jan Seklucjan (1547, 1550, 1558), a popular Cra-

[99] *Akta synodów prowincjonalnych jednoty litewskiej 1626-1637*, p. 54 (canon 21, nr. 4).

cow songbook printed in 1558, and the Nyasvizh *Catechism* from 1563.[100] At the time there were no printing houses in Vilnius, but by the end of the century the situation had changed. The Calvinist *Katechizm wileński* (Vilnius Catechism) in Polish, from 1594, after an outline of the Christian faith provides songs and translations of the psalms in a total number of *c.* 215 pieces,[101] including well-known songs such as a translation of the song *Wesel się tej to chwile* (Enjoy This Moment) from the songbook of Jakub Lubelczyk (Cracow, 1556)[102] or the hymn *Czego chcesz od nas, Panie* (What Do You Want from Us, Lord, for Your Generous Gifts) by Jan Kochanowski.[103] The Polish poetical paraphrase of the Psalter by Kochanowski[104] was used as a popular songbook by various confessional communities. Just like the hymn, the Psalter by Kochanowski was interconfessional, sung by Catholics, Protestants, Orthodox and Uniates. This is very visible in the Lithuanian translations of some of Kochanowski's psalms published in Vilnius. In 1598 they were included in a Calvinist *Katechizm* by Melchior Pietkiewicz, the minister of the Vilnius congregation. It is worth adding that the Catholics also published Kochanowski's psalms. For instance, in 1646 a student of the papal seminary, Salomon Mozer-

[100] J. Seklucjan, *Pieśni chrześcijańskie dawniejsze i nowe…*, ed. A. Kalisz (Cracow, 2007); *Psalterz i kancjonał z melodiami drukowany w 1558 roku – Polish Psalter and Hymnbook with Melodies Printed in 1558*, ed. J.S. Gruchała and P. Poźniak (Cracow, 2010); *Pieśni z katechizmów Ewangelików Reformowanych (1558-1600) – Hymns from the Catechisms of the Reformed Protestants (1558-1600)*, part 1, *Katechizm krakowski i królewiecki*, ed. M. Komorowska, M. Malicki, and P. Poźniak, with an Introduction by B. Chlebowski, M. Korzo, and P. Poźniak (Cracow, 2018); *Pieśni z katechizmów Ewangelików Reformowanych (1558-1600) – Hymns from the Catechisms of the Reformed Protestants (1558-1600)*, part 2, *Katechizm nieświeski i wileński*, ed. M. Komorowska and P. Poźniak (Cracow, 2018).

[101] A. Kalisz, "Wstęp", in: Seklucjan, *Pieśni chrześcijańskie*, p. 22.

[102] J. Lubelczyk, *Pieśń o zmartwychwastaniu Pańskim Wesel się tejto chwile ludzkie pokolenie etc. Druga Krystus Pan zmartwychwstał Zwycięstwo otrzymał* (Cracow, 1556).

[103] The hymn by Kochanowski was used by all Christian Churches in the Polish-Lithuanian Commonwealth. See J. Pelc, "Teksty Jana Kochanowskiego w kancjonałach staropolskich xvi i xvii wieku", *Odrodzenie i Reformacja w Polsce* 8 (1963), p. 222. English translation by Michael J. Mikoś: J. Kochanowski, *Trifles, Songs, and Saint John's Eve Song*, ed. and trans. M.J. Mikoś, with a foreword by M. Hanusiewicz-Lavallee (Lublin, 2018), pp. 165-166.

[104] A poetic paraphrase of the Psalter by Jan Kochanowski was published for the first time in 1579 (J. Kochanowski, *Psałterz Dawidów* (Cracow, 1579)). Mikołaj Gomółka composed 150 melodies to Kochanowski's psalms, which were published in 1580. Kochanowski's work gained immense popularity. Estreicher counted 23 editions in *c.* 11,000 copies of the Kochanowski's Psalter, which were published between 1579 and 1641 (Estreicher, *Bibliographia Polska*, 15 (1897), pp. 71-74). Apart from that, the most important psalms in Kochanowski's adaptation were also published in hymn books, catechisms, and prayer books.

ka Sławoczyński (Saliamonas Mozerka Slavočinskis, *c.* 1630?-1660) published a Lithuanian translation of Kochanowski's Psalms.[105]

In 1623, the Lutheran preacher Samuel Dambrowski composed the prayer book *Paradise for the Souls of Men and Women Composed of Psalms and Prayers with Songs*,[106] which served the Lutheran communities in Lithuania, Poland, and Silesia, including the faithful whom he led in Vilnius. His colleague and successor in the position of Polish preacher in the Vilnius Lutheran church, the reverend Andrzej Schönflissius, also published a prayer book, *The Garden of the Soul for Men*.[107]

The Jews, just as the other inhabitants of Vilnius, were obliged to pray during the day. They were to say prayers in the synagogue, the school, and in their private homes.[108] The prayers were facilitated by prayer books. In early modern times, the *siddur* ('order of prayers') and the *machzor* ('cycle') belonged to the most common books.[109] They were both personal prayer books and liturgical books. The *siddurim* were used for the Sabbath prayers, while the *machzorim* were provided for feast days. In their Ashkenazi versions they were in common use among the Lithuanian Jews. There are no sources from Vilnius that speak about the *siddur* and the *machzor*, however, so we do not know if the Vilnius Jews possessed manuscripts or printed editions. However, it is more likely that they acquired printed copies, published in the printing houses of Poland (Cracow, Lublin),[110] or from Italy and the Netherlands (Venice, Amsterdam).

[105] A. KAUPUŻ, "Kochanowski na Litwie: Przekłady tekstów Jana z Czarnolasu na język litewski", in: *Jan Kochanowski 1584-1984: Epoka – Twórczość – Recepcja*, 2, ed. J. PELC, P. BUCHWALD-PELCOWA, and B. OTWINOWSKA (Lublin, 1989), p. 80; P. BUCHWALD-PELCOWA, "Z dziejów druku kancjonałów litewskich i cenzury kościelnej w XVII wieku", *Rocznik Biblioteki Narodowej* 4 (1968), pp. 181-195.

[106] S. DAMBROWSKI, *Raj duszny męski i białogłowski z psalmów i modlitw z pieśniami* (Toruń, 1623).

[107] A. SCHÖNFLISSIUS, *Wirydarz duszny męski, w którym się zamykają modlitwy i pieśni nabożne z Pisma Świętego i z Doktorów Kościelnych, ludziom chrześcijańskim ku zbawiennemu używaniu zebrane i w druk podane* (Lubcz, 1648).

[108] D.R. KARR, "Judaism in Christendom", in: *The Blackwell Comapnion to Judaism*, ed. J. NEUSNER and A.J. AVERY-PECK (Malden, Mass., and Oxford, 2000), pp. 148-149.

[109] *Ibid.*, pp. 147, 155.

[110] *Drukarze dawnej Polski od XV do XVIII wieku*, 1, *Małopolska*, 1, *Wiek XV-XVI*, ed. A. KAWECKA-GRYCZKOWA (Wrocław, 1983), pp. 379, 381, 388, 390; M.J. HELLER, "Early Hebrew printing from Lublin to Safed: The journeys of Eliezer ben Isaac Ashkenazi", *Jewish Culture and History* 4.1 (2001), pp. 81-96.

As all Muslims, the Vilnius Tartars were obliged to pray five times a day (*salah*). Apart from that, they used prayer books called *khamails*, that is collections of prayers in Arabic supplemented by commentaries in Polish or Ruthenian. Since the Tartars, unlike the Christians and Jews, did not have the means to print their prayer books, they used exclusively handwritten copies. They were used at home, hence their great popularity, but also by the clergy. These collections included prayers pronounced at the ceremony of name-giving, during weddings, funerals, and other religious celebrations, as well as a calendar.[111] They were produced by professional copyists or elderly people, who considered the copying of *khamails* and *kitabs* a pious deed.[112] They almost always bear traces of the personal choice of the maker. Presumably, there are no two identical khamails containing exactly the same prayers, translations, and commentaries.

The Prayer as Poetry

Prayers were supposed to support worship, but, still retaining the function of praising God, they were often also poetic works. They were given a poetic form mainly when they were written by humanists such as Skaryna, professors and students of the Academy of Vilnius, or court poets of Krzysztof II Radziwiłł. Their works were marked by an internal organisation according to the principles of rhetoric, and they could be interpreted on many levels, with references to the Greek and Roman tradition. The odes and Marian epodes of Maciej Kazimierz Sarbiewski are examples among many others, provided in anthologies of his companions in the Jesuit Order. In these works, the boundary between literature and prayer is flexible, and the reader's attitude usually determines whether a text about the Mother of God written in Sapphic stanzas by Sarbiewski is a poem or a prayer. Similarly, an emblem placed on the triumphal arch in honour of St. Casimir could be treated as a masterpiece of the art of poetry or as a text for individual prayer (although it would probably be difficult for the participants of a crowded procession to focus properly).

For most inhabitants of the city this sublime distinction was not important. They normally used prayer texts that did not require good reading skills: it was

[111] Konopacki, *Życie religijne Tatarów na ziemiach Wielkiego Księstwa Litewskiego*, pp. 137, 141.

[112] Kryczyński, *Tatarzy litewscy*, pp. 220-221.

enough to know them by heart. These prayers may have had solid theological foundations or good literary qualities, but often they expressed a simple request, such as in *Modlitwy, gdy się spać masz położyć św. Bazylego* (St. Basil's Prayers for When You Go to Sleep), printed at the end of a primer designed for Orthodox children.

Liturgy and Liturgical Texts

From the point of view of a common lay follower of a religion of a Book, books were not necessary to venerate God. It was enough to learn by heart the most often used prayers and repeat them daily. However, from the point of view of the parish, *qahal*, or local mosque, books were crucial to conduct prayers for the whole community. In the fourteenth century, when Christianity was introduced to Vilnius, the Orthodox and Catholic liturgies were very rich, complex, and without specialised books for the divine offices, divine masses, etc. were impossible to conduct.

The basic Orthodox and Catholic (and later also Uniate) liturgical texts were similar. These denominations employed their own versions of Holy Scripture in the liturgy, and at this level there were some differences as to the canon and language (Church Slavonic and Latin).

As was mentioned before, in the first centuries of the history of Vilnius liturgical books were almost exclusively imported, while at the end of the fifteenth century, under the rule of Alexander Jagiellon, the city became the real capital of the country and the religious centre both for the Orthodox and Catholics. As a result, in the first three decades of the sixteenth century one notices a growing demand for liturgical books. This resulted in increases both in imported liturgical texts and imports and in their production.

There was a great variety in Catholic liturgical books, including gospel books (evangeliaries), psalters, missals, pontificals and rituals, antiphonaries, lectionaries, liturgies of the hours (breviaries), collections of lives of the saints (*passionales*), graduals, and martyrologies. Needless to say, since Vilnius was the capital of the bishopric, the *caeremoniale Episcoporum* was also in use in the local cathedral. In the sixteenth century, after the Council of Trent the

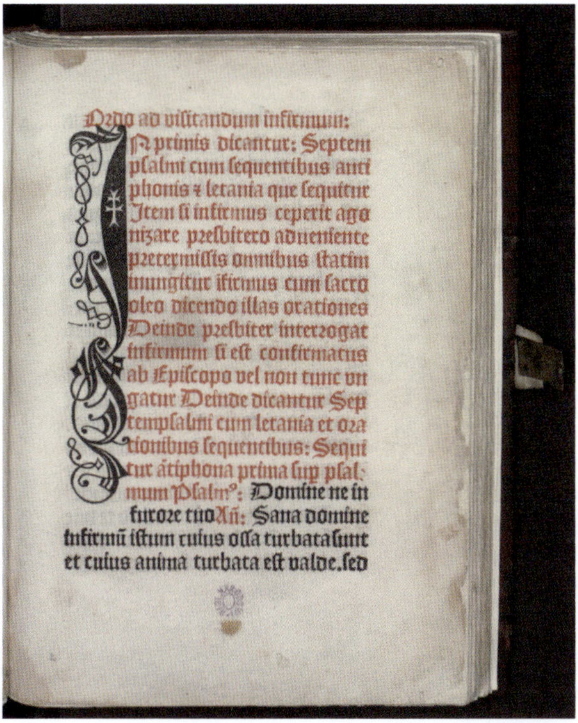

Ordo ad visitandum infirmum:
In primis dicantur: Septem
psalmi cum sequentibus anti
phonis ⁊ letania que sequitur
Item si infirmus ceperit ago
nizare presbitero adveniente
pretermissis omnibus statim
inungitur ifirmus cum sacro
oleo dicendo illas orationes
Deinde presbiter interrogat
infirmum si est confirmatus
ab Episcopo vel non tunc vn
gatur Deinde dicantur Sep
tempsalmi cum letania et ora
tionibus sequentibus: Sequi
tur ãtiphona prima sup psal:
mum Psalm⁹: Domine ne in
furore tuo An̄: Sana domine
infirmũ istum cuius ossa turbata sunt
et cuius anima turbata est valde. sed

Fig. 70 *Agenda, sive exsequiale divinorum sacramentorum*, ed. Martinus canonicus Vilnensis (Gdańsk, 1499), Warsaw, BN, SD Inc. Qu. 141 <https://polona.pl/item-view/2f9e6052-f97f-43a5-be72-0be52a0516ee?page=3> (accessed: 15.07.2023; public domain).

Catholic authorities tended towards the uniformisation of liturgical books Consequently, the older books were gradually replaced by new ones, such as the Roman Ritual (*Rituale Romanum*), the Roman Breviary (*Breviarium Romanum*), or the Roman Martyrology. Copies of all books are listed in the catalogues of the Vilnius Catholic and Orthodox churches.[113]

The first genre to be produced in Vilnius itself was the Vilnius Agenda. At the end of the 1490s, the Vilnius chapter placed an order with Konrad Baumgarten, a travelling printer working first in Gdańsk and then in Royal

[113] See Chapter 2.

Prussia, a fief of the Kingdom of Poland. As a result, in 1499 he had printed a guide on how the parish clergy should administer the sacraments and conduct religious services, the *Agenda or The Funeral Rites of Divine Sacraments*.[114] The *Agenda* was an adaptation of a fourteenth-century French model and differed from the *agenda* of the other dioceses in the Gniezno archbishopric.[115] Its editor was a canon of Vilnius, Marcin of Radom, who acted at the command of bishop Wojciech Tabor. The *Agenda* was intended to enrich the libraries of parish churches both in Vilnius and in the whole diocese, and one of its main goals was to unify the rite.

It is not clear how long the Vilnius Agenda of 1499 was in use. Probably it was replaced in the last decades of the sixteenth century by new agendas provided for the entire Gniezno archbishopric by the synod of Piotrków in 1589.[116] The new agenda, printed in Cracow in 1591,[117] was certainly introduced to the diocese of Vilnius, because in 1613 the bishop of Vilnius, Benedykt Woyna, officially recommended this book.[118] Its main parts were published in Vilnius in 1616 as *The Small Agenda Written for the More Convenient Use of the Priests from the Province of Poland*.[119] The title of the book correctly renders its advantages. It is a small book indeed (in 8°), which facilitated its use. It contains only the most important rites: baptism, communion, the anointing of the sick, marriage, blessing a woman after marriage and after giving birth, the funeral, and several occasional blessings.[120]

These printed books also possessed a particular local feature. In agendas and rituals the rites and prayers are always put in Latin, but some parts of the liturgy were put in the vernacular, for instance the formulas of the marriage

[114] *Agenda sive Exsequiale divinorum sacramentorum per* [...] *Martinum canonicum Vilnensis dioecesis edita* (Gdańsk, 1499). See Z. OBERTYŃSKI, "Agenda Wileńska z 1499 r.", *Przegląd Teologiczny* 10 (1929), pp. 171-191; *Drukarze dawnej Polski od XV do XVIII wieku*, 4, *Pomorze*, pp. 36-37; NOWAK, *Początki sztuki drukarskiej*, pp. 154-155; ID., *Konrad Baumgart*, pp. 133-165; *Nad złoto droższe*, p. 133; *Wszystkie modlitwy*, p. 72.

[115] S. HOŁODOK, "Źródła do dziejów liturgii sakramentów w diecezji wileńskiej (XVI-XVIII w.)", *Studia Teologiczne* 1 (1983), pp. 197-198.

[116] M. MORAWSKI, *Synod piotrkowski w roku 1589* (Włocławek, 1937), pp. 74-75.

[117] *Agenda seu ritus caeremoniarum ecclesiasticarum ad uniformem ecclesiasticarum per universas provincias Regni Poloniae usum, officio Romano conformati, ex decreto Synodi Provincialis Petricoviensis, denuo conscripti et editi*, ed. H. POWODOWSKI (Cracow, 1591).

[118] HOŁODOK, "Źródła do dziejów liturgii sakramentów", p. 198.

[119] *Agenda parva in commodiorem usum sacerdotum Provinciae Polonae conscripta* (Vilnius, 1616; second, enlarged edition, 1630).

[120] *Ibid.* See HOŁODOK, "Źródła do dziejów liturgii sakramentów", p. 199.

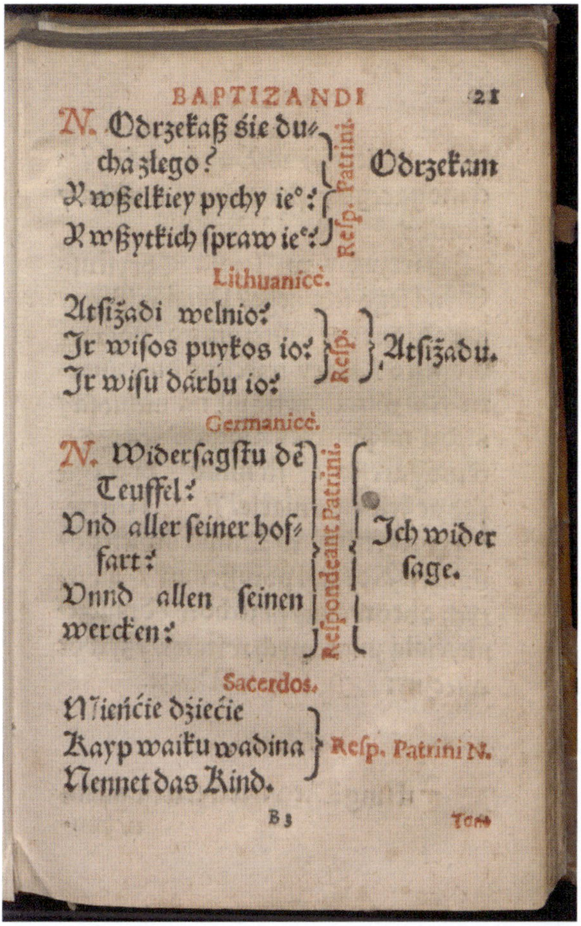
BAPTIZANDI 21

N. Odrzekaß śie du-cha złego? / Y wßelkiey pychy ie°: / Y wßytkich ſpraw ie°: — Reſp. Patrini. — Odrzekam

Lithuanicè.

Atſiżadi welnio: / Ir wiſos puykos io: / Ir wiſu dárbu io: — Reſp. — Atſiżadu.

Germanicè.

N. Widerſagſtu dē Teuffel: / Vnd aller ſeiner hof-fart: / Vnnd allen ſeinen wercken: — Reſpondeant Patrini. — Ich wider ſage.

Sacerdos.

Nienćie dźiećie / Kayp waiku wadina / Nennet das Kind. — Reſp. Patrini N.

B3 Tom

Fig. 71 Rite of baptism in three languages (Polish, Lithuanian, and German) in the Catholic *Agenda parva in commodiorem usum sacerdotum Provinciae Polonae conscripta* (Vilnius, 1630), p. 21. <https:// www.europeana.eu/pl/item/776/_nnsf8fk> (accessed: 15.07.2023; public domain).

oath. In this respect, the agendas printed in Vilnius in the seventeenth century did not differ from other agendas of the region. However, the choice of vernacular languages mirrors the linguistic diversity of Vilnius and the Grand Duchy of Lithuania. For example, the questions to a godparent in the baptism rite are put in three languages, Polish, Lithuanian, and German:[121]

Chcecie dziecię ze krztu podnieść?		*Chcemy.*
Ar norite to wayko iż krixto pakielt?	Responsio	*Norime.*
Wolt ihr das Kind ausz der Tauff heben?	Patrini.	*Ja.*

Mieńcie dziecię	
Kayp wáiku wádino	Responsio Patrini: *N.*[122]
Nennet das Kind	

In the 1630s a new ritual was introduced in the archdiocese of Gniezno.[123] It was published for the first time in Vilnius in 1633, and it was several times reissued later on.[124] The formulae in Polish, Lithuanian, and German are much longer than in the previous *Agendas*. Some Polish texts have the grammatical forms typical for Polish dialects from Lithuania.[125]

Some Catholic priests made manuscript copies of the necessary prayers and liturgical texts for their own use. A small manuscript book from the last two decades of the sixteenth century, written by the Bernardine we have encountered before, Andrew (Andrzej) of Vilnius, contained texts this priest deemed useful, such as the liturgical formula of the baptism or the sacrament of matrimony, with the texts of the vows and questions in Latin and Polish:

> Do you, N., have the good and unforced will to marry N., whom you see before you?
> Response: I do.
> And have you not, N., sworn marital fidelity to another?
> Response: I have not.[126]

[121] In the *Agenda* there is no Ruthenian language because it was reserved for the Uniates (i.e. the Catholics of the Eastern rite) and their Church Slavonic liturgy. The decisions of the Union of Brest (1596), confirmed later by the Pope, stated that the Latin branch of the Church was obliged not to proselytise the Uniate Ruthenians.

[122] *Agenda parva* (1630), p. 20.

[123] HOŁODOK, "Źródła do dziejów liturgii sakramentów", p. 199.

[124] *Rituale sacramentorum ac aliarum Ecclesiae caeremoniarum ex decreto Synodi Provincialis Petricoviensis ad uniformem ecclesiarum Regni Poloniae et Magnus Ducatus Lithuaniae usum recens et in breve opusculum editum* (Vilnius, 1633).

[125] "*N: Nie ślubowałażeś komu innemu wiary małżeńskiej? Resp.: Nie ślubowała*" (*ibid.*, p. 34). In standard Polish the response should have a form: "*Nie ślubowałam*".

[126] MS CZART. 3681 I, p. 143.

Andrew of Vilnius had based his work on existing agendas and the priest who made his own handwritten manual continued the medieval tradition of making such epitomes. In the seventeenth century the printed, unified versions ultimately supplanted the manuscript ones. In some of the printed editions, though, one can encounter manuscript additions, such as the *Benedictio herbarum* (Blessing of the Herbs) written on the last pages of a copy of the *Small Agenda* from 1630, which belonged to the library of the Academy of Vilnius.[127]

The *officia* of the saints held a special position in the Catholic liturgy. This was especially important where relics of the saints were kept and worshipped. Up to the mid-seventeenth century the Holy See canonised or beatified no more than twenty people from the territory of the Gniezno archbishopric, so only a few such places existed there. Cracow and Gniezno were the most important, but from the beginning of the seventeenth century Vilnius was also put on the list. In 1604 St. Casimir was canonised,[128] and the *officium sancti Casimiri* became part of the Catholic liturgy. It was composed originally as early as 1520 by Zacharias Ferreri (1479-1524), the papal legate to King Sigismund I the Old. This *officium* was part of the first, unsuccessful attempt at the canonisation of Prince Casimir in 1516-1521. Ferreri also wrote a first official hagiographical account about St. Casimir, which was published in Rome in 1521.[129] These texts were finally put to use eight decades later. The Latin life of St. Casimir and the *officium* were translated into Polish by Mateusz Chryzostom Wołodkiewicz and were published in Vilnius in 1606.[130] The official worship of St. Casimir, launched in the seventeenth century, has had a great impact on the popular religious life an literature in the city.

As far as the Orthodox Christians are concerned, apart from the whole Bible, Orthodox Christians also used individual parts of it, such as the gospels,

[127] *Agenda parva* (1630), the last two unnumbered pages of a copy from the University Library in Warsaw, shelf mark SD XVII.2.179. The *Blessing of the Herbs* was copied in the *Agenda* from the aforementioned *Rituale* from 1633 (see "In Festo Assumptionis Beatae Mariae Virginis benedictio herbarum et processio", in: *Rituale sarcamentorum*, pp. 99-104).

[128] See Chapter 8.

[129] Z. FERRERI, *Vita beati Casimiri confessoris ex serenimissimis Poloniae regibus et magnis Lithuaniae ducibus clarissimi* (Rome, 1521). Modern editions in: *Ankstyvieji šv. Kazimiero "Gyvenimai"*, ed. M. ČIURINSKAS (Vilnius, 2004) and in: *Żywot przechwalebnego wyznawce świętego Kazimierza królewica polskiego i książęcia litewskiego w Wilnie roku 1606 przez Mateusza Chryzostoma Wolodkiewicza przełożony. Przydane k temu modlitwy nabożne i hymny do św. Kazimierza*, ed. J. OKOŃ, K. GARA, and J. RZEGOCKA (Warsaw, 2016), pp. 129-175.

[130] *Żywot przechwalebnego wyznawce świętego Kazimierza królewica polskiego i książęcia litewskiego (...) Przydane k temu modlitwy nabożne i hymny do św. Kazimierza*, trans. M.Ch. WOŁODKIEWICZ (Vilnius, 1606). A modern edition in: *Żywot świętego Kazimierza* (2016).

the psalter, and the Apostle (Slavonic: *Apostol*) consisting of the Acts of the Apostles and the apostolic letters. Their liturgical books included *Liturgiarions*, the *Octoechos,* and the *Hieratikon*, that is the equivalents of western missals, both *Triodons* (*Triod*), the *Archieratikon* (*Chinovnik*), and the *Minaion* (*Mineya*). A separate group consisted of books which were a combination of biblical and liturgical texts, such as the *Horologion* (*Tchasoslov*; the liturgy of the hours), the *Euchologion* (*Trebnik*), and the *Irmologion*. Additional provisions were contained in the *Typikon* (*Ustav*).[131]

We know three examples of Orthodox liturgical books used in Vilnius in the first decades of the sixteenth century. The first is the *Desatiglav* copied by Matvei Desatyi, which will be presented in the next sub-chapter. In 1518 the splendid fourteenth-century *Kyiv Psalter* was donated to the Orthodox church of St. Nicholas. And finally, in 1525 a printed *Apostle* was published by Skaryna. Certainly, dozens of other liturgical books must also have been in use in Vilnius in that time.

From the mid-1570s, the publishing house run by the Mamonicz family specialised in publishing Orthodox liturgical books; later, their role was taken over by the Brotherhood's printing house. A recent bibliographical survey reveals that between 1575 and 1600 alone in Vilnius at least 27 Orthodox liturgical books were published (evangeliary, liturgy of hours, psalter, octoechos, and apostle).[132] In the last decade of the sixteenth century Vilnius and the Grand Duchy of Lithuania were the biggest centre of production of Church Slavonic liturgical books in Europe.[133] In the next century the number of Church Slavonic liturgical books printed in Vilnius was even greater, because apart from the Orthodox printing house the Basilian (Uniate) printing house produced its own texts.[134]

We know very little about the liturgical texts used before 1611 by the Lithuanian Calvinists.[135] Probably they used *The Form and Rationale* by the Polish

[131] NARBUTT, *Historia i typologia ksiąg liturgicznych bizantyńsko-słowiańskich*, p. 51.

[132] Е.Л. НЕМИРОВСКИЙ, *Славянские издания кирилловского (церковнославянского) шрифта*, 2, part 1: *1551-1592* (Moscow, 2011), pp. 299-312, 315-322, 416-418, 423-425, 443-444, 479-481,493-497, 502-503, (Nos. 144, 146, 147, 172, 176, 187, 202, 206, 207, 208, 211, 212), p. 563 (No. 7); ID., *Славянские издания кирилловского (церковнославянского) шрифта*, 2, part 2 *(1593-1600)*, pp. 21-23, 62-63, 80-83, 90-93, 119-123, 135, 162-163, 167, 172-183, 188-192 (Nos. 214, 215, 225, 231, 232, 234, 235, 242, 247, 259, 262, 264, 266, 267).

[133] See the table in НЕМИРОВСКИЙ, *Славянские издания кирилловского (церковнославянского) шрифта*, 2, part 2, p. 227.

[134] НІКАЛАЕЎ, *Гісторыя беларускай кнігі*, 1, pp. 127-131.

[135] K. BEM, *Calvinism in the Polish-Lithuanian Commonwealth 1548-1648: The Churches*

Calvinist reformer Jan Łaski (John a Lasco, 1499-1560).[136] In 1581, Lithuanian Calvinists published a Polish version of Łaski's work, which was reprinted several times in Vilnius.[137] In 1620 the synod of the Lithuanian Calvinists decided to compose a new agenda:

> When it comes to the eucharistic service, it should be described in two versions. The first one should be codified by those brothers who will be appointed at the next synod. They should improve the version of the old catechism. The other one will be composed by some brothers at this synod. It will be based on the Lithuanian and Polish rite. His Grace the hetman [Krzysztof II Radziwiłł] will choose which one shall be printed. The supervisors of the printing will be rev. Samuel Lenartowicz and rev. Jan Dominik. The costs will be covered by the Vilnius community. The synod will grant to rev. Samuel 30 copies of the book and to rev. Dominik 15 copies as the reward for their efforts. Rev. Ambroży Dąbrowski will check the notes and will be given for this task 15 copies.[138] (original in Polish)

The resolution of the synod was carefully carried out and in the next year a new agenda was published in Lubcz.[139]

The aforementioned survey certainly does not provide an accurate image of the abundance of liturgical books in Vilnius in the sixteenth and seventeenth centuries. However, on the basis of the examples given we can make some assumptions about the 'open' and 'closed' city with respect to liturgical books. Some of them defined both aspects of the city's functioning, for instance the *Agenda* or the *Kyiv Psalter* were produced elsewhere and were later transported to Vilnius for local use. However, Vilnius was a place of book production as well: these books were distributed outside the city, such as *Desatiglav*

and the Faithful (Leiden and Boston, 2020), p. 71.

[136] First edition: J. ŁASKI, *Forma ac ratio tota ecclesiastici ministerii in peregrinorum, potissimum vero Germanorum ecclesia, instituta Londini in Anglia, per ... regem Eduardum eius nominis Sextum anno post Christum natum 1550* (Frankfurt, 1555); M.S. SPRINGER, *Restoring Christ's Church: John a Lasco and the Forma ac ratio* (London, 2007); BEM, *Calvinism in the Polish-Lithuanian Commonwealth*, p. 72, 74.

[137] *Forma albo porządek sprawowania świątości Pańskich, jako chrztu świętego i społeczności wieczerzy Pańskiej, przy tym i inszych ceremoniej albo posługowania Zboru Bożego ku potrzebie pobożnym pasterzom i prawdziwym ministrom Pana Krystusowym znowu wydana i drukowna* (Vilnius, 1600). See BEM, *Calvinism in the Polish-Lithuanian Commonwealth*, p. 74; Łukaszewicz, *Dzieje kościołów wyznania helweckiego w Litwie*, p. 258.

[138] *Akta synodów prowincjonalnych jednoty litewskiej 1611-1625*, p. 55.

[139] *Forma albo porządek sprawowania świętości Pańskich, to jest krztu świętego i świętej wieczerzej Pańskiej, przy tym i inszych cerymonij albo posługowania Zboru Bożego* (Lubcz, 1621).

and Skaryna's booklets. The city was also the seat of ecclesiastical authorities whose role was among other things to decide which books should be used in the city and in other places of worship. For this reason, Vilnius played an important role in the development of religious textual culture in distant churches under the jurisdiction of the Vilnius Catholic bishop and Orthodox archbishop.

This function of Vilnius as a centre of giving authority to liturgical texts became even greater in the second half of the sixteenth century. Several factors determined this. Firstly, the Council of Trent stated that new liturgical books should be introduced in the dioceses, and that the local bishops and chapters were responsible for executing this task. Secondly, the new Reformed Churches, whose communities operated in Vilnius, had their own liturgical texts. The Calvinist synods, which annually gathered in the city, recommended in their canons which books and which forms of rites should be used in the churches of the Lithuanian Calvinist province. Thirdly, from 1588 the Orthodox Brotherhood influenced religious life not only in the city but in other local churches and monasteries as well. Finally, Vilnius became a major centre of the production and distribution of liturgical texts.[140]

Basic and Advanced Religious Teaching: Catechisms and Sermons

We do not know precisely what were the main channels of transmitting knowledge about religion in medieval and early modern Vilnius, but we can make some assumptions. The first and probably the most important place for this was the home. Mothers, who were responsible for bringing up the younger children, taught them their first prayers, usually in the vernacular languages.[141] Next came the institutions, among them the churches and the schools.

From the thirteenth century the authorities of the Catholic Church required catechesis in the cathedral schools and parishes. The synod of the archbishopric of Gniezno, which took place in Łęczyca (Poland) in 1285, stated that during Mass, after singing the Latin *Credo*, a priest was required to say with the parishioners the *Apostles Creed*, the *Lord's Prayer*, and the *Hail Mary*, all in

[140] This has been discussed in Chapter 7.

[141] The acts of the Calvinist Synod held in Vilnius shed some light on this question. Canon 5 from 1612 stated: "those [Calvinists] who allow their wives belonging to other religions [i.e. "the Arrians, Ruthenians, and Papists"] to baptize their children and corrupt them [i.e. teach them the rules of the alien religion]" should be stigmatised. *Akta synodów prowincjonalnych jednoty litewskiej 1611-1625*, pp. 14-15.

Polish.[142] Apart from that, sermons were to be preached in Polish as well. Similar regulations regarding basic catechisation must have been applied also in the Vilnius bishopric, established in 1387 as part of the Archbishopric of Gniezno. This requirement was especially important because of the missionary character of the Vilnius bishopric. The basic prayers and sermons must have played an important role in the evangelisation of the inhabitants of the Grand Duchy of Lithuania, though in towns like Vilnius it certainly had a greater impact than in rural areas.

Certainly at the end of the fourteenth and in the fifteenth centuries there were enough Catholic priests in Vilnius to carry out religious teaching in the four local churches (including the cathedral). If they indeed promoted praying the vernacular Apostolic Creed, Lord's Prayer, and Hail Mary, in which languages were these prayers said? In German, Lithuanian, Polish, or in all three? In the case of German and Polish we know that these prayers were available in vernacular translations. But did Lithuanian have its vernacular version at the turn of the fourteenth and fifteenth century? Were there any standard written versions of the prayers? Was there any competition between vernacular prayers? It would be a fascinating topic to examine how the religious awareness of the inhabitants of Vilnius developed at that time. The lack of sources prevents us, however, to come to any conclusions about this process.

It is an open question what the role of the written word was in this process. The impact of handwritten or printed texts grew in the course of the sixteenth century, mainly because of an increasing number of schools, literate people, and printed texts. Important factors in this process were also the Reformation, the Catholic post-Tridentine Reform, and the reforms introduced by the Orthodox Church in the second half of the sixteenth century.

Another open question is the relations between the written and the spoken word. Large numbers of written texts became secondarily oral, for instance prayers, songs, religious and liturgical formulas, fragments of the Holy Books, etc. However, it will probably be no exaggeration to say that almost all religious texts in early modern Vilnius were rooted in the written word, and consequently in the rules which these texts relied on. This anchoring of religious truths in written texts was the policy of all religions of the Book. Thanks to

[142] I. Skierska, *Obowiązek mszalny w średniowiecznej Polsce* (Warsaw, 2003), pp. 175, 184; J. Rajman, "Wolność Kościoła: xiii wiek", in: *Dzieje Kościoła w Polsce*, ed. A. Wiencek (Cracow, 2008), p. 128.

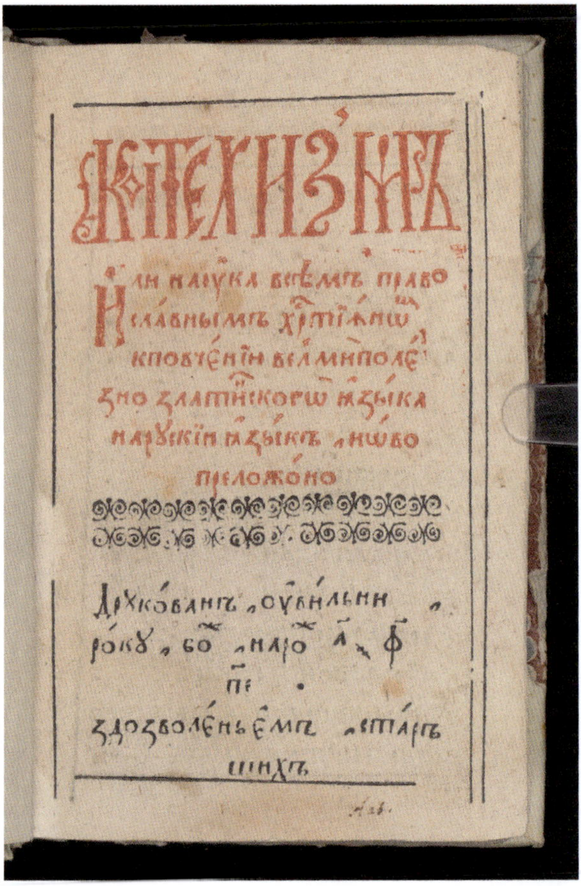

Fig. 72 The Catholic catechism in Church Slavonic: *Кітехизм или наоука всемъ православнымъ хрстїянωм* … (Vilnius, 1585). Uppsala, CR, Litt. Slav. Kyrkslav. 157 (4). <https://www.alvin-portal.org/alvin/view.jsf?dswid=7054&searchType =EXTENDED&query=Litt.Slav.Kyrkslav.+157.4&aq=%5B%5B%7B%7B%22A_FQ%22%3A%22Litt.Slav.KKyrkslav.+157.4%22%3A%22Litt.Slav.Kyrkslav.+157.4%22%7D%5D%&aqe=%5b%5D&af=%5B%5D&pid=alvin-record%3A413166 &c=8#alvin-record%3A413166> (accessed: 15.07.2023; public domain).

writing down the principles of the Faith, a church or synagogue hierarchy could guard and control the orthodoxy of religious practices.[143] This control was always important but became especially urgent in times of religious controversies in the sixteenth century.

Catechisms

In the first half of the sixteenth century educational books, that is catechisms and primers with a religious content, were printed outside the Grand Duchy of Lithuania (in Cracow and Königsberg), but it is certain that they were also imported in Vilnius. Later, primers started to appear also in the capital of Lithuania. On the one hand this is proof that import was not sufficient for the large numbers of students in Vilnius; on the other, it can be considered as part of the process of confessionalisation.

Up to the sixteenth century, in Vilnius, like in other European cities where the Catholic Church operated, the main texts of Catholic catechesis were the Apostles' Creed and the Lord's Prayer. Probably children learnt these prayers at home, but they also formed part of education, namely of learning to read: we can find these texts in the primers. Early Polish manuals of orthography or primers had two functions: as manual of reading and of catechesis.[144] They were printed in the first two decades of the sixteenth century in Cracow, they

[143] E.g. in 1475 in Wrocław (Breslau, Silesia) a volume with the decrees of the diocesan synod was published: *Statuta synodalia episcoporum Wratislaviensium* (Wrocław, 1475). Among Latin decrees, German and Polish prayers were printed in the book. The first official publishing in Polish of the Lord's Prayer, Hail Mary, and the *Apostles' Creed* was an attempt to stabilise and control their form, which varied in different regions of the Gniezno archbishopric. See *Chrestomatia staropolska: Teksty do roku 1543*, ed. W. Wydra and W.R. Rzepka (Wrocław, 1984), pp. 23-28, 305; E. Kaźmierczak, "Ojcze nasz, Zdrowaś Maryjo, Wierzę w Boga", in: *Wszystkie modlitwy Rzeczypospolitej: Katalog wystawy 3 lipca-30 sierpnia 2009*, ed. G. Rolak and D. Sidowicz (Wrocław, 2009), p. 46; A. Knychalska, "Pomnik języka polskiego z xv w.", in: *Wszystkie modlitwy*, p. 45. Other examples of attempts at unification of liturgical texts from the end of the fifteenth century are *The Cracow Missal* (*Missale Cracoviense* (Nuremberg, after 1493) printed at the demand of the bishop of Cracow, cardinal Frederic Jagiellon (1468-1503), the *Cracow Breviary* (*Breviarium secundum usum insignis Ecclesie Cracoviensis* (Lyons?, 1507) commissioned by the bishop of Cracow, Jan Konarski (1447-1525)) and the *Vilnius Agenda* (1499), which will be discussed in this chapter.

[144] F. Pilarczyk, *Elementarze polskie od ich xvi-wiecznych początków do ii wojny światowej: Próba monografii księgoznawczej* (Zielona Góra, 2003), p. 20.

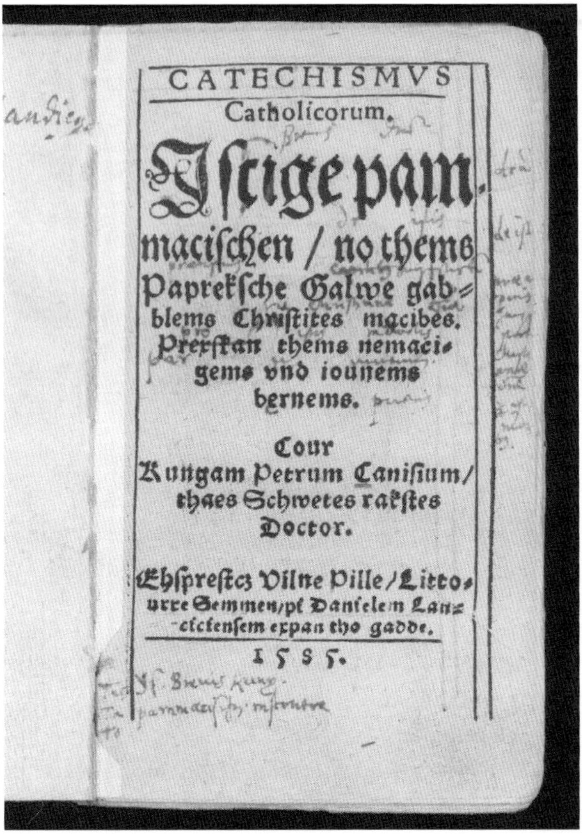
CATECHISMVS
Catholicorum.
Iſcige pam-
maciſchen / no thems
Paprekſche Galwe gab=
blems Chriſtites macibes.
Prerſkan thems nemaci-
gems vnd iounems
bernems.
Cour
Kungam Petrum Caniſium/
thaes Schwetes rakſtes
Doctor.
Ehſpreſtcz Vilne Pille/Litto-
urre Semmen/pt Danielem Lanz-
cicienſem expan tho gadde.
1585.

Fig. 73 Latvian translation of the *Catechism* of Petrus Canisius, *Catechismus catholicorum* (Vilnius, 1585). Uppsala, CR, Utl. Rar. 174 <https://www.alvin-portal.org/alvin/view.jsf?dswid=348&searchType=EXTENDED&query=catechismus+catholicorum&aq=%5b%5b%7B%22A_FQ%22%3A%22catechismus+catholicorum%22%7D%5D&aqe=%5B55D&af=%5B%5D&pid=alvin-record%3A146019&c=2#alvin-record%3A146019> (accessed: 15.07.2023; public domain).

always included the Lord's Prayer, Hail Mary, the Apostles' Creed, the Ten Commandments, the Works of mercy, the Seven deadly sins, and prayers.[145]

[145] The oldest known printed manual of Polish orthography by Stanisław Zaborowski, *Ortographia seu modus recte scribendi et legendi Polonicum idiomaque utilissimus*, appeared in Cra-

In the second half of the sixteenth century a new impulse for catechesis appeared. The Catholic Church in the Polish-Lithuanian Commonwealth released a number of catechisms, translated into the vernacular languages. This was a response to the activity of the Protestants, whose activity in the field of religious education overwhelmed the Catholics. By the middle of the sixteenth century, the difficult situation of the Catholic Church in Lithuania required a new policy on religious education. The Jesuits, especially those from the Academy of Vilnius, played an important role in this process.

Catholic catechisms were published in Vilnius in four languages. The Ruthenian[146] and Latvian[147] ones appeared in 1585. Another one, written by Jacob Ledesma and translated into Lithuanian by Mikołaj Dauksza (Mikalojus Daukša), was published in 1595.[148] Finally a Polish version of Robert Bellarmine's *A Short Companion to Christian Teaching* was printed in 1606.[149] In Jesuit education the Latin catechism of Petrus Canisius was especially important; it was widely used in all Catholic countries after the Council of Trent.[150] Catholic primers, published in Vilnius or imported from Poland, were also in constant use.

cow *c.* 1513. Similar manuals must have been printed in Cracow earlier on. See J. PIROŻYŃSKI, "O poznańskim drukarzu Piotrze Sextilisie z Obrzycka i o polskich elementarzach XVI w.", *Studia Historyczne* 28.1 (1985) p. 8; PILARCZYK, *Elementarze polskie*, pp. 70-71; M.A. KORZO, "O tekstach religijnych w XVI-wiecznych elementarzach polskich", *Pamiętnik Literacki* 106.1 (2015), p. 172.

[146] *Кітехизм или наоука всѣмъ православнымъ хрстїянωм к повученію ввелми полезно з латинского языка и в рускїи языкъ нωво преложоно Друковано оу Вильни року Бож<ого> нарож<енія> а$_{xx}$ ф П є* [=1585] *з дозволеньем старъшихъ*. The only complete extant copy is kept in the University Library in Uppsala, CR 54:315 Kyrkeslav 157; See JAROSZEWICZ-PIERESŁAWCEW, *Druki cyrylickie*, pp. 69-70.

[147] *Catechismus catholicorum: Iscige pammacischen no thems Paprekschе Gawe gabblems Christites macibes: Prexkan thems nemacigems und iounems bernems: Cour Kungam Petrum Canisium thaes Schwetes rakstes Doctor, Ehsprestcz Vilne Pille, Littourre Semmen pi Danielem Lansicinensem expan tho gaddi 1585*; ŚWIERKOWSKI, "Wilno kolebką drukarstwa łotewskiego", pp. 187-190.

[148] M. DAUKŠA, *Kathechismas arba mokslas kiekwienam krikszczionii priwalvs* (Vilnius, 1595). Daukša translated from Jakub Wujek's (?) Polish version, which has not survived. See JOVAIŠAS, *Raštai lietuvių kalba*, pp. 203-204; A. SMETONIENĖ, "The textual influences of Jacob Ledesma's Catechism and the catechism of Mikalojus Daukša on the anonymous Catechism of 1605", *Kalbotyra* 68 (2016), pp. 153-156.

[149] *Krótki zbiór nauki chrześcijańskiej* (Vilnius, 1606). First edition: R. BELLARMIN, *Dichiarazione più copiosa della dottrina cristiana* (Roma?, 1598); See SŁOWIŃSKI, *Katechizmy katolickie w języku polskim od XVI do XVIII wieku*, p. 134.

[150] KASJANIUK, "Katechizm", p. 1041.

The Orthodox responded to the Protestants and Catholics with their own catechisms published in the 1590s and early 1600s.[151] At the end of 1595 or in 1596 Stephan Zizany (*c.* 1570-after 1600), a Ruthenian teacher who came to Vilnius from Lviv in 1593,[152] published his catechism under the patronage of the Orthodox Brotherhood: *Stephan Zizany's Explanation of the Orthodox Faith. For Easier Understanding of Christian Children* [*Organised*] *in Short Questions and Answers: Unorthodox Questions in Bad Faith and Pious Orthodox Answers*.[153] Its publication had two aims. Firstly, it was meant to be a textbook for the Brotherhood school. Secondly, and no less importantly, was the polemical dimension of Zizany's catechism. It was written against the Catholic Church and shortly became also treated as a polemical work against the Union of Brest in 1596.[154] In the first decades of the seventeenth century the next Orthodox polemical catechisms were written, and some of them were printed as well.[155] In 1611, in Vievis (Jewie) the *Catechism or a Short Collection of the Faith* was published as a part of a prayer book.[156] Its intended audience was that of the Orthodox inhabitants of Vilnius and the students of the Brotherhood school.

[151] K. SZCZYPIOR, "Najstarsze katechizmy wschodniosłowiańskie", in: *Święci w kulturze i duchowości dawnej i współczesnej Europy*, ed. W. STĘPNIAK-MINCZEWA and Z.J. KIJAS (Cracow, 1999), pp. 155-161.

[152] ТИМОШЕНКО, *Руська релігійна культура Вільна*, p. 202.

[153] S. ZIZANY, "Стефана Зизаня Изложеше о православной вѣрѣ: Коротким пытаньем и отповѣданьем для латвѣйшаго вырозумѣня христїянским дѣтем: Странный пытает зловѣрный, а православный благовѣрный отповѣдаеть", in: Наука ку читаню, и розумѣню писма словенского ту тыж о Святой Тройци, и овъчловечеи Господни (Vilnius, 1595). A detailed anaysis of Zizany's catechism was presented by Nataliia Harkovich: Н.В. ГАРКОВИЧ, "Катехизис Стефана Зизания (Вильна, 1595 г.)", *Studia Historica Europae Orientalis* 7 (2008), pp. 258-298. See also КОРЗО, *Украинская и белорусская катехетическая традиция*, p. 217; Н.В. ГАРКОВИЧ, *Деятельность Стефана Зизания в контексте православного братского движения в Речи Посполитой Автореферат диссертации на соискание ученой степени кандидата исторических наук по специальности 07.00.03 – Всеобщая история* (Minsk, 2019), pp. 3-4, 18; ТИМОШЕНКО, *Руська релігійна культура Вільна*, p. 217.

[154] N. HARKOVICH, "Sąd cerkiewny nad Stefanem Zyzanią w kontekście stosunków wiernych i hierarchii prawosławnej w Rzeczypospolitej u schyłku XVI wieku", *ΕΛΠΙΣ: Czasopismo Naukowe Katedry Teologii Prawosławnej Uniwersytetu w Białymstoku* 19 (2017), p. 92.

[155] КОРЗО, *Украинская и белорусская катехетическая традиция*, p. 246-291.

[156] "Катехизисъ албо короткое зебранье вѣры и церемонш Святое Соборное Апостолское Всходнее Церкви", in: *Молитвы повседневные от многих святых отец събраные до которыхъ и Катехизм вѣры предан есть вкоропгѣ* (Vievis, 1611). The catechism was discovered by Margarita A. Korzo. See КОРЗО *Украинская и белорусская катехетическая традиция*, p. 272.

Orthodox primers were similar to Catholic and Protestant primers. A good example is a version of the popular primer *Learning to Read for Children* (1633).[157] This primer continued the long tradition of this type of primers; its first edition had been published by Petrus Sextilis in Poznań in 1556.[158]

The Protestants played a leading role in religious teaching by means of books. From the very beginning, the Reformed churches used printed catechisms on a great scale to teach the principles of the Christian religion.[159] This form of teaching, based on questions and answers, had a long history reaching back to late Antiquity. The sixteenth-century leaders of the Reformation gave them a new form. This new invention quickly reached the Polish-Lithuanian state, and the first translations of Luther's Smaller Catechisms appeared in Polish and Lithuanian. They were published in Königsberg under the patronage of Duke Albert of Prussia, the ruler or the first Protestant state in Europe and the protector of the new confession in his country and in Poland and Lithuania. The translators of these catechisms were two Poles and a Lithuanian. Jan Seklucjan published *c.* 1544 *Profession of the Christian Faith* and in 1545 *The Simple Text of Catechism for Simple People*. Jan Malecki, a critic of Seklucjan's work, published his version in 1546: *Catechismus, that is the Christian Learning of the Apostles for Simple People Given in Three Parts*. A Lithuanian version of Seklucjan's catechism, the work of Martynas Mažvydas and incidentally the first printed book in Lithuanian, appeared in 1547 under the title *The Simple Words of the Catechism*.[160] That same year, a new edition of Se-

[157] *Dla dziatek nauka czytania* (Vilnius, 1633). See PILARCZYK, *Elementarze polskie*, pp. 75, 316; КОРЗО, *Украинская и белорусская катехетическая традиция*, p. 491.

[158] P. SEXTILIS, *Nauka ku czytaniu dziatkam małym pisma polskiego* (Poznań, 1556). The only existing copy: Herzog August Bibliothek (Wolfenbüttel, Germany), shelfmark: A:63 Gram. Facsimile and edition in: W. WYDRA, *O najdawniejszej drukowanej książce w Poznaniu* (Poznań, 2003). See also PIROŻYŃSKI, "O poznańskim drukarzu Piotrze Sextilisie", pp. 3-14; KORZO, "O tekstach religijnych", pp. 172, 177; PILARCZYK, *Elementarze polskie*, p. 71.

[159] The most important were the Small and Large Catechisms (German: *Der Kleine Katechismus* and *Der Große Katechismus*), both from 1529. See E. KASJANIUK, "Katechizm (III. W Protestantyzmie)", in: *Encyklopedia katolicka*, 8, *Język-Kino* (Lublin, 2000), p. 1048; КОРЗО, *Украинская и белорусская катехетическая традиция*, p. 13.

[160] J. SEKLUCJAN, *Wyznanie wiary chrześcijańskiej* (Königsberg?, *c.* 1544); ID., *Katechismu tekst prosty dla prostego ludu* (Königsberg, 1545); J. MALECKI, *Catechismus, to jest nauka krześciańska od Apostołów dla prostych ludzi we trzech cząstkach zamkniona* (Königsberg, 1546); M. MAŽVYDAS, *Catechismusa Prasty Szadei* (Königsberg, 1547). See A. BRÜCKNER, "Literatura wyznaniowa litewska", *Reformacja w Polsce* 2 (1922), pp. 125-126; ID., "Z polsko-litewskich dziejów wyznaniowych", *Reformacja w Polsce* 2 (1922), pp. 256-265; ESTREICHER, *Bibliographia Polska*, 27 (1929), p. 358; PILARCZYK, *Elementarze polskie*, pp. 67-70; D.D. POCIŪTĖ-ABUKEVIČIENĖ, "Martynas Mažvydas' Catechism: Tradition and signs of a new consciousness", in:

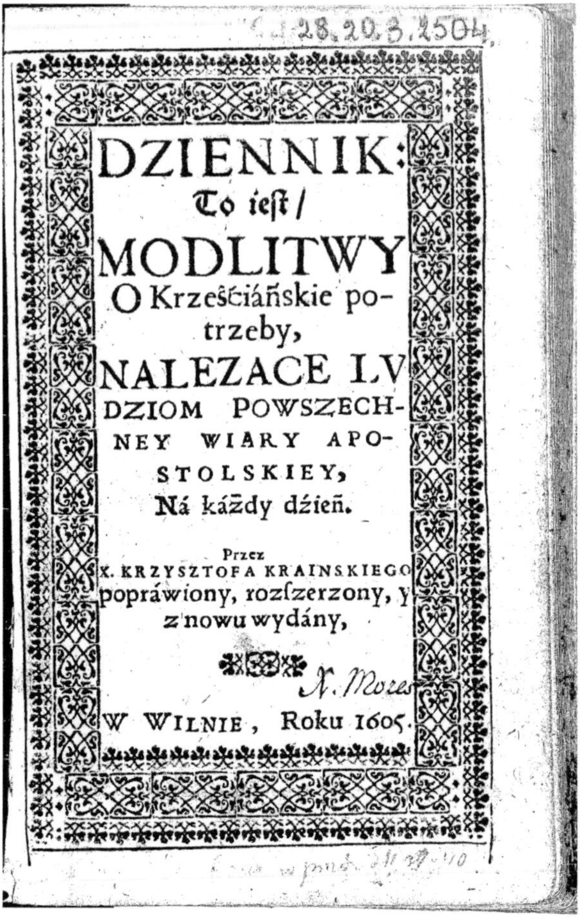
DZIENNIK:
To ieſt /
MODLITWY
O Krześćiáńskie potrzeby,
NALEZACE LVDZIOM POWSZECHNEY WIARY APOSTOLSKIEY,
Ná káżdy dźień.
Przez
X. KRZYSZTOFA KRAINSKIEGO
popráwiony, rozſzerzony, y znowu wydány,
W WILNIE, Roku 1605.

Fig. 74 Title page of a Polish Calvinist catechism by Krzysztof Kraiński, published in Vilnius in 1605 (K. Kraiński, *Dziennik, to jest modlitwy o krześcijańskie potrzeby należące ludziom powszechnej wiary apostolskiej na każdy dzień* (Vilnius, 1605)). Warsaw, BUW, <https:// polona.pl/ item/dziennik-to-iest-modlitwy-o-krzescianskie-potrzeby-nalezace-ludziom-powszechney-wiary, MTE4MTUxMTA/3/#info:metadata> (accessed: 21.05.2022; public domain).

Martynas Mažvydas and Old Lithuania (Collection of Papers), ed. D. KAUNAS *et. al.*, trans. D. BARTKUTĖ (Vilnius, 1998), pp. 141-157; JOVAIŠA, *Raštai lietuvių kalba*, p. 180; КОРЗО, *Украинская и белорусская катехетическая традиция*, pp. 120-130.

klucjan's catechism was also printed in Königsberg.[161] The Lutherans of Vilnius probably used these translations next to the Luther's original catechisms in German from 1529.

The Reformed (Calvinist) Church in Lithuania soon followed in the Lutherans' footsteps, publishing hymn books together with catechisms. The first of them appeared in Polish in Brest in 1553-1554. In Nyasvizh (Nieśwież), a Ruthenian Calvinist catechism was published in 1562[162] and a Polish translation of the Heidelberg Catechism in 1563.[163] The reworked version of the latter was issued in Vilnius in 1594. Other catechisms that appeared in Vilnius included Stanisław Sudrowski's work, published in 1592, and the Polish and Lithuanian ones of Melchior Pietkiewicz, printed in 1598 and again in 1600 under the title *Katechizm zborów Wielkiego Księstwa Litewskiego* (Catechism of the Protestant Churches of the Grand Duchy of Lithuania).[164] Members of both Protestant churches also had catechisms in the original languages, German and Latin, at their disposal, as well as the catechisms printed in Poland by Krzysztof Kraiński.[165] It is supposed that the Lithuanian Protestants also used catechisms printed in Cracow, Königsberg, and more distant places.

Protestant primers, just like the Catholic ones, also contained the basic teaching of doctrine and religious texts, among them fragments of the Bible. As an example may serve *The Basic Instruction of Latin and Christian Piety* from 1603. Its first known version was printed in Cracow before 1575.[166]

[161] J. SEKLUCJAN, *Catechismus to jest nauka naprzedniejsza i potrzebniejsza ku zbawieniu o wierze krześcijańskiej przz Jana Seklucjana nowo wydany* (Königsberg, 1547). See F. PILARCZYK, "Elementarze polskie XVI-XVIII w.", *Dydaktyka Literatury* 13 (1992), p. 89.

[162] НІКАЛАЕЎ, *Гісторыя беларускай кнігі*, 1, p. 161.

[163] A. KAWECKA, "Kancjonały protestanckie na Litwie", *Reformacja w Polsce* 4 (1926), pp. 128-130.

[164] CHEMPEREK, "Środowisko literackie protestantów w Wilnie", p. 47; JOVAIŠAS, *Raštai lietuvių kalba*, p. 210-212; D. KUŹMINA, *Katechizmy w Rzeczypospolitej XVI i początku XVII w.* (Warsaw, 2002), pp. 92, 95-97.

[165] K. KRAIŃSKI, *Katechizm z pieśniami Kościoła powszechnego apostolskiego* (Cracow, 1596).

[166] *Elementaria institutio Latini sermonis et pietatis Christianae* (Vilnius, 1603). The only copy of this edition was discovered in the Gotha Forschungsbibliothek (Erfurt, Germany), shelfmark: Phil 8° 01481/06 (02). The Cracow edition from 1575 is held in the Bulgarian National Library in Sofia. A fragment of an earlier copy was discovered recently by Margarita A. Korzo. See PILARCZYK, *Elementarze polskie*, pp. 71, 217; КОРЗО, *Украинская и белорусская катехетическая традиция конца XVI-XVII вв.*, p. 485; EAD., "O tekstach religijnych", pp. 171-182.

This list of Protestant catechisms alone allows us to see how much emphasis Protestants put on promoting their doctrine in Lithuania. The conclusions of the Calvinist synods speak of the need to translate, publish, and distribute books among the members of the Church.[167]

Some Jewish texts performed a function similar to catechisms. The Jews of Vilnius probably used the extremely popular book *Tseno Ureno* (Yiddish: הנאצ הניארו) by Jacob ben Isaac Ashkenazi from Janów Lubelski (Poland), first published at the beginning of the seventeenth century.[168] It was intended for women, and for this reason Jacob ben Isaac wrote it in Yiddish. It contained explanations of Torah readings for the Sabbaths, taken from the medieval treatises of Rashi and the *midrashim*. An important part of this work is concerned with the rules of conduct in accordance with Halacha, the law derived from the Torah. To the author's dismay, it was also used by men, who were theoretically predestined to study the Hebrew scriptures at a much more advanced level. *Tseno Ureno* was part of a widespread trend whereby religious doctrine was strengthened by the text that popularised it, is written in accessible language, and clearly marks the boundaries of orthodoxy. This was characteristic of all large religions of the Book present in the Polish-Lithuanian Commonwealth.

In case of Muslim education, probably the *kitabs* played the role of manuals of the religious rules. However, we do not know much about their use in Vilnius in the sixteenth and seventeenth centuries.

***

After Zizany had published his work, all the Christian confessions had their own catechisms at their disposal for use in schools. This had important implications. Although literacy and religious education had a medieval or even earlier tradition, in the sixteenth century this union gained yet another dimension. From the end of sixteenth century (and in case of the Protestants even earlier), acquiring basic literacy skills meant at the same time acquiring the

[167] T. GRABOWSKI, "Z dziejów literatury kalwińskiej na Litwie", *Reformacja w Polsce* 6 (1934), pp. 141-143.

[168] SCHIPER, *Język potoczny Żydów polskich i ich literatura*, p. 232; Ch. SHMERUK, *Historia literatury jidysz: Zarys*, ed. M. ADAMCZYK-GARBOWSKA and E. PROKOP-JANIEC (Wrocław, 2007), pp. 20, 131-132. The title of the book is based on the Hebrew version of the Song of Songs 3:11 "Goe foorth, O yee daughters of Zion" (translation after King James Version from 1611, see <https://www.kingjamesbibleonline.org/> (accessed 10.06.2021).

basic religious formation of a specific denomination. Such a double education was always purposely designed by the church authorities. This phenomenon can be called the confessionalisation of literacy.

One may assume that many catechisms, being at the same time hymn books or prayer books printed on an almost massive scale, reached many Vilnius houses. It was the reading matter recommended for everyone by the Catholic, Protestant, and Orthodox Churches, including for women and children, and it was used in schools of all rites as a textbook. Recommendations regarding the use of catechisms appeared in the documents of the church authorities, for instance in the Jesuit *Ratio studiorum* and in the canons of the synods of the Lithuanian Calvinists.[169]

The point of universal catechesis was to instil in people the basic dogmas of a given confession. The simple construction of catechisms, based on a dialogical model of questions and answers, was supposed to facilitate this. Ensuring their survival by means of printing (which was subject to censorship) and by constant repetition were intended to guarantee that orthodoxy would be maintained. To the illiterate, the teachings of the catechism were to be read aloud. In the case of Protestants, the duty to enforce knowledge of dogmas fell on the master of the house, as the Calvinist catechism from 1594 stated it:

> And so each good pious man who wishes to see the progress of Christian teaching in those who live in his home should ask his children and servants at least once a week what they have understood about their different duties which they should learn either through attending school, church [*zbór*], or at home, which should be all the easier if he hammers into their heads this *summarius* of Christian teaching through frequent godly instruction.[170] (original in Polish)

A pocket-sized (*in octavo*) miscellany manuscript (a commonplace book) of the Beranardine friar Andrew of Vilnius (Andreas Vilnensis) provides evidence of very similar Catholic catechesis. The Bernardine worked on it before

[169] *The Jesuit Ratio Studiorum of 1599*, ed. and trans. A.P. Farrell (Washington, DC, 1970), pp. 81, 86, 89, 93, 127; *Akta synodów prowincjonalnych jednoty litewskiej 1611-1625*, pp. 16-17 (1613, canon 6), 19 (1614, canon 5), 29 (canon 5), and 42 (canon 11); *Akta synodów prowincjonalnych jednoty litewskiej 1626-1637*, pp. 53-54 (canon 21, nr. 3 and 4).

[170] *Katechizm albo krótkie w jedno miejsce zebranie wiary i powinności krześcijańskiej z pasterstwem zborowym i domowym, z modlitwami, psalmami i piosnkami na cześć a chwałę Panu Bogu a Zborowi jego ku zbudowaniu teraz znowu za pilnym przejrzeniem i poprawieniem wydany: Nakładem jego m. pana Jana Abrahamowicza na Worniach, wojewody mieńskiego, prezydenta derptskiego, starosty lidskiego i wendeńskiego etc.* (Vilnius, 1594), ff. *Vr-*Vv.

the publication of Dauksza's catechism in Lithuanian. Its order was to facilitate his catechesis work among Lithuanian-speaking people. Andrew included two cards written in Lithuanian in the book, entitled *Suma mokslo krisczioniszko* (A Summary of Christian Teaching). In addition to the Catholic creed, some basic principles of Christian behaviour can be found there, for instance "*Ko ne nori idąnt taw butu darita. To kitām ne darite*" ("Do not do unto others what you would not want done unto thyself").[171]

The texts included in the catechism, which were usually learnt by heart, upheld the unity of the faithful and the one true faith that guaranteed salvation. They played an important role in unifying religious knowledge. At the same time, they contributed to the strengthening of similar mechanisms in a given community for understanding and interpreting the text, and in building a common *episteme*. They set clear norms of conduct in accordance with religious doctrine and, last but not least, made it possible for an average believer to understand what constituted his or her confession as compared to that of others.[172]

Sermons

An important issue in Vilnius was the dissemination and popularisation of interpretations of the Holy Books, as well as the enforcement of their precepts. This was done, first of all, through sermons. Almost all inhabitants of Vilnius had access to this literary genre, but the vast majority of them knew sermons by listening to them and only a few people could read their written versions.

Sermons were usually preached on holy days. For example, on Fridays one could hear commentaries on the Quran in the mosque, during Jewish celebrations on the morning the sabbath, on Fridays, a homiletic Midrash was read as a commentary (*derasha*) on the corresponding extract from the Torah,[173] and on Sundays homilies explaining the Bible and the teachings derived from it were preached in all Christian churches in Vilnius.

We have detailed information only about early modern Christian sermons. It is certain that before the sixteenth century Orthodox and Catholic priests preached sermons, but there are no written sources which tell us more about

[171] MS CZART. 3681 I, pp. 277-280.

[172] GOODY, *The Logic of Writing and the Organization of Society*, pp. 20-21.

[173] S.Ph. DE VRIES, *Obrzędy i symbole Żydów*, trans. A. BOROWSKI (Cracow, 1999), pp. 67-70.

them. We encounter a similar problem in the case of Jewish and Muslim sermons. They were certainly preached and were an important part of the religious life of both communities. We also known some names of Jewish preachers. For instance, in the middle of the seventeenth century Aaron Samuel ben Israel Kaidanover was a valued Jewish preacher.[174] That is all we can say.

On the contrary, the sources about Christian preaching in the sixteenth and seventeenth centuries are abundant.

Preachers

In the first half of the seventeenth century, Vilnius can be called a city of preachers and homiletics. The sermon, because of its universality, became a primary tool for the spiritual and moral control of the faithful by the clergy, that is, an instrument of power. However, looking at this process from a different perspective, one can see that it made possible for the majority of Vilnius residents to get acquainted with the genre of a rhetorised artistic text, the principles of its construction, its topoi, the abundance of its elocutionary means, etc. Through sermons, they had the opportunity to enter into contact with the excerpts of many texts that were included in homilies, starting with the Holy Books, translated for the purposes of preaching, continuing with commentaries on them, and last but not least to the classical authors of pre-Christian Antiquity.

The sermons performed in the Vilnius churches were first of all texts of the 'closed' city. Sermons were usually delivered on the Churches' holy days, as a part of their prayers. In every Christian community good preachers could be found. We know many by name, especially those from the late sixteenth and seventeenth centuries.

Among the Catholics, Piotr Skarga and Stanisław Grodzicki became renowned Polish-language preachers. In the seventeenth century, Marcin Widziewicz, Jakub Olszewski, and Kazimierz Jan Wojsznarowicz, also known as the

[174] TA-SHMA, "Moses ben Isaac Judah", p. 22. On Jewish preaching in early modern times, see SAPERSTEIN, "Education and homiletics", pp. 422-427. We do not know any written Jewish sermons from early modern Vilnius, but some light on their content can be shed by a valuable anthology by Marc Saperstein, who collected information about Jewish sermons from other areas. See *Jewish Preaching, 1200-1800: An Anthology*, ed. M. SAPERSTEIN (New Haven and London, 1989).

author of respected manual of epideictic rhetoric, gained fame.[175] We know also some names of Jesuit priests who preached in the Lithuanian language. Perhaps the aforementioned author of a Lithuanian postil Mikołaj Dauksza (Mikalojus Daukša) was among them. Another Jesuit, Konstanty Szyrwid (Sirvydas), gained great popularity as preacher in the Vilnius parish church of St. John. He preached both in Polish and Lithuanian twice a day for ten years.[176] In the 1640s, yet another Jesuit, Jan Jachnowicz, was a Lithuanian preacher in Vilnius known for the many devotional publications in this language.[177]

Since the mid-1590s we can observe the activity of Orthodox preachers as well. At the time, in the Orthodox community many monks and priests studied in humanist colleges and universities. They became acquainted with the rules of rhetoric, with Latin and Polish rhetorical works, and with Catholic hagiography and sermons;[178] they could apply their expertise in Church Slavonic and Ruthenian sermons. The impulse for this preaching activity were also the controversies related to the Union of Brest.

Stephan Zizany preached in the Orthodox Brotherhood in 1594-1596.[179] At the beginning of the seventeenth century, in the Brotherhood church of the Holy Spirit, preachers of renown were for instance Leonty Karpovych and Melecjusz Smotrycki.[180] Probably Smotrycki's postil was in part based on his preaching activity. Their opponents, the Uniates, settled on the other side of Ostra Street, where they used rhetorical means similar to those used by Karpovych and Smotrycki, but against Orthodox believers. Sermons in the Holy Trinity church were given for instance by Josef Velamin Rutski, Jozafat Kuncewicz, and Leon Kreuza Rzewuski. However, in the first half of the seventeenth century the Vilnius Uniates did not publish a postil similar to that by Smotrycki, perhaps, among other reasons, because they belonged to the Catholic Church and could use the postils of Wujek or Skarga.

[175] K.J. Wojsznarowicz, *Orator polityczny różnym aktom pogrzebowym służący, nowo na świat w roku 1644 wydany* ([Vilnius,] 1644).

[176] V. Biržiška, *Aleksandrynas: Senųjų lietuvių rašytojų, rašiusių prieš 1865 m., biografijos, bibliografijos ir biobibliografijos*, 1, *XVI-XVII amžiai* (Chicago, 1960), pp. 244-254; *Encyklopedia wiedzy o jezuitach*, p. 673.

[177] *XVII a. lietuvos lenkiškos knygos: Kontrolinis sąrašas (Polska książka na Litwie w XVII w. Wykaz kontrolny)*, ed. M. Ivanovič (Vilnius, 1998), pp. 72-74.

[178] Kuczyńska, "Homiletyka cerkiewna pierwszej Rzeczypospolitej", p. 200.

[179] Тимошенко, *Руська релігійна культура Вільна*, p. 165.

[180] Kuczyńska, "Homiletyka cerkiewna pierwszej Rzeczypospolitej", pp. 221-223.

Fig. 75 Konrad Götke, *Andreas Schonflissius Thorunensis Borussus aetatis suae 62 anno Domini 1652* [*Andrzej Schönflissius, A Prussian from Toruń Aged 62 in 1652*], a copperplate (Vilnius, 1652), in: A. Schönflissius, *Postylli chrześcijańskiej z Biblijej świętej i z doktorów kościelnych według starożytnej nauki i zwyczajnego porządku Kościoła Bożego zebranej na niedziele doroczne część pierwsza. Od Adwentu aż do Trójcy Świętej* ([Vilnius?], 1652). Reproduced with the permission of the Museum of Protestantism in Cieszyn. Photo Marcin Gabryś.

In the sermons of Uniate and Orthodox preachers from the end of the sixteenth and the first half of the seventeenth centuries we notice a process of development of a new model for Ruthenian homiletics. Reformation and

Counter-Reformation literature and the rhetorical models for constructing a text that were commonly used at the time had a significant influence on this change.[181] This development is revealed particularly well in Smotrycki's collection and in Polish funeral sermons.

In the Vilnius Lutheran church there were always two preachers working at the same time, one preaching in German and the other in Polish. Two Polish priests gained recognition in the seventeenth century, Samuel Dambrowski, from Greater Poland, who was the superior of the Vilnius Augsburg (Lutheran) Church from 1615 and the superintendent of the Lithuanian churches (*zbór*),[182] and his successor Andrzej Schönflissius, who originated from Toruń.[183] A summa of Dambrowski's activity as a preacher was the *Postylla chrześcijańska* (Christian Postil), published in Toruń in 1621, which gained as much recognition among the Protestants as Jakub Wujek's postil among the Catholics. Dambrowski's success may have been based not only on a clear and accessible source, but also on avoiding open religious polemics and on the universality of his speeches, including in his performances at funerals. Schönflissius was also famous for his funeral sermons. Today we know some twenty such texts, published throughout his lifetime.[184] Among his books printed in Vilnius is the first part of his postil from 1652, which Schönflissius treated as his *opus magnum*.[185]

[181] *Ibid.*, pp. 199-200.

[182] L. PRZYMUSZAŁA, *Struktura i pragmatyka* Postylli *Samuela Dambrowskiego* (Opole, 2003), p. 21.

[183] PAWELEC, *Kazania funeralne Samuela Dambrowskiego*, p. 69.

[184] NIEDŹWIEDŹ, "Wstęp", in: *Dwa kazania wygłoszone*, pp. 8-9, 15-21.

[185] A. SCHÖNFLISSIUS, *Postylli chrześcijańskiej z Biblijej świętej i z doktorów kościelnych według starożytnej nauki i zwyczajnego porządku kościoła Bożego zebranej na niedziele doroczne część pierwsza od Adwentu do Trójcy Świętej na cześć i chwałę wielkiego Boga i Zbawiciela Jezusa Chrystusa w druk podana* (Vilnius, 1652). The other part of the postil was never published as Schönflissius died during the plague in 1654. His manuscripts probably were destroyed during the Muscovite occupation of Vilnius (1655-1658). Schönflussius's printed postil was probably distributed among all Polish-speaking Lutheran communities in early modern times. The only known copy of it is preserved in the Museum of the Reformation in Cieszyn (Poland), which, as the capital of the Cieszyn Principality, was part of the Habsburg Empire until 1918.

Postils

Christians often took care to publish both occasional sermons and homilies. It was easier to print the former, because they were financed by patrons, often for non-religious reasons. Non-occasional homilies usually appeared in the form of more extensive collections, that is postils intended for Sundays and holidays throughout the year. Thanks to these forms of publication, some of these sermons have survived. This was the case also of the sermons of the Lutheran preacher Andrzej (Jędrzej) Schönflissius, who in 1646 published 33 sermons for advent.[186] However, we have to bear in mind that many postils contain written sermons which had not been delivered before, such as the *Postils* by the Jesuit Jakub Wujek, who was a great writer but avoided preaching.[187] Homilies that were not published have been lost, such as Sarbiewski's sermons, which he preached almost daily for four years before King Władysław IV.[188]

The Protestants developed the use of vernacular sermons much earlier than the other Christian communities in Vilnius. First of all, they were texts of the 'open' city. The first Protestant postils were brought to Vilnius from Königsberg, which was an important centre of Protestant publishing. Postils published in Polish and German significantly contributed to the catechesis of the Vilnius Lutherans. Maybe among these books were the postils by Martin Luther (German), and by Grzegorz Orszak and Jan Seklucjan (Polish, 1556).[189] They surely used the Lutheran *Postil* of Mikołaj Rey (Rej)[190] (first edition Cracow 1557) which was extremely popular in the whole

[186] A. Schönflissius, *Wesele wieczne z Ewangelijej o dziesiąci pannach w trzydziestu i we trzech kazaniach zebraniu chrześcijańskiemu w Wilnie w kościele saskim rożnych lat we dni adwentowe pokazane, a teraz wszytkim ludziom pobożnym na to wesele wieczne zaproszonym ku osobliwej pociesze ku zbawiennej nauce i ku życzliwej przestrodze w druk podane* (Vilnius, 1646).

[187] The first two parts of Wujek's *Postil* were printed in 1573: *Postilla catholica, to jest kazania na kożdą niedzielę i na kożde święto przez cały rok* (Cracow, 1573). In the next decades several versions of this work were republished, also in Lithuanian.

[188] Sarbiewski, "List 17 do Łubieńskiego pasterza", p. 62; M. Korolko, "Wstęp", in: Sarbiewski, *Liryki oraz Droga rzymska i fragment Lechiady*, p. xiii.

[189] G. Orszak, *Postylla domowa, to jest kazania na każdą niedziele i święta przedniejsze i na insze pospolite do roku, które niejedno w kościele, ale też i w domu każdy chrześcijański gospodarz może sobie i czeladce swojej kazać abo czytać sam, k oświeconości z Postylle Filipa Melanctona, Spangemberga i inszych zebrane*, ed. J. Seklucjan (Königsberg, 1556). See Estreicher, *Bibliographia Polska*, 27 (1929), p. 361-362.

[190] Mikołaj Rey (Rej) (1505-1569) was a Protestant leader, politician, and a leading writer of the Polish Renaissance. He wrote numerous treatises, plays, sermons, dialogues, satirical

Polish-Lithuanian state, even among Catholic and Orthodox[191] priests. In 1600 a Lithuanian translation of this work was published by Jakub Markowicz in Vilnius.[192] It may have been a Protestant response to the Lithuanian translation of Wujek's postil, printed by Jesuits a year earlier (i.e. Dauksza's postil).

The Calvinists also distributed their postils in Vilnius, and some of them were even printed in the city. The most successful were the works by the Polish preacher Grzegorz of Żarnowiec, who responded to a postil by the Jesuit Jakub Wujek.[193] Jan Karcan's printing house in Vilnius issued *A Defense of Evangelical Postils* (1585-1586) and the second edition of the *Postil* by Grzegorz of Żarnowiec (1597).[194] The proceedings of Calvinist synods say that in 1639 Lithuanian Calvinists decided to contribute to the publication of the translation of a postil in Gdańsk, which their clergy and lay people intended to use.[195]

In the ecclesiastical libraries of the Catholic Church, Latin postils were standard books in the entire period discussed here. For instance in the sixteenth-century library of the chapel of the Holy Cross in the cathedral we encounter *The Sermons upon All the Letters* by a popular Franciscan preacher

poems, emblems, etc. His postil was reprinted four times in the second half of the sixteenth century. The first edition: M. REJ (REY), *Świętych słów a spraw Pańskich, które tu sprawował Pan a Zbawiciel nasz na tym świecie jako prawy Bóg, będąc w człowieczeństwie swoim, Kronika albo Postylla, polskim językiem a prostym wykładem też dla prostaków krótce uczyniona* (Cracow, 1557).

[191] On Catholic priests, see ESTREICHER, *Bibliographia Polska*, 15 (1915), p. 182. On Orthodox priests, see J. JANÓW, "Tłumaczenia i przeróbki z *Postylli* M. Reja w pouczeniach ruskich (Tymczasowy wykaz ok. 50 kodeksów)", *Sprawozdania z czynności i posiedzeń Polskiej Akademii Umiejętności* 48 (1947-1948), pp. 301-306. The fact of using a Protestant writer by the Orthodox clergy was mentioned in 1642 by Kasjan Sakowicz, a convert from Orthodoxy to Catholicism. He recalled the satirical image of an uneducated Orthodox clergyman reading the postil of 'St. Rej' to his parishioners. See FRICK, "Introduction", in: SMOTRYCKI, *Rus' Restored*, p. XXIX.

[192] M. REJ (REY), *Postilla Lietuwiszka tátáy est Iżguldimás prástrás Ewánegeliu ąnt kożnos Nedelios ir Szwentes per wisus metus, kurios págal buda sená Báżniczioy Diewá est skatomos: Nu isż nauia su didżiu perweizdeghimu est iżduotá* (Vilnius, 1600). See A. JOVAIŠAS, "Raštai lietuvių kalba", in ULČINAITĖ and JOVAIŠAS, *Lietuvių literatūros istorija*, p. 213.

[193] Postils by Grzegorz of Żarnowiec were printed in Cracow in 1580 and 1582. In the sixteenth and seventeenth centuries they were reprinted and translated in Czech and German.

[194] Grzegorz z Żarnowca, *Obrona postylle ewanielickiej, to jest odpowiedź na Apologiją jezuicką w Krakowie niedawno wydaną, która odpowiedź w pierwszej części zamyka w sobie dziesięcioro kazań naprzeciwko sześciorgom kazań Apologijej jezuickiej. A w drugiej części okazanie dowodne pobrane prawd ewanielickich w w tejże Apologijej naganiony. Teraz (za niedostatkiem ksiąg) znowu drukowano* (Vilnius, 1591). See R. CZYŻ, *Obrona wiary w edycjach postylli Grzegorza z Żarnowca* (Warsaw, 2008), p. 17.

[195] *Akta synodów litewskich prowincjonalnych 1638-1675*, MS MAB F40-1136, f. 4r, canon 2.

and writer, Jean Royaers (Ioannes Royardus, †1547).[196] However, the publication of the Protestant vernacular postils forced the Catholic authorities to react. To prevent the reading of the Protestant postil by Rey, the Jesuits published their own collections of sermons, which were also available in Vilnius. The most important were Jakub Wujek's *The Catholic Postil* (1573) and Piotr Skarga's *Sermons for Sundays and Holidays*.[197] All these postils were in Polish, but the Jesuits also took care of the Lithuanian-speaking Catholics. In 1599 the Jesuit Mikołaj Dauksza (Mikalojus Daukša) translated and published Jakub Wujek's *Postil* in Vilnius.[198] A couple of decades later, the bilingual Lithuanian-Polish postil *The Abstracts of Sermons* by Konstanty Szyrwid (Konstantinas Sirvydas) were published twice (1629, 1644).[199]

In 1616, Smotrycki published an Orthodox postil, *Evangelie uchitelnoe* (*Instructive Evangeliary*) in the Brotherhood's printing house in Vievis, that is the Ruthenian translation of the homilies then attributed to the fourteenth-century patriarch of Constantinople Callixtus I.[200] Smotrycki introduced significant changes into his version, making it similar to postils written in Polish. The result was a modern Orthodox postil to explain the Holy Scriptures, while it was also the first such extensive collection of his translations into Ruthenian.[201]

Orally Performed vs. Written Sermons

Although the doctrines of the Christian communities in Vilnius differed, their practices of preaching were similar. We can attribute this to the fact that early modern preaching was derived from the medieval *ars praedicandi*. This

[196] First edition: Ioannes Royardus (Jean Royaers), *Homiliae in omnes epistolas dominicales iuxta literam* (Antwerp, 1538); *Altare S. Crucis In Ecclesia Cathedrali Vilnensi*, f. 11r.

[197] P. SKARGA, *Kazania na niedzielę i święta całego roku. Dwa są przy nich regestry, jeden do nauk na umocnienie katolickiej wiary, a drugi do naprawy obyczajów służący: Za dozwoleniem starszych* (Cracow, 1595).

[198] JOVAIŠAS, *Raštai lietuvių kalba*, pp. 204-205.

[199] K. SZYRWID, *Punkty kazań od Adwentu aż do Postu litewskim językiem z wytłumaczeniem na polskie* (Vilnius, 1629).

[200] D.A. FRICK, "Meletij Smotryc'kyj's Ruthenian *Homiliary Gospel* (1616)", in: *The Jevanhelije učitielnoje of Meletij Smotryc'kyj*, introduction by D.A. FRICK (Cambridge, Mass., 1987), pp. IX-X; M. KUCZYŃSKA, "Homiletyka cerkiewna pierwszej Rzeczypospolitej", in: *Między Wschodem i Zachodem. Prawosławie i unia*, ed. M. KUCZYŃSKA (Warsaw, 2017), p. 211.

[201] FRICK, "Meletij Smotryc'kyj's Ruthenian *Homiliary Gospel* (1616)", p. XIV; ID., "Introduction", in: SMOTRYCKI, *Rus' Restored*, pp. XXIX-XXX.

is true even in the case of Orthodox and Uniate sermons, although we have to remember their Byzantine traditions as well. From the second half of the sixteenth century, Orthodox preachers used Catholic and Lutheran models. Some Orthodox and Uniate priests had studied in humanist colleges and universities, where they got a thorough training in how to write sermons following the rules of Latin rhetoric.

Traditionally a sermon, understood as text, is associated with oral performance.[202] However, in the Middle Ages it became a genre in the borderland of oral and written literature.[203] In this respect the sermon is similar to epic poetry, and especially to the epos. The European epic tradition is derived from the *Iliad* and *Odyssey*, and even texts composed in writing, such as the *Aeneid* or *Gerusalemme liberata*, contain a residue of oral epic forms, similar to those which are present in Homer's works. Just so with sermons: even those which from the very beginning were composed as written texts, contain literary devices characteristic of oral literature. It seems, though, that the difference between a written and oral sermon does not lie first of all in their literary structure but in the way they were performed. The oral sermon is by its very nature performative,[204] while the written sermon is discursive. They belong to two different literary orders.

When we think about sermons as texts, in the sixteenth and seventeenth centuries many of them possessed a character of the secondary orality.[205] The residue of this orality is present in two spheres. Firstly, the sermon, whether Christian, Jewish, or Muslim, directly or indirectly referred to the Book or to other authoritative texts.[206] Even when the preacher delivered a sermon without preparing it in writing, it had a background in the form of an earlier text. Secondly, the scheme of a sermon was always based on a textual model. The manner of argumentation, composition, and the linguistic means used all had their

[202] T. SZOSTEK, "Kazanie", in: *Słownik literatury staropolskiej: Średniowiecze – Renesans – Barok*, ed. T. MICHAŁOWSKA (Wrocław, 1998), p. 366; T. MICHAŁOWSKA, *Leksykon: Literatura polskiego średniowiecza* (Warsaw, 2011), p. 424.

[203] On the different concepts of the term 'oral literature' in twentieth-century research, see P. CZAPLIŃSKI, "Słowo i głos", in: *Literatura oralna*, ed. P. CZAPLIŃSKI (Gdańsk, 2010), pp. 5-32.

[204] R. BAUMAN, "Verbal arts as performance", *American Anthropologist* 77.2 (1975), pp. 290-311.

[205] Mutual influences of written and oral sermons are discussed in the recent collected volume *L'Éloquence de la chaire entre écriture et oralité (XIII-XVIIIe siecles): Actes du colloque international de Genève, 11-12 septembre 2014*, ed. G. AUBERT, A. HENEVELD, and C. MELI (Paris, 2018).

[206] E.g. a part of the Muslim *khutbah* consists of reciting the text of Quran.

own written models. The extreme case was that when a sermon was read aloud from someone else's postil.

A sermon was delivered orally, but in early modern times in Lithuania it was the norm to write it down first and later to preach or read it aloud from a manuscript. We have several sources confirming this practice in the seventeenth century, for example the decrees of the Calvinist synod. Before delivering a sermon, the preacher was obliged to write it down and show it to the supervisor of the parish (the minister):

> The catechists [...] in their sermons should not preach on too deep and difficult matters. They should explain the catechism *quam simplicissime* without any deliberations or embarking on deeper *questiae*. They should *show their sermons* to their ministers.[207] [My emphasis.] (original in Polish)

From the correspondence of Maciej Kazimierz Sarbiewski we know that during his service as the royal preacher (1636-1640) he also had to write his sermons down before preaching them.[208] Another example from the second half of the seventeenth century are the manuscripts of funeral sermons of the Vilnius Dominican Michał Woyniłłowicz. His two notebooks document the process of composing sermons which were to be delivered during the funeral service. Later, some of these sermons were printed.[209]

We have to remember though that preaching in the sixteenth and seventeenth century was not a one-way process: from the written word to its oral

[207] *Akta synodów prowincjonalnych jednoty litewskiej 1611-1625*, p. 21 (1614, canon 12).

[208] M.K. SARBIEWSKI, "List 17 do Łubieńskiego pasterza" (Warsaw, 1637), and see: W. SYROKOMLA, *Przekłady poetów polsko-łacińskich epoki zygmuntowskiej*, 6, *Dodatki i uzupełnienia* (Warsaw, 1852), p. 62.

[209] The comparison of Woyniłłowicz's drafts, first manuscript versions and the printed versions can shed new light on how the written and the oral coexisted in the Vilnius republic of letters. See J. NIEDŹWIEDŹ, "Kaznodzieja, lider i ghostwriter: Notatniki Michała Woyniłłowicza (1671-1683) jako ego-dokumenty", in: *Pogranicze czyli polskość: Księga jubileuszowa ofiarowana Profesorowi Andrzejowi Romanowskiemu*, ed. A. BIEDRZYCKA, P. BUKOWIEC, B. KAŁĘBA, and I. WĘGRZYN (Cracow, 2021), pp. 369-395. In many libraries and archives in Belarusia, Lithuania, Poland, Russia, and Ukraine collections of early modern manuscript sermons are preserved. The majority of them were preached in the Catholic, Uniate, and Orthodox churches and were written before the rhetorical action. An example is a vast collection of sermons by a Ukrainian-Russian writer, scholar, and Orthodox Church hierarch Stefan Iavors'kyi (Jaworski, 1658-1722). His sermons (*c.* 4000 pages) are preserved in the Russian State Archive in St. Petersburg (Russia). Many manuscript sermons can be found in church libraries and archives in Cracow (a.o. in those of the Carmelites, Dominicans, Piarists, and Bernardines).

interpretation. The relationship between the oral and the written word was more complex, and this complexity manifests in the traces of orality in sermons.[210] They are present, for example, in a funeral sermon preached on 19 July 1631 by the Jesuit Jakub Olszewski at the *exequiae* mass after death of Queen Constance of Austria. The sermon was printed after the ceremony in numerous copies. In this printed version Olszewski tried to convince the reader that his text is the one he preached in Vilnius cathedral:

> When I recently saw the ancient, excellent, and good coats of arms of the queen's family, I would like to say: *Constantia* or Constance. I cannot, because *I am watching right now* the decorations of the coffin: the skulls and other symbols of the death, I would rather say: *Inconstantia* – Changeability. [...] O miserable condition of our country! To make you better understand the change in your fortune, I will present you firstly, the grief of our Commonwealth, and secondly the grief of each estate. I even show you what is the reason of your mourning. I will be able to do that with your help, Lord Jesus, and because *of your diligence in listening*, my lords. (original in Polish) [My emphasis.][211]

However, Olszewski, professor of rhetoric in the Academy of Vilnius, could easily invent a fictitious situation in a fictitious church. Maybe his words were a kind of dissimulation or, to use the terms from the epoch, *imitatio* or *fictio*? It is highly probable he projected a speech situation before the funeral mass and put this in a written text imitating an oral utterance.

Recapitulation

In Chapters 5 and 7, I tried to answer the question which books inhabitants of Vilnius possessed, read, and used. The inventories of institutional or private libraries shed light also on this issue. However, only an examination of the role of religious texts can help us to better (even if not fully) understand the attitude of the inhabitants of Vilnius to the book and to more complex written texts, by

[210] J. GOEURY, "Des sermons prononcés comme ils ont été écrits, ou bien écrits comme ils ont été prononcés?", in: *L'Éloquence de la chaire*, pp. 131-146.

[211] J. OLSZEWSKI, "Żałoba po śmierci najaśniejszej Konstancyjej, królowej polskiej, księżny litewskiej etc., arcyksiężny rakuskiej, w kościele katedralnym wileńskim 19 Iulii roku Pańskiego 1631 wystawiona przez księdza Jakuba Olszewskiego Societatis Iesu, doktora i dziekana świętej teologijej, kościoła farskiego wileńskiego kaznodzieję", in: *Dwa kazania wygłoszone*, pp. 58-59, 61.

way of the prayers they said and the sermons they heard. It is a highly probable conjecture that in many Vilnius families prayer books were common. This can be confirmed by the number of printed copies available in the city, the customs and the contents of these books. Having a prayer book was both a necessity and a fashion, and not only among the urban elites.[212] In some religious groups, especially among the Protestants, reading and singing pious matter was obligatory. The catechisms, songbooks, and primers-catechisms were also the books most commonly in use.

However, possessing a book and reading it do not exhaust all the possibilities of using pious texts. The inhabitants of Vilnius came into contact with them by listening to these texts or learning them by heart. The vast majority of religious texts were transmitted orally, but we must remember that this was secondary orality or quasi-orality. Sermons and everyday prayers were anchored in previously written texts. One of the tasks of the religious authorities was to guard the orthodoxy of the faith, which usually meant that the oral texts had to agree with their written and approved versions.

The possibility of listening to the written words performed in a church, a synagogue, or a mosque had one more important dimension. Even less educated people, who possessed only pragmatic literacy, had access to the complex rhetorical texts performed by the professionals of the written word. Since the semi-literate people constantly listened to sermons, liturgical formulae, fragments of the Holy Books, songs, and chants, they must have acquired some rhetorical and poetical fluency. This fluency was rather passive. Still, it certainly must have influenced the way people thought, spoke, and used written texts. This must remain a conjecture, because the voices of the inhabitants of Vilnius are irretrievably lost, but at least we have access to some of their texts. Together with our knowledge and imagination, they can help us forge a cultural memory of the rhetorical organisation of the late medieval and early modern societies of Vilnius.

[212] There are scarcely any portraits of the inhabitants of Vilnius from the sixteenth and the first half of the seventeenth centuries, but probably they did not differ from the portraits painted in other cities of the Polish-Lithuanian Commonwealth. Both the men and women represented in them very often hold small prayer books. In such portraits (and also on funeral monuments) the book is a symbol of the piety and social status of the person represented.

Conclusion: The City of Memory

In this book I have referred several times to the memoirs of the royal doctor and mayor (*burmistrz*) of Vilnius Maciej Vorbek-Lettow (1593-1663), entitled *The Support of Recollection, or the Treasury of Memory*.[1] At the beginning of his memoirs, the author provided an essay about the changeability of things (*vicissitudo rerum*) and oblivion. The only thing that rescues our memory and memory about us, Vorbek-Lettow wrote, is script and print:

> If there was no support of print or writing, all knowledge about the memorable deeds and necessary things, that rely only on human recollection, would perish and come to a miserable end. Human memory is like the March snow that vanishes in languid current under the gust of the wind; writing is *oblivionis remedium* [the remedy for oblivion] (Euripides). Only those things and deeds are fully known to future times, which were put on paper by means of writing or print: the most secure and durable *archigraphiarius* [the finest means of recording script]. *Litterarum usu memoriae fulcitur aeternius* [The use of letters supports eternal memory]. Time devours and digests us, *omnes sicut vestimentum veterascent* [all of them shall wax old like a garment] (as King David says in Psalm 101) and all our good and bad deeds and knowledge of all our things would sink into oblivion and an irretrievable loss, if they were entrusted only to memory, without writing and printing. *Perit vox cum sonitu. Lingua mentis vices subit, calamus linguae et verba efformat in char-*

[1] The entire title of this work is very long. Its first part is in Latin, the rest in Polish. See M. Vorbek-Lettow, *Subsidium reminiscentiae abo Skarbnica pamięci różnych spraw domowych jako i potocznych, przypomnienia godnych i potrzebnych, opisanie zachowująca, po wtóre zebrana po zgorzeniu pierwszej w Niepołomicy mil trzy za Krakowem, przy bytności najjaśniejszego Władysława IV, polskiego i szwedzkiego króla etc., pana i dobrodzieja mego miłościwego i ich mości panów senatorów na ten czas przy jego królewskiej mości rezydujących, o czym obszernie informuje manifestacyja z Metryki Wielkiej Koronnej wypisem wyjęta w Krakowie feria quarta post festum Beatissimae Virginis Assumptinis proxima anno 1644*, MS Czart. 1857.

> *ta, quae voce oporteret eloqui* [The voice perishes with the sound. Language follows the mind, the pen follows language and forms the words on a sheet; they in turn ought to be said aloud].[2]

Vorbek-Lettow was not very original in his understanding of the purpose of writing. We can find similar topoi of *scriptura oblivionis remedium* in many ancient and medieval texts, repeated in early modern florilegia and developed in many literary works.[3] The new thing Vorbek-Lettow added to this topos, is the praise of print. The author knew from his own experience that manuscripts do burn, but that printed documents and books are long-lasting. In short, the royal doctor reminds us of the common notion of script and memory in his times.

On the following pages of his diary he wrote the most interesting thing about the practice of memory. He explained the genesis of his memoir. His father, Mateusz Vorbek-Lettow (1558-1624), kept a chronicle of his family, *Subsidium reminiscentiae*, started by one of his ancestors in 1488 and continued by the next generations.[4] Unfortunately, the manuscript burnt in the great fire of Vilnius on 2 July 1610, which was mentioned earlier in this book. Shortly afterwards, seventeen-year-old Maciej decided to reconstruct the chronicle. Because he and his father had read the chronicle many times, they could recall its content. Their memory was trained well enough for this task. Still, it was impossible to remember all the facts and they supplemented the new version with memories from the life of Mateusz.[5]

The next destruction of the chronicle happened a couple decades later. When travelling, Maciej Vorbek-Lettow always took the manuscript with him. In 1645 the laboriously restored chronicle burned with his other manuscripts in the fire of the town of Niepołomice near Cracow, where he was staying.[6] However, the stubborn royal doctor did not give up and wrote the *Subsidium reminiscentiae* once again. In the first part of the manuscript, he reconstructed

[2] VORBEK-LETTOW, *Skarbnica pamięci*, p. 8. The last Latin sentence is a paraphrase of a fragment of the *subscriptio* to emblem 11 by Diego de Saavedra Fajardo (1584-1648). See D. DE SAAVEDRA FAJARDO, *Idea principis Christiano-politici 101 symbolis expressa* (Amsterdam, 1659), p. 83.

[3] DOMAŃSKI, *Tekst jako uobecnienie*, p. 9.

[4] VORBEK-LETTOW, *Skarbnica pamięci*, p. 11.

[5] *Ibid.*, pp. 14-15.

[6] *Ibid.*, pp. 126-130.

the genealogy of his family starting from 1301. In the second, the main part, he focused on his own life. Luckily, this manuscript survived.

The history of Vorbek-Lettow's *Subsidium reminiscentiae* epitomises one of the crucial aspects of Vilnius textuality. From the very beginning of Vilnius, its inhabitants struggled constantly to make and preserve written testimony of their affairs and deeds. The city's written records were destroyed many times by the Teutonic Knights, by fires, floods, religious riots, Muscovite troops in 1655, La Grande Armée of Napoleon in 1812, Russian occupants in the nineteenth century, and by the German Nazis and the Soviets in the twentieth century. As a result, the chances that sources would come down to us were poor. Still, a sufficient number of them survived, and scholars were able to produce an impressive number of studies about the city. It turns out that this struggle for memory, continued from the fourteenth century onwards, has been a victorious one. We have to remember, that the results could be quite different, as the example of the medieval Lithuanian town of Kernavė proves.[7] The success of Vilnius can be ascribed to the particular status of the city as a site of memory.

Throughout this book, I have many times emphasised the economic, political, administrative, educational, and religious functions of the city. However, like other urban settlements, Vilnius was important also as a site of memory (*lieu de mémoire*).[8] The concept of the 'site of memory' is usually associated with twentieth-century societies, their histories and memory practices,[9] but it

[7] The town of Kernavė (Pol. *Kiernów*) can serve as an example of a parallel, but unsuccessful history. Kernavė is a village *c.* 40 km West to Vilnius in the valley of the Neris River. From the first half of the thirteenth century it was one of the main seats of the dukes of Lithuania, a major political and economic centre, whose status was similar to Vilnius. In the fourteenth century it consisted of five settlements and was the capital of a principality. The Teutonic Knights besieged the town several times, and in 1390 they finally took it and burnt it down. After that, Kernavė was never reconstructed and today remains an archeological site. The memory of Kernavė remained in early modern Lithuanian texts, e.g. it was marked on the Radziwiłł Map (1613) as "*Kiernów, primum Duci Lithuaniae domicilium*" (Kernavė, the first seat of the duke of Lithuania); cf. *Magni Ducatus Lithuaniae, et Regionum Adiacentium exacta Descriptio* (the *Radziwiłł Map*) (Amsterdam, 1613) <https://www.sbc.org.pl/dlibra/publication/36243/edition/32908/content> (1631 edition) (accessed: 13.06.2023). However, its symbolic significance cannot be compared to this of Vilnius.

[8] P. NORA, "Mémoire collective", in: *Faire de l'histoire*, ed. J. LE GOFF and P. NORA (Paris, 1974); ID., "Between memory and history: *Les lieux de mémoire*", *Representations* 26 (1989), pp. 7-24; ID., "General introduction: Between memory and history", in: *Realms of Memory: Rethinking the French Past*, 1, *Conflicts and Divisions*, ed. P. NORA (New York, 1996), pp. 1-20; A. SZPOCIŃSKI, "Miejsca pamięci (*lieux de mémoire*)", *Teksty Drugie* 4 (2008), pp. 11-20.

[9] J. WINTER, "Sites of memory", in: *Memory: Histories, Theories, Debates*, ed. S.

can also be linked to earlier times. The French historian Pierre Nora, who introduced the term to the humanities, defined a 'site of memory' as "any significant entity, whether material or non-material in nature, which by dint of human will or the work of time has become a symbolic element of the memorial heritage of any community [...]".[10]

The story about the Iron Wolf from the early sixteenth century, that was recalled at the beginning of this book, shows that already then Vilnius was an important "symbolic element of the memorial heritage" of the early modern Lithuanian nation. However, this symbolic element would not have worked without a longstanding and relentless process of making, reconstructing, accumulating, and preserving texts in Vilnius and about Vilnius. Texts were crucial in making Vilnius a site of memory because, in the late Middle Ages, the written word was the main instrument that constituted the collective memory of European societies. The Grand Duchy of Lithuania and its capital city were also entities that functioned in the realm of script.[11] Their inhabitants relied on writing as the main way of (re-)constructing and preserving memory.

More broadly, as a site of memory Vilnius gave form to a broader category of collective memory, that of thye inhabitants of the city and of the Grand Duchy of Lithuania itself. In order to capture the mechanisms of making this collective memory, we need to return to the seventeenth-century sources. Maciej Vorbek-Lettow and his father Mateusz were convinced that if something was not written down, it would be forgotten. Other inhabitants of Vilnius shared this conviction, although not all of them were able to explain it in such a clear way as the diarist. As we will remember, the archives of the city were lost during the Muscovite occupation,[12] and in 1661 the authorities carefully listed the missing registers. It is obvious that they did this for practical reasons, but there is one more dimension to their attempts. The registers were destroyed and the elites of the city suffered the loss of an important part of the past of Vilnius and of their urban identity. The remedy was the remembrance of the destroyed archives. That is why the Vorbek-Lettows called their own restored family chronicles the *subsidium*, which can mean both 'aid' and 'remedy' or 'cure'. Remembering the loss was both a form of mourning for the irretrievable

RADSTONE and B. SCHWARZ (New York, 2010), pp. 312-324.

[10] P. NORA, "Preface to the English-language edition", in: *Realms of Memory: Rethinking the French Past*, 1, *Conflicts and Divisions*, ed. P. NORA (New York, 1996), p. XVII.

[11] See Parts One and Two of this book.

[12] See Chapter 2. See also *Zbiór praw i przywilejów*, p. 229-230.

loss of the past and a therapeutic gesture of defining and showing the gap. The authorities of Vilnius informed posterity: we used to have huge archives that confirmed our history, we lost them, but we will remember the loss. This remembrance will be a substitute for the archive. Emphasising the gap was yet another form of making a site of memory.

We can find other, similar moments in the texts about Vilnius. Rabbi Moses Ben Naphtali Hirsch Rivkes remembered in his work *The Well of Exile* the treatises *Zebahim* and *Menahot* he had had to leave in Vilnius in the summer of 1655.[13] These treatises contained his extensive manuscript annotations to both texts. After his arrival in Amsterdam, the only result of his longstanding studies was his memory, which he recorded in one of his later works. All what remained was a recollection of a text that had once existed.

Another example from the same time is a story recorded by a Dominican chronicler. When in August 1655 the Dominican provincial, *magister* Tomasz Consoli, escaped Vilnius on foot, the only thing he took with him was the book of the protocols of the gatherings of the Lithuanian province of the Dominicans.[14] It was the only manuscript that the Dominicans rescued; the rest of the archive was lost.

The records of Vorbek-Lettow, the city scribes, Rabbi Rivkes, and the Dominican chronicler remind us of the lost texts about Vilnius and its inhabitants. The city and its people where the final goal of their recollections. In these accounts, the city was no longer (or not only) a real place, but a textual site of collective memory. As was mentioned above, collective memory is predominantly based on material artefacts and texts. Its main substratum is stored memory (*Speichergedächtnis*).[15] Stored memory may include objects, buildings, graves, places, toponyms, pictures, etc., but above all written sources. From the end of the fourteenth century Vilnius was a great depository of such textual

[13] M. Ben Naphtali Hirsch Rivkes, *Be'er ha-Golah* (Amsterdam, 1661), as cited in: Cohen, *History of the Jews in Vilna*, pp. 41-43.

[14] S. Barącz, *Rys dziejów zakonu kaznodziejskiego w Polsce*, 2 (Lviv, 1861), p. 391; J.M.A. Giżycki, *Wiadomości o dominikanach prowincyi litewskiej*, 1 (Cracow, 1917), p. 21.

[15] A. Assmann, *Erinnerungsräume: Formen und Wandlungen des kulturellen Gedächtnisses* (Munich, 1999), pp. 130-145; J. Assmann, "Introduction", in: id., *Religion and Cultural Memory: Ten Studies*, trans. R. Livingstone (Stanford, 2006), p. 25; M. Saryusz-Wolska, "Pamięć magazynująca", in: *Modi memorandi: Leksykon kultury pamięci*, ed. M. Saryusz-Wolska and R. Trąba (Warsaw, 2014), pp. 341-342; J. Assmann, "Collective memory and cultural identity", trans. J. Czaplicka, *New German Critique* 65 (1995), pp. 125-133.

memory.[16] Bearing all this in mind, we have to see this as a phenomenon of communicative memory, that is the oral transmission of textual memory.[17]

Communicative memory reveals itself in an immediate exchange of information between interlocutors. The process of recollection takes place *hic et nunc*, as a real act of encounter and conversation. By its nature, it cannot be widespread or long-lasting, because it is limited to the realm of orality. Communicative memory survives only as long as the persons who participated in the exchange remain alive. It is estimated that in traditional societies recollections transmitted orally, that is living memory, last *c.* eighty years at most.[18] Living memory could be recorded, but when it is written down communicative memory metamorphoses into stored memory.[19]

The moment of the shift from communicative to stored memory was described in several texts we have mentioned just now. For example, in the summer and autumn of 1610, the Vorbek-Lettows composed the *Subsidium reminiscentiae* anew as a written text, but it originated from the conversations between father and son. In the 1660s, after the Muscovite occupation, the authorities of the city summoned the inhabitants to bring documents which had survived the calamity to the town hall. Thanks to this call, the urban scribes were able to reconstruct fragments of the old aldermen's registers. The scribes had access to some preserved books, but most of all they relied on the documents delivered by the inhabitants of the city.[20] The very process of re-writing the old documents by the scribes was also an act of communicative memory. When transcribed, the documents became a fragment of stored collective memory.

The history of Vilnius is based on the tension between stored memory (usually written texts) and communicative memory (direct communication, usually orally). This relation could work in both directions. Vorbek-Lettow wrote the story of his family, and his knowledge was based on conversations

[16] This has been discussed in Chapters 2 and 10.

[17] J. ASSMANN, "Introduction", in: ID., *Religion and Cultural Memory*, p. 25.

[18] J. ASSMANN, *Cultural Memory and Early Civilization*, pp. 34-37, 54.

[19] In the conception of Jan Assmann and Aleida Assmann, cultural memory stands in opposition to personal memory. The centre and source of cultural memory (a form of collective memory) is stored memory: historical accounts, literature, historical sources, pictures, monuments, etc. See A. ASSMANN, "Speichergedachtnis und Funktionsgedachtnis", in: *Wir sind Erinnerung: Referate einer Vorlesungsreihe des Collegium generale der Universität Bern im Sommersemester 2001*, ed. P. RUSTERHOLZ and R. MOSER (Berne, 2003), pp. 181-196.

[20] See Chapter 8.

with his father Mateusz (from communicative to stored memory). However, the recollections of Mateusz came from his reading of the first version of the *Subsidium reminiscentiae* (from stored to personal to communicative memory). Both forms of memory merged with each other.

Throughout this book we find traces of similar textual practices which contributed to the formation of the collective memory of the Vilnians and other the inhabitants of the Grand Duchy of Lithuania. For example, I presented the professionals of the written word who were responsible for the production and dissemination of written records, that is the material forms of keeping memory.[21] The places of preserving these texts were described, namely the archives and libraries.[22] I discussed the ways in which Vilnius women dealt with the written word. Apart from many other functions, their texts were to construct female-focused memory, whether in form of a chronicle of a nunnery or a shopping list.[23] We encountered a Jesuit poet, Maciej Kazimierz Sarbiewski, who in his odes and epodes directly wrote about the eternal memory of the capital of Lithuania and constructed a literary myth of Vilnius.[24]

There is no need to extend this list of practices of keeping memory by the former inhabitants of Vilnius. They usually kept written texts motivated by practical reasons, but one has to remember that memory was also a moral obligation. Firstly, Vilnians cultivated *memoria*, the memory of the deceased members of the community.[25] Secondly, keeping memory was commendable *per se*. In the Middle Ages a good personal memory was considered to be a moral virtue.[26] Gradually the virtue of personal memory seems to have shifted towards the obligation of keeping memory in written forms. Vorbek-Lettow understood that recording the history of his family was his moral obligation. Such a written account (and *a fortiori* a printed one) was a shield against the *edax tempus* (voracious time), fate, changing fortunes, and against internal and external foes. Literate activities that resulted in a written text – whether a memoir, a Latin ode, or a book of court records – gave their authors a sense of time-resistance. It can be called an effect of being time-proof.

[21] See Chapter 1.

[22] See Chapter 2.

[23] See Chapter 4.

[24] See Chapter 10.

[25] Discussed in Chapter 10.

[26] M. CARRUTHERS, *The Book of Memory: A Study of Memory in Medieval Culture* (Cambridge, 1993), pp. 9, 13.

At least from the seventeenth century onwards, the elites of the Polish-Lithuanian Commonwealth constantly had to reconstruct their collective memory. After the partitions (1773-1795), this process became a constant imperative that defined the actions of the elites of a non-existing state. They struggled for the preservation of their cultural and national identity. Their newly defined history was written on the basis of the personal memories of the survivors, rescued documents and artifacts. In turn, this written story was transformed into the living (communicative) memory of the five nations that were the heirs of the Polish-Lithuanian federation: Belarusians, Jews, Lithuanians, Poles and Ukrainians. This mechanism (and also a literary topos) of keeping and reconstructing memory was recognised already at the turn of the eighteenth and nineteenth centuries. In the first decades of the nineteenth century, it was expressed in many works of scholars, writers, politicians, journalists, artists and, composers, among whom I mention only Joachim Lelewel, Jan Paweł Woronicz, Izabela Czartoryska, Jean-Pierre Norblin, Adam Mickiewicz, and Frédéric Chopin. In the countries of East Central Europe, the process of healing the 'phantom pain' after the destruction of the country and a great part of its cultural inheritance lasted until recent times,[27] and it seems that it will be lasting yet.[28] It is literature, historiography, and education that construct the collective

[27] A good example is a poem *Report from a Besieged City* by a famous Polish poet Zbigniew Herbert (1924-1998), written after imposing martial law by the Communist authorities in Poland in December 1981:

> Too old to carry arms and to fight like others –
> they generously assigned to me the inferior role of a chronicler
> I record – not knowing for whom – the history of the siege
> […]
> and even if the City falls and one of us survives
> he will carry the City inside him on the roads of exile
> he will be the City

Z. Herbert, "Report from a Besieged City", trans. Cz. Miłosz, *The New York Review*, 18 August 1983 <https://www.nybooks.com/articles/1983/08/18/report-from-a-besieged-city/> (accessed: 13.06.2023).

[28] The topos of remembering lost texts or artifacts is still an important part of the self-preservation mechanisms of several European nations. It is highly probable that it will be used again in Ukrainian literature as a result of the Russian aggression in 2022. The Russian army is purposely destroying Ukrainian sites of memory (historical monuments, works of art, and libraries). See the interactive map of the cultural losses: https://uaculture.org/culture-loss/> (accessed: 22.07.2023).

memory of a nation, but we can also study this process when studying the fashioning of the sites of memory. These sites are often the new ones, remembering the Second World War and the Holocaust, national uprisings, or historical battles. Protheses or surrogates of the lost historical monuments also belong to this category of the new sites of memory.[29] Sometimes, though, the sites of memory are places which have gained such a status long ago that in the twentieth and twenty-first centuries their function as sites of memory has merely been refashioned.

Vilnius became a site of memory for the inhabitants the Grand Duchy of Lithuania and the entire Polish-Lithuanian Commonwealth no later than in the second decade of the sixteenth century. This can be understood in at least a twofold manner. Vilnius as a real city was a visible symbol of state power and authorities. The city revealed itself to those who saw it as the epitome of Lithuania, its past and presence, especially during state ceremonies such as coronations, royal entries, funerals, and canonisations.[30] It reminded one of the history of the country, its military glory, and its former rulers. Vilnians and visitors alike could see its castles, palaces, the town hall, city walls, cathedral, university, churches, synagogue, etc. The chapel of St. Casimir could remind them about the Jagiellonian dynasty, while the medieval keep on castle hill was associated with Duke Gediminas. In the cathedral, the banners of the defeated Teutonic Knights hung, while the Orthodox St. Trinity church was a votive offering of Prince Konstanty Ostrogski after the victory over the Muscovite army at Orsha in 1514. The inscriptions in public spaces, epitaphs, and the magnates' mausolea were also tangible signs of the past. The originals of the royal privileges, the relics of the Vilnius Catholic and Orthodox saints, and the picture of the icon of the Our Lady of the High Gate (*Matka Boska Ostrobramska*) also belong to this category.

Apart from all this, Vilnius was also a site of memory as an entirely textual representation. In this case, the image of the city was detached from the real experience. It was irrelevant whether these texts were physically present in the city or not, because the image of the city belonged to the realm of the imagina-

[29] There are many examples of such reconstructions in East Central Europe, e.g. the royal castle in Warsaw blown up by the German Nazis in October 1944; the Frauenkirche in Dresden destroyed by the Allied carpet bombing in February 1945; St. Michael's Golden-Domed cathedral (*Mikhailovsky Sobor*) in Kyiv blown up by the Soviet Government in 1936; and the Vilnius lower castle demolished by the Russian authorities in 1799-1803.

[30] See Chapter 10.

tion and was based on several types of rhetorical devices. Among the most representative examples of such texts are maps, views, and descriptions of the city, like two of its compatible depictions: the copperplate by Tomasz Makowski (Fig. 1) and the ode by Sarbiewski of the late 1620s:

> Hence from the midst of the hill all Vilna shall
> Our prospect be. Our eye shall lower fall
> On Vilia's cooler streams, that wind
> And with embraces Vilna bind.
> From thence, far off the temples we'll behold,
> And radiant scutcheons all adorned with gold.
> Then we'll look over that double tower
> The extent of great Palaemon's power.[31]

Most of the sources related to Vilnius that have been discussed in this book (and indeed maybe all of them), aided inconstructing the imagined city to some extent. Among such texts are the *Kyiv Psalter*, various court records, the Radziwiłł Map, testaments, Gediminas' letters, the epitaphs cited by Starowolski, Queen Barbara's letters, the poems by Bartoszewski, historical works by Wojciech Wijuk Kojałowicz, Skaryna's printed editions, the chronicle by Sister Katarzyna of Christ (Tyszkiewiczówna), Dambrowski's sermons, and Skarga's lives of saints. Together, these texts and others constitute an imagined Vilnius. All of them are preserved in libraries and archives far away from Lithuania. What is more, all of them are accessible via the Internet, which makes the textual Vilnius even more detached from the very spot of the city.[32] The imagined city exhibits the power of keeping memory in another way than the real one does. This power relies on sources that can be stored anywhere. Thus the city can exist as a site of memory everywhere in the world.[33]

[31] M.K. SARBIEWSKI, *The Odes of Casimire*, trans. G. HILS (London, 1646), p. 101. Original Latin text: M.K. SARBIEWSKI, "Ode IV 35 Ad Paulum Colovium", in: ID., *Liryki oraz Droga rzymska i fragmenty Lechiady*, pp. 420-423, lines 21-28.

[32] Digital sources might constitute a non-place rather than an imagined city. However, a non-place can turn into a site of memory in the process of interpretation, e.g. in literary works, films, or academic papers. About non-places and non-sites of memory, cf. M. AUGÉ, *Non-Places: Introduction to an Anthropology of Supermodernity*, trans. J. HOWE (London and New York, 1995); "Génocides: Lieux (et non-lieux) de mémoire", *Revue d'histoire de la Shoah* 2 (2004) <https://www.cairn.info/revue-revue-d-histoire-de-la-shoah1-2004-2.htm> (accessed: 9.04.2022).

[33] In Mediterranean tradition Troy and Jerusalem became the two archetypical imagined cities. In Jewish collective memory the matrix of Jerusalem was applied to Vilnius, which is often

The detachment of sources from the real spaces that gave rise to them gives the imagined city an important advantage. This city has every chance to survive as a site of memory, even if the real city were to be destroyed and its inhabitants killed or replaced. Vilnius suffered many catastrophes, such as the Russian bombardments, occupations, and deportations or mass-killings of its inhabitants in 1655 and 1939-1945. The destruction of the city and its depopulation resulted in the discontinuity of its collective memory. The history of Vilnius and of other places in the territories of the former Polish-Lithuanian Commonwealth is marked by many periods when their memory was muffled or even discontinued, usually as a result of the turmoils of war. Sometimes there were no survivors who could immediately reconstruct the lost memory:

> Who will honor the city without a name
> If so many are dead and others pan gold
> Or sell arms in faraway countries?
>
> What shepherd's horn swathed in the bark of birch
> Will sound in the Ponary Hills the memory of the absent –
> Vagabonds, Pathfinders, brethren of a dissolved lodge?[34]

Still, the texts about Vilnius that constitute the rhetorical body of the city and survived (that is, as stored memory), have had a potential to make history new once more. New generations of scholars, artists, and writers remember people, buildings, events, and destroyed texts and write their new *Subsidia reminiscentiae.*[35] The history of Vilnius, medieval, early modern, modern, and quite recent shows that two things have a surprisingly strong ability to reconstruct memory: the power of self-preservation and the power of writing. What unites them is the textual nature of the city.

called the Jerusalem of the North. See J. STEELE, "In the Jerusalem of the North, the Jewish story is forgotten", *The Guardian*, 20 June 2008, <https://www.theguardian.com/ commentisfree/2008/jun/20/secondworldwar> (accessed: 9.04.2022).

[34] Cz. MIŁOSZ, *City Without A Name* (1965), trans. R. HASS, Cz. MIŁOSZ, R. PINSKY, and R. GORCZYNSKI, lines 1-6, <https://www.poetryfoundation.org/poems/49752/city-without-a-name> (accessed: 9.04.2022). Polish original: *Miasto bez imienia* in: Cz. MIŁOSZ, *Wiersze wszystkie* (Cracow, 2011), pp. 554.

[35] An interesting example of a successful re-inventing and re-shaping of a part of contemporary Lithuanian collective memory is the cycle of best-selling historical novels by Kristina Sabaliauskaitė. The story is set in seventeenth century Vilnius. See K. SABALIAUSKAITĖ, *Silva Rerum: Romanas* [Silva Rerum: A Novel] (Vilnius, 2008).

Epilogue: The Lost Voices of the Inhabitants of Vilnius

The voices of the former inhabitants of Vilnius are irretrievably lost to us. We may read their written texts, but the truth is that the Vilnians of yesteryear do not speak in such records. They only left material traces in the form of writing, as physical as the Gate of Dawn (High Gate, Aušros vartai) or a Gothic key excavated in the foundations of the lower castle. These traces are mute until *we* interpret them, read them, and translate them into *our* contemporary language and *our* contemporary understanding. For this very reason the voice with which they speak to us seems to be only *our* voice. Nevertheless, if we view these texts from a diachronic perspective, they do not belong solely to our world. Written several centuries ago, they constituted part of the world long before we came into it. The Vilnius notary of the castle court (*pisarz grodzki*) Jan Kolenda once held a certain sheet of hand-made paper with text in the Cyrillic alphabet in his hands; he put his signature to it. This is why today, after almost four hundred years, we may try to trust this sheet and believe that it is a 'conveyor belt' between our here and now and the world of people who lived several centuries ago. Furthermore, we believe that not only the authentic seventeenth-century paper with rows of black characters, but also the meanings of the words and sentences recorded in these characters are types of transmitters. Everything in this book is based on this trust.

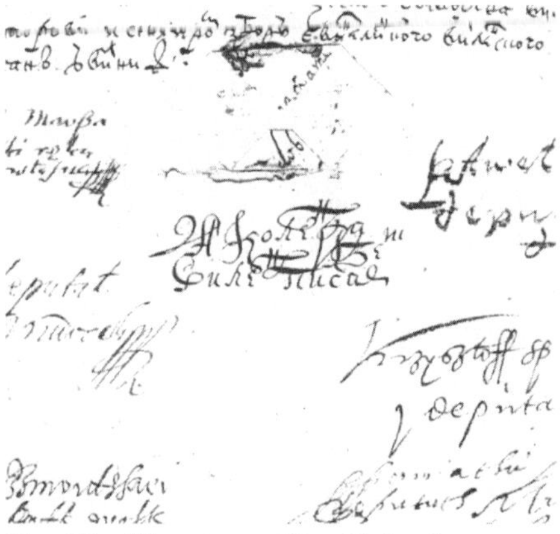

Fig. 76 Signature of Jan Kolenda, notary of Vilnius castle court, 11 July 1611. Vilnius, LNMB, MS F93-1734, p. 2. Photo J. Niedźwiedź.

The Muscovite Invasion

A Secretary of the Vilnius Chapter:

At this point, in August of the same year, a most memorable thing happened to Vilnius and all its surroundings. It was the sudden invasion of the army of the Muscovite Tsar Ivan Vasilyevich, which for three days plundered and slaughtered up to 24,000 men, people who had not escaped, mostly common people, in burnt-down houses, empty churches, and mostly on the main square in front of the town hall, not without inflicting on dissenters who had been spared such atrocities.[1]

***

A Royal Doctor:

On the eighth day of August, both hetmans were positioned on the other side of the Stone Bridge with no chance of following the regiment of his grace the field hetman, which was withdrawing to Paneriai. They gave the order to shoot

[1] *Protokół spraw potocznych przy sądu wielebnej kapituły wileńskiej*, MS MAB, sign. F43-590, f. 80v.

from the bridge at the Muscovites who were murdering our people. Thus they defended the crossing. There was a fusillade of muskets and cannon balls from both sides of the river. Muscovy entered the bridge with five regiments, but the infantry and dragoons of the Prince Great Hetman chased them away from the bridge, took three banners, and defended the area behind the crossing until night fell, while the weaker army and the common people escaped through the woods towards Musninkai. In the night, the hetmans, having left part of the regiments in reserve, ran towards Kumielia. Having conquered the city, the Muscovites burnt the suburbs. [...] As dusk set in, Mr Trop, the Vilnius artillery lieutenant who was staying at my home, took me outside and showed me Vilnius burning. So I went out and, although my estate in Sudervė lies one and a half miles from Vilnius, the flames were blinding. Certainly, Troy did not burn as fiercely.[2]

***

A Bernardine Nun:

This incursion took place during the priorate of the venerable Miss Konstancyja Sokolińska who, seeing their considerable fear, sent some nuns to their relatives, while others remained in the nunnery of their own free will [...]. The venerable sister superior left with eleven other nuns. Of those sisters that stayed in the nunnery, some escaped during the incursion and, having died in exile, lie in Strubnitsa in the Vawkavysk district, while several were tortured by Muscovites (one old Bernardine father saw angels in the clouds above them).[3]

***

A City Dweller:

[...] when in 1655 God's wrath allowed the Muscovite foe with its large and mighty army to invade Vilnius, the capital city of the Grand Duchy of Lithuania, she [Anastazja Pękalska] having left everything, had to escape on foot to save her own life and health as well as her children's in this unfortunate situa-

[2] VORBEK-LETTOW, *Skarbnica pamięci*, pp. 241-242.
[3] *Kronika bernardynek świętomichalskich w Wilnie*, p. 362.

tion. Among various items in the form of products, clothes and house equipment, there were also documents in fascicules, which included the original of the agreement confirming the purchase of the house in St. John's Street, where she lives now.[4]

***

A Merchant:

When escaping the close danger *a foedifrago hoste* [from a traitorous enemy] on the second of August this year, he [Samuel Charytonowicz], having packed his possessions and goods in a large barrel and a chest, put them on a ship called a barge [*wicina*] that belonged to Józef Tukolski, father superior of the Greek (i.e. Orthodox – J.N.) monastery of the Holy Spirit, so they would be shipped as far as Königsberg. Among these things were all of the more valuable Nuremberg trade goods from his stalls located in various Vilnius houses and in the larger and smaller bazaars, such as diverse garments, silverware, brassware, and house equipment, together with pledged goods from various debtors [...]. All these things, as well as documents, placed on this ship of the venerable *ihumen* Tukolski, were seized and looted by the enemy on the banks of the Neris river near Gegužinė on the fifteenth of that month and year. Therefore, since the original documents cannot be issued from the archives of the most respectable capital city Vilnius, now abandoned, the deposition is made at the municipal court of Königsberg.[5]

***

A Carmelite Nun:

The day of our departure was – oh dear God – one of indescribable torment and anguish. We could not have overtaken other people, as there were many carriages not only on the road but also driving through the field. All tried to run in a hurry, while we often stopped on our way, to the great concern of our venerable father abbot and which increased our fear for the following reasons: carriages often broke and not all horses were trained for an equipage: they did not

[4] *Wyjątki z księgi akt sądu wójtowskiego Wilna od 1586*, MS JL 2926, pp. 91-92.
[5] *Ibid.*, pp. 49-50.

go where they should and where the driver drove them, but in random directions. And they often stopped, which seriously worried and distressed our fathers, because we ran in a hurry, but we had to stop for these reasons many a time. [...] On our way, we received different alarming messages, but not until the tenth of August, on St. Laurentius' day, when we arrived at Hrodna, did we hear anything certain about Vilnius. Only there did we learn that the wretched Muscovites had taken Vilnius on the eighth of August. So when we arrived at Hrodna – my dear God – it was such a dismal day, such torment and anguish, screaming and mourning! There were such a large number of people escaping that only miraculously did they not drown because of the pressure to cross the river and they were crossing it throughout the night, with clamour and cries, and we heard it all because we were spending the night in a nearby stable, among the steers, as there was no other inn available due to the number of people.[6]

***

A Jewish Scholar:

On Wednesday, the fifteenth of Tammuz, 5415, almost the whole Jewish community ran for their lives like one man: those who had horses and carts went forth with their wives, sons, and daughters and some of their belongings, and others went on foot, carrying their children on their shoulders.

I went forth with my stick in my right hand, after seizing my bag of phylacteries, and with my left hand I grasped a book on the calendar, murmuring unto myself; "Who knows where I shall find rest in my exile?" I left my house full of good things and abandoned my inheritance, a treasury of all that was desirable, a house full of books, both those which I had inherited from my father of blessed memory and those which the Lord enabled me to buy. Among them were a few books and tractates which I had worked on and annotated, especially the tractates Zebahim and Menahot. Long and wearisomely had I laboured and much time had I spent until I had annotated the two tractates properly; they were all left there. And we went whithersoever we could go, and the earth was rent with the cries and wailing of the fugitives, and from my eyes too poured tears in torrents. We came to the border of the land of Samogitia close to the frontier of Prussia, but there too we found no rest from the sword of war.

[6] *Krótka kronika fundacyi karmelitanek bosych klasztoru św. Józefa w Wilnie*, pp. 76-78.

The hosts of the kingdom of Sweden stripped us to the skin, and after this oppression I and some of the children of my house and also other people entered a ship in the heart of the sea and set our faces towards Amsterdam.[7]

***

A Bernardine Nun:

In turn, the venerable sister superior and her group left Vilnius quickly and headed for Samogitia. But since there was a major threat from the Swedes and other foes, she ran from there to Masovia, where she stayed for three quarters of the year in Wizna. Frome there she went with two companions to Vilnius, because a charter of the Tsar charter allowed everyone to travel. She arrived just after Easter and saw terrible devastation all over the city, heads of dead people were being tossed about on the streets as well as in churches, our church and nunnery were completely ruined. In the church it was pitch black like in a bakery. Crypts were open, the earth had been dug up, the corpses of our founders had been thrown out of their coffins and left in the open. Our venerable sister superior had them properly gathered and buried.[8]

***

Another Merchant:

In 1656, during negotiations between the king, our gracious lord, and the Muscovite tsar, a complainant arrived in Vilnius and found his house utterly desolate and burnt. In his efforts to prevent further ruin to the building and the damage from worsening, he renovated it at his own cost for 388 *złoty* 13 *grosz* and 4 denars. However, for three years, not only could he not have any income from it, but it could not even provide him with a peaceful place of living, as upon the arrival of the Muscovite army in the city the Muscovite soldiers occupied all apartments and drove out their owners. Furthermore, the complainant had not one hour of respite from all kinds of burdens: he paid regular contributions for the construction of fortifications, he sent servants to the city and the castle, provided horses for transport purposes, and served in the guards. And

[7] M. Ben Naphtali Hirsch Rivkes, *Be'er ha-Golah*, pp. 41-43.

[8] *Kronika bernardynek świętomichalskich w Wilnie*, p. 362.

when the Muscovite *voivode* Mishetsky ordered that all the suburbs be burnt down after Mr Lisiecki, the lieutenant of the king withdrew [Lithuanian troops] from Vilnius, the complainant had to escape again, leaving all his possessions to their fate. And when he came here again after the arrival of the king's army with their commander [*regimentarz* Michał Pac], having expected to recuperate quickly, he covered the same house – which had burnt down again – with a roof built on provisional trusses for 34 *złoty* 15 *grosz*. But since the siege of the castle lasted longer than anticipated, the complainant had to reconstruct it again in 1661 for 304 *złoty* 7 *grosz*.[9]

***

A Secretary of the Vilnius Chapter:

And although in the second year the Lithuanian army that had gathered took back the ruins of Vilnius again, the enemy raised the water in the canals from the river Vilnia and thus kept close to the lower castle and the cathedral, as well as in the upper castle, completely destroying the houses of the cathedral chapter in Castle (Pilies) street and all nearby buildings with cannon fire. Not until the end of 1662, partly due to famine and disease, and partly due to constant attacks, bombs exploding from three points, namely St. George's church, Bleak Hill in the Užupis, and the square before the Bernardines' church, but mostly mine attacks under the Castle Hill, did they force the remaining few besieged Ruthenian soldiers and their commander and the tsar's master of the pantry (*stolnik*) Vasilii Mishetsky, called the little *voivode*, to rely on the Lithuanians' mercy. Mishetsky was tried for the terrible atrocities he had committed in Vilnius and, having been severely tortured, he was beheaded on 16 December 1662. Eighty-three defenders were killed during the attack on Castle Hill.[10]

9 *Wyjątki z księgi akt sądu wójtowskiego Wilna*, pp. 96-97.
10 *Protokół spraw potocznych…*, pp. 80v-81r.

Bibliography

Manuscript Sources

AGAD

MS AGAD 1 /7 /0 /1 /23 Archiwum Skarbu Koronnego (The Archive of the Royal Treasury), *Regestrum illustrissimi domini Alexandri magni Litvanie principis per manus magistri Erasmi sue celsitudinis secretarii transierunt*, 1494-1500, <https://www.szukajwarchiwach.gov.pl/jednostka/-/jednostka/17711133> (access: 1.03.2022).

MS AGAD 91 Metryka Koronna <http://agadd2.home.net.pl/metrykalia/MK/0091/> (access: 23.02.2022).

MS AGAD 96 Metryka Koronna <http://agadd2.home.net.pl/metrykalia/MK/0096/> (access: 23.02.2022).

APPD

MS APPD ref. Wd. 1, *Libri Conventus Vilnensis* (1604).

ARSI

MS ARSI Lit. 38F (*Historia seu succincta narratio de origine ac fundatione Collegii Vilnensis Societatis Iesu ab anno 1569 usque ad annum 1611 in Julio*).

MS ARSI Lit. 38f, *Historia seu succincta narratio de origine ac fundatione Collegii Vilnensis Societatis Jesu ab Anno 1569 usque ad annum 1611 in Julio.*

MS ARSI Pol. 75 f. 316.

AS

MS AS 1080, fasc. 1, 48/11, češky cestopis

BJ

MS BJ 177
MS BJ 185, *Anno Domini 1583 Iussu R. P. Provincialis Suffragia scripta Vilnae 1 Februarii.*
MS BJ 2047
MS BJ 2047.
MS BJ 2626
MS BJ 2926
MS BJ 2926
MS BJ 2926.
MS BJ B Slav F 12 and B Slav F 15*Rewizyja gospód dworu jego królewskiego mości w mieście Wilnie pod bytność króla jego mości w roku 1636 i w roku 1639.*

BK

MS BK 2673
MS BK 62, Krzemycki E., *Descriptio Poloniae*, written in Tuchów in 1723.

BN

MS BN 1291.
MS BN in Warsaw 11907 III
MS BN in Warsaw 11924 III

BRAN

MS BRAN, 24.4.28.

CR

MS CR R 380.
MS CR U 271.
MS CR, Carmina Latina et Graeca gratulat. IV. Script. lat. rec., No. 2 (CR 59: 42).*Gratulationes in promotione doctissimi et eruditissimi R. D. Martini Smiglecii Societatis Iesu artium et philosophiae magistri a studiosis Philosophiae amoris ergo et officii in amantissimum Praeceptorem conscriptae*, [Vilnae, 1594].

CZART.

MS CZART. 1063, the ennoblement act of Andrzej Czarnecki (Smolensk, 25 June 1611).
MS CZART. 1320 IV, *Na wjazd jego mości pana Chodkiewicza wojewody wileńskiego witanie*, ff. 44v-45v.
MS CZART. 1320 IV.
MS CZART. 1577 IV, *Triumphus et ingressus regis Vilnam die 24 Iulii 1611 anno*, pp. 478-486.
MS CZART. 1659 IV.
MS CZART. 1662 IV, *Catalogus episcoporum Vilnensium*; *Unde sit origo Lituanorum?*, ff. 413r-414r; 450r-457r.
MS CZART. 1662 IV, *Sententie, które są pisane w Werkach nad Wilnem we dworze biskupim w pokojach, w stołowej izbie i w sieniach* [Sentences written down at Werki near Vilnius, at the episcopal court, in chambers, in the table room and in the hallways], pp. 420-424.
MS CZART. 1814, *Strzelba i municyja własnym nakładem jego królewskiej mości sprawiona MDLXV w Wilnie i na zamki pograniczne rozesłana.*
MS CZART. 2211 IV, *Rod wielkich kniaziej ruskich otkol rodiszasja* oraz *Rod litowskich kniaziej.*
MS CZART. 3681 I, *Explicationes in Librum Tertium de Anima inceptae ad scribendum per me fratrem Andream Vilnensem sub reverendo patre Anibalo Roselo de Calabria lectore generali Crac <oviensi> anno Domini 1583 XI Julii Hor. Oct.*; *Metamorphoseos conceptum super universis sensibus divinae scripturae, quorum primi sunt: historia sive litera; tropologia et mysticus sive spiritualis. Hic vero duplex allegoricus nimirum et anagogicus datur. Ex quibus tanquam fontibus hace transformatio haurietur. Vilnae diei prima Ianuarii anno salutis 1588.*
MS CZART. 3705 I, *Konstytucje panien zakonnych klasztoru wileńskiego przy świętym Michale.*

IMBRAM.

MS IMBRAM. without shelf-mark, David J., *Raj oblubienica i oblubienice, w którym żniwo miry i kwiatków z tajemnic męki Chrystusowej jest zebrane, łacińskim stylem przez wielebnego księdza Jana Dawida S.J. w roku Pańskim 16*[0]*7, a zaś w roku Pańskim 1671 na polski język przetłumaczone* (MS in
MS IMBRAM. without shelf-mark, *Poczet imion w Panu Bogu odpoczywających braci i sióstr po wszytkich klasztorach premonstratu polskiego zmarłych pod szczęśliwą władzą najprzewielebniejszej w Chrystusie panny jej mości panny Zofii z Przyłęka Grotówny, zakonu przeświętnego Norberta św. konwentu przewielebnych panien imbromowskich zasłużonej ksieni przez wielebne księdza Hermana Zawarskiego, tegoż zakonu profesa Chebdowskiego* (sic!) *a na ten czas wikaryjego zwierzynieckiego z pilnością należytą sporządzany i dla wspólnego tych dusz poratowania konwentowi imbramowskiemu aplikowany 1718.*

LNMB

MS LNMB F101-41. <http://pergamentai.mch.mii.lt/IstoriniaiLietDok/istoriniailietdok_5lt.pl.htm> (access: 15.02.2022).

MS LNMB F93-791.

MS LNMB F93-1688, *Kopia listu króla Stefana do nieboszczyka pana wojewody smoleńskiego strony palenia ksiąg w Wilnie ewangelickich 1581 in septembre.*

MS LNMB F93-1688, *Kopia listu króla Stefana do nieboszczyka pana wojewody smoleńskiego strony palenia ksiąg w Wilnie ewangelickich 1581 in Septembre.*

MS LNMB F93-1688, *Kopia listu króla Stefana do nieboszczyka.*

MS LNMB F93-1688.

MS LNMB F93-1689.

MS LNMB F93-1690.

MS LNMB F93-1691.

MS LNMB F93-1699

MS LNMB F93-16*Porządki kościelne*, 1648.

MS LNMB F93-1701, *Kopia relacji miesckiej o wyznaniu niektórych burzycielów zboru wileńskiego 1639 d. 9 Octobra.*

MS LNMB F93-1707.

MS LNMB F93-1715, *List upominalny Władysława IV, króla polskiego do ks. Woyny, biskupa wileńskiego o prześladowanie ewangelików w Wilnie. Niecały, na pół przedarty* z grudnia 1646, excerpt from the books of the Vilnius voivodeship from 7 February 1647.

MS LNMB F93-1716.

MS LNMB F93-1729, *Z listu pana Siesickiego, podwojewodzego mego wileńskiego de data z Wilna 3 Julii 1611.*

MS LNMB F93-1729, *Z listu pana Siesickiego, podwojewodziego mego wileńskiego de data z Wilna 3 Julii 1611.*

MS LNMB F93-1730.

LVIA

MS LVIA F1135, ap. 2, No. 24.

MS LVIA F1135, ap. 2, No. 30.

MS LVIA F1135, ap. 4, No. 471, pp. 36-40 *Index Librorum in Bibliotheca Ecclesiae Cathedralis Vilnensis*,1598

MS LVIA F1135, ap. 4, No. 472.

MS LVIA F20, ap. 1, No. 4563, *Księgi sądowe jurysdykcyjej horodnictwa wileńskiego roku 1619 od dnia 2 marca roku mienionego.*

MS LVIA F22, ap. 1, no 5333.

MS LVIA F22, ap. 1, no 5334.

MS LVIA F23, ap. 1, No. 5096.

MS LVIA F23, ap. 1, No. 5099.

MS LVIA F694, ap. 1, No. 3322. documents from the St. John's Church,

MS LVIA F694, ap. 1, No. 3338

MS LVIA SA 5337, *Testament Jakuba II Dessausa, mieszczanina wileńskiego z 13 listopada 1675 roku* [The last will of Jakub II Dessaus, burgher of Vilnius, 13 November 1675], ff. 107-108.

MAB

MS MAB F264-1381, [*Rhetorica*].

MS MAB F40-1136, *Akta synodów litewskich prowincjonalnych 1638-1675.*

MS MAB F40-1157, *Akta synodów litewskich prowincjonalnych 1611-1637.*

MS MAB F40-12, *Rewizje archiwum prowincjalnego* 1669-1753.

MS MAB F40-148 (*Album profesorów i studentów gimnazjum słuckiego, 1640-1782*), ff. 39r-54r.

MS MAB F40-148, *Specimen profectuum I classis me Johanne Cień rectore a die 11 Augusti ad diem 14 Novembris factorum exhibitum examine publico, quod anno 1693 post festum S. Martini debus 17, 18, et 19 Novembris habebatur in illustri Gymnasio Radziwilliano Słucensi*, ff. 67r-68r.

MS MAB F40-546.

MS MAB F40-833, *Unia ichmościów panów senatorów stanu rycerskiego greckiego i ewangelickiego nabożeństwa Obojga Narodów Korony Polskiej i Wielkiego Księstwa Litewskiego przy prawie i wolnościach in casu religionis oponujących się w Wilnie zawarta anno 1599*, ff. 2r-3v.

MS MAB F41-612, *Quincunx rhetoricus in libros quattuor ad Caium Herennium, Marci Tulii Ciceronis, Aristotelis, Quintiliani et aliorum doctrinis illustrantes.*

MS MAB F43-19347 (VKF1422).

MS MAB F43-19455, *Ordinatio Magistri Ceremoniarum Ecclesiae Cathedralis Vilnensis* (1651).

MS MAB F43-19840, *Przychód pieniędzy na budynek szkoły katedralnej w zamku wileńskim, 7 marca 1632.*

MS MAB F43-210/01, *Akta kapituły wileńskiej 1502-1533*) [*Registers of the Vilnius chapter*].

MS MAB F43-21018 (VKF1637): *Liber magistralis in quo fundationes, confirmationes, summae tam capitales, quam censuales, lapideae, domus, fundi, iurisdictio, incolae necnon inventaria munimentorum totiusque suppellectilis ecclesiae et conventus S. Georgii Vilnae cura et diligentia reverendi ac venerabili patris Francisci Gorzynski interea v. Prioris per r.p. Anselmum Smieszkowic sanctae theologiae baccalaureati, concionatori ordinis conscripta, ordinata et confecta anno Domini 1677.*

MS MAB F43-211 (VKF445), *Akta kapituły wileńskiej 1550-1560* [*Registers of the Vilnius chapter*].

MS MAB F43-212 (VKF446) *Akta kapituły wileńskiej 1561-1570* [*Registers of the Vilnius chapter*].

MS MAB F43-212 (VKF446): A.D. *1603 Libri reverndi domini Ambrosii Beynarti canonici Vilnensis et Samotitiensis post mortem eiusdem Bibliothecae Ecclesiae Cathedralis Vilnensis donati, in Regestr apparatów i inszego sprzętu*, ff. 86r-87r.

MS MAB F43-212 (VKF446: *Akta kapituły wileńskiej 1561-1570*) *Propositio magistri scholae occasione deffectum eiusdem scholae*, ff. 101v-102.

MS MAB F43-212 (VKF446: *Akta kapituły wileńskiej 1561-1570*): *Tractatus et conclusio occasione librorum post mortem olim reverendi domini Georgii Albini iuris utriusque doctoris Dei gratia episcopi Metonensis suffraganei et cantoris Vilnensis intestati decessi*, , ff. 251v-252r.

MS MAB F43-215 (VKF449), *Akta kapituły wileńskiej 1585-1601* [*Registers of the Vilnius chapter*].

MS MAB F43-218 (VKF452), *Akta kapituły wileńskiej 1632-1643* [*Registers of the Vilnius chapter*], "*De scamnis pro schola cathedrali. Pro sua liberalitate asseres seu tabulas siccas promiserunt, specifice vero R. Dominus Decanus unum asserem, R. D. Nieborski duos, R. D. Szulc unum, R. D. Sczyt unum. Reliqua R. D. Cantor obtulit se propositurum*", ff. 18v-19.

MS MAB F43-218 (VKF452; *Akta kapituły wileńskiej 1632-1643*), *Pro bacalaureo scholae Cathedralis*, ff. 142r-142v.

MS MAB F43-26613.

MS MAB F43-26648.

MS MAB F43-26666, *Testament Zuzanny Chreptowiczówny Połubińskiej z 1639*.

MS MAB F43-26717, *The testament of archdeacon of Vilnius Grzegorz Święcicki from 1617*.

MS MAB F43-26739.

MS MAB F43-426 (VKF5938), *Potestas episcopo Vilnensi circa fidem in haereticos*.

MS MAB F43-443/8.

MS MAB F43-451, *Regestr kapituły roku 1577 i roku 1578* [The register of the chapter, 1577 and 1578], f. 21v.

MS MAB F43-452, *Regestr kapituły za rok 1579 i za rok 1580* [The register of the Vilnius chapter].

MS MAB F43-492, *Inwentarz wszytkich pozostałych rzeczy nieboszczyka księdza Ambrożego Beinarta kanonika wileńskiego*, ff. 2r-2v.

MS MAB F43-590, *Protokół spraw potocznych przy sądu wielebnej kapituły wileńskiej za urzędu jego mości księdza Wawrzyńca Mocarskiego kanonika wileńskiego, prokuratora kapitulnego roku 1648 miesiąca Octobra sprawiony*, 1648-1662, ff. 48v-49r.

MS MAB F43-590, *Protokół spraw potocznych przy sądu wielebnej kapituły wileńskiej za urzędu jego mości księdza Wawrzyńca Mocarskiego kanonika wileńskiego, prokuratora kapitulnego roku 1648 miesiąca Octobra sprawiony*, f. 36r.

MS MAB K 71, *Altare S. Crucis in Ecclesia Cathedrali Vilnensi in medio templi situm, fundationis et erectionis S. Reverendissimi in Christo patris d. Domini Valeriani Dei gratia Episcopi Vilnensis*, f. 11r.

MNW

MS MNW 1793, the ennoblement act of Jan Januszowski (Cracow, 24 January 1588).

NGAB

MS NGAB Ф 694 оп. 1 ед. 1, Dowgird S., *Genealogia albo krótkie opisanie wielkich książąt litewskich*; A. Wargocki, *Dom oświeconych książąt na Bierżach i Dubinkach opisany anno Domini 1621* [The House of the Most Illustrious Princes [Radziwiłł] of Biržai and Dubingai], ff. 1r-14v.
MS NGAB Ф 694 оп. 1 ед. 450.
MS NGAB Ф 694 оп. 1 ед. 450, f. 60r.
MS NGAB Ф 694 оп. 1 ед. 450.

RGADA

MS RGADA, Lithuanian *Metrica*, F 389, b. 106, Central Archives of Historical Records in Moscow.

SLUB

MS SLUB G 258, *Dies triumphi in faustissmum reditum serenissimi ac invictissimi domini, domini Sigismundi Tertii Poloniae et Sveciae regis de Smolensko ab ipsius maiestate expunato Vilnae XXIV Iulii celebrata anno Domini 1611.*

VUB

MS VUB F3-1067, *Regni rhetorici leges.*
MS VUB F3-1067, *Tyrocinium eloquentiae.*
MS VUB F3-1375, *De legibus Tullianae Reipublicae Heliconium consilium concernentibus.*
MS VUB F3-1395, [*Rhetorica*].
MS VUB F3-1427, [*Rhetorica*].
MS VUB F3-2037, M.K. Sarbiewski, *In primam partem Summae Theologicae divi Tomae Aquinatis doctoris Angelici Commentarius in certos de Deo uno, et trino tractatus distributes* and *Commentarius in reliquam primam D. Thomae Aquinatis Summae Theologicae a questione L. Partem de angelis.*
MS VUB F3-2171, *Prologomena logica* (1580s?).
MS VUB F3-2199, [*Rhetorica*].
MS VUB F4- 35808 (A2472), *Regestr apparatów i inszego sprzętu, złota i srebra w kościelie św. Stanisława katedralnym na zamku wileńskim spisany i rewidowany*, 1596-1626.

MS VUB F4-11440 (A-157), *Regestr spisania towarów jej mości paniej wileńskiej pokupionych* (*Register of things bought by Mrs Voivode of Vilnius*)
MS VUB F4-18345.
MS VUB F4-2624, *Kronika Kościoła Parafialnego w Goldingen, położonego w Diecezyi Wileńskiej, Gubernii Kurlandskiej, Powiecie Goldyngskim, Dekanacie Kurlandzkim 1849.*
MS VUB F4-35808 (A2472), *Index Librorum in Bibliotheca Ecclesiae Cathedralis Vilnensis*, pp. 78-80.
MS VUB F4-35808 (A2472), *Spisanie srebra w Kaplicy Królewskiej przy grobie św. Kazimierza od różnych osób ex voto zawieszonych od roku Pańskiego 1603 [from 1627]*, pp. 94-118.
MS VUB F4-35808 (A2472).

Printed Sources

Abrogatio abusuum in iudicio scabinali (Cracow, 1547).
Agenda parva in commodiorem usum sacerdotum Provinciae Poloniae conscripta (Vilnius, 1616).
Agenda parva in commodiorem usum sacerdotum Provinciae Poloniae conscripta (Vilnius, 1630).
Agenda seu ritus caeremoniarum ecclesiasticarum ad uniformem ecclesiasticarum per universas provincias Regni Poloniae usum, officio Romano conformati, ex decreto Synodi Provincialis Petricoviensis, denuo conscripti et editi, ed. H. POWODOWSKI (Cracow, 1591).
Agenda sive Exsequiale divinorum sacramentorum per (...) *Martinum canonicum Vilnensis dioecesis edita* (Gdańsk, 1499).
Akta Aleksandra króla polskiego, wielkiego księcia litewskiego itd. (1501-1506), ed. F. PAPÉE (Cracow, 1927).
Akta synodów prowincjonalnych Jednoty Litewskiej 1611-1625, ed. B. GRUŻEWSKI and H. MERCZYNG (Vilnius, 1915).
Akta synodów prowincjonalnych jednoty litewskiej 1626-1637, ed. M. LIEDKE and P. GUDZOWSKI (Warsaw, 2011).
Akta zjazdów stanów Wielkiego Księstwa Litewskiego, 2: *Okresy panowań królów elekcyjnych XVI-XVII wiek* [The Acts of the gatherings of the States of the Grand Duchy of Lithuania, 2: The Periods of the Elective Kings: The Sixteenth and Seventeenth Centuries], ed. H. LULEWICZ (Warsaw, 2009).
Akty cechów wileńskich 1495-1759, ed. H. ŁOWMIAŃSKI, M. ŁOWMIAŃSKA, and S. KOŚCIAŁKOWSKI (Poznań, 2006).
Andrzejowicz, W., *Ogród różany abo opisanie porządne dwu szczepów wonnej różej hierychuntskiej, to jest o dwu świętych różańcach dwojga bractw Błogosławionej Panny Maryjej i Naświętszego Imienia Pana Jezusowego w Zakonie Kaznodziej-*

skim szczepionych k woli braciej i promotorom obojga bractw świętych przez wielebnego ojca brata Waleryjana Lithuanidesa, prezydenta bractw pomienionych tegoż zakonu (Cracow, 1627).

Ankstyvieji šv. Kazimiero "Gyvenimai" [The Early Lives of St. Casimir], ed. M. ČIURINSKAS (Vilnius, 2004).

Annibale a Capua, *Listy Annibala z Kapui nuncyjusza w Polsce o bezkrólewiu po Stefanie Batorym i pierwszych latach panowania Zygmunta III do wyjścia arcyksięcia Maksymiliana z niewoli*, trans., ed. and commentary M. CYTOWSKA (Warsaw, 1952).

Antigraph albo odpowiedź na skrypt uszczypliwy, przeciwko ludziom starożytnej religijej greckiej od apostatów Cerkwie wschodniej wydany, któremu tytuł: "Heresiae. ignoranciae i politika popów i mieszczan Bractwa Wileńskiego", tak też i na książkę rychło potym ku objaśnieniu tegoż skryptu wydaną nazwiskiem "Harmoniją". Przez jednego brata Bractwa Cerkiewnego Wileńskiego religijej greckiej w porywczą dana (Vilnius, 1608).

Apologeticus to jest obrona Konfederacyjej: Przy tym seditio albo bunt kapłański na ewanieliki w Wilnie z wolej a łaski miłego Boga przed harapem wynurzony, ed. E. BURSCHE (Cracow, 1932).

Aristotle, *Commentaria in libros Physicorum Aristotelis in gymnasio Coloniensi quod Bursam Laurentii vocant novissime edita* [per Joannem de Nurtingen]. *Divi Alberti Magni sententias et interpretationes in eodem una cum questionibus disputabilibus ac dubijs textualibus* (Cologne, 1506).

Aristotle, *On Rhetoric: A Theory of Civid Discourse*, ed. and trans. G.A. KENNEDY (New York and Oxford, 2007).

Artykuły zastanowienia pokoju pospolitego po zejściu króla Stefana (Vilnius, 1586).

Assertiones theologicae et philosophicae, in Collegio Vilnensi Societatis Iesu, sub renovationem autumnalem deiendendae anno Domini 1574 (Cracow, 1574).

Augustinus, Aurelius, *Opera*, 1 (Leiden, 1586).

Bartoszewski, W., *Dowody procesyjej nabożnej i poważnego tryumfu w dzień roczny przenaświętszego Ciała Bożego jaśnie wielmożnemu panu jego mości panu panu Chrisztofowi Słuszcze wojewodzie wendeńskiemu na ten czas marszałkowi trybunalskiemu wileńskiemu ofiarowane* (Vilnius, 1615).

Bartoszewski, W., *Parthenomelica albo Pienia nabożne o Pannie Naświętszej, które poważny Senat miasta wileńskiego spólnym a porządnym obywatelów swoich i innej młodzi nabożeństwem i kosztownym apparatem, czasu pożądanego adwentu Pańskiego, na roraciech przystojnie co rok odprawuje. Niektóre poprawione, niektóre z łacińskiego na polskie przełożone, niektóre nowo teraz złożone. Na cześć i chwałę wcielenia Pańskiego i na wielbienie Bogarodzicy* (Vilnius, 1613).

Bartoszewski, W., *Pobudka na obchodzenie świątości rocznej tryumfu i pompy Ciała Bożego dana a jaśnie oświeconemu i najwielebniejszemu w Panu Chryście ojcowi i panu, panu Benedyktowi Woynie z łaski bożej biskupowi wileńskiemu ofiarowana* (Vilnius, 1614).

Bartoszewski, W., *Utwory poetyckie*, ed. M. KARDASZ (Warsaw, 2019).

Bellarmin, R., *Dichiarazione più copiosa della dottrina cristiana* (Roma?, 1598).

Biblia sacra vulgatae editionis Sixti Quinti pontificis maximi iussu recognita atque edita (Antwerp, 1618).

Biblia to jest księgi Starego i Nowego przymierza znowu z języka hebrayskiego, greckiego i łacińskiego na polski przełożone, trans. Sz. Budny (Zaslawye, 1572).

Bielski, M., *Kronika, to jest historyja świata*, ed. D. Śnieżko, D. Kozaryn, and E. Karczewska, 3 (Szczecin 2019).

Bielski, M., and J. Bielski, *Kronika polska* (Cracow, 1597).

Bildziukiewicz, H., *Divi Tutelaris Patrii Casimiri insigne virtutum hieroglyphicis emblematum figuris adumbratum: Poloniarum Riginae Constantiae ... deusta observantia humiliter oblata* (Vilnius, 1610).

Boierus, L. (W. Bojer), *Carolomachia* (Vilnius 1606).

Borasta, G.B. (Borastius G.L.), *Panegyricus Sigismundo III, Poloniae et Sveciaer regi etc. etc invictissimo* (Vilnius, 1611).

Baroffi, C., *In triumpho serenissimi ac potentissimi principis Sigismundi III Poloniae et Sveciae Regis etc. etc. e Moscovia post insinges gloriosae partas victorias feliciter redenuntis oratio* (Vilnius, 1611).

Breviarium secundum sum insignis Ecclesie Cracoviensis (Lyon?, 1507).

Broniewski, M., *АПОКРІΣΙΣ abo odpowiedź na książki o synodzie brzeskim imieiem ludzi starożytnej religijej greckiej* (Raków, 1597).

Catechismus catholicorum: Iscige pammaciscchen no thems Paprekscher Gawe gabblems Christites macibes: Prexkan thems nemacigems und iounems bernems: Cour Kungam Petrum Canisium thaes Schwetes rakstes Doctor, Ehsprestcz Vilne Pille, Littourre Semmen pi Danielem Lansicinensem expan tho gaddi 1585 (Vilnius, 1585).

Caussinus, N., *De eloquentia sacra et humana libri XVI* (Paris, 1643).

Chądzyński, J., *Relacyja a oraz suplika zboru wileńskiego saskiego do hern Martyna Lutra za predykantem Burchardym ministrem swoim, który roku 1623, dnia 14 Octobra, w sobotę, dla traktamentu gości, miłych swoich protestantów, po kury łażąc, z drabiny spadł i szyję szczęśliwie złamać raczył, od wiernych owieczek na piersiach onemu w trunnie położona* (Vilnius, 1624).

Chartularium Lithuaniae res gestas magni ducis Gedemine illustrans. Gedimino laiškai [Letters of Gediminas], ed., trans., and commented by S.C. Rowell (Vilnius, 2003).

Chrestomatia staropolska: Teksty do roku 1543, ed. W. Wydra and W.R. Rzepka (Wrocław, 1984).

Cicero, M.T., *O powinnościach wszech stanów ludzi ... księgi troje*, trans. S. Koszutski (Łosk, 1583).

Cicero M.T., *The Letters to His Friends*, trans. W. Glynn Williams, 1 (London and Cambridge, Mass., 1928).

Cnoglerus, Q., "Pompa Casimiriana sive de labaro d. Casimiri, Casimiri Regis Poloniae et F. Iagellonis N.M.D. Lithuaniae principis etc. a Leone X pontifice maximo in divos relati, ex urbe transmisso et Vilnam Lithuaniae metropolim solenni pompa ad

6 Idus Maii anno MDCIV illato Quirini Cnogleri Austrii sermo panegyricus", in: G. Święcicki, *Theatrum s. Casimiri, in quo ipsius prosapia, vita, miracula et illustris pompa in solemni eiusdem apotheoseos instauratione, Vilnae Lithuaniae metropoli, VI Idus Maii anno Domini MDCIV instituta graphice proponuntur* (Vilnius, 1604).

Codex epistolaris Vitoldi magni ducis Lithuaniae 1376-1430, ed. A. PROCHASKA (Cracow, 1882).

Cracovia impressorum XV et XVI saeculorum, ed. J. PTAŚNIK (Lviv, 1922).

Dambrowski, S., *Raj duszny męski i białogłowski z psalmów i modlitw z pieśniami* (Toruń, 1623).

Daphnogenetica praeclaris et nobili genere natis iuvenibus d. Matthaeo Newe, d. Friderico Kostkae a Skothow, Prutenis, Quo die in alma, quae Vilnae est, Societatis IESV Academia, liberalium Artium ac Philosophiae Magisterij insignibus supremaque solenniter laurea sunt adornati. Amici et in Seminario Pontificio contubernales gratulabundi dd VII Idus Octobris anno Domini 1595 (Vilnius, 1595).

Das Pressburger Protocollum Testamentorum 1410 (1427)-1487, ed. J. MAJOROSSY and K. SZENDE, 1, *1410-1487* and 2, *1467-1529* (Vienna, 2010-2014).

Daukša, M., *Kathechismas arba moksłas kiekwienam krikszczionii priwalvs* (Vilnius, 1595).

Daukša, M., "Przedmowa do czytelnika łaskawego", in: J. Wujek, *Postilla katholicka, tai esit išguldimas ewangelių kiekvienos nedėlios ir šventės per visus metus*, trans. M. DAUKŠA (Vilnius, 2000), p. 42-45.

Dla dziatek nauka czytania pisma polskiego (Vilnius, 1633).

Dowgird, S., *Genealogia albo krótkie opisanie wielkich książąt litewskich i ich wielkich a mężnych spraw wojennych uczynione niegdy przez Matysa Strykowskiego, teraz odnowione i znowu na świat wydane przez Samuela Dougirda z Pogowia* [Genealogy or The Short Description of the Grand Dukes of Lithuania and Their Brave Military Deeds, Written Formerly by Maciej Stryjkowski and Now Renewed and Published by Samuel Dowgird of Pogowie] (Lubcz, 1626).

Dowgird, S. (S. Daugirdas), *Genealogija, arba Trumpas didžiųjų Lietuvos kunigaikščių ir jų didžių bei narsių žygių aprašymas, kadaise Motiejaus Strijkovskio sukurtas, o dabar atnaujintas ir vėl išleistas Samuelio Daugirdo iš Pagaujo* [The Genealogy or Short Description of the Grand Dukes of Lithuania and Their Brave Military Deeds, Written Formely by Maciej Stryjkowski and Now Renewed and Published by Samuel Dowgird of Pogowie], ed. and trans. R. KOŽENIAUSKIENĖ, commentaries by K. GUDMANTAS (Vilnius, 2001).

Dramaty eucharystyczne jezuitów. XVII wiek, ed. J. OKOŃ (Warsaw, 1992).

Du laiškai: popiežiaus nuncijaus Luigi Lippomano ir kunigaikščio Mikalojaus Radvilo Juodojo polemika (1556) [Two Letters: a Controversy between Papal Nuncio Luigi Lippomano and Duke Nicolaus Radvilas the Black (1556)], ed. D. POCIŪTĖ (Vilnius, 2015).

Dubowicz, A., *Kazanie na pogrzebie jaśnie wielmożnego pana p. Teofila Tryzny wojewody brzeskiego, wołkowyskiego, błudnieńskiego etc. starosty, miane w cerkwi by-*

teńskiej zakonu św. Bazylego dnia Februarii roku 1645 przez ks. Aleksego Dubowicza, archimandrytę wileńskiego zakonu św. Bazylego (Vilnius, 1645).
Dubowicz, J., *Kazanie na pogrzebie jaśnie wielmożnej paniej jej mości paniej Barbary Naruszewiczowej Januszowej Skuminowej Tyszkiewiczowej, wojewodzinej trockiej, jurborskiej, nowowolskiej etc. etc. starościny, miane w cerkwi wileńskiej Trójce Przenaświętszej 2 dnia września roku Pańskiego 1627 przez o. Jana Dubowicza Ordinis S. Basilii* (Vilnius, 1627).
Dubowicz, A., *Pióro lekkie ciężki świat noszące na pogrzebie jego mości pana Jana Kolendy, województwa wileńskiego, trybunalskiego, ziemskiego pisarza, w Wilnie, w cerkwi Św. Trójce ojców bazylianów w jedności św. będących, roku 1636, dnia 18 miesiąca decembra wystawione* (Vilnius, 1637).
Dwa kazania wygłoszone po śmierci Katarzyny Habsburżanki i Zygmunta III Wazy, ed. J. Niedźwiedź (Warsaw, 2016).
Elementaria institutio Latini sermonis et pietatis Christianae (Vilnius, 1603).
Ewangelie polskie i litewskie tak niedzielne, jako i wszytkich świąt, które w Kościele katolickim według rzymskiego porządku przez cały rok czytają (Vilnius, 1647).
Ferreri, Z., *Vita beati Casimiri confessoris ex serenimissimis Poloniae regibus et magnis Lithuaniae ducibus clarissimi* (Rome, 1521).
Forma albo porządek sprawowania świątości Pańskich, jako chrztu świętego i społeczności wieczerzy Pańskiej, przy tym i inszych ceremoniej albo posługowania Zboru Bożego ku potrzebie pobożnym pasterzom i prawdziwym ministrom Pana Krystusowym znowu wydana i drukowna (Vilnius, 1600).
Forma albo porządek sprawowania świętości Pańskich, to jest krztu świętego i świętej wieczerzej Pańskiej, przy tym i inszych cerymonij albo posługowania Zboru Bożego [The Form and Order of the Rites of the Lord, i.e. Baptism, Eucharist, and Other Ceremonies of the Church of the Lord], (Lubcz, 1621).
Formularz Jerzego, pisarza grodzkiego krakowskego ok. 1399-1415 [Formulae by George, the Notary of the Castle Court in Cracow, *c.* 1399-1415], ed. K. Górski (Toruń, 1950).
Fortka niebieska, to jest dzielne ćwiczenia żywota duchownego, w których kto się będzie chciał ćwiczyć, doskonałości chrześcijańskiej snadnie może dostąpić. TE złożyła i w nich się ćwiczyła panna niektóra zakonna we Włoszech, które naprzód językiem włoskim z rozkazania biskupa kremońskiego napisano, po tym w rozmaite języki dla pożytków ich, które w ludziach czyniły przełożono, na ostatek i na polskie przez jednego kapłana Societatis Iesu przetłomaczono z dozwoleniem starszych. Przydano niektóre nabożne ćwiczenia, a osobliwie przez cały tydzień o męce Pańskiej rozmyślania, ed. and trans. Sz. Wysocki (Vilnius, 1588).
Frycz Modrzewski, A., *Mowy*, ed. Ł. Kurdybacha and K. Koranyi, trans. E. Jędrkiewicz (Warszawa, 1954).
Funebris laudatio et threnodiae in exequias ornatissimi et lectissimi adolescentis Ioannis Barscii a studiosa iuventute conscriptae in Academia Vilnensi Societatis Iesu (Vilnius, 1595).

Gedimino laiškai [The Letters of Gediminas], ed. V. PAŠUTA and I. ŠTAL (Vilnius 1966) (<http://viduramziu.istorija.net/ru/s1283.htm>, accessed 22.11.2021).

Gertich, M.G., *Protestacyja przeciwko niesłusznej chlubie tych, co za przyczyną disputacji ks. Marcina Śmigleckiego z ks. Danielem Mikołajewskim ministrem Ewangelii P.N.J. Krystusa o widzialnej głowie Kościoła Bożego etc. przed zwycięstwem triumfują* (Vilnius, 1599).

Gminy żydowskie w dawnej Rzeczypospolitej Wybór tekstów źródłowych, ed. and trans. A. MICHAŁOWSKA, (Warsaw, 2003).

Golliusz, J., *Pamiętnik Jana Golliusza, mieszczanina polskiego (1650-1653)*, ed. J. KALLENBACH (Cracow, 1892).

Górnicki, Ł., *Dworzanin polski* [The Polish Courtier] (Cracow, 1566).

Górnicki, Ł., *Dzieje w Koronie Polskiej*, ed. H. BARYCZ (Wrocław, 2003).

Gradowski, F., *Hodoeporicon Moschicum illustrissimi principis ac domini domini Christophori Radiwilionis, ducis in Birża et Dubinga* (Vilnius, 1581).

Gratulatio illustrissimo ac reverendissimo D.D. Benedicto Woynae episcopos Vilnensi a Sodalitate B.V. Mariae Annunciatae S.I. Academica Vilnensi, (Vilnius, 1600).

Gratulationes neomysticae reverendo ac erudito viro d. Francisco Sucholewski Pontificis Maximi alumno, s. theologiae in Academia Vilnensi S.I. auditori, sacri primum operanti. A nonnullis eiusdem Academiae studiosis amoris et observantiae ergo oblatae (Vilnius, 1593).

Gratulationes serenissimo ac potentissimo principi Sigismundo III D. G. regi Poloniae magnoque duci Lithuaniae etc. etc. in optatissimo et felicissimo S.R.M. suae Vilnam adventu factae ab Academia Vilnensi Societatis Iesu (Vilnius, 1589).

Grodzicki, S., *Kazanie na pogrzebie Oświeconej Księżny J.M. Paniej P. Katarzyny z Tęczyna Radziwiłowej, wojewodzinej wileńskiej etc. etc. miane w kościele tumskim wileńskim dnia 20 Julii roku Pańskiego 1592 (...) A przy tym Trutina psychotropii przeciw temu kazaniu przez ministwa dadwornego wydanej* [The Sermon for the Funeral of Her Grace Princess Katarzyna of Tęczyn Radziwiłłowa, the Wife of Mr Voivode of Vilnius, Preached on 20 July 1592 in the Cathedral of Vilnius (...). Together with *Trutina Psychotropii* Published against this Sermon written by the Court Protestant Priest] (Vilnius, 1592).

Grodzicki, S., *O jednej osobie w używaniu Sakramentu Ciała Pańskiego w Kościele Bożym zwyczajnej. Kazań sześć* [Six Sermons about Ordinary Holy Communion in the Church of God, that is Under One Kind] (Vilnius, 1589).

Grodzicki, S., *O czyścu kazanie wtóre ks. d. Stanisława Grodzickiego, theologa Societatis Iesu 26 dnia stycznia miane w kościele ś. Jana. Przy pogrzebie Jego Ks. M. Pana Pana Olbrichta Radziwiła na Ołyce i Nieświeżu W. Ks. Litewskiego wielkiego marszałka, starosty rowieńskiego, samborskiego etc. etc.* (Vilnius, 1593).

Grodzicki, S., *O poprawie kalendarza kazanie dwoje* [Two Sermons about the Reform of the Calendar] , ed. S. MŁODECKI (Vilnius, 1589).

Grodzicki, S., *Prawidło wiary haeretyckiej. To jest okazanie, iż wodzowie kacerscy nie Pismo św. ale własny mózg swój za regułę albo prawidło wiary sobie mają. A przy tym pierwsza centuria albo sto jawnych fałszerstwa w wierze z obrony Postylle ka-*

cerskiej od fałecznego proroka Grzegorza Żarnowca wydanej zebranych (Vilnius, 1592).

Groicki, B., *Artykuły prawa majdeburskiego, które zowią Speculum Saxonum* (Cracow, 1558).

Groicki, B., *Ustawa płacej u sądów w prawie majdeburskim tak przed burmistrzem a rajcami, jak przed wójtem* (Cracow, 1568).

Groicki, B., *Porządek sądów i spraw miejskich prawa majdeburskiego w Koronie Polskiej* (Cracow, 1559).

Groicki, B., *Postępek sądów około karania na gardle* (Cracow 1559).

Groicki, B., *Tytuły prawa majdeburskiego* [The Titles of the Magdeburg Law], ed. K. KORANYI (Warsaw, 1953).

Grothówna, Z., *Kronika klasztorna sióstr norbertanek w Imbramowicach, 1703-1741*, ed. W. BIELAK and W.W. ŻUREK (Kielce, 2011).

Grzegorz z Żarnowca, *Obrona postylle ewanielickiej, to jest odpowiedź na Apologiją jezuicką w Krakowie niedawno wydaną, która odpowiedź w pierwszej części zamyka w sobie dziesięcioro kazań naprzeciwko sześciorgom kazań Apologijej jezuickiej. A w drugiej części okazanie dowodne pobrane prawd ewanielickich w w tejże Apologijej naganiony. Teraz (za niedostatkiem ksiąg) znowu drukowano* (Vilnius, 1591); <https://www.postkomsg.com/reading_room/227714/?fbclid=IwAR1BpDrq5H5X5V5a7K4SPNjsSfAvfjgzCFuvS7TE0iVAYsX1Aq7t0CoKdIE> (accessed 05.02.2022).

Hymny, prozy i cantica kościelne cokolwiek sie ich w brewiarzach i we mszałach rzymskich teraz znajduje i niektóre insze z dawniejszych co przedniejsze, zwłaszcza prozy i hymny, trans. S. GROCHOWSKI (Cracow, 1599).

"Idyllum albo akt o porwaniu Heleny", in: *Dramaty staropolskie: Antologia*, ed. J. LEWAŃSKI, 5 (Warsaw, 1963), pp. 49-57.

Imagines Mortis: His Accesserunt Epigrammata, e Gallico idiomate a Georgio Aemylio in Latinum translata: Ad Haec, Medicina Animae tam iis, qui firma, quam qui adversa corporis valetudine praediti sunt, maxime necessaria, (Cologne, 1555).

Inscriptiones ecclesiarum Vilnensium: Inskrypcje z wileńskich kościołów: Vilniaus bažnyčių įrašai, 1. ed. W. APPEL and E. ULČINAITĖ (Vilnius, 2005).

Institoris, H., and J. Sprenger, *Malleus maleficarum*, ed. Ch.S. MACKAY (Cambridge, 2006).

Jan Ursyn z Krakowa, *Modus epistolandi cum epistolis exemplaribus et orationibus annexis: O sposobie pisania listów wraz z wzorami listów i mowami*, ed. L. WINNICZUK (Wrocław, 1957)

Jan z Komorowa, "Memoriale Fratrum Minorum a fr. Ioanne de Komorowo compilatum", ed. K. LISKE and A. LORKIEWICZ, in: *Monumenta Poloniae Historica*, 5 (Lviv, 1888), pp. 1-418.

Jarzębski, A., *Gościniec abo krótkie opisanie Warszawy* (Warsaw, 1900).

Jaskier, M., *Iuris municipalis Maideburgensis liber vulgo Weichbild nuncupatus ex vetustissimis exemplaribus vigilanti opera nuper latinitate datus, aummaq* (Cracow, 1535).

Jaskier, M., *Promptuarium iuris provincialis Saxonici, quod Speculum Saxonum vocatur tum et municipalis Maideburgensis summa diligentia recollectum* (Cracow, 1535).

Juan de de Jesús María, *Zegar serdeczny, w którym Jezus godziny wybija w sercu grzesznika, aby go do pokuty nawrócił*, trans. P. Domiechowski (Cracow, 1651).

Jurgiewicz, A., *Anatomia libelli famosi et scurrilis Andreae Volani Lwowcoviensis apostate et prafecti Synagogae Calvinisticae Vilnensis* (Vilnius, 1591).

Jurgiewicz, A., *De pio et in sancta Ecclesia iam inde ab apostolis receptissimo sacrarum imaginum usu, deque sacrilega novorum Iconoclastarum in exterminandis illis per summam Christi contumeliam, immanitate. Itemque de sanctorum veneratione et invocatione theses in Academia Vilnensi disputandae, adversus impium et famosum libellum a Volano quodam recenti Iconomachorum Archiministro editum*. Propugnatore Andrea Iurgevicio, sancte theologiae candidato et artium liberalium et philosophiae magistro, praeside R. P. Emanuele a Vega in eadem Academia sanctissimae theologiae professore ordinario, ([Vilnius], 1586).

Jurgiewicz, A., *Mendacia et convitia evangelica Andreae Volani Lwowkoviensis, secretarii, si diis placet, Magni Ducatus Lituaniae, ex ipsius scriptis fideliter collecta et breviter refutata: per Andream Iurgeuicium Canonicum Vilnensem. Additi sunt in fine turpissimi errores eiusdem Volani in grammatica*, (Vilnius, 1588).

Jurgiewicz, A., *Quaestiones de haeresibus nostri temporis Andreae Volano et Lithuaniae Ministris: Per Andream Ivrgielevicivm Canonicvm Vilnensem propositae. Iussu et Authoritae Illustrissimi et Reuerendissimi in Christo Patris et Domini D. Georgii D.M. Tituli S. Sixti, S.R.E. Praesbiteri Cardinalis Radziwił nuncupati, Episcopatus Vilnensis perpetui administratoris etc. in lucem editae* (Vilnius, 1590).

Kal, J., "Religionis, Reipublicae, Vilnae, Collegii et omnium ordinum ex fortunatissimo Sacrae Regiae Maiestatis adventu laetitia et gratulatio / Radosne powinszowania Religii, Rzeczypospolitej, Wilna, Kolegium oraz wszystkich stanów z okazji najszczęśliwszego przybycia Jego Królewskiej Mości", ed. E. Buszewicz and J. Niedźwiedź, in: "*Umysł stateczny i w cnotach gruntowny": Prace edytorskie dedykowane pamięci Profesora Adama Karpińskiego*, ed. R. Grześkowiak and R. Krzywy (Warsaw, 2012), pp. 17-39.

Kalbų varžybos: Lietuvos Didžiosios Kunigaikštystės valdovų ir didikų sveikinimai – Competition of Languages: The Ceremonial Greetings of the Grand Duchy of Lithuania's Rulers and Nobles – Koncert języków: Pozdrowienia władców i magnatów Wielkiego Księstwa Litewskiego, ed., trans., and introduced by E. Ulčinaitė (Vilnius, 2010).

Karmanowski, O., *Wiersze i listy* [Poems and Letters], ed. R. Grześkowiak (Warsaw, 2010).

Karpowicz, L., *Przemowa i napomnienie do oblubieńców w stan św. małżeński wstępujących. Przy szlubie jego mości kniazia Samuela Ogińskiego, podkomorzyca trockiego ... i jej mości panny Zofijej Billewiczówny, ciwunówny szandowskiej ... Przy znamienitym zgromadzeniu tak niektórych ich mości panów senatorów, książąt, paniąt, urzędników ziemskich, jako i wielu innych zacnego szlacheckiego stanu osób czynione* ... (Vilnius, 1619).

Katalog rękopisów kapitulnych Katedry Krakowskiej, 1, *Kodeksa rękopiśmienne*, ed. I. POLKOWSKI (Cracow, 1884).

Katechizm albo krótkie w jedno miejsce zebranie wiary i powinności krześcijańskiej z pasterstwem zborowym i domowym, z modlitwami, psalmami i piosnkami na cześć a chwałę Panu Bogu a Zborowi jego ku zbudowaniu teraz znowu za pilnym przejrzeniem i poprawieniem wydany: Nakładem jego m. pana Jana Abrahamowicza na Worniach, wojewody mieńskiego, prezydenta derptskiego, starosty lidskiego i wendeńskiego etc. (Vilnius, 1594).

Kiszka J., and S. Kiszka, *In auspicatum illustrissimi ac reverendissimi Domini D. Benedicti Woynae D.G. Episcopi Vilnensis ad suam sedem ingressum Gratulatio a Stanislao et Ioanne Kiszka fratribus, in Academia Vilnensi Societatis Jesu studiosis, oblata* (Vilnius, 1600).

Klasztory karmelitanek bosych w Polsce, na Litwie i Rusi: Ich początek, rozwój i tulactwo w czasie rozruchów wojennych w XVII w., 1, *Wilno*, ed. R. KALINOWSKI (Cracow, 1900).

Knapiusz, G., *Tragoediae: Philopater, Faelicita, Eutropius*, ed. and introduced by L. WINNICZUK (Wrocław, 1965).

Kobiety za murem: Antologia tekstów lubelskich karmelitanek bosych XVII i XVIII wieku [The Women Behind the Wall: An Anthology of Writings of Discalced Carmelite Nuns in Lublin from the Seventeenth-Eighteenth Centuries], ed. A. NOWICKA-STRUSKA (Lublin, 2021).

Kochanowski, J., *Trifles, Songs, and Saint John's Eve Song*, ed. and trans. M.J. MIKOŚ, foreword by M. HANUSIEWICZ-LAVALLEE (Lublin, 2018).

Kodeks dyplomatyczny katedry i diecezji wileńskiej, 1 *(1387-1507)*, ed. J. FIJAŁEK and W. SEMKOWICZ (Cracow, 1938-1994).

Kodeks dyplomatyczny Litwy wydany z rękopismów w Archiwum Tajnem w Królewcu zachowanych, ed. E. RACZYŃSKI (Wrocław, 1845).

Kopie listów jezuity Sarbiewskiego oraz księcia Janusza Radziwiłła (1612-1655) [Copies of the Letters of the Jesuit Sarbiewski and Prince Janusz Radziwiłł (1612-1655)], ed. M. JARCZYKOWA, trans. A. GOLIK-PRUS, *Terminus* 12.1 (2010), pp. 231-242.

Korespondencja Hieronima Rozrażewskiego [The Correspondence of Hieronim Rozrażewski], 1, *1567-2 VII 1582*, ed. P. CZEPLEWSKI (Toruń, 1937).

Korespondencja Macieja Kazimierza Sarbiewskiego ze Stanisławem Łubieńskim [The Correspondence of Maciej Kazimierz Sarbiewski with Stanisław Łubieński], ed. and trans. J. STARNAWSKI (Warsaw, 1986).

Kościół zamkowy, czyli katedra wileńska w jej dziejowym, liturgicznym, architektonicznym i ekonomicznym rozwoju, 2, *Źródła historyczne*, ed. J. KURCZEWSKI (Vilnius, 1910).

Koszutski, S., "Epithalamion in nuptiis Sigismundi Augusti Regis Poloniae et Barbarae", in: *Szesnastowieczne epitalamia łacińskie w Polsce,* ed. J. NIEDŹWIEDŹ, trans. J. BROŻEK (Cracow, 1999), pp. 318-341.

Kraiński, K., *Katechizm z pieśniami Kościoła powszechnego apostolskiego* (Cracow, 1596).

Kromer, M., *De origine et rebus gestis Polonorum libri XXX* (Basel, 1555).

Kromer, M., "Oratio in funere optimi et maximi principis Sigismundi, eius nominis primi, Polonorum, Lituanorum, Russorum, Prussorum et Masoviorum regis etc. 1548 Calendis Aprilis defuncti", in: M. Kromer, *De origine et rebus gestis Polonorum libri XXX* (Basel, 1555).

Kromer, M., *Polonia, czyli o położeniu, ludności, obyczajach, urzędach i sprawach publicznych Królestwa Polskiego księgi dwie*, ed. and introduction by R. MARCHWIŃSKI, trans. S. KAZIKOWSKI (Olsztyn, 1984).

"Kronika bernardynek świętomichalskich w Wilnie", ed. M. KAŁAMAJSKA-SAEED, *Nasza Przeszłość*, 101 (2004), pp. 331-435.

"Krótka kronika fundacyi karmelitanek bosych klasztoru św. Józefa w Wilnie, która stanęła w roku 1638, 18 Decembra", in: *Klasztory karmelitanek bosych w Polsce, na Litwie i Rusi. Ich początek, rozwój i tułactwo w czasie rozruchów wojennych w XVII w.*, 1, *Wilno*, ed. R. KALINOWSKI (Cracow, 1900), pp. 19-124.

Krótki zbiór nauki chrześcijańskiej (Vilnius, 1606).

Krzycki, A. (A. Cricius), *Carmina*, ed. K. MORAWSKI (Cracow, 1888).

Kulvietis, A., *Pirmasis Lietuvos Reformacijos paminklas / The First Recorded Text of the Lithuanian Reformation: Abraomo Kulviečio* Confessio fidei *ir Johanno Hoppijaus* Oratio funebris *(1547) –* Confessio fidei *by Abaromas Kulvietis and* Oratio funebris *by Johann Hoppe (1547)*, ed. D. POCIŪTĖ (Vilnius, 2011).

Łacińskie dialogi Kaspra Pętkowskiego, ed. A. SOCZEWKA (Niepokalanów, 1978).

Łaski, J., *Commune incliti Polonie Regni privilegium, constitutionum et indultuum publicitus decretorum, approbatorumque cum nonnullis iuribus tam divinis quam humanis per serenissimum principem et dominum dominum Alexandrum, Dei gratia Regem Poloniae, magnum ducem Lithwanie, Russie, Prussieque dominum et haeredem etc.* (Cracow, 1506).

Łaski, J., *Forma ac ratio tota ecclesiastici ministerii in peregrinorum, potissimum vero Germanorum ecclesia, instituta Londini in Anglia, per ... regem Eduardum eius nominis Sextum anno post Christum natum 1550* (Frankfurt am Main, 1555).

Lauxmin, S., *Praxis oratoria sive praecepta artis rhetoricae, quae ad comparandum orationem necessaria sunt* (Frankfurt am Main, 1665).

Lauxmin, S. (Ž. Liauksminas), *Rinktiniai raštai – Opera selecta*, ed. B. GENZELIS (Vilnius, 2004).

Liber cancellariae Stanislai Ciołek: Ein Formelbuch der polnischen Königskanzlei aus der Zeit der Husitischen Bewegung, ed. J. CARO, 1-2 (Vienna, 1871-1872).

Liber formularum ad ius Polonicum necnon canonicum spectantium in codice Regiomontano asservatum, ed. B. ULANOWSKI (Cracow, 1895).

Lietuvos metrika: Knyga Nr. 4 (1471-1491): Užrašymų knyga 4, ed. L. Anužytė (Vilnius, 2004).

Lietuvos metrika: Knyga Nr. 5 (1427-1506): Užrašymų knyga 5 [The *Lithuanian Metrica*: Book 5 (1427-1506)], ed. A. Baliulis, A. Dubonis, and D. Antanavičius (Vilnius, 2012).

Listy polskie XVI wieku: Listy z lat 1525-1548 ze zbiorów Władysława Pociechy, Witolda Taszyckiego i Adama Turasiewicza [Polish Letters from the Sixteenth Century: Letters form 1525-1548 from the Collections of Władysław Pociecha, Witold Taszycki and Adam Turasiewicz], 1, ed. K. Rymunt (Cracow, 1998).

Listy polskie XVI wieku, 2, ed. K. Rymunt: *Listy z lat 1548-1550 ze zbiorów Władysława Pociechy, Witolda Taszyckiego i Adama Turasiewicza* (Cracow, 2001).

Lorich, R., *Księgi o wychowaniu i o ćwiczeniu każdego przełożonego*, trans. S. Koszutski (Cracow, 1558).

Lubelczyk, J., *Pieśń o zmartwychwastaniu Pańskim Wesel się tejto chwile ludzkie pokolenie etc. Druga Krystus Pan zmartwychwstał Zwycięstwo otrzymał* (Cracow, 1556).

Maggio, G. (Iunianus Maius), *De priscorum verborum proprietate* (Trier, 1477).

Malecki, J., *Catechismus, to jest nauka krześciańska od Apostołów dla prostych ludzi we trzech cząstkach zamkniona* (Königsberg, 1546).

Małkot, F., *Tureckich i iflanskich wojen o sławnej pamięci Janie Karolu Chodkiewiczu głos – Karų su turkais ir Livonijoje balsas apie šlovingo atminimo Joną Karolį Chodkevičių* [The Voice of the Turkish and Livonian Wars of Jan Karol Chodkiewicz of Famous Memory] ed. D. Antanavičius, D. Chemperek, and E. Patiejūnienė (Warsaw, 2016).

Materiały do historii drukarstwa i księgarstwa w Polsce, ed. A. Benis (Cracow, 1892).

Materiały do historyi stosunków kulturalnych w XVI w. na dworze królewskim polskim, ed. S. Tomkiewicz (Cracow, 2015).

Mažvydas, M., *Catechismusa Prasty Szadei* (Königsberg, 1547).

Meditatio in Epistolam divi Pauli ad Ephesios (Vilnius, 1592).

Mercator, G., *Atlas minor Gerardi Mercatoris a Iudoco Hondio plurimis aeneis tabulis auctus atque illustrates* (Amsterdam, 1610).

Metryka Uniwersytetu Krakowskiego z lat 1400-1508. Biblioteka Jagiellońska rkp. 258, II, *Indeksy*, ed. A. Gąsiorowski, T. Jurek, and I. Skierska (Cracow, 2004).

Mikołajewski, D., *Dysputacyja wileńska, którą miał ks. Marcin Śmiglecki Societatis Iesu z ks. Danielem Mikołajewskim, sługą Słowa Bożego, de primatu Petri, a o jednej widomej głowie Kościoła Bożego dnia 2 czerwca w roku 1599. Od samego autora cale i szczyrze wydana. Nie zaniechały się i przysadki ks. Śmigleckiego z odpowiedzią na nie tegoż ks. Daniela Mikołajewskiego* (Toruń, 1599).

Missale Cracoviense (Nuremberg, after 1493).

Modlitewnik Olbrachta Gasztołda, kanclerza wielkiego litewskiego 1528 r. Facsimile, ed. W. Wydra (Poznań, 2015).

*Modlitwy z doktorów św. według św. wschodniej Cerkwie obrane, do których Akafist Panu Jezusowi i Kanon do Przenaświętszego Ducha Boga i Akafist Naświętszej

Pannie Maryjej i inne wielce nabożne prośby teraz nowo przyłożone i na świat wydane (Vilnius, 1650).

Monumenta Medii Aevi Historica res gestas Poloniae illustrantia, 2, *Codex epistolaris saeculi decimi quinti 1384-1492*, ed. A. SOKOŁOWSKI and J. SZUJSKI (Cracow, 1876).

Moravus, J., *Quaestiones de primis grammatices rudimentis, ex quibusque probatis auctoribus in usum secundae classis gymnasi Wilnensis apud orthodoxos collectae* (Vilnius, 1592).

Morochowski, J.A., *ПАРНГОРІА abo kamień z procy prawdy Cerkwie święterj prawosławnej ruskiej na skruszenie fałecznociemnej Perspektywy albo raczej paszkwilu od Kassjana Sakowicza* (Kyiv, 1644).

Olszewski, J., *Tryumf przesławnej Akademii Wileńskiej S.I. po zwycięstwie otrzymanym od Władysława IV króla polskiego, wielkiego książęcia litewskiego, kiedy 24 dnia lutego roku tego zwyciężywszy wojsko moskiewskie pod Smoleńskiem obóz nieprzyjacielski z armatą wzięli: Kazaniem przy podziękowaniu Panu Bogu wystawiony: Per eundem Jacobum Olszewski S.I., sanctae theologiae doctorem, almae Academiae Vilnensis procancellarium et ordinarium ecclesiae parochialis Vilnensis concionatorem w kościele farskim św. Jana wileńskim 12 dnia marca* (Vilnius, 1634).

Olszewski, J., *Tryumf przezacnej konwokacyjej wileńskiej ich mościów panów senatorów i posłów Wielkiego Księstwa Litewskiego po zwycięstwie otrzymanym od ... Władysława IV ..., kiedy 24 dnia lutego roku tego zwyciężywszy potężne wojsko z wielu narodów zacnych zebrane pod Smoleńskiem obóz nieprzyjacielski z armatą wzięli: Kazaniem przy podziękowaniu Panu Bogu stawiamy per Jacobum Olszewski ... w kościele katedralnym wileńskim 7 dnia marca* (Vilnius, 1634).

Olszewski, J., *Żałoba po śmierci najjaśniejszej Konstancjej królowej polskiej, księżny litewskiej etc., arcyksiężny rakuskiej w kościele katedralnym wileńskim 19 iulii 1631 wystawiona przez ks. Jakuba Olszewskiego Soc<ietatis> Iesu doctora i dziekana św. teologijej, kościoła farskiego wileńskiego kaznodzieje* [Mourning after the Death of Her Majesty the Polish Queen Constance, Duchess of Lithuania, etc., Archduchess of Austria, in Vilnius Cathedral Church on 19 July 1631, Delivered by Father Jakub Olszewski Soc<ietatis> Iesu, Doctor and Dean of Holy Theology, and a Preacher in Vilnius Parish Church] (Vilnius, 1631).

Olszewski, J., "Żałoba po śmierci najaśniejszej Konstancyjej, królowej polskiej, księżny litewskiej etc., arcyksiężny rakuskiej, w kościele katedralnym wileńskim 19 Iulii roku Pańskiego 1631 wystawiona przez księdza Jakuba Olszewskiego Societatis Iesu, doktora i dziekana świętej teologijej, kościoła farskiego wileńskiego kaznodzieję", in: *Dwa kazania wygłoszone po śmierci Katarzyny Habsburżanki i Zygmunta III Wazy*, ed. J. NIEDŹWIEDŹ (Warsaw, 2016).

Orszak, G., *Postylla domowa, to jest kazania na każdą niedziele i święta przedniejsze i na insze pospolite do roku, które niejedno w kościele, ale też i w domu każdy chrześcijański gospodarz może sobie i czeladce swojej kazać abo czytać sam, k oświeconości z Postylle Filipa Melanctona, Spangemberga i inszych zebrane*, ed. J. SEKLUCJAN (Königsberg, 1556).

Panegyrica ... Nicolao Christophoro Radzivilo ... post Auspicatissimum initium Vilnae Palatinatum, ab ... Nicolao Christophoro, Ioanne Alberto, Alberto Stanislao Radzivilis, & quibusdam aliis bonarum artium cultoribus, nomine totius Academiae Vilnensis Societatis Iesu, summa fide & observantia (Vilnius, 1604).

Parentalia in obitum illustris et magnifici domini d. Georgii Chodkievicii, generalis capitanei Samogitiae etc. etc. a sodalibus Congregationis Parthenicae Academiae Vilnensis Societatis Iesu mortem sodalis sui et moderatoris quondam vigilantissimi deflentibus conscripta (Vilnius, 1595).

Pasek, J.Ch., *Pamiętniki*, ed. R. POLLAK (Warsaw, 1987).

Pętkowski, K., "Dialog o pokoju dla króla Stefana" [A Dialogue about Peace for King Stephen], trans. H. SZCZERKOWSKA, in: *Dramaty staropolskie. Antologia* [Old Polish Drama: An Anthology], ed. J. LEWAŃSKI, 4 (Warsaw, 1961), pp. 365-418.

Pętkowski, K., *Łacińskie dialogi Kaspra Pętkowskiego*, ed. A. SOCZEWKA (Niepokalanów, 1978).

Piasecki, P.P., *Kronika* [Chronicle] (Cracow, 1870).

Pielgrzymowski, E., *Poselstwo i krótkie spisanie rozprawy z Moskwą. Poselstwo do Zygmunta Trzeciego*, ed. R. KRZYWY (Warsaw, 2010).

Pieśni z katechizmów Ewangelików Reformowanych (1558-1600) / Hymns from the Catechisms of the Reformed Protestants (1558-1600), part 1, *Katechizm krakowski i królewiecki*, ed. M. KOMOROWSKA, M. MALICKI, and P. POŹNIAK, Introduction: B. CHLEBOWSKI, M. KORZO, and P. POŹNIAK (Cracow, 2018).

Pirmasis Lietuvos Statutas, 1, *Dzialinskio, Lauryno ir Ališavos nuorašų faksimilės*; 2, *Tekstai senąja beltarusių, lotynų ir senąja lenkų kalbomis*, ed. S. LAZUTKA, I. VALIKONYTĖ, and E. GUDAVIČIUS (Vilnius, 1991).

Pociej, H., *Antirresis abo apologija przeciwko Krzysztofowi Philaletowi, który niedawno wydał książki imieniem starożytnej Rusi, religiej greckiej, przeciw książkom o synodzie brzeskim, napisanym w Roku Pańskim 1597*, ed. J. BYLIŃSKI and J. DŁUGOSZ (Wrocław, 1997).

Pociej, H., *Synopsis zawierający w sobie opisanie synodu brzeskiego* (1596 – today unknown) *abo apologija przeciwko Krzysztofowi Philaletowi, który niedawno wydał książki imieniem starożytnej Rusi, religiej greckiej, przeciw książkom o synodzie brzeskim, napisanym w roku Pańskim 1597* (Vilnius, 1600).

Pontanus, L. (Luis de la Puente), *Rozmyślania o tajemnicach wiary naszej, żywocie i męce Pana Jezusowej i błogosławionej Maryjej Panny, świętych bożych i ewangelijach przypadających. Z naukami dostatecznymi około nich i około rozmyślnej modlitwy, na sześć części rozdzielone* (Vilnius, 1647).

Possevino, A., *Moscovia* (Vilnius, 1586).

Prawa, przywileje i statuty miasta Krakowa (1507-1795), ed. F. PIEKOSIŃSKI, and S. KRZYŻANOWSKI, 2, *1587-1696* (Cracow, 1909).

Priscianus Caesariensis, *Praeexercitamina. Retoryczne ćwiczenia wstępne*, trans. J. NIEDŹWIEDŹ, introduction A. Gorzkowski, *Terminus* 2.1-2 (2000), pp. 197-227.

Privilegia typographica Polonorum. Polskie przywileje drukarskie 1493-1793, ed. M. JUDA (Lublin, 2010).

Promptuarium iuris provincialis Saxonici quod Speculum Saxonum vocatur, tum et municipalis Maideburgensis summa diligentia recollectum et ad communem editum utilitatem, ed. M. JASKIER (Cracow, 1535).

Psalmy Dawidowe [The Psalms of David], trans. M. RYBIŃSKI (Raków, 1605).

Psałterz Dawidów: Teraz znowu z łacińskiego, z greckiego i z żydowskiego na polski język przełożony i argumentami i annotacyjami objaśniony ... Z dozwoleniem starszych: Pod rozsądek Kościoła świętego powszechnego rzymskiego wszystko niech podlęże, trans. J. WUJEK (Cracow, 1594).

Psałterz Dawidów z łacińskiego, z greckiego i żydowskiego na polski język z pilnością przełożony ... teraz znowu na żądanie wiela panien zakonnych łacińskiego języka nieumiejących a Psałterz mówić pragnących bez argumentów i annotacyj przedrukowany, trans. J. WUJEK (Cracow, 1616).

Rachunki dworu Zygmunta Augusta spisane przez Stanisława Włoszka (1544-1548), in: *Źródła do dziejów historyi sztuki i cywilizacyi w Polsce*, 1, ed. A. CHMIEL (Cracow, 1911).

Radwan, J. (J. Radvanas), *Raštai / Opera*, ed. and trans. by S. NARBUTAS (Vilnius, 2009).

Radziwiłł, A.S., *Pamiętnik o historii w Polsce*, 2, *1637-1646*, trans. and ed. A. PRZYBOŚ and R. ŻELEWSKI, (Warsaw, 1980).

Ratio atque institutio studiorum, czyli Ustawa szkolna Towarzystwa Jezusowego (1599), intro. and ed. K. BARTNICKA and T. BIEŃKOWSKI (Warsaw, 2000).

Regiomontanus (Johannes Müller von Königsberg), *Calendarium* (Venice, 1485).

Reguła świętego ojca Benedykta z łacińskiego przetłumaczona i z reformacyją porządków chełmieńskiego, toruńskiego, żarnowieckiego nieświeskiego i inszych wszystkich w Królestwie Polskim tejże refromacyjej i reguły św. Benedykta, które teraz są i na potym zjednoczone będą klasztorów panieńskich (Cracow, 1606).

Rej, M., *Postilla Lietuwiszka tátáy est Iżguldimás prástrás Ewánegeliu ąnt kożnos Nedelios ir Szwentes per wisus metus, kurios págal buda sená Bážniczioy Diewá est skatomos. Nu isż nauia su didżiu perweizdeghimu est iżduotá* (Vilnius, 1600).

Rej, M., *Świętych słów a spraw Pańskich, które tu sprawował Pan a Zbawiciel nasz na tym świecie jako prawy Bóg, będąc w człowieczeństwie swoim, Kronika albo Postylla, polskim językiem a prostym wykładem też dla prostaków krótce uczyniona* (Cracow, 1557).

Rej, M., *Źwierzyniec, w którym rozmaitych stanów ludzi, źwirząt i ptaków kstałty, przypadki i obyczaje są właśnie wypisane. A zwłaszcza ku czasom dzisiejszym naszym niejako przypadające* (Cracow, 1562).

Rituale sacramentorum ac aliarum Ecclesiae caeremoniarum ex decreto Synodi Provincialis Petricoviensis ad uniformem ecclesiarum Regni Poloniae et Magnus Ducatus Lithuaniae usum recens et in breve opusculum editum (Vilnius, 1633).

Rościszewski, W., *Ad orationem Andreae Volani, qua et errores in Ecclesia Romana si diis placet reprehendit et Pontificem ad deserendum pontificatum adhortatur Ioannis Bobola, in Academia Vilnensi Societatis Iesu studiosi responsio* (Vilnius, 1587?).

Royardus, I. (J. Royaers), *Homiliae in omnes epistolas dominicales iuxta literam* (Antwerp, 1538).

Ruiz de Moros, P. (P. Rojzjusz), *Decisiones* [...] *de rebus in sacro auditorio* [...] *Lithuanico ex appellatione iudicatus* (Cracow, 1563).

Ruiz de Moros, P., *Petri Royzii Maurei Alcagnicensis Carmina*, 1, ed. B. KRUCZKIEWICZ (Cracow, 1900).

Ruiz de Moros, P. (Petrus Royzius), *Petri Royzii Maurei Alcagnicensis Carmina. Vol 2 carmina minora continens*, ed. B. KRUCZKIEWICZ (Cracow, 1900).

Ruiz de Moros, P. (Petrus Royzius, Petras Roizijus), *Rinktiniai eliėraščiai* [Selected Poems], ed. and trans. S. NARBUTAS, E. PATIEJŪNIENĖ, and E. ULČINAITĖ (Vilnius, 2008).

Ruiz de Moros, P., *Decisiones Petri Royzii de rebus in sacro auditorio Lituanico ex appellatione iudicatis* (Cracow, 1563).

Russia seu Moscovia itemque Tartaria commentario topographico atque politico illustratae (Leiden, 1630).

Rymsza, A., *Deketeros akroama albo Dziesięcioroczne powieści wojennych spraw książęcia Krzysztofa Radziwiłła* (Vilnius, 1585).

Rysiński, S. (S. Risinskis), *Trumpas pasakojimas apie garsiuosius šviesiausiojo didiko, Biržų ir Dubingių kunigaikščio Kristupo Radvilos žygius* [A Short Story about the Famous Military Marches of His Grace the Prince of Biržai and Dubingiai], ed. S. NARBUTAS (Vilnius, 2000).

Rysiński, S., *Proverbiorvm Polonicorvm collectorum centuriae decem et octo* (Lubcha / Lubcz, 1618).

Sarbiewski, M.K., *Epigrammatum liber. Księga epigramatów*, ed. M. PISKAŁA and D. SUTKOWSKA (Warsaw, 2003).

Sarbiewski, M.K., *Laska Marszałkowska albo kazanie na pogrzebie Jana Stanisława Sapiehy* (Vilnius, 1635).

Sarbiewski, M.K., *Lemties žaidimai. Poezjijos rintkinė. Ludi Fortunae. Lyrica selecta*, ed. E. ULČINAITĖ (Vilnius, 1995).

Sarbiewski, M.K. *Liryki oraz Droga rzymska i fragment Lechiady*, trans. by T. KARYŁOWSKI, ed. M. KOROLKO and J. OKOŃ (Warsaw, 1980).

Sarbiewski, M.K., *O poezji doskonałej, czyli Wergiliusz i Homer* (*De perfecta poesi, sive Vergilius et Homerus*), ed. S. SKIMINA, trans. M. PLEZIA (Wrocław, 1954).

Sarbiewski, M. K., *Oratio panegyrica habita in praesentia serenissimi ac invictissimi Vladislai IV Poloniae et Sueciae regis a r. p. Matthia Casimiro Sarbiewski Societatis Iesu s. theologiae doctore et sacrae regiae maiestatis concionatore in solenni corporis C. Casimiri translatione, priusquam publica processione per urbis Vilnae plateas in regium cathedralis templi sacellum deferretur anno 1636 14 Augusti* (Vilnius, 1636).

Sarbiewski, M.K., *Wykłady poetyki (Praecepta poetica)*, trans. and ed. S. SKIMINA (Wrocław, 1958).

Scaliger, J.C., *Poetices libri septem* (Lyon, 1561).

Schönflissius, J., *Antidotum spirituale to jest lekarstwo duchowne na truciznę srogiej śmierci przy obchodzie pogrzebu niegdy pobożnego i szlachetnego męża jego mości pana Jakuba Gibla burmistrza wileńskiego. W Wilnie na cmyntarzu saskim anno 1637. 2. Decemb. pokazane przez ks. Jędrzeja Schönflissiusa kaznodzieję polskiego Confess<ionis> August<anae>* (Königsberg, 1638).

Schönflissius, J., "Kazanie pogrzebne królewskie", in: *Dwa kazania wygłoszone po śmierci Katarzyny Habsburżanki i Zygmunta III Wazy*, ed. J. NIEDŹWIEDŹ (Warsaw, 2016), pp. 147-182.

Schönflissius, A., *Korona na szczęśliwą koronacyją najaśniejszego Władysława IV* [The Crown on the Fortunate Head of His Royal Majesty Władysław IV] (Lubcz, 1633).

Schönflissius, J., *Legat prętko przychodzący i zbawienne poselstwo przynoszący. Na pogrzebie niegdaj cnej i pobożnej matrony, Wielmożnej Pani, Jejmości Pani Zuzanny Nunhartównej Chreptowiczowej w roku 1645 9 Decembra w Wilnie zmarłej kazaniem pogrzebnym pokazany* (Lubcz, 1646).

Schönflissius, A., *Postylli chrześcijańskiej z Biblijej świętej i z doktorów kościelnych według starożytnej nauki i zwyczajnego porządku kościoła Bożego zebranej na niedziele doroczne część pierwsza od Adwentu do Trójcy Świętej na cześć i chwałę wielkiego Boga i Zbawiciela Jezusa Chrystusa w druk podana* (Vilnius, 1652).

Schönflissius, A., *Wesele wieczne z Ewangelijej o dziesiąci pannach w trzydziestu i we trzech kazaniach zebraniu chrześcijańskiemu w Wilnie w kościele saskim rożnych lat we dni adwentowe pokazane, a teraz wszytkim ludziom pobożnym na to wesele wieczne zaproszonym ku osobliwej pociesze ku zbawiennej nauce i ku życzliwej przestrodze w druk podane* (Vilnius, 1646).

Schönflissius, A., *Wirydarz duszny męski, w którym się zamykają modlitwy i pieśni nadbożne z Pisma Świętego i z Doktorów Kościelnych, ludziom chrześcijańskim ku zbawiennemu używaniu zebrane i w druk podane* (Lubcz, 1648).

Seklucjan, J., *Catechismus to jest nauka naprzedniejsza i potrzebniejsza ku zbawieniu o wierze krześcijańskiej przz Jana Seklucjana nowo wydany* (Königsberg, 1547).

Seklucjan, J., *Katechismu tekst prosty dla prostego ludu* (Königsberg, 1545).

Seklucjan, J., *Pieśni chrześcijańskie dawniejsze i nowe ...*, ed. A. KALISZ (Cracow, 2007); *Psałterz i kancjonał z melodiami drukowany w 1558 roku / Polish Psalter and Hymnbook with Melodies Printed in 1558*, ed. J.S. GRUCHAŁA and P. POŹNIAK (Cracow, 2010).

Seklucjan, J., *Wyznanie wiary chrześcijańskiej* (Königsberg?, *c.* 1544).

Sextilis, P., *Nauka ku czytaniu dziatkam małym pisma polskiego* (Poznań, 1556).

Shabbatai ben Meir Ha-Kohen, ןהכ יתפש (Cracow, 1646)

Skarga, P., *Kazania na niedziele i święta* (Cracow, 1597).

Skarga, P., *Kazania na niedzielę i święta całego roku. Dwa są przy nich regestry, jeden do nauk na umocnienie katolickiej wiary, a drugi do naprawy obyczajów służący. Za dozwoleniem starszych* (Cracow, 1595).

Skarga, P., *O jedności Kościoła Bożego pod jednym Pasterzem i o greckim od tej jedności odstąpieniu* (Vilnius, 1577).

Skarga, P., *O jedności Kościoła bożego pod jednym pasterzu i ruskiem od tej jedności odstąpieniu. Synod brzeski i Obrona synodu brzeskiego*, ed. S. ZAŁĘSKI (Cracow, 1885).

Skarga, P., *Pro Sacratissima Eucharistia contra haeresim Zvinglianum ad Andream Volanum praesentiam corporis Domini nostri Iesu Christi ex eodem sacramento auferentem libri tres* (Vilnius, 1576).

Skarga, P., *Siedm filarów, na których stoi katolicka nauka o Przenaświętszym Sakramencie Ołtarza, postawione przeciw nauce zwingliańskiej, kalwińskiej Jędrzeja Wolana i przeciw pedagogijej teraz po polsku wydanej jednego ciemnego ministra z ciemnej drukarnijej, przez księdza Piotra Skargę, kapłana Societatis Iesu, który to, co po łacinie przeciw temuż Wolanowi dwakroć pisał, dla pojęcia pospolitego po polsku zebrał* (Vilnius 1582).

Skarga, P., *Synod brzeski* (Cracow, 1597).

Śmiglecki, M., *Absurda synodu toruńskiego, który mieli ewangelicy w Toruniu roku pańskiego 1595 mense Augusto i teraz do druku podali* (Vilnius, 1596).

Śmiglecki, M., *Dysputacyja wileńska, którą miał ks. Marcin Śmiglecki Societatis Iesu z ministrami ewanjelickiemi 2 Iunii w r. 1599 o jednej widomej głowie Kościoła Bożego*, published by Mr Paweł Wołowicz, a judge of the Lithuanian Tribunal, and reprinted with a reply to the protest (*protestacja*) against (the first edition) of this book (Vilnius, 1599).

Śmiglecki, M., *Logica ... selectis disputationibus et quaestionibus illustrate* (Igolstadt, 1618).

Śmiglecki, M., *O bóstwie przedwiecznym Syna Bożego. Świadectwa Pisma świętego do trzech przedniejszych artykułów zebrane. Przeciwko wszystkim Pana Jezusa Chrystusa nieprzyjacielom. Gdzie się też odpowiada na refutacją od Refutarza jakiegoś nowokrzczeńca przeciw ks. d. Jakubowi Wujkowi wydaną* (Vilnius, 1595).

Śmiglecki, M., *Zachariae prophetae pro Christi divinitate illustre testimonium adversus Fausti Socini anabaptistae cavillationes propugnatum* (Vilnius, 1596).

Smotrycki, M., *Apologia peregrinatiej do krajów wschodnich przez mię, Meletiusza Smotrzyskiego, M. D. archiepiskopa połockiego, episkopa witebskiego i mścisławskiego, archimandrytę dermańskiego roku P<ańskiego> 1623 i 24 obchodzonej przez fałszywą Bracią słownie i na piśmie spotwarzonej do przezacnego Narodu Ruskiego obojego stanu duchownego i świetskiego sporządzona i podana A<nno> 1628 Augusti die 25 w Monasteru w Dermaniu*, (Lviv, 1628).

Smotrycki, M., *ГРАММАТІКН Славенския правилное Сүнтагма* (Vievis, 1618).

Smotrycki, M., *Paraenesis abo napomnienie od Bogu wielebnego Melecyjusza Smotrzyskiego, rzeczonego archiepiskopa połockiego, episkopa witepskiego i mścisławskiego, archimandryty wileńskiego i dermańskiego do Przezacnego Bractwa Wileńskiego Cerkwie Św. Ducha a w osobie jego do wszystkiego tej strony Narodu Ruskiego uczynione* (Cracow, 1629).

Smotrycki, M., *Threnos (ΘΡΕΝΟΣ), to jest lament jedynej św. powszechnej apostolskiej wschodniej Cerkwie ... pierwej z greckiego na słowieński, a teraz z słowieńskiego na polski przełożony* (Vilnius, 1610).

Sozzini, F., *Refutacyja książek* (no location, 1593).

Sozzini, F., *Refutatio libelli quem Jacobus Vuiekus Iesuita anno 1590 Polonice edidit de divinitate Filii Dei et Spiritus Sancti* (no location, 1593).

Sozzini, F. (Socinius), *Responsio ad libellum J. Wuieki Iesuitae Polonice editum De divinitate Filii Dei et Spiritus Sancti ubi* EAD. *opera refellitur quicquid Robertus Bellarminus itidem Iesuita disputationum suarum tomo primo, secundae controversiae generalis libro primo de* EAD. *re scripsit* (Raków, 1624).

Stanisława Orzechowskiego i Augustyna Rotundusa debata o Rzeczypospolitej, ed. and introduction K. KOEHLER (Cracow, 2009).

Statuta synodalia episcoporum Wratislaviensium (Wrocław, 1475).

Stebelski, I., *Chronologia albo porządne według lat zebranie znaczniejszych w Koronie Polskiej i w Wielkim Księstwie Litewskim, a mianowicie na Białej Rusi w Połocku dziejów i rewolucyi, zwłaszcza tych, które się tyczą tak starodawnego Monastyru Św. Spasa za Połockiem, niegdyś przez św. Panny i Matki Ewfrozynę i Parascewię Hegumenie rządzonego, jako też teraźniejszego klasztoru na Zamku Połockim założonego* (Vilnius, 1782).

Syrokomla, W., *Przekłady poetów polsko-łacińskich epoki zygmuntowskiej*, 6, *Dodatki i uzupełnienia* (Warsaw, 1852).

Szczerbic, P., *Ius municipale, to jest prawo miejskie magdeburskie nowo z łacińskiego i niemieckiego języka z pilnością i wiernie przełożone* (Lviv, 1581).

Szczerbic, P., *Ius municipale to jest prawo miejskie majdeburskie, nowo z łacińskiego i z niemieckiego na polski język z pilnością i wiernie przełożone*, ed. G.M. KOWALSKI (Cracow, 2011).

Szczerbic, P., *Speculum Saxonum, albo prawo saskie i majdeburskie porządkiem obiecadła z łacińskich i niemieckich egzemplarzów zebrane, a na polski język z pilnością i wiernie przełożone*, 2, ed. G.M. KOWALSKI (Cracow, 2016).

Szczerbic, P., *Speculum Saxonum albo prawo saskie i magdeburskie porządkiem abecadła z łacińskiego i niemieckich egzemplarzów zebrane* (Lviv, 1581).

Szczerbic, P., *Speculum Saxonum, albo prawo saskie i majdeburskie porządkiem obiecadła z łacińskich i niemieckich egzemplarzów zebrane, a na język polski z pilnością i wiernie przełożone*, 1, ed. G.M. KOWALSKI (Cracow, 2016).

Szesnastowieczne epitalamia łacińskie w Polsce, in *Szesnastowieczne epitalamia łacińskie w Polsce*, trans. M. BROŻEK, introduction and ed. J. NIEDŹWIEDŹ (Cracow, 1999).

Szyrwid, K., *Punkty kazań od Adwentu aż do Postu litewskim językiem z wytłumaczeniem na polskie* (Vilnius, 1629).

Tajemna rada abo exorbitantiae niektóre Samuela Dambrowskiego supersuspendenta konfusyi szachskiej od pewnych osób tejże sekty do pospólstwa luterskiego we zborze miane i od nichże naganione, in: Z. NOWAK, *Kontrreformacyjna satyra obyczajowa w Polsce* XVII *wieku* (Gdańsk, 1968).

Testament kanonika wileńskiego Wojciecha Grabowskiego z Sierpca, ed. W. PAWLIKOWSKA-BUTTERWICK, *Studia Pedagogiczno-Artystyczne*, 4 (2004), pp. 116-131.

Testamenty chłopów polskich od drugiej połowy XVI do XVIII wieku [Last Wills of Polish Peasants from the Second Half of the Sixteenth Century], ed. J. Łosowski (Lublin, 2016).

Testamenty z ksiąg sądowych małych miast polskich do 1525 roku [Last Wills from the Court Registers of the Small Polish Towns up to 1525], ed. A. Bartoszewicz, K. Mrozowski, M. Radomski, and K. Warda (Warsaw, 2017).

"Teksty opisowe Wilna" [Texts Describing Vilnius], ed. J. Fijałek, *Ateneum Wileńskie*, 1.3-4 (1923), pp. 506-526.

The Constitutions of the Society of Jesus and Their Complementary Norms: A Complete English Translation of the Official Latin Texts (Saint Louis, 1996).

The Jesuit Ratio Studiorum of 1599, trans., ed. A.P. Farrell (Washington, D.C., 1970).

Thomás de Jesús, *Modlitw wnętrznej droga krótka i bezpieczna ... z łacińskiego przetłumaczona* (Vilnius, 1640).

Threni in exequias illustrissimae Catharinae Radivilae de Tenczyn ducis in Byrże et Dubingi, palatinae Vilnensis etc. etc. nomine Parthenicae Sodalitatis in Academia Vilnensi Societatis IESV institutae, a praecipua iuventute eiusem Sodalitatis conscripti (Vilnius, 1592).

Triumfo diena: 1611 m. birželio 13 d. Smolensko pergalė ir iškilmingas Zigmanto Vazos sutikimas Vilniuje 1611 m. liepos 24 d. Dies Triumphi. Victoria Sigismundi III die XIII Junti A.D. MDCXI Smolensco expugnato et triumphalis ingressus Vilnom die XXIV Julii A.D. MDCXI celebratus. Day of Triumph. The victory at Smolensk on June 13, 1611 and the ceremonial reception of Sigismund Vasa in Vilnius o July 24, 1611, ed. E. Ulčinaitė and E. Saviščevas (Vilnius, 2011).

Tyszkiewicz, S., *Nowy patron Polski* [The New Patron of Poland, the Blessed Stanisław Kostka] (Vilnius, without date).

Ugniewski, Sz., *Żywot św. Władysława króla węgierskiego* (*The Life of St. Vladislaus the King of Hungary*) by (Vilnius 1630).

Ursinus, J., *Modus epistolandi cum epistolis exemplaribus et orationibus annexis* (*O sposobie pisania listów wraz z wzorami listów i mowami*), ed., trans., and introduction by L. Winniczuk (Wrocław, 1957).

Ver Lukiskanum ad serenissimarum maiestatum præsentiam efflorescens, publicæ felicitatis amaenitatem et minimae Societatis Jesu venerabundam hilaritatem iisdem serenissimis Vladislao IV, et Ludovicæ Marae Poloniarum maiestatibus typo exibet (Vilnius, 1648).

Vilniaus ir Žemaičių katedrų kapitulų statutai [The Statutes of the Chapters of the Bishoprics of Vilnius and Samogitia], ed. W. Pawlikowska-Butterwick and L. Jovaiša (Vilnius, 2015).

Vilnius akademijos spaustuvės šaltiniai XVI-LXIX a. [Sources of the Vilnius Academy Printing House, Sixteenth-Nineteenth Centuries], ed. I. Petrauskienė (Vilnius, 1992).

Volumina legum: Przedruk zbioru praw staraniem księży pijarów w Warszawie od roku 1732 do roku 1782 wydanego, 3 (St Petersburg, 1859).

VORBEK-LETTOW, M., *Skarbnica pamięci: Pamiętnik lekarza króla Władysława IV*, ed. E. GALOS and F. MINCER (Wrocław, 1968).

Vossius, G., *Rhetorices contractae, sive partitionum oratoriarum libri V* (Amsterdam, 1655).

Wigand von Marburg, *Nowa kronika pruska* [The New Chronicle of Prussia], ed. S. ZONENBERG and K. KWIATKOWSKI (Toruń, 2017).

Wijuk Kojałowicz, W., *Copiarum Magni Ducatus Lituaniae adversus Zaporowianos Cozacos anno 1648 et 1649 gesta compendiario narrate* (Vilnius, 1651).

Wijuk Kojałowicz, W., *Fasti Radiviliani gesta illustrissimae domus ducum Radziwił compendio continents* (Vilnius, 1653).

Wijuk Kojałowicz, W., *Institutionum rhetoricarum pars I-II* (Vilnius, 1654).

Wijuk Kojałowicz, W., *Miscellanea rerum ad statum ecclesiasticum in Magno Lituaniae Ducatu pertinentium collecta* (Vilnius, 1650).

Wijuk Kojałowicz, K., *Panegyrici heroum varia antehac manu sparsi nunc ab auctore proprio p. Casimiro Wijuk Kojałowicz Societatis Iesu, sanctae theologiae doctoris in gratiam iuventutis studiosae in unum collecti* (Vilnius, 1668).

Wijuk Kojałowicz, W. (A. Vijūkas-Kojalavičius), *Lietuvos istorijos įvairenybės* [Miscellanies of Lithuanian History], 1, ed. D. KUOLYS, trans. D. ANTANAVIČIUS and S. NARBUTAS (Vilnius, 2003).

Wijuk Kojałowicz, W. (A. Vijūkas-Kojalavičius), *Lietuvos istorijos įvairenybės* [Miscellanies of Lithuanian History], 2, ed. D. KUOLYS, trans. R. Jurgelėnaitė (Vilnius, 2004).

Witanie na pierwszy wjazd z Królewca do Kadłubka Saskiego Wileńskiego Iksa hern Lutermarchra. Drukowano w Witembergu roku 1642 dnia wczorajszego (Vilnius, 1642).

Wituński, A., *Okowy nieśmiertelnej sławy i chwały jego mości pana p. Jerzego Deszpota Zienowicza, starosty opiskiego, pułkownika mężnego i sławnego w dzień pogrzebu ciała jego w kościele wileńskim Franciszka świętego ojców bernadynów praesentowane przez ks. Augustyna Wituńskiego tegoż zakonu i kościoła lektora i kaznodzieje, ojca prowincyi polskiej, dnia 15 Martii 1649* (Vilnius, 1649).

Wituński, A., *Przywilej nieśmiertelności jaśnie wielmożnego i przewielebnego jego mości ks. Abrahama Woyny, biskupa wileńskiego w kościele katedralnym wileńskim w dzień pogrzebu ciała jego tłumaczony przez ks. Augustyna Wituńskiego zakonu Franciszka świętego bernardynów mianowanego prowincyi polskiej ojca i kaznodzieje wileńskiego. Dnia 14 maja roku 1649* (Vilnius, 1649).

Wojsznarowicz, K., *Orator polityczny różnym aktom pogrzebowym służący, nowo na świat w roku 1644 wydany* ([Vilnius], 1644)

Wolan, A., *Ad scurillem et famosum libellum Iesuiticae Scholae Vilnensis et potissimum maledici conviciatoris Andreae Iurgevitii, sacrificuli et canonici Vilnensis* (Vilnius, 1589).

Wolan, A., *Apologia Andreae Volani ad calumnias et convitia pestiferae hominum sectae, qui se falso Iesuitas vocant* (Vilnius, 1587).

Wolan, A., *Assertionum de Eucharistia falsarum cum doctrina apostolica et sententia veteris Ecclesiae pugnantium ab Immanuele Vega Vilnensi Iesuita publicatum confutatio* (Vilnius, 1586).

Wolan, A., *De libertate politica sive civili. O wolności rzeczypospolitej albo ślacheckiej*, ed. M. EDER and R. MAZURKIEWICZ (Warsaw, 2010).

Wolan, A., *Defensio verae orthodoxae veterisque in Ecclesia sententiae de Sacramento Corporis et Sanguinis Domini nostri Iesu Christi, veraque eius in Coena sua praesentia contra novum et commentitium Transubstantionis dogma, aliosque errores ex illo natos ad Petrum Scargam Iesuitam Vilnensem, vanissimi huius commenti propugnatorem (...). Respondentur quoque obiter Francisco Turriano ex* EAD. *factione monacho, qui duobus libris, altero Florentiae, altero Romae publicatis, Scargam sibi suscepit contra Volanum defenendum* (Łosk, 1579).

Wolan, A., *Epistolae Aliquot Ad Refellendum Doctrinae Samosatenianae errorem, ad astruendam Orthodoxam de Divina Trinitate sententiam, hoc tempore lectu non inutiles. Ab Andrea Volano scriptae* (Vilnius, 1592).

Wolan, A., *Idololatriae Loiolitarum Vilnensium oppugnatio. Itemque ad nova illorum obiecta responsio, nunc primum in lucem edita* (Vilnius, 1583).

Wolan, A., *Libri quinque contra Scargae Iesuitae Vilnensis Septem missae sacrificiique eius columnas et librum 12 artium Zwingliocalvinistarum, quibus is, veritatem doctrinae apostolicae et sanctae veteris Ecclesiae de sacramento Coene Domini evertere studet. Adiectae est tam Volani, quam purae religionis sectatorumque eius adversus Antonium Possevinum Iesuitam Romanum defensio, ubi Roma Babylon esse ostenditur*, auctore Iohanne Lasicio Polono ad Medicinae Docorem Hieronimum Filipowski (Vilnius, 1584).

Wolan, A., *Panegyricus illustrissimi principi domino d. Nicolao Christphoro Radivillo. Panegirika Mikalojui Kristupui Radivilai*, trans. E. Ulčinaitė, in: A. Wolan (A. Volanas), *Rinktiniai raštai*, ed. I. LUKŠAITĖ and M. ROČKA (Vilnius, 1996), pp. 241-275.

Wolan, A., *Vera et orthodoxa veteris ecclesiae sententia de Coena Domini ad Petrum Skarga* (Łosk, 1574).

Wujek, J., *Postilla catholica, to jest kazania na kożdą niedzielę i na kożde święto przez cały rok* (Cracow, 1573).

Wykład liturgiej świętej i modlitwy z doktorów św. według św. wschodniej i apostolskiej Cerkwie zebrane i na wielu miejscach z pilnością poprawione. Przydane są do tego i inne modlitwy na kożdy dzień św. ojca naszego Cyrilla i kalendarz dni przez rok idących z Paschalią (Vilnius, 1624).

Zaborowski, S., *Ortographia seu modus recte scribendi et legendi Polonicum idiomaque utilissimus* (Cracow, *c.* 1513).

Zajączkowski, R., *Klucz herbowy w domu Pawłowiczowskim marsowa buława z serca żelaznego jego mości pana pana Adama Łukijańskiego Pawłowicza, rotmistrza i pułkownika odważnego, na karkach nieprzyjacielskich ukowany, a na otwarcie skarbnice wiekuistej tego męża chwały. Na wyprowadzeniu ciała jego z kościoła ojców dominikanów w Wilnie ogłoszony dnia 28 Junii roku Pańskiego 1650 przez ks. Rajmunda Zajączkowskiego dominikona, świętej teologiej stud. fr. et decan* (Vilnius, 1650).

Zajączkowski, W. (M. Śmiglecki?), *Opisanie dysputacyjej nowogródzkiej, którą miał ks. Marcin Śmiglecki Societatis Iesu z Janem Licyniuszem, ministrem nowokrzczeńskim o przedwiecznym bóstwie Syna Bożego. 24 i 25 Ianuarii w roku 1594, wydane przez ks. Wojciecha Zajączkowskiego* (Vilnius, 1594).

Zbiór praw i przywilejów miastu stołecznemu Wielkiego Księstwa Litewskiego Wilnowi nadanych, na żądanie wielu miast koronnych jako też Wielkiego Księstwa Litewskiego ułożony i wydany, ed. P. DUBINOWSKI (Vilnius, 1788) (*The Collection of the Laws and Privileges Granted to the Capital City of the Grand Duchy of Lithuania, Edited and Printed on Demand of Many Towns of the Polish Crown and the Grand Duchy of Lithuania*).

Zizany, S., "Стефана Зизаня Изложеше о православной вѣрѣ. Коротким пытаньем и отповѣданьем для латвѣйшаго вырозумѣня христїянским дѣтем. Странный пытает зловѣрный, а православный благовѣрный отповѣдаеть", in: Наука ку читаню, и розумѣню писма словенского ту тыж о Святой Тройци, и овъчловечеши Господни (Vilnius, 1595).

Żywot przechwalebnego wyznawce świętego Kazimierza królewica polskiego i książęcia litewskiego w Wilnie roku 1606 przez Mateusza Chryzostoma Wolodkiewicza przełożony. Przydane k temu modlitwy nabożne i hymny do św. Kazimierza, ed. J. OKOŃ, K. GARA, and J. RZEGOCKA (Warsaw, 2016).

Żywot przechwalebnego wyznawce świętego Kazimierza królewica polskiego i książęcia litewskiego (...) *Przydane k temu modlitwy nabożne i hymny do św. Kazimierza*, trans. M. Ch. Wołodkiewicz (Vilnius, 1606).

Акты относящіеся к исторіи западной Россіи собраные и изданные Археографическую комиссею, 1-4 (St. Petersburg, 1846-1851).

Акты, издаваемые Виленскою Археографическою коммиссиею, 1-39 (Vilnius, 1865-1915).

Библия Матфея Десятого 1507 года. Из собрания Библиотеки Российской академии наук, 1-2 (Санкт-Петербург, 2020). <https://www.postkomsg.com/reading_room/227714/?fbclid=IwAR1BpDrq5H5X5V5a7K4SPNjsSfAvfjgzCFuvS7TE0iVAYsX1Aq7t0CoKdIE> (accessed 05.02.2022).

Библия Матфея Десятого 1507 года. Из собрания Библиотеки Российской академии наук, 1-2 (Санкт-Петербург, 2020).

Кітехизм или наоука всѣмъ православнымъ хрстїянωм к повученію ввелми полезно з латинского языка и в рускїи языкъ нωво преложоно (Vilnius, 1585).

Катехизисъ албо короткое зебранье вѣры и церемонш Святое Соборное Апостолское Всходнее Церкви", in: *Молитвы повседневные от многих святых отец събраные до которыхъ и Катехизм вѣры предан есть вкоропгѣ* (Vievis, 1611).

Киевская псалтырь 1397 года из Государственной Публичной библиотеки имени М. Е. Салтыкова-Щедрина в Ленинграде [олдп F 6] (Москва, 1978).

Летапісы і хронікі Белорусі. Средневечча і раньемодэрны час (Smolensk, 2013).

Молитви повседневні (Vilnius, 1595).

Областный пинкос еврейских общин Литвы (1623-1761), ed. S. DUBNOW, trans. I. TUVIM, *Еврейская старина*, 1 (St. Petersburg 1909), 2 (St. Petersburg 1912).

Памятники изданные временною коммиссіею для разбора древнихъ актовъ высочайше учрежденною при Кіевскомъ военномъ, Подольскомъ и Волынскомъ Генералъгубернаторъ, 1.1 (Kyiv, 1845).

Сборник палеографических снимков с древних грамот и актов храневшихся в виленском центральном архиве и виленской публичной библиотеке (Vilnius, 1884).

Сборник Русского исторического общества, 35, *Памятники дипломатических сношений древней России с державами иностранными. 1. Памятники дипломатических сношений Московского государства с Польско-Литовским государством в царствование Великого Князя Ивана Васильевича. Part 1 (годы с 1487 по 1533)*, ed. Г.Ф. КАРПОВ (Санкт-Петербург, 1882).

Скарына, Ф., *Малая подорожная книжка* (Vilnius, 1522?).

Собрание древних грамот и актов городов: Вильны, Ковна, Трок, православных монастырей, церквей, и по разным предметам: с приложением трех литографированных рисунков / Zbiór dawnych dyplomatów i aktów miast: Wilna, Kowna, Trok, prawosławnych monasterów, cerkwi i w różnych sprawach, z przyłożeniem trzech rysunków litografowanych, 1 (Vilnius, 1843).

Статут Велікого Князства Літовского от наяснейшего господаря короля его мости Жикгимонта Третего на коронацыи въ Кракове выданы року 1588; digital editions: a) <https://pravo.by/pravovaya-informatsiya/pomniki-gistoryi-prava-belarusi/kanstytutsyynae-prava-belarusi/statuty-vyalikaga-knyastva-litoskaga/statut-1588-goda/po-naya-versiya-tekstu-pdf/>; b) <http://starbel.narod.ru/sapeh1.htm> (accessed 08.12.2021).

Тастаменты шляхты і мяшчан Беларусі другой паловы XVI ст. (з актавых кніг Нацыянальнага гістарычнага архіва Беларусі) [Testaments of the Nobility and Burghers of Belarus from the Second Half of the Sixteenth Century (from the Registers Kept in the National Historical Archives of Belarus], ed. А.Ф. АЛЯКСАНДРАВА, В.У. БАБКОВА, and І.М. БОБЕР (Minsk, 2012).

Literature

ADAMCZYK ,W., *Ceny w Lublinie od XVI do końca XVIII wieku – Les prix à Lublin dès le XVIe siècle jusqu' à la fin du XVIIIe siècle* (Lviv, 1935).

ADAMCZYK, W., *Ceny w Warszawie w XVI i XVII wieku* [Prices in Warsaw in the Sixteenth and Seventeenth Centuries] (Lviv, 1938).

ADAMOWICZ, A.F., *Kościół augsburski w Wilnie: Kronika zebrana na obchód trzechwiekowego istnienia Kościoła w roku 1855 w dzień św. Jana Chrzciciela*

[The Lutheran Church in Vilnius: A Chronicle Created to Celebrate Three Hundred Years of Its Existence in 1855 on St. John Baptist's Day] (Vilnius, 1855).

ADAMSKA, A., *Arengi w dokumentach Władysława Łokietka: Formy i funkcje* [The Arengae in the Charters of Władysław Łokietek: Forms and Functions] (Cracow, 1999).

ADAMSKA, A., L'*Ars dictaminis* a-t-elle été possible en langue vernaculaire? Quelques sondages", in: *Le dictamen dans tous ses états: Perspectives de recherches sur la théorie et la pratique de l'ars dictaminis (XIe-XVe siècle)*, ed. B. GRÉVIN and A.-M. TURCAN-VERKERK (Turnhout, 2015), pp. 389-414.

ADAMSKA, A., Mostert M., "Introduction", in: *Writing and the Administration of Medieval Towns: Medieval Urban Literacy I*, ed. M. MOSTERT and A. ADAMSKA (Turnhout, 2014), pp. 1-10.

ADAMSKA, A., "Słowo władzy i władza słowa: Język polskich dokumentów monarszych doby średniowiecza" [The word of power and the power of the word: The language of Polish monarchic charters in the Middle Ages] , in: *Król w Polsce XIV i XV wieku* [The King in Poland in the Fourteenth and Fifteenth Centuries], ed. A. MARZEC and M. WILAMOWSKI (Cracow, 2007), pp. 57-88.

ADAMSKA, A., "Średniowiecze na nowo odczytane.: O badaniach nad kulturą pisma [The Middle Ages read anew: On the study of written culture]", *Roczniki Historyczne*, 65 (1999), pp. 129-154.

ADAMSKA, A., "Stąd do wieczności: Testament w perspektywie piśmienności pragmatycznej na przełomie średniowiecza i epoki nowożytnej" [From here to eternity: Last wills from the perspective of pragmatic literacy at the turn of the medieval and early modern periods], *Kwartalnik Historii Kultury Materialnej* 61.2 (2013), pp. 185-200.

ADAMSKA, A., "Studying preambles today: A paradigm shift in diplomatic?", in: *Urkundenformeln im Kontext: Formen der Schriftkultur im Ostmitteleuropa des Mittelalters (13.-14. Jahrhundert)*, ed. S. ROSSIGNOL and A. ADAMSKA (Vienna, 2016), pp. 35-45.

ADAMSKA, A., "The Jagiellonians and the written word: Some preliminary remarks about royal literacy in the later Middle Ages", in: *Hofkultur der Jagiellonendynastie und verwandter Fürstenhäuser – The Culture of the Jagiellonian and Related Courts*, ed. U. BORKOWSKA and M. HÖRSCH (Ostfildern, 2010), pp. 153-169.

ADAMSKA, A., "Treści religijne w preambułach polskich dokumentów średniowiecznych" [Religious ideas in the preambles of Polish medieval charters], *Studia Źródłoznawcze* 38 (2000), pp. 1-33.

ADOMAITIS, N., "Jews protest to Lithuania over ancient cemetery", *Reuters*, 22 August 2007, 4:12 PM https://www.reuters.com/article/us-lithuania-jews-idUSL2183316620070822 (accessed: 12.05.2021).

Album zabytków ewangelickich w Wilnie wydany przez Towarzystwo Miłośników Reformacji Polskiej im. Jana Łaskiego [The Album of Lutheran Monuments in Vilnius, Edited by the Jan Łaski Society of Amateurs of the Polish Reformation] (Vilnius, 1929).

ALEXANDROWICZ, S., "Osadnictwo żydowskie na ziemiach litewsko-białoruskich od XV do XIX w. (Cechy szczególne)" [Jewish settlement in the Lithuanian and Bielorusian lands from the fifteenth till the nineteenth century], in: *Świat nie pożegnany: Żydzi na dawnych ziemiach wschodnych Rzeczypospolitej w XVIII-XIX wieku*, ed. K. JASIEWICZ (Warsaw, 2004), pp. 45-63.

ALEXANDROWICZ, S., *Rozwój kartografii Wielkiego Księstwa Litewskiego od XV do poł. XVIII wieku* [The Development of the Cartography of the Grand Duchy of Lithuania from the Fifteenth until the Middle of the Eighteenth Century] (Poznań, 1989).

Alma Mater Vilnensis*: Vilniaus universiteto istorijos bruožai: Kolektyvinė monografia* [*Alma Mater Vilnensis*: Features of the History of Vilnius University: A Collective Monograph] (Vilnius, 2012).

Along the Oral-Written Continuum: Types of Texts, Relations and their Implications, ed. S. RANKOVIC, L. MELVE, and E. MUNDAL (Turnhout, 2010).

ALTBAUER, M, "O języku dokumentów związanych z samorządem żydowskim w Polsce" [On the language of documents relative to Jewish self-government in Poland], in: *Żydzi dawnej Rzeczypospolitej: Materiały z konferencji "Autonomia Żydów w Rzeczypospolitej szlacheckiej"* (Wrocław, 1991), pp. 15-22.

ALVAREZ, L.M., "Convivencia", in: *The Oxford Dictionary of the Middle Ages*, ed. R.E. BJORK (Oxford, 2010) [unpaginated online version].

AMOŠIŪNIENĖ, A., "Roizjaus poetinio talento savitumas" [The peculiarity of Royzius' poetical talent], in: P. RUIZ DE MOROS (Petrus Royzius, Petras Roizijus), *Rinktiniai eilėraščiai* [Selected Poems], ed. and trans. S. NARBUTAS, E. PATIEJŪNIENĖ, and E. ULČINAITĖ (Vilnius, 2008), pp. 19-47.

Ankstyvieji šv. Kazimiero "Gyvenimai" [Early "Lives" of St. Casimir], ed. M. ČIURINSKAS (Vilnius, 2004).

ANTANAVIČIUS, D., "*Cnotliwy Litwin* z 1592 roku. Autorstwo i prowieniencja tekstów źródłowych" [The "*Virtuous Lithuanian*" of the year 1592: Authorship and origins of the sources], *Miscellanea Historico-Archivistica* 21 (2014), pp. 63-91.

ANTANAVIČIUS, D., "Vilniaus vyskupo Valerijono Protasevičiaus 1579 m. kovo testamentas" [The testament of bishop of Vilnius Walerian Protasewicz from March 1579], *Lietuvos istorijos metraštis* 1 (2006), pp. 123-144.

ANTANAVIČIUS, D., "Originalių Lietuvos Metrikos XVI a. knygų sąrašas" [The original *Lithuanian Metrica* of the sixteenth century: The list of registers], *Istorijos šaltinių tyrimai* 4 (2012), pp. 157-184.

ANTONIEWICZ, M., "Pochodzenie episkopatu litewskiego XV-XVI wieku w świetle katalogów biskupów wileńskich" [The social origins of the Lithuanian bishops in the light of the catalogues of the bishops of Vilnius], *Studia Źródłoznawcze* 59 (2001), pp. 47-68.

ARIÈS, Ph., *The Hour of Our Death: The Classic History of Western Attitudes Toward Death over the Last One Thousand Years*, trans. H. WEAVER (New York, 2013).

ASSMANN, J., *Cultural Memory and Early Civilization: Writing, Remembrance, and Political Imagination* (Cambridge, 2011).

AUGUSTYNIAK, U., *Dwór i klientela Krzysztofa Radziwiłła (1585-1640): Mechanizmy patronatu* [The Court and the Clients of Krzysztof Radziwiłł (1585-1640): The Mechanisms of Patronage] (Warsaw, 2001).

AUGUSTYNIAK, U., *Informacja i propaganda w Polsce za Zygmunta III* [Information and Propaganda in Poland during the Reign of Sigismond III] (Warsaw, 1981).

AUGUSTYNIAK, U., *Testamenty ewangelików reformowanych w Wielkim Księstwie Litewskim* [Last Wills of the Reformed Calvinists in the Gand Duchy of Lithuania] (Warsaw, 1992).

AUGUSTYNIAK, U., "Wizerunek Krzysztofa II Radziwiłła jako magnata-ewangelika w świetle jego testamentów" [The image of Krzysztof II Radziwiłł as a Reformed Protestant magnate in the light of his testaments], *Przegląd Historyczny* 81.3-4 (1990), pp. 461-477.

AWIANOWICZ, B.B., "Co faktycznie przedstawiają ilustracje w IX księdze *De perfecta poesi* Macieja Kazimierza Sarbiewskiego?" [What had been really depicted in the illustration of Book IX of *De perfecta poesi* of Maciej Kazimierz Sarbiewski?] , *Barok* 12.1 (2006), pp. 129-142.

AWIANOWICZ, B.B., *Progymnasmata w teorii i praktyce szkoły humanistycznej od końca XV do połowy XVIII wieku: Dzieje nowożytnej recepcji Aftoniosa od Rudolfa Agricoli do Johanna Christopha Gottscheda* [The *Progymnasmata* in the Theory and Practice of the Humanist School from the End of the Fifteenth until the Middle of the Eighteenth Century: The History of the Modern Reception of Aftonios, from Rudolf Agricola until Johann Christoph Gottsched] (Toruń, 2008).

AXER, J., "Problemy kompozycji makaronicznej: Poprzedzający *Pieśni trzy* list Kochanowskiego do Zamoyskiego" [The problem of macaronic composition: The letter of Kochanowski to Zamoyski preceding the *Pieśni trzy*], *Pamiętnik Literacki* 76.3 (1985), pp. 123-134.

BADECKI, K., *Literatura mieszczańska w Polsce XVII wieku: Monografia bibliograficzna* [Urban Literature in Poland in the Seventeenth Century: A Bibliographical Monograph (*sic!*)] (Lviv, 1925).

BAKER, P., *Italian Renaissance Humanism in the Mirror* (Cambridge, 2015).

BAŁABAN, M., *Dawid ben Samuel ha-Lewi*, in: *PSB* 4 (1938), p. 461.

BAŁABAN, M., "Drukarstwo żydowskie w Polsce w XVI w." [Jewish Printing in Poland in the sixteenth century], in: *Pamiętnik Zjazdu Naukowego im. Jana Kochanowskiego w Krakowie 8 i 9 czerwca 1930* (Cracow, 1931), pp. 108-112.

BAŁABAN, M., *Historia Żydów w Krakowie i na Kazimierzu* [The History of the Jews in Cracow and in Kazimierz] (Cracow, 1931).

BALIŃSKI, M., "Andrzej Wolan: Jego życie uczone i publiczne" [Andrzej Wolan: His intellectual and public life], in: M. BALIŃSKI, *Pisma historyczne*, 3 (Warsaw, 1843), pp. 3-136.

BALIŃSKI, M., *Historia miasta Wilna* [History of the City of Vilnius], vols. 1-2 (Vilnius, 1836).

BALIŃSKI, M., "Wielkie Księstwo Litewskie opisane" [A description of the Grand Duchy of Lithuania], in: M. BALIŃSKI and T. LIPIŃSKI, *Starożytna Polska pod względem historycznym, jeograficznym i statystycznym opisana* (Warsaw, 1846), pp. 123-200.

Balsys, R., *Paganism of Lithuanians and Prussians*, 1 (Klaipeda, 2020).

Banionis, E., "Pratarmė" [Foreword], in: *Lietuvos Metrika (1427-1506)* [The *Lithuanian Metrica*], *Knyga no. 5, Užrašymų knyga 5*, ed. E. Banionis (Vilnius 1993), pp. 1-29.

Baranowski, H., *Uniwersytet Wileński 1579-1939: Bibliografia za lata 1945-1982* [The University of Vilnius 1579-1939: Bibliography for the Years 1945-1982] (Wrocław, 1983).

Bardach, J., "Bractwa cerkiewne na ziemiach ruskich Rzeczypospolitej w xvi i xvii wieku" [The Orthodox brotherhoods in the Ruthenian lands of the Polish-Lithuanian Commonwealth in the sixteenth and seventeenth centuries], *Kwartalnik Historyczny* 74.1 (1967), pp. 77-82.

Bardach, J., "O praktyce kancelarii litewskiej za Zygmunta i Starego" [On the work of the Lithuanian chancery in the reign of Sigismund the Old], in: *Studia z ustroju i prawa Wielkiego Księstwa Litewskiego, xiv-xvii w.* (Warsaw and Białystok, 1970), pp. 351-378.

Bardach, J., B. Leśnodorski, and M. Pietrzak, *Historia ustroju i prawa polskiego* [History of the Polish Political System and Law] (Warsaw, 2005).

Baronas, C., and S.C. Rowell, *The Conversion of Lithuania: From Pagan Barbarians to Late Medieval Christians* (Vilnius, 2015).

Baronas, D., "Christians in late pagan, and pagans in early Christian Lithuania: The fourteenth and fifteenth centuries", *Lithuanian Historical Studies* 22 (2018), pp. 161-169.

Bartoszewicz, A., "Kobieta a pismo w miastach późnośredniowiecznej Polski" [Women and the written word in the urban settlement of late medieval Poland], in: *Per mulierem ... Kobieta w dawnej Polsce – w średniowieczu i w dobie staropolskiej*, ed. K. Justyniarska-Chojak and S. Konarska-Zimnicka (Warsaw, 2012), pp. 117-126.

Bartoszewicz, A., *Urban Literacy in Late Medieval Poland*, trans. A.B. Adamska (Turnhout, 2017).

Barycz, H., "Agryppa czy Niniński" [Agryppa or Niniński], *Reformacja w Polsce* 7-8 (1935-1936), pp. 434-437.

Barycz, H., "Daniel z Łęczycy", in: *psb* 4 (1938), pp. 405-406.

Barycz, H., "Kulwieć Abraham (ok. 1510-1545)", in: *psb* 16 (1971), pp. 165-167.

Barycz, H., "Z dziejów jednej książki" [From the history of one book], in: H. Barycz, *Z epoki renesansu, reformacji i baroku: prądy, idee, ludzie, książki* (Warsaw, 1971), pp. 656-660.

Baryczowa, M., "Augustyn Rotundus Mieleski, wójt wileński, pierwszy historyk i apologeta Litwy" [Augustyn Rotundus Mieleski, the *Voigt* of Vilnius, the first historian and apologist of Lithuania], *Ateneum Wileńskie* 10 (1935), pp. 71-96, and 11 (1936), pp. 117-172.

Baryczowa, M., "Rotundus Augustyn", in: *psb* 32 (1989-1991), pp. 315-318.

BAUM, M., "Struktura społeczna wspólnoty benedyktynek poznańskich w XVII-XIX wieku" [The social structure of the sisters of the Poznań Benedictine community in the seventeenth-nineteenth centuries], in: *Nad społeczeństwem staropolskim*, 2, *Polityka i ekonomia – społeczeństwo i wojsko – religia i kultura w XVI-XVIII wieku*, ed. D. WEREDA (Siedlce, 2009), pp. 249-266.

BAUMAN, R., "Verbal arts as performance", *American Anthropologist* 77.2 (1975), pp. 290-311.

BEDNARCZUK, L., *Języki Wielkiego Księstwa Litewskiego na tle porównawczym* [The Languages of the Grand Duchy of Lithuania in a Comparative Perspective] (Vilnius, 1993).

BEDNARCZUK, L., "Nazwy Wilna i jego mieszkańców w dokumentach Wielkiego Księstwa Litewskiego (WKL)" [The names of the city of Vilnius and of its inhabitants in the documentation from the Grand Duchy of Lithuania], *Annales Universitatis Paedagogicae Cracoviensis: Studia Linguistica* 5 (2020), pp. 3-18.

BELZYT, L., *Kraków i Praga około 1600 roku. Porównanie topograficznych i demograficznych aspektów dwóch metropolii Europy Środkowo-Wschodniej* [Cracow and Prague around 1600: A Comparison of the Topography and Demography of Two Metropoles of East Central Europe] (Toruń, 1999).

BEM, K., *Calvinism in the Polish-Lithuanian Commonwealth 1548-1648: The Churches and the Faithful* (Leiden and Boston, 2020).

BENEVOLO, L., *The European City*, trans. C. IPSEN (Oxford and Cambridge, Mass., 1993).

BERENSMEYER, I., *Literary Culture in Early Modern England, 1630-1700: Angles of Contingency* (Berlin and Boston, 2020).

BERKOVITZ, J.R., "Rabbinic culture and halakhah", in: *The Cambridge History of Judaism*, 7, *The Early Modern World, 1500-1815*, ed. J. KARP and A. SUTCLIFFE (Cambridge, 2018), pp. 349-377.

BERNATOWICZ, T., Miles christianus et peregrinus*: Fundacje Mikołaja Radziwiłła "Sierotki" w ordynacji nieświeskiej* [*Miles christianus et peregrinus*: The Pious Foundations of Mikołaj Radziwiłł "The Orphan" in the Estate of Nieśwież] (Warsaw, 1998).

BERSOHN, M., *Słownik biograficzny uczonych Żydów polskich XVI, XVII i XVIII wieku* [Biographical Dictionary of Learned Polish Jews from the Sixteenth, Seventeenth, and Eighteenth Centuries] (Warsaw, 1906).

Bibliotheca Sapiehana *Vilniaus universiteto bibliotekos rinkinys: Katalogas* [The *Bibliotheca Sapiehana* in the Collection of the University Library in Vilnius: A Catalogue], ed. A. Rinkūnaitė (Vilnius, 2010).

BIEŃKOWSKI, T., "*Bibliotheca selecta de Ratione studiorum* Possewina jako teoretyczny fundament kultury kontrreformacji" [The *Bibliotheca selecta de Ratione studiorum* of Antonio Possevino as a theoretical framework of the culture of the Counter-Reformation], in: *Wiek XVII – Kontrreformacja – Barok: Prace z historii kultury*, ed. J. PELC (Wrocław, 1970), pp. 191-207.

BIRŽIŠKA, V., *Aleksandrynas: senųjų lietuvių rašytojų, rašiusių prieš 1865 m., biografijos, bibliografijos ir*, 1, *XVI-XVII amžiai biobibliografijos* [Aleksandrynas: Biographies, Bibliographies and Bio-Bibliographies of Old Lithuanian Authors Who Wrote before 1865, 1, Biograms from the Sixteenth and Seventeenth Centuries] (Chicago, 1960).

Biskupstwo, wileńskie od jego założenia aż do dni obecnych, zawierające dzieje i prace biskupów i duchowieństwa diecezji wileńskiej oraz wykaz kościołów, klasztorów, szkół i zakładów dobroczynnych i społecznych [The Bishopric of Vilnius from Its Foundation until Today, Including History and Works of the Bishops and the Diocesan Clergy as well as the List of the Churches, Monasteries, Schools and Charitable and Social Institutions], ed. J. KURCZEWSKI (Vilnius, 1912).

BRIEDIS, L., *Vilnius: City of Strangers* (Vilnius, 2010).

BŁASZCZAK, G., "Regesty dokumentów diecezji wileńskiej z lat 1507-1522 Jana Fijałka i Władysława Semkowicza"[The regesta of charters of the Vilnius bishopric from the period 1507-1522 prepared by Jan Fijałek and Władysław Semkowicz], *Lituano-Slavica Posnaniensia* 9 (2003), pp. 247-299.

BOGDAŃSKA, A.M., "Studium cmentarza żydowskiego Galicji Wschodniej na przykładzie kirkutu w Lutowiskach" [A study of a Jewish cemetery in Eastern Galicia on the example of the cemetery of Lutowiska] , in: *Pogranicza Galicji. Studia*, ed. T. BUJNICKI and J. NIEDŹWIEDŹ (Bielsko-Biała, 2005), pp. 7-23.

BOGUCKA, M., *Kazimierz Jagiellończyk i jego czasy* [Kazimir Jagiellon and His Times] (Warsaw, 1981).

BOGUCKA, M., and H. SAMSONOWICZ, *Dzieje miast i mieszczaństwa w Polsce przedrozbiorowej* [A History of Towns and Town-Dwellers in Poland before the Partitions] (Wrocław, 1986).

BÖMELBURG, H.-J., *Polska myśl historyczna a humanistyczna historia narodowa (1500-1700)* [Polish Historical Thinking and the Humanist National Historiography (1500-1700), trans. Z. OWCZAREK, with an introduction by A. LAWATA (Cracow, 2011); trans. of: ID., *Das polnische Geschichtsdenken und die Reichweite einer humanistischen Nationalgeschichte (1500-1700)* (Wiesbaden, 2007).

BORAWSKI, P., *Tatarzy w dawnej Rzeczypospolitej* [Tatars in the Polish-Lithuanian Commonwealth] (Warsaw, 1986).

BORAWSKI, P., and A. DUBIŃSKI, *Tatarzy polscy: Dzieje, obrzędy, legendy, tradycje* [The Tatars in Poland: History, Rituals, Legends, Traditions] (Warsaw, 1986).

BORAWSKI, P., W. SIENKIEWICZ, and T. WASILEWSKI, "Rewizja dóbr tatarskich 1631 r. – sumariusz i wypisy" [The scrutiny of the Tatar Properties of 1631: Summary and excerpts], *Acta Baltico-Slavica* 20 (1991), pp. 59-135.

BORKOWSKA, M., "Córki chłopskie w polskich klasztorach epoki potrydenckiej" [Daughters of peasants in the Polish monasteries in the post-Tridentine period] , *Nasza Przeszłość* 101 (2004), pp. 315-330.

BORKOWSKA, M., *Dekret w niebieskim ferowany testamencie*: *Wybór testamentów z XVII-XVIII wieku* [A Sentence Pronounced in the Heavenly Will: A Selection of Last Wills from the Seventeenth and Eighteenth Centuries] (Warsaw, 1984).

BORKOWSKA, U., *Dynastia Jagiellonów w Polsce* [The Jagiellon Dynasty in Poland] (Warsaw, 2011).

BORKOWSKA, U., "Edukacja Jagiellonow" [The Education of the Jagiellonian Dynasty], *Roczniki Historyczne* 71 (2005), pp. 99-119.

BORKOWSKA, U., *Królewskie modlitewniki: Studium z kultury religijnej epoku Jagiellonów (XV i początku XVI wieku)* [Royal Prayer Books: A Study of the Religious Culture in the Jagiellonian Period (the Fifteenth and Early Sixteenth Century] (Lublin, 1999).

BORKOWSKA, M., *Panny siostry w świecie sarmackim* [The Sisters in the Sarmatian World] (Warsaw, 2002).

BORKOWSKA, M., "Problemy siedemnastowiecznych fundacji benedyktynek na Litwie w świetle korespondencji. Wybór listów" [Issues of the seventeenth-century foundations of Benedictine nuns in Lithuania: A selection of letters], *Nasza Przeszłość* 80 (1993), pp. 285-307.

BORKOWSKA, U., "*Theatrum Ceremoniale* at the Polish court as a system of social and political communication", in: *The Development of Literate Mentalities in East Central Europe*, ed. A. ADAMSKA and M. MOSTERT (Turnhout, 2004), pp. 431-450.

BORKOWSKA, M., *Życie codzienne polskich klasztorów żeńskich w XVII-XVIII wieku* [Daily Life of the Polish Female Monasteries in the Seventeenth and Eighteenth Centuries] (Warsaw, 1996).

BOURDIEU, P., *Distinction: A Social Critique of the Judgement of Taste*, trans. R. NICE (Cambridge, Mass., 1984).

BOURDIEU, P., *The Rules of Art: Genesis and Structure of the Literary Field*, trans. S. EMANUEL (Stanford, 1996).

BOWDEN, C., "Women in educational spaces", in: *The Cambridge Companion to Early Modern Women's Writing*, ed. L. LUNGER KNOPPERS (Cambridge, 2009), pp. 85-96.

BRAGONE, M.C., "Introduzione", in: *Alfavitar radi učenija malych detej – Un abbecedario nella Russia del Seicento*, ed. M.C. BRAGONE (Florence, 2008), pp. 11-22.

BRAZIŪNIENĖ, A., "*Bibliotheca Sapiehana* – europinės LDK kultūros veidrodis: *Bibliotheca Sapiehana* as a mirror of European culture of Grand Duchy of Lithuania", in: *Bibliotheca Sapiehana Vilniaus universiteto bibliotekos rinkinys. Katalogas* [*Bibliotheca Sapiehana* in the Collection of the Vilnius University Library: A Catalogue], ed. A. RINKŪNAITĖ (Vilnius, 2010), pp. VII-XLIII.

BRENSZTEJN, M., *Zarys dziejów ludwisarstwa na ziemiach b. Wielkiego Księstwa Litewskiego* [A Sketch of the History of the Foundry in the Grand Duchy of Lithuania] (Vilnius, 1924).

BRÜCKNER, A., "Literatura wyznaniowa litewska" [Lithuanian religious literature], *Reformacja w Polsce* 2 (1922), pp. 125-126.

BRÜCKNER, A. "Z polsko-litewskich dziejów wyznaniowych" [From Polish-Lithuanian Religious History], *Reformacja w Polsce* 2 (1922), pp. 256-265.

BRÜCKNER, A., "Z literatury sowizdrzalskiej" [From the chapbook literature], *Pamiętnik Literacki*, 12 (1913), pp. 99-102.

BRZOZOWSKA, A., *Biskup płocki Erazm Ciołek (1474-1522)* [Erazm Ciołek, bishop of Płock (1474-1522] (Cracow, 2017).

BRZOZOWSKA, A., "Erasmi Vitellii, episcopi Plocensis et oratoris regis Poloniae, litterae binae ad Bernardinum Clesium nunc primum editae", *Humanistica Lovaniensia* 62 (2013), pp. 281-296.

BUCHWALD-PELCOWA, P., "Z dziejów druku kancjonałów litewskich i cenzury kościelnej w XVII wieku" [From the history of printing of the Lithuanian hymnals and ecclesiastical censorship in the seventeenth century], *Rocznik Biblioteki Narodowej* 4 (1968), pp. 181-195.

BUEL, L., *New England Literary Culture: From Revolution through Renaissance* (Cambridge and New York, 1986).

BUJNICKI, T., "Miasto w tyglu kultur" [A city in the melting-pot of cultures], in: *Wilno literackie na styku kultur*, ed. T. BUJNICKI and K. ZAJAS (Cracow, 2007), pp. 5-10.

BUJNICKI, T., *W Wielkim Księstwie Litewskim i w Wilnie* [In the Grand Duchy of Lithuania and in Vilnius] (Warsaw, 2010).

BUKOWIEC, P., "From Baranowski to Baranauskas, From James to Ngũgĩ: Post-colonial aspects of linguistic switch", *Studia Interkulturowe Europy Środkowo-Wschodniej* 13 (2020), pp. 219-243.

BUKOWIEC, P., "Mała tożsamość: Esej na marginesie *Leśnika* Marii Kuncewiczowej" [A micro-scale identity: An essay in the margin of the "Leśnik" of Maria Kuncewiczowa], in: *Etniczność, tożsamość, literatura*, ed. P. BUKOWIEC and D. SIWOR (Cracow, 2010), pp. 246-258.

BUKOWIEC, P., "O potrzebie ujęć subwersywnych w badaniach nad pograniczem" [On the need for subversive approaches to the study of borderlands], *Wielogłos* 20.2 (2014), pp. 81-90.

BUKOWIEC, P., *Różnice w druku: Studium z dziejów wielojęzycznej kultury literackiej na XIX-wiecznej Litwie* [Differences in Print: A Study from the History of Multilingual Literary Culture in Nineteenth-Century Lithuania] (Cracow, 2017).

BUOŽYTĖ, (Terleckienė) E., "Kodėl vystyklėliuose jo kiaulės nesurijo: Balcerio Wilkowskio laiškas sūnui (1584)" [Why Have the Swines not Devoured Him in His Swaddling Clothes? A Letter Sent by Balcer Wilkowski to His Son (1584)], *Literatūra*, 60.1 (2018), pp. 142-160.

BURCKHARDT, J., *The Civilization of the Renaissance in Italy*, trans. S. MIDDLEMORE (New York, 2010).

BURGERS, J., and M. MOSTERT, "O fałszerstwach dokumentów w średniowiecznej Holandii" [On the falsifications of charters in medieval Holland], trans. A. ADAMSKA, *Roczniki Historyczne* 69 (2003), pp. 49-70.

BURKE, M.E., J. DONAWERTH, L.L. DOVE, and K. NELSON, "Introduction", in: *Women, Writing and the Reproduction of Culture in Tudor and Stuart Britain*, ed. M.E. BURKE, J. DONAWERTH, L.L. DOVE, and K. NELSON (Syracuse, 2000), pp. XVII-XXX.

BURKE, P., *The Italian Renaissance: Culture and Society in Italy* (Princeton, 1986).

BURSCHE, E., "Nieznany poemat wileński o konfederacji warszawskiej" [An unknown narrative poem from Vilnius about the Confederation of Warsaw], *Reformacja w Polsce* 3 (1924), pp. 271-291.

BUSZEWICZ, E., *De acuto ac arguto / O poincie i dowcipie* [*De accuto ac arguto*: On the punchline and humor], In: *Lektury polonistyczne: Retoryka a tekst literacki*, 1, ed. M. HANCZAKOWSKI and J. NIEDŹWIEDŹ (Cracow, 2003), pp. 23-52.

BUSZEWICZ, E., *Sarmacki Horacy i jego liryka: Imitacja – Gatunek – Styl: Rzecz o poezji Macieja Kazimierza Sarbiewskiego* [The Sarmatian Horace and His Lyric Poetry: Imitation – Genre – Style: A Study about Poetry of M.K. Sarbiewski] (Cracow, 2006).

BURSCHE, E., "W sprawie autorstwa *Apologeticusa*" [On the authorship of the "*Apologeticus*"], *Reformacja w Polsce*, 7-8 (1935-1936), pp. 428-434.

BUSZEWICZ, E., and J. NIEDŹWIEDŹ, "Wstęp" [Introduction] to: J. KAL, "*Religionis, Reipublicae, Vilnae, Collegii et omnium ordinum gratulatio*: Radość i powinszowania Religii, Rzeczypospolitej, Wilna, Kolegium oraz wszystkich stanów", in: *"Umysł stateczny i w contach gruntowny": Prace edytorskie poświęcone profesorowi Adamowi Karpińskiemu*, ed. R. GRZEŚKOWIAK, R. KRZYWY, and A. MASŁOWSKA-NOWAK (Warsaw, 2012), pp. 17-22.

CAMARGO, M., *Ars Dictaminis, Ars Dictandi* (Tunhout, 1991).

CAMARGO, M., "Epistolary declamation: Performing model letters in medieval English classrooms", *Huntington Library Quarterly* 79.3 (2016), pp. 348-351.

CAMMAROSANO, P., "L'éloquence laïque dans l'Italie communale (fin du XIIe-XIVe siècle)", *Bibliothèque de l'École des Chartes* 158.2 (2000), pp. 431-442.

CANNON, C., "Enclosure", in: *The Cambridge Companion to Medieval Women's Writing*, ed. C. DINSHAW and D. WALLACE (Cambridge, 2003), pp. 109-123.

ČAPAITĖ, R., *Gotikinis kursvas Lietuvos dzidžiojo kunigaikščio Vytauto raštinėje* [Gothic Cursive in the Chancery of Grand Duke Vytautas] (Vilnius, 2007).

ČAPAITĖ, R., "XV-XVI amžiaus humanistinio kursyvo terminijos problemos" [Terminological problems of the Humanist cursive of the fifteenth and sixteenth centuries], *Praeities pėdsakais* 52 (2007), pp. 83-99.

ČAPLINSKAS, A.R., *Vilniaus gatvių istorija: Šv. Jono, Dominikonų, Trakų gatvės* [The History of the Streets of Vilnius: St John, Dominican, and Trakai Streets] (Vilnius, 1998).

ČAPLINSKAS, A.R., *Vilniaus gatvių istorija: Valdovų kelias: Pirma knyga: Rūdninkų gatvė* [The History of the Streets of Vilnius: Part One: The Royal Route: Rūdninkai Street] (Vilnius, 2001).

ČAPLINSKAS, A.R., *Vilniaus gatvių istorija: Valdovų kelias: Antra knyga: Didžioji gatvė* [The History of the Streets of Vilnius: Part Two: The Royal Route: Great Street] (Vilnius, 2002).

ČAPLINSKAS, A.R., *Vilniaus gatvių istorija: Valdovų kelias: Trečia knyga: Pilies gatvė* [The History of the Streets of Vilnius: Part Three: The Royal Route: Castle Street] (Vilnius, 2005).

ČEPIENĖ, K., and I. PETRAUSKIENĖ, *Vilniaus Akademijos spaustuvės leidiniai 1576 1805. Bibliografija* [Publications of the Vilnius Academy Printing House 1576-1805: A Bibliography] (Vilnius, 1979).

CHEMPEREK, D., "Jan Karol Chodkiewicz – *miles Christianus* i obrońca ojczyzny: Wstęp historycznoliteracki" [Jan Karol Chodkiewicz – *miles Christianus* and defender of the homeland: Historical and literary introduction], in: F. MAŁKOT, *Tureckich i iflanskich wojen o sławnej pamięci Janie Karolu Chodkiewiczu głos – Karų su turkais ir Livonijoje balsas apie šlovingo atminimo Joną Karolį Chodkevičių*, ed. D. ANTANAVIČIUS, D. CHEMPEREK, and Ė. PATIEJŪNIENĖ (Warsaw, 2016), pp. 47-61.

CHEMPEREK, D., "Siedm filarów Piotra Skargi: Geneza i aspekt retoryczny" [The seven pillars of Piotr Skarga: Their origins and rhetoric], *Ruch Literacki* 54.4-5 (2013), pp. 425-437.

CHEMPEREK, D., "Środowisko literackie protestantów w Wilnie pierwszej połowy XVII wieku.: Krąg pisarzy zborowych" [The literary environment of Vilnius Protestants in the first half of the seventeenth century: The circles of writers from the Protestant congregations], *Wschodni Rocznik Humanistyczny* 4 (2007), pp. 43-52.

CHEMPEREK, D., "Wileńscy luteranie w świetle XVII-wiecznych satyr jezuickich (1620-1642): Wydarzenia, bohaterowie, autorzy" [The Lutherans in Vilnius in the light of the seventeenth-century Jesuit satirical texts], *Terminus* 19.2 (2017), pp. 277-308.

CHORĄŻYCZEWSKI, W., "Kancelarie centralne państwa w XIV-XVIII wieku" [The central chanceries of the State in the fourteenth-seventeenth centuries], In: *Dyplomatyka staropolska*, ed. T. JUREK (Warsaw, 2015), pp. 145-188.

CHROŚCICKI, J.A., *Sztuka i polityka: Funkcje propagandowe sztuki w epoce Wazów, 1587-1668* [Art and Politics: The Propaganda Functions of Art in the Period of the Wasa dynasty, 1587-1668] (Warsaw, 1983).

CHYNCZEWSKA-HENNEL, T., *Nuncjusz i król: Nuncjatura Maria Filonardiego w Rzeczypospolitej 1636-1643)* [The Nuntio and the King: The Nuncio Period of Mari Filonardi in the Polish Republic, 1636-1643] (Warsaw, 2006).

CHYNCZEWSKA-HENNEL, T., "'Ruś zostawić w Rusi': W odpowiedzi Sławomirowi Gawlasowi i Hieronimowi Grali" ["'To leave Rus' in Rus'": In response to Sławomir Gawlas and Hieronim Grala], *Przegląd Historyczny* 78.3 (1987), pp. 533-546.

CICĖNIENĖ, R., "Rankraštinė knyga – Istorijos šaltinis: Vieno LDK kodekso istorija" [A manuscript book – A historical source: The history of one codex from the Grand Duchy of Lithuania], *Knygotyra* 63 (2014), pp. 99-128.

CIESIELSKI, S., and A. SREBRAKOWSKI, "Przesiedlenie ludności z Litwy do Polski w latach 1944-1947" [The resettlement of the population from Lithuania to Poland in the period 1944-1947], *Wrocławskie Studia Wschodnie* 4 (2000), pp. 227-253.

CIEŚLA, M., "The other townsfolk: The legal status and social positions of the Jews in cities of the Grand Duchy of Lithuania in the seventeenth and eighteenth centuries". In: *Religion in the Mirror of Law Eastern European Perspectives from the*

Early Modern Period to 1939, ed. Y. KLEINMANN, S. STACH, and T.L. WILSON (Frankfurt am Main, 2016), pp. 307-328.

CIEŚLA, M., "Żydzi a Rzeczpospolita" [Jews and Poland], in: *Społeczeństwo nowożytnej Rzeczypospolitej wobec państwa*, ed. W. KRIEGSEISEN (Warsaw, 2016), pp. 259-285.

CLANCHY, M.T., *From Memory to Written Record: England 1066-1307*, second edn. (Oxford, 1993).

CLANCHY, M., *Looking Back from the Inventing of Printing: Mothers and the Teaching of Reading in the Middle Ages* (Turnhout, 2018).

CLASSEN, A., *The Power of a Woman's Voice in Medieval and Early Modern Literatures: New Approaches to German and European Women Writers and to Violence Against Women in Premodern Times* (Berlin and New York, 2007).

COHEN, I., *History of the Jews in Vilnius* (Philadelphia, 1943).

COLE, J., "Cultural clientelism and brokerage networks in early modern Florence and Rome: New correspondence between the Barberini and Michelangelo Buonarroti the Younger", *Renaissance Quarterly* 60 (2007), pp. 729-788.

CUBRZYŃSKA-LEONARCZYK, M., "O początkach drukarstwa w Supraślu" [On the beginnings of the printing press in Supraśl], in: *Z badań nad dawną książką: Studia ofiarowane profesor Alodii Kaweckiej-Gryczowej w 85-lecie urodzin*, 1, ed. P. BUCHWALD-PELCOWA (Warsaw, 1991), pp. 173-202.

CUBRZYŃSKA-LEONARCZYK, M., *Oficyna supraska 1695-1803: Dzieje i publikacje unickiej drukarni ojców bazylianów* [The Printing House of Supraśl 1695-1803: The History and Publications of the Uniate Printing House of the Basilian Monks] (Warsaw, 1993).

Cultures of Religious Reading in the Late Middle Ages, ed. S. CORBELLINI (Turnhout, 2013).

CURTIUS, E.R., *European Literature and the Latin Middle Ages*, trans. W.R. TRASK, introduction C. BURROW (Princeton and Oxford, 1983).

CYGIELMAN, Sz.A.A., "Zagadnienia organizacji i programów nauczania szkolnictwa podstawowego w krakowskiej gminie żydowskiej na przełomie XVI i XVII w." [The question of the organisation and teaching programs of the elementary schools of the Jewish community in Cracow at the turn of the seventeenth century], in: *Żydzi w dawnej Rzeczypospolitej: Materiały konferencji "Autonomia Żydów w Rzeczypospolitej szlacheckiej": Międzywydziałowy Zakład Historii i Kultury Żydów w Polsce: Uniwersytet Jagielloński, 22-26 IX 1986*, ed. A. LINK-LENCZOWSKI and T. POLAŃSKI (Wrocław, 1991), pp. 284-296.

CYTOWSKA, M., *Bibliografia druków urzędowych XVI wieku* [Bibliography of the Official Prints from the Sixteenth Century] (Wrocław, 1961).

CZAPLIŃSKI, P., "Słowo i głos" [Word and Voice], in: *Literatura oralna*, ed. P. CZAPLIŃSKI (Gdańsk, 2010), pp. 5-32.

CZYŻ, R., *Obrona wiary w edycjach postylli Grzegorza z Żarnowca* [The Defence of the Faith in the Postils of Grzegorz of Żarnowiec] (Warsaw, 2008).

DAINORA POCIŪTĖ-ABUKEVIČIENĖ, D., "Martynas Mažvydas' Catechism: Tradition and signs of a new consciousness", In: *Martynas Mažvydas and Old Lithuania (Collection of Papers)*, ed. D. KAUNAS *et al.*, trans. D. BARTKUTĖ (Vilnius, 1998), pp. 141-157.

DANBURY, E., "The study of illuminated charters, past, present and future: Some thoughts from England", in: *Illuminierte Urkunden: Beiträge aus Diplomatik, Kunstgeschichte und Digital Humanities – Illuminated Charters: Essays from Diplomatic, Art History and Digital Humanities*, ed. G. BARTZ and M. GREIß (Cologne, 2018: *Archiv für Diplomatik: Beihefte* 16), pp. 259-280.

DANYLENKO, A., "A missing chain? On the sociolinguistics of the Grand Duchy of Lithuania, *Acta Baltico-Slavica* 41 (2017), pp. 31-57.

DAROWSKI, R., "First Aristotelians of Vilnius", *Organon* 15 (1979), pp. 71-91.

DAROWSKI, R., "Pedro Viana SJ (1549-1609) et son activité de philosophie en Lituanie", *Forum Philosophicum* 3 (1998), pp. 199-201.

DAUKŠIENĖ, O., "Sigismundus Laetus – Žygimantas Liauksminas? Apie kai kuriuos paslaptingus Sarbievijaus odžių adresatus" [Sigismundus Laetus – Sigismundus Lauxmin? About some mysterious recipients of Sarbiewski's odes], *Senoji Lietuvos Literatūra* 44 (2017), pp. 53-72.

DAWIDOWICZ, L.S., *From That Place and Time: A Memoir, 1938-1947* (New York, 1989).

DE VRIES, S.Ph., *Obrzędy i symbole Żydów* [Rituals and Symbols of the Jews], trans. A. BOROWSKI (Cracow, 1999).

DEL BARCO, J., "From scroll to codex: Dynamics of text; Layout transformation in the Hebrew Bible", in: *From Scrolls to Scrolling: Sacred Texts, Materiality, and Dynamic Media Cultures*, ed. B.A. ANDERSON (Berlin and Boston, 2012), pp. 91-118.

DELIMATA-PROCH, M., "Choroby w świetle księgi cudów i łask Matki Bożej Świętogórskiej (XVI-XVIII w.)" [Ilnesses in the light of the Book of Miracles and Graces by the Virgin Mary of Święta Góra], *Kwartalnik Historii Kultury Materialnej*, 66/3 (2018), pp. 271-287.

DELLE DONNE, F., "Dalle lettere cancelleresche ai dictamina: Processi di finzionalizzazione e tradizione testuale", in: *Medieval Letters Between Fiction and Document*, ed. Ch. HØGEL and E. BARTOLI (Turnout, 2015), pp. 393-405.

DEROLEZ, A., *The Palaeography of Gothic Manuscript Books: From the Twelfth to the Early Sixteenth Century* (Cambridge, 2006).

DILYTĖ, D., "Alberto Vijūko-Kojalavičiaus Lietuvos istorijos kalbos" [Speeches in the *History of Lithuania* by Wojciech Wijuk Kojałowicz], *Senoji Lietuvos literatūra* 27 (2009), pp. 118-133.

DIRSYTĖ, R., "Kolekcja pergaminów ze zbiorów Litewskiej Biblioteki Narodowej im. Marynasa Mažvydasa" [The collection of parchment documents in the Martynas Mažvydas National Library of Lithuania], *Biliotheca Nostra: Śląski Kwartalnik Naukowy* 41.3 (2015), pp. 10-44.

DMITRUK, K., "Kultura literacka" [Literary culture], in: *Słownik literatury staropolskiej. Średniowiecze, renesans, barok* [Dictionary of Old-Polish Literature:

Middle Ages, Renaissance, Baroque], ed. T. MICHAŁOWSKA, B. OTWINOWSKA, and E. SARNOWSKA-TEMERIUSZ (Wrocław, 1998), pp. 426-440.

DMITRUK, K., *Literatura – społeczeństwo – przestrzeń: Przemiany układu kultury literackiej* [Literature – Society – Space: Changes in the Structure of Literary Culture][(Wrocław, 1980).

DMITRUK, K.M., "Wokół teorii i historii mecenatu" [Concerning the theory and history of patronage], in: *Z dziejów mecenatu kulturalnego w Polsce*, ed. J. KOSTECKI (Warsaw, 1999), pp. 11-31.

DOMAŃSKI, J., *Tekst jako uobecnienie: Szkic z dziejów myśli o piśmie i książce* [Text as Presence: An Essay from the History of Ideas about Script and Book] (Warsaw, 1992).

DOVILĖ, K., "*Desiderium videndi*: Barboros Zapolijos ir Žygimanto Senojo korespondencija" [*Desiderium videndi*: Correspondence of Barbara Zápolya and Sigismund the Old], *Senoji Lietuvos Literatūra* 47 (2019), pp. 15-55.

DRĖMA, V., *Vilniaus bažnyčios: Iš Vlado Drėmos archyvų* [The Churches of Vilnius: From the Archive of Vladas Drėma](Vilnius, 2008).

DROB, J., "Drukowane kazania franciszkańskie w XVI-XVII wieku" [Printed Franciscan sermons in the sixteenth and seventeenth centuries], In: *Franciszkanie w Polsce XVI-XVIII wieku*, 1, ed. H. GAPSKI and C.S. NAPIÓRKOWSKI (Niepokalanów, 1998), pp. 320-338.

Drukarze dawnej Polski od XV do XVIII wieku [The Printers of Old Poland from the Fifteenth to the Eighteenth Centuries], 1, *Małopolska* [Little Poland], 1, *Wiek XV-XVI* [The Fifteenth and Sixteenth Centuries], ed. A. KAWECKA-GRYCZKOWA (Wrocław, 1983).

Drukarze dawnej Polski od XV do XVIII wieku [The Printers of Old Poland from the Fifteenth to Eighteenth Centuries], 4, *Pomorze* [Pomerania], ed. A. KAWECKA-GRYCZOWA and K. KOROTAJOWA (Wrocław, 1962).

Drukarze dawnej Polski od XV do XVIII wieku [The Printers of Old Poland from the Fifteenth to Eighteenth Centuries], 5, *Wielkie Księstwo Litewskie* [The Grand Duchy of Lithuania], ed. A. KAWECKA-GRYCZOWA, K. KOROTAJOWA, amd W. KRAJEWSKI (Wrocław, 1959).

DRZYMAŁA, K., "Lata szkolne i profesorskie ks. Marcina Śmigleckiego T.J." [The period of school and professorial work of the venerable Marcin Śmiglecki, SJ], in: *Sprawozdanie Dyrekcji Zakładu Naukowo-Wychowawczego OO. Jezuitów w Bąkowicach pod Chyrowem za rok szkolny 1937/38* [Report of the Directorate of the Jesuits Fathers' Teaching and Educational Institutiom in Bąkowice near Chyrów for the School Year 1927/38] (Bąkowice, 1938), pp. 37-38.

DUBONIS, A., "Duomenys apie mokslo kainą Vilniuje (XVI a. pradžia)" [Sources for the study of the costs of education in Vilnius (the beginning of the sixteenth century)], in: *Lietuvos miestų istorijos šaltiniai* [Sources for Lithuanian Urban History], 3, pp. 255-257.

DUBONIS, A., D. ANTANAVIČIUS, R. RAGAUSKIENĖ, and R., ŠMIGELSKYTĖ-STUKIENĖ, *Susigrąžinant praeitį: Lietuvos Metrikos istorija ir tyrimai* [Recovering the Past: The History and Study of the *Lithuanian Metrica*] (Vilnius, 2016).

DUBONIS, A., D. ANTANAVIČIUS, R. RAGAUSKIENĖ, and R. ŠMIGELSKYTĖ-STUKIENĖ, *The Lithuanian Metrica: History and Research* (Boston, USA, 2020).

DÜRR-DURSKI, J., *Daniel Naborowski: Monografia z dziejów manieryzmu i baroku w Polsce* [Daniel Naborowski: A Monograph from the History of Mannerism and Baroque in Poland] (Łódź, 1966).

DYJAKOWSKA, M., "*Decisiones Lituanicae* Piotra Rojzjusza – Przykład renesansowego źródła poznania stosowania prawa rzymskiego przed sądem asesorskim w Wilnie: Problemy badawcze i translatorskie" [The *Decisiones Lituanicae* of Piotr Rozjusz – An example of a Renaissance source for the investigation of the practice of Roman Law in the assessor court in Vilnius: Issues of research and translation], *Krakowskie Studia z Historii Państwa i Prawa* 13.1 (2020), pp. 1-15.

DYJAKOWSKA, M., "Prawo rzymskie jako kryterium interpretacyjne w *Decisiones Lituanicae* Piotra Rojzjusza" [Roman law as a factor of interpretation in the *Decisiones Litanicae* of Piotr Rozjusz], *Z Dziejów Prawa* 12 (2019), pp. 109-123.

Dyplomatyka staropolska [Old Polish Diplomatic], ed. T. JUREK (Warsaw, 2015).

DZIĘGIELEWSKI, J., *Pociej Adam Hipacy (1541-1613)*, in: PSB 27 (1982-1983), pp. 18-34.

ECO, U., "Introduction: The role of the reader", in: U. ECO, *The Role of the Reader: Explorations in the Semiotics of Texts* (Bloomington, 1979), pp. 200-260.

Encyclopedia wiedzy o książce [The Encyclopedia of the Sciences of Book], ed. A. KAWECKA-GRYCZOWA, H. WIĘCKOWSKA, and S. PAZYRA (Wrocław, 1971).

Encyklopedia wiedzy o jezuitach na ziemiach Polski i Litwy 1564-1995 [The Encyclopedia of Jesuits in the Polish and Lithuanian Lands, 1564-1995] , ed. L. GRZEBIEŃ (Cracow, 1996).

Epistolografia w dawnej Rzeczypospolitej [Epistolography in the Polish-Lithuanian Commonwealth], ed. P. BOREK and M. OLMA (Cracow, 2014).

FABIANI, B., *Życie codzienne na Zamku Kólewskim w epoce Wazów* [Daily Life at the Royal Castle [of Warsaw] in the Vasa period] (Warsaw, 1996).

FABRE, P. A., "Dépouilles d'Egypte: L'expurgation des auteurs latins dans les collèges jésuites", in: *Les jésuites à la Renaissance: Système éducatif et production du savoir*, ed. L. GIARD (Paris, 1995), pp. 55-73.

FABRE, P.-A., "The writings of Ignatius of Loyola as seminal text", in: *A Companion to Ignatius of Loyola: Life, Writings, Spirituality, Influence*, ed. R.A. MARYKS (Leiden, 2014), pp. 103-122.

FALNIOWSKA-GRADOWSKA, A., "Wstęp" [Introduction], in: *Testamenty szlachty krakowskiej XVII-XVIII w.: Wybór tekstów źródłowych z lat 1650-1799* [The Last Wills of the Nobility of the Cracow Voivodeship from the Seventeenth and Eighteenth Centuries: A Selection of the Sources from 1650-1799], ed. A. FALNIOWSKA-GRADOWSKA (Cracow, 1997), pp. V-XXII.

FAULHABER, Ch.B., "The letter-writer's rhetoric: the *Summa dictaminis* of Guido Faba", in: *Medieval Eloquence: Studies in the Theory and Practice of Medieval Rhetoric*, ed. J.J. Murphy (Berkeley, Los Angeles, and London, 1978) , pp. 85-111.

FAVREAU, R., *Épigraphie médiévale* (Turnhout, 1997).

FEIGELMANAS, N., "Apie Vilniaus universiteto bibliotekos XV-XVII a. knygų proveniencijas ir jų mokslinę reikšmę" [About the provenances and research significance of the books from the fifteenth-seventeenth centuries in Vilnius University Library], in: *Iš lietuvos bibliotekų istorijos* [From the History of Lithuanian Libraries], ed. V. BULAVAS (Vilnius, 1985), pp. 13-16.

FIJAŁEK, J., "Kościół rzymskokatolicki na Litwie: Uchrześcijanienie Litwy przez Polskę i zachowanie w niej języka ludu po koniec Rzeczypospolitej" [The Roman Catholic Church in Lithuania: The Christianisation of Lithuania by Poland and the preservation of the popular vernacular till the end of the Old Poland], in: *Polska i Litwa w dziejowym stosunku* (Warsaw, 1914), pp. 37-333.

FIJAŁEK, J., "Opisy Wilna aż do połowy wieku XVII" [The descriptions of Vilnius till the middle of the seventeenth century], *Ateneum Wileńskie* 1.3-4 (1923), pp. 313-336 and 2.5-6 (1924), pp. 121-158.

FILIPCZAK-KOCUR, A., "Kancelaria podskarbich litewskich w pierwszej połowie XVII wieku" [The chancery of the Lithuanian treasurers in the first half of the seventeenth century], in: *Dzieje biurokracji na ziemiach polskich*, 1, ed. A. GÓRAK (Radzyń Podlaski, 2008), pp. 47-64.

FINDLEN, P., "Introduction: With a letter in hand – Writing, communication, and representation in Renaissance Italy", in: *The Renaissance of Letters: Knowledge and Community in Italy, 1300-1650*, ed. P. FINDLEN and S. SUTHERLAND (London and New York, 2020), pp. 1-20.

FISH, S., "Demonstration vs. persuasion: Two models of critical activity", in: S. FISH, *Is There a Text in this Class? The Authority of Interpretive Communities* (Cambridge, Mass. and London, 1980), pp. 356-372.

FISH, S., "How to recognize a poem when you see one", in: S. FISH, *Is There a Text in this Class? The Authority of Interpretive Communities* (Cambridge, Mass. and London, 1980), pp. 322-337.

FISH, S., *Is There A Text in This Class? The Authority of Interpretative Communities* (Cambridge, Mass., and London, 1980).

FISH, S., "Rhetoric", in: S. FISH, *Doing What Comes Naturally: Change, Rhetoric, and the Practice of Theory in Literary and Legal Studies* (Durham and London, 1989), pp. 485-494.

FISHER, S., and J.E. HALLEY, "Introduction: The lady vanishes: The problem of women's absence in late medieval and Renaissance Texts", in: *Seeking the Women in Late Medieval and Renaissance Writings: Essays in Feminist Contextual Criticism*, ed. S. FISHER and J.E. HALLEY (Knoxville, 1989), pp. 1-17.

FISHMAN, I., *The history of Jewish Education in Central Europe, from the End of the Sixteenth to the End of the Eighteenth Century* (London, 1944).

FOWLER, A., *Triumphal Forms: Structural Patterns in Elisabethan Poetry* (Cambridge, 1970).

FOXMAN, A.H., I. KLAUSNER, and I.O. LEHMAN, "Vilna", in: *EJ*, 20, pp. 528-534.

FRANCZAK, G., "*Faex gentium*: Polacy w Moskwie wobec rosyjskiej 'mniejszości' (1606-1612)" [*Faex gentium*: The Poles in Moscow towards the Russian 'minority'], in: *Etniczność, tożsamość, literatura: Zbiór studiów*, ed. P. BUKOWIEC and D. SIWOR (Cracow, 2010), pp. 45-67.

FRANCZAK, G., "*Polotia recepta*: Mapa Księstwa Połockiego – Teksty i preteksty sporu o władzę" [*Polotia recepta*: The Map of the Duchy of Połock – Texts and pretexts of the struggle for power], *Terminus* 23.2 (2021), pp. 97-133.

FRANKLIN, S., "Mapping the graphosphere: Cultures of writing in early 19th-century Russia (and before)", *Kritika: Explorations in Russian and Eurasian History* 12.3 (2011), pp. 531-560.

FRANKLIN, S., *The Russian Graphosphere, 1450-1850* (Cambridge, 2019).

FRANKLIN, S., *Writing, Society and Culture in Early Modern Rus, c. 950-1300* (Cambridge, 2002).

FREJLICH, K., *Pod przysądem horodnictwa wileńskiego: O jurydyce i jej mieszkańcach w XVII wieku* [Under the Jurisdiction of the Vilnius Burgrave: About the *Jurydyka* and its Inhabitants in the Seventeenth Century] (Toruń, 2021).

FRENKEL, J., "Literatura rabiniczna Żydów w dawnej Rzeczypospolitej" [The rabbinic literature of Jews in Old Poland], in: *Żydzi w Polsce odrodzonej*, 1, ed. I. SCHIPER, A. TARTAKOWER, *and* A. HAFFTKA (Warsaw, 1932), pp. 213-224.

FRICK, D.A., "Introduction", in: *Rus' Restored: Selected Writings of Meletij Smotryc'kyj 1610-1630*, ed., trans. and introduction D.A. FRICK (Cambridge, Mass., 2005), pp. XV-LXIX.

FRICK, D.A., "Jews and others in seventeenth-century Wilno: Life in the neighborhood", *Jewish Studies Quarterly* 12 (2005), pp. 8-42.

FRICK, D.A., *Kith, Kin, and Neighbors: Communities and Confessions in Seventeenth-Century Wilno* (Ithaca and New York, 2013).

FRICK, D.A., *Meltij Smotryćkyj* (Cambridge, Mass., 1995).

FRICK, D.A., "Meletij Smotryćkyj's Ruthenian *Homiliary Gospel* (1616)", in: *The Jevanhelije učitielnoje of Meletij Smotryćkyj*, ed. D.A. FRICK (Cambridge, Mass., 1987), pp. IX-X.

FRICK, D.A., *Polish Sacred Philology in the Reformation and the Counter-Reformation: Chapters in the History of the Controversies (1551-1632)* (Berkeley, 1989).

FRICK, D.A., "*Słowa uszczypliwe, słowa nieuczciwe*: The language of litigation and the Ruthenian polemic", *Paleoslavica*, 10.1 (2002), pp. 121-138.

FRICK, D.A., "The bells of Vilnius: Keeping time in a city of many calendars", in: *Making Contact: Maps, Identity, and Travel,* ed. L. CORMACK, N. PYLYPIUK, G. BERGER, and J. HART (Edmonton, 2003), pp. 23-59.

FRICK, D.A., "The councilor and the baker's wife: Ruthenians and their language in seventeenth-century Vilnius", in: *Speculum Slaviae Orientalis: Muscovy, Ruthenia and Lithuania in the Late Middle Ages*, ed. V.V. IVANOV and J. VERKHOLANTSEV (Moscow, 2005), pp. 45-67.

FRIEDRICH, K., "Royal entries into Cracow, Warsaw and Danzig: Festival culture and the role of the cities in Poland-Lithuania", in: *Europa Triumphans: Court and Civic Festivals in Early Modern Europe*, ed. J.R. MULRYNE, H. WATANABE-O'KELLY, and M. SHEWRING, 1 (Cambridge, 2004), pp. 386-392.

FROST, R., *The Oxford History of Poland-Lithuania*, 1, *The Making of the Polish-Lithuanian Union, 1385-1569* (Oxford, 2015).

FULIŃSKA, A., *Naśladowanie i twórczość: Renesansowe teorie imitacji, emulacji i przekładu* [Imitation and Creativity: Renaissance Theories of Imitation, Emulation and Translation] (Wrocław, 2000).

FUMAROLI, M., *L'École du silence: Le sentiment des images au XVIIe siècle* (Paris, 1998).

FUMAROLI, M., *L'età dell'eloquenza: Retorica e "res literaria" dal Rinascimento alle soglie dell'epoca classica*, trans. E. BAS, M. BOTTO, and G. CILLARIO (Milan, 2002).

GANSINIEC, R., "*Sbigneis* Mikołaja Kotwicza" [*Sbigneis* by Mikołaj Kotwicz], *Pamiętnik Literacki* 48.1 (1957), pp. 123-125.

GARBACIK, J., "Helena (1476-1513)", in: *PSB*, 9 (1960-1961), pp. 359-362.

GĘBAROWICZ, M., "Na śladach polskich bibliotek królewskich" [On the tracks of the Polish royal book collections], *Roczniki Biblioteczne*, 14.1-2 (1970), pp. 113-137.

Geschichtspolitik und demokratische Kultur: Bilanz und Perspektiven, ed. B. BOUVIER and M. SCHNEIDER (Bonn, 2008).

GIARD, L., "Le devoir d'intelligence ou l'insertion des jésuites dans le monde du savoir", in: *Les jésuites à la Renaissance: Système éducatif et production du savoir*, ed. L. GIARD (Paris, 1995), pp. XI-LXXIX.

GIEYSZTOR, A., *Zarys dziejów pisma łacińskiego* [A Sketch of the History of the Latin Script] (Warsaw, 2009).

GINSBURG, C., *The Cheese and the Worms: The Cosmos of a Sixteenth-Century Miller*, trans. J. TEDESCHI and A. TEDESCHI (Baltimore, 1980).

GLEMŽA, L., "Vilniaus miesto ir pilies ryšiai XVI-XVIII a." [Relations between the city and the castle of Vilnius in the sixteenth-eighteenth centuries], In: *Vilniaus Žemutinė pilis XIV a.-XIX a. pradžioje: 2005-2006 m. tyrimai* [The Vilnius Lower Castle, Fourteenth-Beginning of the Nineteenth Centuries: 2005-2006 Research], ed. L. GLEMŽA (Vilnius, 2007), pp. 69-78.

GLIŃSKA, A., "Przyczynek do dziejów poezji karmelitańskiej: Charakterystyka i wybrane wiersze z rękopisu o sygn. 3643 I ze zbiorów Biblioteki Jagiellońskiej" [A contribution to the history of the poetry of the Carmelites: An analysis and selected poems from MS 3643 I from the Jagiellonian Library], *Barok* 5.2 (1998), pp. 185-194.

GODEK, S., *Elementy prawa rzymskiego w III Statucie litewskim (1588)* [The Elements of Roman Law in the Third Statute of Lithuania] (Warsaw, 2004).

GOEURY, J., "Des sermons prononcés comme ils ont été écrits, ou bien écrits comme ils ont été prononcés?", in: *L'Éloquence de la chaire entre écriture et oralité (XIIIe-XVIIIe siècles): Actes du colloque international de Genève, 11-12 septembre 2014*, ed. G. AUBERT, A. HENEVELD, and C. MELI (Paris, 2018), pp. 131-146.

GOŁASZEWSKI, Ł., "Knyszyńskie testamenty składane ustnie wobec władz miejskich na przełomie XVII i XVIII wieku: Teksty autorstwa umierających, czy też pisarzy miejskich?" [Last wills from Knyszyn delivered orally before urban authorities at the turn of the eighteenth century: Texts of dying testators or of the municipal scribes?], *Kwartalnik Historii Kultury Materialnej* 62.3 (2014), pp. 345-366.

GOODY, J., *The Domestication of the Savage Mind* (Cambridge, 1977).

GOODY, J., *The Interface Between the Written and the Oral* (Cambridge, 1987).

GOODY, J., *The Logic of Writing and the Organization of Society* (Cambridge, 1996).

GOODY, J., and I. WATT, "The consequences of literacy", *Comparative Studies in Society and History*, 5.3 (1963), pp. 304-345.

GÓRSKI, Z., "Organizacja kancelarii miejskiej Starej Warszawy i system pracy pisarzy miejskich" [The structure of the municipal chancery of Old Warsaw and the system of work of its notaries], *Archeion* 76 (1984), pp. 19-36.

GÓRSKI, K., "Wstęp" [Introduction], in: *Formularz Jerzego, pisarza grodzkiego krakowskego ok. 1399-1415* [The Book of Formulae by George, the Notary of the Castle Court in Cracow, *c.* 1399-1415], ed. K. GÓRSKI (Toruń, 1950), pp. IX-XX.

GORZKOWSKI, A., *Paweł z Krosna: Humanistyczne peregrynacje krakowskiego profesora* [Paulus Crosnensis: the Humanistic Peregrinations of a Cracow Scholar] (Cracow, 2000).

GRABOWSKI, T., "Z dziejów literatury kalwińskiej na Litwie" [From the history of Calvinist literature in Lithuania], *Reformacja w Polsce* 6 (1934), pp. 141-143.

GRENDLER, P.F., *Jesuit Schools and Universities in Europe 1548-1773* (Leiden and Boston, 2019).

GRENDLER, P.F., *Schooling in Renaissance Italy: Literacy and Learning, 1300-1600* (Baltimore and London, 1991).

GRÉVIN, B., "Le dictamen dans tous ses états: Perspectives de recherches et la pratique de l'*ars dictaminis* (XIe-XVe siècle)", in: *Le dictamen dans tous ses états: Perspectives de recherches sur la théorie et la pratique de l'ars dictaminis (XIe-XVe siècle)*, ed. B. GRÉVIN and A.-M. TURCAN-VERKERK (Turnhout, 2015), pp. 9-25.

GRICKEVIČIUS, A., *Vilniškė popiežiškoji seminarija 1583-1655 metais* [The Vilnius Papal Seminary in 1583-1655] (Vilnius, 2008).

GRISWOLD, W., "Recent moves in the sociology of literature", *Annual Review of Sociology* 19 (1993), pp. 455-467.

GRUCHAŁA, J.S., Iucunda familia librorum*: Humaniści renesansowi w świecie książki* [*Iucunda familia librorum*: Renaissance Humanists in the World of Books] (Cracow, 2002).

GRUCHAŁA, J.S., and S. GRZESZCZUK , "Staropolska poezja ziemiańska" [The Old Polish poetry of the gentry], in: *Staropolska poezja ziemiańska: Antologia*, ed. J.S. GRUCHAŁA and S. GRZESZCZUK (Warsaw, 1988), pp. 5-83.

GRULKOWSKI, M., "Definicja i klasyfikacja ksiąg miejskich: Księgi w kancelariach miast obszaru Hanzy" [Definition and typology of urban registers: Urban chancery registers in the Hanseatic area], in: *Nauki pomocnicze historii: Teoria, metody badań, dydaktyka*, ed. A. JAWORSKA and R. JOP (Warsaw, 2013), pp. 119-148.

GRZEBIEŃ, L., "Biblioteki jezuickie w Krakowie od XVI do XVIII wieku" [Jesuit libraries in Cracow from the sixteenth till the eighteenth century], in: *Librorum amatori: Księga pamiątkowa ofiarowana ks. Czesławowi Michalunio SJ na 50-lecie ofiarnej pracy w Bibliotece Filozoficznej Towarzystwa Jezusowego w Krakowie*, ed. A.P. BIEŚ (Cracow, 2004), pp. 29-55.

GRZEBIEŃ, L., "Chronologia pobytu i działalności Piotra Skargi w Wilnie (1573-1584)" [The Chronology of the sojourn and activities of Piotr Skarga in Vilnius (1573-1584)], *Senoji Lietuvos Literatūra* 35-36 (2013), pp. 15-41.

GRZEBIEŃ, L., "Organizacja bibliotek jezuickich w Polsce od XVI do XVIII wieku" [The organisation of the Jesuit libraries in Poland from the sixteenth till the eighteenth century] (part 1), *Archiwa, Biblioteki i Muzea Kościelne* 30 (1975), pp. 246-264.

GRZEBIEŃ, L., "Organizacja bibliotek jezuickich w Polsce od XVI do XVIII wieku" [The organisation of the Jesuit Libraries in Poland from the sixteenth till the eighteenth century] (part 2), *Archiwa, Biblioteki i Muzea Kościelne* 31 (1975), pp. 225-281.

GRZELCZAK-MIŁOŚ, I., *Mieszczaństwo poznańskie w świetle Libri testamentorum* [The Inhabitants of Poznań in the Light of the *Libri Testamentorum*] (Poznań, 2011).

GRZEŚKOWIAK, R., J. GWIOŹDZIK, and A. NOWICKA-STRUSKA, *Karmelitańskie adaptacje* Pia Desideria *Hermana Hugona z XVII i XVIII w.* [The Carmelite Adaptations of the *Pia Desideria* of Herman Hugo from the Seventeenth and Eighteenth Centuries] (Warsaw, 2020).

GRZEŚKOWIAK, R., and J. NIEDŹWIEDŹ, "Nieznane polskie subskrypcje do emblematów Ottona van Veen i Hermana Hugona: Przyczynek do funkcjonowania zachodniej grafiki religijnej w kulturze staropolskiej" [The unknown Polish *subscriptiones* to the emblems by Otton van Veen and Herman Hugon: Some remarks on how western sacred engravings functioned in Old Polish culture], *Terminus* 14.25 (2012), pp. 54-62.

GRZEŚKOWIAK, R., and J. NIEDŹWIEDŹ, "Wstęp", [Introduction], in: M. MIELESZKO, *Emblematy*, ed. R. GRZEŚKOWIAK and J. NIEDŹWIEDŹ (Warsaw, 2010), pp. 7-70.

GRZYBOWSKI, S., "Epitafia żydowskie w Polsce doby sarmatyzmu: Studium porównawcze" [Jewish epitaphs in Poland in the Sarmatian period: A comparative study], in: *Żydzi w Małopolsce: Studia z dziejów osadnictwa i życia społecznego*, ed. F. KIRYK (Przemyśl, 1991), pp. 49-58.

GUMOWSKI, M., "Wileńska szkoła medalierska w XVI i XVII wieku" [The Vilnius school of medallist art in the sixteenth and seventeenth century], *Ateneum Wileńskie* 6.1-2 (1933-1934), pp. 72-87.

GWIOŹDZIK, J., *Kultura pisma i książki w żeńskich klasztorach dawnej Rzeczypospolitej XVI-XVIII wieku* [The Culture of Writing and the Book in the Nunneries of the Polish-Lithuanian Commonwealth from the Sixteenth till the Eighteenth Centuries] (Katowice, 2015).

GWIOŹDZIK, J., "Kultura umysłowa benedyktynek kongregacji chełmińskiej" [Intelectual culture of the Benedictine sisters of the congregation of Chełmno], in: Sanctimoniales*: Zakony żeńskie w Polsce i Europie Środkowej (do przełomu XVIII i XIX wieku)*, ed. A. RADZIMIŃSKI, D. KARCZEWSKI, and Z. ZYGLEWSKI (Bydgoszcz, 2010), pp. 481-489.

GWIOŹDZIK, J., *Wileńskie mniszki w kręgu kultury słowa w dobie staropolskiej* [The Nuns of Vilnius in the Literary Culture of the Old Polish Period], in: *Kultura i języki Wielkiego Księstwa Litewskiego*, ed. M.T. LIZISOWA (Cracow, 2005), pp. 259-276.

HANUSIEWICZ, M., *Święte i zmysłowe w poezji religijnej polskiego baroku* [Sacral and Sensual in the Religious Poetry of the Polish Baroque] (Lublin, 1998).

HANUSIEWICZ-LAVALLEE, M., "Prywatność w rękopiśmiennej poezji polskich karmelitanek" [Privacy in the handwritten poetry of the Polish Carmelite nuns], *Barok* 18.2 (2011), pp. 11-22.

HANUSIEWICZ-LAVALLEE, M., "Wyobraźnia i erudycja w karmelitańskich pieśniach o Miłości Bożej" [Imagination and erudition in the Carmelite songs of God's love], *Barok* 5.1 (1998), pp. 191-201.

HARKOVICH, N., "Sąd cerkiewny nad Stefanem Zyzanią w kontekście stosunków wiernych i hierarchii prawosławnej w Rzeczypospolitej u schyłku XVI wieku" [The ecclesiastical trial of Stefan Zyzania in the context of the relationships between the believers and the Orthodox hierarchy in Poland in the late sixteenth century], in: *ΕΛΠΙΣ: Czasopismo Naukowe Katedry Teologii Prawosławnej Uniwersytetu w Białymstoku* 19 (2017), pp. 85-95.

HARRIS, S.J., *Les chaires de mathématiques*, in: *Les jésuites à la Renaissance: Système éducatif et production du savoir*, ed. L. GIARD (Paris, 1995), pp. 244-251.

HEDEMANN, O., *Testamenty brasławsko-dziśnieńskie XVII-XVIII wieku jako źródło historyczne* [Last Wills from Brasław and Dzisna from the Seventeenth and Eighteenth Centuries as a Historical Source] (Vilnius, 1935).

HELLER, M.J., "Early Hebrew printing from Lublin to Safed: The journeys of Eliezer ben Isaac Ashkenazi", *Jewish Culture and History* 4.1 (2001), pp. 81-96.

HERNAS, Cz., *Barok* [Baroque] (Warsaw, 1972).

HIRSCH, R., *Printing, Selling and Reading, 1450-1550* (Wiesbaden, 1974).

HŁASKO, E., "Stosunek jednoty litewskiej do arian w świetle kanonów wieku XVII" [The attitude of the Lithuanian Evangelical-Reformed Church to the Polish Brethren in the light of legal texts of the seventeenth century], *Ateneum Wileńskie* 11 (1936), pp. 283-290.

HÖFLER, J., "Še enkrat o tako imenovanem "češkem cestopisu" v zbirki Arhiva Republike Slovenije" [Once again about the so-called "Bohemian Travelogue" in the collections of the archive of the Republic of Slovenia], *Acta historiae artis Slovenica* 6 (2001), pp. 17-31.

HOŁODOK, S., "Źródła do dziejów liturgii sakramentów w diecezji wileńskiej (XVI-XVIII w.)" [Sources for the history of the liturgy of the sacraments in the diocese of

Vilnius (sixteenth-eighteenth centuries)], *Studia Teologiczne* 1 (1983), pp. 197-198.

HOŃDO, L., *Hebrajska epigrafika nagrobna w Polsce* [Hebrew Tomb Epigraphy in Poland] (Cracow, 2014).

HOŃDO, L., "Tytuły osobowe na nagrobkach na przykładzie starego cmentarza żydowskiego w Krakowie" [Personal designations on the funeral stones on the example of the old Jewish Cemetery in Cracow], in: *Żydzi i judaizm we współczesnych badaniach polskich*, 2, *Materiały z konferencji, Kraków 24-26 XI 1998*, ed. K. PILARCZYK and S. GĄSIOROWSKI (Cracow, 2000), pp. 161-177.

HORODYSKI, B., *Podręcznik paleografii ruskiej* [Manual of Ruthenian Palaeography] (Cracow, 1951).

ILARIENĖ, I., "1388 m.-XVI a. Lietuvos Didžiosios Kunigaikštystės vyskupijų viešieji notarai" [The diocesan public notaries in the Grand Duchy of Lithuania, 1388-sixteenth century], *Istorijos šaltinių tyrimai* 5 (2014), pp. 147-169.

ILJASZEWICZ, T., *Drukarnia domu Mamoniczów w Wilnie (1575-1622)* [The Printing House of the Mamonicz Family in Vilnius (1575-1622] (Vilnius, 1938).

IMAŃSKA, I., "Katalog toruńskiego księgarza Samuela Janssona Möllera z 1738 roku w zbiorach Biblioteki Katedralnej w Gnieźnie" [The book catalogue of Samuel Jansson Möller, a bookseller from Toruń (1738) in the collection of the Cathedral Library of Gniezno], *Archiwa, Biblioteki i Muzea Kościelne* 113 (2020), pp. 205-220.

IMAŃSKA, I., "Kilka uwag i spostrzeżeń o katalogach aukcyjnych jako źródle do badań księgozbiorów prywatnych" [Some remarks on auction catalogues as sources for the study of private book collections], *Z Badań nad Książką i Księgozbiorami Historycznymi* 9 (2015), pp. 241-254.

INGLOT, M., *Polska kultura literacka Lwowa lat 1939-1941: Ze Lwowa i o Lwowie: Lata sowieckiej okupacji w poezji polskiej: Antologia utworów poetyckich w wyborze* [Polish Literary Culture of Lviv in 1939-1941: From Lviv and about Lviv: The Years of the Soviet Occupation in Polish Poetry] (Wrocław, 1995).

Iter Italicum: Accedunt Alia Itinera: *A Finding List of Uncatalogued or Incompletely Catalogued Humanistic Manuscripts of the Renaissance in Italian and Other Libraries*, 5, ed. P.O. KRISTELLER (London, 1993).

JABLONSKIS, K., "1510 m. Albrechto Goštauto biblioteka" [The library of Olbracht Gasztołd from 1510], in: *Lietuvių kultūra ir jos veikėjai* [Lithuanian Culture and Its Actors] (Vilnius, 1973), pp. 353-357.

JABLONSKIS, K., "Lietuvos rusiškųjų aktų diplomatika" [Lithuanian diplomatic of Ruthenian charters], in: *Istorija ir jos šaltiniai*, ed. V. Merkys (Vilnius, 1979), pp. 219-298.

JACKIEWICZ, M., "Blinstrubowie i Janczewscy z Blinstrubiszek" [The Blinstrub family and the Janczewski family of Blinstrubiszki], *Przegląd Wschodni* 13.4 (2014), pp. 1133-1146.

JAGLARZ, M., *Księgarstwo krakowskie XVI wieku* [Bookselling in Cracow in the Sixteenth Century] (Cracow, 2004).

JANICKI, M.A., "Grób i komemoracja wielkiego księcia Aleksandra Witolda w katedrze wileńskiej w kontekście upamiętnienia Władysława Jagiełły w katedrze krakowskiej i propagandy jagiellońskiej XIV-XVI w." [The tomb and commemoration of Grand Duke Alexander in the cathedral of Vilnius in the context of the commemoration of King Jogaila (Władysław Jagiełło) in Cracow cathedral and Jagiellonian propaganda in the fourteenth-sixteenth centuries], *Przegląd Historyczny* 111.4 (2020), pp. 769-814.

JANICKI, M.A., "Inskrypcja w przestrzeni publicznej – przykład Krakowa i Małopolski w XIV-XV wieku" [Inscriptions in public space – The example of Cracow and Lesser Poland in the fourteenth-sixteenth centuries], in: *Historia społeczna późnego średniowiecza*, ed. S. GAWLAS (Warszawa, 2011), 245-273.

JANICKI, M.A., "Willa Eustachego Wołłowicza w Werkach pod Wilnem i jej epigraficzny program ideowy" [The villa of Eustachy Wołłowicz in Verkiai near Vilnius and its epigraphic ideological programme], *Barok* 4.2 (1998), pp. 139-149.

JANIK, M., "Wśród form popularyzacji historii w XVII wieku" [Among the ways of the popularisation of history in the seventeenth century], in: *Staropolskie kompendia wiedzy*, ed. I.M. DACKA-GÓRZYŃSKA and J. PARTYKA (Warsaw, 2009), pp. 203-224.

JANKOWICZ, G., and M. TABACZYŃSKI, "Socjologia literatury jako nieodzowne źródło cierpień" [Sociology of literature as an indispensable source of suffering], in: *Socjologia literatury: Antologia*, ed. G. JAKOWICZ and M. TABACZYŃSKI (Cracow, 2015), pp. 12-13.

JANÓW, J., "Tłumaczenia i przeróbki z *Postylli* M. Reja w pouczeniach ruskich (Tymczasowy wykaz ok. 50 kodeksów)" [Translations and redactions of the *Postil* by Mikołaj Rej in Ruthenian educational works (a provisional list of *c.* fifty codices)], *Sprawozdania z czynności i posiedzeń Polskiej Akademii Umiejętności* 48 (1947-1948), pp. 301-306.

JANUSZEK-SIERADZKA, A., "Dwór królowej od kuchni, czyli o zaopatrzeniu stołu Barbary Radziwiłłówny (1548-1551)" [The queen's court as seen from the kitchen, or about the provisions for the table of Barbara Radziwiłłówna], In: *Jagiellonowie i ich świat*, ed. B. CZWOJDRAK, J. SPERKA, and P. WĘCOWSKI (Cracow, 2015), pp. 75-88.

JARCZYKOWA, M., "Listy z XVI i XVII wieku w obiegu czytelniczym" [Sixteenth- and seventeenth-century letters and their circulation among readers], in: M. JARCZYKOWA, *Korespondencja i literatura okolicznościowa w kręgu magnaterii Wielkiego Księstwa Litewskiego* [Correspondence and Occasional Literature among the Magnates of the Grand Duchy of Lithuania] (Katowice, 2019), pp. 34-40.

JARCZYKOWA, M., *"Papierowe materie" Piotra Kochlewskiego: O działalności pisarskiej sekretarza Radziwiłłów birżańskich w pierwszej połowie XVII wieku* [The "Paper Matter" of Piotr Kochlewski: On the Writing Activity of the Secretary of the Radziwiłł Family of Biržai] (Katowice, 2006).

JAROSZEWICZ-PIERESŁAWCEW, Z., *Druki cyrylickie z oficyn Wielkiego Księstwa Litewskiego w XVI-XVIII wieku* [Cyrillic Prints from the Printing House in the Grand Duchy of Lithuania in the Sixteenth-Eighteenth Centuries] (Olsztyn, 2003).

JAWOR, G., "Stałe formuły w testamentach polskich" [The permanent formulae in Polish last wills], *Rozprawy Komisji Językowej: Wrocławskie Towarzystwo Naukowe* 12 (1981), pp. 217-233.

JAWORSKI, I., "Przywileje miejskie na prawo niemieckie w Wielkiem Księstwie Litewskiem" [Urban privileges of the German Law in the Grand Duchy of Lithuania], *Rocznik Prawniczy Wileński* 3 (1929), pp. 48-61.

JAWORSKI, I., *Zarys historii Wilna* [Sketch of the History of Vilnius] (Vilnius, 1929).

JĘDRZEJCZYK, D., *Geografia kulturowa miasta* [The Cultural Geography of a City] (Warsaw, 2004).

Jewish Preaching, 1200-1800: An Anthology, ed. M. SAPARSTEIN (New Haven and London, 1989).

JEZIERSKI, A., and C. LESZCZYŃSKA, *Historia gospodarcza Polski* [Economic History of Poland] (Warsaw, 1998).

JOVAIŠAS, A., and E. ULČINAITĖ, *Lietuvių literatūros istorija: XIII-XVIII amžiai* [A History of Lithuanian Literature: Thirteenth-Eighteenth Centuries] (Vilnius, 2003).

JUDA, M., *Pismo drukowane w Polsce XV-XVIII wieku* [The Fonts of Prints in Poland, Fifteenth-Eighteenth Centuries] (Lublin, 2001).

JULIA, D., "Génèalogie de la *Ratio studiorum*", in: *Les jésuites à l'âge du baroque (1540-1640)*, ed. L. GIARD and L. DE VAUCELLES (Grenoble, 1996), pp. 115-130.

JURGELĖNAITĖ, R., *Lotyniškoji laidotuvių poezija: XVI amžiaus pabaigos Vilniaus Akademijos tekstų retorinė analizė* [Latin Funeral Poetry: Rhetorical Analysis of Texts from the Academy of Vilnius from the End of the Sixteenth Century] (Vilnius, 1998).

JURGINIS, J., V. MERKYS, and A. TAUTAVIČIUS, *Vilniaus miesto istorija (nuo seniausių laikų iki Spalio revoliucijos)* [The History of the City of Vilnius (from Ancient Times to the October Revolution)] (Vilnius, 1968).

JUSTYNIARSKA-CHOJAK, K., *Testamenty i inwentarze pośmiertne z ksiąg miejskich województwa sandomierskiego* [Last Wills and *Post Mortem* Inventories from the Municipal Registers of the Voivodeship of Sandomierz] (Kielce, 2010).

KACZMARCZYK, B., *Język polski w kancelarii królewskiej w pierwszej połowie XVI wieku* [Polish Language in the Royal Chancery in the First Half of the Sixteenth Century] (Wrocław, 2003).

KALĘBA, B., *Rozdroże: Literatura polska w kręgu litewskiego odrodzenia narodowego* [The Crossroads: Polish Literature in the Milieu of the Lithuanian National Revival] (Cracow, 2016).

KALINOWSKI, R., "Klasztor karmelitanek bosych pw. św. Józefa w Wilnie: Pogląd ogólny" [The monastery of the Discalced Carmelite nuns of St. Joseph in Vilnius: A general sketch], in: *Klasztory karmelitanek bosych w Polsce, na Litwie i Rusi: Ich początek, rozwój i tułactwo w czasie rozruchów wojennych w XVII w.*, 1, *Wilno*, ed. R. KALINOWSKI (Cracow, 1900), pp. 1-17.

KAMUNTAVIČIENĖ, V., "The religious faiths of Ruthenians and Old Lithuanians in the seventeenth century according to the records of the Catholic Church visitations of the Vilnius diocese", *Journal of Baltic Studies* 46.2 (2015), pp. 157-170.

KANIEWSKA, I., "Jerzy Podlodowski", in: *PSB* 27 (1982-1983), pp. 130-131.

KANTAK, K., "Najważniejsze rękopisy franciszkańskie bibliotek wileńskich" [The most important Franciscan manuscripts from the libraries of Vilnius], *Ateneum Wileńskie* 5 (1928), pp. 175-184.

KARALIUS, L., "Testamentai" [Last wills], in: *Lietuvos Didžiosios Kunigaikštijos kultūra: Tyrinėjimai ir vaizdai* [The Culture of the Grand Duchy of Lithuania: Analyses and Images] ed. V. ALIŠAUSKAS *et al.* (Vilnius, 2001), pp. 714-723.

KARPIŃSKI, A., *Kobieta w mieście polskim w II poł. XVI i w XVII wieku* [Woman in Polish Towns in the Second Half of the Sixteenth and in the Seventeenth Century] (Warsaw, 1995).

KARPOWICZ, M., *Baroque in Poland* (Warsaw, 1991).

KARPOWICZ, M., "Giovanni Battista Gisleni i Francesco de'Rossi" [Giovanni Battista Gisleni and Francesco de'Rossi] , in: *Lietuvos dailė europiniame kontekste*, ed. E. ALEKSANDRAVIČIUS, M. KARPOWICZ, and R. JANONIENĖ (Vilnius, 1995), pp. 176-190.

KARPOWICZ, M., *Matteo Castello: Architekt wczesnego baroku* [Matteo Castello: An Architect from the Period of the Early Baroque] (Warsaw, 1990).

KARR, D.R., "Judaism in Christendom", in: *The Blackwell Comapnion to Judaism* ed. J. NEUSNER and A.J. AVERY-PECK (Oxford, 2000), pp. 142-161.

KASJANIUK, E., "Katechizm (III. W Protestantyzmie)" [The Catechism (III. In Protestantism), in: *Encyklopedia katolicka* 8 (Lublin, 2000), cols. 1048-1049.

KASPERAVIČIENĖ, A., *Evangelikų liuteronų ir evangelikų reformatų kapinės Vilniuje* [The Evangelical Lutheran and Evangelical Reformed cemeteries in Vilnius] (Vilnius, 1996).

KASZLEJ, A., *Wpływ cerkiewnosłowiańskiej książki drukowanej na rękopiśmienną (na podstawie zbiorów Biblioteki Narodowej w Warszawie)* [The Influence of the Church Slavonic Printed Books on Handwritten Books (On the Basis of the Collection of the National Library in Warsaw)], in: *Najstarsze druki cerkiewnosłowiańskie i ich stosunek do tradycji rękopiśmiennej: Materiały z sesji: Kraków 7-10 XI 1991*, ed. J. RUSEK, W. WITKOWSKI, and A. NAUMOW (Cracow, 1993), pp. 167-178.

KASZOWSKA-WANDOR, B., *Respublica [post] litteraria: Od poetyki wspólnoty do postliteratury* Respublica (post) letteraria [*Respublica [Post] Litteraria*: From the Poetic of Community to (Post-)Literature] (Cracow, 2020).

KATALYNAS, K., *Vilnaius plėtra XIV-XVII a.* [The Development of Vilnius in the Fourteenth-Seventeenth Centuries] (Vilnius, 2006).

KATALYNAS, K., and G. VAITKEVIČIUS, "Rozwój Wilna w XIV wieku w świetle badań archeologicznych" [The development of Vilnius in the fourteenth century in the light of the archaeological research], *Kwartalnik Historii Kultury Materialnej* 50.1 (2002), pp. 3-10.

KATZ, D., *Lithuanian Jewish Culture* (Vilnius, 2004).

KAUPUŻ, A., "Kochanowski na Litwie: Przekłady tekstów Jana z Czarnolasu na język litewski" [Kochanowski in Lithuania: The translations of the texts of Jan Kochanowski of Czarnolas into Lithuanian], in: *Jan Kochanowski 1584-1984: Epoka – Twórczość – Recepcja*, 2, ed. J. PELC, P. BUCHWALD-PELCOWA, and B. OTWINOWSKA (Lublin, 1989), pp. 79-95.

KAWECKA, A., "Kancjonały protestanckie na Litwie" [Protestant song books in Lithuania], *Reformacja w Polsce* 4 (1926), pp. 128-130.

KAWECKA-GRYCZOWA, A., *Biblioteka ostatniego Jagiellona: Pomnik kultury renesansowej* [The Book Collection of the Last Jagiellon King: A Monument of Renaissance Culture] (Wrocław, 1988).

KAŽURO, I, *Vilniaus bazilijonų vienuolyno spaustuvės veikla 1628-1839 m.* [The Activities of the Printing House of the Vilnius Basilian Monastery in 1628-1839] (PhD, Vilnius, 2019).

KEMPA, T., *Konflikty wyznaniowe w Wilnie od początku reformacji do końca XVII wieku* [Religious Conflicts in Vilnius from the Beginning of the Reformation until the End of the Seventeenth Centuries] (Toruń, 2016).

KEMPA, T., "Prawosławie i unia w Polsce i na Litwie: Sytuacja prawna, polityka władców i rola świeckich" [Orthodoxy and the union of the Churches in Poland and Lithuania: The legal status, royal politics, and the role of lay people], in: *Między Wschodem a Zachodem. Prawosławie i unia*, ed. M. KUCZYŃSKA (Warsaw, 2017), pp. 41-46.

KENNEDY GRIMSTED, P., "Introduction", in: *The "Lithuanian Metrica" in Moscow and Warsaw: Reconstructing the Archives of the Grand Duchy of Lithuania. Including An Annotated Edition of the 1887 Inventory Compiled by Stanisław Ptaszycki*, ed. P. KENNEDY GRIMSTED and I. SUŁKOWSKA-KURASIOWA (Cambridge, Mass., 1994).

KĘTRZYŃSKI, S., *Zarys nauki o dokumencie polskim wieków średnich* [Outline of the Science of Medieval Polish Charters] (Poznań, 2008).

KETTERING, S., "Patronage in early modern France", *French Historical Studies* 4.17 (1992), pp. 839-850.

KIAUPIENĖ, J., "*Theatrum ceremoniale* w barokowym Wilnie" [The *theatrum ceremoniale*' in baroque Vilnius] , in: *Wokół Wielkiego Księstwa Litewskiego i jego tradycji*, ed. B. MANYŚ and M. ZWIERZYKOWSKI (Poznań, 2016), pp. 105-109.

KIERSNOWSKI, R., "Funkcje dydaktyczne monet średniowiecznych" [Educational functions of medieval coins], in: *Nauczanie w dawnych wiekach: Edukacja w średniowieczu i u progu ery nowożytnej. Polska na tle Europy*, ed. W. IWAŃCZAK and K. BRACHA (Kielce, 1997), pp. 228-229.

KILIAŃCZYK-ZIĘBA, J., "On the diploma of nobility of Jan Januszowski and a portrait of a Renaissance printer", *Terminus: Special Issue* 1 (2019), pp. 81-105.

KIRKOR, A.H., *Przechadzki po Wilnie i jego okolicach* [Promenades in Vilnius and Its Neighborhoods] (Vilnius, 1856).

KIRKOR, A.H., *Przewodnik historyczny po Wilnie i jego okolicach* [A Historical Guide of Vilnius and its Neighborhood] (Vilnius, 1880).

KIRKOR, A.H., *Wilno i koleje żelazne z Wilna do Petersburga i Rygi oraz do granic na Kowno i Warszawę: Przewodnik z planem, widokami Wilna i mappą kolei żelaz-*

nych [Vilnius and the Railway from Vilnius to Petersburg and Riga towards the Frontier in the direction of Kaunas and Warsaw: A Guide with a Map of the City, Images of Vilnius, and a Railway Map] (Vilnius, 1862).

KLAUSNER, I., *History of the Old Jewish Cemetery in Vilnius* (Vilnius, 1935).

KLEMENSIEWICZ, Z., *Historia języka polskiego* [History of the Polish Language] (Warsaw, 1976).

KLIMECKA, G., *Z historii tworzenia języka dokumentu polskiego wieków średnich: Formularz ciechanowski* [From the History of Creating the Language of the Polish Medieval Charters: The Ciechanów Formulary] (Warsaw, 1997).

KLIMOWICZ, M., *Oświecenie* [The Enlightenment] (Warsaw, 1998).

KLOVAS, M., *Privačių dokumentų atsiradimas ir raida Lietuvos Didžiojoje Kunigaikštystėje XIV a. pabaigoje – XVI a. pradžioje (1529 m.). Daktaro disertacija* [The Emergence and Development of Private Documents in the Grand Duchy of Lithuania from the End of the Fourteenth Century to the Beginning of the Sixteenth (1529): A Doctoral Thesis] (Vilnius, 2017).

KNOLL, P.W., *A Pearl of Powerful Learning: The University of Cracow in the Fifteenth Century* (Leiden and Boston, 2016).

KNYCHALSKA, A., "Pomnik języka polskiego z XV w." [A monument of Polish language from the fifteenth century], in: *Wszystkie modlitwy Rzeczypospolitej: Katalog wystawy 3 lipca-30 sierpnia 2009*, ed. G. ROLAK and D. SIDOWICZ (Wrocław, 2009), p. 45.

KOCHANOWICZ, P., *Inwentarze bibliotek jezuickich 1570-1820: Próba rekonstrukcji* [The Inventories of the Jesuite Libraries 1570-1820: An Attempt at Reconstruction], in: *Librorum amatori: Księga pamiątkowa ofiarowana ks. Czesławowi Michalunio SJ na 50-lecie ofiarnej pracy w Bibliotece Filozoficznej Towarzystwa Jezusowego w Krakowie*, ed. A.P. BIEŚ (Cracow, 2004), pp. 163-178.

KOEHLER, K., *Stanisław Orzechowski i dylematy humanizmu renesansowego* [Stanisław Orzechowski and the Dilemmas of the Renaissance Humanism] (Cracow, 2004).

KOEHLER, K., "Wstęp" [Introduction], in: *Stanisława Orzechowskiego i Augustyna Rotundusa debata o Rzeczypospolitej*, ed. K. Koehler (Cracow, 2009), pp. 7-16.

KOHEN, I., *Vilna* (Philadelphia, 1943).

KÖHN, R., "Correspondence", In: *Brill's Encyclopedia of the Middle Ages* (2016) <http://dx-1doi-1org-1lk0ibnmn0110.hps.bj.uj.edu.pl/10.1163/2213-2139_bema_SIM_033808> (accessed: 27.02.2022).

KOŁOS, A., "Poetyka konceptu Macieja Kazimierza Sarbiewskiego w kręgu historii idei" [Maciej Kazimierz Naborowski's poetics of conceit in the context of the history of ideas], *Forum Poetyki* 2017.1, pp. 6-17.

KON, P., "Odnaleziona część archiwum dawnego kahału wileńskiego" [The retrieved part of the archives of the ancient Jewish community in Vilnius], *Ateneum Wileńskie* 5(15) (1928), pp. 151-166.

KONECZNY, F., *Dzieje administracji w Polsce w zarysie* [Outline of the History of Administration in Poland] (Vilnius, 1924).

KONOPACKI, A., *Życie religijne Tatarów na ziemiach Wielkiego Księstwa Litewskiego w XVI-XIX wieku* [Religious Life of the Tatars in the Grand Duchy of Lithuania in the Sixteenth-Nineteenth Centuries] (Warsaw, 2010).

KORCZAK, L., *Monarcha i poddani: System władzy w Wielkim Księstwie Litewskim w okresie wczesnojagiellońskim* [The Ruler and His Subjects: The System of Power in the Grand Duchy of Lithuania in the Early Jagiellonian Period] (Cracow, 2008).

KÖRNER, A., "Transnational history: Identities, structures, states", in: *Internationale Geschichte in Theorie und Praxis – International History in Theory and Practice*, ed. W.D. GODSEY, B. HAIDER-WILSON, and W. MUELLER (Vienna, 2017), pp. 265-290.

KOROLKO, M., *Seminarium Rzeczypospolitej Królestwa Polskiego: Humaniści w kancelarii królewskiej Zygmunta Augusta* [The Seminary of the Commonwealth of the Polish Kingdom: Humanists in the Royal Chancery of Sigismund August] (Warsaw, 1991).

KOROLKO, M., *Sztuka retoryki: Przewodnik encyklopedyczny* [The Art of Rethoric: An Encyclopedic Guide] (Warsaw, 1998).

KORZO, M.A., "O tekstach religijnych w XVI-wiecznych elementarzach polskich" [On the religous texts in sixteenth-century Polish primers], *Pamiętnik Literacki* 106.1 (2015), pp. 169-182.

KOSIŃSKI, D., *Teatra polskie: Historie* [Polish Theatres: Stories] (Warsaw, 2010).

KOSMAN, M., "Wpływ unii jagiellońskiej na przemiany kulturalne w Wielkim Księstwie Litewskim w XV-XVI wieku" [The influence of the Jagiellonian Union on cultural developments in the Grand Duchy of Lithuania in the fifteenth-sixteenth centuries], in: *Kultura i języki Wielkiego Księstwa Litewskiego*, ed. M.T. LIZISOWA (Cracow, 2005), pp. 111-120.

KOSMAN, M., *Zmierzch Perkuna, czyli ostatni poganie nad Bałtykiem* [The Twilight of Perkūnas, or the Last Pagans on the Shores of the Baltic Sea] (Warsaw, 1981).

KOSMAN, M., *Orzeł i Pogoń: Z dziejów polsko-litewskich XIV-XX w.* [The Eagle and the Pogoń: From Polish-Lithuanian History of the Fourteenth-Twentieth Centuries] (Warsaw, 1992).

KOWALENKO, W., "Geneza udziału stołecznego miasta Wilna w sejmach Rzeczypospolitej" [The origins of the participation of the capital city of Vilnius in the sessions of the Parliament of the Polish-Lithuanian Commonwealth], *Ateneum Wileńskie*, 4.12 (1927), pp. 79-137.

KOWALSKI, W., *Wielka imigracja: Szkoci w Krakowie i Małopolsce w XVI – pierwszej połowie XVII wieku* [A Great Immigration: The Scots in Cracow and Lesser Poland in the Sixteenth and in the First Half of the Seventeenth Century], second edn. (Kielce, 2014).

KOZAKIEWICZ, H., and S. KOZAKIEWICZ, *The Renaissance in Poland* (Warsaw, 1976).

KOZŁOWSKA, A., "Ceny książek ręcznie pisanych" [The prices of manuscript books], *Biuletyn Biblioteki Jagiellońskiej* 49 (1999), pp. 49-52.

KRAMPEROWA, M., and W. MAISEL, "Księgozbiory mieszczan poznańskich w drugiej połowie XVI wieku" [Book collections of the town dwellers of Poznań in the second half of the sixteenth century], *Studia i Materiały do Dziejów Wielkopolski i Pomorza*, 11 (1960), pp. 257-308.

KRĄPIEC, M.A., "Materia i forma: Ich różne rozumienie w historii filozofii" [Matter and form: Varieties of their understanding in the history of philosophy], *Roczniki Filozoficzne* 16.1 (1968), pp. 55-65.

KRAS, P., "Od represji do kompromisu; Edykty antyprotestanckie Zygmunta I i Zygmunta II Augusta" [From Repression to Compromise: The anti-Protestant legislation of Sigismund I and Sigismund II August], in: *Jagiellonowie i ich świat*, ed. B. CZWOJDRAK, J. SPERKA, and P. WĘCOWSKI (Cracow, 2015), pp. 361-367.

KRASZEWSKI, J.I., *Wilno od początków jego do roku 1750* [Vilnius from Its Origins till 1750], 1-2 (Vilnius, 1840), 3 (Vilnius, 1841), and 4 (Vilnius, 1842).

KRAUS, M., "Aphthonius and the *Progymnasmata* in rhetorical theory and practice", in: *Sizing Up Rhetoric*, ed. D. ZAREFSKY and E. BENACKA (Long Grove, Illinois, 2008), pp. 52-67.

KRAWCZUK, W., "Metryka Koronna i Metryka Litewska" [The Polish and Lithuanian *Metrica*], in: *Dyplomatyka staropolska*, ed. T. JUREK (Warszawa, 2015), pp. 206-212.

KRISTELLER, P.O., "Humanism and scholasticism in the Italian Renaissance", *Byzantion* 17 (1944), pp. 346-374.

KRÓL, B., S. MROZIŃSKA, and Z. RASZEWSKI, "Inscenizacja '*Iudicium Paridis*' na Wawelu w r. 1522" [The staging of the '*Iudicium Paridis*' at the Wawel castle in 1522], *Pamiętnik Teatralny* 3.1 (1954), pp. 3-22.

KRUCZKIEWICZ, B., "De Royzii vita operibusque", in: P. RUIZ DE MOROS, *Petri Royzii Maurei Alcagnicensis Carmina*, 1, ed. B. KRUCZKIEWICZ (Cracow, 1900), pp. IX-LXXIX.

KRUG, G., *Myśli o ikonie* [Thoughts on Icons], trans. R. MAZURKIEWICZ (Białystok, 1991).

KRYCZYŃKI, S., *Historia meczetu w Wilnie (próba monografii)* [The History of the Mosque in Vilnius (A Monographic Attempt)] (Warsaw, 1937).

KRYCZYŃSKI, S., *Tatarzy litewscy: Próba monografii historyczno-etnograficznej* [Lithuanian Tatars: An Attempt at a Historical and Etnographical Monograph] (Warsaw, 1938).

KRYNICKA, M., "Oprawy książkowe z herbami ostatnich Jagiellonów w zbiorach Muzeum Narodowego w Krakowie" [Book covers bearing coats of arms of the last Jagiellonian kings in the collection of the National Museum in Cracow], *Rozprawy i Sprawozdania Muzeum Narodowego w Krakowie* 12 (1980), pp. 21-83.

KRZYWY, R., "*Reges et principes Regni Poloniae* Adriana Kochana Wolskiego jako przykład wierszowanego katalogu władców" [*Reges et principes Regni Poloniae* by Adran Kochan Wolski as an example of a rhymed catalogue of rulers], *Acta Sueco-Polonica* 10-11 (2001-2002), pp. 95-104.

KRZYŻANIAK, B., *Kantyczki z rękopisów karmelitańskich (XVII-XVIII w.)* [Christmas Carols and Songs from the Manuscripts of the Carmelites] (Cracow, 1977).

KUBICKI, R., *Testamenty elbląskie: Studium z dziejów miasta i jego mieszkańców w późnym średniowieczu* [Last Wills from Elbląg: A Study from the History of the Town and its Inhabitants in the Late Middle Ages] (Gdańsk and Sopot, 2020).

KUBILIUS, J., *A Short History of Vilnius University* (Vilnius, 1979).

KUCHOWICZ, Z., *Barbara Radziwiłłówna* (Łódź, 1985).

KUCZYŃSKA, M., "Homiletyka cerkiewna pierwszej Rzeczypospolitej" [Orthodox homiletics in Old Poland], in: *Między Wschodem i Zachodem: Prawosławie i unia*, ed. M. KUCZYŃSKA (Warsaw, 2017), pp. 196-237.

KUHN, T.S., *The Structure of Scientific Revolutions* (Chicago, 1996).

KUKLO, C., *Demografia Rzeczypospolitej przedrozbiorowej* [The Demography of Old Poland] (Warsaw, 2009).

KULICKA, E., "Legenda o rzymskim pochodzeniu Litwinów i jej stosunek do mitu sarmackiego" [The legend of the Roman origins of the Lithuanians and its relationship with the myth of Sarmatia], *Przegląd Historyczny* 71.1 (1980), pp. 1-21.

Kultura i języki Wielkiego Księstwa Litewskiego [Culture and Languages of the Grand Duchy of Lithuania], ed. M.T. LIZISOWA (Cracow, 2005).

Kulturowa teoria literatury: Główne pojęcia i problemy [The Cultural Theory of Literature: Main Concepts and Problems], ed. M.P. MARKOWSKI and R. NYCZ (Cracow, 2006).

KULWICKA-KAMIŃSKA, J., *Dialogue of Scriptures: The Tatar Tefsir in the Context of Biblical and Qur'anic Interpretations* (Berlin, 2019).

KULWICKA-KAMIŃSKA, J., "Projekt Tefsir – wydanie krytyczne XVI-wiecznego przekładu Koranu na język polski / The Tefsir Project – Critical edition of the sixteenth century Polish translation of Koran", *Nurt SVD* 2 (2017), pp. 211-212.

KUNIGIELIS, J., "Organizacja funkcjonowania mostów i grobli w Wielkim Księstwie Litewskim – zarys problematyki" [Organization of the functioning of bridges and dikes in the Grand Duchy of Lithuania from the second half of the fifteenth to the end of the sixteenth century: Preliminaries], *Rocznik Lituanistyczny* 7 (2021), pp. 39-58.

KUOLYS, D., "Alberto Vijūko-Kojalavičiaus istorinis pasakojimas: Respublikos kūrimas" [The historical narrative of Wojciech Wijuk Kojałowicz: The creation of the commonwealth], in: A. VIJŪKAS-KOJALAVIČIUS (W.W. KOJAŁOWICZ), *Lietuvos istorijos įvairenybės* [Miscellanies of Lithuanian History], 2, ed. D. KUOLYS, trans. R. JURGELĖNAITĖ (Vilnius, 2004), pp. 391-397.

KUOLYS, D., "Motiejus Kazimieras Sarbievijus politiniame Lietuvos Didžiosios Kunigaikštystės teatre" [M.K. Sarbiewski at the political theatre of the Grand Duchy of Lithuania], in: *Motiejus Kazimieras Sarbievijus lietuvos, lenkijos, europos kultūroje: Tarptautinės mokslinės konferencijos, skirtos poeto 400-ųjų gimimo metinių jubiliejui, medžiaga, Vilnius, 1995, spalio 19-21*, ed. E. ULČINAITĖ (Vilnius, 1998), pp. 318-326.

KUPISZ, D., *Połock 1579* [Polatsk 1579] (Warsaw, 2003).

KURCZEWSKI, J., *Kościół zamkowy, czyli katedra wileńska w jej dziejowym, liturgicznym, architektonicznym i ekonomicznym rozwoju* [The Castle Church i.e. Vilnius

Cathedral in Its Historical, Liturgical, Architectural, and Economic Development], 1 (Vilnius, 1908), 2 (Vilnius, 1910), and 3 (Vilnius, 1910).

KURZOWA, Z., *Język polski Wileńszczyzny i kresów północno-wschodnich XVI-XX w.* [Polish Language of the Vilnius Region and North-Eastern Polish Borderlands in the Sixteenth-Twentieth Centuries] (Warsaw, 1993).

KURZOWA, Z., "Z badań and polszczyzną północnokresową XVII i XVIII w. (Uwarunkowania historyczne: Opis systemu fonetyczno-fonologicznego. Perspektywy rozwojowe)" [From the studies of the Polish language in the Northern part of the Eastern Borderlands (Historical preconditions: The description of the phonetic and phonologic system: Prospects of development)], in: Z. KURZOWA, *Ze studiów nad polszczyzną kresową. Wybór prac* (Cracow, 2007), pp. 192-220.

KURZOWA, Z., *Ze studiów nad polszczyzną kresową: Wybór studiów* [From the Studies of the Polish Language (Cracow, 2007).

KUŹMINA, D., *Katechizmy w Rzeczypospolitej XVI i początku XVII w.* [Catechisms in Old Poland in the Sixteenth and Early Seventeenth Centuries] (Warsaw, 2002).

KVIETKAUSKAS, M., *Vilniaus literatūrų kontrapunktai: Ankstyvasis modernizmas 1904-1915* [Literary Counterpoints of Vilnius: Early Modernism 1904-1915] (Vilnius, 2007).

L'Éloquence de la chaire entre écriture et oralité (XIII-XVIIIe siecles): Actes du colloque international de Genève, 11-12 septembre 2014, ed. G. AUBERT, A. HENEVELD, and C. MELI (Paris, 2018).

LAUCEVIČIUS, E., *Knygų įrišimai Lietuvos bibliotekose* [Book Bindings in Lithuanian Libraries] (Vilnius, 1976).

LAUCEVIČIUS, E., Popierius Lietuvoje XV-XVIII a. [Paper in Lithuania in the Fifteenth-Eighteenth Centuries] (Vilnius, 1967).

LAUSBERG, H., *Handbook of Literary Rhetoric: A Foundation for Literary Study*, with a Foreword by G.A. KENNEDY, trans. M.T. BLISS, A. JANSEN, and D.E. ORTON (Leiden, Boston, and Cologne, 1998).

LEGOFF, J., *Medieval Civilization: 400-1500 A.D.*, trans. J. BARROW (Oxford and Cambridge, Mass., 1988).

LELEWEL, J., *Bibliograficznych ksiąg dwoje* [Bibliography in Two Books], 2 (Vilnius, 1826).

LESIAK, A., "Kobiety z rodu Radziwiłłów w świetle inwentarzy i testamentów (XVI-XVIII w.)" [Women from the Radziwiłł family in the light of inventories and last wills (sixteenth-eighteenth centuries)], in: *Administracja i życie codzienne w dobrach Radziwiłłów XVI-XVIII wieku*, ed. U. AUGUSTYNIAK (Warsaw, 2009), pp. 131-138.

LEŚNIEWSKI, S., *Jan Zamoyski: Hetman i polityk* [Jan Zamoyski: The Hetman and Politician] (Warsaw, 2008).

LIEDKE, M., "Wykorzystanie akt synodów prowincjonalnych Jednoty Litewskiej z XVII wieku w badaniach historycznych" [The use of records of the provincial synods of Lithuanian Calvinists from the seventeenth century in historical research], *Bialostocczyzna* 59-60.3-4 (2000), pp. 9-17.

Lietuva, medaliuose XVI a.-XX a. pradžia [Lithuania in Medals: Sixteenth-Early Twentieth Century], ed. V. RUZAS (Vilnius, 1998).

Lietuvos jėzuitų teatras: XVI-XVIII amžiaus dramų rinktinė [Lithuanian Jesuit Theatre: A Collection of Plays from the Sixteenth-Eighteenth Centuries], ed., trans., and with an introduction by E. ULČINAITĖ (Vilnius, 2008).

Literary Cultures and Public Opinion in the Low Countries, 1450-1650, ed. J. BLOEMENDAL, A. VAN DIXHOORN, and E. STRIETMAN (Leiden and Boston, 2011).

LIZISOWA, M.T., "O języku kancelarii Wielkiego Księstwa Litewskiego" [On the language of the chancery of the Grand Duchy of Lithuania], in: *Wilno i kresy północno-wschodnie: Materiały II Międzynarodowej Konferencji w Białymstoku 14-17 IX 1994 r. w czterech tomach*, 3, *Polszczyzna kresowa*, ed. E. FELIKSIAK and B. NOWOMIEJSKI (Białystok, 1996), pp. 63-78.

LOACH, J., "The teaching of emblematics and other symbolic imagery by Jesuits within town colleges in seventeenth and eighteenth century France", in: *The Jesuits and the Emblem Tradition: Selected Papers of the Leuven International Emblem Conference 18-23 August, 1996*, ed. J. MANNING and M. VAN VAECK (Turnhout, 1999), pp. 161-186.

Loca scribendi: Miejsca i środowiska tworzące kulturę pisma w dawnej Rzeczypospolitej XV-XVIII stulecia [*Loca Scribendi*: Places and Milieus of Circles of the Production of the Written Word in the Polish-Lithuanian Commonwealth in the Fifteenth-Eighteenth Centuries], ed. A. ADAMSKA, A. BARTOSZEWICZ, and M. PTASZYŃSKI (Warsaw, 2017).

ŁAPICZ, Cz., "Trzy redakcje językowe muzułmańskiej legendy w piśmiennictwie Tatarów litewsko-polskich" [Three linguistic redactions of the Muslim legend in the writings of Lithuanian-Polish Tartars], *Acta Baltico-Slavica* 20 (1991), pp. 155-168.

ŁAPICZ, Cz., "Zawartość treściowa kitabu Tatarów litewskopolskich" [The contents of the 'kitab' of the Polish Tartars], *Acta Baltico-Slavica* 20 (1991), pp. 169-191.

ŁAPSZEWICZ, B., "Ratusz wileński, który pamięta średniowiecze" [The City Hall of Vilnius which remembers the Middle Ages], *Kurier Wileński* 18 (52), 11-17.05.2019 <https://kurierwilenski.lt/2019/05/18/ratusz-wilenski-ktory-pamieta-sredniowiecze/> (accessed: 7.11.2021).

ŁATYSZONEK, O., "Polityczne aspekty przedstawienia średniowiecznych dziejów ziem białoruskich w historiografii Wielkiego Księstwa Litewskiego XV-XVI w." [Political aspects of the representations of medieval history of the Belarusian parts of the Grand Duchy of Lithuania in the fifteenth-sixteenth centuries], *Białoruskie Zeszyty Historyczne – Беларускі гістарычны зборнік* 25 (2006), pp. 22-35.

ŁOPATECKI, K., "Ideowa wymowa ozdób armatnich z przełomu XVI i XVII wieku" [Ideological meaning of the cannon ornaments from the turn of the seventeenth century], in: *Nad społeczeństwem staropolskim*, 1, *Kultura – instytucje – gospodarka w XVI-XVIII stuleciu*, ed. K. ŁOPATECKI and W. WALCZAK (Białystok, 2007), pp. 249-270.

Łopatecki, K., "Konwokacja litewska 1615 roku: Z badań nad procedurą przyjmowania uchwał konwokacyjnych" [The 1615 Lithuanian *convocatio*: Some remarks on how the resolutions of the convocatio were cccepted], *Krakowskie Studia z Historii Państwa i Prawa* 12.4 (2019), pp. 493-522.

Łosowska, A., *Kolekcja Liber legum i jej miejsce w kulturze umysłowej późnośredniowiecznego Przemyśla* [The Text-Collection *Liber legum* and Its Place in the Intellectual Culture of Late Medieval Przemyśl] (Warsaw and Przemyśl, 2007).

Łosowski, J., "Akta sądów i urzędów szlacheckich w xiv-xviii wieku" [The documentation of the courts and offices for the noblemen in the fourteenth-eighteenth centuries], in: *Dyplomatyka staropolska*, ed. T. Jurek (Warsaw, 2015), pp. 253-338.

Łossowski, P., *Konflikt polsko-litewski 1918-1920* [The Conflict between Poland and Lithuania in 1918-1920] (Warsaw, 1996).

Loveridge, J., "The practice of the *Progymnasmata* in the Middle Ages: Ancestry and probability in Alan of Lille's *Anticlaudianus*", in: *Les* progymnasmata *en pratique, de l'Antiquité à nos jours*, ed. P. Chiron and B. Sans (Paris, 2020), pp. 203-217.

Łowmiańska, M., "Udział *communitatis mercatoriae* w samorządzie wileńskim" [The participation of the *communitas mercatoria* in the self-government of Vilnius], *Lituano-Slavica Posnaniensia* 9 (2003), pp. 75-108.

Łowmiańska, M.,*Wilno przed najazdem moskiewskim 1655 roku* [Vilnius before the Moscovite Invasion of 1655] (Vilnius, 1929).

Łowmiańska, M., "Wilno przed najazdem moskiewskim 1655 roku" [Vilnius before the Moscovite invasion of 1655], in: *Dwa doktoraty z Uniwersytetu Stefana Batorego w Wilnie: H. Łowmiański, Wchody miast litewskich: M. Łowmiańska, Wilno przed najazdem moskiewskim 1655 roku* (Poznań, 2005), pp. 149-330.

Łowmiański, H., "Agresja zakonu krzyżackiego na Litwę w wiekach xiii-xv" [The aggression of the Teutonic Order against Lithuania in the thirteenth-fifteenth centuries] , *Przegląd Historyczny* 45.2-3 (1954), pp. 338-371.

Łowmiański, H., "Papiernie wileńskie xvi wieku: Przyczynek do ich dziejów" [The paper mills in Vilnius in the sixteenth century: A contribution to their history], *Ateneum Wileńskie* 2.7-8 (1924), pp. 409-422.

Łowmiański, H., and J. Tumelis, "Bibliografia zawartości Ateneum Wileńskiego" [Bibliography of the contents of the *Ateneum Wileńskie*], *Pamiętnik Biblioteki Kórnickiej* 20 (1983), pp. 227-259.

Luciński, J., "Formularze czynności prawnych w Polsce w wiekach średnich: Przegląd badań" [The formularies of legal actions in medieval Poland: A research review], *Studia Źródłoznawcze* 18 (1973), pp. 149-179.

Łukaszewicz, J., *Dzieje kościołów wyznania helweckiego w Litwie* [The History of the Churches of the *Confessio Helvetica* in Lithuania], 1 (Poznań, 1842) and 2 (Poznań, 1843).

Lukšaitė, I., "Biblioteka Salomona Rysińskiego" [The book collection of Salomon Rysiński], *Odrodzenie i Reformacja w Polsce* 30 (1985), pp. 191-206.

LUKŠAITĖ, I., *Lietuvos publicistai valstiečių klausimu XVI a. pabaigoje – XVII a. pirmojoje pusėje* [Lithuanian Political Writers on the Issue of Peasants at the End of the Sixteenth and in the First Half of the Seventeenth Centuries] (Vilnius, 1976).

LUKŠAITĖ, I., *Radikalioji reformacijos kryptis Lietuvoje* [The Radical Direction of the Reformation in Lithuania] (Vilnius, 1980).

LUKŠAITĖ, I., *Reformacja a przemiany kulturowe w Wielkim Księstwie Litewskim* [Reformation and the Cultural Change in the Grand Duchy of Lithuania] (Poznań, 2003).

LUKŠAITĖ, I., *Reformacija Lietuvos Didžiojoje Kunigaikštystėje ir Mažojoje Lietuvoje XVI a. trečias dešimtmetis – XVII a. pirmas dešimtmetis* [Reformation in the Grand Duchy of Lithuania and Lithuania Minor, from the 1530s to the 1610s] (Vilnius, 1999).

LUKŠAITĖ, I., "Risinskis – lietuvos reformacijos veikėjas ir humanistinė kultura" [Rysiński – A Figure in the Lithuanian Reformation and Humanistic Culture], *Lietuvos Istorijos Metraštis* (1984), pp. 5-19.

LUKŠAITĖ, I., "Salomono Risinskio bibliotekos Vilniuje sąrašas" [The register of the Vilnius Book collection of Salomon Rysiński], in: *Iš lietuvos bibliotekų istorijos* [From the History of Lithuanian Libraries], ed. V. BULAVAS (Vilnius, 1985), pp. 17-45.

ŁUKSZA, W., "W sprawie prawosławnych bractw miodowych w Wilnie" [On the Orthodox mead brotherhoods in Vilnius], *Ateneum Wileńskie* 13.2 (1938), pp. 288-290.

LULEWICZ, H, "Rysiński Salomon", in: *PSB* 33 (1991-1992), pp. 553-557.

LUPESCU, M.M., "Spoken and written words in testaments: Orality and literacy in last wills of medieval Transylvanian burghers", in: *Uses of the Written Word in Medieval Towns. Medieval Urban Literacy II*, ed. M. MOSTERT and A. ADAMSKA (Turnhout, 2014) , pp. 273-286.

Maciej Kazimierz Sarbiewski i jego epoka: Próba syntezy [Maciej Kazimierz Sarbiewski and His Times: An Attempt at Synthesis], ed. J.Z. LICHAŃSKI (Pułtusk, 2006).

MACK, P., "Humanist rhetoric and dialectic", in: *The Cambridge Companion to Renaissance Humanism*, ed. J. KRAYE (Cambridge, 2010), pp. 82-99.

MĄCZAK, A., *Klientela: Nieformalne systemy władzy w Polsce i Europie XVI-XVIII w.* [The Patronage System: Informal Systems of Power in Poland and Europe, Sixteenth-Eighteenth Centuries] (Warsaw, 1994).

MAJOROSSY, J., "Archives of the dead: Administration of last wills in medieval Hungarian towns", in: *The Public (in) Urban Space: Papers from the Daily Life-Strand at the International Medieval Congress (Leeds, July 2003)*, ed. J. RASSON and G. JARITZ (Krems, 2003), pp. 21-27.

MALECZYŃSKI, K., *Zarys dyplomatyki polskiej wieków średnich* [An Outline of Polish Medieval Diplomatics], 1 (Wrocław, 1951).

MALECZYŃSKI, K.M., M. BIELIŃSKA, and A. GĄSIOROWSKI, *Dyplomatyka wieków średnich* [Diplomatic of the Middle Ages], (Warsaw, 1971).

MALICKI, J., *Kultura literacka renesansowego Śląska* [The Literary Culture of Renaissance Silesia] (Katowice, 1985).

MALICKI, M., "Nieznany dotychczas polski katechizm kalwiński ze zbiorów Biblioteki Księcia Augusta w Wolfenbüttel" [An as yet unknown Polish Calvinist catechism from the collection of the Prince August Library in Wolfenbüttel], *Biuletyn Biblioteki Jagiellońskiej*, 43.1-2 (1993), pp. 47-64.

MANGUEL, A., *A History of Reading* (London, 1997).

MANYŚ, B., "The pupil in handicraft guilds: The education and development system of boys in craft guilds of Vilnius in early modern times, in light of guild bylaws", *Biuletyn Historii Wychowania* 40 (2019), pp. 7-22.

MAROSZEK, J., "Ulice Wilna w XIV-XVIII wieku" [The streets of Vilnius in the fourteenth-eighteenth centuries], *Kwartalnik Historii Kultury Materialnej* 47.1-2 (1999), pp. 163-186.

MAROSZEK, J., and W.F. WILCZEWSKI, "Archiwa kapituły i kurii diecezjalnej wileńskiej, dzieje i współczesne miejsca przechowywania w zbiorach litewskich i polskich" [The archives of the Vilnius cathedral chapter and episcopal curia, their history and current places of preservation in Lithuanian and Polish collections], *Białostocczyzna* 4 (1998), pp. 3-9.

MAROTTI, A.F., "Patronage, poetry, and print", in: *Politics, Patronage and Literature in England 1558-1658*, special issue of *The Yearbook of English Studies* 21 (1991), pp. 1-26.

MARTYNAS, Jakulis, "Vilniaus katedros kapitulos pajamos XVI a. antroje pusėje-XVIII a. pajamų-išlaidų registrų duomenimis" [Incomes of the Vilnius cathedral chapter in the sixteenth-late eighteenth century based on the data of income-expenditure registers], *Istorijos šaltinių tyrimai* 5 (2014), pp. 171-191.

MARTZ, L., *The Poetry of Meditation: A Study in English Religious Literature of the Seventeenth Century* (New Haven, 1954).

MASLAUSKAITĖ-MAŽYLIENĖ, S., *Dzieje wizerunku św. Kazimierza od XVI do XVIII wieku. Między ikonografiją a tekstem* [History of the Effigy of St. Casimir from the Sixteenth until the Eighteenth Century: Between Iconography and Text] (Vilnius, 2013).

MATUŠAKAITĖ, M., *Išėjusiems atminti: Laidosena ir kapų ženklinimas LDK* [In Memory of the Departed: Burial and Grave Marking in the Grand Duchy of Lithuania] (Vilnius, 2009).

MAZURKIEWICZ, R., "Wstęp" [Introduction], In: A. WOLAN, *De libertate politica sive civili: O wolności rzeczypospolitej albo ślacheckiej*, ed. M. EDER and R. MAZURKIEWICZ (Warsaw, 2010), pp. 9-53.

MAZURKIEWICZ, R., "Zapomniane polonicum w zbiorach Biblioteki Watykańskiej" [A forgotten Polonicum in the collection of the Vatican Library], *Terminus* 3.1-2 (2001), pp. 172-174.

Medieval Letters Between Fiction and Document, ed. Ch. HØGEL and E. BARTOLI (Turnhout, 2015).

MEILUS, E., "The history of Vilnius Old Jewish Cemetery at Šnipiškės in the period of the Grand Duchy of Lithuania", *Lithuanian Historical Studies*, 12 (2007), pp. 63-92.

MEILUS, E., "Życie codzienne w Wilnie w czasie okupacji moskiewskiej 1655-1661" [Daily life in Vilnius during the Moscovite occupation of 1655-1661], in: *Litwa w epoce Wazów*, ed. W. KRIEGSEISEN and A. RACHUBA (Warsaw, 2006), pp. 129-144.

MELLER, K., *"Noc przeszła, a dzień się przybliżył": Studia o polskim piśmiennnictwie reformacyjnym XVI wieku* ["The Night Has Passed and the Day has Approached": Studies on Polish Reformation Literature of the Sixteenth Century] (Poznań, 2004).

MELNYK, M., *Pre-ekumenizm i konfesjonalizm: Prawosławne dążenia zjednoczeniowe w Pierwszej Rzeczypospolitej (1590-1596)* [Pre-Ecumenism and Confessionalism: Orthodox Aspirations for the Unification in the Polish-Lithuanian Commonwealth (1590-1596)] (Cracow, 2018).

MERCZYNG, H., "Czterokrotne zburzenie zboru ewangelickiego w Wilnie" [The fourfold demolition of the Protestant church in Vilnius], in: W. GIZBERT STUDNICKI, *Zarys historyczny wileńskiego kościoła ewangelicko-reformowanego i jego biblioteki* (Vilnius, 1932), pp. 23-31.

MICHAŁOWSKA, T., "Epistola dedicatoria", in: T. MICHAŁOWSKA, *Literatura polskiego średniowiecza* [Polish Medieval Literature] (Warsaw, 2011), pp. 239-243.

MICHAŁOWSKA, T., *Leksykon: Literatura polskiego średniowiecza* [A Lexicon: Polish Literature of the Middle Ages] (Warsaw, 2011).

MICHAŁOWSKA, T., *Średniowiecze* [The Middle Ages] (Warsaw, 1995).

MICHAŁOWSKA, T., *Staropolska teoria genologiczna* [The Old Polish Theory of Literary Genres] (Wrocław, 1974).

MICHAŁOWSKA, *Średniowieczna teoria literatury w Polsce: Rekonesans* [Literary Theory in Medieval Poland: An Exploration] (Toruń, 2016).

MICHAŁOWSKA-MYCIELSKA, A., "The council of Lithuanian Jews (1623-1764): Lithuania's central Jewish representation", *Biuletyn Polskiej Misji Historycznej – Bulletin der Polnischen Historischen Mission* 9 (2014), pp. 51-69.

MICHAŁOWSKA-MYCIELSKA, A., *Sejm żydów litewskich (1623-1764*) [The Parliament of Lithuanian Jews (1623-1764)] (Warsaw, 2014).

MIKUŁA, M., *Municipal Magdeburg Law (*Ius municipale Magdeburgense*) in Late Medieval Poland: A Study on the Evolution and Adaptation of Law*, trans. A. BRANNY (Leiden – Boston, 2021).

MIKUŁA, M., "Statuty prawa spadkowego w miastach polskich prawa magdeburskiego (do końca XVI wieku)" [The statutes of inheritance law in Polish towns under the Magdeburg Law (until the end of the sixteenth century)], *Z Dziejów Prawa* 7 (2015), pp. 33-63.

MIKUŁA, M., "Tradycje prawne w regulacjach testamentowych w miastach Królestwa Polskiego XIV-XVI wieku: Prawo sasko-magdeburskie, prawo kanoniczne i rzymskie oraz prawodawstwo lokalne" [Legal traditions in the testamentary regulations in the towns of the Kingdom of Poland in the fourteenth-sixteenth centuries: The Saxon-Magdeburg law, canon and Roman law, and the local legislation], *Kwartalnik Historii Kultury Materialnej* 68.2 (2020), pp. 131-158.

MIRONOWICZ, A., *Bractwa cerkiewne w Rzeczypospolitej* [Orthodox brotherhoods in the Polish-Lithuanian Commonwealth] (Białystok, 2003).

MIRONOWICZ, A., "Drukarnie bractw cerkiewnych" [Printing houses of the Orthodox brotherhoods], in: *Prawosławne oficyny wydawnicze w Rzeczypospolitej*, ed. A. MIRONOWICZ, U. PAWLUCZUK, and P. CHOMIK (Białystok, 2004), pp. 52-68.

MIRONOWICZ, A., *Józef Bobrykowicz, biskup białoruski* [Józef Bobrykowicz, a Belarusian Bishop] (Białystok, 2003).

MIRONOWICZ, A., "Kościół prawosławny i unicki w Rzeczypospolitej w latach 1596-1648" [The Orthodox and Uniate Church in the Polish-Lithuanian Commonwealth in the period 1596-1648], *Беларускі Гістарычны Зборнік – Białoruskie Zeszyty Historyczne* 5 (1995), pp. 23-55.

MIRONOWICZ, A., "O parafii kornińskiej, ikonie łaskami słynącej i księdze cudów" [On the parish of Kornin, the miraculous icon and the Book of Miracles], in: *Księga cudów przed ikoną Matki Bożej w Starym Korninie dokonanych*, ed. A. MIRONOWICZ (Białystok, 1997), pp. 5-17.

MIRONOWICZ, A., "Szkolnictwo prawosławne na ziemiach białoruskich w XVI-XVIII wieku" [The Orthodox school system in the Belarusian lands in the sixteenth-eighteenth centuries], *Беларускі Гістарычны Зборнік – Białoruskie Zeszyty Historyczne*, 1994, no 2 (2), pp. 20-34.

MIŠKINIENĖ, G., *Seniausi lietuvos totoriu rankraščiai: Grafika, transliteracija, vertimas, tekstu struktura ir turinys* [The Oldest Lithuanian Tartar Manuscripts: Graphics, Transliteration, Translation, Structure, and Content of Texts] (Vilnius, 2001).

MOLENDA, M., Splendide vestitus*: O znaczeniu ubiorów na królewskim dworze Jagiellonów w latach 1447-1572* [*Splendide vestitus*: On the Meaning of Clothes at the Jagiellonian Royal Court in the Period 1447-1572] (Cracow, 2012).

MOLNÁR, F., "Isabella and her Italian Connections", in: *Isabella Jagiellon, Queen of Hungary (1539-1559): Studies*, ed. Á. MÁTÉ and T. OBORNI (Budapest, 2020), pp. 163-172.

MONIUSZKO, A., "Wybrane aspekty ekonomicznego funkcjonowania sądownictwa grodzkiego i ziemskiego na Mazowszu w pierwszej połowie XVII wieku" [Some economic aspects of the castle and land courts in Masovia in the first half of the seventeenth century], in: *Nad społeczeństwem staropolskim*, 2, *Polityka i ekonomia – społeczeństwo i wojsko – religia i kultura w XVI-XVIII wieku*, ed. D. WEREDA (Siedlce, 2009), pp. 41-61.

MORAWSKI, K., *Andrzej Petrycy Nidecki: Jego życie i dzieła* [Andrzej Petrycy Nidecki: His Life and Works] (Cracow, 1892).

MORAWSKI, M., *Synod piotrkowski w roku 1589* [The Synode of Piotrków of 1589] (Włocławek, 1937).

MOSS, A., *Printed Commonplace-Books and the Structuring of Renaissance Thought* (Oxford, 1996).

MOSTERT, M., *A Bibliography of Works on Medieval Communication* (Turnhout, 2012).

MOSTERT, M., "Forgery and trust", in: *Strategies of Writing: Studies on Text and Trust in the Middle Ages*, ed. P. SCHULTE, M. MOSTERT, and I. VAN RENSWOUDE (Turnhout, 2008), pp. 37-59.

MOSTERT, M., "Introduction", in: M. MOSTERT, *A Bibliography of Works on Medieval Communication* (Turnhout, 2012), pp. 1-27.

MOSTERT, M., "New approaches to medieval communication?", in: *New Approaches to Medieval Communication*, ed. M. MOSTERT, Introduction M.T. CLANCHY (Turnhout, 1999), pp. 15-37.

Motiejus, Kazimieras Sarbievijus lietuvos, lenkijos, europos kultūroje. Tarptautinės mokslinės konferencijos, skirtos poeto 400-ųjų gimimo metinių jubiliejui, medžiaga, Vilnius, 1995, spalio 19-21 [Maciej Kazimierz Sarbiewski in Lithuanian, Polish and European Culture: Proceedings of the International Research Conference Dedicated to the Poet's 400th Birthday, Vilnius, October 19-21, 1995], ed. E. ULČINAITĖ (Vilnius, 1998).

MURPHY, J.J., *Rhetoric in the Middle Ages: A History of Rhetorical Theory from Saint Augustine to the Renaissance* (Berkeley, Los Angeles, and London, 1974).

Nad złoto droższe: Skarby Biblioteki Narodowej [More Precious than Gold: The Treasures of the National Library], ed. H. TCHÓRZEWSKA-KABATA and M. DĄBROWSKI (Warsaw, 2003).

NARBUTIENĖ, D., "LDK latyniškoji knyga asmeninėse XVI-XVII a. bibliotekose" [Latin books of the Grand Duchy of Lithuania in the personal libraries from the sixteenth-seventeenth centuries], *Knygotyra* 37 (2001), pp. 138-152.

NARBUITENĖ, D., *Lietuvos Didžiosios Kunigaikštijos lotyniškoji knyga XV-XVII a.* [Latin Books of the Grand Duchy of Lithuania of the Fifteenth-Seventeenth Centuries] (Vilnius, 2004).

NARBUTT, O., *Historia i typologia ksiąg liturgicznych bizantyńskosłowiańskich. Zagadnienie identyfikacji według kryterium treściowego* [History and Typology of the Byzantine-Slavic Orthodox Books: The Problem of Their Identification According to the Criterion of Contents] (Warsaw, 1979).

NARBUTT, T., *Pomniejsze pisma historyczne szczególnie do Litwy odnoszące się* [Minor Historical Studies, Especially Concerning Lithuania] (Vilnius, 1856).

NATOŃSKI, B., *Humanizm jezuicki i teologia pozytywno-kontrowersyjna od XVI do XVIII wieku: Nauka i piśmiennictwo* [The Humanism of the Jesuits and the Apologetic-Controversial Theology from the sixteenth till the eighteenth Century: Learning and Texts] (Cracow, 2003).

NATOŃSKI, B., "Szkolnictwo jezuickie w dobie kontrreformacji" [Jesuit Schools in the period of the Counter-Reformation], in: *Z dziejów szkolnictwa jezuickiego w Polsce: Wybór artykułów*, ed. and with an introduction by J. PASZENDA (Cracow, 1994), pp. 34-62.

NAUMOW, A., "Biblia i liturgia w systemie wartości kultury ruskiej" [The Bible and liturgy in the system of values of Ruthenian Culture], In: Między Wschodem i Zachodem: Prawosławie i unia, ed. M. Kuczyńska (Warsaw, 2017), pp. 121-140.

NAUMOW, A., Domus divisa*: Studia nad literaturą ruską w I Rzeczypospolitej* [*Domus divisa*: Studies on Ruthenian Literature in the First Polish Republic] (Cracow, 2002).

NAUMOW, A., *Wiara i historia: Z dziejów literatury cerkiewno-słowiańskiej na ziemiach polsko-litewskich*: *Studia slawistyczne krakowsko-wileńskie 1* [Faith and History: From the History of the Church Slavonic Literature in the Polish-Lithuanian Lands:Cracow-Vilnian Slavic Studies 1] (Cracow, 1996).

NAWROCKA-BERG, M., "Dziwne światy karmelitanek: Próba czytania zakonnych kantyczek" [The peculiar worlds of the Carmelite nuns: An attempt at reading the monastic songs], in: *Koncept w kulturze staropolskiej*, ed. L. ŚLĘK, A. KARPIŃSKI, and W. PAWLAK (Lublin, 2005), pp. 273-285.

Necessitas et ars: Studia staropolskie dedykowane Profesorowi Januszowi Pelcowi [*Necessitas et ars*: Old Polish Studies offered to the Professor Janusz Pelc], 1, ed. B. OTWINOWSKA *et al.* (Warsaw, 1993).

NEDZINSKAITĖ, Ž., "A quest for originality in Latin poetry of the Grand Duchy of Lithuania observed in manuscripts of the seventeenth-eighteenth centuries", *Interlitteraria* 23.2 (2018), pp. 278-294.

NEDZINSKAITĖ, Ž., "'*Finis epigrammatis est anima eius*': Transformations of the content of the Latin epigram in the epoch of the Baroque", *Interlitteraria* 19.2 (2014), pp. 276-292.

NEKRAŠEVIČ-KAROTKAJA, Ž., "Latin epic poetry and its evolution as a factor of cultural identity in Central an Eastern Europe in the sixteenth and seventeenth centuries", in: Latinitas *in the Polish Crown and the Grand Duchy of Lithuania: Its Impact on the Development of Identities*, ed. G. SIEDINA and M. GARZANITI (Florence, 2014), pp. 21-33.

NEUMANN, N.P., "Kronikarze poznańskiego klasztoru karmelitów bosych i ich dzieło w okresie staropolskim" [The chroniclers of the monastery of the Discalced Carmelites in Poznań and their work in the Old Polish period], *Karmelitańskie Studia i Materiały Historyczne* 1 (1993), pp. 113-146.

New Approaches to Medieval Communication, ed. M. MOSTERT (Turnhout, 1999).

NIEDŹWIEDŹ, J., "Autobiografia Biernata z Lublina (1516)" [The autobiography of Biernat of Lublin], in: *Biernat z Lublina a literatura i kultura wczesnego renesansu w Polsce*, ed. J. DĄBKOWSKA-KUJKO and A. NOWCKA-STRUSKA (Lublin, 2015), pp. 17-26.

NIEDŹWIEDŹ, J., "Cyrillic and Latin script in late medieval Vilnius", in: *Uses of the Written Word in Medieval Towns. Medieval Urban Literacy II*, ed. M. MOSTERT and A. ADAMSKA (Turnhout, 2014), pp. 99-116.

NIEDŹWIEDŹ, J., "How did Virgil help forge Lithuanian identity in the sixteenth century?", in: Latinitas *in the Polish Crown and the Grand Duchy of Lithuania. Its Impact on the Development of Identities*, ed. G. SIEDINA and M. GARZANITI (Florence, 2014), pp. 35-47.

NIEDŹWIEDŹ, J., "Humanitas na styku kultur: Kwestia dyskursów kolonialnych we wschodniej Europie" [*Humanitas* at the junction of cultures: The issue of colonial discourses in Eastern Europe], in: *Humanizm: Historie pojęcia*, ed. A. BOROWSKI (Warsaw, 2009), pp. 199-248.

NIEDŹWIEDŹ, J., "Jesuit education in the Polish-Lithuanian commonwealth (1565-1773)", *Journal of Jesuit Studies*, 5.3 (2018), pp. 441-455.

NIEDŹWIEDŹ, J, "Kaznodzieja, lider i ghostwriter: Notatniki Michała Woyniłłowicza (1671-1683) jako ego-dokumenty" [The preacher, the leader, and ghostwriter: The notebooks of Michał Woyniłłowicz (1671-1683) as ego-documents], in: *Księga jubileuszowa ofiarowana Profesorowi Andrzejowi Romanowskiemu*, ed. A. BIEDRZYCKA, P. BUKOWIEC, and I. WĘGRZYN (Cracow, 2022), pp. 369-395.

NIEDŹWIEDŹ, J., *Kultura literacka Wilna 1323-1655: Retoryczna organizacja miasta* [The Literary Culture of Vilnius 1323-1655: The Rhetorical Organization of the City] (Cracow, 2012).

NIEDŹWIEDŹ, J., "Mercator's Lithuanian-Russian borderlands: *Russiae pars amplificata* (1595) and its Polish sources", *Imago Mundi* 2 (2019), pp. 151-172.

NIEDŹWIEDŹ, J., "Multiscripturality in the Grand Duchy of Lithuania: New research approaches", trans. D.A. Frick, *East European Politics and Societies and Cultures*, 33 (2019), pp. 3-16.

NIEDŹWIEDŹ, J., *Nieśmiertelne teatra sławy: Teoria i praktyka twórczości panegirycznej na Litwie w XVII i XVIII w.* [The Immortal Theatres of Glory: The Theory and Practice of Panegyric Literature in Lithuania in the Seventeenth and Eighteenth Centuries] (Cracow, 2003).

NIEDŹWIEDŹ, J., "Polska szesnastowieczna propaganda wojenna w działaniu: Przypadek Atlasu Księstwa Połockiego (1580)" [Polish sixteenth-century wartime propaganda in action: The case of the Atlas of the Principality of Polatsk (1580)], *Terminus* 19.2 (2017), pp. 477-510.

NIEDŹWIEDŹ, J., "Rapport of research in the Latvian Academic Library and the Latvian National Library in Riga, 2005", in: K. ZAJAS, *Absent Culture: The Case of Polish Livonia* (Frankfurt am Main, 2013), pp. 377-389.

NIEDŹWIEDŹ, J., "Strzała w nodze świętego Michała: Daniel Naborowski i wileńskie narracje sądowe z XVII w." [The arrow in St. Michael's leg: Daniel Naborowski and narrations from Vilnius courts from the seventeenth century], in: *Daniel Naborowski: Krakowianin – Litwin – Europejczyk*, ed. K. GAJDKA and K. FOLLPRECHT (Katowice and Cracow, 2008), pp. 83-101.

NIEDŹWIEDŹ, J., "Sultzer Salomon (ok. 1564 lub 1566-przed 29 IX 1603)", in: *PSB* 45 (2007-2008), pp. 503-504.

NIEDŹWIEDŹ, J., "Sylabotonizm Jana Kochanowskiego i teoria wersyfikacji polskiej w XVII w." [The accentual-syllabic versification of Jan Kochanowski and the theory of Polish versification in the seventeenth century], *Terminus* 8.1 (2006), pp. 173-187.

NIEDŹWIEDŹ, J., "Sylwa retoryczna: Reprezentacja kultury literackiej XVII i XVIII w." [The Rhetorical *silva rerum*: A representation of literary culture in the seventeenth and eighteenth centuries], in: *Staropolskie kompendia wiedzy* [The Old-Polish

Compendia of Knowledge], ed. I. DACKA-GÓRZYŃSKA and J. PARTYKA (Warsaw, 2009), pp. 87-89.

NIEDŹWIEDŹ, J., "Twardowski w szkole XVII i XVIII wieku. (*Quae rapiet sub nubae vetustas minimae molles Tvardovii Musas?*)" [Twardowski in school in the seventeenth and eighteenth centuries (*Quae rapiet sub nubae vetustas minimae molles Tvardovii Musas?*)] , In: *Wielkopolski Maro: Samuel ze Skrzypny Twardowski i jego dzieło w wielkiej i małej Ojczyźnie*, ed. K. MELLER and J. KOWALSKI (Poznań, 2002), pp. 352-359.

NIEDŹWIEDŹ, J., "Wielopiśmienność Wielkiego Księstwa Litewskiego: Nowe perspektywy badawcze" [Multiscriturality in the Grand Duchy of Lithuania: New perspectives of research], *Wielogłos* 2014.2, pp. 11-21.

NIEDŹWIEDŹ, J., "Zbigniew Oleśnicki i jego listy do humanistów" [Zbigniew Oleśnicki and his letters to the humanists], *Terminus* 1.1 (1999), pp. 188-193.

NIENDORF, M., *Das Großfürstentum Litauen 1569-1795: Studien zur Nationsbildung in der Frühen Neuzeit* (Wiesbaden, 2006).

NIEZNANOWSKI, S., "Barokowe kolędy polskie" [Polish Baroque Christmas carols] , in: Necessitas et ars*: Studia staropolskie dedykowane Profesorowi Januszowi Pelcowi*, 1, ed. B. OTWINOWSKA *et al.* (Warsaw, 1993), pp. 113-121.

NOWAK-DŁUŻEWSKI, J., *Okolicznościowa poezja polityczna w dawnej Polsce: Dwaj młodsi Wazowie* [Occasional Political Poetry in Ancient Poland: Two Younger Vasa Kings] (Warsaw, 1972).

NOWAK-DŁUŻEWSKI, J., *Okolicznościowa poezja polityczna w dawnej Polsce: Pierwsi królowie elekcyjni* [Occasional Political Poetry in Ancient Poland: The First Elected Kings] (Warsaw, 1969).

NOWAK-DŁUŻEWSKI, J., *Okolicznościowa poezja polityczna w dawnej Polsce: Zygmunt III* [Occasional Political Poetry in Ancient Poland: Sigismund III] (Warsaw, 1971).

NOWAK, T.M., "O 'mówiących działach' artylerii polskiej XVI-XVIII wieku" [About the 'talking cannons' of the Polish artillery in the sixteenth-seventeenth centuries], *Napis* 12 (2006), pp. 379-393.

NOWAK, T.M., „Sprzęt artylerii polskiej XVI wieku w świetle inwentarza z lat 1551-1565" [The equipment of the Polish artillery of the sixteenth century in the light of the inventory from the years 1551-1565], *Studia i Materiały do Historii Wojskowości* 9.2 (1963), pp. 281-302.

NOWAK, Z., *Konrad Baumgart i początki sztuki drukarskiej w Gdańsku w XV wieku* [Konrad Baumgart and the Beginnings of the Art of Printing in Gdańsk in the Fifteenth Century] (Gdańsk, 1998).

NOWAK, Z., "Literatura sowiźrzalska wobec reformacji" [The attitude of chapbook literature towards the Reformation], *Pamiętnik Literacki* 66.3 (1965), pp. 17-32.

NOWAK, Z., *Początki sztuki drukarskiej na Pomorzu w XV wieku* [The Beginnings of the Printing Art in Pomerania in the Fifteenth Century] (Gdańsk, 1976).

NOWAKOWSKA, N., *Church, State and Dynasty in Renaissance Poland: The Career of Cardinal Fryderyk Jagiellon (1468-1503)* (Abingdon, 2007).

NOWICKA-STRUSKA, A., "Za murami klasztoru: Historiografia lubelskich karmelitanek bosych" [Behind the walls of a nunnery: Historigraphy of the Discalced Carmelite nuns in Lublin], *Acta Universitatis Lodzensis: Folia Litteraria Polonica*, 2.53 (2019), pp. 79-116.

NOWOROLSKA, B., *Kultura literacka Podlasia: Szkice* [The Literary Culture of the Podlasie Region: Sketches] (Białystok, 2017).

NUOVO, A., *The Book Trade in the Italian Renaissance* (Leiden and Boston, 2013).

OBERTYŃSKI, Z., "Agenda Wileńska z 1499 r." [The liturgical agenda of the Vilnius bishopric of 1499] , *Przegląd Teologiczny* 10 (1929), pp. 171-191.

OBREMSKI, K., *Panegiryczna sztuka postaciowania: August II Mocny (J. K. Rubinkowski,* Promienie cnót królewskich ...*)* [A Panegyric Art of Depicting Characters: Augustus II the Strong (J.K. Rubinkowski, "The rays of royal virtues)] (Toruń, 2003).

OCHMAN, J., *Peryferie filozofii żydowskiej* [Peripheries of Jewish Philosophy] (Cracow 1997).

OCHMAŃSKI, J., "Najdawniejsze księgozbiory na Litwie od końca XIV do połowy XVI wieku" [The oldest book collections in Lithuania from the end of the fourteenth until the mid-sixteenth century], in*:* Europa orientalis*: Polska i jej wschodni sąsiedzi od Średniowiecza po współczesność: Studia i materiały ofiarowane Profesorowi Stanisławowi Alexandrowiczowi w 65 rocznicę urodzin*, ed. Z. KARPUS, T. KEMPA, and D. MICHALUK (Toruń, 1996), pp. 73-84.

OCHMAŃSKI, J., "Najdawniejsze szkoły na Litwie od końca XIV do połowy XV wieku" [The oldest schools in Lithuania from the end of the fourteenth until the middle of the fifteenth century], in: *Dawna Litwa*, ed. J. OCHMAŃSKI (Olsztyn, 1986), pp. 113-133.

OCHMAŃSKI, J., "Ruskie wzory organizacyjne w państwie litewskim XIV-XV wieku" [The Ruthenian patterns of the organisation of the Lithuanian State in the fourteenth and fifteenth centuries], in: *Dawna Litwa*, ed. J. OCHMAŃSKI (Olsztyn, 1986), pp. 75-82.

OEXLE, O.G., "Die Gegenwart der Lebenden und der Toten: Gedanken über *Memoria*", in: *Gedächtnis, das Gemeinschaft stiftet*, ed. K. SCHMID (Munich, 1985), pp. 74-107.

OEXLE, O.G., "Memoria als Kultur", in: *Memoria als Kultur*, ed. O.G. OEXLE (Göttingen, 1995), pp. 9-78.

OEXLE, O.G., "Memoria und Memorialbild", in: Memoria*: Der geschichtliche Zeugniswert des liturgischen Gedenkens im Mittelalter*, ed. K. SCHMID and J. WOLLASCH (Munich, 1984), pp. 384-440.

OKO, J., "Un commentaire inconnu de Sarbiewski de la Somme de Saint Thomas d'Aquin", *Humanitas* 1 (1930), pp. 15-32.

OKOŃ, J., *Dramat i teatr szkolny: Sceny jezuickie XVII wieku* [Drama and School Theatre: The Jesuit Stage of the Seventeenth Century] (Wrocław, 1970).

OLSON, D.R., *The World on Paper: The Conceptual and Cognitive Implications of Writing and Reading* (Cambridge, 1995).

ONG, W.J., *Orality and Literacy: The Technologizing of the Word* (New York, 2013).

ORŁOWSKA, A.P., "Kontakty handlowe Gdańska i Wilna w świetle piętnastowiecznej księgi kupieckiej" [Commercial contacts between Gdansk and Vilnius in the light of a fifteenth-century merchant book], *Rocznik Lituanistyczny* 7 (2021), pp. 59-91.

OSIEWICZ, M., "Cechy dialektyczne *Szczytu dusznego* z 1528 r. (modlitewnik Olbrachta Gasztołda)" [Dialectical characteristics of the *Szczyt duszny* of 1528 (the Prayer Book of Olbracht Gasztołd)], *LingVaria* 15.1 (2020), pp. 163-175.

OTWINOWSKA, B., "Imitacja" [Imitation], in: *Słownik literatury staropolskie: Średniowiecze – Renesans – Barok*, ed. T. MICHAŁOWSKA (Wrocław, 1998), pp. 344-349.

OTWINOWSKA, B., "Elogium – *flos floris, anima et essentia* poetyki siedemnastowiecznego panegiryzmu" [Elogium – *flos floris, anima et essentia* of the poetics of the seventeenth-century panegyrics], in: *Studia z teorii i historii poezji* [Studies from the Theory and History of Poetry], series I, ed. M. GŁOWIŃSKI (Wrocław, 1967), pp. 148-184.

OZOROWSKI, E., "Knogler Kwiryn", in: *Słownik polskich teologów katolickich*, 2, ed. H.E. WYCZAWSKI (Warsaw, 1982), pp. 308.

PACEVIČIUS, A., "Bibliotekos" [Libraries], in: *Lietuvos Didžiosios Kunigaikštijos kultūra: Tyrinėjimai ir vaizdai* [The Culture of the Grand Duchy of Lithuania: Analysis and Images], ed. V. ALIŠAUSKAS *et al.* (Vilnius, 2001), pp. 96-97.

PACEVIČIUS, A., "Szkolnictwo" [Education], in: *Kultura Wielkiego Księstwa Litewskiego*: *Analizy i obrazy*, ed. V. ALIŠAUSKAS, L. JOVAIŠA, M. PAKNYS, R. PETRAUSKAS, and E. RAILA, trans. P. BUKOWIEC, B. KALĘBA, and B. PIASECKA (Cracow, 2006), pp. 724.

PAKNYS, M., *Vilniaus miestas ir miestiečiai 1636 m.: Namai, gyventojai, svečiai* [Vilnius City and Its Dwellers in 1636: Houses, Residents, Guests] (Vilnius, 2006).

PAPÉE, F., *Aleksander Jagiellończyk* [Alexander Jagiellon] (Cracow, 1949).

PARTYKA, J., *Żona wyćwiczona: Kobieta pisząca w kulturze XVI i XVII wieku* [A Well-Educated Wife: Writing Women in the Culture of the Sixteenth and Seventeenth Centuries] (Warsaw, 2004).

PASEK, M. (Kardasz M.), "'Bezoar z łez ludzkich czasu powietrza morowego' by Walenty Bartoszewski as an Example of *A Prescription for the Soul and the Body* in Time of the Plague", *Tematy i Konteksty* 2020.1 (special issue in English), pp. 121-149.

PASEK, M., "Słowo – obraz – spektakl: Korespondencja sztuk w opisach wileńskich procesji na Boże Ciało autorstwa Walentego Bartoszewskiego" [Word – image – performance: Interconnection of the arts in the descriptions of the Corpus Christi processions in Vilnius by Walenty Bartoszewski], *Zeszyty Naukowe Towarzystwa Doktorantów UJ Nauki Społeczne*, 2016.3, pp. 69-83.

PASZENDA, J., "Pomieszczenia biblioteczne u jezuitów polskich" [Library accomodations by Polish Jesuits], In: *Librorum amatori: Księga pamiątkowa ofiarowana ks. Czesławowi Michalunio SJ na 50lecie ofiarnej pracy w Bibliotece Filozoficznej Towarzystwa Jezusowego w Krakowie*, ed. A.P. BIEŚ (Cracow, 2004), pp. 111-118.

PASZKIEWICZ, U., *Inwentarze i katalogi bibliotek z ziem wschodnich Rzeczypospolitej (spis za lata 1553-1939)* [Inventories and Catalogues of the Libraries from the Eastern Parts of the Polish-Lithuanian Commonwealth (The List from the Years 1553-1939)], (Warsaw, 1996).

PATIEJŪNIENĖ, E., Brevitas ornata*: Mažosios literatūros formos XVI-XVII amžiaus Lietuvos Didžiosios Kunigaikštystės spaudiniuose* [*Brevitas Ornata*: Small Literary Forms in Publications from the Grand Duchy of Lithuania in the Sixteenth-Seventeenth Centuries] (Vilnius, 1998).

PAULOUSKAYA, H., *Grodzieńskie kroniki klasztorne XVII i XVIII wieku. Formy gatunkowe i aspekty komunikacyjne* [Chronicles of the Convents of Hrodna from the Seventeenth and Eighteenth Centuries: The Genres and Communication Aspects] (Warszawa, 2016).

PAULOUSKAYA, H., "O czym milczą kroniki klasztorów grodzieńskich (II połowa XVII-XVIII wiek)" [What the chronicles of the convents of Hrodna do not tell us (The second half of the seventeenth Century – the Eighteenth Century)], *Rocznik Lituanistyczny* 2 (2016), pp. 93-106.

PAWELEC, M., "Kazania funeralne Samuela Dambrowskiego: Z dziejów protestanckiego kaznodziejstwa XVII w." [The funeral sermons of Samuel Dambrowski: From the history of the Protestant preaching in the seventeenth century], in: *Kultura funeralna ziemi wschowskiej*, ed. P. KLINT, M. MAŁKUS, and K. SZYMAŃSKA (Wschowa, 2010), pp. 55-58.

PAWLIKOWSKA, W., "A 'foreign' elite? The territorial origins of the canons and prelates of the cathedral chapter of Vilna in the second half of the sixteenth century", *Slavonic and East European Review* 92.1 (2014), pp. 44-80.

PAWLIKOWSKA, W., "Znaczenie szlachectwa i wykształcenia przy obejmowaniu przez cudzoziemców wyższych godności kościelnych na Litwie w drugiej połowie XVI wieku" [The importance of noble origin and education for obtaining higher ecclesiastical dignities in Lithuania by foreigners in the second half of the sixteenth century], *Wschodni Rocznik Humanistyczny* 12 (2015), pp. 25-26.

PAWLIKOWSKA-BUTTERWICK, W., "Kanonik Wojciech Grabowski z Sierpca – zapoznana postać szesnastowiecznego Krakowa i Wilna" [Canon Wojciech Grabowski of Sierpc – a forgotten person of sixteenth-century Cracow and Vilnius], *Lituano-Slavica Posnaniensia* 11 (2005), pp. 177-179.

PAWLIKOWSKA-BUTTERWICK, W., "Księgozbiór biblioteki katedralnej w Wilnie z końca XVI wieku" [The book collection of the cathedral library of Vilnius from the end of the sixteenth century], *Odrodzenie i Reformacja w Polsce* 56 (2012), pp. 162-191.

PAWLIKOWSKA-BUTTERWICK, W., "Księgozbiory prywatne w Wielkim Księstwie Litewskim XVI stulecia: Postulaty metodyczne w rozpoznaniu problemu" [Private book collections in the Grand Duchy of Lithuania of the sixteenth century: Methodological suggestions for the investigation of the problem], *Nasze Historie* 8 (2007), pp. 7-15.

PAWLIKOWSKA-BUTTWERWICK, W., "Regarding the sixteenth-century statutes of the cathedral chapters of Vilna and Samogitia", in: W. PAWLIKOWSKA-BUTTERWICK and L. JOVAIŠA, *Vilniaus ir Žemaičių katedrų kapitulų statutai – The Statutes of the Chapters of Vilna and Samogitia* (Vilnius, 2015), pp. 133-141.

PELC, J., "Teksty Jana Kochanowskiego w kancjonałach staropolskich XVI i XVII wieku" [Texts of Jan Kochanowski in the Old Polish hymnals of the sixteenth and seventeenth centuries], *Odrodzenie i Reformacja w Polsce* 8 (1963), pp. 211-247.

PERCZYŃSKA, G., "Kobiety Iszkołci, czyli dzieje zarządzania majętnością" [Women of Ishkalds or the history of the administration of the estate], in: *Administracja i życie codzienne w dobrach Radziwiłłów XVI-XVIII wieku*, ed. U. AUGUSTYNIAK (Warsaw, 2009), pp. 7-109.

PERZANOWSKA, A., *Najjaśniejszym. Panegiryki i utwory pochwalne poświęcone królom i krolowym polskim w zbiorze starych druków Muzeum Narodowego w Krakowie* [To the Most Illustrious: Panegyric and Eulogistic Works Adressed to the Polish Kings and Queens in the Collection of Old Prints of the National Museum of Cracow] (Cracow, 2018).

PETERS, E.J., "Printing ritual: The performance of community in Christopher Plantin's *La Joyeuse et Magnifique Entrée de Monseigneur Francoys ... d'Anjou*", *Renaissance Quarterly* 61 (2008), pp. 370-413.

PETKŪNAS, D., "1585 metų Vilniaus kolokviumas – kunigaikščio Kristupo Radvilos Perkūno pastangos išsaugoti ekleziastinę bendrystę tarp LDK Liuteronų ir Reformatų bažnyčių" [The Vilnius colloquium of 1585: The efforts of Prince Krzysztof Radziwiłł 'the Thunderbolt' to preserve the ecclesiastical unity between the Lutheran and Reformed Churches in the Grand Duchy of Lithuania], in: *Colloquium habitum Vilnae die 14 Iunii, anno 1585 super articulo de Caena Domini*, ed. J. GELUMBECKAITĖ and S. NARBUTAS (Vilnius, 2006), pp. 181-204.

PETKŪNAS, D., "Wilno 1585 Colloquium – Lutheran and Reformed discord over sacramental theology in Lithuania", *Odrodzenie i Reformacja w Polsce* 49 (2005), pp. 17-34.

PETRUCCI, A., *Public Lettering: Script, Power, and Culture*, trans. L. LAPPIN (Chicago and London, 1993).

PETRYSZAK, B., "Sporządzanie testamentów we Lwowie w późnym średniowieczu – pisarze, ceny, okoliczności" [Composing last wills in late medieval Lviv: Scribes, prices, circumstances], *Kwartalnik Historii Kultury Materialnej* 62.3 (2014), pp. 329-336.

PIDŁYPCZAK-MAJEROWICZ, M., *Bazylianie w Koronie i na Litwie: Szkoły i książki w działalności zakonu* [The Basilian Monks in the Polish Crown and Lithuania: Schools and Books in the Activities of the Order] (Warsaw, 1986).

PIDŁYPCZAK-MAJEROWICZ, M., *Biblioteki i bibliotekarstwo zakonne na wschodnich ziemiach Rzeczypospolitej w XVII-XVIII wieku* [Libraries and Librarianship of the Religious Orders in the Eastern Parts of the Polish-Lithuanian Commonwealth in the Seventeenth and Eighteenth Centuries] (Wrocław, 1996).

PIDŁYPCZAK-MAJEROWICZ, M., "Język ksiąg religijnych Kościoła unickiego" [The language of the religious books of the Uniate Church], in: *Kultura i języki Wielkiego Księstwa Litewskiego*, ed. M.T. LIZISOWA (Cracow, 2005), pp. 213-222.

PIECHNIK, L., "O bibliotekach i najważniejszych podręcznikach u początku działalności Towarzystwa Jezusowego" [On the libraries and most important manuals in the early period of the activity of the Jesuit Order], in: *Librorum amatori: Księga pamiątkowa ofiarowana ks. Czesławowi Michalunio SJ na 50lecie ofiarnej pracy w Bibliotece Filozoficznej Towarzystwa Jezusowego w Krakowie*, ed. A.P. BIEŚ (Cracow, 2004), pp. 105-110.

PIECHNIK, L., *Początki Akademii Wileńskiej 1570-1599* [The Beginnings of the Academy of Vilnius, 1570-1599], with a preface by J.W. WOŚ (Rome, 1984).

PIECHNIK, L., *Powstanie i rozwój jezuickiej „Ratio studiorum" (1548-1599)* [The Emergence and Development of the Jesuit "*Ratio studiorum*" (1548-1599)] (Cracow, 2003).

PIECHNIK, L., *Rozkwit Akademii Wileńskiej w latach 1600-1655* [The Flowering of the Academy of Vilnius in the Period 1600-1655] (Rome, 1983).

PIECHOCKI, K.N., *Cartographic Humanism: The Making of Early Modern Europe* (Chicago and London, 2019).

PIEKARSKI, K., *Superexlibrisy polskie od XV do XVIII wieku* [The Polish Supralibros from the Fifteenth till the Eighteenth Century] , 1, tabs. 1-40 (Cracow, 1929).

PIEKOSIŃSKI, F., "Statut litewski, 1, Powstanie trzech redakcyj Statutu" [The Statute of Lithuania, 1, Drafting three editions of the Statute], in*: Rozprawy Akademii Umiejętności Wydział Historyczno-Filozoficzny*, 2nd Series, 14 (Cracow, 1900).

PIETKIEWICZ, K., *Cyrylica: Skrypt do nauki odczytywania pisma staroruskiego i rosyjskiego dla studentów archiwistyki* [The Cyrillic Script: A Manual for Learning to Read the Old Ruthenian and Russian Script for the Students of Archival Studies] (Poznań, 1996).

PIETKIEWICZ, K., *Paleografia ruska* [Ruthenian Paleography] (Warsaw, 2015).

PIETKIEWICZ, K., *Wielkie księstwo litewskie pod rządami Aleksandra Jagiellończyka: Studia nad dziejami państwa i społeczeństwa na przełomie XV i XVI wieku* [The Grand Duchy of Lithuania under the Rule of Alexander Jagiellon: Studies in the History of the State and Society at the Turn of the Sixteenth Century] (Poznań, 1995).

PIETRZAK, J., "*Ciało umarłe większego wymaga opatrzenia* – sekcja zwłok polskich królów i królowych od XVI do XVIII wieku w kontekście przygotowań do ceremonii pogrzebowej" ["A deceased body requires greater care – The postmortem of Polish kings and queens in the context of preparations for the funeral], in: *Śmierć, pogrzeb i upamiętnianie władców w dawnej Polsce*, ed. H. RAJFURA, P. SZWEDO, B. ŚWIADEK, M. WALCZAK, and P. WĘCOWSKI (Warsaw, 2020), pp. 142-170.

PIETRZKIEWICZ, I., "Teksty historiograficzne w środowisku dominikanów Prowincji Litewskiej – wybrane przykłady" [Hagiographical texts in the milieu of the Dominicans in the Lithuanian province – Selected examples], *Annales Universitatis*

Paedagogicae Cracoviensis: Studia ad Bibliothecarum Scientiam Pertinentia 14 (2016), pp. 328-346.

PILARCZYK, F., *Elementarze polskie od ich XVI-wiecznych początków do II wojny światowej: Próba monografii księgoznawczej* [Polish Primers from Their Beginnings in the Sixteenth Century up to the Second World War: A Sketch for a Monograph of Book Science] (Zielona Góra, 2003).

PILARCZYK, F., "Elementarze polskie XVI-XVIII w." [Polish primers of the sixteenth-eighteenth centuries], *Dydaktyka Literatury* 13 (1992), pp. 89-112.

PILARCZYK, K., "Rozpowszechnianie Talmudu w Polsce w XVI i XVII w. a duchowość żydowska" [Dissemination of the Talmud in Poland in the sixteenth and seventeenth centuries in the context of Jewish spirituality], in: *Duchowość żydowska w Polsce: Materiały z międzynarodowej konferencji dedykowanej pamięci profesora Chone Shmeruka: Kraków 26-28 kwietnia 1999*, ed. M. GALAS (Cracow, 2000), pp. 49-59.

PILARCZYK, K., *Talmud i jego drukarze w pierwszej Rzeczypospolitej* [The Talmud and Its Printers in the First Polish Republic] (Cracow, 1998).

PIOTROWSKI, K.J., *Studia nad dziejami poczt w Polsce XVI-XVIII w.* [Studies on the History of the Polish Postal Services in the Sixteenth-Eighteenth Centuries] (Łódź, 1962), <http://hdl.handle.net/11089/17158> (accessed: 27.02.2022).

PIRAMIDOWICZ, D., *Feniks świata litewskiego: Fundacje i inicjatywy artystyczne Kazimierza Leona Sapiehy (1609-1656)* [A Phoenix of the Lithuanian World: Foundations and Artistic Enterprises of Kazimierz Leon Sapieha (1609-1656)] (Warsaw, 2012).

PIROŻYŃSKI, J., "O poznańskim drukarzu Piotrze Sextilisie z Obrzycka i o polskich elementarzach XVI w." [On Piotr Sextilis of Obrzycko, a print master in Poznań, and on the Polish primers of the sixteenth century], *Studia Historyczne* 28.1 (1985), pp. 1-14.

PLATT, D., *Kazania pogrzebowe z przełomu XVI i XVII wieku: Z dziejów prozy staropolskiej* [Funeral Sermons from the Turn of the Sixteenth and Seventeenth Centuries] (Wrocław, 1992).

POCIŪTĖ, D., "Abraomas Kulvietis and the first Protestant *Confessio fidei* in Lithuania", in: Abraomas Kulvietis, *Pirmasis Lietuvos Reformacijos paminklas – The First Recorded Text of the Lithuanian Reformation: Abraomo Kulviečio* Confessio fidei *ir Johanno Hoppijaus* Oratio funebris *(1547) –* Confessio fidei *by Abaromas Kulvietis and* Oratio funebris *by Johann Hoppe (1547)*, ed. D. POCIŪTĖ (Vilnius, 2011), pp. 37-65.

POCIŪTĖ, D., *La Riforma in Lituania*, trans. E. RANOCCHI (Turin, 2021).

POCIŪTĖ, D., *Maištininkų katedros: Ankstyvoji reformacija ir lietuvių-italų evangelikų ryšiai* [Lecterns of the Rebels: The Early Reformation and Lithuanian-Italian Evangelical Relations] (Vilnius, 2008).

POCIŪTĖ, D., *Nematomos tikrovės šviesa: Reformacijos Lietuvoje asmenybės ir idėjos* [The Light of Invisible Reality: Personalities and Ideas of the Reformation in Lithuania] (Vilnius, 2017).

POLAK, E.J., *Medieval and Renaissance Letter Treatises and Form Letters*, 1, *A Census of Manuscripts Found in Eastern Europe and the Former USSR* (Leiden, 1993).

POLAŃSKI, W., *Jak przewożono pocztę polską w dawnych czasach. Szkic historyczny z ilustracjami* [How the Polish Post Was Transported in the Past: A Historical Account with Illustrations] (Toruń, 1925).

POMIAN, K., *Collectors and Curiosities: Paris and Venice, 1500-1800*, trans. E. WILES-PORTIER (Cambridge, 1991).

POMIAN, K., *Przeszłość jako przedmiot wiedzy* [The Past as an Object of Knowledge] (Warsaw, 2010).

POMORSKA, J., *Artyści włoscy w Polsce* [Italian Artists in Poland] (Warsaw, 2004).

POPIOŁEK, B., *Woli mojej ostatniej testament ten... Testamenty staropolskie jako źródło do historii mentalności XVII i XVIII wieku* [This My Last Will and Testament ... Polish Testaments as a Source for the History of Mentalities in the Seventeenth and Eighteenth Centuries] (Cracow, 2009).

POPLATEK, J., "Powstanie Seminarium Papieskiego w Wilnie (1582-1585)" [The creation of the papal seminary in Vilnius (1582-1585)], *Ateneum Wileńskie* 6.1-4 (1933-1934), pp. 47-71, 429-455.

POPLATEK, J., "Wykaz alumnów seminarium papieskiego w Wilnie 1582-1773" [List of the alumni of the papal seminary in Vilnius, 1582-1773], *Ateneum Wileńskie* 11 (1936), pp. 218-282.

POPŁAWSKA, H., *Kultura literacka karmelitanek bosych w Polsce* [The Literary Culture of the Discalced Carmelite Nuns in Poland] (Gdańsk, 2006).

POPŁAWSKA, H., "Rękopiśmienne kantyczki po polsku z XVII wieku – problemy prowieniencji i autorstwa" [Manuscript Christmas carols and songs in the Polish language from the seventeenth century – Issues of provenance and authorship], *Napis* 9 (2003), pp. 79-91.

POPŁAWSKA, H., "Zabawa wesoło-nabożna przyszłych obywatelów nieba: Nad siedemnastowiecznymi sylwami karmelitanek bosych" [A joyful and pious play of future citizens of Heaven: Reading the seventeenth-century miscellanies of the Discalced Carmelite Nuns], in: *Literatura polskiego baroku w kręgu idei*, ed. A. NOWICKA-JEŻOWA, M. HANUSIEWICZ, and A. KARPIŃSKI (Lublin, 1995), pp. 133-159.

POPRAWA-KACZYŃSKA, E., "Ignacjański '*modus meditandi*' w kulturze religijnej późnego baroku: Rekonesans [The *modus meditandi* of Ignatius of Loyola in the religious culture of late Baroque: A survey], in: *Religijność literatury polskiego baroku*, ed. Cz. HERNAS and M. HANUSIEWICZ (Lublin, 1995), pp. 259-270.

POTKOWSKI, E., "Kathedrales at the court of Queen Hedwig", *Codices Manuscripti* 13 (1987), pp. 79-85.

POTKOWSKI, E., "Katedralisi na dworze królowej Jadwigi: Z dziejów kultury książki w Polsce schyłku średniowiecza" [*Kathedrales* at the court of Queen Jadwiga of Poland: From the history of book culture in late medieval Poland], in: *Miscellanea historico-archivistica* 1 (1985), pp. 225-241.

Potkowski, E., *Książka rękopiśmienna w kulturze Polski średniowiecznej* [The Manuscript Book in the Culture of Medieval Poland] (Warsaw, 1984).

Potkowski, E., "Monarsze dary książkowe w polskim średniowieczu – pogrunwaldzkie dary Jagiełły" [Royal gifts of books in the Polish Middle Ages: The gifts of King Jogaila after the Battle of Grunwald], in: *Ojczyzna bliższa i dalsza. Studia historyczne ofiarowane Feliksowi Kiryk owi w sześćdziesiątą rocznicę urodzin*, ed. J. Chrobaczyński, A. Jureczko, and M. Śliwa (Cracow, 1993), pp. pp. 181-198.

Potkowski, E., "Podpisy królów polskich" [The signatures of the Polish kings], *Miscellanea historico-archivistica* 2 (1987), pp. 5-37.

Potkowski, E., "Produkcja książki rękopiśmiennej w Polsce w XV stuleciu" [The production of the manuscript book in Poland in the fifteenth century], in: *Z badań nad polskimi księgozbiorami historycznymi: Książka rękopiśmienna XV-XVII w.*, ed. B. Bieńkowska (Warsaw, 1980), pp. 9-67.

Prejs, M., *Oralność i mnemonika: Późny barok w kulturze polskiej* [Orality and Mnemonics: The Late Baroque in Polish Culture] (Warsaw 2009).

Prokop-Janiec, E., "Kategoria pogranicza we współczesnych studiach żydowskich" [The category of the borderland in contemporary Jewish studies], in: *Na pograniczach literatury*, ed. J. Fazan and K. Zajas (Cracow, 2012), pp. 134-146.

Proot, G., "Prices in Robert Estienne's booksellers' catalogues (Paris 1541-1552): A statistical analysis", in: *Selling and Collecting: Printed Book Sale Catalogues and Private Libraries in Early Modern Europe*, ed. G. Granata and A. Nuovo (Macerata, 2018), pp. 171-210.

Przeździecki, A., *Jagiellonki polskie w XVI wieku* [Women from the Dynasty of the Polish Jagiellons in the Sixteenth Century], 1 (Cracow, 1868).

Przymuszała, L., *Struktura i pragmatyka* Postylli *Samuela Dambrowskiego* [The Structure and Pragmatics of the *Postil* of Samuel Dambrowski] (Opole, 2003).

Ptaśnik, J., *Z dziejów kultury włoskiego Krakowa* [From the Cultural History of Italian Cracow] (Cracow, 1906).

Ptaszycki, S., *Описание книгъ и актовъ Литовской Метрики* [Description of the Books and Acts of the *Lithuanian Metrica*] (St Petersburg, 1887).

Puchowski, K., *Edukacja historyczna w jezuickich kolegiach Rzeczypospolitej 1565-1773* [The Historic Education in the Jesuit Colleges of the Polish-Lithuanian Commonwealth 1565-1773] (Gdańsk, 1999).

Quirini-Popławska, D., "Sebastiano Montelupi, toscano, mercante e maestro della posta reale di Cracovia: Saggio sulle comunicazioni PoloniaItalia nel '500", trans. M. Olszańska and S. Esposito, *Quaderni di Storia Postale* 13 (1989), pp. 39-66.

Rachuba, A., "Kancelarie pieczętarzy WKL w latach 1569-1765" [The chanceries of the seal masters of the Grand Duchy of Lithuania in the Period 1569-1765], in: *Lietuvos Metrika: 1991-1996 metų tyrinėjimai* [The *Lithuanian Metrica*: Research from 1991-1996] (Vilnius, 1998), pp. 256-271.

Radoń, S., *Z dziejów polemiki atyariańskiej w Polsce XVI-XVII wieku* [From the History of Polemics against the Polish Brethren] (Cracow, 1993).

RAGAUSKAS, A., "1650 m. kovo 30 d. Vilniaus suolininkų teismo įrašų knygų aprašas" [A description of the records of the Vilnius aldermen court from 30 March 1650], in: *Lietuvos miestų istorijos šaltiniai* [Sources for Lithuanian Urban History], 3, ed. A. DUBONIS (Vilnius, 2001), pp. 260-266.

RAGAUSKAS, A., *Vilniaus miesto valdantysis elitas XVII a. antrojoje pusėje (1662-1702 m.)* [The Ruling Elites of Vilnius in the Second Half of the Seventeenth Century (1662-1702)] (Vilnius, 2002).

RAGAUSKAS, A., "Źródła do historii urzędu wójta wileńskiego (koniec XIV w.-koniec XVII w.): Czy istniały księgi sądu wójtowskiego?" [Sources for the history of the *Voigt*'s office of Vilnius (end of the fourteenth-end of the seventeenth century): The registers of the *Voigt*'s court: Did they exist at all?], in: *Lietuvos Didžiosios Kunigaištystės istorijos šaltiniai: Faktas: Kontestas: Interpretacija*, ed. A. DUBONIS *et al.* (Vilnius, 2006), pp. 395-417.

RAGAUSKIENĖ, R., "The marriage of Catherine Jagiellon and John III Vasa in Vilnius (1562)", in: *Lithuania-Poland-Sweden: European Dynastic Unions and Historical-Cultural Ties*, ed. E. SAVIŠČEVAS and M. UZORKA (Vilnius, 2014), pp. 82-121.

RAGAUSKIENĖ, R., "XVI a. Lietuvos Didžiosios Kunigaikštystės didikų archyvo atvejis: Dubrovnos linijos Hlebavičių dokumentų aprašai Lietuvos Metrikoje [A case from the noblemen's archive in the Grand Duchy of Lithuania in the sixteenth century: An inventory of the documents of the Dubrovna line of the Hlebowicz family in the *Lithuanian Metrica*], *Istorijos šaltinių tyrimai* 4 (2012), pp. 109-131.

RAGAUSKIENĖ, R., and A. RAGAUSKAS, *Barboros Radvilaitės laiškai Žygimantui Augustui ir kitiems* [The Letters of Barbara Radziwiłłówna to Sigismund Augustus and Other People] [(Vilnius, 2001).

RAGAUSKIENĖ, R., and A. RAGAUSKAS, "Vieną ar dvi žmonas turėjo Augustinas Rotundas Meleskis (apie 1520-1584 m.)? Nauji duomenys įžymiojo Vilniaus vaito biografijai" [Did Augustyn Rotundus Mieleski (*c.* 1520-1584) have one or two wives? New data for the biography of the famous *Voigt* of Vilnius], *Lietuvos istorijos metraštis* 2000, pp. 20-54.

RAJCHEL, J., *Kamienny Kraków* [Cracow in Stone], second corrected edition (Cracow, 2005).

RAMBALDI PEYRONEL, S., "Introduzione: Per una storia delle donne nella Riforme", in: R.H. BAINTON, *Donne della Riforma in Germania, in Italia e in Francia*, trans. F. SARNI (Turin, 1992), pp. 37.

RANOCCHI, E., "In search of origins: *Bogurodzica*", in: *The Routledge World Companion to Polish Literature*, ed. M. POPIEL, T. BILCZEWSKI, and S. BILL (Abingdon-on-Thames, 2022), pp. 9-19.

RASZEWSKI, Z., *Krótka historia teatru polskiego* [A Short History of Polish Theatre] (Warsaw, 1978).

REICHARDT, D., "On the theory of a transcultural Francophony: The concept of Wolfgang Welsch and its didactic interest", *Novecento Transnazionale: Letterature, arti e culture* 1 (2017), pp. 40-56.

Renaissances Before the Renaissance: Cultural Revivals of Late Antiquity and the Middle Ages, ed. W.T. TREADGOLD (Stanford, 1984).

RESNICK, I.M., "The codex in early Jewish and Christian communities", *The Journal of Religious History* 17.1 (1992), pp. 1-17.

RODKIEWICZÓWNA, J., *Cech introligatorski w Wilnie: Zarys historyczny* [The Bookbinders Guild in Vilnius: A Historical Outline] (Vilnius, 1929).

ROMANOWSKI, A., *Młoda Polska wileńska* [Young Poland Movement in Vilnius] (Cracow, 1999).

ROPA, A., and E. ROPS, "The functions of illuminated charters from Latvian and Lithuanian Archives in a European Context", in: *Illuminierte Urkunden: Beiträge aus Diplomatik, Kunstgeschichte und Digital Humanities – Illuminated Charters: Essays from Diplomatic, Art History and Digital Humanities*, ed. G. BARTZ and M. GNEIß (Cologne, 2018), pp. 431-451.

RORTY, R., "The pragmatist's progress", in: *Interpretation and Overinterpretation*, ed. S. COLLINI (Cambridge, 1992), pp. 89-108.

ROSENWEIN, B.H., *Emotional Communities in the Early Middle Ages* (Ithaca and London, 2006).

ROSTOWSKI, S., *Lituanicarum Societas Jesu historiarum libri decem*, ed. J. MARTINOV (Paris, 1877).

ROSZKOWSKA, W., "Od '*Iudicium Paridis*' (1502) do '*Sądu Parysa*' (1542): Glosa do dziejów staropolskiej kultury teatralnej" [From the *Iudicium Paridis* (1502) to the *Judgment of Paris* (1542): A gloss on the history of Old Polish theatrical culture], in: *Literatura staropolska i jej związki europejskie: Prace poświęcone* XVII *Międzynarodowemu Kongresowi Slawistów w Warszawie w roku 1973*, ed. J. PELC (Wrocław, 1973), pp. 175-176.

ROTT-ŻEBROWSKI, T., *Gramatyka historyczna języka białoruskiego* [Historical Grammar of the Bielarusian Language] (Lublin, 1992).

ROVELLI, C., *Seven Brief Lessons on Physics*, trans. S. CARNELL and E. SEGRE (London, 2015).

ROWELL, S.C., "Vilniaus pirklių partnerių tinklas XV a. viduryje: Šaltiniotyrinis aspektas" [The trade network of the merchants of Vilnius in the mid-fifteenth century: An aspect of examining the sources], *Vilniaus istorijos metraštis*, 1, 2007, pp. 19-27.

"Royal Academy of Inscriptions and Literature", in: *The Encyclopedia of Diderot and d'Alembert Collaborative Translation Project*, trans. R. BENHAMOU (Ann Arbor, 2003) <http://hdl.handle.net/2027/spo.did2222.0000.217> (accessed: 08.04.2021)

RÓŻYCKI, E., *Z dziejów książki we Lwowie w* XVII *wieku* [From Book History in Lviv in the Seventeenth Century] (Katowice, 1991).

RUBIKAUSKAS, P., "Przywileje fundacyjne Akademii Wileńskiej" [The foundation charters of the Academy of Vilnius], in: *Z dziejów Almae Matris Vilnensis: Księga pamiątkowa ku czci 400-lecia założenia i 75 wskrzeszenia Uniwersytetu Wileńskiego*, ed. L. PIECHNIK and K. PUCHOWSKI (Cracow, 1996), pp. 19-31.

RUDNICKA, J., *Bibliografia katalogów księgarskich wydanych w Polsce do końca wieku XVIII* [The Bibliography of the Booksellers' Catalogues Issued in Poland until the End of the Eighteenth Century] (Warsaw, 1975).

RUTKOWSKA, G., "Kościół w życiu Heleny moskiewskiej, żony Aleksandra Jagiellończyka" [The Church in the life of Helena of Moscovy, the spouse of Alexander Jagellon], ed. A. KOZAK, *Średniowiecze Polskie i Powszechne* 12.16 (2020), pp. 261-307.

RYBARSKI, R., *Handel i polityka handlowa Polski w XVI stuleciu* [Commerce and Commerce Politics of Poland in the Sixteenth Century], 1, *Rozwój handlu i polityki handlowej* [Development of Trade and Trade Policy] (Poznań, 1928).

RYNDUCH, Z., *Nauka o stylach w siedemnastowiecznych retorykach polskich* [The Discourse on Styles in Seventeenth-Century Polish Manuals of Rethoric] (Gdańsk, 1967).

RYSZKA-KURCZAB, M., "'May every lover of truth find it through reading': Manners of authenticating the message in sixteenth-century accounts of Polish religious isputations, *Terminus* 20 (2018), special Issue, pp. 113-144.

RYSZKA-KURCZAB, M., *Retoryka polskich dialogów polemicznych doby Renesansu* [The Rhetoric of Polish Polemic Dialogues of the Renaissance Period] (Cracow, 2009).

SAENGER, P., "Books of Hours and the reading habits of the later Middle Ages", in: *The Culture of Print*, ed. R. CHARTIER (Cambridge, 1989), pp. 141-173.

SAKS, W., "Zbiory rękopiśmienne synodu ewangelickoreformowanego w Wilnie" [The manuscript collection of the Evangelical Reformed community in Vilnius], *Reformacja w Polsce* 5.1 (1928), pp. 151-155.

SAPERSTEIN, M., "Education and homiletics", in: *The Cambridge History of Judaism*, 7, *The Early Modern World, 1500-1815*, ed. J. KARP and A. SUTCLIFFE (Cambridge, 2018), pp. 407-436.

SAPIRO, G., "The literary field between the state and the market", *Poetics* 31 (2003), pp. 441-464.

SARCEVIČIENĖ, J., "*Bene vixit ideo bene mortua est:* Śmierć kobiety w kazaniach pogrzebowych Wielkiego Księstwa Litewskiego pierwszej połowy XVII wieku" [*Bene vixit ideo bene mortua est*: The death of a woman in the funeral sermons from the Grand Duchy of Lithuania from the first half of the seventeenth century], *Barok* 13.1 (2006), pp. 79-93.

SARYUSZ-WOLSKA, M., *Pamięć zbiorowa i kulturowa: Współczesna perspektywa niemiecka* [Collective Memory and Cultural Memory: The Contemporary German Perspective] (Cracow, 2009).

SCHAEKEN, J., *Voices on Birchbark: Everyday Communication in Medieval Russia* (Leiden and Boston, 2018).

SCHALL, J., *Historia Żydów w Polsce, na Litwie i Rusi z 25 ilustracjami* [A History of Jews in Poland, Lithuania, and Ruthenia, with 25 pictures] (Lviv, 1934).

SCHIPER, I., "Język potoczny Żydów polskich i ich literatura w dawnej Rzeczypospolitej" [Everyday language of Polish Jews and their literature in the Polish-Lithuanian

Commonwealth], in: *Żydzi w Polsce odrodzonej*, 1, ed. I. SCHIPER, A. TARTAKOWER, *and* A. HAFFTKA (Warsaw, 1932), pp. 229-230.

SCHOPENHAUER, A., *Die Kunst, Recht zu behalten*, ed. F. VOLPI (Frankfurt am Main and Leipzig, 1995) (the German text with an English translation: <http://coolhaus.de/art-of-controversy/>, accessed: 07.06.2021).

SELIGMAN, J., "Between Yerushalayim DeLita and Jerusalem – The memorial inscription from the *bimah* of the Great Synagogue of Vilna", *Arts* 9.2 (2020), pp. 1-18.

Selling and Collecting: Printed Book Sale Catalogues and Private Libraries in Early Modern Europe, ed. G. GRANATA and A. NUOVO (Macerata, 2018).

SEMKOWICZ, W., "Hanul, namiestnik wileński (1382-1387) i jego ród" [Hanul, the governor of Vilnius (1382-1387), and his family], *Ateneum Wileńskie* 7.1-2 (1930), pp. 3-4.

SEMKOWICZ, W., *Paleografia łacińska* [Latin Paleography] (Cracow, 2007).

SHMERUK, Ch., *Historia literatury jidysz. Zarys* [A History of Jewish Literature: An Outline], ed. M. ADAMCZYK-GARBOWSKA and E. PROKOP-JANIEC (Wrocław, 2007).

SHULVASS, M.A., "The story of Torah study in Eastern Europe," in: M.A. SHULVASS, *Between the Rhine and the Bosporus: Studies and Essays in European Jewish History* (Chicago, 1964), pp. 70-128.

SIRUTAVIČIUS, M., "Maskvos pasiuntinių priėmimo ceremonialas lietuvos valdovo dvare Vilniuje XV a. pabaigoje – XVI a. viduryje" [The ceremony of reception of the Muscovian envoys at the Lithuanian Court in Vilnius, middle of the fifteenth-end of the sixteenth centuries], in: *Vilniaus Žemutinė pilis XIV a.- XIX a. pradžioje 2005-2006 m. tyrimai* [[Vilnius Lower Castle, Fourteenth-Beginning of the Nineteenth Centuries: 2005-2006 Research], ed. L. GLEMŽA (Vilnius, 2007), pp. 8-33.

SKIBIŃSKI, E., Stróżyk P., "Epigrafika jako problem badawczy: Tezy metodyczne" [Epigraphy as a subject of investigation: Methodological remarks], *Studia Epigraficzne* 1 (2014), pp. 21-27.

SKIERSKA, I., *Obowiązek mszalny w średniowiecznej Polsce* [The Obligation of Sunday Service in Medieval Poland] (Warsaw, 2003).

SKUPIEŃSKI, K., *Notariat publiczny w średniowiecznej Polsce* [Public Notaries in Medieval Poland] (Lublin, 1997).

SKWARCZYŃSKA, S., "O pojęcie literatury stosowanej" [On the concept of practical literature], *Pamiętnik Literacki* 28.1-4 (1932), pp. 1-24.

SKWARCZYŃSKA, S., *Teoria listu* [The Theory of Letters] (Białystok, 2005).

SŁAWIŃSKI, J., "Socjologia literatury i poetyka historyczna" [The sociology of literature and historical poetics], in: *Problemy socjologii literatury*, ed. J. SŁAWIŃSKI (Warsaw, 1971), pp. 45-52.

ŚLEDZIEWSKI, P., "Kościół św. Anny-św. Barbary intra muros castri vilnensis" [The church of. St. Anna – St. Barbara *intra muros castri vilnensis*], *Ateneum Wileńskie* 9 (1933-1934), pp. 1-32.

ŚLĘK, L., "Wiersze Samuela Twardowskiego pod wjazd pisane" [The poems of Samuel Twardowski written for the ceremonial entry], In: *Wielkopolski Maro: Samuel ze*

Skrzypny Twardowski w wielkiej i małej Ojczyźnie, ed. K. Meller and J. Kowalski (Poznań, 2002), pp. 76-88.

Ślękowa, L., "Przeszłych wieków sprawy jako przedmiot poetyckiego przedstawienia w literaturze xvi w." [The past as an object of poetic representation in sixteenth-century literature], in: *Dawna świadomość historyczna w Polsce, Czechach i Słowacji*, ed. R. Heck (Wrocław, 1978), pp. 83-101.

Słowiński, J., *Rozwój pisma łacińskiego w Polsce xvi-xviii wieku* [The Development of Latin Script in Poland in the Sixteenth-Eighteenth Centuries] (Lublin, 1992).

Smetonienė, A., "The textual influences of Jacob Ledesma's *Catechism* and the *Catechism* of Mikalojus Daukša on the Anonymous *Catechism* of 1605", *Kalbotyra* 68 (2016), pp. 153-156.

Smosarski, J., "Religijne widowiska parateatralne w Polsce xvii wieku: Kilka przykładów" [Religious para-theatrical performances in seventeenth-century Poland: A few examples], in: *Dramat i teatr sakralny*, ed. I. Sławińska *et al.* (Lublin, 1988), pp. 107-132.

Śnieżko, A., *Cmentarz ewangelicki w Wilnie 1806-1956* [The Lutheran Cemetery in Vilnius 1806-1956] (Wrocław, 1972).

Snook, E., "Reading women", in: *The Cambridge Companion to Early Modern Women's Writing*, ed. L. Lunger Knoppers (Cambridge, 2009), pp. 40-53.

Snopek, J., *Prowincja oświecona: Kultura literacka Ziemi Krakowskiej w dobie Oświecenia 1750-1815* [The Enlightened Province: The Literary Culture of the Land of Cracow in the Age of Enlightenment, 1750-1815] (Warsaw, 1992).

Snyder, T., *The Reconstruction of Nations: Poland, Ukraine, Lithuania, Belarus, 1569-1999* (New Haven and London, 2003).

Sołtan-Kościelecka, K., "Stilusy późnośredniowieczne z terenu obecny Polski" [The late medieval stiluses from the area of contemporary Poland], *Kwartalnik Kultury Materialnej* 50.2 (2002), pp. 123-132.

Speičytė, B., *Poetinės kultūros formos: ldk palikimas xix amžiaus Lietuvos literatūroje* [Forms of Poetic Culture: The Legacy of the Grand Duchy of Lithuania in Nineteenth-Century Lithuanian Literature] (Vilnius, 2004).

Springer, M.S., *Restoring Christ's Church: John a Lasco and the* Forma ac ratio (London, 2007).

Srebrna biblioteka i inne cymelia królewieckie ze zbiorów Biblioteki Uniwersyteckiej w Toruniu [The Silver Library and Other Treasures from Königsberg in the Collections of the University Library of Toruń] (Toruń, 2005).

Staniszewski, A., "Nieobecna 'książka białogłowskiego konceptu': Kobiety, kanon i badania literatury dawnej" [The absent book "penned by one of the fairer sex": Women, the literary canon, and the study of early modern Polish literature], *Terminus* 16.2 (2014), pp. 205-208.

Staniszewski, A.T., *Historyje krakowskie: Funkcjonowanie narracyjnych tekstów popularnych we wczesnonowożytnej aglomeracji krakowskiej* [Stories from Cracow: The Functioning of Narrative Popular Literature in the Early Modern Agglomeration of Cracow] (Cracow, 2020).

STARNAWSKI, J., "O korespondencji poety z biskupem Stanisławem Łubieńskim" [About the correspondence between a poet and bishop Stanisław Łubieński], in: J. STARNAWSKI, *W świecie barokowym* [In the Baroque World] (Łódź, 1992), pp. 24-30.

Staropolska kultura rękopisu [Old-Polish Manuscript Culture], ed. H. DZIECHCIŃSKA (Warsaw, 1990).

STARZYŃSKI, M., "Last tribute to the king: The funeral ceremony of the Polish King Kazimierz the Jagiellon (1492) in the light of an unknown description", *Viator* 45.2 (2014), pp. 289-302.

STARZYŃSKI, M., "Wiersze na śmierc króla w późnośredniowiecznej Polsce" [Poems for the death of the king in late medieval Poland], In: *Śmierć, pogrzeb i upamiętnianie władców w dawnej Polsce*, ed. H. RAJFURA, P. SZWEDO, B. ŚWIADEK, M. WALCZAK, and P. WĘCOWSKI (Warsaw, 2020), pp. 77-87.

STAWECKA, K., "Maciej Kazimierz Sarbiewski jako prozaik" [Maciej Kazimierz Sarbiewski as author of prose], *Roczniki Humanistyczne* 31.3 (1983), pp. 101-123.

STEFANOWSKA, L., "*Thrēnos* Meletija Smotryckiego: Funkcja retoryki w tekście polemicznym" [The *Thrēnos* of Meletij Smotrycki: A function of rhetoric in a polemic text], in: *Ukraina: Teksty i konteksty: Księga jubileuszowa dedykowana profesorowi Stefanowi Kozakowi w siedemdziesiątą rocznicę urodzin*, ed. B. NAZARUK, W. SOBOL, and W. ALEKSANDROWYCZ (Warsaw, 2007), pp. 143-144.

STERCZEWSKA, L., "Głośny rezon ... Edycja kolęd z osiemnastowiecznych rękopisów Biblioteki Karmelitanek bosych w Krakowie na Wesołej" [A loud sound ... Editing the Christmas carols from the eighteenth-century manuscripts of the Discalced Carmelite Nuns at Wesoła quarter in Cracow], *Terminus* 12.1 (2010), pp. 151-177.

STOBERSKI, Z., *Między dawnymi i młodszymi laty: Polsko-litewskie związki literackie* [Between Old and More Recent Times: Polish-Lithuanian Literary Connections] (Łódź, 1981).

STOPKA, K., *Języki oswajane pismem: Allografia kipczacko-ormiańska i polsko-ormiańska w kulturze dawnej Polski* [Languages Domesticated by Script: The Kiptchak-Armenian and Polish-Armenian Allography in the Culture of Old Poland] (Cracow, 2013).

STOPKA, K., *Szkoły katedralne metropolii gnieźnieńskiej w średniowieczu: Studia nad kształceniem kleru polskiego w Wiekach Średnich* [The Cathedral Schools of the Archbishopric of Gniezno in the Middle Ages: Studies on the Education of the Medieval Polish Clergy] (Kraków, 1994).

STOPKA, K., "Zakres i program nauczania *septem artes* w szkołach katedralnych" [The scope and the programme of instruction in the *septem artes* in the cathedral schools], in: Septem artes *w kształtowaniu kultury umysłowej w Polsce średniowiecznej: Wybrane zagadnienia*, ed. T. MICHAŁOWSKA (Wrocław, 2007), pp. 125-136.

STRADOMSKI, J., "Polemika religijna okresu unii brzeskiej a rozwój drukarstwa prawosławnego w Rzeczypospolitej" [Religious polemics in the period of the Union of Brest and the growth of Orthodox printing in the Polish Republic], in:

Prawosławne oficyny wydawnicze w Rzeczypospolitej, ed. A. MIRONOWICZ, U. PAWLUCZUK, and P. CHOMIK (Białystok, 2004), pp. 69-76.

STRADOMSKI, J., *Spory o „wiarę grecką" w dawnej Rzeczypospolitej* [Controversies around the "Greek Faith" in the Polish-Lithuanian Commonwealth] (Cracow, 2003).

STRUMIŃSKI, B., "Foreword", in: L. Krevza, *A Defense of Church Unity* – Zakharia Kopystens'ky, *Palinodia*, 1, trans. and foreword B. STRUMIŃSKI, ed. R. KOROPECKYJ, D.R. MILLER, and W.R. VEDER (Cambridge, Mass., 1995), pp. I-XIV.

STUDNICKI, W.G., "Biblioteka Wileńskiego Synodu Ewangelicko-Reformowanego" [The library of the Evangelical synod of Vilnius], *Ateneum Wileńskie* 8 (1931-1932), pp. 205-214.

STUDNICKI, W.G., "Biblioteka Wileńskiego Synodu Ewangelicko-Reformowanego (II)" [The library of the Evangelical synod of Vilnius, part II], In: *Biblioteki wileńskie*, ed. A. ŁYSAKOWSKI (Vilnius, 1932), pp. 99-101.

STUDNICKI, W.G., *Zarys historyczny wileńskiego kościoła ewangelicko-reformowanego i jego biblioteki* [Historical Outline of the Evangelical Church in Vilnius and Its Library] (Vilnius, 1932).

SUŁKOWSKA-KURASIOWA, I., *Dokumenty królewskie i ich funkcja w państwie polskim za Andegawenów i pierwszych Jagiellonów 1370-1444* [Royal Charters and Their Function in the Polish State in the Period of the Anjou and Jagiellonian Dynasties, 1370-1444] (Warsaw, 1977).

SUMOWSKI, M., "Duchowni w testamentach mieszczańskich – mieszczanie w testamentach duchownych: Zapisy ostatniej woli jako źródła do badania powiązań (Prusy, XV-początek XVI wieku)" [Clergymen in burghers' testaments – Burghers in clergymen's testaments: Last wills as a source for the study of their relationships (Prussia, fifteenth-early sixteenth centuries)], *Kwartalnik Historii Kultury Materialnej* 68.3 (2020), pp. 315-334.

ŚWIERKOWSKI, K., "Wilno kolebką drukarstwa łotewskiego" [Vilnius as a cradle of Livonian printing], *Ateneum Wileńskie* 8 (1931-1932), pp. 184-204.

SYTA, K., "Archiwa szlachty żmudzkiej w II poł. XVI wieku" [The archives of the Samogitian nobility], in: *Studia o bibliotekach i zbiorach polskich*, 8, ed. B. RYSZEWSKI (Toruń, 1997), pp. 29-47.

SZABELSKA, H., "Między tęczą a kryształem: Echo u Macieja Kazimierza Sarbiewskiego jako gatunek odbicia w świetle jego komentarza do Summy teologicznej Akwinaty" [Between the rainbow and the crystal glass: Echo in the works of Maciej Kazimierz Sarbiewski as a species of refraction in the light of his commentary to the *Summa theologica* of Thomas Aquinas], *Terminus* 23.1 (2021), pp. 25-53.

SZAPSZAŁ, H.S., "O zatraceniu języka ojczystego przez Tatarów w Polsce" [About the loss of the material language by the Tartars in Poland], *Rocznik Tatarski* 1 (1932), pp. 34-48.

SZCZYPIOR, K., "Najstarsze katechizmy wschodniosłowiańskie" [The oldest East Slavic catechisms], in: *Święci w kulturze i duchowości dawnej i współczesnej Europy*, ed. W. STĘPNIAK-MINCZEWA and Z.J. KIJAS (Cracow, 1999), pp. 155-161.

SZEGDA, M., *Metropolita Józef Welamin Rutski (1613-1637)* [The Metropolite Józef Welamin Rutski (1613-1637)], in: *Unia brzeska: Przeszłość i teraźniejszość 1596-1996: Materiały międzynarodowego sympozjum, Kraków 19-20 listopada 1996*, ed. P. NATANEK and R.M. ZAWADZKI (Cracow, 1998), pp. 291-319.

SZELIŃSKA, W., *Biblioteki profesorów Uniwersytetu Krakowskiego w XV i początku XVI wieku* [The Book Collections of the Professors of Cracow University in the Fifteenth and Early Sixteenth Century] (Wrocław, 1966).

SZENDE, K., *Trust, Authority and the Written Word in the Royal Towns of Medieval Hungary* (Turnhout, 2018).

SZMYTKA, R., "Kultura literacka Antwerpii w XVI wieku" [The literary culture of Antwerp in the sixteenth century], in: *Literatura renesansowa w Polsce i Europie: Studia dedykowane Profesorowi Andrzejowi Borowskiemu* [Renaissance Literature in Poland and Europe: Studies Devoted to Prof. Andrzej Borowski], ed. J. NIEDŹWIEDŹ (Cracow, 2016), pp. 274-291.

SZOSTEK, T., "Kazanie" [The sermon], in: *Słownik literatury staropolskiej: Średniowiecze – Renesans – Barok*, ed. T. MICHAŁOWSKA (Wrocław, 1998), p. 366.

SZWYKOWSKA, A., "Imprezy baletowe na dworze Władysława IV" [Ballet performances at the court of Wladislaw IV], *Muzyka* 45.2 (1967), pp. 11-23.

SZYNKIEWICZ, J., "Literatura religijna Tatarów litewskich i jej pochodzenie" [Religious Literature of the Lithuanian Tartars and its sources], *Rocznik Tatarski* 2 (1932), pp. 138-144.

TANDECKI, J., "Dokumenty i kancelarie miejskie" [Urban documentation and chancery], in: *Dyplomatyka staropolska*, ed. T. JUREK (Warsaw, 2015), pp. 442-445.

TARGOSZ, K., "Jedność nauki i sztuki w dziele dzieła Jana Heweliusza" [Unity of science and art in the works of Johannes Hevelius], *Quarterly of the History of Science and Technology*, 4.21 (1976), pp. 634-640.

TARGOSZ, K., "Oprawa artystyczno-ideowa wjazdów weselnych trzech sióstr Habsburżanek (Kraków 1592 i 1605, Florencja 1608)" [The artistic and ideological features of the solemn entrances at the weddings of three sisters from the Habsburg dynasty (Cracow 1592 and 1605, Florence 1608)], in: Theatrum ceremoniale *na dworze książąt i królów polskich: Materiały konferencji naukowej zorganizowanej przez Zamek Królewski na Wawelu i Instytut Historii Uniwersytetu Jagiellońskiego w dniach 23-25 marca 1998*, ed. M. MARKIEWICZ and R. SKOWRON (Cracow, 1999), pp. 207-244.

TARGOSZ, K., *Piórem zakonnicy: Kronikarki w Polsce XVII w. o swoich zakonach i swoich czasach* [With the Nun's Pen: Female Authors of Chronicles on Their Communities and Their Times] (Cracow, 2002).

TARGOSZ-KRETOWA, K., *Teatr dworski Władysława IV (1635-1648)* [The Court Theatre of Władisław IV (1635-1648)] (Warsaw, 1965).

TAUBER, J., and R. TUCHTENHAGEN, *Vilnius: Kleine Geschichte der Stadt* (Cologne, Weimar, and Vienna, 2008).

TAZBIR, J., "Państwo bez stosów" [A country without pyres], in: J. TAZBIR, *Państwo bez stosów i inne szkice* (Cracow, 2000), pp. 5-254.

TAZBIR, J., "Roizjusz Piotr", in: *PSB* 31 (1988), pp. 499-503.

TAZBIR, J., *Piotr Skarga – szermierz kontrreformacji* [Piotr Skarga – A Champion of the Counter-Reformation] (Warsaw, 1983).

TAZBIR, J., *Szlachta i teologowie: Studia z dziejów polskiej kontrreformacji* [The Nobles and Theologians: Studies on the History of the Polish Counter-Reformation] (Warsaw, 1987).

Tefsir Tatarów Wielkiego Księstwa Litewskiego: Teoria i praktyka badawcza – Тафсир Татар Великого княжества Литовского: Теория и практика исследования – The Tafsir of the Tatars of the Grand Duchy of Lithuania: Theory and Research, ed. J. KULWICKA-KAMIŃSKA and Cz. ŁAPICZ (Toruń, 2015).

TĘGOWSKI, J., *Rodowód kniaziów Świrskich do końca XVI wieku* [The Genealogy of the Princes Świrski till the End of the Sixteenth Century] (Wrocław, 2011).

TĘGOWSKI, J., "Rodzina Łoknickich herbu Nieczuja na Podlasiu i w powiecie brzesko-litewskim do połowy XVII wieku" [The Łoknicki family with the Nieczuja coat of arms at Podlasie and in the district of Brest until the mid-seventeenth century], *Rocznik Lituanistyczny* 5 (2019), pp. 121-144.

TEMČINAS, S., "Języki kultury ruskiej w Pierwszej Rzeczypospolitej" [Languages of Ruthenian culture in the Polish-Lithuanian Commonwealth], in: *Między Wschodem a Zachodem: Prawosławie i unia*, ed. M. KUCZYŃSKA (Warsaw, 2017), pp. 81-120.

The "Lithuanian Metrica" in Moscow and Warsaw: Reconstructing the Archives of the Grand Duchy of Lithuania: Including an Annotated Edition of the 1887 Inventory Compiled by Stanisław Ptaszycki, ed. P. KENNEDY GRIMSTED and I. SUŁKOWSKA-KURASIOWA (Cambridge, Mass., 1994).

The Cambridge Companion to Early Modern Women's Writing, ed. L. LUNGER KNOPPERS (Cambridge, 2009).

The Cambridge Companion to Medieval Women's Writing, ed. C. DINSHAW and D. WALLACE (Cambridge, 2003).

The Catalogue of the Book Collection of the Jesuit College in Braniewo Held in the University Library in Uppsala – Katalog księgozbioru Kolegium Jezuitów w Braniewie zachowa nego w Bibliotece Uniwersyteckiej w Uppsali, 2, ed. J. TRYPUĆKO, M. SPANDOWSKI, and S. SZYLLER (Warsaw, 2007).

The Development of Literate Mentalities in East Central Europe, ed. A. ADAMSKA and M. MOSTERT (Turnhout, 2004).

The Great Synagogue and Shulhoyf of Vilna (Vilnius): A Research, Excavation, Preservation and Memorial Project <http://www.seligman.org.il/vilna_synagogue_home.html> (accessed: 02.06.2021).

TOPOLSKA, M.B., *Czytelnik i książka w Wielkim Księstwie Litewskim w dobie Renesansu i Baroku* [Readers and Books in the Grand Duchy of Lithuania in the Periods of Renaissance and Baroque] (Wrocław, 1984).

TOPOLSKA, M.B., "Mecenasi i drukarze ruscy na pograniczu kulturowym XVI-XVII w." [Ruthenian printers and their patrons in the cultural borderland in the sixteenth-seventeenth centuries], in: *Prawosławne oficyny wydawnicze w Rzeczypospolitej*, ed. A. MIRONOWICZ and U. PAWLUCZUK (Białystok, 2004), pp. 33-51.

TORÓJ, E., *Inwentarze książek lubelskich introligatorów z pierwszej połowy XVII wieku* [The Inventories of Books of Bookbinders from Lublin from the First Half of the Seventeenth Century] (Lublin, 2000).

TORÓJ, E., *Inwentarze księgozbiorów mieszczan lubelskich z latach 1591-1678* [The Inventories of Book Collections of the Burgers of Lublin in the Period 1591-1678] (Lublin, 1997).

TÓTH, I.G., "Illiterate and Latin-speaking gentlemen: The many faces of the Hungarian gentry in the early modern period", in: *The Development of Literate Mentalities in East Central Europe*, ed. A. ADAMSKA and M. MOSTERT (Turnout, 2004), pp. 519-530.

TÓTH, I.G., *Literacy and Written Culture in Early Modern Central Europe* (Budapest, 2000).

TRĘBSKA, M., "Oskarżenia i apologie w staropolskich wzorach korespondencji z synami marnotrawnymi i ich dyrektorami" [The accusations and apologies in the Polish formularies of correspondence of fathers with their prodigal sons and their tutors], in: *Epistolografia w dawnej Rzeczypospolitej, 5 (stulecia XVI-XIX): Nowa perspektywa historycznoliteracka*, ed. P. BOREK and M. OLMA (Cracow, 2015), pp. 173-191.

TRILUPATIENĖ, J., "*Dramma per musica* in early seventeenth-century Vilnius", trans. V. AGLINSKAS and R. KONDRATAS, in: *Opera Lietuvos didžiųjų kunigaikščių rūmuose* (Vilnius, 2010), pp. 120-129.

TRZCIŃSKI, A., *Hebrajskie inskrypcje na materiale kamiennym w Polsce w XIII-XX wieku: Studium paleograficzno-epigraficzne* [Hebrew Stone Inscriptions in Poland from the Thirteenth till the Twentieth Century: A Palaeographico-Epigraphical Study] (Lublin, 2007).

TRZCIŃSKI, A., and M. WODZIŃSKI, *Cmentarz żydowski w Lesku*, 1, *Wiek XVI i XVII* [The Jewish Cemetery in Lesko, 1, Sixteenth and Seventeenth Centuries] (Cracow, 2002).

TURSKA, H., *O powstaniu polskich obszarów językowych na Wileńszczyźnie* [On the Emergence of Areas of Polish Language in the Vilnius region] (Vilnius, 1995).

TYGIELSKI, W., *Listy, ludzie, władza. Patronat Jana Zamoyskiego w świetle korespondencji* [Letters, People, Power: The Patronage of Jan Zamoyski in the Light of His Correspondance] (Warsaw, 2007).

TYMIAKIN, L., "O formułach w XVII-wiecznym testamencie przemyskim" [About the formulae in the seventeenth-century testaments from Przemyśl], *Rocznik Przemyski* 27 (1990), pp. 141-145.

TYMIAKIN, L., "Religijność siedemnastowiecznych przemyślan w świetle leksyki testamentowej" [The religious practices of the seventeenth-century inhabitants of Przemyśl in the light of the vocabulary of their testaments], *Rocznik Przemyski* 42.3 (2006), pp. 95-112.

ULČINAITĖ, E., *Lietuvos Renesanso ir Baroko literatūra* [The Lithuanian Renaissance and Baroque Literature] (Vilnius, 2001).

ULČINAITĖ, E., "Mokyklinė Baroko drama: Antikinės dramos tradicijos ir aktualijų atspindžiai" [Baroque school drama: Reflections on ancient drama traditions and their modernization], in: *Lietuvos jėzuitų teatras: XVI-XVIII amžiaus dramų rinktinė* [The Lithuanian Jesuit Theatre: A Collection of Plays from the Sixteenth-Eighteenth Centuries], ed., trans. and introduction by E. ULČINAITĖ (Vilnius, 2008), pp. 11-36.

ULČINAITĖ, E., "Szkoła poetycka Sarbiewskiego na Litwie w XVII-XVIII wieku" [The poetic 'school' of Sarbiewski in Lithuania in the seventeenth and eighteenth centuries], in: Corona scientiarum*: Studia z historii literatury i kultury nowożytnej ofiarowane profesorowi Januszowi Pelcowi*, ed. J. A. CHROŚCICKI *et al.*, (Warsaw, 2004), pp. 373-401.

ULČINAITĖ, E., *Teoria retoryczna w Polsce i na Litwie w XVII wieku. Próba rekonstrukcji schematu retorycznego* [The Theory of Rhetoric in Poland and Lithuania in the Seventeenth Century: An Attempt of Reconstruction of a Rhetorical Model] (Wrocław, 1984).

ULČINAITĖ, E., "The triumph of Sigismund Vasa in the context of ceremonial greetings offered to other rulers of the Grand Duchy of Lithuania", in: *Triumfo diena: 1611 m. birželio 13 d. Smolensko pergalė ir iškilmingas Zigmanto Vazos sutikimas Vilniuje 1611 m. liepos 24 d. Dies Triumphi: Victoria Sigismundi III die XIII Junii A.D. MDCXI Smolensco expugnato et triumphalis ingressus Vilnom die XXIV Julii A.D. MDCXI celebratus – Day of Triumph: The victory at Smolensk on June 13, 1611 and the ceremonial reception of Sigismund Vasa in Vilnius on July 24,1611*, ed. E. ULČINAITĖ and E. SAVIŠČEVAS (Vilnius, 2011), pp. 73-84.

ULČINAITĖ, E., "Utwory powitalne na cześć władców i magnatów w literaturze Wielkiego Księstwa Litewskiego XVI-XVIII wieku: Tradycje a specyfika lokalna" [The welcome poems in honour of rulers and magnates in the literature of the Grand Duchy of Lithuania from the sixteenth until the eighteenth century: Traditions versus local specificity], trans. B. PIASECKA, in: *Kalbų varžybos: Lietuvos Didžiosios Kunigaikštystės valdovų ir didikų sveikinimai – Competition of Languages: The Ceremonial Greetings of the Grand Duchy of Lithuania's Rulers and Nobles – Koncert języków: Pozdrowienia władców i magnatów Wielkiego Księstwa Litewskiego*, ed., trans. and introduction by E. ULČINAITĖ (Vilnius, 2010), pp. 41-45.

Unia brzeska: Geneza, dzieje i konsekwencje w kulturze narodów słowiańskich: Praca zbiorowa [The Union of Brest: Its Origins, History and Consequences in the Culture of the Slavic Nations], ed. R. ŁUŻNY, F. ZIEJKA, and A. KĘPIŃSKI (Cracow, 1994).

Unia brzeska: Przeszłość i teraźniejszość: 1596-1996: Materiały międzynarodowego sympozjum, Kraków 19-20 listopada 1996 [The Union of Brest: Its Past and Present: 1596-1996], ed. P. NATANEK and R.M. ZAWADZKI (Cracow, 1998).

URBAN, W., "Ceny książek w Polsce XVI-XVII w." [The prices of books in Poland in the sixteenth and seventeenth centuries], *Biuletyn Biblioteki Jagiellońskiej* 46 (1996), pp. 61-67.

URBAN, W., "Małopolskie szkoły parafialne w świetle akt sądowych krakowskiej kurii biskupiej z drugiej połowy XVI w." [Parish schools of Lesser Poland in the light of the legal records of the Cracow episcopal curia from the second half of the sixteenth century], *Przegląd Historyczno-Oświatowy* 36.1-2 (1993), pp. 5-14.

URBAN, W., "Szkolnictwo małopolskie od XVI do XVIII wieku" [The education system of Lesser Poland from the sixteenth till the eighteenth century], in: *Nauczanie w dawnych wiekach: Edukacja w średniowieczu i u progu ery nowożytnej: Polska na tle Europy*, ed. W. IWAŃCZAK and K. BRACHA (Kielce, 1997), pp. 67-70.

URBAN, W., "Umiejętność pisania w Małopolsce w II połowie XVI wieku" [Writing skills in Lesser Poland in the second half of the sixteenth century], *Przegląd Historyczny* 68.2 (1977), pp. 231-257.

URBAN, W., and S. LŪŽYS , Cracovia Lithuanorum saeculis XIV-XV – *Lietuvių Krokuva XIV-XVI amžiais* (Vilnius, 1999).

URBAN, W., and A. ZAJDA, "Wstęp wydawców" [Editorial introduction], in: *Zapisy polskojęzyczne w księgach sądów szlacheckich województwa krakowskiego* [Polish-Language Entries in the Registers of Courts of the Nobility of the Cracow Voivodeship], ed. W. URBAN and A. ZAJDA (Cracow, 2004), pp. 7-28.

URBAŃCZYK, S., "W sprawie polskiego języka literackiego" [On the Polish literary language], in: S. URBAŃCZYK, *Prace z dziejów języka polskiego* (Wrocław, 1979), pp. 160-187.

Urzędnicy centralni i dygnitarze Wielkiego Księstwa Litewskiego XIV-XVIII wieku. Spisy [The Officials of the Central Administration and the Dignitaries of the Grand Duchy of Lithuania from the Fourteenth till the Eighteenth Century: The Registers], ed. H. LULEWICZ and A. RACHUBA (Kórnik, 1994).

Urzędnicy Wielkiego Księstwa Litewskiego. Spisy, 1, *Województwo wileńskie XIV-XVIII wiek* [The Officials of the Grand Duchy of Lithuania: The Registers, 1, The Voivodeship of Vilnius, from the Fourteenth till the Eighteenth Century], ed. H. LULEWICZ, A. RACHUBA, and P. ROMANIUK (Warsaw, 2004).

Uses of the Written Word in Medieval Towns: *Medieval Urban Literacy II*, ed. M. MOSTERT and A. ADAMSKA (Turnhout, 2014).

VAITKEVIČIŪTĖ, V., "Inkunabulų sklaidos ir funkcionavimo ypatumai: Lietuvos atminties institucijų rinkinių atvejai" [Peculiarities of the dissemination and functioning of incunabula: Cases of collections of Lithuanian institutional memorials], *Knygotyra* 74 (2020), pp. 7-34.

VALIKONYTĖ, I., "Struktura i zasady kompletowania ksiąg sądowych Metryki Litewskiej Zygmunta Augusta" [The structure and principles of collection of the court registers of the *Lithuanian Metrica* under Sigismund Augustus], *Rocznik Lituanistyczny* 4 (2018), pp. 7-23.

VENCLOVA, T., *Vilnius: A Guide To its Names and People* (Vilnius, 2008): the Lithuanian edition was published in Vilnius, in 2006.

VENCLOVA, T., *Vilnius: City Guide* (Vilnius, 2001).

Vernacularity in England and Wales, c. 1300-1550, ed. E. SALTER and H. WICKER (Turnhout, 2011).

VETEIKIS, T., *Greek Studies and Greek Literature in the Sixteenth-Seventeenth Century in Lithuania: A Summary of a Doctoral Dissertation* (Vilnius, 2004).

Vilniaus žemutinės pilies rūmai (1996-1998 metų tyrimai) [Vilnius Lower Castle, from the Fourteenth until the Beginning of the Nineteenth Century: 2005-2006 Research], ed. V. URBANAVIČIUS (Vilnius, 2003).

VLADIMIROVAS, L., "Georgijaus Albinijaus knygų kolekcijos likimo klausimu" [On the fate of the book collection of Jerzy Albinus], in: *Apie knygas ir bibliotekas: Straipsnių rinkinys* [About Books and Libraries: A Collection of Papers], ed. A. GLOSIENĖ and G. RAGUOTIENĖ (Vilnius, 2002), pp. 217-224.

WALAWENDER, A., *Kronika klęsk elementarnych w Polsce i krajach sąsiednich w latach 1450-1586*, 2, *Zniszczenia wojenne i pożary* [A Chronicle of Natural Disasters in Poland and Neighboring Countires in the Period 1450-1586, 2, Destructions by War and Fires] (Lviv, 1932).

WALCZAK, W., "O kształceniu duchowieństwa unickiego w Rzeczypospolitej w XVII-XVIII wieku" [About the instruction of the Uniate clergy in the Polish-Lithuanian Commonwealth in the seventeenth and eighteenth centuries], in: *Nad społeczeństwem staropolskim*, 1, *Kultura – instytucje – gospodarka w XVI-XVIII stuleciu*, ed. K. ŁOPATECKI and W. WALCZAK (Białystok, 2007), pp. 483-491.

Wilnianie: Żywoty siedemnastowieczne [Burghers of Vilnius, Seventeenth-Century Biographies], ed., introduction, and comments, D.A. FRICK (Warsaw, 2008).

"Wilno" [Vilnius] in: *Wirtualny Sztetl* <https://sztetl.org.pl/pl/miejscowosci/w/1044-wilno/114-cmentarze/38803-cmentarz-zydowski-na-pioromoncie-w-wilnie-juozapaviciaus-g> (accessed: 12.05.2021).

WINIARSKA, A, "Rola Heleny Rurykowiczówny w świetle stosunków litewsko-moskiewskich na przełomie XV i XVI w." [The role of Helena of Moscow from the perspective of the relationships between Poland and Moscovy at the turn of the fifteenth and sixteenth centuries], *Rocznik Naukowo-Dydaktyczny WSP w Krakowie: Prace Historyczne* 4.32 (1968), pp. 5-30.

WINNICZUK, L., "Wstęp" [Introduction], in: Jan Ursyn z Krakowa, *Modus epistolandi cum epistolis exemplaribus et orationibus annexis: O sposobie pisania listów wraz z wzorami listów i mowami*, ed. L. WINNICZUK (Wrocław, 1957), pp. VII-X.

WINNYCZENKO, O., "Dwa tatarskie testamenty wojskowych z pierwszej połowy XVIII wieku" [Two last wills of Tartar soldiers from the first half of the eighteenth century], *Rocznik Lituanistyczny* 3 (2017), pp. 259-273.

WISŁOCKI, W., *Incunabula typographica Bibliothecae Universitatis Jagellonicae Cracoviensis inde ab inventa arte imprimendi usque ad ad A. 1500* (Cracow, 1900).

WISNER, H., *Janusz Radziwiłł, 1612-1655: Wojewoda wileński, hetman wielki litewski* [Janusz Radziwiłł, 1612-1655: Voivode of Vilnius, Great Hetman of Lithuania] (Warsaw, 2000).

WISNER, H., "Likwidacja zboru ewangelickiego w Wilnie (1639-1646): Z dziejów walki z inaczej wierzącymi" [The liquidation of the Evangelical church in Vilnius (1639-1646): From the history of struggle against religious dissenters], *Odrodzenie i Reformacja w Polsce* 37 (1993), pp. 89-102.

WISNER, H., *Rzeczpospolita Wazów, 3, Sławne Państwo: Wielkie Księstwo Litewskie* [The Commonwealth of the Vasa Dynasty, 3, The Glorious State, the Grand Duchy of Lithuania] (Warsaw, 2008).

WISNER, H., *Władysław IV Waza* (Wrocław, 2009).

WISNER, H., *Zygmunt III Waza* (Wrocław, 2006).

WITT, R., "*Ars Dictaminis*: Victim of *Ars Notarie*?", In: *Medieval Letters Between Fiction and Document*, ed. Ch. HØGEL and E. BARTOLI (Turnout, 2015), pp. 359-368.

WITT, R., "Medieval '*ars dictaminis*' and the beginnings of Humanism: A new construction of the problem", *Renaissance Quarterly* 35.1 (1982), pp. 1-35.

WŁODARSKI, M., "Wstęp" [Introduction], in: *Polska poezja świecka XV wieku* [Polish Secular Poetry in the Fifteenth Century], ed. M. WŁODARSKI (Wrocław, 1997), pp. III-CXVIII.

WŁODARSKI, M., "Wstęp" [Introduction], in: *Średniowieczna poezja łacińska w Polsce* [Medieval Latin Poetry in Poland], ed. M. WŁODARSKI (Wrocław, 2007), pp. V-CXVIII.

WNUK, A., "Mieszczanie lubelscy przełomu XVI/XVII wieku a książka" [The town dwellers of Lublin at the turn of the seventeenth century and the book], in: *Lublin a książka: Materiały z konferencji naukowej Lublin – Pszczela Wola, 6-7 listopada 2002 roku*, ed. A. KRAWCZYK and E. JÓZEFOWICZ-WISIŃSKA (Lublin, 2002), pp. 73-89.

WNUK, A., "Szlachta w testamentach i inwentarzach mieszczan lubelskich z końca XVI i pierwszej połowy XVII wieku" [The nobility in the last wills and post mortem inventories of the inhabitants of Lublin from the end of the sixteenth and the first half of the seventeenth centuries], *Klio* 42.3 (2017), pp. 129-157.

WODZIŃSKI, M., *Hebrajskie inskrypcje na Śląsku XIII-XVIII wieku* [Hebrew Inscriptions in Silesia from the Thirteenth till the Eighteenth Century] (Wrocław, 2003).

WOJCIECH-MASŁOWSKA, G., "Dwa krakowskie *libri formularum* z XV wieku" [Two *libri formularum* from the fifteenth century from Cracow], *Studia Źródłoznawcze* 17 (1972), pp. 119-131.

WÓJCIK, R., *Opusculum de arte memorativa Jana Szklarka: Bernardyński traktat mnemotechniczny z 1504 roku* [The *Opusculum de arte memorativa* by Jan Szklarek: A Mnemotechnic Treatise by a Bernardine Friar from 1504] (Poznań, 2007).

WÓJCIK, R., "Uwagi na marginesie książki Marka Prejsa Oralność i mnemonika: Późny barok w kulturze, Wydawnictwa Uniwersytetu Warszawskiego (Warsaw, 2009)" [Remarks on the book by Marek Prejs, Orality and Mnemonic: the Late Baroque in Polish Culture], *Terminus* 13.2 (2011), pp. 127-142.

WOLFE, H., "Reading bells and loose papers: Reading and writing practices of the English Benedictine nuns of Cambrai and Paris", In: *Early Modern Women's Manuscript Writing: Selected Papers from the Trinity / Trent Colloquium*, ed. V.E. BURKE and J. GIBSON (Burlington, 2004), pp. 135-156.

WOLFE, H., "Women's handwriting", in: *The Cambridge Companion to Early Modern Women's Writing*, ed. L. LUNGER KNOPPERS (Cambridge, 2009), pp. 27-35.

WOŁKANOWSKI, W., "Pamięć ludzka jest krucha … Dawne cmentarze ewangelickie w Wilnie" [Human memory is fragile ... Old Lutheran cemeteries in Vilnius], *Przegląd Bałtycki* 8.11.2017 <https://przegladbaltycki.pl/6256,pamiec-ludzka-krucha-dawne-cmentarze-ewangelickie-wilnie.html> (accessed 16.04.2021).

Writing and the Administration of Medieval Towns: Medieval Urban Literacy I, ed. M. MOSTERT and A. ADAMSKA (Turnhout, 2014).

Wszystkie modlitwy Rzeczypospolitej: Katalog wystawy 3 lipca-30 sierpnia 2009 [All Prayers of the Polish-Lithuanian Commonwealth], ed. G. ROLAK and D. SIDOWICZ (Wrocław, 2009).

WYDRA, W., *O najdawniejszej drukowanej książce w Poznaniu* [On the Oldest Printed Book in Poznań] (Poznań, 2003).

WYROZUMSKA, B., *Kancelaria miasta Krakowa w średniowieczu* [The Chancery of the City of Cracow in the Middle Ages] (Cracow, 1995).

WYSŁOUCH, S., *Posługi komunikacyjne w miastach W. Ks. Litewskiego na prawie magdeburskiem do połowy XVI w.* [The Communications Services in the Towns of the Magdeburg Law in the Grand Duchy of Lithuania until the Mid-Sixteenth Century] (Vilnius, 1936).

WYSMUŁEK, J., *Testamenty mieszczan krakowskich (XIV-XV wiek)* [Last Wills of the Inhabitants of Cracow (the Fourteenth-Fifteenth Centuries] (Warsaw, 2015).

WYSMUŁEK, J., "Urban testaments in Poland: Research present and future", in: *Uses of the Written Word in Medieval Towns: Medieval Urban Literacy II*, ed. M. MOSTERT and A. ADAMSKA (Turnhout, 2014), pp. 299-312.

XVII a. lietuvos lenkiškos knygos. Kontrolinis sąrašas [Polish Books in Lithuania in the Seventeenth Century: A Register], ed. M. IVANOVIČ (Vilnius, 1998).

XV-XVI, a. lietuvos lotyniškų knygų sąrašas: Index librorum latinorum Lituaniae saeculi quinti decimi et sexti decimi, ed. D. NARBUTIENĖ and S. NARBUTAS (Vilnius, 2002).

XVII, a. lietuvos lotyniškų knygų sąrašas: Index librorum Latinorum Lituaniae saeculi saeculi septimi decimi, ed. D. NARBUTIENĖ and S. NARBUTAS (Vilnius, 1998).

ZACHARA-WAWRZYŃCZYK, M., "Geneza legendy o rzymskim pochodzeniu Litwinów" [The origin of the legend on the Roman origins of the Lithuanians], *Zeszyty Historyczne Uniwersytetu Warszawskiego* 3 (1963), pp. 5-35.

ZACHARA-ZWIĄZEK, U., "Dwór królowej jako locus scribendi: Analiza wybranych aspektów funkcjonowania na przykładzie korespondencji Elżbiety Habsburżanki z Zygmuntem Augustem" [The queen's court as a *locus scribendi*: An analysis of selected aspects of selected aspects of its functioning on the example of the correspondence between Elisabeth of Austria and Sigismund Augustus], in: *Loca scribendi: Miejsca i środowiska tworzące kulturę pisma w dawnej Rzeczypospolitej XV-XVIII stulecia*, ed. A. ADAMSKA, A. BARTOSZEWICZ, and M. PTASZYŃSKI (Warsaw, 2017), pp. 171-182.

ZACHARA-ZWIĄZEK, U., *Łacina późnośredniowiecznych ksiąg ławniczych Starej Warszawy* [Latin of the Late Medieval Aldermen Registers of Old Warsaw] (Warsaw, 2019).

ZACHARA-ZWIĄZEK, U., "Legaty testamentowe mieszczan krakowskich na rzecz kościoła i klasztoru bernardynów na Stradomiu w drugiej połowie XV wieku" [The legacies of Cracow burghers to the Bernardine church and convent in Stradom from the second half of the fifteenth century], *Kwartalnik Historii Kultury Materialnej* 63.1 (2015), pp. 29-40.

ZAHORSKI, W., *Przewodnik po Wilnie* [A Guide to Vilnius] (Vilnius, 1921).

ZAJĄC-GARDEŁA, Z., *Wariantywność i normalizacja polszczyzny literackiej XVI wieku na podstawie Ksiąg o wychowaniu i o ćwiczeniu każdego przełożonego, nie tylko panu ale i każdemu ku czytaniu barzo pożyteczne: Teraz nowo z łacińskiego języka na polski przełożone Reinharda Lorichiusa w tłumaczeniu Stanisława Koszuckiego: Fonetyka i fleksja: Praca napisana pod kierunkiem prof. dra hab. Bogusława Dunaja* [Variance and Standardization of the Polish Literary Language of the Sixteenth Century based on "The Books about the Upbringing and Education of Supervisors, Very Useful for Everybody, not Only for a Lord, now Translated from Latin into the Polish Language" of Reinhard Lorichius, by Stanisław Koszucki: Phonetics and Inflection: A Doctoral Thesis written under the supervison of professor Bogusław Dunaj] (Cracow, 2020).

ZAJIC, A., "Aufgaben und Stand der mittelalterlichen und frühneuzeitlichen epigraphischen Forschung in Österreich: Mit einem Schwerpunkt auf inschriftenpaläographischen Fragestellungen", in: *The History of Written Culture in the "Carpatho-Danubian" Region I. (Latin Paleography Network – Central and Central East Europe)*, ed. H. PÁTKOVÁ, P. SPUNAR, and J. ŠEDIVÝ (Bratislava and Prague, 2003), pp. 79-90.

ZAJIC, A., "Texts on public display: Strategies of visualising epigraphic writing in late medieval Austrian towns", In: *Uses of The Written Word in Medieval Towns: Medieval Urban Literacy II*, ed. M. MOSTERT and A. ADAMSKA (Turnhout, 2014), pp. 389-426.

ZAKRZEWSKI, A.B., "O kulturze prawnej Wielkiego Księstwa Litewskiego XVI-XVIII wieku – uwagi wstępne" [On the legal culture of the Grand Duchy of Lithuania, sixteenth-eighteenth centuries: Preliminary remarks], In: *Kultura i języki Wielkiego Księstwa Litewskiego*, ed. M.T. LIZISOWA (Cracow, 2005), pp. 33-63.

ZAKRZEWSKI, A.B., "Osadnictwo tatarskie w Wielkim Księstwie Litewskim – Aspekty wyznaniowe" [The Tartar settlement in the Grand Duchy of Lithuania – Some confessional aspects] , *Acta Baltico-Slavica* 20 (1991), pp. 137-153.

ZAKRZEWSKI, A.B., *Wielkie Księstwo Litewskie (XVI-XVIII w.): Prawo – ustrój – społeczeństwo* [The Grand Duchy of Lithuania (Sixteenth-Eighteenth Centuries): Law – Political System – Society] (Warsaw, 2013).

ZAŁĘSKI, S., *Jezuici w Polsce*, 1, *Walka z różnowierstwem 1555-1608*, 1, *1555-1586* [The Jesuits in Poland, 1, The Struggle against Religious Dissidents, 1, 1555-1586] (Lviv, 1900).

ZAREMSKA, H., "Procesje Bożego Ciała w Krakowie w XIV-XVI wieku" [The Corpus Christi procession in Cracow in the fourteenth-sixteenth centuries], in: *Kultura elitarna a kultura masowa w Polsce późnego średniowiecza*, ed. B. GEREMEK (Wrocław, 1978), pp. 25-40.

Zasady wydawania tekstów staropolskich: Projekt [The Rules for Editing Old-Polish Texts], ed. K. GÓRSKI and J. WORONCZAK (Wrocław, 1955).

ZAWADZKA, K., "Ze źródeł i stanu badań dotyczących dawnych klasztornych bibliotek dominikanów w polskich prowincjach" [From the sources and scholarly discussion concerning old libraries of the Dominicans from their Polish provinces], *Nasza Przeszłość* 39 (1973), pp. 213-228.

Zbiór pomników reformacji Kościoła polskiego i litewskiego: Zabytki z wieku XVI [The Collection of Monuments of the Reformation of the Polish and the Lithuanian Church] (Vilnius, 1925).

ZDAŃKOWSKIA, M., *Rolka sztokholmska: Skarb Zamku Królewskiego w Warszawie – The Stockholm Scroll: A Treasure of the Royal Castle in Warsaw* (Warsaw, 2019).

ZDANOWICZ, J., *Sarbiewski na tle kontrowersyj teologicznych swojego wieku* [Sarbiewski against the Theological Controversies of His Period] (Vilnius, 1932).

ZECHENTER, K., "Dzieło Hipacego Pocieja o Unii Brzeskiej" [The Work of Hipacy Pociej on the Union of Brest, *Analecta Cracoviensia* 20 (1988), pp. 501-516.

ZIOMEK, J., *Renesans* [The Renaissance] (Warsaw, 1973).

ŻÓŁKIEWSKI, S., "Badania kultury literackiej i funkcji społecznych literatury" [The study of literary culture and the social functions of literature], in: *Problemy socjologii literatury*, ed. J. SŁAWIŃSKI (Warsaw, 1971), pp. 53-77.

ŻÓŁKIEWSKI, S., *Kultura literacka 1918-1932* [Literary Culture 1918-1932] (Warsaw, 1973).

ŻÓŁKIEWSKI, S., "Kultura literacka: instytucje" [Literary culture: Institutions], in: *Słownik literatury polskiej XX wieku*, ed. A. BRODZKA *et al.* (Wrocław, 1995), pp. 499-518.

ŻÓŁKIEWSKI, S., *Kultura, socjologia, semiotyka literacka* [Culture, Sociology, Literary Semiotics] (Warsaw, 1979).

ŻÓŁKIEWSKI, S., *Wiedza o kulturze literackiej* [The Research of Literary Culture] (Warsaw, 1980).

ZUJIENĖ, G., "Ceremoniał ingresu biskupów wileńskich w XVII-XVIII wieku" [The ceremonial of the entry of the bishops of Vilnius in the seventeenth-eighteenth centuries], *Barok* 13.1 (2006), pp. 59-71.

ŽUKAS, S., *Vilnius: The City and Its History*, trans. L. BLAŽEVIČIŪTĖ (Vilnius, 2002).

ŻUKOWSKI, J., "Balety królowej Cecylii Renaty" [The ballets of queen Cecilia Renata of Austria], in: *Pasaż wiedzy Muzeum Pałau Króla Jana III w Wilanowie*, <http://www.wilanow-palac.pl/balety_krolowej_cecylii_renaty.html> (accessed 17.07. 2023).

ZUPKA, D., *Ritual and Symbolic Communication in Medieval Hungary under the Árpád Dynasty (1000-1301)* (Leiden, 2016).

ŻURKOWA, R., *Księgarstwo krakowskie w pierwszej połowie XVII wieku* [Cracow Bookselling in the First Half of the Seventeenth Century] (Cracow, 1992).

ŻURKOWA, R., "Księgozbiory mieszczan krakowskich w XVII wieku" [Book collections of the town dwellers of Cracow in the seventeenth century], *Rocznik Biblioteki PAN* 13 (1967), pp. 21-51.

ŻURKOWA, R., "Udział Żydów krakowskich w handlu książką w pierwszej połowie XVII wieku" [Participation of Jews in the book trade in the first half of the seventeenth century], in: *Żydzi w Małopolsce: Studia z dziejów osadnictwa i życia społecznego*, ed. F. KIRYK (Przemyśl, 1991), pp. 59-78.

ZWOLSKI, B., *Sprawa zboru ewangelicko-reformowanego w Wilnie w latach 1639-1641* [The Issue of the Evangelical-Reformed church in Vilnius in the Period 1639-1641] (Vilnius, 1936).

ZWOLSKI, B., "Zburzenie zboru ewangelicko-reformowanego w Wilnie w 1682 r." [The demolition of the Evangelical-Reformed church in Vilnius in 1682], *Ateneum Wileńskie* 12 (1937), pp. 482-514.

БЕРШАДСКИЙ, С.А., *Документы и регесты к истории Литовских евреев* [Documents and Registers for the History of the Lithuanian Jews] (St Petersburg, 1882).

БЕРШАДСКИЙ, С.А., "История виленской еврейской общины с 1593 до 1648 гг." [History of the Vilnius Jewish community from 1593 to 1648], *Восход* 6.10 (1886), pp. 125-138, 6.11 (1886), pp. 145-154, 7.3 (1887), pp. 81-98, 7.4 (1887), pp. 65-78, 7.5 (1887), pp. 16-32, 7.6 (1887), pp. 58-73, 7.8 (1887), pp. 97-110.

БЕРШАДСКИЙ, С.А., *Литовские евреи. История их юридического и общественного положения в Литве, 1388-1569* [Lithuanian Jews. The History of their Legal and Social Status in Lithuania, 1388-1569) (St. Petersburg, 1883).

БІЛОУС, Н., "Вызнаваю сим моим тастаменътом и ѡстатнею волею своею. Тестаменти волинських міщанок кінця XVI-XVII ст." [Testaments of women in Volhynian towns in the sixteenth and seventeenth centuries], *Соціум: Альманах соціальної історії* 13-14 (2017), pp. 127-160.

БІЛОУС, Н., *Тестаменти киян середини XVI – першої половини XVII ст.* [The Testaments of the Inhabitants of Kyiv, Mid-Sixteenth-First Half of the Seventeenth Centuries] (Київ, 2011).

БОНДАР, Н.П., "До історії друкування 'вільнюських' аркушів 1595 р.: філігранологічний аналіз примірників" ["On the history of the printing of the 'Vilnius Leaves' of 1595: A philigranological analysis"], *Наукові праці Національної бібліотеки України імені В.І.Вернадського* 31 (2011), pp. 203-213.

БОНДАР, Н.П., "Острожская Библия с 'виленскими листами' из собрания НБУВ" [The Ostrog Bible with "Vilnius pages" from the NBUV collection], in: *Книга и мировая цивилизация: Материалы 11 Международной книговедеческой научной конференции по проблемам книговедения, (Москва, 20-21 апреля 2004 г.)* [The Book and Global Civilisation: Materials of the Eleventh International Bibliological Scientific Conference on the Problems of Bibliology (Moscow, 20-21 April 2004)], 2 (Moscow, 2004), pp. 355-359.

БОНДАР, Н.П., "Экземпляры кириллических изданий вильнюсских типографий из фондов Национальной библиотеки Украины имени В. И. Вернадского как источник историко-книговедческих и филигранологических исследований"

[Copies of the Cyrillic prints from printing houses of Vilnius from the funds of the V.I. Bernad'sky National Library of Ukraine as a source of historico-bibliographical and philigranological research], *Vilniaus universiteto bibliotekos metraštis* (2015), pp. 403-432.

ВАРОНІН, В., "Прадмова" [Foreword], in: *Летапісы і хронікі Белорусі: Средневечча і раньемодэрны час* [Records and Chronicles of Belarus: The Medieval and Early Modern Periods] (Smolensk, 2013).

ВЗДОРНОВ, Г., *Исследование о Киевской псалтыри* [A Study of the Kyiv Psalter] (Moscow, 1978).

ВОЗНЕСЕНСКИЙ, А., "Сведения и заметки о кириллических печатных книгах, 1, Малая подорожная книжка Франциска Скорины" ["Notes and comments on Cyrillic printed books, 1, The little travel book of Francysk Skaryna] in: *Труды Отдела древнерусской литературы* [Works of the Department of Old Russian Literature] 51 (St Petersburg, 1999), pp. 331-341.

ГАЛЕЧАНКА, Г.Я., *Невядомыя и малавядомыя помнікі духоўнай спадчыны і культурных сувязей Беларусі XV – сярэдзіны XVII ст* [Unknown and little-known monuments of the spiritual heritage and cultural ties of Belarus, fifteenth-mid-sixteenth centuries] (Minsk, 2008).

ГАРКОВИЧ, Н.В., *Деятельность Стефана Зизания в контексте православного братского движения в Речи Посполитой Автореферат диссертации на соискание ученой степени кандидата исторических наук по специальности 07.00.03 – Всеобщая история* [The Activities of Stefan Zizany in the Context of the Orthodox Brotherhood Movement in the Polish-Lithuanian Commonwealth: Abstract of a Dissertation for the Degree of Candidate of Historical Sciences in the Specialty 07.00.03 – General History] (Minsk, 2019).

ГАРКОВИЧ, Н. В., "Катехизис Стефана Зизания (Вильна, 1595 г.)" [The catechism of Stefan Zizany (Vilnius, 1595)]" *Studia Historica Europae Orientalis* 7 (2008), pp. 258-298.

ГРУША, А.І., *Белоруская кірылычна палеаграфія. Вучэбны дапаможнік для студэнтаў гістарынага факультэта* [Belarusian Cyrillic Paleography: A Study Guide for Students of the Historical Faculty] (Minsk, 2006).

ГРУША, А.І., "Гісторыя вывучэння белорускай і ўкраінскай кірылычнай палеаграфіі да 1928 гг." [The history of the study of Belarusian and Ukrainian Cyrillic palaeography before 1928], *Белорускі археаграфічны штогоднік* 7 (2006), pp. 95-108.

ГРУША, А. И., *Документальная письменность Великого Княжества Литовского (конец XIV – первая треть XVI в.)* [Documentary Literacy of the Grand Duchy of Lithuania (End of the Fourteenth-First Third of the Sixteenth Centuries)] (Minsk, 2015).

ГУСЕВА, А.А., *Издания кирилловского шрифта второй половины XVI в.: Сводный каталог* [Editions in Cyrillic Script of the Second Half of the Sixteenth Century: A Synoptic Catalogue], 1 (Moscow, 2003).

ГУСЕВА, А.А., *Издания кирилловского шрифта второй половины XVI в.: Сводный каталог* [Editions in Cyrillic Script of the Second Half of the Sixteenth Century: A Synoptic Catalogue], 2 (Moscow, 2003).

ДУБНОВ, С.М., "Разговорный язык и народная литература польсколитовских евреев в XVI и первой половине XVII века" ["The conversational tongue and popular literature of Polish-Lithuanian Jews in the sixteenth and in the first half of the seventeenth centuries"], *Еврейская Старина* 1 (1909), pp. 10-14.

ДУМИН, С.В., "Татарские князья в Великом княжестве литовском" ["Tatar princes in the Grand Duchy of Lithuania"], *Acta Baltico-Slavica* 20 (1991), pp. 9-10.

КАЙДАНОВЕР, Арон, <https://be.wikipedia.org/wiki/%D0%9A%D0%B0%D0%B9%D0%B4%D0%B0%D0%BD%D0%BE%D0%B2%D0%B5%D1%80> (accessed on 17.07.2023).

Кириллические рукописные книги, хранящиеся в Вильнюсе: каталог, [The Cyrillic Manuscript Books Kept in Vilnius: A Catalogue], ed. Н. МОРОЗОВА (Vilnius, 2008).

КИСЕНБАУМ, Ш.В., *Еврейские надгробные памятники города Люблина (XVI-XIX в): Приложение к "Еврейской Старине"* [Jewish Funerary Monuments of the City of Lublin (Sixteenth-Nineteenth Centuries): Addition to *Jewish Antiquity*] (St Petersburg, 1913).

КОРЗО, М.А., *Украинская и белорусская катехетическая традиция конца XVI-XVII вв: Становление, эволюция и проблема заимствований* [The Ukrainian and Belarusian Catechistic Tradition of the End of the Sixteenth-Eighteenth Centuries: Establishment, Evolution and the Problem of Borrowings] (Moscow, 2007).

КРАЛЮК, П., "Острозька Біблія та філософська й богословська думка в Острозькій академії", *Наукові записки: Серія "Філософія* [The Ostroh Bible and Philosophical and Theological Thought in the Ostroh Academy], 4 (2008), pp. 3-13.

МАГГИД, Д., "Вильна" [Vilnius], in: *JEBE* 5, cols. 572-597**check**.

МАГГИД, Х.Н. (H.N. MAGGID-STEINSCHNEIDER), אנליוו ריע Матеріалы къ исторіи Виленской еврейской общины въ краткихъ біографическихъ очеркахъ ея дѣятелей с разными генеалогическими и біографическими заметками [Materials on the History: Materials on the History of the Vilnius Jewish Community in Short Biographical Descriptions of its Actors with Various Genealogical and Biographical Notes] (Vilnius, 1900).

МИШКИНЕНЕ, Г., "Полемика между мусульманами и иудеями (на материале арабскалфавитных рукописей литовских татар середины XVII в.)" ["Polemics between Muslims and Jews (on the basis of manuscripts in Arabic script of Lithuanian Tartars in the mid-seventeenth century"], *Krakowsko-wileńskie studia slawistyczne*, 4, ed. M. KUCZYŃSKA, W. STĘPNIAK-MINCZEWA, and J. STRADOMSKI (Cracow, 2009), pp. 234-249.

МЯКИШЕВ, В., *Кириллические издания Литовского Статута 1588 года* [Cyrillic Editions of the Lithuanian Statute of 1588] (Cracow, 2014).

НЕМИРОВСКИЙ, Е.Л., "Заметки о старопечатных изданиях" ["Notes on early printed editions"], *Україна: культурна спадщина, національна свідомість, державність* [Ukraine: Cultural Heritage, National Consciousness, Statehood] 15 (2006-2007), pp. 186-188.

НЕМИРОВСКИЙ, Е.Л., *Славянские издания кирилловского (церковнославянского) шрифта* [Slavic Editions in Cyrillic (Church Slavonic) Script], 2.1, *1551-1592* (Moscow, 2011).

НЕМИРОВСКИЙ, Е.Л., *Славянские издания кирилловского (церковнославянского) шрифта* [Slavic Editions in Cyrillic (Church Slavonic) Script], 2.2, *1593-1600*, (Moscow, 2011).

НЕМИРОВСКИЙ, Е. Л., *Славянские издания кирилловского (церковнославянского) шрифта: 1491-2000, Инвентарь сохранившихся экземпляров и указатель литературы* [Slavic Editions in Cyrillic (Church Slavonic) Print: 1491-2000: An Inventory of Surviving Examples and an Index of Literature], 1, *1491-1550* (Moscow, 2009).

НЕМИРОВСКИЙ, Е.Л., "Острожская Библия: Как находили и вводили в оборот самое знаменитое издание Ивана Федорова" [The Ostroh Bible: How the most famous edition of Ivan Fedorov was found and entered into virculation"], in: *Федоровские чтения 2005* [Fedorov Readings 2005] (Moscow, 2005).

НЕМИРОВСКИЙ, Е.Л., *Франциск Скорина: Жизнь и деятельность белорусского просветителя* [Francysk Skaryna: Life and Activities of a Belorusian Enlightener] (Minsk, 1990).

НІКАЛАЕЎ, М.В., *Гісторыя беларускай кнігі* [The History of the Belarusian Book] 1, *Кніжная культура Вялікага Княства Літоўскага* (Minsk, 2009).

НІКОЛАЕЎ, М.В., *Палата кнігопісаная: Рукапісная кніга на Беларусі ў X-XVIII стагоддах* [The Writing Quarters: The Manuscript Book in Belarus in the Tenth-Eighteenth Centuries] (Minsk, 1993).

ПУЦКО, В.Г., "Сюжетная гравюра в виленских изданиях Петра Тинофеева Мстиславца" [Subject Engravings in the Vilnius Editions of Petr Tinofeev Mstislavets], in: *Беларуская кніга ў кантэксце сусветнай кніжнай культуры* [The Belarusian Book in the Context of Global Book Culture], ed. M.A. БЯСПАЛАЯ *et al.* (Minsk, 2006), pp. 5-9.

Русско-еврейский архив: Документы и материалы для истории евреев в России, 1, *Документы и регесты к истории литовских евреев (1388-1550)* [Russian-Jewish Archive: Documents and Materials on the History of the Jews in Russia], 1, ed. С.А. БЕРШАДСКИЙ (St Petersburg, 1882).

Статут Вялікага Княства Літоўскага, Рускага і Жамойцкага 1588 г.: да 430-годдзя выдання. Зборнік навуковых артыкулаў па матэрыялах канферэнцыі. У аўтарскай рэдакцыі [The Statute of the Grand Duchy of Lithuania, Ruthenia, and Zamość of 1588: on the 430th Anniversary of Publication: Collection of Scientific Articles from the Materials of the Conference In the Authors' Redaction] (Minsk, 2018).

Собраніе древнихъ грамотъ и актов городовъ: Вильны, Ковна, Трокъ, православныхъ монастырей, церквей и по разнымъ предметамъ [Collection of

Ancient Charters and Acts of Cities: Vilnius, Kovno, Trokiai, of Orthodox Monasteries and Churches, and on Various Subjects], 2 (Vilnius, 1843).

ТЕМЧИН, С.Ю. (Temčinas S.), "Функционирование руськой мовы и ие-рархия церковных текстов" [The functioning of the Ruthenian language and the hierarchy of ecclesiastical texts], *Studia Russica* 23 (2009), pp. 226-234.

ТЕМЧИН, С.Ю., "Роль Матвея Десятого в православной культуре Великого княжества Литовского" [The role of Matvei Desatyi in the Orthodox culture of the Grand Duchy of Lithuania], in: *Latopisy Akademii Supraskiej*, 1, *Prawosławni w dziejach Rzeczypospolitej*, ed. U. PAWLUCZUK (Białystok, 2010), pp. 27-35.

ТИМОШЕНКО, Л., *Руська релігійна культура Вільна. Контекст доби: Осередки: Література та книжність (XVI-перша третина XVII ст.)* [The Ruthenian Religious Culture of Vilnius: Context of the Epoch, Hubs, Literature and the Book (the Sixteenth to the First Third of the Seventeenth Century)] (Дрогобич, 2020).

ТИХОМИРОВ, М.Н., and А.В. МУРАВЬЕВ, *Русская палеография* [Russian Palaeography] (Moscow, 1966).

ТОПОРОВ, В.Н., "Vilnius, Wilno, Вильна: Город и миф" [Vilnius, *Wilno*, Wilna: City and myth], in: *Балто-славянские этноязыковые контакты* [Balto-Slavic Ethnolinguistic Contact], ed. Т.М. СУДНИК (Moscow, 1980), pp. 3-72.

УСПЕНСКИЙ, Б.А., *История русского литературного языка (XI-XVII вв.)* [The History of the Russian Literary Language (Eleventh-Seventeenth Centuries)] (Budapest, 1988).

ФЛЕРОВ, Ё.О., *О православных церковных братствах, противоборство-вавших Унии в югозападной России, в XVI, XVII, XVIII столетиях* [On Orthodox Church Brotherhoods which Resisted the Unia in Southwestern Russia in the Sixteenth, Seventeenth and Eighteenth Centuries] (St Petersburg, 1857).

ШМАТАЎ, В., *Мастацтва белорускіх старадрукаў (XVI-XVIII стст.)* [The Art of Belarusian Old Prints, Sixteenth-Eighteenth Centuries] (Minsk, 2000).

Indices

Index of Personal Names

Abraham, Joshua ben Jacob Heschel 543
Abraham of Seliszewo 137
Abrahimowa 362
Abramowicz, Jan Stanisławowicz 234
Abszamiecirowicz, Islam 362
Adalbert, St. (Wojciech św.) 506, 549
Adam of Vilnius – see: Jakubowicz Adam of Kotra
Adamczyk, Władysław 23, 40, 80, 317, 319
Adamczyk-Garbowska, Monika 580
Adamowicz, Adam Ferdynand 15, 104, 143, 172
Adamska, Anna XIV, 4, 13, 33, 41, 48, 61, 113-115, 187, 188, 191, 192, 199, 226 , 241, 322, 325, 355, 356, 359, 360, 361, 433, 460
Adomaitis, Nerijus 450
Aesop, 122
Aglinskas, Vaiva 486
Agricola, Rudolf 122, 153, 359, 438,
Agryppa, Wacław 74, 244, 402
Alabiano, Garcia 295, 296
Aland, Jan 480
Albert of Prussia (Hohenzollern) 117, 128, 203, 284, 285, 577
Albertus Magnus 119
Albinus, Jerzy 100, 106, 110
Aleksandravičius, Egidijus 117
Aleksandrowycz, Wołodymyr 423
Alexander I Jagiellon 9, 59, 73, 112, 113, 126, 137, 141, 144, 241, 271, 340, 493, 518
Alexander of Villedieu 135
Alexander the Great 115, 413, 544
Alexandrowicz, Stanisław 148, 176, 255
Alginus, Olaus 101
Algirdas (Olgierd) 6, 92, 164
Ališauskas, Vytautas 139, 282, 355
Altbauer, Moshé 275
Alvares (Álvares), Manuel 152, 320
Alvarez, Lourdes María 370
Ambrosius, St. 99
Ambroży of Kłodawa 282
Anatavičius, Darius XV
Anderson, Bradford A. 537
Andriush (a goldsmith) 306
Andrzej (Andrew) of Vilnius (Andreas Vilnensis) 541, 566, 567, 581
Andrzej (bishop of Vilnius) 69, 75, 97, 98, 110, 351
Andrzejewicz, Fiedorek (Theodor) 140, 162, 164
Andrzejowicz, Walerian 550, 551
Anglés, José (Angles, Josephus) 121
Anna Jagiellon 45, 106, 199, 340

Anna Vasa of Sweden 174, 500, 501
Annibale a Capua 173, 174
Antanavičius, Darius 20-22, 24, 71, 76, 83, 201, 247, 362, 513
Antiochus 413
Antoni Włoch (Anthony the Italian) 447
Antoniewicz, Marceli 134
Anužytė, Lina 54
Aphthonius 103, 122, 359, 432
Aphthonius of Antioch 103, 122, 432
Appel, Włodziemierz 442
Aquaviva, Claudio 148, 295, 320
Arcias, Antonio 540
Argenti, Giovanni 156
Ariès, Philippe 442, 443, 459, 460
Aristotle 27, 99, 121, 122, 316, 325, 429, 438, 472, 520, 541
Aruncok 227
Assmann, Aleida 599, 600
Assmann, Jan 34, 599, 600
Aubert, Gabriel 590
Augé, Marc 604
Augustinus, St. (Augustinus, Aurelius) 95, 99, 116
Augustyniak, Urszula 104, 105, 124, 173, 176, 193, 220, 353, 355, 509
Awianowicz, Bartosz B. 153, 359, 438, 489
Axer, Jerzy 204
Azarich (Azaricz), Semen Ivanovich 118, 127
Babich (Babicz), Yakov 288, 309
Bainton, Roland H. 186
Baker, Patrick 40
Bałaban, Meir 312, 384, 536
Balaszkowa, Dorota Demerówna 189
Balcerowa, (an apothecary) 377
Baliński, Michał 13, 64, 85, 86, 92, 114, 191, 421
Baliulis, Algirdas 201
Balsys, Rimantas 526
Banionis, Egidijus 84
Barącz, Sadok 599
Baranowski, Henryk 18, 31
Barbara, Zápolya (Szapolyai) 199, 460
Barco, Javier del 537
Bardach, Juliusz 71, 76, 164, 263
Baronas, Darius 6, 525
Baronio (Baronius), Cesare 119, 208
Barszcz, Jan 474
Bartkutė, Diana 578
Bartłomiej of Biecz 98
Bartnicka, Kalina 150
Bartoli, Elisabetta 324
Bartosz (tailor) 376
Bartoszewicz, Agnieszka 12, 30, 31, 33, 51, 64, 65, 75, 119, 140, 141, 191, 199, 226, 259, 283, 324, 330, 335, 337, 352, 353
Bartoszewicz, Jan – see: Walenty Bartoszewski
Bartoszewski, Walenty (Bartoszewicz, Jan) 20, 236, 494, 495, 496, 497, 549, 604
Bartz, Gabriele 334
Barycz, Henryk 171, 237, 295, 310, 402, 494
Baryczowa, Maria 17, 60, 146
Bas, Emma 155
Báthory, Griselda (Batorówna, Gryzelda) 485
Báthory, Stephen – cf. Stephen I Báthory
Baum, Marzena 207
Bauman, Richard 590
Baumgarten, Konrad 285, 563
Bednarczuk, Leszek 7, 250, 255
Bednarski, Stanisław 148
Beer, Moshe 178
Bejnart, Ambroży 101, 111
Bekier, Ludwik 317, 318
Bellarmine, Robert 297, 372, 575
Belzyt, Leszek 38
Bem, Kazimierz 568, 569
Bembus, Mateusz 480, 540
Benacka, Elizabeth 359
Benedict (a municipal notary) 66

Benevolo, Leonardo 492
Benhamou, Reed 439
Benis, Artur 121
Berensmeyer, Ingo 29
Berezhsky, Joseph 96
Berger, Glenn 11
Bergman, Daniel 198
Bergmanowa, Mrs 198
Bergmanówna, Krzysia 198
Berkovitz, Jay R. 543
Bernard (Biernat) of Lublin 547
Bernard of Vilnius 136
Bernard, St. (Bernard of Clairvaux) 209, 270, 401
Bernardoni, Giovanni Maria 491
Bernart, Carulus 250
Bernatowicz, Tadeusz 491
Bershadski, Sergei A. – see: Бершадский Сергей Александрович
Bersohn, Mathias 542
Beynart, Samuel 79
Beynart, Stanisław 79
Bialecka, Mirka XV
Biedrzycka, Agnieszka 591
Bielak, Włodzimierz 223
Bielińska, Maria 325
Bielski, Joachim 441, 485
Bielski, Marcin 441, 485
Bieńkowska, Barbara 97
Bieńkowski, Tadeusz 150, 155
Bieś, Andrzej Paweł 106
Bilczewski, Tomasz 549
Bildziukiewicz, Hieronim 552, 553
Bill, Stanley 549
Billewiczówna, Zofia – see: Ogińska Billewiczówna, Zofia
Birkowski, Fabian 542
Biržiška, Vaclovas 584
Bitner, Marcin 105
Bittner, Krzysztof 481
Bjork, Robert E. 370
Błaszczak, G. 138
Blaževičiūtė, Laura 13
Blinstrub, Dawid 466, 467
Blinstrub family 467
Blinstrubowa Wiekowicz, Helena 466, 467
Blinsturbowa, Helena (the older) 467
Bliss, Matthew T. 5
Bliziński, Krzysztof 318
Bloemendal, Jan 29
Bobola, Andrzej 501
Bobola, Ioannes 413, 476
Bobrowicz, Jan Nepomucen 467
Bobrykowicz, Józef (Bobrikovich, Josif) 166, 169, 300, 382, 398, 541
Bogdan, Stanisław 310
Bogdańska, Anna Maria 451
Bogucka, Maria 33, 38, 64, 140, 281, 337
Boierus, Laurentius (Bojer Wawrzyniec) 520
Boissard, Jean Jacques 122
Bojer, Wawrzyniec – see: Boyer, Laurentius
Bolimowski, Krzysztof 242
Bolognetti, Alberto 488
Bömelburg, Hans-Jürgen 22, 522
Bona, Sforza 36, 55, 114, 199, 205, 241, 346, 457, 485
Bonaventure, St. 209
Borasta, Grzegorz Wawrzyniec (Borastius Gregorius Laurentius) 504
Borawski, Piotr 179, 277, 537
Borecki, Hiob 382
Borek, Piotr XV, 323, 328
Borgia, Francesco 133, 146
Borkowska, Małgorzata 77, 196, 197, 206, 207, 208, 211, 214, 215, 218, 219, 222, 324, 361
Borkowska, Urszula 113, 114, 202, 203, 241, 346, 433
Borowski, Andrzej XV, 29, 221, 265, 582
Borussus, Federicus 408
Bosgrave, James 148
Bothdivius, Johannes 108
Botto, Margherita 155

Bourdieu, Pierre 34, 35, 186
Bowden, Caroline 195, 198
Boyer, Laurentius (Bojer, Wawrzyniec) 159, 520
Bracha, Krzysztof 272
Brądzberska, Dorota 222
Braga, Antoni 455, 456
Braga, Atanazy 455, 456
Bragone, Maria Cristina 167
Brandt, Jan 372
Branny, Andrzej 354
Braun, Georg 125
Braun, Konrad (Brunus, Conradus) 100
Braziūnienė, Alma 108, 117
Brensztejn, Michał 464-466
Breutelt, Michael 464, 466, 467
Brocus, Adam (Broke) 295, 297, 320
Brodzka, Alina 28
Broniewski, Marcin (Philalet, Christopher) 382, 420-422
Brook-Rose, Christine 472
Brożek, Mieczysław 202
Brückner, Aleksander 416, 577
Bruno, Christian 163
Brunus, Conradus – see: Braun, Konrad
Brzozowska, Ałła 70
Buchanan, George 125
Bucher, Matheus 331, 332
Buchner, Marcin 317, 318
Buchnerówna, Miss 317, 318
Buchwald-Pelcowa, Paulina 274, 560
Budny, Bieniasz 297
Budny, Szymon 535, 544, 549
Buel, Lawrence 29
Bujnicki, Tadeusz XV, 31, 451
Bukowiec, Paweł XV, 31, 139, 282, 509, 591
Bulavas, Vladas 18, 110
Buonaccorsi, Filippo (Callimachus) 113
Buožytė (Terleckienė), Eleonora XV, 19
Burba, Jan 477
Burchard, Mikołaj 415
Burckhardt, Jacob 127
Būrė, Dainius 486
Burgers, Jan 225
Burke, Mary E. 184
Burke, Peter 40, 127
Burke, Victoria E. 215
Burrow, Colin 27
Bursche, Edmund 310, 402, 403, 405
Buszewicz, Elwira 20, 21, 434, 494, 507, 514, 521
Byliński, Janusz 422
Byliński, Stefan Karol 79, 86, 87
Caesar, Caius Iulius 122, 154
Calepino, Ambrogio (Calepinus, Ambrosius) 100, 103, 122, 307, 308
Callixtus I 589
Calvin, John 89, 125, 515
Camargo, Martin 341
Cammarosano, Paolo 341
Canisius, Petrus (Peter) 121, 142, 144, 152, 296, 528, 574, 575
Cannon, Christopher 221
Čapaitė, Rūta 22, 271, 273
Čaplinskas, Antanas Rimvydas 13, 16, 65
Carnell, Simon 244
Carney, Guy XIV
Carruthers, Mary 601
Casimir IV Jagiellon 59, 72, 96, 112, 113, 136, 241, 257, 271
Casimir Jagiellon (St. Casimir, św. Kazimierz) 19, 39, 53, 54, 87, 100, 101, 127, 134, 235, 430, 432, 437, 439, 442, 457, 460-462, 463, 470, 492, 495, 497, 504, 505, 506, 510, 518, 523, 550, 553, 561, 567, 603
Casimir, St. – see: Casimir Jagiellon
Cassian, John 207
Castello, Matteo 454, 455, 457
Castiglione, Baldassare 242, 393
Catherine Jagiellon 199, 433, 494, 509, 518
Catherine of Austria 199
Caussinus, Nicolaus (Caussin, Nicolas) 438

Cebulka, Mikołaj 72, 242
Cecilia Renata of Austria 199, 431, 486
Celtis, Conrad 325
Čepienė, Konstancija 17, 26, 320
Chądzyński, Jan 414, 415
Chalecki family 207, 477
Chalecki, Krzysztof 477
Charles Ferdinand Vasa (Karol Ferdynand Waza) 519
Chartier, Roger 208
Charytonowicz, Samuel 610
Chemperek, Dariusz xv, 20, 22, 383, 420, 421, 579
Chiron, Pierre 359
Chlebowski, Bronisław 559
Chmiel, Adam 304
Chmieleski, Marcin 172
Chodkiewicz, Jan Karol 22, 197, 520
Chodkiewicz, Jerzy 474
Chodkiewicz, Krzysztof 551
Chodkiewiczowa, Zofia (née Drucka Horska) 196, 197, 551
Chojecka, Ostrowska Zofija 376, 377
Chojecki, Jan 376
Chojecki, Jerzy 376
Chomik, Piotr 21, 169
Chopin, Frédéric 602
Chorążyczewski, Waldemar 71, 72, 73, 77
Chreptowiczowa, Zuzanna Nonhartówna 194
Christ – see: Jesus Christ
Chrobaczyński, Jacek 245
Chrościcki, Juliusz A. 12, 491, 492, 498, 506, 518, 522
Chwalba, Andrzej 463
Chynczewska-Hennel, Teresa 235, 422, 487, 497, 510
Chytraeus, David 179, 537
Cicėnienė, Rima 281
Cicero (Marcus Tullius) 27, 50, 103, 116, 122, 142, 154, 159, 202, 231, 297, 347, 425
Ciesielski, Stanisław 17
Cieśla, Maria xv, 275
Cillario, Graziella 155
Cini, Giovanni of Pisa 273, 452
Ciołek, Erazm 70, 73, 109, 283
Čiurinskas, Mintautas xv, 19, 567
Clanchy, Michael Thomas 32, 34, 127, 141, 184, 195, 198, 208, 226, 257, 276
Classen, Albrecht 220
Clingius, Conrad 100
Cnapius, Gregorius – see: Knapiusz Grzegorz
Cnoglerus, Quirinus (Knogler, Kwiryn) 176, 177, 438, 506, 507, 523
Cohen, Israel 15, 90, 125, 255, 275, 277, 384, 397, 449, 542, 543, 599
Cole, Janie 473
Collini, Stefan 472
Comuleus, Alexander (Komulović, Aleksandar) 144
Consoli, Tomasz 599
Constance of Austria 45, 199, 469, 482, 499, 500, 508, 553, 592
Corbellini, Sabrina 33
Cormack, Lesley B. 11
Corvinus, Laurentius 325
Cubrzyńska-Leonarczyk, Maria 274, 460
Culler, Jonathan 472
Curtius (Quintus Curtius Rufus) 122, 154
Curtius, Ernst Robert 27, 221, 484
Cygielman, Szmuel Artur 179
Cyryl of Głubczyce 65, 75, 330
Cytowska, Maria 174, 402
Czaplicka, John 599
Czapliński, Przemysław 590
Czarnecki, Andrzej 334
Czartoryska, Izabela 602
Czechowic, Marcin 392, 408, 411
Czeplewski, Paweł 339
Czwojdrak, Bożena 197, 399
Czyrek, Wacław 48
Czyż, Michał 189
Czyż, Renata 368, 588

Czyżowa, Anna Prokopowiczówna Aleksandrowa 189, 356
Dąbkowska-Kujko, Justyna 138
Dąbrówka, Jan 315
Dąbrowski, Ambroży 569
Dąbrowski, Maciej 286
Dacka-Górzyńska, Iwona M. 283, 523
Daldianus, Artemidorus 122
Dambrowski, Samuel 104, 297, 377, 378, 386, 414, 481, 560, 586, 604
Danbury, Elizabeth 335
Daniel, of Łęczyca 289, 294-296, 298, 300, 310, 402
Dantiscus, Ioannes (Dantyszek, Jan) 344
Danylenko, Andrii 22, 181
Darowski, Roman 385
Daukša, Mikalojus (Mikołaj Dauksza) 45, 144, 159, 297, 575, 582, 584, 588, 589
Daukšienė, Ona 20
Dauksza, Mikołaj – see: Daukša, Mikalojus
David ha-Levi Segal 384
David, Jean 209, 210
Dawidowicz, Lucy S. 464
De Guevara, Antonio 122
De la Puente (Pontanus), Luis 211, 212
De Soarez, Cypriano 153, 320
De Vaucelles, Louis 150
De Vega, Emmanuel 372, 407, 412-413
De Vries Simon Philip 582
Decjusz, Mikołaj 110
Delimata-Proch, Małgorzata 460
Delle Donne, Fulvio 343
Demeszko, Andreas 331
Demosthenes 155
Der Weduwen, Arthur 43
Derolez, Albert 271
Desaus, Anna 317
Deszczek, Nicolaus 331
Devochka, Onisiphor 165
Dido 155
Dilytė, Dalia 513
Dinshaw, Carolyn 30, 221
Dirsytė, Rima 334
Długosz, Jan 97, 98, 113, 422, 521
Długosz, Józef 422
Dłużewski, Juliusz Nowak 18, 432, 508, 511
Dmitruk, Krzysztof 28, 473
Dobry (Dobro), Petrus 331
Doktor Hiszpan – see: Ruiz de Moros Pedro
Domanowski, Jan 59, 393
Domański, Juliusz 443, 596
Domiechowski, Przemysław 209
Dominik, Jan 569
Donatus, 135, 142, 390
Donawerth, Jane 184
Dorofiejewicz, Paweł 445
Dorofiejewiczowa, Akwilina Stryludzianka 45, 189, 446
Dorohostajski, Krzysztof 501
Dove, Linda L. 184
Dowgird, Samuel 298, 513, 522, 523
Dowgirdowicz, Andrzej (Dougirdovich, Andriuška) 264
Drėma, Vladas V. 92, 142, 143
Drob, Janusz 478
Drublański, Rev. 119, 129
Drzymała, Kazimierz 369
Dubinowski, Piotr 24
Dubiński, Aleksander 537
Dubonis, Artūras 143, 201, 247
Dubowicz, Aleksy 78, 82, 479, 481
Dubowicz, Jan 481
Dubowicz, Stefan 229, 317
Dunaj, Bogusław 202
Duns Scotus 385
Dygoń, Marcin 190
Dygoniowa, Anna 190
Dyjakowska, Marzena 49
Dymmel, Piotr 318
Dymus, David 147
Dziechcińska, Hanna 285
Dzięgielewski, Jan 170
Eck, Johann 111

Eco, Umberto 472
Eder, Maciej 20, 128
Eidelberg, Shlomo 384, 542, 543
Elisabeth of Austria 36, 199, 202, 205, 433
Emanuel, Susan 34
Engelbrecht family 190
Engelke, Adrian 175
Ephraim ben Jacob HaKohen 542, 543
Erasmus of Rotterdam 121, 122, 159, 297, 325
Eric XIV of Sweden
Esposito, Salvatore 337
Estreicher, Stanisław 26, 60, 389, 407, 413, 535, 551, 559, 577, 587, 588
Eufrazja of St. Casimir (Helena Sanguszkówna) 214
Eufrazja of St. John (Teodora Piaseczyńska) 220
Euripides 595
Eysmont, Jan 477
Ezofowicz, Jan Abraham 94, 126
Faber, Ioannes 128
Fabre, Pierre-Antoine 155, 371
Fabritius, Franciscus 147
Falniowska-Gradowska, Alicja 324, 357, 362
Farrell, Allan P. 158, 581
Fatio, Giulio 208
Faulhaber, Charles B. 341
Favreau, Robert 436
Fazan, Jarosław XV, 31
Federico da Montefeltro 127
Fedor (*diak*) 282
Fedorov, Ivan 274, 532
Feigelmanas, Nojus 110
Feliksiak, Elżbieta 22, 258
Fenig, Jerzy 447
Ferreri, Zacharias 529, 567
Ficino, Marsilio 443
Fijałek, Jan 17
Filipczak-Kocur, Anna 74, 79, 80
Filipowicz, Joannes 332
Filipowski, Hieronim 414, 426
Filonardi, Mario 487, 497
Findlen, Paula 342
Fish, Stanley 28, 178, 323, 437, 472, 512, 514
Fisher, Sheila 184, 186
Fishman, David 178, 449
Flaminio, Marcantonio 121
Flavius Josephus 297
Florentius Ioannes Stockholmiensis 476
Follprecht, Kamilla 20, 378, 401
Förster, Georg 311, 314
Fowler, Alastair 491
Franczak, Grzegorz XV, 470, 486, 509
Franklin, Simon 34, 225, 254
Frederic Jagiellon 493, 573, 201
Frejlich, Kamil 26, 57, 58, 71, 377
Frenkel, Jeremiasz 542
Frez, Jachim 188
Frezowa, Regina Lewonowiczówna Jachimowa 188
Frick, David A. XV, 10-12, 15, 21, 24, 32, 39, 42, 51, 58, 121, 138, 169, 172, 194, 210, 255, 259, 261, 262, 265, 275, 293, 355, 362, 365, 368, 373, 397, 398, 422, 481, 492, 515, 531, 533, 535, 549, 588, 589
Friedrich, Karin XV, 12, 502
Frölich (a bookseller) 310
Frost, Robert 6, 201, 202
Fuerst, Aharon 542
Fulińska, Agnieszka 159, 205, 325
Fumaroli, Marc 155, 159, 438
Gail, Andreas von 122
Gajdka, Krzysztof 20, 378, 401
Galas, Michał 312
Galos, Ewa 103
Gansiniec, Ryszard 493
Gapski, Henryk 478
Gara, Katarzyna 567
Garbacik, Józef 199
Garzaniti, Marcello 519
Gąsiorowski, Antoni 136, 325, 451

Gastold Albertus – see: Gasztołt, Olbracht
Gasztołd family 344, 458, 521
Gasztołd, Marcin 314
Gasztołt, Olbracht (Albertus Gastold, Albertas Goštautas) 2, 45, 98, 114, 115, 171, 241, 264, 344, 368, 546, 547, 548
Gawlas, Sławomir 422, 436
Gębarowicz, Mieczysław 114
Gediminas, 1, 3, 6, 7, 41, 52, 53, 74, 255, 271, 327, 518, 519, 524, 526, 603, 604
Gediminids 522
Gelumbeckaitė, Jolanta 386
Geneshkovych family 232, 235
Geneshkovych, Yakhiata Girevych 232
Genzelis, Bronislovas 514
Geremek, Bronisław 494
Gertich, Marcin Gracjan 389
Giard, Luce 150, 151
Gibel, Jakub 481
Giblowa, Anna 190
Gibson, Jonathan 215
Giedroyć, Kazimierz 188
Giedroyc, Melchior 251
Gieysztor, Aleksander 252
Gil, Czesław 214
Gilewiczowa, Anastasia Witkowska Janowa 91
Gilowa, Regina Parkiewiczówna Bartłomiejowa 188
Ginzburg, Carlo 373
Gisleni, Giovanni Battista 117
Giżycki, Jan Marek Antoni 599
Glemža, Liudas 244, 492
Glińska, Anna 214
Gliński, Michał 115, 241
Glosienė, Audronė 106
Głowiński, Michał 454
Gneiß, Markus 334
Godek, Sławomir 48, 59
Godsey, William D. 32
Goeury, Julien 592
Gołaszewski, Łukasz 359
Golik-Prus, Aleksandra 20, 348
Golliusz, Jan 198, 582
Gomółka, Mikołaj 559
Gonzaga, Marie Louise – see: Marie Louise Gonzaga
Goody, Jack 4, 30, 32, 236, 257, 472, 527
Górak, Artur 74
Gorczynski, Renata 605
Górecki, Stanisław 358
Gorlaeus, Abraham 125
Górnicki, Łukasz 74, 116, 125, 238, 242, 243, 244, 493, 494
Górski, Jan 222
Górski, Karol 323, 337
Górski, Zbigniew 353
Gorzkowski, Albert 325, 432
Gorzkowski, Mikołaj 136
Goštautas, Albertas – see: Gasztołt Olbracht
Gotthard Kettler – see: Kettler, Gotthard
Grabowski, Tadeusz 580
Grabowski, Wojciech z Sierpca 112, 238
Grącki, Piotr 477
Gradowski, Franciszek 520
Grajewska, Halszka 186
Granata, Giovanna 314
Gregory of Nazianzus 154
Gregory XIII 144, 148, 418
Grendler, Paul F. 12, 34, 141, 142, 145, 147, 149, 151, 152
Gretser, Jacob 152
Grévin, Benoît 324
Griswold, Wendy 28
Grochowski, Stanisław 209
Grodzicki, Bartłomiej 357
Grodzicki, Jan 110
Grodzicki, Stanisław 159, 368, 382, 408, 418, 419, 425, 426, 479, 515, 540, 583
Grodziński, Mikołaj 508
Groicki, Bartłomiej 51, 56, 81, 354, 357
Groterus, Joannes 174
Grotówna (Grothówna), Zofia 219, 223
Grotówna, Miss 223

Gruchała, Janusz S. XV, 5, 34, 116, 127, 129, 130, 559
Grulkowski, Marcin 66, 76
Grużewski, Bolesław 162, 345, 517
Grużewski, Jan 152, 345, 517
Grzebień, Ludwik 87, 93, 106, 107, 108, 401
Grzegorz de Guraw (Grzegorz of Góra) 137
Grzegorz of Ejszyszki (Eišiškės) 143
Grzegorz of Żarnowiec 368, 413, 515, 588
Grzelczak-Miłoś, Iwona 353
Grześkowiak, Radosław XV, 21, 152, 175, 209, 213, 347, 434, 553, 554
Grzeszczuk, Stanisław 5
Grzybowski, Stanisław 276, 450
Guagnini (Gwagnin), Alessandro 129
Gucewicz, Wawrzyniec 65
Gudavičius, Edmundas 59
Gudmantas, Kęstutis 514
Gumowski, Marian 306, 470
Gustavus Adolphus (Gustav II Adolf) 108
Guzowski, Piotr 25
Gwioździk, Jolanta 30, 206-211, 213, 218, 219
Hafftka, Aleksander 536
Haider-Wilson, Barbara 32
Hajek (Gajka), Jan 203
HaKohen, Ephraim ben Jacob – see: Ephraim ben Jacob HaKohen
Halley, Janet E. 184, 186
Hanul (Hans, Hannike) of Riga 7, 327, 329, 335
Hanusiewicz-Lavallee, Mirosława XV, 214, 242, 553, 559
Harkovich, Nataliia – see: Гаркович Наталья Викторовна
Harris, Steven J. 151
Hart, Jonathan 11
Hartleb, Kazimierz 114-117
Hartlib, Mr 174
Hasjusz, Jakub 480
Haslerus, Matthias 147
Hass, Robert 605
Hauenstein, Johann Friedrich 314
Hay, John 147, 385
Haydonenius 163
Hayes, Yitzhak 450
Hedemann, Otton 324, 358
Helena (a maid) 316, 318
Helene (Helena) of Moscow 36, 199, 201
Heller, Marvin J. 560
Heneveld, Amy 590
Henry of Valois
Herbert, Zbigniew 602
Herburt, Jan Szczęsny 122
Hercules 488
Hermogenes of Tarsus 432
Hernas, Czesław 18, 553
Hesiod 155
Hessus, Eoban 125
Hils, George 604
Hippocrates 103
Hirsch, Rudolf 313
Hłasko, Edward 383
Hlebowicz, Jan 220
Höfler, Janez 7
Høgel, Christian 324
Hogenberg, Frans 125
Hołodok, Stanisław 88, 564, 566
Holszański, Paweł 58, 111, 171, 344, 452
Holy Virgin (Mary) 8, 207, 211, 358, 391, 411, 430, 461, 462, 476, 545, 547, 548, 549, 550, 557, 570, 571, 573, 574
Homer 416, 520
Hońdo, Leszek 451
Horace (Quintus Horatius Flaccus) 154, 155, 156, 159, 440
Horodyski, Bogdan 269, 270
Hörsch, Markus 113
Hosius (Hozjusz), Ulrich 100, 242, 250
Hostounský, Baltazar 133, 146, 147, 540
Howe, John 604
Hozjusz, Stanisław 44
Hrusha, Aliaksandr I. – see: Груша

Аляксандр I.
Hugo, Herman 209, 554
Hugona (Marianna Prawda) 219
Hurin 81
Ibińska, Cecylia 374, 376
Iljaszewicz, Teodor 168, 291
Imańska, Iwona 314
Inglot, Mieczysław 29
Institoris, Henricus 410
Ipsen, Carl 492
Isaac ben Yacub 374, 580
Isner, Jan 136
Isocrates 155
Ivanov, V.V. 259
Ivanovič, Marija 26, 584
Ivanovych, Grisha 201
Iwańczak, Wojciech
Iwanowicz, Jakub 94
Izheritskaya, Maria Ondreevna Ivanovicha 332
Jablonskis, Konstantinas 71, 76, 114
Jachno, *Voigt* of Vilnius 331,
Jachnowicz, Jan 531, 584
Jackiewicz, Mieczysław 467
Jackowicz, mayor 119
Jacob ben Isaac Ashkenazi 312, 580
Jacob of Varagin (Jacob of Voragine) 97
Jadwiga (Hedwig) of Poland 6, 97, 136, 245
Jagiełło – see: Jogaila
Jagiellonian dynasty – see: Jagiellonians
Jagiellonians (Jagiellonian dynasty) 241, 518
Jaglarz, Monika 309, 310
Jakimyszyn, Anna 178
Jakowicz, Luca 331
Jakubowicz, Adam of Kotra (Adam z Wilna, Адам Іакоубович съ Котьри) 73, 110, 138, 330
Jan of Komorowo (Komorowski) 88, 282
Jan of Koźmin (Kuźma) 115, 304
Jan of Vilnius 136
Janczewski family 467
Janicki, Marek A. 436, 437, 440, 452, 457, 463, 468, 470
Janik, Maciej 523
Janko Maćkowicz 331
Jankowicz, Grzegorz 28
Janonienė, Rūta 117
Janów, Jan 588
Janowicz of Nosek, Paweł 445
Janowiczowa, Janowna Katarzyna 445
Jansen, Annemiek 5
Janusz III of Masovia 445
Januszek-Sieradzka, Agnieszka 197
Januszowicz, Zygmunt 341
Januszowski, Jan 334, 335
Japlko Hieronimus (Jabłko Hieronim) 462
Jarczykowa, Mariola 19, 20, 91, 251, 323, 344, 347, 348
Jaritz, Gerhard 352
Jarmołowa, Juliana 331
Jaroszewicz-Pieresławcew, Zoja 254, 274, 289,291-293, 575
Jarzębski, Adam 444
Jasiewicz, Krzysztof 255
Jasiński, Józef 102, 110, 111, 227
Jaskier, Mikołaj 51, 191
Jawor, Grażyna 357
Jaworska, Aleksandra 66
Jaworski, Iwo 13, 53, 54
Jędrkiewicz, Edwin 425
Jędrzejczyk, Dobiesław 33
Jeremiah 483
Jeremiah II 165
Jerome, St. 99
Jesus Christ 78, 207, 211, 212, 214, 221, 225, 270, 383, 408, 411, 413, 419, 495, 496, 554, 592
Jezierski, Andrzej 40
Joannes de Nurtingen 99
Job, Tomasz XIV
Jogaila (Władysław Jagiełło) 6, 7, 39, 45, 52, 53, 69, 97, 98, 136, 191, 255, 327, 329, 518, 519, 525, 526

John a Lasko – see: Łaski Jan
John Chrysostom, St. 99, 154, 546
John I Albert Jagiellon 493
John II Casimir Vasa 90, 307, 518
John III of Sweden (John, Duke of Finland) 494, 509
John of the Lithuanian Dukes (Jan z Książąt Litewskich) 85, 114
John Vasa 199, 494, 509
John XXII 52
John Zápolya 493
Jonah ben Isaac 374
Jonston, Jan 122
Jop, Robert 66
Joseph II Sołtan
Joshua Heschel ben Joseph 178, 543
Joshua Heschel Zoref 178, 543
Jovaiša Liudas 25, 59, 139, 282, 578, 579
Jovaišas Albinas 19, 432, 575, 579, 588, 589
Józef the Brewer 316
Józefowicz-Wisińska, Elżbieta 120
Juan de Jesús María 209
Juda, Maria 166, 274
Juda Moses ben Isaac 179, 542, 543, 583
Julia, Dominique 150
Juraj, Šedivý 436
Jureczka, Andrzej 245
Jurek, Tomasz 71, 136, 247, 283
Jurgelėnaitė, Rasa 20, 21, 523
Jurgiewicz, Andrzej 129, 296, 300, 382, 407, 408, 410-412, 414, 422, 424, 425
Jurginis, Juozas 7, 13, 165
Jurski, Jan 88, 105
Justyniarska-Chojak, Katarzyna 31, 352, 357, 360, 362
Kaczmarczyk, Beata 364
Kaidanover, Aaron Samuel ben Israel 125, 542, 583
Kal (Koll) Jakub 21, 197, 434
Kałamajska-Saeed, Maria 216
Kalęba, Beata XV, 31, 139, 282, 591
Kalinowski, Rafał 213, 217, 219
Kalisz, Anna 559
Kallenbach, Józef 198
Kamieński, Petroniusz 480
Kamuntavičienė, Vaida 526
Kaniewska, Irena 202
Kantak, Kamil 282
Karalius, Laimontas (Каралюс Л.) 114, 115, 355
Karcan, Jan 175, 260, 274, 289, 294, 296-298, 300, 310, 312, 534, 588
Karcan, Józef 274, 296, 297
Karcans 295-297, 320
Karczewska, Elena 493
Karczewski, Dariusz 206
Kardasz, Monika 20
Karmanowski, Olbrycht 346, 347
Karo, Joseph 382, 383, 543
Karol Ferdynand Waza – see: Charles Ferdinand Vasa
Karp, Jonathan 178
Karpiński, Adam 21, 186, 189, 195, 196, 214, 352, 353, 434
Karpiński, Andrzej 186, 189, 195, 196, 352, 353
Karpovych (Karpowicz), Leonty 263, 264, 300, 382, 481, 483, 584,
Karpowicz, Mariusz 117, 455-459, 483, 518
Karpus, Zbigniew 237
Karr, David R. 560
Kasjaniuk, Elżbieta 575, 577
Kasperavičienė, Audronė 15, 448
Kaszlej, Andrzej 288
Kaszowska-Wandor, Barbara 478
Katalynas, Kęstutis 7, 526
Katarzyna of Christ (Felicjanna Tyszkiewiczówna) 213, 217, 604
Katerle, Paweł 103
Katherle, Jan 309
Katz, Dovid 255, 275
Kaunas, Domas 578
Kaupuż, Anna 560
Kawecka-Gryczowa, Alodia 17, 18, 34,

108, 114-117, 274, 285, 289, 297, 560, 579
Kazikowski, Stefan 76
Kaźmierczak, Ewa 573
Kazubek, Andrzej 227
Kažuro, Ina 21, 26
Kempa, Tomasz 11, 15, 16, 237, 293, 397, 398, 401
Kennedy, George A. 5
Kennedy, Grimsted Patrick 84
Kępiński, Andrzej 166
Keršienė, Dovilė 199
Kętrzyński, Stanisław 325
Kettering, Sharon 473
Kettler, Gotthard 433
Kettler, Jacob
Kettler, Wilhelm
Khmelnytsky, Bohdan 44
Kiaupienė, Jūratė 469
Kiersnowski, Ryszard 272
Kiewlicz, Jakub 118, 119, 126, 129
Kiewlicz, Marcin 434, 471, 473, 482, 511
Kiewliczowa, Marta Janówna Marcinowa 189, 363
Kijas, Zdzisław J. 576
Kiliańczyk-Zięba, Justyna XV, 335
Kirkor, Adam Honory 13, 448
Kiryk, Feliks 276
Kiszka, Mikołaj 359
Klausner, Izrael 178, 255, 449, 450, 451
Kleinmann, Yvonne 275
Klemens of Moskorzew 97
Klemensiewicz, Zenon 344
Kliczewski, Mikołaj 228
Kliczewski, Piotr 124
Klimecka, Grażyna 323
Klimowicz, Mieczysław 425
Klint, Paweł 481
Kłodziewska, Mrs 377
Klovas, Mindaugas 14, 22, 70, 75, 330, 346
Kluczata, Jan 84
Kmita, Piotr Blastus 289, 294
Knapiusz (Cnapius), Grzegorz 159, 488, 489, 517
Knogler, Kwiryn – see: Cnoglerus, Quirinus
Knoll, Paul W. 136, 137
Knoppers, Laura Lunger 30, 229
Knychalska, Agnieszka 573
Koch, Gregorius 476
Koch, Wawrzyniec 476
Kochanowski, Jan 74, 125, 155-157, 204, 242, 244, 312, 403, 406, 536, 558-560
Kochański, Teodor 118, 168
Kochlewski, Piotr 347
Koehler, Krzysztof 43, 514, 522
Kohen, Israel 15
Köhn, Rolf 343
Kojelavičius-Vijūkas, Albertas – see: Wijuk Kojałowicz Wojciech
Kojelavičius-Vijūkas, Kazimieras – see: Wijuk Kojałowicz Kazimierz
Kolenda, Jan 78, 79, 82, 481, 607, 608
Kołodziński, Mikołaj Gałązka 110
Kołos, Anna 516
Komorowska, Magdalena 559
Komulović, Aleksandar – see: Comuleus, Alexander
Kon, Pinkas 90
Konarska-Zimnicka, Sylwia 31
Konarski, Jan 573
Kondratas, Ramūnas 486
Koneczny, Feliks 60
Konopacki, Artur 180, 544, 538, 561
Konrat (a salt merchant) 316
Konrat, Marcin (Conrat Martinus) 304
Kopysteński, Zachariasz 170, 382, 421
Koranyi, Karol 354, 425
Korczak, Lidia 53, 59, 71, 72
Körner, Axel 32
Korolko, Mirosław 73, 74, 77, 151, 202, 340, 511, 587
Koropeckyj, Roman 170
Korotajowa, Krystyna 18, 34, 274, 285
Korycki, Nicolaus 476

Koryl, Jakub xv
Koryzna, Mikołaj 101, 111
Korzo, Margarita A. – see: Корзо, Маргарита А.
Kościałkowski, Stanisław 25
Kosiński, Dariusz 486, 491
Kosman, Marceli 53, 71-73, 76, 96, 136, 137, 242, 250, 255, 278, 327, 525
Kossobucki (Kossobudzki), Józef 119
Kossobucki (Kossobudzki), Paweł 119
Kostecki, Jakub 105, 473
Kostecki, Janusz 473
Kostka, Fryderyk 474
Kostka, Jan 341
Kostka, Stanisław 299
Koszutski, Stanisław 74, 116, 202-204, 238, 243, 346, 369, 452, 454, 466
Kowalenko, Władysław 244
Kowalowicz, Jan Stanisławowicz 143
Kowalski, Grzegorz M. 191, 354
Kowalski, Jacek 157, 491
Kozak, Adam 201
Kozakiewicz, Helena 458
Kozakiewicz, Stefan 458
Kozaryn, Dorota 493
Koženiauskienė, Regina 513
Kozłowska, Anna Z. 315
Kraiński, Krzysztof 578, 579,
Krajewski, Wojciech 18, 34, 274
Kramperowa, Maria 119, 125
Krąpiec, Mieczysław A. 467
Krąpnicki, Jan 497
Kras, Paweł 399
Krasnodomski, Łukasz 413
Kraszewski, Józef Ignacy 13, 16, 63, 86, 114, 441, 455, 456
Kraus, Manfred 359
Krawczuk, Wojciech 83, 247, 283
Krawczyk, Antoni 120
Kraye, Jill 341
Kreuza, Rzewuski Leon – see: Krevza, Leon
Krevza, Leon (Kreuza, Rzewuski Leon) 170, 300, 368, 382, 542, 584
Kriegseisen, Wojciech 103, 275
Kristeller, Paul Oskar 40, 176
Król, Barbara 485
Krolang, Joachimus 331
Kromer, Marcin 76, 102, 103, 122, 126, 328, 339, 344, 493
Krośniewicki, Baltazar 172
Krośniewicz, Rev. 383
Kroszyński, Jerzy 477
Kroszyński, Mikołaj 477
Kroszyński, Piotr 435
Krotowicjusz, Jan 392, 393
Kruczkiewicz, Bronisław 48
Krug, Grigorij (Gregory) 446
Kruncius, Jakub 313
Krusius, Dawid 415
Kryczyński, Stanisław 15, 179, 180, 252, 255, 256, 266, 538, 543, 544, 561
Krynicka, Maria 304
Kryski, Feliks 501, 509
Krzemycki, Emil (Aemilianus) 113
Krzycki, Andrzej 199, 460, 470
Krzywy, Roman 21, 434, 492, 522
Krzyżaniak, Barbara 214
Krzyżanowski, Stanisław 308
Kubicki, Rafał 352
Kubilius, Jonas 18
Kuczkowska, Marianna 196, 197, 215, 222, 348
Kuczyńska, Marzanna 21, 293, 550, 584, 589
Kuhn, Thomas S. 512
Kuklicki, Mikołaj 477
Kuklo, Cezary 255
Kulicka, Elżbieta 2
Kulvietis, Abraomas (Kulwieć, Abraham) 20, 45, 133, 171, 172, 399
Kulwicka-Kamińska, Joanna 538
Kulwieć, Abraham – see: Kulvietis, Abraomas
Kunigielis, Joanna xv, 60
Kuolys, Darius 20, 21, 513, 520, 523

Kupisz, Dariusz 322
Kupisz, Łukasz 311
Kurczewski, Jan 14, 70
Kurdybacha, Łukasz 425
Kurkleczyński, Stanisław 477
Kurylovych, Khotei 361
Kurzowa, Zofia 22, 260, 373
Kuzmin, Dyonisius 331
Kvietkauskas, Mindaugas 11, 31
Kwiatkowski, Krzysztof 329
Łachman, Rabin 416
Łachmowicz, Symon 188
Łada-Palusińska, Maria XIV
Łącka, Miss 223
Lampartowicz, Albertus 310
Langurga (Lang), Feliks 64, 121, 319
Łapicz, Cezary 268, 538, 543, 544
Łapszewicz, Brygita 65
Lasek, Piotr XV
Łasicki, Jan 408, 426
Łaski, Jan (John a Lasco) 51, 113, 115, 549, 569
Laskowska, Katarzyna 186
Łatyszonek, Oleg 521
Laucevičius, Edmundas 17, 34, 100, 109, 111, 114, 128, 250, 251, 301, 304, 306, 307
Lauksmin, Zygmunt – see: Lauxmin, Sigismundus
Laurentius, Olaus Gothus 476
Laurer, Johann Christian 314
Laurinus, Mr 330
Lausberg, Heinrich 5, 27, 37, 151, 321, 429, 432
Lauxmin, Sigismundus (Lauksmin Zygmunt) 159, 297, 480, 508, 514, 516
Lawata, Andreas 522
Lazutka, Stanislovas 59
Le Goff, Jacques 597
Lebiedzicz, Stefan 91, 120-122, 125, 126, 128, 130, 169, 237, 283, 318, 523
Łęczycki, Mikołaj 107
Ledesma, Jacob 575
Lelewel, Joachim 114, 602
Lenartowicz, Samuel 569
Leontowicz, Teofil 169
Leopolita, Jan 261, 531
Lesiak, Anna 193
Leśniewski, Sławomir 485
Leśnodorski, Bogusław 71
Leszczyńska, Cecylia 40
Lewański, Juliusz 20, 486, 508
Lewicki, Paweł 140
Lewonowicz, Szymon 316
Lichański, Jakub Zdzisław 20
Licyniusz, Jan 367, 383, 391
Liedke, Marzena 25, 89, 176
Lilley, David XIV
Lima, Moses Judah 179, 542, 543
Link-Lenczowski, Andrzej 179
Lipsius, Justus 122, 159
Lisiecki (a lieutenant) 613
Livingstone, Rodney 599
Livy (Titus Livius) 154, 513
Lizdeika, 1
Lizisowa, Maria Teresa 22, 255, 258
Loach, Judi 496
Lobwaser, Ambrosius 536
Locci, Agostino 487
Lombard, Peter 100
Łopatecki, Karol XV, 170, 322, 465
Lorich, Reinhard 202
Łosowicz, Jan 136
Łosowska, Anna 50
Łosowski, Janusz 71, 283, 357
Łossowski, Piotr 17
Louis of Granada (Granatens) 207
Loveridge, Jordan 359
Łowmiańska, Maria 13, 14, 25, 38, 39, 63, 65, 66, 91, 205, 250, 251, 353
Łowmiański, Henryk 17, 25, 54, 75, 250
Loyola, Ignatius 370, 371
Lubelczyk, Jakub 559
Łubieński, Stanisław 348, 587, 591
Luciński, Jerzy 323
Ludwik (a painter) 358

Ludwik, of St. Florian 213
Łukaszewicz, Józef 14, 152, 174, 175, 176, 177, 569
Łukomska, Helena 361
Lukšaitė, Ingė 18, 19, 124, 174, 414
Lulewicz, Henryk 64, 73, 124, 322
Lupesku, Makó Mária 352
Luria, Salomon 374
Luther, Martin 171, 317, 318, 411, 418, 515, 528, 535, 577, 587
Łużny, Ryszard 166
Lūžys, Sigitas 110, 136, 137
Lwówek, Marcin 139
Łysakowski, Adam 89
Łysznanka, Elisabetha 331
Macewicz, Hanko 331
Mack, Peter 341, 343, 359
Mackay, Christopher S. 410
Mackiewicz, Hilary 551
Mączak, Antoni 473
Mączyński, Jan 80
Maffon Pietro of Brescia 339
Mafon, Wojciech 331
Maggid, David Gilelevich – see: Маггид, Давид Гилелевич
Maggid-Steinschneider, Hillel Noah – see: Маггид Хиллел Ноах
Maggio, Giuniano (Iunianus Maius) 138
Maggio, Lorenzo (Laurentius) 146
Maisel, Witold 119, 125
Majer, Adam 124
Majorossy, Judit 352
Makowiecki, Jan 102, 106, 110
Makowski, Tomasz 8, 145, 173, 553, 604
Maksentówna, Barbara 462
Malaspina, Germanico 144
Malczowski, Stanisław Jan 142
Małdrzyk, Mikołaj 72
Malecki, Jan 577
Maleczka (trumpeter) 358
Maleczyński, Karol 325
Malicki, Jan 29
Malicki, Marian 383, 559
Małkus, Marta 481
Mamonicz family (Mamoniczs) 82, 95, 118, 237, 250, 254 289, 290, 296, 312, 533, 556, 568
Mamonicz, Kuźma 60, 168, 291, 293, 300
Mamonicz, Łukasz 250, 251
Manguel, Alberto 135
Manish, Menahem son of Yitzhak Hayes 450
Manning, John 496
Manyś, Bernadetta 113, 469
Marchocka, Marianna Anna (Teresa of Jesus)214
Marchwiński, Roman 76
Marcin (a soap maker) 358
Marcin of Radom 563, 564
Marcinkiewicz, Mr 119, 129
Marcinowa, Połonia 377
Marcurialis, Hieronimus 122
Marcus (a goldsmith) 330
Maria of Viciebsk 92
Marian of Jeziorko 112, 113
Marie Louise Gonzaga 487, 503, 507
Markiewicz, Maciej Daubor 188
Markiewicz, Mariusz 502
Markowicz, Jakub 289, 294, 300, 588
Markowski, Michał Paweł 33
Maroszek, Józef 7
Marotti, Arthur F. 473
Martial (Marcus Valerius Martialis) 154
Martin V 136, 137
Martynov, Joanne 379
Martz, Louis 553
Maryks, Robert Aleksander 371
Marzec, Andrzej 326
Maslauskaitė-Mažylienė, Sigita 553
Masłowska-Nowak, Ariadna 434
Máté, Ágnes 340
Matthias Corvinus 127, 325
Matušakaitė, Marija 459
Matvei (ierei) 109
Matvei, Desatyi 43, 281, 282, 531, 532,

568
Mazurkiewicz, Roman 20, 128, 407, 446, 550
Mažvydas, Martynas (Marcin Mażwid) 45, 334, 577, 578
Mażwid, Macin – see: Mažvydas Martynas
Meilus, Elmantas 14, 103, 449, 450
Melanchthon, Philip 122, 125, 316, 318
Melecius, Michał Brokard 209
Meli, Cinthia 590
Meller, Katarzyna 157
Melnyk, Marek 418, 420
Melve, Leidulf 33
Mercator, Gerardus 524
Mercenich, Franciszek Jakub 311
Merczyng, Henryk 25, 401
Merkys, Vytautas 7, 13, 71, 165
Miakishev, Vladimir – see: Владимир Мякишев
Michałowska (Michałowska-Mycielska), Anna 248, 275
Michałowska, Teresa 28, 135, 154, 323, 324, 341, 344, 590
Michaluk, Dorota 237
Mickiewicz, Adam 32, 602
Mickūnaitė, Giedrė 463
Middlemore, Samuel George Chetwynd 127
Międzyleski, Wawrzyniec 110
Mieleski, Augustyn – see: Rotundus Augustyn Mieleski
Mieleszko, Mikołaj 152
Mikhailovich, Pavel 361
Mikita (painter) 227
Mikołaj of Błażejowice 72
Mikołajewicz, Andreas 332
Mikołajewski, Daniel 367, 386, 387, 389, 392, 393, 394, 413, 535
Mikoś, Michael J. 242, 559
Mikosz, Mikołaj 138
Mikuła, Maciej XV, 51, 192, 354
Milewska, Aleksandra (Alesieńka) 196, 197
Milewska Halszka z Podolskich 196, 197, 348
Miller, Dana R. 170, 373
Miłosz, Czesław 602, 605
Mincer, Franciszek 103
Minkiewicz, Jan 229
Mirandola, Giovanni Pico della 159, 324
Mironowicz, Antoni 21, 121, 165-169, 263, 398, 460
Mishetsky, Vasilii 613
Miškinienė, Galina (Мишкинене Галина) 538, 544, 549
Mistakowska, Dorota 377
Modrzewski, Andrzej Frycz 425
Molenda, Maria 432
Möller, Samuel Jansson 314
Mollerus, Ciriacus 174
Molnár, Mónika F. 340
Moniuszko, Adam 81
Montaigne, Michel de 5
Montana family 195
Montanus, Jakub 195
Montelupi family 339
Montelupi, Sebastiano de 339
Moravus, Joannes 174-176
Morawski, Kazimierz 116, 470
Morawski, Michał 564
Morochowski, Joachim Eliasz 422
Mortęska, Magdalena 206, 214
Moser, Rupert 600
Moses ben Naphtali Hirsch Rivkes 125, 543, 599, 612
Mostert, Jan XIV
Mostert, Marco XIV, 4, 13, 33, 41, 48, 61, 187, 192, 225, 226, 322, 433, 460
Mróz, Mirosław 214
Mrozińska, Stanisława 485
Mrozowski, Krzysztof 354
Mstislavets, Piotr (Mstislavets Pyotr) 95, 254, 274, 289
Mueller, Wolfgang 32
Müller, Johannes von Königsberg – see:

Regiomontanus
Mulryne, J.R. 12
Mundal, Else 33
Münster, Sebastian 307, 308
Muntholt, Alexander 87
Muntholt, Bartłomiej 87
Muntholt, Helena 87
Muntholt, Jan 87
Muntholt, Konrad 87
Muntholt, Michał 87
Murphy, James J. 324, 341
Mycawka, Mirosława XV, 202
Mylonius, Udalricus 476
Myszkowski, Jan 227, 228
Myszkowski, Piotr 74
Naborowski, Daniel 18, 78-79, 177, 238, 243, 447, 456, 536
Nagórko, Anna 249, 288, 309
Nalewajko, Sieńko 416
Namysłowski, Jan Licyniusz 367, 383, 386
Napiórkowski, Celestyn Stanisław 478
Napoleon Bonaparte 597
Narbutas, Sigitas 19, 20, 386, 413, 513
Narbutienė, Daiva 19, 114, 320
Narbutt, Oskar 93, 568
Narbutt, Teodor 441, 442
Narkiewicz, Simon 189
Narkuski, Stanisław 59
Naruszewiczówna, Barbara – see: Tyszkiewiczowa, Barbara
Natanek, Piotr 10, 21, 177
Natoński, Bronisław 149, 176, 367, 371, 372, 389, 407, 540
Naumow, Aleksander 257, 259, 262, 289, 526, 555
Nawrocka-Berg, Magdalena 214
Nazaruk, Bazyli 423
Nedzinskaitė, Živilė 20
Nekraševič-Karotkaja, Žanna 519
Nelson, Karen 184
Nero (Nero Claudius Caesar Augustus Germanicus) 519
Neumann, Piotr Franciszek 216
Newe, Mateusz 474
Niavis, Paulus 340
Nice, Richard 35
Nicolas (*civis* of Toruń) 335
Nicolas of Cracow (Nicolaus Nicolai de Cracovia) 75, 351
Nidecki, Andrzej Patrycy 116
Nieborski 140
Niedźwiedź, Dominika V, XV
Niemojewski, Jan 392, 411
Niendorf, Mathias 22, 520
Niesiecki, Kasper 467
Nieznanowski, Stefan 214
Nikalaeŭ, Mikalai – see: Мікалай, Нікалаеў
Nikolaev, Sergei I. – see: Николаев, Сергей И.
Nipszyc, Mikołaj Nipszyc 344
Nonhart, Piotr 194, 376
Nora, Pierre 597, 598
Norblin, Jean-Pierre 602
Nowak, Tadeusz Marian 465
Nowak, Zbigniew 285, 378, 414, 415, 417, 564
Nowak-Dłużewski, Juliusz – see: Dłużewski Juliusz Nowak
Nowakowska, Natalia 201
Nowicka-Jeżowa, Alina 214
Nowicka-Struska, Anna 31, 208, 209, 213, 216
Nowodworski, Bartłomiej 499, 501
Nowomiejski, Bogusław 22, 258
Noworolska, Barbara 29
Nuovo, Angela 314
Nycz, Ryszard 33
Obdezakovych, Jamaget 232
Obertyński, Zdzisław 564
Oborni, Teréz 340
Oborski, Jan 106
Obremski, Krzysztof 432, 484
Obryński, Stanisław Florian 508
Ochman, Jerzy 543

Ochmański, Jerzy 18, 34, 101, 110, 114, 132, 135, 137, 139, 237, 329
Oexle, Otto Gerhard 12, 34, 443, 446
Ogińska, Billewiczówna Zofia 264, 483
Ogiński, Samuel 264, 483
Oko, Jan 540
Okoń, Jan 489, 494, 496, 511, 567
Oleśnicki, Zbigniew (cardinal) 342, 443
Olma, Marceli 323
Olson, David R. 33
Olszańska, Maria 337
Olszewski, Jakub 20, 159, 478, 480, 504, 508, 510, 583, 592
Ong, Walter Jackson 32, 257
Onkov, Bogdan 288
Onkov, Ivan 288
Origen of Alexandria 99
Orlik, Joanna XV
Orłowska, Anna Paulina XIV, 259
Orszak, Grzegorz 587
Ortelius, Abraham 125, 176, 316
Ortholog, Theophil – see: Smotrycki Meletius
Ortiz, Jacobus 540
Orton, David E. 5
Orzechowski, Stanisław 43, 100, 125, 243, 369, 453, 514, 522
Osiewicz, Marek 547
Osmanovych, Olikhno 232
Ostrogski, Konstanty 94, 532, 603
Ostrogski, Konstanty Wasyl (Ostrozkyi Kostiantyn Vasyl) 532
Ostrowicki, Paweł 59, 332
Oświęcim, Stanisław 232
Otwinowska, Barbara 28, 40, 214, 454, 560
Ovid (Publius Ovidius Naso) 154, 159
Owczarek, Zdzisław 522
Ozorowski, Edward 177
Pac, Michał 613
Pac, Samuel 455
Pac, Stefan 509
Pacevičius, Arvydas 139, 282
Pacewicz, Stanisław 358
Paknys, Mindaugas 39, 92, 139, 172, 282, 512
Pakosz, Wacław 105, 294
Palemon (Palaemon) 519, 520, 604
Papée, Fryderyk 114, 201
Pareus, Johann Philipp 122
Partyka, Joanna 30, 183, 185, 190, 196, 205, 206, 211, 215, 218, 283, 523
Pasek, (Kardasz) Monika 494
Pasek, Jan Chryzostom 217, 494
Paszenda, Jerzy 107, 149
Paszkiewicz, Urszula 99, 101
Paszkowska, Anna 358
Paszkowska, Dorota 358, 359
Paszkowski, Krzysztof 358
Patiejūnienė, Eglė 22, 48
Pátková, Hana 436
Paul, St. 78, 121, 167, 408, 495
Paul the Deacon 100, 115
Paul V 170
Paulouskaya, Hanna 206, 216, 218, 220
Paweł of Krosno (Paulus Crosnensis) 325
Pawelec, Mariusz 481, 586
Pawlak, Wiesław 214
Pawlikowska-Butterwick, (Pawlikowska) Wioletta 21, 25, 58, 59, 85, 100, 101, 112, 128, 134
Pawłowicz Łukijański, Adam 480
Pawluczuk, Urszula 21, 169, 532
Pazyra, Stanisław 17
Pedanius (Dioscorides Pedacius) 103
Pękalska, Anastazja 609
Pelc, Janusz 155, 485, 495, 553, 559, 560
Perczyńska, Gabriela 193
Perzanowska, Agnieszka 504
Peter (Petrus) of Kaunas 138
Peters, Emily J. 507
Pętkowski, Kacper 20, 488, 489, 508
Petkūnas, Darius 386
Petrarch (Francesco Petrarca) 324, 341, 443
Petrauskas, Rimvydas 139, 282

Petrauskienė, Irena 17, 25, 26, 320
Petronell, Joachim 147
Petrucci, Armando 273, 436, 456, 492
Petrus (*civis Vilnensis*) 330
Petrus, Aurifaber 331
Petryszak, Bogdana 353
Peyronel Rambaldi, Susanna 186, 198
Philalet, Christopher – see: Broniewski, Marcin
Piasecka, Anna Ciołkówna 461
Piasecka, Beata 139, 282, 488
Piasecki, Paweł 518
Piaseczyńska, Teodora – see: Mother Eufrazja of St. John
Piccolomini, Enea Silvio 443
Pidłypczak-Majerowicz, Maria 93, 95, 102, 104, 170, 292, 481
Piechnik, Ludwik 18, 34, 106, 132, 133, 142-149, 152, 155, 156, 158, 180, 240, 295, 301, 372, 385, 434, 488, 508, 540
Piechocki, Katharina N. 31
Piekarski, Kazimierz 306
Piekosiński, Franciszek 59, 308
Pielgrzymowski, Eliasz 243, 492, 508, 520
Pietkiewicz, Krzysztof 22, 113, 201, 255, 269, 270, 278
Pietkiewicz, Melchior 177, 289, 559, 579
Pietrzak, Jarosław 493
Pietrzak, Michał 71
Pietrzkiewicz, Iwona 216
Pilarczyk, Franciszek 573, 575, 577, 579
Pilarczyk, Krzysztof 312, 461
Pilnik, Jan 376
Pinsky, Robert 605
Piotr of Zambrzec 137
Piotrkowczyk, Andrzej 311
Piotrowicz, Benedykt 508
Piotrowicz, Józef 79, 119, 508
Piotrowski, Kazimierz Józef 339
Piramidowicz, Dorota 108, 117
Pirożyński, Jan 574, 577
Pisarek, Izabela XIV
Piskała, Magdalena 20
Piso, Jacobus 529
Pister, Aleksandra 503
Pizylewicz, Jerzy 378
Plat, Hieronim 207
Platinius, P. 305
Plato 514
Platt, Dobrosława 482
Plautus 316
Plezia, Marian 416
Pliny the Younger 103
Pociej, Hipacy (Hypatius) 95, 170, 382, 398, 420, 422
Pociūtė, Dainora 19, 20, 171
Podlodowski, Jerzy 202
Pogorzelski, Paweł 348
Polak, Emil J. 340
Polański, Tomasz 179, 384
Poliziano, Angelo 324
Polkowski, Ignacy 99
Pollak, Roman 217
Połubińska, Zuzanna Litaworówna Chreptowiczówna Aleksandrowa 353, 360
Pomian, Krzysztof 84, 130
Pomorska, Joanna 447
Pontano, Giovanni 125
Pontanus (Spanmüller), Jacobus 153, 320, 456
Pontanus, Ludvicus – see: De la Puente, Luis
Popiel, Magdalena 549
Popiołek, Bożena 355
Poplatek, Jan 144, 158, 488, 490, 508
Popławska, Halina 214
Poprawa-Kaczyńska, Ewa 553
Porfiry (a bookbinder) 301
Porzecki, Tomasz 522
Possevino, Antonio 145, 155, 159, 180, 244, 296, 297, 366, 407, 426, 513
Potkowski, Edward 34, 97, 98, 241, 245
Powodowski, Hieronim 393, 564
Poźniak, Piotr 559

Prejs, Marek 285
Priscianus (Caesariensis) 432, 438, 484
Probulski, Andrzej XV
Prochaska, Antoni 340
Prochownik, Andrzej 233
Prokop-Janiec, Eugenia 31, 580
Prometheus 488
Proot, Goran 314
Protasewicz, Walerian 74, 99, 100, 101, 106, 111, 115, 146-148, 244, 362, 379, 519
Przeciszowski, Jan 476
Przeciszowski, Stanisław 476
Przerębski, Jan 74
Przeździecki, Aleksander 203, 346, 494
Przymuszała, Lidia 386, 586
Ptaśnik, Jan 98, 337
Ptaszycki, Stanisław 84
Ptaszyński, Maciej 33
Puccitelli, Virgilio 487
Puchowski, Kazimierz 22, 148, 523
Pylypiuk, Natalia 11
Quintilian (Marcus Fabius Quintilianus) 27, 40, 103, 432
Quirini-Popławska, Danuta 337, 339
Rabinowitz, Louis Izaak 383
Rabka, Ivan 118
Rachuba, Andrzej 21, 64, 71-73, 76, 80, 82, 103
Raczyński, Edward 271
Radau, Michał 320
Radomski, Maciej 352
Radoń, Sławomir 409
Radoński, Aleksander 508
Radstone, Susannah 597-598
Radwan, Jan 19, 408, 413, 441, 519, 520
Radwan, Marian 441
Radzimiński, Andrzej 206
Radziwiłł, Albrycht Stanisław 84, 232, 394, 486, 497, 503, 510, 518, 519
Radziwiłł, Bogusław 91
Radziwiłł family (Radziwiłłs) 8, 19, 89, 91, 117, 124, 176, 177, 207, 336, 344, 346, 348, 386, 426, 491, 503, 513, 519, 522
Radziwiłł, Janusz 20, 221, 348, 492
Radziwiłł, Jerzy 173, 174, 264, 390, 411, 454, 488
Radziwiłł, Krzysztof I "the Thunderbolt" 174, 194, 386, 402
Radziwiłł, Krzysztof II 45, 79, 105, 124, 162, 176, 234, 242, 342, 344-346, 513, 561, 569
Radziwiłł, Mikołaj "the Black" 59, 172, 173, 204, 244, 491, 522, 535
Radziwiłł, Mikołaj "the Red" 202-204, 348, 519
Radziwiłł, Mikołaj Krzysztof "the Orphan" 122, 204, 241, 274, 289, 294, 296, 389, 398, 401, 418, 428, 474, 477, 491, 552
Radziwiłł, Mikołaj Mikołajewicz 70, 115, 241, 281
Radziwiłłowa, Hanna 216-217
Radziwiłłowa, Katarzyna (née Sobieska) 285
Radziwiłłowa, Katarzyna (née Tęczyńska) 194, 195, 426, 474, 551
Radziwiłłówna, Barbara 18, 36, 197, 199-205, 243, 346, 348, 369, 452, 453
Radziwiłłówna, Halszka (Elżbieta) 194
Radziwiłłówna, Zofia Konstancja 217
Radzymiński, Mr 162
Ragauskas, Aivas 16, 50, 64, 65, 66, 67, 79, 86, 87, 194, 195, 202-204, 330, 346
Ragauskienė, Raimonda 16, 21, 24, 71, 76, 83, 194, 195, 199, 202-204, 247, 346, 494
Raguotienė, Genovaitė 106
Raila, Eligijus 139, 282
Rajchel, Jacek 447
Rajfura, Hanna 493
Ranković, Slavica 33
Ranocchi, Emiliano XV, 19, 549
Rapagelonis, Stanislaus (Rafajłowicz, Stanisław) 172

Rashi, 178, 508
Rassius, Adamus (Raszewski, Adam) 172, 383, 517
Rasson, Judith 352
Raszewski, Adam – see: Rassius, Adamus 383
Raszewski, Zbigniew 485, 509
Ratdolt, Erhard 115
Ravisius, Ioannes 122
Reck, Gothard (Rek, Gotard) 307, 311
Regiomontanus, (Johannes Müller von Königsberg) 115
Reichardt, Dagmar 32
Rej (Rey), Mikołaj 381, 387, 388
Rek, Gotard – see: Reck Gothard
Reks, Adam 415
Resnick, Irven M. 527
Reuchlin, Johannes 115
Rey (a municipal scribe) 65, 75, 587-589
Richter, Gregorius 122
Richter, Mikołaj 229
Rinkūnaitė, Aušra 26, 108
Rivkes – see: Moses ben Naphtali Hirsch Rivkes
Robortello, Francesco 325
Ročka, Marcelinas 414
Rodian, Leonard 141
Rodkiewiczówna, Janina 304
Rojzjusz, Piotr – see: Ruiz de Moros Pedro
Rolak, Grażyna 573
Romaniuk, Przemysław 64
Romanowski, Andrzej XV, 31, 591
Romulus 413
Ropa, Anastasija 334
Rops, Edgars 334
Rorty, Richard 472
Rościszewski, Wojciech 413
Rosenwein, Barbara H. 449
Rosochacki, Mr 395
Rosselli, Hannibal 541
Rossignol, Sébastien 325
Rostowski, Stanisław 379, 385
Roszkowska, Wanda 485
Rott-Żebrowski, Teatyn 269
Rotundus, Augustyn Mieleski 17, 43, 59, 60, 63, 64, 74, 116, 128, 146, 194, 242, 332, 407, 453, 522
Rotundusowa, Zofia Mieleska Montanówna 194, 195
Rotundusówna, Elżbieta 195
Rotundusówna, Regina 195
Rovelli, Carlo 244
Rowell, S.C. 6, 9, 14, 52, 53, 74, 328
Royaers, Jean (Royardus, Ioannes) 589
Royzius, – see: Ruiz de Moros, Pedro
Rozbicki, Stanisław 110
Rozdrażewski, Hieronim 339
Rozdrażewski, Krzysztof 441
Rozmusewicz, Sebastian 476
Różycki, Edward 119
Rubikauskas, Paulus 148
Rudenko, Oleksii – see: Руденко, Олексій
Rudnicka, Jadwiga 314
Rudomina, Maciej 360
Ruiz de Moros, Pedro (Piotr Rojzjusz, Roiziusz, Royzius, Doktor Hiszpan, Doctor Spaniard) 18, 19, 45, 48, 49, 59, 60, 110, 112, 116, 242, 244, 305, 379, 380, 381, 453
Rurikids 522
Rusek, Jerzy 289
Rusterholz, Peter 600
Rutkowska, Grażyna 201
Rutski, Józef Welamin (Rutsky, Josyf Velamyn) 89, 95, 170, 177, 292, 398, 399, 584
Ruzas, Vincas 470
Rybarski, Roman 251
Rybiński, Maciej 316, 535, 536
Rymsza, Andrzej 258, 520
Rymunt, Kazimierz 203, 264
Ryś, Aleksandra XV
Rynduch, Zbigniew 154, 438
Rysiński, Salomon (Rysinskis, Salomo-

nas) 20, 79, 123, 124, 125, 128, 130, 316, 517, 536
Ryszewski, Bohdan 91
Ryszka-Kurczab, Magdalena XIV, 150, 384, 393, 516
Ryszkowski, Jan 101, 111
Rywocki, Jan 508
Rządziewicz, Thomas 230, 231
Rzegocka, Jolanta 567
Rzepka, Wojciech Ryszard 573
Rzewuski, Leon Kreuza 170, 300, 368, 382, 542, 584
Sabaliauskaitė, Kristina 605
Sabinka, Stanisław 64
Saenger, Paul 208
Sakowicz, Kasjan 588
Sala, Sebastian 459
Salinariusz (Salinarius), Wojciech 105
Sallust (Gaius Sallustius Crispus) 154
Salter, Elizabeth 33
Samostrzelnik, Stanisław 115, 547
Samsonowicz, Henryk 33, 38, 64, 140, 337
Sanguszko family 344
Sanguszkówna, Helena – see: Eufrazja of St. Casimir
Sans, Benoît 359
Saperstein, Marc 178, 583
Sapieha, Aleksander 477
Sapieha, Dorota (Sapieżyna, née Firlej) 198
Sapieha, Elżbieta (Sapieżyna, née Radziwiłł) 458
Sapieha (Sapiehas) family 344, 455, 458
Sapieha, Iwan Semenowicz 201
Sapieha, Jan Stanisław 408, 477, 479
Sapieha, Kazimierz Lew 51, 108, 117, 149, 459
Sapieha, Krzysztof Mikołaj 459
Sapieha, Lew 49, 60, 73, 76, 84, 198, 205, 221, 243, 258, 291, 306, 390, 458, 501
Sapieha, Mikołaj 508
Sapieha, Paweł (of Kodeń) 441
Sapieha, Teodora Krystyna (Sapieżyna, née Tarnowska) 458-459
Sapiro, Gisèle 34
Sarbiewski, Maciej Kazimierz 19, 20, 156, 159, 160, 297, 311, 348, 372, 416, 479, 480, 489, 504, 510, 511, 514, 516, 520-522, 540, 561, 587, 591, 601, 604
Sarcevičienė, Jolita 482
Sarni, Flavio 186
Sarnowska-Temeriusz, Elżbieta 28
Saryusz-Wolska, Magdalena 42, 599
Saviščevas, Eugenijus 199, 469, 498
Scacchi, Marco 487
Scaliger, Julius Caesar (Giulio Cesare della Scala) 430, 472, 520
Schall, Jakub 178
Schedel, Krzysztof 311
Schiper, Ignacy 536, 580
Schlieben-Lange, Brigitte 225
Schmid, Karl 12, 34, 446
Schmissius, Mathias 174
Schönflissius, Andrzej (Jędrzej) 20, 104, 194, 481-483, 542, 560, 585-587
Schopenhauer, Artur 392, 393
Schottus, Franciscus 122
Schulte, Petra 225
Schwarz, Bill 598
Sczyt, 140
Sebastian (a cartwright) 574
Segre, Erica 244
Seklucjan, Jan 558, 559, 577, 579, 587
Seligman, Jon 464
Semkowicz, Władysław 7, 25, 88, 138, 271, 327, 329, 335
Seneca (Lucius Annaeus Seneca the Younger) 121, 154
Sextilis, Piotr z Obrzycka 577
Shabbatai ben Meir HaKohen 179, 384, 542, 543
Shakhovsky, Mikhail 103
Shewring, Margaret 12
Shmeruk, Chone 580

Shulvass, Moses A. 539
Sidowicz, Dorota 573
Siebeneicher, Jakub 310
Siedina, Giovanna 519
Siemiaszko, Jędrzej 230, 231
Sienicki 306
Sienkiewicz, Witold 179
Siesicki, Jan 163, 428
Siestrzencewicz, Piotr 174
Sigismund I the Old Jagiellon 52, 55-57, 59, 85, 98, 114, 126, 142, 171, 192, 199, 241, 256, 272, 273, 278, 354, 399, 433, 458, 466, 518, 548, 567
Sigismund II Augustus Jagiellon 10, 48, 51, 54, 57-59, 73, 77, 106, 115-117, 127, 128, 146, 172, 199, 202-205, 241-244, 272, 275, 285, 290, 302, 303, 328, 337, 340, 341, 343, 346, 348, 368, 380, 433, 465, 466, 493
Sigismund III Vasa 39, 54, 55, 57, 60, 64, 89, 165, 166, 173, 174, 197, 199, 241, 293, 296, 301, 322, 398, 399, 416, 430, 434, 449, 457, 466, 469, 470, 471, 482, 488, 491, 498, 501, 503, 504, 506, 509-511, 518, 520
Sigismund of Luxembourg 242
Simon, Dubnow – see: Семён Маркович Дубнов
Simonetta, Francesco 501
Sirutavičius, Marius 492
Sirvydas, Konstantinas – see: Szyrwid Konstanty
Siwor, Dorota 31, 509
Skarga, Piotr 18, 45, 129, 159, 208, 234, 237, 263, 295, 300, 305, 315, 379, 382, 401, 404, 406-408, 413, 417, 418, 420-428, 479, 542, 583, 584, 589, 604
Skaryna, Fracysk (Franciszek Skoryna) 45, 95, 118, 121, 236, 240, 242, 249, 254, 273, 274, 286-289, 309, 532, 548, 549
Skierska, Izabela 136, 571
Skimina, Stanisław 156, 416
Skoryna, Franciszek – see: Skaryna, Francysk
Skowron, Ryszard 502
Skrzetuski, Wawrzyniec 376
Skupieński, Krzysztof 324, 325
Skwarczyńska, Stefania 38, 322, 323
Sławińska, Irena 496
Sławiński, Janusz 27, 28
Ślęk, (Ślękowa) Ludwika 214, 430, 491
Śliwa, Michał 245
Słowakowa, Małgorzata 143
Słowiński, Jan Zbigniew 252, 273, 297, 575
Smetonienė, Anželika 575
Šmigelskytė-Stukienė, Ramunė 21, 24, 71, 76, 83, 247
Śmiglecki, Marcin 159, 283, 285, 300, 365-367, 369, 372, 382, 386, 388, 389, 391-394, 406, 408-410, 475, 476, 514, 516, 517, 540, 541
Smosarski, Józef 496
Smotrycki, Meletius (Ortholog Theophil) 32, 51, 96, 168-170, 258, 261-263, 265, 292-294, 300, 368, 382, 399, 421-424, 481, 492, 498, 509, 535, 541, 549, 584, 586, 588, 589
Smuglewicz, Franciszek 179
Śnieżko, Aleksander 15, 448
Śnieżko, Dariusz 493
Snook, Edith 184, 229
Snopek, Jerzy 29
Snyder, Timothy 17
Sobieski, Sebastian 500, 501
Sobol, Walentyna 423
Socyn, Faust – see: Sozzini, Fausto
Soczewka, Aleksander 20, 489, 490
Sokolińska, Anna 435
Sokolińska, Konstancyja 609
Sokołowski, August 340
Solomonio (Solomone), Ruggiero 500, 503
Soltan, Alexandr Alexandrovych 94
Soltan, Ivan 282

Sołtan-Kościelecka, Klara 253
Sommerfeld (Aesticampianus), Jan the Elder 325, 340
Sophia Jagiellon 199
Sophia Palaiologina 201
Sozzini, Fausto (Socyn, Faust) 366, 367, 382, 408-411
Spandowski, Michał 99
Speičytė, Brigita 31
Sperka, Jerzy 197, 399
Spiridon (a monk) 94
Sprenger, Jacobus 410
Springer, Michael S. 569
Spunar, Pavel 436
Srebrakowski, Aleksander 17
Sroczyński, Aleksander XV
Stabrowski, Piotr 334
Stach, Stephan 275
Stanisław III of Masovia 445
Stanisław of Niemenczyn 110
Stanisławska (Zbąska), Anna 222
Staniszewski, Andrzej Tadeusz 120, 126, 222, 314
Starnawski, Jerzy 348
Starowolski, Szymon 273, 441, 442, 452, 453, 459, 462, 604
Starzyński, Marcin 493
Statorius, Piotr 392
Stawecka, Krystyna 479
Stebelski, Ignacy 398
Steele, Jonathan 605
Stefanowska, Lidia 423
Stephen I Báthory 54, 60, 76, 89, 148, 165, 204, 234, 241, 249, 263, 295, 322, 339, 385, 395, 402, 406, 433, 468, 469, 488, 494, 503, 507, 508, 515
Stępniak-Minczewa, Wanda 550, 576
Sterczewska, Lucyna 214
Stoberski, Zygmunt 17, 171, 172, 523
Stoiński, Stanisław 311
Stopka, Krzysztof 12, 34, 135, 266
Stor, Anna 191, 192, 360
Stor, Jan 192, 360
Strietman, Elsa 29
Stróżyk, Paweł 436
Strubicz, Maciej 74, 117, 284, 285
Strumiński, Bohdan 170, 399
Stryjkowski, Maciej 110, 119, 513, 522
Strzałkowski, Andrzej 318, 319
Studnicki, Wacław Gizbert 14, 15, 17, 89, 105, 401
Sturm, Johannes 103
Suabius, Martinus 147
Sucholewski, Franciszek 474, 475
Sudrowski, Stanisław 109, 297, 408, 579
Sudymantowicz, Olehna (Olechno; Alekhna Sudzimontavych, Sudymuntowicz) 53, 72
Sułkowska-Kurasiowa, Irena 84, 325, 327, 341
Sultzer, Salomon 254, 300
Sumowski, Marcin 352
Sunyer, Francisco 145, 146, 385, 508
Sutcliffe, Adam 178
Sutherland, Suzanne 342
Sutkowska, Dorota 20
Švitrigaila 340
Świadek, Barbara 493
Święcicki, Grzegorz 101, 359, 438, 470, 550
Świerkowski, Ksawery 296, 575
Świrski, Andrzej 138
Syrokomla, Władysław 591
Syta, Krzysztof 91
Szabelska, Hanna 516
Szajna, Maria XIV
Szapszał, Hadży Saraja 537
Szarfenberger, Jan 310
Szarfenberger, Mikołaj 310
Szarfenbergers, 310
Szczawieński, Tomasz 377
Szczerbic, Paweł 51, 191, 354
Szczerkowska, H. 20, 508
Szczypior, Konsuela 576
Szegda, Mirosław 170, 177, 398
Szeliga, Andrzej 96, 113

Szelińska, Wacława 315
Szende, Katalin 276, 352
Szklarek, Jan 282
Szkolnik, Leib 416
Szmytka, Rafał 29
Szostek, Teresa 590
Szpociński, Andrzej 597
Szujski, Józef 340
Szulc 140
Szwedo, Patrycja 493
Szweykowska, Anna 431, 486
Szwykowski, family 467
Szydłowski, canon 222
Szyller, Sławomir 99
Szymańska, Kaja XIV
Szymańska, Kamila 481
Szymonowic, Szymon 125, 316, 318
Szynkiewicz, Jakub 15, 543, 544
Szyrwid, Konstanty (Sirvydas Konstantinas) 159, 517, 584, 589
Szystowski, Franciszek 188
Tabaczyński, Michał 28
Tabor, Bartłomiej 137
Tabor, Wojciech (Albertus) 109, 564
Tacitus (Publius Cornelius Tacitus) 154
Taliat, Jerzy 48
Talwosz, Adam 348, 349, 367
Talwoszowa, Maria Radzimińska 367
Tandecki, Janusz 283
Targosz (Targosz-Kretowa), Karolina 30, 205, 206, 213, 216-218, 486, 487, 502, 506, 509, 512
Tartakower, A. 536
Ta-Shma, Israel Moses 583
Tauber, Joachim 13, 14
Tautavičius, Adolfas 7, 13, 165
Taxis, Cristoforo de 339
Tazbir, Janusz 49, 152, 379, 401, 425, 428
Tchórzewska-Kabata, Halina 286
Tedeschi, Anne 373
Tedeschi, John 373
Tęgowski, Jan 138, 195
Temčinas, Sergijus (Темчин, С.Ю.) 22, 532
Tencalla, Costante 455, 458
Terence 122
Terleckienė, Eleonora – see: Buožytė (Terleckienė), Eleonora
Theresa of Ávila 209
Thomas à Kempis 207, 443
Thomas Aquinas 121, 160, 225, 514, 516, 540
Thomás de Jesús 209
Tobiasz (tailor) 358
Tolgsdorf, Erdman 144
Tolsorykowicz, Petrus 331
Tomaszewski 468
Tomaszewski, Rev. 105
Topolska, Maria Barbara 18, 109, 119, 124, 207, 250, 251, 291-294, 296-298, 301, 307, 309, 473
Torój, Elżbieta 119, 125, 299, 301, 315, 528
Torres, Francisco 407
Tostius, Jan 408, 412
Tóth, István G. 185, 187, 190
Trąba, Robert 599
Trask, Willard R. 27
Treadgold, Warren T. 27
Trębska, Małgorzata 328
Trębusiewicz, Małgorzata XIV
Trevisanus, Bernardus 122
Trilner (Trylner), Hanus 306, 470
Trilupatienė, Jūratė 486
Trotz, Michał Abraham 1
Trypućko, Józef 99
Tryznina (Tryzna), Izabella Lacka 479
Trzciński, Andrzej 277, 451, 452
Trzebuchowski, Mikołaj 74
Trzecieski, Andrzej (the Older) 115
Trzecieski, Andrzej (the Younger) 115, 369
Tuchtenhagen, Ralph 13, 14
Tukolski, Józef 610
Tumelis, Józef 17

Turcan-Verkerk, Anne-Marie 324
Turska, Halina 255, 256
Tuvim, I. 276
Tuvim, Wojciech 264, 344
Tymiakin, Leszek 355, 357
Tymirszyc, Abrahim 278
Tymoshenko, Leonid – see: Тимошенко, Леонід
Tyszkiewicz family 455, 456
Tyszkiewicz, Jerzy 179, 207, 213, 492, 497, 519
Tyszkiewicz, Stanisław 299
Tyszkiewiczowa, Barbara (née Naruszewicz) 454, 455, 458, 481,
Tyszkiewiczówna, Felicjanna – see: Katarzyna of Christ
Udbynaeus, Ioannes Duns 477
Ugniewski, Szymon 299
Ugoski, Wojciech 110
Ulana of Tver – see Uliana of Tver
Ulanowski, Bolesław 323
Ulčinaitė, Eugenija XV 18-21, 48, 154, 416, 432, 438, 442, 469, 488, 494, 498, 500, 506-508, 514, 520, 522, 588
Uliana of Tver 92, 441, 526
Uliana Olshanska 113
Urban VIII 155
Urban, Wacław 110, 186, 187, 198, 315, 319, 373
Urbanavičius, Vladas 7
Urbańczyk, Stanisław 344
Urmański, Antonis K. 14
Ursinus, Ioannes (Ursyn, Jan (z Krakowa)) 325, 343
Uspienski, Boris – see: Успенский Борис Андреевич
Uzorka, Marijus 199
Vadianus, Joachim 103
Vaenius, Otto 125
Vaitkevičius, Gediminas 7, 314
Vaitkevičiūtė, Viktorija 314
Valikonytė, Irena 59, 247
Valionienė, Oksana 14
Valla, Lorenzo 324
Van Dixhoorn, Arjan 29
Van Linschoten, Johannes 125
Van Renswoude, Irene 225
Van Vaeck, 496
Vas'ka (scribe) 281
Vasa dynasty (Vasas) 44, 434, 458, 491, 506, 509, 510, 518
Vasa, Charles Ferdinand – see: Charles Ferdinand Vasa
Vasili III of Russia 201
Veder, William R. 170
Venclova, Tomas 13
Venclovienė, Ana
Verkholantsev, J. 259
Veteikis, Tomas 154
Viana, Pedro 385
Victor III 207
Virgil (Publius Vergilius Maro) 154, 159, 403, 520
Vladimirovas, Levas 106
Vladislovas II – see: Władysław IV Vasa
Vladislovas Vasa – see: Władysław IV Vasa
Volanus, Andreas – see: Wolan, Andrzej
Volpi, Franco 392
Vorbek-Lettow, Maciej 45, 103, 124, 128, 163, 172, 178, 232, 415, 447, 448, 514, 517, 542, 595-600, 609
Vorbek-Lettow, Mateusz 447, 596, 598, 601
Vossius, Gerardus 438
Vytautas (Witołd) 39, 45, 72, 113, 134, 136, 179, 242, 248, 255, 271, 278, 281, 327, 340, 452, 457, 465, 498, 519
Walawender, Antoni 98, 102, 147
Walczak, Marek 493
Walczak, Wojciech 170, 465, 493
Walenty (carpenter) 377
Wallace, David 30, 221
Warda, Katarzyna 352
Warecki, Krzysztof 550
Wargocki, Andrzej 522

Warszewicki, Krzysztof 508
Warszewicki, Stanisław 106, 147, 382
Wasilewicz, Raphael 476
Wasilewska, Mrs 188
Wasilewski, Tadeusz 179
Watanabe-O'Kelly, Helen 12
Watt, Ian 32
Weaver, Helen 442
Węcowski, Piotr 197, 399, 493
Węgrzyn, Iwona 591
Weiss, Paul 383, 387
Welzjusz, Andrzej 105
Wereda, Dorota 207
Wicker, Helen 33
Widziewicz, Jan 480
Widziewicz, Marcin 583
Więckowska, Helena 17
Wied, Anton
Wiekowicz family 467
Wiekowicz, Helena – see: Binstrubowa, Helena
Wieliczko, Jan 78
Wierciński, Marcin 477
Wiewiórka, Jan 110
Wigand von Marburg 329
Wijuk Kojałowicz, Wojciech (Albertas Kojelavičius-Vijūkas) 20, 45, 92, 159, 312, 480, 513, 514, 518, 519, 521-523, 604
Wilamowski, Jan 143, 171
Wilamowski, Maciej 326
Wilczewski, Waldemar F. 85
Wiles-Portier, Elisabeth 130
Williams, W. Glynn 347
Wilson, Tracy 275
Winiarska, Agnieszka 201
Winniczuk, Lidia 325, 343, 488
Winnyczenko, Oksana 353, 362
Winter, Jay 597
Wirzbięta (Wierzbięta), Maciej 309
Wisłocki, Władysław 138
Wisner, Henryk 256, 401, 492, 493, 498
Witkowski, Wiesław 289
Witold – see: Vytautas
Witt, Ronald 324
Wituński, Augustyn 480
Wiżgajło, Mikołaj 48
Władysław III Jagiellon 241
Władysław IV Vasa (Vladislovas Vasa, Vladislovas II) 44, 103, 107, 124, 166, 199, 241, 307, 311, 378, 394, 395, 415, 430-432, 434, 444, 466, 478, 486, 491, 493, 500, 501, 503, 504, 507, 509-511, 518-520, 525, 542, 587, 595
Władysław Jagiełło – see: Jogaila
Włodarski, Maciej 135, 344
Włoszek, Stanisław 304
Wnuk, Anna 119, 124, 126, 313, 353, 356
Wobolewicz, Krzysztof 79, 87, 268
Wodziński, Marcin 451
Wojciech (blacksmith) 376
Wojciech of Brudzewo 112
Wojciech of Stopnica 139
Wojciech-Masłowska, Genowefa 323
Wójcik, Rafał 135, 285
Wojda, Aleksandra XV
Wojewodziński, Mr 82
Wojsznarowicz, Kazimierz Jan 514, 583, 584
Wolan, Andrzej (Volanus Andreas) 19, 20, 74, 128, 129, 295, 297, 300, 382, 383, 385, 386, 404, 405-408, 410-414, 417, 420-422, 425, 476
Wolfe, Heather 191, 215
Wolkanowski, Stanisław 222
Wołkanowski, Waldemar 448
Wollasch, Joachim 446
Wołłowicz, Eustachy 106, 198, 215, 258, 389, 390, 457, 458, 463
Wołłowicz family 258, 458
Wołłowicz, Paweł 389
Wołoch, Dorota 330
Wołoch, Martinus 330
Wołodkiewicz, Mateusz Chryzostom 567
Wolski, Jeremiasz 227
Woronicz, Jan Paweł 602

Woś, J.W. 18
Woyna, Abraham 395, 397, 408, 446, 480, 492
Woyna, Benedykt (Benedictus) 106, 176, 232, 444, 454, 501, 504, 506, 564
Woyna, Stanisław 476
Woyniłłowicz, Michał 112, 481, 591
Wujek, Jakub 119, 144, 159, 210, 238, 297, 368, 382, 409, 531, 533, 575, 584, 586-589
Wyczawski, Hieronim Eugeniusz 177
Wydra, Wojciech 115, 547, 548, 573, 577
Wyrozumska, Bożena 325, 354
Wysmułek, Jakub 192, 352, 353, 357
Wysocki, Abraamus 174
Wysocki, Aleksander Walerian 508
Wysocki, Szymon 551, 552
Yuri of Moscow 201
Zaborowski, Stanisław 574
Zachara-Wawrzyńczyk, Maria 2, 520
Zachara-Związek, Urszula 199, 202, 205, 356, 373
Zadencka, Maria XV
Żagiel, Marcin 140
Zahorski, Władysław 13
Zając-Gardeła, Zofia 202
Zajączkowski, Rajmund 480
Zajączkowski, Wojciech 367
Zajas, Krzysztof 31, 142
Zajda, Aleksander 373
Zajic, Andreas 12, 436, 437, 439, 440, 444, 463, 471
Żak, Elżbieta XV
Zakrzewski, Andrzej B. XV, 21, 50, 59, 73, 179, 247
Załęski, Stanisław 382, 423
Zamorski, Krzysztof 463
Zamoyski, Jan 204, 264, 463, 485
Zarefsky, David 359
Zaremska, Hanna 494
Zawadzka, Krystyna 102
Zawadzki, Roman M. 10, 21, 177
Zawarski, Herman 219
Zawistowski, Matys 363
Zawiszanka, Barbara 452
Zbaraski, Krzysztof 501
Zbroshko of Kotra – see: Зброшко
Zdańkowska, Marta
Zdanowicz, Józef 540
Zdelarič, Thoma 147
Zechenter, Katarzyna 420
Zenowicz family 207
Zenowicz, Krzysztof Deszpot 104
Zenowicz, Mikołaj Deszpot 104
Zenowiczówna, Anna 198
Ziejka, Franciszek 166
Ziomek, Jerzy 18, 425, 485
Zizany, Laurentius (Wawrzyniec Zizani) 167-169, 576, 580
Zizany, Stephen 293, 576, 580, 584
Złotkowski, Jan 114
Złotkowski, Krzysztof 550
Żółkiewski, Stefan 28
Zonenberg, Sławomir 329
Zujienė, Gitana 492, 498
Žukas, Saulius 13
Żukowski, Jacek 486
Zupka, Dušan 491
Żurek, Waldemar Witold 223
Żurkowa, Renata 119, 125, 310-312, 315, 316, 537
Zwierzykowski, Michał 469
Zyglewski, Zbigniew 206
Аляксандрава, А.Ф. 356
Бабкова, В.У. 356
Бершадский, Сергей Александрович (Bershadski, Sergei A.) 15, 95
Білоус, Наталія 356, 357
Бобер, І.М. 533
Бондар, Наталія Петрівна 533
Бяспалая, Марыя Аркадзьеўна 291
Варонін, Васіль 1
Вздорнов, Герольд Иванович 94, 96
Владимир, Мякишев (Miakishev Vladimir) 60
Вознесенский, Андрей 555

Галечанка (Голенченко), Георгий Яковлевич 94, 282
Гаркович, Наталья Викторовна (Harkovich Nataliia) 576
Груша, Аляксандр І. (Hrusha, Aliaksandr I., Груша Александр Иванович) xv, 22, 77, 93, 250, 253, 268, 270, 330, 331
Гусева, Александра А. 532, 533
Дубнов, Семён Маркович 90, 275, 374
Думин, Станислав Владимирович 255
Зброшко, (Zbroszko of Kotra, Zbroshko) 138
Каралюс, Л. – see: Karalius Laimontas
Кисенбаум, Соломон Барух 452
Корзо, Маргарита А. (Korzo Margarita A.) xv, 21, 559, 575-579
Кралюк, Петро 533
Маггид, Давид Гилелевич (Maggid David Gilelevich) 451
Маггид, Хиллел Ноах (Hillel Noah Maggid-Steinschneider) 275, 276, 441, 449, 536
Мишкинене, Галина – see: Miškinienė Galina
Морозова, Надежда 282
Муравьев, Анатолий Васильевич 269, 270
Немировский, Евгений Львович 18, 237, 249, 250, 274, 286, 287, 288, 309, 533, 554, 555, 568
Николаев, Сергей И. (Nikolaev, Sergei I.) xv, 307
Нікалаеў, Мікалай (Ніколаеў Мікола В., Nikalaeŭ Mikalai) xv, 93, 98, 253, 254, 281, 282, 532, 533, 568, 579
Пташицкий, Станислав Львович – see: Ptaszycki, Stanisław
Пуцко, Василий Григорьевич 291
Руденко, Олексій (Rudenko Oleksii) xv
Рычков, Андрей 114, 115
Семён, Маркович Дубнов (Simon Dubnow) 90, 275, 276, 374
Скарына, Францыск – see: Skaryna Francysk 554, 555
Судник, Т.М. 11
Темчин, С.Ю. – see: Temčinas Sergijus
Тимошенко, Леонід (Tymoshenko Leonid) xv, 11, 16, 526, 555, 576, 584
Тихомиров, Михаил Николаевич 269, 270
Топоров, Владимир Николаевич 11
Успенский, Борис Андреевич (Uspienski Boris) 22, 257, 258, 260, 262
Флеров, Ёанн Ефимович 157, 168
Шматаў, Віктар Фёдаравіч 18, 291

Index of Place-Names and Ethnic Names

Alanta 89, 105
Amsterdam 11, 537, 543, 560, 590, 612
Andrusovo 84
Antokol (Antakalnis, Antocole) 331
Antwerp 111, 300, 513, 521
Armenian (Armenians) 133, 266
Ashkenazi (Ashkenazic) 248, 275, 277, 312, 560, 580
Ashkenazy (Ashkenazi) 248, 543
Asians 519
Augsburg 10, 104, 163, 171, 382, 387, 527, 586
Austria (Austrian) 146, 440, 444, 471
Balt (Balts) 255
Baltic Sea 2
Bari 114
Basel 300
Belarus 115, 491, 535

Belarusian (Belarusians) 1, 18, 22, 42, 44, 255, 256-257, 259-261, 266, 287, 307, 462, 537, 602
Belgium 147
Berlin 276
Biržai 124, 176, 386
Bishop's Manor (Palace; Dwór Biskupi) 8, 69, 85, 98, 173
Black Sea 6
Blinstrubiszki (Blinstrubiškiai) 467
Bohemia (Bohemian) 7, 127, 386
Bohoniki 537
Bologna 117, 139
Bordeaux 5
Brandenburg 39, 386
Braniewo (Braunsberg) 99, 108, 476
Braslav 253
Bremen 271
Breslau – see: Wrocław
Brest 166, 169, 173, 236, 251, 253
Bridge – see: Stone Bridge
Brodnica (Strasburg in Westpreußen) 98
Brussels 117
Buffałowa Hill (Pamėnkalnis) 448
Bulgarian 579
Chełm 341
Chełmno 197, 206-207, 209
China 145
Cieszyn 585-586
Cieszyn Principality 586
Cologne 271, 311
Constance 103
Coryst (a field) 331
Cossack 501, 513, 542
Courland 508
Cracow (Kraków) 250-251, 260, 274, 276, 284, 286, 297-299, 588, 595
Croat (Croats) 147
Czech (Czechs) 133, 147, 272, 382, 407
Częstochowa 460
Dalmatia (Dalmatian cities) 279,
Dane (Danes) 144
Danzig – see: Gdańsk; Elbląg 163
Dębnik 459
Dokudów 307
Dorowoda 468
Dresden 498, 603
Dubingai 202
Englishman (Englishmen) 144
Erfurt 579
Europe (European) 2, 6, 9, 11-13, 24, 27, 30, 35-36, 39, 47, 52, 84, 116, 122, 132, 140-141, 145, 147, 149, 159, 185, 198, 226, 245, 250, 272, 276, 278, 297, 312, 324, 329, 333, 342, 358, 365, 370-371, 438, 442, 451, 471, 482, 486-487, 492, 522, 524-525, 527-529, 543, 554, 568, 573, 577, 590, 598, 602; Central 42, 297, 340, 440; East Central 31, 42, 602-603; Eastern 6, 27, 37, 122, 159, 297
Finland 493
Finn (Finns) 144
Foundry (Puszkarnia) 464-465
France 149
Frankfurt am Main 49, 311
French 34, 211, 256, 407, 564, 598
Galvė Lake 83
gate – see subject index
Gaul (Gallic towns) 449
Gdańsk (Danzig) 9, 44, 86, 163, 180, 236, 245, 251, 259, 285, 309, 311-312, 328-329, 445, 502, 506, 513, 521, 548, 563, 588
Gediminas Hill 7
Gegužinė 610
Gelvonai – see: Giełwany 461
German (Germans) 144
German Town 329
Germany 74, 173, 341, 498
Giełwany (Gelvonai) 461
Głogów 251
Głubczyce 330
Gniezno 135, 564, 566-567, 570
Goldingen (Kuldīga) 464
Grand Duchy of Lithuania – see: Lithua-

nia
Grand Duchy of Lithuania 1, 2, 3, 6, 10, 13, 17, 19, 23, 30, 36, 40, 42-44, 47-49, 52-54, 57-58, 61, 66, 70-71, 74-75, 79-80, 82, 84-86, 90, 94, 115, 122, 141, 155, 173-174, 187, 192, 196, 233, 239, 241, 243, 247, 253, 256, 258, 264, 268, 270-271, 276, 281, 287-288, 297-298, 300, 321-322, 330, 334, 340, 347, 362, 366, 368, 372, 374, 390, 433, 436, 453, 464-465, 469, 482, 501, 513, 519, 522-523, 526, 531-533, 543, 549, 555, 565, 568, 571, 573, 579, 598, 601, 603, 609
Greater Poland 369, 412, 568
Grodzisko 223
Grunwald 519, 549
Habsburg Empire 586
Halych 95, 290
Hansa (Hanseatic cities) 6, 30, 41, 52, 66, 271
Haszeny 195
Heidelberg 536, 579
Hill of Three Crosses 7
Holešov 543
Hrodna (Grodno) 44, 201, 222, 400, 611
Grodno Volost 138
Hungary 185, 187, 241, 254, 276, 299,
Iberian Peninsula 370
Imbramowice 209-210, 219, 223, 282
Ingolstadt 117, 366
Irishman (Irishmen) 147
Istanbul 11, 32
Italian (Italians) 117, 133, 256, 447, 452, 459, 487-488, 551
Italian (adj.) 195, 273, 295, 377, 471, 486, 491
Italy 324, 371, 419, 452, 551, 560; Northern 149
Janów 312
Jasna Góra 460
Jerusalem 420, 464, 604-605
Jew (Jews) 10, 23, 31, 25, 58, 71, 92, 133, 233, 235, 243, 255, 272, 277, 308, 374, 397, 416, 430, 432, 437, 450, 510, 527, 529, 536, 538, 544, 560-561, 580, 602
Jewie – see: Vievis
Jewish 10, 15, 24, 36, 90, 99, 125, 133, 178-179, 184, 210, 248, 256, 274-276, 312, 370, 373 – 374, 397-398, 438, 448-450, 536-539, 542-543, 549, 580, 582-583, 590, 611
Kaffa 250
Kaliningrad 44
Kalisz 38, 476
Kėdainiai (Kiejdany) 89, 106, 176-177, 294
Kernavė (Kiernów) 597
Kyivan Rus' 6, 498
Kingdom of Poland – see: Poland
Köln – see: Cologne
Koncowicz (a field) 331
Königsberg (Królewiec) 39, 44, 108, 142, 163, 171, 236, 309, 386, 415, 481-482
Košice 311
Kotra 73, 110, 138, 330
Kraków – see: Cracow
Kražiai 155
Kreva (Krevo) 75
Królewiec – see: Königsberg
Kuldīga – see: Goldingen
Kumielia 609
Kutein 298
Kyiv 44, 94-95, 165, 169, 177, 254, 263, 290, 357, 368
Lach (Lachs) – see: Pole
Latin 47, 421; Southern (South) 130, 151, 300; Western (West) 52, 130, 151, 195, 257-258, 300, 312, 521, 529, 555
Latvia 26, 464, 497
Latvian (Latvians) 142, 144, 155, 266, 274
Łęczyca 81, 289, 294-296, 300, 310, 341, 570
Leiden 531
Leipzig 12, 171, 198, 311, 316

Lesser Poland 185, 187, 209, 219, 298-299, 315, 319, 366, 368, 394, 451, 468
Leuven 117
Lewoniszki 250
Lithuania 2, 7, 10, 12, 19, 22, 25, 33, 36, 39-40, 44, 52, 54, 59, 75-76, 83, 94, 98, 105, 113, 117, 133-134, 136, 138, 145, 147, 159, 172, 176, 223, 228, 236, 249-251, 255, 257, 260, 262, 267, 275, 282, 285-286, 289, 297, 299, 309, 312, 315, 327, 330, 346, 350, 365, 371, 383, 386, 403, 415, 419, 431, 442, 447, 457, 459, 462, 480, 504, 509, 514, 518, 521, 523, 531, 535-537, 548, 560, 566, 575, 577, 579, 591, 601, 603-604; Lithuanian Commonwealth (Republic, Rzeczpospolita Litewska) 522; Lithuanian Soviet Socialist Republic 17; Lithuanian-Polish Commonwealth – see: Polish-Lithuanian Commonwealth; Republic of Lithuania 6, 43-44
Lithuanian (Lithuanians) 1, 2, 3, 9, 10, 13, 18, 19, 21, 22, 25, 26, 32, 35-36, 38, 42, 44, 48-49, 52, 71-72, 76, 80, 83-84, 87-89, 92-94, 102, 104-105, 125, 133, 136-137, 151, 153, 156-157, 164, 176, 180, 194-195, 207, 210, 216, 219, 249, 251, 253-255, 272, 291, 297, 306, 309, 313, 322, 330, 337, 341, 357, 380-381, 383, 389, 433, 453, 469-470, 473, 476, 486, 500, 517-518, 523-524, 529, 535, 544, 547, 550, 560, 568-570, 577, 597-598, 602, 613
Lithuanian (adj.) 52
Little Poland 187
Livonia (Inflanty) 145, 253, 290, 327-328, 335, 469, 476
Livonian 329, 339, 351, 395, 470
London 32, 295, 395
Lorraine 464
Łowicz 341
Lubcz 289, 294, 481, 569
Lublin 38, 80, 124-125, 179, 276, 299, 310-312, 319, 353, 393, 451, 468, 528, 537, 547, 560; Lukiškės (Łukiszki) 179, 537
Lutsk 136, 167
Lviv 12, 167-169, 180, 310-311, 353, 368, 442, 524, 541, 576
Łyntupy 264
Magdeburg 271
Cathedral Square 3
Market Square 65, 84-85, 87, 234, 291, 312-313, 468, 497, 503, 506, 553, 608, 613
Market Square (in Cracow) 485
Malbork (Marienburg) 447
Market Square – see: Square
Mazowsze (Masovia) 290, 328, 612
Mediterranean 3, 527, 604
Minsk 26, 44, 81, 123, 253, 357
Moldova 39, 532
Montowtyszki 267
Moravia 217
Moscow 24, 36, 44, 84, 201, 274
Mstislavl 254
Munich 117, 546, 547
Muscovian – see: Russian
Muscovy – see: Russia
Muscovy (Moscovia); Russian Empire 23
Muslim 10
Musninkai 609
Navahrudak (Nowogródek) 44, 366, 368, 391-392, 400
Neris River (Wilia) 1, 276, 449-450, 524, 537, 610
Netherlands 560
Niepołomice 595-596
Novgorod – see: Veliky Novgorod
Nowogródek – see: Navahrudak
Nuremberg 316, 610
Nyasvizh (Nieśwież) 91, 236, 289, 491, 515, 535, 558, 579
Okole – see: Ruski Koniec
Old Town (Vilnius) 7; Ostroh (Остроr, Ostrog) 169, 368, 374, 384, 532, 541

Opatów 468
Orsha 285, 361, 519, 603
Ostraszyn (Astrashyna) 467
Oszmiana district 196
Padua (Padova) 74, 117, 286
Palermo 279
Pamėnkalnis – see: Buffałowa Hill
Paneriai (Ponary) 608
Paplauja – see: Popławy
Paris 32, 438
Parnawa – see: Pärnu
Pärnu (Parnawa) 194
Pechersk Lavra 94
Peczusy 332
Piltene (Piltyń) 497
Pińczów 535
Pinsk 253
Piotrków (Trybunalski) 564
Poland 12, 26-27, 30-31, 33, 39, 54, 75, 99, 112, 119, 128, 135, 146-147, 191-192, 202, 208, 216, 222-223, 226, 253, 255, 259, 260, 262, 271, 282, 285, 305, 324, 328, 335-336, 342, 346, 351, 354, 386, 420, 440, 451, 458, 460, 464, 469, 482, 486, 499, 506, 535, 538, 548, 553, 560, 570, 575, 577, 579, 580, 586, 591, 602; Polish Kingdom (Polish Crown, Kingdom of Poland) 40, 44, 47, 50, 64, 75, 122, 134-135, 204, 206, 241, 257, 283, 288, 297, 353, 369, 402, 433, 453, 522, 532, 553, 564; Polish People's Republic (Polska Rzeczpospolita Ludowa) 15; Republic of Poland (Rzeczpospolita Polska) 16, 44
Polatsk 94, 149, 156, 198, 245, 253, 286-287, 339, 374, 393, 469, 470, 492, 498, 516, 554
Pole (Poles, Lach, Lachs) 1, 7, 10, 17, 44, 133, 153, 179, 243, 255, 263, 332, 476, 487, 522, 526, 537, 577, 602
Polish Crown – see: Poland
Polish Kingdom – see: Poland
Polish People's Republic – see: Poland
Polish End (Lacki Koniec) 7
Polish Quarter 526
Polish-Lithuanian Commonwealth 10, 23-24, 26, 31, 34, 37, 39, 44, 64, 71-72, 81, 106, 132, 146, 148 -150, 159, 164, 166, 176, 180, 185, 190, 198, 206, 209, 212, 216-217, 222, 240, 247-248, 262, 266, 275, 289, 293, 298, 309-314, 337, 362, 365-366, 368, 370, 386-387, 403, 418, 421, 430, 440, 442, 444, 448, 451, 459, 464-465, 468, 490, 492, 508, 518, 528, 531, 532, 535, 537, 541-542, 550, 559, 575, 580, 593, 602, 603, 605
Pomerania 39
Ponary – see: Paneriai
Popławy 250
Porudomina 331
Powilno – see: Lewoniszki
Poznań 38, 61, 106, 125, 180, 207, 311, 353, 366, 372, 392, 442, 476, 488, 577
Pozwole 315
Prague 12, 38, 39, 61, 249, 274, 286-287, 309, 339, 436, 532
Prussia 9, 39, 142, 203, 290, 314, 328, 351, 386, 476, 611; Ducal 142; Royal 44, 142, 447, 502, 548, 564
Pskov 234, 395, 401, 441
Puszkarnia – see: Foundry
Racibórz 223
Radziwiłowo – see: Kėdainiai
Raižiai 537
Raków 368, 420
Republic of Lithuania – see: Lithuania
Republic of Poland – see: Poland
Riga 61, 108, 142, 327-328, 351
Rome 300
Royal Prussia – see: Prussia
Rukony (Rukonys) 359
Rus 95
Ruski Koniec (Ruthenian End, Okole, *Civitas Ruthenica*) 526
Russia 23, 34, 43, 282, 532; North-West 254

Russian (Russians) 44, 247; Muscovian (Muscovians, Muscovites) 44, 144-145, 218, 464, 492, 609, 611
Ruthenia (Ruthenian lands) 39, 60, 75
Ruthenian (Ruthenians) 6, 10, 25, 36, 38-39, 44, 55, 65-66, 107, 133, 144-145, 169, 332, 418-419, 526, 566, 570
Ruthenian Town (Miasto Ruskie) 7, 329
Ruzhany (Różana) 117
Rykantai 349
Samogitia (Żmudź, Žemaitija) 39, 59, 101, 110, 137, 290, 297, 393, 611-612
Samogitian (Samogitians) 105, 137, 334, 467
Sandomierz 38, 149, 357, 386
Sarmatian (Sauromata, Sarmatians) 453, 520
Sarmatian-Palemonic 520
Scot (Scots, Scotsman) 147, 256, 385
Scotland 43
Scottish 385
Senoji Trakai (Old Trakai, Stare Troki) 83, 134, 137, 162-163, 204, 220, 278, 340, 349, 400, 455, 463
Siberia 23
Sicily 279
Sienno 468
Sieradz 81
Silesia 328, 560, 573
Silesian 330
Skopówka 358
Slav (Slavs) 44, 50, 255, 268
Slovakia – see: Upper Hungary
Slutsk 93-94, 129, 174-176, 253, 341
Smarhon' (Smorgonie) 104
Smolensk 1, 94, 245, 254, 334, 432, 470, 478, 498, 503-504, 508
Šnipiškės (Śnipiszki) 10, 87, 362, 449
Sochaczew 81
Sofia 579
Soviet (Soviets) 15, 17, 42, 440, 450, 462, 597
Soviet Lithuania 17
Soviet Union (USSR, Soviet authorities) 17, 18, 179, 441, 448, 603
Spain 279, 371, 419
St. Andrews 43
Stara Warszawa 353
Stockholm 39
Street: Biskupia (Bishop, Vyskupai) 87; Holendernia (Olandų) 448-449; Jatkowa (Mėsinių) 275; Literatų 400; Niemiecka (German, Vokiečių) 448; Ostra (Ostrobramska, Aušros Vartų) 503; Pylimo 394; Rudnicka (Rūdninkų) 497; Sawicz (Savičiaus) 263; Szklanna (Glass, Stiklių) 275; Św. Jana (St. John, Šv. Jono) 402; Tartar 277; Wielka (Great, Didžioji) 84; Zamkowa (Castle, Pilies) 498; Zaułek Świętomichalski (St. Michael, Šv. Mykolo) 400-401; Zborowa (the Protestant Reformed Church) 400; Żydowska (Jewish, Žydų) 275
Strubnitsa 609
Sudervė 609
Supraśl 93, 282, 532
Šventaragis Valley 1
Swede (Swedes) 108, 144, 476, 612
Sweden 39, 145, 482, 503, 558, 612
Switzerland 250
Tallin 61
Suceava 39
Tartaria (Tartary) 145
Tartar (Tartars) 10, 23, 72, 92, 133, 235, 243, 252, 254-255, 266, 277, 465-466, 501, 525, 527, 529, 549
  Minsk 357
Muslim 10
Vilnius 277, 362, 537, 543, 544, 561
Tartar (adj.) 232, 248, 256, 267, 278, 347
Teutonic Knights 7, 75, 98, 329, 134, 519, 526, 597, 603
Toulouse 488
Trakai Castle 83, 362
Transylvania 39

Transylvanian 352
Trent 206, 215, 310, 494, 549, 562, 570, 575
Troy 604, 609
Tykocin 116, 244-245, 464
Ukraine 23, 32, 44, 266, 532, 591
Union of Soviet Socialist Republics (USSR) – see: Soviet Union
Upper Hungary (Upper-Hungarian) 149, 217, 311
Uppsala 99, 108, 475-476, 489, 558, 572, 574-575
Urbino 127
Užupis (Zarzecze) 196, 205, 377, 613
Vawkavysk (Wołkowysk) 253, 609
Vawkavysk district 609
Veliky Novgorod 250, 254
Novgorod – see: Veliky Novgorod
Venice 10-11, 32, 49, 115, 245, 279, 300, 337, 339, 537, 560
Viciebsk (Vitebsk) 82, 92, 254, 350
Vienna 38, 61, 339, 440
Vievis (Jewie) 168, 261, 289, 293-294, 576, 589
Vilnius Region (Wileńszczyzna) 16
Vilnia River 250, 329, 524, 526, 613
Vilnius 277, 362, 537, 543, 544, 561
Volhynia 32, 532
Volodymyr Volynskyi 95
Warmia 328
Warsaw (Warszawa) 12, 61, 165, 310-312, 319, 337, 339, 350, 353, 448, 486, 518, 544, 567, 603
Warszawa – see: Warsaw
Wiekszwiany 334
Wieliczka 297
Wileńszczyzna – see: Vilnius Region
Wilia – see: Neris River
Wittenberg 171-172, 202,
Wizna 612
Włocławek 339
Włoszczowa 468
Wojnicz 318
Wolfenbüttel 386-387, 577
Wrocław 38, 61, 251, 573
Yalta 17
Zaborze 196
Zamość 198
Zarzecze – see: Užupis
Zator, Duchy of 81
Zavoloche 441
Zwierzyniec (a suburb of Cracow) 223

Subject Index

Academy of Vilnius and the Jesuit college (Vilnius Academy, *Universitas Vilnensis*, 1579–1781) 8, 10, 18, 20, 25, 26, 36, 51, 58, 61, 74, 82, 87, 93, 101, 106-108, 115, 117, 132, 133, 136, 138, 139, 141, 142, 144-163, 180, 209, 232, 238, 240, 244, 256, 283, 285, 295, 312, 319,320, 343, 345, 347, 348, 373, 380, 382, 385, 389, 401, 402, 407, 408, 410, 412, 416, 420, 435, 456, 473, 476, 478, 486, 487-490, 492, 495, 502, 504, 507, 508, 510, 512, 515-517, 519, 523, 539, 540, 550, 553, 561, 567, 575, 592
acrostic 477, 555
agenda (liturgical book) 88, 110, 119, 285, 286, 528, 563-567, 569, 573
akathist 287, 554, 555
album studiosorum 136
alderman (aldermen; see also: court; registers) 43, 50, 63, 66, 81, 241, 355
alexandrine (Polish, *trzynastozgłoskowiec*) 225, 403, 406, 513
allography 266
almanac 115

alphabet (script): Arabic 36, 180, 266, 267, 277, 279, 326, 537; Cyrillic 16, 36, 37, 44, 45, 72, 76, 77, 118, 121, 138, 164, 167, 230, 254, 258, 260, 266, 268, 269, 271, 274, 279, 282, 289, 292, 326, 360, 456, 502, 532, 533, 607; Gothic 270-272, 276, 277, 463; Greek 230, 268, 269, 279, 422; Hebrew 36, 151, 266, 274, 276-279, 326, 451, 464; humanistic 270; Latin 22, 36, 37, 76, 167, 260, 266, 269, 271, 272, 274, 279, 456, 502, 557; post-Gothic 273; Renaissance 272, 273
Alumnat – see: school (papal seminary)
Annal 258
anti-Ciceronianism 159
anti-Lutheran 414, 417
antiphonary 98, 315
Antiqua 168, 254, 272-274
Antiquity 2, 27, 403, 577, 583
applied literature (*literatura stosowana*) 38, 322, 323, 327
archbishopric (archdiocese) of Gniezno 135, 494, 564, 566, 567, 570, 571, 573
Archconfraternity – see: confraternity
archdeacon of Vilnius 101, 102, 110, 111, 227, 359
archdiocese of Gniezno – see: archbishopric of Gniezno
Archieratikon (*Chinovnik*) 568
archimandrite of Vilnius (Orthodox) 78, 96, 165, 169, 170, 263, 264, 293, 368, 382, 398, 483
archimandrite of Vilnius (Uniate) 368, 479, 481
archive: Basilian 87; Bishop 85, 330, 352; Burgrave 24, 84, 85; Bernardine 87; Calvinist 88, 89, 105, 332, 428; Carmelite (nuns) 219; Castle Court 84; Chapter 70, 85, 352; Dominican 87; Franciscan 87; guild 90, 91; Jesuit 87; Jewish 90; St. John Parish Church 87, 88; Lithuanian *Metrica* 35, 54, 61, 72, 73, 75, 83, 84, 89, 90, 114, 143, 245, 247, 250, 352, 283, 307, 330, 352, 400; Lutheran 332; municipal (the city) 23, 35, 85-87, 191, 331, 598; private 91, 334, 346; Uniate 89
arenga 55, 56, 325, 357, 358, 360-362
Arians – see: Polish Brethren
ars dictaminis 135, 324; *epistolandi* 135, 204, 205, 341, 342; *memoriae* (art of memory) 135; *notaria* 324; *rhetoricae* – see: rhetoric
art of memory – see: *ars memoriae*
artes liberales – see: liberal arts
Ashkenazi Hebrew – see: language
assembly (*sejmik*) 156
astronomy 102, 112, 125, 168, 175, 211
autobiography 138, 213, 532
avvisi 433
baccalaureate (*baccalaureus*) 136
baptism 88, 495, 564-566
Basilian (Basilians, Basilian Order) 26, 87, 95, 170, 205, 292, 296, 322, 494, 480, 481, 533
bastarda 271, 273
Belarusian – see: language
Bernardine 8, 36, 88, 102, 112, 144, 173, 196, 198, 205-207, 211, 214, 216, 218, 221-223, 270, 282, 285, 322, 401, 445, 452, 458, 463, 480, 541, 566, 581, 609, 612
Bible (bible; Holy Scripture) 30, 78, 99, 103, 105, 107, 110-112, 119, 121, 126, 129, 175, 210, 211, 223, 257, 282, 287, 304, 307, 315, 316, 408, 409, 528, 528-536, 538, 542, 544, 567, 579, 582; Brest Bible (Radziwiłł's Bible; Pińczów Bible) 173, 317, 318, 515, 535; Budny's Bible (Nieśwież's Bible; Nyasvizh Bible) 515, 535, 544, 549; Gdańsk Bible 387, 389, 535; Leopolita's Bible 261, 531; Ostroh Bible 121, 532, 533; Skaryna's Bible 249, 286, 532; Vulgate 99, 261, 531-533; Wu-

jek's Bible 238, 409, 515, 531, 533
birchbark 254
bishop: Catholic (Vilnius) 54, 58, 69, 70, 75, 85, 96-101, 106, 109-111, 113-115, 134, 136, 137, 139, 146, 147, 162, 171, 173, 176, 179, 198, 213, 215, 227, 232, 242, 273, 297, 309, 349, 351, 362, 379-381, 395, 397, 427, 431, 444, 446, 447, 452, 454, 463, 476-478, 480, 487, 497, 501, 504, 506, 519, 524, 564, 570; of Cracow 573; of Lutsk (Catholic) 136; Orthodox Metropolitan (Kyiv) 89, 95, 165, 282, 570; Uniate Metropolitan (Kyiv) 170, 177, 398; of Płock 348, 519, 520; of Samogitia 59, 393; of Warmia 328; of Włocławek 339
bishopric of Vilnius – see: diocese
book: commerce (selling; see also: bookseller) 37, 101, 308-313, 316; commonplace book (*sylva*) 26, 122, 232, 283, 403, 406, 520, 521, 523, 581; liturgical 4, 99, 103, 109, 110, 127, 128, 209, 240, 245, 250, 253, 257, 270, 274, 277, 281, 282, 300, 529, 549, 560, 562, 563, 568-570; of miracles 298, 414, 460; production – see: printing house
bookbinder (*introligator*, *compactor librorum*) 12, 37, 299, 301, 304-309, 312, 313, 528, 557
bookbinding 301-309
bookseller (*bibliopola*) 101, 121, 324, 240, 301, 306, 309-311, 313, 314, 320, 366, 523, 527, 557
bookshop 5, 10, 298, 299, 312, 313, 553
borderland 10, 11, 31, 32, 34, 37, 255
borderland studies (*studia pograniczne*) 27, 31, 32
Brest Union – see: Union
breviary (liturgy of hours) 97, 99, 101, 110, 112, 206, 238, 307, 528, 562, 563, 573
bridge – see: Stone Bridge
Bridgettine Sisters 205, 218
brotherhood 141, 492; furriers 263, 378; of the Holy Rosary 550; honey (*bractwo miodowe*) 262, 263; Jewish Funeral 449; merchant and tanners 90, 263; Orthodox, stauropegic 21, 93, 95, 96, 121, 133, 164-170, 180, 237, 238, 261-263, 289, 291, 293, 294, 296, 300, 398, 399, 473, 481, 502, 509, 523, 533, 541, 550, 557, 568, 570, 576, 584, 589; Ruthenian 263
burgermeister – see: mayor
burgher 42, 44, 54, 71, 118, 165, 190, 192, 227, 231, 233, 242, 361, 440, 461, 471, 501, 506
burgrave of Vilnius (*horodniczy*) 24, 58, 70, 71, 76, 84, 134, 194, 241, 242, 250, 372, 375, 376, 461
burmistrz – see: mayor
Calvinist – see: Christian
Calvinist Community (*Jednota Litewska*) – see: Church (institution)
cancellaresca (chancery script) 190, 268, 273, 278
canon (a priest) 48, 59, 70, 70, 96, 97, 101, 102, 106, 109, 110-112, 127, 129, 134-140, 168, 222, 238, 239, 252, 264, 286, 341, 358, 359, 382, 407, 412, 424, 495, 497, 550, 563, 564
canonisation 160, 437, 460, 495, 505, 506, 567, 603
capital 35, 127; cultural 35, 36, 186, 229, 235, 238, 243, 314, 318, 443, 529; economic 35, 36, 233, 235, 243, 314, 443, 446, 529; educational 35, 36, 186; political 243; social 35, 36, 243, 443, 446
Carmelite; of Ancient Observance 103; Discalced (nuns) 36, 205, 209, 213, 214, 216, 217, 219, 220, 223; Discalced (monks) 103, 144, 213, 509, 539, 551, 591, 610
castellan: of Polatsk 198; of Samogitia 467; of Vilnius 217, 264
castle of Vilnius; lower 8, 70, 71, 83-85,

115, 139, 171, 253, 449, 452, 463, 486, 498, 500, 503, 508, 603, 607, 613; upper 8, 613
castrum doloris 431, 468, 524
catalogue of the books (inventory, register) 93, 99, 100, 102, 103, 105, 107, 111-116, 120, 121, 123, 125, 128, 208, 237, 299, 553, 592
catechism 21, 121, 142, 144, 152, 156, 163, 177, 198, 236, 237, 239, 292, 294, 296, 297, 299, 315, 319, 383, 528-531, 536, 538, 545, 558, 559, 569, 570, 572-582, 591, 593
cathedral: St. Stanislas in Vilnius (Catholic) 58, 70, 85, 96-102, 134, 135, 139, 163, 232, 233, 271, 273, 306, 315, 379, 382, 426, 433, 439, 442, 444, 452, 454, 455, 457, 458, 460, 462, 463, 470, 476, 493, 497, 503, 510, 526, 530, 571, 588, 592, 603, 613; Theotokos in Vilnius (of Dormition, Orthodox, *sobor*) 92-94, 132, 164, 301, 441, 526; Wawel (Cracow) 99, 102, 315, 454, 493, 518
Catholic – see: Christian
Catholicism 6, 10, 133, 155, 176, 230, 272, 295, 297, 491, 526, 527, 588
cemetery 441; Calvinist 394, 397; St. John's 162; Lutheran 448; Jewish (Old) 276, 397, 449, 450; Jewish (New) 449; Tartar (Muslim) 179
centres-peripheries 32
cera (wax tablet) 253
chancellor: Lithuanian 2, 48, 49, 53, 54, 59, 60, 70-73, 76-78, 83, 84, 113, 143, 149, 198, 205, 221, 264, 281, 291, 344, 368, 390, 458, 486, 501, 509, 519, 521, 546, 547; Polish 51, 204, 485, 501, 549; Polish Deputy (*podkanclerzy*) – see: vice-chancellor; of the queen 201, 202
chancery 47, 61, 70, 76, 78, 80, 91, 205, 239, 241, 248, 254, 273, 322, 344, 346, 347; bishops's 69; of the chapter 35, 48, 70, 239; of the field hetman 74; of the great hetman 74; Lithuanian (of the Grand Duchy of Lithuania, the grand duke, the state) 3, 21, 24, 35, 48, 53, 61, 71-73, 76, 77, 79, 80, 83, 84, 137, 242, 253, 269-271, 274, 283, 321, 323, 324, 327, 340, 347, 360, 361; of the queen 36, 202, 203; royal (Polish) 73, 74, 116, 117, 203, 204, 242, 244, 249, 266, 278, 283, 324, 327, 328, 334, 337, 338, 340, 341, 343, 344, 350, 466, 493; urban (municipal) 12, 35, 61, 63-67, 259, 327, 335, 337, 352; of *Voigt* 64; Vytautas's 72, 248, 271, 278
chapter (cathedral) of Vilnius 21, 25, 35, 48, 50, 52, 54, 58, 58, 59, 61, 69, 70, 72, 75, 77, 80, 81, 85, 95-102, 106, 109, 110, 113, 126, 129, 135, 138, 139, 141, 143, 144, 171, 183, 184, 188, 238, 239, 240, 245, 247, 251, 252, 282, 283, 285, 301, 306, 313, 315, 318, 340, 349, 352, 357, 358, 374, 376, 382, 407, 461, 495-496, 503, 539, 563, 570, 608, 613
Christian (Christians, Christianity) 7, 10, 38, 53, 92, 94, 151-152, 166, 168, 180-181, 184, 223, 229-230, 237, 256, 265, 276, 295, 300, 308, 312, 329, 362-363, 365, 368-369, 381, 397-398, 425, 437, 445, 446, 448, 449-450, 452, 456, 458, 482-483, 490, 510, 516, 526-527, 530, 538-541, 545. 549, 550, 558-559, 561-562, 577, 580-583, 587, 589, 590; Catholic (Catholics, anti-Catholic) 6, 7, 8, 21, 23, 31, 32, 35, 38, 44, 52-53, 55, 58, 61, 72, 74, 91, 93, 96, 101-103, 107, 109, 111, 117, 127, 129, 132-133, 140, 142 -147, 150-152, 155, 158-160, 162, 166-167, 172, 176-177, 186, 190, 196, 206-207, 212, 214, 220, 222-223, 228-230, 232, 234-236, 238, 240, 242, 248, 255, 257, 259, 261, 262, 263, 272-273, 281-282, 291, 293, 295, 297, 300-301, 309-310, 322, 327, 335, 357, 361,

366, 368, 369-371, 379, 381-382, 385-386, 389-394,397-398, 400-402, 405-407, 410, 412-413,415-422, 424, 426-428, 432,434, 440, 442-443, 445-446, 448-449, 452, 459-460, 462-463, 469-471, 474, 479, 481, 486, 490-491, 495, 504, 509-510, 520, 525-527, 529-533, 538-542, 547-551, 553-554, 557, 559, 562-563, 565-567, 570-573, 575-577, 579, 581-584, 586-591, 603; Calvinist 8, 10, 14, 17, 25, 32, 74, 88-89, 92-93, 95, 104-105, 124, 129, 131-133, 145, 162, 173, 174, 176-177, 180, 195, 205, 220, 231, 233-234,236, 238, 289, 294-295, 297, 300, 313, 319, 322, 334, 342, 348, 352, 357, 368, 381-383, 385-387, 389, 391, 394, 396-397, 399, 400-402, 404, 406-408, 411, 414, 420-421,424, 426, 428, 467, 485, 491, 510, 515, 527, 535-536, 538, 542, 557-559, 568-570, 578-579, 580-581, 588, 591; Czech Brethren (Unity of Brethren) 382, 386, 389; Eastern-Christian 16; Lutheran 10, 15, 32, 74, 92-93, 103-104, 132-133, 143, 163, 167, 171, 174, 190, 195, 198, 236, 258, 261, 300, 352, 377, 381-382, 385-387, 394, 399-400, 406-407, 411, 414-417, 445, 448, 481, 485, 527, 535, 542, 560, 579, 586-587, 590; Orthodox (anti-Orthodox) 3, 6-8, 10, 16, 18, 21, 25, 31-32, 150, 166-167, 169, 259, 261, 263, 272, 400, 417-419, 510, 527, 538, 541, 567-568, 570, 571, 573, 576-577, 581-582, 584-585, 588-591, 603, 610; Protestant (anti-Protestant) 10, 18-20, 25, 35-36, 38, 88-89, 99, 104, 109, 129, 131, 133, 141, 147-148, 150, 152, 162, 166, 171-174, 176, 190, 196, 222, 234-236, 294-298, 300, 309, 313, 334, 336, 349, 369, 371, 381-382, 385-393, 397, 399, 400, 402, 406-407, 414-415, 417-418, 420-422, 425-427, 446, 449, 474, 481, 490, 496, 510, 525, 529, 534-536, 539-540, 542, 557-559, 575-577, 579-581, 585-589, 593; Uniate (Uniates, anti-Uniate) 10, 16, 21, 23, 32, 38, 44, 58, 61, 74, 92, 95, 121, 133, 150, 166, 169, 170, 177, 189-190, 257, 261-263, 289, 291, 293-294, 300, 368, 381-382, 394, 398, 399- 400, 417, 420-424, 440-441, 445-447, 454-456, 458, 460, 470, 481, 498, 502-503, 527, 529, 531, 533, 542, 559, 562, 566, 568, 584-585, 590-591

Christianisation 268

Christianitas 159

chronicle 102, 112, 115, 119, 208, 213-218, 220-223, 270, 282, 304, 328-329, 381, 433, 458, 464, 513, 521, 596, 598, 599, 601, 604

church (building): St. Anne 401, 468; Assumption of the Holy Virgin (Franciscan) 8, 530; Calvinist (Evangelical-Reformed) 93, 104, 162, 173, 177, 394, 397, 428, 463, 467, 510; St. Casimir (Jesuit) 87, 442; St. Catherine of Alexandria (of Benedictine nuns) 205; Catholic 92, 103, 109, 248, 255, 379, 440, 442, 462-463, 490-491; St. Francis and St. Bernard (Bernardine) 270, 401; St George (Carmelite) 103; St George (Orthodox) 109; Holy Cross (Brothers Hospitallers' Church) 8, 99-100, 588; Holy Spirit (Catholic, Dominican) 144, 162, 550; Holy Spirit (Orthodox) 95-96, 118-119, 127,133, 164, 166, 170, 205, 262, 445-446, 483, 502, 509, 584, 610; Holy Trinity (Orthodox, Uniate) 78, 89, 93-95, 133, 164-166, 170, 205, 262, 293, 300, 368, 382, 398-399, 441, 446-448, 454-456, 458, 479, 481, 502, 584; St. John Baptist and St. John Evangelist (St. John Parish Church) 8, 87-88, 112, 132, 141-142, 145, 162, 238, 242, 256, 343, 379, 380, 441, 462, 497, 506, 548, 564, 584; St. Joseph's (of Carmelite nuns) 205; Lutheran 32, 104, 133, 163, 172, 176, 195, 258, 352, 448-449, 560, 586; Michael the Archangel (of Bernardine nuns) 173, 205, 288; St. Nicholas's (Catholic) 462; St. Nicholas's (Orthodox) 54, 94, 329, 568; Orthodox 92-93, 94-95, 97, 127, 132-133, 164, 234, 255, 294, 313, 386, 398, 400, 434, 437, 440, 446, 449, 470, 526, 563, 591; St. Paraskeva (Orthodox, Uniate) 7; St. Peter and Paul (Orthodox) 164, 555; St. Raphael (Jesuit) 87; St. Stanislaus – see: cathedral; St. Stephen 108, 497; Theotokos – see: cathedral; Uniate 38, 95, 441, 447, 454-456, 458, 460, 502

Church (institution): Reformed (Calvinist), Lithuanian Calvinist Community (*Jednota*)17, 105, 289, 579; Catholic 10, 20-21, 92, 160, 206, 214, 235, 295, 366, 371, 417, 443, 445, 504, 509, 527, 539, 553, 570, 575-576, 584, 588; Lutheran (Augsburg) 104, 133, 163, 195, 258, 448, 586; Orthodox 25, 38, 78, 145, 164, 166-167, 169, 235, 258, 262-263, 270, 289, 293, 366, 382, 398, 417-419, 424, 441, 498, 529, 531-533, 541, 571, 581, 591; Protestant 35, 38, 89, 109, 129, 235 400, 406, 490, 510, 525, 536, 559, 579; Uniate 10, 23, 166, 170, 368, 440-441, 529

Ciceronianism 159

city: 'closed' 39, 245, 249, 322, 323, 365-369, 372, 436, 470, 471, 473, 517, 569, 583; 'open' 39, 83, 245, 248, 249, 300, 322, 323, 330, 336, 351, 365-369, 379, 381, 421, 470, 471, 473, 492, 517, 569, 587

clergy 21, 40, 71-72, 75, 82, 89, 91, 109, 111, 118, 126, 132, 143, 152, 161, 164, 169, 172, 180, 184, 229, 233, 240, 243, 262, 265, 273, 289, 299, 301, 318, 327-328, 369, 398, 413, 416, 419, 425, 430, 442, 500, 503, 510, 526-527, 529-530, 537-538, 541, 544, 549, 552, 554, 561, 564, 583, 588

clergyman (clergymen) 73-74, 98, 100, 106, 109, 111, 126, 151, 189-190, 233, 237, 239, 241, 309, 379, 382, 400, 530, 541,

client 57, 75, 142, 177, 180, 191, 243, 297, 346, 347, 435, 473, 477, 518

closed city – see: city

codex 96, 112, 527, 537

coin 30, 33, 40, 230, 248, 250, 271-273, 314, 317, 406, 462, 468-469, 484, 511

college – see: school

common people (pospólstwo) 55, 56

common-place book – see: book

Confraternity: Archconfraternity of St. Anne 185-186, 550; Archconfraternity of Corpus Christi 550; Archconfraternity of Mercy 550; of St. John the Baptist 141, 550; of St. Martin 550; of the Name of God 550

Congregation of the Rosary 550

convent – see: monastery

convocation (konwokacja) 322, 492

copperplate 8, 111, 585, 604

copyist (see also: *kathedralis*) 5, 80, 97, 98, 114, 282, 463, 561

coronation 30, 202, 337, 402, 433, 454, 503, 542, 603

Corpus Christi Feast 494

correspondence 36, 52, 66, 89, 146, 194, 199, 203-204, 208, 214-215, 229, 243, 245, 248, 264, 297, 335, 340, 341-342, 344, 346-347, 349, 379, 473, 591

Council (Calvinist, *Synod*) 467

Council 107; of Constance 103; of Trent (Tridentine) 99, 206, 310, 369, 490, 494, 496, 549, 562, 570, 571, 575

council of the city (*rada miejska*) 11, 43, 55, 56, 63-67, 71, 79, 80, 85-87, 89, 118, 142, 143, 161, 192, 236, 250, 276, 307, 319, 330, 337, 342, 416, 495, 502,

548
councillor (*rajca*) 55, 63, 64, 66, 90, 94, 165, 175, 190, 232, 335, 342, 395, 412
Counter-Reformation 111, 263, 295, 382, 458, 491, 494, 586
court (tribunal); of the Aldermen (*Voigt*, Bench, *sąd ławniczy*) 11, 50, 55, 62-66, 79-81, 85-87, 330-332, 337, 352; assessorial (appellate state court; *asesorski sąd hospodarski*) 49, 59; bishop's court (consistory court) 58, 70, 162-163, 256, 372; burgrave's court (*sąd horodniczański*) 58, 84, 461; castle court (*sąd grodzki*) 25, 58, 61, 71, 76, 79, 84, 86, 222, 233, 247, 258, 271, 277, 362, 607-608; chapter court (chapter's court) 58; consistory (*konsystorz*) – see: bishop's court; of the Grand Duke (*sąd hospodarski*) 40; land court (*sąd ziemski*) 25, 58-59, 61, 71, 79, 81, 219, 258; the Qahal (qahal courts, beth din, *kehila*) 90, 248, 275, 373, 374, 562; Polish supreme court of the Magdeburg law 56; royal 30, 57, 199, 203, 239, 313, 334, 432-433, 485, 487, 490, 511; Tribunal of the Grand Duchy of Lithuania (*Trybunał Litewski*) 58, 71, 84, 86, 233, 239, 271, 321, 334, 396
craftsman (artisan) 53, 58, 69, 75, 329, 334, 447, 460, 467, 526
cursive 77, 270-271, 273-274, 276, 278, 315, 537
Czech Brethren – see: Christian
delectare 239, 249, 490
deposition 56, 71, 322, 373-374, 400, 404, 610
Derasha 582
description 26, 99, 179, 297, 303, 326, 344, 359, 367, 427, 492-493, 496, 500, 502, 514
diak (clerk) 3, 43, 65, 201, 282
dialogue 242, 258, 370, 384, 386-387, 393, 402, 416, 443, 487, 488-489, 508, 513, 517, 522, 538, 544, 587
diary 103, 124, 128, 163, 198, 218, 223, 447, 486, 596
disputation 222, 367, 369, 372, 379, 383-394, 400, 420, 425, 428, 517
Dominican 52, 74, 87, 102-103, 112, 132, 144, 162, 223, 322, 382, 480, 539, 542, 550, 591, 599, 614
drama 21, 384, 485, 488-490
dramma per musica 431, 486
elegy (elegiae) 154, 328, 487
entry (ceremonial) 60, 81, 97, 140, 276, 311, 326, 378, 415-416, 431, 484, 491, 498-501, 503, 506, 509-510, 518
epicedion 443
epideictic art 429-433, 436, 482, 484, 491
epigram 48, 137, 154, 242, 258, 412-413, 415-417, 453, 465, 476, 487, 506-507, 518
epistolography 153-154, 156, 194, 199, 205, 215, 245, 248, 323, 325, 340-343, 346, 443
epitaph 4, 39, 132, 154, 225, 232, 248, 271, 273, 439, 440-460, 470, 472, 479, 481, 603-604
epithalamy 435
Eucharist 103, 385, 407, 413, 420
eucharistikon 416
Euchologion (*Trebnik*) 568
ex voto – see: votive offering
exegesis 178, 210, 539, 541
forgery (forged documents) 77
formula (formulae): document 325; letter 335, 337, 340-342; last will 357-358, 362
Fraktur 254
Franciscan 8, 36, 52, 70, 74, 87, 102, 110, 134, 137, 270, 330, 442, 530, 541, 588
funeral 78, 124, 160, 198, 235, 237, 263, 276, 346, 359, 362-363, 397, 400, 402, 426, 430-431, 433-434, 436, 443, 445, 449-450, 452, 471, 474, 478-479, 480-482, 484, 492-494, 497, 508, 511, 561,

564, 586, 591-593, 603
Geschichtspolitik – cf. memory
Gospel 77, 168, 318, 393, 408, 419, 531-532, 535, 562, 567
grammar 40, 108, 116, 135, 142, 161, 163, 168, 170, 175, 181, 190, 257, 265, 291, 293, 308, 319-320, 324-343, 374
gramota 254
graphosphere 34, 234, 273, 326, 467
gravestone – see: tombstone
Greek – see: language
grosz 40, 43, 57, 80-82, 125, 128, 134, 143, 175, 186, 227, 228, 230, 232, 251, 252, 304, 306, 315-319, 334, 350, 355, 377, 541, 612, 613
grzywna 40, 49, 80, 143, 296, 306
guild 25, 30, 52, 54, 55, 58, 69, 90, 91, 141, 226, 262, 301, 304, 307, 308, 337, 378, 428, 441, 469, 495
habitus 31, 35
hagiography (see also: legend) 298, 458, 467, 584
Halakha 52, 365, 542
Hansa 6, 30, 41, 52, 66, 76, 271
hendecasyllabic 477
hetman 43; field 74, 78, 608; great 74, 78, 94, 197, 569, 608, 609
hexameron 554
hexameter 225, 406, 466, 477
hieratikon 568
historian 3, 4, 11, 14, 19, 22, 34, 37, 43, 54, 92, 97,159, 204, 275, 298, 323, 374, 385, 401, 441, 443, 449, 459, 460, 521, 522, 527, 598
historiography 97, 216, 258, 325, 430, 442, 473, 513, 520, 521-524, 602
history: of the Grand Duchy of Lithuania 1, 43, 297, 312, 442, 513, 517-524; of literature 16, 18, 27, 51, 324; of Vilnius 13-16, 52, 61, 254, 511, 597, 600-603, 605
Holy Scripture – see: Bible
homiletics (see also: preaching) 107, 542, 583, 585
Horodnictwo – see: *jurydyka*
horodniczy – see: burgrave of Vilnius
horologion 554, 568
House Słucki (*Kamienica Słucka*) 58, 124, 316; Trybunalski (Poznański) 497; Wirszyłowski (*Kamienica Wirszyłowska*) 334; Żagiel's 497
humaniora – see: humanities
humanism 343, 139
humanist 5, 17-18, 40, 48, 70, 73, 82, 105, 111, 113, 115-116, 121-122,128-129, 130, 132-133, 144, 150-151, 153, 158-159, 161, 166-167, 170, 171-172, 174, 176, 180, 202, 204-205, 240, 242, 249, 257, 270, 273-274, 287, 291, 309, 324-325, 328, 341, 343, 348, 369, 397, 400, 407, 411, 418, 420, 424-425, 436, 456, 466, 485, 493, 494, 513, 518, 522-523, 547, 549, 561, 584, 590
humanities (*humaniora*) 27-28, 32-34, 37, 40, 111, 151-152, 155-156, 158-159, 161, 286, 414, 598
icon 127, 225, 230, 248, 250, 269, 445-446, 448, 553, 603
identity 3, 22, 32, 229, 261, 471, 483, 511, 517, 520, 525, 541, 598, 602
illiteracy 193, 225,
ink 5, 94, 252, 279, 296
inscription 30, 39, 158, 230-233, 235, 248, 250, 269, 271-273, 304, 305, 426, 432, 436-442, 445-447, 449-452, 454, 456-471, 484, 495, 499, 500, 510, 524, 528, 603
interpretative community 220, 323, 437
inventory post mortem 25, 50, 91, 101, 118, 119, 168, 228, 237, 239, 248, 251, 299, 311, 314, 318, 333, 353, 359, 527, 528
irmologion 282, 568
Iron Wolf 1-3, 5, 6, 598
Islam 179, 230, 256, 527, 544
Italic 269, 273, 557

Jesuit (Jesuits; Society of Jesus) 8, 17, 18, 20, 21, 35, 36, 51, 74, 87, 92, 93, 95, 99, 101, 106-108, 115, 117, 119, 132, 133, 139-152, 155-159, 161-163, 167, 168, 170, 173-175, 209, 210, 217, 234, 237, 238, 240, 244, 260, 263, 289, 295-298, 301, 310, 311, 313, 320, 322, 342, 346-348, 366-372, 377, 379-383, 385-389, 391, 392, 399-401, 404, 406-409, 412-414, 416, 419-421, 423, 426, 427, 432, 433, 463, 471, 473, 474, 478-480, 485, 486, 488-491, 494-496, 503, 504, 506-509, 511, 514, 515, 518, 520, 523, 531, 539-542, 550, 551, 561, 675, 581, 584, 587-589, 592, 601

Jesuit college – see: Academy of Vilnius

Judaism 230, 527, 544

jurydyka 57, 58, 61, 69, 354; bishop (Catholic) 58, 69, 85, 227; burgrave's (castle, *Horodnictwo*) 58, 71, 84, 375, 376; chapter of Vilnius 58, 70, 306, 313, 358, 376; Metropolitan of Kyiv (Orthodox/Uniate) 58; Magdeburg (of the city) 91; voivode of Vilnius 58

kathedralis 97, 98, 531

khamail 266, 561

kitab 266, 544, 549, 561, 580

konsystorz – see: court

konwokacja – see: convocation

kopa groszy (shock) 40, 44, 82, 128, 134, 143, 163, 227, 228, 232, 306, 315, 316, 318, 319, 334, 350, 358

Kulturbund ('cultural crossroad') 181

Kyiv-Mohyla Collegium – see: school

language: Arabic 133, 256, 266, 277, 530, 537, 538, 544, 561; Armenian 266; Baltic 44; Belarusian 44, 59, 256, 257, 259, 260, 261, 266, 287, 537; Church Slavonic 36, 45, 59, 121, 122, 164, 167, 168, 170, 240, 249, 255-258, 260, 262, 263, 265, 266, 274, 287, 290, 300, 456, 464, 502, 530-534, 549, 555-557, 562, 566, 568, 572, 584; Czech 339, 407, 588; English 38, 42-45, 339, 494, 507; Estonian 155; French 112, 211, 407; German 36, 44, 65, 66, 72, 126, 142, 236, 240, 248, 255-259, 261, 266, 271, 274, 300, 327, 349, 386, 407, 535, 548, 565, 566, 571, 579, 586-588; Greek 96, 121, 122, 146, 151, 152, 154, 159, 165, 167, 168, 170, 171, 210, 226, 257, 261, 262, 287, 316, 318, 393, 421, 422, 426, 488, 507, 540; Hebrew (Ashkenazi Hebrew) 45, 122, 125, 151, 178, 210, 256, 257, 275-277, 312, 349, 409, 450, 451, 464, 530, 540, 580; Latin 16, 19, 20, 26, 33, 36, 42, 43, 45, 51, 52, 59, 60, 65, 66, 72, 76, 84, 85, 87, 103, 113-115, 121, 122, 126, 135, 137, 138, 140, 142, 146, 150, 151-154, 156, 157, 159, 161, 165, 167, 168, 170, 172, 175, 180, 181, 191, 192, 199, 201-203, 205, 208-210, 215, 217, 221, 225, 226, 231-234 240, 242, 243, 248, 254, 255, 257-259, 262, 264-266, 271, 272, 274-276, 279, 286, 289, 297, 298, 300, 301, 318, 324, 326, 327, 330-333, 338-340, 344, 346, 349, 351, 357, 360, 361, 369, 373, 386, 397, 400, 403, 406-408, 411, 417, 420, 421, 432, 437, 439, 442, 444, 445, 447, 454, 461, 462, 464, 469, 479, 487-490, 498, 502, 505, 507, 513, 521, 530, 531, 547-549, 555, 562, 564, 566, 567, 570, 573, 575, 579, 584, 588, 595, 596, 601, 604; Kipchak 266; Latvian 144, 145, 266, 274, 296, 274, 275; literary 258, 262; Lithuanian 36, 44, 45, 144, 171, 180, 236, 240, 254-256, 260, 261, 264, 266, 274, 286, 486, 488, 513, 565, 566, 571, 575, 577, 582, 584, 587, 589; mother tongue 156, 159, 161, 256, 259; Polish 1, 5, 10, 14, 22, 26, 36, 38, 41-45, 56, 59, 60, 66, 76, 84-86, 90, 96, 103, 114, 121, 134, 140, 142, 152-157, 159, 165, 167, 168, 170, 175, 188, 189, 192, 193, 195-197, 200, 202, 203, 205,

208-214, 216, 217, 220, 221, 228-230, 232-234, 236-238, 240, 242, 243, 248, 250, 255-266, 273-277, 291, 292, 300, 307, 318, 326, 327, 333, 334, 340, 343, 344, 346, 348-350, 353, 354, 356-358, 360-363, 373, 374, 383, 387, 402, 403, 407, 409, 413, 416, 417, 419-424, 426, 426, 461, 462, 479, 481, 482, 489, 490, 507, 515, 531, 532, 535-537, 541, 544, 546-549, 554, 556-559, 561, 565-567, 569, 571, 573, 579, 581, 583, 584, 586, 587, 589, 591, 592, 595; Ruthenian (see also: *prosta mova*); Russian 23; Serbian 114; Slavonic 44, 59, 168, 249, 258-262, 266, 286, 418, 421, 532, ; spoken 44, 256, 256, 260, 262, 374; Ukrainian 16, 44, 257; vernacular 33, 156, 208, 236, 274, 373, 529, 534, 535, 555, 564, 565, 570, 571, 575, 587, 589; written 22, 254, 256, 257, 262, 271, 421; Yiddish 10, 178, 256, 257, 266, 275, 276, 278, 312, 326, 342, 362, 373, 374, 416, 536, 580

Latin – see: language

Latinitas 259, 265, 421

Latvian – see: language

laudatio (laudation) 429, 451, 482, 484

law: canon 51, 58, 97, 404; Culm 53; civil 51, 149, 543; criminal 543; Magdeburg (German, Saxon, ius Saxonicum) 4-5, 7,11, 35, 47, 49-53, 55-58, 60, 65, 81, 85, 100, 119, 129, 191-193, 255, 327, 329, 354, 357; municipal (urban) 4, 57, 60; Roman 115, 322; state 47, 58; *Subiednik* 59

lawyer 5, 48, 49, 59, 64, 124, 191, 379, 381

lectionary 528, 562

lecture 147, 155-160, 171, 213, 283, 372, 408, 489, 490, 515, 516, 517, 540, 541

legacy (*legat*) 98, 110, 188, 241

legend (hagiography) 97, 236, 266, 414

letopis (*letopisets*) 1, 258, 270

letter (*epistola, epistula*; see also: epistolography) 6, 30, 38, 39, 41, 49, 52, 53, 72, 74, 82, 88-90, 96, 98, 111, 121, 132, 133, 135, 136, 146-148, 152-154, 163, 166, 167, 174, 179, 190, 194-197, 199-205, 215, 221-223, 228, 229, 231, 234, 235, 241-243, 245, 248, 248, 254, 258, 263, 269, 271-274, 282, 295, 296, 320, 321, 323-325, 327, 328, 333, 335-351, 381, 383, 389, 392, 394, 395, 397, 399, 406-411, 415, 416, 421, 422, 426, 428, 433, 468, 477, 479, 508, 526, 537, 568, 604

liber cancellariae (*formularum*) 322; *mortuorum* (*necrologia*) 219; *testamentorum* 353

liberal arts (*artes liberales*) 122, 135, 136, 138, 139, 143, 175, 177, 476

library 18, 21, 23, 27, 35, 50, 83, 92, 93-130, 299, 320, 351, 601; *Biblioteka Sapiehana* 51, 108, 117; of the Academy of Vilnius (university) 51, 93, 106-108, 567; Calvinist church and school 17, 93, 104-106; cathedral (chapter) 50, 85, 89, 96-102, 282, 588; Catholic churches, monasteries and nunneries 102-104, 237, 299, 476, 530, 553, 564, 588, 591; of the clergy 108-113; king's 50, 106, 113, 114, 115-117, 126, 285, 302, 304; Lutheran church 93, 104; of nunneries 207-209, 211-213; Orthodox churches and monasteries 93-95, 170; Orthodox Brotherhood 93, 95, 96; private 93, 100, 101, 105, 106, 108-114, 118-126, 128, 138, 168, 285, 309, 318, 319, 523, 536, 553, 555, 592; queen's 201

literacy 5, 16, 23, 27, 30, 33, 36, 48, 55, 82, 141, 161, 184, 226, 231, 235, 241, 255, 352, 467, 528, 580, 581; history of 4, 32, 33; levels of 33, 36, 131, 135, 140, 185, 187, 190, 191, 193, 225, 239, 291, 352, 437, 450, 536; phonetic 208;

pragmatic (*pragmatische Schriftlichkeit*) 36, 38, 57, 79, 82, 119, 141, 167, 180, 183, 187, 219, 225, 228, 234, 241, 283, 327, 335, 351, 353, 593; women's 30, 183-198, 206, 207, 222, 223; urban 12, 13, 33, 327, 351
literary culture 18-21, 23, 27-30, 34, 35, 37, 41, 47, 156, 183, 214, 278, 323, 517
literature: anti-Jewish 99; anti-Protestant 19, 99, 400, 406, 425, 496; Greek 157, 158, 422; Latin 157, 158; Lithuanian 236; neo-Latin 18, 19, 156, 460, 466; Polish 18, 37, 38, 43, 156, 157, 425; rabbinical 178, 312; religious 207, 236, 298, 299; rural (*literatura ziemiańska*) 5
Lithuanian *Metrica* – see: archive
Liturgiarion 568
lives of saints – see: legend
location of the city 7, 52, 53, 64, 65, 75, 327, 351
locus: scribendi 33, 190, 203; *textualis* (textual place), *loci textuales* 11, 27, 33, 35-37, 61, 65, 69, 70, 183
logosphere 234
Lutherans – see: Christian
machzorim 560
Magdeburg (German) law – see: law
magister – see: master of arts
magister (master of arts/theology) 70, 109, 111, 137, 143, 231, 475, 540, 541, 599
manifestation (making present, *uobecnienie*) 443
manuscript 2, 26, 60, 86, 96, 102, 114, 115, 157, 158, 160, 209, 210, 212, 213, 219, 232, 281-285, 288, 314, 315, 319, 328, 340, 343, 384, 386, 394, 402, 433, 470, 476, 489, 498, 516, 517, 522, 523, 527, 532, 537, 538, 540, 541, 543, 547, 566, 567, 581, 591, 596, 597, 599
marginalia, marginal note 138, 341, 534
marriage 10, 15, 88, 143, 195, 202, 243, 368, 369, 433, 492, 564
martyrology 562, 563
master of arts – see: *magister*
matzevah 448, 450, 451
mausoleum 8, 443, 448, 454, 455, 457, 458, 518, 603
mayor of Vilnius (*burgermeister*, *burmistrz*) 24, 54, 55, 63, 85, 90, 91, 118-121, 126, 165, 169, 228, 229, 232, 241, 283, 317-319, 337, 342, 360, 395, 428, 434, 455, 456, 471, 473, 481, 501, 595
meczet – see: mosque
medal 250, 439, 462, 468-470
medicine 64, 102, 108, 115, 122, 124, 195
meditation 103, 108, 121, 206, 211-213, 220, 223, 299, 528, 550, 551, 553
memoir 216, 217, 222, 542, 595-597, 601
memoria 34, 443, 445, 446, 449, 470, 601
memory: collective 2, 12, 22, 223, 430, 440, 443, 460, 598-605; communicative 600-602; cultural 3, 34, 436, 593, 600; memorial heritage 598; personal 600-602; politics of history/memory (*Geschichtspolitik*) 25, 41, 42, 43, 441, 520; reconstruction of 597, 602, 603, 605; site of (*lieu de mémoire*) 597-599, 603-605; stored (*Speichergedächtnis*) 599-601, 605; studies 34; textual 600
Mendicant – see: Franciscan
mentality 355, 460
metaphor 4, 78, 431, 523
Metrica – see: archive
Metropolitan of Kyiv 58, 61, 74, 89, 92, 95, 165, 170, 177, 282, 290, 524
metrykant – see: registrar
midrash 528, 536, 580, 582
Minaion (*Mineya*) 568
miniature 100, 115
minister – see: priest
mint 271, 272, 304-306, 469
minuscule 271, 272, 463
Mishnah 536
missal 99-101, 110-112, 115, 119, 126,

238, 306-308, 315, 497, 528, 562, 568, 573
mnemotechnic, mnemonic 132, 438
monastery: Bernardine 8, 95, 112, 173, 206, 282, 285, 463; Carmelite of Ancient Observance (St. George) 103; Carmelite Discalced (St. Teresa) 509; Dominican 8, 112, 144; Franciscan, 8, 110, 137, ; Holy Spirit (Orthodox) 164, 263, 294, 368, 382, 398, 399, 610; Holy Trinity (Orthodox, Uniate/Basilian) 78, 89, 95, 165, 166, 170, 293, 368, 382, 398, 481, 542; Orthodox in Vievis 293
mosque (*meczet*) 179, 277, 464, 530, 537, 544, 562, 582, 593
most – see: Stone Bridge
mother tongue – see: language
mullah 180
multiscripturality 36, 138, 255
music (musical) 97, 117, 282, 431, 434, 683, 485, 487, 491, 494, 496, 502, 514
Muslim (Muslims) 10, 36, 179, 180, 272, 277, 370, 510, 525, 527, 537, 539, 544, 545, 549, 561, 580, 583, 590
Nazis (German) 42, 274, 450, 597, 603
necrologia – see: *liber mortuorum*
nobility 54, 57, 58, 71, 79, 79, 91, 117, 118, 160, 161, 177, 186, 187, 190, 194, 197, 202, 207, 222, 229, 237, 243, 299, 322, 328, 337, 363, 400, 416, 433, 442, 471, 473, 483, 506, 518, 520
nobleman 5, 44, 58, 71, 79, 86, 106, 24, 143, 175, 187, 190, 233, 328, 334, 339, 412, 431, 442
noblewoman 71, 187, 196-198, 205, 216, 461, 467
non-Christian 6, 235, 427, 525; pagan 131, 411, 525; pre-Christian 236, 525, 583
notary 35, 40, 75, 77, 78, 137, 323, 327, 357, 360; aldermen 66, 79-81, 86, 87, 355; bishop's (consistorial) 69; chapter 70, 77; castle court 79, 80, 607, 608; great notary of the Grand Duchy of Lithuania (*pisarz wielki litewski*) 72, 243, 492; land court 79, 80; mint 304; municipal 65, 66, 77, 79, 80, 86, 119, 268, 330, 335, 337, 360; public (*notarius publicus, clericus publicus*) 12, 69, 75, 324, 327, 351, 358; *Voigt* 66, 81
November Uprising (1830–1831) 23, 441
novice 144, 206, 207
nunnery 437, 601; Benedictine 133, 205-222; Bernardine (Franciscan Observant) 8, 173, 205-222, 458, 609, 612; Carmelite 205-222
oblate (*oblata*) 233, 248, 276
occupation; Muscovite 10, 23, 102, 125, 214, 317, 353, 442, 596, 598, 600; Ottoman 532; Polish 16-17; Russian 442, 605; Soviet 440, 442; Swedish 476
October Revolution 13, 60
octoechos 96, 164, 528, 568
ode 471, 510-511, 601, 604
officium (office, prayers in the church) 206, 567
open city – see: city
opera 431, 486-487, 490
oral, orality 30, 236, 257, 264, 329, 370, 383, 406, 425, 545, 571, 589-593, 600
Orthodox – see: Christian
Orthodox Brotherhood – see: Brotherhood (Orthodox)
pagan – see: non-Christian
panegyric 21, 132, 158, 160, 249, 281, 285, 297, 320, 416, 429-434, 443, 471-475, 478, 480-483, 496, 503, 504, 507-512, 517-521, 523
paper 5, 36, 56, 161, 248, 250-253, 274, 279, 291, 296, 315, 329, 334, 448, 468, 471, 511, 537, 595, 607
paper mill 17, 250,
parchment 78, 94, 97, 98, 100, 112, 250, 253, 315, 334, 470, 532, 537
Parliament (*sejm*) 52, 60, 86, 165, 166,

275, 337, 394, 398, 425
passionale 562
patronage 174, 473, 474, 576, 577
periphery – cf. centre-peripheries
phonetic literacy – see: literacy
pinkas (minute book) 52, 90, 275, 276
pisarz – see: notary *or* scribe
pisarz wielki litewski – see: notary (great notary)
podkanclerzy – see: vice-chancellor
podpisek 66
poem 4, 5, 122, 157, 158, 160, 163, 208, 213, 214, 223, 242, 243, 258, 285, 291, 316, 392, 402, 403, 405, 412, 413, 415-417, 426, 447, 466, 470, 472, 474, 476, 477, 488, 493, 502, 503, 507, 508, 519, 520, 528, 555, 561, 588, 602, 604
poetics 27, 38, 132, 147, 152-154, 156, 157, 211, 285, 319, 320, 335, 456, 460, 472, 489, 520
poetry (poetic genres) 20, 22, 40, 47, 122, 125, 126, 137, 151, 152, 154-159, 161, 175, 214, 238, 241, 295, 297, 324, 344, 363, 403, 412, 416, 430, 440, 457, 483, 494, 508, 516, 520, 555, 561, 590
Pogoń (Pahonia) 271, 503, 506, 519, 520
polemic 21, 43, 102, 129, 150 169, 293, 298, 300, 309, 366-368, 370, 371, 381-383, 398-400, 402, 408, 411, 413, 417, 419-422, 425, 432, 453, 491, 522, 528, 533, 586
półgrosz 230, 271, 272
Polish – see: language
politics of history/memory – see: memory (politics of history, *Geschichtspolitik*)
pospólstwo – see: common people
praeexercitamina – see: progymnasmata
pragmatische Schriftlichkeit – see: literacy
prayer 96, 141, 167, 184, 210, 213, 237, 349, 446, 477, 524, 538, 545, 547, 550, 551, 554, 558, 561, 570, 571, 573, 574
prayer book 12, 113-115, 121, 127, 198, 223, 236, 237, 239, 248, 261, 265, 266, 298, 299, 315, 528, 531, 538, 545-551, 555-561, 576, 581, 593
preacher 82, 93, 104, 112, 159, 163, 240, 258, 304, 348, 349, 382, 415, 427, 478, 479, 481, 482, 504, 542, 560, 583-588, 590, 591
preaching 171, 256, 263, 400, 418, 436, 480, 481, 527, 571, 582-584, 586, 587, 589, 591, 592
priest 30, 184, 220, 240; Catholic 77, 80, 100, 112, 126, 141-144, 164, 172, 176, 202, 209, 211, 213, 221, 223, 242, 251, 295, 296, 318, 359, 372, 388, 403, 410, 479, 480, 530, 539, 548, 553, 566, 567, 570, 571, 582, 584, 588, 591; minister (Protestant) 88, 105, 172, 177, 318, 336, 366, 377, 383, 389-391, 401, 406, 415, 416, 417, 426, 481, 497, 515, 559, 586; Orthodox 109, 170, 419, 582, 584, 588; Uniate 590
primer 167, 168, 190, 299, 530, 538, 545, 554, 562, 573, 575, 577, 579, 593
print, printing 2, 43, 208, 240, 263, 282, 292, 295, 299, 310, 320, 384, 399, 476, 479, 511, 532, 533, 561, 587, 595, 596
printer 30, 40, 169, 240, 242, 249, 250, 254, 260, 274, 285, 288, 291, 294, 295, 296, 300, 301, 310, 311, 312, 366, 402, 477, 478, 532, 548, 563
printing house 5, 10, 17, 21, 28, 30, 37, 47, 101, 240, 248, 254, 282, 289, 298, 300, 301, 304, 366, 406, 420, 460, 481, 531, 535, 559, 560; Academy of Vilnius (Jesuit university) 25, 158, 159, 163, 285, 289, 295-297, 301, 311, 319, 320, 366, 420, 426, 479, 480, 504, 509; Basilian (Uniate) 26, 289, 291-292, 296, 300, 415, 480, 568; Brotherhood (Orthodox) of the Holy Spirit 95, 165, 166, 168, 169, 237, 262, 289, 291-294, 296, 300, 399, 481, 533, 557, 568; Brotherhood (Orthodox) in Vievis 261,

293, 294, 589; Calvinist Church 289, 294, 383; Daniel of Łęczyca's 289, 294, 295, 300, 402; Haraburda's 289; Jewish 312; Karcans's 274, 289, 294, 296-298, 300, 588; Kmita's 289, 294; Mamonicz family 60, 95, 237, 289-291, 296, 300, 533, 556; Markowicz's 289, 294, 300; Mstislavets's 95, 289; Pietkiewicz's 289; Radziwiłł's 'the Orphan' 274, 289, 294-296, 418; Skaryna's 240, 249, 273, 286-289; Sultzers' 289, 300

professional of written word 30, 328

progymnasmata (*praeexercitamina*) 122, 153, 359, 438

prosta mova (simple speech; see also: language: Ruthenian) 45, 256, 275

Protestant – see: Christian

psalter 94, 95, 99, 118, 119, 121, 125, 127, 135, 167, 168, 180, 209, 210, 261, 299, 312, 315, 316, 318, 359, 409, 528, 531, 533, 535, 538, 554, 555, 557, 559, 562, 568, 569, 604

qahal (kehila, kahal) 10, 248, 275, 362, 374, 539, 543, 562

quill 30, 36, 76, 78, 82, 250, 252, 274

Quran 180, 266, 268, 277, 528, 529, 537, 538, 544, 582, 590

reader 30, 36, 37, 45, 75, 126, 204, 207, 213, 217, 218, 225, 232, 235, 245, 279, 286, 288, 301, 370, 392, 393, 394, 406, 409, 410, 422, 424, 427, 431, 433, 438, 472, 512, 521, 530, 534, 547, 551, 553, 555, 561, 592

reading (to read) 5, 29, 31, 36, 49, 57, 81, 104, 113, 114, 121, 126, 130, 131, 140, 141, 142, 150, 154, 155, 161, 164, 167, 168, 172, 175, 178, 180, 183, 184, 186, 187, 190-192, 195, 196, 198, 201, 203, 206, 208, 210, 211, 215, 218, 222, 225, 226, 228, 229, 231-234, 236-239, 259, 263, 271, 299, 316, 326, 437, 340, 343, 344, 391, 409, 423, 431, 438, 450, 459, 464, 529, 530, 536, 538, 553, 561, 573, 577, 588, 589, 593, 601

Reformation 10, 18, 19, 111, 143, 236, 263, 529, 531, 535, 571, 577, 585

registers 3, 4, 38, 39, 56, 80, 81, 83, 84, 91, 97, 191, 233, 248, 282, 326, 373, 374, 378, 598; of aldermen court (*księgi wójtowskie*) 24, 65, 67, 68, 86, 352, 353, 600; of the Archconfraternity of St. Anne 185, 186; of baptism 88; of burgrave court (*księgi horodniczańskie*) 24, 71, 84, 247, 374-377, 461; of the Calvinist church 88, 89, 113, 352; of the Calvinist Synod 294, 352; of the castle court (*księgi grodzkie*) 71, 81, 84, 219, 247, 362; of the chapter (*ksiegi kapitulne*) 70, 81, 85, 98, 101, 135, 247, 251, 252, 283, 306, 315, 352, 357; economic (financial inventory) 4, 55, 86, 87, 101, 197, 203, 219, 251, 283, 304, 310, 334, 223, 306, 553; of the guilds 90-91; of the hospitals 86; of the Jewish court 90, 362; of the land court 71, 81, 219; of the Lutheran church 352; of marriages; municipal (of Vilnius) 4, 23-24, 54, 55, 65, 67, 69, 81, 84-87, 118, 121, 186, 191, 219, 233, 247, 252, 269, 276, 306, 330-332, 352, 354, 361, 363, 395, 397, 400; of nunneries 208, 218, 219; private (inventory) 91, 196, 197, 283, 317, 323, 334; of the quartermaster (*stanowniczy*) 511, 512; student (Slutsk) 174; of testaments (*libri testamentorum*) 353; of the Tribunal of the Grand Duchy of Lithuania 71, 219, 396; of the Holy Trinity Uniate monastery 89; of the *Voigt* office 56

rhetoric 2, 5, 6, 27, 37, 40, 51, 80, 102, 108, 122, 125, 132, 135, 147, 151-154, 156, 158, 176, 181, 211, 213, 218, 221, 232, 242, 262, 283, 285, 316, 318-320, 321, 322, 324, 326, 328, 333, 335, 341, 342, 347, 351, 356, 359, 362, 369, 372,

378, 380, 381, 383, 393, 394, 406, 411, 425, 426, 428, 429, 430, 432, 433, 438, 483, 484, 485, 489, 494, 504, 512, 514, 515, 523, 561, 584, 590, 592
rhetorical organisation of the city 27, 37, 54, 183
riot (tumult) 30, 89, 162, 222, 234, 309, 336, 342, 349, 394, 396-398, 400-403, 412, 414, 417, 420, 424, 428, 450, 510, 597
Ruthenian – see: language
sacramentary 528
school (general) 12, 16, 30, 36, 40, 47, 61, 82, 131-133, 135, 137, 141-146, 154, 157, 159, 167, 168, 171, 172, 176, 178, 180, 181, 190, 196, 199, 228, 229, 231, 240, 248, 257, 263, 283, 341, 370, 440, 456, 485, 523, 530, 550, 570, 571, 580, 581; Academic Gymnasium in Gdańsk 142; Basilian – see: Uniate (below) ; Basilian seminary 170; Benedictine (for girls) 196-198; Bernardine (conventual) 132, 144, 539; Brotherhood (Orthodox) 96, 133, 164-169, 180, 238, 291, 502, 509, 523, 541, 576; Calvinist in Kėdainiai 106, 177; Calvinist in Slutsk 174, 175, 177; Calvinist in Vilnius 8, 93, 105, 106, 132, 133, 173-177, 180, 195, 319, 392, 401, 558; Carmelite (conventual) 144, 539; Cathedral 36, 133-140, 143, 162, 163, 168, 179, 231, 238, 343; Collegium Romanum (Jesuit) 372; dioecesan seminary 133, 144, 209; Dominican (conventual; Studium Generale) 132, 144, 162, 539; for girls 195-196, 206, 229; Holy Trinity (Orthodox) 164; humanist 5, 40, 105, 139, 343, 436, 456, 485, 584, 590; Jesuit in Vilnius – see: Academy of Vilnius and college (Jesuit in Vilnius); Jesuit school/college, *collegium* (general or outside Vilnius) 17, 99, 107, 108, 132, 145, 147, 149, 150, 152, 156, 157, 170, 175, 217, 297, 366, 370-372, 416, 476, 485, 490, 516; Jewish 36, 178-179, 397, 560; St. John Parish (municipal) 12, 36, 132, 134, 140-143, 162, 180, 231, 238, 343, 548; Kulvietis' (Lutheran) 171, 172, 399; Kyiv-Mohyla Collegium; Lutheran 93, 132, 133, 163-165, 172, 195, 258; Muslim (Tartar) 36, 179-180, 539; Orthodox (see also: Brotherhood) 36, 133, 164; papal seminary (*Alumnatus*) 87, 133, 144, 145, 149, 209, 474, 531, 540; St. Peter and Paul (Orthodox) 164; Protestant 36, 131, 172, 539; Theotocos cathedral (Orthodox) 132, 164; Uniate (Holy Trinity, Basilian) 133, 169-171
Schwabacher 168, 254, 274, 557
scribe 3, 28, 35, 40, 56, 65, 66, 69-80, 82, 97, 189, 191, 201, 203, 225, 228, 231, 232, 234, 239, 241, 243, 245, 251, 265, 271, 274, 278, 279, 281, 304, 315, 318, 319, 323, 359, 373, 374, 460, 531, 540, 599, 600
scroll 254, 276, 469, 527, 537
seal (sealing) 5, 55, 56, 73, 78, 80, 81, 187-189, 193, 215, 226-229, 238, 326, 332, 334, 344, 357
secretary 3, 35, 36, 40, 48, 64, 70, 72-74, 76-80, 116, 117, 143, 186, 194, 199, 202-205, 215, 238, 239, 241-243, 251, 252, 273, 327, 333, 339, 340, 343, 344, 346, 369, 379, 386, 460, 493, 553, 608, 613
semi-cursive 276
semi-literacy 193, 225
seminary – see: school
semi-ustav 119, 269, 270, 273, 274
sermon 3, 12, 21, 30, 38, 39, 77, 78, 82, 88, 99, 100, 103, 115, 133, 171, 194, 206, 237, 349, 256, 258, 263, 264, 292, 297, 318, 324, 325, 363, 382, 384, 386, 390, 400, 401, 404, 418, 420, 424-428, 434, 436, 443, 471, 473, 478-483, 504,

508, 528, 539, 542, 570, 571, 582-593, 604
signature 138, 186-190, 194, 198, 200, 203, 226, 228, 229, 230, 232, 252, 267, 276, 277, 326, 357, 358, 467, 607, 608
singing (to sing) 100, 139-142, 164, 206, 208, 232, 236, 402, 411, 502 510, 557, 570, 593
site of memory – see: memory
Society of Jesus – see: Jesuits
Sodality of the Blessed Virgin Mary 476, 550
song 4, 211, 214 236, 236, 258, 266, 402, 415, 499, 502, 508, 528, 536, 545, 549, 555, 557-560, 571, 593
speech 122, 132, 154-156, 160, 218, 229, 235, 256-258, 262, 265, 321, 384, 390, 417, 425, 432, 434, 436, 472, 481, 487, 489, 501-504, 508, 510, 511, 513, 586, 592
street – see: Index of Place-names
student 20, 30, 82, 112, 135, 136-139, 142, 147-149, 151-165, 170, 174, 175, 180, 199, 231, 232, 238, 240, 283, 285, 291, 295, 313, 318-320, 322, 342, 343, 348, 349, 369-372, 385, 394, 402, 408, 410, 412, 413, 431, 435, 456, 474-476, 487, 489, 490, 495, 502, 503, 507-509, 515-517, 520, 540, 553, 558, 559, 561, 573, 576
Studium Generale – see: school (Dominican)
Subiednik – see: law
sufra 537
sura 544
sylva – see: book (common-place)
synagogue (Great Synagogue) 132, 230, 248, 275, 398, 436, 437, 441, 464, 471, 527, 530, 536, 539, 560, 573, 593, 603
synod (Calvinist) – see: Council
tablet (wax tablet) – see: *cera*
Talmud 178, 312, 374, 536, 542, 543
Tanakh 536
teacher 30, 40, 119, 126, 131, 132, 139, 140, 142, 143, 147, 149, 153, 156, 163, 166, 167, 169, 174, 176, 180, 240, 285, 299, 318, 319, 416, 590, 530, 539, 542, 558, 576
testament – see: will
textbook 110, 121, 152, 153, 157, 158, 168, 170, 175, 180, 249, 283, 294, 297, 299, 308, 315, 319, 320, 324, 342, 343, 504, 576, 581
textualis 270, 271, 274
theatre (theatrical) 12, 16, 157, 158, 160, 176, 235, 431, 433, 434, 484-491, 494-497, 502, 504, 506
theology 97, 136-138, 147, 148, 150-152, 156, 159, 170, 175, 208, 257, 283, 285, 369-372, 385, 386, 406, 414, 419, 424, 516, 523, 539-542
tombstone (gravestone) 127, 230, 232, 250, 271, 273, 277, 440-413, 445-452, 455, 456, 459, 471, 524
Torah 178, 253, 276, 312, 464, 527-529, 536, 537, 580, 582
town hall 8, 35, 50, 56, 57, 65, 66, 85-87, 91, 163, 327, 440, 600, 603, 608
tragedy 154, 487, 488
translation (translate) 19, 37, 51, 56, 59, 60, 81, 100, 115, 117, 119, 122, 129, 132, 134, 144, 153, 156, 168, 171, 178, 191, 208-211, 213, 261, 262, 264-266, 285, 285, 287, 296, 297, 316, 339, 354, 360, 367, 373, 387, 407, 409, 421, 422, 438, 479, 515, 528, 529, 531-538, 544, 547, 549, 551, 559-561, 567, 571, 574, 575, 577, 579, 580, 583, 588, 589
Trebnik – see: Euchologion
Tribunal of the Grand Duchy of Lithuania – see: court
Triodon (*Triod*) 96, 568
triumph 433, 469-471, 491, 492, 498-511,
triumphal arch 248, 430, 434, 437, 438, 468-470, 484, 500, 503, 506, 508, 511, 518, 520, 524, 561

trivium 40, 135, 141, 324, 335, 343
tumult – see: riot
Typikon (*Ustav*) 532, 568
Ukrainian – see: language
Uniate – see: Christian
Union: Krevo (1385) 6, 75, 255, 271; Brest (1596) 10, 21, 166, 258, 293, 368, 382, 398, 419, 420, 421, 541, 566, 576, 584; Lublin (1569) 522, 532
university: Cracow University (University of Cracow) 65, 70, 109-113, 133, 134, 136, 240, 242, 315, 330; University of Königsberg 386; University of Vilnius (*Uniwersytet Wileński*, 1803–1832) 23; University of Leizig 198; University of Oxford 516; University of Stefan Batory in Vilnius (1919-1939) 17; Universitas Vilnensis (1579–1781) – see: Academy of Vilnius
uobecnienie – see: manifestation
Urteile 50
ustav 268-270
Vaad (the Lithuanian Jews' parliament) 52, 275, 276
vanitas (vanitative *topoi*) 78
vice-chancellor (*podkanclerzy*) 73, 97, 117, 428, 509
Voigt of Vilnius (*wójt*, *advocatus*) 11, 17, 24, 43, 50, 56, 59, 60, 63-66, 79, 81, 86, 121, 146, 194, 195, 242, 259, 319, 332, 337, 355, 553, 453, 522
votive offering (*ex voto*) 459-462, 603
Vulgate – see: Bible
walls of the city 32, 35, 39, 53, 61, 83, 177, 367, 394, 397, 448, 603
wax tablet – see: *cera*
wedding 161, 237, 264, 433, 435, 436, 478, 481,485, 492, 494, 508, 561
wilkierz – see: statute of the city
will (last will, testament) 3-5, 12, 26, 38, 39, 56, 69, 70, 75, 77, 81, 85, 95, 98, 106, 109, 112, 136, 188, 189, 191-193, 220, 230, 238, 269, 316, 318, 321, 323-325, 328, 330, 350-363, 436, 443, 483, 604; price 355; validity 359
wójt – see: *Voigt* of Vilnius
Yiddish – see: language